ENHANCING URBAN SAFETY AND SECURITY

ENHANCING URBAN SAFETY AND SECURITY

GLOBAL REPORT ON HUMAN SETTLEMENTS 2007

United Nations Human Settlements Programme

London • Sterling, VA

First published by Earthscan in the UK and US in 2007

United Nations Human Settlements Programme (UN-Habitat)
PO Box 30030, GPO Nairobi 00100, Kenya
Tel: +254 20 762 3120
Fax: +254 20 762 3477/4266/4267
Web: www.unhabitat.org

HS/943/07E

ISBN: 978-1-84407-475-4 (hardback)
978-1-84407-479-2 (paperback)
978-92-113-1929-3 (UN-Habitat Series)
978-92-113-1920-0 (UN-Habitat paperback)
978-92-113-1921-7 (UN-Habitat hardback)

Typeset by MapSet Ltd, Gateshead
Printed and bound in Malta by Gutenberg Press
Cover design by Susanne Harris

For a full list of publications please contact:

Earthscan
8–12 Camden High Street
London, NW1 0JH, UK
Tel: +44 (0)20 7387 8558
Fax: +44 (0)20 7387 8998
Email: earthinfo@earthscan.co.uk
Web: **www.earthscan.co.uk**

22883 Quicksilver Drive, Sterling, VA 20166-2012, US

Earthscan publishes in association with the International Institute for Environment and Development

A catalogue record for this book is available from the British Library

Library of Congress Cataloging-in-Publication Data
Enhancing urban safety and security : global report on human settlements 2007 / United Nations Human Settlements Programme.
p. cm.
ISBN-13: 978-1-84407-475-4 (hardback)
ISBN-10: 1-84407-475-7 (hardback)
ISBN-13: 978-1-84407-479-2 (pbk.)
ISBN-10: 1-84407-479-X (pbk.)
1. Urban policy. 2. Housing policy. 3. Eviction. 4. Emergency management. 5. Disasters—Risk assessment. 6. Urban violence—Prevention. 7. Crime prevention. 8. City planning. I. United Nations Human Settlements Programme.
HT151.E64 200
307.76—dc22

2007023425

Printed on elemental chlorine-free paper

FOREWORD

Over the past decade, the world has witnessed growing threats to the safety and security of cities and towns. Some have come in the form of catastrophic events, while others have been manifestations of poverty and inequality or of rapid and chaotic urbanization processes. This publication, *Enhancing Urban Safety and Security: Global Report on Human Settlements 2007*, addresses some of the most challenging threats to the safety and security of urban dwellers today.

As the report tells us, urban violence and crime are increasing worldwide, giving rise to widespread fear and driving away investment in many cities. This is especially true in Africa, Latin America and the Caribbean, where urban gang violence is on the rise. Recent widespread violence in the *banlieus* of Paris and throughout urban France, as well as terrorist attacks in New York, Madrid and London, have all demonstrated that cities within high-income countries are also vulnerable.

Large numbers of people in cities all over the world, including most of the 1 billion currently living in slums, have no security of tenure, while at least 2 million are forcibly evicted every year. Forced evictions predominantly affect those living in the worst housing conditions, especially vulnerable and disadvantaged groups, including women and children. Many such evictions are carried out in the name of urban redevelopment, with little regard for consequences among the poor, who are left without alternative shelter provisions. The resulting social exclusion swells the army of the poor and the angry.

As this report points out, there is a very real nexus between natural events and human safety and security. The vulnerability of cities is increasing due to climate change, which has accelerated extreme weather events and rising sea levels. At the same time, urban slums are expanding into areas vulnerable to floods, landslides, industrial pollution and other hazards.

The report highlights the key role urban planning and governance have to play in making our cities safe and secure for generations to come. Through its documentation of many successful experiences, it promotes learning and sharing of knowledge on urban safety and security. I commend it to all those interested in the health of cities around the world.

Ban Ki-moon
Secretary-General
United Nations

INTRODUCTION

Enhancing Urban Safety and Security: Global Report on Human Settlements 2007 addresses three major threats to the safety and security of cities, which are: urban crime and violence; insecurity of tenure and forced evictions; and natural and human-made disasters. It analyses worldwide conditions and trends with respect to these threats and pays particular attention to their underlying causes and impacts, as well as to the good policies and best practices that have been adopted at the city, national and international levels. The report adopts a *human security* perspective, the concern of which is with the safety and security of people, rather than states, and highlights concerns that can be addressed through appropriate urban policy, planning, design and governance.

The report examines a broad spectrum of crime and violence, all of which are generally on the rise globally. Over the period 1980–2000, total recorded crime rates in the world increased by about 30 per cent, from 2300 to over 3000 crimes per 100,000 people. Over the past five years, 60 per cent of all urban residents in developing countries have been victims of crime. The report shows that while the incidence of terrorist-related violence is quantitatively smaller in relation to other types of violence, it has, however, significantly worsened the impacts of violence on cities in recent years. These impacts include: increased fear among urban residents; falling income resulting from the destruction or flight of businesses from affected areas; growth of the private security industry and of urban gated communities; and the diversion of development resources towards investment in public and private security. The report highlights several policy responses aimed at reducing crime and violence, ranging from effective urban planning, design and governance, through community-based approaches in which communities take ownership of the various crime and violence prevention initiatives, to reduction of risk factors by focusing on groups that are likely to be perpetrators of crime, such as the youth.

Turning to insecurity of tenure and forced evictions, the report estimates that at least 2 million people in the world are forcibly evicted every year. The most insecure urban residents are the world's 1 billion poor people living in slums. Incidents of forced eviction are often linked to bulldozing of slums and informal enterprises in developing countries, as well as to processes of gentrification, public infrastructure development, and urban redevelopment and beautification projects. The report emphasizes that forced evictions are most prevalent in areas with the worst housing conditions; that women, children and other vulnerable and disadvantaged groups are most negatively affected by evictions; and that evictions invariably increase, rather than reduce, the problems that they aim to 'solve'. The report documents a number of recent policy responses to the threat of tenure insecurity, including, at the international level, legislation against forced evictions and secure tenure campaigns and, at the national level, policies on upgrading and regularization, titling and legalization, as well as improved land administration and registration.

With respect to disasters, which are increasing globally, the report shows that, between 1974 and 2003, 6367 natural disasters occurred globally, causing the death of 2 million people and affecting 5.1 billion people. A total of 182 million people were made homeless, while reported economic damage amounted to US$1.38 trillion. The report also shows that the aggregate impact of small-scale hazards on urban dwellers can be considerable. For example, traffic accidents kill over 1.2 million people annually worldwide. Factors rendering cities particularly vulnerable include rapid and unplanned urbanization; concentration of economic wealth in cities; environmental modifications through human actions; expansion of slums (often into hazardous locations); and ineffective land-use planning and enforcement of building codes. An increasingly important factor is climate change. There has been a 50 per cent rise in extreme weather events associated with climate change from the 1950s to the 1990s, and major cities located in coastal areas are particularly vulnerable to sea-level rise. Cities have been able to reduce disaster risk through, among other approaches, effective land-use planning and design of disaster-resistant buildings and infrastructure, improved risk mapping, institutional reform and training, establishment of effective communication and emergency response systems, as well as strengthening of reconstruction capacity. At the national level, governments are putting in place disaster risk reduction legislation, strengthening early warning systems, and instituting inclusive governance and planning in order to strengthen the resilience of cities and communities.

An important socio-economic determinant of vulnerability to the three threats to urban safety and security addressed in the report is poverty. The urban poor are more exposed to crime, forced evictions and natural hazards than the rich. They are more vulnerable to disasters than the rich because they are often located on sites prone to floods, landslides and pollution. The urban poor also have limited access to assets, thus limiting their ability to respond to hazards or manage risk, for example through insurance. Because the poor are politically powerless, it is unlikely that they will receive the necessary social services following disasters. The report therefore highlights the need for policy responses that place people, poverty reduction and community participation at the centre. It is my belief that this report will significantly raise global awareness of the current threats to the safety and security of our cities and assist in the identification of appropriate policy responses at the urban, national and international levels.

Anna Kajumulo Tibaijuka
Under-Secretary-General and Executive Director
United Nations Human Settlements Programme (UN-Habitat)

ACKNOWLEDGEMENTS

The preparation of this issue of the *Global Report on Human Settlements* is the result of the dedicated efforts of a wide range of urban researchers, practitioners and policy-makers. Their knowledge and expertise has been essential to the preparation of this and, indeed, also earlier issues in this biennial series. The current volume — which is concerned with urban security and safety, focusing on crime and violence; security of tenure and forced evictions; and natural and human-made disasters — reflects a fundamental commitment to the goals of sustainable and equitable development of human settlements, as outlined in the Habitat Agenda, the Millennium Declaration and in international law relevant to human settlements.

Enhancing Urban Safety and Security: Global Report on Human Settlements 2007 was prepared under the general guidance of two successive Directors of the Monitoring and Research Division, UN-Habitat, i.e. Don Okpala (till February 2006) and Banji Oyeyinka (from January 2007). Naison Mutizwa-Mangiza, Chief of the Policy Analysis, Synthesis and Dialogue Branch, UN-Habitat, supervised the preparation of the report, and was responsible for the substantive editing and drafting of parts of the two introductory chapters, as well as the overall editing of the report. Ben Arimah, Inge Jensen and Edlam Abera Yemeru (Human Settlements Officers, UN-Habitat) were responsible for the substantive editing and drafting of parts of the chapters on crime and violence; security of tenure; and natural and human-made disasters, respectively. They also reviewed and prepared summaries of the case studies contained in Part VI of the report.

The Executive Director of UN-Habitat, Dr. Anna K. Tibaijuka, and the following members of the UN-Habitat Senior Management Board provided strategic and substantive advice at different stages in the preparation of the report: Subramonia Ananthankrishnan, Nefise Bazoglu, Daniel Biau, Selman Ergüden, Lucia Kiwala, Frederico Neto, Toshiyasu Noda, Lars Reutersward and Farouk Tebbal.

Background papers and drafts of chapters were prepared by a number of eminent experts, some of whom also coordinated and supervised case studies: Michael Cohen, New School University, New York, US (Chapters 1 and 2, as well as supervising case studies on natural and human-made disasters); Richard H. Schneider, Department of Urban and Regional Planning, University of Florida, Gainesville, US (Chapter 3, as well as supervising case studies on crime and violence); Ted Kitchen, Sheffield Hallam University, UK (Chapters 4 and 10, as well as supervising case studies on crime and violence); Scott Leckie, Centre on Housing Rights and Evictions (COHRE) (Chapters 5, 6 and 11, as well as supervising case studies on security of tenure); Mark Pelling, Kings College, University of London, UK (Chapters 7, 8, 9 and 12). Iouri Moiseev, independent consultant, Moscow, Russia, compiled the draft version of the Statistical Annex in Part VII.

The report benefited substantially from the contributions of the members of the Advisory Board of the Global Research Network on Human Settlements (HS-Net). This network was established in 2004 with the primary objective of providing substantive guidance to the preparation of the Global Report series. The members of the Board who contributed to the preparation of the current report, through discussions at Board meetings and/or by providing extensive comments in writing on the first draft of the report itself were: Marisa Carmona, Department of Urbanism, Delft University of Technology, the Netherlands; Nowarat Coowanitwong, School of Environment, Resources and Development, Asian Institute of Technology, Thailand; Suocheng Dong, Institute of Geographic Sciences and Natural Resources Research, Chinese Academy of Sciences, Beijing, China; Alain Durand-Lasserve, Sociétés en Développement dans l'Espace et dans le Temps, Université Denis Diderot, Paris, France; József Hegedüs, Metropolitan Research Institute, Varoskutatas Kft, Budapest, Hungary; Paula Jiron, Housing Institute, University of Chile, Santiago, Chile; Vinay D. Lall, Society for Development Studies, New Delhi, India; José Luis Lezama de la Torre, Centro de Estudios Demográficos, Urbanos y Ambientales, Mexico City, Mexico; Om Prakash Mathur, National Institute of Public Finance and Policy (IDFC), Delhi, India; Winnie Mitullah, Institute of Development Studies (IDS), University of Nairobi, Kenya; Peter Newman, Institute for Sustainability and Technology Policy, Murdoch University, Australia; Peter Ngau, Department of Regional and Urban Planning, University of Nairobi, Kenya; Tumsifu Jonas Nnkya, Institute of Housing Studies and Building Research, University of Dar es Salaam, Tanzania; Carole Rakodi, International Development Department, University of Birmingham, UK; Gustavo Riofrio, Centro de Estudios y Promoción del Desarrollo (DESCO), Lima, Peru; Nelson Saule, Instituto de Estudios Formacao e Assessoria em Politicas Socials (POLIS), São Paulo, Brazil; Mona Serageldin, Centre for Urban Development Studies, Harvard University Graduate School of Design, Massachusetts, US; Dina K. Shehayeb, Housing and Building National Research Centre, Cairo, Egypt; Richard Stren, Centre of Urban and Community Studies, University of Toronto, Canada; Luidmila Ya Tkachenko, Research and Project Institute of Moscow City Master Plan, Moscow, Russia; Willem K.T Van Vliet–, College of Architecture and Planning, University of Colorado, Boulder, US; Vladimer Vardosanidze, Institute of Architecture, Tbilisi, Georgia; Patrick Wakely, Development Planning Unit (DPU), University College of London, UK; and Mustapha Zubairu, Department of Urban and Regional Planning, Federal University of Technology, Minna, Nigeria.

The Advisory Board met in September 2005 in New Delhi, India, to discuss a preliminary outline of the report and a background paper on current issues and trends in urban safety. At this stage, the focus of the report was confined to natural and human-made disasters. The Board met again in June 2006 in Vancouver, Canada, at which time it had been agreed to expand the focus of the report to include urban crime and violence as well as security of tenure and evictions. At this second meeting, the Board members discussed annotated outlines of the report's chapters.

Following expert recommendations, a number of authors were commissioned to prepare case studies on the three themes of the report. Their willingness to give of their time, and their responsiveness to requests for revisions at short notice, is very much appreciated. A major case study on the application of the 'human security' perspective in the implementation of three slum upgrading projects in Afghanistan, Cambodia and Sri Lanka was prepared by Marcello Balbo and Giulia Guadagnoli, Dipartimento di Pianificazione, Università luav di Venezia, Italy, with financial assistance from the Government of Japan. Case studies on crime and violence from the following cities were prepared: Bradford, UK (Ted Kitchen, Sheffield Hallam University, UK); Durban, South Africa (Oliver Zambuko, Community Development Programme, University of KwaZulu-Natal, Durban, South Africa; and Cookie Edwards, KZN Network on Violence against Women, Durban, South Africa); Hong Kong, China (Roderic G. Broadhurst, School of Justice, Queensland University of Technology, Brisbane, Australia; Lee King Wa and Chan Ching Yee, Centre for Criminology, University of Hong Kong, China); Kingston, Jamaica (Sherrian Gray, Jamaica's Solution to Youth Lifestyle and Empowerment, US-AID Project, Kingston, Jamaica); Nairobi, Kenya (Grace Masese, Social Development Section, Ministry of Local Government, Nairobi, Kenya); New York, US (Joseli Macedo, Department of Urban and Regional Planning, University of Florida, Gainesville, US); Port Moresby, Papua New Guinea (Samuel Boamah, Queensland Department of Natural Resources and Water, Brisbane, Australia, and Jane Stanley, Director, FOCUS Pty Limited, Brisbane, Australia); Rio de Janeiro, Brazil (Alba Zaluar, Instituto de Medicina Social, Universidad do Estado do Rio de Janeiro); and Toronto, Canada (Sara K. Thompson; and Rosemary Gartner, Centre of Criminology, University of Toronto, Canada).

Case studies on security of tenure from the following countries/cities were also prepared: Bangkok, Thailand and Cambodia (Graeme Bristol, Centre for Architecture and Human Rights, Bangkok, Thailand); Brazil (Leticia Marques Osorio, COHRE); Canada (J. David Hulchanski, Centre for Urban and Community Studies, University of Toronto, Canada); China (David G. Westendorff, Urbanchina Partners LLC, Shanghai, China); India (Colin Gonsalves, Human Rights Law Network, India); Istanbul, Turkey (Robert Neuwirth, author, New York, US); Lagos, Nigeria (Felix C. Morka, Social and Economic Rights Action Center, Nigeria); South Africa (Steve Kahanovitz, Legal Resources Centre, South Africa).

Finally, case studies on natural and human-made disasters from the following countries/cities or events were also prepared: Cuba (Martha Thompson, Unitarian Universalist Service Committee, Massachusetts, US); Indian Ocean Tsunami (Sara Rowbottom, New School University, New York, US); Kobe, Japan (Bart Orr, New School University, New York, US); Mexico City (Rachel Nadelman, Caroline A. Nichols, Sara Rowbottom, Sarah Cooper, New School University, New York, US); Mozambique (Lillian Wambui Chege, Christina J. Irene and Bart Orr, New School University, New York, US, and Rachel Nadelman, New School University, New York, US, and the World Bank); Mumbai, India (Stacey Stecko and Nicole Barber, New School University, New York, US); the Netherlands (Bart Orr, Amy Stodghill and Lucia Candu, New School University, New York, US); New Orleans, US (Wendy A. Washington, New School University, New York, US); and Tangshan, China, and Cape Town, South Africa (Lyndal Pottier and Tanya Wichmann, Disaster Mitigation for Sustainable Livelihoods Programme (DiMP), University of Cape Town, South Africa; Malika Gujrati, John Lindsay and Bart Orr, New School University, New York, US).

At UN-Habitat, a number of people provided vital support by reviewing and commenting on draft chapters, preparing draft text for the report, or providing other valued contributions. In particular, the following staff provided their time amidst competing demands: Cecilia Andersson, Juma Assiago, Clarissa Augustinus, Szilard Fricska, Sarah Gitau, Carmela Lanza, Dan Lewis, Erika Lind, Jan Meeuwissen, Philip Mukungu, Laura Petrella, Rasmus Precht, Mariko Sato, Ulrik Westman and Brian Williams. Gora Mboup provided inputs to the preparation of the Statistical Annex, while Julius Majale and Ezekiel Ngure provided technical assistance in data checking.

In addition, many other people were helpful in reviewing and commenting on drafts, contributing information and in a variety of other ways. Among them the following names should be mentioned: Annmarie Barnes, Ministry of National Security, Jamaica; Nikita Cassangneres, independent expert, Geneva, Switzerland; Zulma Chardon, University of Florida Student Health Care Center, Gainesville, US; Kate Fox, Department of Law and Society, University of Florida, Gainesville, US; Stina Ljungdell, United Nations High Commissioner for Refugees, Geneva, Switzerland; Diana Clare Mitlin, IDPM (Institute of Development Policy and Management), University of Manchester, UK; Cedrique Mokesun, independent expert, Bangkok, Thailand; Bosibori Nyabate, independent expert, Bath, UK; Pali and Cletus Ponsenby, independent experts, Bangkok, Thailand; Fionn Skiotis, COHRE; A. Graham Tipple, Centre for Architectural Research and Development Overseas, University of Newcastle upon Tyne, UK; and Paul Wheeler, Gestalt Center for Domestic Abuse, Gainesville, US.

Antoine King, Felista Ondari, Karina Rossi, Amrita Jaidka, Mary Dibo and Stella Otieno of the Programme Support Division, UN-Habitat; and Margaret Mathenge and Nelly Munovi of the United Nations Office at Nairobi (UNON), provided administrative support during the preparation of the report. Secretarial and general administrative support was provided by Mary Kariuki, Pamela Murage and Naomi Mutiso-Kyalo of UN-Habitat.

Special thanks are due to the governments of Bahrain and China, for their financial contributions in support of the translation of the Global Report series and to the Government of Japan, for funding a major case study on human seecurity and slum upgrading in Asia.

Special thanks are also due to the people at Earthscan Ltd, in particular Jonathan Sinclair Wilson, Managing Director; Hamish Ironside, Production Editor; Alison Kuznets, Editorial Assistant; and Andrea Service, who copy-edited the Report.

CONTENTS

PART II
URBAN CRIME AND VIOLENCE

PART III
SECURITY OF TENURE

PART IV
NATURAL AND HUMAN-MADE DISASTERS

PART V
TOWARDS SAFER AND MORE SECURE CITIES

PART VI
SUMMARY OF CASE STUDIES

PART VII
STATISTICAL ANNEX

LIST OF FIGURES, BOXES AND TABLES

FIGURES

BOXES

TABLES

LIST OF ACRONYMS AND ABBREVIATIONS

ACHR	Asian Coalition for Housing Rights
ADB	Asian Development Bank
ADPC	Asian Disaster Preparedness Centre
AGFE	Advisory Group on Forced Evictions
AIDS	acquired immuno-deficiency syndrome
ASEAN	Association of Southeast Asian Nations
AU$	Australian dollars
AUDMP	Asian Urban Disaster Mitigation Programme
CBO	community-based organization
CCTV	closed circuit television camera
Cdn$	Canadian dollar
CESCR	United Nations Committee on Economic, Social and Cultural Rights (the 'Committee')
COHRE	Centre on Housing Rights and Evictions
Committee, the	United Nations Committee on Economic, Social and Cultural Rights (unless explicitly stated otherwise)
Covenant, the	International Covenant on Economic, Social and Cultural Rights (unless explicitly stated otherwise)
CPI	Corruption Perceptions Index
CPTED	crime prevention through environmental design
CSI	Community Security Initiative (Jamaica)
CSJP	Citizens Security and Justice Programme (Jamaica)
CSP	Community Safety Plan (Canada)
DDMC	Dominican Disaster Mitigation Committee
DFID	Department for International Development (UK)
DHS	Department of Homeland Security (US)
DMP	Disaster Management Plan (Mumbai)
DoE	UK Department of the Environment
ECOSOC	Economic and Social Council of the United Nations
EIA	environmental impact assessment
EM-DAT, CRED	Emergency Events Database, Centre for Research on the Epidemiology of Disasters (University of Louvain, Belgium)
ERL	emergency recovery loan
EU	European Union
FAO	United Nations Food and Agriculture Organization
FEMA	Federal Emergency Management Administration (US)
FIA	Fédération Internationale de l'Automobile
FIG	International Federation of Surveyors
G8	Group of 8 industrialized nations: Canada, France, Germany, Italy, Japan, Russia, the UK and the US
GCB	Global Corruption Barometer
GDP	gross domestic product
GHI	GeoHazards International
GIS	geographic information systems
GNP	gross national product
GRSP	Global Road Safety Partnership
GTZ	Deutsche Gesellschaft für Technische Zusammenarbeit (German Development Agency)
HDI	Human Development Index
HLP (rights)	housing, land and property (rights)

ICESCR	International Covenant on Economic, Social and Cultural Rights (the 'Covenant')
ICVS	International Crime Victimization Survey
IDB	Inter-American Development Bank
IDP	internally displaced person
IFRC	International Federation of Red Cross and Red Crescent Societies
IIMG	Interagency Incident Management Group (US)
ILO	International Labour Organization
IMF	International Monetary Fund
INS	incident of national significance
Interpol	International Criminal Police Organization
IOM	International Organization for Migration
IPCC	Intergovernmental Panel on Climate Change
IPV	intimate partner violence
ISDR	United Nations International Strategy for Disaster Reduction
km	kilometre
km^2	square kilometre
KMA	Kingston Metropolitan Area (Jamaica)
LDSP	Lagos Drainage and Sanitation Project (Nigeria)
MADD	Mothers against Drunk Driving (US)
MANDISA	Monitoring, Mapping and Analysis of Disaster Incidents in South Africa
MDG	Millennium Development Goal
MEERP	Maharashtra Emergency Earthquake Rehabilitation Programme (India)
NDF	National Development Foundation (St Lucia)
NGO	non-governmental organization
NRP	National Response Plan
OAS	Organization of American States
OCHA	United Nations Office for the Coordination of Humanitarian Affairs
OCPI	Organized Crime Perception Index
OECD	Organisation for Economic Co-operation and Development
OHCHR	Office of the United Nations High Commissioner for Human Rights
OSCE	Organization for Security and Cooperation in Europe
PAHO	Pan-American Health Organization
P-GIS	participatory GIS
PIE	Prevention of Illegal Evictions from and Unlawful Occupation of Land Act (South Africa)
Pinheiro Principles	Principles on Housing and Property Restitution for Refugees and Displaced Persons
PRSP	Poverty Reduction Strategy Paper
RMC	risk management committee
SEEDS	Sustainable Environment and Ecological Development Society (India)
SERAC	Social and Economic Rights Action Center (Nigeria)
SEWA	Self-Employed Women's Association (India)
SKAA	Sindh Katchi Abadis Authority (Pakistan)
UK	United Kingdom of Great Britain and Northern Ireland
UN	United Nations
UNAIDS	Joint United Nations Programme on HIV/AIDS
UNCHS	United Nations Centre for Human Settlements (Habitat) (*now* UN-Habitat)
UNDP	United Nations Development Programme
UNESCO	United Nations Educational, Scientific and Cultural Organization
UN-Habitat	United Nations Human Settlements Programme (*formerly* UNCHS (Habitat))
UNHCR	United Nations High Commissioner for Refugees
UNHRP	United Nations Housing Rights Programme
UNICEF	United Nations Children's Fund
UNMIK	United Nations Interim Administration Mission in Kosovo
UNODC	United Nations Office on Drug and Crime
UNOPS	United Nations Office for Project Services
UNTFHS	United Nations Trust Fund for Human Security
US	United States of America
USAID	US Agency for International Development
WHO	World Health Organization

KEY FINDINGS AND MESSAGES

INTRODUCTION

The theme of 'urban safety and security' encompasses a wide range of concerns and issues. These range from basic needs such as food, shelter and health, through impacts of natural disasters, such as those triggered by earthquakes and cyclones, to collective security needs, such as protection from urban terrorism or war. However, only a few of these concerns and issues can be addressed from a human settlements perspective through appropriate urban policy, planning, design and governance. *Enhancing Urban Safety and Security: Global Report on Human Settlements 2007* focuses on three major threats to the safety and security of cities: crime and violence; insecurity of tenure and forced eviction; and natural and human-made disasters.

Combined, these three threats to the safety and security of urban residents currently pose a huge challenge to both city and national governments, as well as to the international community. The report analyses worldwide trends with respect to urban crime and violence, security of tenure and forced eviction, and natural and human-made disasters. It pays particular attention to the underlying causes and impacts of these three threats to the safety and security of urban residents, as well as to the good policies and practices that have been adopted at the city, national and international levels in response to these threats.

The report places urban safety and security within the wider perspective of human security, which specifically focuses on the security of people rather than states and encompasses a wide range of biological, social, economic and political needs. It shows how poverty exacerbates the impacts on cities of the three threats to urban safety and security addressed in the report by influencing the levels of *vulnerability* and *resilience* of urban-poor communities.

The report illustrates how the poor are disproportionately victimized by the three threats to safety and security that it examines. The urban poor are generally more exposed to risky events (such as crime, forced eviction or disasters) than the rich, partly because of their geographical location within the city. The urban poor are more vulnerable to the outcomes of natural and human-made hazards than the rich because they are often located on sites prone to floods, landslides and pollution. The urban poor also have limited access to assets, thus limiting their ability to respond to hazards or to manage risk – for example, through insurance. Because the poor are politically powerless, it is unlikely that they will receive the social services that they need during disasters.

The report shows that the unequal distribution of risk and vulnerability is an important and growing component of daily urban life. It is often linked to the presence of millions of urban residents in slums, which are environments in which much crime and violence occur, where tenure is least secure, and which are prone to disasters of many kinds. These slums, which are presently home to about 1 billion urban dwellers worldwide, represent one part of what has been termed 'the geography of misery'.

CRIME AND VIOLENCE

Key findings

Global trends indicate that crime rates have been on the increase. For instance, over the period of 1980 to 2000, total recorded crimes increased from 2300 to 3000 crimes for every 100,000 people. This trend is, however, not replicated in all regions of the world. In North America and Western Europe, total crime rates fell significantly over the two decades, whereas in Latin America and the Caribbean, Eastern Europe and Africa, total crime rates increased.

Regional variations in crime and violence are more pronounced when specific types of crime are examined. In the case of homicides, which are indicative of violent contact crimes, Africa and Latin America and the Caribbean report double-digit figures, while significantly lower rates are reported for Southeast Asia, Europe, the Eastern Mediterranean and the West Pacific region. At the national level, Colombia, South Africa, Jamaica, Guatemala and Venezuela have very high homicide rates, while Japan, Saudi Arabia, Qatar, Spain, Cyprus and Norway have considerably low rates.

Crime and violence are typically more severe in urban areas and are compounded by their rapid growth. A recent study has shown that 60 per cent of urban dwellers in developing and transitional countries have been victims of crime, over a five-year period, with victimization rates reaching 70 per cent in parts of LAC and Africa. In Latin America, where 80 per cent of the population is urban, the rapidly expanding metropolitan areas of Rio de Janeiro, São Paulo, Mexico City and Caracas account for over half of the violent crimes in their respective countries. The homicide rate in Rio de Janeiro has tripled since the 1970s, while the rate in São Paulo has quadrupled. In the Caribbean, Kingston, Jamaica's capital, consistently accounts for the vast majority of the nation's murders.

In Africa, cities such as Lagos, Johannesburg, Cape Town, Durban and Nairobi account for a sizeable proportion of their nation's crime. Urban areas in Africa also have the highest reported levels of burglary, with victimization rates of over 8 per cent of the population. Although a non-violent crime, burglary is a serious offence in developing regions such as Africa. Here, burglary tends to be partly motivated by poverty, even though material possessions are fewer.

Robbery also poses a major threat to urban areas in many developing countries. This is because it not only results in injury and property loss, but also increases the general fear of crime and feeling of insecurity. In South Africa, the police in 2000 recorded 460 robberies for every 100,000 people, with 30 per cent of residents in Johannesburg reporting to have been victims of robbery. Regionally, the victimization rates for robbery are much higher in Latin America and Africa than in other regions of the world.

The fear of crime and violence is pervasive in both developed and developing countries. Public opinion surveys in the US and the UK repeatedly show that people rank crime among the top concerns they have in everyday life. In Nairobi, more than half of the citizens worry about crime all the time or very often. Likewise, in Lagos, 70 per cent of respondents in a city-wide survey were fearful of being victims of crime, with 90 per cent being fearful of the prospects of being killed in a criminal attack.

In addition to the above, residents of cities in developing, transitional and developed countries have to contend with increasing levels of domestic violence, child abuse, proliferation of youth gangs, corruption and various forms of organized crime.

Cities are increasingly becoming targets of terrorist attacks. Notable examples include the attack on the World Trade Center in New York on 11 September 2001, the coordinated bombings of Madrid in March 2004, the London bombings of July 2005, and the bombing of commuter trains in Mumbai in July 2006. This Global Report notes that the incidence of terrorist attacks is significantly small in comparison to common crime and other types of violence. For example, the US National Counterterrorism Center reported 13 terrorist incidents in the US between February 2004 and May 2005 and, for approximately the same period, the Federal Bureau of Investigation (FBI) identified 10.32 million property crimes and over 1.36 million violent crimes. However, the impacts of terrorism on cities have been enormous. For example, the attack on New York left about 3500 people dead. It also resulted in the destruction or damage of about 2.8 million square metres of office space in Lower Manhattan and damaged the Port Authority Trans-Hudson train station at the World Trade Center.

A multiplicity of factors underlies the observed trends in crime and violence. These include social and cultural factors that might exacerbate or mediate crime. For instance, in cities such as Kabul, Karachi and Managua, violence is so interwoven into the fabric of daily life that it has become the norm for many slum dwellers. On the other hand, in Hong Kong and other parts of East and Southeast Asia, Confucianism-based family values and a generally compliant 'pro-social' population are major factors in keeping crime and violence low. Other factors associated with urban crime and violence include poverty; unemployment; inequality; intergenerational transmission of violence as reflected in the continuous witnessing of parental abuse during childhood; the rapid pace of urbanization; poor urban planning, design and management; growth in youthful population; and the concentration of political power, which facilitates corruption.

The impacts of crime and violence are multidimensional. Apart from injury and death, victims of crime and violence suffer long-lasting psychological trauma and continuously live with the fear of crime. At the national level, crime and violence are impediments to foreign investment, contribute to capital flight and brain drain, and hinder international tourism. In Jamaica, for instance, high levels of homicide have adversely affected tourism and contributed to brain drain. At the local level, crime and violence result in the stigmatization of neighbourhoods or even entire sections of the city. Such areas become 'no-go' zones and eventually lose out in terms of investment or provision of infrastructure and public services.

Key messages

Policies designed to reduce crime and violence fall into several broad categories. At the local level, these include effective urban planning, design and governance; community-based approaches, in which communities take ownership of the various initiatives; reduction of risk factors by focusing on groups that are likely to be perpetrators and victims of crime; and strengthening of social capital through initiatives that seek to develop the ability of individuals and communities to respond to problems of crime and violence. The combination of several of these approaches – all of which are specially suitable for implementation at the local level into a systematic programme, driven by a broad strategy and based upon a careful understanding of the local context – seems more likely to succeed than the *ad hoc* application of individual initiatives.

The preferred mechanism for supporting such a broad-based approach is usually the partnership mechanism. Local authorities can play an important role in organizing such partnerships, while central governments provide the resources, enabling environment and necessary policy framework. The best institutional structures for implementing such programmes are likely to be those that succeed in getting the key players involved in ways that commit them to the programme. Local authorities will often be the most appropriate leaders of such structures. Local communities need to be as fully involved as possible in these processes, not only in terms of consultation, but also as generators and implementers of such initiatives.

At the national level, there is a need to strengthen the formal criminal justice and policing systems. It is important that the police and the criminal justice systems are 'fit for purpose' in the modern world and are seen as key contributors to the fight against crime. A vital issue is the need for public confidence that the police and criminal justice systems will play their part in this process effectively, and where this is not the case, the problems that give rise to this lack of confidence need to be vigorously addressed. Key elements of such action will include the active participation of senior managers in police and criminal justice organizations, resources and political support, and a willingness to try new approaches where existing approaches are not working.

Programmes aimed at strengthening the police, particularly in developing countries, should also address their welfare and poor conditions of service. In many African countries, the police earn a pittance and often lack the necessary resources and equipment to perform their duties. In countries such as Botswana, Lesotho, Swaziland, South Africa and Kenya, members of the police force have not been spared from the HIV/AIDS pandemic. Furthermore, the living conditions in most of the existing police accommodation are appalling.

Prison reforms are one of the key policy areas through which central governments can contribute to tackling crime. By improving prison conditions and placing more emphasis on rehabilitation, the situation where prisons become finishing schools or 'universities' for criminals can be prevented. It is possible for re-offending, or recidivism, rates to be significantly reduced as a consequence of greater emphasis on rehabilitation. This will have a beneficial impact on crime because a high proportion is committed by previous offenders.

Support at the international level can help cities, particularly in developing and transitional countries, to improve their ability to implement measures effectively that address crime and violence. Such direct assistance should be part of a package that also includes continuing and strengthening international cooperation in tackling various types of organized crime, such as trafficking of drugs, arms and people – all of which have international dimensions. There are several examples of international support that have been of immense importance to particular cities. For example, assistance from the US has been a key factor in recent efforts at tackling crime and violence in Kingston (Jamaica). Likewise, Canada, The Netherlands and Sweden have contributed to Safer Cities projects in several African cities.

One particular type of international support that can be very helpful is in the field of training and staff development. There are already several examples of this practice. As part of its support for the reform of the Jamaica Constabulary Force since 2000, the UK government has been providing financial resources to support international police officers working alongside Jamaica's force in addressing crime. This has included Metropolitan Police officers working directly with their Jamaican counterparts, as well as training being offered by the Metropolitan Police to the Jamaica Constabulary Force.

SECURITY OF TENURE AND FORCED EVICTIONS

Key findings

More than 150 countries have ratified the International Covenant on Economic, Social and Cultural Rights (ICESCR). Governments in all of these countries are legally obliged to collect data and report on the scale and scope of tenure insecurity, forced evictions and homelessness (among other issues) in their countries. Despite this, there is a glaring lack of comprehensive and comparative data on security of tenure and forced evictions, both globally and within most countries.

In the absence of such data, perhaps the best indicator on the scale of urban tenure insecurity is the extent of informal settlements and other slums. Insecure tenure is, in fact, used as one of the indicators defining what constitutes a slum. Today, there are about 1 billion slum dwellers in the world. The vast majority of these, more than 930 million, are living in developing countries, where they constitute 42 per cent of the urban population. In the urban areas of the least developed countries, slum dwellers account for 78 per cent of the population. The proportion of slum dwellers is particularly high in sub-Saharan Africa (72 per cent of the urban population) and in Southern Asia (59 per cent).

The most visible outcome of tenure insecurity is the practice of forced evictions. Based on incidents reported to an international non-governmental organization (NGO) in a limited number of countries, at least 2 million people in the world are forcibly evicted every year. The actual figure is probably significantly higher. In addition, every year, several million people are threatened by forced evictions.

In Nigeria alone, an estimated 2 million people have been forcibly evicted from their homes since 2000. In Zimbabwe, an estimated 750,000 people were evicted in 2005 alone. In China, during the 2001 to 2008 period, it is estimated that 1.7 million people are directly affected by demolitions and relocations related to the Beijing Olympic Games. Evictions are not only found in developing countries, however. Each year, 25,000 evictions, on average, are carried out in New York City alone.

The main causes of large-scale forced evictions are public infrastructure development, international mega events (including global conferences and international sporting events, such as the Olympic Games) and urban beautification projects. Often, such evictions are undertaken with bulldozers, supported by heavy police presence, and the targets of such forced evictions are nearly always the residents of poor informal settlements or slums.

In addition to the millions of people subjected to forced evictions, perhaps an even higher number of people are subject to market-based evictions. This is a phenomenon directly linked to increased globalization and commercialization of land and housing. Through a process commonly known as gentrification, individuals, households or even whole neighbourhoods – most of them urban poor – are forced out of their homes, due primarily to their inability to pay higher rents.

Security of tenure is not necessarily related to specific tenure types. Tenure security is also related to a number of other cultural, social, political and economic factors and processes. A whole range of tenure types may thus offer security of tenure to urban dwellers. Even residents with title deeds living on freehold land may be evicted by the state in legitimate (and sometimes less legitimate) cases of expropriation or compulsory acquisition for the 'common good'.

As noted above, evictions are most prevalent in areas with the worst housing conditions. Furthermore, when evictions do occur, it is always the poor who are evicted. Furthermore, women, children, ethnic and other minorities, and other vulnerable and disadvantaged groups are most negatively affected by evictions. Invariably, evictions increase, rather than reduce, the problems they were aimed at 'solving'.

Just as particular groups are more exposed to tenure insecurity, particular events are also major factors affecting tenure security. Natural and human-made disasters, as well as armed conflict and civil strife, are major factors threatening the security of tenure of a large number of people every year. The groups most vulnerable to tenure insecurity in the aftermath of such events are, again, the poor, women, children, ethnic and other minorities, and other vulnerable and disadvantaged groups.

Lack of security of tenure is not only a problem in itself. It is part of a vicious cycle since it is often accompanied by poor or deteriorating dwellings and infrastructure, which, in turn, may lead to increased exposure to crime and violence, as well as to natural and human-made disasters.

Key messages

When evictions are being considered, it is essential that all alternatives to evictions are considered – in collaboration with the potential evictees themselves – before an eviction takes place. When evictions are unavoidable (e.g. in the case of non-payment of rent), such evictions should only be carried out in accordance with the law, and such evictions should never result in individuals being rendered homeless or vulnerable to the violation of other human rights. Under no circumstance should evictions be undertaken without acceptable relocation sites being identified in close cooperation with the evictees.

Interventions addressing the issue of security of tenure should always ensure that the requirements of all groups are adequately addressed. In essence, it is essential to prevent any detrimental discrimination with respect to housing, land and property. For example, land titles should be issued equally to both men and women. Similarly, slum upgrading programmes should consult with and consider the needs of both 'owners', tenants and sub-tenants.

When developing housing and urban policies, it is essential that governments adopt a framework based on housing, land and property rights, as elaborated in international law. Such a framework should take cognisance of the fact that there is a whole range of tenure types which may offer increased security of tenure to the urban poor. In some cases, perceived security of tenure may even be improved simply through the provision of basic services and infrastructure. Perhaps the most important component of improving the security of tenure in informal settlements and slums is that governments at all levels should accept the residents of such settlements as equal citizens, with the same rights and responsibilities as other urban dwellers.

It is essential that states fulfil their obligations under international law with respect to the collection and dissemination of information regarding the scale and scope of tenure insecurity, forced evictions and homelessness. Without the timely collection of such data, it is, in effect, impossible for governments to verify whether they are contributing effectively to the progressive realization of the right to adequate housing according to their obligations as defined in the ICESCR.

Under international law, forced evictions are regarded as *prima facie* violations of human rights. Despite this, the vast majority of forced evictions carried out in the world are in breach of international law. A global moratorium on forced evictions could be an effective first step towards addressing this recurrent violation of human rights.

Application of international criminal law to violations of housing, land and property rights is also necessary. If such rights are to be taken seriously, there should be strong legal grounds on which to discourage the impunity almost invariably enjoyed by violators of these rights. All of those who advocate ethnic cleansing, those who sanction violent and illegal forced evictions, those who call for laws and policies that clearly result in homelessness, or those who fail to end systematic discrimination against women in the land and housing sphere – and all of those promoting such violations – should be held accountable.

NATURAL AND HUMAN-MADE DISASTERS

Key findings

Between 1974 and 2003, 6367 natural disasters occurred globally, causing the death of 2 million people and affecting 5.1 billion people. A total of 182 million people were made homeless, while reported economic damage amounted to US$1.38 trillion. Since 1975, the number of natural disasters recorded globally has increased dramatically (fourfold), especially in Africa. An even higher tenfold increase in the incidence of human-made disasters has been observed between 1976 and 2000. Between 2000 and 2005, average mortality from human-made disasters was lower (30 per event) than deaths caused by natural disasters (225 per event). A total of 98 per cent of the 211 million people affected by natural disasters annually from 1991 to 2000 were in developing countries.

The catastrophic impact of disasters on individuals has been illustrated in recent years by the toll of death (220,000 people) and homelessness (1.5 million) from the Indian Ocean Tsunami of December 2004 and the Pakistan earthquake of October 2005, which killed 86,000 people and left millions homeless. Moreover, losses during disaster and reconstruction deepen existing socio-economic inequalities, thus creating vicious cycles of loss and vulnerability. Especially in poorer countries, women and children tend to be most affected by disasters, as observed in the aftermath of the 2005 Indian Ocean Tsunami. The elderly and those with disabilities are often among the most vulnerable to natural and human-made hazards.

Economic losses associated with disasters have increased fourteen-fold since the 1950s and, during the last decade alone, disasters caused damage worth US$67 billion per year, on average. Wealthier countries incur higher economic costs due to disasters, while poorer countries face greater loss of human life. By destroying critical urban infrastructure, disasters can set back development gains and undermine progress in meeting the Millennium Development Goals (MDGs). Cities connected to regional or global financial systems have the potential to spread the negative consequences of disaster across the global economy, with huge systemic loss effects.

Large and megacities magnify risk since they concentrate human, physical and financial capital and are frequently also cultural and political centres. The potential for feedback between natural and human-made hazards in large cities presents a scenario for disaster on an unprecedented scale. Large urban economies that have sizeable foreign currency reserves, high proportions of insured assets, comprehensive social services and diversified production are more likely to absorb and spread the economic burden of disaster impacts. Smaller cities (less than 500,000 residents) that are home to over half of the world's urban population are also exposed to multiple risks, but often have less resilience against the economic consequences of disasters.

There has been a 50 per cent rise in extreme weather events associated with climate change from the 1950s to the 1990s, and the location of major urban centres in coastal areas exposed to hydro-meteorological hazards is a significant risk factor: 21 of the 33 cities which are projected to have a population of 8 million or more by 2015 are located in vulnerable coastal zones and are increasingly vulnerable to sea-level rise. Around 40 per cent of the world's population lives less than 100 kilometres from the coast within reach of severe coastal storms. In effect, close to 100 million people around the world live less than 1 metre above sea level. Thus, if sea levels rise by just 1 metre, many coastal megacities with populations of more than 10 million, such as Rio de Janeiro, New York, Mumbai, Dhaka, Tokyo, Lagos and Cairo, will be under threat.

Additional factors rendering cities particularly vulnerable include rapid and chaotic urbanization; the concentration of economic wealth in cities; environmental modifications through human actions; the expansion of slums (often into hazardous locations); and the failure of urban authorities to enforce building codes and land-use planning. The urban landscape, which is characterized by close proximity of residential, commercial and industrial land uses, generates new cocktails of hazard that require multi-risk management. The rapid supply of housing to meet rising demand without compliance with safe building codes is a principal cause of disaster loss in urban areas. Lack of resources and human skills – compounded by institutional cultures that allow corruption – distort regulation and enforcement of building codes.

Small-scale hazards, while less dramatic than major hazards, have serious aggregate impacts. This is illustrated by the incidence and impacts of road traffic accidents, which result in more deaths worldwide each year than any large natural or human-made disaster type. Traffic accidents cause extensive loss of human lives and livelihoods in urban areas, killing over 1 million people globally every year. At least 90 per cent of the deaths from traffic accidents occur in low- and middle-income countries. Young males and unprotected road users are particularly vulnerable to injury or death from traffic accidents. Traffic accidents cause substantial economic costs, amounting to an estimated US$518 billion worldwide every year. If no action is taken, traffic injuries are expected to become the third major cause of disease and injury in the world by 2020.

Key messages

Land-use planning is a particularly effective instrument that city authorities can employ to reduce disaster risk by regulating the expansion of human settlements and infrastructure. Evidence-based land-use planning at the city level requires accurate and up-to-date data. Technological innovation can help to fill part of this gap; but the global proliferation of slums also calls for more innovative and participatory land-use planning procedures.

The design of disaster-resistant buildings and infrastructure can save many lives and assets in urban areas from natural and human-made disasters. The technological and engineering expertise to achieve this is available; but implementation is a major challenge. Interdisciplinary and inter-sectoral training, research and partnerships, especially with the private sector, can enhance implementation capacity at the city level. Interaction between different practitioners is essential to avoid professional separation and to foster the integration of risk reduction within urban development and planning efforts. Governance systems that facilitate local participation and decentralized leadership are more effective, especially in the context of rapid and uncontrolled urbanization where capacities for oversight and enforcement are limited.

Governments need to improve risk, hazard and vulnerability assessment and monitoring capacity through increased investment, with support from the international community, where necessary. In addition to informing policy formulation, assessment data should feed into national initiatives that aim to build a culture of awareness and safety through public education and information programmes. Furthermore, risk knowledge should be communicated to relevant actors through effective early warning systems in order to enable timely and adequate responses to disasters.

It is especially important that disaster risk reduction is mainstreamed within national development and poverty reduction policies and planning. Examples of disaster risk reduction strategies that have been designed purposely to contribute to meeting individual MDG targets are available worldwide. National initiatives should move from managing risk through emergency relief and response towards a more proactive pre-disaster orientation.

Greater partnership between humanitarian and development actors is required during reconstruction in order to reconcile demands for rapid provision of basic services against the more time-consuming aim of 'building back better'. Clear legislative and budgetary frameworks should also be in place to avoid uncoordinated and fragmented reconstruction activities by city governments, local actors, donors and humanitarian agencies.

Drawing on existing international frameworks for disaster risk reduction (e.g. the Hyogo Framework for Action, 2005–2015), national governments should continue putting in place disaster risk reduction legislation and policy; strengthening early warning systems; incorporating disaster risk education within national education curricula; and instituting inclusive and participatory governance and planning in order to strengthen the resilience of cities and communities.

International frameworks are important in focusing the attention of multilateral and bilateral donors, as well as international civil society actors, towards disaster risk reduction. They can also facilitate advocacy and guide the development of disaster risk reduction strategies at national and city levels, including through internationally coordinated early warning systems for hazards such as cyclones and tsunamis.

Furthermore, many governments – especially in developing countries – require assistance from the international community in the form of finance, data and information, and technical expertise to establish or improve their disaster risk reduction systems. International assistance for disaster risk reduction should not focus on recovery and reconstruction efforts alone, but also on longer-term development objectives.

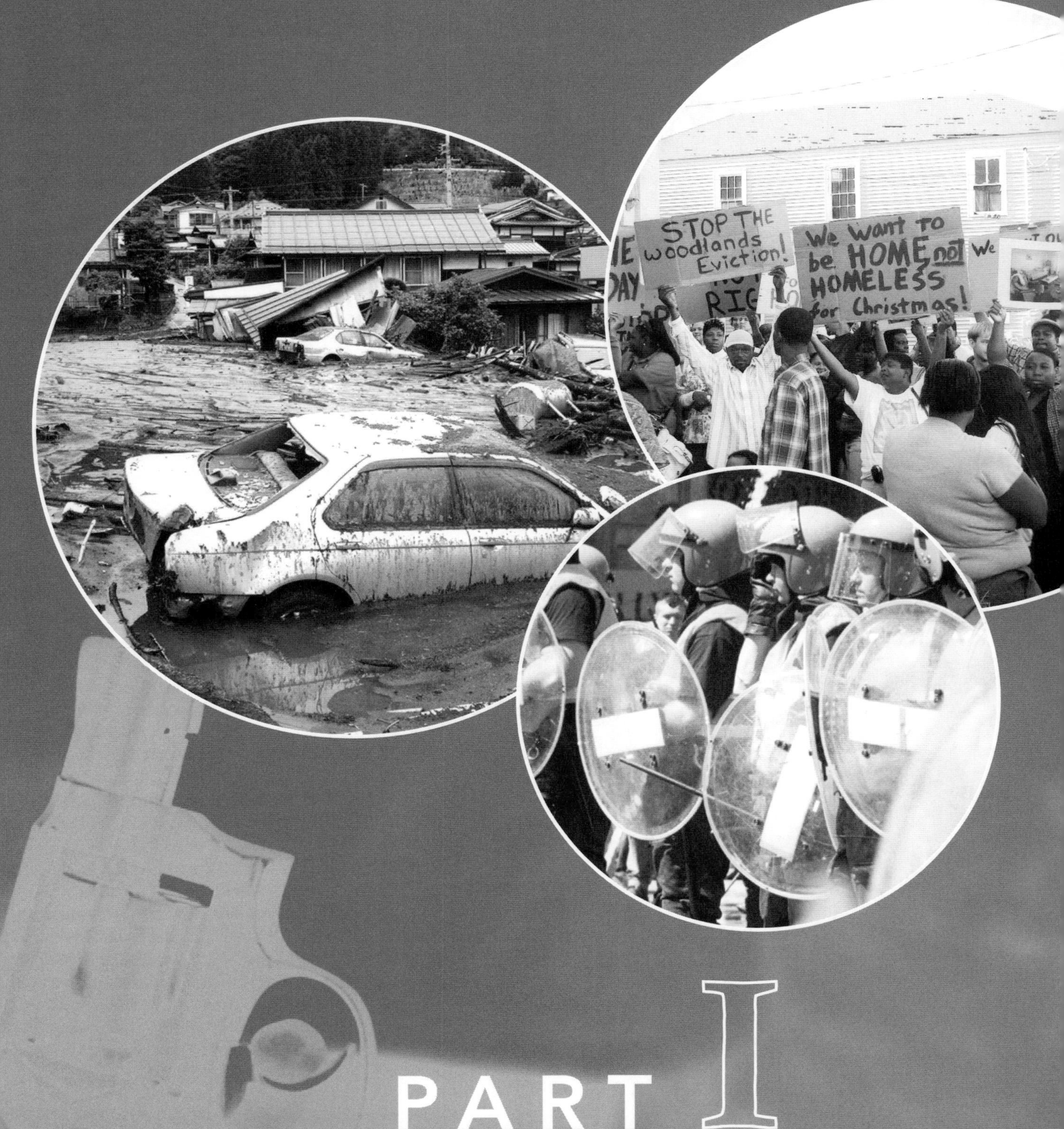

PART I
UNDERSTANDING URBAN SAFETY AND SECURITY

This Global Report on Human Settlements examines some of today's major threats to urban safety and security within the broader frame of rapid urban growth, uneven socio-economic development and the quest for human security.[1] It seeks to review the growing concern about the safety and security of people, rather than states, linking this to the risks and opportunities that accompany increasing social and economic complexity, which is itself a result of growth and development.

In the last decade or so, the world has witnessed increasing numbers of threats to urban safety and security. While some of these threats have taken the form of dramatic events, many have been manifestations of the nexus of urban poverty and inequality with the physical, economic, social and institutional conditions of slums. Urban crime and violence in countries in all regions, regardless of level of development, have led to increasing debate about how to address its origins and impacts. Gang violence in Brazil, Guatemala, Honduras, South Africa and Kenya has affected many people. Dramatic violence in Paris and throughout urban France has demonstrated that such violence could also occur in cities in high-income countries with large disparities in income and opportunity. Many households have faced the threat of insecure tenure and the likelihood of forced evictions. These problems have been evident in cities in Nigeria, Turkey and Zimbabwe, with the case of Harare receiving the most global attention during the last three years. There have also been dramatic impacts of so-called natural disasters, with significant global attention being focused on the Indian Ocean Tsunami affecting Indonesia, Sri Lanka, Thailand and India; monsoon flooding in Mumbai; Hurricane Katrina in New Orleans, US; and earthquakes in Pakistan and Java, Indonesia.

While these 'events' receive media coverage, they are, in fact, symptomatic of deeper and more pervasive processes that affect these cities. While crime and violence are, perhaps, the most obvious of these processes, insecurity of tenure and disasters are also the results of deeper processes and institutional failure. This report seeks to describe these phenomena, to provide a framework for analysis of their causes and impacts, and to suggest a set of recommendations for policy and action that can help to reduce urban insecurity and increase safety.

Growing numbers of urban residents living at increasing densities in horizontal and vertical space necessarily increase opportunities for productive employment and social interaction; but in some situations, particularly in slums, they also increase vulnerability to the harmful consequences of development. In rapidly growing cities, more people need food, housing, water supply, sanitation and employment to generate incomes to buy basic services. This demand, in turn, generates many opportunities for productive, as well as criminal, responses to ever more stimulating and demanding social environments. With opportunities, however, come risks. The social imperative for urban residents to adjust to urban life brings many forms of disequilibria, shortages and, necessarily, differences between the abilities of individuals and households to satisfy their needs and ambitions. Inequalities in opportunities lead to differences in outcomes, perspectives and willingness to live within rules that may appear (particularly for growing numbers of the urban poor) manifestly unjust.

This process of urban social and economic differentiation interacts closely with the physical location and ecological features of cities: their geography, landscape, natural environment and access to specific natural resources, particularly water. Cities historically developed near sources of water supply and water for transport or energy, such as Manchester and Chicago, or on coasts with harbours and colonial *entrepots*.[2] Cities sit on an ecological edge, between solid ground and watersheds. Over time, these historical origins also brought risks such as periodic flooding. Now, there is growing global public awareness that nature itself is no longer inherently stable, but is, rather, at any one time, an outcome of dynamic forces such as climate change or other human-induced pollution or disruption. The physical sites of cities, whether Mumbai or New Orleans, are recognized as dynamic landscapes that can no longer be assumed as benign or as given. The individual circumstances of particular cities fit into a global pattern where 70 per cent of the world's population lives within 80 kilometres of the coast. Land and ocean are thus brought closer together, increasing human vulnerability to the environmental hazards associated with rising sea level.

Within this broader ecological context, cities have always been spaces where many individuals and households have been successful in generating incomes and opportunities for themselves and their families. The differentials between urban and rural incomes explain most of rural to urban migration over the past 50 years. Not surprisingly, successful individuals and households tend to protect their interests in maintaining these prerogatives in the face of the many who have not. History has shown that private interests have public consequences, largely expressed through politics and the resulting public policies and the behaviours of public institutions. If the purpose of government is to provide a set of rules within which individual liberty and private interests can be balanced with the social objectives of enhancing public welfare and equity, it is apparent that the institutional performance of government has frequently been disappointing. What were previously described as growing urban inequalities and differences have now become intergenerational forms of exclusion.

While it is not surprising that urban policies reflect interests, the degree of difference in welfare and opportunities within cities at this time is a matter of growing concern, even at the macro-economic level. Fifty years of efforts by countries and the international community to improve human welfare since the beginning of the United Nations Development Decade of the 1960s have resulted in major improvements in longevity, infant mortality, literacy and income levels in most countries. However, the growing urbanization of poverty, particularly in developing countries, has created a paradox where cities are both the engines of growth in national economies, but also significant loci of poverty and deprivation. If the worst levels of absolute poverty have been somewhat alleviated in some regions, there has been growing evidence of relative poverty or inequality in most countries, particularly in cities. Inequality has become increasingly recognized as an important inhibiting factor to economic growth.[3] It is a significant underlying factor in understanding the mechanisms and processes generating urban insecurity in cities such as São Paulo, Nairobi or Paris. At a more general level, poverty is perhaps the most notable factor in explaining the levels of vulnerability to the urban safety and security threats examined in this Global Report.

The level of urban inequality is not solely the responsibility of national or local governments, but rather is also a result of the interaction of global economic forces and national economies. The mobility of capital, labour and technology has resulted in massive deindustrialization in some countries and the relocation of employment opportunities to other countries where labour costs are lower or factors affecting profitability are more favourable. Debates continue about the costs and benefits of 'free trade', and whether rich countries actually followed the free trade policies they now espouse.[4] But the fact remains that many businesses have voted with their feet, with some relocating, for example, from cities in the US to maquiladoras in northern Mexico, and then later leaving for China in pursuit of lower labour costs and less costly environmental regulations. These global shifts have generated additional uncertainty and insecurity in the lives of many urban income earners. Reduced opportunities for formal employment have also resulted in higher degrees of informality in economies and less application of rules and regulations.

The nature of economic growth itself has therefore changed. Countries which initiated their economic and social transformations during the 1960s on the basis of agriculture and the export of primary commodities have been subject to sharp fluctuations in global commodity prices. The volatility of global markets and, particularly, energy prices has direct impacts on the costs of inputs, prices and market share of local enterprises. Producers of textiles and machinery in many countries have closed down in the face of the higher productivity and lower costs of their Chinese competitors.

There has also been a shift in the definition of wealth during the last 50 years, away from commodities towards information, knowledge, technology and finance. This is a global phenomenon with local consequences. In the midst of the Argentine economic collapse of 2001 to 2002, a Swedish newspaper noted that Argentina had held on to a 19th-century definition of wealth, focused on agricultural commodities and livestock, and had not adjusted to the global economic dynamics of the 21st century.[5] Entering the global markets and building capacity in knowledge-intensive industries is not a short-term venture. It is further complicated by the fact that each of these factors of production is also not evenly distributed across the world; in fact, each is marked by a high degree of centralization and localization in specific countries and cities. Indeed, these patterns of centralization of finance, technology and information are congruent and self-reinforcing. Patterns of income and wealth, therefore, in the 21st century have accentuated the economic vulnerability of developing countries and their populations.

One important consequence of these global forces has been the relative weakening of national and local institutional capacities through the changing distribution of power and authority of public institutions. This has occurred partly through privatization of public services such as water supply, transport, electricity, prison management and many others. In many countries, this has taken place within an overall shrinking of the public sector, mainly on fiscal and institutional grounds. At a time when urban populations are growing and uncertainties have increased, the capacities of these governments to solve specific problems, ensure the security of their populations and control their jurisdictions is considerably less than in previous times in some countries. This reduced capacity of the public sector also contributes significantly to a sense of urban insecurity. It is remarkable that as the process of urbanization continues to grow in scale and importance, the world recognizes few cities in either rich or poor countries as truly replicable examples of 'good practice'.

Within this global and macro-context, this report examines three specific threats to urban safety and security that have become increasingly serious during recent years: crime and violence, insecurity of tenure and evictions, and natural and human-made disasters. While these three phenomena do not account for all of the problems of security and safety facing urban populations, they represent an important share of the public concerns that have been addressed by researchers and practitioners in the human settlements field. When considered within the context introduced above, these threats should not be regarded as 'events', but rather as 'processes' that are tied to underlying social and economic conditions within cities and countries. This rooting in local socio-economic realities is helpful in both understanding them and also finding measures that can help to alleviate their worst consequences.

Threats to urban safety and security are also popularly understood by 'conventional wisdom' in ways that do not readily lead to solutions or assignment of responsibility for them. Upon greater examination, however, these forms of conventional wisdom do not stand up as accurate descriptions of the problems at hand. Natural and human-made disasters are frequently regarded as unpredictable, yet, closer analysis demonstrates that their probabilities are within reasonably tight bounds in time and place – for example, monsoons and hurricanes occur within certain months in specific regions of the world. As such, they are amenable to policy and technical responses that can alleviate their impacts. An analogous approach applies to crime and violence, which tends to occur in specific sites, either directed at persons or property, with a set of motivations that are predictable within individual urban cultures (i.e. to steal property to buy drugs in some cities or to define gang territories in others). Crime and violence are not random; as such, they can be studied in order to address underlying causal factors, as well as through direct measures to confront them. For example, some cities are already known as safe, while others seem to have cultivated 'cultures of fear', frequently with a major role played by the local media. Yet other cities have become 'safer' over the years from crime and violence. It is possible to examine why and how and to use this knowledge to design measures to reduce insecurity. The problem of squatting and evictions is similarly predictable. Indeed, evidence from cities in all countries demonstrates similar behaviour patterns by squatters seeking to reduce the insecurity of their lives, as well as by public-sector authorities seeking to impose order over a rapid and apparently chaotic urbanization process.

This Global Report, therefore, examines these forms of 'conventional wisdom' in some detail to illustrate that the challenges of reducing urban insecurity are not solely 'technical', but rather have much to do with perceptions and popular understanding, as well. In this regard, the report explores the mapping of risk, its predictability and the types of vulnerability that may result. It discusses alternative pathways to resilience: how combinations of institutional behaviour, international legal frameworks such as human rights law, and active recognition of the role of civil society and local cultures can play important functions in anticipating risk and mitigating its negative consequences. By providing a strong description and analysis of these threats to urban safety and security, along with specific recommendations for policy and institutions, the report is intended to contribute to global public awareness of these important issues.

Part I of the report introduces the issues to be discussed and it is divided into two chapters. Chapter 1 frames the problem of urban safety and insecurity within the overall context of human security, and highlights the main problems posed by crime and violence, tenure insecurity and evictions, as well as disasters triggered by natural and human-made hazards. Chapter 2 provides a conceptual analytical framework for the report, which is based on the related ideas of vulnerability and resilience. The ways in which vulnerability and resilience – at the international, national, local, community and household levels – influence urban safety and security are also highlighted.

NOTES

1. Commission on Human Security, 2003.
2. See Harold Platt, 2005.
3. World Bank, 2005.
4. Ha Joon Chang, 2003.
5. *Dagens Nyheter*, 2002.

CHAPTER 1

CURRENT THREATS TO URBAN SAFETY AND SECURITY

The theme of 'urban safety and security' encompasses a wide range of concerns and issues. These range from basic needs, such as food, health and shelter, through protection from crime and the impacts of technological and natural hazards, to collective security needs, such as protection from urban terrorism. However, only a few of these concerns and issues have been, and can be, addressed from a human settlements perspective, mainly through appropriate urban policies, planning, design and governance. For this reason, this Global Report focuses on only three major threats to the safety and security of cities: crime and violence, insecurity of tenure and forced eviction, as well as natural and human-made disasters, including low-level chronic hazards such as road traffic accidents.

These threats either stem from, or are often exacerbated by, the process of urban growth and from the interaction of social, economic and institutional behaviours within cities, as well as with natural environmental processes. They also have impacts which, in turn, affect each other and generate feedbacks that determine subsequent responses to all of them. Each should be understood as an outcome of multiple factors and patterns of causation. Taking a systemic approach to the vulnerability of cities allows one to understand how these dynamics really work.[1] In each case, three issues affect the ability to generate useful policy conclusions and practical approaches to these threats: perception, evidence and methodology.

This chapter introduces the three threats to urban safety and security addressed in this report. It starts by explaining the perspective of urban safety and security taken in the report. It then describes how the current urban context influences the geography of risk and vulnerability. This is followed by a discussion of the main issues characterizing the three threats of urban crime and violence, tenure insecurity and forced eviction, and natural and human-made hazards. Finally, the role of perception, evidence and methodology in improving the understanding of these threats to urban safety and security is examined.

URBAN SAFETY AND SECURITY: A HUMAN SECURITY PERSPECTIVE

The focus of this Global Report on urban safety and security should be placed within the wider concern for human security, which has been recognized by the international community.[2] This concern is specifically focused on the security of people, not states. It was addressed in detail by the United Nations Commission on Human Security, co-chaired by former United Nations High Commissioner for Refugees (UNHCR) Sadako Ogata and Nobel Laureate and economist Amartya Sen. This commission issued its report in 2003 and addressed a wide range of dimensions of human security, including:

> *... conflict and poverty, protecting people during violent conflict and post-conflict situations, defending people who are forced to move, overcoming economic insecurities, guaranteeing the availability and affordability of essential health care, and ensuring the elimination of illiteracy and educational deprivation and of schools that promote intolerance.*[3]

This obviously broad coverage includes several important distinguishing features that are relevant to urban safety and security:

- Human security is focused on people and not states because the historical assumption that states would monopolize the rights and means to protect its citizens has been outdated by the more complex reality that states often fail to fulfil their obligations to provide security.
- The focus on people also places more emphasis on the role of the human rights of individuals in meeting these diverse security needs. There is thus a shift from the rights of states to the rights of individuals.
- Recognizing and enhancing the rights of individuals is a critical part of expanding the roles and responsibilities for security beyond simply the state itself.

The focus of this Global Report on urban safety and security should be placed within the wider concern for human security

- It recognizes that people-centred solutions must be identified and supported to address the range of menaces and risks that they encounter.
- Human security, therefore, goes beyond the security of borders to the lives of people and communities inside and across those borders.[4]

With these concerns in mind, the commission adopted the following somewhat more formal definition of human security:

> *... to protect the vital core of all human lives in ways that enhance human freedoms and human fulfilment. Human security means protecting fundamental freedoms – freedoms that are the essence of life. It means protecting people from critical (severe) and pervasive (widespread) threats and situations. It means using processes that build on people's strengths and aspirations. It means creating political, social, environmental, economic, military, and cultural systems that together give people the building blocks of survival, livelihood and dignity.*[5]

This definition combines descriptive, analytic and normative dimensions in asserting what is 'the vital core', what are 'fundamental freedoms' and what is 'the essence of life'. As a broad and fundamental statement, the concept of human security provides a strong foundation for the conceptual basis of this report.

The human security approach builds upon earlier discussions by the United Nations of basic needs, as discussed in the Copenhagen Declaration

The human security approach builds upon earlier discussions by the United Nations of basic needs, as discussed in the Copenhagen Declaration, adopted at the 2005 World Summit on Social Development, which noted that:

> *... efforts should include the elimination of hunger and malnutrition; the provision of food security, education, employment and livelihood, primary health-care services, including reproductive health care, safe drinking water and sanitation, and adequate shelter; and participation in social and cultural life* (Commitment 2.b).

Another international legal framework is the International Covenant on Economic, Social and Cultural Rights (ICESCR), which states the need to:

> *... recognize the right of everyone to an adequate standard of living for himself and his family, including adequate food, clothing and housing, and to the continuous improvement of living conditions* (Article 11.2).

In the last part of ICESCR, Article 11.2 deals with the progressive realization of these rights, and states that governments are legally obliged, under international law, to take steps to improve living conditions.

Building on these prior statements (and when applied to the world of action and when focused on the security of persons and not states), the human security approach specifically addresses three issues:

- protection of individual security through adherence to declared and legitimate rights, such as those on security of tenure introduced in this chapter and examined in greater detail in Chapter 5;
- freedom of individuals to invoke specific rights in their pursuit of the components of human security, as elaborated above, such as secure tenure or freedom from arbitrary arrest or detention, as elaborated upon in the International Bill of Human Rights;
- freedom of individuals to organize in groups to obtain satisfaction with regard to those components of human security.

While the first of these – protection of individual human security based on international human rights laws – represents a major improvement in the juridical and legal environment at the international level, there remain many difficulties of interpretation and jurisdiction at national and urban levels in using these internationally recognized rights as sufficient protection for individual claims. For example, the great majority of laws governing the administration of justice in cases of daily crime and violence at the national and urban levels depend, first, upon the establishment of law by states or local authorities, as in the cases of local policing or penalties for breaking the law, and then upon their enforcement, which frequently relies upon the jurisdiction in which they are being applied.

The second feature of this framework – that individuals actually have the freedom and capabilities to invoke their rights – depends upon many things, including the political and institutional environments in which they live, but also their wider economic and social contexts. This perspective is derived from the framework developed by Amartya Sen, who emphasizes the importance of ensuring the capabilities and freedoms of people to obtain what they need and to satisfy their material requirements.[6]

The third dimension of the framework – that individuals can organize collectively to obtain their rights and thereby reduce the insecurities that they face – is well exemplified by the 2001 Fukuoka Declaration, which focuses on securing land tenure.[7] The Fukuoka Declaration – adopted by human settlements experts at an international seminar on 'Securing Land for the Urban Poor' – places secure tenure within the broader framework of alleviating poverty and assisting people in the informal sector. It presents a full list of actions that should be taken by governments to ensure that security of tenure is more available to growing urban populations. The declaration, examined in Chapter 11 of this Global Report, is noteworthy because it also seems to assert that security of tenure is both an individual right and a public good worthy of collective public action. It therefore explicitly calls on governments to undertake specific actions to protect both individual rights and the wider public interest while achieving these positive results.

In this context, Box 1.1 illustrates how the human security framework is guiding the implementation of three programmes on slum upgrading in Afghanistan, Cambodia and Sri Lanka.

Considering human security as a public good is useful in providing a common perspective for asserting the need for governments to take responsibility for the three dimensions of urban safety and security addressed by this report: crime and violence, security of tenure, and disasters. While each has specific impacts on individuals and households, they also have a wider set of consequences – what economists call 'externalities' – for society and the economy as a whole, whether at the national or urban levels.

From the perspective of human security, it is clear that threats to urban safety and security are associated with different types of human vulnerability. These can be divided into three broad categories: chronic vulnerabilities, which arise from basic needs, including food, shelter and health; contextual vulnerabilities, arising from the socio-economic and political processes and contexts of human life; and vulnerabilities arising from extreme events, such as natural and human-made hazards. The concept of vulnerability, which is central to the analytical framework of this report, is discussed in Chapter 2.

As mentioned at the beginning of this chapter, of the many threats to urban safety and security, and the associated vulnerabilities, this report addresses only those that can, and have been, tackled from a human settlements perspective (i.e. through urban policy, planning, design and governance). However, this does not mean that the vulnerabilities not discussed in this report are not important. In fact, some of them, especially those chronic and contextual vulnerabilities that collectively influence poverty, are also fundamental determinants of vulnerability and resilience with respect to crime and violence, insecurity of tenure and eviction, as well as to natural and human-made hazards.

Box 1.1 Enhancing urban safety and human security in Asia through the United Nations Trust Fund for Human Security

In March 1999, the Government of Japan and the United Nations Secretariat launched the United Nations Trust Fund for Human Security (UNTFHS), from which the Commission on Human Security prepared the Human Security Now report in 2003, as a contribution to the UN Secretary-General's plea for progress on the goals of 'freedom from want' and 'freedom from fear'. The main objective of the UNTFHS is to advance the operational impact of the human security concept, particularly in countries and regions where the insecurities of people are most manifest and critical, such as in areas affected by natural and human-made disasters.

Growing inequalities between the rich and the poor, as well as social, economic and political exclusion of large sectors of society, make the security paradigm increasingly complex. Human security has broadened to include such conditions as freedom from poverty, access to work, education and health. This, in turn, has necessitated a change in perspective, from state-centred security to people-centred security. To ensure human security as well as state security, particularly in conflict and post-conflict areas where institutions are often fragile and unstable, rebuilding communities becomes an absolute priority to promote peace and reconciliation.

With the rapid urbanization of the world's population, human security as protecting 'the vital core of all human lives in ways that enhance human freedoms and human fulfilment' increasingly means providing the conditions of livelihood and dignity in urban areas. Living conditions are crucial for human security, since an inadequate dwelling, insecurity of tenure and insufficient access to basic services all have a strong negative impact on the lives of the urban population, particularly the urban poor. Spatial discrimination and social exclusion limit or undermine the rights to the city and to citizenship.

In this context, UN-Habitat is coordinating three UNTFHS programmes in Afghanistan, North east Sri Lanka and Phnom Penh, the capital city of Cambodia, all focusing on informal settlements upgrading. On the assumption that community empowerment is crucial for the reconstruction of war affected societies, all programmes have adopted the 'community action planning' method – a community-based consultative planning process – and have established community development councils as the most effective approach to improving living conditions and human security in informal settlements.

Source: Balbo and Guadagnoli, 2007

THE URBAN CONTEXT: GEOGRAPHY OF RISK AND VULNERABILITY

As shown in recent United Nations projections, the world is going through a significant urban transformation (see Table 1.1). The world's population will soon be more than half urban, with projected urban growth in developing countries in the order of 1.2 billion people between 2000 and 2020. This growth increases the pressure on urban residents to earn incomes, and to secure adequate shelter, basic infrastructure and essential social services, such as healthcare and education. Existing backlogs of services – as reflected in the 1 billion people already living in slums – are strong indicators of the weaknesses of both public and private institutions to provide such services (see Table 5.2).[8] These conditions have been well documented in most countries. With more than 2 billion people lacking access to clean water and more lacking sanitation as well, it is clear that the very meaning of 'security' itself needs examination.[9] While cities and towns offer the hope of greater employment, higher wages, and a remedy to poverty,[10] they also bring enormous challenges to human security and safety.

These challenges must be placed within a context of both opportunity and risk. Data from all countries shows that as the share of urban population increases, so does gross domestic product (GDP) and per capita income. These increases reflect increasing productivity and agglomeration economies that make urban-based economic activities highly productive. They now generate more than half of GDP in all countries, with the more urbanized countries in Europe, North America and Asia accounting for up to 80 per cent of their GDP from urban-based activities. The medieval saying that 'city air makes men free' can be complemented with the observation that urban life offers the prospect of greater economic welfare as well.

Table 1.1

Contemporary world urban transformation

	2000 (millions)	2010 (millions)	2020 (millions)	2000 (per cent)	2010 (per cent)	2020 (per cent)
Total world population	6086	6843	7578	100.0	100.0	100.0
Developing countries	4892	5617	6333	80.4 [a]	82.1 [a]	83.6 [a]
Total world urban population	2845	3475	4177	46.7 [a]	50.8 [a]	55.1 [a]
Developing countries	1971	2553	3209	40.3 [b]	45.5 [b]	50.7 [b]
				69.3 [c]	73.5 [c]	76.8 [c]

a: Percentage of total world population; b: Percentage of total population in developing countries; c: Percentage of total world urban population.

Source: United Nations, 2005; UN-Habitat 2006e

This observation, however, must be tempered by the reality of growing numbers of urban residents living in poverty, lacking basic infrastructure and services, housing and employment, and living in conditions lacking safety and security. As Chapters 3, 5 and 7 of this Global Report will illustrate in detail, the poor are disproportionately victimized by the three threats to safety and security examined in this volume: crime and violence, insecurity of tenure, and natural and human-made disasters. This unequal distribution of risk and vulnerability is a major burden for the poor as a whole. It also has a disproportionate impact on groups least able to defend themselves: women, children, the elderly and the disabled.

The poor are disproportionately victimized by the three threats to safety and security examined in this volume

This distribution of risk and vulnerability is an important and growing component of daily urban life. It is often linked to the presence of millions of urban residents in slums, which are environments in which much crime and violence occur, where tenure is least secure, and which are prone to disasters of many kinds. The safety of men, women and children is at risk every day from crime and traffic accidents, violent crime, threats to security of tenure, and natural and human-made hazards. As discussed in Chapter 7, this spatial dimension is reflected in the term 'geography of disaster risk' for which there is extensive data showing what kinds of disasters are occurring in cities in specific regions of the world, as presented in Chapter 7.

Slums are ... the locus of the greatest deprivation in material welfare in societies ... and also lack the institutional and legal framework to guarantee their safety and security

A particularly noteworthy type of challenge to urban safety is the widespread and growing incidence of traffic accidents and related deaths. An estimated 1.2 million people are killed in road traffic accidents each year, and up to 50 million are injured, occupying between 30 and 70 per cent of orthopaedic hospital beds in developing countries.[11] One study of Latin America and the Caribbean concluded that at least 100,000 persons are killed in traffic accidents and 1.2 million are injured each year in that region, with costs measured in lost productivity, hospital bills and other factors estimated at US$30 billion.[12]

Later chapters will present and explain the central significance of slums in this nexus of daily urban risk and vulnerability; but recognizing how the characteristics of slums directly contribute to this nexus is needed to set the context for this report. Slums are at once the locus of the greatest deprivation in material welfare in societies, the weakest human capital in terms of investment in health and education, and also lack the institutional and legal framework to guarantee their safety and security. These forms of deprivation are cumulative and interact with one another. The poorest in most urban areas live in slums lacking both the safeguards for protection from private actions and unjust public policies. Insecurity of tenure – which affects large numbers of poor slum dwellers – itself weakens the possibility of establishing communities, community institutions and cultural norms to govern and regulate behaviour. The slums represent one part of what has been termed 'the geography of misery'.[13]

Global statistical evidence shows strong correlations between level of development and the degree of urban security, as measured by the incidence of disaster and crime and violence

One important dimension of this context is the fact that human life in cities is itself precarious in the absence of basic services such as housing, water supply and sanitation, as well as food. Common waterborne diseases such as cholera or vector-borne diseases such as malaria can quickly reach epidemic proportions in dense underserved urban areas and in the absence of medical prophylaxis. The probabilities of death from health threats such as these constitute the greatest challenges to the security of individuals, especially in urban slums. These health threats to urban safety and security are not discussed in this report; but, as mentioned earlier, they are part of the chronic vulnerabilities that constitute an important dimension of urban poverty.

Lack of basic services, however, is not simply a micro-level issue affecting individuals, households and communities. It also extends to cities and nations as a whole and represents significant macro-economic costs in many societies. This Global Report will present data demonstrating that urban insecurity is a major obstacle to macro-economic growth in some countries and deserves policy attention at the highest levels of government. As shown in Chapter 7, the importance of urban insecurity has already been recognised by the global insurance industry by assigning specific cities around the world to risk categories. Global statistical evidence shows strong correlations between level of development and the degree of urban security, as measured by the incidence of disaster and crime and violence.[14] GDP growth rates, for example, correlate negatively with homicide rates, although this is often offset by income inequality. But, as shown in Chapter 3, this correlation is reversed for property crime, demonstrating other causal mechanisms.

An additional urban dimension of this context is how the scale and density of cities affects urban safety and security. Subsequent chapters will present some aspects of this dimension, especially with respect to the incidence of crime and violence, as well as the impacts of natural and technological hazards, which tend to be higher in larger and denser urban areas. There are important caveats to this conclusion, including, for example, that very high density areas may have lower crime rates, such as New York, while there may also be an increased vulnerability in low density regions, such as isolated areas lacking social and institutional mechanisms for protection. As indicated in Chapter 3, the roles of culture and governance are but two of the factors that mediate these relationships and make clear correlations difficult to establish.

While these caveats apply to the risks of crime and violence, they do not necessarily apply to disasters where the concentration of more people also concentrates and magnifies risk and the likelihood of death, injury and property damage. The case of rapid growth in Dhaka, Bangladesh, illustrates this process of increasing risk in large cities (see Chapter 7). One large risk insurance company has identified the 15 largest cities at high risk due to natural hazards, including earthquakes, tropical storms, tsunamis and volcanic eruptions (also see Table 7.5 in Chapter 7). Smaller cities usually lack the institutional capacity to prepare for and manage risks. In physical terms, urbanization processes at all levels tend to change the risk and hazard profiles of cities. As stated earlier, this concentration of risk is greatest for the urban poor living in slums. All of these issues should focus more attention on urban governance, adding risk management and prevention to the already considerable

Figure 1.1

The violence continuum

Source: Moser and Shrader, 1999; Moser and Winton, 2002.

Road map of types of violence in Central America				
Primary direction of violence continuum	**Category of violence**	**Types of violence be perpetrators and/or victims**	**Manifestations**	**Secondary direction of violence continuum**
↑	Political/ institutional	Institutional violence of the state and other 'informal' institutions Including the private sector	Extra-judicial killings by police State or community directed social cleansing of gangs and street children Lynching	State institutional violence resulting in lack of trust in police and judiciary system ↓
	Institutional/ economic	Organized crime Business interests	Intimidation and violence as means of resolving economic disputes Kidnapping Armed robbery Drug trafficking Car and other contraband activites Small arms dealing Trafficking in prostitutes and USA headed immigrants	
	Economic/ social	Gangs (Maras)	Collective 'turf' violence; robbery, theft	
	Economic	Delinquency/robbery	Street theft; robbery	
	Economic/ social	Street children (boys and girls)	Petty theft	
	Social	Domestic violence between adults	Physical or psychological male–female abuse	
	Social	Child abuse: boys and girls	Physical and sexual abuse	
	Social	Inter-generational conflict between parent and children (both young and adults, particularly older people)	Physical and psychological abuse	
Intra-household social violence results in youths leaving the home and at risk to variety of street violence	Social	Gratuitous/routine daily violence	Lack of citizenship in areas such as traffic, road rage, bar fights and street confrontations	

agenda of policy and programme issues faced by urban managers.

CRIME AND VIOLENCE

The problem of crime and violence in cities has been long recognized as a growing and serious challenge in all parts of the world.[15] Studies of this phenomenon have encompassed the following issues: distribution and incidence across countries and levels of development; distribution and incidence of the impact of crime and violence across different categories of people, specifically by gender, race and age; location of violence by city size; types of violence, perpetrators and victims; economic and financial costs of violence; and diverse theories of causation – from the ecological model of violence, through more psycho-cultural explanations, to broader macro-economic and developmental frameworks. Some of these theories are reflected in what has been described as the 'violence continuum' (shown in Figure 1.1), which categorizes different types of crime and violence by perpetrators, victims and manifestations.

There are many dimensions of urban crime and violence. What is dramatic is its widespread existence in countries in all regions and at all levels of development. While there is considerable variation across countries, the problem is clearly shared. Chapter 3 presents data showing that violent crime increased worldwide from 1990 to 2000, from 6 to 8.8 incidents per 100,000 persons. The data demonstrates that over the past five years, 60 per cent of all urban residents have been victims of crime, with 70 per cent in Latin America and Africa. A recent comparative assessment of homicide across continents shows that the highest rates are found in developing countries, and particularly in sub-Saharan Africa and Latin America and the Caribbean. Studies by the International Crime Victimization Survey report that Africa's cities have the highest burglary and assault rates and the second highest rates of robberies. While crime appears to correlate with national income, there are important exceptions – for example, Russia and the US, which also have particularly high murder rates.[16]

Violent crime increased worldwide from 1990 to 2000, from 6 to 8.8 incidents per 100,000 persons

60 per cent of all urban residents have been victims of crime, with 70 per cent in Latin America and Africa

The World Health Organization (WHO) has estimated that 90 per cent of violence-related deaths in the year 2000 occurred in low- and middle-income countries, with violent deaths at 32.1 per 100,000 people, compared to 14.4 per 100,000 in high-income countries.[17] European murder rates have declined steadily from the 11th century to the present.[18] Indeed, European and US homicide rates have gone in opposite directions.[19] US rates are about 5 per

100,000 people, while the rates for other 'established market economies' are around 1 per 100,000.[20] These rates are interesting because they suggest cultural and institutional differences surrounding violent behaviour.[21]

Further variation in crime rates is found within countries, between rural areas and cities, and between cities of different sizes, with higher rates within larger cities. Cities such as Los Angeles and New York have much higher homicide rates than other cities. All of this data is illustrative, but must also be qualified in terms of the well-known difficulties of obtaining reliable data concerning crime and violence, not only in one city, but even more so when any effort is made to compare across cities, within countries and even on a global basis. Such data and methodological issues will be addressed in later sections of this Global Report.

Rates of violent crime across neighbourhoods within most cities vary considerably, with higher rates correlated with lower incomes and, increasingly, with drug-related behaviour

Within this context, additional threats to individual security are cumulative and exist on top of chronic patterns. For example, the incidence of death that can be attributed to crime and violence among young males in most cities has increased significantly over the past two decades. Figure 1.2 compares death rates among young men (from deprived and non-deprived neighbourhoods) in São Paulo (Brazil), New Orleans (US) and US urban centres as a whole. The figure suggests that male adult longevity rates reflect growing deaths from violent crime in cities in both rich and poor countries. The highest cause of death of African–American males in US cities is from violent crime, with rising rates of imprisonment as well. Death rates in cities such as gang-ridden San Salvador in El Salvador or São Paulo in Brazil are similarly high. Death rates from violent crime in the Middle East and Asia are generally lower, while violence in African cities such as Cape Town, Johannesburg or Lagos is quite high. An important threshold is crossed when crime and violence show up in health statistics. A key point here is that local cultural factors play a significant role in explaining local variation.

The hypothesis that cities would experience violent crime is of long historical origin. In a classical essay of 1903, the sociologist Georg Simmel argued that the anomie in cities and poverty resulting from the industrial revolution explained increasing urban violence.[22] This, in fact, did not happen in Europe; but it seems to have occurred in another context, in cities in developing countries where recent migrants often find themselves in contexts lacking communal values governing individual and collective behaviours. If Simmel's hypothesis did not hold at the city level in Europe, it is probably more robust when tested across various neighbourhoods within cities. Rates of violent crime across neighbourhoods within most cities vary considerably, with higher rates correlated with lower incomes and, increasingly, with drug-related behaviour.

Figure 1.2

Violence-related deaths among young men

Source: Stephens, 1996, p21

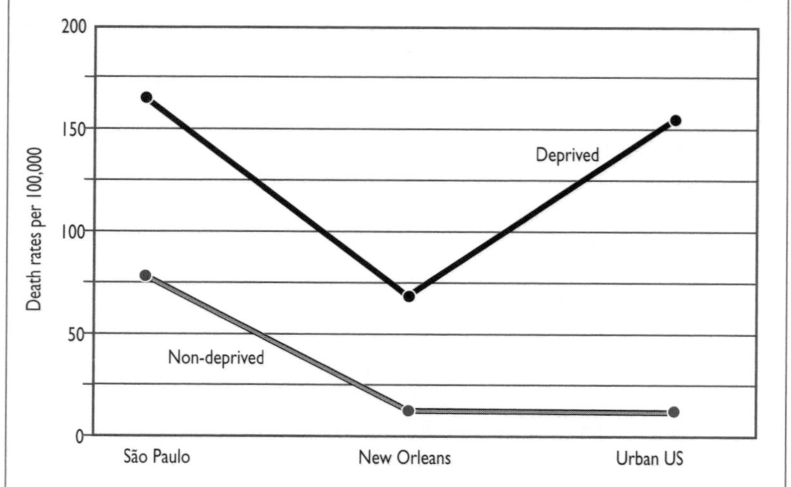

Studies of the origins and motivations for crime and violence have covered a wide spectrum. On one side, there are many psycho-social theories and explanations focusing on the socialization of individuals, including intra-family dynamics and violence, to the birth of aggression and lack of self-esteem, and to peer experiences in school, in gangs and in the streets, much of this captured in the notion of the ecological model.[23] This model connects four analytic levels in explaining interpersonal violence: individual, social relationships, community and society.[24] As shown in Chapter 3, there are also opportunity and place-based models within this broader ecological perspective.

The interactions between these levels are well reflected in a chapter title 'The family as a violent institution and the primary site of social violence' in a recent book.[25] The authors quote a young boy in Bogotá who says: 'Violence begins at home, and it is one of the most important factors in the harmony of the community, and this brings about lack of respect in everyone.'[26] The problem of intra-family violence includes domestic and sexual abuse of women and young girls. As the quotation from the boy in Bogotá suggests, intra-family dynamics carry out to the street as well, as behaviours learned or accepted at home become socialized and directed, often randomly, at the society at large. These include behaviours directly connected to gender, as shown in studies of violence and 'manliness' in the southern US.[27]

Other less psychological but significant explanations of violence and crime are more socially based understandings, seeking to identify societal forces and place-based factors that generate violent responses to relative deprivation. These explanations are well captured in the observation that 'in reality, violence is constructed, negotiated, reshaped and resolved as perpetrators and victims try to define and control the world they find themselves in'.[28] From this perspective, crime and violence may be quite functional to urban survival.[29] In this regard, crime and violence can also be politically and socially constructed.

There are many cases where downturns in the economy lead to attacks by local residents on foreign workers – for example, in Ghana during economic recession in the 1970s when Beninois and Nigerians were sent out of Ghana back to their own countries in convoys of trucks. This episode was followed by retaliatory measures by the Nigerian government in the 1980s. In some cases, socially and racially excluded groups strike back, as in the riots in London in 1981, Los Angeles in 1992 or in Paris and in many other French urban areas in 2006, where several weeks of burning of cars, arson and attacks on property reflected years of frustration with French government policies and with the complicated mechanisms of social and economic exclusion.

The emergence of ethnic identity as the basis of ethnic conflict and nationalist aspirations in the post-Cold War years has been widely noted, with the case of the break-up of the former Yugoslavia into several independent states being one of the most bloody, and with the tragic histories of Bosnia and, later, Kosovo. A study of indigenous populations in 160 countries shows that countries have an average of 5 indigenous ethnic groups, varying from an average of 3.2 per country in the West to 8.2 per country in Africa. Ethnic diversity is more common in Africa, South Asia and Southeast Asia (see Chapter 3).

Within this larger picture, the cases of nationalist movements in Chechnya, East Timor, Kurdistan and Georgia, to cite a few, have all emerged with great force, to the surprise of many people who did not understand the strength of these ethnic identities and their nationalist objectives.[30] These dynamics have been closely connected with the issue of minority status and conditions. A contemporary anthropologist writes about 'the civilization of clashes', playing with the title of the well-known book by Samuel Huntington.[31] He notes that there have been more wars in the nation than wars of the nation.[32]

These wars in the nation have also been closely related to the many cases of state-sponsored violence in many countries over the past few decades, whether in military dictatorships in Argentina, Chile, El Salvador or Guatemala during the 1970s and 1980s, or in Ethiopia, Rwanda or Burundi during the 1980s and 1990s, or in Myanmar over the last decade. The 2005 case of squatter evictions and demolitions in Harare, Zimbabwe, is a recent instance where the government continued despite international attention and calls for restraint. The ongoing case of Darfur in western Sudan has been seen as an example of state-sponsored violence at a regional level.

Studies of crime and violence suggest interesting contradictions, such as the fact that the poorest members of society are rarely the perpetrators of violence; rather, the perpetrators are frequently individuals and groups who have enjoyed some prior upward social mobility or economic improvement and then find themselves blocked from further improvement. These individuals and groups often express their frustrations through violence. This phenomenon was observed in the location of riots during the 1960s in the US, where violence occurred in those cities with the most successful anti-poverty programmes (i.e. Chicago, Detroit and Los Angeles).[33] It also reflects experience in Mumbai and other cities, where recent poor rural–urban migrants who are entering the labour force are rarely involved in violence.[34]

While these theories and cases offer complementary and related evidence about the understanding of crime and violence, they are a backdrop to the daily lived experience of residents of Rio de Janeiro, São Paulo, Mexico City, Johannesburg or Manila, to name a few of the many cities in developing countries where growing crime and violence are perceived as a major problem affecting all strata of society.

During the late 1990s, the Government of Mexico began to publicly discuss urban crime as a problem with macro-economic consequences. This was an interesting development because, in relative terms, Mexico had a comparatively low level of loss of GDP due to violence, at 1.3 per cent in 1997, compared to other Latin American countries such as Colombia and El Salvador, which both lost an estimated 25 per cent.[35] In contrast, the US, with a much larger GDP, had estimates of the costs of violence reaching 3.3 per cent of GDP.[36] This staggering amount has many interesting components, such as the estimated cost of a homicide in the US valued at US$2 million, while estimates were US$15,319 in South Africa and US$602,000 in Australia, respectively, reflecting foregone income.[37] Analytically, the WHO has distinguished between direct and indirect costs of violence in its review of 119 studies of the economic dimensions of interpersonal violence. Figure 1.3 presents these different costs.[38] The financing of these costs is a considerable weight on poor economies. Studies of Jamaica found that 90 per cent of the costs of treating victims of violence at the Kingston Public Hospital were paid by the government.[39]

The emergence of ethnic identity as the basis of ethnic conflict and nationalist aspirations in the post-Cold War years has been widely noted

In this regard, it is interesting to observe differences between cities within countries, such as the reductions in crime and violence achieved in Medellin, Colombia, where a strong mayor and civil society were determined to overcome drug violence and dominance of 'drug lords',[40] compared to continued problems in Cali, where the drug cartels continue to exercise effective power. A third Colombian city, Bogotá, the national capital, has dramatically reduced crime and violence.[41] And yet, although Colombia is globally perceived as a violent country, more people died in armed violence in the *favelas* of Rio de Janeiro (49,913) from 1978 to 2000 than in all of Colombia (39,000).[42]

In Brazil, more than 100 people are killed by guns every day, and the gun-related death rate in Rio de Janeiro is more than double the national average.[43] Organized crime demonstrated its great power in São Paulo during May and June 2006 with its well-orchestrated attacks on police, followed by bloody retribution by the police. Press reports on São Paulo following this episode noted some startling data (see Box 1.2). Chapter 3 presents the drug dimensions of

Figure 1.3

Costs and benefits of interpersonal violence

Source: WHO, 2004, p6

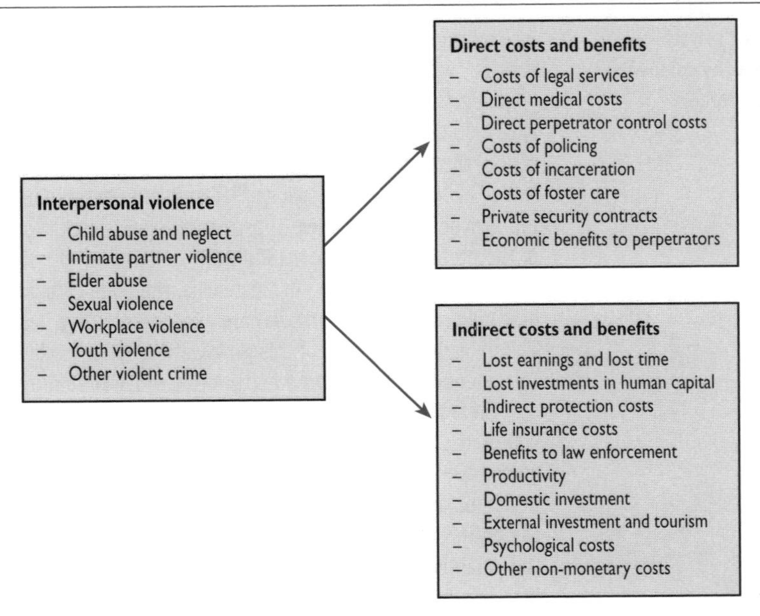

Box 1.2 Startling data on crime and violence in Brazil (2006)

- São Paulo, Brazil, had 1 per cent of the world's homicides, but only 0.17 per cent of the world's population.
- At least 25,000 homes in São Paulo had security cameras to monitor entrances and exits from their grounds,
- There were 35,000 armed cars in Brazil.
- Since the well-orchestrated attacks on police during May to June 2006, there was a 33 per cent increase in armed windshields sales.
- The Brazilian security market had reached some US$49 billion, about 10 per cent of gross domestic product (GDP), of which 60 per cent were private expenditures.
- In 2006, private security companies employed 1.5 million individuals in Brazil.

Source: Esnal, 2006, p4

this problem, showing that some 200 million people are drug users, a slight reduction over the last few years. The impact of specific drugs on these patterns is startling, with cocaine deaths increasing, while the global market for marijuana is about 162 million users.

An important aspect of urban crime and violence has been the role of youth

An important aspect of urban crime and violence has been the role of youth. The WHO reports that during 2000, some 199,000 youth homicides were committed globally, or 9.2 per 100,000 individuals. This is equivalent to 500 people between 10 and 29 dying each day in youth homicides, varying from 0.9 per 100,000 in high income countries to 17.6 in Africa and 36.4 in Latin America. For every fatality, there are from 20 to 40 victims of non-fatal youth violence.[44] In some cases, these high numbers are the results of gang violence in specific cities. In Africa, with nearly 75 per cent of the urban population living in slums and 44 per cent of the population below 15 years of age, the conditions for gang formation are prevalent. This also highlights what is called 'child density' within a population (see Chapter 3). For example, in Cape Flats, Cape Town, South Africa, there are an estimated 100,000 gang members who are considered responsible for 70 per cent of the crime.[45] The case of South Africa is particularly interesting because high rates of urban violence involving youth have their origins in the apartheid period and in patterns of policing and segregation.[46] Data on Nairobi, Kenya, shows similar results, with very high crime rates and high rates of violence.[47] Much of this crime originates from slum areas where 60 per cent of Nairobi's population lives on only 5 per cent of the city's land.[48] Mexico City is divided into zones by some 1500 competing gangs.[49] Gang membership is a problem across many cities. These estimates suggest the size of the problem: El Salvador (35,000), Guatemala (100,000) and Honduras (40,000).[50] In Guatemala, there are estimates of 20,000 murders in gang warfare over the past five years. The following definition of this gang warfare helps to clarify this phenomenon: 'children and youth (who are) employed or otherwise participating in organized armed violence where there are elements of a command structure and power over territory, local population or resources'.[51] Given the dominant role of media and perception of these issues, the definitions of various forms of crime and violence and the establishment of useful comparative categories about both origins and impacts are important foundational steps in developing useful policies and approaches to address these problems. In-depth empirical studies on neighbourhood violence in Kingston, Jamaica, demonstrated that many different forms of violence can operate concurrently, with diverse causes, mechanisms and outcomes.[52] Definitions and categories of crime and violence will be discussed in some depth in Chapters 3 and 4 of this Global Report. It is important to note, however, that there are great differences between so-called 'top-down' perceptions of the problem, and the consequent policy approaches, and other more participatory 'bottom-up' perspectives and suggested remedies.[53] Notions such as 'zero tolerance', as promulgated by a former New York mayor a few years ago, ignore the important differences between the origins and the sites of crime. It is not surprising that the 'zero tolerance' approach found little support in Mexico City when its supporters tried to export the model.

Almost every city in the world has developed private security companies and forces

While this overview has provided a picture of the global situation in cities, another dimension also deserves attention: the response to crime and, specifically, prevention. Beyond the strengthening of policing and the judicial system that will be discussed at length in later chapters, two specific responses have become increasingly common: the privatization of security and the role of community groups. Both of these responses come, in part, from the inadequacy of the police and criminal justice system to address these problems. Almost every city in the world has developed private security companies and forces. An estimate in 2000 indicated that the annual growth of private security was 30 per cent and 8 per cent, respectively, in the developing and developed countries.[54] One study of South Africa reported that the number of private security guards has increased by 150 per cent from 1997 to 2006, while the number of police decreased by 2.2 per cent in the same period.[55] The question of the balance between public and private crime prevention is a major issue.

A second and related aspect of private or 'non-public' security is community security, where community groups decide to maintain security in their neighbourhoods. This process, involving what might be called 'community buy-in' or, more dramatically, 'vigilantism', in some countries has its roots in traditional culture and notions of justice in many cities. It also has become a widespread contemporary phenomenon whereby specific crimes or outbreaks of crime lead to neighbourhood and community efforts, whether citizens patrol their communities or groups are designated to perform this and other functions, such as the Young Lords in New York City. One well-documented case is a group called People against Gangsterism and Drugs (PAGAD), which was formed in Cape Town to murder gang leaders in order to stop violence. This violent approach, however, led to attacks on PAGAD and actually increased the violence,[56] illustrating how such efforts can become out of control. Beyond these dramatic examples, the issue of community responsibility for urban security is a broad concern to be addressed by this Global Report. Indeed, as will be suggested in subsequent chapters, the role of civil society at a general level and of specific communities is an essential part of achieving resilience in the face of these challenges.

TENURE INSECURITY AND FORCED EVICTION

The second threat to urban safety and security that this report examines is the growing worldwide problem of insecure tenure of the urban poor and the threat of forced eviction from public and private land, which they occupy with or without legal permission. While this problem has been studied for many years and considered in the analysis of land use and housing, more recently, freedom from forced eviction has become recognized as a fundamental human right within human rights law.[57] This important advance has fundamentally changed the debate about this subject, shifting it from an issue of technical legal status to one of a legally recognized right. This shift has changed the legal position of households lacking secure tenure. In theory, households are now legally protected from administrative decisions of local or national governments to bring in the bulldozers. The challenge, now, is to identify appropriate alternative forms of security of tenure within a specific locality.

Chapters 5, 6 and 11 of this report are devoted to security of tenure. They review the wide range of tenure options that currently exist in different parts of the world and discuss what makes tenure secure or insecure. The discussion is based on the increasing recognition that security of tenure is a basic human right. This approach also fits within the concept of human security, as presented earlier in this chapter, and thus takes a more all-encompassing vision of human rights as they relate to the tenure issue.

As noted in Chapter 5, security of tenure has been defined as 'the right of all individuals and groups to effective protection by the state against forced evictions'. In this context, it is important to distinguish forced evictions from market-driven evictions. Market-based evictions are much larger in scale and frequency than public expropriations of land.[58] It has been emphasized that 'Eviction mechanisms and trends must be analyzed with reference to the global context of the persistent imbalance between demand and supply of land for housing, the scarcity of prime urban land for development, increases in the market value of urban land, and increasing commodification of informal land markets.'[59] A useful typology of these situations has been developed (see Box 1.3).

What is the scale of insecurity of tenure? As noted earlier, there are already more than 1 billion people living in slums, and many more are expected in the projected urban expansion to come over the next few decades. Chapter 5 suggests that many slums in developing country cities are often characterized by insecurity of tenure and that the scale of insecurity of tenure is growing, along with urban demographic growth. Furthermore, current evidence suggests that there is deterioration in tenure status as expanding urban populations are forced into unplanned or illegal settlements.

Estimates cited in Chapter 5 note that, in most developing country cities, between 25 and 70 per cent of the urban population are living in irregular settlements, including squatter settlements and rooms and flats in dilapidated buildings in city centre areas. In spite of the many existing poverty alleviation initiatives and safety-net programmes, the total number of people living in informal settlements is increasing at a faster rate than the urban population.[60] According to one analyst, an additional 2.8 billion people will require housing and urban services by 2030, with some 41 per cent of humanity possibly living in slums.[61] Another finds that informal land occupation in urban areas remains large scale: 51.4 per cent in sub-Saharan Africa; 41.2 per cent in East Asia and the Pacific; 26.4 per cent in Latin America and the Caribbean; 25.9 per cent in the Middle East and North Africa; and 5.7 per cent in Eastern Europe and Central Asia.[62] At the national level, the pattern is the same, with between 40 and 70 per cent of the population of Brazil's main cities living in irregular settlements and some 58 per cent of all households in South Africa living without security of tenure.[63] Data also shows that tenure problems exist in developed countries as well, such as in the UK and the US.

Beyond the difficulties of estimating the scale and complexity of the tenure insecurity problem, Chapter 5 also presents a range of existing tenure and occupancy options. What is clear is that no one alternative is appropriate for all circumstances. Security of tenure depends upon what kind of land and/or housing is being occupied (public or private), and whether the occupant has some form of legal contract or lease, or not. While protection from forced evictions has been accepted in international law, the fact is that evictions are nevertheless increasing. The challenge, therefore, is to understand why and to identify measures to reduce this form of urban insecurity.

Freedom from forced eviction has become recognized as a fundamental human right within human rights law

Box 1.3 Forced eviction: A typology

- A landowner who has, in the past, authorized tenants to settle on his land now wants to develop it or to sell it to a developer. He refuses to collect rent and asks the occupants to move out (this has been a common case within inner-city slums in Bangkok during the last 30 years).
- An investor buys land suitable for development from a private landowner with the intention of developing it. If tenants or squatters already occupy the land, and if the investor cannot persuade them to leave through negotiation, he may obtain an eviction order from a court.
- Public authorities launch an expropriation procedure, by power of eminent domain, in order to build infrastructure or carry out urban renewal, or a redevelopment scheme, or a beautification project.
- Public authorities sell land to private investors which is already occupied by tenants or squatters (this is common in cities in transition, where land is being privatized with the pressure of emerging land markets). The sale of public land aims to increase their revenues in the absence of land taxation and other fiscal resources.
- Public authorities recover land that had been allocated to occupants under a temporary 'permit-to-occupy' regime in order to carry out a development project, usually in partnership with private investors (this is common in sub-Saharan African cities, where the 'permit-to-occupy' regime still prevails).

In all of these cases, occupants of the land will ultimately be exposed to forced evictions. However, *de facto* security of tenure in informal settlements usually provides protection against forced evictions, which may compromise the success of legal actions to evict occupants, and may force private investors or public authorities to negotiate.

Source: Durand-Lasserve, 2006

Within the field of urban policy and research, insecurity of tenure has long been recognized as a constraint to the physical improvement of low-income communities through investment in housing and infrastructure.[64] Households lacking some guarantee of occupancy simply have not invested in housing improvements. As a result, the actual condition of housing has not always reflected the income level of its inhabitants and frequently is considerably worse than it could be if some security of tenure existed. Studies in many urban slums in developing countries demonstrate that residents often have more money than the quality of their shelter would suggest. The absence of secure tenure has also inhibited the granting of mortgage and home improvement loans by public and private financial institutions, even when these same individuals might have the income and assets to serve as forms of collateral for housing loans.[65] This significant depressive impact on the housing sector in many developing country cities has largely been the result of inadequate public policies regarding housing, land and urban infrastructure.

Insecurity of tenure is at once a cause and an outcome of poverty and inequality

This leads to the conclusion that insecurity of tenure is at once a cause and an outcome of poverty and inequality. People are poor because they have inadequate living conditions and, at the same time, they are also unable to improve their living conditions due to the tenure arrangements under which they live. Among the victims of tenure insecurity are particular groups such as women, indigenous peoples, ethnic minorities, refugees, tenants, the displaced and the disabled. Their problems are elaborated upon in Chapters 5 and 6. What is apparent is that tenure insecurity is a significant component of the numerous disadvantages facing the poor.

At least 2 million people are forcibly evicted every year, while a similar number is threatened by evictions

Several important examples of forced evictions are well known. In Zimbabwe, *Operation Murambatsvina* displaced an estimated 700,000 urban residents in 2005. Soon after this operation by the Government of Zimbabwe, thousands of people faced forced evictions in Nigeria and, more recently, in Zambian cities in early 2007. Data collected by the Centre on Housing Rights and Evictions (COHRE) suggests that at least 2 million people are forcibly evicted every year, while a similar number is threatened by evictions (see Chapter 5).

Tenure insecurity increases the vulnerability of the urban poor to natural hazards

The scale of insecurity of tenure and forced evictions is largely a result of public policies and private-sector behaviours. Urban growth places great demands on public policies and strategies to enable the provision of shelter, whether by the public or private sectors. Many governments often argue that they need to displace urban residents from locations planned for other uses. In some cases, these actions simply reflect official intentions to eliminate 'eyesores', often around the time of major international events bringing important guests and tourists. In some cities, governments view slum areas as threats to public health or as the breeding ground for urban crime.

These arguments in favour of forced evictions, however, can also be seen within the larger picture that most government policies have not been effective in providing an adequate legal framework for the rapid provision of legal options for shelter and occupancy of land. Constraints such as ineffective land tenure and administration systems, poor infrastructure design and construction, as well as lack of finance, have limited the availability of legally accessible land and shelter options for growing urban populations. Providers of infrastructure services such as water supply or public transport use the absence of tenure as excuses for not providing services to low-income communities.[66] As noted earlier, with a backlog of 1 billion people living in slums and another 1.2 billion expected urban residents in developing countries by 2020, this problem is acute (see Table 1.1).

Insecurity of tenure contributes significantly to other problems as well. By seriously undermining the performance of the housing sector in many countries, tenure issues limit the overall supply of housing, thereby raising both prices and costs. These, in turn, contribute to homelessness and the pressure on the urban poor to find whatever land is available for squatting, whether between railroad tracks in Mumbai, on dangerously unstable hillsides in Ankara or Caracas, or alongside canals filled with human waste in Bangkok or Jakarta. The plight of these people is well captured in the terms 'pavement dwellers' in India or in '*villas miserias*' (villages of misery) in Buenos Aires. It is also clear from this that tenure insecurity increases the vulnerability of the urban poor to natural hazards.

Despite 50 years of public and, indeed, global debate on these issues, it is remarkable that many national and local governments continue to believe in the bulldozer as the preferred instrument of public policy in the clearance of these slums and slum populations, whether in Harare or Mumbai.[67] In addition to the direct impact of slum clearance on the urban poor, it should also be recognized that the social and economic exclusion of this large and growing population – more than 1 billion people worldwide and 6 million people in greater Mumbai alone – has a negative impact on local finance and economic productivity. A total of 1 billion people living in slums is not only a severe social problem, but also a major drain on urban-based economic activities since slum dwellers are likely to be less healthy and less productive than more fortunate urban residents.[68] Sending the urban poor to remote locations on the peripheries of cities further inhibits their opportunities for earning incomes and meeting their own basic needs. Indeed, studies of these phenomena in many cities such as Abidjan, Lagos or Rio de Janeiro demonstrate conclusively that urban relocation reduces incomes and further impoverishes already poor people.[69] If the importance of security of tenure should not be minimized, it is also possible to assign a disproportionate influence to this constraint on the quality of human settlements. Experience in many cities demonstrates that security of tenure is a necessary, but insufficient, condition for housing investment and housing quality. Access to residential infrastructure such as water supply, sanitation and other environmental infrastructure, such as drainage, is equally if not more important in ensuring the basic needs of individuals and households. Having a title to a plot of land without reasonable access to water supply does not solve the housing problems of an urban household.[70]

Tenure, therefore, should be recognized as a legal protection and human right against uncertainty about whether public authorities will bulldoze so-called illegal settlements and forcibly evict households from their shelter. It operates on both sides of the supply-and-demand equation, constraining the supply of investment in new housing and the demand for new housing and improvements to existing housing.[71]

With these concerns in mind, Chapters 5 and 6 of this Global Report will examine the problem of insecurity of tenure, assessing the scale of urban evictions and their distribution around the world, as well as examining the range of remedies to insecurity of tenure. These remedies include full ownership to varying forms of short- and longer-term occupancy permits. One important issue here involves the identification of housing units and plot boundaries themselves. An interesting experiment has been the street addressing programme undertaken in Dakar, Senegal, where housing units are given addresses, which offers some form of legal recognition and, hence, a degree of security; but having an address does not, by itself, imply legal ownership or unlimited occupancy.[72]

NATURAL AND HUMAN-MADE DISASTERS

The third threat to urban safety and security addressed in this Global Report is the growing frequency of natural and human-made disasters. The number of major disasters in the world grew from under 100 in 1975 to almost 550 in 2000 (see Figure 1.4)[73] The economic costs of natural disasters have also grown, some 14 times more than during the 1950s, with the International Monetary Fund (IMF) estimating material losses to be US$652 billion during the 1990s (see Figure 1.5).[74] Studies estimate that a total of 4.1 billion people in the world were affected from 1984 to 2003, with 1.6 billion affected from 1984 to 1993, and the number growing to almost 2.6 billion from 1994 to 2003.[75] These numbers have increased, as well, with the increased frequency and scale of natural disasters during the 2004 to 2006 period, including the toll of death (220,000 people) and homeless (1.5 million) from the Indian Ocean Tsunami of December 2004 and the Pakistan earthquake of October 2005, which killed 86,000 people and left millions homeless.[76] It is important to note that 98 per cent of the 211 million people affected by natural disasters annually from 1991 to 2000 were living in developing countries.[77]

The location of these disasters in developing countries is particularly important because of the impact on their already low levels of income and poverty. Data on the distribution of these disaster 'hotspots' is presented in Chapter 7. While the tsunami reduced Indonesia's GDP growth only marginally, by 0.1 to 0.4 per cent, the province of Aceh lost capital stock equivalent to 97 per cent of its GDP. The Kashmir earthquake caused estimated losses of US$5 billion, or roughly equivalent to total development assistance to Pakistan, a large country of over 150 million people, for the previous three years. The periodic floods affecting Bangladesh and Mozambique continue to wipe out the agriculture and infrastructure in two of the world's poorest countries. These differences in country circumstances mean a lot. Landslides in Venezuela and storms in France in December 1999 both caused about US$3 billion in damages; but France is much richer than Venezuela, with the costs of individual buildings also likely to be higher. Similarly, Venezuela lost 50,000 people, while the death toll in France was only 123.[78] An Organisation for Economic Co-operation and Development (OECD) study concluded that outside post-disaster financing and donations usually represent less than 10 per cent of the disaster losses, so the event is 'a permanent loss of development momentum.'[79]

The increasing frequency of these events, therefore, is a matter of great concern. Patterns of climate change resulting from global warming, rises in sea temperatures and resulting weather patterns have all contributed to a 50 per cent increase in extreme weather events from the 1950s to the 1990s.[80] This includes heat waves that have produced dramatic losses of life in Chicago, France and south India (see Chapter 7). For example, during the last 15 years, more people have died in the US from heat stress than from all

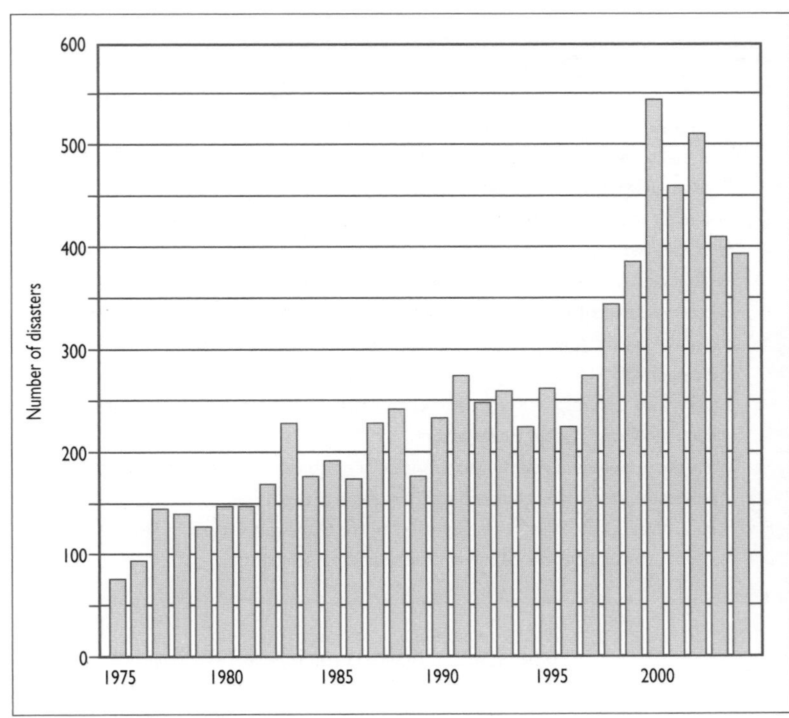

Figure 1.4

Natural disasters are increasing

Source: World Bank, 2006a, p4

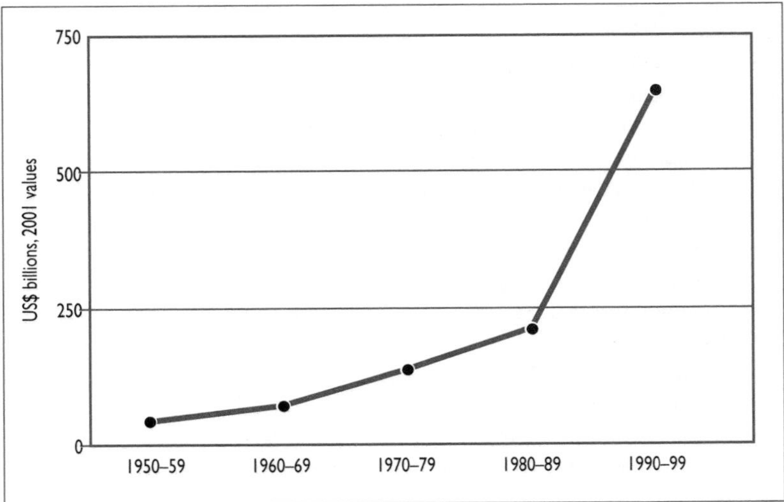

Figure 1.5

The rising cost of disasters

Note: The data is for 'great' disasters in which the ability of the region to help itself is distinctly overtaxed, making interregional or international assistance necessary.

Source: World Bank Independent Evaluation Group, 2006, p5.

Box 1.4 Conventional wisdom about natural and human-made disasters

- Natural and human-made disasters are not predictable.
- They are indeed largely 'natural' (i.e. caused by changes in nature).
- Their occurrence is independent of human behaviour.
- As a result of the above, the major issues for policy concern are preparedness, mitigation, relief and recovery.
- Disasters can occur anywhere; they are largely independent of locality.
- Recovery from disasters means restoring the conditions existing before the disaster, and not addressing the conditions that may have contributed to the disaster.
- The responsibility of government is largely immediate relief, risk management and providing insurance. The response of government is usually to 'manage the problem' and not to undertake steps to remedy causal factors.
- While the responses of government and voluntary organizations are helpful, they are usually inadequate in relation to the scale and depth of needs.
- Political reactions to disasters rarely go beyond 'the blame game', assigning responsibility rather than mobilizing political support for sustainable solutions.

other forms of disasters combined.[81] The heat wave in south India in May 2002 was also very dramatic, with temperatures of up to 50 degrees Celsius. Increased frequency of extreme weather events has been particularly evident in Central America and the Caribbean: Hurricane Mitch affected Honduras and Nicaragua in 1998; landslides and flooding killed many people in Guatemala in 2005; and Caribbean hurricanes during the period of 2002 to 2005 hit the whole region, particularly Cuba, Haiti, Jamaica, and the Yucatan Peninsula in Mexico.

Conventional wisdom at the global level about natural and human-made disasters, described in Box 1.4, contributes little towards alleviating growing threats to urban safety and security from such disasters.

In contrast, detailed descriptions and analyses of individual natural and human-made disasters suggest insights that directly challenge conventional wisdom and tenets (see Box 1.5).

The conclusions in Box 1.5 suggest alternative policies and approaches to conventional wisdom. Two principal policy messages emerge: first, it is important to better understand how human behaviour contributes to disasters; and, second, more needs to be done to prevent disasters from happening.

These messages also focus more attention on the distinction between natural and human-made (including technological) disasters. Major industrial accidents – such as the Union Carbide accident in Bhopal, India, during the 1980s; the Chernobyl nuclear disaster of 1986 in the then Soviet Union; an oil pipeline explosion in Lagos in 2006; a chemical plant explosion in Jilin, China, in 2005; and a fertilizer plant explosion in Toulouse, France, in 2001 – all demonstrate that technologically induced disasters can occur in all regions of the world, regardless of income level (see Chapter 7). Indeed, analysis of the location of technological disasters concludes that greatest risk has accumulated in

Box 1.5 Disaster experiences that challenge conventional wisdom

- Natural and human-made disasters are largely predictable within historical patterns of probability and within specific regions and locations. These predictable patterns suggest that some regions are highly susceptible to these events, even though the specific location and timing of such events may be predictable only within wider parameters of time. An example would be the likelihood of hurricanes in countries bordering the Gulf of Mexico during the period of June to October each year.
- The locus of the impact of natural and human-made disasters is closely related to pre-disaster conditions – for example, mudslides and flooding are likely to occur in valleys where deforestation has occurred, as in the cases of Haiti and Guatemala.
- Individual large-scale disasters fit into broader regional patterns of specific types, death and injury tolls, homeless and affected, and financial and economic losses.
- The performance of infrastructure – roads, drains, bridges, electricity networks or water supply systems – in withstanding disasters is a good indicator of the pre-disaster capacity of institutions to manage, operate and maintain infrastructure. An example would be insufficient maintenance of the drainage system of Mumbai prior to the annual monsoon season (June to September).
- The risk profiles of increasingly large and dense urban centres of all sizes indicate that the vulnerability of urban populations can be enormous, as demonstrated by the large numbers of victims of earthquake events, such as the 250,000[82] death toll of the Tangshan earthquake of 1976 in northeast China, as well as the 86,000 deaths and destruction of millions of homes resulting from the 2005 earthquake in Pakistan.
- The profile of victims of disasters shows a disproportionate share of women, children, elderly and disabled populations. This is well illustrated in the case of the Indian Ocean Tsunami, where female victims outnumbered male victims in a number of places, as shown in Chapter 7.
- Natural and human-made disasters are not events, but processes, in which previous historical responses to events contribute heavily to the degree of preparedness and the extent and nature of impacts. The impacts of hurricanes on the Florida coast have been relatively contained as experience has grown about preparedness and evacuation procedures.
- The extent of the impact of a disaster is closely related to the capacity of institutions and the public to learn and adjust from previous experiences. The national mobilization in The Netherlands following the 1953 floods created an enduring model of public education, which is now being applied to preparations to confront the anticipated rise in sea levels due to global warming. The more that people understand likely impacts, the more likely they will prepare for and/or evacuate situations of increasing risk. The differences in evacuation experiences between New Orleans and Houston in 2005 in anticipation of Hurricanes Katrina and Rita demonstrate the importance of public awareness.
- Rather than assume that the impacts of disasters are independent of politics, it is apparent that political will plays a large role in the degree of preparedness, the nature of the short-term public response, and the medium- and longer-term processes of recovery.
- Recovery from disasters offers important opportunities to address underlying causes, problems and institutional incapacities. Reform during recovery from disaster has a greater chance of success than reform during periods of 'business as usual'. This experience is well illustrated by the way in which new women's non-governmental organizations (NGOs) and community groups assumed a larger role in community decision-making in the relief and recovery process following earthquakes in Bursa (Turkey) and Surat (India).

cities of richer countries. This reflects the logic of concentration and economies of scale. The complex patterns of causation affecting technological disasters will be examined in greater detail in Chapter 4.

THE CHALLENGE OF IMPROVING UNDERSTANDING: PERCEPTION, EVIDENCE AND METHODOLOGY

Taken together, the three threats to urban safety and security examined in this report pose many challenges for understanding and action. Of particular importance in this respect are the effects, or implications, of perception, evidence and methodology. While these three threats to urban safety and security are intrinsically different in character, they all share the fact that their underlying causes are popularly misunderstood. Not surprisingly, it is difficult to mobilize sustained political support for their remedy, whether at the international, national or local levels. The assertion, for example, that crime and violence or disasters are frequently predictable is upsetting, even shocking, to the public; yet, evidence presented in this report would support this conclusion. To characterize some disasters as 'disasters by design', in terms of the inadequacies of infrastructure design and weak institutional capacity to address them, has produced important political reactions in places such as New Orleans or Mumbai. Yet, as shown in the previous section, in-depth analyses of cases demonstrate that conventional wisdom is frequently misinformed about the origins and mechanisms of these three threats to urban safety and security.

The role of perception

The perception of insecurity in cities depends largely upon the substantial amount and constant flow of information that urban residents receive from many sources. This information directly challenges the reality that most places in most cities are safe, at least from crime and violence. The media plays a critical role in this process. As noted in Chapter 3, studies in the UK have demonstrated that readers of 'tabloids' were twice as likely to be worried about violent crime, burglary and car crime as readers of 'broadsheets'. The content and style of the media, whether newspapers or television, have an enormous impact on public perception of the conditions that people believe are prevalent in their cities. Whether these perceptions are exaggerated or not, they depend upon individual media sources, how stories are communicated and how public authorities respond.

In the era of global communications, the role of the media is central to both local and international perceptions of safety and security in specific cities: for example, whether it was dangerous to visit New York in the 1980s, but safer today, or whether there is a greater likelihood of crime in Rio de Janeiro or São Paulo today. While terrorism has become a major preoccupation in many cities around the world since 11 September 2001, media attention seems to focus on crime and violence. Globally, media practices seem to build upon promoting a 'culture of fear' in order to sell newspapers or to guarantee television audiences. These practices generate what one report has called 'fearscapes': public spaces where people fear the lack of urban security.[83] In contrast, in other cities, the media tries to actively play down such sensational news. Responsible reporting and coverage can play a major role in promoting urban security and safety.

The importance of media was visible at a global scale in the perception of poor governmental response to Hurricane Katrina in New Orleans and the subsequent crime and violence. It was striking for the world to see governmental ineffectiveness and the concurrent outbreak of crime and violence among the poor in New Orleans. A global and, indeed, national audience was given the impression that a significant outbreak of crime and violence had occurred in New Orleans, a subject that is still a matter of debate. There is little doubt, however, that media coverage of some incidents and their repeated televising all over the world certainly created the impression of lawlessness in New Orleans.

The perception of insecurity in cities depends largely upon the substantial amount and constant flow of information that urban residents receive from many sources

At the same time, intensified media coverage also suggested that the impact of Hurricane Katrina had been predicted and could have been largely avoided through better preparedness. It helped to challenge the global conventional wisdom about natural disasters being neither 'human made' nor 'predictable'.

In addition to media, the personal experiences of individuals and households, and word-of-mouth communication among people within and across neighbourhoods, comprise a central process in describing threats to security. Individual experience confirms apparently similar events reported in the media, leading to a broader sense of vulnerability even if statistical evidence does not confirm such a trend.

A potentially useful approach to assess the level of urban insecurity in specific cities and/or neighbourhoods would be to ask the residents of a particular area for their assessment of specific threats. This has been done in some cities struck by a disaster. In most cases, residents are able to use their local knowledge to identify the origins of the problem and where the risks lie. They usually conclude that the event was 'human made'. This is certainly the case in New Orleans, but also in Mumbai.[84] It also applies quite forcefully in the case of fears of evictions. Municipal authorities in some cities repeatedly issue warnings of eviction against squatters and slum dwellers, regardless of the state of legal appeals and procedures. They create climates of fear and apprehension. In Lima, Peru, there are stories of women fearing to leave their homes vacant in order to avert demolition and destruction of their belongings. Indeed, one of the benefits of secure title in some of the *barriadas*, or slums, of Lima has been the increased mobility of women.

Judged by coverage in the media, crime in some cities is rapidly growing, with the sense of insecurity very present and constantly reinforced by individual stories

Judged by coverage in the media, crime in some cities is rapidly growing, with the sense of insecurity very present and constantly reinforced by individual stories. Yet, in comparative terms, it is frequently difficult to see how one city is 'more dangerous' than another. For example, by 2000, citizens in Buenos Aires, a metropolitan area of 12 million people, were outraged by growing crime and, later in 2004, by kidnappings and murder of young men and women. More than 150,000 people marched on the Plaza de Mayo in central Buenos Aires in 2004 to protest insufficient government attention to crime and insecurity. A murder a month at that time had captured the media and fed people's sense of insecurity. But during the same period, Washington, DC, a city of 600,000 people (or 5 per cent of Buenos Aires), had 1.5 murders per day. Nevertheless, the public mood and outcry was much less in Washington than in Buenos Aires. Perception and visibility of the problem is thus a major issue. It may also reflect who is being murdered. In the case of Buenos Aires, the victims were frequently middle-class people; while in Washington, the victims were almost always African–Americans, the crimes were usually drug related, and they occurred in the poorer neighbourhoods of the city: areas that received less coverage in the media.

In all three areas – crime and violence, insecurity of tenure and disasters – there are significant problems in finding reliable and useful data

The role of evidence

Perceptions and expectations of urban insecurity also depend upon the availability of evidence. This chapter has presented examples of the evidence on the three threats to urban safety and security addressed in this Global Report. Here, trends in data are important to assess. In all three areas – crime and violence, insecurity of tenure, and disasters – there are significant problems in finding reliable and useful data. For example, definitions of each of these phenomena vary across cities and countries. They do not involve only big events such as hurricanes, but also small events in daily life: car robberies, muggings, evictions of individual families or traffic accidents. Systems for collecting such data are well developed in developed countries; but even in these cases there are problems of definition and comparison. In developing countries, in the absence of institutions responsible for the effective collection and analysis of statistical data, it is harder to establish data and examine trends.

Quantitative definitions in most cases badly need to be complemented by qualitative case studies

Each of the three threats to urban safety and security addressed in the report poses specific sets of difficulties with regard to measurement. For the area of crime and violence, these include the following:

- Differences in the legal definitions of various kinds of crime make international comparisons problematic. Similarly, differences occur with regard to recording practices, and precise rules for classifying and counting crime incidents.
- Inadequacy/inaccuracy of official crime data, particularly data recorded by the police. This is partly because police records often depend upon reporting by victims. Consequently, differences in the propensity to report crime will undermine the comparability of the incidence of crime.
- The comparison of crime data across countries or societies that are fundamentally different might ignore key issues that affect levels of reporting. For instance, in certain societies, social norms make it virtually impossible for women to report cases of rape, while in others, they are encouraged to report. This certainly will affect the accuracy of such comparisons.
- The reporting of crime tends to vary with the level of development. Factors such as the number and accessibility of police stations and the number of telephones will be positively correlated with levels of reporting. In societies where there is distrust of the police by the population, reporting levels are likely to be lower than where the police are trusted.

It has been documented that with the recent reduction in crime within the US, pressure is being placed on senior police officials to manipulate or under-report crime data in order to significantly reduce reported crime in areas under their control.

Attempts to overcome these methodological challenges include the introduction of national incident-based reporting systems, self-report crime surveys and crime victimization surveys. These are discussed in Chapter 3.

Similar problems of measurement exist regarding insecurity of tenure. As discussed in Chapter 5, there are many different forms of tenure, varying not only in the degree of security and duration, but also depending upon individual national legal systems. To measure the lack of security, therefore, poses the challenge of measuring the probability of violations of tenure arrangements, whether, for example, as threats by local government to bulldoze a slum, or whether the action to be counted is the actual bulldozing itself (i.e. whether threats as intentions are to be measured). This is quite complicated in an individual context, but even worse when the effort is intended to be comparative (e.g. to show that one country has more secure tenure for its urban residents than another). While it is possible to estimate the numbers of people with insecure tenure through surrogate indicators, such as occupancy of slums, as discussed in Chapter 5, inferences from such estimates have to be taken cautiously.

These issues also apply with regard to natural and human-made disasters. Normally, the characterization of an event as a 'disaster' or as a 'catastrophe' is made on common sense grounds in terms of the number of people or land area affected. This is a relatively easier data problem than in the case of crime and violence or tenure security because the event to be measured is less subject to different local definitions and meaning. It can be asserted that a flood is a flood, even if the people directly affected by the flood experience it differently and may argue that if the flood is 'catastrophic' for one family, it may be less so for another.

This example leads to the issue of the stage at which quantitative data takes on qualitative characteristics, an issue that relates to the difference between quantitative and qualitative information. Definitions of events vary because they reflect different cultural and contextual perceptions of events and behaviours in different locations. As such, quantitative definitions in most cases badly need to be complemented by qualitative case studies. The latter, however, are complicated to undertake and again depend upon what is to be studied. For example, the last thing the criminal desires is to be an object of study. The clandestine character of criminal behaviour therefore 'masks' much of the important data about motivation and dynamics of crime itself. The impact of individual crimes on victims is easier to document.

All of this suggests that devoting more effort to understanding the contexts in which challenges to urban safety and security occur would be a significant first step towards improving evidence. Here it should be possible to build on already shared conclusions about existing trends. For example, if it is known that increased demographic growth will create a growing housing shortage in cities in developing countries, there should be no surprise that more and more people will illegally occupy public and private land (some of it vulnerable to natural hazards) because they have no legal alternatives. This will exacerbate the problem of insecurity of tenure. It can be expected that people do not break rules and risk punishment if they have other ways of meeting their needs.[85] Unless sound policy is developed to increase access to tenure security, it is reasonable to expect more difficulties for the urban poor and the increasing probability of more forced evictions.

Methodologies and public understanding

While perception and evidence can be obstacles to improving public understanding, there are also significant problems in methods of analysis, as discussed later in this Global Report. Methodological problems can be grouped into the following categories:

- defining issues relevant to discussing the three threats to urban safety and security addressed in this report;
- specifying origins and sequences of causation;
- describing agents, whether perpetrators of crime; individuals or institutions affecting security of tenure or carrying out evictions; or individuals or institutions involved in preparedness, mitigation or recovery from disasters;
- identifying victims;
- measuring impact;
- establishing typologies of impact;
- identifying loci of responsibility;
- establishing the basis for comparative analysis; and
- identifying effective forms of prevention or good practice.

All three of these challenges to urban safety and security reflect policy failures, inadequate institutional capacity at both national and local government levels, and insufficient public education for analysis of risk and probabilities of threats to urban safety and security, preparedness, response and remedy. The responsibility for these inadequacies, however, is not strictly limited to urban policies directly concerned with human settlements, and particularly slums, but also reflects constraints imposed by macro-economic policies and, indeed, the impacts of the global economy.

The issues, however, go far beyond financial resources. They are rooted in ideas, public perceptions of these issues, and cultural values and understandings of how the world works. Everyone thinks that they understand these three issues; therefore, conventional wisdom develops and becomes the basis for public action. Unfortunately, that conventional wisdom is not always correct and may, in fact, inhibit finding effective solutions. Indeed, it remains to be seen whether conventional wisdom itself is correctible by forceful public leadership and effective public education. This Global Report seeks to present an analytic framework and policy recommendations to address these problems.

While perception and evidence can be obstacles to improving public understanding, there are also significant problems in methods of analysis

CONCLUDING REMARKS

This chapter has provided an overview of the three threats to urban safety and security that constitute the theme of this report. It is apparent from experiences in cities around the world that some cities are able to stand up and respond to these threats better than others. Chapter 2 will present a conceptual framework based on the two ideas of vulnerability and resilience, which are useful in explaining threats to urban safety and security and in developing public policy options for enhancing urban safety and security, respectively. Societies can build the needed resilience required to overcome crime and violence, insecurity of tenure and disasters. Some cities such as Medellin (Colombia), Daidema (Brazil), or New York (US) have demonstrated that crime and violence can be reduced. Increased global recognition of the human right to secure tenure represents a large step forward towards reducing tenure insecurity. The success of grassroots movements in many countries, notably the Slum Dwellers Federation, which started in India, and is now active in South Africa and the Philippines, among other countries, shows that citizen action can play a critical role in this process. Similarly, the experiences of countries after disasters demonstrate that knowledge and education can enhance preparedness. The experience of The Netherlands since the flooding of 1953 shows that it is possible to anticipate flooding through building dikes and investing in institutional and societal learning.[86] Likewise, the response of Kobe to the 1995 Great Hanshin Earthquake demonstrates how rebuilding can provide the opportunity to achieve a much higher level of security through attention to building methods and a stronger building code.[87] Cuba has developed effective procedures for quick evacuation of Havana[88] and other urban areas in the face of repeated hurricanes. Women's organizations in disaster-affected areas have all demonstrated that they can respond to the disaster, but also advance the cause of social and community reform.[89] Each of these areas of risk and vulnerability also contain what has been called 'spaces of hope'.[90]

Societies can build the needed resilience required to overcome crime and violence, insecurity of tenure and disasters

NOTES

1 Pelling, 2003.
2 United Nations Commission on Human Security, 2003.
3 *Ibid*, piv.
4 *Ibid*, pp4–6.
5 *Ibid*, p4.
6 Sen, 2000.
7 UN-Habitat and ESCAP, 2002.
8 UN-Habitat, 2003d, 2006e.
9 UN-Habitat, 2003f.
10 Tannerfeldt and Ljung, 2006.
11 Mohan, 2002a.
12 Gold, 2000a.
13 Appadurai, 2006.
14 UNDP, 2004.
15 There is a large literature on urban crime and violence. A useful overview and set of case studies on this subject is in *Environment and Urbanization* (2004) vol 16, no 2, October.
16 Reza et al, 2001.
17 WHO, 2004a.
18 Gurr, 1981.
19 Monkkonen, 2001a, p81.
20 Reza et al, 2001, Figure 1.
21 This work has been extended more recently in Eisner, 2003.
22 Simmel, 1903.
23 Bronfenbrenner, 1988.
24 WHO, 2004a, p4
25 Moser and McIlwaine, 2004, p99.
26 *Ibid*.
27 Nisbett and Cohen, 1996.
28 Robben and Nordstrom, 1995, p8, quoted in Moser and McIlwaine, 2004.
29 Simone, 2005.
30 Chua, 2003.
31 Huntington, 1996.
32 Appadurai, 2006, pp15–16; see also Huntington, 1996.
33 Balbus, 1973.
34 Appadurai, 2006.
35 WHO, 2004a, Table 1, p14.
36 *Ibid*, 2004a, p13.
37 *Ibid*, 2004a, px.
38 *Ibid*, 2004a, p6.
39 *Ibid*, 2004a, p27.
40 Sanin and Jaramillo, 2004.
41 Boisteau and Pedrazzini, 2006.
42 Ministry of Foreign Affairs, Canada, 2006, p12.
43 Viva Rio, 2005.
44 *Ibid*, p24.
45 Ministry of Foreign Affairs, Canada, 2006, pp2–3.
46 Shaw, 2002.
47 UN-Habitat and UNDP, 2002.
48 Ministry of Foreign Affairs, Canada, 2006, p7.
49 *Ibid*, 2006, p8.
50 *Ibid*, 2006, p12.
51 Dowdney, 2005, quoted in Ministry of Foreign Affairs, Canada, 2006, p12.
52 Moser and Holland, 1997b.
53 See, for example, the bottom-up research methodology proposed by Moser and McIlwaine, 1999.
54 Vanderschueren, 2000, p2.
55 Ministry of Foreign Affairs, Canada, 2006, p9.
56 Ministry of Foreign Affairs, Canada, 2006, p10.
57 UN-Habitat and OHCHR, 2002.
58 Durand-Lasserve, 2006.
59 *Ibid*, p3.
60 Durand-Lasserve and Royston, 2002, p3.
61 UN-Habitat, 2005c, p4; UN Millennium Project, 2005.
62 Durand-Lasserve and Royston, 2002a.
63 Royston, 2002, p165.
64 See, for example, Turner and Fichter, 1972; World Bank, 1975.
65 UN-Habitat, 2005c.
66 Hardoy and Satterthwaite, 1989.
67 See Tibaijuka, 2005.
68 World Bank, 1993b.
69 There is a long tradition of these studies going back to the 1960s – for example, Marris, 1961; Haeringer, 1969; Cohen, 1974.
70 See, for example, case studies in *Environment and Urbanization* (2003) vol 17, no 1; or Payne, 2005.
71 Angel, 2000.
72 Farvacque-Vitkovic et al, 2005.
73 World Bank, 2006a, p3; Guha-Sapir et al, 2004.
74 *Ibid*.
75 Guha-Sapir et al, 2004.
76 World Bank, 2006a, p3.
77 IFRC, 2001, quoted in World Bank, 2006a, p11. Additional data is presented in Chapter 7.
78 World Bank, 2006a, p5.
79 Linnerooth-Bayer and Amendola, 2000.
80 Guha-Sapir et al, 2004.
81 Klinenberg, 2002b.
82 Other, non-official, estimates put the death toll of the Tangshan earthquake as high as 655,000 (see Wikipedia, http://en.wikipedia.org/wiki/List_of_natural_disasters_by_death_toll, table titled 'Ten deadliest natural disasters').
83 Ministry of Foreign Affairs, Canada, 2006, p7.
84 See Washington, 2007.
85 This argument may not always apply to urban crime and violence, which, while considerably more complicated, both at the individual and societal level, is nevertheless not a preferred occupation if people have other opportunities that allow them to earn incomes to meet their needs.
86 See Orr et al, 2007.
87 See Orr, 2007.
88 Thompson, 2007.
89 See Rowbottom, 2007.
90 Harvey, 2000.

CHAPTER 2

VULNERABILITY, RISK AND RESILIENCE: TOWARDS A CONCEPTUAL FRAMEWORK

This chapter presents a conceptual framework for understanding urban safety and security issues that relies on the concept of *vulnerability*. Vulnerability, as an analytical framework, has during recent years been increasingly used in a number of disciplines, including economics (especially in the study of poverty, sustainable livelihoods and food security), sociology and social anthropology, disaster management, environmental science, and health and nutrition.[1] In these disciplines, vulnerability is often reduced to three fundamental elements – namely, *risk*, *response* and *outcome*, while the last two elements, in particular, are determined by the extent of *resilience* at various levels (i.e. individual, household, community, city and national levels).

This chapter starts by defining and discussing the concept of vulnerability, together with its components of risk, response and outcome, as well as the related concept of resilience. Together, these ideas constitute the building blocks towards a conceptual framework for analysing the three threats to urban safety and security addressed in this Global Report – that is, crime and violence, insecurity of tenure and forced eviction, as well as natural and human-made disasters. This is followed by a discussion of the risk factors underlying these threats to urban safety and security, which are examined at various geographic or spatial levels: global, national, urban, neighbourhood or community, household and individual. Thereafter, the concept of resilience is discussed in relation to the three threats to urban safety and security that constitute the theme of this report. Of particular importance in this section is the identification of the challenges of overcoming institutional weaknesses and building capacity, and how this can be achieved through what might be called 'pathways to resilience'. A clear understanding of the risk factors at various geographic levels, in relation to the concept of resilience, is essential for the formulation and implementation of effective policies for enhancing urban safety and security. Finally, the role of urban policy, planning, design and governance in enhancing urban safety and security is discussed briefly, thus providing a rationale for the choice of 'urban safety and security' as a theme for a Global Report written from a human settlements perspective.

VULNERABILITY AND RELATED CONCEPTS

Vulnerability may be defined as the probability of an individual, a household or a community falling below a minimum level of welfare (e.g. poverty line), or the probability of suffering physical and socio-economic consequences (such as homelessness or physical injury) as a result of risky events and processes (such as forced eviction, crime or a flood) and their inability to effectively cope with such risky events and processes. The logical sequence is that individuals, households and communities are vulnerable to suffering negative outcomes or consequences, and the level of vulnerability (which is sometimes measurable) comes from exposure to risk and the ability or inability to respond to or cope with that risk. Distinctions can be made between physical vulnerability (vulnerability in the built environment) and social vulnerability (vulnerability experienced by people and their social, economic and political systems). Together they constitute human vulnerability.[2]

As pointed out earlier, the concept of vulnerability is better understood by dividing it into the 'risk chain' elements of risk, risk response and outcome.[3] *Risk* refers to a known or unknown probability distribution of events – for example, natural hazards such as floods or earthquakes. The extent to which risks affect vulnerability is dependent upon their size and spread (magnitude), as well as their frequency and duration.

The concept of vulnerability is better understood by dividing it into the 'risk-chain' elements of risk, risk response and outcome

Risk response refers to the ways in which individuals, households, communities and cities respond to, or manage, risk. Risk management may be in the form of *ex ante* or *ex post* actions – that is, preventive action taken *before* the risky event, and action taken to deal with experienced losses *after* the risky event, respectively. *Ex ante* actions taken in advance in order to mitigate the undesirable consequences of risky events may include purchase of personal or home insurance to provide compensation in case of theft, injury or damage to property; building strong social networks able to cope with risky events or hazards; and effective land-use planning and design of buildings and infrastructure able to withstand natural hazards such as floods, tropical storms and earthquakes. *Ex post* actions may include evacuating people from affected areas; selling household assets in order to deal with sudden loss of income; providing public-sector safety nets, such as food-for-work programmes; or reconstructing damaged buildings and infrastructure.

From the point of view of policy-making, the challenge with respect to risk response is to find ways of addressing the constraints faced by individuals, households, communities and cities in managing risk. These constraints may be related to poor information, lack of finance or assets, inability to assess risk, ineffective public institutions and poor social networks.[4] All of these constraints are among the determinants of *resilience*, a concept that reflects the quality or effectiveness of risk response. Resilience has been defined as the capacity of an individual, household or community to adjust to threats, to avoid or mitigate harm, as well as to recover from risky events or shocks. Resilience is partly dependent upon the effectiveness of risk response, as well as the capability to respond in the future.[5] The concept of resilience, which is discussed in more detail later in this chapter, has been increasingly used during the last decade to characterize societies and institutions that are able to adjust to change or to bounce back from problems.

One of the most important socio-economic determinants of vulnerability is poverty

Outcome is the actual loss, or damage, experienced by individuals, households and communities due to a risky event or risky process – for example, physical injury, death and loss of assets resulting from crime and violence; falling below a given poverty line and loss of income as a result of forced eviction from informal housing or informal sources of livelihood; as well as damage to buildings and infrastructure resulting from natural or human-made hazards. The outcome of a risky event is determined by both the nature of the risk as well as the degree of effectiveness of the response of individuals, households, communities and cities to risky events.

Another very important determinant of vulnerability is the capacity of institutions

A recent paper has provided a good interdisciplinary working concept of vulnerability at the household level, which can be extended to the individual, community, city and national levels as well:[6]

> *A household is said to be vulnerable to future loss of welfare below socially accepted norms caused by risky events. The degree of vulnerability depends on the characteristics of the risk and the household's ability to respond to risk. Ability to respond to risk depends on household characteristics – notably their asset base. The outcome is defined with respect to some benchmark – a socially accepted minimum reference level of welfare (e.g. a poverty line). Measurement of vulnerability will also depend on the time horizon: a household may be vulnerable to risks over the next month, year, etc.*

One of the most important socio-economic determinants of vulnerability is poverty.[7] It has even been suggested that, because of their close correspondence, poverty should be used as an indicator of vulnerability.[8] The urban poor are generally more exposed to risky events (such as crime, forced eviction or disasters) than the rich, partly because of their geographical location. With respect to disasters, the urban poor are more vulnerable than the rich because they are often located on sites prone to floods, landslides and pollution. The urban poor also have relatively limited access to assets, thus limiting their ability to respond to risky events or to manage risk (e.g. through insurance). Because the poor are politically powerless, it is unlikely that they will receive the necessary social services following disasters or other risky events. In addition, the urban poor are more vulnerable to the undesirable outcomes of risky events because they are already closer to or below the threshold levels of these outcomes, whether they are income poverty or tenure insecurity. Particularly affected in this respect are the least advantaged groups in society, such as women, children, the elderly and the disabled.

Another very important determinant of vulnerability is the capacity of institutions. This influecnes the *response* and *outcome* elements in the *risk chain* discussed above – in terms of effectiveness and severity, respectively. For the purposes of the conceptual framework currently under discussion, the term *institution* refers to any structured pattern of behaviour, including informal institutions or behaviours, which communities and households may use to maintain their equilibrium in the face of dynamic conditions such as crime and violence or disasters. Given the weakness of formal institutions in many developing countries, it is instructive to approach this question from the level of social organization, rather than only from the perspective of formal institutions such as municipalities, police or emergency preparedness agencies, which are usually the focus of technocratic approaches to these problems. This broader definition thus allows the recognition of 'informal' institutions as legitimate participants and stakeholders in addressing threats to urban safety and security. Both formal and informal institutions can be characterized by their degree of resilience in the face of threats and uncertainty.

Vulnerability may be used as a general framework for conceptualizing and analysing the causal relationships between risk, responses and outcomes of risky events and processes, as in much of the work on sustainable livelihoods and also as used in this report. However, some applications of the vulnerability concept have been quite precise and have sought to measure vulnerability in quantitative terms. The main challenge has been to identify measures of vulnerability to different outcomes of risky events and processes and, sometimes, to find a common metric that is applicable across different outcomes.[9] Another approach has been that of *vulnerability mapping*.[10] This has been used predominantly in food security and disaster management studies. The objective of vulnerability mapping is to identify spatially vulnerable areas by overlaying maps of different vulnerability factors (or variables) and of population distribution by socio-economic class in order to identify the extent of vulnerability of populations residing in high risk areas.

Clearly, the concept of vulnerability provides a useful framework for understanding the nature of risk and risky

Table 2.1

Vulnerability as a conceptual framework: Risk, response and outcome

Threat to urban safety and security	Risk	Response	Outcome
Crime and violence	Specific risky events are the various types of crime and violence, such as burglary, assault, rape, homicide and terrorist attacks.	Responses may include more effective criminal justice systems, improved surveillance, community policing, better design of public/open spaces and transport systems, improved employment for youth, development of gated communities, and provision of private security services.	Key outcomes include loss of assets, injury, death, damage to property, emotional/ psychological suffering or stress, fear, and reduced urban investment.
Tenure insecurity and forced eviction	Specific risky event is forced eviction, while risky socio-economic processes and factors include poverty, social exclusion, discriminatory inheritance laws, ineffective land policies, as well as lack of planning and protection of human rights.	Examples of risk responses at the individual and household levels include informal savings and social networks, and political organization to resist forced eviction and to advocate for protection of human rights. At the institutional level, responses include more effective land policies and urban planning, as well as housing rights legislation.	Outcomes include homelessness, loss of assets, loss of income and sources of livelihood. May also include physical injury or death if eviction process is violent.
Natural and human-made/technological disasters	Specific risky events (or hazards) include floods, earthquakes, hurricanes, volcanic eruptions, technological disasters and war.	Examples of major responses include *ex ante* measures such as more effective spatial design of cities and the design of individual buildings, as well as home insurance; and *ex post* measures such as emergency response systems, reconstruction of buildings and infrastructure, as well as rehabilitation of institutions in war-torn countries.	Key outcomes may include physical injury, loss of income and assets, damage to buildings and infrastructure, as well as emotional/psychological stress.

events, the impacts or outcomes of risky events, as well as responses to risky events at various levels. Within the context of this report, risk refers to both risky events (such as natural and human-made disasters), as well as risky socio-economic processes (such as crime, violence and the kind of social exclusion that leads to tenure insecurity and forced eviction). Outcomes of risky events and processes are the undesirable consequences of crime and violence (such as loss of assets, injury and death), of tenure insecurity and forced eviction (such as homelessness and loss of livelihoods), as well as of natural and human-made disasters (such as injury, death and damage to property and infrastructure). The chapters in Parts II, III and IV discuss the nature and global incidence of the major risky events, or threats to urban safety and security, addressed in this report. The chapters also discuss the impacts or outcomes of (as well as the responses to) these major threats or risks. Table 2.1 is a schematic representation of how the concept of vulnerability is used in this report as an analytical framework.

Human life is inherently vulnerable and susceptible to a wide range of risks or hazards that can threaten urban safety at the individual, household, community or neighbourhood, city and national levels. While the sources of human vulnerability are multiple, they can essentially be divided into three broad categories:

- The first category includes *chronic vulnerabilities* associated with biological necessities such as food, water, shelter and health. People must have these needs met to some minimal degree in order to survive. Significant disruptions to satisfying these needs can result in ill health and death. In many cases, these vulnerabilities are persistent and of a long-term nature.
- The second category includes *contextual vulnerabilities* arising from the social, economic, political and environmental contexts of human life, including the density of interactions between and among people, which surround the life of one individual. These can include harm from ethnic violence, loss of income and employment due to deindustrialization, drug-induced crime, or unjust policies of government to bulldoze slums, thereby increasing insecurity of tenure. While these vulnerabilities are the consequences of contextual processes, they may take the form of infrequent incidents or events.
- A third category includes vulnerability from major unusual, but periodic, events such as natural or human-made disasters, including hurricanes, earthquakes or wars. They are distinguished from the second category by their magnitude and depth of impact. As suggested in the introduction to Part IV, they are notable by their scale of loss, which exceeds the resilience, or overwhelms the ability, of a household, community or city to cope.

The extent of the impact of catastrophic events depends upon the presence and force of chronic underlying conditions

Assessments of threats to urban safety and security must include all three categories and, indeed, some are interdependent, such as satisfaction of basic needs requiring income and employment to sustain access to those services. The key distinction here, however, is between *underlying chronic conditions* resulting from the level of development and per capita income of countries and the frequency of either minor or major *significant or catastrophic events* that occur with low probabilities in the same locations. Analytically, the conceptual frameworks for these categories have been traditionally distinct, although experience, especially with the application of the vulnerability framework, demonstrates that they are increasingly interactive. An example is that many communities face land tenure conflicts in their recovery from disasters (see Box 2.1). A tenure insecurity problem, such as forced eviction, may result in serious violence, while a natural disaster may result in crime and a general breakdown of law and order.

It is now understood that the extent of the impact of catastrophic events depends upon the presence and force of chronic underlying conditions. In this sense, in many (although not all) cases, these events may be more of a process than an event. A clear example is the performance of infrastructure during a disaster since this is a strong indicator of institutional capacity, as is the maintenance of order by

Box 2.1 The 2004 Indian Ocean Tsunami: Victims and land tenure

Land tenure is another institution which, if weak or corrupt, can increase vulnerability to hazard. For individuals or families living in insecure land tenure situations (e.g. squatting on privately owned land or on land for which a title does not exist), once displaced they may be unable to return. For some people, assistance to rebuild may require documentation, or one or more other parties may claim that the land is theirs. Beyond being poor and living in structurally weak homes close to the sea, many tsunami-struck communities lived on government or privately held land, or land with multiple claims. Land grabs plagued coastal communities where undocumented and uncertain land status provided government and private landowners opportunities to evict residents. In other cases, ownership documents were destroyed and physical property lines were non-existent. Still others faced discrimination by regulations instituted post-tsunami under the pretext of reducing vulnerability, such as banning rebuilding within certain distances of the sea.

These situations plague thousands of tsunami survivors across the affected region; but many communities are seeking ways of rebuilding their lives, including improving land tenure security. New strategies are emerging across the region. To begin, many communities are simply going back to their land to rebuild, even without permission, or while the land is still being disputed. This was the strategy of the Aceh's *Udeep Beusaree* network of villages and Thai communities, who then used their solidarity and occupation as a negotiation tool. These and other communities also mapped their settlements, collected information on historical ownership and prepared redevelopment plans. Two important solutions have transpired and are a result of communities coming together, as well as networking with other communities: land sharing and collective land tenure arrangements. Land sharing entails disputed land being shared by both parties. The community rebuilds on one portion of the land with legal and secure rights, and the landowner develops the other portion commercially. Collective land tenure includes collective leases, collective title and collective user rights. The community is the unit of ownership/lease holding, which can fend off challenges and manipulation more easily than individuals can. Plots cannot be sold independently. In this way, solutions are being found to institutional problems that have made communities vulnerable for generations. Many previously vulnerable residents now have a base from which to lobby government and to fight private interests. With legal rights to their land, they will be able to more securely invest in their homes and property, improving their human and physical security, and more easily access assistance in the event of hazardous events.

Source: Rowbottom, 2007

normal police presence. Similarly, studies of the health impacts of urban environmental problems are closely tied to the availability and condition of infrastructure. Indeed, they show patterns of causation that clearly demonstrate how various types of infrastructure can alleviate specific health risks.[11]

Threats to urban safety and security ... are closely linked to many factors at different geographic levels of analysis: global, national, urban, neighbourhood or community, household and individual

RISK FACTORS AT DIFFERENT LEVELS OF ANALYSIS

As introduced in Chapter 1, the threats to urban safety and security addressed in this Global Report are closely linked to many factors at different geographic levels of analysis. In order to identify the location of risks as well as the multiple levels of causation, this section examines risk factors at the following analytic levels: global, national, urban, neighbourhood or community, household and individual. Special attention is paid to underlying patterns of causation, highlighting the cumulative impact of the identified factors, as well as their interdependence in several spheres of activity: social, economic and environmental. As many studies of urban safety and security suggest, there are multiple forms of interaction that operate simultaneously to create risks and condition the vulnerabilities experienced by nations, cities, communities, households and individuals. The conceptual task is how to describe and distinguish these different interactions and to assess their relative weights. In this regard, it is important to stress that factors beyond the urban level have considerable impact on conditions of urban safety and security.

Global forces

Three aspects of global forces are likely to have significant impacts on urban safety and security: the global economy and, particularly, financial markets; the global environment and the likely impacts of climate change; and increased uncertainty due to the interaction of global forces and the consequent weakening of the capacity of national and local institutions to manage risks and reduce vulnerabilities. Each has direct and indirect impacts on the three threats to urban safety and security addressed by this report: crime and violence, forced evictions and insecurity of tenure, and natural and human-made disasters.

■ The global economy

The processes of globalization of the world economy have significantly reduced the independence of national and local economies. The formation of a global capital market, the diffusion and dominant role of technology in information flows and decision-making, and the liberalization of these flows through the application of neo-liberal economic policies at the global and national levels have introduced new actors into the world of national and local policymakers. No longer can governments manage their economies (i.e. interest rates, flows of private investment now known as foreign direct investment, trade projections, and commodity and energy prices) without daily attention to global markets and the behaviours of major players such as China, the European Union (EU), the Organization of the Petroleum Exporting Countries (OPEC), Japan and the US. The importance of decisions in distant locations is reflected in the 24-hour operations of global and national institutions and their increased surveillance of the behaviour of overseas markets. No longer are these developments monitored only by ministries of finance, central banks and major financial institutions on Wall Street, the City in London or the stock market in Tokyo, but they are actively included in national and local public and private economic decisions on a daily basis.

Global information flows do not necessarily bring increased stability. Global markets have carefully followed developments in individual national economies and produced significant shared reactions, such as capital flight, or alternatively, in-pouring of funds in search of quick profits following the Asian financial crisis of 1997 and later in Brazil, Russia and Argentina. These effects are considerable and are reflected in dramatic changes in country risk ratings. Finance ministers may seek to protect their economies from such processes; but this ability to manage risks and uncertainty is limited in an increasingly interdependent world.

An important aspect of this contagion is increased volatility. There is now a clear recognition that the volatility of the global economy creates additional uncertainties and insecurities for national and local economic actors.[12] This volatility does not just have impacts on financial markets, but can also have specific impacts on, for example, whether private water companies will invest in extending water supply services to underserved neighbourhoods on the peripheries of cities.[13] Increases of 0.25 per cent in world interest rates can upset investment plans at the city level. This fact becomes particularly salient when considered in light of the additional 2 billion expected urban residents by 2030.

If national and local shortages of finance for urban shelter and infrastructure were serious problems before the globalization of financial markets,[14] these shortages will be increasingly exacerbated by the interdependence and volatility of these markets. There is great sensitivity of urban investment decisions to changes in interest rates. When a decision to invest in housing or shelter in Guadalajara or Istanbul is connected to whether interest rates increase as a result of decisions by Chinese monetary authorities to reduce inflation in China, new degrees of uncertainty have begun to affect local markets and the quality of urban shelter and infrastructure.

Global finance is already affecting the cost and availability of capital for investment and job creation in urban areas. These pressures have direct impacts on many aspects of the national and urban economy. For example, changes in the cost of capital can affect public investment programmes from urban infrastructure to crime prevention, in both cases affecting the safety and security of urban residents, as well as prospects for employment and incomes, particularly for the poor whose incomes are closely tied to the demand for unskilled labour. Changes in interest rates also directly provoke changes in the prices of housing and land, and thus affect the circumstances of security of tenure for the poor. Positive and negative changes in urban inequality and economic opportunity, in turn, provoke new forms of crime and violence. A study of macro-economic changes and urban poverty in Latin America in the late 1990s showed that while the incomes of middle- and upper-income groups are sensitive to upturns in macro-economic performance, those of the urban poor drop disproportionately lower in times of recession and improve at a much slower rate than do those of middle- and upper-income groups.[15]

A study on these patterns at the national level in the US in 1999 showed how cumulative causation operates through marginal changes in interest rates, translated into housing prices and rent levels, local finance, school expenditures and the social conditions of neighbourhoods.[16] When global forces are added to the mix, they will be increasingly present at local levels.[17]

The volatility of the global economy creates additional uncertainties and insecurities for national and local economic actors

The global environment

Another global force that directly affects local safety and security is the global environment. Scientific evidence of global warming and climate change is helping to explain the increased frequency of extreme weather events and changes in the normal patterns of regional and national weather (see Figure 2.1). These events, such as hurricanes, violent storms, increased rainfall in some locations and decreased rainfall in others, all serve to upset historical patterns of cultivation and economic activity, as well as place new physical strains on infrastructure. These have been well illustrated by the effects of El Niño in Latin America, which has brought drought in some areas and intensive rainfall in others. In both cases, agricultural output has been damaged in Argentina and the Andean countries. The distinctions between so-called category 3 and 4 hurricanes in the Gulf of Mexico that were previously largely meteorological notions with technical implications for engineering standards for levees have now become household words as the public learns more about what happened in New Orleans and what will happen with subsequent hurricane seasons.

Scientific evidence of global warming and climate change is helping to explain the increased frequency of extreme weather events and changes

Scientific and public debate on climate change has intensified during the last several years as scientific evidence of climate change has been confirmed in many forms, as a recent observation states:

> *Multiple lines of evidence indicate that the Earth's climate is nearing, but has not passed a tipping point, beyond which it will be impossible to avoid climate change with far-ranging undesirable consequences.*[18]

The increased frequency of severe weather events, however, is only part of the global environment threat to safety and urban security. Global warming contributes to the melting of ice caps and glaciers and results in rising sea levels. These phenomena have recently been described in the following terms:

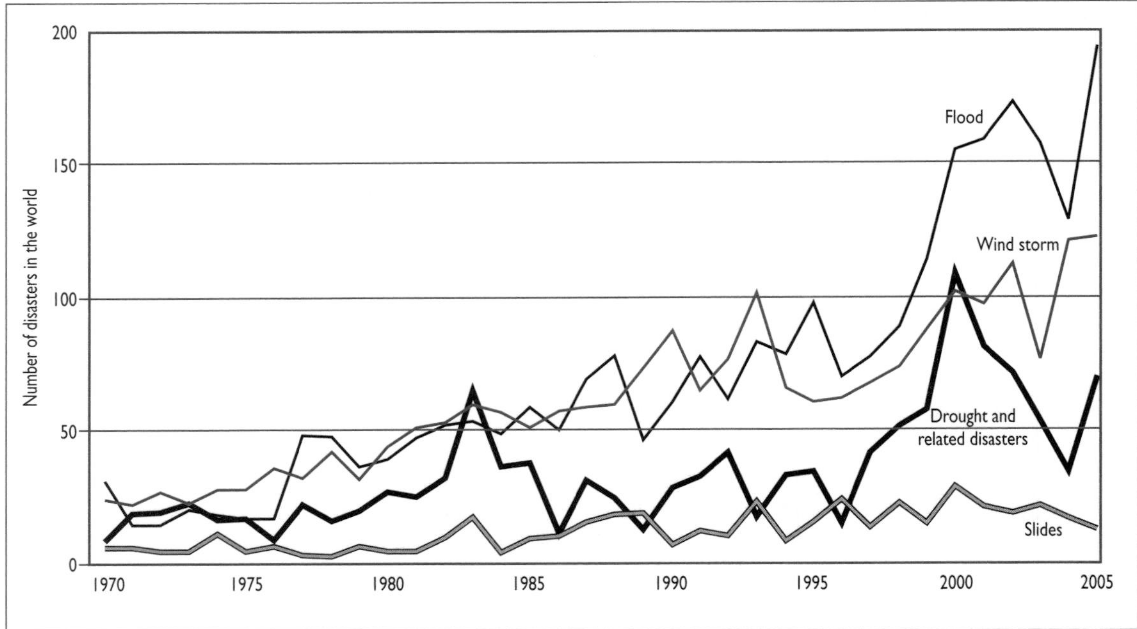

Figure 2.1

Global warming and meteorological disasters

Source: United Nations International Strategy for Disaster Reduction, Disaster Statistics, www.unisdr.org/disaster-statistics-occurence.pdf

> *Kilimanjaro's ice cloak is soon to disappear, the summertime Arctic Ocean could be ice free by century's end, 11,000-year-old shelves around Antarctica are breaking up over the course of weeks, and glaciers there and in Greenland have begun galloping into the sea. And the receding glaciers, at least, are surely driving up sea level and pushing shorelines inland... Rising seas would push half a billion people inland.*[19]

The declining effectiveness of government and public authority is a potentially devastating result of global environmental trends

This frightening prospect makes flooding in Mumbai or New Orleans appear quite limited in impact and significance. A large share of the world's total stock of wealth, including fixed public assets such as infrastructure, private investments in production capacity and cultivation, not to speak of the heritage of cities themselves as the crucibles of civilization, are located in coastal areas (see Figure 2.2). The issue of sea-level rise therefore deserves special attention. Recent estimates show dramatic economic losses in countries as diverse as Japan, Egypt and Poland, all in different ecological zones and climates, but all facing potential impacts on millions of people and losses in the many billions of US dollars.[20]

In this context, these global environmental forces completely change the meaning of urban safety and security. Table 2.2 presents some of this data. One can wonder when 'the rich' will begin to buy 'safe' inland locations and how such changes in investment will affect normal patterns of urban life. Such change does not occur overnight; but one can imagine that a few major events could easily spark behaviour changes on a worldwide level. Speculation about the impacts of such changes is beyond the scope of this Global Report; but it deserves attention from researchers.

Table 2.2

Distribution of world population as a function of distance from the nearest coastline

Source: Gommes et al, 1998

Distance from the coast (km)	Population (million)	Accumulated population (million)	Accumulated percentage
Up to 30km	1147	1147	20.6
>30 to 60km	480	1627	29.2
>60 to 90km	327	1954	35
>90 to 120km	251	2205	39.5
Beyond 120km	3362	5567	100

Global uncertainty and weakening of national institutions

A third type of global factor is the increased uncertainty arising from the interaction of global forces and the consequent weakening of national and local institutions to manage risks and reduce vulnerabilities. Uncertainty reduces the capacity to plan and to prepare for change. When the probability of events does not depend upon the actions of the party likely to be affected, or in this case national or local governments, it weakens the status and authority of government when it seeks to manage risks and reduce vulnerabilities. The public at large can ask why they should accept the advice of government if the latter does not have either better information about a probable event or any means to mitigate its impact. In fact, anticipation is the first step towards mitigation and, therefore, anticipation does reduce risks and vulnerabilities by removing the role of surprise and allowing the possibility of some degree of preparedness.

The declining effectiveness of government and public authority is a potentially devastating result of global environmental trends. The constructive responses and solidarity among victims of flooding in Mumbai in July 2005 may be interpreted as socially and culturally responsible behaviour in the absence of effective action by the Maharashtra State Government and the Municipal Corporation of Mumbai. The opposite seems to have occurred in New Orleans as federal, state and local authorities were unable to protect the New Orleans population, and particularly the poorest people among them, following Hurricane Katrina in 2005.[21] In both cities, a legacy of the disaster is growing scepticism about the capacity of public institutions to solve problems. This can easily become a self-fulfilling prophecy as public officials

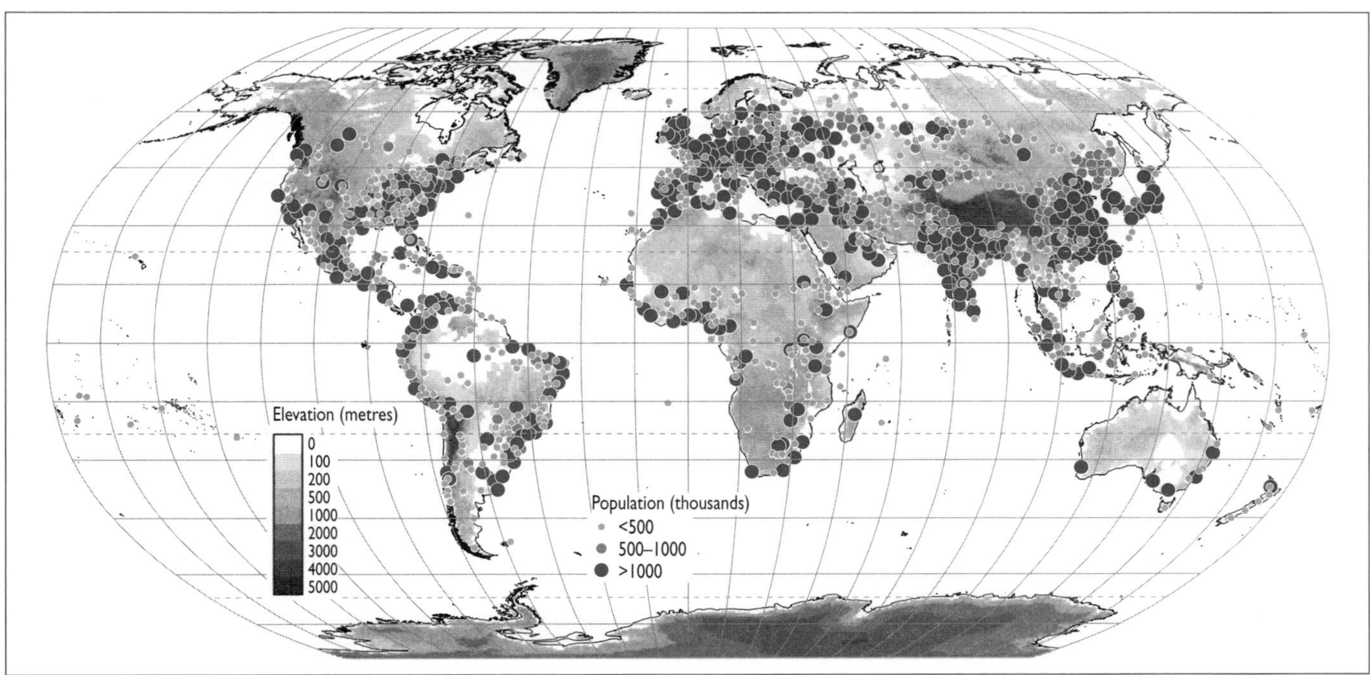

Figure 2.2

Location of major population centres

Source: United Nations, 1997

simply 'give up' in the face of risks they feel they are unable to manage. The latter behaviours fall within the self-destructive behaviours of institutions and societies which have declined and, in some cases, disappeared.[22] Both of these cases, however, demonstrate the importance of local culture and civil society, subjects that will be treated later in this chapter – as well as in Chapters 7 and 8 – in relation to the issue of resilience.

It is also important to stress that the responses of government to disasters are now themselves globally visible. The leadership of the mayor of New York after 11 September 2001 was widely praised and considered as an example of effective government. In contrast, the mayor of Mumbai, at risk of losing his job after having been sharply criticized for the Mumbai Municipal Corporation's weak response to the monsoon flooding in July 2005, remarked some months later, after the world saw the poor performance of US institutions in responding to Hurricane Katrina in New Orleans: 'Thank heavens for New Orleans.' Confidence in public institutions is therefore itself at risk, with major implications in other arenas as well. Dozens of articles appeared in the Indian press asking why public institutions had not been better prepared to deal with the extreme impacts of largely predictable monsoon rains.[23]

Indeed, there is evidence that political changes are common following disasters as questions are raised about the effectiveness of government responses and the capacities of leadership. Some of the cases of political change following disasters, including Turkey, Mexico, Chile, Nicaragua and Guatemala, are presented in Chapter 7.

These three examples of global forces – the impact of the global economy, the global environment, and the interaction of global uncertainty with the weakening of national and local institutions – are illustrative of the linkages between global, national and urban levels. Each demonstrates how vulnerability to threats to urban safety and security can be affected by forces that previously were not considered to be so significant in reducing local risks. The global level, therefore, must now be considered in the mapping of urban risk.

National level

A wide spectrum of national factors affects vulnerability to problems of urban safety and security and, specifically, the problems of crime and violence, security of tenure, and natural and human-made disasters. These problems start with the level of income of individual countries and societies. In general, data shows that richer countries have lower levels of crime and violence, although there are many exceptions to this pattern, such as the higher homicide levels in the US or in Russia. Chapter 3 presents evidence on the incidence of different types of crime and violence by region of the world and examines the correlations with various socio-economic, political, demographic and cultural factors.[24] The importance of national cultural factors deserves special mention because, for example, the availability and use of firearms is highly cultural, as illustrated in the large differences between the UK, the US and Canada.

In general, data shows that richer countries have lower levels of crime and violence, although there are many exceptions to this pattern

Insecurity of tenure and the likelihood of illegal occupancy of public and private land are also highly negatively correlated with national income. So, too, is vulnerability to natural and human-made disasters, as demonstrated by the fact cited in Chapter 1 that 98 per cent of the victims of disasters since 1990 have been in developing countries. National per capita income, therefore, seems to be a robust and significant, if not entirely determinant, proxy for vulnerability to these three threats to urban safety and security. However, this statement also requires some qualification reflecting local cultural differences across cities.

This finding also correlates strongly with the general finding that many attributes of welfare – longevity, literacy, health status, housing quality, access to water supply and sanitation, among others – correlate positively with national per capita income. Each of these indicators reflects both the resources available in the societies to provide needed services and the institutional capacity to formulate and implement effective public policies. They also correlate (negatively) with levels of absolute poverty, as well as (in many cases) levels of inequality and exclusion.

The following question, therefore, arises: when national per capita income is held constant, how can differences in performance in reducing vulnerability to urban safety and security threats between two countries be explained? This issue is addressed in Chapter 3. This type of question, well answered in the context of the housing sector, suggests the importance of comparative analysis in developing theories of performance on these issues.[25] In the case of housing, local policy variables such as building codes, zoning and the processes to obtain construction permits all have specific impacts on the performance of the housing sector in individual cities. This is well illustrated by the comparison between Bangkok and Kuala Lumpur, where the first city is considerably poorer than the second, but has nevertheless produced a greater quantity of housing at reasonable quality and cost, all due to the differences in the regulatory framework for housing.[26]

National income and national development of countries are strong predictors of vulnerability

This suggests that while levels of national income and national development of countries are strong predictors of vulnerability, they are necessary, but not sufficient, conditions to explain local performance in managing challenges to urban safety and security. As the list of 'conventional wisdom' in Chapter 1 (see Box 1.4) suggests, these challenges are profoundly linked to their urban contexts – whether in relation to environmental, institutional, economic or social dimensions. The level of penetration of 'national' factors into urban performance depends upon the sector (e.g. criminal justice or infrastructure management), as well as the country and the historical development of its institutions. Former French colonies in West Africa such as Côte d'Ivoire or Senegal continue to be institutionally centralized, where the policies and approaches of ministries of interior will determine the responses of local institutions. The weight of central institutions is likely to be less in countries with more decentralized traditions such as Ghana, Nigeria or Tanzania.

It is important to also understand how macro-economic policies concerning expenditures on infrastructure, social services, police and emergency services play critical roles

Influence of national macro-economic factors

For the purpose of this Global Report, within the national level, the role of the macro-economy also deserves further specificity with regard to the impacts of certain policies directly affecting urban safety and security. While the previous discussion linked urban security to levels of national income and development in a general sense, it is important to also understand how macro-economic policies concerning expenditures on infrastructure, social services, police and emergency services play critical roles in this arena. As noted earlier, urban security can also be understood as a 'public good' generated by explicit public policies, investments and current expenditures.

Countries and localities without such expenditures for these public goods will be more vulnerable to threats to safety and security addressed by this report. For example, recent research in Africa shows that 29 per cent of businesses surveyed reported that, in the absence of effective policing, crime was a significant business constraint – 50 per cent more than the global average.[27] Similar studies have been carried out in Jamaica and Papua New Guinea, as well as in cities in parts of the US and the UK.[28]

Such public goods, however, are not so easily created. Indeed, in cities experiencing rapid demographic and spatial growth, it is frequently difficult to convince government authorities that public goods – whether environmental quality or green space – are priorities for public expenditures. These can be reinforced when supported by the broader frameworks of human security and human rights. The ability to provide public goods, however, depends not only upon juridical frameworks, but is also a direct result of the macro-economic patterns of savings and expenditures.

The issues of crime and disaster preparedness are very interesting in this regard. When crime becomes a national issue, or is perceived as a macro-economic problem in terms of its inhibiting impact on tourism and direct financial losses, as in the Mexico City case described in Chapter 1, there is a greater likelihood that the Ministry of Finance will allocate funds to public institutions responsible for fighting crime. Similarly, when countries in the path of recurrent hurricanes in the Caribbean or monsoon rains in South Asia realize that these events have major macro-economic impacts, they will invest in preparedness to reduce these impacts, as the effectiveness of Cuban preparedness for hurricanes and subsequent relief measures demonstrate.[29] Examples also exist in the field of land tenure, for example with respect to stabilization of the location of urban slums. Rather than evict large numbers of people with the attendant economic, financial, social and political costs, national and local authorities can work with communities, private landowners and public authorities to find solutions. While the international community may have a useful role to play in these issues in some circumstances, ultimately the allocation of resources for these purposes is a national macro-economic responsibility.

These examples raise the question of what would be reasonable levels of expenditure to address these challenges. How much, for example, can a developing country afford to maintain urban safety and security? Given the high financial and economic costs of disasters as estimated by the World Bank (presented in Chapter 1), as well as the costs of evicting large urban communities, it would seem that governments should consider allocating considerable investments to strengthening preparedness and urban planning. The economic rates of return of such investments should be very high. One study of costs and benefits of preparedness for disasters concluded that losses could have been reduced by US$20 billion if only US$40 million had been invested in mitigation and preparedness.[30]

The issue of who finances such investments, however, also needs to be examined. What is the balance between international, national and urban responsibility for maintenance of urban safety and security? In conditions of disasters there is generally the expectation that national governments will provide some relief services and also contribute to recovery. But their ability to do so depends both upon national fiscal capacity, as well institutional and technical capacity. Nevertheless, in many cases the causes of these problems may lie outside national boundaries – for example, from political problems such as the settling of political refugees from Darfur in Chad or Rwandans in Congo. The issue of refugees also intersects with the issue of security of tenure because, in many cases, refugees occupy land on a temporary basis, and often for extended periods of time, regardless of its legal status.

A similar case is the losses from periodic floods in Mozambique even though the rivers originate in neighbouring countries. As noted in Chapter 1, even with major international assistance, aid levels have never covered the costs of more than 10 per cent of the losses. This conclusion suggests that countries, particularly the poorest, will have to simply absorb these losses and accept that progress in improving the welfare of their populations will once again be held back. 'Living with the floods', a phrase from the public debate in Mozambique, reflects this resignation in the face of the repeated force of nature.[31]

As noted earlier, from a macro-economic perspective, urban safety and security are also private goods that are consumed by individuals and households. Indeed, there is growing evidence that safety and security from crime in some cities and from natural disasters in other cities are major private priorities for many households. Comparative studies of the effects of structural adjustment in developing countries demonstrate that the impacts of macro-economic change through changes in prices, job opportunities and public expenditures have enormous cumulative impacts on urban households, and particularly the poor. A comparative study of Guayaquil, Manila, Lusaka and Budapest demonstrated how these impacts increased the vulnerabilities of the poor by undercutting important household and community assets,[32] including labour, economic and social infrastructure, housing, household relations, and social capital at the community level. As macro-economic conditions deteriorated and poverty deepened at the community level, urban security became a high priority for poor households as crime and violence dramatically increased, from domestic violence to drug-related crime.

An additional aspect of crime that affects the macro-economic level is the issue of corruption, which is addressed in Chapter 3. Extensive evidence now exists on the impact of corruption on macro-economic performance. Indices of corruption developed by Transparency International have been extended through surveys of individual regions and countries to assess the impact of perceptions of corruption on business practices and levels of investment. Business Environment and Enterprise Performance Surveys are being conducted by the European Bank for Reconstruction and Development, as well as the World Bank, since 1999 in 27 countries, mostly in Central and Eastern Europe and the countries of the former Soviet Union.[33] Analytic work in other regions has advanced as well, with institutions such as the World Bank hardening its approach to this controversial issue.

If corruption refers mostly to crime involving public institutions and officials, another prevalent and growing criminal phenomenon affecting the macro-economic level is organized crime, which is discussed in Chapter 3. While it is difficult to assess the scale and penetration of organized crime into national economies, there are some areas, such as the drug trade, where organized crime is a major force. One study by the United Nations Drug Control Programme estimated that US$1 billion of illicit capital circulates every day in the world's financial institutions.[34]

The urban level

The next level of analysis at which urban safety and security can be assessed is the urban level itself. The essence of the urban is its relation to context: physical, spatial, environmental, social, cultural, economic and political. The meaning of urban safety and security is highly contextual because, while it is indisputably affected by global and national factors, the most institutionally meaningful unit of analysis, as well as arena for action, is the urban region or city.

Urban safety and security are also private goods that are consumed by individuals and households

One of the discourses on urban safety has been the design of 'defensible space' (i.e. how cities and neighbourhoods can be designed to reduce the factors that contribute to crime and violence itself). This includes neighbourhood layouts, the integration of public space with other uses, such as shopping, in order to increase circulation of people at various times in the day, or how transit systems can reduce the isolation of specific transit stops and locations. Extensive studies have been undertaken in the US and major European cities on the relation between transit and security.[35] These issues are discussed in some detail in Chapter 3.

While it is difficult to assess the scale and penetration of organized crime into national economies, there are some areas, such as the drug trade, where organized crime is a major force

Security of tenure is an interesting case at the urban level because the occupancy of land is a central fact in the urban landscape, with implications for poverty, inequality, human rights and discrimination against specific groups, including non-enforcement of internationally recognized rights, as well as national law. The urban context is important here, as illustrated in Chapter 6, which shows how various countries have addressed insecurity of tenure and the safeguarding of human rights. The South Africa case, for example, shows that formalization may be hard to achieve even with legislation, and that such formalization can impose significant costs on the poor. Brazil, too, has made an effort to enact legislation; but the scale and depth of both urban poverty and intra-urban inequality inhibits increasing access to security of tenure. The Indian case is also contradictory, with rights protected by law and the courts; yet, state and local government policy is much more politicized and influenced by political and economic interests, such as the real estate industry.

One of the discourses on urban safety has been the design of 'defensible space'

As noted earlier in this chapter, vulnerability to disasters at the urban level is unevenly distributed and reflects historical settlement patterns, as well as varying degrees of preparedness and attention given to different classes of people. It has been observed that the New Orleans experience demonstrated, to a global audience, visible discrimination in the immediate responses to the security needs of African–American, white and Creole residents, in

Box 2.2 Urban land-use processes and dynamics

A private investor in a city of 3 million people builds a factory in 1960 to produce a chemically based product. Following municipal zoning procedures and industrial safety regulations, the factory is located on the far periphery of the metropolitan area, outside the borders of the central municipality, allowing the noxious fumes to blow far away from any residential areas. Each year, however, the expansion of the built-up urban area reaches closer to the factory.

Eventually, the land near the factory becomes an unregulated residential area for poor households who had been evicted from downtown locations. Having been evicted once, the poor wisely do not invest heavily in their homes. Similarly, the poor municipality on the periphery of the city has no interest or feels no political pressure to provide water supply and other infrastructure to the illegally occupied area. Households drill their own wells or use water from nearby waterways, both of which are probably polluted by the factory. The incidence of disease and other health problems is significant, affecting employment and incomes. A consequence is that the area becomes known for drug dealing and crime.

By 1980, however, the location of this residential land is increasingly considered to be in the first ring of the metropolitan area or central zone of a rapidly expanding city. The now wealthier and politically more important municipality then decides to evict the poor, clearing out 'undesirable elements', and announces that it will provide infrastructure for a 'proper' residential neighbourhood. However, having failed to secure international funding, on environmental and other grounds, the municipality had to mobilize resources for this from the area's new and wealthier residents. Five years later, the factory is surrounded by a mixed residential area of 50,000 people working in the formal sector. Residents form a strong neighbourhood organization to ensure the security of the area and, among other tasks, to keep the drug dealers out.

In 1990, with machinery in the factory now 30 years old, there is a serious industrial accident with escaping chemical fumes killing hundreds of people living near the factory grounds and affecting thousands in the neighbourhood. Fortunately for the poorest households who had been forced to leave the area ten years earlier, they have escaped the effects of the accident and live in a squatter area 16 kilometres to the west of the factory. Many residents of the neighbourhood are gravely injured and are unable to work. Neither the company nor public authorities at the municipal or national level are able to provide much compensation to cover medical costs or unemployment insurance.

Postscript. In some European capital, thousands of kilometres away, the head of the Urban Development Division of the International Aid Agency thanked his or her lucky stars that, despite the intense lobbying efforts of the government of the city, the housing project had been turned down for financing in 1980. Perhaps there will now be an opportunity for a new development project including environmental cleanup, showing the agency's new 'green awareness'.

particular, as well as those of the elderly and the disabled, before and at the time of Hurricane Katrina and later in relief and recovery efforts.[36]

The cases of Mumbai and New Orleans are also very instructive about general patterns of the complex multiple factors that operate at the urban level. Vulnerabilities appear to be cumulative; yet they also interact with one another, exacerbating safety and security. For example, the poor occupy the most hazardous sites in most cities, such as the *gecekondus* and *barrios* on the hillsides of Ankara and Caracas, respectively, or in the *kampungs* along the canals in Jakarta, or between the railway lines in Mumbai. They are unable to find 'safe' land in cities where land prices are high or where public policy is not intended to allow the poor to occupy central or desirable locations. So they are forced to accept the risk of physically dangerous sites in order to avoid the risk of forced evictions if they settle in other 'safer', but prohibited, locations. In the event of a flood, their homes on the banks of canals are the first to be flooded, with the risk that they will lose everything.

Aerial photography of most cities vividly shows that the poorest and most fragile quality of housing and infrastructure is coincident with physical and natural risks

These patterns explain, for example, the origins of settlements such as Mathare Valley, an undesirable location in Nairobi, or in the desert areas of metropolitan Lima. Nezahualcoyotl, a large settlement distant from employment in central Mexico City, initially grew spontaneously in unhealthy, dusty and dry conditions, but is now home to more than 2 million residents just across the border of the Federal District of Mexico City.[37]

The development of these settlements is essentially determined by the distribution of risk in space. Aerial photography of most cities vividly shows that the poorest and most fragile quality of housing and infrastructure is coincident with physical and natural risks. If household decisions about urban location are generally determined by price and access, for the poor these decisions increasingly include weighing the probability of risks from different forms of hazard. It is possible to identify a typology of preferences among the poor in individual cities according to such hazards, from living near waste disposal facilities, to living near waterways, to settling between railway tracks, to choosing between air pollution and the likelihood of injuries to children playing near passing trains or traffic.

This distribution of risk in space is intensified by the growing proportion of slums in cities, such as Mumbai, with more than 6 million people living in slums,[38] or São Paulo, Lagos and other cities, where slum dwellers are more than half the population. As their number increases, the poor seek any available locations that offer cheaper access to employment opportunities, including on environmentally marginal land that no one else wants. A particularly dramatic example of this scenario is the estimated 500,000 people living in the City of the Dead in Cairo.[39] Cultural or religious taboos about occupying cemeteries are at risk of being overridden in many cities.

When considering the urban level as the unit of analysis, it is easier to include the role of various forms of externalities that operate at the urban and the metropolitan scale. The prototypical fictitious example presented in Box 2.2 illustrates the various dynamics and processes found in many cities, involving shifts in land-use patterns over time and exposure to industrial hazards.

The fictitious story in Box 2.2 unfortunately captures a set of realistic cumulative dynamics through which efforts to manage urban safety are overwhelmed by shifting maps of risk over 30 years. The capacity of public institutions to manage these processes is limited, although the decision to build a residential neighbourhood close to a factory could be questioned. However, given the property values of land inside the first ring of the metropolitan area, the housing project made sound economic sense and allowed the taxation of property to help finance the public infrastructure.

Two dimensions of the urban level deserve special attention in regard to the challenges of urban safety and security: urban spatial processes and institutional capacity at the metropolitan and municipal levels.

Urban spatial processes

As suggested in the story in Box 2.2, the major fact about urban land use is that it changes. The functions performed in any given location shift over time. These functions, whether residential, productive or administrative, depend upon many factors, including those at the global and national levels.[40] Patterns of spatial change and land use frame the context in which urban safety and security issues actually exist, thus emphasizing the importance of urban planning.

One of the most noted changes in urban space over the last two decades has been the growth of private urban space in the form of gated communities, a logical conclusion to the argument for defensible space. While these communities have, in part, been a response to growing urban crime and concerns about security, their impacts are far greater, leading to an increasing polarization of urban space and segregation between urban poor and middle- and upper-income groups.

The case of metropolitan Buenos Aires is a good example of this phenomenon. Studies of the growth of gated communities show that, by 2000, there were 434 private communities in metropolitan Buenos Aires. By August 2000, some 500,000 people lived in an area of 323 square kilometres, or an area 1.6 times larger than the downtown federal capital area, which houses 3 million people.[41] This level and disproportionate land share of gated communities is more intense than similar developments in other Latin American cities; but it shares common features.[42] Analytically, these areas can be differentiated by their date of settlement, the level of income of the population and, as a result, the scale and costs of residential plots and housing.[43] Most significantly, they represent a segregation and privatization of urban space. They are also direct consequences of the widening gap in incomes and wealth within the metropolitan population and are reflected in the growing social exclusion of large numbers of people.[44] This is well captured in the phrase '*la construccion del nosotros y de los otros*' (meaning 'the construction of ourselves and the others') in a study of the lifestyles of the gated communities.[45] This phrase also describes the psychological and cultural basis of fear that led to, and then is reinforced by, the privatization of urban space.

The socio-spatial fragmentation within one city is well illustrated in a description that links intra-urban inequality to the different velocities of mobility and connectivity of three households living in metropolitan Buenos Aires: one leaving their computer at home in a gated community, driving in their car along a highway to downtown white collar employment, probably in the financial sector, talking on their cell-phones; a second leaving their neighbourhood and taking a bus to work downtown in the service economy unconnected to computer technology; and a third not leaving their neighbourhood at all.[46]

Urban spatial change, therefore, frames the vulnerability of urban groups to various risks in specific locations, whether from crime, evictions or disasters. As noted below, location in space is not necessarily coincident with the jurisdictions of urban institutions responsible for ensuring safety and security.

One of the most noted changes in urban space over the last two decades has been the growth of private urban space in the form of gated communities, a logical conclusion to the argument for defensible space

Metropolitan and municipal institutional capacity

While the issue of institutional capacity is important at all levels, it is particularly lacking at both the metropolitan and municipal levels, especially in developing countries. The institutional framework governing cities is complex, with national institutions often establishing norms – for example, for infrastructure standards – or providing federal revenue through states or provinces to the municipal or urban level. Municipal institutions are usually dependent upon these revenue flows, are often weak technically, except in large cities with long traditions of technical and professional training, and normally spend most of their resources on personnel expenditures followed by the costs of waste collection. Local institutions in developing countries rarely have the capital for investment in large-scale infrastructure provision such as water supply or electricity.

Within a multilevel institutional framework and frequently overlapping jurisdictions, urban safety and security are important responsibilities, but most capacities in policing or disaster preparedness are notoriously weak. These problems are described in some detail in Chapters 4 and 8.

Institutional capacity ... is particularly lacking at both the metropolitan and municipal levels, especially in developing countries

One aspect of weak institutional capacity is the frequent lack of effective institutions at the metropolitan level. Very few cities have managed to establish metropolitan-level capacity to manage the positive and negative externalities of urban population density and habitat. These externalities affect the environment, the design and management of infrastructure, or the multiple flows that come in and out of a metropolitan area, to name a few.[47] The historical dominance of downtown municipalities and their unwillingness to give up their long-held prerogatives in order to build metropolitan forms of cooperation is a major problem at the urban level, whether in Buenos Aires, Dakar, Lagos or São Paulo. Despite the great claims made for decentralization of responsibility to peripheral municipalities, this process also does not guarantee effective capacity and performance. Responsibility without adequate financial resources – the problem of mandate without resources – often results in poor performance. This has direct consequences for urban governance and public-sector management of the three challenges to urban safety and security addressed by this Global Report.[48]

The neighbourhood or community level

Ultimately, the context where vulnerability and impact are felt most heavily is the community level

Ultimately, the context where vulnerability and impact are felt most heavily is the community level, which itself varies considerably between countries and even within countries. While there is, indeed, a set of cascading factors that generate cumulative and interacting impacts at the community level, there are also community structures and behaviour patterns which, in turn, interact with urban safety and security risks. These include location and spatial patterns of settlement; the historical origins and development of specific communities; structures of community power, authority and solidarity; levels and differences in income and wealth; and the perceived justice or injustice in the distribution of various conditions or privileges within the community. Just as there is increasing awareness of intra-urban differences, analysis of communities needs to take into account intra-community differences. The interactions of these factors and the differences within communities condition how urban safety and security is experienced.

One of the most significant changes in security at the community level has been the recent acknowledgement of individual rights against the threat of forced evictions

The degree of safety and security felt within communities depends upon both exogenous and endogenous factors, as with other levels. This makes it difficult to explain the impact of specific assaults on security by a single factor. Outcomes depend upon intervening factors that may well determine institutional performance – for example, whether federal revenue-sharing formulae encourage the steady flow of resources for community policing, resolving tenure disputes through land registration systems and legal support, or disaster preparedness. Causation is complicated. In cases of communities that experience a high incidence of crime and violence, it is likely that high incidence is a function of cumulative impacts. Weak community authorities may be unable to enforce order and prevent criminal and violent behaviour, which, in turn, may have increased as a result of macro-economic changes, such as a reduced urban labour market, or sharply increased prices for essential products or services. In contrast, there may be other communities where leaders and the community are able to act together to patrol streets and reduce the likelihood that pedestrians will be accosted by delinquent youth. Explanations of these differences come from diverse factors; but it is important to acknowledge that many – though not all – of these originate at the community level.

It is at the household level that the effects of poverty on risk response and on vulnerability ... are ... most magnified and ... best analysed

As noted in Chapter 1, one of the most significant changes in security at the community level has been the recent acknowledgement of individual rights against the threat of forced evictions. In some communities in which occupancy is legalized for the majority of residents, there is often little sympathy for people vulnerable to evictions. Squatters are regarded as security threats and as illegal occupants who undermine the stability of neighbourhoods. In other communities inhabited mostly by squatters, in which there is empathy and solidarity among households in a shared status, the threat of evictions is largely perceived as an external threat unlikely to be acted upon if community members consolidate their communities as much as possible. In so doing, they try to send a strong and aggressive signal to public authorities to desist from even considering evictions.

Both circumstances, however, have slowly begun to change since households lacking secure tenure, whether as a minority within a community or as members of the majority in a community of squatters, may now appeal to new legal frameworks and have been able in some cases cited in Chapters 5 and 6 to find alternative tenure arrangements or to postpone immediate eviction until some form of resettlement solution can be found.

Household and individual levels

The household is an important locus of threats to security and safety. First, individual household dwellings are often the sites of many types of crime and violence. The dwelling itself is also frequently the site of burglary and robbery. But at the same time, the security of the occupancy of the dwelling itself – containing the household – is very much under threat. This is particularly so in the case for the urban poor living in slums, as indicated in Chapter 1.

Understanding security of households, therefore, requires both social analysis – what is happening *to* the household, as well as *within* the household – and a broader physical and juridical analysis, including the degree of security of tenure that a specific household has achieved. As suggested in Chapter 3, there is extensive data on the likelihood of crime and violence against individual households in slums in cities such as Nairobi. In Australia, there are estimates of the average financial loss coming from household burglaries and vandalism. At the same time, evidence from many countries shows that violent physical abuse within households against the most vulnerable members, such as women, children, the elderly and the disabled, is common. This intra-household violence is yet another dimension of widespread intra-household inequality in which women and girls frequently receive less food, access to education and healthcare than male family members.

Vulnerability at the household level is partly determined by obstacles to effective risk response. These are generally tied to poverty, including lack of assets. A poor household with insecure residential tenure, and therefore likely to be forcibly evicted, is, in the first place, in that situation mainly because of poverty. Such a household – often located in an area prone to natural or industrial hazards – is not likely to be able to afford insurance against a natural disaster or burglary, nor is it likely to be able to evacuate family members and household effects on the sudden occurrence of a catastrophic hazard, such as a hurricane. It is at the household level that the effects of poverty on risk response and on vulnerability, in general, are perhaps most magnified and certainly best analysed.

The issues raised in the preceding section might also be considered from the perspective of an individual. While intra-household violence is addressed at specific individuals, in some cases there are, in fact, 'generic victims', who may be 'gendered victims', such as women and girls. Other kinds of generic victims exist in cities – for example, street children who may be abused, maimed and even killed by public authorities to rid the city of so-called nuisances, or by private individuals or gangs who assume that attacking street children can be done with impunity. If these victims are vulnerable to crime and violence, they are also vulnerable to forced evictions and are likely to be the least protected during natural disasters. These individuals are, therefore, likely to be cumulatively vulnerable to risks and hazards.

FORMS OF INTERDEPENDENCE

The above analysis demonstrates that urban safety and security are dependent upon complicated patterns of cumulative causation and multiple impacts. An added dimension to this complexity is a pattern of interdependence, as well. Distinct spheres of action – social, economic and environmental – interact in ways that demonstrate the high degree of interdependence among them. Indeed, it is these myriad forms of interdependence which form a central part of the argument about various forms of resilience and sustainability.[49]

So far, examples in which social, economic or spatial outcomes have depended upon multiple factors have been presented. These factors have been described as contributing to cumulative causation. The chains of causation, however, do not move only in one direction. For example, the high crime in Mexico City may be, in part, a result of macro-economic changes affecting the availability of employment. But high crime, as suggested earlier, also has a significant cost for the macro-economy and contributes to low levels of foreign direct investment or tourism. High crime at the community level can also reduce the rate of savings or asset accumulation of households who have been robbed. As a result, they are unable to invest in improving their homes. Therefore, even though their investment is modest, their victimization by crime has inhibited economic multipliers within their community. This micro-example is repeated many times over in countries such as Colombia or El Salvador, where households may be wary to reveal any wealth for fear of robbery. The causes of insecurity, therefore, may come from different origins.

The complexity of these patterns of causation suggests that simple explanations or single-issue recommendations to improve urban safety and security are likely to be of limited value. This observation sets up the normative framework in the following section.

PATHWAYS TO RESILIENCE

Previous sections of this chapter have proposed a conceptual framework for understanding the origins, causation and impacts of the three threats to urban safety and security addressed in this report: crime and violence, insecurity of tenure, and disasters. Risk factors underlying these threats have also been discussed at different geographical and analytical levels. This discussion has demonstrated that single-cause explanations are insufficient representations of the complexity of these phenomena. In normative terms, three arenas have been identified that have the potential to remedy some of the worst impacts of these problems: institutions and policy, the juridical framework of international law, and civil society and culture.

While each of these arenas will be presented in detail in subsequent chapters of this report in relation to each of the three threats to urban safety and security, the following sub-sections suggest that, individually and together, the arenas offer alternative and complementary pathways to the *resilience* required to alleviate some of the worst impacts of these problems. For the purposes of this chapter, as noted earlier, resilience is defined as the capacity to adjust to threats, to mitigate or avoid harm, and to bounce back from shocks.

The complexity of ... patterns of causation suggests that simple explanations or single-issue recommendations to improve urban safety and security are likely to be of limited value

Institutions and policy

As suggested in previous sections of this Global Report, one dimension of the urban safety and security challenges requiring direct attention is the role of institutions. Examples have been provided showing how various factors at the global and national levels have affected national institutions and, in turn, their influence on the capacity of urban and community institutions to respond to these challenges. While it is relatively easy to identify and document these institutional impacts, it is much harder to improve institutional performance on managing, for example, crime and violence in the short, medium and even the long term. Indeed, the weakness of urban institutions is itself a vulnerability that allows these threats to security to be so heavy in their social and economic impacts in the first place.

As noted above, the term 'institution' refers to any structured pattern of behaviour, including 'informal' institutions or behaviours, that communities and households may use to maintain their equilibrium in the face of dynamic conditions such as crime and violence or disasters. The value and utility of this sociological definition of 'institution' is illustrated in the following examples. Recent experiences have demonstrated that in disasters in many countries, such as after earthquakes in Surat in India and Bursa in Turkey, or in recovery from tsunami-affected areas in India or Sri Lanka, women's groups are usually the best informed about community conditions and about the mapping of facilities, households and community hazards.[50] It should not be surprising that they also are effective in determining the priorities for relief and recovery, as international aid organizations have now come to recognize and appreciate.

Resilience is ... the capacity to adjust to threats, to mitigate or avoid harm, and to bounce back from shocks

The issue of information is critical in this context: normally male-dominated public institutions seek to control information before and after disasters, using such events as opportunities to assert power or to have a privileged claim on the flow of new resources destined for relief and recovery. Women's groups as informal institutions, therefore, should be central to any mapping of institutional actors involved in maintaining urban safety and security. The importance of gender in this regard directly contradicts what is normally a male-dominated, top-down, technical approach of institutions involved in managing safety and security. In many contexts, women have either been 'ignored' by these institutions or 'protected', rather than allowed to be active participants in the processes that directly affect them.

In contrast, it is apparent that the weaknesses and lack of financial capacity of formal municipal, state or provincial institutions are important underlying contributors to the chronic condition affecting vulnerability of individual communities. These weaknesses are actually amplified by the fact that they frequently refuse to recognize and/or cooperate with community-level institutions. The strategic question, therefore, is how this gap can be bridged to strengthen urban institutional capacities, whether to reduce crime and violence, to regulate housing and land markets so that people's rights to secure tenure are honoured, or to anticipate and mitigate the impacts of disasters.

Informal community institutions have a critical and central role to play in preparedness to address future problems as much as during immediate emergencies

This Global Report will suggest that each of these threats to urban safety and security represents a major opportunity to reform and strengthen institutions. In the case of disasters, this means not returning to the *status quo ante*, but rather seeking new forms of representation, decision-making and accountability in formal institutions, as well as the recognition that informal community institutions have a critical and central role to play in preparedness to address future problems as much as during immediate emergencies. In a word, disasters may represent a political and economic opportunity for the poor.[51] This opportunity has been amply demonstrated in the myriad efforts by disaster victims in Sri Lanka and India to use disaster recovery efforts to address security of tenure issues.

This insight has profound implications in developing an effective analytic and policy approach to the issues of urban safety and security. For many years, international institutions, following national and local practices around the world, took the position that responses to disasters were not the right time to undertake institutional reform. They argued that victims had immediate material needs for food, medicine and shelter, and that the institutions best suited to providing those services were existing institutions. Institutional reform or strengthening was viewed as a medium- or long-term goal to be addressed after short-term priorities were met. The problem with this perspective is that, in most cases, considerable responsibility for the disaster in the first place lay with the practices of existing institutions. It makes little sense to give them more resources to distribute and to manage in ways that have previously proven to be ineffective. It is the classic case of 'throwing good money after bad'.

Disasters offer an opportunity for institutional change

Finding an effective and sustainable institutional solution to critical problems does not mean accepting the *status quo ante* as desirable or even as second best. Rather, as a growing body of case experience is showing – for example, in communities who survived Hurricane Mitch in Guatemala and Honduras – disasters offer an opportunity for institutional change.[52]

As subsequent chapters will present in some detail, institutional strengthening covers a wide spectrum of subjects, from clarifying institutional mandates, ensuring budgetary resources, improving personnel practices, building leadership, requiring accountability, improving processes of formulating policies and regulations, designing effective work programmes, and sensibly allocating institutional capacities. With respect to each of the three threats addressed by this report, these institutional challenges have different technical meanings and priorities. Their urgency differs from city to city and from country to country, depending upon existing local institutional capacities as well as the significant threats to security. The critical questions to pose are: what should be changed? How much time is there? Who is responsible for making change happen? Clearly, one size does not fit all.

Juridical framework of international law

A second pathway to social resilience is the emerging juridical framework of human rights as elaborated upon in the international instruments cited in Chapters 5, 6 and 11. In the context of this Global Report, international law and emerging human rights mean different things in each of the three challenges to urban safety and security. For example, in the arena of tenure security, emerging rights refer to the rights of urban residents to protection from eviction in the absence of prior alternative housing arrangements. What is noteworthy and new is that the juridical framework of human rights adopted at the international level – the process of establishing legal norms – is increasingly being applied to local urban circumstances, including in the areas of crime and basic needs. This might also be applied in some countries as the right to effective governance and delivery of services. The existence of human rights, therefore, can empower urban residents to 'claim' and/or defend their rights when these rights are under threat. This changes the political environment in which they live.

While the outcomes of appropriate institutional behaviour addressing urban safety and security are critical determinants of the impacts of hazards and risks of various kinds, they also need to be understood as highly transitory and dependent upon political circumstances at a particular historical moment. Institutional responses to urban crime during the term of one mayor may be effective and have an appropriate balance between prevention and punishment; but the next mayor can have an altogether different approach. It is therefore critically important to establish enduring norms of behaviour that can guide institutional behaviour and protect the citizenry over time. In this regard, the growing body of human rights laws relating to diverse aspects of human security should be seen as 'emerging rights', not yet fully acquired or even accepted in some countries, but of growing importance.

The concept of emerging rights is important because it signifies a process by which a 'right' comes to be recognized as legitimate and judiciable in a court of law, or as coined in several legal instruments: 'the progressive realization' of various rights. This covers a wide and ever expanding range of human behaviour across countries – for example, the emerging rights of producers of intellectual property such as recorded music, or the emerging rights of prisoners in jail for common crimes, or the rights of people with disabilities to access public space, or the right not to be discriminated against on the basis of race, ethnic identity or gender.

The presence and weight of human rights is directly applicable to the problem of insecurity of tenure and forced evictions. Because freedom from forced evictions is now included in international human rights law, as mentioned earlier and explained in greater detail in Chapters 5 and 6, citizens fearing such evictions can invoke this legal framework in order to avoid such evictions or to claim compensation. While these processes are tedious and often do not provide compensation in a timely manner, the right to invoke legal protection has had a dramatic effect on many people and institutions planning new projects on already occupied land in cities, and for which new projects would require resettlement of existing occupants. It has led to formulation and wide publication of new guidelines for official practice in city agencies, as well as international institutions such as the World Bank,[53] whose policies then must be aligned with those of the cities and countries receiving international assistance, thereby multiplying the impact of such guidelines.

An important dimension of these new guidelines is the requirement for public consultation. While such requirements have been in force in many developed countries for many years, this step in approving planning and construction projects represents a major new departure in developing countries, opening up further possibilities for political empowerment.[54]

The existence of human rights for secure tenure and against forced eviction is also related to the important subjects of inheritance and property rights. In many countries, women are denied such rights even though they are the effective managers of household resources. If women have a right not to be evicted, this fact immediately has implications for who is entitled to security of tenure. This does not apply only to the case of evictions, but is common, for example, in cases of who is entitled to receive recovery or reconstruction assistance or compensation following disasters. In most cases, these forms of assistance are allocated to 'property owners', frequently recognized only as the male 'head of household', ignoring the fact that in most cities there is a significant proportion of female-headed households. But if this bias did not in the past reflect the role of women in rebuilding communities after disasters, now such bias is increasingly a legal issue, as well, for those women able to present such cases to judicial authorities.

Human rights, in this sense, is a powerful pathway for helping women and other disadvantaged groups to obtain their lawful status and rights, but also to be effective participants in the reconstruction of infrastructure, shelter and community services. This implies a much broader view of the process of change where women's groups actually establish precedents and protocols for community recovery. This has two important dimensions: women's participation and, hence, their recognition as legitimate community actors, and the likelihood of community outcomes being different – indeed, being more sustainable – if they are involved.

Several examples of women's mobilization emphasize this point. The most effective campaigns against driving under the influence of alcohol and juvenile delinquency in the US have been organized by women such as Mothers against Drunk Driving (MADD), whose right to protect their children could not be opposed by anyone. Similarly, in Kingston, Jamaica, women's groups analysed the nature of neighbourhood violence and organized different approaches to managing it.[55] In Gujarat State in India, the Self-Employed Women's Association (SEWA) has built a major organization over 35 years that has significantly enhanced their participation in development and is now active in providing community finance as well. Women's groups in Latin America have also been proactive and have changed the political landscape in these areas (see Chapter 8). All of these cases suggest that recognition of the right to participate in ensuring safety is a major asset in helping to build social resilience at the community and, eventually, the urban level.

The presence and weight of human rights is directly applicable to the problem of insecurity of tenure and forced evictions

Civil society and culture

The third pathway to resilience is through civil society and culture. While the previous examples highlight the role and mobilization of women in addressing problems of urban safety and security, these efforts need to be placed within the wider context of civil society as a whole. Clearly, one of the legacies of the fall of the Berlin Wall and the end of the Cold War has been the legitimacy given to civil society. If civic participation had been caught in the ideological battles of the Cold War, it is now understood as a desirable and, indeed, necessary component of societal decision-making and problem-solving, regardless of what definition or form of democracy is adopted. The diversity and capacity of civil society organizations at both the global and national levels have expanded many fold.[56]

The three threats to urban safety and security discussed in Chapter 1 represent increasingly serious hazards to society. Crime and violence, forced evictions and disasters destroy existing forms of social capital, as well as injure individuals and households. This social capital, in the form of formal and informal institutions, social knowledge and problem-solving capacity, is a critical ingredient in protecting individuals and groups from threats to urban security.

Social capital ... is a critical ingredient in protecting individuals and groups from threats to urban security

The role of social capital, as distinct from individual capacity, is very important. Experience in confronting these hazards has demonstrated that individuals cannot withstand such risks by themselves. Rather, there is strength in numbers. It is, therefore, critical to determine what are the capacities and rights needed to strengthen civil societies in the face of such threats. These capacities depend, first, upon a set of rights, including the right to anticipate the future,[57] the right to information about such threats, the right to organize, and the right to participate in decisions affecting prevention, mitigation, relief, recovery and redevelopment. Building capacities to exercise those rights is much more complicated and will be discussed in some detail in subsequent chapters of this report.

An important theoretical insight by Amartya Sen about famines is relevant here. Sen observed in 1982 that no famine had ever occurred in a democracy.[58] He explained the societal and economic adjustments to shortage of food as highly dependent upon the free flow of information within a democratic society. Similarly, the ability to anticipate a threat to safety and security, such as a tsunami or a flood, depends heavily upon the flow of information, in time, to people likely to be affected by such an event. If information on an impending hurricane is available, as in the case of Havana, people can make precautions or evacuate. In either case, the disaster is not a surprise, becomes more of a process than an event and is therefore possibly more manageable in some of its impacts.

Preventing or mitigating the impacts of threats to urban safety and security hinges upon allowing civil society to play an active, informed role

It is important, therefore, to acknowledge that preventing or mitigating the impacts of threats to urban safety and security hinges upon allowing civil society to play an active, informed role. What this means, however, in specific places depends heavily upon culture. The meaning of culture here is closely tied to values and perceptions of key factors, such as authority, identity, status, risk, costs, participation and impact. The contextual meaning of these concepts shapes the content of human behaviour in these situations. For example, how women communicate and work together within tsunami-affected villages in southern India depends heavily upon caste. The modes and style of women's participation in community recovery groups after the earthquake in Bursa, Turkey, were contingent upon whether they were highly religious. Responses to gangs in Guatemala or Honduras must be highly conditioned by an understanding of what are the issues facing the identity of young male gang members and why they join such violent gangs in the first place.

Narratives of resilience are necessary for public education, as well as for political leaders

An important part of this engagement by civil society is the nature of participation itself. There are three aspects of the participatory claim that deserve attention: the procedural aspect, the methodological dimension and the ideological position. Participation can have very different functions, outputs and outcomes. It is clear that in each of the three threats to security considered in this Global Report, there is an important role for citizen participation in mitigating the worst effects of these phenomena, as demonstrated by the participatory risk assessments in South Africa or Peru. The Asian Coalition for Housing Rights (ACHR) has demonstrated that citizen participation in the aftermath of the Indian Ocean Tsunami has made an enormous difference in the rate and quality of recovery in the local areas of India, Indonesia, Sri Lanka and Thailand affected by this tragedy.

Disasters reveal the resilience and capacity of governments. The performance of infrastructure is a reliable indicator of how well public agencies are doing their jobs

If culture is important as a factor in explaining behaviour, it is also central to identifying normative approaches to ensuring urban safety and security. There are many examples of communal – not just community – responses to these issues. Communal identities and values, whether religious or ethnic, play a major role in determining what behaviours are acceptable and what are not. So, too, do they determine what is popularly regarded as 'justice' in the prevention of violence and punishment.

Lessons learned on the pathways to resilience

Taken individually, institutions and policy, the human rights legal framework, and civil society and culture each represent pathways to strengthening social resilience in cities. Taken together, they are highly interdependent and are integral, interwoven fibres in the texture of social resilience.

In suggesting that building social resilience should be a core social and development objective for all countries, regardless of income level, it is also important to acknowledge that scholars and practitioners have been working with this concept and applying it in both the natural and social sciences for several decades. This work has been collected and summarized in various volumes and websites.[59] Much of this work is useful in understanding how the concept of resilience can be an effective normative objective for policy and the international community. In this regard, several key lessons deserve attention.

Some of these lessons come from studies of response to disaster,[60] but also apply to other threats to urban safety and security. These can be described as follows:

- Narratives of resilience are necessary for public education, as well as for political leaders. While these stories are not always universally accepted and, in fact, are usually highly contested, as the cases of Mumbai and New Orleans suggest, they provide an important role in building resilience itself. Telling the stories of how security of tenure was achieved in Klong Toey in Bangkok or the *barriadas* of Lima helps to build popular understanding and support for other efforts. Similarly, the stories of the Young Lords in helping to control violence in New York or how crime in Medellin was stopped all help to build a popular image in urban culture about what is possible.
- Disasters reveal the resilience and capacity of governments. The performance of infrastructure is a reliable indicator of how well public agencies are doing their jobs. Similarly, the performance of departments within government, as well the performance of leaders, is deeply revealing of the strength and character of public institutions. One former government official has noted that 'adversity does not build character; it reveals it'.[61] Whether institutions have been working together prior to a disaster is a critical determinant of performance. As the mayor of Baltimore bluntly commented in a seminar on disaster preparedness: 'You don't want to be exchanging business cards on the scene.'[62]
- Similarly, if the municipal police are able to contain a criminal problem in one neighbourhood without unnecessary violence, they are able to demonstrate capacity, which enhances their credibility for the next time. Furthermore, in cases where relocation of people from their homes is unavoidable, such relocations can be handled with sufficient advance notice, following appropriate consultation and participation of the people concerned. There is a much greater likelihood that the process can occur smoothly and lead to real improvements for the people affected.

- Local resilience is linked to national capacity, but is site specific. National recovery and efforts support and reinforce local efforts; but local resilience is contextually specific. As one observer has commented: '911 is a local call.'[63] This is well illustrated in the case of Catuche in Caracas, Venezuela, where a local community organization saved thousands of lives in flooding and landslides in 1999.[64]
- Resilience and physical rebuilding benefit from prior investment. These processes are historically cumulative and build upon one another. Capacity to address one threat to urban security is transferable to addressing other threats. Social learning occurs within cities and communities. This is well illustrated in the case of Cuba's response to hurricanes, where being highly organized in public health and education carry over to preparedness for tropical storms in Havana and other Cuban cities.
- Resilience is built on the past, but anticipates the future. The capacity for a city to 'get on with its life' is a strong indicator of how it values its past, but also how it can imagine and work towards its future.[65]

Finally, in normative terms, learning how to build resilience is important because cities are experiencing shifting patterns of risk and vulnerability. These shifting patterns reflect dramatic changes at multiple levels: global, national, urban, local, community, household and individual. All of these levels depend upon one another and feel the impacts of patterns of causation that do not simply go in one direction, but rather have feedback loops and generate other impacts. Some of these loops actually contribute to resilience through social learning at the urban level. Learning about environmental justice in one city can be applied to other cities, as the experience of the US illustrates. In other cases, there are severe obstacles to building capacity to absorb and manage risks and challenges to urban safety and security.

In a world of rapidly expanding information flows and exchange of experience, the process of peer learning – South–South and South–North, as well as the North–South and North–North – can produce impressive results. Indeed, as the experience of Hurricane Katrina illustrates, some countries of the North have much to learn from the South. In this regard, there are some cases such as The Netherlands' response to the floods of 1953 that laid the foundation for several generations of institutional learning and public education, preparing the country probably best of all for the anticipated sea-level rise expected from global warming.[66] Recent experience as well as projections of future urban growth suggest that this learning will need to rapidly accelerate since demographic, social, economic and environmental pressures will all intensify dramatically. The conceptual framework and discussion presented in this chapter is intended to help identify a language and an analytical framework for understanding these phenomena.

CONCLUDING REMARKS: THE ROLE OF URBAN POLICY, PLANNING, DESIGN AND GOVERNANCE IN ENHANCING URBAN SAFETY AND SECURITY

Chapters 1 and 2 have provided an overview of the three threats to urban safety and security: crime and violence, insecurity of tenure, and natural and human-made disasters. Both chapters have been descriptive and analytic: identifying problems, as well as providing a conceptual framework that helps to understand their origins and how they are embedded in urban areas and urban processes. From the perspective of each of these three broad threats to urban safety and security, there is an evident need to improve preparedness, to reduce risks and vulnerabilities, to increase the capacity for response, and to take advantage of the opportunities for positive urban reform and social change during the process of recovery.

Resilience and physical rebuilding benefit from prior investment. ... Resilience is built on the past, but anticipates the future

It should be asked, however: what is the role of the human settlements perspective (i.e. urban policy, design, planning and governance) in guiding these steps towards positive change? How can the impact of urban policy, planning, design and governance on these three very difficult sources of insecurity be enhanced? This concluding section addresses these questions, signalling further discussions of these issues in subsequent chapters of the report.

For the purposes of this Global Report, urban policy is understood as all those explicit decisions intended to shape the physical, spatial, economic, social, political, cultural, environmental and institutional form of cities..

In terms of improving urban safety and security, urban policy is translated into urban design, programmes, and operating procedures and measures that can directly affect social behaviour. For example, urban policy could include the strategic decision to decentralize urban governance in order to multiply and increase the density of public institutional contacts with the citizenry in a rapidly expanding city. Increased public presence could serve to inhibit neighbourhood crime and violence. It could include attaching community policing measures to decentralized municipal structures for paying taxes, obtaining permits, and resolving neighbourhood conflicts, such as land tenure disputes. It entails decision-making about the spatial-physical form, social and economic goals and institutional organization of the city.

As the experience of Hurricane Katrina illustrates, some countries of the North have much to learn from the South

Planning, for the purposes of this Global Report, is the assembly and analysis of information, the formulation of objectives and goals, the development of specific interventions intended to improve urban safety and security, and the organizational processes needed to bring them to fruition. Planning takes the decisions of urban policy-makers and transforms them into strategy and measures for action.

Urban design, as used in this report, involves the design of buildings, groups of buildings, spaces and landscapes in towns and cities, in order to create a sustainable, safe and aesthetically pleasing built environment. It is limited to the detailed physical structure and arrangement of buildings and other types of physical development within space. This includes the use of building codes, for example to mandate earthquake-proof or flood-proof buildings. Urban design is narrower than urban planning, and is often seen as part of the latter. While subsequent chapters of this report present problem-oriented planning solutions, this section will highlight some of the approaches deserving consideration.

The first challenge of planning to improve urban safety and security is the assembly of information to correctly frame the problem

The first challenge of planning to improve urban safety and security is the assembly of information to correctly frame the problem. In the area of crime and violence, this calls for increased efforts, mostly but not entirely in developing countries, to collect reliable data on crime and violence. This varies tremendously across countries and even cities within countries; but better information allows a clearer and more detailed assessment of threats, risks and vulnerabilities. A similar exercise is required to reduce the problem of insecurity of tenure. Surveys of land occupancy and housing in cities could help to identify the scale of the tenure problem and on what types of land it is most prevalent. The assembly of data on settlement patterns should be related to processes of spatial expansion, not simply demographic growth.[67] In the field of disaster preparedness, there exists a body of good practice in mapping hazards and developing risk profiles, as shown in the cases of hazard mapping and risk assessment in India, described in Chapter 8. Risk assessments must include collection and analysis of multiple types of information and address complex issues of multiple hazards, cumulative risk, and primary, secondary and tertiary consequences (see Chapter 8).

The second challenge of planning ... is in the formulation of objectives

The second challenge of planning in relation to urban safety and security is in the formulation of objectives. In the field of crime and violence, a major issue is whether substantial resources can be devoted to the prevention of crime and violence and, if so, how? Cities have historically vacillated between sending strong signals to discourage potential perpetrators of crimes through heavy sentences and punishments for crime and more socially oriented 'softer' approaches, including community policing and expanding civil society involvement. A parallel example in the tenure field is whether governments will recognize the impressive list of human rights that have been declared by the international community and, therefore, desist from bulldozing homes and neighbourhoods in the name of land-use and zoning regulations. With respect to disasters, a number of thematic areas for urban planning (including urban design) have been identified in Chapter 8: mapping hazard, vulnerability and risk; strengthening local capacity for resilience; land-use management and urban planning; building codes, regulation and disaster-resistant construction; planning to protect critical infrastructure and services; early warning; financing urban risk management; disaster response and recovery.

A third challenge is the formulation and enforcement of norms and codes of behaviour

A third challenge is the formulation and enforcement of norms and codes of behaviour. It is generally understood that prevention of crime and violence requires publicly established sentences and penalties for crimes committed. This issue, however, is heavily affected by the concept of mitigating circumstances that lead judges to either increase or decrease sentences. Norms have gradually become codified regarding land tenure issues; but these arrangements can be so complicated that simply understanding them is far beyond the educational level of the poor people most affected by them. Codes with regard to building construction or land use to avoid natural disasters are more easily understood; but even here, the issues of enforcement to reduce risk are complicated in local environments. This affects the levels of preparedness that are possible in different environments – for example, using people-centred preparedness systems or focusing more on local government procedures.[68]

Both the processes of urban policy, as broadly defined, and planning are integral parts of the governance process. As the previous section on pathways to resilience suggests, each of the different components of the governance process has important roles to play: institutions and policy, the juridical framework of international law, and civil society and culture. Governance is more than government, whether institutions or forms of public authority: it is an all-encompassing process by which official and non-official actors contribute to management of conflict, establishment of norms, the protection of the common interest, and the pursuit of the common welfare.

During the 21st century, urban growth has contributed to increasing concentrations of hazards and risk for growing urban populations. While much of the responsibility to reduce these risks is at the urban and national level, the international community has also accepted some responsibilities for specific aspects of these challenges. Part I of this Global Report has framed the problem. Subsequent parts will examine each of the challenges to urban safety and security in greater depth and suggest positive approaches for reducing these risks as cities continue to grow.

NOTES

1 Alwang et al, 2001; Bankoff et al, 2004.
2 *Ibid.*
3 Alwang et al, 2001, p2.
4 Holzman and Jorgensen, 2000.
5 Alwang et al, 2001, p10; Pelling, 2003.
6 Alwang et al, 2001, p4.
7 Sharma et al, 2000; Devereux, 1999; Moser, 1998.
8 Adger, 1999.
9 Alwang et al, 2001, p5.
10 Bankoff et al, 2004.
11 Stephens et al, 1994.
12 Pettis, 2003.
13 Stiglitz, 2002.
14 See UN-Habitat, 2005c.
15 Morley, 1998.
16 Galster, 1999.
17 Cohen et al, 1996.
18 Hansen, 2006.
19 Kerr, 2006.
20 See Chapter 12.
21 Davis, 2006b.
22 See, for example, Diamond, 2005.
23 See, for example, articles in *DNA, The Times of India, Indian Express* and *Hindustan Times* during July 2005, and Stecko and Barber, 2007.
24 See Chapter 3.
25 See Angel et al (2005) for an excellent analysis explaining the differences in the performance of the housing sector across countries.
26 Angel et al, 2005.
27 United Nations, 2001a.
28 See Chapter 3.
29 See Thompson, 2007.
30 DFID, 2005; also see Box 12.7 in this report.
31 See Chege et al, 2007.
32 Moser, 1996.
33 See Chapter 3.

34 See Chapter 3; Thachuk, 2001.
35 See Chapter 3.
36 Davis, 2006b. See also Hartman and Squires, 2006.
37 Ziccardi, 1991.
38 Bombay First, 2003.
39 Nedoroscik, 1997.
40 Soja, 2001.
41 Svampa, 2001, p57.
42 Caldeira, 2000.
43 Svampa, 2001, pp61–82.
44 Svampa, 2005.
45 Arizaga, 2005, p105.
46 Cicolella, 1999.
47 Sivaramkrishnan, 1986; Rojas et al, 2006.
48 There is now a large literature on urban governance. A useful set of cases is included in McCarney and Stren, 2003.
49 Stren and Polese, 2000.
50 Yonder et al, 2005.
51 Sandy Schilen, cited in Yonder et al, 2005, p1.
52 *Ibid.*
53 See World Bank, 2001, and www.worldbank.org/safeguards .
54 Friedmann, 1992.
55 Moser and Holland, 1997b.
56 Kaldor et al, 2004.
57 Gutman, 2006.
58 Sen, 1982.
59 Vale and Campanella, 2005. For many references see, http://urban.nyu.edu/catastrophe/index.htm; see also documentation of United Nations Disaster Decade.
60 Vale and Campanella, 2005, pp330–353.
61 Fred Hochberg, dean of the Milano School of Management and Urban Policy, New School University, comment at Symposium on Cities at Risk, New School University, 7 April 2006.
62 Martin O'Malley, mayor of Baltimore, comment at Symposium on Cities at Risk, New School University, 7 April 2006.
63 Fred Hochberg, dean of the Milano School of Management and Urban Policy, New School University, comment at Symposium on Cities at Risk, New School University, 7 April 2006.
64 Jeffrey, 2000, cited in Sanderson, 2000, pp93–102.
65 Vale and Campanella, 2005, pp330–353.
66 See Orr, et al, 2007.
67 See Angel et al, 2005.
68 See Chapter 8.

PART II

URBAN CRIME AND VIOLENCE

Part II of the Global Report on Human Settlements analyses the global conditions and trends of urban crime and violence, and examines policy responses designed to reduce the incidence and impacts of crime and violence. In particular, Chapter 3 assesses global trends in the incidence of urban crime and violence by type, the factors that determine levels of vulnerability to crime and violence, and the impacts of urban crime and violence. Chapter 4 identifies the range of policy responses at the local, national and international levels designed to tackle urban crime and violence.

Crime and violence are fundamental threats to human security and safety from crime, and violence – including the resulting fear and insecurity – is increasingly being acknowledged internationally as a public good, as well as a basic human right. Although found in virtually all cities across the world, most places are safe and most citizens are neither perpetrators nor victims of crime and violence. Rather, crime tends to be concentrated in certain parts of the city and in neighbourhoods that are known to the police and citizens. Fear of crime, whether linked to these specific 'hotspots' or more general in nature is often exacerbated by the media and may spread quickly as information is communicated by cell phones, email and through the internet.

As shown in this part of the report, global crime incidence has steadily increased over the 1980–2000 period, rising about 30 per cent, from 2300 to over 3000 crimes per 100,000 inhabitants. However, crime incident rates have fallen significantly in some regions, such as North America. This is in contrast to Latin America and the Caribbean, where crime incidence rose during this period, reflecting, in part, political transitions from autocracy to democracy and localized civil conflicts. Globally, there is little indication that crime rates will decrease in the near future.

Homicide, a significant type of violent crime, is discussed in detail in this part of the report. Homicide rates for cities are extremely variable, with Asian cities demonstrating generally low rates compared to cities in Africa, Latin America and the Caribbean, Eastern Europe and North America. Interpersonal violence is widespread, with women and children being the main victims. While the private setting of the home is often the venue for child abuse and interpersonal violence, many victims experience these crimes at public institutions such as schools, hospitals or in other public facilities.

Another type of crime examined is organized crime, which is often linked to corruption. It is estimated to account for US$1 billion in illicit capital that is circulated daily by criminal groups among the world's financial institutions. Findings show comparatively high levels of perceived organized crime in Africa, Central Asia, and Latin America and the Caribbean, while low levels are reported for Canada, Australia and Northern Europe. Drug, arms and human trafficking are among the principal activities of organized crime. Women and girls are especially vulnerable to human trafficking. It is estimated that between 700,000 and 1 million persons are trafficked around the world each year. Human traffickers often exploit children and young, uneducated and unemployed women from rural areas. The prevalence of as many as 100 million street children in cities around the world is also associated with drug and human trafficking, along with interpersonal violence, child abuse and poverty, among other factors. Youth gang membership is also estimated to be in the millions worldwide, with institutionalized youth gangs concentrated in cities that have high violence rates.

With respect to the factors underlying crime and violence, which are examined at length in this part of the report, informal social, cultural and religious values are generally more powerful motivators or constraints than formal legal rules or regulations. Poverty has long been recognized as an important factor associated with increased crime and violence. While crime may be seen as a survival alternative in the face of grinding poverty, there are poor communities where crime levels are low because behaviour is constrained by informal social and cultural values. Inequality may be a more important underlying factor in the perpetration of crime and violence than poverty *per se*.

An important issue explored in this part of the report is the relationship between city size, density and crime incidence. The rapid pace of urbanization in many developing countries, and the resulting increase in city size and density, is associated with increased crime and violence. Poor urban planning, design and management have increasingly been cited as playing a role in the shaping of urban environments that put citizens and property at risk. Thus, the physical fabric and layout of cities have a bearing on the routine movements of offenders and victims and on opportunities for crime. In response, a number of crime prevention strategies through environmental design have emerged, especially in developed countries.

The proportion and growth of youthful populations have long been connected with increased crime and violence rates. Unemployment is a fundamental risk factor related to

Box II.1 Nairobi: A city under siege by murderous gangs

They shot my 19-year-old nephew Jaimeen last week. I don't know who 'they' were; but I do know they were young men barely out of their teens who felt no qualms about killing someone for a few shillings, a mobile phone or a car. 'They' are the face of Kenya today: ruthless, lacking in compassion or ethics, totally devoid of feeling, worshippers of only one god – money. The bullet entered my nephew's intestine, where it left 16 gaping holes, finally lodging itself in his thigh. Luckily he survived. But though the wounds have been stitched and he is healing, the trauma of the event has left him permanently scarred.

The same day that my nephew was shot, 'they' invaded parts of Nairobi's Kangemi slums, not far from where my nephew lives, and tore down *mabati* shacks so they could steal the few possessions of Nairobi's dispossessed. This was a less ambitious group of criminals; but sources tell me that the fear they instilled in the slum was so widespread that no one slept that night. Neither the near-fatal shooting of my nephew nor the slum robbery was reported in the press. Nor were the cases of the many women and girls who have been violated and tortured by robbers in front of their husbands, fathers and sons in the last few years. Their tragedies are being played out every single day in this city gone mad. And no one, except maybe the Nairobi Women's Hospital and some good cops, cares.

Every day, and today is no exception, someone somewhere in this city of dread will be killed, raped, robbed or carjacked. It wasn't always so. When I was growing up, most people in the city didn't have *askaris* guarding the gates to their homes. The windows in houses lacked grills and the remote alarm was something we only saw in James Bond movies. Dogs in those days were pets, not man-eating beasts trained to maim intruders. Most children walked to school without ever wondering if they would be raped or molested on the way.

In my family home in Parklands, we often left the house door open, even at night. People drove with their car windows open and their car doors unlocked. If your car broke down in the middle of the road, someone would stop and give you a lift, and even take you home.

The security business was virtually non-existent. There was crime, but the benign kind: an odd jewellery snatching here, a pick-pocketing there. The men with guns had not yet arrived. Then it all changed, suddenly and without warning. A financial scandal of monstrous proportions was revealed. It emerged that the people we feted as heroes were, in fact, thieves, smugglers and con men. Kenyans lost faith in the system. Overnight, the money they carried in their pockets wasn't worth the paper it was printed on. Inflation soared, banks collapsed. Middle-class Kenyans moved to slums. Slum dwellers struggled to survive. Kenya joined the ranks of the most unequal societies in the world.

As neighbouring Somalia descended into anarchy, a culture of impunity set in. AK-47s were being sold openly in Nairobi's Eastlands for less than 500 Kenyan shillings (US$7.58) each. Police officers looked the other way. Well-off Kenyans sent their children abroad in the hope that they would never return. Skilled professionals left the country in droves, to the US and Europe. The brain drain became an epidemic.

Meanwhile, back home, security firms flourished. Night guards became mandatory in all housing estates. Construction companies began building homes with window grills, barricades and electrical fences. Gated communities became the norm rather than the exception. Nairobians began to believe that it was normal to have 'safe havens' in their homes, three locks on their front doors and alarms next to their beds.

Fear, the biggest inhibitor to freedom of movement, ruled the streets and invaded our houses. We became hostages … of the thugs who roamed freely on the streets with their guns. One foreign correspondent even compared Nairobi to Mogadishu, where lawlessness and violence were the order of the day.

Nairobians have now learned to live in fear. They envy people in other cities who can walk alone at night or who sleep without worrying about the safety of their children. They dream of escape – to Europe, America, Australia, even Asia, where living in a city does not mean always wondering if or when you will be killed or maimed. The ones who get away never come back. Those of us who stay out of misguided patriotism, lack of resources or just plain bad luck do the only thing we can in these circumstances – we come home from work before dark, lock ourselves in our homes and pray.

Source: Warah, 2007

crime and violence rates among both young males and females. Furthermore, the globalization of markets threatens employment opportunities for many young people, especially in transitional and developing nations. The deportation of criminals to their countries of origin, particularly from the US to Latin America and the Caribbean, accounts for increasing levels of youth crime and gang-related activities in the region.

The transition towards democratization often brings social and economic disruption that may be associated with increased crime and violence, at least in the short term. Findings suggest that some nations undergoing transition from autocratic governance to democracy have had significant increases in homicide rates. These include countries in Eastern Europe and in the Latin American and Caribbean region.

This part of the report also addresses the impacts of urban crime and violence, from the local to the global levels. Findings suggest that in 2000, more than 500,000 people across the globe were victims of homicide. Crime negatively affects economic and health systems at the national and regional levels. It has been identified as an impediment to foreign investment and a cause of capital flight and brain drain. High homicide and violent crime rates are also associated with increased healthcare and policing costs. The collapse of the Brazilian public hospital system during the 1980s and 1990s has been attributed to large numbers of homicides and criminal injuries.

Local impacts of crime and violence include the flight of population and businesses from central city locations. There is also evidence that rising levels of crime tend to depress property values – an important economic variable bearing on investment decisions and the creation of wealth. The impact of robberies and burglaries in cities of developing countries manifests in the growing demand for private security and the proliferation of gated communities. In South Africa, for instance, the number of private security guards has increased by 150 per cent since 1997.[1] The increased privatization of security and public space is an indication of the loss of confidence in the ability of the relevant authorities to cope with the growing levels of crime and violence. When confidence in public authorities and processes is low and cultures of fear are high, citizens may resort to vigilante or rough justice.

No current discussion of urban safety and security would be complete without mention of terrorism. Recent attacks in Nairobi, Dar es Salaam, Bali, New York, Madrid, London, Colombo and Mumbai, as well as the daily attacks in Baghdad, have all had specific and more general impacts on urban centres, including a significant shift in public perceptions of the safety and security of cities. However, this part of the report does not address the origins, motives or instruments of terrorism – rather, it focuses on the impacts of terrorism-related violence on cities, as well as on city-level responses designed to mitigate these impacts. Indeed, it is apparent that responses to terrorism in cities such as New York and London have influenced the debates about and responses to urban insecurity in other cities. A few cases of urban terrorist attacks and responses of the targeted cities are described in this report in order to illustrate the impacts of this extreme type of urban violence on cities, as well as the vulnerability, resilience and preparedness of these cities.

Some of the issues relating to the trends, factors and impacts of crime and violence discussed in this part of the report are illustrated by the case of Nairobi (Kenya), described in Box II.1.

Finally, several policy initiatives have emerged in response to the trends, factors and impacts of crime and violence sketched in the preceding paragraphs, as shown in this part of the report. Since a high proportion of crime takes place in specific locations, the most significant of the levels of response is the local level. But much crime can also be organized across much broader spatial scales, and so responses at levels that are broader than the local are important if crimes of this nature are to be addressed effectively. Evidence suggests that the most successful policy responses to prevent and reduce the incidence and impacts of crime and violence are those that take cognisance of the local context, rather than those based on the experience of other places.

The policy initiatives at the local level to address issues of urban crime and violence have been grouped into six broad categories:

- enhancing urban safety and security through effective urban planning, design and governance;
- community-based approaches to enhancing urban safety and security;
- strengthening formal criminal justice systems and policing;
- reducing risk factors;
- non-violent resolution of conflicts; and
- strengthening social capital.

Many of these policy responses have been attempted in combination with others, and it is becoming increasingly common to find that several of these are constituent elements of formal programmes. In addition, there are many examples of targeted single initiatives that seek to address particular types of crimes.

Enhancing urban safety and security through effective urban planning, design and governance starts from the proposition that there is a relationship between the characteristics of the built environment and the opportunity to commit crime. It therefore seeks to manipulate the built environment in ways that are intended to reduce or even to eliminate the opportunity to commit crimes. Key to this notion is the role of the planning system since it is through the planning system that most development is mediated. Available evidence from countries that have attempted this is that it can undoubtedly add value to the range of methods available to tackle crime.

Community-based initiatives cover a broad spectrum of approaches, including information-gathering, processes for determining policies and projects, implementation, and creating opportunities for communities to take initiatives themselves. The essence of these approaches is that initiatives to tackle crime and violence should be 'done with' local communities rather than 'done to' them. Central to this approach is the need to recognize that the people who are the intended beneficiaries of projects must contribute fully to shaping them, implementing them and, often, taking ownership of them.

In this context, a widespread response examined in this part of the report is the strengthening of social capital. This entails not only improving the ability of groups and communities to respond positively to problems of crime and violence, but is also about the creation of assets that assist in enhancing the resilience of communities. Available evidence suggests that stronger communities are better able to fight crime and violence than are weaker communities, and so initiatives which build the capacity of communities to respond and which provide community assets that reinforce this process are of huge value.

Strengthening formal criminal justice systems and policing have traditionally been the main tools for responding to crime and violence. However, problems have been experienced in this context in some parts of the world. These include corruption in such systems, inflexibility of response to changing criminal circumstances, limited resources and skills in relation to the needs of the job, and ineffective practices. The problem of corruption in criminal justice systems and in the police is a particularly corrosive one in terms of public confidence since the public at large relies on these agencies to do their traditional jobs of apprehending and sentencing criminals.

To date, policy responses focusing on reducing risk factors seem to have concentrated on tackling violence against women and trying to prevent young people from drifting into a life of crime. An important part of work to tackle problems of violence against women is the need to fully engage families, households and local communities since in some instances violence against women seems to be deeply entrenched in local cultures. Strategies to prevent young people from drifting into a life of crime typically employ a wide range of initiatives, including employment creation. The non-violent resolution of conflicts, which is more of a philosophical idea than a specific policy to address crime and violence, is yet another response. As a philosophy, it has much more to offer in tackling problems of crime and violence than has yet been appreciated – not only in helping to address immediate problems, but also in teaching valuable life skills.

Finally, the role of institutions is highlighted. Institutional responses from all levels of the hierarchy of government, as well as partnerships that serve as a viable mechanism to encourage interested parties and stakeholders, are crucial for the success of the various approaches to reducing urban crime and violence.

NOTES

1 See www.humansecurity-cities.org, 2007, p27.

CHAPTER 3

URBAN CRIME AND VIOLENCE: CONDITIONS AND TRENDS

This chapter documents global conditions and trends with respect to urban crime and violence. It forms the basis for the policy responses that are presented in Chapter 4 and recommendations as to ways forward that are advanced in Chapter 10. In examining crime and violence, the analytical framework presented in Chapter 2 is used by focusing on vulnerability, risk factors and impacts at the global, national, local urban, community, household and individual levels. It must be emphasized from the outset that the topic areas covered in this and the other chapters on crime and violence involve vast and rapidly evolving literatures. This is one measure of the importance of the subjects to individuals, states and the global community. This also means that comprehensive review of the field is not feasible in a few chapters, nor is this the intent. Rather, the aim is to provide an assessment of conditions and trends, as well as policies and strategies, which are fundamental to the creation of safer and more secure cities relative to the prevention, reduction and mitigation of crime and violence. The chapter is divided into five sections.

The first section describes the analytical framework and orientation of the chapter. It also identifies key concepts and terms, and makes observations about the quality and availability of crime data. The section on 'The incidence and variability of crime and violence' discusses the incidence of crime at the global, regional, national and local levels. The factors that trigger crime and violence are discussed in 'Factors underlying crime and violence'. The impacts of crime and violence are then addressed in a fourth section. This is followed by the final section, which provides brief concluding remarks.

ANALYTICAL FRAMEWORKS FOR THE CHAPTER

Crime and violence as predictable phenomena

Like natural disasters, crime and violence are predictable phenomena variably affecting cities of all sizes across the globe. Often seen as discrete events, crime and violence are the result of processes and choices that have long-term underlying roots, including those related to global economic changes, national conditions and to the level and pace of urban development. Crime and violence are also associated with more immediate risk factors, such as the ready availability of drugs and guns.

'Common' or conventional crimes and violence are socio-pathologies that are traditionally and often automatically associated with cities. But it should be clear that *most* places in *most* cities are safe and that most types of common street crime tend to reoccur at certain locations – hotspots – that are venues known to citizens and to public officials. They are therefore reasonably predictable events; indeed, some research suggests that, relative to crime prevention, the question that could best be asked first is not *who* committed the crime but *where* it happened.[1]

Conventional crimes and violence are socio-pathologies that are traditionally and often automatically associated with cities

Cultures of fear and the media

While the issues are complex, it is clear that fear of crime, violence and terrorism are global concerns, made increasingly salient by all forms of media, including that provided by the internet and sensationalized press reports. For instance, the media in Latin America plays a key role in constructing images of fear, insecurity and violence due to the phenomenal and, at times, sensational coverage given to youth violence and youth gangs.[2] Similarly, the British Crime Survey found that readers of national 'tabloids' were twice as likely to be worried about violent crime, burglary and car crime as people who read 'broadsheets', although it is not clear whether such readers were more predisposed to worry about crime in the first place.[3]

Fear of crime, violence and terrorism are global concerns, made increasingly salient by all forms of media

The flood of information (and misinformation) reaches residents of megacities at an astonishing rate, especially as the internet, email and cell phones knit together more of the world. The rapid diffusion of information is now the lifeblood of industrialized and democratized market economies where both conflict and enterprise are generally constrained by law. But the media also affects that half of the world's population that is described by some as falling within the unregulated 'shadow economy', in which violence rather than the state's rule of law is the ultimate 'arbiter' of disputes. As discussed below, burgeoning criminal networks – called by some the 'sinister underbelly of globalization'[4] – have helped to nurture shadow economies in many nations and cities. It is ironic, but not unpredictable, that media portrayals of this sector have never stoked the same level of fear that it has about terrorism, which is far less pervasive and arguably less serious than either common or organized crime.

Since the media is the key vehicle of globalized fears, it also has an important role in the construction of the perceptions of local insecurities, in terms of issues that are highlighted and the way actors are depicted. Cultures of violence do permeate many media reports, and impact on the way violence against women or police brutality or youth gangs are understood in society. The importance of understanding and considering fear in analysing impacts and responses to crime and violence has to be acknowledged, as it points to the need to address not only crime and violence as phenomena, but also the sentiments of fear and insecurity in a broader sense.

Formal and informal institutions play important roles in mediating or exacerbating the impacts of crime and violence

International legal frameworks and trends

The discussion in this chapter is also guided by the view that safety from crime and violence, including the fear and insecurity that flow from these disturbing events, are public goods and basic human rights, not unlike the right to clean water, air and shelter. These principles have been embraced at the international level and are increasingly being acknowledged by national and local governments, as well as by local community organizations. In concert with this, crime *prevention* approaches have gained credibility and momentum, as demonstrated by the development and reaffirmation of the United Nations Economic and Social Council Resolution 1995/9 of 24 July 1995, the United Nations Guidelines for Crime Prevention,[5] by the entry into force of the United Nations Convention against Transnational Organized Crime and its three protocols,[6] and by the promulgation of the United Nations Anti-Corruption Toolkit as part of the Global Programme Against Corruption,[7] to name but a few of the relatively recent initiatives.

Crime is fundamentally defined as an antisocial act that violates a law and for which a punishment can be imposed by the state or in the state's name

Formal and informal institutions

It is clear that formal and informal institutions play important roles in mediating or exacerbating the impacts of crime and violence insomuch as victims and perpetrators are affected by rules, decisions and programmes that flow from public policy, as well as by 'socially shared rules, usually unwritten, that are created, communicated and enforced outside of officially sanctioned channels'.[8] In many instances, informal institutions trump the policies made by formal institutions, as suggested in the examples from Brazil and Russia below.

Formal institutional rules are epitomized in a variety of interventions at all levels across the developed and developing world and will be discussed in more detail. They include some recurring themes based upon conditions and trends in crime and violence, and can encompass social and economic, situational and law enforcement interventions, or combinations of these. For instance, based on what is known about the linkages of employment, youthful populations and the risks of crime, a major strategy of public and private crime prevention programmes – from Kenya and Papua New Guinea to the US – is targeting unemployed urban youths, especially males, by providing training and job opportunities.[9] Such programmes are variably effective, given local implementation strategies; but their desirability is almost universally embraced.

Informal institutions are cultural norms that are not sanctioned by official programmes or public policy (although they may be influenced by them). For example, while extrajudicial killings are prohibited by Brazilian law, the police are sometimes encouraged by informal norms, pressures and incentives within the security system to execute suspected criminals who might otherwise escape prosecution. In the former Soviet Union, although not approved by the state, the '*blat*' system was widely used to obtain commodities not provided by the Soviet command economy. It was a 'prohibited but possible' means of receiving goods and favours that would otherwise not be available.[10]

There are instances where informal institutions play vital and positive roles, for example in providing mediation mechanisms that resolve conflicts within a community before resorting to the formal justice system, therefore providing diversion channels for minor offenders. There are examples of informal institutions that are supported and sanctioned by public policy, and do contribute to safety and security in neighbourhoods. For example, the *Sungusungu* of Tanzania are organized groups of people (neighbourhood watch) operating with the authority and protection of the government for law enforcement and protection of people and property. *Sungusungu* are legally recognized through the Peoples' Militia Laws (Miscellaneous Amendment) Act, 1989 (No. 9 of 1989). The powers granted to *Sungusungu* are similar to those vested in police officers of the rank of Police Constable[11]. The *Sungusungu* groups are established by the communities and recruit unemployed youth who receive militia training and various forms of support from the communities and municipalities. The communities sometimes provide financial support, while the municipalities usually provide material support, such as uniforms.

There are also instances where distinctions between formal and informal institutions blur. This is evident in the violence in Darfur and Iraq. In these circumstances, it is not easy to distinguish between formal and informal institutions that are perpetrating violent acts against citizens. In other instances, where legitimate state force – in the way of the *realized* protection of law and regulation – is lacking or ineffective, criminal enterprises often fill the vacuum, as exemplified by the expansion of the Russian mafia following the fall of the Soviet Union and by burgeoning gangs in lawless areas of Latin America's megacities.

Key concepts and terms

A crime is fundamentally defined as an antisocial act that violates a law and for which a punishment can be imposed by the state or in the state's name; the resulting range of punishable acts is extraordinary and varies across jurisdic-

Table 3.1

Roadmap of categories, types and manifestations of violence in urban areas

Category of violence	Types of violence by perpetrators and/or victims	Manifestations
Political	• State and non-state violence	• Guerrilla conflict • Paramilitary conflict • Political assassinations • Armed conflict between political parties
Institutional	• Violence of state and other 'informal' institutions, including the private sector	• Extra judicial killings by the police • Physical or psychological abuse by health and education workers • State or community vigilante-directed social cleansing of gangs and street children • Lynching of suspected criminals by community members
Economic	• Organized crime • Business interests • Delinquents • Robbers	• Intimidation and violence as a means of resolving economic disputes • Street theft robbery and crime • Kidnapping • Armed robbery • Drug trafficking • Car theft and other contraband activities • Small arms dealing • Assaults including killing and rape in the course of economic crimes • Trafficking in prostitutes • Conflict over scarce resources
Economic/social	• Gangs • Street children • Ethnic violence	• Territory- or identity-based turf violence • Petty theft • Communal riots
Social	• Intimate partner violence inside the home • Sexual violence (including rape) in a public area • Child abuse: boys and girls • Intergenerational conflict between parent and child • Gratuitous/routine daily violence	• Physical or psychological male–female abuse • Physical and sexual abuse particularly evident in the case of stepfathers, but also uncles • Physical and psychological abuse • Incivility in areas such as traffic, road rage, bar fights and street confrontations • Arguments that get out of control

Source: Moser, 2004, p5

tions and cultures. Within this context, crime prevention approaches and classification schemes have focused on offenders, on punishment, on policing, on corrections, on victims, and on sociological, cultural and economic contexts of the criminal event. These emphases have produced an extensive literature[12] of prevention strategies relative to addressing offenders' moral, psychological, economic and social conditions, devising police tactics, assessing the efficacy of prisons and correctional systems, remedying urban slums and addressing physical and management issues relative to urban planning and design.

Violence has multiple definitions and is subject to numerous classification schemes. The World Health Organization (WHO) defines violence as 'The intentional use of physical force, threatened or actual, against oneself, another person, or against a group or community that either results in or has a high likelihood of … injury, death, psychological harm, mal-development or deprivation.' The WHO further categorizes violence relative to whether it is self-directed, interpersonal or collective.[13] It is also possible to identify broad categories of violence, types of violence by perpetrators or victims, and manifestations.[14] This typology is illustrated in Table 3.1.

The typology is quite inclusive and focuses attention beyond types of violence receiving media attention to more specific forms, including those specifically directed at women and children, as well as those originating from the state. In addition to the above, the notion of *structural violence* has been identified.[15] This relates to non-physical acts or indirect forms of violence that have emerged from historical experiences and are woven into social, economic and political systems. In this context, violence is 'built into the structure of society … and shows up as unequal power and consequentially as unequal life chances'.[16] Such implicit forms of violence include exploitation, exclusion, injustice inequality and discrimination.

The linkage of crime and violence

Crime and violence are related issues, although many crimes may not entail violence (such as theft and drug-related offences) and some acts of violence may not be crimes (such as those committed pursuant to law or those embedded in cultural norms. However, there are significant overlaps between crime and violence, such as in the cases of murders, armed robberies and assaults, including sexual assault. Violence is one feature that distinguishes types of crime within the broad categories of crimes described below. Certain types of violence may not be considered as crime in some jurisdictions or may be illegal but tolerated within the context of overriding religious or cultural frameworks. In these cases, violence is so embedded in norms that it is part of the accepted structure of life.

There are significant overlaps between crime and violence, such as in the cases of murders, armed robberies and assaults, including sexual assault

Although the International Crime Victimization Survey (ICVS) uses 11 types of conventional crime on which overall victimization rates are based,[17] crimes may also be grouped into three broad descriptive categories that affect people throughout the world: personal or contact (violent) crimes; property offences; and crimes against public order and welfare.

Contact crimes

The first category of crimes includes violent acts against persons, which are considered to be the most serious offences. Sometimes called personal crimes,[18] this group of offences generally includes homicides, assaults (including those suffered as a result of domestic violence), robbery (including armed robbery), rape and, in some jurisdictions, kidnapping. It may also include some relatively minor offences, such as pick-pocketing. Though usually less frequent than property crimes, personal crimes such as homicides and robberies imperil individuals and communities, with significant social and economic impacts to families, cities and states. They often have significant long-term impacts on the way in which urban areas are perceived and used by residents and outsiders, and how they are regenerated (or ignored) by public agencies. Contact crimes jeopardize the physical and psychological well-being of victims, with potentially devastating results. This chapter focuses on homicides and robberies as some of the most well documented of these crimes in more detail below.

Contact crimes jeopardize the physical and psychological well-being of victims, with potentially devastating results

Property crimes

Property offences constitute the second category of crime and are considered less serious than personal crimes. Nonetheless, they significantly affect individual victims and negatively influence the overall quality of urban life. Across *all* crime categories, larceny and thefts are generally the most frequent individual offences, with rates that usually far exceed either violent crimes or those of other types of property crime. The vast majority of all crimes are, indeed, minor in most places. There are, of course, exceptions to this, such as in Accra, Ghana, where assaults were the highest individual category of offences reported between 1980 and 1996.[19] There are a considerable number of 'lesser' property crimes, including vandalism and 'quality of life' crimes, such as graffiti and damage to property.

The most serious property crimes generally include burglary, larceny and theft (the latter two are often, but not always, synonymous with each other depending upon jurisdiction), arson and other property-related offences that are specific to localities. Of all property crimes, burglary is probably the most invasive offence, often carrying with it long-term psychological impacts on victims, stigma for neighbourhoods and districts, and implications for planning and design. Burglary is considered in more detail below.

Of all property crimes, burglary is probably the most invasive offence, often carrying with it long-term psychological impacts on victims, stigma for neighbourhoods and... implications for planning

Crimes against public order

A third broad category includes moral infractions and crimes against public order and welfare and may include anti-social behaviour, as well as some types of sexual offences and infractions, such as corruption, trafficking of human beings, firearms and drugs. As an example of the wide range of offences in this category, Ghana includes currency offences, treason, sedition, mutiny, rioting, publication of false rumour, evasion of military service, prostitution and food safety violations, among others.[20] Other much less serious offences and disorder in this category of crime can include public intoxication and criminal damage. Fraud, cyber-crime (including identity theft), other so-called 'white collar' crimes and environmental offences may be variably included in the crimes against public order category or even fall within the civil law domain as distinct from criminal offences, depending upon jurisdiction, seriousness or other factors related to the specific circumstance. Trafficking offences are often the province of organized and relatively sophisticated groups at global, national and urban levels. The growth of international criminal enterprises, such as trafficking, is associated with broader global trends, facilitated by weak or failing formal institutions and abetted by complicit or fragile civil societies.

Data issues

There are several important caveats to interpreting the data that follows. These include:

- Methods of recording and counting crime vary from country to country, and there are no accepted universal standards on producing and presenting crime statistics.
- Crime reporting is related to the prevalence of law enforcement and to peoples' willingness to come forward, both of which vary by country – in virtually all jurisdictions many crimes are not reported to authorities.
- Crime victimization data obtained through surveys tends to be higher quality than police reports, even though they, too, rely on people's memories and willingness to cooperate.
- Definitions of what constitutes a crime differ widely and may not be comparable by virtue of cultural, social and legal system differences.
- Crime data quality diverges widely and is related to resource availability – hence, poor nations are less likely than wealthy ones to have complete and accurate crime data.

Comparisons of crime data between and among regions, countries and cities should therefore be seen in light of these limitations. Moreover, it is important to note that trends can be best understood in terms of a long-term perspective as a means to understanding regional and national differences.

Although there are differences among countries, four general approaches are commonly used to count crime. These include: crimes that are reported or known to the police; information gathered on the arrest of persons; data based on convictions for crimes; and crime rates obtained from victim surveys audits. Offender interviews and hospital admission records are also employed to collect crime data, although their use is not as widespread as police reports, arrest and conviction rates and victim survey data. While each of these measures offers insights into crime conditions and trends, all crime data must be carefully balanced against the numerous data collection problems noted above.

Recognizing these issues, attention is paid to certain conventional crimes that research and victim surveys suggest as having significant impact on urban dwellers, with compounding effects on the larger communities of which they are a part. These include contact crimes such as homicides (an indicator of violent crime, generally) and robbery, as well as property crime, indicated by burglary – a non-violent but nonetheless serious crime. Furthermore, this chapter considers a variety of public order offences, such as corruption, organized crime and trafficking offences, including drugs, arms and human trafficking.

THE INCIDENCE AND VARIABILITY OF CRIME AND VIOLENCE

Crimes and violence are unevenly distributed across the globe and within nations and cities. Nevertheless, they are pernicious, continuing threats to human security, generally, and especially for the poor, who are disproportionately victimized as individuals and whose communities are strongly affected. While crime and violence must be considered through the lens of unique local contexts and circumstances, trends in crime and violence can also be seen at much broader levels. This section reviews some of the global, regional, national and city data for serious contact, property and public order crimes.

Global and regional crime conditions and trends

Figure 3.1, based on United Nations surveys, shows that crime rates at both the global and regional levels have increased steadily over the period of 1980 to 2000, rising about 30 per cent from 2300 crimes per 100,000 to over 3000 per 100,000 individuals.[21] But this is not the case for all regions. Some crime rates, such as those in North America, fell significantly over these two decades even though the general level of crime was higher there than for other regions, except for the European Union (EU) beginning in approximately 1999. Crime in Latin America and the Caribbean regions rose during this period, reflecting, in part, political transitions from autocracy to democracy and civil conflict. Data for the EU disguises the fact that states have experienced variable crime rates, with increases in some Eastern European nations and decreases in some Western European nations. African data has been excluded since only a relatively few African states provided crime survey data for the indicated period.

Comparatively high general crime levels in higher-income regions of North America and Europe are explained by the greater propensity of people to report crimes of all types to the police, whereas in middle- and lower-income nations, serious offences, such as violent contact offences, are more often reported than property crimes. Crime rates in middle-income nations are likely to increase as the spread of technology offers more opportunities for things to steal and as people have increased abilities to report crimes to the police.[22]

Although the levels of crime are higher in North America, this is also where the most significant declines are evident. Despite many competing explanations for the decrease, one suggestion attributes this to countermeasures that have been enacted, especially in the US.[23] Nonetheless, much of the decline in crimes in North America is due to the decrease in property crimes, which constitute the vast bulk of crimes and are more likely to be reported in industrialized countries vis-à-vis developing ones.

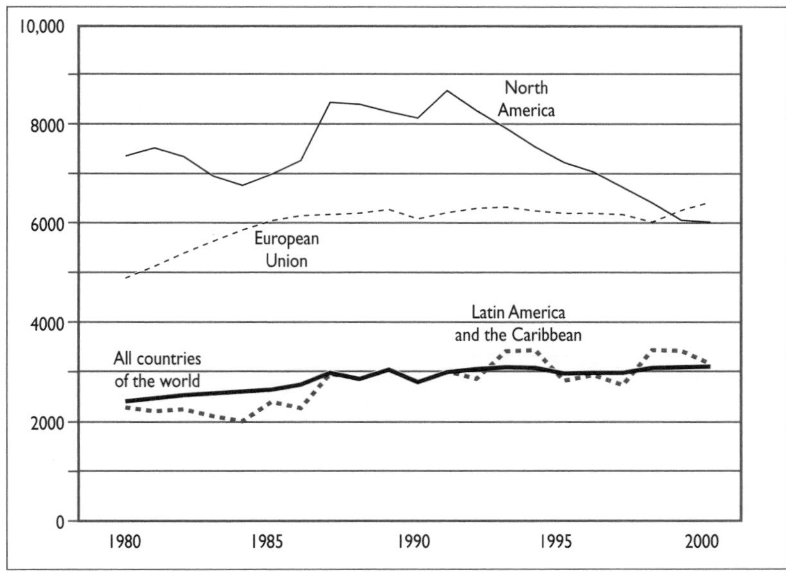

Figure 3.1

Total recorded crime trends per 100,000 individuals in selected regions of the world

Source: Shaw et al, 2003, p42

National crime conditions and trends

When various types of crimes for all income groups are aggregated cross-nationally, the sums are staggering. For example, there were almost 50 million property and violent crimes recorded by police in 34 industrialized and industrializing countries in 2001 alone.[24] These nations account for less than one fifth of the world's population according to 2006 estimates,[25] which makes the numbers even more compelling when it is considered that many crimes are not reported. Moreover, crime statistics routinely undercount poor victims and those from marginalized communities, where crime is likely to be more pervasive. Large nations such as the US, Russia and the UK consistently account for a major share of crime incidents, although their rates have varied considerably within each country over the past decade. Moreover, crime rates differ significantly between countries and are not always explained by sheer population size. For example, based on 2001 data, the US had about six times the crime rate of Cyprus (3658 crimes per 100,000 versus 595 crimes per 100,000 individuals), but 383 times

Crime statistics routinely undercount poor victims and those from marginalized communities, where crime is likely to be more pervasive

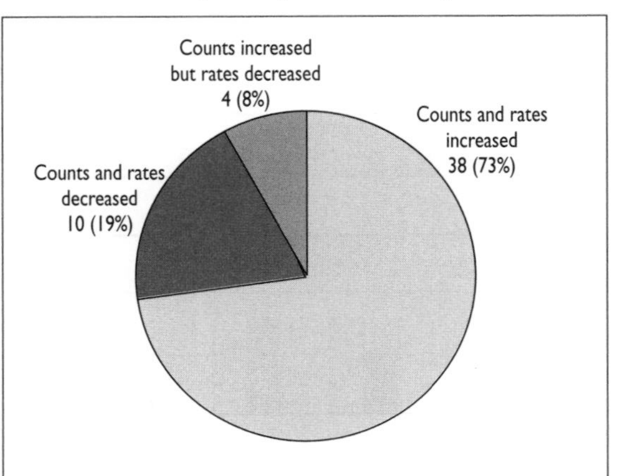

Figure 3.2

Police-recorded crimes and attempts for 52 countries: Changes in counts and rates (2001–2002)[26]

Source: Adapted from UNODC, 2005a, Table 2.1

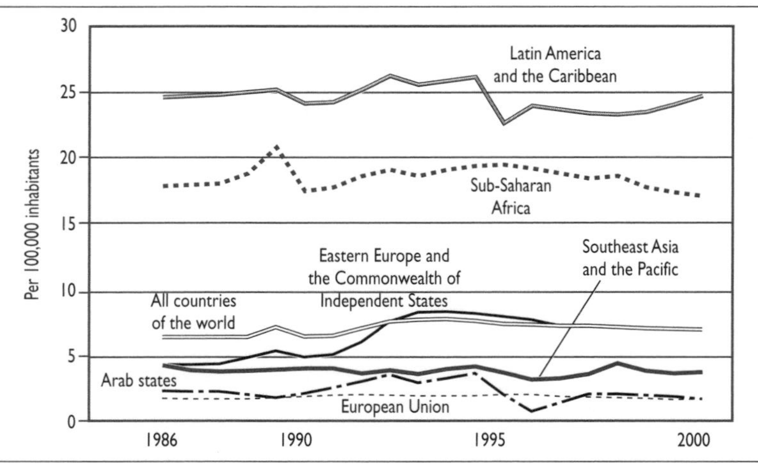

Figure 3.3

Rates of homicides: Selected regional trends (1986–2000)

Source: Shaw et al, 2003, p48

the population (300 million versus 784,000). Although it is important, there are many other factors at work besides population size that explain crime counts and rates. Not the least of these is how data is reported and recorded at local and national levels.

Using another sample, Figure 3.2 shows that 73 per cent of the mostly industrialized nations (38 out of 52) providing information on crimes reported to the police showed an increase in both crime counts and rates between 2001 and 2002, while 19 per cent experienced decreased counts and rates, and 8 per cent higher counts but reduced rates.[27] The overall increase in counts and rates is generally consistent with victim survey data for this time period. However, this data includes 'crime attempts' that make it difficult to compare with other official crime data sets. Given the very short interval, no trends can be clearly discerned.

Homicides at global and regional levels

Homicides are considered in terms of global, regional and national levels since in many cases the data overlaps. Homicides are violent contact crimes. The definition of homicide generally includes intentional and non-intentional homicide. Intentional homicide refers to death deliberately inflicted on a person by another person, including infanticide. Non-intentional homicide refers to death that is not deliberately inflicted on a person by another person. This includes manslaughter, but excludes traffic accidents that result in the death of a person.[28] Homicide is widely considered the single most important indicator of violent crime, and there are often many other lesser crimes (such as robbery) that are associated with it. Moreover, it is the offence that is most likely to be reported. Consequently, homicides are likely to be recorded by the police.[29] Despite this, it should be clear that homicide is a rare crime, especially when compared with property crimes such as larceny and theft.

Homicide rates are associated with combinations of social, economic, cultural and political factors that are unique to localities, even though similar underlying risk factors tend to be found globally, such as poverty, unemployment, and cultural and social norms that may encourage violence as a way of settling disputes. These risk factors are discussed in more detail in the section 'Factors underlying crime and violence'. Figure 3.3 provides a picture of homicide rates for selected global regions. It clearly shows that Latin America and the Caribbean region and sub-Saharan Africa have the highest rates of homicides, while the EU and the Arab States have the lowest rates. For the period of 1990 to 2000, WHO data shows that violent crime, including homicide, grew globally from about 6 incidents per 100,000 to 8.8 per 100,000 individuals.[30]

Figure 3.4 includes homicide and war casualty rates for various regions. It shows double-digit homicide rates for Africa and the Americas, and significantly lower rates in Southeast Asia, Europe, the Eastern Mediterranean and especially the Western Pacific. Although there are many factors at work, some of the divergence between regions reporting high and low homicide rates is associated with broad socio-cultural constraints on violence and the development and perceived efficacy of criminal justice systems. High war casualty rates for Africa reflect large numbers of localized conflicts that have taken place there over the last decade. Research suggests that the deadly after effects of civil wars linger for about five years after combat itself stops, increasing the per capita rate of homicide by about 25 per cent irrespective of changes to income levels, equality or the nature of state institutions.[31]

Figure 3.5 reports the same homicide data regionally, but also shows suicide rates. Suicide is considered an intentional crime in many countries. With the exception of the Eastern Mediterranean region, suicide rates are almost the inverse of homicide rates in other regions. Among other things, this data suggests that poverty is less of a risk factor associated with suicide than cultural and social values and norms that discourage (or support) self-harm as a viable solution to problems. Interpreted this way, it reinforces the fundamental importance that informal institutions play in shaping behaviour.

Figure 3.4

Homicide rates and war casualties

Source: UNODC, 2005b, p54

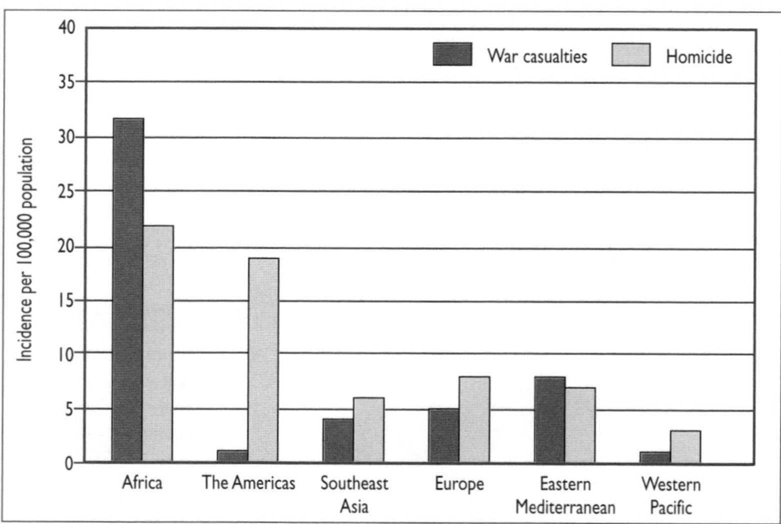

Homicides trends in cities

Homicide rates for 37 selected cities drawn mainly from developed countries and based on police reports are presented in Figure 3.6. Also shown is the EU average for the same period. EU city averages are significantly higher (2.28 per 100,000) compared to the matching *country* homicide rate average (1.59 per 100,000). High murder rates (near or above 5 per 100,000 individuals) are apparent for cities in countries undergoing civil strife, such as Belfast (Northern Ireland) and in cities that are in the midst of transitions between political and economic systems, such as Tallinn (Estonia), Vilnius (Lithuania) and Moscow (Russia). The highest reported murder rate is in Washington, DC, which equals or exceeds rates in developing nations. This city has a number of converging risk factors, including significant social and economic inequality, a high proportion of impoverished citizens and widespread availability of guns.

While crime rates vary significantly within regions and countries, over a recent five-year period, it has been estimated that 60 per cent of all urban dwellers in developing countries have been crime victims, with rates of 70 per cent in parts of Latin America and Africa.[32] Crime and violence are typically more severe in urban areas and are compounded by their rapid growth, especially in developing and transitional nations. In Latin America, where 80 per cent of the population is urban, the rapidly expanding metropolitan areas of Rio de Janeiro, São Paulo, Mexico City, Lima and Caracas are responsible for over half of the homicides reported in their respective countries.[33] The homicide rate in Rio de Janeiro has tripled since the 1970s, while the rate in São Paulo has quadrupled. In the Caribbean, Kingston, Jamaica's capital, consistently accounts for the vast majority of the nation's murders.[34]

At the global level, discerning violent crime trends is complicated by the significant variability across regions (as seen above), within nations and between areas within cities. For example, as is evident in Figure 3.6, violent crime rates for some American cities, such as Washington, DC, and San Francisco, are widely divergent and Washington's homicide rate is more comparable to that of Rio de Janeiro's, which was about 45 per 100,000 in 2001. Tokyo's and Rome's rates are about the same, although they are cultures and continents apart.[35]

Within cities, homicide rates vary significantly. In São Paulo, crude homicide rates in 2001 ranged from 1.2 per 100,000 in the Jardim Paulista district to 115.8 per 100,000 individuals in the Guaianazes district.[36] The reasons for such variations are subject to much debate, with rationales variously attributed to differences in local drug markets, policing strategies and contextual community cultural and social values.

More recently, violent crimes, such as homicides and assaults, have been increasing in the US, particularly in medium-sized cities of between 500,000 and 1 million people.[37] Despite this recent upsurge in violent crime, overall crime rates in North American cities had been generally declining. Large and rapidly growing cities in Asia and the Middle East, which are constrained by a variety of formal and informal forces, consistently report significantly lower crime rates than urban places elsewhere. These variable trends, admittedly based on imperfect statistics, suggest that while crime and violence may be predictable phenomena in cities and regions, they are not necessarily their unalterable fates.

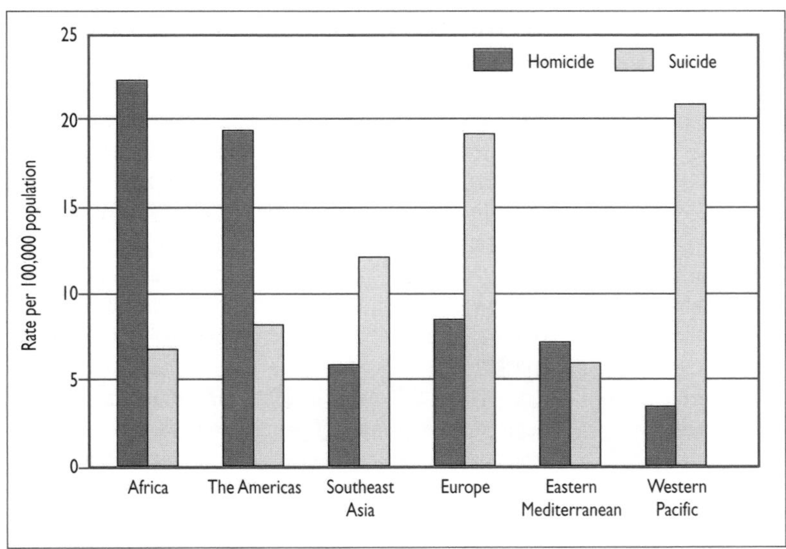

Figure 3.5

Homicide and suicide rates by World Health Organization region (2000)

Source: Krug et al, 2002, p11

Fear of crime and violence

Cultures of fear of crime and violence are widespread, both in the developed and developing world. Public opinion surveys in the US and the UK repeatedly show that people rank crime among the top concerns that they have in everyday life. It should be noted that fear of crime is different from the perception of crime, which is the recognition and knowledge that crime occurs.

These concerns are also found in developing countries, as evidenced in Nairobi (Kenya), where survey

Figure 3.6

Recorded homicides in selected cities

Source: adapted from Barclay et al, 2003

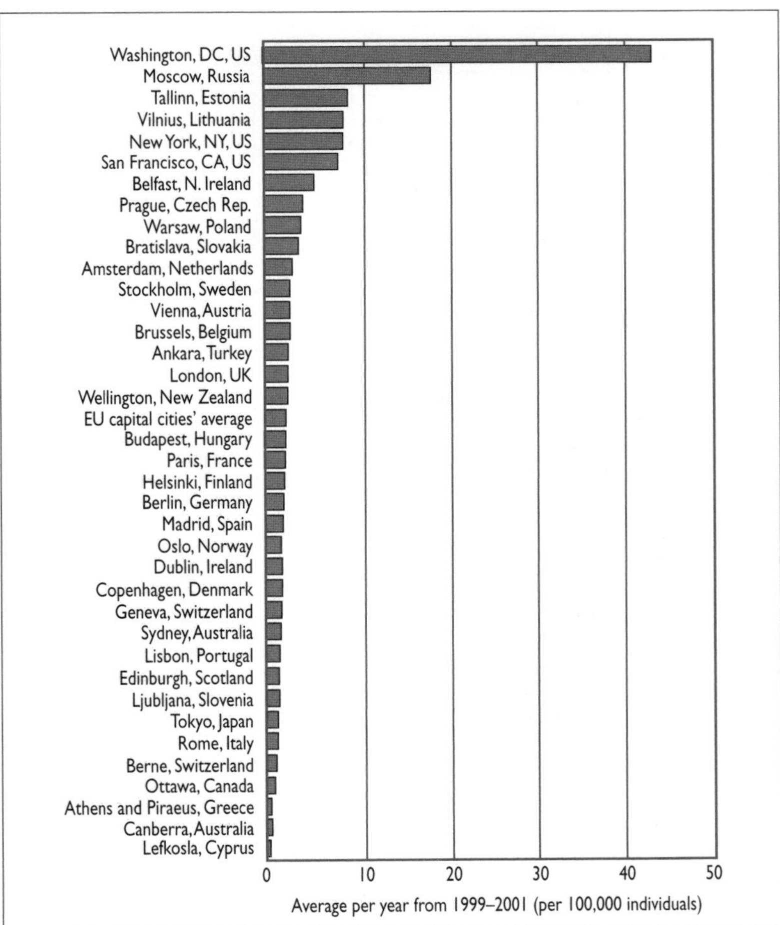

data reveals that more than half of the citizens worry about crime all the time or very often.[38] A national survey conducted in South Africa found that about 25 per cent of respondents indicated that concerns about crime prevented them from starting their own businesses and interfered with everyday transportation decisions.[39] Likewise, a World Bank study in Zambia uncovered significant fear of crime that manifested itself in the work decisions of teachers.[40] In Lagos (Nigeria), 70 per cent of respondents in a city-wide survey were fearful of being victims of crime, while 90 per cent were fearful of the prospect of being killed in a criminal attack.[41]

Burglary is the most common property crime connected to local built environmental and design features

Figure 3.7, based on ICVS and United Nations data, depicts the responses of people from 35 developing and industrialized nations when asked how safe they felt walking home at night. It is obvious that although the fear of crime is pervasive, it is also extremely variable, with the highest levels of fear reported being in Brazil, where 70 per cent of respondents felt unsafe walking home at night, and the lowest in India, with 13 per cent. Latin American and African nations rank among the top ten. Regionally, the fear of crime and violence tends to correlate with police-recorded crime and victimization surveys of crime and violence.

Robbery

Robbery may be defined as the taking of property through the use of violence or threat of violence.[42] Primarily a contact crime, robbery is often classified as both a violent crime and a property crime in many jurisdictions. Consequently, it is more likely to be reported to police than lesser crimes. Robbery is a major security threat and a special concern in developing countries. This is because it not only results in injury and property loss to victims, but also increases the general fear of crime.[43]

Figure 3.8 suggests that global robbery trends have increased between 1980 and 2000 from about 40 incidents per 100,000 individuals to over 60. Data for Eastern Europe, Latin America and Africa (primarily from South Africa) is grouped into 'Selected countries with high robbery rates'.[44] North America witnessed a remarkable decline from 200 per 100,000 recorded cases in 1992 to about 120 in 2000. Victimization rates for robbery based on United Nations survey results are presented in Figure 3.9. It shows much higher rates for robbery in Latin America and Africa than in other regions of the world. Although of a shorter period, it corroborates the information presented in the police-reported data.

Figure 3.10, based on Crime Trends Survey data, shows that South America has the highest robbery rates, with 442 incidents per 100,000 individuals. This is followed by Southern Africa, with 349 cases. The regions with the lowest rates of robbery are South Asia and the Middle East, with 3 and 2 incidents per 100,000 inhabitants, respectively.

Although the findings are generally comparable, some differences between this data can be attributed to collection procedures and differences in the specificity of the various sub-regions. As noted earlier, victimization surveys tend to yield more reliable data, especially when compared to police reports that depend upon the willingness of victims to come forward.

Burglary

Although often targeted against vehicles, burglary is the most common property crime connected to local built environmental and design features. It may be generally defined as the unlawful entry into someone else's property with the intention to commit a crime. Like other crimes, the elements that constitute a burglary are different across the world. For example, in some localities, theft from a car would not be considered a burglary. In other places, the required elements of a burglary include forced entry or the taking of property, whereas other jurisdictions do not have these requirements. High burglary rates have implications for neighbourhoods, cities and nations. Commercial and residential properties are frequent targets for burglaries and data shows that, on average, one out of five urban residents worldwide report being victimized within a five-year period.[45]

Regional trends in burglary, robbery and assaults between the period of 1996 to 2000, based on victim reports, are shown in Figure 3.11. The data includes 31 countries that participated in the ICVS sweeps in 1996 and 2000. Owing to differences in the number and distribution of countries analysed based on the 2000 ICVS survey, caution should be exercised in discerning the patterns, especially relative to developing nations.[46]

Figure 3.7

Percentage of respondents stating that they 'feel unsafe walking home at night'

Source: Nuttall et al, 2002, p40

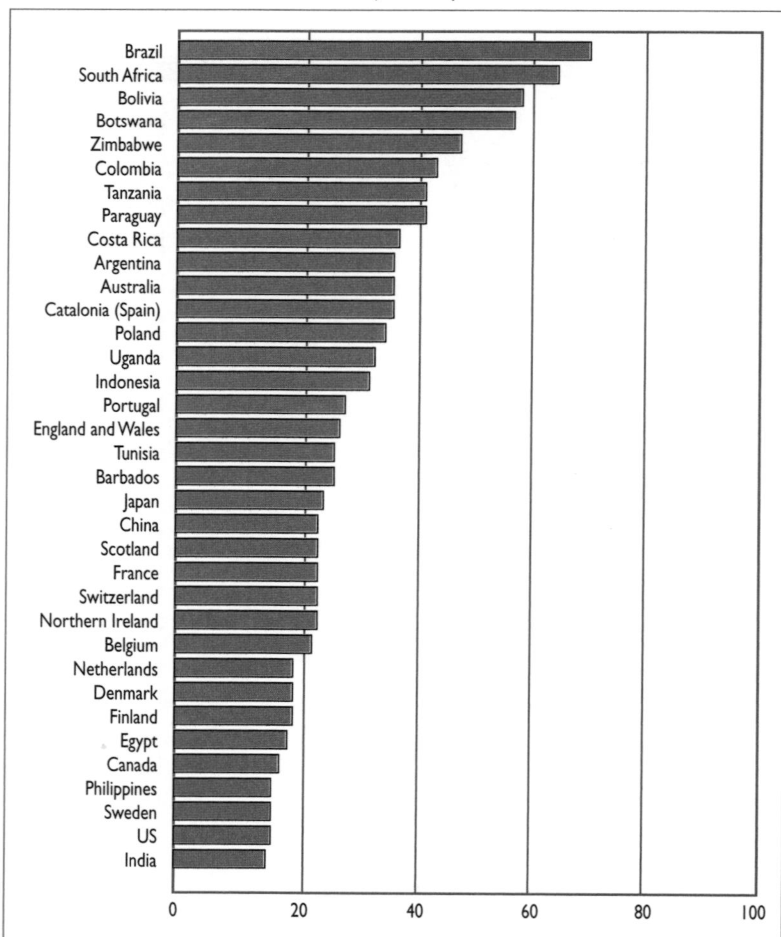

The survey data generally shows declining rates of burglary for all regions, with the exception of Western Europe, with relatively dramatic drops in Africa, Asia and Latin America. Police-reported data for EU countries shows an average decrease of 10 per cent in domestic burglaries for the period of 1997 to 2001, and no change in burglaries for the period of 2001 to 2002.[47] Despite the reported decreases, African nations, and especially African urban areas, still have the highest reported overall levels of burglary, with victimization rates of over 8 per cent of the population in sub-Saharan Africa (see Figure 3.12).

Although a non-violent crime, burglary is a very serious offence in developing regions such as Africa, given the fact that people generally have fewer goods in the first place. More Africans believe that they will be victimized by burglary than people in any other region. Nonetheless, the reporting rate for burglary in Africa is 55 per cent, with only Asia reporting a lower rate of 40 per cent. Other reporting rates are 84 per cent for Oceania, 72 per cent in Europe and 59 per cent in the Americas.[48] Reporting rates for burglary, like many other crimes, tend to be related, in part, to the perceived competence and integrity of the police and public authorities by citizens.

Intimate partner violence and child abuse

Intimate partner violence (IPV) has global, national and local significance as a type of contact crime that may culminate in homicide, assaults and property damage or public order offences. It is aggressive, violent, coercive and threatening behaviour from a spouse, dating partner or ex-partner that often entails psychological abuse. Also known as *domestic abuse*, IPV negatively affects many intimate relationships and families worldwide. Due to the sensitive and personal nature of exposure to domestic violence, many victims do not report the crime to authorities.[49] Surveys in the UK show there were almost 500,000 official reports of domestic violence in 2000. Furthermore, 4 per cent of women and 2 per cent of men were victims of non-sexual domestic violence during 2001.[50] A national study within the US estimates that 29 per cent of women and 22 per cent of men are victimized by IPV (including physical, sexual and psychological abuse) during their lifetime.[51]

Globally, women are significantly more likely than men to be victims of IPV. A recent international study by the WHO interviewed over 24,000 women from ten different countries about their experiences with intimate partner violence. The majority of women (between 51 and 71 per cent) from Peru, Ethiopia, Tanzania and Bangladesh reported experiencing physical or sexual violence from an intimate partner. Women in other countries reported less physical or sexual violence from a partner, such as Brazil (29 per cent), Namibia (36 per cent) and Japan (15 per cent). Sexual victimization was less common than physical abuse by an intimate partner for most women. However, between 30 and 56 per cent of victimized women experienced *both* physical and sexual assaults from a partner.[52] Box 3.1 illustrates the plight of women in South Africa, including some of the underlying risk factors associated with IPV.

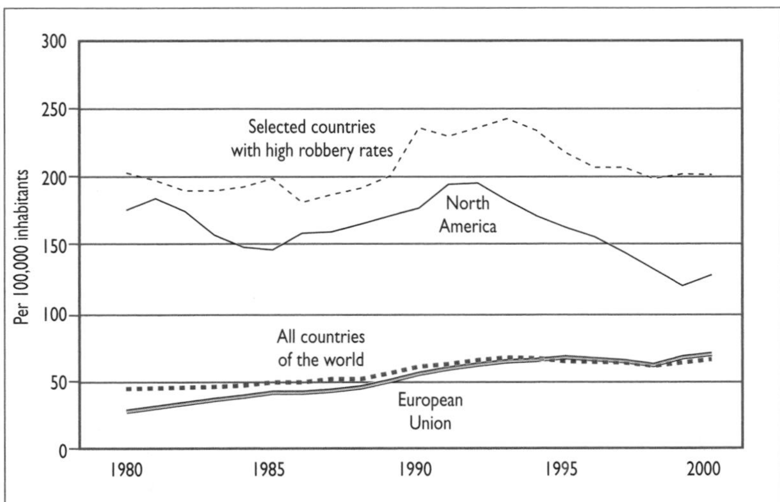

Figure 3.8

Trends in reported robbery per 100,000 individuals (selected regions)

Source: Shaw et al, 2003, p.50

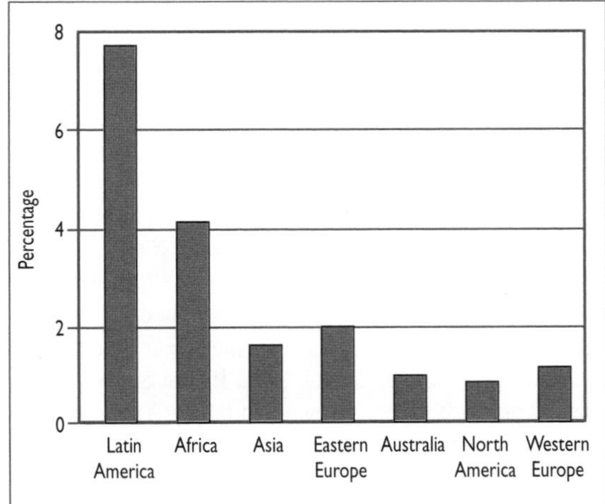

Figure 3.9

Victimization rates for robbery (one-year period)

Source: adapted from del Frate, 2003, p132

Note: Data indicates percentage of population robbed during a one-year period. Data recorded in years between 1989 and 2000.

Factors predictive of women's increased likelihood of being victimized by an intimate partner include age (younger women are at a higher risk); lower socio-economic status; less education; childlessness; less social support; and exposure to abuse in the family of origin. Factors predictive

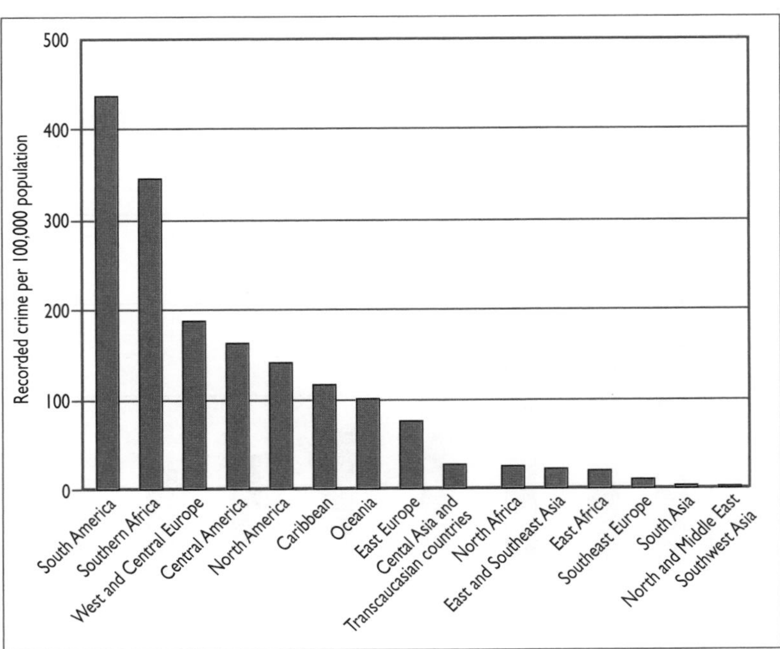

Figure 3.10

Police-recorded robbery

Source: UNODC, 2005b, p60

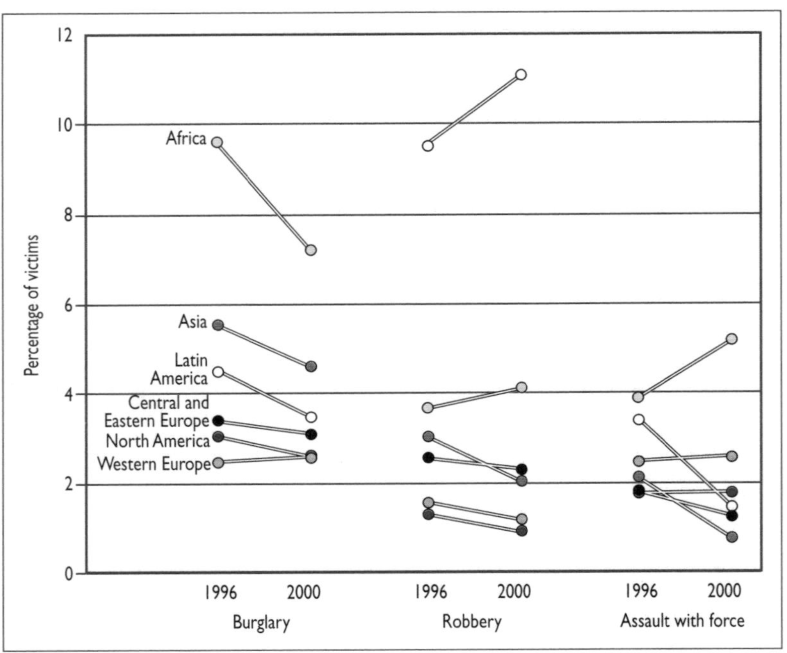

Figure 3.11

Trends in victimization, selected crimes (1996–2000)

Source: del Frate, 2003, p135

of a woman's male partner to become abusive include use of drugs/alcohol; unemployment status; economic pressures; and witnessing parental violence during childhood.[53] In some settings, local cultures, community attitudes and social norms significantly influence the likelihood of violence taking place between intimate partners. For instance, in Zambia, the 2002 Demographic and Health Survey shows that 79 per cent of married women believe that domestic violence is justified when a woman goes out without the permission of her husband.[54] Similarly, in India, married women with low dowries expect to be victims of domestic violence, not only at the hands of their husbands, but also at the hands of their inlaws.[55]

Violent households are often venues for child abuse. Child abuse includes physical abuse, sexual abuse, psychological/verbal abuse, commercial or other exploitation of children, as well as neglect and negligent treatment of children. As with many crimes, there is no 'universal' definition of child abuse. For example, some definitions include witnessing parental violence as child maltreatment, whereas others do not. Vast numbers of children are exposed to violence each year. The United Nations estimates that between 133 million and 275 million children experience violence at home annually, with the largest proportion in South, Western and Eastern Asia, as well as in sub-Saharan Africa.[56] Boys and girls are often equally subjected to child abuse by family members and are equally victimized by child labour exploitation. However, globally, girls make up 98 per cent of children who are sexually exploited.[57]

Figure 3.12

Survey respondents who have suffered burglary during the previous year

Source: UNODC, 2005b, p63

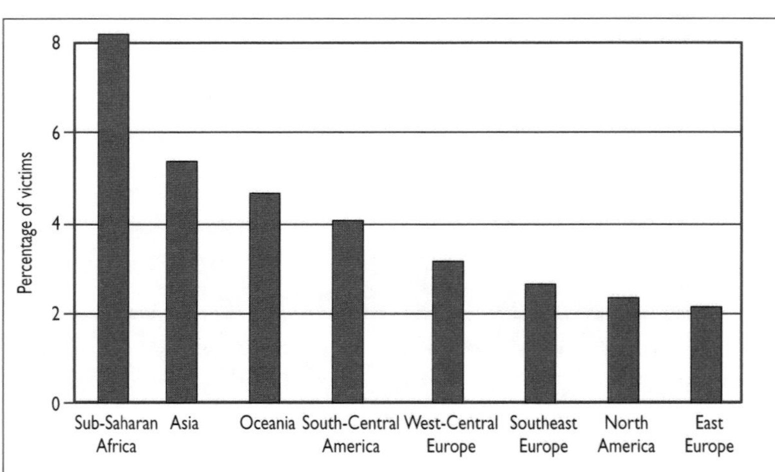

Most children experience abuse at the hands of their primary caregivers – parents and step-parents – with abuse largely taking place within the home. Consequently, some children either run away from home or are removed by authorities and placed in foster care or orphanages. In 2003, 12 per cent of children in sub-Saharan Africa, 7 per cent in Asia and 6 per cent in Latin America and the Caribbean were living in orphanages.[58] A major factor contributing to the high rates of children in orphanages is the death of parents largely attributable to the HIV/AIDS pandemic. Many orphaned children are at great risk of abuse and exploitation.[59] Early marriage is also used by victimized children as a means of escaping abuse. It is important to note that there are other reasons why youths may marry early, including cultural tradition, religious reasons or to obtain financial security.

Children are increasingly being victimized outside their homes – in schools and hospitals and by individuals other than primary caregivers, such as teachers, police or clergy in the workplace and in community settings at large.[60] The *World Report on Violence and Health* reports that 57,000 children were murdered internationally in 2000. Aside from the fundamental violations of human rights that these cases present, child abuse often has been cited as a major risk factor linked to future criminal behaviour, and recent research firmly supports that contention.[61]

Street children

Interpersonal violence, child abuse, family disintegration and poverty contribute to the growing numbers of street children and families across the world. Recent global estimates indicate there are likely to be tens of millions of street children, and some estimates place the number as high as 100 million.[62] Other more localized studies point to 250,000 street children in Kenya, 150,000 in Ethiopia, 12,000 in Zimbabwe, 445,226 in Bangladesh, 30,000 in Nepal and 11 million in India.[63] The United Nations Children's Fund (UNICEF) estimates there are more than 6000 street children in the Central African Republic.[64] It is estimated that there are hundreds of thousands of street children in Latin America, with a significant proportion in Brazil.[65] Future approximations project increasing numbers of street children, growing especially with the pace of urbanization.[66] The growth in the numbers of street children is illustrated by the situation in Kenya, where the numbers of street families and children have developed almost exponentially, as discussed in Box 3.2. In the absence of any form of formal assistance, many street children turn to crime as a survival strategy and eventually become easy targets for membership of youth gangs.

Corruption

Although it comes in many forms, corruption is generally classified as a crime against public order. There is no universally accepted definition of corruption; but it has been summarized as the abuse of public power for personal gain.[67] It constitutes a growing threat to human security and plays a significant role in urban development, planning, management, and programme design and policy. Corruption may be found at the 'grand scale', penetrating the highest policy-making organs of government, or it may be seen at 'petty' or street-scale levels, which involve day-to-day public and social transactions. It often involves soliciting, giving or taking bribes and is sometimes categorized by levels of 'infiltration' within the public sector. While grand corruption has the broadest impacts on societies, corruption in any form helps to destroy public confidence in the fairness of government, the rule of law and economic stability.[68] There are several measures of corruption. Among the most widely used are the Corruption Perceptions Index (CPI) and the Global Corruption Barometer (GCB), both developed by Transparency International. Each is discussed briefly below.

■ The Corruption Perceptions Index (CPI)

The Corruption Perceptions Index calculates a score on the perceived levels of corruption in a given country, based on the responses of business people and analysts around the world, including local experts resident in the country being evaluated. The CPI has a range of between 10 (highly clean) and 0 (highly corrupt). A higher score means less perceived corruption. The map in Figure 3.13 shows the ranking for 158 countries. It indicates that the top ten ranked countries (least corrupt countries) are wealthy European and Oceanic nations, headed by Iceland. The bottom ten ranked countries consist largely of poor and developing nations of Eastern Europe, Asia, Africa and the Caribbean, with Bangladesh and Chad being the lowest ranked.[71]

■ The Global Corruption Barometer (GCB)

The Global Corruption Barometer provides an indication of the extent and nature of corruption from the perspective of ordinary people or the general public around the world. Findings from the 2005 GCB based on a survey of 54,260 people in 69 countries noted that political parties, parliaments, the police and the judicial system were the most corrupt.[70] Figure 3.14 illustrates the distribution of responses among sectors in this regard. Religious bodies, non-governmental organizations (NGOs) and registry and permit services are considered the least corrupt sectors.

Although the responses vary by region, 62 per cent of the countries surveyed reported that political parties were the most corrupt sector. This trend has increased since 2004, when 58 per cent of nations saw political parties as the most corrupt. As Table 3.2 indicates, when considered on a regional basis, Asian, Western European and Latin American citizens saw their political parties as the most corrupt, while African respondents judged their police to be the sector most corrupt. In Central and Eastern Europe, political parties and the police tied for first place as the most corrupt sectors.

Box 3.1 Violence against women in South Africa

South Africa has one of the highest incidences of violence against women (and children) in the world. United Nations Office on Drugs and Crime (UNODC) data on crimes reported by the police indicate that 123.84 rapes per 100,000 individuals were committed in 2000. This is one of the saddest and most alarming manifestations of violence in a society generally regarded as traumatized and wracked by violent crime and (very often) violent interpersonal and public behaviour. Although the causes of the high levels of violence in South African society are manifold and complex, they broadly relate to the country's violent history of colonialism and apartheid. One can also safely assume that the high levels of poverty and unemployment in the country and the resultant economic hardships and frustrations add to the already volatile social and political atmosphere. In addition, patriarchal attitudes, which we share with other societies, make it particularly difficult for women to attain economic independence. As a result, many women are unable to permanently leave their abusive partners, thus failing to protect themselves and their children from physical, sexual, emotional, economic and other forms of abuse.

Source: Zambuko and Edwards, 2007

Petty corruption in the way of bribery is widespread, but affects poorer countries more significantly than richer ones, with some families in Cameroon, Ghana and Nigeria reporting that they spend at least the equivalent of 20 per cent of gross domestic product (GDP) per capita on bribery 'taxes'. Of special significance to urban dwellers are the bribes paid for services that they would normally be entitled to receive since they tend to be larger recipients of services than rural residents. Figure 3.15 shows the variation in service bribery among surveyed nations. Former socialist nations such as Lithuania, Romania, Russia and Ukraine tend to top the lists.

Petty corruption in the way of bribery is widespread, but affects poorer countries more significantly than richer ones

Corruption is closely linked with organized crime. Indeed, the two have been characterized as 'two sides of the same coin'.[71] Research on the connections between corruption and organized crime suggests that socio-economic factors such as poverty, unemployment, societal wealth, income inequality, the pattern of public investment that benefits citizens' quality of life, levels of judicial independence, independence of civil servants, and the strength of

Box 3.2 Street families and street children in Nairobi

One of the major challenges facing urban development in Kenya is the growing number of street families. It is estimated there were approximately 115 street children in 1975. By 1990 this number had grown to 17,000 and by 1997 over 150,000.[72] In 2001, the number was estimated to be 250,000 street children countrywide.[73] With older street dwellers included, the total population of street persons was estimated at approximately 300,000. The bulk of such street dwellers are found in Nairobi, which at present has approximately 60,000 street persons. Street families live permanently or part time in the central business district area streets, bonded by a common identity and involved in organized street survival activities within given operational 'territories'. These families operate in environments that lack protection and supervision mechanisms available in normal social settings.

The survival activities include begging, albeit forcefully, pick pocketing and stealing, child prostitution, and the use and trafficking of drugs. Consequently, the public generally perceives street persons as criminals, thieves, drug addicts and eyesores that should be removed from the streets. Citizens feel that most ills are the responsibility of criminals who were previously street children. The public has no mechanisms to respond to the manifestations and causes of crime by street children – hence, their fear and over-generalizations.

Source: Masese, 2007

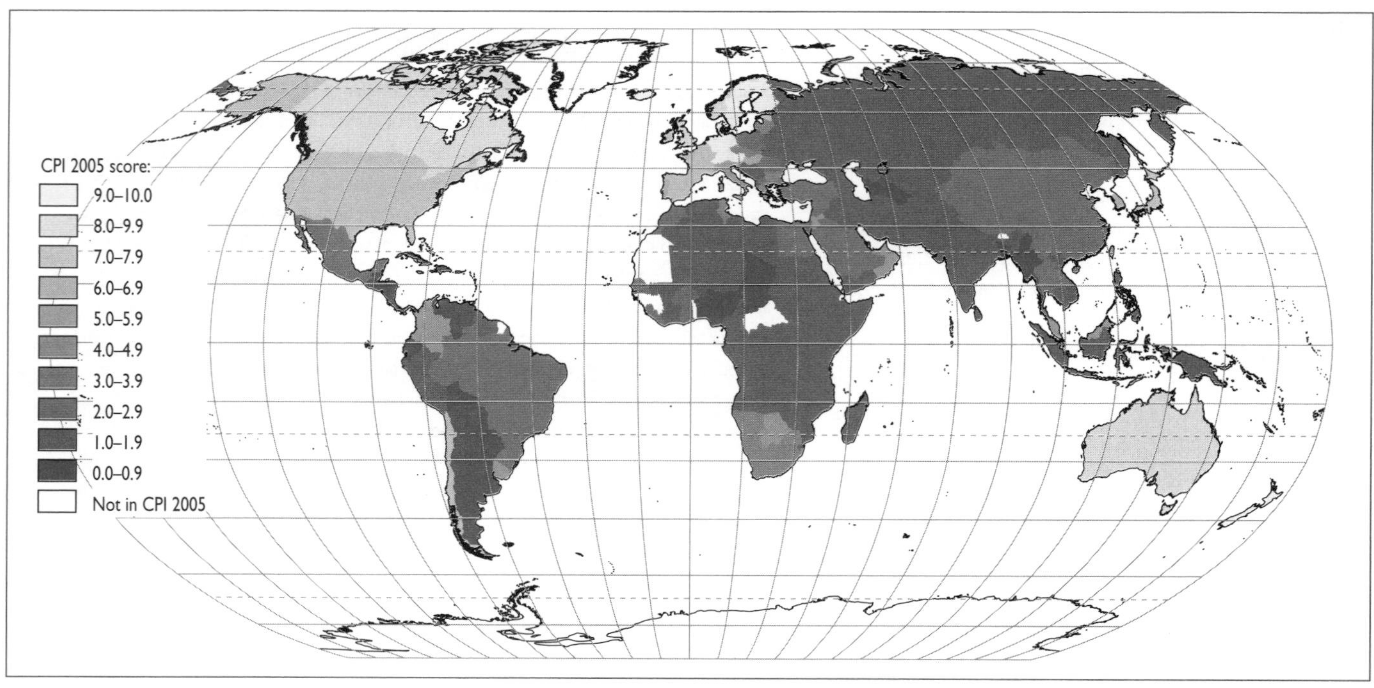

Figure 3.13

Transparency International Corruption Perceptions Index (2005)

Source: Transparency International, 2005b

Figure 3.14

Sectors and institutions most influenced by corruption

Note: 1 = not at all corrupt; 5 = extremely corrupt.

Source: Transparency International, 2005a

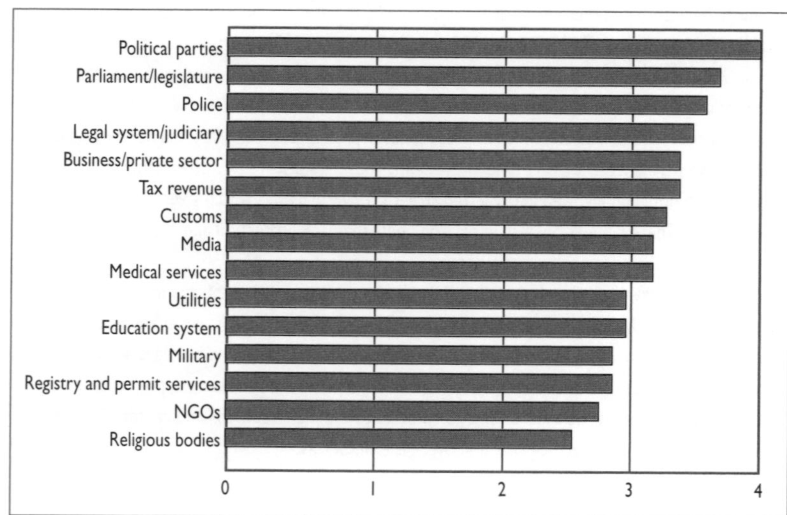

democratic institutions explain the occurrence of corruption among countries.[74] The likelihood of corruption taking place is also high where significant natural resources are extracted in environments that are relatively free of state oversight, including effective judiciaries. For instance, in 2004, Transparency International noted that many oil-producing states in the developing and transitional world have low CPI scores since these industries provide significant opportunities for bribery, embezzlement and cash skimming.[75] Such circumstances also provide the recipe for civil unrest and urban warfare insomuch as they 'provide fuel for both greed and grievance'.[76] The following sub-section considers the various conditions and trends associated with organized crime.

Organized crime

The United Nations Convention against Transnational Organized Crime defines organized crime to mean 'a structured group of three or more persons existing for a period of time and acting in concert with the aim of committing one or more serious crimes or offences established pursuant to this Convention in order to obtain, directly, or indirectly, a financial or other material benefit'.[77] As one of the major threats to human security, transnational organized crime has been characterized by the United Nations Office on Drugs and Crime (UNODC) as 'impeding the social, economic, political and cultural development of societies worldwide'. An enormously diverse series of enterprises, organized crime profits from drug trafficking, trafficking in human beings, trafficking in firearms, smuggling of migrants and money laundering, among others. As one measure of its profitability, the United Nations Drug Control Programme has estimated that US$1billion in illicit capital is circulated daily by criminal groups among the world's financial institutions. These groups thrive in political and social contexts where traditional values have given way to 'a mentality of individual advancement at any price'.[78] Fed by market forces, and especially by globalization, organized crime groups have adapted to changing economic and social conditions faster than the abilities of most states to constrain them.

Assessing the conditions and trends of international criminal organizations is challenging for many reasons. Chief among them are the different scales at which the various groups operate (from the local to the international level); the fundamental data collection hurdles relative to crime, generally, and to the secretive nature of the groups, in particular; and the highly adaptive structures and dynamic nature of the groups. To overcome some of these problems, a recent analysis of the prevalence and global distribution of organized crime has been conducted using 'statistical markers' based on data from World Economic Forum surveys (1997 to 2003) and an international crime assessment group representing 156 countries.[79]

One of these markers is the Organized Crime Perception Index (OCPI), which is a composite score that refers to the 'levels of different types of organized crime activities, such as extortion and drugs, arms and people trafficking, as perceived by potential victim groups and experts'.[80] That marker and four others – the extent of the shadow economy; the percentage of unsolved homicides; the high level of corruption among public officials; and the extent of money laundering – are used in Table 3.3 to rank regions of the world on the basis of their levels of organized crime activities. Table 3.3 shows that Oceania/Australia has the lowest composite rank (least), while the Caribbean has the highest (most) in terms of organized crime activity.

Although there is general consistency between regional scores and the rank order, a cautionary note is necessary with regard to these numbers, given that data is missing for some countries. Nevertheless, the data is suggestive of regional differences that tend to be consistent with country data. Figure 3.16 illustrates the manifestations of organized crime in various nations of the world using the OCPI.

The index shows low levels of organized crime in Canada and Australia. The same is true for Northern Europe, with levels increasing as one moves south and east into Italy, Spain and especially into Eastern European nations such as Russia and Ukraine. South Asia, particularly Pakistan and Bangladesh, stand out with comparatively high levels of organized crime, while India and China are seen as having higher activity than some southern European countries, such as Italy. The African nations of Nigeria, Angola and Mozambique have the highest composite scores. In Latin America and the Caribbean, the countries of Haiti, Guatemala, Paraguay, Venezuela, Colombia and Jamaica stand out with the highest composite index scores.[81]

Conditions supporting the growth of organized crime, such as globalization of markets and increasingly sophisticated communications technology, are not likely to diminish in the near future. Facilitated by developments in these areas, organized crime has flourished in urban drug trafficking and trafficking in arms and in people. The following sub-sections describe global, regional and national conditions and trends related to these facets of organized crime.

Illicit drug trafficking and use

Drug trafficking, simply defined as buying and selling illegal drugs, is a huge worldwide industry that is often the province of organized crime. Moreover, drug trafficking and drug use are fundamental risk factors underlying crime and violence at global, national and local levels. Drug addiction, particularly in urban areas, fuels crime and violence, increases policing and healthcare costs, disintegrates families and generally diminishes the quality of life. While long-term overall trends point to some successes in combating the availability of drugs, such as the reduction of coca cultivation in the Andean region and the decline of opium production in Asia's Golden Triangle, these gains may be offset by setbacks elsewhere, such as the increasing demand for cocaine in parts of Europe, amphetamines in Asia and the US and new transit routes for illicit drugs that have opened in West Africa. The extent of global illicit drug use is depicted in Figure 3.17. This is estimated to be 5 per cent of the worlds' population aged 15 to 64, or 200 million people.

Asia (12 countries)	Political parties 4.2	Parliament/legislature 3.9	Police 3.9	Tax revenue 3.5
Africa (8 countries)	Police 4.4	Political parties 4.2	Customs 4.0	Parliament/legislature 3.8
Western Europe (16 countries)	Political parties 3.7	Parliament/legislature 3.3	Business/private sector 3.3	Media 3.3
Central and Eastern Europe (14 countries)	Political parties 4.0	Police 4.0	Parliament/legislature 3.9	Legal system/judiciary 3.9
Latin America and the Caribbean (15 countries)	Political parties 4.5	Parliament/legislature 4.4	Police 4.3	Legal system/judiciary 4.3

Table 3.2

The most corrupt sectors by region

Note: 1 = not at all corrupt; 5 = extremely corrupt.

Source: Transparency International, 2005a, p5

Trafficking is one of the major components of the illicit drug problem. The other components are cultivation, production, retailing and consumption. Of these components, the least is known about trafficking, although information can be obtained indirectly through studies of criminal group activities and through estimates of drug supplies, areas under cultivation and drug seizures. Seizure and trafficking routes for drugs vary by region, by nation and by the type of drug in question.[82]

There are three major destinations for cannabis resin: West and Central Europe (transiting Spain and The Netherlands); the Near and Middle East/Southwest Asia region (with supplies originating in Afghanistan and Pakistan); and North Africa. Much of the cannabis resin supplied to West and Central Europe and to North Africa is produced in Morocco. In 2004, more cannabis resin was seized in Spain in 2004 than in any other nation.

Drug addiction, particularly in urban areas, fuels crime and violence ... disintegrates families and generally diminishes the quality of life

The world's main cocaine trafficking routes continue to run from the Andean region, notably Colombia, to the US, with Europe as the second most important destination for cocaine produced in the Andean region. The trafficking and use of cocaine in Asia and Oceania is low compared to the rest of the world, while the use in West and Central Africa increased in 2004 on account of the region being a transshipment point to European markets.

Trafficking illicit drugs is a major profit generator for organized crime groups, who often plough their profits into the purchase and subsequent marketing of illegal weapons and engage in trafficking people. The connections between drugs, arms and human trafficking are complex and not

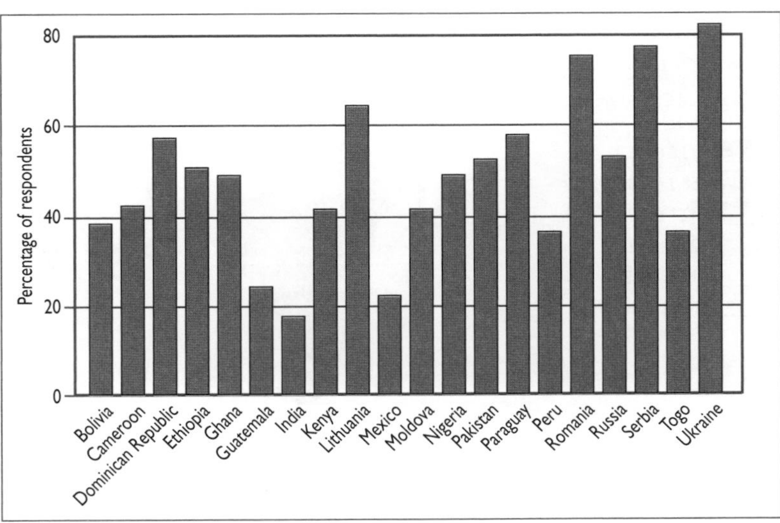

Figure 3.15

Bribes for public services

Note: Percentage of respondents who paid a bribe for public services they were entitled to.

Source: Transparency International, 2005a, p15

Table 3.3

Regional mean scores and ranks on the Organized Crime Perception Index (OCPI) (rank numbers of regions)

Source: van Dijk and van Vollenhoven, 2006, p5

	Average of the OCPI and rank	OCPI (rank)	Informal sector (rank)	Unsolved homicides (rank)	High-level corruption (rank)	Money laundering (rank)
Oceania/Australia	33 (1)	1	1	1	2	1
West and Central Europe	35 (2)	2	2	2	4	3
North America	44 (3)	4	4	4	6	4
East and Southeast Asia	45 (4)	5	3	7	3	6
Central America	50 (5)	4	13	3	8	13
Near and Middle East	50 (6)	7	6	11	1	2
World	54					
South Asia	54 (7)	14	8	8	7	11
North Africa	55 (8)	6	5	6		5
East Africa	55 (9)	12	9		11	9
Southern Africa	56 (10)	10	12	5	12	10
South America	58 (11)	11	14	10	13	12
Southeast Europe	58 (12)	15	10	12	9	14
West and Central Africa	60 (13)	13	11	15	5	8
East Europe	70 (14)	17	16	14	14	16
Central Asia and Transcaucasian	70 (15)	16		13	15	
Caribbean	70 (16)	9	15		16	15

completely understood because of the dynamic and inherently secretive nature of these groups and transactions. Other aspects of organized crime – arms and human trafficking – are discussed below.

Arms trafficking

Easy access to illegal weapons is a major risk factor driving crime and violence rates. Like drug trafficking, arms trafficking is often the focus of organized crime. Access is facilitated by the trafficking of small arms and light weapons, characterized as the weapons of choice of youth gangs, organized criminal groups, paramilitary groups, rebel forces and terrorists. Defined as weapons that 'one or two people can carry, can be mounted on a vehicle, or loaded onto a pack animal', they are easy to obtain as pilfered or legally sold remnants of stockpiles left behind after wars and civil unrest.[83] They are also relatively cheap, lethal, portable, concealable and durable, and their use can be disguised under many legal pretences. Probably most important from a control standpoint is that they are in high demand as the means and motivations for personal security, especially in the absence of effective policing or public protection. For these reasons, small arms are widely trafficked and they are prime facilitators of common crime and violence around the globe.

Research suggests that, overall, weapons tend to move from unregulated jurisdictions to regulated ones.[84] This has become more of an issue as trade of all goods increasingly globalizes. The illegal trade in small arms is much harder to document than the legal trade, but it is thought to be worth about US$1 billion a year.[85] According to the Small Arms Survey, the latter sales account for an estimated 60 to 90 per cent of the 100,000 combat deaths that occur each year and thousands more that take place outside of war zones. It is estimated that there are more than 640 million small arms

Figure 3.16

Organized Crime Perception Index

Source: van Dijk and van Vollenhoven, 2006, p6

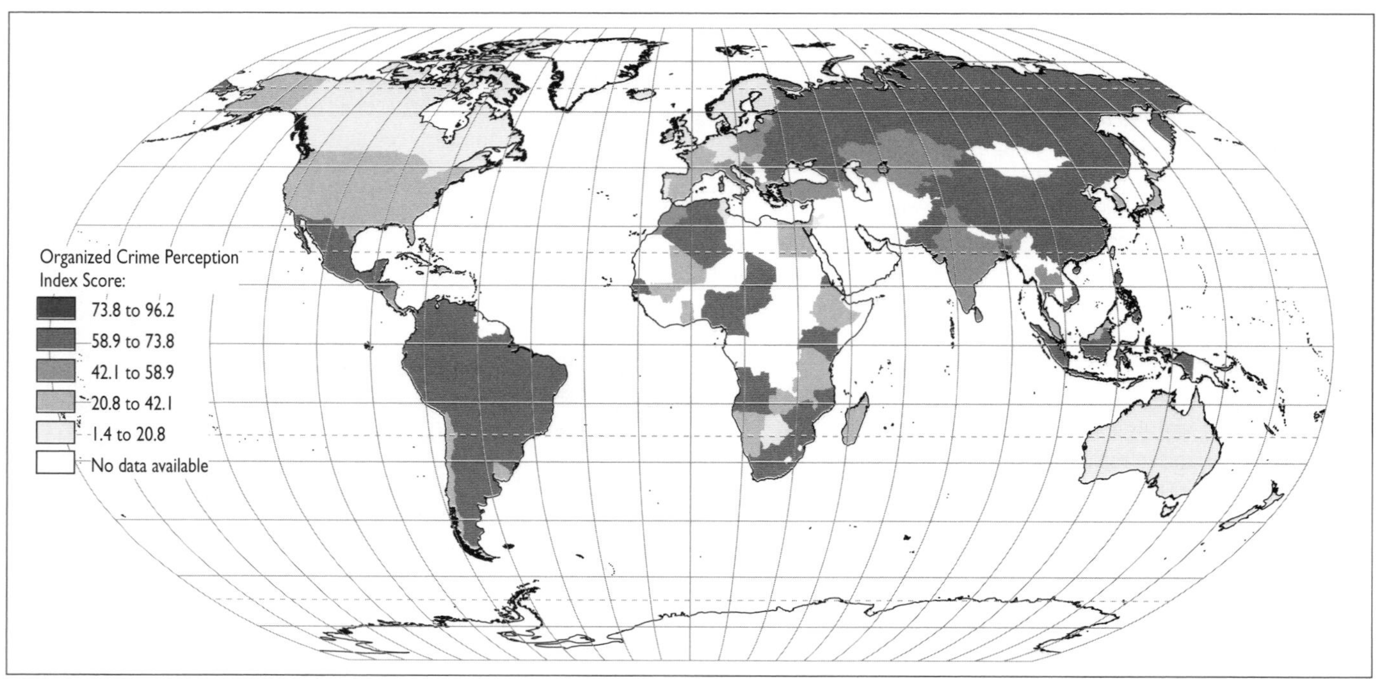

available worldwide, or enough to arm one in every ten persons, and that 1000 individuals each day are murdered by guns worldwide.[86]

Many legal and illicit arms arriving in West Africa from Central and Eastern Europe, Russia, China and other African nations become converted by brokers and private sellers who reap the profits. In Brazil, the 'leakage' of arms from military arsenals has been one of the prime ways in which weapons get into the hands of *favela*-based gangs.[87] The upsurge in violent crimes in Kenya, particularly in Nairobi over the last few years, has, in part, been attributed to the influx of illegal arms from war-torn neighbouring countries, particularly Somalia.[88] Recent estimates for Kenya show that there is one illegal firearm for every 300 citizens.[89] This is likely to be much higher in Nairobi, where gangs 'provide a deep and widening market for illegal weapons' and where an illegal firearm can be hired for as little as US$15.[90] Within the Economic Community of West African States (ECOWAS), the problems of arms trafficking and availability of small arms are vastly compounded by the proliferation of non-state armed groups. According to the United Nations Development Programme (UNDP) and the US State Department, there are at least 8 million illicit small arms in West Africa, with about half in the hands of criminals or insurgents. These represent most of all illegal weapons on the continent.[91] The problems have been particularly severe in Liberia, Sierra Leone and Guinea, which were wrecked by protracted civil wars.

Human trafficking

Like the trade in drugs and arms, human trafficking is a global problem that involves organized criminal groups and that disproportionately affects women and children. Human trafficking is defined as:

> *The recruitment, transportation, transfer, harbouring or receipt of persons, by means of the threat or use of force or other forms of coercion, of abduction, of fraud, of deception, of the abuse of power or of a position of vulnerability or of the giving or receiving of payments or benefits to achieve the consent of a person having control over another person, for the purpose of exploitation. Exploitation includes, at a minimum, the exploitation of the prostitution of others or other forms of sexual exploitation, forced labour or services, slavery or practices similar to slavery, servitude or the removal of organs.*[92]

Although accurate data is unavailable, it is estimated that between 700,000 and 1 million persons are trafficked around the world each year.[93] Trafficking people is big business that generates enormous revenues for traffickers. Human trafficking adds to urban service provision problems, already overburdened in many nations by waves of legal and illegal immigrants, by creating new crime and violence targets largely unprotected by formal institutions that are underserved by informal institutions. Trafficking people

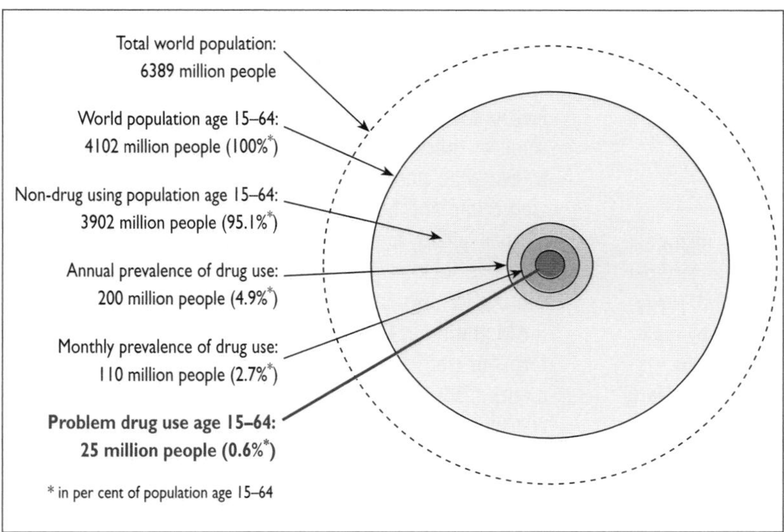

Figure 3.17

Illegal drug use at the global level (2004)

Source: UNODC, 2006a, p8

violates a wide array of national laws and contravenes United Nations protocols that have been adopted as part of the Convention against Organized Crime.[94] Like other crimes, it is best characterized as a complex process, rather than in terms of discrete incidents.

The trafficking process involves at least four phases – recruitment, transportation, exploitation and profit laundering – that take place in many countries and regions. Women and children, especially girls, living in poverty and without economic prospects are particularly vulnerable to traffickers, with bogus promises of jobs and financial security being prime lures. Although sexual exploitation is by far the most frequently reported type of exploitation, forced labour is also a major component of the problem. Trafficking is often confused with smuggling of human beings, which may entail elements of consent, whereas trafficking involves compulsion and criminal victimization.[95] Nevertheless, there can be a fine line between the two depending upon circumstances, and the results can be equally disastrous for individuals, especially when transportation arrangements go awry, as in the case of 58 Chinese migrants who died in an airtight truck on their way to the UK in 2001, or 19 Mexican migrants who suffocated in similar circumstances trying to enter the US in 2003.[96]

Human trafficking is a global problem that involves organized criminal groups and that disproportionately affects women and children

Origin, transit and destination points

UNODC data reveals 127 countries in which trafficking reportedly originates and 137 destination countries.[97] Some of the 98 countries that are identified as transit points overlap those identified as points of origin. The main countries of origin include those in Central and Southeastern Europe, the Commonwealth of Independent States and Asia. These regions are then followed by nations in Western Africa, Latin America and the Caribbean. The regions of origin tend to be economically poorer, rank higher on corruption indices, have had more recent political transitions, civil wars and civil disruptions, and (with the exception of Latin America) are generally more rural than destination regions.

Some of the main transportation paths for human trafficking include countries within Central, Southern and

Western Europe, and nations within Southeast Asia, Central America and Western Africa. Corruption and weak state institutions have been identified as some of the principal risk factors associated with the prevalence of transit routes in some of these regions and nations. In one of the highest transit zone states – Bulgaria – corruption linked to organized crime and human trafficking were cited as principal reasons initially hindering its accession to the EU.[98]

Youth gangs are found throughout the world, partly spurred by rapid urbanization, exclusion, poverty and the enactment of repressive public policies towards marginalized groups

Trafficking people is a relatively low-risk, low-cost venture for organized crime. The International Organization for Migration (IOM) notes that 'compared with other illicit forms of trafficking such as drugs or weapons, the investments made by the traffickers in a victim are limited to transportation and, sometimes, documentation, bribes, protection and marketing'.[99] Moreover, unlike other illegal commodities such as drugs, which can generally be sold only once to a consumer, human contraband can be sold several times over.

The regions that are the most common destinations include countries within Western Europe, East and Southeast Asia, and some countries in the Western Asia subregion, such as Turkey. The US and Canada, respectively, are identified as very high and high destinations for human trafficking. Germany is the highest destination nation for women and children trafficked for sexual purposes.[100]

There are two prime reasons underlying trafficking to destination countries: the first is the demand for cheap labour in destination nations; the second is the perception of greater economic and living opportunity in destination nations by victims from origin nations. These beliefs are easily exploited by traffickers who typically prey on poorly educated individuals from distressed social and economic backgrounds. For example, a United Nations Interregional Crime and Justice Research Institute (UNICRI) study that documents women trafficked from Romania to Germany notes that:

Many young men from marginalized communities join gangs who help to replace the extended family and who provide economic and social values not found in mainstream society

> *Recruiters targeted young women (17 to 28 years old) from rural areas with a low level of education and no employment. While being recruited, 95 per cent of victims were lied to regarding the nature of the work they were going to perform in Germany, the working conditions and the living conditions in Germany.*[101]

Trafficking often involves the movement of persons, especially females, from rural to urban areas across borders, as well as within their own nations. Victims are lured to cities with promises of work or marriage, such as in Lao PDR, Viet Nam and Indonesia, where many are later exploited in factories, for sexual purposes or domestic servitude. In Ecuador, some poor farm families have been forced to sell their children to work in the cities, and in Cambodia, traffickers move large number of rural women to cities to take advantage of the demand for cheap labour and sex.[102] Indeed, serving the urban sex industry is a primary reason for trafficking women and girls.

Youth and territory-based gangs

Like organized crime, youth gangs are found throughout the world, partly spurred by rapid urbanization, exclusion, poverty and the enactment of repressive public policies towards marginalized groups. Some gangs, such as the Crips found in the US and Europe, have international reach and have become 'institutionalized' by virtue of persistence over time, complex organizational composition, adaptive survival strategies and the ability to meet some local community needs. In the US, increase in gang violence has been popularly linked to the growth in cocaine markets beginning during the 1980s, although empirical studies do not clearly support causal connections.[103] In Latin America, youth gangs constitute key features on the urban violence landscape, and are variously known as *pandillas*, *maras*, *bandas*, *galeras*, *quadrilhas*, *barras* and *chapulines*.[104] Examples include the youth gangs of Rio de Janeiro and São Paulo, Brazil, whose violence is legendary throughout Latin America, even spawning an internationally acclaimed movie entitled *Cidade de Deus* (*City of God*). In Brazil, two-thirds of all homicides involve youths,[105] where children as young as six years are drawn into gangs to serve as lookouts and carriers of hard drugs.[106] Apart from drug trafficking, youth gangs in Guatemala regularly engage in pick pocketing, mugging, theft and bus robberies, kidnapping and arms trafficking, as well as various forms of social violence such as territorial conflict, rape and vandalism.[107] In sub-Saharan Africa, where the impacts of rapid urbanization and poverty have been particularly severe, many young men from marginalized communities join gangs who help to replace the extended family and who provide economic and social values not found in mainstream society.

Although seen as a reaction to economic conditions, one research stream suggests that institutionalized urban youth gangs have evolved as avenues through which resistance identities have been forged as a means for marginalized young people to stand against prevailing cultures and the instability of modernizing societies.[108] In this context, youth gangs may be distinguished from organized crime groups, which have been described as primarily profit driven. While no reliable numbers exist, it has been estimated that, worldwide, membership of youth gangs runs into millions – spreading throughout both high and low crime cities. While the direction of causality is arguable, recent research suggests that cities that have high violence rates tend to have institutionalized youth gangs, and this includes Chicago, Los Angeles, Rio de Janeiro, Medellin, Caracas, Kingston, Lagos, Mogadishu and Belfast.[109]

Although youth gangs often become involved in common crime and violence, their enterprises also intertwine with mainstream community life, thus making suppression especially challenging. While this involvement may include politics, one trend has been away from politicization, especially as left-wing movements declined during the 1990s. A recent study quotes a Central American journalist in this regard, who notes: 'Until recently, a rebellious youth from Central America would go into the mountains and join the guerrillas. Today, he leaves the

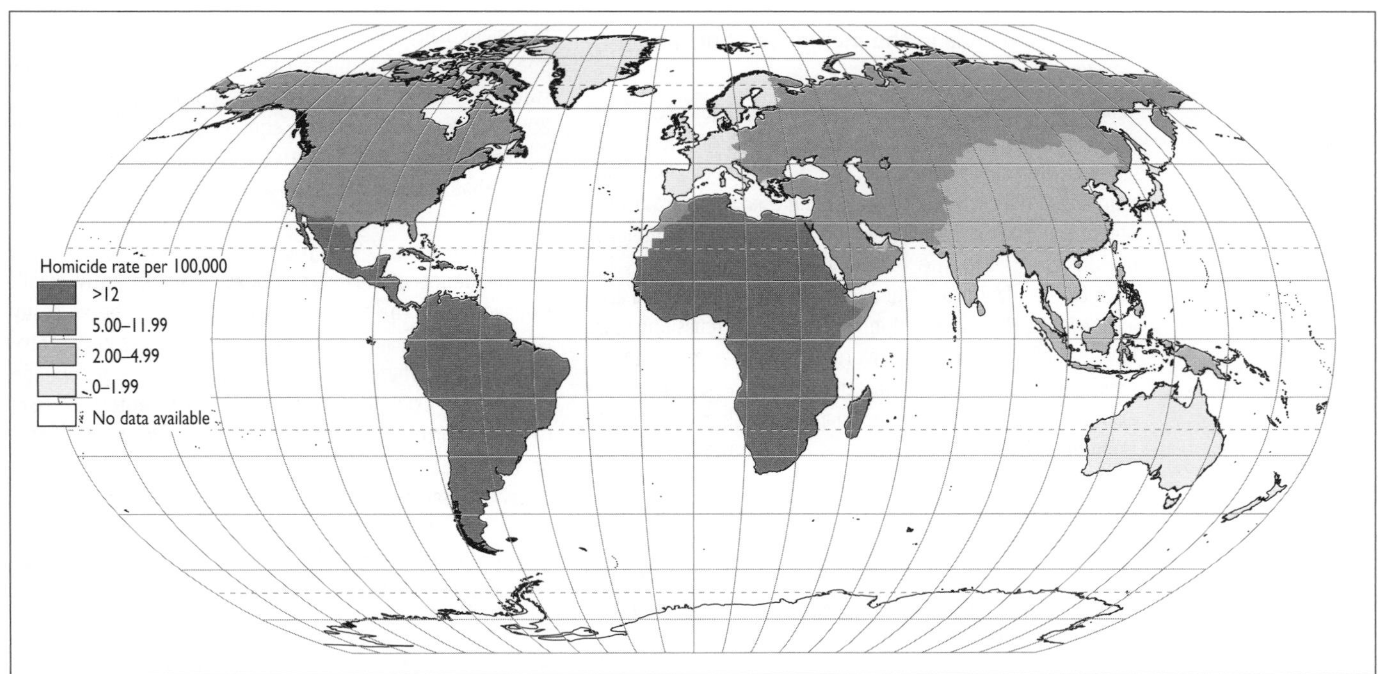

Figure 3.18

Estimated homicide rates among youths aged 10 to 29 (2000)

Source: Krug et al, 2002, p26

Note: Rates were calculated by WHO region and country income level and then groups according to magnitude.

countryside for the city and joins one of the street gangs engaged in common crime without political objectives.'[110]

Youth homicides

Closely related to youth gangs is the issue of youth homicides. According to WHO data, about 199,000 youth homicides took place globally in 2000, implying an average of 565 young people aged between 10 and 29 dying daily due to various types of violence.[111] Regional variations show that youth homicide rates were lowest in Western Europe and in the high-income countries of the Pacific. The highest rates are found in Latin America, the Caribbean and Africa, as shown in Figure 3.18. This coincides with regions where there are large bulges in the youthful population. Countries with very low rates include Japan (with 0.4 per 100,000 individuals); France (0.6 per 100,000); Germany (0.8 per 100,000); and the UK (with 0.09 per 100,000). The countries having high rates of youth homicide include Colombia (with 84.4 per 100,000 individuals); El Salvador (50.2 per 100,000); Puerto Rico (41.8 per 100,000); and Brazil (with 32.5 per 100,000). Other countries with high rates are the US (11 per 100,000); Russia (18 per 100,000); and Albania (with 28.2 per 100,000). The high rate in the US reflects, in part, gun policies and inequality, while that of Russia can be linked to its economic transition.

Urban terrorism

Urban terrorism is one type of violence that has serious consequences for cities in both developed and developing countries. Acts of terrorism fall within the ambit of 'spectacular violence', which derives from the deliberate attempt to unsettle and disrupt urban populations, in contrast to 'everyday violence'.[112] In this report, terrorism is seen as violent *acts* that are deliberately targeted at civilians and urban infrastructure. The report does not examine the perpetrators of acts of terror, their origins or their motives – all of which lie outside the scope of this report. This approach is adopted due to the contentious and complex nature of what constitutes terrorism, since terrorism itself could have different meanings depending on the perspective from which it is viewed. While this approach might have certain shortcomings, it clearly avoids the problematic issue of 'when one person's "terrorist" becomes another's "freedom fighter"', and escapes the essentialist categories associated with the discourse on the current 'war on terror'.[113]

The terrorist attacks on New York of 11 September 2001 have brought to the fore in vivid terms the vulnerability of cities to terrorism. Cities make attractive targets for terrorist attacks due to several reasons. Cities are built-up agglomerations with high densities, and, as such, the impact of an explosion increases with density — thereby maximizing the impact of an attack or destroying a large amount within a short time. This is often referred to as the 'target effect'[114] — implying that the large size and dense agglomeration of cities make them ideal targets for terrorist attacks. Furthermore, given the role of cities in terms of their administrative, economic, social, cultural and political functions, as well as the fact that the influence of cities transcends their national boundaries,[115] attacks on cities provide a high degree of visibility. Within cities themselves, infrastructure and services such as mass transit and communication systems, as well as commercial areas and shopping malls, restaurants, sports stadia, hotels, theatres and other places where large numbers of people gather, form the key targets of terrorist attacks because of the likelihood of greater devastation. For instance, the suburban train system in Mumbai, India which carries more than 6 million commuters daily, and one of the busiest in the world[116] has been the target of a series of terrorist attacks over the last decade because of the enormous consequences of such attacks.

Urban terrorism is one type of violence that has serious consequences for cities in both developed and developing countries

Within cities ... infrastructure ... such as mass transit and communication systems... and other places where large numbers of people gather, form the key targets of terrorist attacks because of the likelihood of greater devastation

Recent trends in the incidence of urban terrorism

Table 3.4 shows major terrorist incidents that have taken place since 1997, which include: the attack on the World Trade Center in New York, US, on 11 September 2001; the bombing of holidaymakers in Bali, Indonesia; the coordinated bombings in Madrid in March 2004; the London bombings of July 2005; and the bombing of commuter trains in Mumbai in July 2006. Although these acts of terrorism are local events, they have had international repercussions that have ricocheted across the world. Therefore they tend to receive greater media and international coverage than, for example, riots or disturbances in an urban slum that might claim more lives. Although not indicated in the table, most terrorist-related attacks and subsequent loss of human lives that have occurred in 2007 are linked to the situation in Iraq, where deaths from car bombing have remarkably increased. It is pertinent to note that a greater proportion of recent terrorist attacks have taken place in developing countries (see Table 3.4). If the situation in Israel is left out, the lowest level of terrorist attacks occurs in developed countries.[117] Colombia, more than any other country, experienced a total of 191 terrorist attacks in 2001 alone.[118]

Although mass transit systems, particularly commuter trains, are frequently targeted, recent international research that compares several modes of travel has shown that mass transit systems are extremely safe and that other travel modes, such as the automobile, represent a far greater risk to society than does transit terrorism.[119] For example, while not intending to minimize the horror of the events, this study notes that the 56 deaths resulting from the 7 July 2005 London bombings were equivalent to about six days of normal British traffic fatalities and that the 9/11 attacks killed about as many as die in a typical month of US traffic accidents.

In relation to 'everyday violence' or common crime, the incidence of terrorist attacks is significantly small. Consequently, the risks of terrorism cannot be as easily calculated, since such small numbers of attacks defy probability analysis when compared to huge numbers of common crimes. For example, the US National Counterterrorism Center reported 13 terrorist incidents in the United States between February 2004 and May 2005 and, for approximately the same period, the Federal Bureau of Investigation identified 10.32 million property crimes and over 1.36 million violent crimes.[120] Nonetheless, the impacts of terrorism on cities have been enormous in recent years.

Table 3.4

Examples of major terrorist incidents since 1997

Source: http://en.wikipedia.org/wiki/List_of_terrorist_incidents

Date	Incident	Number of people killed	Number of people injured
17 November 1997	Gunmen attack tourists in Luxor, Egypt	62	24
7 August 1998	US embassy bombings in Dar es Salaam, Tanzania and Nairobi, Kenya	225	> 4000
18 October 1998	Blowing up of the Ocensa pipeline near Machuca in Antioquia, Colombia	84	100
11 September 2001	A series of hijacked airliner crashes into the World Trade Center in New York City and The Pentagon in Arlington, Virginia, USA	3500	
9 May 2002	Bomb explosion in Kaspiisk in Dagestan, Russia during Victory Day festivities	42	130
12 October 2002	Bombing of holidaymakers Bali, Indonesia	202	
23–27 October 2002	Moscow theatre hostage crisis, Russia	160	
27 December 2002	Truck bombing of the Chechen parliament in Grozny	83	
7 February 2003	El Nogal Club bombing in Bogotá, Colombia	36	150
12 May 2003	A truck bomb attack carried out on a government building in the Chechen town of Znamenskoye	59	
25 August 2003	South Mumbai bombings: Gateway of India and Zaveri Bazaar	48	150
6 February 2004	Bombing of Moscow Metro, Russia	41	
27 February 2004	Bombing of Superferry 14 in the Philippines	116	
11 March 2004	Coordinated bombing of commuter trains in Madrid, Spain	191	1500
24 August 2004	Terrorist attack on two domestic Russian aircraft in Moscow, Russia	90	
7 July 2005	London bombings: Bombs explode on three underground trains and on one double-decker bus	56	700
23 July 2005	Bombing of tourist sites in Sharm el-Sheikh, Egypt	88	> 100
29 October 2005	Multiple bomb blasts in markets in Delhi, India	61	200
9 November 2005	Three explosions at hotels in Amman, Jordan	60	120
11 July 2006	A series of explosions rock commuter trains in Mumbai, India	209	714

FACTORS UNDERLYING CRIME AND VIOLENCE

This section discusses some of the factors associated with criminal and violent activities. Crime and violence are life-changing events that are often facilitated by the convergence of several risk factors. These include the immediate availability of guns, drugs and alcohol. The last two serve as triggers, rather than the causes of violence. These facilitators play off individual and relationship characteristics, such as personality traits, histories of abuse and neglect, dysfunctional family settings, age and gender, and risky lifestyles. At broad national and societal (macro) levels, crime and violence are linked to a range of long-term underlying economic, social, cultural and political circumstances that produce opportunities and incentives for criminal behaviour and violent acts, as well as the situations that frame victimization. Some of these factors are described in the following sub-sections.

Social and cultural factors

Globally, informal forces embedded in social and cultural values are arguably the most powerful factors acting to encourage or discourage crime and violence. In some societies, crime and violence are common components of daily life and are accepted social and cultural norms, or (in the case of 'structural violence') are built into, or encouraged by, law. For example, in Kabul, Karachi and Managua, violence is so interwoven into the fabric of daily life that it has become 'routinized', or normalized, as 'terror as usual' for many slum dwellers.[121] Structural violence helps to legitimize other forms of ethnic- and gender-based domestic physical and sexual assault that have immediate impacts on individuals, and which may result in re-victimization. For instance, between 70 and 90 per cent of Pakistani women suffer from domestic violence incidents, many of which have resulted in other victimizations such as rape and murder.[122]

Almost half of Pakistani women who report rape to authorities are jailed as a result of the Hudood Ordinances, which criminalize sexual relationships (including rape) outside of marriage. Pakistani women are also victims of honour killings, which are private acts condoned by social and cultural norms. Hundreds of women are victimized and killed each year by burnings or acid attacks from their intimate partners.[123] A sizeable majority of women in Ethiopia, Thailand, Samoa, Peru and Bangladesh view IPV as acceptable behaviour from their partner in response to unfaithfulness. Between 60 and 80 per cent of women in Ethiopia believe that enduring violence at the hands of their intimate partner is an acceptable consequence for failing to complete housework or for disobeying one's husband.[124]

Cultural and social expectations of violence, coupled with young male 'hyper masculinity' values, pervade many Brazilian *favelas*, Colombian *barrios*, Jamaican slums and North American ghettos – where marginalized young men are expected to revenge insults with injury or death, often using guns. On the other side of the spectrum, culture can mediate crime. For example, in Hong Kong, Confucianism-based family-oriented values, extended kinship structures and a generally compliant 'pro-social' population, who favours a government hostile to crime and corruption, are seen as major factors in keeping crime and violence rates low.[125] Similarly, in the Middle East and Arab states, the comparatively low homicide and crime rates are, in part, attributed to the religious and social values prevalent in such cultures. Crime and violence is thus significantly influenced by prevailing social and cultural norms, including religious values, which often overpower official and legal pronouncements. But, they may also be encouraged by legislation, as in the case of the Hudood Ordinances noted above.

Poverty

It is clear that crime is a survival strategy for many urban dwellers whose attitudes and perceptions are shaped by poverty. For example, a survey of residents of the South African town of Greater East London suggests that unemployment and marginalization have dramatic impacts on attitudes towards violent crime.[126] A significantly larger proportion of unemployed respondents were more tolerant of crime than those who were employed. Murder, theft from vehicles and domestic violence were considered by more than half of the unemployed respondents not to be taken seriously. While some of the tolerance for violence is attributed to the residual climate of the anti-apartheid era, a possible rationale for the tolerance of domestic violence is attributed to tensions between jobless men and women.[127] Women are often employed in domestic work, a sector that is not equally available to men. In Jamaica's poorest neighbourhoods, young people are accustomed to seeing violence at home and on the street. The high homicide rates in Jamaica are partly due to urban poverty and gang warfare, as well as political parties arming young men with guns in their struggle for political control.[128]

At the global level, rates of violent death generally vary with income. The WHO estimates presented in Table 3.5 show that in 2000, the rates of violent death for high income countries (14.4 per 100,000 individuals) were less than half that of low- to middle-income countries (32.1 per 100,000).[129] Survey data from Brazil, as indicated in Figure 3.19, show that as family income increases, residents are less likely to have relatives that have been murdered.

While economic prosperity is associated with lower death and homicide rates, income inequality, as discussed below, is likely to be a more salient operative factor affecting crime rates. Indeed, a body of international evidence connects poverty levels as well as income inequality to crime and violence rates, although the connections are still subject to debate in the literature.[130] The direction of the causal link between poverty and violence has been questioned, with some researchers noting that violence promotes poverty since it degrades the physical and social capital in affected areas. This is borne out by studies on the concentration of firearms and violence-related property crimes in the *favelas* of Brazil. At the national level, economic data suggests that violence drives out capital and depresses economic growth so that it further impoverishes poor nations and communities. Moreover, there are desperately poor communities throughout all regions of the world where crime rates are constrained by prevailing cultural and social values. This is the case in parts of Ghana and Indonesia, where powerful informal social control mechanisms serve to keep crime rates low.[131] The same is true for Hong Kong and Japan, where the influence of informal and cultural systems tends to moderate many risk factors that are normally associated with crime.[132] Evidence from poor Latin American communities in the US suggests that community characteristics that stress protective norms and building social capital can help to protect adolescents from the negative effects of poverty, including crime.[133]

A body of international evidence connects poverty levels as well as income inequality to crime and violence rates

There are desperately poor communities throughout all regions of the world where crime rates are constrained by prevailing cultural and social values

Inequality

The relative distance between the richest and poorest members of society is as important as, or even more important than, levels of poverty in affecting crime and violence. Closely associated with inequality are key exclusionary factors relating to unequal access to employment, education, health and basic infrastructure.[134] Research has consistently found that income inequality measured by the Gini coefficient (a measure of the inequality of a distribution) is strongly correlated with high homicide rates.[135] For example, two major comparative studies – one of 18 industrialized nations using data for 1950 to 1980 and the other of 45 industrialized and developing countries with data between 1965 and 1995 – concluded that income inequality had a significant and positive effect on homicide rates.[136]

Growth in GDP has been found to be negatively correlated with homicide rates, although this was offset by income inequality. This has been the general finding for violent crimes, although the reverse holds true for property crimes: the higher the growth in GDP, the higher the level of property crime rates. This indicates that increasing levels of

Type of violence	Number[a]	Rate per 100,000 individuals[b]	Proportion of total (percentage)
Homicide	520,000	8.8	31.3
Suicide	815,000	14.5	49.1
War related	310,000	5.2	18.6
Total[c]	1,659,000	28.8	100.0
Low- to middle-income countries	1,510,000	32.1	91.1
High-income countries	149,000	14.4	8.9

Table 3.5

Table 3.5 Estimated global violence-related deaths (2000)

Notes: a Rounded to nearest 1000.

b Age standardized.

c Includes 14,000 intentional injury deaths resulting from legal intervention.

Source: Krug et al, 2002, p10

prosperity are associated with increasing levels of property crimes. Similarly, within cities, more prosperous areas or neighbourhoods often account for a larger proportion of property crimes. Relative to individual prosperity, recent research suggests that the wealth of an individual is closely connected to the risk of becoming a crime victim. In countries with high levels of income inequality, the risk of individual crime victimization is higher than in countries with less inequality.[137]

Gender, racial, ethnic and religious inequalities are also major factors in violence perpetrated against women and minorities. While the venue of violence against women and children is often the home, racial, ethnic and religious inequality generally plays out in community settings. In this context, an egregious example is the atrocities committed in Rwanda by ethnic Hutu groups against Tutsis, where it is estimated that as many as 800,000 people were massacred.

The speed of urbanization is significantly associated with increased crime rates in some of the world's regions

Pace of urbanization

While early research failed to substantiate a relationship between crime and the pace of urbanization,[138] more recent studies have found that the speed of urbanization is significantly associated with increased crime rates in some of the world's regions. For instance, results from a survey of 17 Latin American countries indicate that households located in areas experiencing high levels of growth are more likely to be victimized than those in communities with stable populations.[139] In Latin America, city growth is seen as a very stronger indicator of crime rates.[140] These findings suggest that there may be a wider association between urbanization and crime in certain high-growth regions.

The impacts of rapid urbanization also extend beyond direct victimization. People in rapidly growing cities of Latin America have diminished confidence in police officials and the judiciary to resolve problems.[141] Thus, rapid development places increased pressures on the ability of authorities to meet public security and safety demands. When expectations are not met, citizens become cynical and distrustful of public institutions. This is especially important since almost all of the world's urban growth in the next two decades will be absorbed by cities of the developing world, whose public institutions are least equipped to deal with the challenges of rapid urbanization.

Moreover, the rate of urbanization is related to the pace at which people change households – population instability – which is strongly associated with crime. Rapidly growing urban centres are typically places where there is a high turnover of people and where social coherence is less stable and 'protective' as an informal social control for criminal behaviour. Thus, being 'transient' is a significant risk and an enabling factor associated with organized and common crime in urban areas and especially where 'illegal immigrants, drug dealers and sex workers tend to congregate'.[142] For instance, almost half of Port Moresby's (Papua New Guinea) urban population of 330,000 live in squatter settlements most are relatively recent in-migrants to the city. These settlements are considered to be the main sources of criminal activity in the city. The problems are compounded by poverty, the lack of formal-sector employment, low confidence in public authorities to provide protection and justice, and the destabilization of traditional social and cultural systems found in village councils and courts.[143] The burgeoning growth of São Paulo, Brazil, offers another example of the disruptive effects of rapid population growth and change, as shown in Box 3.3.

Projections indicate that the pace of urbanization is most rapid in the less developed regions of Africa and Asia. Smaller urban settlements of less than 500,000 and medium-sized cities between 1 million and 5 million are growing faster than megacities. Existing urban areas of Africa, Asia and Latin America are projected to have the largest increases in urban populations by 2030. Yet, these are regions whose institutions – including planning, criminal justice, social service and infrastructure systems – are least equipped to deal with rapid urbanization. All of this invariably suggests impacts in terms of increases in slum and squatter settlements, street children and crime within urban centres struggling to provide adequate public services (including security and justice systems) to existing residents.

Figure 3.19

Family income and relatives murdered (Brazil)

Note: MW = minimum wage: approximately US$175 per month at time of publication.

Source: Zaluar, 2007

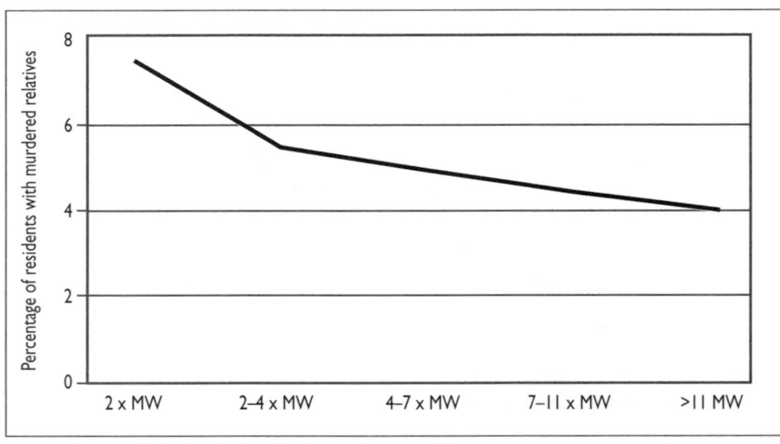

City size and density

If the relationship between the pace of urbanization and crime is not completely understood, the same can be said about the highly complex connections between city size, density and crime. Nevertheless, there is little question that more people are increasingly vulnerable to crime and violence in many large urban areas than ever before. A fundamental theory is that city size and density are in themselves directly associated with social pathologies, including crime.[144] There is evidence that city size and crime rates are related.[145] However, this relationship is likely to be more pronounced in developing countries vis-à-vis developed countries. For instance, while in Latin America, a household living in a city of 1 million or more people is 78 per cent more likely to be victimized by crime than a household living in a city of between 50,000 and 100,000 people, the corresponding figure for the US is 28 per cent.[146] The link between crime and city size in developing countries can be explained by three factors.[147] First, returns on crime are likely to be higher in larger cities due to the greater concentration of wealthier victims, more opportunities to commit various types of crime, and a more developed second-hand market for the disposal of stolen items. Second, the chances of arresting a criminal might be lower in larger cities because large cities spend less on law enforcement per capita, or have lower levels of community cooperation with the police, or require more police officers per inhabitant to effect an arrest. Finally, larger cities have a greater proportion of crime-prone individuals/potential criminals.

The blanket association between size, density and crime has been the basis of attempts to stop or limit the size of new residential developments in many cities and to halt the expansion of existing residential areas, especially slums. As suggested by cities such as Cairo, New York, Hong Kong and Singapore, there are many exceptions when urban areas are compared on the basis of population size alone. Differential crime rates suggest that city size alone does not 'cause' crime and violence since some of the largest cities such as New York have comparatively low rates, thus disproving conventional wisdom.[148] Although vastly different in scale, a study of Madagascar communes suggested that crime was positively associated with low population densities and feelings of insecurity and isolation, contrary to expectations about the link between urban size, density and crime.[149]

There are many dimensions to connections between population density and crime. Confounding factors such as culture, socio-economic development, governance and the strength of civil society controls are arguably as important determinants of crime and violence rates as population density. Within cities of all sizes, crime is concentrated within certain, generally known, geographic areas and population density is just one of many variables that play a role in its occurrence. There is evidence that population density is variably related to the occurrence of different types of crimes. For example, some US-based research suggests that high-density cities have fewer burglaries than lower-density cities. According to this research, motor vehicle thefts are also higher in denser cities.[150] Reasons for the differential effects are ascribed to opportunity, risk, effort and reward factors that are related to residential structural type and the opportunity for surveillance of property that may be planned or fortuitous. For example, because high-density residences are typically located in apartment complexes, they are more risky and difficult for burglars to enter than detached suburban houses with rear doors and windows, which burglars favour because of reduced surveillance possibilities.

In sum, city size and density measures are important relative to predicting crime rates, but are incomplete determinants of criminal or violent behaviour, and may be overshadowed by other, more local, social and environmental factors and by qualitative and economic forces relating to social inclusion and cohesion.

Box 3.3 Rapid urban growth and crime: The example of São Paulo, Brazil

São Paulo's population exploded at an annual rate of 5 per cent from 1870 to 2000, with the city and its peripheral areas now hosting over 18 million people. The population of central São Paulo expanded by 171 per cent between 1940 and 1960, and its suburban areas grew by 364 per cent in the same period, largely due to rural in-migration. Existing civil institutions were overwhelmed by the pace and size of population growth and were incapable of dealing with demands for services in the hundreds of illegal subdivisions that sprang up, where standards of due process of law are low or non-existent and levels of retributive justice and vigilantism are high. Crime increased along with the rapid pace of urbanization, such that in 1999, the city recorded 11,455 murders, more than 17 times that of New York City's 667 murders. One of São Paulo's rapidly growing suburban municipalities, Diadema, reached a murder rate of 141 per 100,000 individuals in 2003, one of the world's highest rates.[151]

Poor urban planning, design and management

Only relatively recently has research pointed to the urban environment as posing risk factors associated with crime and violence. There is increasing evidence that poor planning, design and management of the urban environment puts citizens at risk of death, injury and loss of property. Place-based crime prevention and reduction theories of defensible space,[152] crime prevention through environmental design (CPTED),[153] situational crime prevention[154] and environmental criminology[155] have increasingly been supported by empirical research suggesting that physical design and management of the built environment play a role in facilitating or diminishing opportunities for crime and violence. While there is no way of accurately counting the number of incidents related to physical design or management, it has been estimated that 10 to 15 per cent of crimes have environmental design and management components.[156]

There is increasing evidence that poor planning, design and management of the urban environment puts citizens at risk of death, injury and loss of property

Globally, this amounts to millions of incidents each year. Thus, land-use juxtapositions, street layouts, building and site design, transportation system planning, infrastructure improvements – especially lighting and facility and landscape maintenance, as well as activity and space scheduling – have been shown to have variable impacts on crime opportunity and on the subsequent incidence and fear of crime.[157] The lack of integration of crime prevention strategies within comprehensive city planning practices has been cited as a factor in facilitating opportunities for urban crime.[158] Physical planning can make a difference in terms of crime prevention/reduction, to more effective policing, to informal surveillance and to the protection of persons and property. For example, street widening programmes can open up previously impenetrable urban areas to police and emergency service vehicles, and the creation of new housing or commercial developments can change traffic generation patterns and may provide increased economic and residential opportunities. Site design that provides increased prospects for people to observe their surroundings can reduce criminal opportunity.

It has been estimated that 10 to 15 per cent of crimes have environmental design and management components

Evidence also suggests that permeable street layouts that encourage vehicular traffic flows across the urban fabric tend to enhance certain crime opportunities since more potential offenders will see more potential targets. This is said by some to increase the cost of policing.[159] On the one hand, access and escape routes for offenders are facilitated by gridiron-based patterns, reducing the risk of being caught, as well as facilitating the efforts to commit robberies and burglaries.[160] On the other hand, permeable street patterns knit cities together in the face of increasingly privatized gated communities and tend to reduce dependence upon the automobile, especially when urban mass transit is utilized.[161] While the evidence is not conclusive and the mechanisms are imperfectly understood, studies have linked these elements with the routine movement, behaviour and interactions of offenders and targets in cities.[162]

From a planning and public policy standpoint, then, where crimes occur and how places are designed and managed are at least as important as who the perpetrators are

From a planning and public policy standpoint, then, *where* crimes occur and *how* places are designed and managed are at least as important as *who* the perpetrators are. This is so because crime and violence tends to reoccur in relatively limited numbers of places in cities that provide niches for offending. Moreover, these places are generally known to citizens and police, and occurrences are therefore reasonably predictable. Most other places are reasonably safe. Chapter 4 identifies some of the approaches that cities across the world have taken in integrating place-based crime reduction strategies within existing or new planning and public policy processes in attempting to grapple with these challenges.

Demographics: Youthful population growth

A wealth of international data suggests that crime and violence are strongly associated with the growth and proportion of youthful populations and, especially, young males. Cross-national research using data on 44 countries from 1950 to 2000 reveals that 'the percentage of young people in the populations and prosperity are jointly more important in explaining the variability of homicide'.[163] The number of children under 16 years per area (child density) has been noted as the single most important variable in explaining vandalism in certain housing estates in the UK.[164] In Nairobi (Kenya), where bank robbery, violent car robbery, house breaking, and street muggings and snatching are the main criminal activities, a distinctive attribute of the perpetrators is their youthfulness – criminals in their teens and 20s.[165]

Crime and violence are strongly associated with the growth and proportion of youthful populations and, especially, young males

For people between the ages of 14 and 44 years old, violence has been identified as a major cause of death,[166] and in some distressed communities it is the primary cause of mortality of young people. This is a particularly salient issue for young males. Chapter 1 noted, for example, that violence was among the highest causes of death among African–American males in the US; the homicide death rate for African–American males aged 15 to 24 is 12 times the rate for white males in the same age category and twice the rate for Hispanic males.[167] The firearm-related death rate for African–American males aged 15 to 19 is four times the rate for white males in the same category.[168] Age and gender are fundamental factors in determining vulnerability to small arms violence, generally. These risk factors are particularly significant when comparing firearms-related homicides among nations as shown in Figure 3.20.

Across countries, Small Arms Survey and WHO data report that males aged 15 to 29 account for about half of all firearm-related homicides and, as Figure 3.20 indicates, rates tends to be much higher for them than for the general population in the top five selected nations. This trend is consistent over time. The Small Arms Survey estimates the total number of annual global deaths from gun-related homicides for men aged 15 to 29 as falling between 70,000 and 100,000.[169]

Other factors associated with youth crime

Youth crime and violence rates are associated with other factors, such as level of policing, conviction and imprisonment rates, drug cultures and a host of situational elements that condition people, especially young men, to their surrounding world. For example, the Small Arms Survey concludes that youth demographics alone are insufficient in explaining the variability of rates of violence among nations.[170] It cited a US study suggesting that more and better trained police, increased prison populations, the ebbing crack epidemic and the effects of legalized abortions have had more impact on crime rates than youthful populations.[171] For young males, local situational factors related to masculine identity, achievement of status, prestige and social and economic empowerment are important elements in explaining the variability of violent crime rates around the world.[172]

■ Youth unemployment

In addition to the risk factors described above, unemployment is a fundamental issue related to crime and violence rates among young people. The World Bank estimates that 74 million people between the ages of 15 and 24 are unemployed, which accounts for 41 per cent of all unemployed persons.[173] In connecting these dots, most research suggests that unemployed youths are disproportionately more likely to be perpetrators, as well as victims, of crime and violence. Unemployment, and especially long-term unemployment, undermines human capital so that work abilities and motivations 'atrophy'. Unemployment is also correlated with other aspects of social disadvantage, such as low socio-economic status, family dysfunction and prior criminal history. In this sense, the link between employment, youth and criminal behaviour is part of a process and a constellation of issues rather than the mark on a line as an incident or event.[174]

Few factors have affected the prospects of young people more than the globalization of employment markets. A recent address to the Goethe-Institut in Johannesburg claimed that 'supply shock' has affected world labour markets, and especially youthful job-seekers, as millions of new workers have been added to world job markets due to the influx of new labour from nations of the former Soviet Union, the restructuring of China's economy, India's opening of new economic frontiers, and pressures brought to bear on developing nations to cut back bureaucracies while increasing private-sector involvement in state enterprises.[175] The resulting destabilization has led to widespread job insecurity and increasing social fragmentation among young people, especially those living in distressed communities in developed and developing nations. Gang membership thereby provides alternative avenues relating to illicit economic gains from robbery, extortion and other types of crime, with violence being used as a resource to obtain social identity.[176] Although there is variability among regions and nations, this overall trend is not likely to be reversed in the foreseeable future.

Deportation of offending criminals

Closely related to globalization is the deportation of criminals to their countries of origin. This phenomenon, which is quite common in Latin America and the Caribbean, where offenders are deported from the US, in part accounts for increasing levels of youth crime and gang-related activities in the region. In Central America, the phenomenal growth in youth gangs has been attributed to the deportation of young Salvadorans from the US. This has resulted in the 'transfer' of gang wars from the ghettos of Los Angeles to the streets of El Salvador.[177] Similarly, in Jamaica, where gangs have a stranglehold on society and are at the centre of most murders, the feeling is rife that deportees are a major part of the crime problem. Indeed, the deportation of criminals has been linked to escalating gang violence, extortion and drug-related murders experienced over the past five years.[178] In 2001, 'an analysis by the Jamaican police concluded that deportees, many of them gang members from the north-eastern US, were involved in 600 murders, 1700 armed robberies and 150 shoot-outs with police'.[179] The effect of deportees on the Jamaican crime scene is further highlighted in a survey of deported criminals, which revealed that 53 per cent had been involved in criminal activities since deportation.[180] Such crimes include those not reported to the police. Among those reporting involvement in crime, 78 per cent had committed more than one crime, and another 35 per cent indicated that they had been involved in drug-related offences.

Transition towards democratization

As violent crime rates have variably increased over the past half century, cross-national, longitudinal research paints a picture of this as an outcome, at least in part, of broad international trends in governance. In this context, homicide rates are used as an indicator of violent crime. Reporting on observed trends in 44 mostly industrialized countries over a 50-year period, research indicates that global homicide rates have grown at about the same time as there have been significant increases in political democratization.[181] Evidence to support this contention comes from researchers tracking significantly increased homicides in Latin America following widespread democratization of the region during the 1990s. Democratization is broadly characterized as the spread of governments that are put into power by majority vote and supported by civil societies that 'encourage citizen participation, public deliberation and civic education'.[182] Three principal theories have been elaborated upon in this context. They are the 'civilization perspective', the 'conflict perspective' and the 'modernization perspective'. Figure 3.21 summarizes the expected relationships between democracy and crime based on these theories.

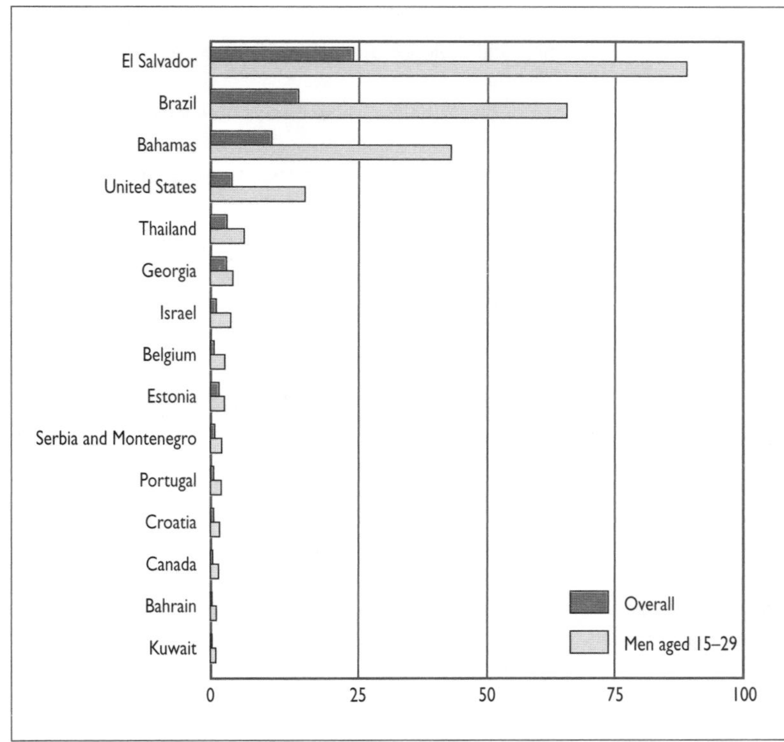

Figure 3.20

Firearm homicide rates: Victims per 100,000 individuals among men aged 15 to 19 compared with the overall population (selected countries, latest year available)

Source: Small Arms Survey, 2006a, p297

Results of statistical analysis suggest that nations undergoing transition from autocratic governance to democracy exhibit the most significant increases in homicide rates (modernization perspective). These include countries in Eastern Europe and the Latin America and Caribbean region. As such nations move towards full democracy, their rates may begin to decline, even though they will not disappear and may, indeed, creep upward as evidenced by the data from full democracies. Evidence to support the decline in rates commensurate with democratization may be found in South Africa's murder rates, which have been declining as it has been consolidating democratic governance. In 1995, its murder rate was 68 per 100,000 individuals, which dipped to 50 per 100,000 and then 48 per 100,000 in 2002. During 2003 to 2004, the rate dropped to 44 per 100,000 – still extremely high, but an impressive 35 per cent improvement in less than a decade. Other evidence comes from the reduction of the murder rate in Diadema (Brazil), which has slowly consolidated a democratic response to crime as it has evolved from a community based on frontier justice standards. Although still high, its murder rate has fallen twice as fast as that of neighbouring São Paulo's between 1999 and 2003.[183] It should be noted that the latter trends are short term and may not be indicative of causal relationships. Indeed, there are democratic states where violence rates are extremely high, such as Colombia and Jamaica.

In Central America, the phenomenal growth in youth gangs has been attributed to the deportation of young Salvadorans from the US

What this implies is that connections between democratization and violence are extremely complex and not easily explained.

Nevertheless, some groups have used high violence rates as political arguments against democratization and as a rationale for segregating distressed populations and carving up urban territories into gated privatized enclaves. Such approaches have been particularly evident in São Paulo (Brazil) and Johannesburg (South Africa)[184] and are implicit in strategies used elsewhere to privatize security and territory.

IMPACTS OF CRIME AND VIOLENCE

This section addresses some of the social, psychological and economic impacts of crime and violence at the global, national, local and individual levels. These impacts are complex, interconnected and not easily separable. Nevertheless, some of the conditions and trends are sketched here relative to homicide, robbery, burglary and corruption. Owing to data availability, the discussion focuses more on local impacts relative to robbery and burglary. The section starts by distinguishing between primary, secondary and tertiary victims of crime and violence.

One violent crime can have many victims, including shattered families

Impacts of crime and violence: Victim categories

At the global level, homicide and other violent crimes have obvious and significant impacts, which include loss of life and physical and psychological injury to the primary victims. Data from the WHO suggests that almost one third of the estimated global violence-related deaths in 2000 were due to homicides. In some countries with easy access to weapons, the tolls have been particularly high. For example, Colombia has experienced over 500,000 deaths due to common and organized crime since 1979, which amounts to 17,600 deaths per year. Over 80 per cent of these have been due to gun violence.[185] The incidence of homicide is often exacerbated by civil conflicts that make weapons more available to the general population.

Figure 3.21

Expected relationship between democracy and violent crime from different perspectives

Source: LaFree and Tseloni, 2006, p33

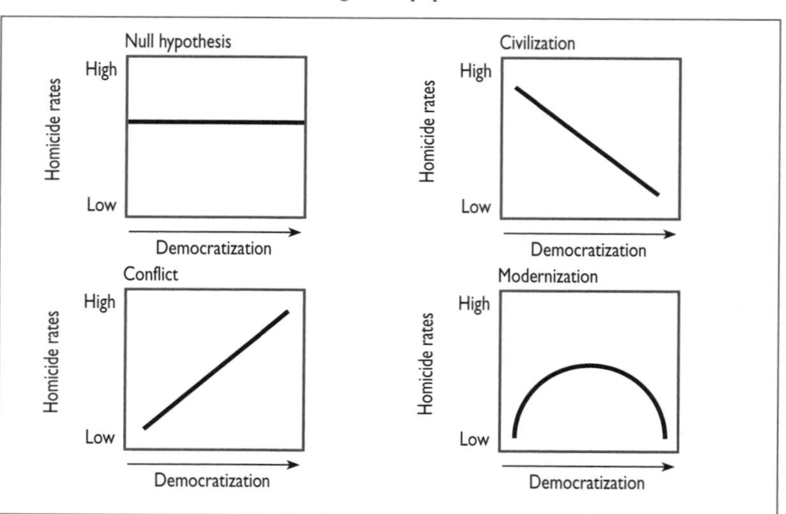

Secondary victims include family and friends, often referred to as homicide survivors, who often experience negative psychological and physical effects, including intense grief and impairment of social functioning. These impacts are borne out by recent research on the clinical implications of homicide to surviving family and friends. They suggest staggering psychological costs that require long-term professional treatment. Worldwide, homicide survivors often experience post-traumatic stress disorder, with significant impacts on the children of homicide victims. It is clear, therefore, that one violent crime can have many victims, including shattered families.

Tertiary victims include communities and society, generally, which can experience profound shocks to healthcare, social services and economic systems. The costs of crime play out very differently for individuals and their families across the world, especially when compared between developed and developing nations. For example, UNOCD compared the discounted value of the lost economic productivity costs of a typical homicide victim in Cape Town (South Africa) as US$15,319 relative to a typical homicide in New Zealand as US$829,000, with the difference stemming from the much higher predicted income for the latter individual. However, the death or injury of the individual in Cape Town is liable to be economically profound since there are likely to be more family members directly dependent upon the victim than in New Zealand, which also has more public and private safety nets.[186]

Impacts on most vulnerable victims

Violent crimes such as homicide and armed robbery eat away at the social and cultural fabric of communities by threatening the covenant of trust binding people together. This is often manifested in the isolation of individuals from each other and from work, educational and healthcare opportunities, all necessary elements to building social and human capital. The most vulnerable citizens, such as the poor, elderly, women and children, are victimized in multiple ways: some become stranded in their own homes at night, some retreat into depression, while others give up life and career opportunities. For example, one author describes the experience of her neighbours in Guayaquil (Ecuador) having to live with the daily terror of violent robbers such that in one six-month period 'one in five women had been attacked by young men armed with knives, machetes or hand guns'. In speaking about the impacts of these acts, she notes that 'the streets were no longer safe after dark, so girls and young women were dropping out of night school, exacerbating their social isolation'.[187] In this way, violent crime tends to compound already existing patterns of discrimination against women and girls. As Box 3.4 suggests, violent crime often highlights social justice gaps between the wealthy and the vulnerable poor, and tests citizens' confidence in the willingness of public authorities to listen to them.

Some groups, such as women and those living in impoverished communities, are particularly vulnerable to violent crime. While men are the primary users of guns, women suffer disproportionately from gun violence as they are rarely gun purchasers, owners or users. The International Action Network on Small Arms estimates that, globally, 30,000 women and girls are murdered by small arms each year, while millions of others are injured by guns and sexually abused at gun point.[188] Even if they are not directly victims, women become indirectly victimized when male relatives who are economic providers are murdered. This undermines families, and the effects ripple throughout communities and, ultimately, through states and globally. When viewed in psychological and economic terms, the direct and indirect impacts on children are incalculable, with many killed, injured or left economically adrift. Thus, it is worth restating that a single incident can have an enormous multiplier effect.[189]

Economic studies suggest that domestic violence has negative impacts on productivity at broad scales. A study calculating the costs of domestic violence in terms of lost productive capacity for women found that the extrapolated total costs were US$1.73 billion in Chile (1 per cent of GDP in 1997) and US$32.7 million in Nicaragua (1.4 per cent of GDP in 1997).[190] In subsequent research, the direct medical costs plus lost productivity were calculated at being equivalent to 2 per cent of GDP in Chile and 1.6 per cent of GDP in Nicaragua.[191] As might be expected, the costs of IPV are considerably higher in low- to moderate-income nations than in high-income countries. Unlike wealthy nations where costs of violence can be absorbed by resilient social and economic structures, in low- to moderate-income nations, the costs of violence are likely to be absorbed through direct public expenditures and negative effects on investments and economic growth.

Impacts of the fear of crime

Increased fear of crime of all types, but particularly violent crimes such as murder, has a major impact and can be even more paralysing and costly than actual criminal events. For instance, a World Bank study in Zambia found that fear of crime in one poverty-stricken community was preventing teachers from showing up at work.[192] Similarly, a study of the 'timing' of work concluded that higher homicide rates reduced the propensity of people willing to work evenings and nights in large American metropolitan areas.[193] In South Africa, about 24 per cent of respondents to a national crime survey reported that fear of crime stopped them from using public transportation systems, with more than 25 per cent indicating that they were reluctant to allow their children to walk to school, while more than 30 per cent stopped using public parks.[194]

Although not easily quantified, these decisions translate into social quality of life and economic costs to individuals in terms of lost opportunities and added day-to-day expenditures for transportation and educational and urban services. Other 'hidden' costs of the fear of crime affecting the quality of urban life play out in the choices that individuals make in seemingly mundane decisions, such as deciding whether to walk somewhere at night, or in more fundamental ways, such as choosing where to live. In Nairobi, survey data reveals that more than half of the citizens worry about crime all the time or very often.[195] In a national survey conducted in South Africa, 26 per cent of respondents stated that concerns about crime prevented them from starting their own business. Such psychological impacts obviously affect individuals, but also drain resources from social service and healthcare systems.

Box 3.4 Serial murder in a New Delhi slum

The vulnerability of the poor is illustrated by a recent case in New Delhi (India), where an alleged serial murderer is reputed to have killed and dismembered as many as 17 women and children and disposed of their body parts in a sewer drain behind his home. The victims were all impoverished and the alleged killer is a wealthy businessman living in an upscale suburb. Police reportedly discounted reports by relatives about their missing family members until a public outcry was raised after some of the bodies were discovered behind the reputed murderer's home. One resident, who came from a nearby slum, came looking for her 16-year-old son, who had been missing for four months, and said: 'When I told the police he had disappeared, they told me to look for myself. Things would have been different if I'd been rich. Then I could have bribed them to make them investigate.'

Source: Gentleman, 2007

The impacts of these decisions do not fully take into account the social and economic costs of lost work productivity, access to markets, urban sprawl (especially in developed nations) or losses incurred from misused public infrastructure, all by-products of work timing and travel decision-making. These costs are compounded in developing and transitional nations, where crime and violence can have disastrous effects on victims who are unable to access effective criminal justice or insurance systems that are widely available in industrialized countries. Both systems provide measures of indemnification against crime and violence that, in personal and financial terms, are crucial components of human resilience or the ability of people to successfully adapt to elemental life disruptions.

Increased fear of crime of all types, but particularly violent crimes such as murder, has a major impact and can be even more paralysing and costly than actual criminal events

National impacts of crime and violence

At national levels, high homicide and violent crime rates have multiple impacts. Some of these may be illustrated by economic and healthcare indicators. The former is demonstrated in Kingston (Jamaica), where rising urban homicide rates have been cited as a factor affecting national tourism, with negative economic consequences at every level of society. The World Bank has identified the impact of crime on business as one of the major reasons for Jamaica's weak economic development.[196] The upsurge in violence and insecurity that characterized Kenya during the 1990s resulted in the reduction of both the influx of tourists and the contribution of tourism to foreign exchange earnings.[197] A similar phenomenon is noted in Papua New Guinea, where violent crime, particularly in some suburbs of Port Moresby, discourages tourists from exploring the country.[198] Urban crime in Papua New Guinea is seen as the most important of all business costs.[199] Much of the brain drain in Latin American and Caribbean nations has been attributed to fear of crime and insecurity, compounded by the lack of effective responses from state or civil society.[200] Countries such as the Dominican Republic, El Salvador, Guatemala, Guyana,

Haiti, Jamaica and Mexico have been hard hit, as a large proportion of educated individuals migrate to North America and the UK.[201] Similarly, increasing levels of crime and violence played a key role in the emigration of many South African professionals to countries such as Australia, New Zealand, the UK and Canada during the 1990s.

Impacts of contact crimes on economic and health systems

At national levels, high crime rates are identified as major impediments to foreign investment, and also affect capital flight and the reluctance of people to invest in their own countries. Recent research in Africa showed that more than 29 per cent of business people surveyed report that crime was a significant investment constraint.[202] Investors generally worry about violent crime and corruption since they fear direct losses to enterprises, and about the safety of their expatriate employees. They are also concerned about the impacts of corruption on business investment.[203] Findings from Latin America show that the financial burden of violence is equivalent to 25 per cent of the GDP in Colombia and El Salvador; 12 per cent in Mexico and Venezuela; 11 per cent in Brazil; and 5 per cent of the GDP in Peru.[204] Other research in Latin America concludes that crime has substantially reduced the performance of enterprises and has had a particularly serious impact on sales growth.[205]

High homicide and violent crime rates are also associated with increased healthcare costs and social services costs

High homicide and violent crime rates are also associated with increased healthcare costs and social services costs. For example, the collapse of the Brazilian public hospital system in the 1980s and 1990s has been attributed to the weight of the high number of homicides and criminal injuries. The 'combination of mental health, social work, physical rehabilitation and surgeries' overwhelmed the system's resources.[206] High homicide and violent crime also affect the provision of police services. These incidents are generally expensive and time-consuming crimes for police to investigate, and add further stress to many overburdened and under-resourced national criminal justice systems.

Impacts of property crime on buildings and property values

The impacts of crime on urban society are also manifested in damage to buildings and infrastructure. Together, these costs represent a significant, albeit incalculable, economic loss worldwide. To understand the full cost of property damage requires knowledge of the total number of crimes actually committed. This is not possible. Consequently, indirect methods that use survey data, multipliers to adjust differences between police data and survey results, and data extrapolation are commonly employed to provide estimates of the extent of the problem.

High rates of robbery ... serve as a deterrent to investment, thereby leading to greater levels of poverty and deprivation

Research on the economic impacts of crime on property values in London found that criminal damage (graffiti, vandalism and arson) had a negative effect on property prices.[207] Using UK-based multipliers, Australian estimates of the costs of burglaries drawing on police data and surveys suggest an average property loss and damage of AU$1100 for residential burglaries and AU$2400 for non-residential incidents, for total losses estimated at AU$1.3 billion, of which AU$0.9 billion was identified for residential burglaries alone.[208] Including lost output (but not medical costs), the total costs of burglaries for the country were estimated at AU$2.43 billion. Cost for other property crimes, such as criminal damage (vandalism) and arson total almost AU$2.7 billion, including lost output, intangible costs and the costs of fire protection and ambulance services. One point that is clear from the existing evidence is that the true costs of property crime damage are complex insomuch as they involve many associated costs, such as work output, municipal services, decreased property values and quality of life, which are all challenging to quantify.

Local impacts of crime and violence

While crime and violence have global, regional and national impacts, the impacts are very much manifested and felt at the city and neighbourhood levels. The impact of crime and violence at such local levels relates to the 'defensible space' and provides insights into how cities and neighbourhoods can be better designed to reduce the factors that contribute to crime and violence.

Impacts of crime on urban flight

In terms of the impacts on cities, there is convincing evidence that rising crime rates, especially violent crime, influence population and commercial flight from central city locations, with more affluent households and those with children more likely to leave.[209] Also known as 'human capital flight', the educated and employed middle classes flee sections of the city with high crime rates. This perpetuates an environment in which the proportion of law-abiding citizens is diminished compared to those individuals regularly engaged in criminal activity. Similarly, many businesses have left central city locations because of crime. Although substantial, the costs of such losses have rarely been quantified. On the opposite side of the equation, there is evidence that reduced crime rates are significantly associated with rising property values in some cities, an important economic variable bearing on investment decisions and the creation of societal wealth.[210]

Impacts of robbery

As suggested above, the flight of the middle class from sections of the city affected by crime leaves impoverished populations often concentrated in such areas. The effects are cumulative since crimes, such as robbery and armed robbery, are associated with the number of motivated offenders in any one area. Furthermore, high rates of robbery contribute to a downward spiral of low property values and serve as a deterrent to investment, thereby leading to greater levels of poverty and deprivation. The result is that poor neighbourhoods are the hardest hit by a range of crimes. In this context, a connection between lesser property crimes, such as theft, and more serious crimes, such as armed robbery in poor neighbourhoods, has been proposed in the following sequence:

- Poor areas provide customers, who, for economic reasons, are willing to purchase second-hand and questionable goods.
- Because there are willing customers, poor areas provide places to sell secondhand and questionable goods.
- Markets for such goods encourage property offenders to be active in poor areas.
- Proceeds from property offences are used in drug or other illegal transactions.
- Such transactions fuel more serious crimes, such as armed robbery and assaults.[211]

Besides the effects on specific victims, high robbery and violent crime rates affect cities by leaving some areas desolate, especially in the evenings, thereby adversely affecting the local economy. In communities, generally, but especially in high crime risk areas, fear of violence discourages pedestrians and reduces the attractiveness of public spaces. As such, it has a cumulative effect by diminishing surveillance possibilities, or 'eyes on the street', which increases risks to offenders of being observed, caught, prosecuted or, in informal systems, retaliated against. Although there remains significant debate on its efficacy, depending upon other circumstances, increased surveillance may discourage street crime generally, including contact crimes such as armed robbery.

Impacts of burglary

Although often committed against vehicles, burglary is the most common property crime connected to the built environment. High burglary rates have implications for neighbourhoods, cities and nations. Commercial and residential properties are frequent targets for burglaries, and data shows that, on average, one out of five urban residents worldwide report being victimized within a five-year period.[212] Burglaries have significant direct and indirect consequences for victims, especially where there are no indemnification systems and where victims suffer significant long-term psychological effects. In one study, nearly 40 per cent of burglary victims stated that they had been very much affected and 68 per cent indicated that they felt angry as a result of burglaries and attempted burglaries. Shock, fear and difficulty in sleeping were also fairly common experiences of burglary victims.[213] The enduring psychological effects of burglary on its victims are just as severe as the effects related to violent crimes, such as assault and robbery.

Evidence suggests that burglars target properties that are expected to yield loot with the highest market value and some neighbourhoods become known for burglary incidents, which may depress property values, although this relationship is quite complicated. Some research has shown that other property crimes, such as criminal damage to buildings in the form of vandalism, graffiti and arson, have a larger negative impact on property values than burglary insomuch as they are overt indicators of community deterioration that generate fear and drive off investment.[214]

One manifestation of the failure of public agencies to adequately address the fear and incidence of serious property and contact crimes, such as burglary and robbery, is the global explosion of privatized gated areas and private security forces. Many cities in developing countries have witnessed the proliferation of private security as a means of safeguarding residences and commercial enterprises. In Caracas, 73 per cent of the population have private security for their homes, while 39 per cent made contributions in terms of money and time to community and neighbourhood watch initiatives designed to reduce crime.[215] In South Africa, the number of private security guards has increased by 150 per cent since 1997, while the number of police officials has declined by 2.2 per cent during the same period.[216] In Kenya, the private security industry is one of the fastest growing businesses.[217] The proliferation of private security firms in Kenya coincides with the upsurge in crime, particularly in Nairobi during the mid 1980s. Prior to then, private security firms were a rarity. It is important to note that the use of private security in cities of developing countries is no longer the sole preserve of wealthy households: it is becoming increasingly common in informal and low-income settlements where crime is widespread.

Characterized as a 'common interest' approach to security, guarded and gated communities are found in developed nations such as the US, where they are prevalent across the south, southwest and west,[218] and in the UK, where they are growing at a significant pace in the London Metropolitan area and in the southeast of England.[219] They are also increasingly found in transitional and developing nations. Indeed, the high rates of violent crimes and the fear of crime are important in explaining the emergence of gated communities in Latin American and Caribbean cities.[220] While security concerns have been advanced as a primary rationale for their increase, they are certainly not the sole reasons. Prestige, lifestyle choice, perceived urban service delivery advantages (including better policing), as well as increased land and home values, are also identified as factors contributing to their growth, depending upon local contexts.[221]

One manifestation of the failure of public agencies to adequately address the fear and incidence of serious property and contact crimes... is the global explosion of privatized gated areas and private security forces

Definitions of gated communities vary widely, but they tend to share the following functional characteristics: separation from neighbouring land by fences, walls, or by other constructed or natural obstructions, including symbolic barriers; filtered entry using mechanical, electronic or human guardianship as access-control elements; and, generally, privatized internal gathering areas and circulation systems, which may include roads, sidewalks and footpaths.

As noted, a primary rationale for gated and guarded communities is enhanced security, and some studies suggests that gating has limited short-term benefits in reducing specific crimes.[222] But research also indicates that the effects of gating tend to decay over time as offenders adapt and as environmental and social conditions change.[223] More significant impacts of gating are seen in the real and potential spatial and social fragmentation of cities, leading to the diminished use and availability of public space and increased socio-economic polarization. In this context, gating has been characterized as having counterintuitive impacts, even increasing crime and the fear of crime as the middle classes abandon public streets to the vulnerable poor, to street children and families, and to the offenders who prey on them. Such results also tend to broaden gaps between classes insomuch as wealthier citizens living in relatively homogeneous urban enclaves protected by private security forces have less need or opportunity to interact with poorer counterparts.

Despite these generally negative assessments and impacts, the growth of gated, privately guarded enclaves remains a fact of life. Some states and communities have regulated gating through planning and design ordinances or though general law, as in South Africa's Gauteng Province.[224] Whether regulated or not, it is clear that the global expansion of guarded and bounded private communities is sobering evidence that citizen confidence in the power of the state to ensure security is, at best, fragile, especially in places where fear of crime is high, where public authorities are seen as ineffectual and where economic factors favour self-help solutions.

Abused children and those who grow up in violent family settings stand a much greater risk of becoming offenders than those who have not had such experiences

Neighbourhoods seen as high risk for burglaries, robberies and other forms of violence gain reputations that impede outsiders' desire to travel, work and live there, and lessen the ability of residents to receive social services, such as a decent education or healthcare, which are fundamental to the building of human capital. Moreover, residents of such neighbourhoods become stigmatized and may be excluded from outside employment opportunities. In some instances, communities are isolated from the outside world, as in the case of *favelas* in Brazil whose drug bosses cut off territorial access to outsiders, and especially those from 'enemy' *favelas*.[225] Distressed communities such as these tend to aggregate pathologies, such as the concentration of offenders, which contribute to long-term stigmatization of areas and unsustainable conditions.

■ Impacts of intimate partner violence and child abuse

While the aggregate effects on cities are difficult to measure, it is clear that IPV and child abuse destroy social and human capital and contribute to the rising numbers of street families and children in transitional and developing nations. Many women who are victims of IPV not only experience negative physical and psychological effects, but are also affected financially due to lost productivity from paid work, medical care costs, mental healthcare costs, property loss and legal costs. They are also likely to earn less than women who suffer no such violence.[226] Abused children and those who grow up in violent family settings stand a much greater risk of becoming offenders than those who have not had such experiences. Furthermore, abused children often perform poorly in school, thereby adversely affecting their lifetime opportunities.[227] Thus, the impacts of IPV and child abuse violence reverberate across time and affect the economic prospects of families and communities for generations. By diverting resources to public and private policing and to incarceration, communities are less able to mobilize sustained collaborative efforts to grapple with the needs of battered and abused children and IPV victims. Furthermore, children who are exposed to IPV are more likely to abuse drugs and alcohol, run away from home, join gangs and commit crimes. This ultimately diverts resources from social and human capital building programmes and services in terms of schools, libraries and medical facilities into criminal justice operations, such as increased policing and incarceration.

■ Impacts of the prevalence of street children

Street children are both victims and perpetrators of crime in cities due to survival needs and exposure to cultures of violence, including deviant peer behaviour. There is evidence that their increasing numbers in some cities are related to trafficking and organized crime. For instance, a study on beggars in Bangkok (Thailand) revealed an organized racket of child beggars built on children from poor families trafficked from Cambodia and Burma, who are forced to beg by their brokers.[228] The children make nothing from their takings and are sometimes beaten. This example highlights the economic exploitation of street children, and implies that the growth in the number of street children has an economic dimension.

Street children have little education, are sexually active at a very early stage and, as such, stand a high risk of contracting sexually transmitted diseases, including HIV/AIDS. The females among them fall victims to teenage pregnancy, thus becoming teenage mothers and perpetuating a cycle of life on the streets. Street children are also at a higher risk than other children of abusing drugs, especially inhalants such as paint, glue, solvents or aerosols, which are inexpensive, readily available and generally legal substances.[229] Street children have contributed to increasing the levels of crime and notoriety of the areas where they are found. In Kenya, they have made the streets of Nairobi highly insecure, where they specialize in mugging, purse and jewellery snatching, pick pocketing, removing of side mirrors from slow-moving or stationary vehicles in traffic hold-ups, and the extortion of money from passers-by with the threat to smear them with human waste should they refuse.[230]

From the foregoing, it is therefore not surprising that public opinion of street children is overwhelmingly negative, with many viewing street children as criminals, unsightly and a menace to society. Public attitudes are often reflected in abuses by police, and violence against street children is reportedly widespread in several countries, including Bulgaria, Brazil, Guatemala, India and Kenya.[231] Their growing numbers and needs in terms of healthcare, education, social services and security dwarf the capacities of urban governmental agencies in most developing and transitional nations.

Impacts of organized crime

As noted in the section on 'The incidence and variability of crime and violence', corruption and organized crime, especially at the grand scale, are often connected. Moreover, the impacts of organized crime vary from global to local levels, and data availability and format do not offer easy ways of separating these distinctions. In the following subsections, the interconnected impacts on cities of organized crime in terms of corruption, as well as drug, arms and human trafficking are examined. Thereafter, the impacts of youth gangs on city spaces and services are briefly reviewed. It is difficult to disentangle these subjects (e.g. the prevalence of youth gangs in some cities is related to the supply of illicit weapons and drugs supplied by adult-organized gangs), and while separating them may be useful analytically, this can only provide a hint as to how they actually interact in cities across the globe.

Impacts of corruption

According to the World Bank, corruption is the largest single obstacle to development. In Africa, corruption is perceived to be even more important than other types of crime and violence as a disincentive to entrepreneurial investment.[232] Corruption subverts the ability of governments and city authorities to provide fair municipal services by distorting planning and allocation processes. It is a significant factor for those living in informal settlements since residents are generally not recognized by urban authorities as having rights to basic services, such as water, sanitation and electricity. Access to such amenities is therefore often dependent upon negotiations, which entail the paying of bribes or favours to local officials.[233] Urban residents generally bear the brunt of corruption because they require more services from officials.

The impact of corruption is also evident in the registration of land and construction of housing. In many cities of developing countries, the registration of land, the planning approval process and the inspection of housing construction are fraught with numerous bureaucratic bottlenecks. For instance, in Nigeria, the process of registering a property is circuitous, involving 21 procedures, which takes about 274 days.[234] At each juncture, this process provides ample avenues for government officials to extract bribes from prospective builders. This has resulted in the approval of shoddy plans and ineffective inspection during the construction process, during which many deficiencies are overlooked. This phenomenon partly accounts for the frequent collapse of buildings that have occurred in cities such as Lagos and Nairobi.

Corruption in many countries is particularly evident in large-scale infrastructure projects, such as the construction of roads, bridges and dams. These provide multiple opportunities for both grand and petty corruption and many entry points for organized crime. In this context, it has been suggested that:

> *Bribes are paid to secure concessions and kickbacks are provided in exchange for contracts. Bid rigging occurs, shell companies are established and procurement documents are falsified. Sub-standard materials are used in construction, regulators are paid off, and prices for infrastructure services are inflated. Compensation for forcibly displaced communities ends up in the pockets of bribe-seeking local officials.*[235]

The operation and maintenance of existing infrastructure, which is a crucial aspect of urban management, can be harmed by corruption. Expenditures that would normally be used in maintaining existing facilities are directed towards new infrastructure projects. In extreme cases, the maintenance of existing infrastructure is deliberately neglected so that it falls into a state of disrepair to the point that it has to be rebuilt, thereby providing the opportunity for highly placed officials to extort kickbacks from enterprises that will rebuild the infrastructure.[236] The question arises as to whether balanced local and community planning can take place in an environment skewed to new infrastructure that continually funnels cash into new projects at the expense of maintaining existing infrastructure.

Corruption subverts the ability of governments and city authorities to provide fair municipal services by distorting planning and allocation processes

Impacts of drugs on neighbourhoods and livelihoods

Organized drug trafficking reaches into communities where local settings for transactions may include outdoor drug markets on street corners or other public places that provide ideal environments for recruiting new drug users. Easy access, escape routes and vantage points from which to survey the surroundings are common environmental attributes. Such areas often provide physical and place management cues to offenders and to residents, and they attain reputations for criminal activity, often becoming no-go zones. For these reasons, the neighbourhoods in which they are located may be excluded from, or demoted on redevelopment priority lists. In other cases, such as in the *favelas* of Rio de Janeiro, drug bosses actively restrict the mobility of residents, police and public officials, cutting off access to justice systems, schools, health agencies and recreational centres.[237] They accomplish this by the use of physical barriers, intimidation and death threats, with the latter enforced against residents of 'enemy' *favelas* who trespass.

Drug distribution networks in cities are varied and range from centralized complex organizations to relatively simple decentralized ones, such as those common in Central America. In a growing number of cases, such networks illustrate the evolution of gangs that have moved from being structured around identity and territory issues to those that are primarily profit-driven, highly organized criminal enterprises, whose activities include not only retail drug distribution, but also other aspects of the trade, including smuggling, transportation and wholesale distribution. Such schemes provide varying levels of income to participants and even provide benefits to some communities, particularly in the absence of assistance from formal institutions. For example, drug trafficking was a major factor accounting for infrastructure improvements in a Managua *barrio*, and was crucial to its economic survival beyond the 'mere subsistence' level.[238] But drug trafficking was also responsible for significantly increased violence in the neighbourhood and increased urban segregation from below, as distinct from that prompted by elites from above.[239] This illustrates the more general point that drug trafficking is often a double-edged sword from the points of view of many distressed communities. It provides benefits, including economic survival options for some residents, while simultaneously

Drug distribution networks in cities are varied and range from centralized complex organizations to relatively simple decentralized ones, such as those common in Central America

contributing to neighbourhood deterioration through increased violent crimes, which also acts to distance these communities from mainstream urban society.

Impacts of arms trafficking on violence in cities

The impact of the widespread availability of arms on cities is variable, although reasonably predictable relative to distressed communities globally. In some nations, such as the US, legal gun ownership is widely dispersed throughout urban neighbourhoods, while in the UK, legal gun ownership is far more restricted. In Brazil, gun ownership is relatively restricted among the general population; but some dangerous *favelas* have significant numbers of small arms that are illegally purchased, pilfered from government arsenals or traded among drug gangs.[240] Generally, the use of both legal and illicit firearms in the commission of violent crime is more likely to take place in, or adjacent to, distressed low-income neighbourhoods rather than high-income areas. Such incidents tend to increase compartmentalization and the segregation of the former neighbourhoods as a result of fear generated by perceptions and realities of gun crime. Urban spaces that may be shunned as being dangerous are made more undesirable by the belief that weapons are available and used in such areas. This further discourages private investment, new business and the social integration of such neighbourhoods within the wider urban community, heightening cycles of violence and impoverishment.

Generally, the use of both legal and illicit firearms in the commission of violent crime is more likely to take place in, or adjacent to, distressed low-income neighbourhoods rather than high-income areas

The spatial and temporal distribution of gun violence contributes to its perception as an issue by the general public and the media in many nations. While gun violence may be concentrated in certain neighbourhoods, it also typically spreads over time and space within these areas, especially when compared with other hazards that attract public attention. India reports that more than 6000 individuals per year are killed by small arms – twice the death toll of the 11 September 2001 attacks,[241] and in the US, more than 30,000 persons each year are killed by guns. While major catastrophes galvanize media and public attention, ongoing diffused ones, such as those related to gun violence, are more costly in terms of lives and, arguably, the social and economic well-being of communities and states. Moreover, since the victims and perpetrators of gun violence tend to be the poor and marginalized, there is less sustained public and media focus directed towards this issue, at least until it rises to the level of perceived national crisis, as it has in Jamaica.

Impacts of human trafficking

The impacts of human trafficking at local and community levels are difficult to sort out from those at national levels since there is little research that clearly draws this distinction. It is certain, however, that there are multiple and very costly consequences for cities based on the sheer numbers of people trafficked globally and their transit routes, often taking them through or to cities. The role of organized criminal elements is clearly seen in this activity, although in many cases, this is aided and abetted by normal labour migration patterns, by local norms and values, and by crushing levels of poverty affecting the families of trafficking victims.[242]

Beyond the incalculable costs to trafficked individuals, who are denied their basic human rights, there are health and urban service costs to cities that can only be approximated. For example, human trafficking greatly increases prospects for prostitution and sex tourism, especially in large cities where rural women and girls are often transported by traffickers. Such activities hasten the spread of disease and crimes associated with the sex industry. A recent study by an Indian NGO, the Nedan Foundation, suggests that increased human trafficking in India's northeast region 'opens up huge possibilities for the spread of HIV'.[243] Human trafficking also increases the costs of policing and the provision of social services since many victims have no resources, little education and cannot sustain themselves without government or private assistance when (and if) they are set free.

Human trafficking not only increases the healthcare costs of cities in developing countries that are already overstressed, it threatens the building of human and social capital by playing a key role in the destabilization of families. For instance, there is evidence linking child trafficking with the breakdown of family units resulting from divorce or death of a parent. Children from such families in some West African countries are at higher risk of being trafficked than children from two-parent households. Studies of trafficked children in Togo and Cameroon found that significant proportions were from households where one or both parents had died. This evidence has prompted some researchers to suggest a connection between child trafficking and HIV/AIDS – a rapidly increasing cause of orphanage in sub-Saharan Africa.[244] Thus, trafficking is an important link in a pernicious cycle of family and, ultimately, community devastation.

Impacts of youth gangs on city spaces and services

Within cities, youth gangs often help to shape and redistribute urban space, dividing city territories into zones using real and symbolic markers

Within cities, youth gangs often help to shape and redistribute urban space, dividing city territories into zones using real and symbolic markers. This is one thread in the splintering of urban landscapes, which has left some cities with a net loss of truly public space, balanced between the private enclaves of the wealthy and the no-go zones of the poor. Urban youth gangs protect and defend their territories, giving renewed emphasis to the notion of defensible space as predicated by some crime prevention theorists.[245] For example, Nicaraguan *pandillas*, or youth gangs, are associated with particular urban neighbourhoods throughout the nation's cities and, especially, in Managua. They consist of age and geographical subgroups and are associated with significant violence in defence of their perceived neighbourhoods. One rule shared among the many *pandillas* is to not prey on local neighbours and to protect them from outside harm. One gang member is quoted as saying:

> *You show the neighbourhood that you love it by putting yourself in danger for people, by protecting them from others... You look after the neighbourhood; you help them keep them safe.*[246]

But gangs are not limited by local territorial concerns or identity issues. For instance, local gang membership may be a portal through which members gain entry to inter-city and even international membership. This is the case with the Mara Salvatrucha gang, also known as MS-13, which originated in the US, but is now active in many Central American countries as well. The *Mungiki* movement in Kenya, as described in Box 3.5, offers an example of a complex combination of territorial, mythical, economic and political dimensions in a group that has attracted many disaffected urban youth. Inspired by the *Mau Mau* movement and by anti-Western, anti-colonialist sentiment, the *Mungiki* are reputed to be engaged in forcefully managing Nairobi's public transport system and in offering protection to large swathes of the informal settlements that make up 60 per cent of the city. The movement is organized and large enough to attract the attention of politicians by providing security services that are perceived by residents to be better than those available through public agencies. This has potentially dire implications for citizens' confidence in public justice systems and for the provision of public services throughout city districts.[247]

Impacts of terrorism on cities

'Urban acts of terror ... destroy what development has built, in relation to both the physical and social fabric and cause cities to regress in development terms'.[248] The current documentation and analytical focus of the impacts of terrorism tend to be skewed towards developed countries, especially since the events of 9/11. However, the impacts of the 9/11 attack on New York City, shown in Table 3.6, provide a good example of the economic impacts of acts of terror within cities – in terms of the loss of jobs and damage to physical capital and infrastructure – whether in developed or developing countries. The table shows that the total labour and capital loss in monetary terms to New York City as of June 2002 amounted to between US$33 and US$36 billion.

Although not clearly understood or documented, as in the case of developed countries, the effects of terrorism on cities in developing countries are likely to be exacerbated by high levels of poverty, rapid pace of urbanization and unplanned expansion of cities, as well as the inability to effectively respond to, and recover after severe terrorist attacks.[249]

One of the most profound impacts of urban terrorism is the loss of lives. Estimates for the attacks of 9/11 reveal a death toll of over 3,500.[250] The March 2004 bombings of Madrid resulted in 191 deaths, while that of Mumbai in July 2006 led to the loss of 209 lives. In situations where victims are breadwinners and have dependants, the effects are further compounded, as secondary victims – family members and friends – experience economic loss and adverse psychological effects. In the more developed countries, part of the economic loss suffered by victims' families is covered by private insurance, given that many primary victims would have taken life-insurance policies.[251] This is not the case in developing countries, where very few people take out life-insurance policies, and, as such, it is highly unlikely that families of the bomb blast victims in Mumbai or Baghdad would have benefited from any form of indemnity on account of the death of their breadwinner.

Physical infrastructure plays a fundamental role in development. Its destruction during acts of terrorism therefore reduces the productive capacity of cities. The damage and destruction of physical capital and infrastructure constitutes one of the most important or direct impacts of acts of terrorism in urban areas. With respect to 9/11, the most direct impact was the destruction of Lower Manhattan. Specifically, the following were destroyed or damaged: 2.8 million square metres of office space — representing 30 per cent of class-A real estate; more than 100 retail stores in the World Trade Center area; subway tunnels (Lines 1 and 9); the Port Authority Trans-Hudson train station; the streets within the vicinity of the attack sites; and parts of the telecommunication and power infrastructure, including a switching facility and substations.[252] The extent of the physical destruction that followed the 9/11 attack has been likened to that of an earthquake or a similar major natural disaster.[253] Table 3.6 shows that in monetary terms, the

The damage and desstruction of physical capital and infrastructure constitutes one of the most important or direct impacts of acts of terrorism in urban areas

Box 3.5 The *Mungiki* movement in Nairobi, Kenya

In Nairobi, the *Mungiki* movement has an important political dimension, in part owing to the sheer numbers involved in the movement. The movement is estimated to have anywhere between 200,000 and 2 million members (the actual number is difficult to assess given the movement's secretive nature). However, it is clear that the movement commands enough numbers to draw the attention of politicians. In some constituencies, where there are large numbers of *Mungiki* members, capturing the movement's votes is a clear attraction to politicians.

For example, during the 2002 general elections in Kenya, *Mungiki* members thronged the streets of Nairobi to express solidarity with one of the candidates for presidency. The police stood by as the crude weapons-wielding *Mungiki* members took charge of the central business district. This is a clear pointer to the likelihood of politicians enlisting *Mungiki*'s support to terrorize opponents into submission. Prominent politicians were reported in the press as having called on the sect's members to 'parade up and defend' the ruling party, causing worry to members of the public, and this is part of the reason why there was widespread fear of electoral violence in 2002. The involvement of *Mungiki* in the political process is mainly because of the more insidious aspect of the movement's political cum 'protection' dimension. Anecdotal evidence suggests that in the informal settlements where the group has controlled security arrangements, local residents actually benefited from improved security. The movement's rough form of justice appears to serve as a deterrent to criminals.

What *Mungiki* has been able to do is to step into a power vacuum and demonstrate an ability to deliver a vital security service better than state agencies, at least from some locals' perspectives, even though they have to pay *Mungiki* some 'taxes' for this. In addition to providing security, it is alleged that the group makes illegal connections of electricity and water, which they force inhabitants of informal settlements to buy. They also constitute kangaroo courts for dispensing their own idea of justice. During the second week of November 2006, the group allegedly unleashed mayhem and untold violence in Mathare slum in Nairobi, which led to several deaths, displacement of many people, wanton destruction of property and disruption of livelihoods.

The entrenchment of such a situation has uncertain implications for society and therefore calls for serious reflection and intervention on the part of government and concerned citizens. The issue should be viewed not as a matter relating only to *Mungiki*, but more importantly to the conditions in society that give rise to similar situations. Mob justice is such a case: citizens take the law into their own hands because of an apparent vacuum in the existing criminal justice system; but such circumstances increasingly lead to repression and are inefficient in the long term.

Source: Masese, 2007

Table 3.6

Impact of the World Trade Center attack on New York City as of June 2002

Source: Bram et al, 2002, p12

Impact	Estimated magnitude	Notes
Labour market		
Loss of human life	Estimated 2780 workers, US$7.8 billion lifetime-earnings loss	Losses estimated as present discounted value of lifetime earnings; federal Victim Compensation Fund set up to help offset earnings losses and psychological impacts on families
Net job losses	38,000–46,000 in October 2001, rising to 49,000–71,000 by February 2002, diminishing to 28,000–55,000 by June 2002	Most of the employment losses related to the attack were in finance, airlines, hotels and restaurants
Net earnings losses	US$3.6 billion to US$6.4 billion between September 2001 and June 2002	Based on estimates of net job losses and reduced hours
Attack-related productivity effects	Some increase in post-traumatic stress disorder and alcohol and drug use three months after attack	Difficult to quantify attack's impact on workers' mental and physical disabilities
Total labour loss	US$11.4–14.2 billion	
Physical capital		
Cleanup and site restoration	US$1.5 billion	Completed June 2002; expenses covered by the Federal Emergency Management Agency (FEMA)
Destroyed buildings in World Trade Center complex	Approximately 14 million square feet, US$6.7 billion to rebuild	Book value of towers at $3.5 billion; complex privately insured
Damaged buildings in World Trade Center area	Approximately 15 million square feet, US$4.5 billion	Inclusion of damage to Class B and C space raises estimate to 21 million square feet
Contents of buildings in World Trade Center complex	US$5.2 billion	Significant offset from private insurance
Public infrastructure		
Subway	US$850 million	Estimated repair cost; significant offset from private insurance and/or FEMA for repair to all three components of infrastructure
PATH train station	US$550 million	
Utilities	US$2.3 billion	
Total capital loss	US$21.6 billion	
Total (labour, capital) loss	US$33–36 billion	

Notes: The rounding of the total (labour and capital) loss figure acknowledges imprecision in the estimates. On the one hand, estimates of the labour loss may be understated, primarily for two reasons: the June 2002 cutoff for estimating earnings impacts and the possible earnings reductions due to a drop in the number of hours worked (in industries other than apparel and restaurants). In addition, attack-related declines in worker productivity (due, for example, to stress) may have affected employed workers and are not captured in our estimated earnings losses associated with declines in employment and hours. On the other hand, estimates of the labour loss may be overstated, because of the double counting of the earnings losses of some of the deceased workers and the assumption that the deceased workers would have worked in New York City until retirement. Furthermore, although this earnings-loss tally corresponds to New York City proper, these figures will overstate the net impact on the broader metropolitan area and the nation because many of the job 'losses' reflect job relocations from the city to the suburbs – largely northern New Jersey. Because these are aggregate loss estimates, the issue of distributional impacts is not addressed.

estimated magnitude of the loss of physical capital and infrastructure, including the cost of cleanup and restoration, was US$26.1 billion. A significant proportion of the cost of destruction and damage has been offset by private insurance, while the Federal Emergency Management Agency covered the cost of cleanup and restoration. All these have contributed to reducing the long-term effects of the destruction of physical capital and infrastructure on New York City.

Terrorist attacks have resulted in new and tightened security measures on public transportation systems in cities across the world

The impacts of terrorist attacks on physical infrastructure in cities of developing countries are equally devastating and the long-term effects are likely to be more pronounced, given the inadequate condition of such infrastructure in the first place. For example, it has been observed that the effects of the various violent assaults on Baghdad's infrastructure have been to reduce what was once a fairly advanced economy to 'pre-industrial age'.[254] Furthermore, the poor state of the economy of many developing countries and the absence of indemnity to cover the cost of destruction on such a massive scale imply that recovery from severe terrorist attacks is likely to be very difficult, if not impossible.

The loss of urban employment on account of terrorist attacks is more documented in the case of developed countries, particularly in the aftermath of 9/11. Sources of livelihood have also been lost in cities of developing countries following terrorist attacks, and their effects are likely to be exacerbated, given the relatively low levels of formal sector employment. The events of 9/11 have had a disruptive effect on employment in New York City. In particular, Table 3.6 shows that the number of private sector job losses varied between 38,000 and 46,000 in October 2001, and had increased to between 49,000 and 71,000 by February 2002. These job losses varied across industries, as indicated in Box 3.6, with the most affected being financial services, restaurant, hotel, and air transportation. Other industries that were affected include business services, apparel manufacturing, printing and publishing – due to their strong concentration in Lower Manhattan.

Terrorist attacks have resulted in new and tightened security measures on public transportation systems in cities across the world. With respect to air transport in the US, some of these measures include:[255]

- About 5000 members of the US National Guard, dressed in camouflage and with M-16 rifles in hand, deployed to some 422 airports around the country.
- More (private) security personnel deployed at airports.
- Allowing only ticketed passengers in the departure gate areas.
- Better screening of passengers at airport checkpoints, for knives, cutting instruments, guns and other weapons.
- More random checks of passengers, their shoes and their carry-on luggage.
- X-raying of carry-on lap-top computers and other baggage.
- More detailed background checks on all aviation

Box 3.6 Examples of employment disruptions by industry due to the 9/11 attack, New York City, US

The **financial services industry** appears to have been the most directly affected sector by far. In New York City, the number of jobs in the securities industry fell by 12,000, or 7 per cent, in October 2001, and by an additional 6000 from October 2001 to June 2002. In addition, the banking industry saw a net job loss of 8000, or 8 per cent, in October and lost another 1000 jobs through June 2002. Net job losses in these key financial industries totalled 20,000 in October and another 7000 through June 2002.

The **restaurant industry** also sustained steep job losses immediately following the attack. For the city overall, the number of jobs at bars and restaurants – which was imperceptibly affected at the national level – fell by an estimated 9000 (6 per cent) in October, but rebounded fully by December and held steady up to June 2002. However, these are net changes and do not capture the geographical distribution of employment in this industry. Thus, it is not clear if restaurant employment in the areas closest to the World Trade Center – the Financial District, Tribeca and Chinatown – has fully rebounded to pre-attack levels.

The **hotel industry** lost an estimated 6000 jobs, or 15 per cent, city-wide between September 2001 and March 2002. This reflected the drop-off in tourism, although 5000 of those jobs were lost in October alone.

The steep decline in the number of people travelling also led to job losses in areas away from the World Trade Center site – in particular, at John F. Kennedy International Airport and LaGuardia Airport, both in the borough of Queens. The number of jobs in the city's **air transportation industry** fell by about 11,000, or 20 per cent. Almost all of this decline occurred in October and November 2001.

Although other industries, such as business services, apparel manufacturing, printing and publishing, were also presumably affected, largely because of their strong concentration in Lower Manhattan, there is no indication of any significant shift in employment trends following 11 September. However, it should be noted that many business owners and workers who did not lose their jobs evidently suffered income losses because of the disruptions in the weeks and months immediately following the attack. This is of particular concern in the restaurant and apparel industries, where workers' pay depends on business volume.

Source: Bram et al, 2002, p8

employees, and increasing restrictions on their movements on the ramps, in baggage areas and in the terminals.
- Purchasing, by airlines, of more powerful scanners that can detect explosives in baggage.
- Deployment of armed, plain clothes, Sky Marshals (security guards) on some domestic and international flights.
- Increased surveillance of baggage and baggage handlers at airports.

Increased security measures that have been undertaken with respect to seaports, bus stations and train stations are:

- Installation of more surveillance cameras to monitor daily activities.
- Deployment of more armed security guards (with guns, tear gas, pepper spray and clubs).
- Establishment of more checkpoints to scan and examine people and baggage.

Other impacts of urban terrorism include the development of an atmosphere of fear, which might be exacerbated by terror alert levels adopted in affected countries; post-traumatic stress disorder and increased depression experienced by victims of terrorist attacks; and increased spending on public security, especially in terms of surveillance, emergency planning and training of operatives in counter-terrorism. In the case of cities in developing countries, such increased spending diverts scarce resources away from productive investment in areas designed to promote growth, poverty eradication and sustainable urban development.

CONCLUDING REMARKS

Although crime and violence are found in virtually all cities across all global regions, most places are safe and most citizens are neither perpetrators nor victims of crime and violence. Crime, and especially street crimes such as robbery and assaults, tends to be concentrated in certain city areas and neighbourhoods, which are often the 'worst' urban locations in terms of property value and environmental risks from disasters and hazards. Nevertheless, even though localized, crime, violence and the fear of crime remain fundamental threats to urban safety and security and to the sustainability of urban places. They are predictable and especially problematic challenges to vulnerable populations – the poor, young males, minorities, women and children – in distressed neighbourhoods, generally, and in developing and transitional countries of Latin America and Africa, where crime rates have grown dramatically within burgeoning urban centres. In this context, crime and violence rates are associated with the pace of urbanization and the size of urban populations, although these are variable predictors relative to changes in crime and violence, particularly when specific types of crimes are taken into account. Nevertheless, increasing urbanization in regions of the world that are least able to cope with existing problems portends the need for new or reinvigorated policy and programme directions to cope with crime and violence.

To be effective, these policies and programmes will need to recognize the dimensions of crime and violence at all levels and to take into account the complex risk factors that underlie them, as discussed above. Among responses that are possible in framing strategies are those aimed at better urban planning, design and governance, which incorporate crime prevention and reduction approaches. Some of the problems and possibilities of currently used crime prevention policies and programmes are detailed in Chapter 4, while Chapter 10 provides a view of the way forward in this field.

NOTES

1 Eck, 1997.
2 Moser et al, 2005.
3 Walker et al, 2006.
4 Thachuk, 2001.
5 United Nations, 2002, Guidelines for Crime Prevention, 2002, and 11th United Nations Congress on Crime Prevention and Criminal Justice, Bangkok, 18–25 April 2005.
6 UNODC (2000) 'Convention against transnational organized crime', General Assembly Resolution 55/25.
7 UNODC, 2004.
8 Helmke and Levitsky, 2004.
9 International Labour Organization (ILO), Papua New Guinea Red Cross Society and the US National Crime Prevention Council.
10 The *blat* system relies on the complex exchange of personal favours within the context of personal networks; see Butler and Purchase, 2004.
11 Hampton, 1982.
12 Schneider and Kitchen, 2007; UNODC, 2005b; Moser and McIlwaine, 2004; Levitt, 2004; ODPM (Office of the Deputy Prime Minister), 2004; Felson, 2002; Schneider and Kitchen, 2002; Monkkonen, 2001b; Clarke, 1997; Sherman et al, 1997; Clarke and Felson, 1993; Barr and Pease, 1990; Brantingham and Brantingham, 1991; Newman, 1973; Jacobs, 1961; Burgess and McKenzie, 1925.
13 WHO, 2002, p5.
14 Moser, 2004.
15 *Ibid*; Eversole et al, 2004.
16 Galtung, 1969, p171.
17 These include theft of car, theft from car, theft of motorcycle, theft of bicycle, burglary, attempted burglary, robbery, theft of personal property, sexual offences, sexual incidents against women, and assault/threat. Victims cannot, of course, report their own homicides, so this important index is not part of the International Crime Victimization Survey (ICVS).
18 Mboya, 2002. This general typology is also used by the US National Crime Victimization Survey: see www.ojp.usdoj.gov/bjs/cvict.htm#ncvs.
19 Appiahene-Gyamfi, 2003.
20 *Ibid*.
21 Shaw et al, 2003.
22 *Ibid*.
23 *Ibid*.
24 Aggregated from data compiled by Barclay et al, 2003.
25 World Fact Book, 2006.
26 *Counts and rates increased*: (38 countries, 73 per cent: Albania, Argentina, Austria, Azerbaijan, Belarus, Belgium, Canada, Chile, Croatia, Cyprus, Czech Republic, Denmark, Finland, Germany, Iceland, Italy, Japan, Lithuania, Luxembourg, Maldives, Malta, Morocco, The Netherlands, Northern Ireland, Oman, Peru, the Philippines, Poland, Saudi Arabia, Scotland, Slovakia, Slovenia, South Africa, Sweden, Switzerland, Tunisia, the UK, Uruguay).
   Counts and rates decreased: (10 countries, 19 per cent: Bolivia, Costa Rica, El Salvador, Hungary, Kuwait, Latvia, Moldova, Myanmar, Nepal, Panama).
   Counts increased, rates decreased: (4 countries, 8 per cent: Canada, Mexico, Portugal, US).
   Adapted from UNODC, 2005a, Table 2.1.
27 UNODC, 2005a.
28 See the Urban Indicators Guidelines, UN-Habitat, 2004a. The definition is used by the United Nations Statistics Division.
29 While homicides are violent crimes, they are not included in ICVS reports since these are self-reported incidents. While definitions of what constitutes a homicide differ (e.g. all murders are homicides, but not all homicides are considered murders), homicide rates are, nevertheless, used as the international comparative standard for violent crime.
30 WHO, 2002.
31 Collier and Hoeffler, 2004, cited in UNODC, 2005b.
32 UN-Habitat, 2006c.
33 Briceno-Leon, 1999.
34 See Lemard and Hemenway, 2006.
35 Hagedorn and Rauch, 2004.
36 *Morbidity and Mortality Weekly Report*, 2004.
37 US Department of Justice, 2006.
38 Institute for Security Studies, 2002.
39 UNDOC, 2005b.
40 Moser and Holland, 1997b.
41 Alemika and Chukwuma, 2005.
42 Shaw et al, 2003.
43 *Ibid*.
44 *Ibid*.
45 van Ness, 2005, based on ICVS data.
46 del Frate, 2003.
47 Barclay et al, 2003.
48 UNODC, 2005b.
49 WHO, 2005.
50 Kershaw et al, 2001.
51 Coker et al, 2002.
52 WHO, 2005.
53 *Ibid*; Koenig et al, 2006.
54 Mboup and Amuyunzu-Nyamongo, 2005.
55 Jejeebhoy and Cook, 1997; Rao, 1997.
56 UN Secretary General's Study on Violence against Children, 2006.
57 UNICEF, 2006.
58 *Ibid*.
59 *Ibid*.
60 WHO, 2005.
61 Currie and Tekin, 2006; WHO, 2002.
62 UNICEF, 2006.
63 Consortium for Street Children, 2003.
64 Willemot, 2006.
65 Volunteer Brazil, undated, and Casa Alianza UK, undated.
66 UNICEF, 2006.
67 Anti-Corruption, undated; Anti-Corruption Gateway for Europe and Eurasia, undated; Transparency International, undated.
68 UNODC, 2004.
69 Transparency International, 2005b.
70 *Ibid*.
71 van Dijk and van Vollenhoven, 2006, p.11.
72 Shorter and Onyancha, 1999.
73 Kenya Government Position Paper, August 2001.
74 Buscaglia and van Dijk, 2003.
75 Transparency International, 2005a.
76 UNODC, 2005b, p20.
77 UNODC, 2000.
78 Thachuk, 2001.
79 van Dijk and van Vollenhoven, 2006.
80 *Ibid*, p3.
81 *Ibid*, p6.
82 See UNODC, 2006a, for maps of seizure and trafficking routes for amphetamine-type stimulants (ATS) (such as methamphetamine and amphetamine), ecstasy, heroin and other opiates, and cocaine.
83 Stohl, 2005.
84 Cukier and Seidel, 2005.
85 Small Arms Survey, 2002.
86 See International Action Network on Small Arms, undated a.
87 The case of Rio de Janeiro, prepared for this Global Report by Zaluar, 2007.
88 Gimode, 2001.
89 Okwebah and Wabala, 2007.
90 *Ibid*.
91 UNDP, 2006a; US State Department, 2001.
92 UNODC, 2006b, p7.
93 Office on Violence against Women, 2000; Schauer and Wheaton, 2006.
94 Protocol to Prevent, Suppress and Punish Trafficking in Persons, Especially Women and Children, 2003.
95 Schauer and Wheaton, 2006.
96 BBC News, 2001; La Oferta, 2006.
97 UNODC, 2005b.
98 Sofia Echo.com, 17 May 2006. Note that Bulgaria was admitted to the EU on 1 January 2007.
99 IOM (undated).
100 Schauer and Wheaton, 2006.
101 Cited in UNODC, 2006b, p61.
102 See www.humantrafficking.org.
103 Howell and Decker, 1999.
104 Rodgers, 1999.
105 Zaluar 1997, cited in Rodgers, 1999.
106 Moser et al, 2005.
107 Winton, 2004.
108 Hagedorn, 2005.
109 *Ibid*, p162.
110 *Ibid*, p161.
111 Krug et al, 2002.
112 Goldstein, 2004.
113 Beall, 2006, p106.
114 Glaeser and Shapiro, 2002.
115 Beall, 2006.
116 BBC News, 2006b.
117 Beall, 2006, p111.
118 Barker, 2003, cited in Beall, 2006.
119 Litman, 2005.
120 National Counterterrorism Center, 2006; FBI, 2004.
121 Moser, 2004.
122 HRW (undated a).
123 *Ibid*.
124 WHO, 2005.
125 Broadhurst et al, 2007.
126 Haines and Wood, 2002.
127 *Ibid*.
128 Lemard and Hemenway, 2006.
129 WHO, 2002.
130 Gartner, 1990; Unnithan and Whitt, 1992; Hsieh and Pugh, 1993; Fajnzylber et al, 2002.
131 UN-Habitat, 2003a, pp75–77.
132 Broadhurst et al, 2007.
133 Denner et al, 2001.
134 Moser et al, 2005.
135 Unnithan and Whitt, 1992.
136 Gartner, 1990; Fajnzylber et al 1999.
137 Andrienko, 2002.
138 Cornelius, 1969; Lodhi and Tilly, 1973.
139 Gaviria and Pages, 2002.
140 Moser et al, 2005.
141 Gaviria and Pages, 2002.
142 UNODC, 2005b, p8.
143 Boamah and Stanley, 2007.
144 Weber, 1899; Wirth, 1938.
145 Glaeser and Sacerdote, 1999.
146 Gaviria and Pages, 2002; Glaeser and Sacerdote, 1999.
147 Gaviria and Pages, 2002.
148 Monkkonen, 2001a.
149 Fafchamps and Moser, 2003.
150 Decker et al, 1982; Felson, 2002.
151 Manso et al, 2005.
152 Newman, 1973.
153 Originated by Jeffrey, 1977. The theory has undergone

significant change.
154 Clarke, 1997.
155 Brantingham and Brantingham, 1991.
156 Schneider and Kitchen, 2002, 2007.
157 There is a large and growing literature in this field providing empirical research to support place- and opportunity-based crime prevention/reduction theories. For overviews, including discussions of theory, empirical work and practical applications, see Poyner, 1983; Felson, 1986; Brantingham and Brantingham, 1991; Taylor, 1999; Felson, 2002; Schneider and Kitchen, 2002, 2007; Colquhoun, 2004; Cozens et al, 2004; ODPM and the Home Office, 2004. For some examples and evaluations of specific empirical work, see Newman, 1973; Beavon et al, 1994; Sherman, 1995; Eck and Wartell, 1996; La Vigne, 1996; Clarke, 1997; Sherman et al, 1998; Loukaitou-Sideris, 1999; Schweitzer et al, 1999; Farrington and Welsh, 2002; Hillier, 2004.
158 Schneider and Kitchen, 2002, 2007.
159 Knowles, 2003a, 2003b.
160 Schneider and Kitchen, 2007.
161 Kitchen, 2005.
162 Schneider and Kitchen, 2002, 2007.
163 LaFree and Tseloni, 2006.
164 Wilson, 1978.
165 Gimode, 2001.
166 WHO, 2002.
167 Center for Family Policy and Research, 2006.
168 *Ibid*, 2006.
169 Small Arms Survey, 2006a, p297.
170 *Ibid*.
171 Levitt, 2004.
172 Small Arms Survey, 2006a.
173 World Bank, 2003c.
174 Saunders and Taylor, 2002.
175 Lock, 2006.
176 Moser et al, 2005; Briceno-Leon and Zubillaga, 2002.
177 De Cesare, 1997, cited in Moser et al, 2005.
178 Rose, 2006.
179 Sinclair and Mills, 2003.
180 Rose, 2006.
181 LaFree and Tseloni, 2006.
182 LaFree, 2002.
183 Manso et al, 2005.
184 Caldeira, 2000; Rodgers, 2003; Blandy et al, 2003.
185 Small Arms Survey, 2006b.
186 UNODC, 2005a.
187 Moser, 2004.
188 See International Action Network on Small Arms, undated b.
189 While women are extremely vulnerable to gun crimes, statistically, marginalized young men are the most likely victims of small arms violence. They can be caught up in a range of socio-cultural pressures where guns become status symbols of masculinity and power, especially in the absence of political and economic opportunities. For example, in the *favelas* of Rio de Janeiro, the combination of availability of guns, drugs and cultural values dictating that men do not accept insults have helped to push the city's homicide rates for young low-income males to record heights over the past 25 years; see Zaluar, 2007.
190 Morrison and Orlando, 1999.
191 Buvinic and Morrison, 1999.
192 Moser and Holland, 1997b.
193 Hamermesh, 1998.
194 UNODC, 2005b.
195 Institute for Security Studies, 2002.
196 World Bank, 2003a; Krkoska and Robeck, 2006.
197 Gimode (2001) notes that in 1996, tourism accounted for 13 per cent of total revenue in Kenya, which was a far cry from the preceding decades.
198 Boamah and Stanley, 2007.
199 *Ibid*.
200 Tewarie, 2006; Adams, 2003.
201 Adams, 2003.
202 UNODC, 2005b; Brunetti et al, undated.
203 UNODC, 2005b.
204 Londono and Guerrero, 1999, cited in Moser et al, 2005.
205 Gaviria, 2002.
206 Zaluar, 2007, p.15.
207 Gibbons, 2002.
208 Mayhew, 2003.
209 Sampson and Wooldredge, 1986.
210 See Schwartz et al, 2003.
211 This sequence is derived from Felson, 2002.
212 van Ness, 2005, based on ICVS data.
213 Budd, 1999.
214 Gibbons, 2002.
215 Moser et al, 2005.
216 www.humansecurity-cities.org, 2007, p27.
217 Gimode, 2001.
218 Blakely and Snyder, 1997.
219 Blandy et al, 2003; Blandy, 2005.
220 Mycoo, 2006.
221 Blakeley and Snyder, 1997; Blandy, 2005.
222 Atlas and LeBlanc, 1994.
223 Clarke, 2003; Schneider and Kitchen, 2007.
224 See the Gauteng Provincial Legislature, which passed the Rationalization of Local Government Affairs Act in 1998.
225 Zaluar, 2007.
226 Buvinic et al, 1999, cited in Moser et al, 2005.
227 *Ibid*, 2005.
228 Humantrafficking.org, 2005.
229 WHO, 2001.
230 Gimode, 2001.
231 HRW, undated b.
232 UNODC, 2005b.
233 See United Nations, undated, 'Backgrounder 8', www.un.org/cyberschoolbus/habitat/background/bg8.asp.
234 World Bank, 2006d.
235 Bosshard and Lawrence, 2006.
236 Tanzi and Davoodi, 1997; Tanzi, 1998; Wei, 1999; Arimah, 2005.
237 Zaluar, 2007.
238 Rodgers, 2003.
239 *Ibid*.
240 Zaluar, 2007.
241 See *Times of India*, 2006.
242 See Humantrafficking.org, undated.
243 *IRIN News*, 2007a.
244 According to joint estimates developed by UNAIDS, UNICEF, USAID and the US Bureau of Census in 2002, the total number of living children under age 15 whose mother, father or both parents have died of AIDS in sub-Saharan Africa is 11 million (Synergy Project, 2002). See HRW, undated a.
245 Newman, 1973.
246 Rodgers, 2003.
247 Masese, 2007.
248 Beall, 2006, p114.
249 Beall, 2006.
250 Glaeser and Shapiro, 2002.
251 Bram et al 2002.
252 *Ibid*, p11.
253 *Ibid*.
254 Banarji, 1997 cited in Beall, 2006.
255 These measures are taken from Goodrich, 2002, p57.

CHAPTER 4

URBAN CRIME AND VIOLENCE: POLICY RESPONSES

Chapter 3 has described in some depth the nature of urban crime and violence as they are experienced across the world. The purpose of this chapter is to examine some of the policy responses to these problems, and to explore some of the available evidence on how successful these initiatives have been. It needs to be understood, from the outset, that a high proportion of these initiatives have not been fully or properly evaluated, and that a further proportion have either not had the results of such evaluations made public at all or have done this in ways that are not readily accessible. It is also the case that much of the evidence that is available and accessible comes from the developed world, rather than from the developing world, and it should not be automatically assumed that conclusions from the former context will automatically apply to the latter. Consequently, the evidence based on what works is much thinner than the plethora of initiatives to be found.

This situation gives rise to one important policy recommendation (i.e. the importance of developing a learning culture in this field) since the absence of meaningful and publicly accessible evaluation is a major flaw with many projects. The absence of a learning culture has two clear consequences. One of these is that it becomes very difficult in these circumstances to be clear about how successful a project has been, although there are many examples of projects that have been declared successes without any effective evaluation to demonstrate the truth of this claim. A second is that the opportunity for both the participants in the project and others elsewhere to learn from this experience is undermined by the lack of effective and accessible evaluation. This latter point is of particular importance when the opportunity to learn from demonstrated good practice elsewhere is greater now than it has ever been. Both of these issues are returned to in greater depth in Chapter 10.

Although this chapter draws heavily on the base established by Chapter 3, it does not follow the same structure because in many instances the policy responses that are identifiable represent a means of approaching a range of criminal activities and not each of the types that are separately identified in Chapter 3. Two examples will serve to make this point. One of the most common responses to the problems of urban crime and violence is through the formation of partnerships that are designed to bring together the key players involved in tackling such problems. Typically, partnerships will seek to address a range of criminal activities, usually focusing on those that are of greatest prominence or the cause of greatest public concern in their localities. There are many things that can be said about partnerships and they take many different forms; but the approach adopted here is to discuss this phenomenon in a freestanding section rather than as a component of many responses to many different types of crime.

The same argument applies to efforts to combat corruption, which is of fundamental importance to this particular field. Although tackling crime and violence is widely recognized as being about much more than just the work of police forces, for example, there is no doubt that police work of many kinds remains central to this task. Corrupt police operations, or police operations that are perceived by the public as being corrupt, are therefore very likely to undermine other efforts in this field. The same broad arguments apply to corrupt processes of political decision-making and corrupt planning processes. Since the elimination of corruption in areas such as these is a fundamental part of many attempts to tackle urban crime and violence, this, too, is the subject of a single discussion in this chapter as part of a broader examination of how tackling problems of crime and violence relates to urban governance structures and processes.

The approach that has been adopted is to address the field of policy responses to urban crime and violence in seven parts:

- levels of responses, from the global downwards;
- the significance of stages of development;
- urban governance structures and processes;
- types of policy responses to problems of crime and violence;
- institutional and community responses;
- partnerships;
- some emerging policy trends.

The greatest amount of attention is devoted to the types of policy response to problems of crime and violence since this is the core of the chapter. In effect, the first three of these sections are about contextual issues, the second group of three sections covers policy and organizational responses, and then the final section identifies some emerging trends.

There is one overarching point that needs to be fully appreciated before the examples in the sections that follow can be understood in their proper context. In this field, the evidence points overwhelmingly to the fact that very many initiatives depend upon local circumstances and cultures.[1] What this means is that what works well in one locality will not necessarily work in another because initiatives need to be tailored to the particular circumstances in which they will be applied. So, a particular initiative drawn from the urban governance practices in the Western world could not necessarily be transplanted without considerable thought and adaptation to a developing country, where the processes, cultural norms and expectations, as well as skills available, are likely to be different.

This does not mean that it is impossible to learn from experiences elsewhere, or that initiatives that appear to have worked in one location cannot be successfully adapted to another. Rather, considerable care needs to be exercised in doing this to ensure that what is being tried relates effectively to local circumstances.

LEVELS OF RESPONSES

Much crime is characterized by the fact that it takes place in specific locations and affects specific individuals or groups, either because they have been specifically targeted or because an opportunistic offender takes advantage of a particular situation. As Chapter 3 has already pointed out, one of the most important questions in this situation needs to be about the characteristics of the locality *where* the incident took place. The *where* is as important a question as *who*, *what* or *how*. The characteristics of place can make a big difference to the opportunity to commit a crime, as can the behaviour of human beings in particular places; so efforts to understand these relationships in order to make the process of offending harder and the perception of the balance between risk and reward by a potential offender less attractive are important components in many initiatives to reduce crime.

Chapter 3 also suggests that poor planning, design and management of urban places and spaces are factors associated with crime and violence. This implies that responses at the local level are especially significant, since it is at this spatial scale that the impact of planning decisions and many crimes are most felt.[2] Similarly, social factors associated with crime, as indicated in Chapter 3, can also be addressed at the local level, through social policies and through interventions that involve communities or local actors. Often, even if social policies are formulated and implemented at various levels, local implementation ensures that targeted vulnerable groups are reached. Similarly, it is at the local level that integration of policies is best achieved. Nevertheless, not all crimes can be ameliorated by local action as some need to be tackled on a much broader scale. Examples include drug trafficking,[3] arms trafficking[4] and human trafficking,[5] most of which involve illegal movements across national boundaries, which, as a consequence, require cooperation between all the nations involved if they are to be tackled effectively.

In addition, policy and financial frameworks that govern what can be done at the local level are often put in place at higher levels of the governance hierarchy. For example, many police forces operate over much broader areas than individual cities, as do laws and many practices. Sometimes the resources needed to tackle crime problems at a local level are not available from within that locality, and so higher levels of governance have a role to play in making resources available. While the main focus of this chapter is on what happens at the urban scale and more locally, it is important to recognize the contributions that are made at broader governmental scales and to acknowledge that multi-level approaches to issues of crime and violence are an inevitable consequence of multilevel governmental structures. This section, therefore, provides a series of examples of different kinds of contributions from the international level to the sub-national level. The remainder of the chapter will then concentrate on the urban and more localized levels and on community activities. This is a vast area and it is not possible to cover it comprehensively here; but the examples discussed should give an indication of the range of possible activities and policy trends in tackling urban insecurity.

Not all crimes can be ameliorated by local action as some need to be tackled on a much broader scale

International cooperation

International cooperation and mechanisms have an important part to play in efforts to combat certain crimes in particular – for example, the United Nations Convention against Transnational Organized Crime, the International Criminal Police Organization, and programmes and projects supported by international and regional organizations. They also have an important role in setting principles and guidelines, as in the case of the UN-Habitat Safer Cities Programme, which provides an integrative approach for addressing issues of crime and insecurity at city level, through city-wide processes and strategies, and for supporting local initiatives and international exchanges and learning.

International cooperation and mechanisms have an important part to play in efforts to combat certain crimes

■ United Nations Convention against Transnational Organized Crime

The United Nations Convention against Transnational Organized Crime was signed by just under 150 member states between December 2000 and December 2002.[6] The convention seeks to standardize terminology and concepts in order to create a common basis for national crime-control frameworks, and commits signatories to a series of actions. These include adopting domestic laws and practices designed to prevent or suppress organized crime; confiscating illegally acquired assets; adopting an approach to extradition that avoids the creation of 'safe havens'; mutual legal assistance; the adoption of measures to protect victims and witnesses; programmes of technical cooperation; financial and material assistance to help developing nations implement the convention; and the establishment of a regular conference to review progress.

For present purposes, it is important to note three characteristics of this convention: the commitment to specific actions that signature entails; the recognition that not all nations are equally well placed to implement the convention and, thus, the creation of a mechanism to help developing nations; and the recognition of the need for a standing review mechanism. There is no suggestion that a framework of this nature will of itself resolve all the difficult problems associated with tackling transnational crime; but there can be little doubt that such a mechanism as a vehicle for encouraging appropriate cooperation between nations is of considerable importance. It could also be argued that signing a convention of this nature is the easy part, and that what really matters is what governments do over time. The convention also has a role to play in setting standards for governments to maintain and, indeed, to improve upon over time.

International Criminal Police Organization

Another international initiative is the International Criminal Police Organization (Interpol), which has 186 member countries.[7] A key role of Interpol is to increase and improve international law enforcement in order to combat all forms of organized crime, including illicit drug production and trafficking, weapons smuggling, trafficking in human beings, money laundering, child pornography and white collar crime, as well as high-tech crime and corruption. Its functions entail the creation and operation of secure global police communications services; the maintenance and development of operational databases and data services for police organizations; and the provision of operational police support services. As many aspects of crime have become internationalized, so the need for police forces to be well connected internationally and to work harmoniously with other police forces in seeking to address common problems has become more significant. Interpol plays an important role in supporting and facilitating these processes. As well as providing support through its incident response teams at the scenes of disasters, terrorist attacks and large-scale events that required additional security, Interpol's operational support services were particularly active in 2005 in five priority crime areas: public safety and terrorism; drugs and criminal organizations; trafficking in human beings; financial and high-technology crime; and fugitives. The importance of much of this work for urban areas is that cities bear the brunt of crimes of this nature. It seems likely that, in a globalizing world, more crime will have international dimensions, and so the need for police responses which not merely range from the local to the international but which also link these effectively will become more important.

UN-Habitat Safer Cities Programme ... tackles crime and violence as issues of good urban governance... which ... recognizes that crime and insecurity have been strongly affected by the impact of urbanization

UN-Habitat Safer Cities Programme

A further example of a form of international cooperation mechanism of direct relevance to the concerns of this chapter is the UN-Habitat Safer Cities Programme[8], which tackles crime and violence as issues of good urban governance, in response to a United Nations Economic and Social Council resolution of 1995.[9] The programme, which was launched in 1996, recognizes that crime and insecurity have been strongly affected by the impact of urbanization, and as such, have become a major preoccupation for many countries in Africa, Asia, Latin America and the Caribbean, and the Pacific. In this context, the issue of urban crime prevention, which is the focus of the Safer Cities Programme, represents a key challenge for the sustainable development of cities and human settlements in general. A number of countries are in the process of reforming their police and justice systems with a greater appreciation of the urban environment, and inspired by international standards that increasingly recognize the central role of municipalities as key actors in coalitions and in the development of community-wide planning strategies for addressing crime and violence prevention. The prevention of crime has received more sustained attention, not only in relation to the integration of socially excluded groups, but also for victims of crime.

The programme's initial focus was on Africa, at the request of a group of African city mayors who were concerned about the extent of violence in their cities and wanted help with the development of prevention strategies. This provided a learning ground upon which the programme adapted, piloted and tested various tools within an internationally recognized municipal framework and approach to crime prevention. To date, Safer Cities initiatives are well under way in several African cities (Johannesburg, Durban, Dar es Salaam, Abidjan, Antananarivo, Dakar, Yaoundé, Douala, Nairobi), and are also being replicated at the national level in some of the pilot countries in Africa. The programme has been extended to Latin America, Asia and Port Moresby, Papua New Guinea in order to cater for an increasing need for exchange of information, knowledge and good practice between national, regional and local governments as well as civil society and non-government organizations, but also at the international level.

Although the programmes vary according to the characteristics and requirements of the particular locality, the essence of the approach is broadly common, with emphasis on attitudinal change and governance processes. Its key activities are:

- strengthening the capacities of local authorities to address urban safety issues and reduce delinquency and insecurity;
- promoting holistic crime prevention approaches implemented in collaboration with central and local authorities, the criminal justice system, the private sector and civil society;
- developing tools and documentation to support local initiatives
- encouraging city networks in order to exchange experiences;
- preparing and implementing capacity-building programmes, and bringing in qualified and experienced partners from elsewhere to help;
- focusing on three main action areas, in particular: developing social crime prevention approaches targeting groups at risk, developing situational crime prevention approaches targeting public spaces, and supporting reform of the criminal justice system.[10]

Box 4.1 The Safer Nairobi Initiative

The strategy involves a two-year action plan based upon four pillars:

- better enforcement of existing laws and by-laws;
- improvement of urban design and the environment;
- community empowerment; and
- socially oriented measures providing support for groups at risk, including children, youth, women and street families.

The major elements of the strategy are:

- the adoption and implementation of a local safety action plan;
- local diagnoses of insecurity, involving a crime victimization study, youth offender profiling and a study of violence against women;
- extensive discussion of survey findings with stakeholders groups, including communities, the private sector, women groups;
- a city-wide residents convention held in 2003 that approved the city-wide crime prevention strategy, later endorsed by the City Council;
- the establishment of an interdepartmental committee on safety and security within the city council under the auspices of the mayor;
- safety audits conducted in key locations;
- launch of a Safer Spaces and Streets Campaign with two pilot projects;
- publication of a quarterly newsletter on city safety and security;
- establishment of a local coordinating team and office;
- progressive development of action-oriented partnerships;
- broad-based stakeholder consultations and reviews;
- training and exchange visits; and
- lighting up of Nairobi's slums and streets.

It is still too early to draw overall conclusions on the success of the programme since it is trying to combat what are, in some cases, quite long-term trends and since it is seeking not merely to undertake specific projects targeted at specific problems, but also to change the ways in which crime and public safety issues are tackled in Nairobi. But what is already clear is that there have been some specific successes – for example, the programme of lighting Nairobi's streets and slums is seen as a success both in aesthetic terms and in addressing some of the people's fear of crime and violence. In addition, the problems of youth-related crime (including its street-life elements) are not only better understood, but are also being tackled through a longer-term strategy.

Source: Masese, 2007

Safer Cities programmes in individual cities have been developed within a democratic framework in the fight against crime based on three principles: law enforcement for all, solidarity and crime prevention. This has tended to proceed through a six-step approach, as follows:

1. diagnosis of problems;
2. mobilization and building of a coalition of partners;
3. developing a crime prevention strategy;
4. developing and implementing an action plan;
5. mainstreaming and institutionalizing the approach; and
6. continuous monitoring and evaluation.

The experience of Nairobi (Kenya) with the Safer Cities Programme has been captured in one of the case studies for this Global Report, and the main elements of the Safer Nairobi Initiative are summarized in Box 4.1.

The Safer Cities Programme is an example of an international initiative that is locally applied, and which is essentially about improved local governance, as opposed to just local government, and which includes local capacity-building and providing a framework within which the ability of local communities to tackle their own problems is improved over time. It is also about the establishment of a culture of prevention so that key issues are identified and tackled through activities that engage a wide range of key partners and local residents. In other words, its focus is not just on immediate problems, but is also on the longer term. UN-Habitat provides an integrated model, a relevant knowledge resource, much encouragement, some resources and access to a range of contacts willing and able to help; but the main task is addressed locally in the light of local conditions and aspirations. The approach itself appears to be robust in terms of both the basic structure that it offers and the strategic approach to problems of crime and violence that it advocates. The main issues in terms of its success are likely to be more local ones, around resources, people and commitment to the long haul. It can also be seen as offering something positive where previously very little seemed to be available to many cities to help them tackle problems of crime and violence.

It is important to stress that the Safer Cities Programme is not a 'one-size-fits-all' solution to the problems of urban crime, and that many cities in the world have made progress in tackling crime and violence using a similar approach but outside the realm of the UN-Habitat Safer Cities Programme. Indeed, the number of cities participating in the UN-Habitat Safer Programme today is very small in comparison with those that have or are seeking to address these issues in other ways. One of the key characteristics of the Safer Cities Programme is that it encourages documentation, evaluation and reporting of what is being done so that there is an evidence base in relation to these activities – which is often lacking in similar programmes and projects.

It is important to stress that the Safer Cities Programme is not a 'one-size-fits-all' solution to the problems of urban crime

Although mainly concerned with local impacts of crime prevention and capacity development, the Safer Cities Programme maintains a global outlook, as it supports global and regional debate and exchange of experiences and the development of policy guidance and generic reference

Box 4.2 The key propositions in the European Pre-Standard on Urban Planning and Crime Prevention

Key propositions

- Urban planning can affect different types of crime and the fear of crime by influencing both the conduct and the attitudes of key people, such as offenders, victims, residents and the police.
- Some types of crime, such as burglary and vandalism, are particularly amenable to urban planning activities.
- Crime and the fear of crime need to be seen as different but related phenomena.
- Fear of crime is an important issue in its own right; but to be tackled effectively, it needs to be separated out from a much broader range of feelings that people have about their living environments.
- Strategic approaches to the creation of securer and safer cities and neighbourhoods that examine the physical and social environments can be successful.
- As well as looking at planning and design issues, policy-makers and practitioners must also focus on maintenance issues.

Appropriate strategies

Planning strategies: include respecting existing physical and social structures, creating liveliness, creating mixed-status areas, and achieving reasonable urban densities.

Urban design strategies: include achieving visibility, addressing issues of accessibility, creating a sense of territory, making environments attractive, and ensuring that basic artefacts (such as windows, doors and street furniture) are robust.

Management strategies: include target hardening, maintenance, surveillance, rules for the conduct of the public in public places, the provision of infrastructure for key groups (such as youth), and good communication with the public.

Source: CEN, 2003, pp5–6, 15–17

tools in support of the crime prevention processes it promotes.

European Pre-Standard on Urban Planning and Crime Prevention

A final example of a form of international cooperation that is different from the first three is the work which has been done to create a European pre-standard for the reduction of crime and the fear of crime through urban planning and building design. Essentially, a technical committee reviewed both the available literature and the current practice within current and aspiring European Union (EU) member countries, paying particular attention to project evaluations where these existed and drawing on several important applied traditions, including, in particular, CPTED and situational crime prevention. This resulted in the publication of the urban planning component of the European pre-standard in 2003.[11] This identified six broad propositions about the field, and fifteen types of strategies that might be applied, grouped together under three broad headings: planning, urban design and management. The six broad propositions and the underlying strategies are summarized in Box 4.2.

In effect, this is a distillation of good practice across Europe as perceived by the technical committee, recognizing, as it did, that practice in this field was very variable. As such, its particular value in the short term is probably in the help that it offers to those parts of the EU and to countries aspiring to membership where practice is less well developed. In the long term, the pre-standard may play a more formal role in helping to develop EU policy and practice in this field. It should be noted that some of the strategy recommendations in the European pre-standard are not without controversy.[12] For present purposes, though, this serves as a useful example of one of the particular ways in which international cooperation can be very valuable.

These four examples – the United Nations Convention against Transnational Organized Crime, the work of Interpol, the UN-Habitat Safer Cities Programme and the European Pre-Standard on Urban Planning and Crime Prevention – show something of the variety to be found in forms of international cooperation and in the purposes behind initiatives of this nature.

National level

At the national level, responsibilities and involvement in relation to crime and violence issues vary remarkably

At the national level, responsibilities and involvement in relation to crime and violence issues vary remarkably. This is largely due to the structure of government responsibilities in each country. Key elements of the differences relate to the level of guidance or policy initiative that is provided by the national level even for local intervention, and the level of decentralization of responsibilities in this field. The US and the UK, for example, have many matters in common in relation to this field; but one of the most striking differences between them relates to the respective roles of the national government in both countries.[13]

Examples from the UK and the US

During recent years, the UK has seen a strong policy drive from the national government level to get crime prevention concerns embedded within the planning process, supported by extensive central government published advice.[14] This process is summarized in Box 4.3 and reflects the gradual development of policy over a period of some 11 years, during which there was a change of government in 1997. The British model would not necessarily be appropriate for other countries; but what is interesting about this example is not merely its contents, but the process of policy development that has led up to the current situation.

In the US, on the other hand, where initiatives of this kind exist it is because action has been taken at the state or local level. The US constitution makes clear the respective roles of the various levels of government and in this field the main rights reside at state and local levels rather than at the federal level. Nevertheless, national security concerns will always be a matter of considerable importance to national governments, and in the US, particularly since the events of 11 September 2001, the federal government has played a leading role in addressing the threat of terrorist attacks. Interestingly, much of the work undertaken under this banner seems to have come from the stable of CPTED and so it can be argued that the national thrust to address the threat of terror has advanced the cause of CPTED in the US further and faster than had a series of more localized initiatives during the last couple of decades.[15]

Example from Jamaica

The third example of the role of national governments in addressing urban crime and violence is taken from a developing country – Jamaica. Since Jamaica became independent in 1962, it has experienced significant growth in violent crimes. For instance, murder rates rose from 8.1 per 100,000 people in 1970 to 40 per 100,000 in 2002, and 64 per 100,000 in 2005, making Jamaica one of the nations with the highest murder rates in the world.[20]

In response to escalating levels of violent crimes, the Ministry of National Security embarked on a major process of developing the necessary law enforcement infrastructure required to tackle the problem of crime and violence. A multilevel approach is being used that involves new crime fighting initiatives, legislative reform, modernization of the police, and social intervention programmes at the community level. For instance, modernization of police services includes improving the professional standards of the police; improving their investigative capacity, specifically using an intelligence approach to operations; introduction of new technology; and utilization of personnel from overseas. The latter has entailed forging links with Scotland Yard, UK, in which training is provided for members of the Jamaica Constabulary Force. This is in addition to seconding high-ranking police officers from Scotland Yard to work with their local counterparts in Jamaica.

In 2004, the Jamaica Constabulary Force launched *Operation Kingfish* as a major anti-crime initiative. The purpose of the operation was to dismantle criminal networks within Jamaica and to disrupt illegal trafficking of drugs and firearms throughout the central and western Caribbean, with the assistance of international partners. In this regard, *Operation Kingfish* can be considered a partnership between the Jamaica Constabulary Force and international police agencies. The operation has targeted gangs, crime bosses, extortion rackets and narcotics trafficking. One major accomplishment of *Operation Kingfish* has been the dismantling of gangs within the Kingston corporate area. The initiative has also led to the recovery of numerous illegal firearms and equipment used in the illicit drug trade. The first major drug bust of *Operation Kingfish* came in 2004 when American law enforcement agents, assisted by Jamaica and British counterparts, intercepted cocaine valued at Jamaican $4 billion (US$59 million) destined for Jamaica.[21]

The envisaged changes in the crime fighting initiatives of the Jamaica Constabulary Force are meant to work in tandem with other initiatives, such as community-based policing and several social and crime prevention initiatives

Box 4.3 Getting the English planning system to engage with crime prevention

- *1994:* UK Department of the Environment (DoE) Circular 5/94[16] encouraged planners to consult with police architectural liaison officers.
- *1998:* Section 17 of the Crime and Disorder Act placed a statutory duty on local planning authorities to take account of crime prevention issues in their work.
- *2000:* The Urban Policy White Paper[17] undertook to review Circular 5/94 and to make crime prevention a key objective for planning.
- *2004:* The new national guidance on planning for crime prevention,[18] to replace Circular 5/94, was published.
- *2005:* Planning Policy Statement 1,[19] the government's statement about the main purposes and responsibilities of the planning system described the primary task of planning as the delivery of sustainable development and saw safety as one of the key characteristics of a sustainable community.

implemented by the Ministry of National Security. These initiatives – specifically the Citizens Security and Justice Programme (CSJP) and the Community Security Initiative (CSI) operate predominantly within the Kingston Metropolitan Area. The former is funded through a partnership between the Government of Jamaica and the Inter-American Development Bank (IDB), and the latter by the UK Department for International Development (DFID). These programmes were initiated to enhance community safety and security. The CSI was established to ensure efficient and effective 'joined-up action' between existing programmes on improving security and safety, reducing poverty and strengthening social development. CSJP operates in 15 violence-prone communities in Kingston and has been instrumental in providing support to residents and developing legitimate community leadership and structures.

In the US, particularly since the events of 11 September 2001, the federal government has played a leading role in addressing the threat of terrorist attacks

Before moving away from the roles of national governments, it is important to note that over and above specific initiatives, the ongoing work of national governments has a huge impact on crime and violence in urban areas and how these problems are tackled.[22] Three examples that relate to themes introduced in Chapter 3 are given to emphasize this point.

First, national governments often have a major role to play in providing policy, legal and financial frameworks for the work of local authorities, and so the ability of local authorities to address problems of crime and violence in their localities can be very heavily influenced by these factors. In particular, national governments often encourage local authorities and other bodies to do more in particular areas of concern by providing funding and other types of resources for these purposes. An example of this is the work of the National Crime Prevention Centre in Canada, which supports crime prevention activities through three funding programmes: the Crime Prevention Action Fund; the Policing, Corrections and Communities Fund; and the Research and Knowledge Development Fund.[23] It should be noted that some governments are active not just in providing funding internally, but also in providing funding for such projects in other countries.

Second, national governments often have a major role to play in relation to military, security and police forces in

Box 4.4 The government of Western Australia's Community Safety and Crime Prevention Strategy

Western Australia's Community Safety and Crime Prevention Strategy is guided by seven principles: sustainability; working better together; inclusiveness; targeted efforts; evidence-based decision-making; focusing on results; and sharing knowledge. It is driven by five key goals, and under each a set of priority actions is identified. The five key goals are:

- supporting families, children and young people;
- strengthening communities and revitalizing neighbourhoods;
- targeting priority offences;
- reducing repeat offending; and
- designing out crime and using technology.

The other two primary components of the strategy involve the development of partnership processes, and the establishment of various forms of grant funding which are targeted at helping with the implementation of the priority actions. Partnerships between communities, police, local government and other public agencies are encouraged at local level throughout the state to develop local Community Safety and Crime Prevention Plans, with both state advice and resources being available to assist with this process. The strategy also identifies five specific funds that will be established as part of a total spending of AU$15 million on grants over four years in order to take this process forward. These five funds are the:

- Local Government Partnership Fund, which will help local partnerships to get established and produce local Community Safety and Crime Prevention Plans;
- Community Partnership Fund, which will give small grants for community crime initiatives being undertaken with, or supported by, the police;
- Indigenous Partnership Fund, which is specifically for supporting work on community safety and crime prevention in indigenous (Aboriginal) communities;
- Research and Development Fund, which is about supporting targeted and evidence-based approaches through research and related activities; and
- Crime Prevention Through Environmental Design (CPTED) fund, which will support the adoption of CPTED principles in the planning of new development and infrastructure improvements.

Source: Government of Western Australia, 2004

National governments often have a major role to play in relation to military, security and police forces in terms of policy, funding and disposition

terms of policy, funding and disposition. All of these elements impact both directly and indirectly upon the experience of crime and violence in cities. In particular, the ways in which police services are directed and managed are of particular significance in this context, and so it is very common to see city political and executive leaders wishing to engage in a regular dialogue about these matters, not only with national government, but also with the senior officers responsible for police operations in cities.

Third, while there is often an important local dimension in campaigns to tackle corruption of various kinds, the role of national governments is absolutely vital since the legal and judicial systems will both have important parts to play in such initiatives. National governments can also set the tone for drives against corruption, as part of a commitment to good governance. It is important that this is done otherwise individual local initiatives can quickly lose momentum.

Sub-national level

Governance arrangements vary remarkably at the sub-national level. Consequently, it is difficult to generalize about this level of activity, except to note that where it exists, and depending upon its powers, it is quite likely that important components of initiatives to tackle urban crime and violence will be found. To illustrate this, three examples of initiatives at sub-national level are described below. The first is the approach to tackling crime prevention in Western Australia, where the state has significant powers and sees the process on which it is embarking as being strategy led. In the second approach – a less direct example – the sub-national level is responsible for putting in place tools that can provide a framework within which crime and violence are looked at alongside other elements that determine public policy priorities in municipalities. This is the process of preparing integrated development plans in the province of KwaZulu-Natal (South Africa). The third example relates to the role that legislative processes at the state level can play in crime prevention through the Safe Neighborhood Act in Florida (US).

Community safety and crime prevention strategy: Western Australia

The lead in developing policies and practices on crime prevention in Western Australia is taken by the Office of Crime Prevention.[24] It has six key tasks:

- initiating crime prevention public-awareness campaigns;
- developing and coordinating strategic and holistic policy;
- providing advice to state and local government;
- undertaking research to establish best practice to be utilized in community safety and crime prevention strategies;
- informing about relevant training and development programmes; and
- providing grant funding for community safety and crime prevention initiatives.

The state's Community Safety and Crime Prevention Strategy[25] is summarized in Box 4.4.

One of the most interesting elements of this example is its use of grant funding to implement the strategy. One of the difficulties with strategies produced for large and diverse areas can be finding mechanisms that enable priorities to be pursued and actions targeted in ways that not only meet strategy objectives, but that are also appropriate on the ground. This particular example of a set of grant programmes is an interesting way of trying to address this particular issue.

Integrated development plans in the province of KwaZulu-Natal, South Africa

The second example is the process of preparing integrated development plans in the province of KwaZulu-Natal (South Africa).[26] This is not specifically a crime prevention initiative as such, but a process of integrating crime prevention issues within the planning process in order to improve quality of life and enhance the safety and security of citizens. Here the responsibility for preparing integrated development plans rests with the 61 municipalities rather than with the province. However, the province performs a variety of functions to support municipalities and to guide the process. The integrated development plan is essentially a management tool that sets out the municipality's vision, objectives, strategies and key projects, and the intention of the act establishing this process is that the provisions of the integrated development plan will shape the way in which the local authority performs.

The importance of this example is that it demonstrates two characteristics that are not always to be found in work at this level of government: the commitment to a strategic approach, and the importance of thinking holistically about problems, rather than seeking to tackle them through independent streams of action. In addition, it is now a requirement throughout KwaZulu-Natal that integrated development plans covering the major urban areas must include both crime prevention policies and women's safety audits.[27] Integrated development plans offer a strategic vehicle for taking a holistic view of crime and violence, for embedding the actions needed to address it in the everyday work, and for mainstreaming these activities as part of agreed priorities. For example, the integrated development plan for the eThekwini Municipality for 2002 to 2006 sought to commit its community services plan to facilitate the implementation of the Durban Safer Cities strategy by ensuring that:

- The council facilitates intergovernmental cooperation with regard to the design and implementation of a Safer City Plan to be operationalized at the local level.
- Effective social crime prevention programmes exist.
- A security-conscious environmental design is adopted.
- A highly visible and effective policing service exists.
- Partnerships to increase community involvement in crime reduction are supported.
- Community education regarding crime prevention is improved and expanded upon.
- Security in targeted areas (such as transport routes and tourist areas) is improved through various measures, including surveillance cameras.[28]

The integrated development plan initiative in KwaZulu-Natal offers an example of how government at provincial level guides and assists the review of a strategic process in order to make the end product as appropriate and effective as possible. It is also an interesting example of how tackling crime prevention and public safety needs to be seen in a broad strategic context as an integral element of the process of municipal management.

State of Florida: Safe Neighborhood Act

The final example relates to the role of state legislation in providing for needs that are specific to a given area. The State of Florida has enacted Chapter 163.501, Florida Statutes, commonly called the Safe Neighborhood Act. It is based on legislative findings that the 'proliferation of crime' is one of the principal causes of the deterioration in business and residential neighbourhoods in the state. The act further declares that the safe neighbourhoods are 'the product of planning and implementation of appropriate environmental design concepts, comprehensive crime prevention programmes, land use recommendations and beautification techniques'.[29] Under the provisions of the act, local governmental entities are empowered to develop, redevelop, preserve and revitalize neighbourhoods using public funds that may be 'borrowed, expended, loaned and granted'.[30] For implementation purposes, the act defines a safe neighbourhood as falling within an 'improvement district', which means an area in which more than 75 per cent of the land is used for residential purposes, or in an area in which more than 75 per cent of the land is used for commercial, office, business or industrial purposes, excluding the land area used for public facilities.

It is now a requirement throughout KwaZulu-Natal that integrated development plans covering the major urban areas must include both crime prevention policies and women's safety audits

To be eligible for funding, the district must include a plan to reduce crime through the implementation of CPTED, environmental security or defensible space techniques, or through community policing innovations. The act provides districts with corporate powers, including the ability to enter into contracts, to accept grants and property, to make street and infrastructure improvements, and to raise funds by special assessments (following referendum), and provides other powers and responsibilities normally given to governmental agencies. Matching grants are available to the districts from the state up to US$100,000. Neighbourhood councils comprised of local citizens are authorized to monitor the implementation of improvement plans and to report violations to the governing bodies (which may be city or county commissions). Furthermore, the act requires that all improvement districts:

- Collect crime data in the district using surveys and other research techniques.
- Provide an analysis of crimes related to land use and environmental and physical conditions of the district, giving particular attention to factors that support or create opportunities for crime.
- Formulate and maintain short-range and long-range projects and plans that crime-to-environment analysis, including surveys and citizen participation data, has determined are applicable.

- Prepare and implement safe neighbourhood improvement plans, including modifications to existing street patterns and removal, razing, renovation, reconstruction, remodelling, relocation and improvement of existing structures and facilities.
- Coordinate with other agencies providing relevant informational, educational and crime prevention services.
- Ensure that all capital improvements within the district are consistent with the capital improvement elements of the applicable local government comprehensive plans (Florida requires all local governments to prepare comprehensive plans).[31]

Legislation by itself is often not enough, and that attention needs to be paid to the processes of implementation and to the resource needs that these imply

This example illustrates two points that are particularly significant. The first is the importance of legislative powers wherever they sit in the structure of governance within a country. The second is that legislation by itself is often not enough, and that attention needs to be paid to the processes of implementation and to the resource needs that these imply. The latter arises because sufficient funds have not been made available to implement the provisions of the act.[32] Indeed, the implementation of the act has been hampered by low levels of funding from the Florida Legislature. Consequently, only a relatively few communities across the state have been able to take advantage of its provisions. Nevertheless, its comprehensive crime prevention elements serve as a model for other jurisdictions in the US and elsewhere.

It is important to recognize that these examples show many levels and a wide range of possibilities at each level. Under these circumstances there is clearly scope for confusion about who does what, and room for under-performance created by inadequate liaison, coordination and communication. Multilayered approaches exist for good reasons and are an inevitable consequence of multilayered governmental structures; but it is important that the scope for approaches of this nature to create barriers and to underachieve is recognized and is vigorously addressed.

One of the biggest issues facing cities in developing countries where crime and violence are major problems is their capacity to cope

THE SIGNIFICANCE OF STAGES OF DEVELOPMENT

As Chapter 3 has demonstrated, it is rather simplistic to equate the level of development of a country with the existence of a problematic scale of urban crime and violence. The examples discussed above show that crime and violence can be a major problem in the urban areas of the developed world. To this, it should be added that this is often the perception of their citizens, even when, in comparison with other countries, crime and violence may not be particularly high.[33] Similarly, while it is clear that in some developing countries urban crime and violence are a major problem, this is by no means always the case in all developing countries. Nevertheless, there are several examples of developing countries where urban crime and violence are not only a major problem, but affect economic development. It is also the case that the level of development in a country (e.g. in terms of its processes of governance and the availability of skilled staff to operate them effectively) may affect the ability of that country to tackle problems of this nature, which creates a vicious circle requiring systematic intervention. One of the biggest issues facing cities in developing countries where crime and violence are major problems is their capacity to cope. This sense of having the 'capacity to cope', which is part of resilience, can be seen in several dimensions, some examples of which are as follows:

- Are the police and the judiciary willing and able to do their classic jobs of law enforcement so that the rule of law generally prevails?
- Does the political process (the nature of which varies hugely in cities across the world) recognize the range of functions that need to be involved in addressing crime and violence issues, and is it committed to doing so?
- Are the functions noted above broadly free from corruption, and where there is evidence that corruption might exist, is there a clear commitment to tackling it?
- Are the skills needed to support initiatives of this kind available to the process of governance in the city, and where there are shortfalls of this nature, are these identified and addressed?
- Is there a willingness to recognize the importance of community-based initiatives in tackling crime and violence issues, and a consequent willingness to make resources available to support community-level activities and to consult with communities fully and openly?
- Do agencies and communities work in genuine partnership with each other to ensure that their combined efforts work to maximum effect, preferably driven by a clear and agreed strategy?
- Is there an acknowledgement that tackling urban crime and violence has to be seen as a long-term commitment and is not the territory of 'quick fixes'?

These are not the only questions that arise when thinking about the 'capacity to cope' and resilience of systems of urban governance in this context; but the studies that have been done to date suggest that they are the kinds of questions that many cities in the developing world have struggled to answer in the affirmative. If this is not done, the gains will, at best, be short term since fundamental problems of lack of capacity in urban systems of governance will continue to cause problems that will probably undermine short-term achievements. It should also be remembered that there is a lot of evidence from studies, mainly in the Western world, that many elements of the criminal fraternity are highly adaptive.[34]

What this means, in practice, is that it cannot be assumed that gains in terms of improvements in tackling crime and violence on the part of the process of local governance will not be matched by adaptive responses by local criminal elements. This is one consideration that needs to be factored into the notion of improving local capacity as being a long-term commitment. Many of the examples that are used in the rest of this chapter are, therefore, about (or incorporate elements of) improving the capacity of processes of governance at the urban level to address issues of crime and violence since the evidence suggests that this may well be one of the most important needs in the urban areas of the developing world.

One of the ways in which these processes can be helped is through partnering with cities in other parts of the world that have relevant experience to offer in order to learn from that experience and also to speed up processes of capacity development. An important issue here is the need to borrow from experiences that are appropriate to local circumstances. A good illustration of this is the discussion of the extent to which planning systems (mainly) in the developed world are beginning to address crime prevention as an issue where they can have an impact through their control over physical development.

Even so, there were still many worries about how effective and how efficient the planning systems were,[35] and clear evidence that not all planners have responded constructively to messages about the role of planning in tackling issues of crime prevention.[36] These facts alone would suggest the need for a degree of caution before much younger, much less well-established, and much less well-staffed planning systems attempt to do what the British system is trying to do (see Box 4.3), even if they felt it was wholly appropriate to their local situations. Indeed, it may well be the case that one of the important issues in this field is the extent to which planning systems in the developing world are able to build concerns for crime prevention into their work. If they do not encompass crime prevention concerns, then that is one of the potential tools available for tackling crime and violence issues that will not be used. But clearly there are significant issues to be addressed before such practices are part of the planning lexicon in most parts of the world. This is further addressed in Chapter 10.

URBAN GOVERNANCE STRUCTURES AND PROCESSES

Tackling crime and violence is an issue of good urban governance. This section focuses on three issues. First, it examines some of the influences which affect the ability of processes of urban governance to address issues of crime and violence in their localities, when they are not in control of all the programmes or agencies that might need to contribute to such an effort. Therefore, it is about some of the challenges that crime and violence issues pose for urban governance. Second, it looks at two examples of efforts to undertake programmes of this nature in localities that have been very seriously affected by crime and violence: Diadema in the São Paulo metropolitan area of Brazil, and Port Moresby in Papua New Guinea. Finally, it discusses one of the big challenges that efforts of this kind too often face, which is the problem of corruption, both in the process of municipal government and directly in police operations.

It is important to note that in most cases the processes of urban governance involve exercising various types of control or influence over many of the levers that are available for use in tackling crime and violence. For example, while the arrangements for controlling the work of the police service vary from one country to another, and often involve structures covering much wider areas than individual cities, it is not unusual to see within such structures arrangements that acknowledge the particular issues experienced in the city and that provide for close working links between the police and the local authority. Similarly, attempts to get planning systems, by virtue of their control over new development, to consider crime prevention as part of this process almost always, in practice, happen at local authority level since this is the level at which most such decisions are taken and since it is usually at this level that planning services are controlled. Getting planning and police services to work together on crime and violence issues is still relatively new.[37]

Getting planning and police services to work together on crime and violence issues is still relatively new

It needs to be remembered that although this is a new field for planners, it is also very much a 'non-traditional' activity for the police. Available evidence suggests that only a limited number of police work in this kind of crime prevention activity compared with more traditional police operations.[38] It is also the case that local authorities will see issues of crime and violence as affecting two of their primary concerns: the quality of life of their citizens and the ability of their city to develop its economy. If these two factors are seen as being adversely affected by issues of crime and violence, then there is increased likelihood that the process of urban governance will seek to address this problem area as a major priority. So, while local authorities are, to a large extent, involved in dealing with crime and violence by virtue of their mainstream activities, there clearly are circumstances that can cause this issue to rise to, or near, the top of the agenda of urban priorities.

It can also be argued persuasively that the need to ensure that levels of crime and violence are low and that fear of crime does not intrude in any significant way into the life decisions that citizens make is an integral element in good urban governance:

Public safety is one of the necessities of urban life to which all citizens have the right of access

> *Urban governance is inextricably linked to the welfare of the citizenry. Good urban governance must enable women and men to access the benefits of urban citizenship. Good urban governance, based on the principle of urban citizenship, affirms that no man, woman or child can be denied access to the necessities of urban life, including adequate shelter, security of tenure, safe water, sanitation, a clean environment, health, education and nutrition, employment and public safety, and mobility. Through good urban governance, citizens are provided with the platform which will allow them to use their talents to the full to improve their social and economic conditions.*[39]

Public safety is one of the necessities of urban life to which all citizens have the right of access. But it is clear that this desirable goal is not attained in many cities in the world. It is also clear that local authorities cannot rely simply on exercising their mainstream functions efficiently and effectively in order to change this situation. So, what is needed over and above what might be described as the qualities of good public administration in order to move in this direction? Three qualities, in particular, seem to stand out in this context: political will, sustained commitment to action, and strong and visible leadership.

Some examples of the application of these qualities are given in the following sub-sections, which utilize two cases, in particular, where major efforts have been made or are in the process of being made to tackle very high levels of crime and violence. These are Diadema, a suburb in the São Paulo urban region of Brazil and Port Moresby in Papua New Guinea.

Diadema, São Paulo

Diadema is a relatively recent creation as a suburb of São Paulo (Brazil). Its population grew at an annual average rate of 16 per cent between 1950 and 1980, before slowing to an annual average rate of 2.2 per cent over the next two decades.[40] These growth rates are well in excess of those experienced by São Paulo. Consequently, Diadema has become the second most densely developed location in Brazil. This rapid growth, much of it caused by in-migration of some of Brazil's poorest people, seems to have overwhelmed the capacity of civic institutions to cope, and one of the consequences of this was the emergence of 'frontier violence'.[41] This relates to the fact that Diadema's high level of violence had features in common with some periods of pioneer settlement in the history of other parts of the world – precarious forms of territorial occupation, absence of government and poor local organization.

By the1990s, Diadema experienced murder rates which were among the highest in the world – 141 per 100,000 individuals in 1999. Gang violence and intense inter-gang rivalry were widespread. This period was characterized by anarchy and complete breakdown of law and order. The inability of the police and legal system to tackle crime and violence meant that a group of people called the *justiceiros* dished out their own version of law and order, which included killings. All of this had a generally negative impact on the quality of life of the people and on the opportunities available to them. Problems of this magnitude are clearly not going to be tackled by a single initiative; but critical to the process of turning this situation around was the desire of some of the mayors of Diadema over a period of time to make a difference. The progress that Diadema has experienced over the past decade or so is described as follows:

> *We easily can exaggerate the progress in Diadema. Its broad central avenues, with bus terminals, supermarkets, fast food restaurants and automobile distributorships, no longer create the impression of a poor city... However ... homicide rates are still high, despite their reduction in recent years. The average monthly income of family heads in Diadema in 2000 was half the average for the municipality of São Paulo. But the combined effect of its political structure, of the strengthening of its public institutions and the expansion of commerce has been very positive, showing how much its people value stability. Diadema has also shown that the problem of homicides can be reduced fairly quickly with a political effort based on a community consensus and more effective action by the authorities. Four decades after the start of the migratory surge of precarious settlement, Diadema no longer is a city trapped in a downward spiral of apparently insoluble crises. Instead, it is showing the strength of democracy and is emerging on the crest of a process of civilization.*[42]

One initiative that seems to have been important in this process was the enactment and the enforcement of a law to close all bars in the city after 11.00 pm. The reason for this was that a high proportion of the murders in the city took place in or near these bars between 11.00 pm and 2.00 am.[43] The process of making this happen involved a protracted period of discussion in the city council around three issues, in particular. These were a recognition of the need to confront many vested interests if such a new law was not going to be undermined by exceptions;[44] the need for an intense campaign of publicity and persuasion; and then the need to commit to a major enforcement effort which would have to involve partnership between several public institutions that had not always worked in the past. This seems to have had an immediate effect since the monthly homicide rate in the first month of enforced closures fell to eight from previous figures that were typically four or five times higher than this.[45]

One element in this process may well be the fact that homicide rates in the Greater São Paulo area were falling anyway during the early years of the 21st century, with Diadema being both a leading element in this process and a beneficiary of the general economic forces that seem to have been helping it. One of the particular characteristics of this process is that locations that were once crime hotspots are being turned over to new forms of economic activity that are pushing out crimes and criminals, as the following assessment illustrates:

> *The public space exposed to violence is shrinking. As in the rest of Greater São Paulo, few streets in Diadema remain without paving and lighting. In the periphery, a spontaneous quarantine is developing that tends to isolate bandits from citizens who want to live in peace and avoid problems. Each group recognizes and respects the sphere of the other, but keeps its distance. A force reducing the space for violence is the expansion of commerce at all levels, from the new supermarkets to street sellers and small neighbourhood repair shops, to women selling candy and cake out of their homes. At the edge of Jardim Campanario, a vacant municipal lot used to be a killing ground*

Box 4.5 Key conclusions from the 2003 Port Moresby survey of people aged 15 to 35, undertaken for its Safer Cities Programme

The key action points were summarized according to the following four headings:

Law enforcement:

- Improve professionalism, transparency, effectiveness, efficiency and accountability in government, police and criminal justice systems.
- Focus more attention on crime prevention and restorative justice, and on the re-socialization and rehabilitation of offenders.
- Link traditional village courts and mediation structures to the criminal justice system.
- Strengthen coordination among law enforcement agencies.

Community development:

- Improve community access to basic urban services.
- Involve youth and marginalized groups in decision-making.
- Strengthen the family–community–church partnership to engage youths at risk.

Urban management and planning:

- Principles of safety, convenience and sustainability should be integral features of a functioning urban environment.
- Improve urban governance through broad-based partnerships.
- Include squatter settlements in planning and management, including a review of land tenure opportunities.
- Strengthen the participation and coordination capabilities of the staff involved in planning and management.

Culture and family:

- Promote social cohesion through programmes aimed at maintaining social harmony.
- Educate communities on the benefits of crime prevention.
- Encourage mediation and conflict resolution at the family level.

A key need was seen to be the *strengthening of institutional capacity*. Further recommendations in this regard included:

- Strengthen the ability of existing institutions to manage urban safety and security issues.
- Promote public, private and community interfaces to address safety and security issues.
- Improve the capacity of community groups to prepare and implement crime prevention action plans.
- Improve coordination of the roles and responsibilities of the institutions involved in urban safety and security.

Source: Boamah and Stanley, 2007

> *and a dump for corpses and the carcasses of stolen cars after their saleable parts were removed. Now this space is occupied by SESI, a sports and swimming complex used by local families, with new high-rise apartments for the middle class in the background.*[46]

The case of Diadema illustrates what can be achieved by political will, sustained commitment to action, effective partnership, and strong and visible leadership, starting off from a very poor position where crime and violence were clearly impeding the progress of the settlement and its people. Nevertheless, Diadema still has a long way to go before its homicide rates are down to what would be regarded as 'normal' rates in many other parts of the world. For example, its 2003 homicide rate of 74 per 100,000 people, while being little more than half the rate that it had experienced four years previously, was still 50 per cent larger than that for Greater São Paulo and more than ten times the rates experienced in many other world cities.[47] Clearly, the need here is to continue with the sustained commitment to action that has been exhibited in recent years, and to recognize that this will need to be seen as a long-term initiative.

Port Moresby, Papua New Guinea

Port Moresby in Papua New Guinea has several themes in common with Diadema. Probably the most significant is the very high crime rates that the city has experienced, particularly the high levels of violence associated with criminal activities – 48 per cent of crimes in Port Moresby involve a high level of violence. The city has a population of over 330,000, which makes it the biggest urban centre in Papua New Guinea. Its population is characterized by a rapid growth rate of 3.6 per cent per annum, a high proportion of migrants, high cultural and ethnic diversity, and a very young structure.[48] The rapid rate of urban growth, coupled with inadequate land legislation, has resulted in the creation of some 40 squatter settlements around the city, which house about 50 per cent of its population. These areas are regarded as havens of criminal activity. Another characteristic that appears to be a significant factor in the city's experience of crime and violence is its very high reliance on the informal economy for employment, given limited opportunities in the formal sector. This means that young men often have little experience of employment and resort to other means of making a living, often in association with gang membership. Box 4.5 summarizes the key points from a survey of 1500 young people aged between 15 and 35, undertaken in 2003 as part of the process of establishing Port Moresby's Safer Cities Programme.

The points summarized in Box 4.5 undoubtedly represent a huge agenda, and the Port Moresby Safer Cities Programme is only in the early stages of tackling it. At present, it can only be seen as a useful case study of what is involved in establishing a sound basis of understanding in order for a start to be made in such a difficult situation. But this is of value in itself because sometimes the process of making a start can appear bewildering given the nature and intensity of the problem. Inevitably, the first phase of this programme has concentrated on the things needed to get it started and running effectively.

There can be little doubt that if the Port Moresby Safer Cities Programme is to succeed, it will need to be seen as a relatively long-term activity, and to sustain such a programme successfully over such a period will require the three characteristics noted earlier: political will, sustained commitment to action, and strong and visible leadership. Early signs indicate that these characteristics will be present in the Port Moresby initiative.

Corruption

Campaigns to reduce and, if possible, eliminate corruption are of considerable importance to the prospects for success in tackling crime and violence

Another frequent problem in developing countries is corruption, especially in the various arms of municipal government and the police. In essence, the very organs that citizens should be looking up to in tackling problems of crime and violence are not trusted because they are corrupt, or at least are seen as having very questionable linkages with criminal elements. Where this is the situation, it seems likely that efforts to tackle crime and violence will be undermined by relationships of this nature. It is clear that the process of rebuilding citizens' trust of their local government structures and police services is fundamental to any campaign against crime and violence. For these reasons, campaigns to reduce and, if possible, eliminate corruption are of considerable importance to the prospects for success in tackling crime and violence. These, too, require the same characteristics as noted above – political will, sustained commitment to action, and strong and visible leadership.

Although in both cases it is clear that wide-ranging programmes of action were necessary in Diadema and will be necessary in Port Moresby, it is difficult to see how problems on the scales exhibited in these two cities can be tackled without strong political support from the outset, and sustained for significant periods of time. Another necessary condition for success appears to be that efforts need to be made to ensure that the implementing arms of the local authority and other public agencies are fully behind action programmes and are pulling in the same directions. In order to achieve this, the role of the decision-making processes is crucial: the link between a local diagnosis or audit, the development of a strategy, possibly through consultation and involvement of different actors, and its implementation through targeted actions should support buy-in and involvement of different departments and actors, including communities. Partnership mechanisms are one of the most important tools available to achieve these latter objectives, and this is the subject of a fuller discussion later in the chapter.

The key point to emphasize is that the actions described in this section have to be seen as part of a long-term commitment on the part of local authorities, as well as central and regional/provincial/state governments, to reducing crime and violence to the point where their effects upon the lives of citizens and the prosperity of the city are under control. The kind of leadership role needed to sustain this is likely to fall to the city's political leaders. This also needs to be complemented by sustained support and commitment from the heads of local authorities and key programme areas. This does not in any way denigrate the contribution of community-based initiatives or deny the necessity of full community engagement with processes of this nature. But experience suggests that there is an essential role for political leaders committed to the view that safer cities are an essential aspect of good governance and that good governance is a fundamental key to successful crime prevention initiatives.

TYPES OF POLICY RESPONSE TO PROBLEMS OF CRIME AND VIOLENCE

There are many kinds of responses to issues of crime and violence, with evidence suggesting that the most successful ones are those that are tailored to the particular circumstances being addressed

There are many kinds of responses to issues of crime and violence, with evidence suggesting that the most successful ones are those that are tailored to the particular circumstances being addressed, rather than those that are essentially standardized based upon experience elsewhere. It is possible to classify these responses into six broad groups of approaches as follows:

1 *Enhancing urban safety and security through effective urban planning, design and governance.* Poor planning, design and management have been identified as among the constellation of factors associated with crime and violence. This group of activities is therefore mainly about manipulating and maintaining the physical environment, which is the setting within which most crimes take place.
2 *Community-based approaches to enhancing urban safety and security.* Activities of this nature are essentially about getting communities to take ownership of initiatives. Very often this will mean that community groups or individuals will either be the source of project ideas or will play leading roles in implementing them.
3 *Strengthening formal criminal justice systems and policing.* This could be seen as the 'classical' approach to problems of crime and violence, regarding them as being the primary territory of the police and the criminal justice system. Initiatives in this area are also often undertaken at the city or even broader scale.
4 *Reduction of risk factors.* These approaches tend to focus on groups that are likely to be perpetrators of crime or on groups that are at risk of being victims of crime. The aim here is either to reduce the likelihood of such groups getting involved in criminal activities or to reduce the problems faced by victims.
5 *Non-violent resolution of conflicts.* This essentially is about seeking to manage situations in which conflicts often arise in order to reduce the likelihood of this happening or to find solutions to the problems that do not result in violence.
6 *Strengthening of social capital.* This includes improving the ability of people, groups and communities as a whole to challenge the problems of crime and violence and the provision of community facilities that facilitate or provide more opportunities for processes of this nature.

There are two points that need to be made about these policy responses. First, they are not watertight compartments but involve considerable areas of overlap. A simple illustration of this is the fact that a programme targeting young men because this group commits a high proportion of crime will often seek to deflect their activities in more acceptable directions, including investing in strengthening social capital in areas such as education, sport and recreation, and cultural activities. Second, it is not necessarily a question of choosing between these approaches because it is possible to combine elements of several or all of them. Indeed, available evidence suggests that a carefully managed programme that combines several elements of these approaches in ways that recognize the connections between them and their appropriateness to the local context has a better chance of success than merely focusing on a single element. This is because deeply-embedded problems of crime and violence are rarely amenable to simple, one-dimensional solutions. Programmes of this nature are often generated and promoted through partnerships of various kinds.

Enhancing urban safety and security through effective urban planning, design and governance

The process of enhancing urban safety and security through effective urban planning, design and governance is still in its infancy in many parts of the world, although in some countries such as the UK, the US and Canada it is more advanced. The attempts of the UK government to get the planning system to regard crime prevention as one of its major objectives in the drive to secure sustainable development have already been referred to earlier. But such a 'top-down' process would be of little value by itself unless it is accompanied by effective action at the local level. The Bradford case study prepared for this Global Report[49] explores this area (see Box 4.6). It is clear from this case that key issues here include the following:

- An important role for the police service based upon its experience in handling crime is providing advice to the key players in the development process about how the opportunity to commit crimes can be reduced or eliminated through the ways in which buildings and spaces are designed.
- There should be a recognition of the opportunity provided by the development control part of the planning service to ensure that crime issues are carefully considered in approving development proposals, including the possibility that projects that do not do this might be refused planning permission.
- Since the planning system in the UK is 'plan led',[50] appropriate policies need to be in the development plan to provide a formal basis for this activity.
- Effective working relationships must exist between all of the key players in the development process and, in particular, in this context between planners and police architectural liaison officers.[51]

Deeply-embedded problems of crime and violence are rarely amenable to simple, one-dimensional solutions

The Bradford case study demonstrates that much has been achieved in moving towards a situation where crime prevention is well integrated within the planning process. However, it also shows that there is still work to be done in developing effective working relationships and agreed stances between the key players. This is clearly one of the important lessons that can be drawn from this case – the major elements can be in place, but a lot still depends upon effective working relationships between the key players.

Available evidence shows that CPTED-based approaches to the processes of shaping new development

Box 4.6 The Bradford Unitary Development Plan on planning for crime prevention

The Bradford Unitary Development Plan (which is the formal development plan for the City of Bradford) was adopted in October 2005. It includes Policy D4, which is its most specific policy on planning for crime prevention, and its central message is that 'Development proposals should be designed to ensure a safe and secure environment and reduce the opportunities for crime.' At its heart, what this is seeking to do is to get developers to think about crime prevention as part of the design process, rather than as a later add-on, so that when proposals are presented to the planning system for formal approval, crime prevention is already integral to them. As such, it draws heavily on the traditions of CPTED, as expressed through the British police's Secured by Design scheme. To this end, developers are expected to think, in particular, about the following issues:

- natural surveillance of public and semi-private spaces, especially in relation to entrances to developments, paths, play spaces, open spaces and car parks;
- defensible space, which should be created with the clear definition, differentiation and robust separation of public, private and semi-private space so that all spaces are clearly defined and adequately protected in terms of use and ownership;
- lighting of the development and, in particular, of streets and paths;
- design and layout of pedestrian, cycle and vehicular routes into and within the site, including how these integrate with existing patterns;
- landscaping and planting, especially to avoid the creation of hiding places and dark or secluded areas.

The policy also advises developers to make early contact with the police architectural liaison officer for Bradford when considering significant development proposals, and it promises that more detailed guidance will be published in future to supplement the outline provided by Policy D4.

Source: Kitchen, 2007

have an important contribution to make to crime prevention.[52] This approach, which focuses on the setting of crime, links crime prevention and reduction to changes in physical design. To date, most of the experience of applying this approach has been in the developed world. But subject to two important conditions, there is no reason why approaches of this nature cannot be successful in developing countries. The first of these conditions is the need for support for these approaches to be generated among the development communities of such localities so that attempts to apply them do not become a running battle between developers, planners and the police. The second condition is that appropriately trained staff must be available in order to put these approaches into practice. These issues are further taken up in Chapter 10.

Available evidence shows that crime prevention through environmental design-based approaches to the processes of shaping new development have an important contribution to make to crime prevention

A final example of a type of initiative that is common in many parts of the world is the use of closed circuit television cameras (CCTVs). The UK is an example of a country which has deployed CCTV cameras widely during recent years, not just in public places such as shopping centres and car parks, but also in some residential areas.[53] This latter element has been very controversial in the US because of the implications for civil liberties of installing cameras in residential areas. There are other areas of controversy, such as who owns and operates CCTV cameras and what uses those responsible are allowed to make of the pictures taken. But the biggest controversy probably centres on the question of whether or not they work as crime prevention tools. Do they actually deter people from committing crimes, or do they just make the subsequent process of tracking down perpetrators easier? Do they ease people's fears of crime in public places, or after a while do people get used to the presence of cameras and take little or no account of them? Do they encourage adaptive behaviour by criminals, which might include the displacement of crime into other areas where cameras are not ubiquitous? These are questions that are still hotly debated; but what is clear is that CCTV cameras have now become a commonplace part of initiatives against crime and violence in many parts of the world.[54]

Planning and design interventions are generally geared towards reducing vulnerability of targets (people and property) by increasing protection and discouraging delinquents. They also reduce general risk factors by reducing opportunities for violence. Finally, they favour the development of other resilience factors, linked to socialization, community involvement and policing. They are therefore largely overlapping and contributing to other types of interventions.

Community-based approaches clearly have an important role to play in the litany of responses to crime and violence

Community-based approaches to urban safety and security

Community-based approaches clearly have an important role to play in the litany of responses to crime and violence. It is, however, important to understand that this can mean a wide range of possible ways in different local circumstances. At one end of the spectrum, some approaches are about helping the development and implementation of initiatives where the main impetus is from the community itself, and where community members will have an ongoing responsibility for the initiative. In such instances, the role of the public sector is likely to be primarily an enabling one. At the other end of the spectrum, community involvement in place-based initiatives mounted by the local authority seems to be essential if they are to have the maximum chance of success: such initiatives should be 'done with' communities rather than 'done to' them. Communities may not be the initiators; but they still have a central role to play in shaping initiatives based both upon their local knowledge and upon the fact that, in their daily lives as residents, what they do or do not do can make a difference to what happens on the ground. It is also possible that the role of communities and their representatives may grow throughout the life of a project, so that they may take over as local wardens or stewards once community acceptance has been secured. So a wide range of project types might fit under this heading; but central to all of them is the concept of community engagement as being vital to the success of such projects.

It is also important to understand that community responses to crime and violence are not just about communities banding together to tackle problems, whether or not this involves working in partnership with the state. People, where they have or can put together the financial resources, also respond to problems of crime and violence through increasing urban segregation, with the affluent often choosing to live in gated communities or closed condominiums which they regard safer than the rest of the city. This has been extensively studied in Latin American cities, where the leading work has traced how rising crime and insecurity in São Paulo transformed it from a city characterized by open circulation to one with a large number of 'fortified enclaves'.[55] This came about not so much through any act of deliberate public policy, but rather through the exercise of individual and community choices on a considerable scale by those who were rich enough to make such choices. While this is wholly understandable from the point of view of such individuals, the effect on both the physical and the social functioning of the city can be very negative.

The above discussion is largely about how relatively wealthy elites in São Paulo have chosen to segregate themselves physically from the problems being experienced in the rest of the city. The conclusion should not be drawn that processes of this nature inevitably leave the urban poor in such cities helpless and unable to do anything about their circumstances. For example, the story of how crime and violence have been addressed in Diadema is about taking positive action to tackle crime and violence in part of the same São Paulo conurbation of 'fortified enclaves'. It is mainly about the importance of political leadership, about the process of partnership between key agencies, and about determined action to tackle deep-seated problems.[56]

But one element of the Diadema story is also about the community itself, and about the desire of that community to see the extreme problems being tackled and to take advantage of the new opportunities being provided in order to build better ways of life. What is illustrated here are two sets of phenomena that appear to exist side by side: private action by elites to insulate themselves from what they see as unacceptable levels of crime and violence in the city, and public and community action in some or all parts of those cities designed to tackle these problems.

Community involvement in Toronto, Canada

A good example of a city where several different forms of community involvement exist in its approaches to crime prevention and safety is the city of Toronto (Canada).[57] Toronto is one of the world's most ethnically diverse cities, with people from over 200 nations who speak more than 100 languages. As such, it epitomizes the point that 'community' means very many different things when looking at large cities. One of the most striking elements of the 2004 Toronto Community Safety Plan 2004[58] is the emphasis on crime prevention through social development. This is the idea that spatially targeted or area-based interventions are necessary to tackle the particular problems of specific neighbourhoods. The approach recognizes the different social and structural factors at work in each of these neighbourhoods, and programmes seek to build on the strengths of the neighbourhoods.

At the time that the Toronto case study for this Global Report was being drafted in 2006, 13 'at-risk' neighbourhoods[59] had been identified both for preparing crime prevention programmes and for securing the resources to support them. The approach adopted in each of these areas was to develop a Neighbourhood Action Plan through partnership between the city council, residents, community leaders, the police and relevant local agencies. The intention behind this process is that the interventions that are considered to be appropriate in each case should build the local community's capacity to improve safety and to prevent crime, especially violent crime. Examples of these initiatives are summarized in Box 4.7.

Although this approach appears to have considerable potential to reduce crime, it is too early in the life of this initiative to offer much by way of evaluation. But three elements stand out: its wide-ranging and imaginative nature; the various ways in which local communities are directly involved in programme delivery; and the targeted nature of what is being attempted. This set of activities also illustrates the point made earlier about not seeing initiatives as if they are in tightly sealed compartments because the examples in Box 4.7 illustrate a range of ways in which communities can get involved and could also be seen as illustrating initiatives on reduction of risk (particularly the emphasis on activities to keep youth away from crime) and strengthening of social capital.

Classical response to crime and violence: Strengthening formal criminal justice systems and policing

Strengthening formal criminal justice systems and policing could be seen as the classical response to problems of crime and violence. This is because the criminal justice systems and policing were seen to be the main societal tools designed to address this issue before the broadening of the response agenda in recent years. However, criminal justice and police systems are often perceived by the public at large as being part of the problem rather than part of the solution. Many people would like to be in the position of being able to engage in discussions with their local police force about crime prevention initiatives in their areas, but feel unable to do so because either they do not trust the police or they feel that there are protective links between the police and criminal groups.[60]

The case of Diadema discussed earlier contains elements of this in the days when its streets were characterized by lawlessness. One of the issues that this initiative had to tackle was the need to develop more positive relations between the police and the local communities.[61] In this case, improvements to policing, in particular through the efforts of a charismatic senior police officer (who himself was subsequently murdered), were very important in securing the success of the initiative to close bars in the city much earlier than previously. Therefore, improving the performance of these 'classical' services that tackle crime and violence has an important part to play; in particular, actions to tackle corruption are central to efforts to improve the confidence that communities have in these services. This requires implementation of initiatives that improve the ability of the police to respond to community needs and priorities and the ability of those communities to participate in prevention efforts. It is difficult to imagine measures to tackle crime and violence being successful if they have to try to bypass criminal justice and police systems, even where they are seen as uncooperative or operating in ways that support criminal activities.[62]

Criminal justice and police systems are often perceived by the public at large as being part of the problem rather than part of the solution

Changing approaches to policing in Hong Kong

The Hong Kong case study undertaken for this report[63] suggests that changes in styles and processes of policing since the 1960s appear to have been an important factor in the achievement and maintenance of Hong Kong's low crime rates. The essential change here has been a move away from a traditional 'command-and-control' approach and towards the evolution of a more community-based approach to policing. The various stages of this process are summarized in Box 4.8.

It is difficult to imagine measures to tackle crime and violence being successful if they have to try to bypass criminal justice and police systems

This story of a change process over a protracted period of time illustrates the point that significant adaptations to complex structures such as police forces are unlikely to be accomplished quickly, partly because there is likely to be intense debate about what the right steps are in the particular circumstances and partly because the task of 'winning the hearts and minds' of all the staff members involved is a large one. Nevertheless, it is of fundamental importance that changes of this nature can and do happen if police forces are to play their full part in the fight against crime and violence.

Guardianship approaches in New York City's Bryant Park

One related type of initiative that seems to be becoming more common, and can work well in appropriate circum-

Box 4.7 Examples of initiatives undertaken as part of the Crime Prevention through Social Development programme of Toronto's Community Safety Strategy

Youth Opportunity Initiatives: Training
This initiative is about providing opportunities for young people to develop employment-related skills and to obtain relevant experience through activities such as internships and apprenticeships. It involves close cooperation with community organizations, businesses and trade unions.

Youth Opportunity Initiatives: Jobs for Youth
The provincial government has provided Cdn$28.5 million in funding over three years so that the city can offer summer employment opportunities to youth from the priority neighbourhoods. Community-based organizations administer the funds, recruit and select job candidates, and work with employers. In 2004, over 300 young people living in Toronto's 'priority' neighbourhoods secured summer employment.

Youth Challenge Fund
The Province of Ontario has a Cdn$15 million fund to support local programmes, training and jobs for youth living in Toronto's 13 'at-risk' neighbourhoods. In particular, this supports ideas for community safety that come from people living in these areas, and community organizations are encouraged to apply for funds that will enable projects of this nature to be implemented. In April 2006, the premier of Ontario challenged the private sector to match this public investment and promised that if that happened, further private-sector contributions up to a maximum of another Cdn$15 million would then be matched over the next three years, taking the total up to a potential Cdn$60 million.

The Community Crisis Response Programme
This programme focuses on getting city services to respond in a coordinated manner to support neighbourhoods following 'trauma-inducing events', such as killings or violent assaults. Programme staff work with neighbourhood residents to identify and implement appropriate and culturally sensitive interventions that are intended to facilitate the recovery process.

Community Use of Schools
This recognizes that there is often a very valuable resource locked up in schools during evenings, weekends and the summer months, and so schools have been opened in a number of neighbourhoods to provide free access to community and recreation programmes. The aim of this is to break down financial barriers and to promote participation in a range of community activities.

Grassroots/Community-Based Youth Services
These services are essentially about providing support for not-for-profit community-based agencies to provide programmes and services for youth in at-risk neighbourhoods. These include violence prevention, anger management, conflict resolution, mentorship and peer support, individual and family counselling, academic programming, life skills training, and gang prevention/exit programmes.

Expanded Healthcare Centres
Healthcare facilities are being improved in at-risk neighbourhoods to ensure that teams with a wide range of skills are available locally to deliver a range of programmes and support services for youth, young children and families.

Source: Thompson and Gartner, 2007

One related type of initiative that seems to be becoming more common, and can work well in appropriate circumstances, is the use of uniformed security staff

Uniformed staff can convey to the public the same sense of presence as police officers do and, in practice, can provide a level of visibility that stretched policing resources are unable to achieve

stances, is the use of uniformed security staff. There is an example of this initiative in the New York case study for this Global Report, which examined the regeneration of Bryant Park. This had become a major problem area during the 1980s, described by local businesses as being a 'war zone';[64] but a series of physical and social improvements has turned around both public perception of the park and its economic impact on the surrounding area. One of these improvements has been the establishment of a visible security presence in the park, which is particularly important because while physical improvements tend to take place at a particular point in time, an ongoing security presence helps in maintaining the quality of what has been achieved and therefore its attractiveness to the general public. In addition, the visible presence of uniformed security staff can change public perception of how safe a place is. Both of these elements seem to have been important in the Bryant Park case.

Strictly speaking, uniformed security staff are not part of the police force, although there are various forms of relationships here. For instance, some of them are former police officers. The important point is that uniformed staff can convey to the public the same sense of presence as police officers do and, in practice, can provide a level of visibility that stretched policing resources are unable to achieve. This may well be the kind of measure which is more limited in its value when it is undertaken by itself; but in the Bryant Park case, this was undertaken alongside other types of activities. It must be emphasized that uniformed security staff operate in cities of developing countries as well. They are quite visible in 'public spaces' in cities such as Kingston, Johannesburg, Lagos and Nairobi. It is also important to acknowledge that such arrangements do not always make a positive contribution to tackling problems of crime and violence. But in appropriate circumstances, initiatives of this kind can add considerable value to what the police and criminal justice systems would otherwise achieve.

Informal and formal approaches to policing and conflict management

The emergence of vigilante groups is a very common way in which poor and not so poor community groups respond to escalating levels of crime and violence in the perceived absence or ineffectiveness of the police and judicial system.

Box 4.8 Changing styles of policing in Hong Kong since the late 1960s

The process of shifting from a traditional 'command-and-control' form of policing in Hong Kong, where the priority of the colonial government (including the police) was to provide an environment where trade could be conducted smoothly, to one which is much more community based, has taken place over a period of 40 years. One key element in this process of change is that the police force has become very largely a force drawn from local communities, rather than one that was more typical of a colonial military organization housed in barracks – and the likelihood is that this major change in the composition of the police force has been an important element in the growing public acceptance of the police force in Hong Kong over this period.

A trigger for change appears to have been the recognition during the late 1960s that the traditional style was a factor in three major civil disturbances during that decade, and that it had also contributed to much public hostility to the police. A factor that was clearly of considerable importance in this particular case was the reversion of Hong Kong from British colonial to Chinese control in 1997, not only in the sense that this date was a watershed in its own right, but also because the fact that this change was due to happen clearly influenced events during the preceding years. The major phases of change are as follows:

- A tentative start was made between 1968 and 1973, where the main focus was on improved communications with the public.
- From the early to mid 1970s, this process was intensified, with an emphasis on promoting police–community relationships as a two-way process and on involving the public in the fight against crime. This included major campaigns such as the Fight Violent Crime Campaign, the establishment of the Police Community Relations Officer Scheme in 1974 and the creation of neighbourhood police units. By 1983, 90 neighbourhood police units were in operation throughout Hong Kong. A major effort was also put into liaison with schools, and today the Junior Police Call Scheme is still the largest youth organization in Hong Kong, with 505 primary school clubs, 383 secondary school clubs, and 144,203 members territory wide.
- There was an element of retrenchment in the community relations efforts of the police in the 1980s, where the emphasis during a period of reorganization was on trying to use limited resources as effectively as possible. Neighbourhood police units were scrapped; but to help make up for this loss, Neighbourhood Watch schemes were piloted during the mid 1980s in two public estates that had experienced a surge of burglaries and sexual offences. It was evident during this period that there were some tensions among police senior managers between those who favoured more conservative approaches and those who favoured approaches based on community policing; but by the late 1980s it had become clear that the latter was the preferred model.
- In the period of the run-up to the reversion to Chinese control in 1997, 1989 saw the appointment of the first Chinese commissioner of police and the last British governor, who brought with him in 1992 the idea of a customer-based service culture. The development of a culture of service throughout Hong Kong government activities as a whole included a public pledge to transform the then Royal Hong Kong Police into a 'service of quality'.
- The final stage, which continues, has been the adoption of more localized perspectives and the promotion of a new image of a people's force with its citizen-centred slogan of serving the community, including embracing modern information technology. This process has had to cope with a less quiescent public than in the past; and so periodically there are still tensions between the police and groups in the community which continue to raise questions about the balance being struck between serving the community and fighting crime.

Source: Broadhurst et al, 2007

The emergence of vigilante groups is a very common way in which poor and not so poor community groups respond to escalating levels of crime and violence in the perceived absence or ineffectiveness of the police and judicial system

This has become an increasingly familiar phenomenon in Brazil, Ghana, Jamaica, Kenya, Nigeria, Peru, South Africa and Tanzania.[65] Vigilante groups have also started to emerge in many other countries for the same reasons. Though well-intentioned initially, vigilantism has obvious limitations. The activities of vigilante groups have often been abused in that they have the tendency to degenerate into anarchy and become extra legal, whereby innocent persons are assaulted, maimed or even killed in cases of mistaken identity or false accusations. In addition, vigilante groups have been used to settle personal and political scores. All of this further exacerbates the problems of violence and lawlessness. The solution to problems of this nature is for the state to examine why vigilante groups have come into being, and to see whether this reflects a failure of formal systems of policing and criminal justice that should be addressed.

In terms of changes to the justice system, one development that has been visible in several parts of the world is the idea of restorative justice. This is based on ideas that were originally part of tribal or clan-based cultures that stand the risk of disappearing in the face of modernization. For example, with respect to Port Moresby, Box 4.5 indicates that there is significant public support for reconnecting with former tribal systems of justice. The idea here is that the harm caused by criminal behaviour is emphasized, and, as a consequence, restorative justice models encourage communication between the crime victim and the offender in order to facilitate healing, reconciliation and rehabilitation. A similar system known as penal mediation was established in France in 1992.[66] It entails finding a negotiated solution to conflicts, where perpetrators are made to face their victims; if restitution is made, the case is not taken to court. Another example of this is the idea of family group conferences, which have been part of Maori culture in New Zealand for centuries and were adopted by Israel during the 1980s as part of the development of that country's restorative justice strategies. Several Latin American countries have also implemented projects of this

The activities of vigilante groups have often been abused in that they have the tendency to degenerate into anarchy ... whereby innocent persons are assaulted, maimed or even killed nature. For example, in 1995 the Colombian government launched two *Casas de Justicia* (Houses of Justice), which are based on face-to-face meetings between parties in conflict and which include the provision of access to legal services for low-income families.

Strategies aimed at reducing risk factors

The main elements in strategies designed to achieve the reduction of risk factors appear to be measures to tackle violence against women, programmes to prevent youth (particularly young males) from slipping into a life of crime, as well as programmes to help people in both of these groups who have become victims of crime.

In some parts of the world violence against women appears to be deeply etched in society; but it is also clear that there is growing pressure for this to be ended

Focusing on violence against women

In some parts of the world violence against women appears to be deeply etched in society; but it is also clear that there is growing pressure for this to be ended as part of securing basic human rights for women. One publication seeking to offer practical advice to this end in Eastern and Southern Africa notes:

> *The call for an end to violence against women is growing ever louder. Increasingly, women's rights are seen as a cornerstone in the promotion of human rights and the realization of social justice. Clearly, women cannot live free, safe and dignified lives when violence, or the threat of violence, pervades their public and private experiences. Without the basic right to live free from fear, all other gains are compromised… The challenge for activists now is to translate these visions of women's rights into practical projects and activities that promote meaningful change in the lives of women, men, families and communities.*[67]

The process of tackling domestic violence requires long-term commitment since it often seeks to address cultural habits and practices that are deeply ingrained

The approach suggested for tackling domestic violence against women has five phases:

1. *Community assessment:* gathering information about attitudes and beliefs, and beginning to build relationships with community members.
2. *Raising awareness:* increasing awareness of domestic violence and its consequences, not just among the community at large, but specifically with various governmental and professional sectors.
3. *Building networks:* encouraging and supporting community members and professional sectors to begin considering action and changes that uphold women's right to safety.
4. *Integrating action:* making action against domestic violence part of everyday life and of the policies and practices of institutions.
5. *Consolidating efforts:* strengthening activities in order to ensure their sustainability, continued growth and progress. Such actions might well include gathering data to provide evidence of what has been achieved since positive evidence of this nature can of itself provide a stimulus to further action.[68]

This is just one example of an initiative to offer practical advice and support in tackling domestic violence in a part of the world where this is a major problem. The process of tackling domestic violence requires long-term commitment since it often seeks to address cultural habits and practices that are deeply ingrained. This requires committed leadership and the ability to keep going in the face of setbacks. An important element that has been promoted widely and increasingly by both activists and municipalities is the development of partnerships and joint initiatives, in which voluntary work, institutional support and access to networks and infrastructures is facilitated by pulling together resources and capacities. One of the trends during recent years in this context has been that what were often previously isolated initiatives of this kind have not only been supported by international organizations, but have also been able to link with other groups in other parts of the world for advice, support and encouragement. Initiatives of this nature are much facilitated by the development of electronic communication, including the internet,[69] and by the ability of groups to come together at major world events to exchange experiences.[70]

Women's safety audits

A starting point for many projects that seek to tackle violence against women is the use of women's safety audits. Essentially, these involve exploratory walks by groups of three to six people, mainly women designed to identify specific problems in the local environment from a woman's safety perspective. At each specific site, participants identify where the potential for crime is high or where women, or others, may feel unsafe. This helps to suggest appropriate corrective action. Women's safety audits not only provide valuable information, but also increase awareness of violence against vulnerable groups, and help decision-makers to understand how men and women experience their environments.[71] Box 4.9 summarizes the experience of Durban in this regard.[72]

Grappling with youth crime

The fact that cities as different as Port Moresby (see Box 4.5) and Toronto (see Box 4.7) both recognize the need to pay particular attention to youth crime is suggestive of the ubiquitous nature of this problem. A significant proportion of the crimes that occur in cities across the world are perpetrated by young males.[73] In many instances, this is because they have few options. Consequently, strategies designed to show young people that there are better alternatives and to encourage them to experience employment opportunities or engage in sporting or cultural activities in preference to a life of crime are increasingly becoming popular. The value of such strategies can be seen in both their short- and long-term effects. In the short term, strategies of this nature can deflect young people away from criminal activities and therefore can positively affect one of the groups most prone to crime. There are examples of short-term successes of this nature in Kingston (Jamaica), where in the Grants Pen area the creation of a peace park has provided recreational opportunities for young people that were previously absent and contributed to a lowering of the murder rate in the area.[74] In the long term, such strategies offer the possibility that individuals who benefit from them will contribute more fully and effectively towards the development of their community and society than would otherwise have been the case, thus becoming much less of a burden on overstretched police and criminal justice systems.

One of the major problems in this area is the extent to which young people see criminals as role models and thus seek to emulate them. For example, a study of a poor community in Managua[75] has argued that the most ostentatiously wealthy people in that community (as reflected in the quality of their houses, clothes and cars) are those involved in drug trafficking.[76] Under these circumstances, it is not wholly surprising that some young people see this as something to be aspired to. This is particularly the case when it is associated with a culture where the macho-type behaviour often exhibited by such people is seen as evidence of their significance in the community. This is apparently the case in many Latin American cities, where attitudes of this nature help to encourage the recruitment of child soldiers to gangs at a relatively young age.[77]

From the policy perspective, the problem of youth crime underscores two points. First, the problem of disaffected young people who see themselves as being largely outside the formal economy and who turn to crime and violence in preference to the other alternatives can rank among the most intractable issues that national and city authorities have to contend with. Second, the response to problems of this nature goes beyond a concern with crime and violence – a holistic perspective is necessary. The establishment of good governance, with comprehensive national and urban policies that pay specific attention to the needs of children and youth, is essential. It is likely that encouraging participation in economic activity will constitute a large part of this kind of response, with job-related training and experience being made available and major efforts being made to ensure that beneficiaries are able to move into employment. The response will also involve investing in alternative activities such as sporting and cultural activities. But it will also need to offer to young people a vision of what life as a member of the community can be like, a vision that is able to compete successfully with what other visions can offer to them. Finally, it is important to realize the potential of the youth themselves, and to engage their participation in the development of appropriate responses and solutions. All of these are likely to be challenging and to require significant inputs of resources over significant periods of time.

Non-violent resolution of conflicts

The non-violent resolution of conflicts is perhaps more of an approach to issues based upon a particular moral philosophy[78] than a specific policy response to crime and violence. It, however, deserves a short discussion given its potential to contribute to the range of ways of thinking about what can be very difficult problems.[79] This idea can also be linked with the earlier discussion on restorative justice since elements of that approach which emphasize involving families of both perpetrators and victims seeking solutions also highlight non-violent methods of resolving difficulties. Put simply, this approach is about achieving results by means other than violence. It has been extensively used as a philosophical idea by the labour, peace, environmental and women's movements. It has also been extensively employed in political actions, especially against repressive regimes in several parts of the world. It is also an important philosophy in relation to education, where conflict resolution education is part of the curriculum in many schools and where conflict resolution techniques are applied to the resolution of many of the difficulties experienced by pupils.[80]

Box 4.9 The role of the women's safety audit in Durban (eThekwini), South Africa

The inspiration for undertaking a women's safety audit in Durban came from the discussion of best practice in this area at the first International Women Seminar held in Montreal in 2002. The pilot project was conducted in KwaMakutha, a peri-urban area experiencing both high levels of social crime and unemployment. The process entailed going out and identifying problems on site, as well as a needs assessment and a strategic planning workshop undertaken with service providers. The key environmental factors that were taken into account in this process were lighting, signage, isolation, movement predictors, entrapment sites, escape routes, maintenance and overall design. Since the pilot project was undertaken, this process has been extended to other parts of the city as part of Durban's partnership approach to tackling rising levels of crime and violence. Although this approach has not eradicated crime, it has managed to contain it in comparison with previous experiences.

The key challenges that the auditing process faced included getting local authorities to buy into it; establishing and developing the necessary relationship between local authorities and local communities; and effective implementation. This latter point was seen to be particularly significant. This is because of the risk of disillusion and eventual apathy on the part of the community if nothing happened after all the effort that had been expended in the process. Much of the action that was identified in specific localities involved applying the principles of CPTED, and thus one of the important tasks was the need to train city employees who would need to be involved in the implementation of the principles of CPTED.

Source: Zambuko and Edwards, 2007

It is important to realize the potential of the youth themselves, and to engage their participation in the development of appropriate responses and solutions

The avoidance of violence in schools is an important issue in its own right, not least because of its potential for inculcating appropriate habits among young people, but also because it is central to the effective functioning of the school itself and to the quality of the educational experience that it offers its pupils.[81] In this sense, this concept of non-violent approaches to conflict resolution also relates to the discussion of tackling youth crime, where school experiences can be of vital importance.

There appear to be four broad approaches to conflict resolution education, the last two of which will be taken together because, in principle, they are very similar:

- *Process curriculum:* this is where educators teach the principles and processes of conflict resolution as a distinct lesson or course.
- *Peer mediation:* this is where trained youth mediators work with their peers to find resolutions to conflicts. It

accepts as a fundamental principle that young people are more likely to be comfortable with, and respond positively to, attempts at mediation by other young people rather than adults.
- *Peaceable classroom and peaceable school:* these approaches incorporate conflict resolution within the core subjects of the curriculum and within classroom and institutional management processes. An important feature of approaches of this nature is that they seek to involve everyone connected with the unit of management in question (e.g. individual class or whole school), irrespective of their roles. Peaceable school approaches challenge both youth and adults to act on the understanding that a diverse, non-violent society is a realistic goal.[82]

Initiatives to reduce crime and violence are likely to be of help to the city as a social and economic entity by addressing one of the main barriers that it faces

The US Office of Juvenile Justice and Delinquency Prevention summarized the experience of applying these approaches in 1997 as follows:

> *Most conflict resolution and peer mediation programs, an estimated 7500 to 10,000, have been implemented in our nation's elementary, middle and high schools. However, conflict resolution programs are also a meaningful component of safe and violence-free juvenile justice facilities, alternative education programs, and community mobilization efforts to combat violence.*[83]

During recent years in the US, there have been cases of armed individuals (including students) gaining entry to school grounds and killing or injuring staff and pupils. Typically, this has caused school authorities to revisit issues of school security in order to make entry of this kind more difficult, often including the application of the principles of CPTED.[84] Thus, strategies of this nature can often co-exist alongside the application of non-violent methods of conflict resolution both inside schools and in their surrounding communities.

Young people need to have opportunities for them to participate in, and to contribute to, society that offer them better alternatives than a life of crime

It is probably fair to say that compared with many of the other policy responses discussed in the chapter, this one is still in its infancy in terms of its application to issues of crime and violence. But the evidence from American experience suggests that it has much to offer as an element in the range of responses. For example, an evaluation of the New Mexico Centre for Dispute Resolution's Youth Corrections Mediation Programme found that the recidivism rate among youth trained as mediators was 18 per cent lower during the first six months after returning to the community than for a control group not trained in mediation.[85]

Strengthening social capital

Elements of approaches to the strengthening of social capital can be found in many of the discussions of other policy responses since this seems to be a very common factor in crime prevention programmes that combine several of these approaches. This is particularly the case because the approach adopted earlier in this chapter to the definition of social capital is a broad-based one. It is not only about improving the ability of groups and communities to respond positively to problems of crime and violence, but is also about the creation of community assets that assist with these processes. More broadly still, it can also be argued that the economic prospects of cities, the social welfare of their citizens, and the safety of the public realm are interrelated.

Initiatives to reduce crime and violence are likely to be of help to the city as a social and economic entity by addressing one of the main barriers that it faces. Similarly, measures to improve what the city offers its residents and users in terms of education, employment, sporting and cultural activities are likely to be helpful in tackling crime and violence because they improve opportunities to participate positively in the life of the city, and offer positive lifestyle alternatives to individuals. This approach is reflected in UN-Habitat's Global Campaign on Urban Governance, which takes as its theme the idea of the inclusive city, where all urban inhabitants, regardless of economic means, gender, race, ethnicity or religion, are able to participate fully in the social, economic and political opportunities that cities have to offer.

A particular feature of efforts to improve social capital in many of the case examples is the use of this approach to address issues of youth crime. This is very visible in the Toronto programmes summarized in Box 4.7, where there is a strong emphasis on employment, on appropriate training and on work experience. It is also evident in the Diadema case, through educational opportunities and participation in cultural activities.[86] The argument in both cases is essentially the same: young people need to have opportunities for them to participate in, and to contribute to, society that offer them better alternatives than a life of crime. Therefore, investing in the creation of these opportunities for young people is also investing in the future welfare of the city and its citizens. It is also envisaged that this will develop the willingness in these individuals as adults to contribute positively to the welfare of their communities in the future.

There are several examples in individual UN-Habitat Safer City Programmes that can be seen as including the creation of social capital. These include:

- Durban, where urban renewal efforts have concentrated on areas with the highest rates of poverty, unemployment and violent crime, with several projects in these areas that provide employment opportunities for local youth;[87]
- Dar es Salaam, where pilot projects have included employment creation and skills training for youth;[88] and
- Support for street lighting initiatives, as well as for improvement of community and recreation facilities in slums (Nairobi, Dar es Salaam and Douala).

There can be little doubt about the importance of activities of this nature because they address some of the underlying causes of crime and violence in cities by offering youths a better alternative. But it is also clear that efforts of this nature can be financially demanding, involve a wide range of partners, and be pursued consistently over a period of time if they are to make a significant difference.

INSTITUTIONAL AND COMMUNITY RESPONSES

Institutional and community responses to problems of crime and violence are integral to many of the policy activities reviewed. This section identifies a few key points in this regard. Institutional responses to crime and violence can come from all levels of the hierarchy of governance, and very often this is what is required in a comprehensive response to problems of crime and violence. One of the challenges in these situations is to get the whole range of responses to work together in a coordinated manner, based upon a broad strategy and programmes of action. For cities, a typical problem might be that they do not control the police and criminal justice systems, but want these systems to do particular things to support a city-wide or more localized initiative.

For higher levels of government, they can typically find this kind of spatial differentiation difficult to achieve, either because it challenges their broad policies or organizational structures, or it would involve moving resources around and giving priority to one location over another. Thus, getting all levels of the hierarchy to focus in a coordinated way on a city or more localized initiative can be difficult. This, in turn, explains why the efforts of the various arms of the public sector that are apparently contributing to a project can appear to local people to be less well integrated than would be desirable for the success of the project. This is one of the reasons why the role of the local authority is absolutely crucial in this process.

Local authorities are uniquely placed to take an overview of their locality and its needs, to represent the interests both of the city as a whole and of its individual residents, and to work with others to ensure that an integrated programme of action is drawn up, agreed and implemented. They control many of the services that need to be fully involved in this process, and they have good working relationships with a range of other service providers. Usually, there is no other key player in the process of whom all this could be said, which is why leadership of this process often falls to the local authority. Players should also have one other asset that is fundamental in this process: the strength of their links with local communities.

Many initiatives to combat crime and violence are started and implemented by communities. Where this is the case, the role of local authorities may be limited to issues such as the granting of necessary permissions and offering various forms of assistance. But many initiatives, by their nature, are more likely to be initiated as part of a more comprehensive programme and to be put into practice by one or more partners of that programme. In this case, the community role is more likely to be about any or all of the following:

- consultation and the generation of community support since it is very difficult to mount successful initiatives in the face of community opposition;
- the provision of local information because the knowledge base of local community members is potentially of vital importance; and
- negotiation over the detail, including what the expectations are of local communities and what kind of contributions they are able and willing to make, because even if communities are not project initiators, they can often play important roles in helping projects to succeed.

These are highly important to the success of initiatives in their own right; but community involvement in, and support for, projects is important in another sense as well. For example, an initiative to encourage members of the public to come forward and report crimes to the police depends upon whether or not people are prepared to put aside the reasons for not doing this previously and cooperate, which, in turn, might depend upon many other issues (e.g. trust in the police in relation to matters such as witness protection schemes).

Institutional responses to crime and violence can come from all levels of the hierarchy of governance, and very often this is what is required in a comprehensive response to problems of crime and violence

Many initiatives stand or fall based on their ability to engage local communities as active participants or even as passive participants. Sometimes, the way in which people talk to each other about projects in their areas as part of their daily conversations can make a difference to how positively or negatively people feel about such projects. Failure to engage local communities in the past has stopped many ideas that in their own right may well have been good ones from achieving their full potential. Community engagement is central to initiatives in this field since community members are the ultimate beneficiaries of such initiatives. This being the case, the basic principle here which derives from people's rights as citizens is that initiatives should be 'done with' them rather than 'done to' them.

PARTNERSHIPS

Partnerships can be seen as both a specific mechanism that can be used to encourage interested parties to work together and a more philosophical approach that recognizes the multifaceted nature of the problems of crime and violence. The partnership approach in this latter sense is becoming more frequently utilized in initiatives to tackle urban crime and violence because experience has demonstrated that if such initiatives are to succeed they need to acknowledge the complex and multidimensional nature of the problems they are seeking to address. This inevitably means that a wide range of players will be involved in processes of this nature, which, in turn, creates the requirement for mechanisms to ensure that these contributions operate in integrated and coherent ways.

Partnerships offer both a mechanism of this kind and a framework within which individuals and organizations can commit to holistic approaches. In addition, there is considerable evidence to support the view that initiatives are more likely to be successful if they are part of an integrated programme, supported by a broad strategy and based on an understanding of the local context. Partnerships offer a vehicle for undertaking tasks of this nature and for agreeing on the outcomes of these processes, including tapping into the knowledge and understanding of partners at the appropriate times. These reasons show why both as a mechanism and as a process, partnerships have become so common in this field.

There are, however, some important cautionary words that are necessary, not least because *partnership* is in the same class as *community* when it comes to concepts that are seen in some quarters as being the equivalent of magic dust. In reality, the theoretical virtues of the partnership approach will only materialize if the partnership works effectively, which, among other things, requires a significant commitment of resources by partners. Partnerships can also be exclusive, as well as inclusive: who is not there can be as significant in determining outcomes as who is there, and can often be a controversial issue in a locality. Indeed, achieving a proper level of representation around the partnership table can be a real challenge in its own right, not least because there may well be very different views about what 'proper' means in relation to particular sectors or organizations.

The most important policy trend... has been the move away from the idea that crime prevention and tackling violence are essentially matters for the police and the criminal justice system, and towards the idea that these are complex phenomena which require broad-based responses

The workings of partnerships can also be difficult to understand from the outside, especially if their communication processes are not very effective and their procedures are complex, bureaucratic and difficult for potential participants to follow. Partnerships run the risk of being too cosy in the sense that a relatively small group of people can agree things among themselves without taking account of much wider community views and wishes. Partnerships also need to have an action focus so that they avoid the danger of drifting into becoming mere talking shops that actually do very little. Finally, it is important that a sensible balance is struck between the importance of the leadership role and the absence of the domination that sometimes comes with this. Effective partnerships need good leadership; but partnerships should never become merely a rubber stamp for the views of whoever is in the leading role. These are just some of the dangers that exist in relation to partnerships and, indeed, some of the things that some critics have said about them.[89]

There are many examples of partnerships of all kinds, some of which are good and some of which are not. However, the potential advantages of partnership are very real. Indeed, it is difficult to think of other mechanisms that have the same potential. But it is equally clear that partnership is not a magic formula. It is something that has to be worked at in particular circumstances.

CONCLUDING REMARKS

Inevitably, a discussion of emerging policy trends across as diverse a set of policy responses to crime and violence as reviewed in this chapter involves being selective. Nevertheless, there do appear to be some significant policy trends that are visible. This section discusses what may be the most notable.

The most important policy trend in the field over the past two decades or so has been the move away from the idea that crime prevention and tackling violence are essentially matters for the police and the criminal justice system, and towards the idea that these are complex phenomena which require broad-based responses. The emergence of urban crime prevention as a specific concern of urban policy and urban actors is an indication of such shift. As a result, the range of policy responses described in this chapter has become more commonplace, with, to some extent, each of them seeing significant development as the search for solutions has broadened. This does not imply that the roles of the police and the criminal justice system have become unimportant, or that developments have been mainly in other areas rather than in these. Instead, the historic reliance on a limited number of areas has been replaced by a more broad-based range of responses that recognize the need to find other ways of addressing crime and violence. Four of these areas, in particular, seem to have attracted interest, although the nature and the intensity of this have varied across the world.

First is the idea that through the manipulation of the physical environment it is possible to reduce the opportunity for certain kinds of crimes to be committed. This recognizes the point made in Chapter 3 that the physical environment poses risks of crime and violence and that, as a consequence, the *where* of crime is an important issue which, until recently, was often neglected. There is now an understanding that it is possible to make a difference to the opportunity for crimes such as burglary to be committed by design choices, and that it is possible to make a difference to people's feelings about the safety of the environment in which they move around through similar processes.[90] In particular, much attention has been paid to the residential environment,[91] which is important since housing is by far the most extensive urban land use. This interest has been extended in some areas to an exploration of the role of the planning system through its control of development in addressing these aspects of crime prevention.[92]

The second of the policy responses is the idea that approaches need to be more community based. The broad reasons for this have been discussed. It seems to be the case that this means different things in different parts of the world, and it is an area of considerable controversy since many practices that are claimed as being community based would not be in other areas. There is still considerable scope for further development of this area and for the development, in particular, of a better understanding of what community involvement means. Interestingly, as is demonstrated in the Hong Kong case study,[93] these issues have also affected discussions about appropriate policing strategies, with the process of moving in the direction of community policing taking place over a period of 40 years and being influenced by the major change in 1997 when Hong Kong was returned to China.

The third area relates to the focus on particular groups in society that are either vulnerable to, or perpetrators of, most crimes. This has been a key feature of many UN-Habitat Safer Cities programmes, where the focus has been on women at risk of violence and on young people, especially young men, who commit a larger proportion of crimes.[94]

The final area where there has been significant policy development is in the strengthening of social capital. This represents a recognition of the fact that to deflect youths from a life of crime and to offer them more attractive alternatives, the city needs to become a place where opportunities abound for young people to participate fully in economic, social, cultural and sporting activities. The importance of this is that it is not a traditional 'crime and violence policy', but essentially about addressing the social and economic circumstances that cause young people to choose a life of crime and violence.

Over and above these broad policy trends, there is a further trend that appears significant. This has to do with the processes used. Increasingly, it is being recognized that initiatives need to be part of an integrated and comprehensive programme, backed up by a broad strategy and founded on good understanding of the issues addressed, as distinct from an *ad hoc* basis. Consequently, it is now common to find programmes of this nature containing elements of many of the policy responses discussed in this chapter, which recognize their mutually reinforcing nature. Very often, the mechanism chosen for moving this approach forward is the partnership mechanism, which is often accompanied by an attempt to engage local communities in decision-making and implementation.

There are two final points that also constitute emerging policy trends. The first is the acceptance that solutions cannot simply be borrowed from elsewhere where they may have appeared to have worked, but must be adapted to the local context. This raises important issues for the nature of international assistance in this field since it suggests that it needs to be as much about assisting with this process of adaptation as it is about helping with the application of tried and tested practices from home locations. The second and related point is the need to evaluate what is being done properly and to publicize such evaluations so that others can learn from them. There are still far too many initiatives that are not properly evaluated;[95] but the recognition of the need to do this does seem to be becoming more widespread. In addition, the potential for evaluation to contribute to collective learning is greater than it has ever been by virtue of the spread of internet access.

NOTES

1 See the discussion of this issue in Chapter 3.
2 It is also the case that crime has a very particular impact at the individual level since it is very often individuals and the households of which they are part who are the victims of crime.
3 It should be noted that the consequences of drug trafficking are often experienced locally.
4 A similar issue applies in this case as well. The consequences of the use of such weapons in criminal activities are, of course, felt locally.
5 And the same applies here also since much human trafficking results in illegal activities, such as prostitution in urban areas.
6 See http://untreaty.un.org/English/TreatyEvent2003/Treaty_1.htm.
7 Interpol, 2006.
8 See www.unhabitat.org/programmes/safercities/approach.asp.
9 ECOSOC resolution 1995/9 of 24 July 1995.
10 UN-Habitat, 2005f, p27.
11 CEN, 2003.
12 Schneider and Kitchen, 2007.
13 Kitchen and Schneider, 2005
14 ODPM and the Home Office, 2004.
15 Schneider and Kitchen, 2007, Chapter 7
16 DoE, 1994.
17 DETR, 2000.
18 ODPM and the Home Office, 2004.
19 ODPM, 2005.
20 The discussion of the response of the Government of Jamaica draws heavily from the case study of Kingston prepared for this Global Report by Sherrian Gray (Gray, 2007).
21 See http://en.wikipedia.org/wiki/Jamaica_Constabulary_Force.
22 Most of the evaluative work that has been done on this issue relates to countries in the developed world, and very little such work has been conducted on the specific initiatives undertaken by national governments in the developing and transitional worlds to support efforts at the urban level to tackle problems of crime and violence.
23 National Crime Prevention Centre, 2005.
24 The information utilized here has been taken from the Government of Australia's Office of Crime Prevention's website at www.crimeprevention.wa.gov.au.
25 Government of Western Australia, 2004.
26 Fox, 2002. See also the illustration in UN-Habitat, 2006j, p13.
27 Women's safety audits are discussed in more detail later in this chapter, when measures to address the risk of violence towards women are reviewed. There are several ways in which audits of this nature could be carried out; but, in essence, they involve small groups going out on site and looking at local environments from the perspectives of women's safety (usually including women who can bring some local experience to bear on this process) as part of an intensive process in order to identify potential problems and to suggest solutions to them.
28 UN-Habitat, 2006b, p13.
29 Florida Legislature, 2006.
30 *Ibid.*
31 *Ibid.*
32 Schneider, 2003.
33 For example, in the UK the English Best Value User Satisfaction Survey for 2003/2004 showed that the top response of citizens to a question about what makes somewhere a good place in which to live was a low level of crime (ODPM, 2005a).
34 See, for example, Ekblom, 1997.
35 DTLR, 2001.
36 Morton and Kitchen, 2005
37 Schneider and Kitchen, 2007, Chapter 4.
38 *Ibid.*
39 UN-Habitat, 2006b, p15.
40 These figures, and other material in this section, are taken from Manso et al, 2005.
41 *Ibid.*
42 *Ibid*, p12.
43 *Ibid*, p1.
44 *Ibid*, 2005.
45 *Ibid*, 2005.
46 *Ibid*, 2005, pp11–12.
47 *Ibid*, 2005, p11.
48 The material here and in the paragraphs that follow is taken from Boamah and Stanley, 2007.
49 Kitchen, 2007.
50 This, in essence, means that planning decisions are taken in accordance with the provisions of the development plan unless there are clear, cogent and relevant reasons why this should not be so.
51 In some UK police forces, the officers carrying out this work go by different titles; but for convenience they will all be referred to as architectural liaison officers.
52 Schneider and Kitchen, 2007.
53 Schneider and Kitchen, 2002.
54 For a fuller discussion of many of the issues surrounding CCTVs, see http://en.wikipedia.org/wiki/Closed-circuit_television.
55 Caldeira, 2000.
56 Manso et al, 2005.
57 The material reported here is taken from Thompson and Gartner, 2007.
58 This document can be found at http://www.toronto.ca/safety/sftyrprt1.htm.
59 The basis of the definition of 'at-risk' neighbourhoods was not just their experience of crime and violence, but also their economic and social circumstances.
60 This was noted particularly during much of the discussion in the sessions dealing with crime and violence at the World Urban Forum in Vancouver by delegates from cities in Central and South America and Africa.
61 Manso et al, 2005.
62 Zaluar, 2007, suggests that this was a factor in the high level of shootings that were not properly investigated in that city.
63 Broadhurst et al, 2007.
64 Macedo, 2007.
65 Benevides and Ferreira, 1991; Bukurura, 1993;

Vanderschueren, 1996; Allen, 1997; Baker, 2002; Adinkrah, 2005; Nwankwo, 2005.

66 Vanderschueren, 1996.

67 Michau and Naker, 2003.

68 *Ibid*, 2003.

69 For example, see the Women in Cities International website at www.womenincities.org.

70 For example, Women in Cities International, together with their partners, organized a programme of events across the five days of the World Urban Forum in Vancouver in June 2006, which amounted, in total, to 17 advertised sessions.

71 UN-Habitat, undated, p5.

72 Durban case study undertaken for this Global Report (Zambuko and Edwards, 2007).

73 Reliable international comparisons in relation to this statement are very difficult to find because of differences in the ways in which data is recorded.

74 Kingston case study (Gray, 2007). In this instance, the community of Grants Pen had not recorded a single murder during 2006 until the point when this case study was drafted. This goes against the trend for murders in Jamaica, which rose from 8.1 per 100,000 people in 1970 to 40 per 100,000 in 2002, and 64 per 100,000 in 2005, making Jamaica one of the nations with the highest rates of murders in the world.

75 The community in question is Barrio Luis Fanor Hernandez.

76 Rodgers, 2005.

77 Presentation by Robert Lawson at the networking event Security and Safety: Public Policies, Urban Practices, at the World Urban Forum, Vancouver, 20 June 2006. Lawson suggested that the average age of recruitment to gangs in Colombia was 11 to 14 years, and that the gangs that these young people joined were often better armed than the police.

78 See, for example, the discussion at http://en.wikipedia.org/wiki/Non-violence.

79 Although, as yet, this approach does not seem to have been widely attempted in public programmes designed to address crime and violence, the initial experience of the programmes recently instituted in Kingston (Jamaica) suggests that non-violent processes of conflict resolution can be utilized effectively in such circumstances.

80 UNESCO, 2002.

81 The Rio de Janeiro case study prepared for this volume (Zaluar, 2007) underlines the significance of these considerations when it points to the importance of improving schooling as one of the central themes of efforts to get young people in the city away from a life of crime and violence.

82 US Department of Justice, 1997. See also the discussion paper at http://www.ed.gov/offices/OSDFS/actguid/conflct.html.

83 US Department of Justice, 1997.

84 Florida Department of Education, 2003.

85 US Department of Justice, 1997.

86 Manso et al, 2005.

87 Durban case study undertaken for this Global Report (Zambuko and Edwards, 2007).

88 UN-Habitat, undated, pp11–12.

89 One of the well-known examples of a partnership process in the field of crime prevention are the statutory crime and disorder reduction partnerships introduced in England as a result of the 1998 Crime and Disorder Act.

90 Schneider and Kitchen, 2007.

91 Town et al, 2003; Poyner 2006.

92 Schneider and Kitchen, 2007, Chapter 4.

93 Hong Kong case study prepared by Broadhurst et al, 2007.

94 UN-Habitat, 2006b, p23.

95 Sherman et al, 1997.

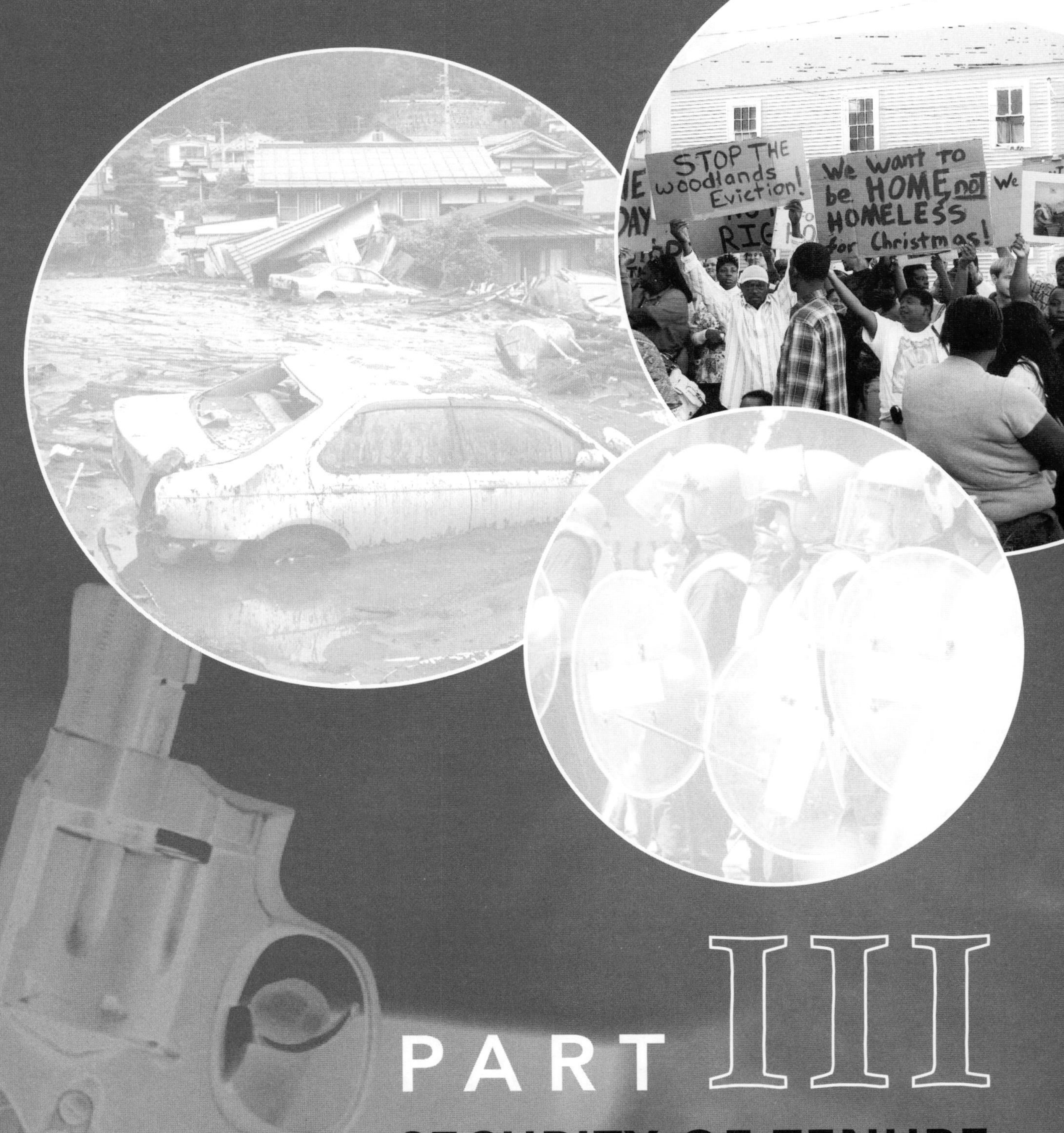

PART III
SECURITY OF TENURE

We further commit ourselves to the objectives of ... providing legal security of tenure and equal access to land to all people, including women and those living in poverty.[1]

Security of tenure – or 'the right of all individuals and groups to effective protection from the State against forced evictions'[2] – is a major concern for hundreds of millions of slum dwellers and other poor people. The possibility that individuals, households or whole communities may be evicted from their homes at any time is a major safety and security threat in urban areas the world over. The following two chapters address a range of issues linked to the increasingly prominent and fundamental issue of security of tenure. The analysis explores a wide range of questions linked to secure tenure from the primary perspective of human rights and good governance, augmented by experiences in various countries. The chapters compare and contrast various initiatives taken by states and analysts on the question of secure tenure, and seek to identify the strengths and weaknesses of the most prevalent approaches taken to procure security of tenure throughout the world. More specifically, Chapter 5 explores the scope and scale of tenure insecurity in the world and trends surrounding tenure, while Chapter 6 provides a review of policies that have been adopted to address tenure concerns.

The analysis treats the concept of security of tenure as a key component of a housing policy built upon the principles of human rights law, which seeks to achieve the goal of adequate housing for all, as elaborated upon in the Habitat Agenda. This raises a number of crucial questions, which are addressed in this part of the report:

- Are all types of housing, land and property tenure capable of providing the degree of security of tenure meant to be accorded to everyone under human rights laws?
- What makes tenure secure and insecure?
- If security of tenure is a right, how can it be enforced?
- Is there an emerging jurisprudence of security of tenure as a human right?
- Is the universal enjoyment of security of tenure as a human right a realistic possibility within a reasonable timeframe?

These and a series of additional questions clearly require greater attention by the research and legal communities, as well as by governments, the United Nations and policymakers. This part of the Global Report thus aims to examine contemporary approaches to security of tenure through the perspective of human rights in order to determine how initiatives in support of tenure security might achieve better outcomes once a human rights approach is embraced.

As noted in Chapter 1, the year 2007 marks a turning point in human history: for the first time there are more people living in cities and towns than in rural areas. While some may argue about the precise date on which city and town residents became a majority, the political, legal and resource implications, coupled with the social and economic consequences of this shift, are widely recognized, even though they may still not be fully appreciated by decision- and policy-makers.

Urbanization brings with it both positive and negative prospects for the world's cities and towns and the existing and new populations of the world's built-up areas. In China alone, the urban population has increased by hundreds of millions of people, and this number is expected to continue to grow in the coming years as the economic boom continues. The Indian capital, Delhi, is growing by about half a million people each year, and similar urban growth is occurring throughout the developing world. Although the major part of urban growth in most cities today occurs through natural population growth or physical extension of urban areas,[3] large numbers of these new urban dwellers are migrants from rural areas. Urban areas will continue to provide employment choices, standards of living and cultural options simply unavailable in the countryside. Cities will continue to exert a considerable pull factor for the world's poor and underemployed as great numbers of people see their aspirations linked to an urban life.

It is now widely known and understood that migrants to the world's cities do not end up as residents in upmarket or even middle-class neighbourhoods. Rather, because very few governments have sufficiently prioritized actions in support of pro-poor housing solutions for the urban poor, the formal, legal and official housing market is neither affordable nor accessible to these groups; as a result, illegal or informal land markets, slums, shanties, pirate subdivisions, pavements and park benches become the new abodes for millions of people every year. These informal self-help solutions have long been the only housing option available to the poorest in most developing world cities and, increasingly, in some developed world cities, as well.

At the same time, however, the sense of urgency

Box III.1 Security of tenure: The triumph of the 'self-service city'

They all laughed: six men laughing because an outsider didn't understand their concept of landownership.

They sat in a teahouse in a dusty patch of Istanbul (Turkey), called Paşaköy, far out on the Asian side of the city.

'*Tapu var?*' a researcher asked. 'Do you have title deeds?'

They all laughed. Or, more accurately, some laughed, some muttered uncomfortably and some made a typical Turkish gesture. They jerked their heads back in a sort of half nod and clicked their tongues. It was the kind of noise someone might make while calling a cat or a bird, but at a slightly lower pitch. This indicates: 'Are you kidding?' or 'Now that's a stupid question' or, more devastatingly, 'What planet are you from, bub?'

The researcher blundered on. 'So who owns the land?' More laughter. More clicking.

'We do,' said Hasan Çelik, choking back tears.

'But you don't have title deeds?' This time they roared.

And somebody whispered: 'Why is this guy so obsessed with title deeds? Does he want to buy my house?'

To understand the squatter communities of Turkey, it is important to accept the existence of a sense of property ownership that is completely different from what exists in Europe and North America. It is a system of land tenure more rooted in the legal rights of communities than in the apparatus of title registration and the clean pieties of private property. While it may seem unruly to outsiders, it has enabled the accommodation of massive urbanization in a sensible and successful way by harnessing the power of self-building and sweat equity.

For instance, it is likely that the land under the seven-storey city hall in the neighbouring Sultanbeyli belongs to thousands of people who have no idea that they own it and have never even heard of this obscure outpost far out on the Asian side of Istanbul. That is because 70 per cent of the land in this squatter metropolis is held under *hisseli tapu* – or shared title. Today, this anachronistic form of landownership exists where parcels of land have never been divided into exact lots and ownership has never been apportioned to individuals.

So, why is this not seen as a problem by Sultanbeyli's 300,000 residents, and why do they not fear eviction at the hands of the rightful owners of their land? Perhaps the best answer is that Istanbul is a 'self-service city', a place where nobody owns but everybody builds. Between 1986 and 1989, people erected 20,000 houses in Sultanbeyli and the city now boasts 150 major avenues, 1200 streets, 30,000 houses, 15 neighbourhoods, 91 mosques, 22 schools and 48,000 students.

Yet, today there is increasing pressure to formalize tenure rights. The mayor of Sultanbeyli is encouraging people to buy private title to the land that they occupy. Many residents, however, are not so sure. Indeed, many in Sultanbeyli are balking at the idea of paying a fee for their land. In the city's Akşemsettin neighbourhood, Zamanhan Ablak, a Kurd who came to Sultanbeyli in the mid 1990s, reports that his family initially paid approximately US$1500 for their land (they registered their new right of possession with the local *muhtar*, an elected official who functions as a kind of justice of the peace). They also paid US$120 for the city's permission to erect a new building, and approximately US$400 towards a neighbourhood fund dedicated to installing drainage culverts and building a mosque and a school. Zamanhan, who works as a waiter in his cousin's kebab restaurant, is already protesting the fact that Sultanbeyli is charging residents US$160 to hook into the water system. He explained his irritation with a little wordplay: the city's fee (*ruhsat* in Turkish), is nothing more than a bribe (*rusvet*). So, Zamanhan asked: '*Ruhsat, rusvet*: what's the difference?' Zamanhan and many of his fellow Akşemsettin residents do not look favourably on the idea of having to shell out more money to purchase a title deed for a parcel that was unused and unwanted when they arrived.

After all, they say, it is through their own work that Sultanbeyli and many other informal settlements have become indistinguishable from many legal neighbourhoods in Istanbul. Through a combination of political protection and dogged building and rebuilding, they have developed their own communities into thriving commercial and residential districts that are desirable places in which to live. Indeed, with Istanbul continuing to grow, it is possible that selling private titles could set off a frenzy of speculation in Sultanbeyli. Informal ownership, while perhaps legally precarious, is perhaps safer for poor people because they do not have to go into debt to formally own their houses. They build what they can afford, when they can afford it.

Source: Neuwirth, 2007

required to ensure adequate housing for all is distressingly absent from most government decision-making bodies. Public expenditure on housing remains minimal in virtually all countries, and private sector-led efforts to provide housing at an affordable cost have generally not achieved results (even when heavily subsidized or provided with tax incentives or other inducements to do so). As a result, governments of all political hues are turning to the market as the source of hope for housing the hundreds of millions of people who today lack access to a safe, habitable and secure home. Indeed, the market can, and must, be a crucial link in any successful housing supply chain. Most commentators are, however, sceptical about the ability of the market alone to provide affordable and accessible homes to all sectors of society. And yet, from an analysis of the latest housing policy trends throughout the world, it is clear that the market – perhaps more than ever before – is seen by many people and governments as the 'only real solution' to solving the global housing crisis.

As a result, the global housing crisis – characterized by ever growing slums, housing price increases, conflict and disaster-induced loss of housing and property resources, and continuing forced evictions and mass displacements – continues to get worse without any sort of positive end in sight. Because of this, an equally massive response by local and national governments to address this crisis, backed by strong efforts of the international community, might be reasonably expected. Intensive building activities of social housing and subsidized housing units, all of which could be accessed by those on low incomes, might also be expected. The activation of policy measures throughout the world specifically designed to ensure that members of particularly vulnerable groups, such as the elderly, the disabled or homeless children, have access to adequate housing which they can afford might be further anticipated. At the very least, given that housing is treated as a right under international human rights law, governments would be expected to accurately monitor the scale of housing deprivation as a first step towards the development of a more effective set of housing laws and policies that would actually result in a fully and adequately housed society. And yet, as reasonable as these and other expectations may be, global housing policy debates today can, in many respects, be boiled down to one key discussion point: the question of tenure and tenure security.

Security of tenure, of course, is crucial to any proper understanding of the housing reality facing every household throughout the world; indeed, the worse the standard of one's housing, generally the more important the question of security of tenure will become. The degree of 'security' of one household's tenure will be instrumental in determining the chances that they will face forced eviction, have access to basic services such as water and electricity, be able to facilitate improvements in housing and living conditions, and be able to register their home or land with the authorities. Indeed, one's security of tenure impacts upon many areas of life and is clearly a fundamental element of the bundle of entitlements that comprise every individual's housing rights. The broad issue of security of tenure has been the subject of extensive analysis during recent years in connection with efforts such as the Global Campaign for Secure Tenure, coordinated by UN-Habitat. There is also a growing realization that the scale of insecure tenure is increasing and is likely to worsen in coming years. It is widely accepted that secure tenure is of vital importance for stability, economic development, investment and the protection of human rights. As stated by the World Bank:

> *Empirical evidence from across the world reveals the demand for greater security of tenure and illustrates that appropriate interventions to increase tenure security can have significant benefits in terms of equity, investment, credit supply, and reduced expenditure of resources on defensive activities.*[4]

At the same time, while a great deal has been written on the clear linkages between security of tenure and the achievement of the goal of access to adequate housing for all, the fact remains that security of tenure often remains underemphasized by policy-makers, perhaps overemphasized by those with large vested interests in land, and, as a concept, all too commonly misunderstood by those with the most to gain from improved access to it. In particular, it is important to note that security of tenure does not necessarily imply ownership of land or housing (see Box III.1).

Thus, the following questions arise: is the renewed focus on tenure a comprehensive enough approach to solve the global housing crisis? Can security of tenure alone be considered an adequate response to the massive growth of slums and illegal settlements in the world's cities? Is the focus on security of tenure likely to be effective in a world where states refuse or are unable to allocate the funds required to house the poor majority? If we focus on security of tenure, which type of tenure provides the best and most appropriate forms of protections? Can a focus on tenure by policy-makers, without a corresponding emphasis on infrastructure improvements, service provision and proper planning, actually yield desirable results? And perhaps the most contentious questions of all: what is the proper role of the state within the housing sector, and is the growing global initiative in support of secure tenure, in practical terms, a sufficient response to the broader aim of adequate housing and housing rights for all? These and related questions are explored in the chapters that follow.

NOTES

1. Habitat Agenda, para 40(b).
2. UN-Habitat, 2006e, p94.
3. UN-Habitat, 2006e.
4. World Bank, 2003b, p8.

CHAPTER 5

SECURITY OF TENURE: CONDITIONS AND TRENDS

> *Access to land and security of tenure are strategic prerequisites for the provision of adequate shelter for all and for the development of sustainable human settlements... It is also one way of breaking the vicious circle of poverty. Every government must show a commitment to promoting the provision of an adequate supply of land ... governments at appropriate levels ... should ... strive to remove all possible obstacles that may hamper equitable access to land and ensure that equal rights of women and men related to land and property are protected under the law.*[1]

Security of tenure is a basic attribute of human security in general

Few issues are as central to the objective of adequate housing for all as security of tenure. While approaches towards achieving this objective vary widely, it is clear that virtually all commentators agree that secure tenure is a vital ingredient in any policy designed to improve the lives of those living in informal settlements throughout the world. Furthermore, security of tenure is a basic attribute of human security in general: a full, dignified life, wherein all human rights can be enjoyed in their entirety. Those on the political 'Left' and those on the political 'Right' may have very different views on how, and on the basis of which policies, security of tenure can best be enjoyed by increasingly large numbers of people. Yet, very few disagree about the central importance of tenure security to the broader question of housing, slum improvement and, increasingly, the protection and promotion of human rights. Indeed, the United Nations has long and consistently expressed its concerns in this regard, repeatedly urging that special attention should be paid to improving the access of the poor to land and housing with secure tenure.[2]

Both the international human settlements community and the global human rights community have devoted increasing attention to ... security of tenure in recent years

And, yet, despite this widespread agreement, security of tenure remains extremely fragile for hundreds of millions of the urban and rural poor. Furthermore, the security of tenure of millions of poor people throughout the world is deteriorating as land values within cities continue to rise, as affordable land becomes increasingly scarce, and as housing solutions are increasingly left to market forces. A number of additional factors contribute to these deteriorating conditions, including the rapid and continuing growth of informal settlements and slums; structural discrimination against women, indigenous peoples and others; and displacement caused by conflict and disaster. If these global *de facto* realities are contrasted against the clear normative framework elaborating rights to secure tenure, the world faces nothing less than a severe security of tenure crisis. With more than 200,000 slums existing today globally,[3] mostly located across the cities of developing countries, and with nearly 80 per cent of urban dwellers in the least-developed countries living as residents of such slums, then questions of tenure security are daily concerns affecting well over one fifth of humanity.[4]

While security of tenure is often perceived primarily as a housing or human settlements issue, interestingly, both the international human settlements community and the global human rights community have devoted increasing attention to the question of security of tenure in recent years. It is true that many housing and urban researchers, as well as local and national government officials, do not initially view tenure concerns necessarily as an issue of human rights. Yet, the human rights movement – judges, United Nations bodies, lawyers, non-governmental organizations (NGOs), community-based organizations (CBOs) and others – have increasingly embraced and considered tenure security. This, coupled with the growing treatment of security of tenure as a self-standing right by a range of international and national legal and other standards, has led to a unique convergence of effort and approach by the global housing community, on the one hand, and the human rights community, on the other. Although the formal links between security of tenure and human rights comprise a reasonably recent policy development, the link between human rights and tenure issues stretches back to the first United Nations Conference on Human Settlements (Habitat) in Vancouver (Canada) in 1976.[5]

Thus, it appears that the difficulties faced by many within the human rights field to fully appreciate the human rights dimensions of poverty, slum life and displacement – as well as the sometimes naive and biased views on the appropriate role of law in human settlements – seem increasingly to be issues of the past. This emerging convergence between fields traditionally separated by artificial distinctions has generated a series of truly historical developments in recent years which, if continued and expanded, could arguably bring the objective of security of tenure for all closer than ever to universal fruition. If a balance can be struck between those favouring free market, freehold title-based solutions to insecure tenure and those who view security of tenure both as an individual and group right, as well as a key component in any effective system of land administration and land registration and regularization, it may be possible to envisage a future of much improved tenure security for the urban poor.

Indeed, viewed through the lens of human rights, among all elements of the right to adequate housing, it is clearly the right to security of tenure that forms the nucleus of this widely recognized norm. When security of tenure – the right to feel safe in one's own home, to control one's own housing environment and the right not to be arbitrarily and forcibly evicted – is threatened or simply non-existent, the full enjoyment of housing rights is, effectively, impossible. The consideration of security of tenure in terms of human rights implies application of an approach that treats all persons on the basis of equality. While it is true that all human rights are premised on principles of equality and non-discrimination, viewing security of tenure as a human right (rather than solely as a by-product of ownership or the comparatively rare cases of strong protection for private tenants) opens up the realm of human rights not merely to all people, but to all people of all incomes and in all housing sectors.

The rights associated with ownership of housing or land tend, in practice, to generally offer considerably higher – and, thus, in legal terms, more secure levels of tenure – protection against eviction or other violations of housing rights than those afforded to tenants or those residing in informal settlements. Thus, the right to security of tenure raises the baseline – the minimum core entitlement – guaranteed to all persons by international human rights standards. While security of tenure cannot always guarantee that forced evictions will be prohibited *in toto* (particularly in lawless situations of conflict or truly exceptional circumstances), perhaps no other measure can contribute as much to fulfilling the promise of residential security and protection against eviction than the conferral of this form of legal recognition.

Examining security of tenure simultaneously as both a development issue and as a human rights theme clearly reveals the multilevel and multidimensional nature of this status and how it relates to people at the individual or household level, the community level, the city level, and at the national and international levels.

This chapter provides an overview of the main conditions and trends with respect to tenure security in urban areas today. It provides a brief outline of various types of tenure, of variations in the levels of tenure security and a discussion of the problems of measuring tenure security. This is followed by an analysis of the scale and impacts of tenure insecurity and various types of evictions. The last sections focus on groups who are particularly vulnerable to tenure insecurity, and the reduction in tenure security often experienced in the aftermath of disasters and armed conflict.

TYPES OF TENURE

Tenure (as distinct from security of tenure) is a universal, ubiquitous fact or status which is relevant to everyone, everywhere, every day. Yet, there is a wide variety of forms, which is more complicated than what the conventional categories of 'legal–illegal' or 'formal–informal' suggest. On the one hand, there is a whole range of intermediary categories, which suggests that tenure can be categorized along a continuum. On the other hand, the types of tenure found in particular locations are also a result of specific historical, political, cultural and religious influences. It is thus essential that policy recognizes and reflects these local circumstances.

When security of tenure ... is threatened or simply non-existent, the full enjoyment of housing rights is... impossible

On a simplified level, any type of tenure can be said to belong to one of six broad categories – namely, freehold, leasehold, conditional freehold ('rent to buy'), rent, collective forms of tenure and communal tenure.[6] In practice, however – and, in particular, with respect to the development of policy – it may be more useful to acknowledge the wide variation in tenure categories that exist globally. Table 5.1 provides an overview of the many forms that tenure (each with varying degrees of security) can take throughout the world.

The broad categories of tenure types identified in Table 5.1 reveal the complex nature of tenure and why simple answers to the question of how best to provide security of tenure to everyone is a complicated process. One-size-fits-all policy prescriptions concerning security of tenure simply do not exist. It is correct and true to assert that all should have access to secure tenure; but determining precisely how to achieve this objective is another story all together.

One-size-fits-all policy prescriptions concerning security of tenure simply do not exist

Box 5.1 presents a brief overview of the variation of tenure categories typically available to the poor in urban areas of developing countries, differentiating between the formality of settlements and the physical location in the city. Yet, the common denominator for most of these tenure categories is inadequate degrees of tenure security.

It is important to note that no one form of tenure is necessarily better than another, and what matters most is invariably the degree of security associated with a particular tenure type. Tenure is linked to so many factors and variables – including, as noted above, political, historical, cultural and religious ones – that proclaiming that the formal title-based approach to tenure alone is adequate to solve all tenure challenges is unlikely to yield favourable results. While complicated from a purely housing policy perspective, it is perhaps even more so from the perspective of human rights. For if human rights protections are meant to be equitable, non-discriminatory and accessible to all, and often capable of full implementation with a reasonably clear set of legal and policy prescriptions, this is certainly not always the case with regard to security of tenure. It can be done; but failing to realize the complex nature of tenure in any effort designed to spread the benefits of secure tenure more broadly is likely be detrimental both to the intended beneficiary and policy-maker alike.

No one form of tenure is necessarily better than another

Table 5.1

A general typology of land tenure and property rights

Source: adapted from Payne, 1997, pp52–54

Customary rights	
Tribal/collective	Members of the group or tribe controlling customary land may be entitled to a variety of rights, such as access, occupation, grazing and development, but not transfer; this can be undertaken only by the group as a whole or its accepted leaders. While rights can usually be inherited, land cannot be used as collateral for loans to individual group members.
Stool land	Allocation by chiefs of unused land near an existing settlement; common in southern Ghana. Access depends upon the chief's approval; secure.
Ejidal land	Land controlled either by a group of people, as in Mexico, or a co-operative.
Individual	In a few cases, as in Burundi and Burkina Faso, customary rights to a family plot may acquire a status akin to individual title. They normally revert to corporate status, however, on the death of the original owner.
Ground rent (e.g. *hekr*)	The charges made for long-term lease of undeveloped land, often by large landholders, who obtained their rights through grants made under feudal concepts. It is also used for any situation in which the rent is payable on the land as distinguished from rent payable on the building. Under the Ottoman Land Law of 1858, it enabled farmers and others to settle and develop unused land for the payment of a ground rent, or *hekr*, on registration of a claim. Secure where traditional writs still apply, but less so where active land markets operate.
Private tenure categories	
Unlimited duration (e.g. freehold, dominium, *mulk*)	Provides for full ownership of unlimited duration and the right to free enjoyment and disposal of objects providing that they are not in any way contrary to laws and regulations. The only restriction is normally that of 'eminent domain', where the state may acquire part or all of a property, provided that due process of law is observed and full compensation paid.
Finite duration (e.g. leasehold, individual)	Provides rights to the exclusive possession of land or property by the landlord (or lessor) to the tenant (or lessee) for a consideration or rent. Leases are normally for a specified period, which may vary from one week to 999 years. Long leases are practically indistinguishable from freehold, while shorter leases may be renewed subject to revised terms. The assignment of a lease by a lessee is normally permitted as with freehold.
Tribal/collective	As above, though usually for shorter periods to enable the terms and conditions to be revised in accordance with market trends.
Condominium	A form of 'horizontal ownership' common in multi-storey developments. Rights may be freehold or leasehold.
Leasehold, rent control	This form of tenure accords tenants full security and restricts the freedom of the freeholder or head leaseholder to increase rents more than a specified amount over a given period. It is extensive in cities with older high-rise apartments, such as Bombay. Since rents do not generate an economic return on investment, maintenance is often poor, and both residential mobility and new supply are limited. Key money may be required for properties that become available and this, in effect, restores a market value that can benefit outgoing tenants as much as the freeholder.
Public tenure categories	
Crown land	Originally intended to acquire for the Crown unused or unclaimed land in parts of British, Spanish, Portuguese and other colonies. Such lands were often extensive (e.g. half the land of Buganda), and were allocated to European settlers and companies with freehold or long leases.
State land	This is not significantly different from Crown land. In private domain, state land may be placed on the market through the award of leases. In public domain, state land is retained by the state for use by public organizations. It is widely used for forests, military camps, roads and other natural resources; but in Namibia, for example, it also applies in urban areas.
Public land	This consists of land acquired by government for public purposes. Compensation may be paid in acquiring it from other owners or those with rights, and sometimes acquisition is simply to enable land to be developed and/or reallocated as freehold or leasehold.
Occupancy certificates	Also known as 'certificates of rights' or '*permit d'habitation*', originally introduced by colonial administrations as a device to deny local populations freehold tenure and to enforce racial segregation. More recently, used by independent governments as a means of providing 'allottees' on housing projects with security of tenure, while restricting the development of freehold land and property markets.
Land record rights	Memorandum of an oral agreement between a local authority and an occupant. Provides for loans to develop the site, providing the occupant pays all dues and builds in conformity to official standards. Duration normally specified.
Islamic tenure categories	
Mulk	Land owned by an individual and over which he has full ownership rights. Most common in rural areas.
Miri	Land owned by the state and that carries *tassruf*, or usufruct, which can be enjoyed, sold, let, mortgaged or even given away. Rights may also be transmitted to heirs (male or female), although the land cannot be divided among them. The state retains ultimate ownership and, if there are no heirs, such land reverts to the state. Also, the state retains the right of supervising all transactions pertaining to the transfer of usufruct rights and their registration.
Musha	Land owned collectively. It originates from the tribal practice of dividing up arable land on which the tribe settles its members and takes account of variations in land quality to ensure equality. Restricted in application to tribal areas with low population densities.
Waqf	Land held in perpetuity as an endowment by religious trusts and therefore 'stopped for God'. Originally established to ensure land availability for schools, mosques and other public buildings, it gradually became a means of keeping land away from extravagant heirs or acquisitive states.
Other formal tenure types	
Co-operatives	In most developing countries, these are often a device to share costs, and transfer is sometimes possible (although this does not conform to the international principles on co-operatives).
Shared equity/ownership	Not common in developing countries: the occupant buys part of the equity (30:70, 50:50, 60:40, etc.) from the freeholder and rents the remaining value. The proportion of mortgage repayments/rent can be amended at a later date, enabling the occupant to eventually acquire the freehold.
Housing association lease	Extensive in the UK, but not common in developing countries. Housing associations are non-profit organizations that provide and manage housing primarily for lower-income groups. Some also offer shared ownership. Tenancies are secure, providing rents are paid and other obligations are met.
Collective, shared or joint ownership	A small, but expanding, form of tenure in which a group pools ownership and allocates rights of alienation and price to a self-created organization. Well established in Ethiopia and Colombia, where it is used to combat external threats to security of tenure. A variation is the land pooling programmes of Thailand and the Philippines in which land parcels are re-subdivided to enable part of the plot to be developed in return for the settlers receiving security of tenure for an agreed share of the land and/or property.
Non-formal tenure types	
Squatter, regularized	Secure, possibly with services and access to formal finance; higher entry cost than before regularization.
Non-regularized	Security depends upon local factors, such as numerical strength and political support; low entry costs and limited services provision.
Tenant	Generally, the most insecure of all tenure categories and also the cheapest. A contract is unlikely. Minimal housing and services standards.
Unauthorized (or illegal) subdivisions	Land subdivision, without official approval, usually by commercial developers for sale to lower-income households seeking plots for house construction. May take place on public or private land. Now commonly the largest single tenure category in the urban areas of many countries. Legal status varies; but most occupants possess some form of title, such as the *hisseli tapu* or shared title, found in Turkey. Entry costs are usually modest due to efficient land development and refusal by developers to follow official standards and procedures. Commonly legalized and serviced after a period.
Unauthorized construction	Development on land that is legally occupied, but for which the occupant does not possess official permission to build. The offence is therefore technical or procedural, but may be classified as illegal. Security can, therefore, be less than indicated by the tenure status *per se*.
Unauthorized transfer	Widespread in public-sector projects, where original allottees transfer their rights, at a substantial profit, to another. The transfer is invariably not permitted by the allottee's contract, but is effected using a secondary contract or power of attorney, which is recognized in law. It is particularly common in Delhi. Secondary allottees are very rarely removed or punished, due to legal complications. Entry costs are relatively high as the transfer is used to realize the full market value for a subsidized unit.
Purchased customary land	In areas where customary tenure is subject to urbanization, such as Southern Africa and Papua New Guinea, illegal sales of land take place to both long-established residents and newcomers, usually kinsmen. Such sales do not enjoy legal or customary approval, but are increasingly accepted by all involved, providing occupants with security of tenure and even *de facto* rights of transfer.

Customary tenure arrangements

The role of customary law in the regulation of tenure and secure tenure rights is far more widespread than is generally understood. This is particularly true in Africa where non-customary (formal) tenure arrangements generally cover less than 10 per cent of land (primarily in urban areas), with customary land tenure systems governing land rights in 90 per cent (or more) of areas.[7] In some countries, the proportions are slightly different; yet, customary land remains by far the largest tenure sector (such as Botswana, where 72 per cent of land is tribal or customary, 23 per cent state land, and freehold some 5 per cent).

One of the characteristics of customary tenure arrangements is that there may be no notion of 'ownership' or 'possession', as such. Rather, the land itself may be considered sacred, while the role of people is one of a steward protecting the rights of future generations. Thus, under customary tenure systems, rights to land may be characterized as:

- *User rights:* rights to use the land for residential or economic purposes (including grazing, growing subsistence crops and gathering minor forestry products).
- *Control rights:* rights to make decisions on how the land should be used, including deciding what economic activities should be undertaken and how to benefit financially from these activities.
- *Transfer rights:* rights to sell or mortgage the land, to convey the land to others through intra-community reallocations, to transmit the land to heirs through inheritance, and to reallocate use and control rights.[8]

Rights are determined by community leaders, generally according to need rather than payment. Customary systems of tenure are often more flexible than formal systems, constantly changing and evolving in order to adapt to current realities. However, this flexibility, as well, can be highly detrimental to the rights of poorer groups and great care must be taken in areas governed by customary land relations to ensure that these groups are adequately protected.[9]

Traditionally, such customary tenure systems have been found mostly in rural areas. Continued population growth in urban areas, however, has often implied that urban areas have spread into areas under customary tenure systems. This influx of migrants has frequently led to conflicts over the role of local chiefs, who traditionally allocate land to members of their community under well-established and officially recognized arrangements. It is not surprising that people living in such areas object to being considered illegal occupants of their land, even though they lack official titles to prove ownership. The inability of the local authorities or governments, as well as the unwillingness of the formal market to increase the supply of planned residential land at prices which the poor can afford, has perpetuated the dependence upon customary tenure arrangements. In many instances, urban sprawl into such areas has even led to the introduction of entirely new tenure arrangements.[10]

Box 5.1 Tenure categories for the urban poor

The table below outlines the main tenure options available to the urban poor. As the table indicates, most urban areas are comprised of an urban core and an urban periphery, both of which may be the location of both formal and informal neighbourhoods.

	Formal neighbourhoods	Informal neighbourhoods
Urban core	Tenements: • Hand-me-downs • Units built for the poor Public housing Hostels, flophouses	Squatters: • Authorized • Unauthorized Pavement dwellers
Urban periphery	Private rental housing Public housing	Illegal subdivisions: • Owner occupied • Rental Squatters: • Authorized (including site and service) • Unauthorized

In addition, it should be noted that in some cities camps for refugees and displaced persons complete the tenure picture.

In the urban core, most of the formal neighbourhoods outlined above do not provide the degrees of security of tenure envisaged under human rights law. Similarly, the informal areas may or may not provide for legal or quasi-legal security of tenure, although in many instances unofficial forms of security of tenure may be in place due to localized political agreements and expediency.

As with the urban core, some individuals residing in the periphery may enjoy a measure of legal or quasi-legal security of tenure; but the norm tends to be a combination of inadequate physical housing conditions coupled with inadequate degrees of tenure sufficiently strong to protect dwellers against forced evictions and secure and stable enough to encourage them to make the necessary investments in their own homes to improve conditions of housing adequacy.

Source: Davis, 2006a, p30

WHAT IS SECURITY OF TENURE?

Each type of tenure provides varying degrees of security. The spectrum ranges from one extreme of no *de facto* or *de jure* security, to the other end of the continuum, where those with legal and actual secure tenure can live happily without any real threat of eviction, particularly if they are wealthy or politically well connected.

So, what is *security* of tenure? It has been described as:

> *... an agreement between an individual or group [with respect] to land and residential property which is governed and regulated by a legal [formal or customary] and administrative framework. The security derives from the fact that the right of access to and use of the land and property is underwritten by a known set of rules, and that this right is justiciable.*[11]

The security of the tenure can be affected in a wide range of ways, depending upon constitutional and legal frameworks, social norms, cultural values and, to some extent, individual preference. In effect, security of tenure may be summarized as 'the right of all individuals and groups to effective protec-

Customary systems of tenure are often more flexible than formal systems

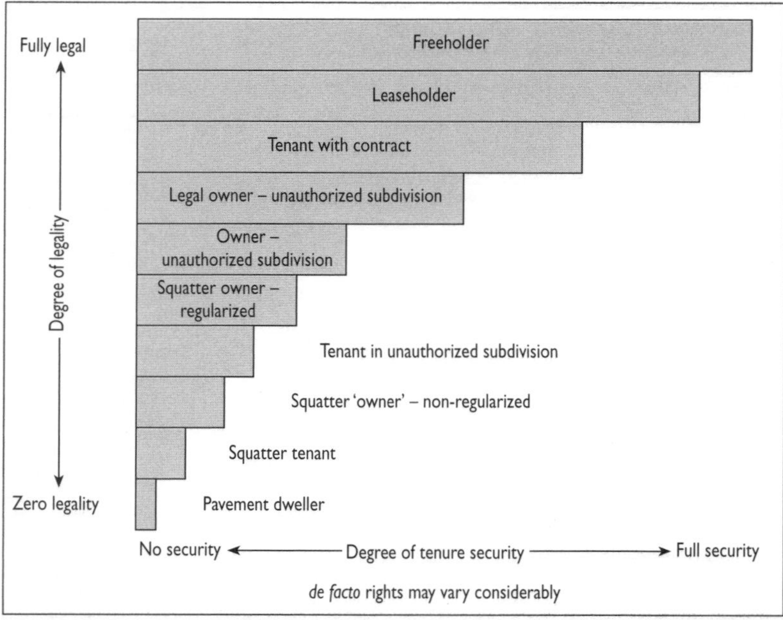

Figure 5.1

Urban tenure categories by legal status

Source: adapted from Payne, 2001e

tion from the State against forced evictions'.[12] Under international law, forced eviction is defined as 'the permanent or temporary removal against their will of individuals, families and/or communities from the homes and/or land which they occupy, without the provision of, and access to, appropriate forms of legal or other protection'.[13]

While all persons reside with one or another form of tenure, not all tenure types are secure. Moreover, security is not necessarily only available through the formalization of tenure rights. As many analysts have asserted, security of tenure often has as much to do with one's *perception* of security as the actual legal status one may enjoy. A variety of tenure arrangements can provide tenure security. People can have *de facto* security of tenure, coupled with varying degrees of legal tenure when, for instance, governments provide assurances against displacement or incorporate a neighbourhood within a special zone protected against evictions, such as is envisaged under the Brazilian City Statute (see Box 11.8 in Chapter 11). Governments can also recognize security of tenure, but without officially regularizing the community concerned, and can also issue interim occupancy permits or temporary non-transferable leases that can provide forms of secure tenure. At the other end of the spectrum, governments can support laws and policies which envisage long-term leases and secure tenure through leasehold or freehold rights. As Figure 5.1 shows, tenure must be viewed as a spectrum with various degrees of security, combined with various degrees of legality.

Security of tenure often has as much to do with one's perception of security as the actual legal status

Box 5.2 Tenure types in Phnom Penh, Cambodia

In the case of Phnom Penh, nine types of tenure have been categorized, from the most to the least secure:

1 certificate of ownership;
2 certificate of possession;
3 government concession;
4 court order after dispute;
5 family registered book;
6 unauthorized occupation of private land;
7 unauthorized occupation of state private land;
8 unauthorized occupation of state public land; and
9 pavement/mobile dweller.

Source: Payne, 1997.

In practical terms, however, the issue of tenure security may be even more complicated than that outlined in Figure 5.1. Security (and insecurity) of tenure takes a plethora of forms, varying widely between countries, cities and neighbourhoods, land plots and even within individual dwellings, where the specific rights of the owner or formal tenant may differ from those of family members or others. As noted above, the figure does not, for example, include customary or Islamic tenure categories, nor does it take into account other specific historical, political or other circumstances. Box 5.2 presents the variation of tenure categories in one specific location, Phnom Penh (Cambodia).

Moreover, it is important to point out that different tenure systems can co-exist next to each other. This is not only the case at the national level where a country may maintain and recognize many different types of tenure, but even at the neighbourhood or household level. It is quite common in the developing world for informal settlements to be comprised of homes that possess varying degrees of tenure security, and that provide differing levels of rights to inhabitants depending upon a variety of factors. The common practice of squatters subletting portions of their homes or land plots to tenants is one of many examples where individuals living on the same land plot may each have distinct degrees of tenure security/insecurity.

This discussion highlights the fact that security of tenure is a multidimensional, multilevelled process that is of universal validity, but which needs to be approached and acted on in a myriad of ways, many or all of which can be consistent with internationally recognized human rights. Understanding the different categories of tenure, the varying degrees of security that each affords dwellers and how the benefits of secure tenure can be spread more extensively and equitably throughout all societies remains a major policy challenge. While human rights law now clearly stipulates that security of tenure is a basic human right, ensuring that all who possess this right enjoy security of tenure remains a major challenge to governments and the broader international community.

At the extreme end of the secure–insecure tenure continuum are the millions of people who are homeless. Even within this group, however, there is a wide range of different tenure types, with different levels on tenure security, or rather, in this case, different levels of tenure insecurity (see Box 5.3). Homelessness is quite often the outcome – for shorter or longer periods of time – when communities, households or individuals are evicted from their homes. However, due to the wide range of definitions of homelessness, general lack of data, and in particular comparative data, this Global Report does not include a specific discussion on the trends and conditions relating to homeless people.

Insecure tenure is not exclusively a problem facing those residing within the informal housing and land sector, but also affects businesses and income-generating activities within the informal enterprise sector. With as little choice within the official employment sector as they have within the official housing sector, hundreds of millions of people subsist within the informal economy, providing vital goods, services and labour to the broader society. Those working within the informal economy are increasingly facing eviction from the markets and kiosks in which they work.

The fact that there are many types of tenure and many degrees of tenure security has important implications for the development of policy and practice, not only in terms of housing policy, but also in terms of human rights and how rights relate to tenure. Having access to secure tenure cannot, in and of itself, solve the problems of growing slums, structural homelessness, expanding poverty, unsafe living environments and inadequate housing and living conditions. Nonetheless, it is widely recognized that secure tenure is an essential element of a successful shelter strategy.

Measuring security of tenure

Despite the fact that an individual's, household's or community's security of tenure is central to the enjoyment of basic human rights and sustainable development, there are currently no global tools or mechanisms in place to monitor security of tenure. So far, it has been impossible to obtain household data on secure tenure; nor has it been possible to produce global comparative data on various institutional aspects of secure tenure.

At the same time, it should be recalled that the 156 governments[14] that have voluntarily bound themselves to promote and protect the rights contained in the International Covenant on Economic, Social and Cultural Rights (ICESCR), which contains the most important international legal source of the right to adequate housing, including security of tenure, are currently required to submit reports 'on the measures which they have adopted and the progress made in achieving the observance of the rights recognized' in the Covenant.[15] States are required to answer a range of specific questions on housing rights under a series of guidelines developed by the United Nations Committee on Economic, Social and Cultural Rights (CESCR) to assist governments with their reporting obligations. Many of these questions are directly linked to security of tenure (see Box 5.4). Because the presentation of such reports is legally required of all states parties to the Covenant every five years, all governments bound by the Covenant should have in place the means and institutions required to collect comprehensive answers to these queries.

Although few, if any, governments actually collect statistics and other data on the many issues linked to security of tenure, it is clear that they are expected to do so. Yet, access to such information is vital in any society if policy and practice are to be successful in addressing realities on the ground. Placing greater emphasis on these legal duties of states could facilitate the collection of more comprehensive and reliable data on security of tenure. Among the initiatives that deserve some attention in this respect is that undertaken by the United Nations Housing Rights Programme (see Box 5.5).

Box 5.3 Defining homelessness

For statistical purposes, the United Nations has developed the following definition of homeless households:

> *households without a shelter that would fall within the scope of living quarters. They carry their few possessions with them sleeping in the streets, in door ways or on piers, or in any other space, on a more or less random basis.*

In terms of national data collection, however, there is no globally agreed definition of homelessness. The result is that those (rather few) countries that are collecting data on homelessness tend to use their own (official and non-official) definitions, usually related to national legislation and policy legacies. In general, the definitions used range from narrow ones of 'rooflessness' – such as the one quoted above, embracing only those sleeping rough – to a wide range of 'broader' definitions which may include a variety of categories, based on the quality of dwellings, the risk of becoming homeless, time exposed to homelessness and responsibilities for taking alleviating action.

'Narrow' definitions are most commonly used in developing countries, while 'wider' ones are more commonly used in developed countries. Among the main reasons for this is the very fact that some of the wider definitions of homelessness used in some developed countries, i.e. defining all those 'inadequately housed' as being homeless, would categorize the vast majority of people in some developing countries as homeless.

Depending on definitions used, the following is a sample of the most common categories of conditions which may or may not be included in a given definition of homelessness: rough sleepers, pavement dwellers, occupants of shelters for homeless persons, occupants of institutions (such as persons in prisons or in long-term stays at hospitals), street children, occupants of un-serviced housing, occupants of poorly constructed and insecure housing (vulnerable sites, precarious tenancy), sharers (people who are 'doubling-up' with friends or relatives, when they really want a place for themselves), occupants of housing of unsuitable cost (i.e. people in danger of being evicted for non-payment), occupants of mobile homes, occupants of refugee and other emergency camps, itinerant groups (nomads, Roma, etc.).

Source: UNCHS, 2000b; United Nations, 1998

A number of global bodies, including UN-Habitat, are wrestling with the problem of measuring the scope and scale of security of tenure, and there is no clear methodology on this yet which could produce robust information. UN-Habitat is currently collaborating with a range of partners to assess the limitations of a common monitoring strategy and to develop a common strategy for an operational method for measuring, monitoring and assessing security of tenure. In the meantime, and for global monitoring purposes, in response to its reporting responsibilities with respect to the Millennium Development Goals (MDGs), UN-Habitat has suggested that people have secure tenure when:

Secure tenure is an essential element of a successful shelter strategy

- There is evidence of documentation that can be used as proof of secure tenure status.
- There is either *de facto* or perceived protection from forced evictions.[16]

Whatever form a global system for monitoring security of tenure may eventually take, it should focus on the issues already identified by the CESCR with respect to security of tenure as a component of the right to adequate housing, as summarized in Box 5.4.

Box 5.4 Security of tenure: State party reporting responsibilities under the International Covenant on Economic, Social and Cultural Rights (ICESCR)

All of the 156 states which have ratified the International Covenant on Economic, Social and Cultural Rights (ICESCR) are legally required to report to the United Nations Committee on Economic, Social and Cultural Rights (CESCR), every five years, on the measures they have taken and the progress made in addressing the rights recognized in the Covenant. Among the more prominent questions which states are required to answer are the following:

> *Please provide detailed information about those groups within your society that are vulnerable and disadvantaged with regard to housing. Indicate, in particular:*
>
> 1 *the number of homeless individuals and families;*
> 2 *the number of individuals and families currently inadequately housed and without ready access to basic amenities, such as water, heating (if necessary), waste disposal, sanitation facilities, electricity, postal services, etc. (in so far as you consider these amenities relevant in your country); include the number of people living in overcrowded, damp, structurally unsafe housing or other conditions which affect health;*
> 3 *the number of persons currently classified as living in 'illegal' settlements or housing;*
> 4 *the number of persons evicted within the last five years and the number of persons currently lacking legal protection against arbitrary eviction or any other kind of eviction;*
> 5 *the number of persons whose housing expenses are above any government-set limit of affordability, based upon ability to pay or as a ratio of income;*
> 6 *the number of persons on waiting lists for obtaining accommodation, the average length of waiting time and measures taken to decrease such lists, as well as to assist those on such lists in finding temporary housing;*
> 7 *the number of persons in different types of housing tenure by social or public housing; private rental sector; owner-occupiers; 'illegal' sector; and others.*
>
> *Please provide information on the existence of any laws affecting the realization of the right to housing, including …*
>
> 3 *legislation relevant to land use; land distribution; land allocation; land zoning; land ceilings; expropriations, including provisions for compensation; land planning, including procedures for community participation;*
> 4 *legislation concerning the rights of tenants to security of tenure, to protection from eviction, to housing finance and rent control (or subsidy), housing affordability, etc;*
> 5 *legislation concerning building codes, building regulations and standards and the provision of infrastructure;*
> 6 *legislation prohibiting any and all forms of discrimination in the housing sector, including groups not traditionally protected;*
> 7 *legislation prohibiting any form of eviction …*
> 9 *legislation restricting speculation on housing or property, particularly when such speculation has a negative impact on the fulfilment of housing rights for all sectors of society;*
> 10 *legislative measures conferring legal title to those living in the 'illegal' sector.*

Source: United Nations Document E/C.12/1990/8, pp88–110

Box 5.5 Measuring the progressive realization of housing rights

The United Nations Housing Rights Programme is a joint initiative of UN-Habitat and the Office of the United Nations High Commissioner for Human Rights (OHCHR). The programme was established in 2002 with the objective of supporting the efforts by governments, civil society and national human rights institutions towards the full and progressive realization of the right to adequate housing. Since its inception, the programme has focused on developing a set of housing rights indicators to facilitate monitoring and evaluating progress in achieving housing rights.

The development of indicators is grounded in the existing reporting responsibilities of states under international law (see Box 5.4) and the clarifications provided by the United Nations Committee on Economic, Social and Cultural Rights (CESCR) in its General Comment No 4. The activities have progressed to the development of a set of 12 housing rights indicators, which address habitability, accessibility to services, affordability, security of tenure, forced evictions, homeless populations, and legal and institutional frameworks. Furthermore, the principles for formulating a global monitoring and evaluation mechanism have been set out and will be used to test the set of indicators in a number of countries.

In the context of the ongoing reform of human rights frameworks and mechanisms within the United Nations system, this initiative seems to hold a lot of promise. In fact, the OHCHR is currently expanding this initiative and assessing the possibility of developing a more comprehensive set of indicators to streamline the reporting responsibilities of states with respect to a whole range of economic, social, cultural, civil and political rights.

Source: UN-Habitat, 2003e; UN-Habitat, forthcoming; United Nations document HRI/MC/2006/7

Realities underlying tenure insecurity

The continuing absence of real household and individual security associated with lack of security of tenure experienced in the world's growing slums and informal settlements has serious consequences for the enjoyment of human rights. But this insecurity does not stop at the doorway of the average slum dwelling. Rather, such insecurity increasingly manifests itself in the creation of conditions that may lead to more destructive forms of political instability. While there may be many other causes, questions of urban crime and insecurity, terrorism, political violence and turmoil cannot be de-linked from the fact that a large portion of humanity does not enjoy levels of security of tenure promised to them under human rights laws, political pronouncements, global campaigns and other initiatives devoted towards these ends.

The consequences of tenure insecurity are by no means peripheral concerns. Living without tenure security can mean the constant threat of (often violent) eviction; limited or no access to basic services, including water, sanitation and electricity; social exclusion and homelessness; human rights violations; reduced revenues for local government; violence against women; particularly severe problems for elderly persons, persons with disabilities, children and other vulnerable groups; reduced investments in housing and distortions in the price of land and services; and an undermining of good governance and long-term planning. Moreover, reduced investments in housing may lead to reduced household and individual security in the home itself as structures become more prone to illegal entry by criminals. Indeed, governments that allow (or encourage) levels of tenure security to decline, that tolerate (or actively support) mass forced evictions, that fail to hold public officials accountable for such violations of human rights, and that place unrealistic hopes on the private sector to satisfy the housing needs of all income groups, including the poor, contribute towards the worsening of these circumstances. The result is even less tenure security and less social (and national) security.

If governments and global institutions are serious about security, then international security needs to be seen less as a question of military balances of power, unlawful acts of military aggression and politics through the barrel of the gun, and more as questions revolving around security at the level of the individual, the home and the neighbourhood. Such a perspective of security is grounded in human security, human rights and – ultimately – security of tenure. If governments long for a secure world, they must realize that without security of tenure and the many benefits that it can bestow, such a vision is unlikely to ever emerge.

SCALE AND IMPACTS OF TENURE INSECURITY

While, as noted above, reliable and comparative data on the scale of tenure insecurity are globally non-existent, few would argue against the fact that the number of slum dwellers is growing, not declining. UN-Habitat has estimated that the total slum population in the world increased from 715 million in 1990 to 913 million in 2001. And the number of slum dwellers is projected to increase even further. Unless MDG 7 target 11 on improving the lives of at least 100 million slum dwellers by 2020 is achieved, the number of slum dwellers is projected to reach 1392 million by 2020 (see Table 5.2).[17] In fact, if no firm and concrete action is taken, the number of slum dwellers may well reach 2 billion by 2030.[18] This dramatic increase in the global slum population should not come as a surprise to anyone, however. Nearly two decades ago, in 1989, a seminal work concluded:

> *If present trends continue, we can expect to find tens of millions more households living in squatter settlements or in very poor quality and overcrowded rented accommodation owned by highly exploitative landlords. Tens of millions more households will be forcibly evicted from their homes. Hundreds of millions more people will build shelters on dangerous sites and with no alternative but to work in illegal or unstable jobs. The quality of many basic services (water, sanitation, waste disposal and healthcare) will deteriorate still further and there will be a rise in the number of diseases related to poor and contaminated living environments, including those resulting from air pollution and toxic wastes.*[19]

Reliable and comparative data on the scale of tenure insecurity are ... non-existent

As indicated in Table 5.2, cities in developing countries are hosts to massive slum populations. The proportion of urban populations living in slums is highest in sub-Saharan Africa (72 per cent) and Southern Asia (59 per cent). In some countries of sub-Saharan Africa, more than 90 per cent of the urban population are slum dwellers. While circumstances vary, a clear majority of those living in slums, squatter settlements, abandoned buildings and other inadequate homes do not possess adequate levels of formal tenure security, or access to basic services such as electricity and water.

More than one quarter of the world's urban population experience various levels of tenure insecurity

Table 5.3 provides rough estimates of the scale of urban tenure insecurity worldwide. While the data should be treated as indicative only, it does provide an approximation of the scale of various forms of tenure insecurity and regional variations. Table 5.3 indicates that more than one quarter of the world's urban population experience various levels of tenure insecurity, although it should be noted that the level of insecurity varies considerably. For example, many of the renters in developing countries may well have quite high levels of tenure security compared to renters in the slums of many developing countries. At the national

	Total slum population (millions)					Slum population as a percentage of urban population	
	1990	2001	2005	2010	2020	1990	2001
World	**715**	**913**	**998**	**1246**	**1392**	**31.3**	**31.2**
Developed regions	42	45	47	48	52	6.0	6.0
Transitional countries*	19	19	19	19	18	10.3	10.3
Developing regions	654	849	933	1051	1331	46.5	42.7
Northern Africa	22	21	21	21	21	37.7	28.2
Sub-Saharan Africa	101	166	199	250	393	72.3	71.9
Latin America and the Caribbean	111	128	134	143	163	35.4	31.9
East Asia	151	194	212	238	299	41.1	36.4
Southern Asia	199	253	276	308	385	63.7	59.0
Southeast Asia	49	57	60	64	73	36.8	28.0
West Asia	22	30	33	38	50	26.4	25.7
Oceania	0	0	1	1	1	24.5	24.1

* Commonwealth of Independent States

Table 5.2

The urbanization of poverty: The growth of slum populations (1990–2020)

Source: UN-Habitat, 2006e, pp188, 190

	Squatters (no rent)	Renters	Other	Total
Southern Africa	8	16	6	29
Rest of Africa	13	30	7	50
China	5	2	8	15
East Asia and Pacific, excluding Australasia	7	26	9	41
South and Southeast Asia	14	31	5	50
Middle East	8	28	6	42
Western Europe	2	19	4	25
North America and Australasia	1	10	4	16
Latin America and the Caribbean	11	17	6	34
World	7	17	4	28

Urban tenure insecurity, by region (percentage)

Source: Flood, 2001

level, the pattern is the same, with between 40 and 70 per cent of the population of Brazil's main cities living in irregular settlements and some 58 per cent of all households in South Africa living without security of tenure.[20]

The situation in Cambodia deserves some special attention since everyone who returned to Phnom Penh after the collapse of the Khmer Rouge regime was a squatter:

> *In 1979, when people first began to emerge from the jungle into an empty, dilapidated city, they camped out in empty buildings and lit open fires to cook their rice. When all the houses and flats had been occupied, newcomers built shelters wherever they could find space, along river banks and railway tracks, on streets, in the areas between buildings and on rooftops.*[21]

Urban spatial growth ... have resulted in ... displacement of farmers, illegal land seizures and growing tenure insecurity

To formalize this situation and provide the residents with security of tenure, a new Land Law was adopted in 1992 and revised in 2001. As a result, any person who had enjoyed peaceful, uncontested possession of land for no less than five years prior to the promulgation of the law had the right to request a definitive title of ownership.[22]

Having the right to request a definitive title and actually getting title are, however, two quite different things. Furthermore, many residents – particularly the poor – may qualify for title under the law but are unaware both of their status and of the procedures for requesting title. While various organizations have been working to increase that awareness, they do not have the resources to reach all of the country's families facing eviction. Even for those who are aware of their rights to possession and who can make a claim, there are further obstructions: 'Corruption has also made land titles difficult to obtain; an application for a land title can cost from US$200 to $700 in informal payments to government officials, a cost that is prohibitive for many.'[23] And then, even where people are aware of their rights, have made their claim and have received official documents to this effect, this does not mean that they have any security of tenure. A half-hour television documentary broadcast in Australia in October 2006 exemplified the insecurity faced by many urban residents in Cambodia (see Box 5.6).

In much of the developing world, it is not solely cities that are host to households without security of tenure. In rural areas, agricultural land provides the sole basis of income for more than half a billion people. About half of these suffer some form of serious tenure insecurity due to their status of tenant farmers, because they are landless, or due to incomplete and dysfunctional land administration systems not suited to the prevailing circumstances.[24] In addition, rapid economic development – leading to urban spatial growth – in countries such as China (see Box 5.7) and India have resulted in massive losses of farmland and the subsequent displacement of farmers, illegal land seizures and growing tenure insecurity. With particular regard to China, from the mid 1980s onward, large swathes of rural land near cities and towns have effectively entered the urban land market, threatening security of tenure to land and housing.[25] Between 1986 and 1996, 31 cities in China expanded their land area by some 50 per cent, most of this former farmland.

Security of tenure problems are by no means isolated to the developing world, and while they may manifest in fundamentally different ways, declines in security of tenure are visible in many of the wealthier countries (see Box 5.8). In the UK, for instance, fewer and fewer people are able to access the property market due to rising costs and continuing declines in buyer affordability.[26] In the US, millions of tenants do not have adequate levels of secure tenure protecting them from possible eviction. Moreover, people facing eviction in the US do not have a right to counsel; as a result, the scale of evictions in the US is far higher than it would be if tenants were provided legal representation in eviction proceedings.[27] According to official figures, some 25,000 evictions are carried out annually in New York City alone.[28] The *Economist* publishes annual figures outlining housing price developments in a range of countries, indicating the upward trend over the past 15 years which, although

Box 5.6 When is tenure secure? The eviction of the Group 78 community in Phnom Penh, Cambodia

Residents of the Group 78 community in Phnom Penh had been living in the same location since the mid 1980s and had proof of their continuous 'peaceful and uncontested possession' of the land, as specified in Article 30 of the 1991 Land Law. Many of the residents had documents issued by the local authorities recognizing their legal occupation of the land. They thus clearly met the requirements of the Land Law. Yet, when they applied for formal title to the land in 2004, their applications were refused. They thus lodged their case to the National Cadastral Commission and the National Authority on Land Dispute Resolution. The verdict was negative. Their application was refused as their land was needed to 'contribute to city beautification and development'. The Group 78 residents were informed by the local authorities in June 2006 that they would have to move to a resettlement area on the outskirts of the city.

While the Land Law does provide for expropriation of land for the public interest, 'it is doubtful whether the purported reason of "beautification" could fulfil this requirement. If acceptable, such vague wording would render the public interest test meaningless.' A more likely explanation may have been that the evictions were related to the increasing value of their land. With land prices soaring, increasing sevenfold since the year 2000, the potential for corruption is considerable. The US ambassador to Cambodia made the following observations:

> *There's too many land disputes, too many rich people, greedy companies. Property is really the key to prosperity and freedom and once people are not secure in what they own, everything else falls apart… Corruption is central to everything, at all levels. I don't know of any case of where a corrupt official has really gone to gaol here – certainly not from the ruling party.*

Source: ABC TV, 2006; Bristol, 2007a

Box 5.7 Increasing tenure insecurity in China

It is not surprising that a low-income country with as huge and diverse a land mass and population, and a history of tumultuous political and economic change, as China would be afflicted with problems stemming from insecure tenure. It is, nonetheless, surprising how quickly China has evolved from a country with relatively secure tenure for all during most of its history to the opposite during the last decade.

China's largely successful transition to a highly globalized mixed economy from a minimally open-command economy during the years since the Four Modernizations were announced in 1978 has much to do with this: land has become a scarce commodity. Prices now more accurately – if still incompletely – reflect the expected return on investment to alternate uses. Land prices have risen dramatically during the past decade, while the development of the legal and administrative infrastructure governing the allocation, transfer and conversion of rural and urban land has only just begun to adapt itself to existing and emerging economic pressures. As urban and industrial development have expanded westward during the past decade, problems of insecure tenure that were originally found only in the fast growing coastal cities and their suburbs can now be found throughout the country. Various groups of dwellers are particularly susceptible to insecurity of tenure to housing in China. These include:

- Farmers, whose insecurity of livelihood in the countryside forces them to migrate to the cities in search of income-earning opportunities. Lacking an urban residence permit, and in the absence of policies supportive towards rural migrants, their security of tenure to housing remains tenuous, at best. Approximately 120 million to 150 million migrant workers live in major metropolitan centres for a large part of the year.
- Former state-sector workers who have been laid off (*xiagang*) or paid off (*maiduan*) by their employers and are living in original 'welfare' housing that they bought from their employer during earlier housing reforms.
- Non-state sector workers holding urban residence permits whose incomes do not allow them secure tenure to housing. These may be long-term city-centre residents who are, or were, employed in either collective or informal enterprises and who have been renting or subletting affordable housing from private parties or local authorities.
- Registered and non-registered urban residents of informal settlements (*chengzhongcun*), dangerous or dilapidated housing (*weijiufangwu*), or housing constructed illegally or without conforming to building codes (*weifaweiguifangwu*).
- Urban workers with adequate incomes and/or political resources to maintain access to adequate housing in the event that their property is expropriated and demolished under the force of 'eminent domain'.

Source: Westendorff, 2007

Security of tenure problems are by no means isolated to the developing world

now moderating in many countries, has resulted in increasing numbers of people being unable to access the owner–occupation sector, particularly in city centres.[29]

These various examples, of course, are a mere sampling of the degree to which security of tenure is not a reality for so many throughout the world today, in rich and poor countries alike. The scale of insecure tenure and the growing prevalence of inadequate housing conditions and slums are clearly daunting in nature and will require considerably larger and better resourced efforts than the world has witnessed to date. While political and economic interests and a range of other causes lie at the heart of the global security of tenure deficit today, the very nature of tenure itself contributes to the difficulties in building a clear global movement to ensure that all can live out their lives with secure tenure.

SCALE AND IMPACTS OF EVICTIONS

While insecure tenure is experienced by many largely in the realm of perceptions – although such perceptions may be experienced as very real fear, and have very concrete outcomes, such as the inability or unwillingness to improve dwellings – evictions are always experienced as very real events, with harsh consequences for those evicted. This

Box 5.8 Erosion of tenure protections in Canada

During the last decade, security of tenure regulations – which is a provincial government responsibility – have been eroded in many of Canada's ten provinces. In Ontario, for example, the largest province with about 40 per cent of Canada's population, 'the entire 50-year evolution of security of tenure legislation was wiped off the statute books in the late 1990s'. In Ontario in 1998, the Tenant Protection Act repealed and replaced the Landlord and Tenant Act, the Rent Control Act and the Rental Housing Protection Act.

The previous legislation had allowed municipalities in Ontario to refuse permission for the demolition or conversion of rental apartment buildings until the rental housing supply and affordability crisis had passed. The adoption of the Tenant Protection Act repealed this provision, and it was replaced by provisions for 'vacancy decontrol'. In practice, the new legislation implies that when a unit is vacated, the rent on the unit can be set at any level: 'This accounts for the steep increases in rents, far outpacing tenant incomes.'

Another important feature of the Tenant Protection Act was that it allowed for quick and easy evictions: a tenant has five days during which to reply to an eviction notice. If tenants do not reply (i.e. they were away or did not realize that they have to submit a written intention to dispute, or if they have language problems or other pressing issues), the landlord can obtain a default order that does not require a hearing. A review of the impact of the legislation found that over half of eviction orders (54 per cent) were issued as the result of a default order. The Tenant Protection Act resulted in the number of eviction orders in the City of Toronto increasing from about 5000 at the time of the new legislation to a peak of 15,000 in 2002. Not all orders result in an eviction. The estimate is that about 3900 tenant households (about 9800 persons) are evicted annually in Toronto as a result of the Tenant Protection Act.

Source: Hulchanski, 2007

section outlines the scale and impacts of three major categories of evictions: forced evictions; market-based evictions; and expropriation and compulsory acquisition. The categories are not mutually exclusive, and the real causes underlying the evictions may be very similar. For example, many cases of so-called 'expropriation for the common good' may well be a convenient way of getting rid of communities who are considered as 'obstacles to development'. Three major causes of large-scale evictions are also discussed below.

At least 2 million people are victims of forced evictions every year

Forced evictions

Large-scale forced evictions and mass forced displacement have been part and parcel of the political and development landscapes for decades as cities seek to 'beautify' themselves, sponsor international events, criminalize slums and increase the investment prospects of international companies and the urban elite. As recognized by the Global Campaign for Secure Tenure, most forced evictions share a range of common characteristics, including the following:

Forced evictions are often accompanied by the use of excessive force ..., such as arbitrary arrests, beatings, rape, torture and even killings

- Evictions tend to be most prevalent in countries or parts of cities with the worst housing conditions.
- It is always the poor who are evicted – wealthier population groups virtually never face forced eviction, and never mass eviction.
- Forced evictions are often violent and include a variety of human rights abuses beyond the violation of the right to adequate housing.
- Evictees tend to end worse off than before the eviction.
- Evictions invariably compound the problem that they were ostensibly aimed at 'solving'.
- Forced evictions impact most negatively upon women and children.[30]

Forced evictions are the most graphic symptom of just how large the scale of tenure insecurity is and how severe the consequences can be of not enjoying tenure rights. Table 5.4 charts a portion of the eviction history during the last 20 years, revealing that forced evictions have often affected literally hundreds of thousands of people in a single eviction operation. The three most common types of large-scale forced evictions – urban infrastructure projects, international mega events and urban beautification – are discussed later in this chapter. Other types of forced eviction may be carried out in connection with efforts to reclaim occupied public land for private economic investment. Conflict and disaster, as well as urban regeneration and gentrification measures, can also be the source of eviction. The most frequent cases of forced evictions, however, are the small-scale ones: those that occur here and there, every day, causing untold misery for the communities, households and individuals concerned.

While forced evictions are certainly the exception to the rule when examining governmental attitudes to informal settlements, it is clear that this practice – though widely condemned as a violation of human rights – is still carried out on a wide scale in many countries. Despite the repeated condemnation of the practice of forced evictions, millions of dwellers are forcibly evicted annually, with hundreds of millions more threatened by possible forced eviction due to their current insecure tenure status and existing urban and rural development plans that envisage planned forced evictions. In the vast majority of eviction cases, proper legal procedures, resettlement, relocation and/or compensation are lacking. The Centre on Housing Rights and Evictions (COHRE) has, over the last decade, collected information about eviction cases from all over the world (see Table 5.5). Its data is not comprehensive since it collects data from a limited number of countries only, and only on the basis of information received directly from affected persons and groups and where the cases at hand are particularly noteworthy. Yet, the data indicates that at least 2 million people are victims of forced evictions every year. The vast majority of these live in Africa and Asia.

Despite the numerous efforts by those in the international human rights community to prevent evictions, the many initiatives to confer secure tenure to slum dwellers and the simple common sense that forced evictions rarely, if ever, actually result in improvements in a given city or country, this practice continues, and is often accompanied by the use of excessive force by those carrying out the evictions, such as arbitrary arrests, beatings, rape, torture and even killings. In a selection of forced evictions in only seven countries – Bangladesh, China, India, Indonesia, Nigeria, South Africa and Zimbabwe – between 1995 and 2005, COHRE found that over 10.2 million people faced forced eviction during this ten-year period.

While all regions have faced large-scale forced evictions, Africa has perhaps fared worst of all during recent years. A new study reveals that the practice of forced evictions has reached epidemic proportions in Africa, with more than 3 million Africans forcibly evicted from their homes since 2000.[31] Some of the cases highlighted in that and other studies include the following:[32]

- In Nigeria, some 2 million people have been forcibly evicted from their homes and many thousands have been made homeless since 2000 (see Box 5.9). The largest individual case occurred in Rainbow Town, Port Harcourt (Rivers State) in 2001, when nearly 1 million residents were forcibly evicted from their homes. In Lagos, more than 700,000 people have been evicted from their homes and businesses since 1990.[33]

Table 5.4

A selection of major urban eviction cases since 1985

Source: COHRE (www.cohre.org/evictions); Davis, 2006a, p102

Year(s)	Location	Number of people evicted
1986–1992	Santo Domingo (Dominican Republic)	180,000
1985–1988	Seoul (Republic of Korea)	800,000
1990	Lagos (Nigeria)	300,000
1990	Nairobi (Kenya)	40,000
1995–1996	Rangoon (Myanmar)	1,000,000
1995	Beijing (China)	100,000
2000	Port Harcourt (Nigeria)	nearly 1,000,000
2001–2003	Jakarta (Indonesia)	500,000
2004	New Delhi (India)	150,000
2004	Kolkata (India)	77,000
2004–2005	Mumbai (India)	more than 300,000
2005	Harare (Zimbabwe)	750,000

Region	Persons evicted 1998–2000	Persons evicted 2001–2002	Persons evicted 2003–2006	Total 1998–2006
Africa	1,607,435	4,086,971	1,967,486	7,661,892
Europe	23,728	172,429	16,266	212,423
The Americas	135,569	692,390	152,949	980,908
Asia and the Pacific	2,529,246	1,787,097	2,140,906	6,457,249
Total	4,294,978	6,738,887	4,277,607	15,311,472

Notes: The data presented in this table is based on information received by the Centre on Housing Rights and Evictions (COHRE) directly from affected persons and groups and where the cases at hand are particularly noteworthy. Moreover, the data is collected from some 60 to 70 countries only (although the population of these countries amounts to some 80 per cent of the total world population). The data is thus not comprehensive in terms of representing the global scale of the practice of forced eviction. Without a doubt, the actual number of forced evictions is considerably higher than what is indicated in the table.

Table 5.5

Estimated number of people subjected to forced evictions by region

Source: COHRE, 2002, 2003, 2006

- In Sudan, more than 12,000 people were forcibly evicted from Dar Assalaam camp in August 2006. The majority of the evictees had been previously displaced through conflict in Sudan and settled in camps in or around the capital, Khartoum. Authorities have forcibly evicted thousands of people from these camps, resettling them in desert areas without access to clean water, food and other essentials. Currently, there are about 1.8 million internally displaced persons (IDPs) in and around Khartoum.[34]
- In Luanda, the capital of Angola, at least 6000 families have been forcibly evicted and have had their homes demolished since 2001. Many of these families, who have received no compensation, have had their property stolen by those carrying out the forced evictions and remain homeless.
- In Equatorial Guinea, at least 650 families have been forcibly evicted from their homes since 2004, when the government embarked on a programme of urban regeneration in Malabo and Bata. What is even more disturbing is that these families had title to their property. Thousands more residents are threatened by forced evictions.
- In Kenya, at least 20,000 people have been forcibly evicted from neighbourhoods in or around Nairobi since 2000.
- In Ghana, some 800 people also had their homes destroyed in Legion Village, Accra, in May 2006, while approximately 30,000 people in the Agbogbloshie community of Accra have been threatened with forced eviction since 2002.

Not all news about evictions in Africa is bad, however. Indeed, there is evidence of a growing movement in Africa opposing evictions. In some instances, support in this regard has come from one of Africa's most important human rights institutions, the African Commission on Human and Peoples Rights, which broke new ground when it held that Nigeria's:

> *...obligations to protect obliges it to prevent the violation of any individual's right to housing by any other individual or non-state actors like landlords, property developers, and land owners, and where such infringements occur, it should act to preclude further deprivations as well as guaranteeing access to legal remedies. The right to shelter even goes further than a roof over one's head. It extends to embody the individual's right to be let alone and to live in peace – whether under a roof or not.*[35]

Forced evictions has reached epidemic proportions in Africa

This juxtaposition, of the large-scale global reality of often violent, illegal and arbitrary forced evictions, on the one hand, and the increasingly strong pro-human rights positions taken against the practice, on the other, captures the essence of the ongoing struggle between those favouring good governance, respect for the rule of law and the primacy of human rights, and those supporting more top-down, authoritarian and less democratic approaches to governance and economic decision-making. Efforts to combine best practices on the provision of security of tenure with the

Box 5.9 Forced evictions: A sample of cases from Nigeria

During the last two decades it appears as if forced evictions have been extensively used in Nigeria as a 'tool of urban engineering' in a (largely counterproductive) effort to eliminate the growth of slums. Poverty and lack of basic services and amenities have been cited as justification for the demolition of entire communities:

- When the government of Lagos State in July 1990 demolished the homes of over 300,000 Maroko residents, it claimed that the community was prone to flooding and 'unfit for human habitation'.
- When the government of Rivers State forcibly evicted over 1 million Rainbow Town residents in 2001, it claimed that the community harboured too many criminals.
- When the government of Lagos State forcibly evicted and burned the homes of over 3000 Makoko residents in April 2005, it claimed that it was helping some private citizens to flush out undesirable squatters.
- The forced eviction of thousands of residents in Abuja by the Federal Capital City Development Authority has been presented as an effort to correct distortions to the Abuja Master Plan.
- The Lagos State government's persistent efforts to forcibly evict the Ijora-Badia community have been explained by the need to rid the community of filth, flooding and prostitution (see Box 6.21).

Additional recent cases of forced evictions have been reported from:

- Aboru Abesan, in Ikeja (Lagos State), where at least 6000 residents were rendered homeless when their homes were demolished by officials of the Federal Ministry of Housing and Urban Development in January 2005;
- Agip Waterside Community in Port Harcourt, where 5000 to 10,000 people were rendered homeless between February and April 2005 when the Rivers State government demolished their homes.

Source: COHRE, 2006, p26; Morka, 2007

position taken on these questions under human rights law may be one way that a new approach to tenure can be encouraged, particularly when these evictions are carried out in ways clearly contrary to human rights law. Reducing or eliminating what are often referred to as 'market evictions', however, presents another set of challenges.

Market-based evictions ... are increasing both in terms of scale ... and as a proportion of the total ... eviction tally

Evictions of those working in the informal economic sector have been registered in a range of countries. *Operation Murambatsvina* (also referred to as *Operation Restore Order*) in Zimbabwe resulted not only in the demolition of housing, but in mass evictions of informal traders as well, which, in turn, drastically increased unemployment and further undermined both the formal and informal economies in the country (see also Box 5.14). Additional large-scale evictions of informal enterprises have been reported in Bangladesh, where at least 10,868 homes and businesses were demolished in 2004, and in Nigeria, where some 250,000 traders, kiosks and residences were destroyed in 1996.[36]

Market-based evictions

> *Moralists used to complain that international law was impotent in curbing injustices of nation-states; but it has shown even less capacity to rein in markets that, after all, do not even have an address to which subpoenas can be sent. As the product of a host of individual choices or singular corporate acts, markets offer no collective responsibility. Yet responsibility is the first obligation of both citizens and civic institutions.*[37]

Market-driven displacements may also result from in situ tenure regularization, settlement upgrading and basic service provision

Another key trend shared by most countries – regardless of income – is the growing phenomenon of market-based evictions. Although precise figures are not available, observers have noted that such evictions are increasing *both* in terms of scale (e.g. the number of persons/households evicted annually) and as a proportion of the total global eviction tally. To cite a not untypical case, it has been estimated that some 80 per cent of households in Kigali, Rwanda, are potentially subject to expropriation or market-driven evictions.[38] Market evictions, most of which are not monitored or recorded by housing organizations, which tend to restrict their focus to forced evictions, are caused by a variety of forces. These include urban gentrification; rental increases; land titling programmes; private land development and other developmental pressures; expropriation measures; and the sale of public land to private investors. Market-driven displacements may also result from *in-situ* tenure regularization, settlement upgrading and basic service provision without involvement of community organizations or appropriate accompanying social and economic measures (such as credit facilities, advisory planning or capacity-building at community level), and this may give rise to increases in housing expenditure that the poorest segment of the settlement population is not able to meet. When combined with increases in land values and market pressures resulting from tenure regularization, the poorest households will be tempted to sell their property and settle in a location where accommodation costs are less. This commonly observed progressive form of displacement results in the gradual gentrification of inner city and suburban low-income settlements.

Market evictions ... can easily generate new homelessness and new illegal settlements

Because market-based evictions are seen as inevitable consequences of the development process in the eyes of many public authorities, and due to the fact that negotiations between those proposing the eviction and those affected are not uncommon, this manifestation of the eviction process is often treated as acceptable and even voluntary in nature. Some may even argue (albeit wrongly, in many cases) that such evictions are not illegal under international law and thus are an acceptable policy option. However, one view suggests:

> *Disguising a forced eviction as a 'negotiated displacement' is usually seen as 'good governance' practice. It is less risky, in political terms, than a forced eviction; it is less brutal and, accordingly, less visible as it can be achieved following individual case-by-case negotiations. Most observers consider that the very principle of negotiating is more important than the terms of the negotiations, especially regarding the compensation issue, even when the compensation is unfair and detrimental to the occupant.*[39]

While all forms of eviction, forced and market based, are legally governed by the terms of human rights law, compensation in the event of market-based evictions tends to be treated more as a discretionary choice, rather than a right of those forced to relocate. Because one's informal tenure status may limit evictees from exercising rights to compensation and resettlement if they are subjected to market evictions, these processes can easily generate new homelessness and new illegal settlements. Even when compensation is provided, it tends to be limited to the value of a dwelling and not the dwelling and the land plot as a whole, with the result being greater social exclusion. In the absence of legal remedies, adequate resettlement options or fair and just compensation, market-based evictions lead to the establishment of new informal settlements on the periphery of cities, and tend to increase population pressure and density in existing informal inner-city settlements. This usually results in deterioration in housing conditions and/or increases in housing expenditure and commuting costs for displaced households.

Expropriation and compulsory acquisition

International human rights standards, intergovernmental organizations, a growing number of governments and many NGOs have embraced the view that forced eviction – or, for that matter, virtually every type of arbitrary or unlawful displacement – raises serious human rights concerns and should be excluded from the realms of acceptable policy. Yet, all states and all legal systems retain rights to expropriate or compulsorily acquire private property, land or housing (e.g.

Box 5.10 Expropriation and compulsory acquisition: Examples of constitutional provisions

The 1957 Constitution of Malaysia states that 'No person shall be deprived of property save in accordance with law' and that 'No law shall provide for the compulsory acquisition or use of property without adequate compensation' (Articles 13(1) and 13)2)).

Similarly, the 1960 Constitution of Nigeria asserts that:

> *No property, movable or immovable, shall be taken possession of compulsorily and no right over or interest in any such property shall be acquired compulsorily in any part of Nigeria except by or under the provisions of a law that (a) requires the payment of adequate compensation therefore; and (b) gives to any person claiming such compensation a right of access, for the determination of his interest in the property and the amount of compensation, to the High Court having jurisdiction in that part of Nigeria. (Article 31(1))*

A different, more nuanced, approach is taken in the 1996 Constitution of South Africa, which is formulated as follows (Article 25):

> *1 No one may be deprived of property except in terms of law of general application, and no law may permit arbitrary deprivation of property.*
>
> *2 Property may be expropriated only in terms of law of general application:*
>
> *(a) for a public purpose or in the public interest; and*
>
> *(b) subject to compensation, the amount of which and the time and manner of payment of which have either been agreed to by those affected or decided or approved by a court.*
>
> *3 The amount of the compensation and the time and manner of payment must be just and equitable, reflecting an equitable balance between the public interest and the interests of those affected, having regard to all relevant circumstances, including:*
>
> *(a) the current use of the property;*
>
> *(b) the history of the acquisition and use of the property;*
>
> *(c) the market value of the property;*
>
> *(d) the extent of direct state investment and subsidy in the acquisition and beneficial capital improvement of the property; and*
>
> *(e) the purpose of the expropriation …*
>
> *5 The state must take reasonable legislative and other measures, within its available resources, to foster conditions which enable citizens to gain access to land on an equitable basis.*

This very carefully worded constitutional provision is indicative of how human rights principles in South Africa have taken on added significance within the context of the recognition of property rights. The provisions attempt to ensure that those holding customary rights will enjoy protection, while reference to the 'history of its acquisition' was enshrined to ensure that land restitution rights emerging from apartheid-era racist land confiscations would not be ignored.

by using the force of 'eminent domain'). Typically, these rights of state are phrased in terms of limitations on the use of property. Box 5.10 provides some examples of how national constitutions allow for the expropriation of private property, provided that such expropriation is undertaken 'in accordance with the law'. Similar provisions are found in all jurisdictions, and even the Universal Declaration of Human Rights includes similar perspectives.

This essential conflict between the right of the state to expropriate and to control the use of property and housing, on the one hand, and land and property rights (including security of tenure), on the other, remains a vitally important issue.[40] For it is in determining the scope of both the rights of individuals and those of the state that it is possible to determine which measures resulting in eviction are truly justifiable and which are not. It is important to note that while expropriation is not in and of itself a prohibited act, under human rights law it is subject to increasingly strict criteria against which all such measures must be judged to determine whether or not they are lawful. The power of states to expropriate carries with it several fundamental preconditions. When housing, land or property rights are to be limited, this can only be done:

- subject to law and due process;
- subject to the general principles of international law;
- in the interest of society and not for the benefit of another private party;
- if it is proportionate, reasonable and subject to a fair balance test between the cost and the aim sought; and
- subject to the provision of just and satisfactory compensation.

Expropriation … is subject to increasingly strict criteria … to determine whether or not they are lawful

Once again, if any of these criteria are not met, those displaced by such expropriation proceedings have a full right to the restitution of their original homes and lands. Recent examples from China exemplify how expropriations 'for the common good' may be misused (see Box 5.11). A fictional case from Australia (see Box 5.12) exemplifies how such expropriations may be successfully challenged in court.

Major causes of large-scale evictions

While the previous sections have discussed the main categories of evictions, this section now takes a closer look at three of the most common causes of large-scale evictions – namely, infrastructure projects, international mega events and urban beautification initiatives.

Box 5.11 Urban growth causes large-scale rural land seizures and relocations in China

Rapid urban growth in China is a major cause of forced evictions and development-related relocations of farmers or other rural dwellers as cities expand into what were previously rural areas. In addition to the development of new infrastructure, three other major causes of such evictions have been highlighted:

Economic development zones

During the early 1990s, many urban authorities set out to replicate the efforts of Shenzhen, Xiamen, Shantou and other successful export processors to attract foreign investment. This resulted in a massive investment in new 'economic development zones'. By 1996, within the areas requisitioned for construction of the zones, approximately 120,000 hectares of land remained undeveloped for lack of investment. Roughly half was agricultural land, of which half could not be converted back to agricultural use. Proper compensation to the farmers was often ignored. Nevertheless, the number of economic development zones continued to grow, exceeding 6000 by 2003. Among these, 3763 had already been ordered shut down after a series of investigations begun in the same year revealed that they had been set up on illegally seized farmland. More closures may result as investigations are pending for many of the remaining more than 2000 zones.

University cities

These are a recent variant of economic development zones in which local authorities and university officials take over suburban agricultural land for the construction of new educational and research facilities. For city officials who preside over the installation of such facilities, demonstrating that they are able to do things on a grand scale while significantly pumping up local gross domestic product is key to gaining promotions. For universities, the attractions include economies of scale in shared educational facilities and urban networks; modernized physical plants; expanded enrolment capacity; and, typically, an opportunity to raise revenue through real estate projects within the zones. By the end of 2003, the 50 university cities already established occupied land surface equal to 89 per cent of the land occupied by all of the other universities in the country. In one of the most egregious land grab cases of this kind, city and provincial officials of Zhengzhou acquired nearly 1000 hectares of agricultural land without payment. They also hid their actions from the city office of the State Bureau of Land and Resources, from whom they were bound by law to seek approval of their planned action. Once caught in the fraud, Zhengzhou city officials directed the city office (of land and resources) to help cover up continuing efforts to bring their project to fruition. Within nine months of acquiring the land, city officials completed construction of the facilities and moved in five universities. Apparently, local officials could count on success: three other university cities had already been built in Zhengzhou City.

Villa and golf course complexes

Exclusive residential complexes have sprung up in the suburbs of China's large cities, and many of the country's 320 golf courses are among their chief amenities. Indeed, the world's largest golfing complex, Mission Hills, is sited just outside the city of Shenzhen, adjacent to Hong Kong. According to official sources, among the first 200 courses completed, only a dozen were built legally. In November 2004, the Ministry of Land and Natural Resources classified golf courses among 'the five most egregious examples of illegal land seizures in China, noting that nearly a third of the land was taken improperly and that compensation had not been paid'.

Source: Westendorff, 2007

Box 5.12 The epic struggle of the Kerrigan family

The popular 1997 Australian cult classic film *The Castle* tells the fictional story of the Kerrigan family and their epic suburban struggle to resist the compulsory acquisition of their home. Through the inimitable legal tactics of solicitor Dennis Denudo and QC Lawrence Hammill, the High Court eventually decides in favour of the Kerrigans and other neighbours similarly threatened with looming eviction, and their tenure remains secure and intact.

While the story that unfolds in *The Castle* is surely one of the best housing rights tales to be told on the big screen, this story of household resistance to expropriation by a small group of homeowners against far more powerful corporate interests is, unfortunately, the exception to a larger global rule: housing or residential justice still all too rarely prevails, even when human rights principles are raised with such eloquence before the highest courts in the land.

Yet, the very fact that such a story became a very popular movie in Australia, with a wide audience, exemplifies how housing rights and the freedom from threats of forced evictions are increasingly being acknowledged around the world. The movie also made important links to the dispossession of Aboriginal populations from their lands and the encroaching powers of big business to move ordinary people from their homes against their will.

Infrastructure projects

As noted above, forced evictions continue to affect millions of people every year and cause considerable human suffering, resulting in what are often gross and systematic human rights violations. Infrastructure projects, in particular, seem to be a major cause of forced evictions. One observer has noted that 'the word infrastructure is the new code word for the unceremonious clearance of the fragile shelters of the poor'.[41] The number of people forcibly evicted by dams in India alone since 1950 has been estimated at 50 million.[42] Similarly, in China, using government figures, it has been estimated that reservoirs displaced 10.2 million people between 1950 and 1989.[43] This figure includes some of the largest single dam eviction totals on record: Sanmenxia with 410,000; Danjiangkou with 383,000 (plans exist to raise the dam height and displace a further 225,000 people, many of whom were displaced by the original reservoir); Xinanjiang with 306,000; and Dongpinghu with 278,000.[44] More recently, and according to official sources, the Three Gorges Dam project has displaced more than 1.2 million people.[45] It has been estimated that some 4 million people are being displaced every year through the construction of large dams, primarily in Asia. In addition, some 6 million people are being displaced annually by urban development and transportation programmes.[46] The compensation provided to the people relocated has often been much less than promised, whether in cash, in kind or employment, and has resulted in worsening impoverishment for many. Quite often, tensions remain high in the regions where relocations for such projects have taken place long after the resettlement officially ends.[47]

Many governments continue to believe that such large-scale mega projects will reduce poverty and raise national incomes. These same projects, however, even if bringing some benefit, are far too frequently the cause of increased poverty and major displacement. A former president of Argentina referred to mega projects as 'monuments to corruption'.[48] In another instance, during the early 1990s, in Karachi, Pakistan, the World Bank was willing to fund an 87 kilometre-long expressway (about one third of it elevated), despite strong opposition that the project design was inappropriate and expensive; would have an adverse environmental impact on the city; cause much dislocation; cause much disruption, especially in the city centre; and affect the historical buildings in the city.[49] After strong resistance by citizens' groups, the World Bank, to its credit, withdrew support for the project.

International mega events

International mega events, including global conferences and international sporting events such as the Olympic Games, are often the rationale behind large-scale evictions. For instance, reports indicate that some 720,000 people were forcibly evicted in Seoul and Inchon (South Korea), prior to the 1988 Olympic Games.[50] Some 30,000 were forcibly evicted in Atlanta prior to the 1996 Olympic Games. The oldest public housing project in the US, Techwood Homes, was deliberately de-tenanted because it stood in the way of a 'sanitized corridor' running through to CNN headquarters and the city centre. Half of the 800 houses were knocked down. Of the remainder, after renovation, only one fifth was reserved for poor families, and strict new credit and criminal record checks excluded many who most needed these units. The other apartments have become middle- to upper-income accommodation. Preparations for the 2004 Olympic Games in Athens were used as a pretext to forcibly evict several Roma settlements located in Greater Athens, ultimately forcing hundreds from their homes.[51]

A further 1.7 million people have reportedly been evicted in Beijing (China) in the run-up to the 2008 Olympic Games (see Box 5.13). Some 300,000 people have been relocated to make room for facilities directly linked to the Olympic Games. These locations have experienced the complete demolition of houses belonging to the poor, who have been relocated far from their communities and workplaces, with inadequate transportation networks. The process of demolition and eviction is characterized by arbitrariness and lack of due process, with courts reportedly often refusing to hear cases of forced evictions because of pressure on judges and lawyers by local officials. In many cases, tenants are given little or no notice of their eviction and never receive the promised compensation, sometimes leaving the evictees homeless because of lack of or inadequate compensation.

In an attempt to reduce the negative housing impacts of the Olympic Games, the International Olympic Committee has been repeatedly urged by NGOs and others to play a firmer role in discouraging host cities from using the games as a pretext for eviction and to take eviction intentions into account in determining future hosts of the Olympics. To date, however, the International Olympic Committee has refused to take any concrete measures to facilitate greater respect for housing rights and security of tenure in connection with the Olympic Games.[52]

1.7 million people have reportedly been evicted in Beijing (China) in the run-up to the 2008 Olympic Games

Urban beautification

Another common type of forced evictions is carried out in the name of urban beautification, or simply cleaning up a city, often in conjunction with investment inducements. Urban beautification is in itself used as justification and legitimization of such evictions. The forced eviction operation carried out in May 2005 in Zimbabwe is a case in point. The United Nations Special Envoy described *Operation Murambatsvina* as follows in the report of the fact-finding mission to Zimbabwe to assess the scope and impact of the

Box 5.13 Forced evictions caused or 'facilitated' by the 2008 Beijing Olympics

The mayor of Beijing has said that some 300,000 people will be relocated from sites where facilities for holding the 2008 Summer Olympics are to be constructed. This includes competition venues, the athlete's village, management facilities, green spaces, transport lines, hubs and amenities for visitors. However, if the standard for assessing the impact of the 2008 Olympics on relocations is widened to include urban development activities that were either speeded up, enlarged or facilitated by the politics of 'holding the best Olympics ever', then the impact will be much larger. Among the projects 'helped along' by the Olympics are the expansion of the capital's transportation network – including the airport, subway and light rail network; extensive demolitions in the Qianmen quarter and its planned reconstruction; the approval and construction of a central business district on the city's east side; a new round of massive public contracts and investments in the high-tech corridor of Zhongguancun; the clearance of old work unit (*danwei*) housing in the central east corridor between the second and fourth ring roads to make room for high-end residential developments, luxury shopping complexes and entertainment districts; and large environmental remediation projects, including the rustication to Hebei Province of the main facility of the Capital Steel Factory.

It has been estimated that some 1.7 million people are directly affected by demolitions/relocations in Beijing for the period of 2001 to 2008 – the high tide of Olympic preparations. This includes the mayor's estimate of those moved because of Olympic construction. By comparison, for the nine years of 1991 to 1999, demolitions/relocations directly affected 640,000 persons, or roughly 70,000 persons annually. The average for the pre-Olympic period is nearly three times larger (or 200,000 annually). Whether the 400,000 migrant workers living in the informal settlements (*chengzhongcun*) within the capital's fourth ring road have been included in the mayor's relocation estimate is unclear. In all likelihood they have not because very few migrant workers own property legally in Beijing. Moreover, because they are renters in illegally constructed buildings, they have virtually no protection against eviction or the right to a resettlement allowance. The total direct costs of holding the 2008 Olympic Games have been estimated at US$37 billion. The actual cost is likely to be considerably higher if losses to individuals are included.

Source: Westendorff, 2007

eviction operation on human settlements issues in Zimbabwe (see also Box 5.14):

> *On 19 May 2005, with little or no warning, the Government of Zimbabwe embarked on an operation to 'clean-up' its cities. It was a 'crash' operation known as* Operation Murambatsvina... *It started in the ... capital, Harare, and rapidly evolved into a nationwide demolition and eviction campaign carried out by the police and the army... It is estimated that some 700,000 people in cities across the country have lost either their homes, their source of livelihood or both. Indirectly, a further 2.4 million people have been affected in varying degrees. Hundreds of thousands of women, men and children were made homeless, without access to food, water and sanitation, or health-care... The vast majority of those directly and indirectly affected are the poor and disadvantaged segments of the population. They are, today, deeper in poverty, deprivation and destitution, and have been rendered more vulnerable.*[53]

Operation Murambatsvina ... was raised repeatedly before the United Nations Security Council as a possible threat to international peace and security

What was unique about the Zimbabwe evictions was the scale of international outcry that emerged from many parts of the world, strenuously opposing the eviction. For perhaps the first time ever, the issue of this mass forced eviction was raised repeatedly before the United Nations Security Council as a possible threat to international peace and security. Equally noteworthy was the appointment (also a first) by the United Nations Secretary General of a Special Envoy to examine the forced eviction programme in Zimbabwe and to suggest ways of remedying the situation. That a Special Envoy was appointed is yet another indication of the growing seriousness given to the human rights implications of forced evictions, particularly when these are large scale in nature. It remains to be seen if other Special Envoys will be appointed in the future to deal with mass forced evictions in other countries.

In one particularly large forced eviction effort, the Government of Myanmar forcibly evicted more than 1 million residents of Yangon (Rangoon). In preparation for the Visit Myanmar Year 1996 undertaken in Rangoon and Mandalay, some 1.5 million residents – an incredible 16 per cent of the total urban population – were removed from their homes between 1989 and 1994. The evictees were moved to hastily constructed bamboo-and-thatch huts in the urban periphery.[54]

GROUPS PARTICULARLY VULNERABLE TO TENURE INSECURITY

While tenure insecurity may, in principle, affect anyone living in urban areas, in practical terms particular groups are more exposed than others. As noted above, it is always the poor who are evicted, and similarly it is primarily the poor who perceive lack of security of tenure as a threat to urban safety and security. In addition, many social groups are

The people and Government of Zimbabwe should hold to account those responsible for the injury caused by the Operation

Box 5.14 Recommendations by the United Nations Special Envoy on *Operation Murambatsvina*

The first ever appointment by the United Nations of a Special Envoy to address the consequences of mass forced evictions in Zimbabwe in 2005 was widely welcomed by the world's human rights community as an important precedent. The recommendations of her report were seen by many commentators to be both firm and constructive:

> *Recommendation 1: ... The Government of Zimbabwe should immediately halt any further demolitions of homes and informal businesses and create conditions for sustainable relief and reconstruction for those affected.*
>
> *Recommendation 2: There is an urgent need for the Government of Zimbabwe to facilitate humanitarian operations within a pro-poor, gender-sensitive policy framework that provides security of tenure, affordable housing, water and sanitation, and the pursuit of small-scale income-generating activities in a regulated and enabling environment.*
>
> *Recommendation 3: There is an immediate need for the Government of Zimbabwe to revise the outdated Regional Town and Country Planning Act and other relevant Acts to align the substance and the procedures of these Acts with the social, economic and cultural realities facing the majority of the population, namely the poor.*
>
> *Recommendation 5: The Government of Zimbabwe is collectively responsible for what has happened. However, it appears that there was no collective decision-making with respect to both the conception and implementation of Operation Restore Order. Evidence suggests it was based on improper advice by a few architects of the operation. The people and Government of Zimbabwe should hold to account those responsible for the injury caused by the Operation.*
>
> *Recommendation 6: The Government of Zimbabwe should set a good example and adhere to the rule of law before it can credibly ask its citizens to do the same. Operation Restore Order breached both national and international human rights law provisions guiding evictions, thereby precipitating a humanitarian crisis. The Government of Zimbabwe should pay compensation where it is due for those whose property was unlawfully destroyed.*

Source: Tibaijuka, 2005, pp8–9

subjected to various forms of discrimination that may impact upon their security of tenure and/or their exposure to various forms of evictions. Moreover, the consequences of evictions may be harder to bear for some groups. What follows is a brief overview of the conditions experienced by some such vulnerable groups.

The urban poor

Poverty and inequality remain the key determinants of vulnerability from tenure insecurity. Generally, the poorer a person or household is, the less security of tenure they are likely to enjoy. Despite a variety of well-intentioned efforts – such as campaigns to end poverty and the MDGs – all relevant indicators point to poverty levels increasing in much of the world. Likewise, global income inequalities seem to be at the highest level since measurements began. The richest 2 per cent of adults in the world now own more than half of global household wealth, and the richest 1 per cent of adults alone owned 40 per cent of global assets in the year 2000. The richest 10 per cent of adults accounted for 85 per cent of the world's total wealth, while, by contrast, the bottom half of the world's adult population owned barely 1 per cent of global wealth.[55]

While national GDP levels have increased in many nations, this has not always resulted in improved housing and living conditions for lower-income groups. In fact, there is some evidence that society-wide economic progress can actually reduce tenure security for the poorer sections of society as land values, speculation and investment in real estate all collude to increase the wealth of the elites, thus making it much more difficult for the poor to have access to housing that is secure and affordable. The widespread housing price boom of the past 15 years in many countries, for instance, certainly benefited existing owners of homes and those able to obtain mortgages in many countries, but also priced millions out of the housing market.

At the national level, the economic boom in China, for instance, has significantly reduced security of tenure. Some 50 million urban residents in China (not including migrant workers) are now highly vulnerable, often subject to eviction from the affordable homes they have occupied for decades. Few of these residents can afford to buy or rent new housing in the districts where they now reside, given recent property price increases, and new and affordable rental units are far scarcer than the numbers needed.[56]

In recognition of the fact that rising real estate prices have made the dream of homeownership increasingly distant for many lower-income groups, access to security of tenure takes on added significance. In many settings, enjoying tenure security is far more important to dwellers than homeownership or being providing with a title to a land plot. During recent years, there has been a major policy shift away from more conventional approaches, to informal settlements, to more simplified, innovative, cost-effective and locally driven efforts to procure security of tenure. With governments unable and/or unwilling to commit the resources required to raise levels of housing adequacy, and civil society and NGOs largely sceptical of any efforts by the state or private sectors to improve housing conditions, it is not difficult to see how the international community has reached the view that the provision of security of tenure should be seen as a cornerstone of efforts to reduce poverty.

Tenants

If there is any particular group of urban dwellers who is under-protected and under-emphasized and frequently misunderstood, it is surely the world's tenants. While precise figures are lacking, the number of the world's tenants may well be measured in billions. In terms of security of tenure, tenants most certainly can be provided with levels of tenure security protecting them from all but the most exceptional instances of eviction; but all too rarely are the rights of tenants and the rights of title holders to secure tenure treated equitably under national legal systems. However, if the question of tenure is viewed from the perspective of human rights, it is clear that tenants, owners and, indeed, all tenure sectors – formal and informal – should enjoy equitable treatment in terms of tenure security and protection against eviction.

There would seem, as well, little justification for treating tenants in a fundamentally different way from owners or title holders when regularization processes are under way within a given informal settlement. Such processes should be fair, equitable and of benefit to all of the lower-income groups. In Kenya, for example, the Mathare 4A slum upgrading programme fell short of its objectives because of the lack of considering the impact of upgrading on the security of tenure of tenants.[57] In terms of rental markets, there is a growing appreciation that tenure security can assist, and not hinder, in increasing the prospects of long-term rental contracts, which, in turn, can strengthen security of tenure rights in this sector. The insecurity of tenure prevalent throughout much of Latin America, for instance, is seen as a key reason why long-term tenancy arrangements are so rare in the region.

Tenants are rarely a topic of focus within global human settlements circles. Moreover, when they are, they are frequently neglected (or even treated with disdain) in the context of urban development and slum regularization initiatives, and also in the context of post-conflict housing and property restitution programmes.[58] Although faced with precisely the same circumstances that lead to their displacement (which can include crimes such as ethnic cleansing, etc.), some restitution measures have clearly favoured the restitution rights of owners over those of tenants when the time to return home arrives. While the procedures under the Commission on Real Property Claims that emerged from the Dayton Peace Accords in Bosnia-Herzegovina gave fully equal rights to both formal property owners and those holding social occupancy rights to their original homes, as did the restitution regulations of the Housing and Property Directorate in Kosovo, it remains common for former owners to be treated more favourably than tenants despite the similarity of the origins of their displacement.[59]

The issue of tenants and security of tenure is also vital when examining the various policy debates under way on the

Generally, the poorer a person or household is, the less security of tenure they are likely to enjoy

Society-wide economic progress can actually reduce tenure security for the poorer sections of society

Tenants ... are frequently neglected ... in ... urban development and slum regularization initiatives, and ... in ... post-conflict housing and property restitution programmes

question of how best to ensure that tenure security can be accessible to all. For example, policies that focus on the possession of freehold title as a means of increasing security of tenure[60] tend, effectively, to leave out those who do not wish to, or who cannot, become possessors of freehold title. It is important to recall, however, that a nation's wealth is not invariably linked to the percentage of those owning property. For example, during the early 20th century when the power of the UK was at its peak, up to 90 per cent of its population were tenants. Similarly, tenants today form the majority among the population in some of the world's wealthiest countries, including Germany, Sweden and Switzerland. Tenants in these and similar countries have substantial security of tenure protections, grounded in enforceable law before independent and impartial courts, which may be a reflection of their overall share of the total population and corresponding political influence.

Control of land is particularly important for women

Women

Beyond the trends of increasing poverty and inequality, continued discrimination against women also contributes to tenure insecurity and resultant forced evictions. The World Bank notes that 'control of land is particularly important for women... Yet traditionally, women have been disadvantaged in terms of land access.'[61] In many (if not most) countries, traditional law implies that women's relationship to men defines their access to land. 'Legal recognition of women's ability to have independent rights to land is thus a necessary, though by no means sufficient, first step toward increasing their control of assets.' Without such independent recognition, including structural discrimination in the areas of inheritance and succession rights, women experience constant insecurity of tenure (as well as that of children). This is particularly highlighted in the context of the HIV/AIDS epidemic as the death of a husband (or father) may lead to the eviction of the rest of the household. Although women's equal rights to housing, land, property and inheritance are well established under international human rights law, major obstacles are still inherent in policies, decision-making and implementation procedures in realizing these rights. Hence, women are disproportionately affected by gender-neutral approaches to land inheritance and are often unable to access their formal rights (see Box 5.15).

Moreover, when the lack of secure tenure facilitates the carrying out of forced evictions, women are disproportionately affected, as noted by the Advisory Group on Forced Evictions (AGFE):

> *Indeed, for most women, the home is the single most important place in the world. Beyond shelter, it is a place of employment, where income is generated; it is a place to care for children; and it provides respite from violence in the streets. Evictions often take place in the middle of the day, when the men are away from home. Women are left to fight to defend their homes, and the evictors meet such resistance with violence, beating, rape, torture and even death. Violence and discrimination against women are not only the result of evictions; rather, they are often the cause. Domestic violence frequently drives women out of the home, effectively forcibly evicting them. In all situations, women forced from their homes and lands are further robbed of economic opportunities, ability to provide for their families' stability and means of autonomy. Women often experience extreme depression and anger in the aftermath of forced evictions. As a result of a lack of autonomy or stability, women become even further marginalized.*[62]

In many parts of Africa, for instance, women have access to land so long as they remain within their husband's and/or parents' land because 'traditional law implies that women's access to land is mediated through their relationships with men'.[63] Achieving security of tenure rights without a formal link to a male relative can thus still be impossible in a number of countries. Women often face disproportionate challenges in landownership even in cases where their spouses have died and they should be the *bona fide* owners (see also Box 5.16). Yet, it should be noted that legal recognition of women's ability to have independent rights to land is a necessary, although by no means sufficient, first step towards increasing their control of assets.

Box 5.15 Inheritance and gender

Inheritance is often treated as peripheral to, or semi-detached from, general debates and policy formation concerning security of tenure, land rights, land reform or regularization. However, inheritance is one of the most common ways of women acquiring land or access to land. Since women in many countries have not generally been able to purchase property or benefit from land reforms, in many cases a woman could only become a landowner by inheriting land from her husband or companion on his death.

Issues related to succession and inheritance are regulated through the civil codes in most Latin American countries, with the exception of Costa Rica and Cuba, where these have been laid down in family codes. In countries such as Panama, Honduras, Mexico and Costa Rica, absolute testamentary freedom leaves the surviving spouse defenceless in a marriage under a separate property regime.

In the Balkans, Serbia Montenegrin inheritance laws identify the surviving spouse and his/her children as the heirs of the first inheritance degree who inherit in equal parts per person. The laws also protect the spouse through a lifetime right to use the deceased's real property, or a part thereof if such request is justified by the spouse's difficult living conditions.

Under compulsory Islamic law, only one third of an estate can be bequeathed, with the remaining subject to compulsory fixed inheritance rules that generally grant women half of that which is granted to males in a similar position.

Most of Southern Africa has a dual legal system where inheritance is governed by both statutory and customary laws. In a number of countries, including Lesotho, Zambia and Zimbabwe, the constitution still allows the application of customary law in inheritance matters and courts have upheld discriminatory practice. Under customary law and with only a few exceptions, inheritance is determined by rules of male primogeniture, whereby the oldest son is the heir (the oldest son of the senior wife, in case of polygamy).

Property grabbing from widows of HIV/AIDS-affected husbands is a particularly acute problem in Southern Africa, although the act of dispossessing widows of property is a criminal offence in most countries of the region.

Source: UN-Habitat, 2006f

Other vulnerable and disadvantaged groups

A number of other groups suffer detriment and discrimination in terms of access to secure tenure and the benefits that such access can bestow. Such groups include children (including orphans, abandoned children, street children and those subjected to forced/child labour), the elderly, the chronically ill and disabled, indigenous people, members of ethnic and other minorities, refugees, internally displaced persons, migrant workers, and many others. Such groups often suffer discrimination with respect to their ability to own and/or inherit land, housing and other property (see also Box 5.16). While this Global Report does not attempt to describe the problems faced by each of these groups, Box 5.17 provides an example of the particular problems faced by migrant workers in the rapidly expanding urban areas of China.

Box 5.16 Forced evictions and discrimination in international law

The most authoritative international instrument on forced evictions, United Nations Committee on Economic, Social and Cultural Rights (CESCR) General Comment No 7 on forced evictions, has the following to say about discrimination against women and other vulnerable individuals and groups:

> *Women, children, youth, older persons, indigenous people, ethnic and other minorities, and other vulnerable individuals and groups all suffer disproportionately from the practice of forced eviction. Women in all groups are especially vulnerable given the extent of statutory and other forms of discrimination which often apply in relation to property rights (including homeownership) or rights of access to property or accommodation, and their particular vulnerability to acts of violence and sexual abuse when they are rendered homeless. The non-discrimination provisions of Articles 2.2 and 3 of the Covenant impose an additional obligation upon governments to ensure that, where evictions do occur, appropriate measures are taken to ensure that no form of discrimination is involved.*

Source: CESCR, General Comment No 7, para 11

Box 5.17 Security of tenure for migrant workers in China

The size of the migrant workforce in China, the so-called floating population (*liudongrenkou*), may today be as high as 150 million to 200 million. It is likely to increase further to reach 300 million by 2020. With the rapid expansion of the migrant workforce, affordable housing options in the city centre or on work sites have become scarce. The overflow is now taking refuge in informal settlements (*chengzhongcun*) or urban villages. More and more, these resemble in size and form peri-urban settlements that characterized rapid urbanization processes in other developing countries during the 1950s and 1960s. The earliest of these were developed during the 1980s on the peripheries of China's faster growing major cities (i.e. Guangzhou, Shenzhen, Shanghai and Beijing).

At first, when they grew large enough to draw the attention of local authorities, they were suppressed and eventually torn down. Among the largest and most famous of these cases was *Zhejiangcun* (Zhejiang village). Before its demolition in December 1995, Zhejiang village housed a population of some 100,000 individuals and thousands of enterprises. The village governed itself, establishing health clinics, water and sanitation systems, recreational facilities, schools, etc. It also proved itself to be a major boon to Beijing residents who rented land to the village and who bought the village's prodigious output of low-cost fashionable clothing.

By 2002, more than 1 million people were living in Beijing's 332 informal settlements. The 2002 census estimated that some 80 per cent of these were migrants. Today the numbers are thought to be much larger. What is sure is that many cities around China are planning to suppress or redevelop informal settlements. In Beijing's case, the 2008 Olympics are adding urgency to this task (see Box 5.13). Since 238 of these settlements for migrant workers are being demolished before 2008, it still remains unclear where the residents will be relocated.

While these migrant workers have contributed greatly to urban development in China over the last two decades, the formal housing provision system has made little or no provision for them. Even in Shanghai, where policies towards migrants have been relatively progressive, employment and lengthy employment tenure in the city had not yet freed the migrant workers from insecurity of tenure to housing.

It is no exaggeration to say that once in the city, migrants continue to be on the move. But such mobility is not necessarily driven by the need for tenure or even amenity. Few migrants make the transition from bridge headers to consolidators after years of living in the city, a trend in migrant settlement seen elsewhere in other developing countries. Instead, most remain trapped in the private rental sector or stay in dormitory housing. Homeownership is yet to become attainable for migrants, and self-help housing is largely absent, primarily because of the attitudes of municipal authorities.

Source: Westendorff, 2007

SECURITY OF TENURE IN THE AFTERMATH OF DISASTERS AND ARMED CONFLICT

Just as particular *groups* are more exposed to tenure insecurity, particular *events* are also major factors affecting security. Natural and technological disasters, as well as armed conflict and civil strife, are major factors threatening the security and safety of large urban populations every year. This section highlights the links between security of tenure and such disasters and conflicts.

Disasters and secure tenure

Natural and technological disasters – including earthquakes, tsunamis, storms and floods – often result in the large-scale displacement of people from their homes, lands and properties (see Part IV of this Global Report). Earthquakes alone destroyed more than 100 million homes during the 20th century, mostly in slums, tenement districts or poor rural villages.[64] In some settings, the displaced are arbitrarily and/or unlawfully prevented from returning to, and recovering, their homes, and/or are otherwise involuntarily relocated to resettlement sites despite their wishes to return home and to exercise their security of tenure rights.

This remains the case, for instance, in Sri Lanka where large numbers of those displaced by the tsunami in late 2004 are still prevented from returning to their original homes and lands.[65] Tenants and other non-owners are also facing discriminatory treatment in Aceh (Indonesia), and are not being allowed to return to their former homes and lands, even while owners are able to exercise these restitution rights. Housing and property restitution measures can be used as a means of ensuring secure tenure and facilitating the return home of all persons displaced by disaster, should this be their wish.

Box 5.18 Security of tenure-related challenges in occupied Iraq

Shortly after the US-led occupation of Iraq in 2003, a number of challenges related to security of tenure were identified, including:

- housing, land and property disputes;
- illegal and arbitrary forced evictions and displacement without any effective remedies;
- homelessness and inadequate housing and living conditions;
- housing, land and property registration and titling systems;
- unauthorized or irregular occupation of abandoned private and public land, housing and property;
- inequality facing women in the exercise of housing, land and property rights;
- housing and property damage;
- pending housing privatization; and
- lack of a clear institutional framework and response.

Source: Leckie, 2003a

Conflict, peace-building and security of tenure

Security of tenure rights are increasingly seen as a key area of concern in post-conflict settings

Security of tenure and related housing, land and property rights issues also arise in the contexts of conflict and post-conflict peace-building. Security of tenure rights are increasingly seen as a key area of concern in post-conflict settings. In Iraq, for example, a range of such challenges was identified in the immediate aftermath of the US-led occupation of the country (see Box 5.18). The situation with respect to most, if not all, of these challenges has worsened since 2003. By December 2006, the already disastrous situation in Iraq had become far worse, resulting in a housing crisis leading to a massive growth in slums and squatter settlements, with nearly 4 million people facing displacement.[66]

While the housing and tenure insecurity issues facing the people of Iraq are particularly severe, these types of issues occur in most countries engaged in, or emerging from, conflict. Consequently, addressing housing, land and property rights challenges in the aftermath of conflict is of vital importance for reconstruction and peace-building efforts.[67] This includes:

Security of tenure is a key element for the integration of the urban poor within the city

- attempting to reverse the application of land abandonment laws and other arbitrary applications of law;
- dealing fairly with secondary occupants of refugee or IDP land or housing;
- developing consistent land, housing and property rights policies and legislation;
- redressing premature land privatization carried out during conflict;
- reversing land sales contracts made under duress;
- protecting women's rights to inherit land; and
- ensuring that owners, tenants and informal occupiers of land are treated equitably.[68]

The United Nations and other actors have a vital role to play in ensuring that these issues are adequately and comprehensively addressed since security of tenure rights challenges are common to all post-conflict countries and territories, as noted by the United Nations Food and Agriculture Organization (FAO):

> *Providing secure access to land is an important part of dealing with emergency humanitarian needs, as well as longer-term social and economic stability. Secure access to land helps victims of conflicts to have a place to live, to grow food and to earn income. Security of tenure, without fear of eviction, allows people to rebuild economic and social relationships. More broadly, it allows local regions and the country to establish their economies. It supports reconciliation and prospects for long-term peace.*[69]

International peace initiatives, both large and small, increasingly view these concerns as essential components of the peace-building process and as an indispensable prerequisite for the rule of law. Yet, much remains to be done in the area of developing a comprehensive United Nations policy on these concerns.[70] As a result, citizens in some countries or territories have seen their tenure rights taken very seriously by peace operations, while in other countries or territories, citizens facing precisely the same tenure predicaments that face victims of conflict everywhere have seen their security of tenure rights effectively overlooked.

THE GROWING ACCEPTANCE OF THE 'INFORMAL CITY'

Perhaps the key trend at both the international and national levels is the growing recognition that informal settlements and the informal or so-called 'illegal' city hold the key to finding ways of conferring security of tenure on all of the world's dwellers. While, to a certain degree, due to default – given the massive scale and lack of other options to address these massive political challenges – the international community has clearly recognized that informal settlements are here to stay, that they are important sources of employment and economic growth, and, in fact, that they are likely to grow in coming years. While the squatter invasions of unused public land so commonplace during the 1960s and 1970s have largely ceased, the existence of informal settlements is a social phenomenon few are willing to deny. Linked to this, there has been a growing recognition of a 'right to the city' as one antidote to the neglect shown towards the informal city by policy-makers the world over.

There is also growing agreement, on all points of the political spectrum, that secure tenure is a multifunctional instrument in everything, from poverty alleviation, through the protection of human rights, to the generation of assets and capital. An emerging consensus that security of tenure is a key element for the integration of the urban poor within the city can also be discerned, as can the realization that – given that security of tenure is multidimensional in nature, often varying widely between countries and within countries, cities and even neighbourhoods and streets, as well as between and within households – 'one-size-fits-all' approaches to security of tenure will simply not work and should not even be attempted.[71]

Along with the recognition that it is within the informal sector that solutions to the global tenure crisis will need to be found, there is also a growing acceptance of the informal city by most local and national governments. While some governments – particularly those of an authoritarian or less than democratic tilt – are willing to violate international human rights norms and wantonly evict hundreds of thousands of people in a single eviction operation, this remains the exception to the rule. Of the 1 billion people living in slums today (see Table 5.2), it is likely that well under 1 per cent face forced eviction in a given year. This is certainly 1 per cent too many; but this fact shows that governments now generally accept the inevitability of the informal city much more than ever before, in spite of (or, perhaps, because of) the reality that these cities are beyond the reach of the law in so many ways. In most instances, a sense of benign neglect exists, sometimes side by side with concrete and tested policies that actually succeed in providing secure tenure and broader neighbourhood-wide improvements; but often it is simply acceptance of the inevitable, and the political consequences of choosing a more active policy opposing these developments, that dominates local government approaches to these questions.[72]

This begrudging acceptance of the informal or 'illegal' city, however, has almost invariably fallen short of what would be considered an adequate response to the social and economic conditions that lead to the emergence of such communities. For if law is meant to be a reflection of the society that it is designed to order and arrange, then legal systems the world over are also falling far short of their expectations. Legal systems cannot aspire to legitimacy if they exclude the majority of their population:

> *... laws are unjust when the poverty of the majority of people makes it impossible for them to comply with them. If, for most urban citizens, the basic tasks of daily life – building or renting a shelter, earning an income, obtaining food and water – are illegal, it would be wise for governments to change the legislation or simply to eliminate unrealistic laws. Urban legislation should be more flexible in adapting to the great variety of circumstance and the rate at which these can change.*[73]

Governments can rather easily – for a variety of reasons, most importantly the high political costs of forcibly evicting entire neighbourhoods – allow the informal city to exist. Responsible governments, however – who are actively seeking to comply with human rights obligations – need to do much more than simply accept that a growing portion of their populations are forced by circumstance to find housing options outside of the legally recognized realm. Governments need to acknowledge that the poor choose such options precisely because the legal housing sector does not provide them with access and options that they can afford, and which are located near employment and livelihood options.

Laws are unjust when the poverty of the majority of people makes it impossible for them to comply with them

CONCLUDING REMARKS

As has been outlined in this chapter, the question of security of tenure is by its very nature complex, diverse and often comprised of unique attributes depending upon the particular settings considered. That security of tenure can be developed, albeit with varying degrees of protection, within all tenure types is evidence of the need for flexible policy approaches geared towards ensuring that everyone, within every society, has a sufficient degree of the security of tenure that all of their rights directly linked to their tenure status can be enjoyed in full. To a degree, this needed flexibility is now at least rhetorically apparent within the various international discussions on security of tenure policy and, to a greater or lesser degree, is equally apparent at the national level in those states that have consciously chosen to treat tenure issues increasingly in human rights terms. While many trends can be identified, the growing acceptance of the informal or 'illegal' city perhaps best encapsulates many of the converging trends that simultaneously seek to achieve greater degrees of tenure security, while economic and geopolitical forces that threaten security of tenure continue to dominate.

Security of tenure can be developed, albeit with varying degrees of protection, within all tenure types

The preceding analysis reveals the challenges in determining the most effective ways of merging human rights law and principles with the practical steps, both political and legal, that will allow increasingly larger and larger numbers of people to enjoy security of tenure as a practical, legal and enforceable human right. Clearly, international human rights law now recognizes that all rights holders possess the right to security of tenure, both as a core element of the right to adequate housing and also as a key feature of a series of additional rights that are not always viewed as necessarily relevant to security of tenure, but which, in practice, very much are. To this list, of course, should be included rights to privacy, rights to the peaceful enjoyment of possessions, rights to security of the person, rights to housing and property restitution and a range of others. What is needed, therefore, in policy terms at the international and national levels is a new vision of security of tenure that combines the best practices and experiences of the housing world intrinsically with the best that can be offered by the world of human rights law and practice. The emergence of such an integral approach will most likely be beneficial to both sectors and, ultimately, to the hundreds of millions of urban dwellers who do not at present enjoy rights to secure tenure. The contours of such an integral vision are explored in the next chapter.

International human rights law now recognizes that all rights holders possess the right to security of tenure

NOTES

1 Habitat Agenda, para 75.
2 Global Strategy for Shelter to the Year 2000.
3 Davis, 2006a.
4 UN-Habitat, 2003d, ppvi, 107.
5 See, for instance, Vancouver Declaration on Human Settlements, Recommendation B.8.c.iii; and Vancouver Action Plan, para A.3.
6 See, for example, UN-Habitat, 2004b, pp33–41.
7 World Bank, 2003b, pxxi.
8 FAO, 2005, p21.
9 Kanji et al, 2005, p3.
10 Payne, 2001c, p51.
11 UN-Habitat, 2004b, p31.
12 UN-Habitat, 2006e, p94.
13 CESCR, General Comment no 7.
14 As of 19 April 2007. For the latest ratification status, see www.unhchr.ch/tbs/doc.nsf/StatusfrsetOpen?FrameSet.
15 ICESCR, Articles 16 and 17.
16 UN-Habitat, 2006e, p94.
17 *Ibid*, p190.
18 UN-Habitat, 2003d, pxxv.
19 Hardoy and Satterthwaite, 1989, p301.
20 Royston, 2002, p165.
21 ACHR, 2001, p66.
22 Cambodia Land Law (revised 2001), Article 30; available at http://cb2.mofcom.gov.cn/aarticle/?lawsofhost?country/investmenthost/200612/20061203917903.html.
23 Pawlowski, 2005.
24 Huggins and Ochieng, 2005, p27.
25 Cai, 2003, pp662–680.
26 BBC News, 2006a.
27 Scherer, 2005.
28 New York City, undated.
29 See www.economist.com.
30 UN-Habitat, 2004b, p50.
31 Amnesty International and COHRE, 2006.
32 For a more comprehensive overview of eviction cases in Africa (and other regions), see COHRE, 2002, 2003, 2006.
33 COHRE, 2006, p26; Morka, 2007.
34 *IRIN News*, 2007b.
35 *Social and Economic Rights Action Center and the Center for Economic and Social Rights* versus *Nigeria*, para 63.
36 For more information on such evictions, see www.cohre.org/evictions.
37 Barber, 1996, p16.
38 Durand-Lasserve, 2006, pp2, 4.
39 *Ibid*, p4.
40 Allen, 2000.
41 Seabrook, 1996, p267.
42 Roy, 1999.
43 World Bank, 1993a, p72.
44 *Ibid*. See also Tyler, 1994.
45 See, for example, Haggart and Chongqing, 2003.
46 Cernea, 1996, p1517.
47 Jing, 1997.
48 Caulfield, 1998, p247.
49 See Hasan, 2003.
50 Asian Coalition for Housing Rights and Third World Network, 1989.
51 COHRE, 2003.
52 *Ibid*.
53 COHRE, 2005.
54 Davis, 2006a, p107.
55 Davies et al, 2006.
56 Westendorff, 2007.
57 Ngugi, 2005.
58 Although there are exceptions: see UN-Habitat, 2003c.
59 Leckie, 2003b.
60 de Soto, 2000.
61 World Bank, 2003b, pxx.
62 UN-Habitat, 2005d.
63 World Bank, 2003b, pxx.
64 Hewitt, 1997, pp217–218.
65 Leckie, 2005b, pp15–16.
66 Luo, 2006.
67 See also UN doc S/2004/616, which explicitly recognizes this point.
68 FAO, 2005, p32.
69 FAO, 2005, p1.
70 Leckie, forthcoming.
71 Payne, 2001c.
72 Hardoy and Satterthwaite, 1989.
73 *Ibid*, p35.

CHAPTER 6

POLICY RESPONSES TO TENURE INSECURITY

Chapter 5 provided a brief overview of security of tenure and the many complex definitions and localized meanings that are associated with this term. The chapter examined the scale and impacts of tenure insecurity, the reasons why security of tenure is not yet universally enjoyed, and the social groups who are particularly affected by conditions of tenure insecurity, with a key focus on those driven from their homes by forced eviction, market evictions and other causes, including armed conflict and disaster. The analysis concluded with coverage of the ways in which the 'illegal' or informal city is now an increasingly accepted reality in much of the developing world. It is in these 'illegal cities' – now home to perhaps one quarter of humanity – that security of tenure conditions are at their worst.

As Chapter 5 showed, security of tenure is complex, multifaceted and difficult to define purely in terms of formality or informality, legality or illegality, or modern or customary law. The United Nations has grappled with the complexities of security of tenure since its earliest years as part of its broader efforts in support of peace, security, poverty reduction and human rights. Although attention was placed more on rural than urban areas during the early years, a resolution on land reform adopted in 1950, for instance, speaks of 'systems of land tenure' that impede economic development and 'thus depress the standards of living especially of agricultural workers and tenants'. The resolution also urges states to institute appropriate forms of land reform and to undertake measures to 'promote the security of tenure and the welfare of agricultural workers and tenants'.[1]

The debate has moved on considerably since 1950, and there has been an ever growing recognition of the problem and how best to address it, particularly concerning urban land. Security of tenure issues are now routinely examined as a core concern and component, not just of sustainable human settlements and urban policies, but also as a fundamental concern of human rights. This increasingly expansive approach, where questions of tenure, rights, policies and laws converge, contributes to the emergence of more integral or multidimensional approaches to security of tenure. This, in turn, can lead to the identification of more nuanced, practical and appropriate measures designed to ensure that ever larger numbers of urban (and rural) dwellers are protected by adequate degrees of secure tenure.

As discussed in Chapter 5, cities are characterized by a wide range of tenure categories, from legal categories based on statutory, customary or religious law, to extra-legal ones, such as squatting, unauthorized land subdivisions and houses constructed in contravention of official norms. In practical terms, this implies that most people in the cities of developing countries live within a continuum in which some aspects of their housing are legal, while others are not. The existence of such a continuum has serious consequences for the development and implementation of urban policy: 'It is essential to identify the range of statutory, customary and informal tenure categories in a town or city so that the consequences of urban policy on different tenure sub-markets can be anticipated.'[2] Governments and international agencies have undertaken a wide range of policies to redress problems of tenure insecurity and to remedy the often deplorable living conditions found in the world's informal settlements.

Most people in the cities of developing countries live within a continuum in which some aspects of their housing are legal, while others are not

This chapter builds on Chapter 5 and turns to the question of how national and local governments, the international community and civil society have attempted to grapple with tenure insecurity, both through policy and legal measures. Several key policy and legal responses on questions of tenure security are examined, including upgrading and regularization; titling and legalization; land administration and registration; legal protection from forced eviction; and addressing violations of security of tenure rights. This is followed by a discussion of the roles and potential contributions of civil society and the international community. The final section contains a more in-depth review of how three countries – South Africa, Brazil and India – have approached the question of security of tenure in terms of both policy and human rights.

Governments and international agencies have undertaken a wide range of policies to redress problems of tenure insecurity

UPGRADING AND REGULARIZATION

Slum upgrading and tenure regularization are perhaps the most common policy responses to illegal settlements throughout the developing world. Such processes, when

Box 6.1 The Millennium Development Goals (MDGs) and security of tenure

Goal 7, target 11 of the Millennium Development Goals (MDGs) expresses the aim of achieving 'significant improvement in the lives of at least 100 million slum dwellers by 2020'. In terms of monitoring, the 'proportion of people with secure tenure' was selected as one of the indicators to measure progress in the implementation of this goal. Other indicators are related to access to safe water and adequate sanitation, as well as the structural quality of dwellings and overcrowding.

The MDGs are an important attempt to set global targets to achieve improvements in the lives of a portion of the world's slum dwellers. The global recognition of the need for such improvements and the inclusion of security of tenure issues within the monitoring process are, indeed, welcome developments.

Yet, how does this goal measure up within a human rights framework, which is based on principles of entitlement, equity and non-discrimination? It is clear that in a world of 1 billion slum dwellers, improving the lives of only 10 per cent of the world's poorest citizens has to be seen as the barest minimum that governments should aim at achieving .

Furthermore, the number of slum dwellers is not static. Projections indicate that the number of slum dwellers is set to increase to some 1.3 billion by 2020, even if MDG 7, target 11 is achieved (see Table 5.2).

Forced evictions, demolition of slums and consequent resettlement of slum dwellers create more problems than they solve

carried out successfully, can result in the provision of infrastructure, urban services and security of tenure for residents. Slum upgrading is also very much an approach that is in line with the Millennium Development Goal (MDG) on improving the lives of slum dwellers (see Box 6.1). The Cities Alliance, which through its Cities without Slums initiative, is directly linked to the quantification of this target,[3] has developed a set of essential guidelines for the implementation of slum upgrading programmes (see Box 6.2).

Onsite upgrading is now seen as a far better option than improvements requiring relocation and eviction. In fact, there seems to be wide agreement that forced evictions, demolition of slums and consequent resettlement of slum dwellers create more problems than they solve. Such activities tend to destroy, unnecessarily, housing that is affordable to the urban poor. Meanwhile, the new housing provided has frequently turned out to be unaffordable. The result has been that relocated households move back into slum accommodation elsewhere. Perhaps even more serious, resettlement frequently destroys the proximity of slum dwellers to their employment sources. Thus:

> *Relocation ... of slum dwellers should, as far as possible, be avoided, except in cases where slums are located on physically hazardous or polluted land, or where densities are so high that new infrastructure ... cannot be installed.* In-situ *slum upgrading should therefore be the norm.*[4]

Box 6.2 Essential ingredients for slum upgrading

The Cities Alliance notes that slum upgrading consists of a whole range of physical, social, economic, organizational and environmental improvements undertaken cooperatively and locally among citizens, community groups, private-sector actors and local authorities. It has identified the following essential ingredients for any successful national slum upgrading programme:

1. *Demonstrate political will:* both national and local governments must provide the vision, commitment and leadership required to sustain nationwide upgrading.
2. *Set national and city targets:* set clear targets and ensure public-sector accountability by engaging stakeholders in planning and monitoring results.
3. *Put it in the budget:* support slum upgrading as part of core business, nationally and locally.
4. *Implement policy reforms:* ensure necessary reforms dealing with land, finance and institutional frameworks.
5. *Ensure open and transparent land markets:* reform closed and opaque land markets that encourage corruption, patronage and exploitation of the urban poor, as well as constrain capital markets.
6. *Mobilize non-public-sector resources:* engage slum dwellers themselves, who have both the ability and the interest in promoting upgrading, and the private sector, which should be engaged as a risk-sharing partner rather than a mere contractor to the public sector.
7. *Prevent the growth of new slums:* facilitate access to land and services by planning realistically for future growth.

Source: Cities Alliance, 2003, p37

Regularization and upgrading can, of course, take various forms, and initiatives that provide some measure of security without necessarily involving the provision of individual freehold titles are commonplace. For instance, some regularization efforts simply recognize the *status quo*, thus removing the threat of eviction, but not providing formal security of tenure to dwellers in the community. Such efforts, which are often more motivated by the possibility of a positive political spin for the government concerned than the rights of those affected, can be easily overturned and generally can only offer temporary protection, without the accrual of legally recognized rights. A second form of regularization is the recognition of various forms of interim or occupancy rights without the provision of formal tenure. This is a more intensive approach, which provides a higher degree of protection than simply recognizing current realities and also strengthens the negotiating possibilities of the residents of the settlement concerned.

Third, more official processes of regularization that recognize the legitimacy of the process by which the urban poor have acquired land for housing (without necessarily providing legal tenure rights) are also increasingly commonplace. Such an approach focuses on negotiations between landowners and residents, rather than government regulation. Furthermore, the approach requires simplification of procedures for registering land rights. The main characteristic of this approach is that property 'becomes a political right: a right to build, a "right to the city"'.[5] A major component of this approach is the involvement of local authorities in approving the use, location and layout of a particular residential area.

Regularization efforts that protect people against eviction, even if this falls short of legal protection and is purely political in nature, can sometimes be the preference of communities. In Karachi during the 1970s, for example, the initiation of public works in low-income settlements led to major investments in houses in expectation of regularization and the receipt of long-term leases. In many of the settlements, however, once the threat of eviction was removed, people refused to pay for land title documents.

The work of the Sindh Katchi Abadis Authority (SKAA) in Karachi has been widely heralded for its unique approaches to regularization (see Box 6.3). Removing the fear of eviction was seen by settlers to have a much greater value than obtaining formal property documents. Similar experiences have been reported from many other locations, as informality 'does not necessarily mean insecurity of tenure'.[6] In some countries in sub-Saharan Africa, for instance, communal or customary land delivery systems may not be formally recognized by the state, yet they still guarantee a reasonably good level of security. The perception of security offered through the recognition by the community itself and by the neighbourhood is often considered more important than official recognition by the state.

The city government of Brazil's largest city, São Paulo, has pursued particularly constructive policies on providing secure tenure to the urban poor for several years in a manner combining the various approaches just noted. The city government has developed a legal allotment programme that assists slum dwellers to obtain rights and register their homes. This programme sought to benefit 50,000 families in some of the poorest neighbourhoods of this city.[7]

The upgrading and regularization process, combined with the understanding of the importance of the informal sector and a growing acceptance of the informal city, together point to another trend in the security of tenure policy discussion that places considerable responsibility on community-level organizations and poor individuals to solve the often severe residential problems confronting them on a daily basis. The *Baan Mankong* (Secure Housing) programme in Thailand, for instance, enables poor communities to influence a national process of forging comprehensive solutions to problems of housing, land tenure and basic services in Thai cities. The programme, which was initiated in 2003,

Box 6.3 The Sindh Katchi Abadis Authority (SKAA)

The Sindh Katchi Abadis Authority (SKAA) is responsible for the implementation of the Katchi Abadis Improvement and Regularization Programme (KAIRP) in Pakistan. This important government poverty alleviation programme has, over the years, faced a number of constraints that SKAA has successfully overcome. Among these constraints has been the lack of funds for upgrading initiatives, forcing SKAA to depend upon large foreign loans from the World Bank and the Asian Development Bank (ADB). Other constraints have been excessive costs of overheads for infrastructure developments, complicated regularization procedures and an absence of community participation.

To combat these constraints (and other obstacles), SKAA undertook a series of measures, including decentralization of the entire upgrading and regularization process; focus on user friendliness; transparency; community participation; affordable lease rates; and flexibility in designs. In SKAA's view, the three major starting points for a successful policy for low-income land supply can be summarized as:

- Low-income people are often characterized by having irregular incomes and can thus only build their dwellings in a flexible and incremental manner. This has to be acknowledged in policy and programme design. As a result, traditional standards for construction are meaningless and often directly harmful to the aspiration of the poor.
- It is essential that ways are found to identify who should be the beneficiaries of land allocations. Only those who really need plots for their own dwellings should benefit, while those who want plots for investment or speculation purposes should be excluded.
- Procedures for allocation of land should be simple, straightforward, transparent and efficient.

Source: Ismail, 2004

Box 6.4 Upgrading with community empowerment

A comparative analysis of upgrading projects undertaken by UN-Habitat in Afghanistan, Cambodia and Sri Lanka has shown that the upgrading interventions provided people with a 'secure place to live with dignity' by improving the physical conditions and by establishing the institutional framework necessary for communities to plan future activities in a sustainable manner. All of these projects – which were supported by the United Nations Trust Fund for Human Security (see Box 1.1) – have focused on the empowerment of communities using an approach involving community action planning, community development councils and the community contracts system.

The projects had the following impact on security of tenure in the three countries:

- Increased investments in the settlements (indicating a perceived increase in security and future prospects).
- Increased ownership of the work done in the settlements (high community contributions and vigilant community surveillance).
- The involvement of registered community development councils legitimized occupancy rights (it provided a sense of belonging and confidence as well as a sense of responsibility).
- Dialogue among community development councils has strengthened the opposition to forced evictions, and has increased demands for policies focusing on the allocation of land to the poor and regularization of tenure.

The projects have demonstrated that the use of upgrading as an entry point to the empowerment of communities is effective where institutions have been fragile and unstable in post-conflict situations, and where there is no conducive environment for providing protection.

For instance, in the case of Afghanistan, a community development council was established in a settlement which did not even appear on the city map before the project started, and was later named Majboorabad 2. Residents had been threatened of evictions several times in the past, both by warlords and by the Ministry of Interior which claims the land. As the community is located near a military area, residents had been fined and even imprisoned for their 'illegal' building activities. When the residents had their community development council registered by the municipality this seemed to increase the confidence of the community at large. It implied that the government now formally accepted their former 'illegal settlement' as an 'informal settlement'.

Source: Balbo and Guadagnoli, 2007

Removing the fear of eviction was seen ... to have a much greater value than obtaining formal property documents

channels government funds, in the form of infrastructure subsidies and soft housing loans, directly to poor communities. These communities are then responsible for the planning and carrying out of improvements to their housing, environment and basic services and manage the budget themselves.[8]

As argued in Chapter 5, while the question of security of tenure and access to the registration system can be complex and cumbersome for poor communities, *in-situ* upgrading of settlements has been widely used as an entry point for improving living conditions. The practical negotiations, dialogues and interfaces undertaken between authorities and communities in a number of such settlements upgrading initiatives have in fact contributed to exploring and establishing more acceptable and viable tenure systems at the country level (see Box 6.4).

It would be foolish to pass from one distortion – that the slums are places of crime, disease and despair – to the opposite that they can be safely left to look after themselves

Limits of community-based upgrading and regularization

In the decades to come, programmes similar to those described above may or may not prove to have been the wisest policy route. But whether it succeeds or fails, this approach arose due to the historical and (perhaps even) structural inabilities of either the state or the market to provide safe, secure, affordable and accessible housing to everyone within a given society. Again, as if by default, governments now turn to the people themselves as the only sources of energy and resources that can hope to transform the informal city into an increasingly desirable place in which to live and work. To a degree, such an approach has much to offer: it can empower people and communities to determine their own fate; it can ensure that people are active participants within an increasingly democratic urban development process; and it can 'enable' them to build housing and communities that best suit their needs and wishes.

Legalization through amnesties ... provide varying degrees of political security of tenure, rather than legal security of tenure

And yet, it can also be simply that neither the state nor the private sector are sufficiently interested in undertaking legal reforms and making the infrastructure and other investments needed to actually transform poor communities. Thus, the poor have no other option than organizing and pooling their common resources and resolving to improve the places where they reside. It would, however, be unwise to disregard the reservations raised to increasing emphasis on sweat equity: 'It would be foolish to pass from one distortion – that the slums are places of crime, disease and despair – to the opposite that they can be safely left to look after themselves.'[9] It is widely recognized that the withdrawal of the state from many of the public provision sectors, coupled with the privatization of previously public goods, has had a major impact on increases in poverty and inequality during the 1980s and 1990s. The growing weakness (or unwillingness) of central and local governments in many countries means that good governance with respect to securing housing, land and property rights for all, including security of tenure, is increasingly absent. When this is combined with a lack of democratic decision-making and democratic participation, as well as inappropriate regulatory frameworks that are increasingly anti-poor in orientation, the result is the cities we see today in most developing countries (i.e. in which growing numbers of people are forced into informality simply because they have no other option). In such contexts, upgrading and regularization will be of limited assistance.

Within a truly democratic city, existing in a truly democratic nation, where the rule of law and human rights flourish and are taken as seriously as they are intended to be, the importance of community-based action is, of course, beyond question. However, there is a danger in relying too heavily on the poor to help themselves without a corresponding increase in commitment by governments and the international community to develop legal and regulatory frameworks that are appropriate, that are consistent with the scale of the problem and which actually succeed in providing security of tenure for everyone, everywhere. This will only result in current trends of slum growth continuing into the future. Involving the community in the security of tenure process is one thing; but supporting policies that place an over-reliance on the community, however, is another issue entirely.

TITLING AND LEGALIZATION

During the last few years there has been an increasing focus on titling to achieve the goal of security of tenure for all. The primary argument has been that the provision of property titles to the world's slum dwellers and those living 'illegally' will not only give them rights to land and property, but because of the ability to use land as collateral, will also facilitate their access to credit.[10] Issuing of freehold titles is, however, not the only way to achieve security of tenure in informal settlements. Many countries have years of experience with simpler and less expensive responses.

Countries such as Turkey, Egypt and Brazil, in particular, have seen years of official tolerance of illegal settlements followed by periodic legalization through amnesties (see Box 6.5). Such approaches are often quite pragmatic responses to political problems. Moreover, they provide varying degrees of political security of tenure, rather than legal security of tenure. In practice, however, the perception within the communities concerned may well be that their level of security of tenure is quite high (see Box III.1). However, without simultaneous regularization measures being undertaken, such legalization does not generally result in greater access to services and infrastructure, nor does it simplify the registration of housing, land and property rights.[11]

Land titling with the provision of freehold title is closely linked to the commonly recognized process of adverse possession (see Box 6.6). This is a mechanism for awarding secure land tenure in a way that is associated with minimal institutional requirements. The requirement that a beneficiary has to have had possession and use of the land for a specified period of time has several positive consequences. It eliminates the risk of past owners suddenly surfacing and claiming the land, while at the same time ensuring that valuable land is not left vacant. Furthermore, it ensures the exclusion of land investors and speculators. The formalizing of adverse possession rights in the way undertaken under the City Statute in Brazil, conferring security of tenure to long-time residents, may serve as a model for other countries, as well, in their efforts to reduce price speculation in land by making the conferral of such rights easier and less controversial.

There is no doubt that there are a number of advantages to formalizing housing through titling approaches, and that many of the characteristics of legalizing what are presently informal arrangements can have considerable benefits. This approach enables households to use their property titles as collateral in obtaining loans from formal-sector finance institutions in order to improve their homes or develop businesses. Moreover, it helps local authorities to increase the proportion of planned urban land and provide services more efficiently; it enables local governments to integrate informal settlements within the tax system; and it improves the efficiency of urban land and property markets.[12] It has also been argued that such formalization will empower poor households; give them additional political influence and voice, thus strengthening democratic ideals; and may also increase the land user's investment incentives.[13]

Titling is seen as the strongest legal form that the registration of tenure rights can take, with titles usually guaranteed by the state. It is also, however, the most expensive form of registration to carry out, requiring formal surveys and checking of all rival claims to the property. In many developing countries, local governments may be unable to muster the resources required to establish the land management and regulatory frameworks as well as institutions required to make the provision of freehold titles to all a realistic endeavour. Many observers have thus noted that

Box 6.5 The legalization of Turkey's *gecekondu*

During close to 500 years of Ottoman rule, all land in Turkey was held by the Sultan. Private ownership simply meant the right to collect taxes on a particular parcel. This tradition continues in many of Turkey's cities today, and huge tracts of land remain either under federal control or owned through an ancient tradition called *hisseli tapu* (shared title) (see also Box III.1). This ownership system is, however, quite outmoded today and shares have not been apportioned; most share owners have no idea even how many other shareholders there are.

Millions of people who came to Turkey's cities over the last 50 years made use of this tradition. They took advantage of an ancient Turkish legal precept: that no matter who owns the land, if people get their houses built overnight and move in by morning, they cannot be evicted without being taken to court. This is why squatter housing in Turkey is called *gecekondu*, meaning 'it happened at night'. Many such communities have thrived under this arrangement and feature well-developed infrastructure and popularly elected governments. Today, almost half of the residents of Istanbul (perhaps 6 million people) dwell in homes that either are *gecekondu* or were when they were first constructed.

Gecekondu land invasions became a noticeable phenomenon in Turkey during the early 1940s. By 1949, the Turkish government made its first attempt to regulate such constructions by passing a law requiring municipalities to destroy the illegal dwellings. But this proved to be politically unpalatable. Only four years later, the government modified the law, allowing existing *gecekondu* to be improved and only mandating demolition of new developments. This was effectively the first *gecekondu* amnesty in Turkey. In 1966, the government rewrote that law again, granting amnesty to all *gecekondu* houses constructed over the 13 years since the previous law had been enacted. At the same time, they introduced new programmes to promote development of alternatives to *gecekondu* housing.

By 1984, the government essentially gave up the fight against already existing squatters. It passed a new law that again gave amnesty to all existing *gecekondu* communities and authorized the areas to be redeveloped with higher-density housing. Even without planning permission, squatters quickly realized that they could take advantage of the new law. They began ripping down their old-fashioned single-storey homes and building three- and four-storey ones of reinforced concrete and brick. In 1990, the government issued a new *gecekondu* amnesty, again essentially accepting all of the illegal neighbourhoods that had already been built.

Source: Neuwirth, 2007

Box 6.6 Adverse possession

Adverse possession is a legal doctrine under which a person or community in possession of land owned by someone else can acquire legal rights, including title to it, as long as certain legal requirements are complied with and the adverse possessor is in possession for a sufficient period of time, which can range anywhere from 5 to 20 years. While specific requirements may differ between countries and different legal regimes, adverse possession generally requires the actual, visible, hostile, notorious, exclusive and continuous possession of another's property, and some jurisdictions further require the possession to be made under a claim of title or a claim of right. In simple terms, this means that those attempting to claim the property are occupying it exclusively (keeping out others) and openly as if it were their own. Generally, possession must be continuous without challenge or permission from the lawful owner for a fixed statutory period in order to acquire title.

While often associated with the squatting process within the informal settlements of the developing world, adverse possession claims exist in developed countries as well. For instance, the Land Registry in the UK receives an average of 20,000 applications for adverse possession registration every year, 75 per cent of which are successful. Under law binding until 2003, squatters in the UK could claim adverse possession of land or property following 12 years of possession. A new Land Registration Act of 2002 did not abolish adverse possession rights, but created a mechanism whereby the owner of the land concerned has a right to evict a squatter before the current possessors can gain title.[a]

Similarly, adverse possession was also the main mechanism whereby most settlers in the US acquired their land.[b] Today, all US states retain legal provisions upholding the ability of squatters to acquire ownership rights through continued possession of a property in good faith for a specified period.[c]

Moreover, the process of adverse possession is also included in the City Statute in Brazil (see Box 11.8) as a constructive means of establishing secure tenure and enforcing social equity in the use of urban property. Such rights (called *usucapião*) are defined as the right to tenure acquired by the possession of property, without any opposition, during a period established by law.[d]

Sources: a) Parker, 2003; b) de Soto, 2000; c) Deininger, 2003; d) Imparto, 2002.

Adverse possession ... is a mechanism ... ensuring that valuable land is not left vacant

Box 6.7 Land titling programmes and internal conflict

Land titling programmes commonly involve formalization and registration of rights to land through systematic adjudication, surveying and (if necessary) consolidation of boundaries. While these titling programmes are useful in certain contexts, they often fail to increase certainty and reduce conflict. In some cases, these programme failures have resulted from the distributional consequences of land titling itself. Long-term conflict has resulted because poor or otherwise vulnerable land occupiers have been dispossessed by wealthier and more powerful groups; yet the new titleholders and state enforcement mechanisms have been unable to prevent encroachment by the former occupiers.

This state of grievance and incomplete exclusion then tends to become cyclical in environments of political instability. When a regime changes in circumstances of historical grievance, old claims often reassert themselves through acts of violence, land invasion or state-sanctioned evictions. This phenomenon challenges the economic conception that once property rights are established, there is relatively little likelihood of reversion to open access. In other cases, titling programmes provoke long-term conflict due to the fluid nature of non-state systems of land tenure. In these systems, multiple overlapping rights often co-exist in an uneasy balance, and programmes to define and regularize these rights have caused dormant internal disputes to emerge in the form of open conflict.

Source: Fitzpatrick, 2006, pp1013–1014

Local governments may be unable to muster the resources required ... to make the provision of freehold titles to all ... realistic

other forms of registration are also possible, such as title deeds registration, and documentation of secondary use rights and other claims to land and natural resources. These may not have the same state backing but are cheaper to undertake and maintain, and may be sufficient to protect rights at the local level.[14] Furthermore, it has been noted that issuing freehold titles may lead to conflicts between individuals and communities, as 'land registries are so incomplete and inaccurate that moves to provide titles in urban or peri-urban areas may encourage or intensify disputes over who has the primary claim' (see also Box 6.7).[15]

Large-scale granting of freehold title to residents of slum settlements ... may facilitate dispossession

Other observers argue that tenure regularization and titling approaches can be detrimental to some households living in informal settlements, especially those who have the most vulnerable legal or social status. Among the groups most likely to face the negative consequences of such approaches are tenants or sub-tenants on squatter land; newly established occupants who are not considered eligible for regularization (or title); single young men and women; and female heads of households. Furthermore, such approaches can also dramatically increase rent levels, which may displace tenants to other more affordable neighbourhoods or force them to create new slums and squatter settlements.[16]

The most effective ... implies implementing an incremental approach, focusing on increasing the short- and medium-term security for those living in informal settlements

It is, in fact, the very informality of informal settlements that has enabled growing urban populations to find a place in which to live. In a situation where urban populations continue to grow and urban areas expand, some observers point to potential entry problems of new urban dwellers in a formalized housing market: 'Will the new urban poor that will settle in newly urbanized areas benefit from the formalization of the land market on the urban periphery?' There is a danger that they will be confronted by a much more rigid, more regulated and better enforced pattern of landownership. It is questionable whether such new entrants into the housing market will already have the access to credit necessary to purchase land (and housing) in the open market at market prices.

Perhaps one of the most obvious objections to the large-scale granting of freehold title to residents of slum settlements is that it may facilitate dispossession. Few observers disagree with the fact that 'tenure has invariably proved to be an important factor in stimulating investment and it may serve as the foundation for developing credit mechanisms, mortgage markets and revenues for urban development'.[17] The main problem occurs when one borrows money and uses the title as collateral. If 'circumstances arise that prevent repayment, the money lender has a viable claim against the asset denoted by the title'.[18] Many developing countries have relatively dysfunctional states, where powerful politicians or others may bring about dispossession of land in a variety of ways. In situations like this, the provision of titles may, in fact, reduce rather than increase security of tenure. It has been argued that the provision of formal title to the poor 'means that they must ... decide to exchange their embeddedness in one community for an embeddedness in another community'.[19] It is not immediately obvious in many countries that the government is able to provide the poor with more effective protection against dispossession than what was traditionally provided through membership in a family, clan or village. Furthermore, 'experience has shown, time and again, that the urban poor either willingly sell or otherwise lose their land when given individual title'.[20]

There is also increasing empirical evidence that 'full, formal tenure is not essential – or even sufficient, on its own – to achieve increased levels of tenure security, investment in house improvements or even increased property tax revenues'.[21] For instance, a study of legislation introduced to enable low-income tenants to purchase their dwellings in Colombo (Sri Lanka) concluded that the residents were too poor to benefit from the initiative. They could not afford to undertake the necessary improvements without external assistance, regardless of their level of tenure security.[22] Others point out that it is possible – as has been realized in India, Indonesia and Peru – to redefine the objectives of legalization since guaranteeing security of tenure does not necessarily require the formal provision of individual land titles.[23]

To a certain extent, all of these views are correct. Few would argue against the aims and objectives associated with providing some form of official recognition of rights to slum dwellers who do not currently enjoy such protection. What is fundamental is not so much this objective, but how it is pursued and, ultimately, achieved. The most effective approach may thus be to broaden the range of legal options available. This implies implementing an incremental approach, focusing on increasing the short- and medium-term security for those living in informal settlements. The most obvious way to initiate such an approach is to ban forced evictions for a minimum period (see below). This moratorium on forced evictions should be followed by the gradual introduction of some form of statutory tenure.[24] Again, in practice, perceived tenure security in informal settlements is much more important than the precise legal status of the land.

Box 6.8 The Global Land Tool Network

The Global Land Tool Network was initiated in 2004 with the twin objectives of increasing global knowledge, awareness and tools to support pro-poor and gender-sensitive land management; and working in selected countries to apply pro-poor and gender-sensitive tools in line with the United Nations recommendations on reform and aid effectiveness. Its broad aims are to:

- Promote a continuum of land rights, from perceived security of tenure to intermediate forms of tenure such as certificates, and including individual freehold title.
- Improve and develop pro-poor tools on land management and land tenure.
- Assist in unblocking existing initiatives.
- Assist in strengthening existing land networks.
- Improve global coordination on land.
- Assist in the development of gendered tools that are affordable and useful to the grassroots.
- Improve the general dissemination of knowledge about how to achieve security of tenure.

The network works through a series of partners to develop innovative, affordable and scaleable land tools. Eight priority areas have been identified for its activities, namely:

- affordable national land records management (land access and land reform);
- land administration and land governance;
- land administration approaches for post-conflict societies;
- land-use planning at the regional, national and city-wide levels;
- affordable gendered land tools (e.g. on adjudication);
- affordable and just estates administration (especially for HIV/AIDS areas);
- pro-poor expropriation and compensation; and
- pro-poor regulatory frameworks for the private sector.

Source: Global Land Tool Network, www.gltn.net

As noted above, there are few more contentious and complex problems in the world than those dealing with land and secure tenure. At the same time, very few pro-poor, gender-sensitive tools exist to address land issues. As a result, while many excellent land policies have been drafted, implementation of these policies remains a profound barrier to poverty reduction and the achievement of the MDGs. The Global Land Tools Network, initiated by UN-Habitat, is a recent initiative that seeks to respond to this challenge (see Box 6.8).

LAND ADMINISTRATION AND REGISTRATION

The question of land administration and registration is also vital in any attempt aimed at ensuring that security of tenure will best serve the interests of the urban and rural poor. Land administration can be defined as the way in which security of tenure rules are actually made operational and enforceable, and while linked to titling, it deals more with the administrative aspects of how tenure rights are accorded and managed by the civil authorities concerned. These processes can involve allocating rights in land, determining

Box 6.9 The importance of efficient land administration systems

In a recent study on access to land and land administration, focusing on rural land after violent conflict, the United Nations Food and Agriculture Organization (FAO) makes a number of observations that are relevant to urban areas as well:

> *... land registration is not inherently anti-poor in its impacts and ... the distributional consequences of land registration depend on the design of the registration process and of the institutions responsible for its management. Land registration systems can be set up so as to address the risk of bias against poorer and marginalized groups by considering issues of language, cost and accessibility and by recording secondary rights. Attention also needs to be paid to establishing effective accountability mechanisms for the institutions implementing land registration programmes, as well as for oversight and dispute settlement institutions.*
>
> *Our work demonstrates the limitations of those approaches that assume that the 'legal empowerment of the poor' may be promoted simply by providing land titles. In reality, different models of land registration exist, local contexts vary substantially, and overlapping rights on the same piece of land may coexist. Therefore, the real issue is not embracing readily available blueprint solutions based on Western models, but rather learning how to design land registration systems that secure the land rights of poorer and more marginalized groups in specific geographic and historical contexts.*
>
> *In addition, whether land titles or other registration documents improve land tenure security of local land users depends on the existence of strong local institutions that are able to uphold and defend the rights embodied in those documents. Building the capacity of local land institutions over time is therefore a key challenge.*

Source: FAO, 2005, p27

Box 6.10 What are cadastres and land registries?

Cadastres and registries are key land administration instruments:

- A land registry handles information on landownership and transactions.
- The cadastre contains information on the boundaries of parcels as defined by surveys and recorded on maps. It also contains any additional information about the parcels. The cadastre provides the basis for a number of other functions, such as land-use planning, management and disposal of public lands, land valuation and taxation, provision of other public services, and generation of maps.

Source: World Bank, 2003b, p70

boundaries of land, developing processes for exchanging land, planning, valuation and the adjudication of disputes (see Box 6.9).[25]

Comprehensive and regularly updated housing, property and land registration systems are a crucial element of … security of tenure

While there are many views on the importance of land registration and administration, few would disagree with the proposition that some appropriate, affordable, reasonably simple to update and administer, and culturally sensitive form of registering lands and homes, and of delineating land property boundaries, must be in place if security of tenure is to be treated as a right and if the quest for expanding the enjoyment of this right is to ever bear fruit. This is a view widely shared and one that is clearly consistent with the existing and longstanding approaches of states the world over. All countries have systems in place (even if desperately outdated, under resourced and not properly administered) for the registration of housing, land and residential property. Once again, the systems exist and are part and parcel of every culture and society; but what matters is how these processes are undertaken, to what extent they facilitate security of tenure, and whether they are consistent with the relevant human rights issues involved.

However, … land registration does not automatically provide security of tenure

Although virtually never examined for their human rights components, comprehensive and regularly updated housing, property and land registration systems are a crucial element of the security of tenure process. Through registration, the legal conferral of security of tenure is made possible, a public and transparent record of ownership and dweller rights exists, and all rights relating to housing can be protected. And yet, hundreds of millions of urban dwellers the world over do not, at present, have their housing, land and property rights registered within an appropriate documentation system. Equal numbers rely on informal tenure arrangements that may give them some measure of protection against eviction and abuse, but may not provide them with any type of enforceable rights. As noted above, evidence from a number of countries indicates that new creative, innovative and process-oriented approaches seem to have considerable merit compared to those that focus on large-scale provision of freehold titles. Indeed, registering currently unregistered land has proven destabilizing in many countries and can quickly turn from a hopeful gesture to a source of conflict and disputes if carried out in an inappropriate manner.[26]

Once land is registered, it is entered into cadastres and registries; these documents then become vital tools for the enforcement of rights, urban planning measures and taxation (see Box 6.10). In principle, land registries can become human rights tools as well, playing a vital role in ensuring the full enjoyment of rights to housing and security of tenure. Indeed, it is through regularly updated and properly maintained land registries – which can function equally well in both systems of formal and customary land administration – that rights can gain recognition and, thus, stand a greater chance of enforcement in the event of competing claims or disputes over the land in question. The World Bank, among others, argues strongly for the registration of all land where previous records are out of date or do not exist at all:

> *… a systematic approach, combined with wide publicity and legal assistance to ensure that everybody is informed, provides the best way to ensure social control and prevent land grabbing by powerful individuals, which would be not only inequitable, but also inefficient.*[27]

It also highlights the importance of registering all urban land as 'a precondition to the establishment of effective urban management'.[28]

It is important to reiterate, however, that land registration does not automatically provide security of tenure. Growing evidence points to registration processes actually contributing to a redistribution of assets towards wealthier segments of society. Or, as noted by one observer: 'As land becomes scarcer, poorer and more vulnerable groups may see their claims weakened and lose access to land, leading to their increasing marginalization and impoverishment.'[29] Moreover, in countries such as Ghana, which has had registration systems in place for well over a century, the cumbersome nature of the registration process has led to very few people actually registering land claims. This has been acknowledged by many observers, who note that registration of urban land may not be feasible in the short and medium term in many countries due to the lack of resources among local authorities and the observed inability of registries to keep pace with developments on the ground. Thus, the World Bank has noted that in 'cases where land registers are not operational or effective, it may, therefore, be desirable to establish land inventories which simply record claims of landownership and property rights without the legal authority to determine them'.[30]

Many have thus pointed to the need for new and more appropriate forms of land registration, which, in turn, can facilitate the provision of security of tenure. The main components of such a new and more flexible approach are outlined in Box 6.11. There are many dangers associated with such processes of registration. But there are also major dangers now in a world where so many people are not able to have their rights – even informal rights – properly recognized.

Perhaps one of the strongest arguments in favour of developing proper housing, land and property registration systems hinges on the vital role that these institutions can play in remedying severe human rights violations, such as ethnic cleansing, arbitrary land confiscations, forced evictions and other crimes. Fortunately, such crimes are not committed against all of the world's urban poor; but they are, tragically, very widespread and constitute the most severe outcomes of practices that run counter to a world governed by, and based on, the principles of human rights. It is important to recall that it is through the existence of, and reliance on, such records that the housing and property restitution rights of refugees can be secured. As the ethnically driven forced displacements in Bosnia-Herzegovina, Kosovo, Tajikistan and elsewhere have made clear, removing people forcibly from their homes, confiscating personal housing and property documents, destroying housing and property and cadastral records have all been used by ethnic cleansers in their attempts to alter the ethnic composition of territory and permanently prevent the return of those they forcibly expelled from their homes. While little gain emerged from the Balkan wars of the past decade, the international community was at least unambiguous about the need to reverse ethnic cleansing and to ensure the right to housing and property restitution for everyone displaced during the conflicts in the region. Intractable political considerations aside, whenever such records are available following conflict, the task of determining housing and property rights is far easier and far more just.

Where tenure rights were taken seriously, displaced persons were able to reclaim their homes or find some sense of residential justice, indicating that restitution may not be as infeasible as it may at first appear. For instance, an important restitution programme in Kosovo, coordinated by the United Nations Housing and Property Directorate, has provided legal clarity regarding tenure and property rights to 29,000 disputed residential properties in the disputed province since 2000. All but 6 per cent (1855 claims) had been fully implemented by 2006. Some 68 per cent of all claims were decided within three years.[31] Security Council Resolution 1244, which established the United Nations Interim Administration Mission in Kosovo (UNMIK), placed a high priority on property restitution for refugees and internally displaced persons (IDPs). The resolution of property issues was also considered vital to ensuring restoration of the rule of law and stimulating economic growth and stability in Kosovo and the wider region. Early initiatives in the property rights sector culminated in the establishment, in 1999, of the Housing and Property Directorate and its independent quasi-judicial body, the Housing and Property Claims Commission, which aimed to achieve 'an efficient and effective resolution of claims concerning residential property'.[32] This comprised a relatively novel development in international post-conflict peace-building operations and represented a significant step forward for the restitution of property rights of refugees and IDPs. It constituted a mass claims-processing mechanism, designed to resolve high numbers of property claims through the application of standardized proceedings.

The process was goal oriented in that its procedures and evidentiary rules were designed to facilitate optimal efficiency in the resolution and implementation of decisions in a cost-efficient manner in order to meet with the urgent desire of refugees and IDPs to return to their homes, while at the same time preserving compliance with fair procedures and due process guarantees.

Box 6.11 Towards a new approach to land registration

A new and more appropriate land registration system should include the following components:

- decentralized technical processes that are transparent and easily understood by local people;
- land information management systems that can accommodate both cadastral parcels and non-cadastral land information;
- new ways of providing tenure security to the majority through documentation of rights and boundaries for informal settlements and/or customary areas, without using cadastral surveys, centralized planning and transfer of land rights by property lawyers;
- accessible records, both in terms of their location and their user friendliness; and
- new technical, administrative, legal and conceptual tools.

Source: Fourie, 2001, p16

LEGAL PROTECTION FROM FORCED EVICTION

> *... the issue of forced removals and forced evictions has in recent years reached the international human rights agenda because it is considered a practice that does grave and disastrous harm to the basic civil, political, economic, social and cultural rights of large numbers of people, both individual persons and collectivities.*[33]

The resolution of property issues was ... considered vital to ensuring restoration of the rule of law ... and stability in Kosovo

Parallel to the policy discussions on provision of freehold title versus other forms of tenure, various debates have been under way within the human rights community on related questions, focusing primarily on the issue of forced evictions and the human rights and security of tenure impacts that this can have upon the urban poor. This process has resulted in the practice of forced evictions moving from being viewed and acted upon almost solely as an act synonymous with apartheid-era South Africa (but largely neglected elsewhere), to a globally prohibited practice that has received considerable attention by human rights bodies. In fact, during the past 20 years, forced evictions have been the subject of a range of international standard-setting initiatives, and an increasing number of planned and past evictions carried out or envisaged by governments have been widely condemned. In the past few years, governments ranging from the Dominican Republic, Panama, the Philippines and South Korea, to Turkey, Sudan and others have been singled out for their poor eviction records and criticized accordingly by United Nations and European human rights bodies. In 1990, in the first declaration that a state party had violated the International Covenant on Economic, Social and Cultural Rights (ICESCR), the United Nations Committee on Economic, Social and Cultural Rights (CESCR) decided that the evictions that were attributable to the Government of the Dominican Republic were not merely failures to perform

Box 6.12 Evictions as violations of international law

In its first ruling that a state party had violated the International Covenant on Economic, Social and Cultural Rights (ICESCR), the United Nations Committee on Economic, Social and Cultural Rights (CESCR) famously decided that:

> *The information that had reached members of the Committee concerning the massive expulsions of nearly 15,000 families in the course of the last five years, the deplorable conditions in which the families had had to live, and the conditions in which the expulsions had taken place were deemed sufficiently serious for it to be considered that the guarantees in Article 11 of the Covenant had not been respected.*

Source: UN Document E/C/12/1990/8, 'Concluding observations to the initial periodic report of the Dominican Republic', para 249

obligations, but, in fact, violations of internationally recognized housing rights (see Box 6.12).

This decision was followed a year later with a similar pronouncement concerning forced evictions in Panama, which had not only infringed upon the right to adequate housing, but also on the inhabitants' rights to privacy and security of the home. Subsequently, the Committee has decided that many state parties had, in fact, violated the terms of the ICESCR. In addition, international standards addressing the practice of forced evictions grew considerably during the 1990s, both in terms of scope, as well as in the consistent equation of forced evictions with violations of human rights, particularly housing rights. In one of its first of what have become regular pronouncements on forced evictions, the CESCR has declared that 'instances of forced eviction are *prima facie* incompatible with the requirements of the Covenant and can only be justified in the most exceptional circumstances, and in accordance with the relevant principles of international law.'[34] Similarly, the former United Nations Commission on Human Rights has declared forced evictions as 'gross violations of human rights, in particular the human right to adequate housing',[35] a perspective echoed on numerous occasions by various United Nations human rights bodies and other human rights institutions.[36] Perhaps the most significant development occurred in 1997, when the CESCR adopted what is now widely seen to be the most comprehensive decision yet under international law on forced evictions and human rights. Its General Comment No 7 on forced evictions significantly expands the protection afforded dwellers against eviction, and goes considerably further than most previous pronouncements in detailing what governments, landlords and institutions such as the World Bank must do to preclude forced evictions and, by inference, to prevent violations of human rights (see Box 6.13).

Instances of forced eviction ... can only be justified in the most exceptional circumstances

As noted earlier, a series of international standards, statements and laws has widely condemned forced evictions as violations of human rights. General Comment No 7 goes one step further in demanding that 'the State itself must refrain from forced evictions and ensure that the law is enforced against its agents or third parties who carry out forced evictions'. Furthermore, it requires countries to 'ensure that legislative and other measures are adequate to prevent and, if appropriate, punish forced evictions carried out, without appropriate safeguards by private persons or bodies'.[37] In addition to governments, therefore, private landlords, developers and international institutions such as the World Bank and any other third parties are subject to the relevant legal obligations and can anticipate the enforcement of laws against them if they carry out forced evictions. The rules plainly require governments to ensure that protective laws are in place domestically and that they punish persons responsible for forced evictions carried out without proper

The State itself must refrain from forced evictions and ensure that the law is enforced against its agents or third parties who carry out forced evictions

Box 6.13 Are evictions ever legal?

This is perhaps the most frequently raised question with respect to housing rights under international law. For example, when taking a human rights or human security perspective, what is expected from governments and what is legally allowed when people are squatting on public lands, such as that intended for schools or some other public purpose? In practice, in some cases, proper slum upgrading initiatives cannot be carried out unless some dwellings are demolished:

- Are governments not entitled (or perhaps even required) to evict people and communities from marginal land or dangerous locations such as floodplains or landslide-prone hillsides, all in the interest of public health and safety?
- How far do the rights of governments stretch in this regard?
- To what extent can the urban poor and other dwellers, within both the informal and formal housing sectors, anticipate a social and legal reality that does not envisage the practice of forced evictions?
- When does an eviction become a forced eviction?

General Comment No 7 provides some guidance in this regard. While it does not ban outright every possible manifestation of eviction, it very clearly and strongly discourages the practice and urges states to explore 'all feasible alternatives' prior to carrying out any forced evictions, with a view to avoiding or at least minimizing the use of force or precluding the eviction altogether. It also provides assurances for people evicted to receive adequate compensation for any real or personal property affected by an eviction.

In paragraph 12 of General Comment No 7, the text outlines the specific types of evictions that may be tolerated under human rights law:

> *Where some evictions may be justifiable, such as in the case of the persistent non-payment of rent or of damage to rented property without any reasonable cause, it is incumbent upon the relevant authorities to ensure that those evictions are carried out in a manner warranted by a law that is compatible with the Covenant and that all the legal recourses and remedies are available to those affected.*

Box 6.14 Procedural protections when forced evictions are unavoidable

When forced evictions are carried out as a last resort and in full accordance with the international law, affected persons must, in addition to being assured that homelessness will not occur, also be afforded eight prerequisites prior to any eviction taking place. Each of these might have a deterrent effect and result in planned evictions being prevented. These procedural protections include the following:

- an opportunity for genuine consultation with those affected;
- adequate and reasonable notice for all affected persons prior to the scheduled date of eviction;
- information on the proposed evictions and, where applicable, on the alternative purpose for which the land or housing is to be used, to be made available in reasonable time to all those affected;
- especially where groups of people are involved, government officials or their representatives to be present during an eviction;
- all persons carrying out the eviction to be properly identified;
- evictions not to take place in particularly bad weather or at night unless the affected persons consent otherwise;
- provision of legal remedies; and
- provision, where possible, of legal aid to persons who are in need of it to seek redress from the courts.

Source: CESCR, General Comment No 7, para 15

safeguards. While extending protection to all persons, the General Comment gives particular mention to groups who suffer disproportionately from forced evictions, including women, children, youth, older persons, indigenous people, and ethnic and other minorities. With respect to the rights of women, the text asserts that:

> *Women in all groups are especially vulnerable given the extent of statutory and other forms of discrimination which often apply in relation to property rights (including home ownership) or rights of access to property or accommodation, and their particular vulnerability to acts of violence and sexual abuse when they are rendered homeless.*[38]

One of the more precedent-setting provisions of General Comment No 7 declares that 'evictions should not result in rendering individuals homeless or vulnerable to the violation of other human rights'.[39] The General Comment makes it incumbent on governments to guarantee that people who are evicted – whether illegally or in accordance with the law – are to be ensured of some form of alternative housing. This would be consistent with other provisions (i.e. that 'all individuals have a right to adequate compensation for any property, both personal and real, which is affected', and that 'legal remedies or procedures should be provided to those who are affected by eviction orders').[40] If governments follow the provisions of the General Comment, therefore, no one should ever be forced into the realms of homelessness or be subjected to violations of their human rights because of facing eviction, notwithstanding the rationale behind such evictions.

The Committee is also critical of the involvement of international agencies in development projects that have resulted in forced evictions, and stresses that:

> *... international agencies should scrupulously avoid involvement in projects which, for example ... promote or reinforce discrimination against individuals or groups contrary to the provisions of the Covenant, or involve large-scale evictions or displacement of person without the provision of all appropriate protection and compensation.*[41]

While the overall position of the General Comment is to discourage the practice of forced evictions, it does recognize that in some exceptional circumstances, evictions can be carried out. However, for these evictions to be legal and consistent with human rights, a lengthy series of criteria will need to be met in full (see Box 6.14).

Evictions should not result in rendering individuals homeless or vulnerable to the violation of other human rights'

In essence, therefore, General Comment No 7 and the numerous international standards preceding and following it recognize that forced evictions are not an acceptable practice under human rights law. At the same time, the international legal instruments realistically acknowledge that under truly exceptional circumstances, after having considered all possible alternatives and in accordance with a detailed series of conditions, some types of eviction may be permissible. It is to this question that we now turn.

Many states have enacted domestic legislation reflecting the sentiments of standards such as those found in international law as a means of implementing their various international obligations in recognition of housing rights and security of tenure. National constitutions from all regions of the world and representing every major legal system, culture, level of development, religion and economic system specifically address state obligations relating to housing. More than half of the world's constitutions refer to general obligations within the housing sphere or specifically to the right to adequate housing (see Box 6.15). If human rights linked to and indispensable for the enjoyment of housing rights are considered,[42] the overwhelming majority of constitutions make reference, at least implicitly, to housing rights.

Domestic laws also increasingly recognize rights linked to security of tenure. The Republic of the Philippines' Urban Development and Housing Act provides an example of national legislation dealing with the discouragement of forced evictions, the due process necessary to ensure that an

Box 6.15 Constitutional recognition of housing rights

Constitutional clauses from a cross-section of countries reveal that national laws can, and often do, recognize and enshrine housing rights:

Armenia (Article 31): every citizen is entitled to an adequate standard of living for himself or herself and his or her family, to adequate housing, as well as to the improvement of living conditions. The state shall provide the essential means to enable the exercise of these rights.

Belgium (Article 23(3)): everyone has the right to enjoy a life in conformity with human dignity… These rights include, in particular, the right to adequate housing.

Honduras (Article 178): all Hondurans have the right to decent housing. The state shall design and implement housing programmes of social interest.

Mexico (Article 4): every family has the right to enjoy decent and proper housing. The law shall establish the instruments and necessary supports to reach the said goal.

Nicaragua (Article 64): Nicaraguans have the right to decent, comfortable and safe housing that guarantees familial privacy. The state shall promote the fulfilment of this right.

The Philippines (Article 13(9)): the state shall by law, and for the common good, undertake, in cooperation with the private sector, a continuing programme of urban land reform and housing which will make available at affordable cost decent housing and basic services to underprivileged and homeless citizens in urban centres and resettlement areas.

Portugal (Article 65(1)): everyone shall have the right for himself and his family to a dwelling of adequate size satisfying standards of hygiene and comfort and preserving personal and family privacy.

Russian Federation (Article 40(1)): each person has the right to housing. No one may be arbitrarily deprived of housing.

South Africa (Article 26(1)): everyone has the right to have access to adequate housing. The state must take reasonable progressive legislative and other measures to secure this right.

Spain (Article 47): all Spaniards have the right to enjoy decent and adequate housing.

eviction is not arbitrary, and the requirement that relocation and resettlement be offered to evictees (see Box 6.16). The legislation in a number of other countries has similar provisions. The following list comprises a small sample of the many diverse ways in which governments have legislated in favour of security of tenure rights:

- *Brazil:* the Statute of the City is grounded in the 'social function of the city' and guarantees 'the right to sustainable cities, understood as the right to urban land, housing, environmental sanitation, urban infrastructure, transportation and public services, to work and leisure for current and future generations' (see also Box 11.8).[43]
- *France:* the 1990 Law 90/449 on the right to housing provides an example of how national legislation mandates public provision of affordable housing for those in need.
- *India:* The 1984 Madhya Pradesh Act No 15 (Slum Dwellers Protection Act) confers tenure to landless persons in urban areas who had settled on land plots of less than 50 square metres for a prescribed period.
- *Tanzania:* the 1999 Land Act recognizes the tenure rights of those residing in informal settlements. Residents in unplanned urban settlements have their rights recorded and maintained by the relevant land allocating authority and that record is registered. All interests on land, including customary land rights that exist in the planning areas, are identified and recorded; the land rights of peri-urban dwellers are fully recognized and rights of occupancy issued; and upgrading plans are prepared and implemented by local authorities with the participation of residents and their local community organizations. Local resources are mobilized to finance the plans through appropriate cost-recovery systems.[44]
- *Trinidad* and *Tobago:* the 1998 Regularization of Tenure Act establishes a Certificate of Comfort that can be used to confer security of tenure on squatters as the first step in a process designed to give full legal title to such persons.[45]
- *Uganda:* the 1995 Constitution and the 1998 Land Act together confer security of tenure through ownership rights (including customary law ownership) or perpetual lease rights on lawful and *bona fide* occupiers of land. Certificates of occupancy of the land are also made accessible under the laws.[46]
- *United Kingdom:* the 1977 Protection from Eviction Act creates various offences for anyone who unlawfully evicts residential occupiers from their homes, and provides an example of how a government can protect housing rights from forms of interference other than interference by the state.

ADDRESSING VIOLATIONS OF SECURITY OF TENURE RIGHTS

… our level of tolerance in response to breaches of economic, social and cultural rights remains far too high. As a result, we accept with resignation or muted expressions of regret, violations of these rights… We must cease treating massive denials of economic, social and cultural rights as if they were in some way 'natural' or inevitable.[47]

Box 6.16 The Republic of the Philippines' Urban Development and Housing Act

Eviction or demolition as a practice shall be discouraged. Eviction or demolition, however, may be allowed under the following situations:

- when persons or entities occupy danger areas such as *esteros*, railroad tracks, garbage dumps, riverbanks, shorelines, waterways and other public places, such as sidewalks, roads, parks, and playgrounds;
- when government infrastructure projects with available funding are about to be implemented; or
- when there is a court order for eviction and demolition.

In the execution of eviction or demolition order involving underprivileged and homeless citizens, the following shall be mandatory:

- notice upon the affected persons or entities at least … 30 days prior to the date of eviction or demolition;
- adequate consultations on the matter of resettlement with the duly designated representatives of the families to be resettled and the affected communities in the areas where they are to be relocated;
- presence of local government officials or their representatives during eviction or demolition;
- proper identification of all persons taking part in the demolition;
- execution of eviction or demolition only during regular office hours from Mondays to Fridays and during good weather, unless the affected families consent otherwise;
- no use of heavy equipment for demolition except for structures that are permanent and of concrete materials;
- proper uniforms for members of the Philippine National Police who shall occupy the first line of law enforcement and observe proper disturbance control procedures; and
- adequate relocation, whether temporary or permanent.

Source: Republic of the Philippines, 1992 Urban Development and Housing Act (Republic Act No 7279), Section 28

Although the development of effective remedies for the prevention and redress of violations of economic, social and cultural rights, including security of tenure, has been slow, several developments in recent years have added to the seriousness given to these rights and are graphic evidence of the direct linkages between human rights and security of tenure. The 1997 Maastricht Guidelines on Violations of Economic, Social and Cultural Rights, for instance, provide a great deal of clarity as to which 'acts of commission' (see Box 6.17) and 'acts of omission' (see Box 6.18) would constitute violations of the ICESCR. Based on these guidelines, it is possible to develop a framework for determining the compatibility of national and local law and policy on aspects of tenure security with the position of human rights law.

Because security of tenure and the rights forming its foundation continue to grow in prominence at all levels, it should come as no surprise that official human rights bodies, including courts, at the national, regional and international levels are increasingly scrutinizing the practices of governments with respect to security of tenure. This is a positive development and, yet, is one more additional indication that a combined approach to this question between the human settlements and human rights communities is beginning to bear fruit. Much of the pioneering work in this regard has been carried out by the CESCR. As mentioned earlier, since 1990 the Committee has issued dozens of pronouncements about security of tenure conditions in different countries. Box 6.19 provides an overview of a cross-section of these statements to give an idea of the extent of progress made in addressing security of tenure as a core human rights issue.

Official human rights bodies … are increasingly scrutinizing the practices of governments with respect to security of tenure

Despite the work of the CESCR, the human rights dimensions of security of tenure are not yet widely enough

Box 6.17 Violations of economic, social and cultural rights through 'acts of commission'

Violations of economic, social and cultural rights can occur through the direct action of states or other entities insufficiently regulated by states. Examples of such violations include:

- The formal removal or suspension of legislation necessary for the continued enjoyment of an economic, social and cultural right that is currently enjoyed;
- The active denial of such rights to particular individuals or groups, whether through legislated or enforced discrimination;
- The active support for measures adopted by third parties which are inconsistent with economic, social and cultural rights;
- The adoption of legislation or policies which are manifestly incompatible with pre-existing legal obligations relating to these rights, unless it is done with the purpose and effect of increasing equality and improving the realization of economic, social and cultural rights for the most vulnerable groups;
- The adoption of any deliberately retrogressive measure that reduces the extent to which any such right is guaranteed;
- The calculated obstruction of, or halt to, the progressive realization of a right protected by the Covenant, unless the state is acting within a limitation permitted by the Covenant or it does so due to a lack of available resources or *force majeure*;
- The reduction or diversion of specific public expenditure, when such reduction or diversion results in the non-enjoyment of such rights and is not accompanied by adequate measures to ensure minimum subsistence rights for everyone.

Source: Maastricht Guidelines on Violations of Economic, Social and Cultural Rights, Guideline 14

Box 6.18 Violations of economic, social and cultural rights through 'acts of omission'

Violations of economic, social and cultural rights can also occur through the omission or failure of States to take necessary measures stemming from legal obligations. Examples of such violations include:

- The failure to take appropriate steps as required under the Covenant;
- The failure to reform or repeal legislation which is manifestly inconsistent with an obligation of the Covenant;
- The failure to enforce legislation or put into effect policies designed to implement provisions of the Covenant;
- The failure to regulate activities of individuals or groups so as to prevent them from violating economic, social and cultural rights;
- The failure to utilize the maximum of available resources towards the full realization of the Covenant;
- The failure to monitor the realization of economic, social and cultural rights, including the development and application of criteria and indicators for assessing compliance;
- The failure to remove promptly obstacles which it is under a duty to remove to permit the immediate fulfilment of a right guaranteed by the Covenant;
- The failure to implement without delay a right which it is required by the Covenant to provide immediately;
- The failure to meet a generally accepted international minimum standard of achievement, which is within its powers to meet;
- The failure of a State to take into account its international legal obligations in the field of economic, social and cultural rights when entering into bilateral or multilateral agreements with other States, international organizations or multinational corporations.

Source: Maastricht Guidelines on Violations of Economic, Social and Cultural Rights, Guideline 15

Of all … domestic-level judicial approaches to … security of tenure, … South African courts that have taken the most interesting route

understood by those making international and national policies in this area. Furthermore, a range of courts have been addressing these links for decades. For instance, although under the European Convention on Human Rights there is no general right to a home, as such, many cases have dealt with the question of forced evictions and issues of security of tenure (see Box 6.20). These and related sentiments can also be found in the decisions of national courts in many countries. Of all the domestic-level judicial approaches to the question of security of tenure, it is the South African courts that have taken the most interesting route. A number of recent court cases in South Africa exemplify how the right to security of tenure is increasingly gaining recognition at the national level internationally (see Box 6.26).

Box 6.19 United Nations Committee on Economic, Social and Cultural Rights (CESCR) statements on state compliance with the right to security of tenure

Canada (1993): the CESCR is concerned that the right to security of tenure is not enjoyed by all tenants in Canada. The Committee recommends the extension of security of tenure to all tenants.

Mexico (1993): the CESCR recommends the speedy adoption of policies and measures designed to ensure adequate civic services, security of tenure and the availability of resources to facilitate access by low-income communities to affordable housing.

Dominican Republic (1994): the government should confer security of tenure to all dwellers lacking such protection at present, with particular reference to areas threatened with forced eviction. The CESCR notes that Presidential Decrees 358-91 and 359-91 are formulated in a manner inconsistent with the provisions of the Covenant and urges the government to consider the repeal of both of these decrees within the shortest possible timeframe.

The Philippines (1995): the CESCR urges the government to extend indefinitely the moratorium on summary and illegal forced evictions and demolitions and to ensure that all those under threat in those contexts are entitled to due process. The government should promote greater security of tenure in relation to housing in accordance with the principles outlined in the CESCR's General Comment No 4 and should take the necessary measures, including prosecutions wherever appropriate, to stop violations of laws such as RA 7279.

Azerbaijan (1997): the CESCR draws the attention of the state party to the importance of collecting data relating to the practice of forced evictions and of enacting legislation concerning the rights of tenants to security of tenure in monitoring the right to housing.

Nigeria (1998): the CESCR urges the government to cease forthwith the massive and arbitrary evictions of people from their homes and take such measures as are necessary in order to alleviate the plight of those who are subject to arbitrary evictions or are too poor to afford a decent accommodation. In view of the acute shortage of housing, the government should allocate adequate resources and make sustained efforts to combat this serious situation.

Kenya (2005): the state party should develop transparent policies and procedures for dealing with evictions and ensure that evictions from settlements do not occur unless those affected have been consulted and appropriate resettlement arrangements have been made.

Source: Office of the United Nations High Commissioner for Human Rights, www.ohchr.org/english/bodies/cescr/index.htm

Box 6.20 Security of tenure case law: European Court of Human Rights

Among the many cases addressed by the European Court of Human Rights, perhaps the most prominent is the inter-state complaint case of *Cyprus* versus *Turkey* (1976) which addressed evictions as a violation of the right to 'respect for the home', and thus provided significant protection against this violation of internationally recognized housing rights.

In *Akdivar and Others* versus *Turkey* (1996), the court found that 'there can be no doubt that the deliberate burning of the applicants' homes and their contents constitutes ... a serious interference with the right to respect for their family lives and homes and with the peaceful enjoyment of possessions'.

In the case of *Spadea and Scalabrino* versus *Italy* (1995), the court opined that the failure of the public authorities to evict elderly tenants from the homes owned by the applicants was not a violation of the right to peaceful enjoyment of possessions – in effect, protecting the rights of the tenants to remain in the accommodation.

In *Phocas* versus *France* (1996), the court held that there had been no violation of Article I of Protocol No I in the case where the applicant's full enjoyment of his property had been subjected to various interferences due to the implementation of urban development schemes since the said interference complied with the requirements of the general interest.

In *Zubani* versus *Italy* (1996), a case concerning expropriation, the court held that there had been a violation of Article I of Protocol No I since no fair balance had been struck between the interest of protecting the right to property and the demands of the general interest as a result of the length of the proceedings, the difficulties encountered by the applicants to obtain full payment of the compensation awarded and the deterioration of the plots eventually returned to them.

In *Connors* versus *United Kingdom* (2004), the court stated clearly that:

> *... the eviction of the applicant and his family from the local authority site was not attended by the requisite procedural safeguards ... and consequently cannot be regarded as justified by a 'pressing social need' or proportionate to the legitimate aim being pursued. There has, accordingly, been a violation of ... the Convention.*

CIVIL SOCIETY RESPONSES TO SECURITY OF TENURE AND FORCED EVICTIONS

A growing number of non-governmental organizations (NGOs) at international, national and local levels have become involved in efforts to support the provision of security of tenure and opposing forced evictions in recent years. Their efforts have ranged from lobbying national governments and delegates at international conferences and meetings, to providing advice or direct support to local communities. Among the most prominent NGOs that have been working at the international level for several years are the Asian Coalition for Housing Rights (ACHR), the Centre on Housing Rights and Evictions (COHRE) and the Habitat International Coalition (HIC). At the national level, the efforts of NGOs have often been supplemented by those of other civil society actors, including local universities, as in the case of Pom Mahakan in Bangkok (see Box 11.6).

Acts of forced eviction – whether carried out to construct a large dam or a new road, in the context of ethnic cleansing or simply to gentrify a trendy neighbourhood – are almost invariably accompanied by attempts by those affected to resist the eviction and to stay in their homes. Although perhaps most initiatives to stop forced evictions before they occur eventually fail, there are no shortage of inspiring and courageous cases where planned evictions have been revoked and the people allowed to remain in their homes on their lands.

A few examples of strategies against planned evictions are summarized below. Any number of additional examples of strategies against planned evictions could be provided; but even this cursory examination reveals that evictions can be prevented by using a wide range of measures, all of which are premised on the human rights of the persons and communities affected:[48]

Acts of forced eviction ... are almost invariably accompanied by attempts by those affected to resist the eviction and to stay in their homes

- *Zambia.* Some 17,000 families (at least 85,000 people) were spared planned eviction in 1991 due to the efforts of a local women's rights organization, the Zambia Women and Shelter Action Group (ZWOSAG). Basing claims on international human rights standards on eviction in negotiations with government officials, ZWOSAG was able to obtain a suspension order from the minister for local government and housing, who went on national television and radio to announce the suspension, and who urged local authorities throughout Zambia to refrain from carrying out forced evictions.
- *Nigeria.* The Social and Economic Rights Action Center submitted complaints to the World Bank Inspection Panel, attempting to prevent mass evictions in Lagos that would result from the World Bank-funded Lagos Drainage and Sanitation Project (see also Box 6.21).
- *Brazil.* As discussed in Chapter 11, anti-eviction campaigners utilize 'special social interest zones' (urban areas specifically zoned for social housing) as a means of preventing evictions. Moreover, the efforts of the national housing movements have also had a major impact on policies related to security of tenure (see Box 6.27).
- *The Philippines.* Various strategies have been employed to halt evictions before they are carried out. In addition to community organizing and popular mobilization, the use of the media, lobbying efforts, the use of human rights arguments based on international law and other measures, as well as legal strategies based on the 1992

Urban Development and Housing Act have occasionally been successful.

- *Thailand.* Several evictions have been prevented or considerably reduced in scale through an eviction prevention technique referred to as 'land sharing', where the land owner of a slum agrees to resettle the current residents onsite in exchange for full use of a large segment of the land concerned.
- *Pakistan.* The Urban Resource Centre regularly prepares alternative plans to government plans involving eviction as a means of preventing evictions.

RESPONSES OF INTERNATIONAL ORGANIZATIONS TO TENURE INSECURITY AND FORCED EVICTIONS

The Global Campaign for Secure Tenure ... facilitates efforts ... to replace the practice of unlawful evictions with negotiation with affected populations and their organizations

In addition to the numerous efforts of civil society actors, a range of international organizations have also been focusing increasing attention on security of tenure during recent years. The Global Campaign for Secure Tenure was initiated in 1999 by UN-Habitat and has two main objectives: slum upgrading through negotiation, not eviction; and monitoring forced evictions and advancing tenure rights. So far, the campaign has been introduced in cities across the world, including Casablanca, Durban, Manila, Mumbai, Kingston (Jamaica), and Ouagadougou (Burkina Faso).

The campaign facilitates efforts by many member states to replace the practice of unlawful evictions with negotiation with affected populations and their organizations. Moreover, it supports the introduction of tenure systems that are favourable to the urban poor, while at the same time being feasible for local land administration authorities. The campaign is built around a series of organizing principles. These include protecting and promoting housing rights for all; opposing forced evictions; secure residential tenure; gender equity; partnership; negotiated resettlement; open land markets; promoting legislative reform and sustainable shelter policies; and land availability.[49]

The campaign works on the basis of encouraging national-level campaigns for secure tenure that focus on concrete steps to increase the enjoyment of tenure rights by those currently living in informal settlements. The campaign's guidelines on undertaking national campaigns for secure tenure[50] provide a useful synopsis of the steps required for successful local-level activities. These include, for instance, initial consultations with stakeholders, diagnosis of local tenure security (including the preparation of city protocols, situation analyses and security of tenure action plans), launching of national campaigns, media activities and, finally, implementation of national security of tenure action plans. Despite the widespread support given to the campaign by civil society actors, donor nations have so far shown considerable reluctance to support this innovative approach. While it may be too soon, therefore, to determine how successful the campaign has been in expanding the enjoyment of secure tenure, the concentrated and coordinated efforts of the campaign – the first initiative of its kind –

Box 6.21 Resisting forced evictions: The Ijora-Badia community in Lagos, Nigeria

In July 1996, residents of 15 Lagos slum communities, with a total population of 1.2 million people, learned of plans by the Lagos state government to forcibly evict them from their homes and businesses as part of the Lagos Drainage and Sanitation Project. Evictions started in the Ijora-Badia community in 1997, when bulldozers demolished the homes of more than 2000 people.

Prior to the July 1996 eviction announcement, the Social and Economic Rights Action Center (SERAC) was already working within the Ijora-Badia community, providing basic human rights education and improving the community's capacity to communicate with various government institutions. In an effort to address the eviction threat, SERAC increased its support to the targeted slum communities. Working with community leaders, women, youth and associations, SERAC organized a number of initiatives, including outreach and sensitization meetings; group discussions; a legal clinic; training workshops; and disseminated information material within and beyond the target communities. Experienced leaders and organizers from other communities with first-hand experience in resisting evictions were brought in to share their knowledge and experience.

Following a series of consultations and investigations, the Lagos state government renewed its effort to forcibly evict the Ijora-Badia community on 29 July 2003, with the demolition of another part of the Ijora-Badia settlement. Now, however, the residents were better organized, mobilized and determined to keep their homes, and the demolitions were halted due to vehement resistance.

On 1 August 2003, SERAC filed a lawsuit on behalf of the Ijora-Badia residents, also seeking an order of injunction restraining the relevant authorities from continuing the demolitions pending a resolution by the courts. In disregard of the pending lawsuit and the order of injunction (which was granted by the court on 19 August), the demolitions continued on 19 October 2003, leaving over 3000 people homeless, mostly women and children.

In a dramatic turn of events, however, research revealed that a significant portion of the Ijora-Badia lands had been acquired by the federal government of Nigeria in 1929. This finding had profound implications for the community. In a SERAC-backed petition to the federal government, the Ijora-Badia community demanded immediate action to save their homes and land. As a result, the Minister of Housing and Urban Development notified the Lagos state government of its legal ownership of the Ijora-Badia land and directed it to keep away from the Ijora-Badia land while accepting responsibility to upgrade and redevelop Ijora-Badia for the benefit of its people.

Source: Morka, 2007

Box 6.22 The Advisory Group on Forced Evictions (AGFE)

The Advisory Group on Forced Evictions (AGFE) was established in 2004 following a resolution of UN-Habitat's Governing Council. The AGFE reports directly to the executive director of UN-Habitat, and provides advice on alternatives to forced evictions. In its first two biannual reports, the AGFE has documented more than two dozen cases of imminent or ongoing unlawful evictions in several countries and has successfully engaged in conciliatory activities to propose alternatives.

During the first four fact-finding and conciliatory missions undertaken by the AGFE, it was instrumental in developing alternatives to unlawful evictions:

- In Rome, the authorities set a moratorium on forced evictions.
- In the Dominican Republic, a commission was established to discuss the enactment of an eviction law.
- In Curitiba, the AGFE was requested by the municipality to assess housing rights violations, advise stakeholders on practices in line with international human rights laws and standards, and develop an action plan to prevent further evictions. The AGFE organized a public hearing on unlawful evictions that put pressure on stakeholders to find alternative solutions. As a consequence, the local authorities began to resettle families and provide them with alternative sites and building materials.
- In Ghana, the AGFE supported the government's plan to relocate the Old Fadima slum community, which had been threatened with forced eviction for a long time, and to build low-cost housing for them based on the beneficiaries' consent. The AGFE helped pave the way for the recently launched intervention of UN-Habitat's Slum Upgrading Facility that will enable 1000 poor families to get better housing.

Source: UN-Habitat, 2005d, 2007

towards achieving security of tenure for all have to be seen in a positive light.

Closely linked to the Global Campaign for Secure Tenure, the Advisory Group on Forced Evictions (AGFE) was established in 2004. The objective of the AGFE is to monitor forced evictions and to identify and promote alternatives, such as *in-situ* upgrading and other alternative options. Evictions and relocations, if unavoidable, must be undertaken in a manner that conforms to international human rights standards and the United Nations guidelines on development-based displacement[51] (i.e. such relocation should only be undertaken following negotiated settlements with the individuals and communities concerned, and should include provision of alternative land with long-term security of tenure). The AGFE is comprised of individuals from civil society organizations, local authorities, central government and professionals in developing and developed countries. It is supported by a network of representatives from organizations in the fields of human settlement, law, tenure policy and human rights (see Box 6.22).

Approaching the security of tenure question from a slightly different perspective, the Commission on Legal Empowerment of the Poor was established in 2005 and seeks to promote the extension of formal legal rights and protections to marginalized groups (see Box 6.23). Its stated aim is to 'explore how nations can reduce poverty through reforms that expand access to legal protection and economic opportunities for all'.[52] The commission organizes national and regional consultations all over the world to learn from the experiences of those who live and work in slums and settlements, and is thus partnering with grassroots organizations, governments and institutions. One major goal that has emerged through these discussions is how to transform the legal system from an obstacle to an opportunity for poor and otherwise disempowered communities.

The Commission on Legal Empowerment of the Poor ... seeks to promote the extension of formal legal rights and protections to marginalized groups

The Cities Alliance is another institution that continues to promote improved security of tenure conditions across the world. A global coalition of cities and their development partners committed to scaling up successful approaches to poverty reduction, the alliance brings cities

Box 6.23 The Commission on Legal Empowerment of the Poor

The Commission on Legal Empowerment of the Poor is the first global initiative to focus specifically on the link between exclusion, poverty and law. The commission was launched in September 2005 by a group of developing and industrialized countries, including Canada, Denmark, Egypt, Finland, Guatemala, Iceland, India, Norway, Sweden, South Africa, Tanzania and the UK, and has a mandate to complete its work in 2008.

The commission focuses on four thematic issues: access to justice and the rule of law; property; labour rights; and entrepreneurship. Its working methods include:

- compiling an inventory of lessons learned from those governments that have sought to extend legal protection to the informal sector;
- generating political support for broad reforms that will ensure legal inclusion and empowerment;
- exploring reforms that will underpin the broadening of access to property rights;
- examining which structures can best promote economic growth;
- identifying ways to support other development approaches; and
- producing a comprehensive set of practical and adaptable tools that will guide reforms at the country level.

Source: Commission on Legal Empowerment of the Poor, 2006a, 2006b; www.undp.org/legalempowerment

Box 6.24 Land-sector harmonization, alignment and coordination for poverty reduction in Kenya

The Development Partners Group on Land in Kenya brings together the government, bilateral donors, and a range of United Nations and civil society organizations for the purpose of developing a common approach to some of the most challenging land-related issues in Kenya. The main reason for the establishment of the group was the realization that there was an urgent need for harmonization among the various programmes undertaken in the land sector in Kenya in order to avoid overlapping or divergent approaches among development partners. The group was officially formed in July 2003 and channelled support to the National Land Policy Formulation Process through a basket fund arrangement.

In line with this new agenda on aid effectiveness, the Development Partners Group on Land aims to deliver and manage aid to the land sector in Kenya and to meet the principles of harmonization, alignment and coordination. In its activities and cooperation with other stakeholders, the group strives to achieve consensus and support around the policy direction of the government instead of pursuing diverging agendas. The emphasis of the group is on three areas:

- strengthening government capacity to develop and implement land-related policies and programmes;
- aligning donor support with government priorities as set out in its poverty reduction strategy; and
- avoiding duplication and overlap in aid initiatives.

The support of the group is now expanding to cover the main activities run by the Ministry of Land, such as the land policy process, the development of a pro-poor land information management system, the implementation of the recommendations of the Ndungu Commission on illegal allocation of public land, and the development of forced eviction guidelines in Kenya. Since its establishment, the donor group has supported the government with investments worth US$10 million in the land sector.

Source: UN-Habitat, www.unhabitat.org/content.asp?typeid=24&catid=283&id=1603

together in a direct dialogue with bilateral and multilateral agencies and financial institutions, promotes the developmental role of local governments and helps cities of all sizes to obtain more coherent international support. By promoting the positive impacts of urbanization, the alliance helps local authorities to plan and prepare for future growth, assists cities in developing sustainable financing strategies, and attracts long-term capital investments for infrastructure and other services. Cities Alliance supports cities to prepare city development strategies, which are action plans for equitable growth in cities and their surrounding regions, developed and sustained through participation, to improve the quality of life for all citizens.

South Africa has few parallels when it comes to prohibiting and regulating the practice of evictions

Another initiative that deserves some attention is the work of the Development Partners Group on Land in Kenya. The group focuses on promoting secure tenure for disadvantaged groups and the development of sustainable land information management systems. It also supports productive investments in urban and rural areas. The group represents an innovative approach to land-sector coordination in line with international declarations calling for greater harmonization, alignment and coherence in the field of international technical cooperation (see Box 6.24).

Box 6.25 Key legislation on security of tenure adopted in South Africa since 1996

- Restitution of Land Rights Act (No 22 of 1994)
- Land Reform (Labour Tenants) Act (No 3 of 1996)
- Communal Property Associations Act (No 28 of 1996)
- Interim Protection of Informal Land Rights Act (No 31 of 1996)
- Extension of Security of Tenure Act (No 62 of 1997)
- Housing Act (No 107 of 1997)
- Prevention of Illegal Eviction from and Unlawful Occupation of Land Act (No 19 of 1998)
- Communal Land Rights Act (No 11 of 2004)

SECURITY OF TENURE AND HUMAN RIGHTS: EXAMPLES FROM SOUTH AFRICA, BRAZIL AND INDIA

All countries have policies and laws in place that affect the degree to which the population concerned has access to legal security of tenure. In some countries, the explicit human rights dimensions of security of tenure have become part and parcel of the prevailing laws, practices and values. Recent developments in three developing countries that stand out in this respect – South Africa, Brazil and India – are discussed below.

South Africa

In terms of legal frameworks recognizing the importance of security of tenure, South Africa has few parallels when it comes to prohibiting and regulating the practice of evictions. South Africa's first democratic election took place in 1994. The newly elected government, under an interim constitution, set up the Land Claims Court with a Land Commission to replace an Advisory Commission. This meant that black South Africans who had been forcibly removed and been dispossessed of their land during the apartheid era could institute a claim for the return of their land or compensation.[53]

The new 1996 South African Constitution contains several important provisions relating to tenure that became contested litigation areas during the last ten years.[54] These include:

- section 25, which provides for protection of property rights, protection against arbitrary deprivation of property, compensation for expropriation of property

Box 6.26 Security of tenure case law in South Africa

In terms of national-level judicial approaches to the question of security of tenure, three recent court cases in South Africa stand out.

In *Grootboom*, the first case under the South African Constitution to address the complex questions of forced eviction, relocation and security of tenure, the Constitutional Court asserted in 2001 that:

> 1 *The state is required to take reasonable legislative and other measures. Legislative measures by themselves are not likely to constitute constitutional compliance. Mere legislation is not enough. The state is obliged to act to achieve the intended result, and the legislative measures will invariably have to be supported by appropriate, well-directed policies and programmes implemented by the executive. These policies and programmes must be reasonable both in their conception and their implementation. The formulation of a programme is only the first stage in meeting the state's obligations. The programme must also be reasonably implemented. An otherwise reasonable programme that is not implemented reasonably will not constitute compliance with the state's obligations.*
>
> 2 *In determining whether a set of measures is reasonable, it will be necessary to consider housing problems in their social, economic and historical context and to consider the capacity of institutions responsible for implementing the programme. The programme must be balanced and flexible and make appropriate provision for attention to housing crises and to short-, medium- and long-term needs. A programme that excludes a significant segment of society cannot be said to be reasonable. Conditions do not remain static and therefore the programme will require continuous review.*
>
> 3 *Effective implementation requires at least adequate budgetary support by national government. This, in turn, requires recognition of the obligation to meet immediate needs in the nationwide housing programme. Recognition of such needs in the nationwide housing programme requires it to plan, budget and monitor the fulfilment of immediate needs and the management of crises. This must ensure that a significant number of desperate people in need are afforded relief, though not all of them need receive it immediately. Such planning, too, will require proper cooperation between the different spheres of government.*

In what has been described as a win–win case, in *Modderklip* (in 2004), the Supreme Court of Appeal held that the state had breached its constitutional obligations to both the landowner and the unlawful occupiers by failing to provide alternative land to the occupiers upon eviction. The court thus consolidated the protection extended to vulnerable occupiers in the *Grootboom* case by stipulating that they were entitled to remain on the land until alternative accommodation was made available to them.

In the *Port Elizabeth Municipality* case, the South African Constitutional Court (in 2005) ruled that:

> *It is not only the dignity of the poor that is assailed when homeless people are driven from pillar to post in a desperate quest for a place where they and their families can rest their heads. Our society, as a whole, is demeaned when state action intensifies rather than mitigates their marginalization. The integrity of the rights-based vision of the constitution is punctured when governmental action augments rather than reduces denial of the claims of the desperately poor to the basic elements of a decent existence. Hence the need for special judicial control of a process that is both socially stressful and potentially conflicutal* (para 18)
>
> *Section 6(3) [of the Prevention of Illegal Eviction from and Unlawful Occupation of Land Act, which gives effect to sec 26(3) of the constitution] states that the availability of a suitable alternative place to go to is something to which regard must be had, not an inflexible requirement. There is therefore no unqualified constitutional duty on local authorities to ensure that in no circumstances should a home be destroyed unless alternative accommodation or land is made available. In general terms, however, a court should be reluctant to grant an eviction against relatively settled occupiers unless it is satisfied that a reasonable alternative is available, even if only as an interim measure pending ultimate access to housing in the formal housing programme.* (para 28)

and (in section 25(5)) requires that 'the state must take reasonable legislative and other measures, within its available resources, to foster conditions which enable citizens to gain access to land on an equitable basis';

- section 25(6), which provides that 'A person or community whose tenure of land is legally insecure as a result of past racially discriminatory laws or practices is entitled, to the extent provided by an Act of Parliament, either to tenure which is legally secure or to comparable redress.'

Furthermore, and responding to the fact that many millions of South Africans had been forcibly removed from their homes during the apartheid period, section 26 of the constitution now provides that:

> 1 *Everyone has the right to have access to adequate housing.*
>
> 2 *The state must take reasonable legislative and other measures, within its available resources, to achieve the progressive*

> *realization of this right.*
>
> 3 *No one may be evicted from their home, or have their home demolished, without an order of court made after considering all the relevant circumstances. No legislation may permit arbitrary evictions.*

Moreover, during the years since the adoption of the 1996 South African Constitution, the South African Parliament has adopted a series of key legislation dealing with various aspects of security of tenure (see Box 6.25). Accordingly, those suffering in circumstances of insecure tenure are in a dramatically stronger position legally than they were a decade ago. Court decisions have given them substantive protection under the constitution and an ability to obtain orders that the authorities produce constitutionally viable and acceptable plans for fulfilling their obligations. Eviction law has changed dramatically and new cases are developing a substantive rights jurisprudence and not merely interpreting procedural protections.

The state is obliged to act to progressively improve the housing conditions in South Africa. It is also required to ensure that policies and programmes are well directed and that they are well implemented

The next key shift occurred with the so-called *Grootboom* case, when the Constitutional Court[55] – while not following the High Court's order that shelter should be mandatory for children[56] – held that in failing to provide for those most desperately in need, an otherwise reasonable local authority housing policy was still in breach of the constitution. Thus, the decision stressed that the state is obliged to act to progressively improve the housing conditions in South Africa. The state is not only required to initiate and implement programmes, it is also required to ensure that policies and programmes are well directed and that they are well implemented. Other recent cases, such as the *Port Elizabeth Municipality* and *Modderklip* cases, build on this case and highlight the goal of avoiding evictions and stress the obligations to provide alternative and appropriate accommodation when evictions are unavoidable (see Box 6.26).

Municipalities ... are required to formulate master plans incorporating the constitutional principles linked to the 'right to the city'

These legislative efforts, however, have not always succeeded in achieving the results sought. Besides the fact that forced evictions have clearly not been eradicated from South Africa, efforts to provide security of tenure through the formalization process have also clearly fallen short of expectations. One analysis points out the following lessons from South Africa's experience with formalization to date:

- *Formalization of property rights through titling does not necessarily promote increased tenure security or certainty and in many cases does the opposite.*
- *Formalization of property rights does not promote lending to the poor.*
- *Rather than giving their property the character of 'capital', formalization could expose the poor to the risk of homelessness.*
- *The urban and rural poor already have some access to credit.*
- *Formalization through registered title deeds creates unaffordable costs for many poor people.*
- *Informal property systems currently support a robust rental market that is well suited to the needs of the poor.*
- *Formalization via title deeds for individual property can very quickly fail to reflect reality.*
- *The poor are not homogenous and those in the extra-legal sector should be differentiated according to income and vulnerability status.*[57]

Moreover, and tellingly, during recent years South Africa has witnessed accelerated urbanization and increased rural impoverishment, in addition to substantial increases in the price of land in the main urban areas where people are looking for houses and seeking jobs. The post-apartheid state deserves credit for a housing programme that has provided in excess of 1 million houses since 1994. The extent of the continuing challenge with respect to providing secure tenure is apparent from a recent survey, which records that notwithstanding the number of houses built, the number of households in the nine largest urban areas without formal shelter has increased from 806,943 in 1996 to 1,023,134 in 2001 and 1,105,507 in 2004.[58]

Brazil

The approval of the new democratic Constitution of Brazil in 1988 and the collapse of the national social housing system in 1996 led to the development of new policies and programmes targeting the situation of the population living in informal urban settlements. The promotion of the 'right to the city' and the right to housing were major components of these new initiatives.

Under the constitution, all municipalities of more than 20,000 residents are required to formulate master plans incorporating the constitutional principles linked to the 'right to the city'. These norms were significantly bolstered by the adoption in 2001 of the innovative City Statute (see Box 11.8). Property rights are regulated according to the special constitutional provisions addressing rural and urban land, indigenous peoples' and Afro-descendants' lands, and private and public land. As for property rights over urban land, the municipalities have jurisdiction to issue laws supplementing state and federal legislation as applied to local matters, such as environment, culture, health and urban rights. All municipalities are required to develop a master plan as the basic legal instrument for urban development and to ensure that both the city and the property owners fulfil their legal and social functions according to the law. The municipalities may also promote legislation and/or regulations as required for control, utilization, urbanization and occupation of urban land.

National programmes to support the production of social housing, land regularization and slum upgrading have been implemented by the Ministry of the Cities created in 2003. Civil society, social movements and NGOs have been leading the implementation of such policies together with the federal government, and consistent with the principles and instruments provided by the City Statute. The process of

Box 6.27 Participatory housing policies and legislation in Brazil

Various groups in Brazil have carried out innovative, independent and self-organized efforts to address housing and land rights. The most common experiences involve co-operatives, associations or other self-help efforts aimed at building or improving housing in urban areas. Since the 1980s, such efforts have been organized under the National Forum on Urban Reform, which is an umbrella organization of popular movements, professional organizations and non-governmental organizations (NGOs) in the areas of housing, urban management, urban transportation and sanitation. Among the major achievements of the forum is the development of a Platform for Urban Reform, which seeks to realize housing and land rights and to combat poverty and social inequalities. This platform was underwritten by 131,000 voters and presented by various organizations to Congress in 1987 as part of the process leading up to the adoption of the new constitution of 1988.

In some cities, the forum is represented through local or regional forums, which deals with the following issues:

- actions in the defence of the 'right to the city' and of communities whose housing rights are threatened with forced displacement by the implementation of projects for development or the promotion of tourism and/or infrastructure construction or improvement;
- participation in programmes and projects for land regularization in informal and irregular urban settlements;
- organization of counselling and capacity-building on public rights and policies for popular leadership and organizations; and
- participation in city management processes.

Among the major achievements of the National Forum was the approval of the City Statute and its contribution to the establishment of the Ministry of Cities in 2003. The National Forum also played a major role in both the first and the second National City conferences, held in 2003 and 2005, respectively. The first conference led to the establishment of the National City Council in 2004. The council is a consultative body responsible for proposing guidelines and goals for public policies addressing national urban development, housing, sanitation and transportation. It also provides guidelines and recommendations for the application of the City Statute and initiates national and regional plans for territorial organization.

Another result of the organization of the urban social movements was the approval of a bill creating the National Social Housing System and the National Fund. The proposal for this new law was presented in 1988 and was signed by 1 million voters, as is required for such popular initiatives. It proposed the creation of an articulated national housing system composed of an executive public authority: the Ministry of the Cities; the Federal Savings Bank as its operational agent; the National City Council and the National Social Housing Fund; housing councils and funds created at the municipal and state levels; and housing co-operatives and community associations. The law reflecting the demands of this popular initiative was approved by the Federal Senate in 2005 (Law No 11.124/2005) and established the National Housing System to facilitate access to rural and urban land and adequate housing by the poor people through implementation of a policy of subsidies. This law provides for the transfer of funds now used to repay the foreign debt to municipal and state programmes to subsidize housing and land for the low-income population.

The National Social Housing Fund is managed by a council composed of 22 representatives, of whom 10 are from the governmental sector and 12 are from the non-governmental sector (social movements, the private housing sector, trade unions, professional entities, universities and NGOs). The council members are entitled to approve the annual plan of financial investment for housing programmes, considering the resources available in the National Fund; to establish criteria for the municipalities, states, housing co-operatives and associations to access these financial resources; and to monitor the full application of such resources.

Source: Marques, 2007

There are still many structural obstacles of a conceptual, political, institutional and financial nature to be overcome before the legal concessions become a reality

implementing national policies and legislation concerning the promotion of land and housing rights by the federal government and the civil society is assisted by specific policies and programmes, such as the National Policy to Support Sustainable Urban Land Regularization, established in 2003 by the Ministry of the Cities; the National Social Housing System and its Social Housing Fund, approved in 2005; and the National City Conferences, held in 2003 and 2005 (see Box 6.27).[59]

Brazil continues to face serious land-access problems both in urban and rural areas, as can be seen from the many and varied conflicts over land possession. Despite the fact that the federal government has managed to advance significantly in formulating comprehensive national housing and land policies and in creating the essential legal–institutional bases, some programmes are isolated and ineffective, and have little significant impact on the Brazilian reality.

There are still many structural obstacles of a conceptual, political, institutional and financial nature to be overcome before the legal concessions become a reality. Recent statistics show that the Brazilian housing deficit has increased over the last decade from 5.4 million housing units in 1991 to 6.7 million in 2000 – an increase of 22 per cent in only ten years. Furthermore, it continues to grow at a rate of 2.2 per cent per year. In 2000, the urban housing deficit was estimated at 5.4 million units. Paradoxically, according to the 2000 census, there are 4.8 million unoccupied residences in the cities.[60]

India

In India, the national housing policy of 1994 states that central and state governments must take steps to avoid forced evictions. Moreover, they must encourage *in-situ* upgrading, slum renovation and other initiatives with the provision of occupancy rights. When evictions are unavoidable, the policy states that the government 'must undertake selective relocation with community involvement only for

Box 6.28 Security of tenure case law: India's Supreme Court

In 1978, the Supreme Court first found in the case of *Maneka Gandhi* versus *Union of India* that the right to life provisions in the Indian Constitution (Article 21) must be taken to mean 'the right to live with dignity'.

Building on this conclusion, in the 1981 case of *Francis Coralie Mullin* versus *Union Territory of Delhi*, the Supreme Court asserted that: 'We think that the right to life includes the right to live with human dignity and all that goes along with it, namely the bare necessities of life such as adequate nutrition, clothing, and shelter over the head.'

In what has become clearly the most celebrated Indian case in this regard, known colloquially as the Bombay Pavement Dwellers Case, the Supreme Court expanded further on the right to life provisions in the constitution, even while the decision ultimately allowed the eventual eviction of the pavement dwellers concerned. In the 1985 case of *Olga Tellis* versus *Bombay Municipal Corporation*, a constitutional bench of the Supreme Court declared that 'Eviction of petitioners from their dwellings would result in the deprivation of their livelihood... The right under Article 21 is the right to livelihood because no person can live without the means of living'.

Reaching a similar conclusion, in the case of *Ram Prasad* versus *Chairman, Bombay Port Trust*, the Supreme Court directed the relevant public authorities not to evict 50 slum dweller families unless alternative sites were provided for them.

In the case of *Ahmedabad Municipal Corporation* versus *Nawab Khan Gulab Khan and Ors*, in 1997, the Supreme Court stated that it:

> *is the duty of the State to construct houses at reasonable rates and make them easily accessible to the poor. The State has the constitutional duty to provide shelter to make the right to life meaningful ... the mere fact that encroachers have approached this court would be no ground to dismiss their cases. Where the poor have resided in an area for a long time, the State ought to frame schemes and allocate land and resources for rehabilitating the urban poor.*

Housing rights in India are an extraordinary example of practice departing sharply from the law

the clearance of sites which take priority in terms of public interest'. Work has been ongoing for the development of a national slum policy.[61] Added to these favourable policies, a series of judicial decisions in India has also been supportive of housing rights and tenure claims. For more than two decades, the Indian Supreme Court has issued a range of far-reaching decisions relying both on the right to life provisions found in the constitution, as well as other norms to protect the housing rights of dwellers (see Box 6.28).[62]

Law, policy and jurisprudence do not always mesh with reality. One third of Mumbai's slum dwellers are evictees,[63] and, clearly India's recent economic boom has not distributed the benefits equally. Housing rights in India are an extraordinary example of practice departing sharply from the law. India has ratified the ICESCR without any reservation, and the ICESCR has been referred to in scores of judgements of India's Supreme Court. Furthermore, there is no doubt whatsoever that it is enforceable in Indian courts. Nevertheless, wave after wave of brutal demolitions have taken place, without notice or justifiable reason, in inclement weather, and without compensation or rehabilitation. The Commonwealth Games proposed to be held at Delhi in 2010 initiated the largest ever displacement from Delhi in the year 2000. There are no records available of the number of homes demolished; but NGOs estimate that over 200,000 people have been evicted. From the Yamuna Pushta area alone, 150,000 people were brutally evicted in order to create parks and fountains.[64]

For decades, the quest for security of tenure has ... been an illusive one

With a population of about 15 million people, Mumbai has half of its population living in slums. They occupy only 8 per cent of the city's land. Formally, those who were listed in the 1976 census of slums were eligible to be covered by slum improvement schemes and also eligible for an alternative plot in case of evictions. This introduced the concept of a cut-off date. Later, the electoral rolls of 1980 were adopted as the cut-off. This was then shifted to 1985, to 1990 and later to 1995. In 2003, 86,000 families in and around the Sanjay Gandhi National Park were evicted despite being covered by the cut-off dates under the orders of the High Court, which took the extreme step of using helicopters and deploying retired military officers to evict the poor inhabitants.[65] Along these lines several massive demolitions took place in Mumbai. Between November 2004 and February 2005 alone, more than 300,000 people were rendered homeless when over 80,000 homes were smashed.

CONCLUDING REMARKS

This chapter has provided a brief overview of some of the most prevalent types of policy responses that have been employed towards the objective of enhancing security of tenure. The overview yields a range of conclusions. One is perhaps more notable than the others: in spite of all the various approaches taken over the past decades, there can be no doubt that failure, rather than success, has been the norm with respect to addressing the goal of security of tenure for all. Were it otherwise, the world would not face a security of tenure crisis where hundreds of millions of people live without any form of officially recognized or legally secure tenure.

For decades, the quest for security of tenure has, in many respects, been an illusive one. Though all political creeds adhere to views supporting the opinion that security of tenure must lie at the centre of any realistic efforts to improve the lives of the world's 1 billion slum dwellers, the policies that intend to achieve this aim vary widely. Views focusing on titling propose that formalizing slums through the provision of individual land titles will be the most effective way of raising standards of living, of creating assets and of improving housing conditions. Another view is that title-based approaches are far too expensive to undertake, and when they are attempted, they have the net result of reducing rather than increasing tenure security. Still others favour maintaining customary land tenure arrangements because they are seen as culturally appropriate, grounded deeply in the history of the area concerned, and because they work and are more equitable than approaches based on modern law and private property rights.

Clearly, one of the key challenges for policy-makers is sifting through these and many other views on security of tenure and divining the best approach to a given situation. Before looking at several approaches, it is important to point out that just as formality of tenure does not unequivocally guarantee secure tenure, informality does not necessarily mean insecure tenure. As seen above in the context of regularization, some forms of informality can provide a reasonable degree of tenure security. This is not to say that this approach should necessarily be favoured; but it goes to the core of the issue at hand, which is essentially that much of the strength of tenure security comes in the form of one's *perception* of the security of tenure that they believe they have.

This may appear difficult to fit together with the principles and rights of human rights law; but this may not necessarily be the case. Perhaps perception and rights can go hand in hand, with the objective being a process, perhaps even a lengthy one, whereby the personal or community perception of security can slowly and steadily be transformed into a form of tenure – possibly based on freehold title and possibly not – but whereby those currently residing firmly in the informal sphere, without formal protection from eviction, gradually accrue these rights in a progressively empowering way. In this connection, it is important to remember that the *de facto* and *de jure* status of a given parcel of land may be markedly different:

> *A squatter, or resident of an illegal subdivision, for example, may enjoy no legal rights of occupation, use or transfer, but can still feel physically sufficiently secure, because of numerical strength or political support, to invest in house building and improvement.*[66]

Four major factors seem to contribute to people's perception of the level to which they are protected from eviction. These include the:

Just as formality of tenure does not unequivocally guarantee secure tenure, informality does not necessarily mean insecure tenure

- length of occupation (older settlements enjoy a much better level of legitimacy and, thus, of protection than new settlements);
- size of the settlement (small settlements are more vulnerable than those with a large population);
- level and cohesion of community organization; and
- support that concerned communities can get from third-sector organizations, such as NGOs.[67]

Security of tenure must be seen as a prerequisite, or an initial step, in an incremental tenure regularization process, focusing particularly as it does on the protection, as opposed to the eviction, of the irregular settlement occupants and not on their immediate regularization in legal terms. Approaches that try to achieve security of tenure are the only ones that will meet the immediate and longer-term needs of the populations. As these varying points of view conclusively show, the security of tenure debate is alive and well. Realistically speaking, the main point for the hundreds of millions of people currently living without security of tenure is, perhaps, not whether they are the owners of freehold title to a piece of land or not. More importantly, it is about being able to live a life where their rights to security of tenure are treated as seriously as human rights law says that they should be.

Much of the strength of tenure security comes in the form of one's perception of ... security

NOTES

1 General Assembly Resolution 401(V).
2 Payne, 2001d.
3 See Millennium Declaration, Article 19.
4 UN-Habitat, 2003d, pxxviii.
5 Durand-Lasserve, 1998, p245.
6 Durand-Lasserve and Royston, 2002, p6.
7 Prefecture of São Paulo, 2003, p8.
8 See Boonyabancha, 2005; Shack and Slum Dwellers International, 2004.
9 Seabrook, 1996, p197.
10 de Soto, 2000.
11 Durand-Lasserve, 1998.
12 Payne, 2001c, p51.
13 Cousins et al, 2005.
14 Kanji et al, 2005.
15 Payne, 2001a, p23.
16 Payne, 1997, p46.
17 *Ibid*, p26.
18 Bromley, 2005, p6.
19 *Ibid*, p7.
20 Payne and Majale, 2004, p54.
21 Payne, 1997, p26.
22 Payne, 1997.
23 Durand-Lasserve, 1998, p244.
24 Payne and Majale, 2004.
25 FAO, 2005, pp22–24, 26.
26 Cousins et al, 2005; Huggins and Clover, 2005.
27 World Bank, 2003b, pxxix.
28 *Ibid*, p50.
29 Kanji et al, 2005, p3.
30 World Bank, 2003b, p50.
31 Housing and Property Directorate/Housing and Property Claims Commission, 2005.
32 UNMIK Regulation 1999/23, Preamble.
33 UN doc E/CN.4/Sub.2/1993/8.
34 CESCR, General Comment No 4, para 18.
35 Commission on Human Rights, Resolution 1993/77.
36 See COHRE, 1999; UN-Habitat and OHCHR, 2002; UN-Habitat, 2002, 2005a, 2005b.
37 CESCR, General Comment No 7, paras 8–9.
38 *Ibid*, para 10.
39 *Ibid*, para 16.
40 *Ibid*, para 13.
41 *Ibid*, para 17; and CESCR, General Comment No 2, para 6 and 8(d).
42 Including the right to freedom of movement and to choose one's residence; the right to privacy and respect for the home; the right to equal treatment under the law; the right to human dignity; the right to security of the person; certain formulations of the right to property or the peaceful enjoyment of possessions.
43 Polis, 2002.
44 McAuslan, 2002, pp34–35.
45 *Ibid*, p36.
46 *Ibid*, p36.
47 Alston, 1993.
48 For more comprehensive survey of strategies, see COHRE, 2000.
49 UN-Habitat, 2003b.
50 *Ibid*.
51 Contained in Annex I of UN Document E/CN.4/Sub.2/1997/7.
52 Commission on Legal Empowerment of the Poor, 2006a.
53 See section 121 of the (interim) Constitution of the Republic of South Africa, Act 200 of 1993; and Restitution of Land Rights Act 22 of 1994.
54 Constitution of the Republic of South Africa, Act 108 of 1993, Chapter 2 (the Bill of Rights).
55 *Government of the Republic of South Africa and Others* versus *Grootboom and Others*.
56 *Grootboom* versus *Oostenberg Municipality and Others*.
57 Cousins et al, 2005.
58 South Africa Cities Network, 2006.
59 Kahanovitz, 2007.
60 Marques, 2007.
61 Banerjee, 2002.
62 Baxi, 1982.
63 See, for instance, Jacquemin, 1999; Eviction Watch India, 2003; Gonsalves, 2005.
64 *Hindustan Times*, 2005.
65 Indian People's Human Rights Commission, 2000.
66 Payne, 1997, p8.
67 *Ibid*, p7.

PART IV

NATURAL AND HUMAN-MADE DISASTERS

Over the last three decades, natural and human-made disasters have claimed millions of lives and caused huge economic losses globally. Cities, where half of humanity currently resides and much of the world's assets are concentrated, are fast becoming the locus for much of this destruction and loss from disasters. Rapid urbanization, coupled with global environmental change, is turning an increasing number of human settlements into potential hotspots for disaster risk. The 2005 South Asian earthquake, in which 18,000 children died when their schools collapsed, and the Indian Ocean Tsunami in 2004 that wiped out many coastal settlements in Sri Lanka, India and Indonesia, are testament to the risk that has accumulated in towns and cities and that is released when disaster strikes. Numerous other cases illustrate the suffering and losses experienced by urban dwellers due to natural and human-made disasters (see Box IV.1).

Part IV of this Global Report examines the consequences of natural and human-made disasters for safety and security in cities, and the policy options for preventing and reducing damage caused by these events. Disasters are defined as those events where human capacity to withstand and cope with a natural or human-made hazard is overwhelmed. The majority of the report focuses on large disasters that register direct impacts at the community level and above. However, the impacts of small-scale hazards, where direct impacts are limited to the individual or household levels, are illustrated through an examination of traffic accidents that result in over 1 million deaths worldwide each year, more than any large natural or human-made disaster type.

As highlighted in this part of the report, cities are particularly vulnerable to the effects of natural and human-made disasters due to a complex set of interrelated processes, including a concentration of assets, wealth and people; the location and rapid growth of major urban centres in coastal locations; the modification of the urban built and natural environment through human actions; the expansion of settlements within cities into hazard-prone locations; and the failure of urban authorities to regulate building standards and land-use planning strategies. As cities grow, disaster risk often increases through the rising complexity and interdependence of urban infrastructure and services, greater population density and concentration of resources. Yet, urban growth need not necessarily result in increased disaster risk.

Inequalities in the distribution of disaster risk and loss in urban areas are evident at the global, national and city levels: poorer citizens in cities of poorer countries are most at risk. Disaster impacts are also varied, depending upon what is considered to be at risk. In terms of absolute mortality and economic loss as a proportion of gross domestic product (GDP), regions dominated by low- and middle-income countries record high losses. Indeed, Africa and Asia have experienced the fastest rate of increase in the incidence of natural and human-made disasters over the last three decades. These are also among the world regions with the highest rates of urban growth, indicating that risk will increase in the future as populations grow. Absolute economic loss from natural and human-made disasters is highest in high-income regions such as North America and Europe, although Asia also records high loss in this respect. Indeed, high levels of economic development and political stability help to shift the impact of disasters from human to physical assets, as is evident in the case of Europe. This illustrates that disaster risk reduction planning, investment and management capacity are critical in shaping vulnerability in human settlements.

Disaster loss is also differentiated at the city level. A city's vulnerability to disaster impacts is shaped by its levels of economic development and disaster preparedness. The structure of the urban economy determines which actors bear the brunt of disasters, while its connectivity influences the global spread of impacts from one economy to another. At the individual level, disaster impacts vary according to social differentiation, with women, children, the elderly and the disabled being most vulnerable. The greatest vulnerability to disaster is, however, experienced by the 1 billion people forced to live in urban slums worldwide. People here are excluded from living and working in places protected by construction and land-use planning regulations and have the least assets to cope with disaster shocks. But the speed of urbanization can spread vulnerability to other social groups. For example, where building codes are not followed because of a lack of enforcement, disaster has claimed the lives of those living in the formal housing sector.

The aggregate impact of small hazards and disasters on urban dwellers can be considerable, as shown in this part of the report. Traffic accidents are the best documented of the small-scale hazards, killing over 1.2 million people annually worldwide. The World Health Organization (WHO) calculates the economic costs of traffic accidents to be 1 per cent of gross national product (GNP) in low-income countries, 1.5 per cent in middle-income countries and 2 per cent in high-income countries. Most deaths and injuries are

Box IV.1 Living through disaster in New Orleans, US

Long before Hurricane Katrina washed ashore, New Orleans was inundated with abject poverty, high crime rates, an inadequate education system and governance failures – or, in other words, high vulnerability. Situated as the city is – below sea level, nestled between Lake Pontchatrain, the Mississippi River and Lake Borgne – New Orleans is one of the most hazard-prone and vulnerable areas in the US. The events stemming from 29 August 2005 only re-emphasized the folklore that defines the character of New Orleans as the 'city that care forgot'. For more than two weeks after Katrina struck, 80 per cent of the city remained under water. In addition to 1300 deaths, 350,000 displaced victims were scattered throughout the US. One citizen described her experience:

> *I knew the world was coming to an end… It was me, my husband and daughter. Water was up to my neck. My husband had my [little] girl on his shoulders and we were just holding on to a tree. The water was flowing so hard, it was gushing and gushing. I just prayed for it all to happen quickly if we were going to die.*

As problems of saving victims or restoring order came to characterize the unfolding events of Hurricane Katrina, government and public agencies ceased addressing and meeting the basic human needs of residents in the Superdome and Convention Center to employ tactical response to civil unrest, further thwarting and prolonging safety and security measures designed to protect and assist citizens. As one citizen (a white male, aged 62) explained:

> *Of this whole frightening catastrophe, the police and the military soldiers had me more afraid than anything. I was in a boat trying to help people to the foot of the bridge, when someone said: 'Don't move!' They pointed their rifles at me and asked what was I doing in New Orleans and told me I had to immediately leave the city. I just went home and sat by the door with my wife and my guns. I never would have stayed if I knew that water would get that high all over the city.*

Whether trying to remember or forget, the New Orleans community persists in seeking innovative tactics to return home and find home elsewhere. Seeing that residents remain plagued with no definitive plan from city and state government, nor direct consistent assistance from the federal government, they have assembled and created networks and communities committed to returning home and rebuilding. An African–American female waiting for the possibility to return commented:

> *I know the city will never be the same. But this [is] all I know. I can't wait to get out of Dallas. Those people are tired of helping us. I was able to gut out my house in the east; but who knows when they're going to put on electricity. All my clothes were destroyed. The only thing I am bringing back is plenty of red beans. I got two suitcases full. Everybody told me: bring back red beans! Bring back red beans!*

Is it smart and safe to rebuild the city considering it is 2 metres below sea level and surrounded by water on three sides? Without adequate technological intervention and government funding, the wetlands continue to erode, levee structures remain weak and the city remains vulnerable to more disasters. Nonetheless, since the onset of this catastrophe, community groups and neighbourhoods are participating in rebuilding and reconstruction efforts, determining their own immediate and longstanding opportunities. For example, residents of the Ninth Ward took the initiative and collectively orchestrated a demonstration that halted demolition and bulldozing of their property. One Ninth Ward resident said:

> *I don't care if the government don't give me a dime to help me rebuild: I got this property from my parents; I lived here my whole life, raised six kids here and I am going to die right here. They can bury me right by mama and daddy in the graveyard five blocks away. I'm staying in a hotel in Metarie now, just waiting for the city to get the electricity on in this area (the Ninth Ward). I'm on the list for my FEMA trailer, so I'll be in good shape with or without help; but I ain't waiting on nobody to ask if I can live on my property. I know this looks real bad; but we gonna make them do right by us. We can't let them destroy a whole city.*

Source: Washington, 2007

caused by motorized vehicles, with other road users – pedestrians and cyclists, in particular – being mostly victims. In cities where vehicle ownership is high, car drivers are also among those suffering high levels of loss.

Despite their destructive powers, disasters in urban areas are yet to receive the attention they merit within the field of urban development planning. Indeed, disasters are neither pure natural events nor acts of God, but, rather, products of inappropriate and failed development. Thus, this report takes a risk reduction approach that calls for both small- and large-scale disasters to be seen as problems of development, requiring not only investments in response and reconstruction, but also changes in development paths to reduce or minimize the occurrence and impacts of disaster *ex-ante*. Building on this understanding, a growing number of community groups, non-governmental organizations (NGOs), urban authorities and governments are active in findings ways of reducing the disaster risk that has accumulated in cities.

Mapping disaster risk and its constituent elements of hazard, vulnerability and resilience, or capacity to cope, is a fundamental element of any strategy to reduce risk. This is the case at local as well as urban and national levels. Risk mapping in urban contexts is complicated by the many overlapping hazard types and the dynamism of the social and economic landscape. Great advances in mapping have been made by the application of remote sensing and geographic information systems (GIS), and by the development of participatory mapping methods. However, great inequalities in hazard assessment capacity are also evident. Poorer countries and urban authorities lack the necessary skills and resources to undertake risk assessments. A lack of data to complement assessment techniques, such as census data, poses an additional challenge to risk assessment. Participatory approaches present opportunities for overcoming some of these challenges by enabling communities to have greater control over information and interventions, thereby enhancing their resilience.

One of the key trends observed in this part of the report is that strengthening local resilience or the capacity of local actors to avoid, absorb or recover from the shock of disasters through targeted interventions is now recognized as a vital component of risk reduction. Resilience is closely linked with access to economic, social, political and physical assets, and is constrained by the institutional environment of the city and its wider political–administrative context. Enhancing social networks of support and reciprocity is one way of improving local resilience. Legal frameworks can also be used to invoke the rights of communities to protection and access to resources during and after disasters. Also important is the strengthening of household economies through finance provision and support of livelihood activities. Challenges to the building of local resilience remain; yet, innovative strategies, such as piggybacking risk reduction onto existing local activities, present opportunities.

The availability of information on hazards and vulnerability enables effective early warning (and its four components of knowledge, monitoring and warning, communication and response capacity) in the face of disaster risk. Although significant gains have been made in collating scientific information on approaching risks and hazards, communicating this information to risk managers in a timely and appropriate manner has not been easy. It is also important that information flows are transparent and clear and help to build trust between those communicating and receiving the information. Where information on imminent hazards has not been available or failed to be communicated, potentially avoidable losses have been magnified unnecessarily. Evidence suggests that the more localized early warning and response knowledge can be, the more resilient these systems are in times of disaster. Successful examples of people-centred early warning systems that build communication systems on top of existing networks used in everyday activities exist and are highlighted in this part of the report.

The concentration of infrastructure and buildings in cities, including their spatial layout, is a key source of vulnerability in the face of disasters. However, with adequate planning and design, capacity for regulation, and commitment to compliance or enforcement, potential risks in the built environment of cities may be reduced. For instance, a fundamental tool for integrating disaster risk reduction within urban development initiatives is land-use planning. Likewise, building codes are essential for ensuring safety standards in components of the urban built environment. Yet, enforcement and implementation of these guidelines and regulations remain problematic. Particularly challenging is planning in small urban centres where resources are limited, but population growth (often into new areas of risk) is rapid, and in informal or slum districts of large cities where there is limited power to enforce land use. In both cases, greater inclusion of those at risk in land-use and planning decision-making offers a way forward. Imaginative thinking to overcome the challenge of land-use planning implementation has included suggestions that, as well as being enforced by law, building codes should operate on a system of incentives and support for training of informal-sector builders.

Protecting critical infrastructure and services will influence response and reconstruction capacity in the period after a disaster has struck a city. The potential for cascading events to affect multiple infrastructure systems makes it paramount that critical infrastructure and services are protected and, where possible, managed independently of each other to prevent contagion effects. However, networks of communication and exchange between such services are vital in ensuring a certain minimum level of functioning during and after a disaster.

In the post-disaster period, municipal authorities and local governments are best placed to coordinate relief and reconstruction efforts. Partnerships with community groups and international development and humanitarian agencies are necessary in pre-disaster planning, which is needed in allocating responsibilities and developing operating guidelines for relief and reconstruction. Reconstruction should also be seen as an opportunity to build risk reduction into development. However, reconstruction programmes may even fail to return survivors to pre-disaster conditions. Useful lessons on integrating long-term development goals within reconstruction work are emerging from recent disasters, such as the 2004 Indian Ocean Tsunami. Where development and humanitarian agencies have worked together, as in the involvement of UN-Habitat in the reconstruction of parts of Pakistan following the 2005 earthquake, there are more grounds for optimism.

The difficulties faced by national and city governments in obtaining funding for risk reduction or reconstruction can (and do) preclude the development of relevant policies in these areas. Moreover, national budgets tend to prioritize relief and reconstruction activities. Likewise, much of the funding provided by international organizations and governments for disasters through bilateral and multilateral channels is mostly for recovery and reconstruction activities. Some governments do not set aside budgets for relief and reconstruction activities, but rather draw on contingency funds in the aftermath of a disaster. During recent years, however, the value of investing in risk reduction is being recognized and reflected in international and national funding for disaster-related interventions. This is partly due to evidence illustrating significant cuts in the economic, social and environmental costs of disaster where a risk reduction approach is adopted.

As in the case of natural and human-made disasters, risks arising from traffic accidents can be prevented and/or minimized through targeted policies and interventions. Transport and urban planning, promotion of safe road-user behaviour and traffic management are some of the key strategies for improving road safety. Without building the necessary institutions and awareness for road safety, however, vulnerability to road traffic accidents cannot be reduced. It is equally important to collect and disseminate traffic accident data in order to formulate relevant policies, legislation and interventions. An important trend in recent years is that road safety has gained prominence globally, as is evidenced by extensive international cooperation in this area.

This part of the report considers the multiple aspects of risk in urban areas today associated with natural and human-made disasters. In doing so, Chapter 7 provides an overview of global trends in the incidence and impacts of natural and human-made disasters, as well as those urban processes that contribute to the generation of risk. Subsequently, Chapter 8 reviews existing policy approaches for reducing disaster risk and incorporating risk reduction within urban management and disaster response and reconstruction. Chapter 9 then examines the trends – including policy trends – and impacts of road traffic accidents as an example of hazards threatening the safety and security of urban dwellers on a day-to-day basis.

CHAPTER 7

DISASTER RISK: CONDITIONS, TRENDS AND IMPACTS

Disasters in urban areas are experienced when life support systems fail in the face of pressure from external stress, resulting in loss of life, damage to property and the undermining of livelihoods. However, they are not natural events or 'acts of God', but products of failed development. For the majority of people at risk, loss to disaster is determined more by processes and experiences of urban development and governance than by the physical processes that shape natural or human-made hazards.

This chapter presents an overview of global trends in the incidence and impacts on cities of disasters associated with natural and human-made hazards. In this context, natural hazards include earthquakes, hurricanes, tsunamis, tornadoes, landslides, floods, volcanic eruptions and windstorms, while human-made hazards encompass explosions and chemical releases. However, the conceptual distinction between disasters associated with natural and human-made hazards is increasingly becoming blurred, as many human actions and practices, such as the construction of human settlements in flood-prone areas or on the slopes of active volcanoes, exacerbate human-made hazards. While the focus here is primarily on large-scale disasters that register direct impacts at the community level and above, the characteristics of small-scale disasters whose impacts are largely felt at the individual or household levels are reviewed.

Epidemic diseases and environmental health are not discussed herewith, nor are acts of war. This is because while these forms of stress impact upon the built environment, human health and political systems, the balance of impact is different in each case. It is natural and human-made hazards that most frequently threaten urban sustainability through damage to buildings and critical infrastructure. The focus on natural and human-made disasters also responds to global trends in increasing numbers of such events, in people affected and made homeless by disaster, and in the economic impacts of disaster, especially on the poor and marginalized.

An overview of the relationships between urbanization and disaster risk, human vulnerability and loss (or outcome) is presented below, once key disaster terms are defined. This is followed by a detailed discussion of the distribution of disaster loss associated with natural and human-made hazards worldwide and across cities. The economic and social outcomes, or impacts, of disasters, including the disproportionate impacts on the poor and marginalized, the aged, the very young and women, are then reviewed. Subsequently, factors generating urban disaster risk and contributing to human vulnerability, including modification of the urban environment, planning and construction techniques, urban finance and poverty, are examined. Finally, a regional comparison illustrates variation in conditions, trends and impacts of urban disaster risk globally.

DISASTER TERMINOLOGY

In addition to the terms introduced in Chapters 1 and 2, terminology specific to disaster risk is first presented here to identify what a disaster is and its component parts, and then to identify elements of disaster risk management (see Box 7.1). It is important not to confuse the definition of terms here with meanings attributed to these terms in sister disciplines. For example, in the international development community, 'vulnerability' is commonly used in reference to economic poverty, whereas here vulnerability refers to exposure and susceptibility to harm from natural or human-made hazards, also referred to as 'risky events' in the conceptual framework presented in Chapter 2.

A disaster is understood here to be the outcome of a vulnerable individual or society being hit by a human-made or natural hazard. The vulnerability of an individual or society is reduced through short-term coping and longer-term adaptation that adjust human actions to minimize risk impacts or outcomes.

Disaster management is seen as best undertaken through a disaster risk reduction approach. Here, disaster risk is addressed at a number of stages. Before hazards occur, underlying physical and technological processes can be contained through mitigation. Unfortunately, in most societies, mitigation is not sufficient and residual hazard remains. Reducing risk from residual hazard requires preparedness, including education, risk assessment and early warning and evacuation planning. Disaster response takes place in the first hours and days after a disaster and

Box 7.1 Key terminology

Disasters and their component parts

Disaster: a serious disruption of the functioning of a community or a society causing widespread human, material, economic or environmental losses that exceed the ability of the affected community or society to cope using its own resources. A disaster is a function of risk processes. It results from a combination of hazards, human vulnerability and insufficient capacity or measures to reduce the potential negative consequences of risk.

Natural disaster: a serious disruption to human systems triggered by a natural hazard causing human, material, economic or environmental losses that exceed the ability of those affected to cope.

Human-made disaster: a serious disruption to human systems triggered by a technological or industrial hazard causing human, material, economic or environmental losses that exceed the ability of those affected to cope.

Natural hazards: natural processes or phenomena occurring in the biosphere that may constitute a damaging event. Natural hazards can be classified by origin (geophysical or hydro-meteorological), and they can vary in magnitude or intensity, frequency, duration, area of extent, speed of onset, spatial dispersion and temporal spacing.

Human-made hazards: danger originating from technological or industrial accidents, dangerous procedures, infrastructure failures or certain human activities that may cause the loss of life or injury, property damage, social and economic disruption, or environmental degradation. Examples of human-made hazard include industrial pollution, nuclear activities/accidents and radioactivity, toxic wastes, dam failures, and industrial or technological accidents (explosions, fires and spills).

Human vulnerability: the conditions determined by physical, social, economic and environmental factors or processes that increase the exposure and susceptibility of people to the impact, or outcomes, of hazards.

Coping capacity: the means by which people or organizations use available resources and abilities to face identified adverse consequences that could lead to a disaster. In general, this involves managing resources, both in normal times as well as during crises or adverse conditions. The strengthening of coping capacities builds resilience to withstand the effects of natural and human-induced hazards.

Adaptation: adaptation refers to human action taken to reduce exposure or sensitivity to hazard over the long term.

Managing disaster risk

Disaster risk reduction: an overarching term used to describe policy aimed at minimizing human vulnerability and disaster risk to help avoid (prevention) or to limit (mitigation and preparedness) the adverse impacts of hazards within the broad context of sustainable development.

Mitigation: structural (e.g. engineering) and non-structural (e.g. land-use planning) measures undertaken to limit the severity or frequency of natural and technological phenomena that have the potential to become hazardous.

Preparedness: activities and measures taken in advance to ensure effective response to the impact of hazards, including the issuance of timely and effective early warnings and the temporary evacuation of people and property from threatened locations.

Response: the provision of assistance or intervention during or immediately after a disaster to meet the life preservation and basic subsistence needs of those people affected. It can be of an immediate, short-term or protracted duration.

Recovery: decisions and actions taken after a disaster with a view to restoring or improving the pre-disaster living conditions of the stricken community, while encouraging and facilitating necessary adjustments to reduce disaster risk. Recovery affords an opportunity to develop and apply disaster risk reduction through rehabilitation and reconstruction measures.

Resilience: the capacity of a system, community or society potentially exposed to hazards to change by coping or adapting in order to reach and maintain an acceptable level of functioning and structure. This is determined by the degree to which the social system is capable of organizing itself to increase its capacity for learning from past disasters for better future protection and to improve risk reduction.

Source: adapted from ISDR, 2004a

addresses the basic needs of survivors. As soon as possible, and often with some overlap, disaster response is followed by the more developmental agenda of recovery.

At all stages, from pre-disaster to relief and recovery, there are opportunities to address the root causes of human vulnerability, such as (among others) unsafe housing, inadequate infrastructure, poverty and marginalization. Bringing these elements of risk reduction together can help to make individuals, groups and cities more resilient.

THE SCALE OF DISASTERS

... cities experience both large and small disasters, but the latter are seldom systematically recorded and often ignored...

Most cities experience both large and small disasters, but the latter are seldom systematically recorded and are often ignored, even by the local news media. More often than not, there is no mention of 'small disasters' in the policy statements of government or non-governmental organizations (NGOs).[1] Yet, for those involved, small events can be as destructive as large events causing injury and death and undermining livelihoods. The impact of small disasters is particularly worrying because, while there is no systematic data, many commentators argue that the aggregate impact of small events in cities exceeds losses to the low-frequency, high-impact hazards that capture news headlines.

There is no agreed upon definition, such as the scale of human or economic loss, for what makes a disaster small or large. In practice, the scale ascribed to a disaster is context dependent. Ten people being killed by a landslide in

Rio de Janeiro might be considered a small event by urban authorities; but the same event in the much smaller city of Castries, Saint Lucia, may well be considered of national significance. Table 7.1 outlines those characteristics that can be used more objectively to identify similarities and differences between small and large disasters.

Human vulnerability also plays a large role in determining the scale of disaster. Small hazard events can be turned into large disasters where high vulnerability means many people are at risk, emergency response is inadequate and critical infrastructure is fragile. Where vulnerability is low, emergency services are adequate and critical infrastructure is resilient, large disasters can be avoided even from large hazards.

Successive disasters can reduce the resilience of people or households to subsequent shocks and stresses. Small disasters can pave the way for large events by eroding people's assets and the integrity of critical infrastructure, progressively lowering society's thresholds of resilience.[2] Large events that damage critical infrastructure or urban economies will similarly undermine the capacity of individuals or emergency services to resist even everyday hazards, potentially making small disasters more frequent.

Everyday hazards may be hard to avoid for those at risk and, indeed, become an intrinsic part of livelihood and survival strategies. In this way, everyday hazards and small disaster losses can mistakenly become accepted as an expected part of life. In turn, this can have the perverse effect of lowering the willingness of individuals at risk or development agencies to invest in risk reduction,[3] thus creating a vicious circle where poverty and marginalization coincide with disaster risk.

Everyday hazards and small disasters differ from large disasters in that they are often seen as a problem of technological efficiency and infrastructure management – in other words, as problems of development. This has two consequences. First, everyday hazards tend to be managed by specialists from diverse fields, including engineering, medicine, land-use planning and chemistry, making integrated risk reduction more difficult. Secondly, social dimensions are easily overlooked by technological professions and planning agencies that dominate these areas of work.

Episodic hazards and large disasters pose an even greater challenge to sustainable urbanization. This is because they are too often seen not as problems of development, but as problems for development. Predominant strategies for dealing with risk and loss from large disasters focus on emergency response and reconstruction – not in addressing underlying failures in development that lead to human vulnerability. The risk reduction approach taken by this Global Report calls for small and large disasters to be seen as problems of development, requiring changes in development paths as well as in disaster response and reconstruction to build resilient human settlements.

Table 7.1

Small and large disasters

	Small disasters	Large disasters
Scale of risk	Individuals and small groups	Communities, city regions, cities, global
Systems at risk	Individual health and livelihoods, subcomponents of critical infrastructure, local economic or ecological systems	Social stability, critical infrastructure, urban economies, ecosystem services
Examples of associated trigger hazard	Localized hazard events such as tidal flooding or irresponsible driving	Widespread hazard events such as a severe earthquake or major release of toxic chemicals
Frequency of hazard event	High ('every day')	Low ('episodic')
Strategic importance to development planning	Aggregate loss high	Huge loss from individual events
Data sources	Emergency services, local news media	National and international emergency relief agencies and news media
Dominant actors in response	Family, neighbours, emergency services	Family, neighbours, emergency services, military or civil defence, national and international humanitarian actors

URBANIZATION AND DISASTER RISK

The last decade has seen an unprecedented number of disaster events unfold worldwide. The global incidence and impacts of disasters from 1996 onwards illustrates extensive damage both in terms of mortality and economic losses (see Table 7.2).[4] Transport accidents[5] and floods were the most frequently reported disasters. Impacts were highest for natural disasters, with earthquakes and tsunamis being the deadliest. Floods and windstorms accounted for the greatest number of disaster events and also affected the greatest number of people. Windstorms were most costly compared to other disaster types. Even with a time span of ten years, comparing the frequency and impacts of disaster types can be problematic. Large infrequent events, such as the Indian Ocean Tsunami, or individual flood or earthquake events can distort aggregate measurements of impacts associated with each hazard and disaster type. Far longer time spans would be needed to capture infrequent disaster types. However, longer time spans would subject disaster impact data to the effects of changing underlying human development contexts, including urbanization.

In the new urban millennium, natural and human-made disasters are likely to have their greatest impact in

In the new urban millennium, natural and human-made disasters are likely to have their greatest impact in cities where half of humanity is expected to reside. The world will become predominantly urban, with the total urban population expected to reach 5 billion by 2030, while rural populations will begin to contract from 2015 onwards.[6] The location of major urban centres in coastal areas exposed to hydro-meteorological hazards and in geologically active zones is an additional risk factor. The concentration of

Table 7.2

Global extent and impacts of disasters by hazard type (total 1996–2005)

	Number of events	Mortality	People affected	Economic damage (US$ millions, 2005 prices)
Avalanches/landslides	191	7864	1801	1382
Earthquakes, tsunamis	297	391,610	41,562	113,181
Extreme temperatures	168	60,249	5703	16,197
Floods	1310	90,237	1,292,989	208,434
Volcanic eruptions	50	262	940	59
Windstorms	917	62,410	326,252	319,208
Industrial accidents	505	13,962	1372	13,879
Miscellaneous accidents	461	15,757	400	2541
Transport accidents	2035	69,636	89	960

Source: EM-DAT, CRED database, University of Louvain, Belgium, www.em-dat.net

Figure 7.1

Recorded disaster events and world urban population (1950–2006)

Data Sources: EM-DAT, CRED database, University of Louvain, Belgium, www.em-dat.net; United Nations, 2005

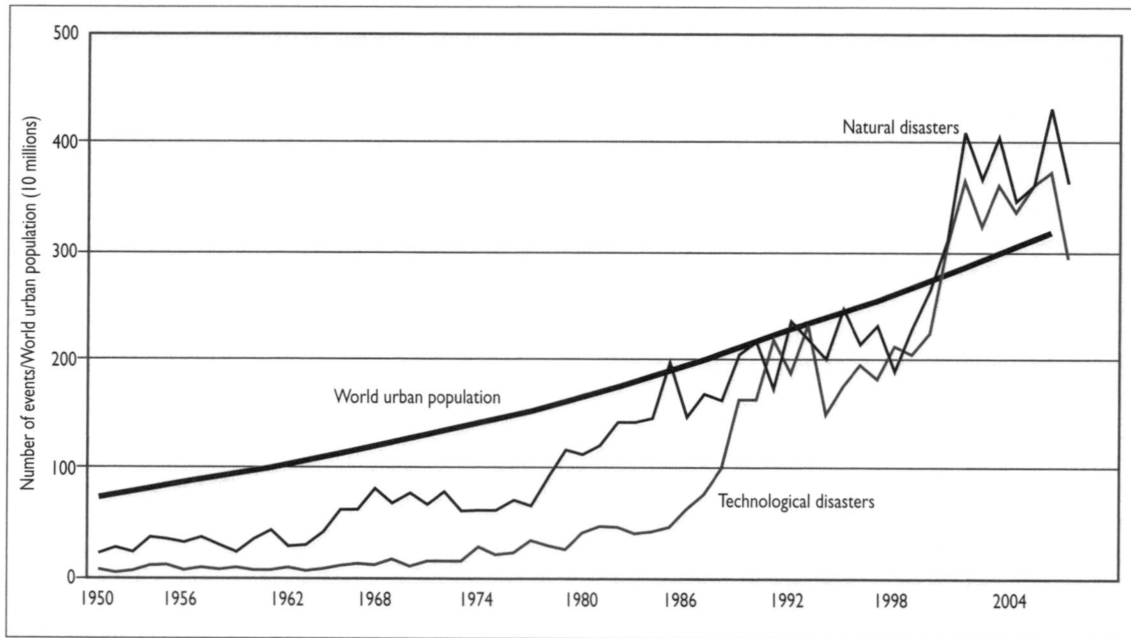

...the 1 billion slum dwellers worldwide, who reside in hazardous locations within cities... are perhaps most vulnerable to the impacts of disasters

economic assets, cultural heritage, infrastructure, services and basic life-support systems, industries and other potentially hazardous establishments in cities further exacerbates disaster risk and impacts. The growing numbers of the urban poor, especially the 1 billion slum dwellers worldwide, who reside in hazardous locations within cities such as industrial waste sites, floodplains, riverbanks and steep slopes, are perhaps most vulnerable to the impacts of disasters. As indicated earlier in Chapter 2, increasing urban poverty and exclusion also worsen the vulnerability of some urban inhab-

Box 7.2 The urban impacts of Mozambique's great flood

In February 2000, floods in Mozambique killed at least 700 people, displaced 650,000 and affected 4.5 million. Arguably, it was Mozambique's small but growing urban populations who were hardest hit, with more than 70 per cent of all flood-related deaths occurring in urban areas.

Extensive deforestation contributed to flood risk in Mozambique, where between 1990 and 2000, an average of 50,000 hectares of forested area were depleted annually. Urban land-use plans and codes in existence prior to the 2000 flood were not adhered to, often resulting in the spontaneous occupation of plots and building of roads in unsuitable areas and, in the long term, a cumulative process of soil erosion. Mozambique's experience during the 2000 floods must also be situated in both its circumstances of significant poverty, debt and post-conflict recovery from the 16-year civil war. The war internally displaced 3 million people and destroyed vital infrastructure, while pushing people towards urban centres.

The urban poor within Maputo, Matola, Xai-Xai and Chokwe suffered the most from the 2000 flood. Exorbitant pricing and highly politicized land distribution force many poor urban residents to live in informal settlements and unregulated slums, known as *barrios*, constructed in undesirable and hazardous locations such as in ravines, slopes susceptible to landslides and low-lying areas prone to flooding. In addition, the majority of *barrios* are constructed with locally accessible materials, such as bamboo and straw, that easily collapse easily beneath torrential rains and get washed away in flooding. The lack of drainage infrastructure in Maputo has also meant that seasonal one-day rain events can result in flooding that lasts for days, and rain over the course of several days can cause flooding that will not subside for a month.

The 2000 flood reached disastrous proportions when torrential rainfall brought on flooding in the Incomati, Umbeluzi and Limpopo rivers that flow within the Maputo and Gaza provinces. Accumulated rainfall, as well as Cyclone Eline, which hit Inhambane and Sofala provinces during the month of February, caused flooding in the cities of Maputo, Matola, Chokwe and Xai-Xai. The flooding of the latter two cities within the Limpopo River basin was responsible for the majority of the fatalities. Post-flood evaluations revealed that within the urban areas affected, flooding and rains had damaged the physical infrastructure and production capabilities of over 1000 shops and wholesalers in the river basins.

The 2000 flood also caused extensive damages to productive sectors in Maputo, the hub of Mozambique's industrial production, and Matola, a major industrial centre and the country's primary port. Destruction in Xai-Xai, the capital of Gaza Province and a coastal city, dealt a blow to fishing and tourism industries. The destruction of roads linking Maputo to neighbouring countries not only halted trade, but prevented the distribution of relief supplies. Across Mozambique's urban economy, food prices rose rapidly in response to losses in the countryside. Yet, by incapacitating Mozambique's transportation infrastructure, the floods had wiped out critical linkages to less affected Mozambican areas, impeding or preventing delivery of available foodstuff to urban areas that had few other options to secure food sources.

Source: Chege et al, 2007

Table 7.3

Selected recent natural disasters affecting human settlements (1972–2005)

Year	Location/area	Country	Hazard	Mortality	Economic losses (US$ billion)	Comment
2005	Northwest Frontier and Pakistan-controlled Kashmir	Pakistan (also affected: India-controlled Jammu and Kashmir and Afghanistan)	South Asian earthquake	73,000 (in Pakistan)	5.2	Collapsed schools killed 18,000 children; 2.8 million made homeless
2005	New Orleans	US	Flood and Hurricane Katrina	1863	81.2	The costliest natural disaster in US history
2004	Banda Aceh	Indonesia	Indian Ocean Tsunami	70,000	–	Complete destruction of coastal settlements
2004	Bam	Iran	Earthquake	31,000	–	World Heritage historic city destroyed
2003	European cities	Europe	Heat wave	35,000 to 50,000	–	Impacts worst in cities; the elderly were most vulnerable
2002	Dresden (and other cities on the Elbe River, as well as the Danube)	Germany (also Hungary, Slovakia and the Czech Republic)	Flood	90	–	30,000 evacuated in Dresden; cultural assets damaged
2002	Goma	Democratic Republic of Congo	Volcanic eruption	47	–	>100,000 made homeless; 25% of city destroyed
2001	Gujarat	India	Earthquake	20,000	5.5	1.2 million made homeless
2000	Maputo, Chokwe, Xai-Xai and Matola	Mozambique	Flooding	700	–	4.5 million affected
1999	Caracas and coastal Venzuela	Venezuela	Flooding and landslides	Up to 30,000	1.9	5500 homes destroyed; rains in 2000 left another 2000 homeless
1999	Orissa and coastal settlements	India	Cyclone	>10,000	2.5	130,000 people evacuated
1999	Izmit	Turkey	Marmara earthquake	15,000	12	Failure to enforce building codes a significant cause
1998	Tegucigalpa, Honduras and many smaller settlements in Honduras and Nicaragua	Honduras and Nicaragua	Hurricane Mitch	11,000–20,000	5.4	Flooding and landslides caused most loss
1998	Dhaka	Bangladesh	Flood	1050	4.3	
1998	Gujarat and coastal settlements	India	Cyclone	Up to 3000		2938 villages affected
1992	South of Miami	US	Hurricane Andrew	65	26	
1991	Coastal settlements	Bangladesh	Cyclone	138,000	–	Three times as many women as men were killed
1988	Spitak and surrounding towns	Armenia	Earthquake	25,000	–	500,000 homeless; Spitak, a city of 25,000, was completely destroyed
1985	Mexico City	Mexico	Earthquake	At least 9000	4	100,000 made homeless
1985	Santiago	Chile	Earthquake	180	1.8	45,000 dwellings destroyed
1976	Tangshan	China	Great Tangshan earthquake	Around 300,000	–	180,000 buildings destroyed
1972	Managua	Nicaragua	Earthquake	>10,000	–	Core of city completely destroyed

...the number of recorded disasters is increasing as the number of people living in cities increases

itants to disaster risk. Such processes underlying the vulnerability of urban areas to disaster are examined in greater detail later in this chapter.

Despite such risk factors, vulnerability to disaster remains largely underestimated in urban development.[7] There is no dedicated global database with which to analyse urban disaster events or losses. Indeed, few countries or cities systematically record disasters. Existing evidence does, however, indicate an upward trend in the annual number of natural and human-made disaster events reported worldwide, and a similar upward trend for global urban population since 1950 (see Figure 7.1).

No simple causal link between urban growth and reported worldwide disaster occurrence can be made from such data; but it is clear that the number of recorded disasters is increasing as the number of people living in cities increases. Given these trends, it is not unreasonable to conclude that, without major changes in the management of disaster risks and of urbanization processes, the number of urban disasters will also increase in the future.

An account of the urban costs of flooding in Mozambique illustrates the complexity of factors exacerbating urban disaster risks (see Box 7.2). The high levels of risk that have already accumulated in urban societies due to a complexity of factors means that, even with risk reduction activity being undertaken today, disaster risk is set to increase in the foreseeable future. Furthermore, recent events continue to show weaknesses in the ability of governments and of the international community to protect their citizens from, and to respond to, disaster. Experience from recent disasters also points to a central role for sustainable human settlements planning and management in risk reduction.

Experience from recent disasters ... points to a central role for sustainable human settlements planning and management in risk reduction

Table 7.4

Selected recent human-made disasters affecting human settlements (1984–2006)

Note: Transport disasters and traffic accidents are included.

Year	Location/area	Country	Hazard	Mortality	Comment
2006	Lagos	Nigeria	Explosion in an oil pipeline	200	
2005	Jilin	China	Explosion in a chemical plant		>10,000 people evacuated; an 80km long toxic slick resulted
2001	Toulouse	France	Explosion in a fertilizer factory	31	650 seriously injured
1999	New Jalpaiguri	India	Two trains collide	>200	
1995	Seoul	South Korea	Department store collapsed	421	>900 injured
1994	Baltic Sea	Estonia	Sinking of ferry	859	Worst post-war European maritime disaster
1993	Bangkok	Thailand	Fire	188	500 seriously injured; most casualties were women
1986	Chernobyl	Russia	Nuclear power plant explosion	56	Evacuation and resettlement of 336,000 people; continental radiation impact
1984	Bhopal	India	Accidental release of toxic gases	>15,000	Up to 60,000 injuries

Since 1975, there has been a fourfold increase in the number of recorded natural disasters globally

INCIDENCE OF NATURAL AND HUMAN-MADE DISASTERS

This section reviews available data in order to assess the distribution of disaster risk, which unfolds at a range of scales, from the global to the local. The lack of data on vulnerability, hazard and disaster loss at the city level means some inference from national data is required. The first level of analysis is at the global scale, followed by a comparison of disaster loss by levels of national development. Differences in city-level risk profiles are then analysed.

The global incidence of disaster risk and loss

Since 1975, there has been a fourfold increase in the number of recorded natural disasters globally. Each of the three years with the highest number of recorded disasters has been during the current decade, with 801 disasters in 2000, 786 in 2002 and 744 in 2005.[8] While all continents now report more natural disaster events, on average, the rate of increase has been highest for Africa, where a threefold increase in natural disaster events has been experienced in the last decade alone.[9] Human-made disasters have seen a tenfold increase from 1975 to 2006, with the greatest rates of increase in Asia and Africa.

An outline of recent natural and human-made disaster incidents that have affected human settlements globally goes some way to indicate their destructive powers (see Tables 7.3 and 7.4). This is by no means a complete list; but, rather, attempts to indicate the scale of loss and diversity in hazard and settlement types that will be examined in detail throughout this Global Report. The best documented are large-scale natural disasters. The great diversity in types of hazards and disaster impacts across various human settlements is evident.

Natural disasters

A global geography of natural disaster risk based on exposed populations and past losses (1980 to 2001) illustrates that both predominantly rural and urban world regions are at risk

Figure 7.2

Global distribution of highest risk disaster hotspots indicated by mortality (1980–2001)[10]

Source: Dilley et al, 2005

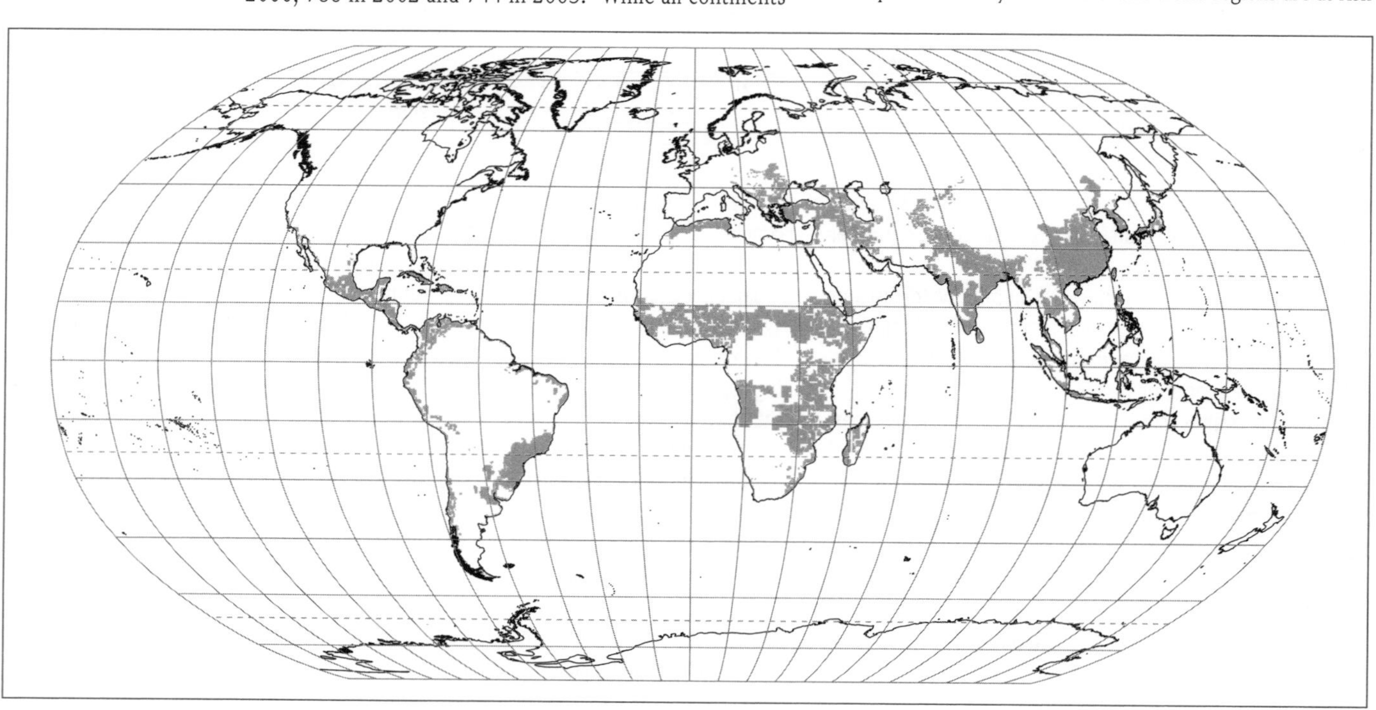

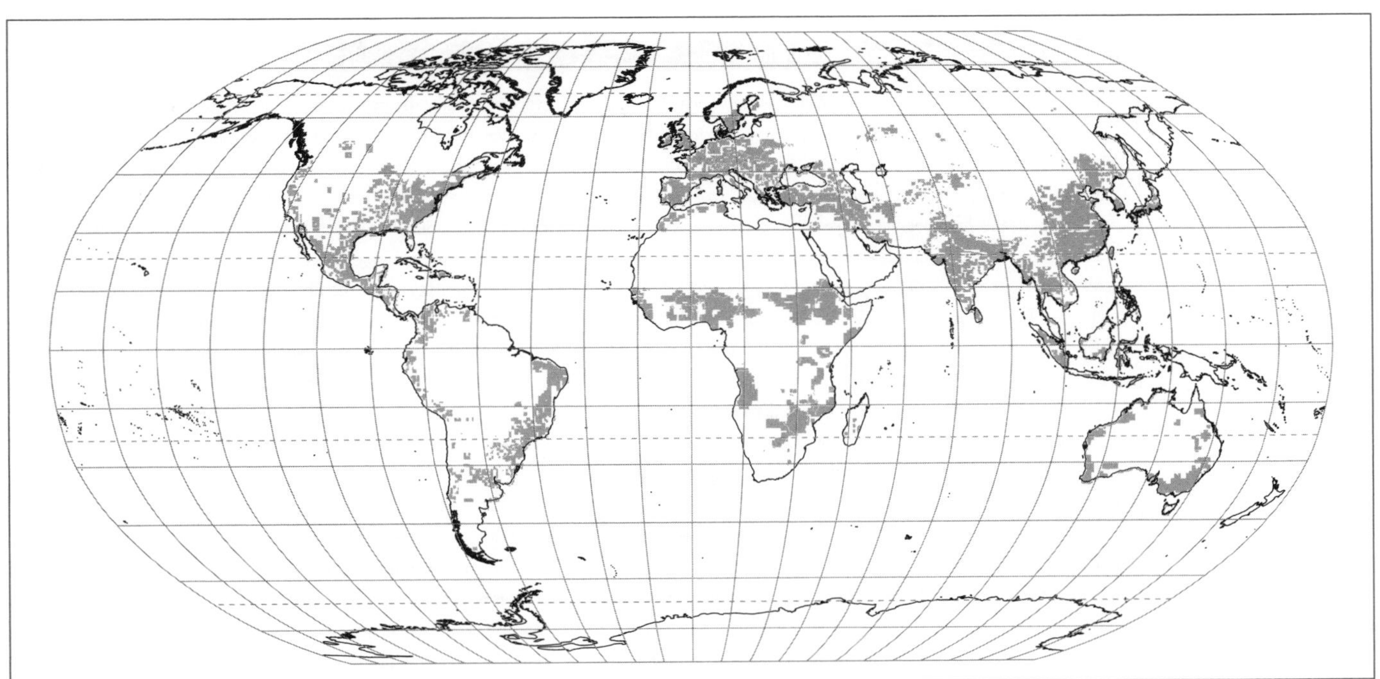

Figure 7.3

Global distribution of highest risk disaster hotspots indicated by total economic loss (1980–2001)[11]

Source: Dilley et al, 2005

(see Figures 7.2 to 7.4). Loss to hydrological (floods, landslides and hurricanes) hazard is most widespread, affecting human settlements in China, Southeast Asia and Central America, and in a band from Eastern Europe through Central and Eastern Asia. Loss to geological hazard (earthquakes and volcano eruptions) is most concentrated in Central Asia and the Mediterranean and Pacific Rim states (e.g. Japan, the US and Central America). The Americas show variable loss, with low levels of loss in North America.

Central Asia is exposed to losses from the greatest number of hazard types. Likewise, the Black Sea region, Central America and Japan face multiple hazards. Disaster risk is, however, distributed differently across specific regions, depending upon what is considered to be at risk. In terms of mortality caused by natural disasters, hotspots include Central America, the Himalaya, South and Southeast Asia, Central Asia and sub-Saharan Africa (see Figure 7.2). Risk of absolute economic loss shows quite a different distribution (see Figure 7.3). Wealthier countries lose the highest value of economic assets in natural disasters. Consequently, hotspots for absolute economic loss include North America, Europe and Central, South and Southeast Asia, with sub-Saharan Africa being less prominent. A third measure – economic loss as a proportion of gross domestic product (GDP) – resembles losses recorded for mortality (see Figure 7.4).

Figure 7.4

Global distribution of highest risk disaster hotspots indicated by economic loss as a proportion of GDP per unit area (1980–2001)[12]

Source: Dilley et al, 2005

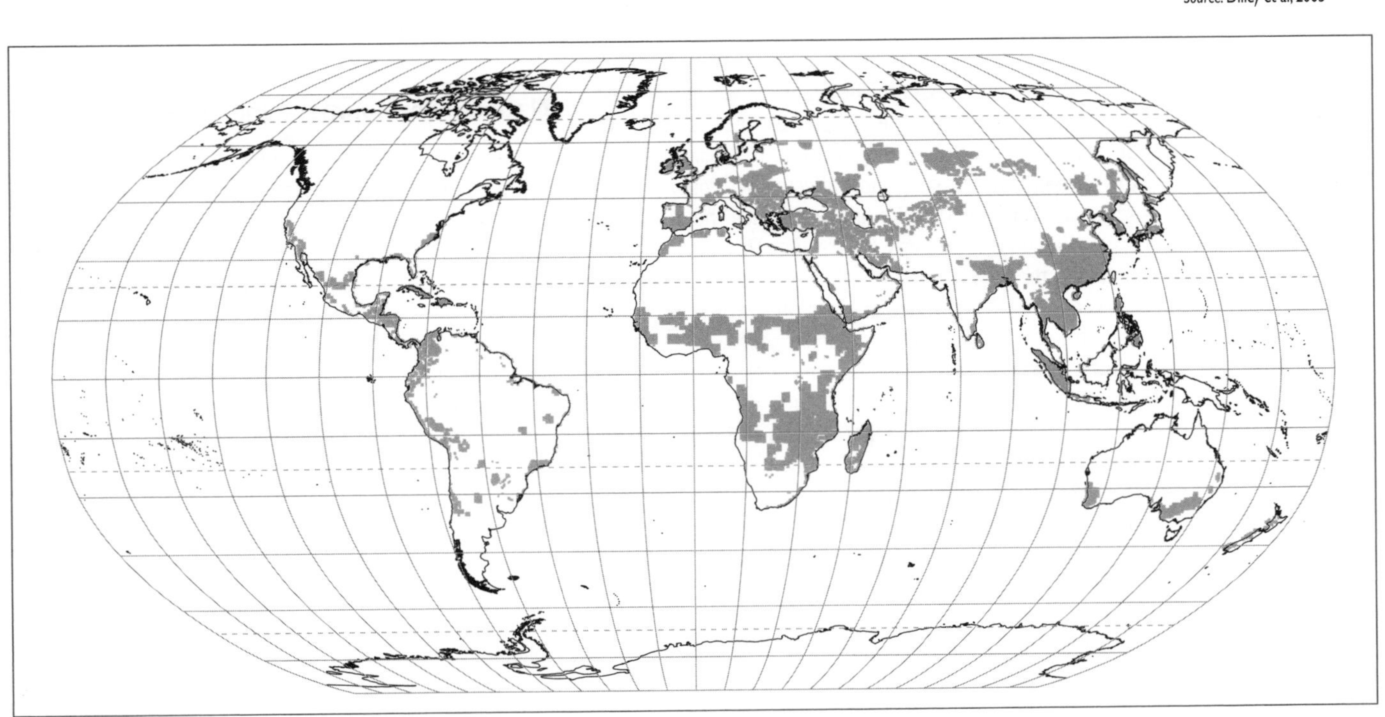

Box 7.3 Bhopal: A deadly human-made disaster

The accident at Union Carbide's pesticide plant in Bhopal, Madhya Pradesh (India), in 1984, exposed 500,000 people, the majority living in low-income settlements close to the plant, to toxic gas. To date, assessments of the death toll vary from 4000 to 20,000. The majority of deaths have been in the years since the disaster, as its chronic health effects unfold. Even by conservative estimates, it remains the worst industrial disaster on record, and the victims are still dying. The company paid US$470 million compensation to a trust in 1989. The survivors say they received around US$500 each and claim the cleanup efforts were inadequate.

The disaster was initiated when a faulty valve let nearly 1 tonne of water being used to clean pipes pour into a tank holding 40 tonnes of methyl isocyanate. The resulting runaway reaction produced a deadly cloud of toxic gas.

The runaway reaction should have been contained but was not, largely because Bhopal had far more limited emergency equipment than was available, for example, in Carbide's sister US plant. Gasses can be contained by being burned off by flare towers or filtered by a scrubber. At the time of the incident, the Bhopal plant had only one flare, shut for repairs. Bhopal's sole scrubber was overwhelmed by the mass of liquids and gases that boiled up at a rate over 100 times for which it was designed.

Bhopal's liquid waste was also poured into open lagoons to evaporate. Recent analyses of groundwater, soil and people near the plant have found high levels of heavy metals, such as mercury and toxic organo-chlorine chemicals.

Responsibility for the Bhopal incident is contested, with Dow Chemical, which took over Union Carbide, insisting that Carbide's Indian subsidiary was wholly responsible for the design and running of the plant. In 1999, Bhopal survivors launched a class action in New York State, which led to the court forcing the company to release internal documents, some of which contradicted its claims.

In the wake of the disaster, almost two dozen voluntary groups formed to cope with medical relief, supporting the families of victims and organizing a political and legal response to the disaster. This is, in part, a reflection on the lack of preparedness and response capacity that served to heighten the vulnerability of those living near the plant.

Sources: Jasanoff, 1994; New Scientist, 2002

Human-made disasters typically cause less direct loss of life than natural disasters

Human-made disasters

Most human-made disasters and the highest numbers of people killed are found in Asia and Africa. Data from the Emergency Events Database, Centre for Research on the Epidemiology of Disasters (EM-DAT, CRED) for 1997 to 2006 shows that 1493 human-made disasters were recorded in Asia and 952 in Africa, compared with only 392 events in the Americas, 284 in Europe and 11 in Oceania. The mean number of deaths during this period per event is highest in Oceania (46 deaths). Asia (34 deaths) and Africa (32 deaths) also have high average deaths per event, and this is especially significant given the high numbers of human-made disasters in these two world regions. The Americas (28 deaths) and Europe (24 deaths) recorded the lowest mean number of deaths per event and also the lowest absolute mortality for this time period. Europe is most affected by economic loss, which at over US$10 billion is greater than the economic loss suffered by any other world region. This demonstrates well both the high level of capital investment in Europe and the knock-on effect this has for loss profiled with low mortality and high economic loss. A similar profile is found for natural disasters where high-income countries and regions shift loss from mortality to economic damage. Outside Europe, economic loss is higher for Asia (US$883 million) and Africa (US$830 million), with lower economic loss in the Americas (US$83 million). No economic loss was recorded for events in Oceania.[13]

...national economic development ...can both reduce and generate risk ... for society

Human-made disasters typically cause less direct loss of life than natural disasters. Worldwide, the mean number of deaths per human-made event (2000 to 2005) is 30, while for natural disasters (excluding drought and forest fire, which are predominantly rural events) this is 225.[14] While direct human loss is lower for human-made disasters, impacts can be felt in the ecosystem and in human health many years after an event, and this loss is seldom recorded in official statistics. One of the most notorious examples of the long-term health consequences of human-made disaster has been the 1984 Bhopal disaster in Madhya Pradesh (India) (see Box 7.3). Here, the accidental release of 40 tonnes of methyl isocyanate from a factory owned by Union Carbide India caused thousands of deaths and injuries. The effects are still being recorded in babies whose parents were exposed to the released gas, so that impacts have crossed generations.

National development and disaster loss

The relationship between national economic development and natural disaster risk and loss is complicated. It is, however, clear that development can both reduce and generate risk for society and determine who in society carries the greatest burden of risk from natural and human-made hazard.

According to an analysis of the influence of development on natural disasters by the United Nations Development Programme (UNDP), countries with a high Human Development Index (HDI) experience low absolute and proportional disaster mortality rates (see Figure 7.5). Small island states such as Vanuatu and St Kitts and Nevis show relatively low absolute mortality, but high mortality as a proportion of population, reflecting the low total populations of these small states. Countries that had experienced a catastrophic disaster during the period for which data were collected (1980 to 2000), such as Armenia and Honduras, also show high losses as a proportion of population.

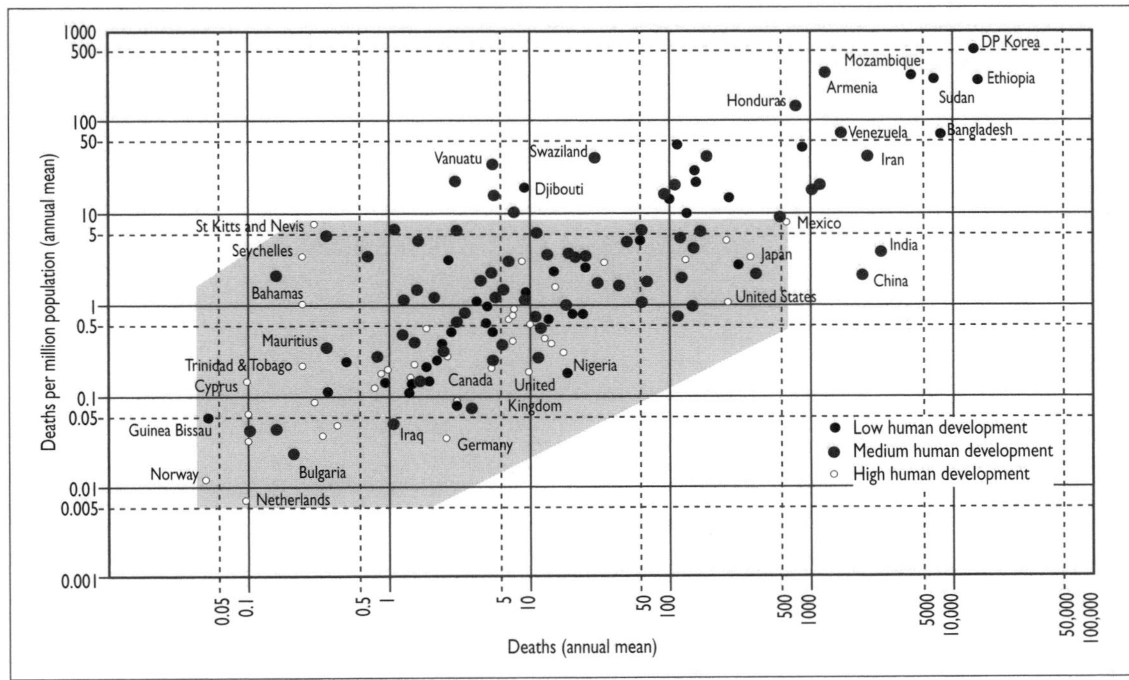

Figure 7.5

National development status and natural disaster mortality (1980–2000)

Source: UNDP, 2004

Note: HDI ranking for Afghanistan, Democratic People's Republic of Korea, Iraq, Liberia and Yugoslavia are from UNDP Human Development report 1996, all others from UNDP Human Development Report 2002.

The UNDP also developed the Disaster Risk Index, a pioneer tool for assessing variations in disaster vulnerability according to levels of development. The index tests 24 socio-economic variables against disaster mortality for earthquakes, flooding and windstorm at the national level to identify those variables that most explained patterns of loss. For all hazard types, exposure of human populations to hazard-prone places was found to be statistically associated with mortality. Urban growth was also found to be statistically associated with risk of death from earthquakes. This work provides statistical support for the large amount of observational data that connects rapid urban growth with disaster risk, and, in particular, with losses associated with earthquakes. Disaster risks and impacts are also differentiated by levels of development and investments in risk reduction at the city level.

City-level comparisons of disaster risk

There have been few studies of the global distribution of disaster risk for individual cities. Munich Re's Natural Hazards Risk Index for Megacities is a rare example (see Table 7.5).[15] The Natural Hazards Risk Index includes 50 participating cities and is primarily designed to compare insurance risk potential. With this caveat in mind, the index database is applied here to build up a picture of disaster risk at the city level.

One achievement of the Natural Hazards Risk Index is its multi-hazard approach, covering earthquake, windstorm, flood, volcanic eruption, bush fires and winter damage (frost). Reflecting Munich Re's business focus, the conceptualization and measurement of vulnerability is restricted to built assets, with an additional measure of financial exposure. The multi-hazard approach is enabled through individual assessments of vulnerability for each hazard type (for building structures and construction and planning regulations), which are then combined with an overall assessment of the general quality of construction and building density in the city to arrive at a risk index. There is some concern over the quality of vulnerability data available for cities; but Munich Re considers the results to be plausible and reflective of expert opinion on city vulnerability and risk.

Using Munich Re's methodology, results show that greatest risk has accumulated in the cities of richer countries. Only one megacity from a non-industrial country, Manila, is in the top ten when cities are ordered by the risk index.[16] With a view to supporting decision-making within the insurance sector, the Natural Hazards Risk Index understandably identifies high exposure in cities with large physical assets and commercial interests. Hence, Tokyo, San Francisco and Los Angeles have the highest Natural Hazards Risk Index values.

From a human settlements perspective, Munich Re's Natural Hazards Risk Index is less instructive than the base data held in Table 7.5. When considering the vulnerability of cities in terms of the sum of different types of natural hazard exposure, high risk becomes associated with Manila, Tokyo, Kolkata, Osaka–Kobe–Kyoto, Jakarta and Dhaka, all cities in excess of 10 million inhabitants and with high exposure to at least two different kinds of natural hazard. There are some counterintuitive results. For example, San Francisco appears low on the list, despite high earthquake exposure, because of low exposure to other hazard types.

Munich Re's data is also useful for identifying those cities where a large natural disaster is most likely to impact negatively upon the national economy. Dhaka, with 60 per cent of national GDP produced within the city, and with high exposure to earthquakes, tropical storms and storm surges, is a strong candidate for a city whose risk has national consequences.

The impact of disaster is … differentiated according to the development paths and levels of disaster preparedness of individual cities

The impact of disaster is further differentiated according to the development paths and levels of disaster

Table 7.5

Comparative exposure to large natural hazards for 50 cities

Source: Munich Re, 2004

Megacity	Country	Sum of natural hazard exposure	Population (million, 2003)	Area (km^2)	City GDP as percentage of national GDP	Individual natural hazard exposure assessment							Munich Re Natural Hazards Risk Index
						E	V	St	So	F	T	SS	
Manila	Philippines	15	13.9	2200	30	3	2	3	2	2	2	1	31.0
Tokyo	Japan	12	35	13,100	40	3	1	2	2	1	1	2	710.0
Kolkata	India	12	13.8	1400	< 10	2	0	3	2	3	0	2	4.2
Osaka–Kobe–Kyoto	Japan	12	13.0	2850	20	3	0	2	2	2	1	2	92.0
Jakarta	Indonesia	12	12.3	1600	30	2	2	1	2	2	2	1	3.6
Dhaka	Bangladesh	12	11.6	1500	60	3	0	3	2	3	0	1	7.3
Hong Kong	China	11	7.0	1100	10	2	0	3	2	2	0	2	41.0
Shanghai	China	10	12.8	1600	< 10	1	0	3	1	2	0	3	13.0
Karachi	Pakistan	10	11.1	1200	20	3	0	1	1	2	1	2	3.1
Mexico City	Mexico	9	18.7	4600	40	3	3	0	2	1	0	0	19.0
Istanbul	Turkey	9	9.4	2650	25	3	0	0	2	2	1	1	4.8
Miami	US	9	3.9	2900	< 5	0	0	3	2	1	0	3	45.0
Lima	Peru	8	7.9	550	50	3	0	0	1	1	3	0	3.7
Los Angeles	US	7	16.4	14,000	< 10	3	0	0	2	2	0	0	100.0
Buenos Aires	Argentina	7	13.0	3900	45	1	0	0	2	2	0	2	4.2
London	UK	7	7.6	1600	15	0	0	0	3	2	0	2	30.0
Randstad	Netherlands	7	7.0	4000	50	0	0	0	3	2	0	2	12.0
Singapore	Singapore	7	4.3	300	100	1	0	1	2	1	1	1	3.5
Alexandria	Egypt	7	3.7	100	Unknown	2	0	0	1	1	2	1	1.4
New York	US	6	21.2	10,768	< 10	1	0	1	2	1	0	1	42.0
Seoul	Korea, Rep. of	6	20.3	4400	50	1	0	2	1	2	0	0	15.0
Mumbai	India	6	17.4	4350	15	2	0	1	1	1	0	1	5.1
Delhi	India	6	14.1	1500	< 5	2	0	0	2	2	0	0	1.5
Tehran	Iran	6	7.2	500	40	3	0	0	2	1	0	0	4.7
Bangkok	Thailand	6	6.5	500	35	1	0	1	2	2	0	0	5.0
Baghdad	Iraq	6	5.6	500	Unknown	2	0	0	2	2	0	0	1.3
St Petersburg	Russia	6	5.3	600	< 5	0	0	0	2	2	0	2	0.7
Athens	Greece	6	3.2	450	30	2	0	0	2	1	0	1	3.7
Medellín	Colombia	6	3.1	250	Unknown	3	0	0	2	1	0	0	4.8
Rio de Janeiro	Brazil	5	11.2	2400	15	0	0	1	2	2	0	0	1.8
Ruhr area	Germany	5	11.1	9800	15	1	0	0	2	2	0	0	14.0
Paris	France	5	9.8	2600	30	0	0	0	3	2	0	0	25.0
Chicago	US	5	9.2	8000	< 5	1	0	0	2	1	0	1	20.0
Washington, DC	US	5	7.6	9000	< 5	0	0	1	2	1	0	1	16.0
Bogotá	Colombia	5	7.3	500	20	3	0	0	1	1	0	0	8.8
San Francisco	US	5	7.0	8000	< 5	3	0	0	1	1	0	0	167.0
Sydney	Australia	5	4.3	2100	30	1	0	0	2	1	0	1	6.0
Cairo	Egypt	4	10.8	1400	50	2	0	0	0	2	0	0	1.8
Beijing	China	4	10.8	1400	< 5	2	0	0	2	0	0	0	15.0
Johannesburg	South Africa	4	7.1	17,000	30	1	0	0	2	1	0	0	3.9
Bangalore	India	4	6.1	300	Unknown	1	0	1	1	1	0	0	4.5
Santiago	Chile	4	5.5	950	15	2	0	0	1	1	0	0	4.9
Milan	Italy	4	4.1	1900	15	1	0	0	2	1	0	0	8.9
Sâo Paulo	Brazil	3	17.9	4800	25	0	0	0	2	1	0	0	2.5
Lagos	Nigeria	3	10.7	1100	30	0	0	0	2	1	0	0	0.7
Moscow	Russia	3	10.5	1100	20	0	0	0	2	1	0	0	11.0
Madrid	Spain	3	5.1	950	20	0	0	0	2	1	0	0	1.5
Berlin	Germany	3	3.3	900	< 5	0	0	0	2	1	0	0	1.8
Abidjan	Côte d'Ivoire	2	3.3	500	50	0	0	0	1	1	0	0	0.3

Notes: Natural hazards key is defined as follows (3 = high; 2 = medium; 1 = low; 0 = none):
E = earthquake;
V = volcanic eruption;
St = tropical storm;
So = other storms (winter storms, hailstorms, tornado);
F = flood;
T = tsunami;
SS = storm surge.

preparedness of individual cities. This is evident when comparing the contrasting cases of Kobe (Japan) (hit by a 7.2 Richter magnitude earthquake in 1995) and Marmara (Turkey) (hit by a 7.4 Richter magnitude earthquake in 1999). The Kobe (or Great Hanshin) earthquake was among the worst disasters to have befallen modern Japan since it claimed 6433 lives. The Marmara earthquake was similarly catastrophic; but with 18,000 lives lost, was three times as deadly as the Kobe earthquake.[17] In Kobe, strong engineering standards reduced losses; but a lack of planning for social systems to identify vulnerable groups and help in response, relief and reconstruction compounded losses. In Marmara, decades of ineffective building and planning regulation meant many modern buildings were not adequately resistant to earthquakes, and accumulated risk translated into high human loss. As in Kobe, failure in social planning also undermined response and reconstruction. The Tangshan earthquake in China in 1976 similarly illustrates how differential vulnerability shapes loss in different human settlements (see Box 7.4).

Box 7.4 The Great Tangshan earthquake, China

The most destructive earthquake of the past 400 years occurred in Tangshan (China) in 1976. The magnitude 7.8 earthquake occurred in the early morning while the majority of the over 1 million residents slept and lasted 14 to 16 seconds. Later in the day, the city was further paralysed by an aftershock with a magnitude of 7.1. The official death toll published by the Chinese government was about 240,000. More recent estimates place the total for casualties at over 0.5 million.

While nearly 50 per cent of the population of the city of Tangshan died during the earthquake, the neighbouring County of Qinglong had only one death out of 470,000 residents. Scientists from the State Seismological Bureau identified six main factors that contributed to the unprecedented destructiveness of the Tangshan earthquake, including high population density, existence of few earthquake-resistant buildings, occurrence of shock while people were sleeping followed by a strong aftershock later, paralysis of critical infrastructures and the geological conditions under the city.[20] Yet, the disparity between the death toll in Tangshan and Qinglong cannot be accounted for by these factors alone since both counties experienced similar vulnerabilities. The divergence in the death toll between Qinglong and Tangshan comes from an additional seventh factor: the difference in earthquake preparedness in the two areas.

Tanghsan's over-reliance on scientific monitoring of seismic activity for national preparedness partly contributed to the massive loss of life during the 1976 earthquake. Two years earlier, a report by the Chinese Academy of Science had advised greater preparedness and monitoring in North China. During the following two years, Qinglong County increased the number of earthquake monitoring stations and intensified public education using pamphlets, films, posters, drills and community discussions, far beyond those reported to have been undertaken in Tangshan. Qinglong's successful disaster mitigation was a best-case outcome of the coordination between public administrators, scientists and the public.

Source: Pottier et al, 2007

DISASTER IMPACTS

This section differentiates between and discusses the main impacts of disasters. The capacity for disaster impacts to cause knock-on consequences and additional risks through secondary human-made disasters and the ecological impacts in the city is also examined.

Although the review of natural and human-made disasters goes some way in indicating their destructive power, it can only show tip-of-the-iceberg losses. Gaps in data and contradictory statements make comprehensive assessment of disaster impacts difficult. Even assessments of disaster incidence, although made easier by global media, are not easily undertaken at the global scale, where there is no standard system for verifying local reports.

Systematic gaps in disaster data collection and presentation mean that loss is underestimated in three different ways:

- Psychological and livelihood impacts are seldom recorded, with the majority of disaster impact data focusing on mortality and economic loss.[18]
- Macro-economic loss estimates cannot easily capture the secondary and knock-on consequences of disaster for economic production and trade.
- Disasters affecting small urban settlements and small-scale disasters in large cities are often overlooked, despite evidence suggesting that, in aggregate, small-scale disasters may be associated with at least as much suffering and loss as the large-scale disasters in cities that make front page news.[19]

At a minimum, psychological trauma, livelihood losses and losses to productive infrastructure should be included in measuring the full impact of disasters.

Direct and systemic impacts of disaster

Disaster impacts can be classified as either direct or systemic. Direct impacts include damages directly attributable to the disaster, including lives lost and injuries and physical damage to infrastructure and buildings. Direct (and other) losses can also be caused by knock-on human-made or natural disasters. For example, an earthquake can trigger chemical fires or liquefaction. If uncontained, direct impacts can be magnified through failures in critical infrastructure and services in the city, leading to systemic impacts such as outbreaks of disease, social violence and lack of access to electricity, potable water or food. For instance, a review of health service infrastructure in Latin America and the Caribbean found that around half of all hospitals are sited in high-risk areas. Perhaps not surprisingly, this report also found that over the 1980s and 1990s, 100 hospitals and 650 health centres have been destroyed in disasters. This is a little over 5 per cent of all hospitals in this region.[21] In turn, such disruptions can lead to instabilities in the political economy of the city and undermine economic development.

Gaps in data … make comprehensive assessment of disaster impacts difficult

Systemic loss can further be differentiated into indirect losses and secondary effects. Indirect losses (sometimes called flow losses) are the costs of goods that will not be produced and services that will not be provided because of a disaster. Secondary effects are generated by macro-economic distortions.[22]

Urban areas are characterized by great diversity in land use as well as environmental variability (e.g. in slope angle and direction, soil properties and land altitude). This

Natural hazard	Primary hazard	Secondary hazard
Cyclone	Strong winds, heavy seas	Flood and sea surge, landslide, water pollution, chemical release
Flood	Flooding	Water pollution, landslide, erosion, chemical release
Tsunami	Flooding	Water pollution, landslide, erosion, deposition, chemical release
Earthquake	Ground motion, fault rupture	Soil liquefaction, fire, flood, landslide, tsunami, water pollution, explosion, chemical release
Landslide	Ground failure	Flooding following river damming, water pollution, debris flow
Volcano	Lava flow, pyroclastic flow, ash fall, gas release	Fire, air pollution, tsunami, water pollution, ground subsidence, explosion, chemical release

Table 7.6

Primary and secondary hazards

Source: Institute of Civil Engineers, 1999

diversity can lead to initial 'primary' natural hazards triggering 'secondary' hazards (see Table 7.6). In many cases, secondary hazards can be as devastating as the primary hazard (or even more). Warnings of this potential include Kobe (Japan) in 1995 and San Francisco (US) in 1906, where earthquakes were followed by urban fires.

Human-made hazards triggered by the impacts of natural disasters are called Natech events. There is little systematically held data on the vulnerability of industrial facilities to natural hazards since assessments are undertaken privately and often considered too sensitive for public access. There is also little recording of Natech incidents, and even less data on near misses. Again, this information is often held privately and is not easily accessible for analysis. The seriousness of the threat posed by Natech events in urban contexts can be seen by the following list of events triggered by the 1999 Marmara earthquake in Turkey:[23]

The potential for feedback between natural and human-made hazards in large cities presents the scenario for a disaster on an unprecedented scale

- leakage of 6.5 million kilograms of toxic acrylonitrile – as a result, contaminating air, soil, water and threatening residential areas;
- the intentional air release of 200,000 kilograms of ammonia gas to avoid explosion;
- the release of 1.2 million kilograms of cryogenic liquid oxygen caused by a structural failure;
- three large fires in Turkey's largest oil refinery, consuming more than 180,000 cubic metres of fuel;
- a release of liquefied petroleum gas, killing two truck drivers.

Powerful players can move indirect economic losses around the urban economy

Human-made hazards can also lead to unexpected secondary hazards, potentially turning minor incidents into major events. On 10 August 1983, a 30 centimetre diameter water main ruptured in New York's Garment District. Water flooded an underground electricity sub-station, causing a fire. The fire was too intense for fire fighters to approach it directly. The blaze ignited the roof of a 25-storey building and took 16 hours to extinguish. Power was not restored for five days. The resulting blackouts hit 1.9 square kilometres of the Garment District, disrupting telephones and an international market week being hosted in the Garment District at the time. The cascading events started by this minor incident caused disruption and loss in increasingly complex systems. Estimated losses were in the tens of millions of dollars.[24]

The potential for feedback between natural and human-made hazards in large cities presents the scenario for a disaster on an unprecedented scale. The economic impacts of such a disaster in a city of regional or global importance could resonate around the world's financial system, with catastrophic consequences worldwide.

Ecological damage and the impacts of recovery

Urban disaster impacts can be significantly compounded by environmental damage, resulting in the loss of ecosystem stability. Perhaps most important is the potential for disaster to result in the pollution of groundwater. Salt water intrusion following storm surges, tsunami and coastal flooding, or the pollution of groundwater from sewerage, petrol and hazardous chemicals, can render aquifers unsafe for prolonged periods. This was the case in Banda Aceh following the Indian Ocean Tsunami.[25]

Disaster impact assessments seldom include damages caused in the process of disaster response and recovery. This is a serious omission. A recent evaluation has suggested that the ecological costs of cleanup and reconstruction following the Indian Ocean Tsunami will compete with or even exceed environmental losses caused by the wave.[26] In the wake of typhoon Tokage, which hit Japan from 19 to 21 September 2004, 44,780 tonnes of waste were produced by the city of Toyooka, composed mainly of forest debris and household goods. Waste treatment took over four months, at an estimated cost of US$20 million – a significant financial burden on the budget of a small city.[27] The use of debris as recycled material in reconstruction is commonplace in local reconstruction efforts, but rare in large contracted reconstruction work.

An account of the Great Hanshin earthquake that hit Kobe City in 1995 concludes that the volume of dioxins released into the atmosphere through the incineration of 2 million tonnes of waste equalled the amount generated by the 1976 industrial disaster in Seveso (Italy), effectively causing a human-made disaster. Other environmental impacts included the scattering of asbestos and concrete particles during demolitions, improper lining of landfills used for hazardous waste, use of tetrachloroethylene, which caused pollution of soil and groundwater, and a missed opportunity to recycle waste.[28]

Economic effects of disasters

The following discussion focuses on the economic effects of disasters. The economic sectors exposed to individual disaster types and the role of land markets are discussed in turn.

■ Economic production and infrastructure

The economic costs of natural and human-made disasters over the past few decades have been phenomenal. Economic losses from natural disasters, for instance, have increased 15-fold since the 1950s.[29] In a matter of two decades between 1974 and 2003, economic damages worth US$1.38 trillion were caused worldwide by natural disasters. In 2006, economic losses from natural disasters amounted to US$48 billion, while human-made disasters triggered economic

Table 7.7

Economic impacts of disasters by hazard type

Source: adapted from UNDRCO, 1991

Impact	Hazard type							
	Flood	Wind	Wave/tsunami	Earthquake	Volcano	Fire	Drought	Human made
Direct: loss of housing	✗	✗	✗	✗	✗	✗		
Direct: damage to infrastructure	✗	✗	✗	✗	✗	✗		
Systemic: short-term migration	✗				✗		✗	
Systemic: loss of business production	✗	✗	✗	✗		✗	✗	✗
Systemic: loss of industrial production	✗	✗	✗	✗		✗	✗	✗
Systemic: disruption of transport	✗	✗		✗				✗
Systemic: disruption of communication	✗	✗	✗	✗				✗

losses worth US$5 billion.[30] Economic losses are regionally differentiated, with the Americas and Asia incurring highest losses from natural disasters[31] and Europe experiencing greatest loss from human-made disasters.

Various hazards have differentiated effects on urban economic systems (see Table 7.7). The scale of economic impact varies according to the spread, intensity and form of the energy released by each hazard type. For example, natural disasters that tend to produce spatially concentrated impacts, such as flows of hot ash and rock fragments from volcanoes, will not usually overwhelm urban transport systems, compared to the more widespread impacts of earthquakes, hurricanes or catastrophic flooding. Drought is more likely to undermine economic activity indirectly rather than lead to property damage and therefore may cause a loss of industrial productivity, but with little impact on productive infrastructure. Human-made disasters tend to have systemic impacts on cities through damage to, or isolation of, critical infrastructure such as transport and communication systems, but are less destructive of housing.

Powerful players can move indirect economic losses around the urban economy. This was the case in Kobe (Japan) following the 1995 earthquake. Here, major producers, such as Toyota Motor Corporation and Kawasaki Heavy Industries Ltd, used a 'just-in-time' stocking approach. Following the earthquake, damage to subcontractors threatened to hold back production. The major producers were able to protect themselves by shifting to new subcontractors within a few days. This strategy passed risk on from the major producers to the subcontractors who had to cope with a double burden of disaster impacts and lost contracts. Many faced bankruptcy as a result.[32]

Larger developed urban/national economies with sizeable foreign currency reserves, high proportions of insured assets, comprehensive social services and diversified production are more likely to absorb and spread the economic burden of disaster impacts. An example of large economic losses in an urban region that were contained comes from the 1999 Marmara earthquake in Turkey. Direct losses were estimated at US$2 billion for industrial facilities, US$5 billion for buildings and US$1.4 billion for infrastructure, including a similar figure for losses generated through lost production during the many months required for factories and industrial facilities to return to their pre-disaster production levels.[33] However, only seven months after the disaster, a downturn in the rate of inflation and declining interest rates for government borrowing indicated that the Turkish economy had made a fast recovery.[34]

There is also growing potential for cities connected to regional or global financial systems (e.g. Mexico City, Rio de Janeiro, Johannesburg, Bangkok, Manila, Seoul and Singapore) to spread the negative consequences of disaster across the global economy, with huge systemic loss effects. Evidence for what has become known as the 'contagion effect' can be seen from the losses incurred following the Kobe earthquake in 1995. While world stock markets were unaffected, the Japanese stock market lost over 10 per cent of its value in the medium term. The duration of negative effects on stock markets depends upon wider consumer confidence. Munich Re considers human-made disasters to be worse than natural disasters for the international market. More catastrophic might be a disaster (or series of disasters) that damages the global trading infrastructure. It is for this reason that financial institutions and businesses invest heavily in back-up systems.[35]

Larger developed urban/national economies ... are more likely to absorb and spread the economic burden of disaster impacts

For urban residents, systemic economic effects may not be felt for some time as businesses restructure, although in the short term, unemployment or livelihood disruption is to be expected and may be prolonged. Shelter and labour power are the two most important assets for low-income urban households. When either is damaged or destroyed in disaster, households are forced to expend savings or borrow to survive and re-establish livelihoods. Relief aid itself can distort local livelihoods and markets as goods and services that can be provided locally are undercut and replaced by externally sourced aid. The result is that local livelihoods and the local economy can be eroded. For households with strong familial or social ties, access to remittances or borrowing money without interest payments is a possibility. Increasingly, access to remittances from overseas is a key indicator of resilience to economic shocks caused by natural and human-made disasters in urban Latin America.

Disaster impacts, risk of disaster impacts and actions taken to protect areas from disaster risk ... have an impact on urban land values

■ Urban land markets

Disaster impacts, risk of disaster impacts and actions taken to protect areas from disaster risk all have an impact on urban land values. As in any urban regeneration or upgrading scheme, urban planning and engineering projects aiming to mitigate disaster exposure can lead to changes in the social geography of communities or city regions.

Investing in mitigation to protect those at risk can result in increases in the value of land and housing, which, in turn, can lead to lower-income households selling to higher-income households. This cycle is a major challenge to the poverty reduction potential of investments in structural mitigation. Informal, illegal and formal/legal land and

Box 7.5 Urban land markets and flooding in Argentina

In Argentina, land market agents have tended to oppose any legislation that might constrain their actions on areas prone to flooding. The consequence has been that across Argentina, in Buenos Aires, Santa Fe and Greater Resistencia, the state has allowed the division of land in flood-prone areas into lots for sale. In Greater Resistencia, despite existing legal instruments, the Resistencia City Council has consistently voted for exceptions to regulations if they hinder construction plans. Development in areas prone to flooding has not only generated new hazard, but has also caused changes to land drainage, placing previously safe developed areas at risk.

Flood risk has had a detrimental effect on land values in Buenos Aires. A study in the Arroyo Maldonado area found that land values in this middle- and low-income community fell by 30 per cent following two years of consecutive flooding. Land at risk from flooding is cheaper and can be purchased by low-income households, as has happened in parts of Buenos Aires such as Matanza-Richuelo and Reconquista, and in Resistencia along the course of the Rio Negro. In Resistencia, middle-income households are also at risk from flooding, but can often evacuate to family or friends in higher (more expensive) neighbourhoods. This option is less available to the poor, who rely on state or non-governmental organization (NGO) shelters.

In middle- to high-income areas, real estate agents have been found to mask flood risk. In housing developments at Colastiné and Rincón, Greater Santa Fe, land was purchased in the belief that it was flood secure. Unfortunately, this was not the case, with purchasers feeling cheated. The state was implicated in this, having failed to regulate against granting development in flood-prone locations. In already built-up areas in Buenos Aires (e.g. Belgrano on Avenida Cabildo), flooding is also effectively masked, with no discernable change in the market price of flats except for temporary decreases following severe flooding.

On the whole, middle- and high-income populations, as well as estate agents and land developers, have successfully masked flooding to avoid possible land and property value losses. This also reflects the higher resilience of areas occupied by middle- and high-income households and associated commercial activities that are able to cope better with flooding than low-income households and marginalized commercial activities.

Source: Clichevsky, 2003

housing market values are equally sensitive to disaster risk (see Part III of this Global Report on security of tenure).

Box 7.5 examines the history of urban land development and the impact of flooding in Argentina. It illustrates the negative spiral of flood-prone land having a reduced value and therefore being affordable to low-income households, but also increasing exposure to flood hazard among this group, who has the least resources to cope with or respond to flood hazard.

Especially in poorer countries, women and children tend to be most affected by disasters

Social and political impacts of disaster

The social and political impacts of disaster are less easy to pin down than the direct economic impacts of disaster. The social impacts of disaster are determined by those institutions and processes in society that shape differential access to resources. These include cultural, ethnic, religious, social, and age- and disability-related causes that lead to segregation and exclusion. Every urban community is structured by a myriad of social relationships, obligations, competitions and divisions that shape the particular social characteristics associated most with vulnerability and loss.[36] Despite checklists of vulnerability routinely including social characteristics, rigorous research is relatively limited, with most of the resulting knowledge focusing on gender inequalities. A common theme is that where inequality has generated disproportionate vulnerability for a specific social group, higher losses during disaster and reconstruction serve to deepen inequality, thus creating vicious cycles of loss and vulnerability.

Political impacts of disaster are often determined by the pre-disaster political context. Post-disaster, political leaders have a remarkable ability to deflect criticisms and survive, or even benefit from disaster notwithstanding any role their decisions might have played in generating disaster risk.

This section examines the ways in which vulnerability to disaster impacts is shaped by gender, age, disability and political systems. On the ground, the many social and economic roots of vulnerability interact. For simplicity, social characteristics are discussed in turn; but any individual may experience more than one form of social exclusion and this, in turn, may be compounded or relieved through economic status. Economic poverty – for example, experienced through homelessness – is not discussed here as a separate social pressure, but is a theme that runs throughout the analysis of disaster risk in this and subsequent chapters.

Gender and disaster

Gender is a social variable that shapes vulnerability and is reflected in disaster impact statistics worldwide. Especially in poorer countries, women and children tend to be most affected by disasters.[37] The 1991 cyclone in Bangladesh killed 138,000 people and mortality among females over ten years of age was over three times that of males over ten years old.[38] Following the Maharashtra earthquake in India, in 1993, while less women than men were affected (48 per cent), more women than men were killed (55 per cent).[39]

In addition to differential death and injury rates from the direct impacts of natural and human-made hazards, women are at risk from indirect impacts. Four pathways for this inequality have been identified:[40]

- *Economic losses* disproportionately impact upon economically insecure women (e.g. when livelihoods traditionally undertaken by poor women rely on assets at risk, such as peri-urban agriculture, or the destruc-

tion of women's home-based businesses, or when women and girls are granted only limited access to post-disaster economic aid).
- *Work load changes* suggest that disasters increase women's responsibilities in the domestic sphere, paid workplace and community.
- *Post-disaster stress* symptoms are often (but not universally) reported more frequently by women.
- *Increased rates of sexual and domestic violence* against girls and women are reported in disaster contexts.

One global study has found that in 42 out of 45 disaster events, women or girls were more adversely affected. The study focused on post-traumatic stress disorder and found that psychological effects were not only stronger among females, but more lasting, as well.[41] Box 7.6 elaborates upon the disproportionate impact on women of the Indian Ocean Tsunami in 2004.

Social and legal systems can discriminate against women during reconstruction. The lack of rights or the ability to exercise such rights can push women closer to vulnerability, particularly in the post-disaster period, and especially if male household heads have been killed. The disproportionate vulnerability of women (and children) to hazards, but also to exploitation during the social disruption that follows disaster, has not been adequately factored into disaster planning. For example, disaster impact assessments are not routinely disaggregated by gender. There are some notable exceptions; but more needs to be done to systematically record gendered vulnerabilities.

Box 7.6 More women than men lost in the Indian Ocean Tsunami

Evidence from Indonesia, India and Sri Lanka illustrates that many more women and children than men died due to the Indian Ocean Tsunami. In four villages in the Aceh Besar district in Indonesia, male survivors outnumbered female survivors by a ratio of almost 3:1. In another four villages in North Aceh district, females accounted for 77 per cent (more than three-quarters) of deaths. In the worst affected village of Kuala Cangkoy, there were four female deaths for every male death.

In Cuddalore in India, almost three times as many women as men were killed, while the only people to die in Pachaankuppam village were women. In Sri Lanka, too, partial information such as camp surveys and press reports suggest a serious imbalance in the number of men and women who survived.

Some of the causes of these patterns are similar across the region: many women died because they stayed behind to look for their children and other relatives; men more often than women can swim; and men more often than women can climb trees. But differences, too, are important. Women in Aceh, for example, traditionally have a high level of participation in the labour force; but the wave struck on a Sunday morning when they were at home and the men were out on errands away from the seafront. Women in India play a major role in fishing and were waiting on the shore for the fishermen to bring in the catch, which they would then process and sell in the local market. In Sri Lanka, in Batticoloa district, the tsunami hit at the hour women on the east coast usually took their baths in the sea.

Source: Oxfam International, 2005a

Age, disability and disaster

The young, the elderly and those with disabilities are often among the most vulnerable to natural and human-made hazards. For example, in the Bangladesh cyclone in 1991, mortality rates for those under 14 and over 50 years of age were more than three times that for the 15 to 49 age group.[42] Since data on age and disability is not routinely collected post-disaster, evidence is limited to accounts of individual events.

Children's lack of physical strength and immature immune systems make them vulnerable to injury and illness following disaster. Where children are separated from parents or carers, their safety is jeopardized during relief and reconstruction. Property rights and personal security of children, as well as women survivors, are not easy to protect during reconstruction. Children and young people may be placed in positions of increased responsibility for household maintenance or at greater risk through lack of familial support. For instance, studies from Cape Town show that children from low-income households face a much higher risk of sustaining fire-related injuries. This is linked to being left alone for long periods.[43]

For the elderly, vulnerability is more ambiguous. In some circumstances, the elderly can acquire resilience through their knowledge and more developed social networks of support. Where this is not the case, the elderly can become a high-risk social group. The heat waves that hit Chicago in 1995 and Paris in 2003 both disproportionately impacted upon the elderly. However, in both cities, it was the socially isolated and unsupported elderly who were most at risk. This underlines the social construction of vulnerability. The physical fragility of senior years itself was not a cause of increased mortality. In Chicago, high death rates were found among the elderly who lived alone and were isolated from the community around them. This has been described as a social process during which some individuals remain living in a transitional urban neighbourhood while the community changes around them, thus making it more and more difficult to sustain supportive social networks.[44]

The young, the elderly and those with disabilities are often amongst the most vulnerable to natural and human-made hazards

Data on the additional vulnerability faced by the disabled is very limited. Occasional anecdotal accounts are available, and these suggest, in some cases, that the disabled might be purposely abandoned during disaster. A news report in 2004 claimed that disabled people were left behind during evacuation in the 2000 floods in Zimbabwe and Mozambique.[45]

The political consequences of disaster

The social and political repercussions of disaster can extend well beyond forcing change in disaster management policy and practice. In extreme cases, disasters can serve as catalysts for political change. That political systems affect disaster risk is also clear. A survey of 89 natural disasters between 1972 and 1976 found that political interference was a regular consequence. The most common problems concerned lack of acknowledgement of the disaster by the government of the affected country, the government's political interference with the response process, and corruption in the distribution of relief.[46] Despite such evidence, there has been little analysis of the impacts of disasters affecting urban areas upon political systems.

A common metric for measuring the impact of disasters upon political systems might be described as political

Table 7.8

Natural disasters and socio-political change

Source: Pelling, 2003; except *: Dill and Pelling, 2006

City (country)	Date of disaster	Disaster trigger	Socio-political reaction
Lice (Turkey)	1972	Earthquake	Discrimination against the minority Kurdish population was blamed for inadequate preparedness before, and relief aid after, the earthquake. Complaints were made by a Kurdish member of parliament to the Turkish Parliament.
Managua (Nicaragua)	1972	Earthquake	The scale of corruption by the Somoza dictatorship united workers, intellectuals, the business community and international popular opinion fuelling a popular revolution that eventually led to a change in regime.
Guatemala City (Guatemala)	1976	Earthquake	Described as a 'classquake' because of its high impact among slum dwellers, this event stimulated popular mobilization and land invasions, which reshaped the geography of the city.
(Chile, nationwide)	1985	Earthquake	A traditional civilian response threatened to undermine a weak dictatorship. The response was demobilized through repression and the state took over.
Mexico City (Mexico)	1985	Earthquake	Inadequate state response. A highly organized civil society-led reconstruction programme emerged, unique in Mexico's modern history of authoritarian state control.
Miami (US)	1992	Hurricane	Broad interest coalitions formed, assisting in the rebuilding of the city. These coalitions have not persisted but have created the potential for cooperation in local politics.
Marmara* (Turkey)	1999	Earthquake	A conspicuous failure in state oversight of the construction industry led to riots and political lobbying for policy change.

space. It may be possible to assess how disaster risk reduction, the hazard events themselves and their aftermath open or close political space. In other words, do the activities conducted during these periods of disaster management provide an opportunity for inclusive governance? Disasters can act as catalysts highlighting underlying inequality, corruption and incompetence that fuels popular unrest; but they can also close political space. More authoritarian political regimes whose legitimacy is built on the control of political power in a national state are likely to feel threatened by any opening of political space through disaster, and so may be expected to act to restrain emerging civil society voices. Entrenched political systems are difficult to change and single disaster events rarely achieve significant political movement, unless this was already entrained before the event.

...political relations at the local level will be tested by disaster events ...

Table 7.8 presents information from studies of disasters that have had a mainly urban impact and were triggered by a natural hazard. In many cases, it was the capital city that was hit, with political consequences for the nation as a whole. In cases where the formal state response has been politically biased (Turkey in 1972) or inadequate (Mexico City in 1985; Turkey in 1999), civil society responses have emerged or even come to dominate disaster relief, recovery (Chile in 1985; Mexico City in 1985) and reconstruction (Guatemala City in 1976). In many cases, civil society efforts can become formalized when interest groups have created coalitions with the state (Miami in 1992; Mexico City in 1985; Turkey in 1999) or protested through formal political or legislative channels (Turkey in 1972). Where political differences between the cooperating groups are too large, collaboration may not last long beyond the disaster reconstruction period (Miami in 1992); but even here the experience is likely to have built up new trust between civil society groups within the city.

State elites can benefit from disaster when, for example, the political function of party networks is adapted for relief distribution or institutional weaknesses allow corruption (Managua in 1972), thus strengthening 'clientalism' in society. This suggests that it can be in the interest of parasitic governing elites to allow degeneration in the institutions overseeing disaster response (providing a space for corruption), while investing in state control over local disaster response strategies (to prevent the emergence of potentially critical civil society organizations). Where states do not benefit from disaster, astute politicians can control potential damage. In 1966, despite having made decisions that directly led to increased vulnerability to flooding in New Orleans, the incumbent mayor was successfully re-elected, having demonstrated leadership in reconstruction.[47]

Beyond the national level, political relations at the local level will be tested by disaster events and also by risk reduction and reconstruction interventions. If disaster risk reduction is to be effective in changing the root causes of risk, then change in local social and political relations – between gender, economic class, cast, and ethnic and religious groups – is a legitimate target for action. Even where change is not intended, this may often be an unplanned outcome of interventions, with positive and negative consequences for those affected. For all disaster types at the local level, periods of disaster and emergency response – especially if these are prolonged – can result in dislocations in the authority of the state and the emergence of, if only temporarily, alternative forms of social organization. Disasters can also lead to more positive social bonding and the building of trust between people forced together by adversity.

Cultural impacts of disaster

Urban areas concentrate cultural assets, including architecturally significant buildings and urban landscapes, but also artworks housed in urban centres. The Jahrhundertflut flood of August 2002 that affected the Czech Republic, Germany and Hungary, is one recent example where cultural assets were at risk. The World Heritage towns of Cesky Krumlov and Prague were damaged and large galleries in Dresden and Prague were flooded. In Prague, flooding in the National Museum and Prague University of Technology caused damage to books, including an archive on Czech architecture. The vulnerability of the historic city of Genoa (Italy) further illustrates the cultural impacts of disasters (see Box 7.7).

The United Nations Educational, Scientific and Cultural Organization (UNESCO) World Heritage List includes 644 cultural and 24 mixed cultural and natural properties (including an additional 162 natural properties, such as nature parks). Many of these sites are located in earthquake-risk hotspots in Central America and Central Asia and flood-risk areas in Central Europe. In Africa, sea-level rise has been identified as a cause of heritage loss in coastal Ghana, where Fort Peasantine in the Volta region has been lost. In Mali, drought has caused the abandonment of areas with significant architectural heritage, placing these buildings at risk from lack of maintenance.[48] The ancient citadel and surrounding cultural landscape of the Iranian city of Bam, where 26,000 people lost their lives in the earthquake of December 2003, was simultaneously inscribed on UNESCO's World Heritage List and on the List of World Heritage in Danger in 2004. World Heritage List status has enabled UNESCO to lead international efforts to salvage the cultural heritage of this devastated city. The potential for protecting global architectural heritage through the inclusion of World Heritage sites in urban disaster management plans has also been realized – for example, in Central Quito (Peru) and Havana (Cuba).[49]

When places of cultural importance are damaged or destroyed by disaster, the impacts go far beyond economic value.[50] Cultural heritage can provide disaster-affected communities with a much needed sense of continuity and identity during reconstruction, as well as a future resource for economic development. Cultural heritage is particularly at risk in the period following a disaster, when the urgency to address the basic needs of the population, combined with the interests of developers and entrepreneurs, often leads to emergency response activities and planning and rehabilitation schemes for recovery that are insensitive to the cultural heritage of the affected areas or the social traditions of their inhabitants. With this in mind, many have called for cultural heritage to be integrated within the general framework of development and planning, as well as within existing disaster management policies and mechanisms.[51]

Box 7.7 Flood hazard threat to cultural heritage in Genoa, Italy

The city of Genoa is located in the Liguria region, in northwest Italy, where earthquakes, landslides and floods represent the major natural hazards being historically experienced. These natural hazards pose a serious threat to the cultural heritage of Genoa, which hosts one of the largest medieval centres in Europe, with about 150 noble palaces and many valuable architectonic evidences. The historic city centre is particularly subject to floods that are produced by the many streams crossing the area and partially conveyed by hydraulic structures built during the last two centuries. Failures in the artificial drainage system are, therefore, the main reason of flooding for the ancient neighbourhoods of the town.

The vulnerability of local monumental heritage against flooded waters was first brought to attention following the 1970 flooding, which caused 19 casualties, 500 homeless and losses of about US$60 million in the productive sector.

An extensive survey of the available records of flooding episodes during the last 100 years was completed in order to derive a map of historically flooded areas. The study concludes that the vulnerability to flooding of cultural monuments can hardly be addressed at the scale of a single monument or art piece. Thus, projects involving the whole area of the historic centre are recommended. Results from the study also illustrate that the problem is mainly of a hydrologic/hydraulic nature; therefore, hydraulic solutions must be at the base of the intervention.

Source: Lanza, 2003

URBAN PROCESSES GENERATING DISASTER RISK

This section presents an examination of the root causes of vulnerability in cities exposed to natural and human-made disaster risk. First, the impact of patterns of growth of mega and large cities and of the many intermediate and smaller human settlements on disaster risk is reviewed. Second, the ways in which urban processes generate risk through modifying the physical environment and through the extent and impact of poverty in urban slums is examined. Third, the role of urban management and, in particular, of building construction, urban planning and the influence of international action on urban development is reviewed. These topics are returned to in Chapters 8 and 11, where experience of, and future potential for, disaster risk reduction is reviewed.

Growth and diversity of urban areas

Rapid urban growth, coupled with geomorphology, hydrology, politics, demography and economics, can create and exacerbate landscapes of disaster risk in a variety of ways (see Box 7.8). Global statistics on urban growth are as impressive as those on disaster loss.[52] UN-Habitat's *State of the World's Cities 2006/2007* shows that during 2000 to 2015, 65 million new urban dwellers will be added annually, 93 per cent of these in developing countries. Asia and Africa are the most rapidly urbanizing regions. In 2005, urban populations were 39.9 per cent in Asia and 39.7 per cent in Africa, increasing to 54.5 per cent and 53.5 per cent, respectively, in 2030.[53] By this time, over 80 per cent of Latin America's population will be urban based.

Rapid urban growth ... can create and exacerbate landscapes of risk in a variety of ways

Urban settlements are becoming larger and more numerous through a combination of natural population growth and in-migration. Political stability and economic opportunity can lead to small rural settlements expanding into towns, as is happening in Central America, and taking on new social and environmental challenges and opportunities in which urban managers might not be experienced. At a larger scale, rapid expansion of urban corridors, such as that along China's seaboard, can reconfigure risk profiles at the regional level.

For cities, there is a constant pressure to keep pace with, if not lead, change in regional and global economic development. This, in turn, can be a force contributing to uncontrollable urban expansion and the generation of more vulnerability to disasters. Mumbai, for instance, shifted its industrial base from import substituting to export orientation in response to changes in the global political economy. This led to industrial relocation from the central city to highways extending beyond the city limits, catalysing massive population growth in the urban periphery. Some settlements reportedly grew to six times their original population, outstripping the capacity of urban planning and infrastructure provision.[54]

Foreign investment can bring new prosperity to a city and its residents and be a resource for risk management. However, competing for foreign capital investment can also

Box 7.8 Rapid urbanization and environmental hazard in Dhaka, Bangladesh

Dhaka has a population of 11.6 million, and this is rising fast. The city is built on alluvial terraces and is exposed to flooding from rivers, direct rainfall, coastal flooding and earthquakes. With so many sources of natural hazard, one might ask how a city came to thrive in such a location.

The city's growth has been tied to its political importance. The city was established as the capital of Bengal in 1610. In 1905, Dhaka became the capital of East Bengal and in 1947 it was designated the capital of East Pakistan, with the greatest growth after independence when Dhaka became the capital of Bangladesh. In 1971, there were between 1 million and 2 million residents. Throughout the modern period, expansion has seen the conversion of marshes and farmland into urban land use. High-rise commercial and residential buildings have become increasingly used to cater for growth and are predominantly located in the higher areas of the city.

Despite its long history, 90 per cent of population growth and associated urban expansion into areas at risk has occurred since 1971. Initial expansion to the north of the city captured higher ground above flood levels or on earth-filled lower-lying sites. More recent expansion has continued northwards over low-lying land. Inequality is extreme in the city, with the richest 2 per cent of the residents occupying 20 per cent of the city's land. Some 30 per cent of the city's population fall below the poverty line and live in increasingly marginalized and hazardous slums and squatter settlements.

The multiple relationships between urbanization and hazard are well exemplified in Dhaka. Rapid population growth is partly fuelled by rural migrants who have been made homeless by flooding, cyclones or shifting river beds in rural districts. The neglect of small towns also increases the pull of Dhaka as a place of economic opportunities. Urban expansion in Dhaka is swallowing adjacent agricultural land, reducing opportunities for sustainable local food production.

Industrial risk has increased as industrial zones that were originally on the outskirts of the city have been swallowed by sprawling residential areas. These residential zones fall outside of land-use planning and regulations. Fire is a problem in these areas and in densely populated slum districts.

Source: Huq, 1999

Increasingly, urban planners are looking for ways in which ... disaster risk-reduction ... can scale down ... to semiautonomous local planning and action zones

be a pressure leading to an increase in vulnerability through the lowering of employment rights or environmental protection legislation. The 3500 deaths from a toxic gas leak in Union Carbide's plant in Bhopal (India) in 1984 can be explained by just such a cocktail of pressures.[55]

Urban populations follow industrial investment, so that large cities also contribute substantially to their country's GDP. For instance, Mexico City is responsible for around one third of Mexico's GDP. Large cities and megacities,[56] in particular, create huge concentrations of people and physical and financial assets, and are frequently also cultural and political centres. They generate the potential for substantial losses from single large disaster events, creating new challenges for risk management. Increasingly, not only the balance of urban populations, but also the world's largest cities, will be found in Africa, Asia and Latin America and the Caribbean.[57]

Not all large urban centres have similar vulnerability profiles. At a broad level, differences exist between those cities that form part of the core global economy (London, Paris, New York and Tokyo) and are globally connected (Mexico City, Johannesburg, Alexandria and Mumbai), on the one hand, and, on the other, those that are large but only loosely connected globally (Lagos, Nairobi and Khartoum). While this division is simplistic, it serves well to illustrate the different economic base, political institutions and management capacity that is found in large cities and megacities worldwide.

Small cities of less than 500,000 are home to the large majority of the world's urban dwellers, with the total population of small urban areas exposed to environmental risk exceeding the total at-risk population resident in megacities.[58] Small cities may be especially susceptible to complete destruction in a single event – for example, a volcanic eruption and mudflow in Amero (Colombia) in 1985 killed most of the city's 25,000 inhabitants.[59] Despite this, the majority of research and investment have, to date, focused on large cities and megacities.

While smaller settlements might, as a last resort, be relocated to avoid hazard risk, this becomes increasingly problematic with large cities. There has been some talk of moving major cities away from zones of earthquake risk, as in the case of Tehran, where a large earthquake could claim 720,000 lives and bring the country to a standstill.[60] Simply scaling up risk management procedures developed for relatively smaller cities might not be the best option for building security into megacities. Increasingly, urban planners are looking for ways in which infrastructure, land-use and disaster risk reduction and response planning can scale down from master plans at the city level to semi-autonomous local planning and action zones. However, experiences of managing disaster risk in larger cities should not be uncritically applied in small urban areas where political, economic, social and environmental contexts and capacities will differ (see Box 7.9).

Even where urban expansion is planned, disaster risk can be generated. In El Salvador, free trade zones in San Bartolo, El Pedregal, Olocuilta and San Marcos were promoted by the government without adequate concern for earthquake hazard. During the 2001 earthquake, large losses were reported from among migrant workers who supplied labour to foreign-owned enterprises in these new towns.[61] Thus, to understand the motors shaping trends in urbanization and disaster risk, it is necessary to look beyond population statistics to changes in the form, composition and governance of human settlements.

Box 7.9 Disaster risk in a small city: Shimla, India

Shimla is a small settlement in India, with a population of 140,000. The city is located in the north Indian Himalayas in an area of high seismic activity. On 4 April 1905, an earthquake of 7.8 on the Richter scale damaged much of the city. While the city was designed for 25,000 occupants, it now houses up to 140,000 as permanent residents and another 100,000 transitory population. Urban development has proceeded apace and without due regard for hazard management. Risk has accumulated as the city has developed.

Capacity for urban planning has not been able to keep pace with development, although recent initiatives have built disaster management capacity. The non-governmental organization (NGO) Sustainable Environment and Ecological Development Society has worked with the municipal corporation of Shimla to build resilience. An earthquake risk assessment has been conducted that has flagged several urban processes as contributing to risk:

- Rapid unplanned growth has occurred so that residential districts – but also critical infrastructure (e.g. hospitals, power stations, telecommunication installations and water supply stations) are located in hazard zones.
- Most buildings are residential (over 75 per cent) and the city is high density. Both of these factors limit the amount of spare capacity space that could be used for public shelter in the event of a large disaster.
- Many of the buildings are not accessible from roads (72 per cent) and many are on steep hill slopes, making evacuation and relief difficult.
- Emergency services are under-funded. Only 100 fire fighters with six fire engines serve the city and its surrounding region.
- The building stock is predominantly of a poor condition. Existing building stock is poorly maintained, particularly in the rental sector, coupled with a preference for building with unsafe material, such as brick or concrete with minimal reinforcement. Some 36 per cent of the city's building stock has been classified by the Sustainable Environment and Ecological Development Society as being of very poor quality.
- Many buildings are inappropriately high for an earthquake region. At least 24 per cent of buildings have three or more stories, 40 per cent of which are built on steep slopes on top of un-compacted soil.
- Around 15 per cent of Shimla's building stock was constructed before 1925 and is built of wood. This is a concern for half of these structures, which have not been properly maintained, leading to decay. In the old districts of the town, the high density of building means that adjoining buildings are put at risk.
- Seismic building codes were introduced in 1971. About 30 per cent of the buildings were constructed before this ordinance was passed; but a lack of regulation enforcement means that some 80 per cent of buildings do not meet standards.

Source: Gupta et al, 2006

Environmental change and poverty in cities

The economic imperatives that drive urbanization also play a large role in determining the status of the urban environment and ecosystems, as well as the extent and depth of poverty, wealth and inequality in the city. This sub-section reviews the ways in which urbanization processes generate risk by shaping the environment of the city and the growth of slums. The role of global environmental change on disaster risk in cities is also considered.

Modifying the hazard environment

Consumption of natural assets (trees for fuel, groundwater, sand and gravel) and the overexploitation of natural services (water systems and air as sinks for sewerage or industrial waste) modify the environment and generate new hazards. These include deforestation and slope instability within and surrounding cities, encouraging landslides and flash flooding. Such changes to the urban environment do not impact upon citizens equally.

Recent evidence illustrates that with increasing affluence and through the use of technology, those who produce waste and risk can avoid the consequences both in time and space. Thus, the environmental costs of over-consumption by the wealthy become burdens for the poor, who are forced to live not only in unsafe and insecure housing, but also with urban pollution and environmental degradation.[62] Climate change is the most extreme example of this thesis. High consumption by the rich and in aggregate by richer cities has contributed 80 per cent of carbon emissions that cause climate change. Yet, it is the less wealthy and the poor in cities, towns and villages who will least be able to cope with and adapt to the local impacts of climate change, either directly or collectively through government or social actions.[63]

Flooding, perhaps more than any other hazard type, has been exacerbated by the physical processes of urbanization. Flood risk has been made worse in urban areas through the silting of natural water courses and the lowering of water tables, followed by salt intrusion or land subsidence. Building roads and houses makes it harder for rainwater to drain through the soil, leading to more frequent flash flooding in cities. The loss of mangrove ecosystems on urban fringes leads to coastal erosion and exposure to storm wind and waves. Similarly, deforestation on hill slopes within and surrounding settled land can create instability and lead to greater landslide hazard. Many losses to Hurricane Mitch, during 1998, in Central America were in small regional towns smothered by mudslides or flash floods caused by deforestation in adjacent agricultural areas.[64] Increased losses to flooding can also be expected as the number and size of urban settlements in coastal areas increases.[65]

Inadequately built multi-storey construction has been a cause of losses in many urban disasters…

The urban landscape itself is changing the context of natural and human-made disasters. Inadequately built multistorey construction has been a cause of losses in many urban disasters, and skyscrapers have also been the site for devastating fires. In São Paulo in 1974, 189 people died in a fire in a 25-storey building.[66] The close proximity of residential, commercial and industrial land uses in a city can generate new cocktails of hazard that require multi-risk management. Calcutta and Baroda are just two cities where the close proximity of manufacturing, hazardous materials storage and residential areas has been a cause for concern.[67] The growth of slums whose residents' livelihoods are tied to solid waste dumps is a similarly common cause of hazard in large cities such as Manila, where 300 people were killed by a landslide in the city's Patayas dump.[68]

Climate change has far reaching consequences for the incidence and impacts of disasters in cities

The impact of climate change

Climate change has far reaching consequences for the incidence and impacts of disasters in cities. Cities are particularly vulnerable to the impacts of climate change, as this is where much of the population growth over the next two decades will take place and where a large and growing proportion of those most at risk from climate change reside.[69]

Rising global temperatures and the resultant changes in weather patterns and sea levels have direct impacts on cities. In particular, cities located along the world's coastlines will face an increased number of extreme weather events such as tropical cyclones, flooding and heat waves.[70] There has been a 50 per cent rise in extreme weather events associated with climate change from the 1950s to the 1990s, and the location of major urban centres in coastal areas exposed to hydro-meteorological hazards is a significant risk factor: 21 of the 33 cities which are projected to have a population of 8 million or more by 2015 are located in vulnerable coastal zones and are increasingly vulnerable to sea-level rise.[71] Around 40 per cent of the world's population lives less than 100 kilometres from the coast, within reach of severe coastal storms. In effect, close to 100 million people around the world live less than 1 metre above sea level. Furthermore, recent research shows that 13 per cent of the world's urban population lives in low elevation coastal zones, defined as less than 10 meters above sea level.[72] Thus, if sea levels rise by just 1 metre, many coastal megacities with populations of more than 10 million people, such as Rio de Janeiro, New York, Mumbai, Dhaka, Tokyo, Lagos and Cairo will be under threat. Indeed, several projections have indicated that sea levels are expected to rise by 8 to 88 centimetres during the 21st century due to climate change.[73]

... if sea levels rise by just one metre, many coastal mega cities with populations of more than 10 million people ... will be under threat

Climate change also has less dramatic and direct effects on cities. In sub-Saharan Africa, climate change and the consequent extreme climatic variations is a key factor which causes rural populations to migrate to urban areas, thereby fuelling rapid and often uncontrolled urban growth.[74] In turn, this exacerbates other disaster risk factors such as the spread of settlements into easily accessible yet hazardous locations and unsafe building practices.

While cities remain vulnerable to the effects of climate change, they are also key contributors to global warming. Cities are responsible for 80 per cent of the carbon emissions that cause climate change through energy generation, vehicles, industry and the burning of fossil fuels and biomass in household and industrial energy consumption.[75] Levels of greenhouse gas emissions are higher in many cities of developed countries than in developing country cities. For instance, emissions from cities in North America and Australia are often 25 to 30 times higher than those of cities in low-income countries.[76]

The vulnerability of urban slums

Some 998 million people lived in urban slums in 2006, and if current trends continue, it is predicted that some 1.4 billion will live in slums by 2020.[77] It is not unusual for the majority of urban residents in cities to be excluded from the formal housing market. In Manila, informal settlements at risk to coastal flooding make up 35 per cent of the population; in Bogota, 60 per cent of the population live on steep slopes subject to landslides; and in Calcutta, 66 per cent of the population live in squatter settlements at risk from flooding and cyclones.[78]

Slums are characterized by inadequate and insecure living conditions that generate hazard...

Slums are characterized by inadequate and insecure living conditions that generate hazard; but they are also home to many people with few resources and, thus, high vulnerability. At an individual and household level, vulnerability to natural and human-made hazard is shaped by the kinds of physical, economic, social and human capital assets that people can command. Capacity to increase, protect or diversify an asset profile is largely determined by cultural, administrative and legal institutions and opportunities, such as security of tenure, access to markets, customary hospitality or the effectiveness of the rule of law. Many people in slums have fewer assets and supporting institutions than those living in formalized residential areas and are consequently highly vulnerable to harm from natural and human-made hazards, as well as from other risks associated with crime, violence and insecurity of tenure. Box 7.10 describes such risk conditions for those living in one of Rio de Janerio's slums.

The most important physical asset for the urban poor is housing. Housing provides personal security, but can also be a livelihood resource if it is the locus of home-based enterprises. Those with no home at all are perhaps the most vulnerable. During Hurricane Mitch in 1998, a disproportionate number of the victims were street children.[79] For those with homes, lack of secure tenure has many consequences for their quality of life.[80]

Lack of secure tenure, discussed in greater detail in Part III of this Global Report, reduces people's willingness to upgrade and therefore mitigate local environmental hazard. Renters as well as those living in squatter settlements are at risk from eviction, generating uncertainty before disaster and often resulting in homelessness post-disaster due to competing higher-value land uses. It is not unusual for disasters to be followed by the redevelopment of inner-city low-income rental or squatter areas during reconstruction, often (and famously, in the case of Mexico City) with widespread protest.

When people are excluded from the formal housing market through poverty, they are forced to live in places of risk. People often choose to face environmental hazards and increase their chances of earning a living than live in a more

Box 7.10 Living with risk in the *favelas* of Rio de Janeiro, Brazil

Rio de Janeiro is home to over 10 million people, of which nearly one third live in slums known as *favelas*. Many *favela* residents were originally squatters and the vast majority lack legal title to their homes. Rocinha, one of Rio de Janeiro's richest and most developed *favelas*, is home to between 100,000 and 150,000 people. Rocinha's highly prized location in the south zone of Rio (*Zona Sul*) includes famous seafront neighbourhoods such as Copacabana, Ipanema and Leblon. In the absence of state presence, except for frequent police incursions, it is controlled by those involved in organized drug trafficking. Violence caused by frequent intra-gang warfare and police invasions, coupled with densely populated living conditions, make the *favela* an undesirable place to live. Most inhabitants dream of saving enough money to move out of the *favela*; but very few ever do. Yet, living in Rochina is an advantage, given its proximity to some of Rio's richest neighbourhoods and, hence, potential sources of employment.

Rocinha's population is home to various social groups, and certain areas of the *favela* are more expensive to live in than others. The very bottom of the *favela*, across the highway from the wealthy neighbourhood of Sao Conrado, is relatively prosperous and many homes have legal titles. Neighbourhoods located further up the mountain are generally poorer and more prone to disaster because of the difficulty of building on a nearly vertical mountain slope. One of these neighbourhoods is Roupa Suja, the top of which is located right below a vertical wall of rock and considered a *Zona de Risco* – or risk area – by the Rio de Janeiro city government. Technically, residents are prohibited from building and living in this area; but many are so poor that they have no alternative place to build. The majority of the residents living in this area immigrated to Rio attempting to escape even greater poverty in the rural drought-stricken northeast. Others immigrated from different *favelas* in Rio after urban renewal campaigns razed many of these. Some also come from poorer *favelas* on the city's periphery.

Several people die every year in mudslides caused by heavy rains in Rio's *favelas*. Deforestation at the edge of Rochina, as it expands into the national forest of Tijuca, has worsened this risk. Rio's municipal government, as well as residents themselves, have built aqueducts to channel the water away from homes; but these do not protect all areas of the *favela*. The danger of falling rocks is perhaps greater than that of rain. Since the homes at the top of the *favela* are directly beneath a vertical overhang, rocks break off due to erosion and fall on the homes below.

Faced each day with multiple types of risk – from natural hazards, violence and disease – the residents of Roupa Suja's *Zona de Risco* lead a precarious and difficult life. Most stay because they have nowhere else to go.

Source: Carter, 2006

Income generation is a more immediate concern for the poor than disaster risk

environmentally secure location, but one that offers limited livelihood opportunities. Income generation is a more immediate concern for the urban poor than disaster risk. For 25 years, the Yemuna River drainage reserve in central Delhi has served as an informal settlement for just this reason.[81] Regular flooding has not reduced the demand for living space in this high-risk location.

The strong social bonds that exist in many slums can be a resource for building resilience; but slum dwellers can also experience social isolation, particularly when they are new to the city. Recent rural migrants are often identified as among the most vulnerable people in cities. In Dhaka (Bangladesh), for example, the urban poor are mainly rural migrants whose lack of access to secure housing and livelihoods is compounded by the absence of familial support.[82] Work in Los Angeles (US) has shown that legal and illegal migrants from Latin America live in the least well-constructed housing built before earthquake codes were introduced.[83]

Building control and land-use planning

A key determinant of the physical vulnerability of buildings and infrastructure in urban areas is the enforcement of building and land-use planning regulations. In the absence of such controls, or a lack of observance of the same, unsafe construction and land-use practices will flourish, generating greater vulnerability. This section examines the effects of safe building construction and land-use planning on urban disaster risk.

Safe building construction

The rapid supply of housing to meet rising demand without compliance with safe building codes is a principal cause of disaster loss in urban areas. The failure of urban administrations to enforce safe building practices exacerbates urban disaster risk in three ways:

- Unsafe housing increases the likelihood of injury and damage to property during a disaster.
- Debris from damaged buildings is a major cause of injury during and after disaster.
- The loss of dwellings through disaster places a major strain on individuals and on the sustainability of communities and cities.

The rapid supply of housing to meet rising demand without compliance with safe building codes is a principal cause of disaster loss in urban areas

There are few urban settlements that are not covered by building codes. However, in order for building codes to work, they need to be appropriate – that is, to be designed in light of prevailing and likely future hazard risks, and to take into account prevalent building materials and architectural customs. In particular, while some core aspects might be retained, the importation of one country's building codes to another requires careful thought. Jamaica's building codes were based on British templates; but these required revision to provide security in a country exposed to hurricanes.[84] In cities exposed to multiple hazards, careful judgement has to be used to balance risks in building design – for example, offsetting the preferred steep roof pitches for volcanic ash fall against the flatter roof design for properties exposed to hurricane-force winds.

Arguably, the most important reason for unsafe construction is the failure to implement and enforce building codes. Failure to enforce regulation was the principal cause of high losses among poor and middle-class households in the 1999 Marmara earthquake in Turkey,[85] and in the collapse of multi-storey buildings in Spitak in the Armenian earthquake in 1988.[86] Even among public buildings and critical infrastructure such as schools, unsafe construction continues in the face of building codes. The 2005 Pakistan earthquake destroyed 4844 educational buildings, 18,000 children were killed by the collapse of school buildings and 300,000 children were still unable to attend school six months after the event.[87] The collapse of schools was presumed to have resulted from poor-quality construction and construction materials, a lack of monitoring in the building processes, and a general lack of awareness of seismic risk and appropriate standards.[88]

Urban land-use planning has not succeeded in separating people from sources of potential human-made or natural hazard

Municipal authorities are normally charged with overseeing construction standards, but are prevented from fulfilling their duty for several reasons. Lack of resources and human skills are perhaps greatest for smaller cities, where land-use or development planning departments may be absent, and responsibilities for overseeing construction standards become added to those of the city engineer or surveyor. In many cities, even these professionals may be absent and construction regulation is, in effect, non-existent. Resource scarcity can be compounded by institutional cultures that allow corruption to distort regulation and enforcement.

While lack of enforcement fails those who can afford to build safely, poverty and exclusion from the formal housing sector consign many, often the majority of urban residents, to living in unsafe dwellings. Unsafe building in slums is compounded by the burden of natural and human-made hazards found in these communities. The result is a deadly cocktail of human vulnerability, unsafe dwellings and high hazard. It is not surprising, then, that the poor, especially those living in slums, bear the brunt of natural disaster losses.

Land-use planning

Urban land-use planning has not succeeded in separating people from sources of potential human-made or natural hazard. In the UK, around 15 per cent of urban land, containing 1.85 million homes and 185,000 commercial properties, is built on land known to be at risk from flooding. Much of this land has been developed since the 1947 Town and Country Planning Act, which gave local authorities power to prevent floodplain development.[93] In this case, as in many others, pressure for local economic development has been given priority over flood risk management, with increasingly disastrous consequences demonstrated by widespread flooding in 1998 and 2000.

In middle- and low-income countries experiencing rapid urbanization, the capacity of town planning departments to measure, let alone manage, the expansion of urban land use is seriously inhibited. This is a major cause for the accumulation of disaster risk in human settlements. The spread of informal and slum settlements has already been identified as an acute concern. These settlements, at best, are only weakly influenced by land-use planning policy, so that internal structure as well as adjoining land uses and characteristics combine to produce disaster risk. Not only are slum settlements located in risky places, but high density also limits access for emergency vehicles and can in itself be a cause of hazard – for example, in spreading house fires.

Even in cities responsive to formal planning control, inappropriate policy can lead to increased risk. In many cities, widespread concretization and the infilling of natural drainage has increased flood hazard. In Bangkok, the conversion of drainage canals into streets now results in regular flooding.[94] In Georgetown, the capital of Guyana, uncontrolled expansion of the built environment, infilling of drainage canals and concretization has similarly increased the speed of runoff and reduced the water storage capacity and speed of natural drainage in the city, contributing to an increase in flooding.[95]

Box 7.11 takes up this theme with regard to Mumbai and looks in some detail at the ways in which poverty has come together with poor planning decisions and hazard management to generate flood risk.

Urban land-use planning is too often left outside of reconstruction planning. When reconstruction is undertaken

Box 7.11 Poverty and flooding in Mumbai, India

The 2005 monsoon brought disastrous flooding to Mumbai (India). Those worst affected were the most vulnerable – slum dwellers living in flood-prone locations and with little capacity to avoid or cope with flood impacts. Over half of Mumbai's 12 million people live in slums.[89] Because the majority of these slums are located on hill slopes, low-lying areas, coastal locations and pavements along water mains and open drainage systems, they are the most prone to flooding during times of heavy rainfall and high tides.

Typically, slum dwellers occupy land that is close to the streets or main transportation hubs, such as railways. These communities are constantly in danger from passing trains and are denied formalized access to water, sanitation and electricity because they build on land owned by the Indian Railways and other public or private companies.[90] Beyond this, encroachment onto this land is in conflict with the need to maintain transport and drainage networks. The survival strategies of Mumbai's poorest populations directly affect the city's ability to maintain disaster management infrastructure. By not addressing chronic housing and infrastructure problems, the entire city is exposed to flood hazard.

A risk analysis was undertaken as part of Mumbai's Disaster Management Plan (DMP) prior to the July 2005 floods. Subsequently, a mitigation strategy that focuses on public information systems, infrastructure and sanitation improvements, as well as land-use policies and planning, was developed. The strategy also includes a plan for coordination between public service providers, emergency personnel and disaster aid non-governmental organizations (NGOs).[91] Despite the DMP, the severity of the 2005 floods indicated just how much risk had accumulated over time in the city, built into the geography of its land use, the inadequacy of drainage, rapid urban expansion and tensions within the urban and state-level administrations, including competing interests of senior politicians who are also real estate developers and owners of commercial land.[92] The neglect of outdated zoning regulations and inflated land markets, in particular, contributed to the overall vulnerability of Mumbai and its inhabitants to flood risk.

The experience of the slum dwellers of Mumbai and their vulnerability to flooding is rooted in the larger socio-economic processes of the city (and beyond); but failure to address this vulnerability threatens the sustainability of the city as a whole – as well as the poor majority.

Source: Stecko and Barber, 2007

in the same sites without risk reduction measures, losses recur. A great lesson was learned in Rio de Janeiro when local landslides caused 1000 deaths in 1966, after which houses were reconstructed at the original sites and 1700 people were killed the following year.[96] Relocating disaster survivors away from hazardous sites is also problematic. Social and economic networks are not easy to maintain after relocation, and the loss of these assets, combined with potentially higher transport costs to find work or education and health services, can put an additional strain on individuals and households, thus undermining resilience.

International development policy and urban disaster risk

Urban planning is influenced by national and international development frameworks and priorities. The Millennium Development Goals (MDGs) have had a great impact on prioritizing the international development agenda. The most urban focused goal, target 11 of MDG 7, demands that a significant improvement in the lives of at least 100 million slum dwellers is achieved by 2020. This is an important motor for pro-poor urban planning, and efforts to improve the lives of slum dwellers should take natural and human-made disaster risk into account. There is scope here for indicators of urban vulnerability to disaster risk to contribute to a more holistic assessment of quality of life.

Meeting other MDGs will also be hindered if disaster risk reduction is not made more prominent in urban planning. The great potential for disasters that hit urban areas to destroy critical infrastructure and set back development gains can undermine progress in meeting MDG 1, which calls for the halving, between 1990 and 2015, of the proportion of people whose income is less than US$1 per day. MDG 2 calls for governments to ensure that, by 2015, children everywhere, boys and girls alike, will be able to complete a full course of primary schooling. A great deal of investment has been made in building new primary schools; but only seldom are they designed to disaster-resistant standards. The result is that more children are placed at risk and development gains are liable to be lost. In the Pereira earthquake in Colombia in 1999, 74 per cent of the region's schools were damaged.[97]

Urban risk accumulation was accelerated by the debt crisis and subsequent structural adjustment programmes of the 1980s and 1990s that forced governments throughout Latin America, Asia and Africa to slash subsidies on food, electricity and transportation and to retrench public-sector workers. The impact of these policies was perhaps most visible in the food riots of sub-Saharan Africa, triggered by the removal of subsidies on the price of food.[98] Poor people responded to the economic downturn by putting more family members (especially women and school-age children) into the labour market and by pulling back from long-term investments in children's education and in housing improvement, in this way reducing long-term resilience to disaster. In addition, the cumulative impact of inequality and privatization may have further removed poor people from accessing legal land markets, leading to the proliferation of informal settlements, often in cheap and hazardous locations.

During the early 21st century, World Bank lending has been repackaged, with the stated aim of enabling greater country leadership through national poverty reduction strategies, initially proposed through national Poverty Reduction Strategy Papers (PRSPs). Yet, little work has examined the consequence of the PRSP framework for natural disaster reduction. One study found that few national plans mentioned disaster risk reduction beyond the need for early warning. With many municipal and city administrations having uncomfortable political relationships with national administrations, the extent to which PRSPs enable or constrain municipal government control over financial budgets and access to international support will have a profound impact on urban development and disaster risk reduction. This falls short of an integrated risk reduction approach.[99]

...efforts to improve the lives of slum dwellers should take natural and human-made disaster risk into account

Half of all post-disaster borrowing provided by the World Bank goes to housing reconstruction. A recent review of reconstruction financing argues that this practice exposes funds to capture by local and national elites, thus contributing to urban inequality and vulnerability in ways that other targets for reconstruction funds that would remain as public goods (such as critical infrastructure) might not.[100]

Opportunities for disaster reconstruction funding to contribute to the building of urban resilience have too often been missed by urban, national and international agencies. Where national catastrophe funds are not available, funds earmarked for development works are vulnerable to being diverted to finance reconstruction. This is a principal pathway for the indirect systemic impacts of disaster. International finance has similarly contributed in the past to the perpetuation of cycles of urban poverty, environmental degradation and disaster through disaster reconstruction loan agreements that have increased indebtedness, reducing options for future economic growth or anti-poverty policy.[101]

Meeting ... MDGs will ... be hindered if disaster risk reduction is not made more prominent in urban planning

COMPARATIVE ANALYSIS OF GLOBAL TRENDS

This section provides a comparative analysis of urban disaster incidence and impact for each world region: Africa, the Americas, Asia, Europe and Oceania. This scale of analysis covers great diversity at the national and sub-national levels, but is useful in flagging the major natural and human-made disasters affecting human settlements and the barriers to disaster prevention and mitigation specific to each region.

Africa

Flooding is the most frequent natural disaster type in Africa and results in the highest mortality (see Table 7.9). Earthquakes, floods and storms cause the greatest economic loss and drought affects the most people. Food insecurity resulting from drought can affect urban societies indirectly through food price fluctuation and the in-migration of refugees. Economic loss to disasters is low for Africa,

Table 7.9

Disaster incidence and impacts in Africa (1996–2005)

Note: For all disaster types, small events with less than 10 mortalities or 100 affected people are not included.

Source: EM-DAT, CRED database, University of Louvain, Belgium, www.em-dat.net

	Number of events	Mortality	People affected (thousands)	Economic loss (US$ million, 2005 value)
Avalanches/landslides	11	251	3	No data
Drought/famines	140	4656	173,979	334
Earthquakes/tsunamis	20	3313	361	5824
Extreme temperatures	7	168	0	1
Floods	290	8183	23,203	1880
Volcanic eruptions	5	201	397	10
Windstorms	74	1535	3902	1082
Industrial accidents	49	2785	10	838
Miscellaneous accidents	94	2847	189	23

compared to other world regions, but is high as a proportion of GDP.

Between 1996 and 2005, more people were killed or affected by volcanic eruptions in Africa than in any other region, despite incidence (five events) being low (see Table 7.9). Low incidence in Africa is explained by the long return periods for volcanic eruptions, unlike in other world regions that are more exposed to volcanic risk. The high loss-to-event ratio indicates low resilience and this was demonstrated in the volcanic eruption of Mount Nyiragongo, which destroyed 40 per cent of buildings and displaced 250,000 persons in Goma (Democratic Republic of Congo) in 2002.[102]

Neo-liberal policies ... have scaled down state responsibilities for risk reduction and response...

African rates of urbanization are the most rapid in the world, albeit from a low base. The poverty of countries in this region severely limits household coping capacity and the capacity of governments to build resilience and undertake risk reduction. There is a growing and, in some cities, strong civil society presence that provides coordination for grass-roots actions. The lack of regional governance for risk reduction is a serious limiting factor preventing South–South learning across the region. Limited capacity to regulate industry also means urban settlements in this region have among the highest rates of industrial disaster worldwide. Widespread poverty and vulnerability make this region highly susceptible to the local impacts of global environmental change. Vulnerability is exacerbated by conflict, chronic disease and weak governance.

North African countries have higher levels of urbanization and development than sub-Saharan Africa. Poverty and inequality remain high; but government risk reduction capacity is stronger than in sub-Saharan Africa, although in some states limited civil society presence constrains the building of resilience outside of state-sanctioned activities. In this sub-region, risk management is led by technological and engineering sectors. For example, great advances have been made in mapping urban earthquake risk and designing earthquake-proof structures. A lack of focus on governance and social development has created challenges for implementing and enforcing codes.

Americas

Across all regions, the Americas experience the greatest economic loss from natural disasters (see Table 7.10). In 2005, Hurricane Katrina alone caused US$81.2 billion in economic damage in the US (see Table 7.3). Windstorms (including hurricanes and tornadoes) are the most frequent type of disaster, affect the greatest number of people and cause the highest total economic costs. In turn, windstorms can trigger flooding and landslides. Indeed, flooding is a high incidence event that causes the greatest number of deaths for any disaster type in the region and also records a high mortality count. In 1998, Hurricane Mitch devastated Honduras and Nicaragua, killing over 9000 people, many of whom lost their lives to landslides.[103] The impacts of volcanic eruptions have been limited despite the region experiencing 46 per cent of the global recorded events from 1996 to 2005. This suggests good levels of resilience to this hazard type.

North America is a wealthy and highly urbanized region. Canada and the US have strong states and active civil societies providing top-down and bottom-up risk reduction capacity. Mexico is a large economy with a strong state and active civil society, but is weakened by extensive poverty and tensions in governance, particularly related to indigenous and marginal urban and rural populations. Neo-liberal policies, particularly in the US and more recently in Mexico, have scaled down state responsibilities for risk reduction and response and placed greater emphasis on the role of private citizens and companies. This has had mixed results for urban

Table 7.10

Disaster incidence and impacts in the Americas (1996–2005)

Note: For all disaster types, small events with less than 10 mortalities or 100 affected people are not included.

Source: EM-DAT, CRED database, University of Louvain, Belgium, www.em-dat.net

	Number of events	Mortality	People affected (thousands)	Economic loss (US$ million, 2005 value)
Avalanches/landslides	42	1632	203	97
Drought/famines	51	54	15,287	4094
Earthquakes/tsunamis	45	2861	3757	7689
Extreme temperatures	33	1597	4037	5620
Floods	281	38,028	9525	27,903
Volcanic eruptions	23	54	283	22
Windstorms	321	28,110	25,278	234,680
Industrial accidents	39	277	576	1245
Miscellaneous accidents	70	2989	12	1609

Table 7.11

Disaster incidence and impacts in Asia (1996–2005)

	Number of events	Mortality	People affected (thousands)	Economic loss (US$ million, 2005 value)
Avalanches/landslides	112	5464	1579	1265
Drought/famines	87	216,923	639,190	16,380
Earthquakes/tsunamis	171	364,651	33,392	70,060
Extreme temperatures	48	9854	895	3650
Floods	472	42,570	1,255,118	129,055
Volcanic eruptions	13	3	211	3
Windstorms	340	31,900	289,215	62,449
Industrial accidents	361	10,056	716	696
Miscellaneous accidents	220	8401	172	14

Note: For all disaster types, small events with less than 10 mortalities or 100 affected people are not included.

Source: EM-DAT, CRED database, University of Louvain, Belgium, www.em-dat.net

resilience to natural and human-made hazards, as was seen in the failed state response and recovery efforts during Hurricane Katrina in 2005. Technical capacity for disaster risk reduction in the region is very high.

South America is highly urbanized and predominantly middle income. There is large aggregate economic capacity, but also great socio-economic inequality in the cities of the region. Financial and political instability have undermined resilience at all scales. Colombia is worst affected and suffers from significant internal conflict. Despite this, the country has also demonstrated regional leadership in urban planning for risk reduction, saving lives from landslide and earthquake hazards, in particular. Technical capacity is high and, in some countries, this is matched by strong civil society action to build physical and social resilience. Where there is state capacity, industrial hazard is contained through regulation. Earthquake, flood, drought, fire, windstorm and temperature shock are the most important natural hazards for this region.

Central America and the Caribbean comprise the poorest sub-region in the Americas. Urbanization levels are high and cities are characterized by high levels of poverty and inequality. Past political tensions have made for strained civil society–state relations; but there is capacity for coordinated top-down and bottom-up risk reduction. Industrialization is high, with potential for industrial hazard, but is spatially disbursed. Resilience comes from a strong regional level of governance, which reinforces state capacity for early warning and response capacity. Earthquakes, hurricanes and flooding are the primary hazards for this region.

Asia

Asia is the most disaster-prone region. The incidence of disasters associated with avalanches or landslides, earthquakes or tsunamis, floods, windstorms and industrial accidents is higher than for any other region. The high density population means that mortality is highest in this region for all disaster types, with the exception of volcanic eruptions. The number of people affected is also highest in this region, with the exception of volcanic eruptions and extreme temperatures (where more people in the Americas are affected). Economic loss is similarly the highest in this region for all disasters, except for extreme temperatures, volcanic eruptions, industrial accidents (Europe has the highest) and miscellaneous accidents (the Americas have the highest).

Table 7.11 shows the diversity of incidence and impacts within the region. Flooding is the most frequent natural hazard affecting the largest number of people and causing the greatest economic losses. Earthquakes and tsunamis cause the greatest mortality, with the 2004 Indian Ocean Tsunami accounting for around 230,000 deaths.[104] Human-made disasters are also high in their incidence and human impact.

Asia is the most disaster-prone region

The region's high economic and population growth rates make it set to be a major net contributor to global environmental change. Inequality in the region means that this is also a region at high risk from the local impacts of global environmental change.

Southeast Asia, from China to Indonesia, is middle income, with high levels of urbanization and urban growth rates. This region contains many countries with the highest levels of exposure to natural and industrial hazards, but also with great experience of risk management. Capacity for building resilience is limited by governance, with tensions between civil society and state actors found across the region. Political tensions, weaknesses in governance, economic inequality and rising levels of chronic illness are the chief barriers to resilience.

South Asia covers the Indian subcontinent and is a middle- to low-income sub-region. Urbanization is variable, with many large cities and megacities, but also with substantial numbers of intermediate and small settlements. With the exception of Afghanistan, strong states with good administrative capacity have led disaster management. During recent years, civil society has gained in strength, and in India, in particular, partnerships with the state have built resilience. Political tensions in the region and within countries constrain risk reduction capacity.

West and Central Asia includes middle-income states, from Turkey to Uzbekistan and Iran, as well as high-income oil-producing Gulf states. Urbanization and industrialization levels are high. The region is characterized by strong states and weak civil societies. A consequence of this is that risk reduction has tended to be delivered in a top-down manner and is dominated by engineering solutions. There is limited scope for bottom-up initiatives that seek to reduce risk through the building of social and economic capacity. Questions of governance constrain the extent to which top-down risk reduction policies have been effective in reaching the poorest and most marginalized populations with the highest levels of vulnerability. Regulation of industrial standards is similarly weakened, increasing risk from industrial hazard.

Table 7.12

Disaster incidence and impacts in Europe (1996–2005)

Note: For all disaster types, small events with less than 10 mortalities or 100 affected people are not included.

Source: EM-DAT, CRED database, University of Louvain, Belgium, www.em-dat.net

	Number of events	Mortality	People affected (thousands)	Economic loss (US$ million, 2005 value)
Avalanches/landslides	18	389	14	20
Drought/famines	14	0	1063	8019
Earthquakes/tsunamis	52	18,584	4016	29,609
Extreme temperatures	79	48,630	771	6706
Floods	229	1422	5048	47,860
Volcanic eruptions	2	0	0	24
Windstorms	110	610	7025	18,138
Industrial accidents	56	844	71	11,100
Miscellaneous accidents	73	1474	14	874

Europe

The role played by relatively high levels of economic development and political stability in shifting the impact of disasters from human to physical assets can be seen most clearly in this region (see Table 7.12). This is exemplified by volcanic eruptions, where Europe suffers the highest economic losses of any region, but no people have been killed or affected. Vulnerability and human loss is highest, compared to other world regions, for extreme temperature events. Between 1996 and 2005, Europe experienced 47 per cent of all extreme temperature events, but 81 per cent of all mortalities. Compared with Europe, the Americas experienced less than half the number of extreme weather events, with comparatively few deaths, but four times the number affected. This reflects the different severity of events, but also greater investment in early warning and response for extreme temperature in the Americas.

Oceania records the lowest incidence of disasters for any region and hazard type…

Within Europe, floods were the most common disaster between 1996 and 2005. Mortality was highest for extreme temperatures, with around 35,000 premature deaths from the 2003 heat wave alone.[105]

Europe is a high-income and highly urbanized region. Risk profiles for this region are split between the east and west. Western Europe has strong states and civil societies providing good capacity for resilience. It is also a region with relatively low levels of hazard exposure. Eastern Europe is more variable, with examples of strong states but weak civil society, and with governance challenges that limit regulation of industrial activity and capacity for top-down programmes aimed at vulnerability reduction. This region is also economically poorer than Western Europe.

Oceania

Oceania records the lowest incidence of disasters for any region and hazard type, with the exception of volcanic eruption (see Table 7.13). This is the only region not to record any industrial accidents from 1996 to 2005. The region had the lowest economic losses and absolute number of people killed and affected by all disaster types. Within the region, disasters are most commonly associated with windstorms, and these result in the greatest economic losses. Earthquakes and tsunamis account for the highest levels of mortality.

The region is of mixed economic status, but with high levels of urbanization. Poorer countries also tend to have greater political tensions, often between indigenous and immigrant populations. Many are small island developing states facing particular governance challenges within a context of limited human resources. Larger countries, especially New Zealand and Australia, have strong states and civil societies, as well as robust economies. Yet, inequality undermines resilience in these multicultural societies. For low-lying small island states, sea-level rise due to climate change will have catastrophic implications.

CONCLUDING REMARKS

Urban disasters are a product of failed urban governance and planning. Wealth is necessary for building resilience at the local and city levels, but is not sufficient in the absence of governance. Without good governance and open participation in urban planning, economic development too often leads to inequality and failures to implement regulation in the industrial and residential sectors.

The relationships between urbanization and disaster risk are dynamic. Past urban civilizations have collapsed

Table 7.13

Disaster incidence and impacts in Oceania (1996–2005)

Note: For all disaster types, small events with less than 10 mortalities or 100 affected people are not included.

Source: EM-DAT, CRED database, University of Louvain, Belgium, www.em-dat.net

	Number of events	Mortality	People affected (thousands)	Economic loss (US$ million, 2005 value)
Avalanches/landslides	8	128	1	No data
Drought/famines	8	88	1083	329
Earthquakes/tsunamis	9	2201	36	No data
Extreme temperatures	1	0	0	221
Floods	38	34	96	1735
Volcanic eruptions	7	4	49	No data
Windstorms	72	255	832	2859
Industrial accidents	0	0	0	No data
Miscellaneous accidents	4	46	12	No data

because of overstretching the ecological basis of their economies, leading to political conflict and terminal decline. Future new risks might include those associated with global environmental change and also with the increasing connectivity of urban centres worldwide that enables the transmission of economic impacts through transport and finance networks.

Global hazard maps can be used to indicate the distribution of risk. Richer countries are most at risk from absolute economic loss, whereas poorer countries suffer more human loss, as well as economic loss, as a proportion of GDP. Human-made risk and recorded loss is greatest in low-income countries, especially in sub-Saharan Africa. The largest concentrations of urban populations, in megacities, represent focal points for urban risk, especially those cities exposed to multiple hazards and with limited capacity for risk management.

Disaster impacts are seldom fully measured. This is a particular problem for cities since they house much of the accumulated cultural heritage of the world. Direct economic loss from damage and human impacts can be accounted for; but longer-term impacts on economies, or individual loss and psychological trauma, are much more difficult to measure. Disaster losses are often compounded when one event triggers a secondary event, or when recovery and reconstruction activities lead to ecological damage and social disruption. The social and political impacts of disasters are especially sensitive to reconstruction, with this being an opportunity for improvements in governance, as well as in basic needs.

This chapter identified the following aspects of urbanization that shape disaster risk:

1 Large cities and megacities concentrate and magnify risk.
2 Smaller cities (less than 500,000 residents) that are home to just over half of the world's urban population also experience exposure to multiple risks, but are likely to have limited formal capacity and organized civil society with which to build resilience.
3 Ongoing demographic and social changes in cities are a challenge since social groups at risk may alter, requiring flexibility in disaster management. Nevertheless, the economically poor, politically marginalized and socially isolated (often women) are consistently the most vulnerable.
4 Urbanization processes modify the hazard profile of the city directly – for example, through the urbanization of hill slopes and floodplains – but also indirectly as the impacts of climate change hit cities (the sites for a large proportion of greenhouse gas emissions).
5 Building standards are in place in almost all cities, but they are seldom implemented. This, more than any other policy challenge, highlights the need for social policy to connect with technical and engineering solutions to risk management.
6 The increasing numbers of urban residents forced to live in slums and squatter settlements is an indication of the depth of failure of urban governance to provide even the most basic needs and to protect the political, social, economic and cultural rights of all. Slums and squatter settlements are places of great hazard, but also of great potential. Governance structures that can partner with this local energy can reduce risk.
7 Urban planning is seriously under capacity in most cities. It is almost impossible for many planning departments to keep pace with rapid urbanization. New techniques in urban planning are needed that can extend formal practices into the informal housing sector. Meeting the MDGs is dependent upon this.

Taking urban disaster risk management seriously requires an integrated approach. For this reason, it is of concern that very few national Poverty Reduction Strategy Papers include risk management. Although it is not unusual for urban plans to integrate hazard mitigation, the next step is to match this with a commitment for vulnerability reduction that includes relevant social and economic policy.

Comparing urban risk at the regional scale re-emphasizes the centrality of urban governance as a driver for urban risk profiles. In those cities where strong government and civil society sectors take risk reduction seriously, great gains can be made.

NOTES

1 One exception is the Australian government, which defines a small disaster as one where state expenditure (on all assistance measures) does not exceed AU$240,000 (US$185,500), roughly equivalent to the cost of repairing 20 houses.
2 Kasperson et al, 1996.
3 Blaikie et al, 1994.
4 Data is drawn from the EM-DAT, CRED database. Only events that exceed a minimum threshold of 10 deaths, 100 people affected or a call for international assistance or declaration of a state of emergency are included. Consequently, many small disasters will have been excluded. This is likely to have affected data on transport and is also reflected in the absence of a category for house fires.
5 This is a term used in EM-DAT, CRED to describe accidents involving mechanized modes of transport. It comprises of four disaster subsets involving air, boat, rail and road accidents.
6 The current millennium has been dubbed the 'urban millennium' given that, in 2007, for the first time in history, the world's urban population will equal the rural population (UN-Habitat, 2006e).
7 Kreimer et al, 2003.
8 IFRC, 2003.
9 *Ibid*.
10 A global geography of natural disaster risk based on exposed populations and past losses (1980 to 2001) illustrates that both predominantly rural and urban regions are at risk worldwide. Loss to hydrological hazard (floods, landslides and hurricanes) is most widespread, affecting human settlements in China, Southeast Asia and Central America, and in a band from Eastern Europe through Central and Eastern Asia. Loss to geological hazard (earthquakes and volcano eruptions) is most concentrated in Central Asia and the Mediterranean and Pacific Rim states (e.g. Japan, the US and Central America). The Americas show variable loss, with low levels of loss in North America. Central Asia is exposed to losses from the greatest number of hazard types. Likewise, the Black Sea region, Central America and Japan face multiple hazards. Data from Dilley et al, 2005; maps also adapted from this source.
11 *Ibid*.
12 *Ibid*.
13 EM-DAT, CRED, University of Louvain, Belgium,

www.em-dat.net/ (includes industrial accidents, miscellaneous accidents and transport accidents).

14 This was calculated using data from EM-DAT, CRED, which only includes loss data for events with at least 10 mortalities, 100 people affected, a national state of emergency or a call for international assistance. Thus, the many smaller natural and human-made disasters were not included in this calculation of mortality per event.
15 Munich Re, 2004.
16 *Ibid.*
17 Özerdem and Barakat, 2000.
18 See Washington (2007) for some insight into the ways in which different psychological orientations influence decision-making.
19 Guha-Sapir et al, 2004.
20 Yong et al, 1988.
21 Conchesco, 2003.
22 McGranahan et al, 2001; Benson and Twigg, 2004; ECLAC, 2004.
23 ISDR, 2003.
24 O'Rourke et al, 2006.
25 Ministry of the Environment, Republic of Indonesia (undated).
26 Tsunami Evaluation Coalition, 2006.
27 UNEP, 2005.
28 Shiozaki et al, 2005.
29 Guha Sapir et al, 2004.
30 Swiss Re, 2007.
31 These are aggregate figures and economic damages per event are higher in the Americas than in Asia, where there is a greater frequency of events.
32 UNCRD, 1995.
33 Özerdem and Barakat, 2000.
34 Pelling et al, 2002.
35 Munich Re, 2004.
36 Wisner et al, 2004.
37 Guha-Sapir, 1997.
38 Bern, 1993.
39 Enarson, 2000.
40 *Ibid.*
41 Norris (undated).
42 Bern, 1993.
43 Delgado et al, 2002.
44 Klinenberg, 2002a.
45 Twigg, 2004.
46 Freudenheim, 1980, cited in Albala-Bertrand, 1993.
47 Abney and Hill, 1966.
48 Taboroff, 2003.
49 UNDP, 2004; UNESCO at http://whc.unesco.org.
50 Vecvagars, 2006.
51 See, for example, debates summarized from the United Nations World Conference on Disaster Reduction, Kobe, 2005, session on Cultural Heritage Risk Management, www.unisdr.org/wcdr/thematic-sessions/thematic-reports/report-session-3-3.pdf.
52 United Nations, 2005; Clark, 2000.
53 UN-Habitat, 2006e.
54 Harris, 1995.
55 Shrivastava, 1996.
56 Cities with 1 million to 5 million inhabitants are defined as intermediate, while cities with more than 10 million inhabitants are referred to as megacities (UN-Habitat, 2006e, p5).
57 UN-Habitat, 2006e.
58 Cross, 2001.
59 Hardoy et al, 2001.
60 Astill, 2004.
61 National Labour Committee, El Salvador, 2001.
62 McGranahan et al, 2001.
63 Tibaijuka, 2006.
64 IFRC, 1999.
65 Nicholls, 2004.
66 Quarantelli, 2003.
67 See www.adpc.net/audmp/India.html.
68 Satterthwaite, 2006.
69 *Ibid.*
70 Klein et al, 2003.
71 McGranahan et al, 2007.
72 IPCC, 2001.
73 Barrios et al, 2006.
74 UNEP and UN-Habitat, 2005.
75 Satterthwaite, 2006.
76 Pelling, 2003.
77 UN-Habitat, 2006e.
78 Blaikie et al, 1994.
79 General Secretariat Central American Integration System, 1999.
80 UN-Habitat, 2003d.
81 Sharma and Gupta, 1998.
82 Rashid, 2000.
83 Wisner, 1999.
84 Brown, 1994.
85 Özerdem and Barakat, 2000.
86 Kreimer and Munasinghe, 1992.
87 Save the Children, 2006.
88 ISDR, 2005a.
89 Revi, 2005.
90 Patel et al, 2002.
91 Government of Maharashtra, Department of Relief and Rehabilitation (undated).
92 Dossal, 2005.
93 Tunstall et al, 2004.
94 Mitchell, 1999.
95 Pelling, 1997.
96 Alexander, 1989.
97 UNDP, 2004; and ISDR at www.unisdr.org.
98 Walton and Seddon, 1994.
99 DFID, 2005.
100 Freeman, 2004.
101 Anderson, 1990.
102 www.volcanolive.com/news16.html.
103 www.nhc.noaa.gov/1998mitch.html.
104 www.oxfam.org.au/world/emergencies/asia_tsunami.html.
105 Bhattachatya, 2003.

CHAPTER 8

POLICY RESPONSES TO DISASTER RISK

A variety of actors, ranging from the international to the local level, have sought to reduce disaster risk in urban areas through policy responses and interventions. While urban risk reduction policies are in their infancy, or altogether absent in some contexts, a number of innovative strategies have been developed and implemented successfully elsewhere. Risk reduction policies are also differentiated in terms of their orientation to shorter-term reconstruction and response needs or development-oriented strategies seeking to reduce vulnerability in the long term. These differences are partly shaped by the resources and technical capacity available to national and local actors, but also by their political will and commitment.

The aim of this chapter is to assess the policy responses of urban local authorities, national governments, civil society and the international community to disasters, both natural and human made. Responses designed to mitigate disaster impacts involve land-use planning, the design of buildings and infrastructure, early warning and emergency response systems. Hazard and vulnerability assessment techniques used to identify the locus and potential impacts of disasters are particularly useful in informing policy priorities and decisions. A critical and increasingly prevalent policy response to disaster risk focuses on strengthening household and local disaster resilience through social, legal and economic pathways. Protecting critical infrastructure and services, without which disaster response and recovery is obstructed, is also recognized as a necessary component of disaster risk reduction in cities. Financing disaster risk management remains a challenge and points to a critical role for the international community.

DISASTER RISK ASSESSMENT

The rapid growth of urban areas has, in many cases, far outstripped national and local capacities for formal data collection or planning services. Thus, a major challenge for responding to disaster risk is to assess human vulnerability, hazard and risk in a way that can enable action from national, international and local actors. Disaster risk assessment encompasses techniques that seek to determine (in quantitative or qualitative terms) 'the nature and extent of risk by analysing potential hazards and evaluating existing conditions of vulnerability that could pose a potential threat or harm to people, property, livelihoods and the environment on which they depend'.[1]

Risk assessment contributes to disaster risk reduction by informing policy priorities and decisions on resource expenditure. To effect change, risk assessment needs to be incorporated within new policies or legislation for disaster risk reduction. If undertaken in a participatory manner, the process of risk assessment can build local capacity and generate shared understanding of common threats and opportunities.[2] Risk assessments also provide information that is useful at all stages of the disaster risk reduction continuum: in everyday development planning, as part of preparedness and prevention pre-disaster, as well as in response and reconstruction post-disaster. There are at least ten kinds of information that risk assessment can provide:[3]

...a major challenge for responding to disaster risk is to assess human vulnerability, hazard and risk...

1 Identify those hazards from which an area is at risk.
2 Identify the location, character and probability of risks for relative risk assessment.
3 Determine who and what are vulnerable, relative vulnerabilities, and pathways that have been generated and maintained by people and places in states of vulnerability.
4 Assess the capacities and resources available for those at risk to ameliorate their vulnerability.
5 Identify perceptions of risk held by those people at risk.
6 Determine levels of risk that are acceptable to those at risk and the wider society.
7 Generate input for forecasting future human vulnerability, hazard and risk.
8 Provide input to decision-making for policy and project decision-making.
9 Generate assessments of the capacity of municipal and national governments to undertake reconstruction following disaster.
10 Catalyse the raising of risk awareness locally and among policy-makers.

Risk assessment involves not only an evaluation of hazards, but also the vulnerability of humans and the built and natural environment vis-à-vis an analysis of exposure to hazard and susceptibility to harm, as well as capacity to respond to disasters. Hazard and risk assessments employ a range of techniques, from quantitative analysis built around scenario modelling and mapping to qualitative, non-technical approaches, depending upon the kinds of data that need to be generated.

Hazard mapping

...technical advances ... for hazard mapping ... are often lacking in developing countries...

Hazard assessment involves an analysis of the likelihood of occurrence of natural or human-made hazards in a specific future time period, including their intensity and area of impact.[4] Data generated through hazard assessments needs to be presented to decision-makers and communities at risk to raise awareness and enable the design of appropriate interventions and policies. One approach is the use of maps to depict the spatial location, size and frequency of hazards. This allows general statements to be made about the exposure of national urban systems and individual cities to hazards.

Mapping natural hazard

At the global scale, hazard mapping is well advanced for volcanic, earthquake, flood, wind and landslide hazards.[5] Many countries also have national hazard maps, particularly of geophysical hazards. While global- and national-scale hazard maps can help to identify national legislative or policy planning priorities, planning at the city level requires more detailed information. Many cities in middle- and high-income countries, particularly those which are administrative or industrial centres, have detailed single and multi-hazard maps. During the last decade, the number of cities with seismic hazard maps has increased.[6] Other hazards, such as flooding and extreme temperatures, vary spatially, requiring more continuous monitoring and mapping, which can be more costly.

The advent of geographic information systems (GIS), coupled with satellite imagery of disaster events, have revolutionized the amount of data that is now available worldwide. While technical advances have increased the potential for hazard mapping, they have also generated inequalities in hazard assessment capacities. Technical approaches require financial investment in hardware and human resources that are often lacking in developing countries and are beyond reach for poorer urban authorities. Partnerships between technical advisory bodies and national centres for disaster management offer a potential mechanism for technology and skill transfer. One example of this is the Government of India–United Nations Development Programme (UNDP) Urban Earthquake Vulnerability Reduction Project, shown in Box 8.1.[7]

Low-impact, high-frequency hazards are less likely to be mapped, despite their erosive impact on human health

Box 8.1 India's national hazard map: A foundation for coordinated disaster risk reduction

An example of cooperation in disaster risk reduction between an international organization and a national government is the Government of India–United Nations Development Programme (UNDP) Disaster Risk Management Programme. A key subcomponent of this programme is the Urban Earthquake Vulnerability Reduction Project, implemented between 2003 and 2007. The project aims to raise awareness of earthquake risk in urban areas among decision-makers and the public and to improve disaster preparedness.

Several of India's populous cities, including the capital, New Delhi, are located in zones of high seismic risk. National data on seismic hazard has been used to identify 38 cities with populations of 500,000 or more that have become the focus for the project. The map in Figure 8.1 was developed by the project and shows four levels of seismic risk and 60 cities from which the 38 partner cities were selected.

Key expected outcomes of the project, among others, include enhanced disaster risk management capacity, effective administrative and institutional frameworks for earthquake risk management in the most exposed urban centres, and development of emergency, preparedness and recovery plans for those urban centres. The project also intends to build local capacity for risk assessment, preparedness and response.

Source: adapted from UNDP India, www.undp.org.in/index.php?option=com_content&task=view&id=?84&Itemid=264

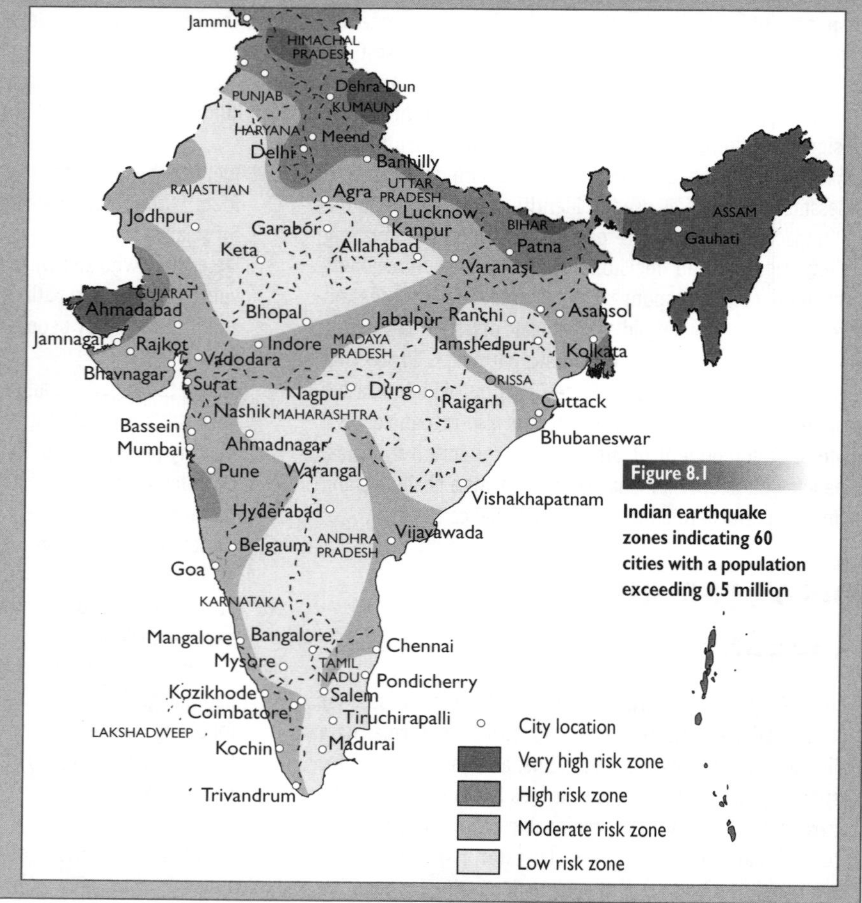

Figure 8.1

Indian earthquake zones indicating 60 cities with a population exceeding 0.5 million

and livelihoods. This gap has been filled in some neighbourhoods by community-based hazard and risk mapping projects. This data, combined with national- and city-level records of past events, can be used to identify priorities for urban planning and construction standards.

Less information is available at the global scale for hazards that affect the lifelines to a city such as drought, or emerging hazards such as heat and cold shocks. Global-scale data can be used to extend analyses of hazard exposure beyond the municipal boundary to demonstrate the vulnerability of cities to disasters affecting their hinterland by disrupting trade, or blocking access and flows of resources and waste.

Mapping human-made hazard

National directories of human-made hazards are becoming more common, and many are open to the public. In the UK, the Environment Agency hosts a pollution and hazardous waste sites inventory. This is searchable by postal code and also provides information on water quality and flood hazard.[8] In the US, Green Media's Toolshed website includes a searchable scorecard, which provides data on chemicals being released from any of 20,000 industrial facilities, or a summary report for any area in the country.[9] More difficult is the mapping of human-made risk associated with industrial facilities, buildings' integrity or transport infrastructure. Much of the information needed to build comparative hazard datasets is commercially valuable and therefore not released to the public.

Local authority land-use planning maps and schedules include information on industrial sites where hazardous activities are undertaken, and can be used as a basis for urban industrial hazard mapping. This is particularly valuable for assessing the risk of human-made disasters caused by natural hazards. More difficult is the acquisition of data on informal-sector industrial activities, such as tanneries or fireworks factories. These might not represent a significant hazard individually; but, in aggregate, unplanned industrial activity is a major risk to health from air, water and ground pollution and from fire and explosion hazards. Risk is heightened because of the unregulated nature of informal industrial activity and its close proximity to densely settled residential areas.

Risk assessments for individual cities

As noted in Chapter 7, there is limited comparative data on natural disaster risk and impacts at the city level. Two initiatives have made major contributions at this level of analysis – namely, the Natural Hazards Risk Index for Megacities by Munich Re (see Chapter 7)[10] and the Earthquake Disaster Risk Index used by GeoHazards International (GHI).

GHI developed and applied an Earthquake Lethality Estimation Method in 2000/2001. The method produces results that indicate the relative severity of earthquake risk, the sources of risk within each city, and the relative effectiveness of potential mitigation options. The same results are also produced for the exposure of school children to collapse of educational buildings. The method was applied to cities in the Americas and Asia, differentiated by city size (see Box 8.2).

Box 8.2 Estimating urban loss of life to earthquakes

GeoHazards International's (GHI) Earthquake Lethality Estimation Method estimates the number of lives that would be lost if all parts of a city experience earthquake shaking at a level that has a 10 per cent chance of being equalled or exceeded in 50 years. The method has been applied to assess the risk of life loss in 22 cities in the Americas and Asia. Deaths caused by building collapse, earthquake-induced landslides and fires are included. Capacity for organized search, rescue and emergency medical care is also considered. Results are validated over time through a comparison of estimates with actual loss. GHI's approach is especially noteworthy because of its emphasis on the safety of school children, which reflects the vulnerability of schools.

Data is collected through meetings with local experts and city officials dealing with seismology, soils and landslides; city planning; building inventory; school buildings; emergency response; medical emergency preparedness; hospital emergency preparedness; and fire preparedness.

Results show great variation in the risk of earthquake-induced loss of life in cities. For example, in the American region, a person living in Mexicali is almost three times more likely to be killed by an earthquake than a person living in Quito, and about ten times more likely than a person living in Santiago. In the Asian region, a person living in Kathmandu is about nine times more likely to be killed by an earthquake than a person living in Islamabad and about 60 times more likely than a person living in Tokyo.

GHI's approach is also able to identify differences in the immediate causes of death and, thus, guide the subsequent development of mitigation strategies and policies. For example, in a comparison between Delhi and San Salvador, while most of the deaths in Delhi will be due to building collapse and earthquake-induced fires, an important fraction of the deaths in San Salvador will be due to earthquake-induced landslides.

The analysis of school risk also shows differentiated vulnerability across cities. A school child in Kathmandu is 400 times more likely to be killed by an earthquake than a school child in Kobe and 30 times more likely than a school child in Tashkent.

Source: GHI, 2001

The philosophy of GHI is that loss estimation is both a process and a product. The process aspect engages decision-makers at the community and city levels and recognizes that data alone is insufficient to effect change in human behaviour. The process of assessment includes local expertise and favours rapid assessment that can feed into ongoing decision-making over possibly more accurate, but also more costly and less participatory, methods. Readily available information is supported with data from local experts. The final results allow a quantitative assessment of the effectiveness of mitigation options under consideration.

...there is limited comparative data on natural disaster risk and impacts at the city level

Including indicators for social vulnerability in risk assessment at the city level is difficult since it requires the availability of relevant data on population and social indicators. For instance, research on risk of heat waves in London has used census data and is appropriate for those countries that have spatially disaggregated and high-quality census data.[11] In the majority of cities, especially those that are rapidly expanding in poorer countries, this is not a reliable source of data. Other methods, such as the use of satellite information on night-time lights and fires, offer an alternative, but still not comprehensive, measurement of population density in rapidly expanding and poor cities.

Comparison of disaster risk between districts within a city has rarely been undertaken. One example of this

Box 8.3 Multidisciplinary assessment of urban seismic risk, Bogotá City, Colombia

The Holistic Vulnerability Index uses a novel methodology for incorporating social as well as physical indicators of vulnerability, and combining these with seismic hazard data to produce an assessment of urban seismic risk. The index has been applied to 19 districts of Bogotá City in Colombia. Four variables are included in the measurement of the physical vulnerability of buildings and public infrastructure:

- damaged area in square kilometres;
- mortality and number of injured;
- ruptures to water mains, gas networks and power lines; and
- number of telephone exchanges and electricity substations affected.

Hazard is measured by combining data on the propensity of each zone for accelerating seismic energy and on soil type influencing proneness to seismic amplification, susceptibility to liquefaction and landslides. Social vulnerability is measured from the sum of three compound indexes:

Exposure: population exposed, density of population exposed, exposed areas, including built areas, industrial areas and areas under government use (health, education, administration, etc.).

Social fragility: areas of illegal or marginal human settlement, annual rate of mortality by natural causes, annual number of crimes per 1000 inhabitants, and level of unsatisfied basic needs.

Resilience: number of hospital beds, number of medical professionals, area of space available for emergency housing, number of emergency and rescue workers, including trained volunteers, overall development level, preparedness, and emergency planning as appraised by a relevant city authority.

Results show the complexity and context specificity of processes leading to seismic risk. Those districts recording the highest levels of calculated risk included the middle-income districts of Tesaquillo, Chapinero and Usaquen, as well as the low-income districts of San Cristóbal, Usme and Ciudad Bolivar.

The advantage of such an approach is that it presents multiple aspects of risk simultaneously to decision-makers. This can be a pressure to put the social as well as the physical aspects of vulnerability centre stage in integrated urban planning. The 2000 Urban Master Plan for Bogotá took the results of this model into consideration.

Source: Carreño, 2007

approach is the Holistic Vulnerability Index,[12] calculated only in relation to seismic risk. It measures disaster risk as the probability of a loss occurring as a consequence of a seismic hazard with a defined magnitude over a given time. It includes indicators for physical and social vulnerability, thus demonstrating to decision-makers the need for work on both fronts. The index has been applied to various districts of Bogotá City (Colombia), and results were considered in the preparation of the 2000 Urban Master Plan for Bogotá (see Box 8.3).

In even the richest countries, there is a lack comprehensive hazards databases

Assessing human-made hazard risk

Human-made hazard risk assessments tend to be driven by a hazards focus and employ GIS software. Vulnerability is sometimes indicated through population distribution, which reflects the limited availability of geo-referenced social data. However, as has been found with urban heat shocks, social variables affecting information flows and access to resources will influence individual exposure and susceptibility through, for example, variable abilities to seek timely medical assistance.

Internet tools have the potential to greatly increase public access to geographical hazard and social data. For example, in the US, the Environmental Protection Agency,[13] the Department of Housing and Urban Development[14] and the New York Public Interest Research Group host internet resources that enable the mapping of hazardous facilities, public projects and Brownfield sites. These become powerful risk-mapping tools when combined with data from other sites that provides demographic and socio-economic characteristics of the proximate populations.[15]

GIS mapping of technological/industrial hazard and social vulnerability is faced with a number of challenges. In even the richest countries, there is a lack of comprehensive hazards databases. In some countries, industrial hazard is hidden behind commercial secrecy. Where point source data for hazards are available, modelling the geographic extent of exposure and the characteristics of affected populations is problematic. Developing models for hazards where there has only been limited experience of the health consequences of exposure is difficult. In many instances, little is known of the long-term health effects of exposure to chemicals that can cross generations. Advances in modelling and the use of proxy data sources provide ways for technological improvement; but the underlying paucity of data is much harder to address without political will.

Participatory risk assessments

Perhaps the most extensive collection of methodologies comes from participatory risk assessments. This includes a variety of approaches, all drawn from the tradition of participatory approaches.[16] Many international and national non-governmental organizations (NGOs) have developed participatory methodologies that aim to provide a structured way for local actors to reflect on the hazards, vulnerabilities and capacities influencing their lives. Examples include the International Federation of the Red Cross and Red Crescent's Vulnerability and Capacity Assessment,[17] as well as ActionAid's Participatory Vulnerability Analysis.[18]

Impetus for promoting participatory approaches in risk assessment has been provided by the Hyogo Framework

Box 8.4 How participatory is urban disaster assessment?

It is possible to assess the extent to which disaster risk assessment methodologies are participatory according to the following three features of participatory approaches:

Procedural
This differentiates approaches according to the relative distribution of power and ownership in the assessment process. At one extreme are approaches that are initiated, planned and conducted by local actors at risk, who might also be the audience for, and owners of, the results. At the other extreme are assessments that include local actors only as subjects of study or as sources of data or future project inputs.

Methodological
The chief distinction here is between the application of methods of data collection, aggregation and analysis that are quantitative or qualitative. It is often assumed that participatory approaches are predominantly qualitative; but this is not always the case. Particularly where some aggregation and up-scaling of local survey results is desired for national policy, the collection of quantitative data is included in participatory approaches. Qualitative methods are useful for collecting information, especially with marginalized populations; but this may, in turn, be aggregated for quantitative analysis.

Ideological
This distinguishes between emancipatory and extractive approaches. Emancipatory approaches tend to see participatory work as a long-term and iterative process, and as a mechanism for participants to reflect on the social, political and physical root causes of their vulnerability and level of resilience. This scope for reflection is sometimes given higher priority as an output than the generation of data for its own sake. Assessments might be initiated and/or facilitated by non-local actors, but would become owned by those at risk as empowerment takes hold. Extractive approaches are concerned primarily with the collection of data to be used by external actors, and are not intended to contribute to learning among respondents.

Source: Pelling, forthcoming

No single definition for participatory, risk assessment exists at present

for Action 2005–2015,[19] which states as a general consideration, that:

> *Both communities and local authorities should be empowered to manage and reduce disaster risk by having access to the necessary information, resources and authority to implement actions for disaster risk reduction.* (Section III A, point 13.f)

Participatory approaches offer specific entry points for this agenda.

No single definition for participatory risk assessment exists at present. Approaches are variously termed participatory, community based or local.[20] The lack of a single nomenclature reflects the diversity of interests and agencies involved with participatory approaches (and also the contentiousness of meanings attributed to terms such as participation and community). However, a lack of common understanding also opens this field of work to misplaced or exaggerated claims of participation, inclusiveness and empowerment.

Some generalizations of contemporary participatory risk assessment can be made. Mainstream extractive approaches (e.g. disaster impact household assessments) tend to be quantitative, owned by the executing or funding agency and not intended to confront existing power inequalities. In contrast, participatory approaches claim to utilize qualitative methods that produce data owned by the subjects of the research and contribute to local empowerment through the research process. However, the loose attribution of participatory status to various assessment methods has meant that this category has also been widely used to describe interventions that may use quantitative methods, where the subjects of the research rarely own the outputs or set the research agenda, and with scant evidence on the contribution of methodologies to the processes of empowerment.

As shown in Box 8.4, three aspects of so-called participatory approaches that allow closer scrutiny of the participatory claim of risk assessment have been proposed.[21] The procedural, methodological and ideological character of an assessment tool will depend upon its strategic use (e.g. is it seen as a stand-alone tool or conceptualized as part of a larger suite of tools?), its conceptual orientation (is the aim to identify local vulnerabilities and capacities with respect to a specific hazard type, or to undertake a more generic assessment?) and the position of the observer (a local resident might perceive the same tool very differently from an external implementer).

Identifying the social, political and economic root cause of vulnerability is the first step in ...risk reduction

Those who employ participatory methodologies that aim towards empowerment should be careful not to raise false expectations among participants. Participatory methods can be counterproductive if they do not point to ways of raising resources to reduce risk. Identifying the social, political and economic root causes of vulnerability is the first step in making change; but resources and skills are needed to build and apply capacity for risk reduction. It might not be possible to resolve a hazard in the short term; but the building of resilience through social capacity, information and risk awareness through local risk assessments are outcomes in themselves. Box 8.5 shows an example from Lima (Peru), where a participatory methodology has contributed to the building of resilience through the strengthening of local capacity to undertake risk assessment.

The range of options for strengthening local resilience, in which participatory risk assessments can play a valuable part, are discussed in more detail later in the section on 'Strengthening local disaster resilience'.

Box 8.5 Risk assessment strengthens local capacity and resilience in Lima, Peru

Located along the boundary of two tectonic plates, Lima is at risk from earthquakes, floods and landslides. One of the city's high-risk zones is Caquetá, a highly congested area with large amounts of waste produced by street traders and an irregular rubbish collection service. An estimated 15,500 people live in Caquetá in 3000 formal and informal dwellings consisting of a mixture of wooden shacks and four- and five-storey concrete frame/brick-infill and rendered houses. The Caquetá ravine, cut through by the Rimac River, is a site for a potentially deadly combination of hazard and vulnerability. Poorly enforced building and planning codes, high densities and rapid urbanization (due to its proximity to commercial locations) combine with frequent landslides to increase the vulnerability of the squatter housing perched on the ravine edge. As a result, shelter damage and collapse are frequent, with losses of investments and sometimes lives.

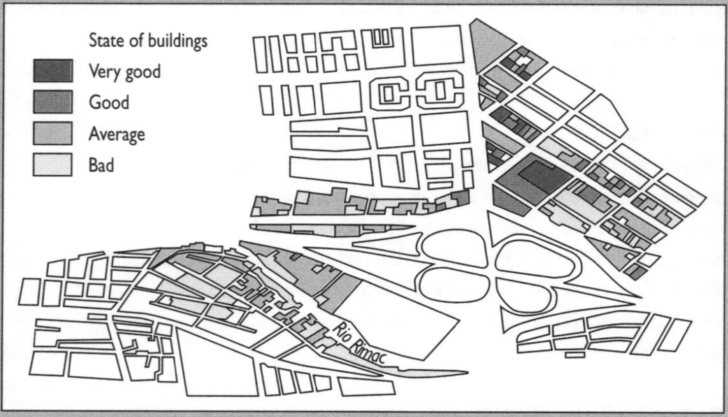

A risk assessment was undertaken – jointly by the Oxford Centre for Disaster Studies and the Peruvian non-governmental organization (NGO) Instituto Para la Democracia Local – to gather data on hazard, vulnerability and capacity to be used for the formulation of 'risk reduction action plans. Data was gathered on the ravine area, informal markets and a consolidated squatter area in Caquetá.

The assessment was undertaken using a combination of research tools. Participatory rural appraisal tools were applied during meetings with housing and market association representatives. Activities included community mapping; time-line development to link the accumulation of risk with local disasters and recovery; the development of disaster matrices recording views of causes and possible solutions; and hazard ranking. Additional research tools included the review of existing research, preparation of maps identifying building and infrastructure standards, and administration of questionnaires with households and organizations.

The assessment helped to build relations with key actors at community, NGO and municipality levels and, importantly, provided credibility for the initiative among authorities. Findings from the assessment and the relationships built up in the process led to a three-day workshop attended by 30 representatives of local associations, municipalities, local NGOs, the fire service and international NGOs. Key problems were presented and participants scoped ideas for workable solutions. These included training for fire awareness, ravine improvement through lobbying, and information exchange. As a result of the workshop, local groups, including communities and the municipality, began to communicate more frequently, and the importance of risk awareness and vulnerability reduction was recognized.

Figure 8.2

Participatory mapping of building quality: Caquetá ravine in Lima, Peru

Source: Sanderson, 1997

Risk, in any one place, is an outcome of decision-making and action – or inaction- at local, municipal, national and international scales

Challenges of urban risk assessments

Risk assessments are undertaken at a range of scales, from the local to the global. There is great diversity in the target of assessments (people, buildings and the urban economy), in the sources of data (interviews, existing datasets, satellite imagery or expert judgements) and in the degree to which they are participatory or extractive in collecting data. In all cases, assessments aim to simplify complicated experiences of risk in order to assist in decision-making. Complexity comes from:

- *The multiple hazards to which people are simultaneously exposed.* Recent and frequently experienced hazard types may be more visible to assessors than others at any one moment. Following the Indian Ocean Tsunami, many assessments of tsunami risk were undertaken despite the likelihood of a future tsunami being much lower than seasonal rainfall flooding or armed conflict.
- *The multiple sectors that are at risk.* It is difficult to aggregate vulnerability across sectors such as housing, communication networks, water and sanitation, education, healthcare infrastructure, power networks, etc. Each sector will have different exposure and susceptibility to risk and capacities and resources for coping and recovery.
- *The multiple scales at which risk is felt and responded to.* Risk, in any one place, is an outcome of decision-making and action – or inaction – at local, municipal, national and international scales. It is challenging to include all of these scales in the analysis of impacts and capacity.
- *The multiple assets to be accounted for in measuring vulnerability and capacity.* This applies to all scales, from the individual to the urban scale. Some assets will be contingent upon the utilization of others and rarely are different types of assets commensurate.

- *The multiple stakeholders with roles to play in shaping risk.* Stakeholders' actions influence the degree to which they, and others, are placed at risk. This can be hard to pin down – for example, when such actions are part of everyday development processes.
- *The multiple phases that disaster cycles pass through.* Perceptions of risk and actions to build capacity and resilience may look very different before and after disaster and during periods of everyday development.

It is precisely in urban centres where these overlapping aspects of risk are most challenging. Thus, urban risk assessment methodologies and programmes need to be multi-sectoral, multidisciplinary and sensitive to differentiated risk, vulnerability and capacity.[22]

Additional challenges of risk assessment include the following:

- While innovations in information technology, including the use of satellite imagery, offer great potential as sources of data for assessments, access to this technology is not equally distributed globally and even within countries. Inequality in the distribution of human resources, as well as hardware, and the ability to buy in data from private sources comprise a challenge for development.
- People are the true wealth of cities. However, many measurements of urban risk, particularly those operating at the urban scale, focus on built assets at risk. This may be a reflection of the economic importance of physical assets. It might also reflect the background of scientists who have led the field of urban risk modelling and assessment, an area dominated until recently by an engineering focus and an interest in earthquake risk. It also reflects the difficulty of measuring human vulnerability, particularly at larger scales.
- The fast pace of change in the physical fabric and social life of slums, and other low-income settlements, is a challenge for risk assessment. Local and participatory methodologies have partly been adopted in response to this challenge as they are easier to manage and less costly and therefore can be undertaken with greater frequency. More problematic, still, is the difficulty of including highly vulnerable people dispersed across the city, such as the homeless and illegal immigrants, in particular. This challenge is proving hard to overcome in even wealthier countries and cities.

Perceptions of risk

Perceptions of risk play an important part in disaster risk reduction. They influence the ways in which risk is measured and the willingness of citizens and authorities to undertake actions to manage risk. Planners and policy-makers often employ expert risk analysis to justify hazard mitigation policies; yet, expert and lay risk assessments do not always concur. This can undermine policy legitimization and compliance.

Perceptions are shaped by a number of factors, including the nature and availability of disaster-related information, past experiences of disaster events, cultural values and the socio-economic status of concerned individuals or households. Perceptions influence the relative importance given to natural or human-made hazards, compared to other competing needs and opportunities. In turn, the importance ascribed to disaster risks determines subsequent efforts to avoid or limit the impacts of those hazards. For instance, research in the US has found that hurricane risk perception is a useful predictor of storm preparation, evacuation and hazard adjustment undertaken by households.[23]

The ability of a household or individual to act on perceived risk is also constrained by their coping and adaptive capacity and by urban governance institutions. Too often, poverty and marginalization force the most vulnerable to accept risk from natural and human-made hazards as a trade-off for access to shelter and work. Risk assessments can help policy-makers understand the multiple risks faced by those in poverty by making perceptions more tangible.

Once individuals have experienced a disaster event, they tend to have an elevated sense of future risk.[24] Without support, this can lead to stress and panic. A number of rumours and false alarms followed in the wake of the Indian Ocean Tsunami. In one instance, a rumour caused 1000 people to flee from the beach area of Pangandaran (Indonesia).[25]

The pace of change in the physical fabric and social life of slums...is a challenge for risk assessment

Perceptions of risk ...influence...the willingness of citizens and authorities to undertake actions to manage risk

...the most vulnerable...accept risk from natural and human-made hazard as a trade-off for access to shelter and work

STRENGTHENING LOCAL DISASTER RESILIENCE

Local disaster resilience refers to the capacity of local actors to minimize the incidence and impacts of disasters, and to undertake recovery and reconstruction activities once disasters occur. In places where hazard and loss are tangible, disaster risk reduction or reconstruction can be opportunities for improving the solidarity, inclusiveness, human skills and confidence of local groups and their leaders. Box 8.6 shows just how effective local capacity-building can be for disaster risk reduction. This section reviews social, legislative and economic pathways for building local resilience and discusses the challenges therein.

Social pathways

Social capital offers a resource upon which to build resilience to disaster shocks, even where economic resources are limited and political systems are exclusionary. Local stocks of social capital – norms and habits of behaviour that support reciprocity and collective action – are resources that can be used to build capacity in the face of multiple development challenges, including disaster risk. This provides a great opportunity for integrating disaster risk reduction and development at the local level.

Building local networks of support and reciprocity can increase self-reliance among households and neighbourhoods and in this way enhance disaster resilience. An example of the benefits to be gained by communities with strong social ties comes from Catuche, Caracas, in

Box 8.6 Community action builds leadership and resilience in Santo Domingo, the Dominican Republic

The Dominican Disaster Mitigation Committee (DDMC) is a national non-governmental organization (NGO) that, with support from the Organization of American States (OAS), has sought to build local capacity as an integral part of its disaster risk reduction work in the city of Santo Domingo.

Activities implemented by the DDMC include community mapping of local hazards, vulnerabilities and capacities, as well as leadership training. Communities are then invited to draw up competitive proposals for hazard mitigation projects where costs are split between DDMC and the local community. This approach generates multiple outputs. At one level, a risk reduction project is supported. More fundamental is the experience gained by grassroots actors of undertaking risk assessments and developing project proposals for external funding. The DDMC will only cover 50 per cent of the costs for any project proposal, requiring the community to raise additional funds or resources in kind through labour. The DDMC will also not provide financial support for any additional projects, thereby encouraging local actors to build on their experience to apply for funding from other NGO or government sources.

Seven communities in Santo Domingo have taken part in the programme, with 2000 people benefiting directly. Activities have included building local sewer systems, storm drains, a flood dike and an anti-landslide wall. Building local capacity in the communities has not only reduced risk, but has also enhanced disaster response. In one community, Mata Mamon, in 1998, Hurricane Georges caused damage to 75 per cent of houses. It was the local community who managed aid distribution when the first supplies arrived after ten days.

Source: Pelling, 2003; see also Dominican Association of Disaster Mitigation, www.desastre.org/home/index.php4?lang=esp

Venezuela. This community was among those exposed to the extreme flooding and landslides of 1999, which killed 30,000 people. According to an official from the organization Ecumenical Action-ACT:[26]

While community solidarity can be an asset for disaster risk reduction, communities are not inherently harmonious…

> *… the organization of the neighbourhood and the solidarity of the people saved hundreds of lives … as the flooding progressed, community members mobilized to assist one another. Neighbours who knew each other and had worked together for years communicated swiftly the news of the rising water. Older residents were helped from their homes by younger neighbours. When a few were reluctant to leave because they didn't believe the threat or because they were afraid their few possessions could be stolen, neighbours broke down doors and carried people forcibly to safety… In one incident where we were trying, unsuccessfully, to kick down the heavy door of a woman who refused to leave her house, a young gang member came along, pulled out a pistol and fired into the lock, allowing the door to be opened. The gang member then pointed his gun at the woman and ordered her out of her house. Seconds after she left the dwelling, the house fell into the raging current … perhaps as few as 15 people died, a very small figure compared to other similar neighbourhoods where hundreds lost their lives.*

The urban population is a key resource during times of disaster, as demonstrated in Mexico City, where, following the 1985 earthquake, up to 1 million volunteers helped in rescue and relief operations.[27]

Where disaster risk is a dominant aspect of everyday life, it can become a concern around which local associations organize and remain engaged with development. A great diversity of local associations can contribute to disaster risk reduction, including kinship, religious and gender- or youth-based groups, as well as groups organized around particular interests, such as sports, environmental or social improvement. All of these groups, and not only those that are development or disaster oriented, can play a role in building networks of support and, thus, disaster resilience. It is those communities who have a rich stock of associations that are also most likely to engage in risk reduction at the local level. Furthermore, local associations can act as intermediaries, conveying information between local residents and external actors seeking to build local resilience. They can also enrich externally funded risk reduction projects by sharing knowledge of local customs, environmental hazards, social vulnerability and capacity.

While community solidarity can be an asset for disaster risk reduction, communities are not inherently harmonious entities. Rather, they are heterogeneous and are often cross-cut by internal competition, information asymmetries and socio-economic inequality. This can undermine community-level risk reduction projects, leading to interventions exacerbating inequalities and undermining collective resilience. For example, in many communities, women may predominate in the membership of community groups, but may be excluded from leadership. This is a missed opportunity.[28] An Indian NGO, Swayam Shiksam Prayong, has attempted to address this concern by enacting a philosophy of not only rebuilding physical structures, but realigning social relations in post-disaster periods. A priority was to work with women to facilitate their visions of life after the earthquake, which included, for example, assigning land titles to both women and men.[29] Box 8.7 offers some examples of ways in which women have taken a lead in reducing local disaster risk.

External agencies seeking to work with community-level partners in disaster risk reduction must also be cautious not to assume that community leaders represent the best interests of local residents. Following the Bhuj earthquake in Gujarat (India) in 2001, international and government aid prioritized speed in distribution of goods, which enabled high-cast groups to capture a disproportionate amount of aid at the expense of lower-cast groups and Muslims.[30] This observation underlines the advantages of disaster risk reduction and response work that is built on sound knowledge of local political and social rivalries, as well as capacities for collective action to build resilience.

Building the capacity of local authorities is also vital for disaster risk reduction. The Asian Urban Disaster Mitigation Program (AUDMP) works to build local- and city-level capacity across Asia. One of its projects in the city of Ratnapura (Sri Lanka) seeks to improve the disaster risk management capacity of local authorities by providing them with improved tools and skills. This involved the development of a methodology for identifying hazards and determining potential losses. Outputs have included the formation of a Disaster Management Council, guidelines for building construction in disaster-prone areas and a Disaster Management and Mitigation Plan for Ratnapura.[31]

Legal approaches

The Universal Declaration of Human Rights already supports the right to personal security and a basic standard of living during periods of unforeseen livelihood disruption.[32] The human rights agenda offers a potentially powerful tool for local actors to argue for increased pre-disaster investment and post-disaster compensation. It offers a moral imperative that could mobilize local political will.[33] Rights-based approaches that seek to justify investment in prevention are increasingly being supported by economic analysis, which shows the financial savings to be made by investing in risk reduction before a disaster, compared to the costs of managing disasters through relief and reconstruction. The UK Department for International Development (DFID) estimates that for every US$1 invested in disaster risk reduction, between US$2 and $4 are returned in terms of avoided or reduced disaster impacts.[34]

The failure of the international community to set a legally binding international treaty on disaster risk reduction in the Hyogo Framework for Action 2005–2015,[35] and the absence of disaster risk targets in the Millennium Development Goals (MDGs), however, limits the international pressure that can be used to support local actors at risk.

Nationally, an increasing number of governments are putting in place disaster risk reduction legislation. While such legislation often does not provide targets for action, it does establish responsible agencies for risk reduction, typically in local and regional government. Where legal systems are robust, legislation has proven a strong weapon to strengthen communities at risk from technological and industrial hazards, and underpins the Environmental Justice Movement. Court action taken by the survivors of the Payatas (Manila) rubbish mountain landslide in 2000 is an example. Some 300 people were killed in this event. In partnership with civil rights lawyers, survivors filed a US$20 million legal claim against the city government for compensatory and moral damages based on the assertion that city authorities were responsible for the Payatas dumpsite. That low-income survivors of an urban disaster could take legal action indicates the strength of community capacity in Payatas, and also a supporting infrastructure of civil rights lawyers, basic conditions not found in every city and especially lacking in smaller urban settlements.[36]

Where the law allows it, and where culpability can be proven, group actions brought by survivors of toxic releases against companies or the state can amount to significant sums and act as a deterrent on other companies. In South Africa, a strong legal system provides for disaster risk reduction to be a shared responsibility between national, regional and municipal governments and, in so doing, provides for collective legal action against state agencies found to be complicit in the generation of disaster risk (see Box 8.8).

Box 8.7 Women lead contributions to local disaster risk reduction in Latin America

The Pan American Health Organization (PAHO) has long worked with women and men to build local capacities for risk awareness and reduction. In a review of the contribution made by women to local resilience, it was concluded that, while women are severely affected by natural disasters, disasters often provide women with an opportunity to challenge and change their status in society.

In many (if not most) cases, women are more effective than men at mobilizing the community to respond to disasters. They form groups and networks of social actors who work to meet the most pressing needs of the community. This kind of community organizing has proven essential in disaster preparedness and mitigation. A review of PAHO field notes illustrates the contribution of women towards disaster risk reduction:

- Following Hurricane Mitch in 1998, women in Guatemala and Honduras were seen building houses, digging wells and ditches, hauling water and building shelters. This shows how willing women are to take on activities traditionally considered to be 'men's work'. Beyond increasing the efficiency and equity in disaster reconstruction, this kind of experience can also help in changing society's conceptions of women's capabilities.
- After the 1985 earthquake in Mexico City, low-income women working in factories organized themselves into the '19 of September Garment Workers' Union', which was recognized by the Mexican government and proved instrumental in lobbying for the recovery of women's employment.
- Following Hurricane Joan in 1988, women in Mulukutú (Nicaragua) organized to develop plans for disaster preparedness that included all the members of a household. Ten years later, Mulukutú was better prepared for Hurricane Mitch and it recovered more quickly than other similarly affected communities.

Source: PAHO (undated)

Economic approaches

Microfinance has a great potential to build community resilience to disasters. The extension of small loans through micro-credit enhances the incomes and assets of urban households and communities, thereby reducing their poverty. In turn, this helps to reduce vulnerability to disasters and develops greater coping capacity. Post-disaster loans and micro-insurance can help poor urban households recover more quickly. Yet, it is only recently that micro-credit and micro-insurance have been applied for building community resilience to disaster risk.

... an increasing number of governments are putting in place disaster risk reduction legislation

To date, microfinance institutions have been involved mostly with post-disaster recovery activities. There is a need, however, for microfinance to be perceived as a potential tool to better prepare communities before natural hazards strike. In particular, the scope for micro-insurance to act as an affordable mechanism for extending risk-sharing into low-income communities has recently received much attention.

Challenges remain for the role of microfinance in strengthening local resilience against disasters. The complexity of livelihoods and social life in urban areas has delayed the development of microfinance schemes, compared to some rural contexts. Disasters can also destroy the very assets in which individuals have invested micro-credit loans, leading to debt as well as loss of assets. Following a disaster, if micro-credit is available, there is a danger that survivors will overextend their ability to repay loans in efforts to re-establish livelihoods. Pre-disaster

Box 8.8 Using the law to fight technological risk in Durban, South Africa

South Durban Community in South Africa is a highly polluted area where 200,000 largely vulnerable and disadvantaged residents live side by side with heavy industries. In 2002, successful legal action was taken by the community to prevent the development of a paper incinerator by Mondi, a paper manufacturing company. This legal case was taken up by the community after the provincial government granted permission to Mondi to construct an incinerator without following proper procedures. The Legal Resources Centre lodged an appeal on behalf of the community in the Durban High Court on 11 October 2002, restraining the Minister of Agriculture and Environmental Affairs, KwaZulu-Natal Province, from approving the Mondi incinerator. The minister was interdicted pending the finalization of a judicial review.

The legal recourse was taken on the grounds that government granted an oral exemption to Mondi from conducting a full environmental impact assessment (EIA). It was argued that this exemption was invalid, according to statutory requirements, and that the failure to appoint an independent consultant, conduct a full IEA and examine the necessary alternatives was in breach of existing legislation. The Legal Resources Centre also pointed out that a proper interpretation of the EIA showed that sulphur dioxide emissions from Mondi's incinerator would exceed World Health Organization (WHO) standards and national guidelines of 1998. This, the community noted, was against their constitutional right to live in a healthy environment.

The verbal exemption from conducting an EIA given to Mondi was overruled by a high court judge and the company's proposal had to be processed again, taking into account the necessary EIA requirements.

Sources: South Durban Community Environmental Alliance, 2003a, 2003b

planning is the best way of protecting households from these and other risks. Box 8.9 presents eight ways in which this can be done.

Box 8.9 Microfinance for disaster risk reduction

It is important that gains made through microfinance are protected from the economic and human impacts of disaster. Here, eight ways of protecting microfinance clients from disaster risk are presented:

1. Meet with clients to discuss preparations for, and responses to, natural disasters.
2. Create accessible emergency funds to provide clients with a financial safety net in times of crisis.
3. Microfinance groups can provide a ready social network for promoting primary healthcare in order to build resilience pre- and post-disaster.
4. Microfinance coordinators can aid in the building of resilience through encouraging clients to diversify into disaster-resistant activities.
5. Housing is arguably the most important asset in urban livelihoods. Microfinance initiatives should consider providing savings or loan products to encourage clients to move to safer areas and to invest in more durable housing.
6. Insurance products provided by multinational financial institutions to their clients are typically designed to protect against individual crisis and not crises that affect the entire portfolio of clients. Some microfinance agencies have begun experimenting with insurance products for disaster response, in some cases turning to the re-insurance market to spread aggregate risks.
7. Microfinance coordinators can disseminate information on providers of emergency services and safe shelter in times of emergency.
8. The social network of the microfinance organization can act as an information conduit for early warning.

Source: Microenterprise Best Practice (undated)

Challenges of building local capacity for risk reduction

Local potential for disaster risk reduction can only be realized in supportive social, economic, legislative and political environments. In a recent study of slum settlements in six African countries, ActionAid found that a lack of collective action to reduce risk was a major determinant in shaping vulnerability and reducing capacity to recover from flooding.[37]

There is also an uneasy tension between the empowering of local actors to confront local causes of risk and the offloading of state or private-sector responsibilities. Decentralization of urban governance has seen many municipalities struggling with a gap between responsibilities that have been devolved from central government and the resources, which have, in many instances, not been made available. There is a danger that the same flow of responsibility without resources will result from the increasing emphasis on local actor involvement in risk reduction.

It is also important not to lose sight of the deeper historical and structural root causes of disaster risk in the national and global political economy. Community-based approaches inherently focus on the concerns of particular places and are often directed by the most immediate local development challenges. On the surface, this is reasonable; but without care, it can mask deeper social and economic structures and physical processes that are the root causes of inequality, vulnerability and hazard.

The challenge of bringing together top-down, scientific and strategic policy-driven risk reduction priorities with bottom-up, experiential and often tactical priorities of grassroots actors lies at the heart of all planned interventions for local capacity-building. Building local capacity is difficult in contexts where disaster risk reduction is not perceived to be a priority by local actors. In areas where disasters are infrequent or have had only a limited impact, it is quite rational for those on a low income, with little time to spare and subject to many hazards – from police harassment and street crime to the threat or reality of homelessness – not to want to participate in disaster risk reduction initiatives as a priority.

The tension between local and external priorities is made especially visible, but also difficult to reconcile, when external actors engage with community actors through participatory methodologies. This can mean that long-term risks, including low-frequency, high-impact hazards and low-level chronic hazards, such as air pollution, are not identified as priorities by local actors and therefore might not be addressed.

Strategies for reconciling local everyday and external strategic visions of risk are needed in order to maximize the potential for local capacity to build resilience to disaster. Three strategies are to:

- Piggyback disaster risk reduction work onto existing activities that are accepted as priorities locally. In Latin America, the Pan-American Health Organization (PAHO) has included risk reduction training and information with family and women's health issues.[38]
- Bring a wide range of actors together to highlight shared (systemic) challenges to development. The AUDMP adopted this approach in the Bangladesh Urban Disaster Mitigation Project, where community-based disaster risk management was enhanced through the wide involvement of urban actors.[39]
- Undertake a staged programme of disaster risk reduction when external agencies are committed to a long-term engagement with a community. CARE Zambia's Programme of Support for Poverty Elimination. and Community Transformation (PROSPECT) sought to confront governance aspects of urban vulnerability to multiple hazards in Lusaka. It was left open for community participants to define priority concerns.[40] As debates unfolded, the linkages between disaster risk and loss from even small events with developmental concerns became more visible.

LAND-USE PLANNING

Land-use planning is perhaps the most fundamental tool for mainstreaming disaster risk reduction into urban development processes. It provides a framework within which interventions to partner local actors for risk mapping and community resilience building can be undertaken. This includes partnerships between the municipal or city government, community groups and the private sector. Familiar planning tools such as zoning, community participation, GIS, and information and education programmes are all integral to mainstreaming risk reduction within local comprehensive land-use planning process.

Mainstreaming risk reduction within strategies that underpin land-use planning is challenging, particularly for authorities with limited human and economic resources and political influence. Perhaps most challenging of all is the aim of including all urban stakeholders in the shaping of planning policy and development decisions, with a rigorous, independent and transparent procedure for overcoming conflicting interests. This requires a multi-scaled approach, as well as one that brings together actors from different policy areas and from public, private and civil sectors. Algeria's National Land-Use Planning Model is a case in point. Developing this national framework in 2005 necessitated coordination between scientists, planners and policy-makers and harmonization with local land-use planning models.[41]

Cuba has one of the best records for integrating disaster risk planning within urban risk management. The Institute for Physical and Spatial Planning has been legally responsible for physical planning for over 40 years. Risk maps have contributed to recommendations for retrofitting, resettlement and urban growth regulation in 107 coastal settlements. In conjunction with the United Nations Educational, Scientific and Cultural Organization (UNESCO), a comprehensive development plan was developed in 1998 for areas of Havana exposed to coastal hazards. Importantly, the agency with responsibility for disaster response – the Civil Defence Service – has participated in developing these plans. Plans have included protection for the Old Town of Havana, a World Heritage site.[42] This is unusual since many places of national and global architectural importance are not adequately considered in disaster planning. The loss of Bam in Iran is only one example.

Land-use planning is perhaps the most fundamental tool for mainstreaming risk reduction into urban development processes

Designing and implementing comprehensive land-use planning is particularly challenging in many smaller cities, where municipal capacity for urban planning is limited. Initiatives that seek to extend risk reduction planning to smaller municipalities have begun to emerge, although there is still much to be done. For instance, in Nicaragua, the Executive Secretariat of the National System for Disaster Prevention, Mitigation and Response, created in 2000 by law, has, together with UNDP Nicaragua,[43] developed a programme to support local capacity-building for risk management in six municipalities. This programme has encouraged local participation in disaster risk planning. This, in turn, has been facilitated through the production of a series of four manuals based on the experience of local actors and designed to be user friendly and non-technical. They contain guidance for building community groups, conducting risk assessments and influencing the municipal government. Through this, local participation and the disaster risk reduction component in land-use decision-making can be enhanced. The success of these plans can be seen in their reaching a third publication run in as many years by 2004.

Urban risk management needs to consider not only the internal, but also the external environment

Planning to manage risk systems in their entirety further complicates land-use planning. Human settlements of all sizes are situated within larger socio-ecological systems that include environmental features (such as watersheds, regimes of coastal land erosion and sediment deposition, or earthquake zones), as well as social and cultural systems. These systems are interdependent, expressed, for example, through migration and economic exchange between rural and urban areas or across urban centres. Urban risk management needs to consider not only the internal, but also the external environment. There are few successful examples of this highly integrated approach; but there are many places where this large-scale planning might bring dividends. Box 8.10 presents an example from The Netherlands, where socio-ecological systems planning has been conducted in an open fashion, thus strengthening democratic culture, as well as reducing risk.

Extending land-use planning to informal settlements and slums

Nearly 1 billion people, or one in every three city dwellers, live in an informal settlement or slum.[44] Such areas are typically cramped, with industrial and residential land uses in close proximity (sometimes in the same building) and exposed to natural hazard through their location on hill slopes or low-lying land subject to waterlogging and flooding. Within a context of rapid urban population growth and physi-

Box 8.10 Managing socio-ecological systems to protect human settlements in The Netherlands

Much of The Netherlands comprises reclaimed lowlands and estuarine systems for the Meuse, Waal and Rhine rivers. Managing flood risk in this country, and protecting urban as well as rural settlements, livelihoods and assets, has required an integrated socio-ecological systems approach. This approach has developed over time until now and each aspect of coastal and riverine risk management can be understood to protect not only local assets, but also those of the linked socio-ecological system, and to take people's changing values into account.

The long timeframe needed to construct the Eastern Scheldt Dam, which was initiated in 1953, led to the project being halted in 1967. Originally intended to protect people against flooding from the sea, the barrier designs took little else into consideration. The original design aim was to create a freshwater lake from the Eastern Scheldt. However, during the late 1960s, new ecological awareness and recognition of the value of coastal resources such as shellfisheries for local livelihoods stimulated redesign. Because of the controversy, and the eventual political willingness to incorporate a dialogue on the process surrounding the project, technical innovations exceeded expectations, and now the barrier is one of the most highly regarded water management structures in the country, if not the world.

A second major technological accomplishment was the Maeslant Barrier, constructed in the New Waterway. The New Waterway was a shipping avenue that had to remain open. One option would have been to raise existing dikes, which had proven costly in the past and had also generated protests from residents. Dikes in The Netherlands can be several metres wide and homes have been constructed upon them, so building higher dikes often means removing property, often at great cost. To come up with a solution that was acceptable across the spectrum of stakeholders, the Ministry of Transport, Public Works and Water Management held a competition for an innovative design for the New Waterway. Like the Eastern Scheldt Dam, the Maeslant Barrier was a technological breakthrough and was completed in 1997.

Both of these technological responses to flood hazard were managed at a national scale and were underpinned by an open approach that enabled multiple stakeholders to debate and shape the final technological outcome. The open process took more time and money, but resulted in better solutions, highlighting how successful engineering-based responses to risk management can benefit from taking wider social and ecological contexts into consideration. The process resulted in a shift in flood management from a perspective that was oriented solely to providing safety, to one that, today, seeks to arrive at compromises with ecological and cultural demands.

Source: Orr et al, 2007

The provision of basic services and security of tenure has many positive consequences, including the reduction of vulnerability to disaster

cal expansion of cities, planners are often unable to keep up with mapping new settlements, let alone planning land use for them. Set against these pressures, the lack of human and financial resources and the low profile often enjoyed by land-use planning in urban planning departments are startling. Innovative methods for reaching populations at risk are thus needed.

Where there is political commitment and resources are made available, slums can be successfully brought into formal planning programmes. In Brazil, Egypt, Mexico, South Africa, Thailand and Tunisia, large-scale commitment to upgrading and service provision has led to an overall reduction in the growth rates of slums.[45] The provision of basic services and security of tenure has many positive consequences, including the reduction of vulnerability to disaster. Households that can access basic needs are not only healthier, but often have more time and, as a consequence, money and energy available for investment in household and, collectively, community improvement.

An emerging alternative to the extension of formal planning into informal settlements at risk is to work with community associations to develop local land-use plans…

If risks are too high or disaster has already struck, re-housing can be an option. However, careful consultation with those to be re-housed and the community into which people will be moved is essential. Box 8.11 provides an example of a re-housing and relocation programme that successfully brought together local government and slum community leaders. Without significant local consultation, re-housing is in danger of leading to the break-up of social networks and livelihood resources upon which the poor and vulnerable rely.[46]

There is an added risk in re-housing programmes if the alternative sites are also disaster prone. Naga City in the Philippines is relatively small (127,000 residents) but has a considerable population of low-income citizens. The Naga City Integrated Disaster Management Plan has had significant consequences for low-income households. Before the plan was instituted, an ongoing slum resettlement programme had identified 33 resettlement areas. However, it was found that 19 of these were in flood-prone areas. In light of this, alternative sites were found that were free of flood hazard, while still offering employment opportunities.[47]

An emerging alternative to the extension of formal planning into informal settlements at risk is to work with community associations to develop local land-use plans that can be extended upwards to meet with the formal planning system. These plans are owned and researched by local communities and have limited legal standing, but provide a mechanism for those left outside of the formal planning process to identify land-use challenges to disaster resilience. Such planning takes place at the micro scale and is most successful in informal settlements that have not yet consolidated. At the pre-consolidation stage, there is some flexibility in land use so that strong community groups can police collective decisions to, for example, leave spaces between housing to allow for access routes for emergency vehicles. The challenge to this approach remains the extent to which community plans can be welcomed by and integrated with formal planning systems. A careful balance has to be met between the strategic emphasis of city-level land-use planning and the more local concerns of community plans.

Unconsolidated informal settlements vary in the strength and character of leadership. Partnerships with local planning authorities can build procedural rigour and provide additional legitimacy. Such partnerships can also be a mechanism for local planning authorities to initiate regularization, which often requires significant land-use decisions to be made that can allow later provision of critical infrastructure, such as water and electricity.

Box 8.11 Relocation planning in Sacadura Cabral, São Paulo, Brazil

In 1997, relocation was proposed as part of a slum upgrading programme in Sacadura Cabral, São Paulo (Brazil). A densely populated *barrio* subject to annual flooding was chosen by city planners for relocation. A total of 200 families were to be relocated from within the settlements to allow redevelopment and upgrading of the site.

The selection of families to be moved was initially controlled by the planning authority; but this met with much local resistance and was eventually replaced by a more communicative strategy built around a series of public meetings with communities and their leaders. Relocation planning was revised as an outcome of these meetings. The new plan included a role for the local community in the selection of families to be relocated. An agreement was reached that families would be housed within 1 kilometre from Sacadura Cabral and be given access to subsidized credit. Local people were to lead the reconstruction and upgrading process, with technical assistance from the local authorities.

A particularly innovative aspect of the project that arose from local consultations was that the selection of families for relocation was not restricted to those living in areas within Sacadura Cabral to be upgraded. Instead, the whole community was included. Thus, some of those who agreed to be relocated were not living in areas to be cleared and upgraded. The relocation of these families provided space within the existing community for some people living in areas to be upgraded to be re-housed within the community.

Source: Olivira and Denaldi, 1999

BUILDING CODES, REGULATION AND DISASTER-RESISTANT CONSTRUCTION

In 2003, an earthquake in the city of Bingol (Turkey) destroyed 300 buildings and damaged more than 5000 others. One of the buildings that collapsed was a school dormitory, killing 84 children. The dormitory had only been built in 1998 and was a modern engineered structure. The fact that this event occurred only four years after the Marmara earthquake reopened the public debate on the prevailing standards and building codes that are applied or (as in the case of the dormitory) not applied.[48]

Most countries have building codes aimed at ensuring that construction meets a minimum standard of disaster resilience. In some cases, codes might not be as appropriate as they could be. For example, in Jamaica, losses to Hurricane Gilbert in 1988 included 30,235 homes. High losses have been blamed on a lack of preparedness in the physical planning and housing sectors and because the 1983 National Building Code of Jamaica was inappropriately modelled on UK standards. In contrast to the housing sector, many small businesses were well prepared and were able to return to work quickly.[49]

The United Nations International Strategy for Disaster Reduction (ISDR)[50] recommends that building codes should be:

- realistic, given economic, environmental and technological constraints;
- relevant to current building practice and technology;
- updated regularly in light of developments in knowledge;
- understood fully and accepted by professional interest groups;
- enforced in order to avoid the legislative system being ignored or falling into disrepute;
- adhered to, with laws and controls based more on a system of incentives rather than punishment;
- integrated fully within a legal system that takes account of potential conflicts between the different levels of administration and government.

The greatest challenge is enforcing adherence to building codes during construction. Failure to comply with codes is a root cause of vulnerability in buildings. Too often, perverse incentives make it more attractive for administrators, architects, builders, contractors and even house owners to circumvent construction standards. This is not simply a product of poverty, but, at heart, is a problem of governance. In Turkey, much of the loss of life associated with the Marmara earthquake in 1999 has been attributed to the ineffective regulation of construction. In this case, risk generated by ineffective governance was compounded by high inflation, which meant that few people had insurance cover. Public outrage at this failing led to a protest and reform of the system of building regulation in Turkey.

Failure to comply with codes is a root cause of vulnerability in buildings

The potential for regulation of building codes to be undertaken by the private sector has been explored in recent research. Although it is argued that it might be cost efficient for a private body to undertake site inspections, it is unclear if a private body would be any less open to the perverse incentives that distort public-sector inspection and enforcement.[51]

Even where external financing might be thought to provide additional incentives for oversight and successful use of standards, this is not always the case. A recent review of World Bank lending during the period of 1984 to 2005 found that 60 per cent of projects receiving disaster financing were damaged by a subsequent event. Of 197 completed projects with a focus on mitigation – designed to use disaster-resistant standards – 26 per cent showed flaws in design, and half had been damaged by a subsequent event. Of the 65 projects in the transportation, urban and water and sanitation sectors approved between 2000 and 2004 in countries identified by the World Bank as disaster hotspots, only 3 projects included any detailed disaster planning.[52]

In cities of lower-income countries, but increasingly also in large cities of middle-income countries, the high proportion of citizens forced to reside in informal settlements where activities operate outside the formal planning and regulatory systems is particularly challenging for build-

Box 8.12 Improving low-income housing construction in Saint Lucia

A substantial portion of the housing stock in the Eastern Caribbean is built through the informal sector and does not meet official building standards. Under the Organization of American States (OAS) Caribbean Disaster Mitigation Project, a National Development Foundation (NDF) was created in St Lucia.

In July 1994, the St Lucian NDF established a revolving loan facility to finance retrofitting for St Lucian homeowners in the low-income sector. This was intended to better enable homeowners, small entrepreneurs, contractors, artisans and non-professional builders to adopt appropriate and cost-effective disaster vulnerability reduction measures in the informal housing sector. Loans were granted to a maximum of 15,000 Euros[53] per project for not more than four years.

Preparation for this programme required marketing in order to establish demand and training of builders to deliver the programme. Demand for the programme was identified through a household survey of two pilot communities at Gros Islet and Dennery. This was followed by a more extensive market study that illustrated the extent and nature of demand and finance required for both hurricane retrofitting and household safety and improvement purposes. Marketing strategies made use of community meetings, radio and television talk programmes, press releases and church notices. Tradespeople and artisans were trained in retrofitting techniques through the Sir Arthur Lewis Community College.

The NDF was able to obtain Group Insurance at reasonable rates through a local insurance broker on the condition that all properties are retrofitted. The project officers of the foundation were trained in property evaluation by the insurer. Furthermore, the NDF agreed to loan money to meet the first year's premium for any household that was unable to pay.

Between 1996 and 2002, 345 house improvement loans had been distributed. While the specific eligibility criteria applied in this case would exclude low-income households from poorer nations, the approach has made a contribution to safety and points the way towards the potential for productive relationships to be built with private-sector insurance companies for proactive risk reduction.

Sources: OAS, 2001, 2003; UNDP, 2004

ing control. There is limited international and governmental action to address this, although some innovative responses have come from non-governmental and research organizations (see Box 8.12).

A number of international initiatives have begun to build frameworks for information exchange and learning in technical aspects of safe construction. This is most developed among the earthquake engineering community. An internet-based encyclopaedia of housing construction is being prepared by the Earthquake Engineering Research Institute in the US[54] and by the International Association of Earthquake Engineering in Japan.[55] The World Seismic Safety Initiative,[56] a coalition of academic and professional engineers, has sought to extend public awareness and government commitment to earthquake safety through working in partnership with national associations such as Nepal's National Society for Earthquake Technology and Uganda's Seismic Safety Association. GHI has applied a Global Earthquake Safety Initiative to 21 urban areas, including regional as well as capital centres and megacities.[57]

...costs of safer building construction are often relatively high

Megacities are the urban centres that have received most coordinated attention at the international level. Prominent is the Earthquakes and Megacities Initiative,[58] linked to the World Seismic Safety Initiative. This was initiated in 1997 to promote comprehensive city-wide disaster management systems in large cities exposed to seismic hazard. The project is noteworthy in advocating for policy on land-use planning and recovery, as well as structural mitigation through construction standards and engineering-based initiatives. City-to-city learning is facilitated through the Cluster Cities Project and a Training and Education Programme directed at professional groups. The holism of this approach can be seen in the Americas Cluster Project Workshop held in Ecuador in 2001, where key areas for collaboration included community-based vulnerability reduction, population needs and healthcare delivery in disasters, and promoting a culture of prevention.[59]

Disaster events often provide an opportunity for training those working in the construction industry in safe construction techniques. This can contribute towards addressing the great gap between construction standards and their implementation if local artisans have the skills and knowledge to build safely. Where the additional costs are minimal, safer building might become more achievable. Yet, costs of safer building construction are often relatively high.

There is much to learn from vernacular building design and practices. Work on vernacular housing, including the training of local builders, has been reported by the ISDR from Bangladesh, China, Colombia, India and Peru.[60] Reports from earthquakes in the Himalayas, in Srinagar, Himachal Pradesh and the Garhwal Highlands, have shown vernacular housing to be the most resistant to earthquake damage.[61]

PLANNING TO PROTECT CRITICAL INFRASTRUCTURE AND SERVICES

Chapter 7 noted how the impacts of a disaster can be magnified through the domino effects of secondary and indirect losses caused when critical infrastructure or services are damaged by disaster. This is, of course, precisely why acts of terror and war are targeted at critical systems. The damage caused by Storm Lothar, which hit France in December 1999, was greatly magnified by the indirect impacts on the 3 million people whose electricity supply was cut.[62]

Critical infrastructure includes:

- electricity (generation, transmission and distribution infrastructure);
- natural gas and liquid fuels (storage, transportation and distribution infrastructure);
- potable water and sanitation (collection, treatment, storage, transportation and distribution infrastructure);
- telecommunications (broadcasting, cable transmission and cellular telephone infrastructure);
- transportation (road systems, mass public transport, and air and sea transport systems).

Critical services include:

- hospitals and access to healthcare;
- police and maintaining the rule of law;
- banks and stability in financial services.

Protecting critical infrastructure and services against all conceivable sources of harm is prohibitively expensive, especially so for countries and cities with small economies. Resilience targets can be used in planning to act as goalposts when determining a minimum level of capacity to be protected in the case of a disaster. These are rough guidelines; but they enhance transparency in priority setting. Such a target could be that for a city there should be a 95 per cent chance that 80 per cent of hospitals can operate at 90 per cent of their capacity within 24 hours of an earthquake of a particular severity. Monitoring performance can include simple metrics. In the case of transport infrastructure, for example, possible criteria could include total vehicle hours travelled post- and pre-earthquake (congestion); total vehicle kilometres travelled post- and pre-earthquake (detour length); time delay between critical origin/destination pairs (e.g. from damaged areas to emergency hospitals); and restoration time to, say, 80 per cent of pre-earthquake capacity.[63]

Critical infrastructure and services share a reliance on networks that allow for the movement of information and commodities. These networks are fundamental in ensuring the health and safety of the population and the functioning of the urban economy. They are interdependent so that a failure in one system can lead to repercussions in associated systems. The links that unite life-support networks and convey vulnerability can also be a source of resilience, offering alternative routes for information flow and feedback in the system or for overlapping functions and spare capacity. In any system, it is important that both direct and indirect links are made visible. Indirect links are those that cascade through intermediary networks and are often hardest to perceive. For example, storm winds toppling power cables will lead to blackouts with direct impacts on business; but business will also be affected if the blackout cuts off power to public mass transport.

There is a large technical literature on risk management for critical infrastructure and services. The majority concerns risk management procedures to be undertaken as part of good management practice. There has been relatively little work on linkages with the urban planning community. The majority concerns internal risk management, with only a relatively small part oriented towards the urban planning community. As shown in Box 8.13, a review of this literature from the perspective of natural disasters argues that risk communication should be a central pillar for building resilience and response capacity.[64]

Protecting critical infrastructure and services against all conceivable sources of harm is prohibitively expensive

PAHO has been a leading organization pushing for health services to be incorporated within disaster planning. It has produced a number of studies on protecting health services through appropriate construction, design and management of health facilities. For example, in Peru, legislation has been drawn up to encourage the inclusion of disaster reduction activities in health-sector action plans.[65]

In the education sector, the goal of meeting the education targets of the MDGs has raised the political impor-

Box 8.13 Risk communication for critical infrastructure and services

A communication system is needed to ensure the transfer of information between linked critical infrastructure and services. It should aim to help in the coordination of risk reduction, the containment of disaster impacts and in speedy recovery. It is recommended that a formally constituted risk management committee (RMC) should be established with representatives from all linked networks and associated local stakeholders who would be affected by decisions, as well as municipal and national authorities with responsibility for overseeing operations in these life-support systems. The RMC would have subcommittees for particular domains of expertise and be driven by four areas of work:

Risk prevention

The first responsibility of the committee is to ensure that vulnerability is adequately reduced to provide an acceptable level of risk. Any residual risk with implications for the population will require a policy on disclosure.

Risk preparation

Each life-support network has the responsibility of reaching a level of preparedness that permits it to maintain or re-establish, in the shortest possible time, the functions that allow it to fulfil its mission during a disaster. Certain elements will need to be planned jointly with the RMC, including early warning criteria; a protocol for exchanges between networks; channels for communication or exchanges; agreements on encoding and decoding transmitted information, as well as feedback processes; the implementation of mitigation measures at the level of operations and infrastructure; and decision-making levels required and involved in these information exchanges.

Risk intervention

Direct links between managers and experts of linked life-support systems must be established for use during a crisis. Preferred channels of communication must transport high-quality, concise, precise and tangible information; transmit information quickly and without distortion; transmit information that sets mitigation measures in motion; transmit information that integrates with the operations of the destination networks, and establish a direct link between personnel of the hierarchical and operational levels; and create robust, redundant and compatible links between the networks. All mechanical and electronic means can be considered. The RMC can provide a review for the system or a reference point for networks seeking advice on how to connect to the system.

State of readiness

The RMC has responsibility for maintaining the system. It must agree on responsibility for maintenance of the communication channels; verification of the robustness of these channels; training of personnel who intervene in emergency situations; and preparation of joint exercises, allowing the readiness of all participants to be verified.

Source: Robert et al, 2003

tance of securing educational facilities from natural disaster risk. The fact that many school buildings also double as shelters in times of emergency also increases the value of investing in secure construction for schools. Nevertheless, many schools are not constructed or retrofitted to safe standards. More than 1000 school children were killed by inadequate school building standards in Spitak (Armenia) in 1988.[66] The Unit for Sustainable Development and Environment of the Organization of American States (OAS), PAHO and ISDR developed a programme,[67] in 1993, to build disaster resilience in educational services. The programme has focal points in Argentina, Costa Rica, Peru, Trinidad and Tobago, the US and Venezuela. In Peru, for example, work on schools in Quito has revealed design weaknesses, such as short columns, inappropriate joint designs and lightweight roofs. In Quebec, the Canadian Red Cross has worked with teachers to help children aged 5 to 16 psychologically prepare for the aftermath of natural disasters.[68]

Early warning is a cornerstone of disaster risk management

Risk to critical infrastructure and service networks in cities of developing countries is exacerbated by the complexity of their evolution and maintenance. Design is often piecemeal, the product of individual infrastructure development projects, with resulting networks being eclectic and varying in age, form and operational criteria. This serves to complicate and delay reconstruction of critical infrastructure as experts are called in from other cities or overseas. This is complicated further by informal-sector provision of critical services, such as potable water and policing. In an increasing number of cities, informal provision of such services is the primary distribution mode for the majority of citizens. The coordinated identification of network vulnerability and subsequent risk mitigation with informal-sector actors outside of regulatory control is challenging.

...translating scientific information on approaching hazard into language that results in action continues to challenge risk managers

EARLY WARNING

Early warning is a cornerstone of disaster risk management. Despite this, few cities have early warning systems or even hold data on past hazards and disaster events. Losses to the Indian Ocean Tsunami in 2004, the 2003 heat wave in Europe and the Bhopal chemical gas release in 1984 have all pointed to gaps in early warning systems that have since become political priorities for action. There are four interdependent components of early warning systems: risk knowledge; monitoring and warning; communication; and response capacity.[69] The capacity of an entire system is threatened if any one of these components is weak. This section reviews policy for early warning, risk knowledge, risk communication and response capacity.

In 2005, the ISDR undertook a survey of capacities and gaps in global early warning systems. The survey found that considerable progress had been made in developing the knowledge and technical tools required to assess risks and to generate and communicate predictions and warnings. Early warning system technologies are now available for almost all types of hazards and are in operation in at least some parts of the world. The weakest elements of warning systems concern warning dissemination and preparedness to act. Early warnings may fail to reach those who must take action, and may not be understood or address their concerns. Root causes appear to be inadequate political commitment, weak coordination among the various actors, and lack of public awareness and public participation in the development and operation of early warning systems.[70]

Risk knowledge and warning

Risk assessment is based on the tracking of information on hazards at a range of scales, from local to global, depending upon the character of the hazard and the nature of the city's vulnerabilities. Many of the techniques discussed earlier in this chapter can be used to generate baseline data against which subsequent assessments can measure risk trends. Shifting social contexts as well as environmental changes can make historical comparisons of risk over time difficult. An additional challenge for the monitoring of technological risk is the secrecy of industrial interests (public as well as private). For example, both the gas release from Union Carbide (India) Ltd's plant in Bhopal in 1984 and the release of radioactive particles from a nuclear power plant in Chernobyl (Ukraine) in 1986 were associated with technical and management failures inside the plants that should have been detected and responded to by a risk management system.[71]

Risks associated with natural hazards can require surveillance of physical phenomena locally – as, for example, in river-level gauges in the city – and at a distance. More distant measurements of risk can provide additional time for defensive action to be taken. Examples include water levels in rivers or dams, satellite tracking of tropical cyclones and storms, or seismic activity, as done by the International Tsunami Information Centre warning system.[72]

Risk communication

Technologically driven systems for risk identification and assessment routinely attract investment, as can be seen from the number of private-sector, national and international scientific bodies working in this field. But translating scientific information on approaching hazard into language that results in action continues to challenge risk managers.

People-centred approaches to risk communication and planning for appropriate response to early warnings require systems of communication to be in place and the use of appropriate language. There are many examples where risk identification has not led to timely warning and action due to a lack of clear lines and methods of communication. Seismic activity resulting in the Indian Ocean Tsunami was detected; but with no established lines of communication at the international level, information was not acted upon. Less well known is the 2002 volcanic lava flow that destroyed 40 per cent of the town of Goma in the Democratic Republic of Congo. This event was predicted by a local academic geologist; but in the absence of a municipal or national early warning system, his information was not acted upon. In response, the NGO Concern initiated a Community Preparedness for Volcano Hazards Programme (2002 to 2004). This programme built local resilience to volcanic risk by strengthening community understanding of risk, information networks and disaster response of partners and communities. This is an example of an early warning project embedded within a wider risk reduction programme. It involved administrative representatives, health and education staff, local Red Cross representatives, and the sub-commissions for education and civil protection set up in the wake of the volcanic eruption of 2002.[73]

Box 8.14 presents a success story of a people-centred early warning experience from Honduras that built local resilience through early warning, even when national early warning systems failed.

Effective early warning requires trust between those giving and receiving information. Some degree of coordination can give legitimacy to national early warning systems, although this is not always the case, especially where past experience of the state has eroded local trust in its institutions. The experience of La Masica is not unique in showing the advantages of decentralized systems. Transparent and clear information flows can help to build trust by constraining opportunities for the concealment of imminent hazards. Local and national governments have sometimes kept the public in the dark when receiving technical information on imminent threats to prevent unease among investors, especially in tourist economies. There are also cases where the public may refuse to heed early warnings from authorities. In both cases, clear and balanced information is critical, even when some level of uncertainty remains.[74]

Communicating risk to the public is less problematic in urban than rural areas because of the high density of communication infrastructure and social networks. This may not hold true for smaller, isolated and informal settlements or slums. Maintaining early warning communication systems where hazards are infrequent but potentially capable of delivering a high impact is especially difficult. Communication infrastructure may not be tested regularly and social contacts might be lost over time. One way around this is to build early warning communication systems on top of everyday communication networks. For instance, where mobile phones are common, they offer a potential network for spreading early warning and preparedness advice.

Box 8.14 People-centred early warning: La Masica, Honduras

The experience of La Masica in Honduras shows that small urban centres can successfully build their own resilience to disaster risk through people-centred early warning. The system developed in La Masica is relatively low cost and operates independently of outside information flows or resources, thus increasing its robustness during times of emergency.

La Masica's early warning system was put to the test during Hurricane Mitch in 1998. Hurricane Mitch killed over 20,000 people in Nicaragua and Honduras. In La Masica, despite flooding and economic damage caused by the nearby River Lean, none of the municipality's 25,000 residents was killed.

The early warning system had been initiated a few years before Hurricane Mitch, with the full involvement of the municipality's residents. The area had suffered in 1974 from Hurricane Fifi, and from smaller flooding incidents. Recognition of the community's high exposure to hazard catalysed the local early warning and preparedness programme. The programme included participatory risk assessments with local people observing river flow, the establishment of a local risk management organization, and the drawing-up of emergency plans for responding to rising water levels. Many of those involved in the programme were women.

The success of La Masica's local early warning system contrasts with the national flood warning system, which was disabled by flood waters and technical difficulties with satellite data. In this case, local organization based on simple technology provided greater resilience than the national high-tech alternative.

Source: Lavell, 2005, in Wisner et al, 2005

Response capacity

More difficult in cities is the coordination of action in response to alerts and early warnings. Pre-planning and clear communication with the public are needed to prevent inappropriate action or panic. In Lagos (Nigeria), a city where trust in officials is strained, more than 1000 people were killed in 2002, most by drowning, while fleeing in panic from an explosion in an army barrack.[75] This contrasts with Hong Kong, where tropical cyclone bulletins include practical advice on securing homes and businesses and how to access more information.[76]

In congested cities with overburdened transport networks, evacuation can be challenging. Cuba has perhaps the best track record on urban evacuation with a well-managed and frequently practised evacuation strategy as part of its risk reduction system (see Box 8.15). Clear lines of authority and cultural acceptance of large-scale public evacuation are elements in this success. In 2004, Hurricane Charley severely damaged 70,000 houses, but killed only four people thanks, in part, to the evacuation of over 2 million people.[77] The Cuban system contrasts with that of the US, which has increasingly relied on individuals to take responsibility for their own evacuation and safety following an early warning. Huge numbers of people successfully do this. Over 2.5 million people were evacuated from Florida following an early warning in advance of Hurricane Charley.[78] But, as was seen in 2005 during Hurricane Katrina, there will always be a sizeable urban population who lacks access to private transportation and will rely upon a well-organized public evacuation service.

Effective early warning requires trust between those giving and receiving information

FINANCING URBAN RISK MANAGEMENT

City authorities seldom generate sufficient funds to meet all their development and risk reduction needs. Thus, they face the twin challenge of attracting finance and balancing the conditionalities that come with this support against local priorities and strategies for disaster risk management. Inefficient or inadequate fiscal decentralization further reduces the financial capacity of local governments. This is especially the case in poorer or rapidly expanding cities where the proportion of residents and organizations who contribute to the city revenue can be low.

National governments finance urban infrastructure works through project grants or line financing through ministries with responsibility for infrastructure in the urban sector. In Guyana, central government is responsible for sea defence and land drainage work, which nonetheless protects

Box 8.15 Lessons in risk reduction from Cuba

Cuba's integrated system of disaster risk management has succeeded in saving many lives and has built resilience beyond the level that might be expected from the country's economic status. Between 1996 and 2002, six hurricanes hit Cuba, causing 16 deaths in Cuba out of the total of 665 deaths they collectively caused. What is Cuba doing right?

Central to Cuba's successful risk reduction is the government's stated priority that its fundamental commitment during a hurricane is to save lives. The country's risk reduction plan and disaster preparedness structures support this commitment to save lives through the following:

- a disaster preparedness plan, which incorporates a specific focus on the most vulnerable, provides for monitoring their situation and adapts plans to address their specific needs;
- the national civil defence structure, which uses sub-national government at the provincial, municipal and local level for disaster preparedness and response (in most disasters, local knowledge and leadership play key but unacknowledged roles in disaster risk reduction; the Cuban model incorporates these as central);
- practical, effective lifeline structures, with particular emphasis on mass evacuation and use of safe secure shelters;
- a 'culture of safety' that creates the trust and awareness necessary to motivate people to cooperate and participate in risk reduction;
- citizen participation by incorporating community mobilization in a three-tiered system of participation in planning, community implementation of lifeline structures and the creation and building of social capital.

Since 75 per cent of Cuba's 11 million people are urban, the country's disaster preparedness plan has a strong focus on being operational in urban areas.

Cuba's model also owes a lot to its unique system of government and its socio-economic model, which has consistently addressed risk reduction through policies of social and economic equity and poverty reduction. These policies have produced 'multiplier effects' that enhance risk reduction in many ways. The adult population is 100 per cent literate and therefore can access educational materials about disasters, and all children are exposed to disaster preparedness in school curricula. There is an adequate road system in the country that facilitates speedy evacuation and building codes are enforced, which reduces the element of highly vulnerable substandard construction. Approximately 95 per cent of the households in the country have electricity and therefore can access information about disasters through radio and television. Finally, the intricate web of social, professional and political organizations in the country provides organizational structures that can be quickly mobilized in disaster. Surprisingly, the economic crisis triggered by the collapse of the Soviet Union has not affected Cuba's success in protecting the lives of its population from hurricanes.

The Cuban government is unique in that it has paid an equal amount of attention to the structural and physical aspects of disaster preparedness, but also created a 'culture of safety' through successful education and awareness campaigns. It has also demonstrated the central importance of management capacity and political will in successful risk reduction. This holds out real possibility and hope for other countries, rich and poor alike, facing the growing dangers of natural hazards.

Source: Thompson, 2007

National budgets for disasters tend to prioritize relief and emergency responses

the capital city, Georgetown, from flooding. Political and personal rivalry between the leaders of city and national governments is, at times, interpreted as a cause for delay or withdrawal of funds.

...bilateral and multilateral donors ... have a history of supporting disaster reconstruction

National budgets for disasters tend to prioritize relief and emergency responses. Prevention and mitigation are less attractive as funding choices. After all, governments get less praise from the electorate and the international community for reducing disaster risk than they do for a speedy and generous emergency response.[79] A number of countries have special calamity funds to cover the additional costs of reconstruction (e.g. India, the Philippines and Colombia), while some in Latin America and the Caribbean make special mention of municipal-level support for risk reduction.[80]

Social funds and public works programmes are more normally associated with large-scale rural disasters as mechanisms for supporting livelihoods; but they have potential for urban areas too. In Nicaragua, following Hurricane Mitch in 1998, social fund financing was released through four regional offices and used to build shelter, water and sanitation systems, and bridges. This was essential for enabling critical services and market access to smaller towns and rural settlements.[81]

Like national governments, bilateral and multilateral donors, including international development banks, have a history of supporting disaster reconstruction. The Asian Development Bank (ADB), the Inter-American Development Bank (IDB), the UNDP, the World Bank and the African Development Bank all have policies covering natural disasters and implement projects in this area. Only the UNDP funds relief; but all are active in reconstruction. With the exception of the African Development Bank, disaster reconstruction can be funded by drawing on funding already allocated to development projects. The World Bank's approach to disasters, for instance, has tended to be reactive rather than tactical (see Box 8.16). Disasters have been treated as interruptions in development rather than as a risk that is integral to development. Few Country Assistance Strategies or Poverty Reduction Strategy Papers (PRSPs) supported by the World Bank mention disaster risk.

Recent initiatives, notably by the IDB, the Caribbean Development Bank, the DFID and the Deutsche Gesellschaft für Technische Zusammenarbeit (GTZ), among others, indicate a reappraisal and recognition of the value of investing in risk reduction. For example, in 2006, the DFID committed to allocating approximately 10 per cent of its

Box 8.16 World Bank funding for disaster risk reduction and reconstruction

As a proportion of World Bank lending, disaster lending has increased from 6 per cent during the period of 1984 to 1988 to 14 per cent from 1999 to 2003. Four times as much disaster lending is spent in rural than urban areas. Emergency recovery loans (ERLs) provided under the World Bank's Emergency Recovery Assistance Policy are made available to countries undertaking disaster reconstruction. ERLs were first adopted during 1970 following an earthquake in Peru. These loans are intended for recovery from natural and human-made disasters, but also economic shocks following biological and political events, such as foot-and-mouth disease outbreaks and political violence, including terrorism. However, a large amount of the World Bank's disaster response lending takes place outside of ERLs. For instance, only 2 out of 95 fire-related projects and 23 out of 59 earthquake-related activities are ERLs.

ERLs are disadvantaged since they are limited to a three-year timeframe. This has led to delays in implementation because projects that could benefit from attention to social and economic concerns have been prepared too quickly. Current policy does not support the purchase of consumables that might be used for disaster relief. This closes an opportunity for supporting countries hit by catastrophic events, such as the incapacitation of major and capital cities, which are beyond the capacity of governments, bilaterals and humanitarians to support. The World Bank has shown some flexibility by financing temporary shelter programmes in Colombia, El Salvador, Honduras, India and Turkey, as well as cash transfers to earthquake-affected populations in Chile in 1985, Turkey in 1999, and in response to the 2004 Indian Ocean Tsunami in Sri Lanka and the Maldives.

In addition to ERLs, World Bank emergency assistance is available through reallocation, redesign of pipeline projects, freestanding mitigation projects and assessments. This provides some useful flexibility for countries. What is missing is a mechanism for providing rapid lending for relief that does not involve opportunity costs over the medium term. The World Bank is good at supporting infrastructure reconstruction, but neglects the support for social organization that is necessary for building sustainability into investments. This observation might be linked to the failure of many projects to incorporate the findings of disaster prevention studies that have been commissioned as part of the project. Of 197 projects focusing on disaster mitigation or prevention, 142 included such studies, but only 54 took these studies into account.

Recent work in the World Bank has moved in a positive direction and begun to embrace prevention and mitigation to include non-structural measures, such as institution building for hazard management, land-use planning, enforcement of building codes and insurance mechanisms. But more work is still to be done. In particular, challenges remain in supporting institutions and developing lending tools that encourage maintenance of investments; in reviewing procurement strategies that do not go through competitive bidding; in coordinating between donors, including non-governmental organizations (NGOs); and in strengthening community level involvement and capacity.

Source: World Bank Independent Evaluation Group, 2006

funding for natural disaster response to prepare for and mitigate the impact of future disasters, where this can be done effectively. The DFID expects this new financial support to be particularly relevant for sudden onset disasters and it will only apply to responses that will cost more than UK£500,000.[82] Large-scale urban disasters are likely to fall within this new scheme. United Nations organizations (notably, the Bureau for Crisis Prevention and Recovery at UNDP and UN-Habitat) and some international NGOs, such as the International Federation of the Red Cross and Red Crescent Societies (IFRC) and Tearfund, have championed the risk reduction agenda. These organizations are active in lobbying internationally for risk reduction and have emphasized the need for risk reduction in urban contexts.

Private sector insurance is important as a means of financing reconstruction

Private-sector insurance is important as a means of financing reconstruction and as a source of foreign currency with which to offset balance of payments deficits during the reconstruction period.[83] Insurance companies have also been active in promoting secure building practices. In areas of high potential loss, private-sector insurance has been underwritten or replaced by government insurance. This is the case in the US, where Florida's catastrophe fund reimburses insurers when disaster losses exceed set levels.[84]

DISASTER RESPONSE AND RECONSTRUCTION

This section reviews the roles played by local authorities and others, including local people and international agencies, during response and reconstruction phases of disaster. In particular, the aim of this section is to review the challenges to 'building back better' during these phases. First, issues of common concern to response and reconstruction are discussed and then each phase is reviewed in more detail.

Municipal authorities and local government are well placed to coordinate emergency response and reconstruction

The role of local authorities

Municipal authorities and local government are well placed to coordinate emergency response and reconstruction. They can link response and reconstruction to pre-disaster development goals and, indeed, can provide a forum for pre-disaster development goals to be reappraised in light of the disaster event. Table 8.1 describes the core activities of local authorities during response and reconstruction phases. There is a good degree of overlap in basic roles such as assessment for planning, coordination with civil society and other government agencies, liaising with international agencies, monitoring progress, establishing lines of finance, reviewing performance and providing public information. The distinction between relief and reconstruction is even less clear on the ground. This is especially the case in urban contexts where many different sectoral actors are involved and disasters have led to different scales of destruction in different parts of a settlement or city. Consequently, some sectors or areas of a city, or individual settlements, may be progressing towards development-oriented reconstruction, while others are still coping with relief work.

During large events, where response and reconstruction involve international actors, it can be hard to retain control over coordination, especially for local authorities with limited capacity. Even where joint coordination systems work, the myriad of smaller agencies (many of which may be new to development and humanitarian work) are often not identified and are not party to management and coordination decisions. Loss of coordination through swamping from international agencies, or as a result of the diversity of small groups, can erode local self-reliance and hinder the integration of development within reconstruction. Pre-disaster planning that includes organizational structures to manage joint action and, as far as possible, to decentralize decision-making to sectoral, regional and community levels is the best way to avoid loss of strategic control.

The building-back-better agenda crystallizes the aim of building development into post-disaster work

Building-back-better agenda

The building-back-better agenda crystallizes the aim of building development into post-disaster work so that vulnerability is reduced and life chances are enhanced as a result. The tension between speed of delivery and the desire for inclusive and participatory decision-making is a theme that runs throughout the integration of development into response and reconstruction. Established cultures of response privilege speed and efficiency in delivery; but this has meant that an opportunity has been lost for furthering development aims through post-disaster action.

A continuum of actions from relief through response to development and preparedness exists. Developmental and emergency thinking and actions are needed at each stage. The emphasis is different at each stage and, in practice, it is proving difficult to integrate the right balance of humanitarian and development actors and ideas; but progress is being made. Innovative planning for shelter reconstruction in Kashmir following the South Asian earthquake in 2005 included not only cash for work, where survivors were paid to clear land, but also cash for shelter. Affected people were provided with building materials and then paid for construction work. The rush to build before the coming winter was made sustainable through designs that could be upgraded to more permanent structures over time. Through these two mechanisms, reconstruction became developmental.[85]

The challenge to 'build back better' confronts a number of dominant practices in reconstruction work. These are well exemplified in experiences that have arisen from planned housing reconstruction in the Andaman and Nicobar Islands after the Indian Ocean Tsunami. After the tsunami, the Government of India offered to replace nearly 10,000 homes. But lack of participation led to inappropriate building design and materials, as well as selection of settlement sites. Moreover, a preference for external contractors missed an opportunity to strengthen local livelihoods. The depth of alienation felt by survivors in this project erupted in protests that left more than 100 people injured.[86]

Capitalizing on the opportunity that disaster presents to build back better requires pre-disaster planning. From the perspective of human settlements, land-use titling and the granting of secure tenure before a disaster occurs make the distribution of recovery support (potentially including relocation or rebuilding) more transparent and efficient. The rationalization of planning and building regulations and administrative approaches that reach the poor will not only reduce loss, but act as benchmarks for reconstruction building. Without the enforcement of such guidelines, risk will be built into new construction.

More generally, reconstruction after the Indian Ocean Tsunami has provided much experience in attempts to build back better. A number of lessons can be learned that will have resonance for all housing and infrastructure reconstruction projects, including:[87]

- A clear policy framework that articulates objectives, entitlements of affected families, decision-making criteria, timetables and grievance-settling procedures helps

Table 8.1

Local authority actions during disaster relief and reconstruction

Local authority role	Relief	Reconstruction
Assessment for planning	Undertake a rapid impact assessment to help judge the scale of response and rehabilitation to be undertaken.	Monitor human and economic impacts as they unfold. A dynamic approach to impact assessment is particularly important to be able to track inflationary consequences of reconstruction materials and any shortages in food supplies.
Coordination	Coordinate administrative and technical aspects of disaster emergency response with emergency services, the armed forces, the Red Cross/Red Crescent and other civil society groups. This work should involve liaison with managers of critical infrastructure and services.	Bring together stakeholders to plan the transition from emergency to reconstruction and from reconstruction to development. Consider to what extent development pathways led to the accumulation of risk and eventual disaster event, and the opportunities for building risk reduction into reconstruction, rehabilitation and post-disaster development.
Liaise with national and international agencies	Determine if national and international assistance is required for emergency response.	Determine if national and international assistance is required for reconstruction and rehabilitation.
Monitor progress	Monitor and review the performance of emergency services.	Monitor and review the performance of reconstruction services.
Seek finance	Facilitate access to finance through access to local and national emergency funds.	Facilitate access to finance through emergency funds and private insurance. Enable private remittance flows.
Review performance	Document decision-making for future analysis and learning.	Review the performance of pre-disaster policy and organization for risk reduction, early warning, disaster response and reconstruction. Document and evaluate the programmes.
Public information	Keep the public informed at all times.	Keep the public informed at all times.

to foster trust and collaboration between stakeholders.
- The criteria for identifying beneficiaries must be clear. In developmental approaches, consideration is given to supporting those vulnerable households who were not affected by the disaster.
- Involving local participation in the selection of resettlement sites improves final choices and increases acceptability.
- Information dissemination systems can regularly report on progress directly to affected families and individuals in order to reduce stress and tension.
- Reconstruction is a prime opportunity to enhance women's property rights. This has been done by giving new ownership titles jointly to husband and wife or in the name of the female head of household in single parent families.
- The best building design is flexible. Families use houses differently and have diverse traditions of design and use. Those who will live in houses should be allowed to contribute in the design stage in order to diversify and make appropriate use of architectural styles. Where vernacular housing design has proven resilient to hazards, this should be given preference.
- Particularly when large contracting firms are used, the most successful projects have built-in mechanisms for community oversight.
- Reconstruction provides a great opportunity to support the local economy. Local craftspeople should be employed or trained in preference over external firms. Traditional materials and technologies can be used.
- The environmental impact assessment (EIA) of reconstruction is seldom taken into account and, in large schemes, can be considerable, including the generation of local hazard (e.g. by felling mangrove stands or construction in low-lying places). The best EIAs include not only damage onsite, but also the carbon costs of sourcing and transporting materials.

The following discussion analyses in greater detail the roles that can be played, in particular, by local authorities in pro-development disaster response and reconstruction.

Disaster response

Effective disaster response rests on having a prepared and rehearsed plan with clearly identified responsibilities. The stakeholders involved in response are broadly similar for natural and human-made disasters. Initial response includes neighbours and community organizations, emergency services and civil defence. Emergency response can overlap with development, so that, increasingly, development actors (including those with experience in urban planning and construction), along with international agencies such as UN-Habitat, become involved.

In those cities and parts of cities where municipal resources are limited, self-organized and community-based response plans can save many lives. Residents of Los Manguitos, an informal settlement in the city of Santo Domingo (the Dominican Republic) did not receive government or NGO support for two weeks following Hurricane Georges in 1998. Pre-disaster social organization enabled community members to undertake social care, policing and housing repairs during this period of uncertainty.[88]

More broadly, the state has responsibility for maintaining the rule of law and to protect property and people from looting and violent crime during disasters. This is a major task during reconstruction. There may be a role for civil society groups or international observers to oversee activities or work in partnership with security agencies, such as the army, police or civil defence. This is particularly the case in cities where the state or para-statal groups have had a violent relationship with citizens pre-disaster.

Reconstruction provides a great opportunity to support the local economy

Some people are more at risk than others of being left out of relief and response programmes. Women, children and orphans, the elderly and those who are marginalized because of language, culture or social class are especially liable to not having their entitlements met during relief and response. The social pressures that create pre-disaster inequality underpin how people fare during disaster response. This is a particular challenge because it means that it is not sufficient to follow local demands and directions on aid distribution. These must be questioned in light of the prevailing development context. Accounts from the South Asian earthquake in 2005 note that women were largely dependent upon men for access to relief. Few women received tents or food or came forward to participate in food or cash work programmes. Even when this gender disparity was recognized by agencies, it was difficult to find skilled women, underlining the influence of pre-disaster inequalities on post-disaster work that aims to build back better.[89]

Security is also a concern if temporary shelter is provided in camps. Women are often most at risk from violence, but also suffer from a lack of privacy and from inadequate provision for personal hygiene.[90] In Sri Lanka, after the Indian Ocean Tsunami, women were seldom found among the managers of camps. Indeed, the Sri Lankan Parliament Select Committee on Natural Disasters, mandated to assess disaster preparedness and mitigation, had only 2 women out of its 22 members. Many tent villages set up after the South Asian earthquake have been reported to have little or no functional security.[91]

...where municipal resources are limited, self-organised and community-based response plans can save many lives

Careful coordination of response activities can help families to stay together, and to protect women, children and the aged. But this relies on pre-disaster registration and on safe record-keeping. Birth registration forms and formal identification documents are often lost in disasters; but are essential tools for protecting individuals' rights, including access to relief and in reuniting families.[92] The best relief is a product of pre-disaster training and preparedness based on local decentralized control.

Reconstruction for risk reduction

Strong local government is needed to oversee reconstruction and to help control profiteering over land held for resettlement.[93] Reconstruction is a period when urban land rights are often contested or fought over by competing interests. It is not uncommon for those with only usufruct or customary rights, or for the poor or tenants, to lose claims over high-value land, and for this to be transferred to speculators and developers in the process of reconstruction. If land titles did not exist before the disaster or have been lost, proxy indicators are useful. Where such measures are not possible, alternative means need to be found to ensure that land is not seized outright or that fraudulent claims are not honoured.

Reconstruction is a period when urban land rights are often contested or fought over by competing interests

Following the Indian Ocean Tsunami in 2004, reconstruction planning for Aceh (Indonesia) recognized the opportunity to build back better through the provision of land titles. Land rights were correctly understood to be the cornerstone upon which communities rebuild their homes and livelihoods. They provide a solid, legal foundation for spatial planning, reconstruction and long-term economic development. Reconstruction has been supported by a multi-donor fund of US$28 million. Under the project, some 600,000 land parcels are to be titled, many for the first time ever, since less than 20 per cent of the landowners in Aceh had legal titles prior to the tsunami. This developmental aspect of reconstruction will enable citizens to use their land as collateral for financing homes and businesses. Yet, a review of progress in December 2006 found that while field-based teams had surveyed and adjudicated over 120,000 parcels of land, bureaucratic obstacles had resulted in the disbursement of only 7700 titles. Political will as well as technical capacity is needed to push forward ambitious programmes for building back better.[94]

The basic need for shelter should not be used as an excuse for overly rapid and socially unsustainable housing reconstruction

The overall aim of building back better is to use reconstruction as an opportunity to improve the economic, physical and social infrastructure, and to support the asset bases of individuals and households at risk. Reconstruction becomes a project for improving survivors' life chances and resilience, not returning them to pre-disaster levels.

If reconstruction programmes are to build back better, they must take into account the needs of families and be sensitive to gender, age and culturally specific needs and norms. The basic need for shelter should not be used as an excuse for overly rapid and socially unsustainable housing reconstruction. Too often, household livelihoods requiring access to external space (such as peri-urban agriculture) are lost when reconstruction planning places excessive emphasis on value for money. The misapplication of a development approach was seen in the Indian Ocean Tsunami in 2004, where efforts were made to strengthen the local livelihood base beyond pre-tsunami levels through the widespread provision of fishing boats. In some communities, this led to a lack of crew and the withdrawal of older male children from school.

...local economic development must be restarted as soon as possible after a disaster

One positive outcome of reconstruction that takes development goals into account can be the strengthening of social capital, which, in turn, builds resilience. In cities were civil society is strong, disasters can be opportunities for pushing reforms in urban planning. Popular action in Mexico City, following the 1985 earthquake, prevented the implementation of city plans to redevelop low-income inner-city tenements for higher-income uses.

The International Labour Organization (ILO) Crisis Response Programme aims to promote social development during reconstruction by helping to save existing jobs and creating new ones through the reconstruction process. The response package to the 2001 Gujarat earthquake in India included a model programme for social and economic reconstruction in ten villages in the Kutch district, funded by the ILO and implemented by the Self-Employed Women's Association (SEWA). In response to the earthquakes in El Salvador and in Peru in 2001, rapid employment impact projects were launched in partnership with the UNDP.[95] In order for households and communities to recover, local economic reconstruction must be restarted as soon as possible after a disaster. This means developing local markets through cash-for-work schemes, as well as direct support for local businesses requiring new premises or tools to restart. Often called 'foundation markets', these include consumer and retail services – stalls and shops.[96]

A final act in the transition to (realigned) development has often been to memorialize a disaster. Memorials can serve to support the healing process and help as a reminder of what can result from inappropriate development. Memorials are especially powerful when they gather together data and experiences – perhaps conflicting – of the event, its causes and consequences.

There is great scope for disaster impacts to be reduced if development actors are invited to contribute to planning reconstruction and rehabilitation. The inclusion of UN-Habitat in planning reconstruction following the earthquake in Bam (Iran) in 2003 led to a policy of supporting residents in reconstructing their own homes, including the incorporation of improved seismic resistance in preference to the established procedure of placing residents in temporary shelters.[97]

CONCLUDING REMARKS

The components of urban risk policy outlined in this chapter are mutually reinforcing. Successful early warning relies upon risk assessment and strong local communities for information transfer and action. Risk assessment feeds directly into land-use planning decisions. These and the other activities outlined in this chapter offer opportunities to build back better when they are considered in reconstruction, as well as in preparedness for disaster. They are key pathways for meeting developmental activities with the humanitarian imperatives of relief and reconstruction and point towards mechanisms for urban disaster risk reduction.

Local authorities are the most important actors in urban disaster risk reduction. Local authorities are the level of government closest to the ground and most directly answerable to those at risk. They occupy a strategic institutional position, mediating between competing interests in the city and beyond, and as a conduit of information and resources between communities and external actors. Their scope for action is, however, often severely limited by lack of finance, human skill shortages, an overburdening of responsibilities and political constraints.

The most successful partnerships for risk reduction invariably include local authorities and communities, often also with civil society organizations involved. Such partnerships can combine the scale of action and resources of government, on the one hand, with sensitivity for local diversity held by community-based organizations and the technical ability of NGOs, on the other. If urban governance systems are to take disaster risk reduction seriously, greater support for multi-stakeholder planning and project implementation is needed. Reforms in international financial organizations indicate greater support in the near future for building risk reduction into development planning and for a reconsideration of reconstruction financing in order to create real opportunities for progressive urban risk reduction.

The following key challenges remain; but progress is being made:

- Urban disaster continues to be predominantly managed in low- and middle-income countries by emergency response and reconstruction, rather than mitigation, preparedness and investing in disaster-resilient development. Changes in international funding regimes can help move the risk reduction agenda forward.
- A lack of routine and rigorous collection of data on city-wide vulnerability and loss contribute to the low policy status of risk reduction.
- Where formal planning capacity is unlikely to meet demand in the foreseeable future, recent innovations in extending urban planning and building construction controls into the informal sector have met with some success and point the way forward in large and small cities alike.
- Early warning continues to be dominated by techno-centric approaches. Technology is a helpful, but partial, solution to early warning. Investment in piggybacking early warning systems onto existing social networks can be a cost-effective and sustainable way forward.
- A lack of transparency in reconstruction can lead, for example, to economic investments being recycled into the international economy, thus missing an opportunity for enhancing local safety, security and long-term development through reconstruction. The rapidity with which reconstruction is undertaken should be more seriously weighed against the potential for more participatory approaches that offer downward accountability.

NOTES

1 ISDR, 2004a.
2 For a discussion and examples of community capacity-building through hazard and vulnerability mapping, see ADPC (2004).
3 This list builds on ISDR, 2004a.
4 ISDR, 2004a.
5 See UNDP, 2004, and www.ldeo.columbia.edu/chrr/research/hotspots/.
6 Seismic hazard maps aim to show the susceptibility of an area to damage from energy waves travelling through the ground caused by earthquakes. They vary in comprehensiveness, from those based on geological information alone to those that incorporate soil properties and building resistance.
7 In 1997, the Government of India produced a national *Vulnerability Atlas*, which has been instrumental in helping state and municipal authorities strengthen land-use and construction codes and mainstream disaster risk reduction into development planning. See www.bmtpc.org/disaster.htm.
8 UK Environment Agency, www.environment-agency.gov.uk/maps/.
9 See www.scorecard.org/index.tcl.
10 Munich Re, 2004.
11 McGregor et al, 2006.
12 Carreno et al, 2007.
13 See www.epa.gov/enviro.
14 See www.cmap.nypirg.org.
15 See www.hud.gov/emaps.
16 For a wealth of theoretical and practical experience on participatory approaches in general, see the International Institute for Environment and Development, Participatory Learning and Action Notes, accessed at www.iied.org/NR/agbioliv/pla_notes/index.html.
17 See www.provention consortium.org/?pageid=39.
18 See www.provention consortium.org/files/tools_CRA/ActionAid_PVA_guide.pdf.
19 See www.unisdr.org/eng/hfa/hfa.htm.
20 For an updated collection of case studies and guidance notes on participatory methods, see www.?provention consortium.org/?pageid=43.
21 Pelling, forthcoming.
22 ADPC, 2005.
23 Peacock et al, 2005.
24 Greening et al, 1996.
25 *Taipei Times*, 2006.
26 Jeffrey, 2000.
27 Cross, 2001.
28 Enarson and Morrow, 1997.
29 See http://sspindia.org.
30 Wisner et al, 2004.
31 Asian Urban Disaster Mitigation Programme (undated).
32 See www.fourmilab.ch/etexts/www/un/udhr.html.
33 Wisner, 2001.
34 See www.dfid.gov.uk/news/files/disaster-risk-reduction-faqs.asp.
35 See www.unisdr.org/eng/hfa/docs/HFA-brochure-English.pdf.
36 Pelling, 2003.
37 ActionAid, 2006.
38 Pelling, 2003.
39 ISDR, 2004a.
40 Hedley et al, 2002.
41 ISDR, 2005b.
42 ISDR, 2004a
43 These plans were also supported by the Swiss Development Cooperation Agency and the Nicaraguan Institute for Municipal Development and implemented in Dipilto, Mozonte, Ocotal, Ciudad Darío, San Isidro and Sébaco. See www.sosnicaragua.gob.ni.
44 UN-Habitat, 2006a.
45 UN-Habitat, 2006a.
46 See Chapter 12 for a more detailed discussion of challenges and good practice guidelines for re-housing.
47 Asian Urban Disaster Mitigation Programme, 2001.
48 See www.info-turk.be.
49 Pelling et al, 2002.
50 ISDR, 2004a.
51 See www.provention consortium.org/.
52 World Bank Independent Evaluation Group, 2006.
53 Around US$6000.
54 See www.eeri.org/.
55 See www.iaee.or.jp/.
56 See www.wssi.org/.
57 See Box 8.2 and www.geohaz.org/project/gesi/GesiOver.htm.
58 See www-megacities.physik.uni-karlsruhe.de/.
59 ISDR, 2004a.
60 *Ibid*.
61 Sharma, 2001.
62 See www.unisdr.org/wcdr/thematic-sessions/presentations/session4-8/buckle.pdf.
63 Robert et al, 2003.
64 *Ibid*.
65 See www.paho.org/english/PED/publication_eng.htm.
66 See www.unisdr.org/wcdr/thematic-sessions/presentations/session 5-1/fsss-mr-wisner.pdf.
67 Known as the *Hemispheric Action Plan for Vulnerability Reduction in the Education Sector to Socio-Natural Disasters* (or *EDUPLANhemisférico*).
68 International Federation of the Red Cross and Red Crescent Societies, www.ifrc.org/Docs/pubs/?disasters/reduction/canada-case-en.pdf.
69 ISDR, 2006a.
70 *Ibid*.
71 See Box 7.3.
72 See http://ioc.unesco.org/iocweb/disaster Mitigation.php.
73 ISDR, 2004b.
74 ISDR, 2006b.
75 BBC News, 2003.
76 WMO, 2002.
77 For more detail on the Cuban risk reduction system, see Box 8.15.
78 Wisner et al, 2005.
79 For a full discussion of the institutional barriers to disaster risk reduction, see DFID, 2005.
80 ISDR, 2004a.
81 UNDP, 2003.
82 DFID, 2006.
83 Pelling et al, 2002.
84 See www.bisanet.org/bism/2004/getting_smart.html.
85 AIDMI, 2006.
86 Rawal et al, 2006.
87 *Ibid*; Christoplos, 2006; Oxfam International, 2005b.
88 Pelling, 2003.
89 Fordham, 2006.
90 Fordham, 2003.
91 Fordham, 2006.
92 Plan International, 2005.
93 World Bank, 2005.
94 Breteche and Steer, 2006.
95 Calvi-Parisetti and Kiniger-Passigli, 2002.
96 Billing, 2006.
97 DFID, 2005.

CHAPTER 9

SMALL-SCALE HAZARDS: THE CASE OF ROAD TRAFFIC ACCIDENTS

As noted in Chapter 7, a hazard is a potentially damaging event that causes loss of life or injury, property damage, social and economic disruption, or environmental degradation.[1] A number of less frequent and smaller-scale hazards influence safety and security in urban areas. Yet, while hazards that trigger large-scale disaster events and thus cause huge losses are well documented, smaller-scale hazards that result in aggregate loss over a longer period of time are often not recorded. Fire, flooding, building collapse and traffic accidents are some of the small-scale hazards common to urban areas.

The significance of small-scale hazards is particularly illustrated by the incidence and impacts of road traffic accidents, which result in more deaths worldwide each year than any large natural or human-made disaster type. Traffic accidents cause extensive loss of human lives and livelihoods in urban areas, killing over 1 million people globally every year.[2] An absence of systematic data collection on the incidence and impacts of traffic accidents, however, leads to their invisibility to urban planners and policy-makers.

This chapter examines the trends and impacts of road traffic accidents in urban areas. The substantial human and economic losses from traffic accidents and their linkages to processes of urbanization are elaborated upon. Traffic accidents are examined here in detail because, in aggregate, they cause more loss of human life and economic productivity than larger-scale natural and human-made disasters. Furthermore, it is important to consider traffic accidents in urban development since they are the products of policy failures and omissions, not of urban life *per se*.

INCIDENCE AND IMPACTS OF ROAD TRAFFIC ACCIDENTS: GLOBAL TRENDS

Traffic accidents, which are reviewed here from a human settlements perspective, include those involving road-based motorized and non-motorized vehicles of various capacities. Traffic accidents range from major events resulting in high loss of human life to everyday incidents whose impacts are only felt at the individual or household level. They pose a serious threat to the safety and well-being of urban households on a daily basis by generating economically and socially unsustainable outcomes. It is thus important to review traffic accidents as a key hazard threatening the safety and security of urban inhabitants.

The following discussion first examines the global and regional incidence and impacts of traffic accidents through lives lost and economic losses. Different vulnerability factors are then explored since the distribution of traffic accident loss in urban areas is not random. In analysing the impacts of traffic accidents, comprehensive and comparative analysis of risk and loss at the national and city levels is difficult since data is not available for some potentially high-risk locations. Mortality should be seen as a tip-of-the-iceberg measure of loss. Data on those injured is less reliable, with many cases not being reported, and therefore has not been used in this report. Indirect impacts are also difficult to analyse with current available data.

Traffic accidents cause extensive loss of human lives and livelihoods in urban areas, killing over 1 million people globally every year

Impacts on human lives

Losses to traffic accidents are commonplace and needlessly deadly aspects of urban life. The scale of impact of traffic accidents at the aggregate level is disturbingly large. The World Health Organization (WHO) estimates that 1.2 million people are killed in road crashes each year, and as many as 50 million are injured.[3] In effect, 3242 individuals die daily from traffic accidents worldwide.[4] Projections indicate that these figures will increase by about 65 per cent over the next 20 years unless there is new commitment to enhance prevention. Indeed, by 2020, road traffic injuries are expected to become the third major cause for disease and injury in the world. Nevertheless, the everyday nature of traffic accidents means that they attract less policy and media attention than the consequent high loss rates deserve.

...a disproportionate 90% of the deaths from traffic accidents worldwide occur in low and middle-income countries

Currently, a disproportionate 90 per cent of the deaths from traffic accidents worldwide occur in low- and middle-income countries.[5] Table 9.1 presents a breakdown of the distribution of reported traffic mortality by world region for the year 2002. Separate data is presented for middle-, low- and high-income countries within each world region. It is the low- and middle-income countries in Africa

World Region	Mortality per 100,000 individuals	
	Low- and middle-income countries	High-income countries
Africa	28.3	–
The Americas	16.2	14.8
Asia (Southeast Asia)	18.6	–
Asia (Eastern Mediterranean)	26.4	19.0
Europe	17.4	11.0
Western Pacific	18.5	12.0

Table 9.1

Traffic accident mortality rates by world region, 2002

Source: WHO, 2004

and Asia that have the highest mortality rates resulting from traffic accidents, with high-income countries in Europe and the Western Pacific having the lowest mortality rates. Studies have shown that traffic accident fatality is high when gross domestic product (GDP) is low and then declines with continued GDP growth.[6]

For those countries where data is available, it is striking that mortality rates are much higher than the regional averages shown in Table 9.1. Some of the highest mortality rates (deaths per 10,000 motor vehicles) worldwide occur in African countries such as Ethiopia (195), Uganda (122) and Malawi (193). Two countries, South Africa and Nigeria, account for more than half of Africa's road fatalities.[7] In the People's Republic of China, despite huge investments to improve road networks, the rapid development and increasing number of vehicles have substantially increased road accidents and loss of life. During the period of 2000 to 2004, over 500,000 people were killed and around 2.6 million injured in road accidents in the People's Republic of China, equivalent to one fatality every five minutes, the highest in the world.[8]

Pro-poor urban policies need to consider traffic accidents as a factor that…can tip households into poverty or collapse

High rates of mortality are also found in some Latin American countries (41.7 per 100,000 individuals in El Salvador; 41 per 100,000 in the Dominican Republic; and 25.6 per 100,000 in Brazil), as well as some countries in Europe (22.7 per 100,000 individuals in Latvia; 19.4 per 100,000 in the Russian Federation; and 19.3 per 100,000 in Lithuania) and Asia (21.9 per 100,000 individuals in the Republic of Korea; 21 per 100,000 in Thailand; and 19 per 100,000 in China).[9]

Mortality rates are high in low- and middle-income countries despite their relatively low levels of vehicle ownership and use (see Table 9.2). For instance, for every 10,000 vehicles in circulation, the average Latin American country registers around 18 traffic fatalities per year. In the US, Canada, Japan and several European countries belonging to the Organisation for Economic Co-operation and Development (OECD), the average is only 2.4 fatalities per 10,000 vehicles.[10] Africa's global road fatality share is three times as large as its motor vehicle share.[11] The Asia–Pacific region has only around 18 per cent of the world's motorized vehicle fleet, but is disproportionately affected by traffic hazards, accounting for around 50 per cent of global road deaths.[12]

This provides a strong indication that the scale of motorization in a country or city's transport system is not of itself a sole indicator for, or a cause of, traffic accidents. The higher number of cars in richer countries means that potential hazard is high; but through road traffic planning, the education of different road users and emergency response teams, risk has been reduced, although it remains a significant challenge. This observation clearly shows the potential for risk management to reduce loss from traffic accidents.

Although a substantial increase in road traffic mortalities is expected over the next 20 years if current policies are not adjusted,[13] these trends vary by region. In Europe and North America, mortality rates have been in decline since the 1960s. Elsewhere, rates have been on the increase, most notably in Latin America and the Caribbean and in the Middle East and North Africa, with a slower increase for sub-Saharan Africa. By 2020, high-income countries are expected to experience a 30 per cent decline in fatalities from traffic accidents, while low- and middle-income countries will record a phenomenal increase of 80 per cent.[14] South Asia alone will experience a 144 per cent rise in fatalities from traffic accidents by 2020.

Economic impacts

Economic costs of traffic accidents are difficult to calculate, given that there are many indirect impacts to consider. The WHO estimates that the total economic cost of traffic accidents is 1 per cent of gross national product (GNP) for low-income countries, 1.5 per cent in middle-income countries and 2 per cent in high-income countries. Low- and middle-income countries lose US$65 billion a year in traffic accidents, more than they receive in development assistance.[15] To put this in perspective, the annual average estimated economic damage due to natural disasters over the 1990s was US$62 billion.[16] The significance of traffic accidents when taken in aggregate is thus very clear.

Table 9.3 presents calculated economic costs of traffic accidents in 1997 by continent. Road accidents cost US$65 billion in developing and transitional countries, and US$453 billion in highly motorized countries (considered equivalent to OECD countries), amounting to a crude estimated total of US$518 billion worldwide.[17] As the analysis uses 1997 loss data, current losses can be expected to exceed these values.

Pro-poor urban policies need to consider traffic accidents as a factor that, like other hazards, can tip households into poverty or collapse. The consequences of traffic accidents extend far beyond the individuals concerned. Loss of an economically productive member of the family, and perhaps one in whom the family has invested valuable

Table 9.2

Motorization rates by Human Development Index (HDI)

Notes: * Data is for 2003 or most recent year available. Motor vehicles include cars, buses and freight vehicles, but do not include two-wheelers. Population refers to mid-year population in the year for which data is available.

Source: UNDP, 2006b; World Bank, 2006c

Country		Human Development Index (HDI)	Number of vehicles (per 1000 persons),* 1990	Number of vehicles (per 1000 persons), 2003
High HDI	Canada	0.950	605	577
	Germany	0.932	405	578
	Japan	0.949	469	582
	Poland	0.862	168	354
	Republic of Korea	0.912	79	304
	UK	0.940	400	442
	US	0.948	758	808
Low HDI	Ethiopia	0.371	1	2
	Kenya	0.491	12	11
	Swaziland	0.500	66	83
	Pakistan	0.539	6	8
	Uganda	0.502	2	5

resources for education, can drive families into poverty (see Box 9.1). Such high economic impact at the household level is explained by most road fatalities and injuries being among young men, the most economically active social group in these societies. In Kenya, for example, more than 75 per cent of road traffic casualties are among economically productive young adults.[18] The impact of accidents is likely to be especially magnified in those societies where there is limited or no state support for medical treatment or social security for those who are unable to work as a result of disability following an accident. The psychological and financial burden of caring for a previously economically active family member who has been disabled through an accident can be even more destabilizing for the household economy. The second leading cause of orphaned children in Mexico is the loss of parents as a result of road traffic accidents.[19]

VULNERABILITY AND CAUSES OF ROAD TRAFFIC ACCIDENTS

Road traffic accidents result from a combination of structural, physical and behavioural factors (see Box 9.2). While the exposure of road users to traffic accidents is shaped by physical aspects of the road environment, individual behaviour, awareness of safety regulations and travel habits also determine vulnerability to traffic accident risks. In addition, the safety and design features of vehicles shape the likelihood of being involved in a traffic accident, as well as the severity of the impact.

World region	Regional GNP	Estimated annual accident costs	
		GNP (percentage)	Cost (US$ billion)
Africa	370	1.0	3.7
Asia	2454	1.0	24.5
Latin America and the Caribbean	1890	1.0	18.9
Middle East	495	1.5	7.4
Central and Eastern Europe	659	1.5	9.9
Highly motorized countries	22,665	2.0	453.0
Total			517.8

Table 9.3

Economic costs of traffic accidents by world region, 1997

Source: Jacobs et al, 1999

Vulnerability to injury and death from traffic accidents also varies according to the mode of transportation used. In societies with high levels of motorization, vehicle users are most vulnerable to accidents (see Figure 9.1). In middle- and low-income countries, vulnerability is highest for unprotected road users – pedestrians, cyclists and motorcyclists. For instance, causalities are highest among two-wheel vehicle users in Thailand, Indonesia and Malaysia (see Figure 9.1). This is not surprising given the dominance of two- and three-wheeled vehicles in the region, accounting for well over 70 per cent of vehicles in countries such as Cambodia, Indonesia, the Lao People's Democratic Republic and Viet Nam.[20]

In Kenya, between 1971 and 1990, pedestrians represented 42 per cent of all traffic accident fatalities, and pedestrians and passengers combined accounted for approximately 80 per cent of all fatalities each year.[21] In Nairobi (Kenya), between 1977 and 1994, 64 per cent of road users killed in traffic crashes were pedestrians.[22] In Beijing (China), about one third of all traffic deaths occur among bicyclists.[23]

Box 9.1 The impact of traffic accidents on the urban poor in Bangladesh and India

A study of the differentiated impacts of road traffic accidents on households in Bangladesh and India clearly illustrates the association between traffic accidents and urban poverty. While the poor were not necessarily at greater risk of death or injury from traffic accidents, many urban households became poor following the death or injury of a member.

Breadwinners were most at risk in urban Bangladesh, where income from the urban poor killed by traffic accidents amounted, on average, to 62 per cent of their household's total income. Likewise, Bangalore (India), poor households suffered disproportionately given that those killed by traffic accidents contributed 59 per cent of the household income.

Road crashes imposed a double financial burden on poor households. At the same time that they faced unexpected medical, if not funeral, costs, they also lost the income of the victim and/or carer. Urban poor households in Bangladesh paid the equivalent of almost three months' household income on funerals, a significantly greater proportion of household income than the non-poor.

Table 9.4 Household impacts of serious traffic accident injury in Bangladesh

Consequence of serious injury		Urban poor* (percentage)	Urban non-poor* (percentage)
Income decreased	Yes	57	33
	No	43	67
Food consumption decreased	Yes	59	25
	No	41	75
Living standards decreased	Yes	58	25
	No	42	75
Arranged loan	Yes	62	35
	No	38	65

In contrast to non-poor households, the majority of urban poor households reported decreased income, food consumption and living standards. Most poor households also borrowed money, thereby facing debt. Almost none of the households received insurance compensation, while only 13 per cent of the urban households received a private settlement.

Source: Aeron-Thomas et al, 2004

Note: * The poor were identified on the basis of official government estimates of poverty, household per capita income (not victim's income alone) and post-crash household income (not pre-crash household income).

Box 9.2 Risk factors determining incidence and severity of traffic accidents

Factors that contribute to the risk of occurrence of a road crash include:

Exposure: amount of travel undertaken, defined as the number of trips, the distance travelled, or time in the road environment.

Behavioural factors: human behaviour, including the extent of knowledge and understanding of traffic systems, driver experience, skill and attitudes to risk, and the relationship between risk and factors, such as speed choice and alcohol consumption.

Vehicle factors: vehicle design and safety features, such as braking systems, lighting and tyre quality.

Road environment: road safety engineering and traffic management make a direct contribution to reducing crash risk. Road design affects road user behaviour and crash risk through the speed that drivers will perceive as appropriate, through detailed design factors such as curves, gradients and road markings, and through failure to provide facilities for vulnerable road users.

The likelihood of injury occurring is determined by the above factors, but also:

Vulnerable road users: road users such as pedestrians, cyclists and motorized two-wheeler riders are especially vulnerable to injury worldwide.

Use of safety devices: these include seat belts and helmet use.

Post-crash medical care: the outcome of a road crash for the victims, in terms of their chance of survival and long-term prognosis, is affected by the level of available medical care.

Source: Commission for Global Road Safety, 2006

Vulnerability to death from traffic accidents is ... differentiated by gender and age

Vulnerability to death from traffic accidents is also differentiated by gender and age. In 2002, 73 per cent of all people who died from road traffic accidents were men.[24] Road traffic mortality rates were found to be higher among men than women in all world regions, regardless of income level, and also across all age groups. This difference is likely to result from a combination of greater exposure to traffic, partly through a gendered division of employment, and also of social factors such as greater risk-taking behaviour among young men.

Age is also associated with vulnerability to traffic accidents. The youth have been recognized as a particularly vulnerable group in a recent report launched during the first United Nations Global Road Safety Week (23–29 April 2007).[25] Worldwide, 30 per cent of those killed by road traffic accidents are under the age of 25. Road traffic accidents are the leading cause of death for young people aged 15 to 19, and the second leading cause of death for those aged 10 to 14 and 20 to 24.[26] Mortality data shows that young men are the most vulnerable to traffic accidents.

Worldwide, injuries among children under the age of 15 present a major problem. The extent and patterns of child road injury are linked to differences in road use. In Africa, children are more likely to be hurt as pedestrians and as users of public transport. In Southeast Asia, it is as pedestrians, bicyclists and, increasingly, as passengers on motor scooters, and in Europe and North America, it is as passengers in private motor cars and as pedestrians, that children are at greatest risk of a road traffic injury. The burden of injury is unequal. More boys are injured than girls, and children from poorer families have higher rates of injury. Even in high-income countries, research has shown that children from poorer families and ethnic minority groups have higher rates of road traffic accident injury, particularly in the case of child pedestrians.[27]

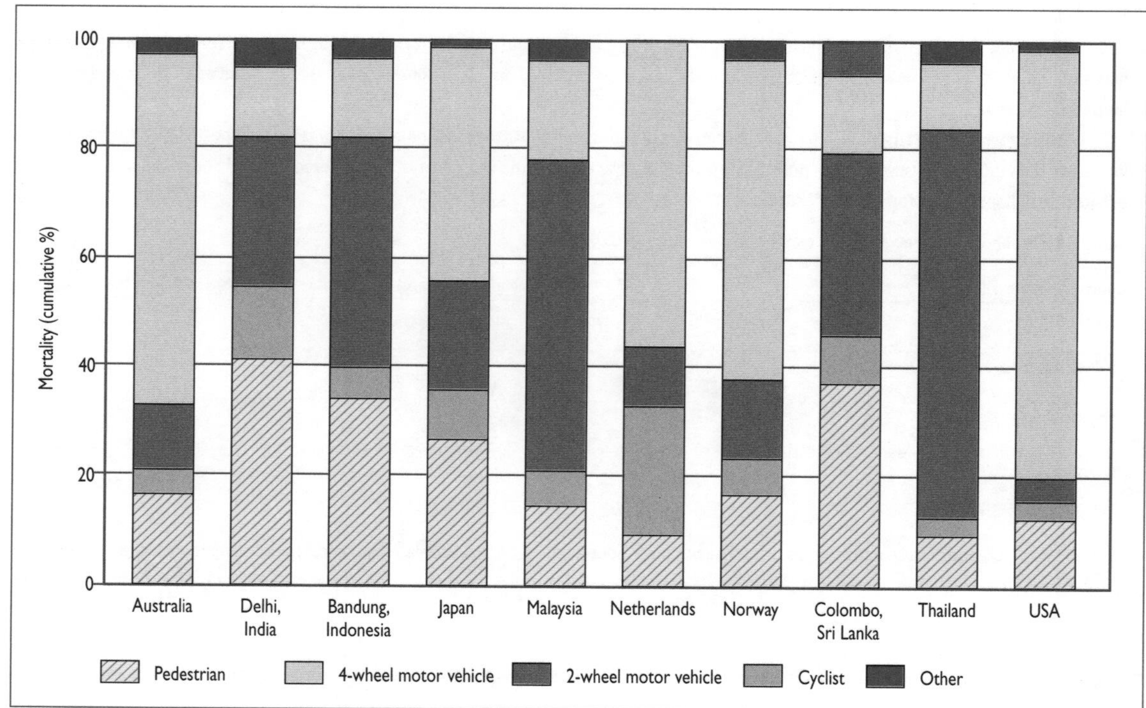

Figure 9.1

Road users killed by transport mode as a proportion of all road traffic deaths

Source: Mohan, 2002b; note that data is from various years

URBANIZATION AND TRAFFIC ACCIDENTS

Urban areas are the main locus of traffic accidents, given the concentration there of vehicles, transport infrastructure and people. For example, in Latin America, about half of all traffic accidents take place in the region's cities, and between one half and one third of those killed are pedestrians. In many cities, high accident rates among pedestrians are related to dense populations and walking as a main form of transport, so that many people are exposed to traffic hazard. Exacerbating this vulnerability in many cities is the failure of transport management systems, which often focus on planning for cars rather than for people.[28]

Uncontrolled and unplanned urban growth can increase the likelihood of occurrence of traffic accidents. This is especially the case in many developing country cities where rapid urbanization and the consequent explosion of motorized vehicles, unplanned settlements and human populations seriously threaten road safety (see Box 9.3). In Europe, urban growth, characterized by geographical dispersal of the territory within which inhabitants carry out their daily activities and greater use of private cars, is thought to increase the risk of traffic accidents, given the diversity of road uses and increase in travel, traffic flows and crossings of these flows.[29]

Across the globe, there is an evident rise in the use of motorized forms of transportation in urban areas, although at differing paces. In particular, with greater affluence, private vehicle ownership and use have increased in cities around the world. For instance, car ownership in the 15 European Union member states (EU-15)[30] has trebled in the last 30 years and continues to rise by 3 million every year.[31] As illustrated by the case of São Paulo Metropolitan Area (Brazil), increased motorization is accompanied by a number of negative externalities, including traffic accidents, congestion and declining use of public transportation (see Box 9.4). While private car ownership may be on the rise in some countries, motorization is characterized by an increase in two- and three-wheeled vehicles elsewhere. For instance, in India, motorcycle ownership increased 16-fold between 1981 and 2002, while private car ownership increased sevenfold during the same period.[32] Rates of motorization are also higher in richer countries, compared with poorer countries, with lower Human Development Index (HDI) levels (see Table 9.2).

Urban poverty and vulnerability to injury from traffic accidents are linked. Although the urban poor have environmentally friendly travel habits through a dependence upon non-motorized and public modes of transportation, they are the main victims of road traffic accidents.[33] Urban transport systems influence patterns of vulnerability in that they can force the poor into choosing high-risk transport options. In Bangladesh and India, a recent study shows that the poor are killed and seriously injured mainly as vulnerable road users (i.e. while walking or using two- or three-wheeled transport, both motorized and non-motorized).[34] In cities where public transport has become unreliable, expensive or does not serve areas of rapidly expanding settlements, privately

Box 9.3 Factors threatening road safety in India's cities

Traffic accidents pose a serious threat to residents of India's cities. Since 1971, traffic fatalities have increased fivefold in India. The massive growth in motor vehicles is thought to be the main factor underlying this rise in traffic accidents. Between 1971 and 2001, there has been a 20-fold increase in the combined number of cars, taxis, trucks and motorcycles. A number of additional factors threaten road safety in India's cities:

- limited network of roads, often narrow, poorly maintained and unpaved;
- unsafe driving behaviour, which results from virtually non-existent driver training, extremely lax licensing procedures and lack of traffic law enforcement;
- unsafe vehicles;
- inadequate or non-existent traffic signals and signage and lack of traffic management;
- almost complete lack of infrastructure for pedestrians and cyclists;
- forced sharing of narrow, crowded rights of way by both motorized and non-motorized vehicles, pedestrians, animals and street vendors; and
- overcrowding of buses, rickshaws and even motorcycles.

Source: Pucher et al, 2005

Box 9.4 Increasing use of the automobile: The case of São Paulo, Brazil

Comprised of 39 cities, the São Paulo Metropolitan Area has a population of 17 million. It has experienced not only rapid urban growth over the last few decades, but also a sixfold increase in its motorized vehicle size between 1970 and 1996. A study of transportation and traffic accidents in the area (for the period of 1967 to 1997) illustrates how increasing use of automobiles is causing a range of negative externalities, such as traffic accidents, congestion and pollution, to sky rocket. The sharp rise in the use of private transportation has been accompanied by a concomitant decrease in the use of public transportation.

Results from the study indicate that the mobility-income paradigm, where those with higher income enjoy greater mobility, has been maintained. The individualization of motorized mobility is evident: between 1987 and 1997 alone, 75 per cent of all additional trips were made by car. An analysis of changes in mobility by income level between 1987 and 1997 illustrated a decrease in mobility based on public modes of transportation.

A number of factors are thought to have contributed to the increasingly unsustainable changes in São Paulo Metropolitan Area's transport systems, including:

- conflict and lack of coordination between institutions concerned with decisions on land use, transport and traffic at both the federal and local levels;
- policies supporting automobile use and less prioritization of public modes of transportation (e.g. 27 per cent of the budget of São Paulo city was used for road construction between 1967 and 1977);
- lack of integration between modes of public transportation (e.g. only 10 per cent of trips between the subway and rail are integrated, while there is no integration between suburban trains and bus services);
- the poor and deteriorating quality of public modes of transportation (service irregularity, unreliability, increased travel time and discomfort), yet increasing cost of fares; and
- inadequate enforcement and safety education and campaigns.

The transformation of the roadway system to accommodate automobile use is thought to have increased the vulnerability of pedestrians and non-motorized transportation modes to traffic accidents.

Source: Vasconcellos, 2005

owned minibuses, trucks or cars have filled the transport gap, often without adequate regulation and consideration of safety measures. Examples of informal or semi-formal transports include the *matatu* in Kenya (minibuses); Manila's *jeepneys* (remodelled trucks); the *dolmus* of Istanbul (minibuses); the *dala dala* of Tanzania (minivans); the *tro-tro* of Ghana (minivans); the Haitian *tap-tap* (remodelled trucks); and the *molue* (large buses, locally known as 'moving morgues') and *danfo* (minibuses, locally referred to as 'flying coffins') in Nigeria.[35] Safety is often compromised by informal transport operators due to competition, lack of awareness or flagrant violation of traffic rules, and poor vehicle maintenance.[36]

Safety is often compromised by informal transport operators...

PREVENTING AND MITIGATING LOSS FROM TRAFFIC ACCIDENTS

Traffic accidents and subsequent loss are the products of human behaviour, but also of urban planning and design, both of which are amenable to development policy. Preventing and mitigating the impact of traffic accidents requires interventions to address the multiple risk factors underlying those accidents (see Box 9.2). This section explores contemporary policies to reduce traffic accidents and improve road safety, in general. These include transport and urban planning; the promotion of safe behaviour; improvement of accident response and recovery; improvements in traffic accidents data collection; traffic management and building institutions; and enhancing awareness of road safety. Other aspects of transport safety that do not touch upon urban planning or social and economic development, such as vehicle design, safety standards and hospital capability, are not discussed in detail.

Road crash injury is largely preventable and predictable...

The WHO recommends that the severity and consequences of injury from traffic accidents can be controlled by acting on four fronts: reducing exposure to risk; preventing road traffic accidents from occurring; reducing the severity of injury in the event of an accident; and reducing the consequences of injury through improved post-accident care. High-income countries have successfully reduced injuries from traffic accidents by adopting such multifaceted policy approaches (see Box 9.5). Policies targeting a single mode of transportation, although effective, need to be supplemented by interventions addressing related factors that reduce road safety. For instance, Box 9.6 describes the experience of transport safety reform targeting minibus taxis in Kenya. It is not unusual for such reforms to be met with resistance from those with a vested interest in the status quo. In cities and countries where the transport sector has political and economic clout, change can be very slow.

The need for innovative and dedicated work to reduce mortality and injury from traffic accidents worldwide has been widely recognized by the international community. The WHO's proposed seven-point plan for understanding and reducing road traffic accidents may be an appropriate starting point in the global fight against traffic accidents:[37]

1. Road crash injury is largely preventable and predictable – it is a human-made problem amenable to rational analysis and counter-measures.
2. Road safety is a multi-sectoral and public health issue – all sectors, including health, need to be fully engaged in responsibility, activity and advocacy for road crash injury prevention.
3. Common driving errors and common pedestrian behaviour should not lead to death and serious injury – the traffic system should help users to cope with increasingly demanding conditions.
4. The vulnerability of the human body should be a limiting design parameter for the traffic system, and speed management is central.
5. Road crash injury is a social equity issue – the aim should be equal protection to all road users since non-motor vehicle users bear a disproportionate share of road injury and risk.
6. Technology transfer from high-income to low-income countries needs to fit local conditions and should address research-based local needs.
7. Local knowledge needs to inform the implementation of local solutions.

Box 9.5 Reducing road traffic injuries: The experience of high-income countries (HICs)

Fatalities from road traffic accidents rose rapidly in high-income countries (HICs) during the 1950s and 1960s, following rapid motorization, eventually peaking in the 1970s. Since the 1980s and 1990s, injuries have been reduced in many HICs by as much as 50 per cent despite continued traffic growth. This has been attributed to a shift from focusing on 'behaviour' alone to safety systems such as good road and vehicle design and traffic management. A combination of measures has been taken by HICs to reduce road injuries, including:

Safe road users: enforcement of laws to moderate the behaviour of drivers, such as speed limits, drink-driving laws, seat belt-use laws and helmet-use laws, have been very effective.

Safer vehicles: improvements in vehicle design have improved the chances of survival in motor vehicle crashes.

Safer road infrastructure: engineering measures such as signs, lane separation, pedestrian crossings and traffic-calming measures have helped to reduce road traffic causalities.

Source: Commission for Global Road Safety, 2006

Improving road safety through transport and urban planning

The urgent need to address transport and road safety concerns in cities is evident; yet, several challenges remain. Rapidly growing megacities are especially constrained in this regard; but medium-sized and small urban centres should not be neglected either. It is particularly important to focus on medium-sized centres, given that these are the cities where future population growth may be most rapid in aggregate and where planning now can potentially avoid some of the problems being experienced by the largest cities.

Recent work on medium-sized cities in Asia shows the potential for coordinating urban and transport planning to simultaneously address road safety, air pollution and pro-

Box 9.6 The struggle for road transport safety in Nairobi, Kenya

In 2006, over 1900 people lost their lives in traffic accidents on Kenyan roads. Only malaria and HIV/AIDS claimed more lives. Public transport in Nairobi and Kenya, more generally, relies primarily upon *matatus*, or minibuses. In October 2003, Legal Notice No 161 was issued to regulate this sector – a comprehensive notice aimed at reducing the danger and insecurity faced by *matatu* users. This was to be achieved through more effective policing of speeding; encouraging greater professionalism and accountability to customers by drivers and conductors; and tighter restrictions on operating routes.

In order to achieve these important goals, specific actions were proposed by the government, including:

- fitting speed governors to limit speed to 80 kilometres per hour;
- fitting seat belts on all vehicles (both public, commercial and private);
- employing drivers and conductors on a permanent basis;
- issuing badges to drivers and conductors;
- issuing uniforms to public service vehicle drivers and conductors;
- indicating route details and painting yellow bands on all *matatus* for the purposes of easy identification;
- re-testing drivers after every two years;
- asking every driver to prominently display their photograph.

Breaches of any regulations were to be punishable by a fine.

The success of this act in road safety terms is clear. The number of traffic-related deaths in 2006 was lower than the World Health Organization (WHO) estimate of average annual mortality from traffic accidents in Kenya (3000 people). Accidents were reduced by 73 per cent in the first six months of implementation, compared to the same time during the previous year. However, the act met a good amount of resistance from the *matatu* lobby. Lack of political will has also threatened advances made in road safety.

Source: WHO, 2004b; Chitere and Kibual, 2006

poor transport. Each of these three critical agendas for sustainable development in cities has common practical solutions. Some solutions are relatively inexpensive, such as separating pedestrian walkways and bicycle lanes from motorized transport. Others, such as the integrated planning of residential and employment space with good quality public transport, require strategic planning. It is in medium-sized cities undergoing rapid population growth where strategic planning that can be proactive may have the most impact with the least cost.[38]

Promoting public and non-motorized transportation

Transport planning too often overlooks the needs of the majority of urban residents for whom non-motorized and public transport may be the norm. Instead, planning models itself on a vision of the city that is firmly tied to the motor-car. As a result, there is a lack of investment in technological support for pro-poor transport, as shown in the case of Delhi (see Box 9.7). In planning decisions, the needs of pedestrians and cyclists come second to those of motorized transport.[39] Low- and middle-income countries seeking to promote economic growth, trade and employment are particularly preoccupied with investments in road infrastructure.[40]

Transport planning…models itself on a vision of the city that is firmly tied to the motor car

Yet, road construction and increasing capacity to accommodate cars may not necessarily reduce the negative externalities of motorization, such as traffic accidents and congestion. For instance, after constructing at least 2 ring roads, over 100 flyovers and almost 200 overpasses, the rush-hour average speed on Beijing's trunk roads remained at 13 to 19 kilometres per hour.[41] Indeed, increased traffic volume resulting from road construction may result in additional traffic congestion.[42] Private cars, in particular, require a great deal of space, both for their movement and parking, when compared with other modes, especially highly space-saving modes of public transport.[43]

For a large majority of the urban poor in developing countries, public transportation and non-motorized transport are the only affordable means of travel.[44] However, the state of public transportation systems in developing countries, often poorly constructed and maintained and heavily burdened by excessive overloading, is itself a risk factor contributing to the rising incidence of traffic accidents.[45] For instance, in India, buses account for 90 per cent of the transport in cities.[46] Yet, India's public modes of transportation are described as being overcrowded, uncomfortable, undependable, slow, uncoordinated, inefficient and dangerous.

Thus, improving the quality and functioning of public transport can enhance road safety and thereby reduce traffic accidents. Mass forms of transportation not only reduce negative externalities of greater motorization, but are able to deliver high-quality mass transportation at a cost that is affordable to most municipalities, including those of low-income countries. One example is the bus rapid transit system, which is growing in popularity globally compared to other forms of mass transit (such as light and heavy rail), especially in Asia, South America and Europe.[47] Bus rapid transit is particularly efficient as it offers greater network coverage, value for money, service capacity and relative flexibility. Widely acclaimed examples include the TranMilenio bus rapid transit system in Bogotá (Colombia) and that of Curitibá (Brazil).

…improving the quality and functioning of public transport can enhance road safety

Improved public transportation may also enable the poor to make choices that improve other aspects of their safety and security. Often, the urban poor have to tolerate poor housing conditions in environmentally or socially hazardous locations due to lack of reliable, affordable and accessible transport.[48] The 'choice', if there is one, is between settlements that are hazard prone, but close to employment and livelihood opportunities, and those that may be less hazardous, but do not meet short-term economic needs.

Box 9.7 Challenges and opportunities for a sustainable transport system in Delhi, India

In some respects, Delhi has led the way in sustainable transport. In others, progress has been less comprehensive. Some 77 per cent of Delhi's population (about 10 million people) live in inadequate housing, many in inner-city slums or peripheral informal settlements. This majority group of the city's population relies mainly on public transport, walking or bicycles for travel. A total of 50 per cent of the city's residents can only afford non-motorized transport. There are estimated to be 1.5 million bicycles and 300,000 cycle-rickshaws in the city. Public transport in Delhi is provided mainly by buses, which make up only 1 per cent of the city's vehicles, but serve about half of all transport demand. Since 1992, the private sector has played an increasing role in bus transport. Privatization has increased the size of the bus fleet; but buses continue to be overcrowded and poorly maintained.

A key challenge within Delhi's transport system is overcoming the negative stereotypes about non-motorized forms of transport that are too easily seen as being anti-modern or as a cause of traffic congestion. On the contrary, non-motorized forms of transport are less dangerous and more sustainable forms of transport. Encouraging non-motorized transport and providing safety from the hazard generated by motor vehicles while preventing congestion is problematic.

Where investments in traffic improvements have occurred, they repeatedly promote mechanized transport and further marginalize more environmentally sustainable and pro-poor modes, such as walking, cycling and good quality public transport. The city government has enhanced its worldwide reputation and markedly improved air quality through the transition of public transport to compressed natural gas; but similar innovation and leadership are harder to see in city transport planning that can serve the poor majority.

Road systems in Delhi and other Indian cities can be redesigned to meet the needs of the poor majority and increase road safety. Road geometry and traffic management can be altered to better reflect the diversity of road users, with an emphasis on the needs of pedestrians, cyclists and public transport users. Delhi is fortunate in having many wide roads with additional service lanes that could be converted into segregated space for pedestrians, bicycles and motorized vehicles. Segregated traffic systems are likely to reduce congestion and ease traffic flow if such a policy is implemented.

Source: ORG, 1994; Tiwari, 2002

...road users may not give up use of private cars easily

Rationalizing road space allocation by accommodating commonly used forms of transportation ... may help to reduce traffic accidents

Promoting public transportation use in place of private vehicles may prove difficult, in practice. In richer countries, a range of techniques are available, often best applied in tandem, to provide disincentives for private car use (such as environmental fuel levies or congestion charges) and incentives for a switch to public transport (such as improved service, park-and-ride schemes, easily available information on timetables, and low fares). Deregulation and the consequent involvement of the private sector in public transport provision have enabled innovation in public transport service provision within European countries.[49] However, even where public transportation infrastructure and services are available in richer countries, road users may not give up the use of private cars easily. For example, a study in London (UK) illustrated how perceptions that alternatives to the car are not viable and long distances between work and home discourage widespread use of these services.[50] Intra-urban economic inequalities within developed country cities may also cause differentiated uptake and implementation of policies seeking to promote non-motorized transport. For instance, a study in Auckland (New Zealand) shows how the Walking School Bus scheme, whereby children are escorted by volunteers between home and school to protect them from traffic accidents, was more widely adopted in affluent neighbourhoods.[51] In poorer countries, public transport systems are often in a state of collapse and may not offer greater safety than private transport options. Furthermore, private vehicle users in developing countries from middle- and high-income groups may not be willing to sacrifice the comforts and convenience of personal transport.[52]

■ Safer transport infrastructure

Road infrastructure design – in terms of road networks, mix of types of traffic and types of safety measures – determines the likelihood of traffic accidents occurring in urban areas. Road design and facilities influence driver behaviour through amenities such as curves, gradients, road markings and the provision of facilities for vulnerable road users. Initiatives that can readily be used without major re-planning of urban neighbourhoods include the installation of traffic lights, pedestrian-only streets, lighting, bus lanes, pedestrian walkways, video monitoring of traffic and speed bumps.[53] It is important to maintain the goodwill of road users when implementing such road safety measures. For example, the importance of drivers' acceptance of automatic speed limiters in order to implement the policy has been illustrated in a study undertaken in Leeds (UK).[54]

Vulnerable road users are disadvantaged in modern road systems, most of which are designed to cater for motor vehicles.[55] If road design does not take into account the needs of pedestrians, bicyclists and public transport vehicles, they will still use infrastructure that is not designed for them – hence, increasing accident risks for all road users.[56] Rationalizing road space allocation by accommodating commonly used forms of transportation, such as two- and three-wheeled vehicles and non-motorized transport, may help to reduce traffic accidents. For instance, the construction of a segregated lane for bicycles in Delhi would increase the road space available for motorized traffic by 50 per cent on three-lane roads while meeting the needs of bicyclists. The provision of a high-capacity bus lane would increase capacity by 56 to 73 per cent; while the inclusion of separate lanes for non-motorized vehicles and bus priority lanes would reduce traffic delays by 80 per cent and reduce injury accidents by 40 per cent and fatalities by 50 per cent.[57]

Road designs that cater for non-motorized and public forms of transportation have been more widely implemented in richer countries. For instance, a review of good practice for safer cycling on UK roads provides some examples of innovative redesign to encourage bicycle use.[58] A danger reduction benchmark was awarded to Devon County Council for experimenting with radical measures to reduce traffic speeds on a high-speed road. Here, a two-lane road has been narrowed to a single track with passing places and the old carriageway surface has been broken up. This has successfully reduced speeds and diverted speeding traffic onto more suitable routes.

The integration of safety concerns within road design and construction is also increasingly evident in developing countries. In one crash hotspot on the main Accra–Kumasi Highway in Ghana, speed bumps have reduced the number of crashes by 35 per cent between 2000 and 2001. Fatalities fell by 55 per cent and serious injuries by 76 per cent. Following on from this success, rumble strips have been constructed on the Cape Coast–Takoradi Highway, the Bunso–Koforidua Highway and the Tema–Akosombo Highway. Speed humps, to slow down vehicles and improve pedestrian safety, have been applied in the towns of Ejisu and Besease on the Accra–Kumasi Highway.[59]

Separating road users has also proven an effective method for reducing traffic accidents. The banning of motorized through traffic from street markets and from high-density residential areas saves lives, reduces local air pollution and can provide a stimulus for economic development. The historic centres of many cities have been 'pedestrianized' to encourage tourism-led regeneration. Giving priority on roads to public transport vehicles or non-motorized transport can help to encourage people onto buses. Curitibá in Brazil, a city often used to exemplify best practice in integrated transport and urban planning, has a high-capacity traffic management system that provides segregated bus lanes, priority at traffic lights for buses, as well as safe and fast access for users.

Land-use planning

Integrated land-use and transport planning may also contribute to reducing traffic accidents by minimizing the number and length of journeys taken. Where safe workplaces and residential and recreational land uses are in close proximity, non-motorized transport or short journeys by car and bus are more likely. This also has a knock-on effect in reducing atmospheric pollution and greenhouse gas emissions and provides a framework for community-building.[60] For instance, Singapore has been successful in cutting car journeys and alleviating severe traffic congestion through its comprehensive and coordinated land transport policy, which combines integrated land-use and transport planning, as well as demand management measures (see Box 9.8).

In Costa Rica, the development of a five-year National Road Safety Plan uses a performance-based incentive scheme to encourage organizations and individuals involved in road-building and transport engineering to adopt better practices. A similar approach is being proposed for medium-sized municipalities in Brazil.[61]

Box 9.8 Reducing traffic congestion by integrating land-use and transport planning, Singapore

Singapore is a densely populated urban area (5900 individuals per square kilometre) and thus faces severe scarcity of land, exacerbated by a growing population. At the same time, increasing affluence and the consequent increase in car ownership and usage during the 1970s and 1980s has resulted in severe congestion in the island. Cognizant of these issues, the government developed a strategic plan in 1972, focusing on land-use–transportation relationships.

A key recommendation of the strategic plan was the development of regional centres to ensure greater employment decentralization, thereby reducing congestion in the central business district and improving home–work relationships. The government has also sought to improve the efficiency of the public transport system by merging private bus companies and rationalizing their services, and later integrating these with a mass rapid transit system introduced in 1987. A number of measures were also put in place to improve traffic management through controlling vehicle ownership and usage, including the Area Licensing Scheme, which was unique in the world when it was introduced in 1975. This scheme required cars entering designated restricted zones during peak hours to pay a fee.

A study of the Tampines Regional Centre (TRC) of Singapore illustrated that regional centres have a great potential for reducing work travel in terms of distance travelled and number of trips generated across the island. In the long term, the promotion of regional centres is likely to result in more efficient land-use relationships and less dependence upon cars. Similarly compact and high-density cities may learn from this strategy; but those facing urban sprawl and low-density suburbs may have to take a different approach.

Source: Sim et al, 2001; Willoughby, 2001

Separating road users has ... proved an effective method for reducing traffic accidents"

Promoting safe behaviour

Promoting changes in behaviour can reduce people's exposure to traffic hazards. This involves, among others, interventions seeking to enhance driver skills and training, to reduce impaired driving and to promote the use of safety equipment. Driver training and licensing are important forms of promoting safe behaviour. The age of qualification and rigour of testing varies greatly from city to city. Malaysia has recently increased the legal riding age for two wheelers from 16 to 18 years and reduced accidents as a result.[62]

Education and legislation are both instrumental in increasing the use of safety equipment in vehicles. The introduction of a helmet-wearing law in Thailand for motorcycles saw helmet use increase fivefold, head injuries decrease by 41 per cent, and deaths decrease by 20 per cent.[63] In the Republic of Korea, seat-belt use rose from 23 per cent in 2000 to 98 per cent in 2001 (sustained during 2002), following a national campaign of police enforcement, a publicity campaign and an increase in fines for non-use. This resulted in a 5.9 per cent decrease in fatal road traffic crashes.[64] Safety equipment can also extend to pedestrians. In South Africa, a pedestrian visibility campaign using reflective material has been added to the uniforms and school bags of 2500 school children.[65]

Education and legislation are both instrumental in increasing the use of safety equipment in vehicles

Driver impairment

Driver impairment leading to dangerous driving may be the result of a number of factors, such as alcohol or drug consumption, injury, infirmity, fatigue, the natural ageing process and distractions including mobile phone use, or a combination of these factors. A recent global review indicates the role of impairment as a cause of traffic accidents.[66] In Bangalore (India), 28 per cent of crashes involving males over the age of 15 were attributable to alcohol. Roadside breath tests conducted as part of the same project concluded that 30 to 40 per cent of night-time drivers were in a state of intoxication. One study in Colombia found that 34 per cent of driver fatalities and 23 per cent of motorcycle fatalities are associated with alcohol. They also report that a study in Argentina found 83 per cent of drivers acknowledge that they drink and drive.

Substance abuse is also a key cause of road accidents. A recent study in France of drivers aged less than 30 and killed through road accidents indicates that as much as 39 per cent of the drivers had consumed cannabis.[67] The study highlights the increasing prevalence of substance abuse among French drivers, especially drugs such as cannabis, amphetamines and cocaine. While legislation against driving under the influence of drugs has been introduced by the French government, the need for greater public sensitization through campaigns and roadside testing is noted.[68] Similarly, a study of fatally injured drivers in Sweden between 2000 and 2002 showed a significant increase in the detection of illicit drugs, from 5.4 to 10 per cent.[69]

Legislation prohibiting drinking and driving is included in most countries' traffic laws; but enforcement is lacking and public awareness is poor

Fatigue caused by overwork, excessive hours of driving, lack of rest and lack of nourishment may also cause driver impairment. In Ghana, demands for increased returns by transport owners force drivers to speed and work when exhausted.[70] In Kenya, on average, a public minibus (or *matatu*) driver works 14 hours a day for seven days a week. Traffic regulations in many countries often limit driving time for commercial drivers, including coach and bus drivers. As with drinking and driving, enforcement is greatly improved by information campaigns.

A global review of alcohol-, drug- and fatigue-related impairment found systematic data collection, comprehensive legislation and rigorous enforcement lacking in most middle- and low-income countries.[71] Only in Latin America was it common to find a government agency with responsibility for coordinating road safety: Colombia, Argentina, Brazil, Chile, Costa Rica and Mexico all have an institutional framework based on a National Road Safety Council, with Costa Rica leading in a national campaign to reduce drinking and driving.

Legislation prohibiting drinking and driving is included in most countries' traffic laws; but enforcement is lacking and public awareness is poor. In many countries, a legal alcohol limit is in force, backed up by frequent public information campaigns and enforcement operations by the police. In Australia, since 1993, random breath testing has led to an estimated reduction in alcohol-related deaths of around 40 per cent. In some countries, such as the US, lower thresholds are in force for younger and inexperienced drivers. Information campaigns are used to increase awareness of the risks of driving after drinking alcohol and of the legal penalties imposed, but can also help to make drinking and driving less socially acceptable. Legislation for other causes of driver impairment is less advanced and, alongside enforcement mechanisms, represents a major area for enhancing road safety.

The limited existing levels of engagement with impaired driving in developing countries suggests that there is significant scope for reducing traffic accidents through controlling drinking, drugs and fatigue through education, legislation and enforcement. Small reductions in the amount of drunk driving can result in significant reductions in the incidence of traffic accidents. Drivers' perceptions of risk, police powers and monitoring equipment all need to play a role in reducing impaired driving. While most countries have legislation in place, coordination that can bring political will to this area is lacking. Political will is needed if the scope of education, legislation and enforcement is to reach beyond drunk driving to include other causes of impairment, such as fatigue, and new causes of distraction, such as mobile phone use.

Accident response and recovery

First responses are critical in reducing loss from traffic accidents. The capacity to respond to traffic accident injury and to minimize bodily harm varies according to levels of economic development. Half of all fatalities in European countries occur at the scene of the traffic accident or on the way to the hospital, while death before arrival at the hospital can be as high as 80 per cent in low- and middle-income countries.[72]

Trained first-aiders not only save lives, but also prevent unnecessary injury sustained through inappropriate action taken following an accident. As with disaster preparedness work, the piggybacking of transport first-aid skills onto more established public service or civil society delivery programmes is cost effective. In low- and middle-income countries, there is little access to emergency vehicles, increasing the benefits from widespread public education programmes in first aid. Such training has been given to police in Uganda and the general public in India.[73]

Traffic management

Basic traffic regulations and signage to manage traffic are essential instruments for enhancing road safety. Enforcement of such regulations remains a key challenge in cities worldwide. Table 9.5 makes a sharp distinction between Kuwait, the US and the UK, where regulation and enforcement for road users is in place, and other countries where road safety is yet to have been addressed comprehensively. Mortality as a proportion of car ownership rates is an order of magnitude lower in the former group of countries. This is a clear indication that traffic mortality is a product of social policy and cultural context as much as engineering.[74] Managing traffic safety in the future will need to consider the specific characteristics of the automobile culture of each country.

The effectiveness of traffic regulation enforcement in promoting road safety has been documented in several low- and middle-income countries. For instance, through the introduction of a new traffic code in January 1998 and heavier penalties for non-compliance, Brazil has succeeded in increasing the use of safety equipment by motorcycle and car drivers.[75] Accordingly, non-use of motorcycle helmets decreased from 62.5 per cent in 1997 to 13.9 per cent in 2000. In Costa Rica, a public awareness campaign was launched between 2003 and 2004 to promote seat-belt use. This was supported by national television adverts and linked to a national seat-belt law. The combined effect of the campaign and enforcement resulted in an increase in seat-belt use from 24 to 82 per cent.[76] In Khon Kaen Province in Thailand, authorities introduced legislation making helmet wearing mandatory for motorcyclists. Together with an awareness campaign, the legislation led to a 90 per cent helmet wearing rate, a 40 per cent reduction in head injuries and a 24 per cent reduction in motorcycle injuries in 1996.[77] Good governance and anti-corruption measures are particularly important in improving the enforcement of traffic and road safety regulations.[78]

Evidence suggests that partnerships between community groups, civil society and organizations and the police can help in enforcing traffic regulations. Barriers to partnerships exist on both sides, with accident victims often anticipating unfair police treatment. Drive Alive, a non-governmental organization (NGO) working on road safety in South Africa, aims to reduce traffic accident deaths and injury through education campaigns, lobbying for stricter legislation against impaired driving and advocating increased traffic laws.[79] In the US, Mothers against Drunk Driving (MADD) has grown substantially since being founded in 1980. Among other objectives, this non-profit organization seeks to stop drunk driving and related injuries.[80] More broadly, four different kinds of community involvement in road traffic policing have been identified:[81]

- partnerships between community groups and local authorities to help identify road hazards;
- volunteer traffic wardens and school patrols;
- formal partnerships between the police and citizen groups (here, citizens partner police in road traffic monitoring exercises);
- higher political attention to advocacy for road safety.

Building institutions and awareness for road safety

Sensitizing road users as well as relevant decision-makers about the causes and consequences of traffic accidents and relevant risk reduction strategies is a key starting point for improving road safety. Once available, information on traffic accidents needs to be communicated to relevant actors through appropriate and effective media. As noted earlier, the availability of road traffic accident data in developing countries is limited, thereby also restricting levels of awareness. Furthermore, the design of policies and interventions is constrained by the lack of adequate data and knowledge on trends and impacts of traffic accidents.

Country	Mortality rate per 100,000 individuals (1998–2003 average)	Car ownership per 1000 individuals (2004)
China	19.0	7
Colombia	24.2	36
Dominican Republic	41.1	44
El Salvador	41.7	20
Peru	17.6	30
Nicaragua	20.1	13
Kuwait	23.7	432
US	14.7	459
UK	6.1	499

Table 9.5

Comparing national car ownership and mortality rates

Source: Wells, 2007

Implementation of road safety measures and policies requires the necessary institutional capacity and resources, which may be absent in poorer cities and countries. The Asian Development Bank (ADB)–Association of Southeast Asian Nations (ASEAN) Regional Road Safety Programme, for instance, aims to build institutional capacity to address issues of road safety in member countries (see Box 9.9). In a bid to improve road safety in the region, the programme identifies key institutional constraints, most of which are shared in common with other developing countries of the

Box 9.9 Association of Southeast Asian Nations' ASEAN's Regional Road Safety Strategy and Action Plan, 2005–2010

The Association of Southeast Asian Nations (ASEAN) Regional Road Safety Strategy and Action Plan recognizes key constraints impeding the development and implementation of interventions and policies to improve road safety in member countries. These include inadequate awareness of the scale of loss on the part of decision-makers; gaps in the knowledge and expertise of local professionals; limited collaboration and knowledge-sharing; and lack of multi-sector and multidisciplinary plans to provide holistic approaches. Accordingly, the strategy focuses on the following key areas:

Analysis and understanding. Significant improvements are needed in all countries in terms of data collection, analysis and systems.

Advocacy and/or awareness-raising. Getting international organizations, development partners and ASEAN governments to recognize the seriousness and urgency of the problem – so that adequate funds are allocated and priority is given to improving road safety in the ASEAN region – is important.

Institutional strengthening. Improved safety management structures and data systems and more effective coordination and funding mechanisms are needed to assist individual countries in implementing safety improvements. Knowledge and skills of key professionals with road safety responsibilities must be upgraded through training.

Cooperation. Regional activities and workshops must be developed to share knowledge and documents, disseminate best practices, develop a knowledge network, and share mechanisms among ASEAN countries. Networks of special interest groups should be created to share, develop and exchange knowledge and experience in each sector.

Collaboration. Greater private-sector, civil society and non-governmental organization (NGO) participation in safety activities should be facilitated, and their active involvement in the national and regional road safety action plans should be encouraged, as should collaboration between central and local governments.

Coordination. Road safety activity has to be orchestrated, developed and managed for it to achieve optimal effectiveness. Regional activity will need to be coordinated with in-country initiatives. Efforts of the private sector, NGOs, governments and international development partners need to be harmonized, and this, if done well, will contribute significantly to improving road safety in the ASEAN region.

Source: Asian Development Bank, www.adb.org/Documents/Reports/Arrive-Alive/default.asp

world.

Engaging multiple stakeholders is particularly essential in raising awareness and institutionalizing road safety among all road users, but especially among drivers of motorized vehicles. Problems of coordination between different governmental bodies at various levels and with private-sector operators of transport services pose a serious challenge for cities of developing countries, such as Seoul and Mexico City.[82] In India, the National Urban Transport Policy proposed the creation of unified metropolitan transport authorities in cities with at least 1 million inhabitants in order to improve interagency cooperation on transport planning.[83]

Traffic deaths and injuries remain largely invisible to society and policy-makers ...

Improving traffic accident data collection

Traffic deaths and injuries remain largely invisible to society and policy-makers because they are mostly scattered individual events with low impact.[84] This is exacerbated by a lack of capacity to collect and compile traffic accident data, especially in developing countries. For instance, only 75 countries report data on traffic mortality to the WHO. Where national-level data on traffic safety is incomplete, it limits strategic planning. Data on mortality is often available; but casualty information is needed for a more comprehensive analysis of the impact of traffic accidents on livelihoods and economies. One way forward is to develop integrated recording systems for police and hospitals. Where national- or city-level data is available, it is not always clear that this has been used in policy development, suggesting a potential opportunity for more evidence-based planning.

Continued international cooperation and support are vital for the reduction of road traffic accidents, especially in developing countries

More work is needed to help understand the full economic costs of road crashes and to assess performance of policies aimed at reducing traffic accident risk. Policy assessments could combine accident statistics with other performance indicators, especially those that can be targeted at improving vulnerable road user safety (such as the number of pedestrian crossings installed, safety audits conducted and hazardous locations improved).[85]

Access to accident statistics is also a critical determinant of risk perception by road users, which, in turn, shapes their behaviour.[86] Moreover, it is an important basis for publicity and education campaigns designed to promote road safety.

INTERNATIONAL COOPERATION IN ROAD SAFETY PROMOTION

A major advancement in the road safety agenda over the last decade has been the growing number of United Nations, multilateral and bilateral donor organizations that have developed road safety policies.[87] In October 2005, the United Nations endorsed a historic Resolution on Improving Global Road Safety in recognition of the limited capabilities of developing countries and countries with economies in transition to address road safety concerns and the need for international cooperation.[88] This led to a call for a Global Road Safety Week, the first of which was held in April 2007 in order to raise awareness on road safety concerns (see Box 9.10). Furthermore, the WHO was mandated to coordinate road safety issues across United Nations agencies and with other international partners through the United Nations Road Safety Collaboration.[89] Since its establishment, this collaboration has been active in the areas of data collection and research, technical support provision, advocacy and policy, and resource mobilization.[90] The collaboration has also established an Annual World Day of Remembrance for Road Traffic Victims.[91]

Another influential international collaborative effort is the Global Road Safety Partnership (GRSP) (see Box 9.11). The GRSP provides non-financial support for country and city governments by improving global dissemination of road safety lessons and through a series of partnership-based road safety projects. The GRSP concentrates its resources among a group of highly vulnerable countries where partnerships for road safety could be built. These are Brazil, Costa Rica, Ghana, Hungary, India (Bangalore), Poland, Romania, South Africa, Thailand and Viet Nam. Initial work has been successful in generating data and raising the profile of road safety, and pilot projects have shown ways of reducing risk.

The work inspired by the GRSP shows that safety can be gained in even the most vulnerable countries. The partnership approach has meant that non-governmental road safety projects do not compete with government schemes. Partners have been varied and the private sector has played a role. In South Africa and Thailand, multinational corporations have been involved in road safety initiatives. In Ghana and India, local business partners are more important. Community actors have also contributed in India and South Africa – for example, in creating 'safe zones' as a public way of generating demand for safer roads. In Poland, the Technical University of Gdansk has become a partner with the GRSP. The key to success in building awareness of, and support for, road safety has been partnerships to institutionalize road safety, an area of work that many other countries could learn from.[92]

A number of other initiatives illustrate the attention that road traffic accidents are receiving internationally. The Commission for Global Road Safety recently established by the FIA Foundation[93] seeks to examine the framework for, and level of international cooperation on, global road safety and to make policy recommendations.[94] The World Bank's Global Road Safety Facility, launched in November 2005, intends to generate increased funding and technical assistance for initiatives aimed at reducing deaths and injuries in low- and middle-income countries.

Continued international cooperation and support are vital for the reduction of road traffic accidents, especially in developing countries. In the 2007 Accra Declaration, African ministers of transport and of health reaffirmed their commitment to road safety and called upon the 2007 G8 Summit to recognize the need to improve road safety in Africa and to incorporate this agenda in development assistance programmes.[95]

CONCLUDING REMARKS

Traffic accidents are the most significant cause of injury and death associated with small-scale hazards in urban areas. Global trends indicate that the incidence and impacts of traffic accidents will increase by 2020 if no action is taken. High-income countries will experience a decline in road traffic accident fatalities, while regions dominated by low-income countries will experience a phenomenal increase in mortality from road traffic accidents. The magnitude of loss both in terms of human life and economic assets is substantial. However, loss and injury vary greatly across countries, cities and within cities. Mortality is highest in Asia and Africa, while Asia and Latin American and Caribbean countries experience the highest economic losses. Within cities of developing countries, unprotected road users (cyclists, pedestrians and motorcyclists) are most vulnerable to death and injury from traffic accidents, while a proportionately higher number of people are injured as users of four-wheel vehicles in developed nations such as the US, Australia and The Netherlands.

A variety of interrelated factors determines the incidence and severity of traffic accidents, including behavioural factors, vehicle factors, road environment, vulnerability of certain road users and post-accident medical services. Reducing the risk of traffic accidents in urban areas thus requires action on a combination of fronts. Successful policies and interventions to reduce the risk of traffic accidents combine legislation, enforcement and public education.

At the international level, frameworks and guidelines are required to support government actions to reduce traffic accident risk. Current international cooperation and lobbying with respect to traffic accidents is encouraging; but low- and middle-income countries require additional support to increase their technical and legislative capacities to reduce risk. At the national level, legislation and policies should be introduced to improve road user behaviour, road safety awareness and transport infrastructure investments. Policies governing levels and rates of motorization at the national level should consider the consequences of increased motorization for traffic accident incidence. City authorities should seek to reduce traffic accident risk through traffic management, road design and safety, road space allocation, land-use planning and accident response capacity.

Box 9.10 The first United Nations Global Road Safety Week, 23–29 April 2007

In October 2005, the United Nations General Assembly invited the United Nations Regional Commissions and the World Health Organization (WHO) to jointly organize the first United Nations Global Road Safety Week. The week was modelled after previous road safety weeks orchestrated by the United Nations Economic Commission for Europe and after World Health Day 2004.

The theme for the week was 'young road users' as young people constitute a major group at risk of death, injury and disability on the road. While the focus was on young road users, the actions resulting from the week are intended to benefit road users of all ages. During the course of the week, a large number of local, national and international events were hosted all over the world. Numerous partners participated in these events, including governments, United Nations agencies, non-governmental organizations (NGOs) and the private sector.

The main objectives of this first United Nations Global Road Safety Week were to:

- raise awareness about the societal impact of road traffic injuries, highlighting the risks for young road users;
- promote action around key factors that have a major impact on preventing road traffic injuries: helmets, seat belts, drink driving, speeding and infrastructure;
- highlight the fact that road safety happens not by accident, but through the deliberate efforts on the part of many individuals and many sectors of society (governmental and non-governmental alike), as emphasized in the slogan for the week: 'Road safety is no accident.'

Sources: WHO, www.who.int/roadsafety/week/en/; General Assesmbly Resolution, 60/5

Box 9.11 The Global Road Safety Partnership (GRSP)

The Global Road Safety Partnership (GRSP) was initiated in 1999 by the World Bank with partners from business and civil society, as well as bilateral and multilateral donors. The secretariat is currently hosted by the International Federation of Red Cross and Red Crescent Societies (IFRC) in Geneva. The GRSP has worked alongside city and national governments seeking to promote road safety. Activities focus on efforts to change the behaviour of road users as a means of reducing risk.

In Ghana, work has focused on a Voluntary Code of Conduct, launched in 2004. The project aims to improve the road safety performance of individuals driving, in particular, for work purposes by asking them to sign up to a Voluntary Code of Conduct. The code of conduct increases drivers' awareness of the primary risk factors involved in crashes, including excessive speed, alcohol, fatigue and mobile phone use.

In Thailand, among a number of initiatives, the Safer Schools Zones project engages most with land use. The project has installed pedestrian crossing signs and undertaken education programmes on road safety with children and local residents, including competitions on road safety for school children. Monitoring shows that safe behaviour is more common among children who completed a road safety education course. The behaviour of parents, however, does not seem to have changed.

In Poland, inadequate pre-hospital care and slow emergency response times lead to complications and increased mortality from traffic accidents. The need for advocacy and training on emergency response was recognized and a workshop held with a small group of decision-makers and experts. The primary goal of the workshop was to generate action on the part of key stakeholders in Poland to increase the effectiveness of the pre-hospital care and emergency preparedness and response systems in Poland. The workshop led to an evaluation of the pre-hospital care system in Poland involving experts from the World Health Organization (WHO), Austrian Red Cross, Holmatro and the World Rescue Organization.

Source: GRSP, www.grsproadsafety.org/

NOTES

1 See www.unisdr.org/eng/library/lib-terminology-eng%20home.htm.
2 WHO, 2004b.
3 WHO, 2007.
4 WHO, 2004b.
5 *Ibid.*
6 Commission for Global Road Safety, 2006.
7 Jacobs et al, 1999.
8 Asian Development Bank, www.adb.org/Projects/PRC RoadSafety/road-safety.asp.
9 WHO, 2004b.
10 Gold, 2000.
11 Jacobs et al, 1999.
12 Asian Development Bank, www.adb.org/Projects/PRC RoadSafety/road-safety.asp.
13 Kopits and Cropper, 2003.
14 WHO, 2004b.
15 *Ibid.*
16 EM-DAT CRED, www.em-dat.net.
17 Jacobs et al, 1999.
18 Odero et al, 2003.
19 Hijar et al, 2003.
20 ADB, 2002.
21 Odero et al, 2003.
22 Khayesi, 2003.
23 WHO, 2004b.
24 *Ibid.*
25 WHO, 2007.
26 *Ibid.*
27 WHO, 2004b.
28 Gold, 2000.
29 Milliot, 2004.
30 The EU-15 includes member countries in the European Union prior to the accession of ten candidate countries on 1 May 2004. The EU-15 is comprised of Austria, Belgium, Denmark, Finland, France, Germany, Greece, Ireland, Italy, Luxembourg, The Netherlands, Portugal, Spain, Sweden and the UK.
31 European Commission, 2001.
32 Pucher et al, 2005.
33 Tiwari, 2002.
34 Aeron-Thomas et al, 2004.
35 WHO, 2004b.
36 UNCHS, 2000a.
37 General Assembly Resolution 58/289 (adopted 11 May 2004).
38 Davis et al, 2003.
39 Barter, 2001.
40 Commission for Global Road Safety, 2006.
41 Tiwari, 2002.
42 *Ibid.*
43 Barter, 2001.
44 Srinivasan and Rogers, 2005.
45 UNCHS, 1993; Pearce et al, 1998.
46 Pucher et al, 2005.
47 Hensher, 2007.
48 Barter, 2001.
49 Ongkittikul and Geerlings, 2006.
50 Kingham et al, 2001.
51 Collins and Kearns, 2005.
52 UNCHS, 1993.
53 Gold, 2000.
54 Comte et al, 2000.
55 Commission for Global Road Safety, 2006.
56 Tiwari, 2002.
57 *Ibid.*
58 Cyclists' Touring Club, 2002.
59 Afukaar et al, 2003.
60 Hummel, 2001.
61 GRSP, undated.
62 GRSP, www.grsproadsafety.org/.
63 GRSP, www.grsproadsafety.org/?pageid=28#GRSP%20in%20Thailand.
64 GRSP, www.grsproadsafety.org.
65 GRSP, www.grsproadsafety.org/?pageid=22&projectid=58#58.
66 Davis et al, 2003.
67 Mura et al, 2006.
68 *Ibid.*
69 Holmgren et al, 2005.
70 Davis et al, 2003.
71 Jacobs et al, 1999.
72 Commission for Global Road Safety, 2006.
73 WHO, 2004b.
74 Tiwari, 2002.
75 Bastos et al, 2005.
76 Commission for Global Road Safety, 2006.
77 *Ibid.*
78 *Ibid.*
79 See www.drivealive.org.za.
80 See www.madd.org.
81 Dimitriou, 2006.
82 Vasconcellos, 2005.
83 Pucher et al, 2005.
84 Commission for Global Road Safety, 2006.
85 Aeron-Thomas et al, 2004.
86 Zheng, 2007.
87 Aeron-Thomas, 2003.
88 United Nations General Assembly Resolution A/RES/60/5.
89 See www.who.int/roadsafety/en.
90 *Ibid.*
91 The third Sunday of November every year has been dedicated to this day of remembrance.
92 GRSP, www.grsproadsafety.org.
93 Fédération Internationale de l'Automobile (FIA) Foundation.
94 See www.fiafoundation.com/commissionforglobalroadsafety.
95 ECA and WHO, 2007.

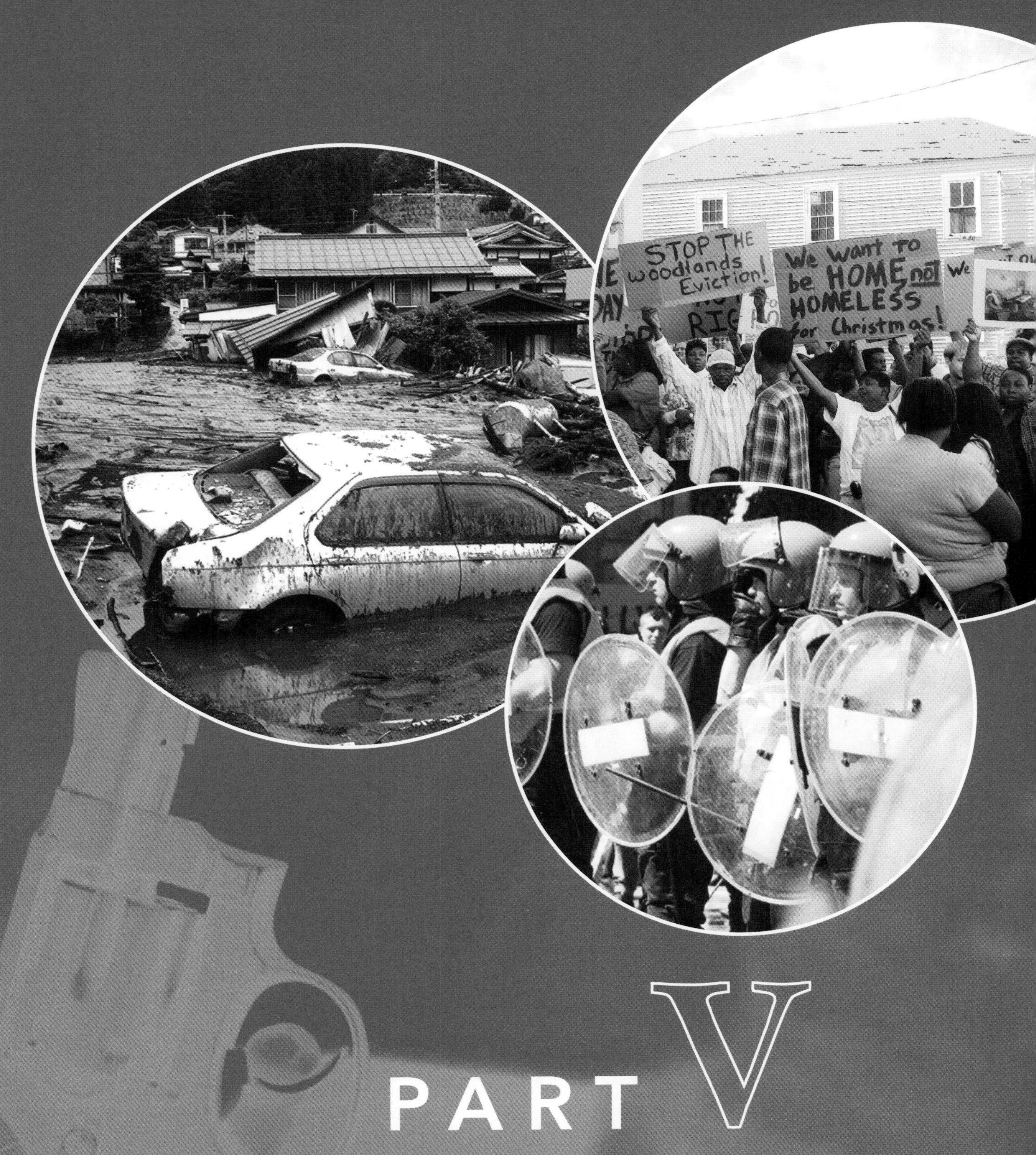

PART V

TOWARDS SAFER AND MORE SECURE CITIES

This part of the Global Report explores promising policy responses to the three major threats to urban safety and security reviewed in Parts II, III and IV. It specifically builds on the international, national and local policy and practice trends identified and discussed in Chapters 4, 6 and 8 – that is, on crime and violence, security of tenure and forced evictions, and natural and human-made disasters, respectively.

There can be little doubt that there is considerable scope for further development in policies and practices for reducing urban crime and violence. Chapter 10, the first in this part of the report, discusses policy responses and practices designed to address the threat of urban crime and violence that, on the basis of experience to date, could be further pursued in the future.

The 'traditional' approach to problems of crime and violence, which is to see them as the primary responsibility of the police and the criminal justice system, is increasingly being replaced by an approach that recognizes that the complexity of the phenomena being addressed requires a broad-based response. There is considerable scope for further development of this approach. Nonetheless, it is important that the police and the criminal justice system are 'fit for purpose' in the modern world, and are seen as key contributors to the fight against crime and violence. Improvements and reforms in these 'traditional' areas are essential and should primarily be driven by central governments in most developing countries. Such improvements should be seen as complementary to the newer approaches being developed in 'non-traditional' fields, and appropriate linkages should be developed between all of these activities.

The main 'non-traditional' or newer approaches explored in Chapter 10 include enhancement of urban safety and security through effective urban planning, design and governance; the development of community-based approaches to enhancing urban safety and security; reduction of key risk factors by focusing on groups most vulnerable to crime; and strengthening of social capital through initiatives that seek to develop the ability of individuals and communities themselves to respond to problems of crime and violence, provide economic, social, cultural and sporting opportunities, and improve the environment in ways that assist these processes. The combination of several of these approaches – all of which are specially suitable for implementation at the local level – into a systematic programme, driven by a broad strategy and based upon a careful understanding of the local context, seems more likely to be successful than the *ad hoc* application of individual initiatives.

The preferred mechanism for supporting this broad-based approach is usually the partnership mechanism; but to be fully effective, partnerships need to address a series of questions about their operation, and partners need to buy fully into the spirit of partnership. Central and local governments can play a key role in providing an enabling environment and framework for partnerships to flourish. The best institutional structures for implementing such programmes or initiatives are likely to be those that succeed in getting the key players involved in delivery together in ways that get them not only to commit to the programme, but also to explore how the mainstream work of their own agencies can contribute to the overall effectiveness of these initiatives. Local authorities will often be the most appropriate leaders of such structures. Local communities need to be as fully involved as possible in these processes, not only in terms of consultation, but also as generators and implementers of projects. Capacity-building is a fundamental part of work to address crime and violence at the local level. The approach adopted towards capacity-building activities needs to be as broadly based as possible, and to respond to the capacity-building needs of professional groups, partnership members and local community members.

The transfer of ideas from elsewhere can be very valuable, but it needs to be thought about carefully in the particular circumstances in which it is intended to apply them. It cannot be assumed that ideas that have worked in one part of the world will necessarily work elsewhere. There are no one-size-fits-all solutions, and there is no substitute for a careful study of the particular situation in order to determine the most appropriate course of action.

There needs to be a greater level of commitment to evaluating crime prevention programmes, as well as more open reporting of evaluation results, including areas where problems have been experienced. This is an area where civil society and independent non-governmental organizations (NGOs) can play a key role. This is because much that is done in the area of crime and violence prevention is either not evaluated, is assessed in the most perfunctory manner, or is declared to be successful without much, if any, evidence to support such claim. An important point that is by no means always recognized is that valuable lessons can be learned from what has not gone well, as well as what has succeeded.

International support of various kinds can help cities,

particularly in developing and transitional countries, to improve their ability to effectively implement measures that address problems of crime and violence. Such direct assistance should be part of a package that also includes continuing and strengthening international cooperation in tackling various types of organized crime, such as trafficking of drugs, arms and people — all of which have international dimensions. There are several examples that have been of immense importance to particular cities. For instance, assistance from the US has been a key factor in recent efforts to mount projects tackling aspects of crime and violence in Kingston (Jamaica). Likewise, Canada, The Netherlands and Sweden have contributed to Safer Cities projects supported by UN-Habitat in several African cities.

One particular type of international support that can be very helpful is in the field of training and staff development. There are already several good examples of this practice. For example, as part of its support for the reform of the Jamaica Constabulary Force since 2000, the UK government has been providing financial resources on a significant scale, mainly to support international police officers working alongside Jamaica's force in addressing issues of serious crime. This latter element has included Metropolitan Police officers working directly with their Jamaican counterparts, as well as training being offered by the Metropolitan Police to the Jamaica Constabulary Force. The relationship between the Jamaica Constabulary Force and the UK's Metropolitan Police suggests that there can be particular advantages in this relationship – on a continuous rather than an *ad hoc* basis – since this offers the opportunity of progressive improvement rather than short-term gains.

The UN-Habitat Safer Cities Programme has much potential for expansion, especially by engaging more cities than it has done to date and, where possible, by helping to speed up the process in cities that have proved to be slow in getting to grips with the problems of crime and violence. There are several things that might help in this context; but one important issue is the availability of resources, both for the programme as a whole and for projects in individual cities. Further international support could be of considerable value in this context as well.

Forced evictions are the most visible manifestation of tenure insecurity. The number of people falling victim to forced evictions each year runs into several millions, and the human costs associated with such evictions are staggering. Evicted people not only lose their homes and neighbourhoods, but they are also often forced to leave behind personal possessions since little warning is given before bulldozers or demolition squads destroy their settlements. And, in many such cases, the entire eviction process is carried out without having been subject to judicial scrutiny. Forced evictions are inevitably traumatic: they cause injury; they affect the most vulnerable; and they place victims at risk of further violence. Evictees often lose their sources of livelihood since they are forced to move away from areas where they had jobs or sources of income. In particular, women evictees face unique challenges, suffering disproportionately from violence before, during and after a forced eviction. Women also often have to manage multiple responsibilities as the primary caretakers of children, the sick and the elderly in situations of forced eviction and homelessness.

All of these consequences of forced evictions are directly linked to the theme of this Global Report: from a range of aspects of physical security of the person, to job security and social security, to the very notion of security of the home itself. Evictions that result in homelessness are a serious threat to most, if not all, aspects of human security. An end to forced evictions is thus a major part of a strategy to enhance urban safety and security. Chapter 11 examines how an approach to security of tenure combining international advocacy with human rights and human security concerns could prove invaluable in preventing the practice of forced evictions.

A large and increasing body of international law now condemns the practice of forced eviction as a gross and systematic violation of human rights. Despite this, evictions are a tragically common feature in all regions of the world. Chapter 11 argues that the right to security of tenure goes beyond a narrow focus on property rights alone, and proposes that it is more appropriate to use the term housing, land and property rights, or HLP rights. Such an approach would contribute to avoiding the exclusion and inequitable treatment of, or outright discrimination against, certain segments of the population, such as tenants, co-operative dwellers, people living and/or working in informal settlements without security of tenure, women, nomads, indigenous peoples and other vulnerable groups.

At the international level, four areas stand out for particular attention. First, there is a need to raise the awareness of governments and other stakeholders with respect to what the already existing body of international law implies at the national and local levels. Chapter 11 suggests the proclamation of a global moratorium on forced evictions as one way of addressing this. Such a moratorium would send a strong signal about the importance of such rights and could enhance the international public debate with respect to the right to security of tenure. Second, Chapter 11 calls for the application of international criminal law to cases of forced evictions. Third, international cooperation activities should increasingly focus on supporting local institutions, including, in particular, NGOs and community-based organizations (CBOs) that are actively involved in awareness-raising about HLP rights at the national and local levels. Fourth, as noted in Chapter 5, there is an immediate need to ensure that governments are fulfilling their obligations with respect to monitoring the progressive realization of the right to adequate housing. Efforts under way to develop indicators for global monitoring mechanisms on security of tenure, evictions and other aspects of HLP rights should thus be actively encouraged and supported.

At the national level, states are obliged to respect, protect and fulfil all human rights, including HLP rights. The obligation to respect requires states to refrain from interfering with the enjoyment of rights, such as when a state engages in arbitrary forced evictions. The obligation to protect requires states to prevent violations of such rights by third parties, such as landlords or private developers. Finally, the obligation to fulfil requires states to take appropriate legislative, administrative, budgetary, judicial and other measures to ensure that all people have access to adequate housing. So, while states are not necessarily required to build homes for the entire population, they are obliged to take a whole range of steps, both positive and negative in nature, grounded in human rights law, which are designed to ensure the full realization of all human rights, including the right to adequate housing.

Chapter 11 provides a whole range of specific recommendations on elements to consider when developing housing and urban policies, taking into account the principles of HLP rights. These include, among other issues, steps to prevent discrimination with respect to housing; to cease the practice of forced evictions; to introduce faster and more affordable measures for conferring security of tenure to people living in informal settlements and slum areas; and to ensure that the obligations of states under international law are incorporated within national legislation. As noted above, in order for national (as well as local) governments to fulfil their obligations with respect to international law, and in order to plan for improving tenure security for all, there is a pressing need for better monitoring and better data on security of tenure and forced evictions.

It is important to note that security is less about which type of tenure an individual community, household or individual enjoys, but rather about the security enjoyed. Even freehold land can be expropriated by the state under the pretext of being 'for the common good'. As noted in Chapters 5 and 6, there is a whole range of tenure options that may (or may not) provide security of tenure. Thus, living in an informal settlement or in a residential area governed by customary or communal law does not inherently mean that a person, household or community will be forcibly evicted from their homes and lands. It has to be recognized that there are no universal solutions to the provision of security of tenure and that challenges in this regard tend to be solved in different ways in different locations. Depending upon circumstances, there are a number of acceptable forms of secure tenure, and the merits of innovative policies are clear. The importance of the urban or local level lies in the fact that evictions are most frequently carried out by local authorities or other local actors. It is thus essential that local authorities, in their development strategies and planning, acknowledge the right to enjoy security of tenure. Likewise, the most important actors in any effort to prevent evictions are those operating at the local level. As noted above, the report thus highlights the importance of supporting the activities of NGOs, CBOs and others engaged in enhancing security of tenure and combating forced evictions.

The extensive impacts of natural and human-made disasters on cities and their inhabitants have been elaborated upon in Part IV of this Global Report. Various actions are currently being pursued at the international, national and local levels to reduce disaster risk in urban areas. Chapter 12 examines key policy areas where future prospects for building resilience against natural and human-made disasters in cities lie.

In view of the increasing numbers of people being affected by disasters globally, risk reduction is now identified as a significant concern in several international frameworks and agreements. Most fundamental are the Millennium Development Goals (MDGs). Although there is no disaster risk reduction MDG, it is recognized that failure to integrate disaster risk reduction within urban, national and regional development policy will undo development gains and thus impede the achievement of other MDGs. Disaster risk reduction is also highlighted in both international frameworks for urban development (the Habitat Agenda) and disaster risk reduction (the Hyogo Framework). Such international frameworks are important in focusing the attention of multilateral and bilateral donors, as well as international civil society actors, towards disaster risk reduction. They can also facilitate advocacy and guide the development of disaster risk reduction strategies at national and city levels. Furthermore, governments require assistance from the international community in the form of funding, data and information and technical expertise to establish or improve their disaster risk reduction systems. International assistance for disaster risk reduction should not focus primarily on recovery and reconstruction efforts, as has been the case in the past, but also on longer-term development objectives.

Chapter 12 identifies a number of policies that, if adopted at the national level, can support city-level risk reduction planning and implementation. It is especially important that disaster risk reduction is mainstreamed within national development and poverty reduction policies and planning. Knowledge of disaster trends and impacts is fundamental in guiding the development of risk reduction policies. Governments thus need to improve risk, hazard and vulnerability assessment and monitoring capacity through increased investments, with support from the international community, where necessary. Technological innovation has greatly improved such assessments, although not equally in all countries. Participatory techniques offer a unique opportunity of generating basic data on hazard, vulnerability and loss where this is not available from centralized databases, as is the case in many low-income countries. In addition to informing policy formulation, assessment data should feed into national initiatives that aim to build a culture of awareness and safety through public education and information programmes. The use of education systems to raise awareness and skills for disaster risk reduction is especially effective in minimizing loss from disasters.

Governments should also seek to build and strengthen national and local early warning systems. Cultural and linguistic diversity or socio-economic inequalities may lead to some people being excluded from early warning information and advice on how to respond to disaster. Involving local communities in vulnerability and hazard assessments can facilitate the dissemination of early warning messages and, thus, enhance local-level preparedness. Indeed, participatory and inclusive strategies that enable the full participation of relevant local actors should guide risk reduction activities at both national and city levels. People-centred early warning systems, which bring together technical expertise for identifying approaching hazard with local expertise, are invaluable in diffusing early warning information and catalysing preventative action. The use of socially acceptable communication media to disseminate early warning information has been found to be particularly effective. Furthermore, knowledge derived from early warning systems should be linked to local-level action plans as these enable timely response and resource mobilization in the face of disasters.

As highlighted in Chapter 12, city authorities can also implement a number of strategies to reduce disaster risk under the auspices of overarching national policies. Disaster risk reduction should become an integral part of urban planning and management, although this is not easy. A key constraint at the city level is a lack of capacity for enforcing regulations and implementation of plans. Differences in professional training and work practices, and budget lines that make a distinction between development and emergency also hamper progress. Interdisciplinary and inter-sectoral training, research and partnerships can be used to enhance implementation capacity at the city level. Involving the private sector in disaster risk reduction efforts can further enhance the capacity of city authorities to reduce loss from disasters.

Land-use planning is a particularly effective instrument that can be employed by city authorities to reduce disaster risk by regulating the expansion of human settlements and infrastructure. Evidence-based land-use planning at the city level requires accurate and up-to-date data, which is lacking in many contexts, especially those with rapidly expanding populations and informal settlements. Technological innovation can help to fill part of this gap. Participatory planning offers opportunities for extending land-use planning into informal settlements and slums. For instance, participatory GIS can be used to identify more subtle local characteristics of places that lead to vulnerability or risk.

Designing disaster-resistant buildings and infrastructure in cities can save many lives and assets from natural and human-made disasters. The technical expertise to achieve this is available; but implementation is a major challenge. The safety standards of buildings and infrastructure can be improved through integrating risk reduction within construction design and project management. Partnerships between engineers, artisans and the public can help to promote disaster-proof construction locally. Increasing the prominence of disaster risk management in relevant academic and training courses has the potential to improve safer design and construction. Even where initial designs or construction methods have not been sound, retrofitting provides an option for ensuring safety standards. Indigenous designs should not be cast aside in the rush to modernize urban settlements, as valuable techniques for safe construction can be lost in the process.

Finally, reconstruction efforts need to balance a range of competing pressures. Hardest to reconcile are demands for rapid provision of basic needs against the more time-consuming aim of 'building back better'. This tension is particularly evident in shelter reconstruction. Greater partnership between humanitarian and development actors is the most likely way beyond this impasse. If humanitarian actors are to integrate development planning within their work, appropriate budgetary and institutional changes are necessary. Clear legislative frameworks should also be in place to avoid uncoordinated and fragmented action by city governments, local actors, donors and humanitarian agencies. Innovative financial programmes, such as microfinance or micro-insurance, are necessary for facilitating the revival of household and community economies, while avoiding the disempowering experience that can come with international humanitarian aid. Mobilizing spare capacity at the city level, such as medical stock and temporary accommodation, can enhance response and recovery efforts.

All of the three chapters in this part of the report do, in fact, propose specific pathways to resilience, as discussed in Chapter 2. While working towards the goal of safer and more secure cities, it is obvious that the efforts undertaken at all of the various levels discussed in this Global Report have to address, often simultaneously, a number of issues in various arenas. Crime and violence cannot be addressed solely through a focus on more police or more jails. Similarly, security of tenure cannot be addressed through the provision of title deeds alone, and people cannot be protected against natural and human-made disasters if all efforts are concentrated at disaster response. Safer and more secure cities can only be realized through comprehensive initiatives that, at the same time, incorporate aspects of institutional and policy development, and international and national law, as well as the potential contributions of all relevant stakeholders, including civil society actors.

CHAPTER 10

REDUCING URBAN CRIME AND VIOLENCE

The primary purpose of this chapter is to explore some of the most helpful ways forward for urban areas in seeking to tackle issues of crime and violence, based on the discussion in Chapter 4 of the policies being applied to this end. In this regard, the chapter is divided into five sections. The first explores the potential of the six groupings of policy responses to crime and violence identified in Chapter 4. The second section examines the emerging policy trends that were also identified in Chapter 4 in terms of their future utility. The third section looks at some of the key issues for implementing policy that have been identified since it is clear that one of the key challenges in this field is the need to find effective ways of putting them into practice. The fourth section pulls together some of the key issues that arise from these discussions for the future of the UN-Habitat Safer Cities Programme. The final section identifies 13 broad propositions that reflect the conclusions of this chapter.

SCOPE FOR THE CONTINUING DEVELOPMENT OF KEY POLICY RESPONSES

Chapter 4 identified six groups of policy responses to crime and violence in urban areas:

1. enhancing urban safety and security through effective urban planning, design and governance;
2. community-based approaches to enhancing urban safety and security;
3. strengthening formal criminal justice and policing;
4. reducing risk factors;
5. non-violent resolution of conflicts; and
6. strengthening social capital.

Each of these is discussed in more detail below in terms of its potential to contribute effectively to addressing crime and violence in urban areas.

Enhancing urban safety and security through effective urban planning, design and governance

Chapters 3 and 4 have shown that poor planning, design and management of cities are among the factors associated with crime and violence. The idea that *where* crimes takes place is something that should be of interest to the processes of planning and urban design is a relatively new idea in terms of its mainstream acceptance. But the reason why this matters is that the work of these disciplines through their manipulation of the physical environment has the potential either to reduce the opportunity for crime to be committed or to create such opportunities. The accumulated experience from several parts of the world suggests that attempts to manipulate the physical environment in order to reduce the opportunity for crime as part of design processes are potentially very useful elements in the fight against crime and violence.[1]

Experience from several parts of the world suggests that attempts to manipulate the physical environment in order to reduce the opportunity for crime ...are potentially very useful elements in the fight against crime and violence

Building crime prevention into new and existing environments

There are usually two primary elements to processes of this nature: building crime prevention considerations into the design processes that shape new development, and revisiting problematic existing built environments where there is the possibility that reshaping these might reduce the crime problems that they are experiencing. This latter element is often given less attention than the former; but in most societies the amount of new development under consideration is on a much smaller scale than the extent of development that already exists. As a result, it is important that attention should not be focused exclusively on new development. Nonetheless, it is essential to get new development right from a crime prevention perspective for three reasons. First, the problems of crime are experienced by the occupants of developments over protracted periods of time, and this can be a major factor in public satisfaction (or otherwise) with these developments. Second, developments that encourage high levels of criminal activity are also likely to put pressure on policing services, which, of course, is a public cost. Third, retrofitting is inevitably a somewhat constrained process; therefore, revisiting developments to correct mistakes is not only expensive and disruptive, it is also unlikely to be as successful as getting it right in the first place.

This makes a powerful case for enhancing urban safety through effective urban planning, design and governance. But making the case and successfully constructing systems and procedures that can enable this opportunity to be taken are two different things. It should also be recognized that this is merely one part of the struggle against crime and violence, which needs to be seen alongside other approaches and not as a universal panacea. But on the face of it, trying to make sure that the process of development does not offer opportunities to commit crimes in future and tie up police resources on an ongoing basis[2] seems to be an approach with much potential. It is therefore not surprising that interest in this, worldwide, seems to have been growing.

Design should not just be about the aesthetics and the functionality of what is being created, but ...about how criminals might abuse it for their own ends

Designing with crime prevention in mind

Perhaps the most basic requirement of an approach of this nature is that the design process needs to think from the outset about the possible criminal use of the buildings and spaces being created. In other words, design should not just be about the aesthetics and the functionality of what is being created, but should also be about how people can occupy and use it safely and about how criminals might abuse it for their own ends. This is probably the right place to start, rather than with planning processes, because planning processes essentially get to deal with designs for development that are often not only already well formed, but also have substantial levels of commitment attached to them. Thus, planning systems would be faced with a difficult challenge if their role was essentially to try to add further design considerations at a relatively late stage into a process that has already in the minds of its promoters reached a satisfactory conclusion. So the starting point must be that it would be highly desirable if design processes took account of safety considerations and of the possibility of criminal misuse from first principles. As illustrated below, this is also one of the reasons why effective planning policies not only indicate what they will do when faced with an unsatisfactory design from a crime prevention perspective, but also seek to put in place basic principles of crime prevention that they want developers and their designers to consider in order to reduce the likelihood of an unsatisfactory submission.

It should not be assumed that an approach of this nature would necessarily be welcomed unreservedly by all designers, especially if they see it as constraining their design freedom and creativity or as challenging particular views about urban design to which they hold strong allegiance. Some of this is undoubtedly controversial,[3] and there is still much work to be done to resolve much of this controversy on the basis of evidence. But one helpful approach to this issue, which does not necessarily require a designer to adopt a particular design perspective, but asks individuals to think strategically about what are key problems in terms of residential burglary as part of their design approach, has been developed (see Box 10.1).[4] This approach appears to be more acceptable to many designers than regulatory standards or guidelines, which they see as being inflexible and constraining, as it puts the onus on them to come up with appropriate solutions to these problems as part of their design processes.

Persuading designers and developers to think about crime prevention as an integral part of the design process would be a huge step forward since there is clear evidence that, in the past, crime can be seen as having been unintentionally designed within some developments[5] – 'unintentionally' because the problem was that designers simply did not think about crime prevention in relation to their designs; rather, they actively 'designed crime in'. There is an argument today, of course, now that much is known about the relationship between design and crime, to the effect that this kind of ignorance is no longer acceptable.[6] The safe use of buildings and spaces, and the reduction of opportunities for crime, now need to be part of basic design thinking.

Box 10.1 Design strategies to tackle residential burglary and related crimes

Barry Poyner argues that the record in the UK shows that there are four main types of crime that affect housing developments, and that designers should develop strategies to address these matters:

Burglary – a strategy to discourage people from trying to break into the house. The key design challenges here are to inhibit the selection of a house as a target for burglary, and to protect, in particular, the rear of the house since a great deal of burglary takes place via access from the back of a house.

Car crime – a strategy for providing a safe place to park cars. The key design challenge here is to create parking within protected boundaries, where possible, or if not, to find safe alternatives. The available evidence suggests that separate parking areas accessible from off-street footpath networks are likely to be the least safe locations in terms both of theft of cars themselves and of theft from cars.

Theft around the home – a strategy for protecting the front of the house and items in gardens, sheds and garages. The key design challenge here is to think about each of these elements as its own location carrying its own particular problems, rather than to see all of these elements simply as parts of one single problem. A particularly important issue in this case will often be the approach that is adopted for the security of the boundaries of the plot on which the property sits.

Criminal damage – a strategy to minimize malicious damage to property. The available evidence about appropriate strategies in this case is not well developed; but a key issue is clearly the relationship between open spaces likely to be used by children or youths and the frontages of houses. In these instances, some thought needs to be given to separating the two uses, perhaps by landscaping or through a residential street or pedestrian route.

Source: Poyner, 2006, pp99–103

Planning with crime prevention in mind

Planning systems can also play an important role in this process through policies and practices that promote thinking about crime prevention and through their role in controlling development. Chapter 4 has demonstrated that the process of getting planning systems to think in this way is relatively recent and far from being straightforward. For example, Box 4.3 shows how the English planning system developed thinking about this in several steps over a period of 11 years. Even then, there were both controversies around the guidance available to planners and doubts about how readily and how fully the planning community picked this guidance up.[7] In many parts of the world, planning systems are relatively recent arms of urban governance, struggling with limited resources and problems of access to sufficient skilled personnel to cope with large-scale development pressures. Many planners, faced with this situation, will undoubtedly be tempted to feel that being expected to start thinking about issues of crime prevention is yet another pressure on them that they do not need.

Nevertheless, planning must surely be concerned with the quality of urban living, as well as coping with the pressures caused by its scale. From this perspective, thinking about how planning can contribute to crime prevention is important because there is ample evidence from citizen feedback studies that crime and safety are top priorities in residential neighbourhoods, especially for the urban poor.[8] This issue is undoubtedly a challenge for planners, their professional bodies and for the process of planning education since crime prevention has not achieved prominence in planning dialogues. But it is also a challenge for urban governance because if planning is to make its full contribution to crime prevention planning systems, and structures are to be properly established and resourced, planning staff need to be properly trained and the political process needs to support planning systems in undertaking these tasks.

Integrating crime prevention within planning policy and practice: The British example

In most planning systems, an important step in the chain of effective action is the need to create planning policy tools that planners can apply consistently and with the expectation that their actions will be supported. The most common form with which this drive to create appropriate tools starts is the need to get basic policies about planning for crime prevention written into development plans and associated documents since both shape how planners deal with submitted applications for permission to develop and send out messages to the development community about what the planning system is looking for.

British practice may offer useful lessons for developments of this kind in two ways. First, it demonstrates a fairly highly structured set of relationships between planners and police architectural liaison officers (these are the staff members in the police service who provide advice about crime prevention in relation to physical developments), which means that there is a process of securing police inputs in development decisions made by the planning service. Second, there is a range of advisory documents available from both national and local government levels setting out what the planning system is trying to achieve in seeing urban safety as an integral element in achieving sustainable development, which is the primary purpose of the UK planning system.[9] All of this does not imply that the British system has solved the problem of integrating crime prevention within planning, or that even if it had, the British system would be capable of being transplanted to other locations. Rather, this is an example of a planning system that has taken work in this field further than many others and thus contains useful examples of tools and approaches that may provide lessons elsewhere.

Integrating urban safety within planning and service delivery: The UN-Habitat Safer Cities Programme example

Approaches of this nature are also typically part of the UN-Habitat Safer Cities Programme. The starting point for this has to be a recognition that, in many instances, the existing structures of urban governance had not done much of this kind of work before. Thus, introducing what are new processes and practices is likely to be a long-term process, raising important issues of skills, resources, training and staff development, as well as causing debates about priorities for planning systems. UN-Habitat has identified a range of planning, design and municipal service delivery initiatives based on the experience of the Safer Cities Programmes in African Cities (see Box 10.2).

Thinking about how planning can contribute to crime prevention is important because there is ample evidence...that crime and safety are top priorities in residential neighbourhoods, especially for the urban poor

The wide range of activities summarized in Box 10.2 provides a good indication of the kinds of initiatives that are possible under the broad heading of environmental stewardship, which is the theme that links these activities. It is crucial that the results of evaluations of how effective initiatives of this kind have been, and under what circumstances, are made widely available. Other cities can then design their programmes with the benefit of this information. There is

Box 10.2 Urban planning and design and municipal service delivery initiatives in Safer Cities programmes in African cities

UN-Habitat's range of planning, design and municipal service delivery initiatives have been grouped together under seven broad headings; the key actions in each instance are summarized as follows:

- Integration of safety principles within the planning or upgrading of neighbourhoods, public places and street furniture, including planning for mixed uses (including, in some cases, a multiplicity of uses) and animation, signage and physical access, vision and lighting, frequency of use and access to help, as well as safety audits.
- Surveillance of streets, equipment and public spaces through formal and informal mechanisms, including CCTV and patrols of various kinds (usually by community-based organizations rather than the police), incentives for increased human presence throughout the day, and partnerships with private security service providers.
- Design and intervention in neighbourhoods, including lighting, access roads, cleaning and waste removal, removal of abandoned vehicles, elimination of graffiti, and the maintenance and repair of street equipment.
- Management of markets and public ways, including updating, integration and enforcement of municipal by-laws, urban renewal of particular areas, and interaction and dialogue with retailers' and hawkers' associations.
- Management of traffic and parking, including updating, integration and enforcement of municipal by-laws, specialized squads and car guards, and sensitization campaigns.
- Control of bars, including the regulation of opening and closing hours, the periodic control both of juveniles and of activities, and promoting the responsibility of owners.
- Securing homes and neighbourhoods, including sensitization campaigns on safety measures, technical assistance to homeowners and tenants, surveillance and mutual assistance between neighbours, neighbourhood watch activities, and access to help.

Source: UN-Habitat, 2006e, p33

some early evidence that these kinds of approaches are beginning to play a part in reducing, or at least containing, crime in African cities.[10] But more still needs to be known not just about what appears to be working, but about why this seems to be the case. Nevertheless, the breadth of this listing does demonstrate the scope for contributions of an environmental stewardship kind to initiatives to tackle crime and violence.

■ Improving places for people through crime prevention design and planning systems

Urban planning systems contribute in important ways to the broader process of environmental stewardship by the opportunity that they provide to think strategically about improving places for people

Urban planning systems contribute in important ways to the broader process of environmental stewardship by the opportunity that they provide to think strategically about improving places for people. If properly done, such processes have the potential to contribute considerably in these terms, especially if they are successful in encouraging the design process to consider crime prevention from the outset. To do this, a critical step is the need to develop appropriate policies and practices about planning for crime prevention. This is a technical challenge for planners individually and collectively; but it is also a major challenge for urban governance since properly resourced and supported planning systems are essential if this potential is to be realized.

There is clear evidence that there are moves taking place in this direction in some parts of the world.[11] But the pace of change needs to be accelerated if this is to be fully integrated within the challenge that planning systems face in coping with the tide of urbanization expected in many parts of the world over the next few decades. This is not just a problem for the developing world since it is clear that the transitional countries of Eastern Europe still have some distance to go before catching up with the work that has been done in other parts of the European Union (EU) to move towards establishing European standards in this field.[12]

Community-based approaches to enhancing urban safety and security

With respect to community-based approaches, Chapter 4 argued that there are two main types: those where the community is not in the lead but is involved in a project in various ways, and those where the community is, essentially, the driving force behind a project and where the public sector plays an enabling role. Although there is no reliable data on this, the probability is that where formal responsibilities for engaging with the public in formulating and implementing public policy are part of the law or expected practice affecting local authorities and other public bodies, the former approach, with its many variations, is much more commonly found. This model is more typical of the developed world[13] than it is of the developing world, where the role of the state at local level in promoting public engagement does not appear to be as fully developed. Nonetheless, there is a wide variation of practices to be found within each of these two broad groupings, and this is affected by several factors. Thus, comparisons between societies are not easy to make meaningfully, and in many ways this might be less helpful than looking at how individual societies and cities develop their own thinking and approaches over time.

■ Changing community-based approaches

There are two other elements that are important in this discussion. One of these is a recognition that the role of community-based approaches is likely to change according to the project in hand. For example, a long-term strategy for tackling crime and promoting public safety across a large urban area is a very different thing from an individual project in a specific locality scheduled to be implemented at a particular point in time. In the former case, a common situation is that the lead on this will be taken by a public-sector agency, probably working with a partnership structure, with the role of the community being essentially around information provision and consultation on drafts. Even here, community representatives can play a more proactive role than this by utilizing their membership of the partnership to raise issues and to promote ideas that emanate from within communities. In the case of a specific project, it is possible that the idea originated within the community and is implemented with community members playing leading roles, with the role of public-sector agencies being that of providing support. Both of these approaches may be perfectly appropriate to the particular situation, although in both instances there is considerable scope to develop the roles of key players and to see each particular initiative as a learning opportunity that can contribute to future developments of this nature.

■ Community types, interests and diversity

The other critical factor is the nature of communities themselves. There is huge scope for discussion about how communities are defined, in the first instance, and given the fluid population structure of many cities, it is important to bear this in mind rather than to treat it as being fixed once geographical definitions have been arrived at. Another way of looking at this is to think not just in terms of geographical communities, but in terms of communities of interest, which may well not correspond to communities defined by residential location. An example here would be work on employment development opportunities for young people, which is likely to transcend particular geographical boundaries. However, this may well need to take account of those localities where youth unemployment is high, and where there is a significant risk that young people will drift into criminal lifestyles.

Many cultural or sporting initiatives are also of this kind since they are often about facilities that can only be in a limited number of locations but draw users from wide areas. Even where this is thought about in terms of residential location, it is not always the case that the communities in these areas are homogeneous. Homogeneous communities do not always show unanimity of view, and so it is important to have processes in place that go beyond relying on a handful of people to say what the 'community view' is since they may only represent part of it. All of this implies that it is important not to take an overly simplistic view of 'community', but rather to understand its diversity and to ensure that the range of views and interests often to be found is not obscured by this process of simplification. All of these factors need to be carefully thought about when considering forms of community involvement, including the role of the public sector as initiator, rather than just playing an enabling role.

It is clear that right across the spectrum of community-based approaches in enhancing urban safety and security, there is considerable scope for beneficial development. This needs to be seen in terms of opportunities, rather than in terms of problems, and must be approached realistically, which means properly understanding the local circumstances. There is no point in drawing idealistic conclusions about what local communities are capable of achieving and then criticizing them for failing to live up to these ideals. However, there is every point in taking the view that community capabilities are not static, but can be developed through appropriate training, information, support and opportunity. Consequently, programmes to develop community capability need to sit alongside appropriate contemporary programmes of community engagement. In particular, if the part of the spectrum which is about direct community action, rather than about information and consultation, is to be developed, it is important that public- and private-sector agencies and partnerships learn to trust communities and to be willing to work with them as equal partners.

The following points need to be made regarding community-based interventions:

- Given the nature of crime and violence, they are by some, not considered very appropriate issues to be dealt with at the community level. The police, for instance, may be reluctant to share data on crime or on their operations with communities and the public at large, for fear that this information may be abused.
- Communities themselves may have their own views of crime and delinquent activities that may not be fully compliant with the definitions and classifications provided by the law. Indeed, in many communities, the lines between legal, formal, informal and illegal activities are blurred. A measure of common ground has to be found before any meaningful engagement can take place.
- Security may be a major issue for mobilizing a community into action, but may not be such a sustaining force; as the problems get solved, the community may shift attention to other issues. It is therefore important to build security and prevention issues into broader communities agendas, and link them with service delivery, management of services, and community development in general. In this way, efforts can be sustained and modulated over time.
- Finally, city strategies need to acknowledge the social mechanisms and knowledge that communities already deploy, possibly in isolation from, or even in contradiction to, official practice to address risk factors and vulnerabilities related to crime and violence. As they have enormous potential to contribute to overall safety, these mechanisms need to be described, discussed and assessed.

Indeed, communities not only have the direct experience of crime and violence, of which they often bear the brunt, but they also often have the understanding of local dynamics and risk factors, as well as of the ideas and mechanisms vital for tackling them. That said, communities have a key role to play in the prevention of crime, both by reducing vulnerabilities and addressing risk factors.

City strategies need to acknowledge the social mechanisms and knowledge that communities already deploy...to address risk factors and vulnerabilities related to crime and violence

■ Community safety approaches: Toronto and Kingston

A good example of an approach described in the preceding section is in the Crime Prevention through Social Development strand of Toronto's Community Safety Strategy, summarized in Box 4.7. Here, there are several instances of individual programmes where, in effect, a policy, financial and administrative framework is provided for community-based initiatives, but where the initiatives themselves come from communities. Examples include:

- youth opportunity initiatives: Jobs for Youth, which provides government funding for community-based organizations to run summer employment projects targeted at youth from priority neighbourhoods;
- the Youth Challenge Fund, which supports community safety ideas that come from people living in Toronto's 13 'at-risk' neighbourhoods, and encourages community organizations to apply for funding in order to implement projects of this nature;
- grassroots/community-based youth services, which provide support for not-for-profit community-based agencies to implement programmes and services for youth in 'at-risk' neighbourhoods.

Communities not only have the direct experience of crime and violence, of which they often bear the burnt, but they also often have the understanding of local dynamics and risk factors, as well as of the ideas and mechanisms vital for tackling them

There are also examples of programmes with some of these characteristics in Kingston (Jamaica), where 'top-down' programmes of the type described in Chapter 4 were accompanied by programmes designed to encourage local communities to play a more active role in some parts of the city in addressing the problems that were contributing to high levels of crime and violence. For instance, in the Fletchers Land community, major efforts were made to encourage better parenting in order to tackle what was seen as a breakdown in family values. The success of this initiative led to its replication in other parts of the city. Similarly, the Grants Pen community in Kingston, which once had a reputation for its volatility, has witnessed significant progress in reducing crime through a range of programmes, which have included a major emphasis on the creation and use of sports opportunities targeted at young people. In both of these cases, important roles were played by formal programmes in terms of the provision of facilities or opportunities; but the local communities also played a major role in determining how these were utilized.[14]

It is, of course, possible to go beyond this and to have a completely open-ended approach to community-based initiatives. However, there are few examples of this since the resources available for community safety initiatives are usually small in relation to the scale of the problem. What is important even when organizations that control funding are not prepared to take an open-ended view of community-based initiatives is that they should be willing to listen to ideas that come from the community sources.

Strengthening formal criminal justice and policing

Although one of the most apparent trends in the response to crime and violence has been the move from sole reliance on the police and the judiciary to the development of more broadly based approaches, this does not detract from the importance of measures to strengthen the formal criminal justice and policing systems in societies where these can be seen as part of the problem. The move towards more broadly based approaches should not be seen as diminishing the importance of the police and the judiciary, but rather as an acknowledgement of the fact that the struggle against crime and violence needs to encompass an ever broader range of approaches. What is important is that these more 'traditional' elements are seen as integral to contemporary comprehensive approaches, rather than as elements standing outside them.

One of the most apparent trends in the response to crime and violence has been the move from sole reliance on the police and the judiciary to the development of more broadly based approaches

An example of a changing police culture: Hong Kong

An interesting illustration of the interdependent nature of these phenomena is provided by the move of the Hong Kong police towards a more community focus for its work, and the development of a community service culture (see Box 4.8 in Chapter 4). Here, the debates about the nature and role of community policing approaches, which had been going on vigorously in police forces across the world over this period,[15] were overlain by major political changes away from a colonialist governmental legacy and towards reintegration with China, which, in turn, recognized that Hong Kong was in some important ways different from the rest of the country.

What was also clear during this process of change was that it did not always take place in a linear or orderly manner. It included significant stages where public responses to what had been done previously shaped events, and where the ebb and flow of ideas were influenced by the views of key personalities at various points in time. It was also a process that took place over a long period. Clearly, there are elements of this story that are particular to the circumstances of Hong Kong; but there are also aspects that offer useful lessons elsewhere about the dynamics of a process of this nature. In particular, this case study illustrates the importance of a process of winning hearts and minds, both within the police service and among the communities for whom it works. This can be among the most difficult and protracted elements of a change process of this nature. But it is vital if the case for change is to be properly developed and then put into effective practice.

Resistance and the inability to change in police and justice systems

One of the most important reasons why changes to police and criminal justice systems need to be an integral part of comprehensive attempts to address crime and violence is because diagnoses of the problems to be faced have often concluded that the operation, in practice, has added to the difficulties. Three paragraphs from the UN-Habitat review of its experiences of Safer Cities projects in Africa summarize this well:

> *Police have traditionally placed more emphasis on major crime at the expense of unrelenting community problems and conflicts. Police are often opposed to the introduction of reforms due to cultural resistance to change, inadequate training offered to its agents and a lack of transparency.*
>
> *The justice system is also being questioned in view of its inability to deal effectively with urban delinquency. The helplessness in dealing with files efficiently, the lack of resources, in some cases a lack of transparency, the myriad of laws that are impossible to implement, and the lack of alternative solutions all account for the inefficiency within the justice system. In Africa, the number of prisoners awaiting trial is twice as high as the number of accused. This number is equal in Latin America and much lower in other regions. This illustrates the slow pace and the lack of efficiency in the justice system.*
>
> *Prisons, with the exception of a few modern and experimental ones, can be considered schools for technical training and network development for delinquents.[16] The worldwide rate of recidivism exceeds 60 per cent. But despite evidence that the restorative function of prison fails, they maintain a symbolic value in the minds of many which renders it an easy solution and clear response, as demonstrated in Africa where the rate of incarceration is similar to Latin America but higher than in other regions in the world.[17]*

Not surprisingly, given this diagnosis, an important component of Safer Cities projects in African cities has been attempts to address such problems. Box 10.3 summarizes the various actions that have been undertaken in this regard.

The importance of public confidence in police and justice systems

As well as the direct benefits that flow from the specific actions summarized in Box 10.3, the public at large also feels confident that the police and the criminal justice systems will do their jobs properly so that their contribution to public safety will be effective. There is clear evidence from the case studies for this Global Report that this is not always the case.

For example, the Port Moresby case study suggests that the police and criminal justice systems' public credibility is poor. This is so for several of reasons, including what is frequently seen as violent behaviour by the police; the failure of the prison system to offer anything much more than an advanced education in crime; and the general failure to effectively address the city's escalating crime problems.

As a consequence, there is a need to 'modernize' these systems if they are to play a key role in tackling the problems of crime and violence in Port Moresby.[18] An important part of initiatives of this nature is the need to address corruption wherever it exists. This is because the widespread belief that corrupt behaviour will enable criminals to avoid capture and sentencing, or to be treated more leniently than would have been the case, is corrosive of public trust and confidence in these services. Where it is clear that confidence and trust are low, an important element in any action would be steps to retrieve this position since it is very difficult for the police and the criminal justice systems to operate effectively without public support and goodwill.

It is important to note that programmes aimed at strengthening the police, particularly in developing countries, should also address their welfare and poor conditions of service. For instance, in Kabul, Afghanistan, the average police officer earns $15 per month.[19] Similarly, in African countries such as Nigeria, Kenya and Ghana, the police earn a pittance, and often lack the appropriate equipment to carry out their duties. In countries such as Botswana, Lesotho, Swaziland, South Africa and Kenya, members of the police force have not been spared from the HIV/AIDS pandemic. Furthermore, the living conditions in most police accommodation are appalling. It was therefore not surprising to observers when, in 2002, junior officers of the Nigeria Police Force threatened to embark on strike action to press for improved working and service conditions.

Box 10.3 Actions to strengthen formal criminal justice and policing in Safer Cities projects in African cities

There are broadly nine types of actions that have been undertaken to date, which are summarized as follows, together with the key specific types of projects that have been carried out under each of these headings:

Decentralized police services: includes strengthening of local police precincts, and creating satellite and mobile police stations.

Collaboration with municipalities: includes improvements to police facilities and equipment, joint analysis of crime problems and identification of priorities, and neighbourhood watch.

Municipal police involvement in by-laws enforcement: enforcement of the traffic code and regulations, and more patrols and greater visibility in problematic neighbourhoods and areas.

Coordination and training: includes liaison with private security agencies, coordination of operations between national and municipal police, and better training of police personnel.

Working closer with the local population: including community, neighbourhood and problem-solving policing approaches, prevention programmes that target youth, victims and retailers, and sensitization campaigns.

Alternative sanctions: including community work and reparations to victims of various kinds.

Neighbourhood justice: including legal education (focusing on rights and responsibilities), ward tribunals, and mediation by neighbourhood and religious chiefs.

Detention oriented towards the social and economic reintegration of young offenders: includes completing school, job training and sensitization to the prevention of health problems.

Partnership with civil society: including the reintegration of young people within their families and training sessions in the workplace.

Source: UN-Habitat, 2006e

Learning from initiatives, finding resources and setting priorities for community safety change

In terms of future action, two points stand out from the material summarized in Box 10.3. First, it represents a lot of initiatives in different cities, and it is critical that when evaluations of these initiatives have been undertaken, the lessons that can be learned from them are publicized so that other cities can see what has worked well and under what circumstances, and can shape their own practices accordingly. Second, many of the actions listed in Box 10.3 require extra resources in order to be undertaken. But some of this is about priorities for the use of existing resources. There is still an opportunity cost issue as time spent doing one thing is time not spent doing something else. It is therefore critical that leaders and senior managers in the police and criminal justice systems participate fully in the debates on community safety strategies, are active members of the partnership arrangements that shape them, and buy into what is being attempted in a manner that recognizes the need to review how they utilize their existing resources in order to find ways in which they can contribute effectively.

All of this pertains to priorities, and experience suggests that it is easier to influence the priorities of the police and the criminal justice services if their leaders and senior managers are active participants in the process of pulling together and implementing community safety strategies than if they stand outside them. This may also be about the willingness to experiment and to try new things, especially when faced with evidence or perceptions that traditional ways of doing things may actually be contributing to the problem. It may well be that leaders and senior managers in the police and criminal justice services will be more willing to look at this positively if it is seen as part of a comprehensive programme of change where others are willing to experiment and try new things.

Programmes aimed at strengthening the police, particularly in developing countries, should also address their welfare and poor conditions of service

The challenges of imprisonment and recidivism

The philosophies and resources that govern prison policy and practices, and the laws that determine the crimes for which offenders are sent to prison are usually controlled at national rather than municipal levels. This is one of the most important policy areas through which central governments – by addressing these issues – can contribute to measures to tackle urban crime. Although this problem is being addressed in some countries by improving prison conditions and by placing more emphasis on rehabilitation, a particular element of these debates is the frequency with which prisons can still easily become finishing schools for criminals. For instance, a similar point is made in the Port Moresby case study, where the Bomana prison is often referred to as 'the university', and where inmates enter without any skills and come out armed with skills and contacts with crime.[20]

There can be little doubt that it is possible for recidivism rates to be significantly reduced as a consequence of a much greater concentration on rehabilitation during periods in prison

There can be little doubt that it is possible for recidivism rates to be significantly reduced as a consequence of a much greater concentration on rehabilitation during periods in prison. This will have a beneficial impact on urban crime because a high proportion of crime is committed by previous offenders. This will be a huge challenge to governments, not least because there might well be public and media opposition to an approach of this nature as being 'soft on crime', and because of the resource implications in terms of the need for new and improved prison facilities and more investment in staff training and development. But the potential benefits of a changed approach to the experience and circumstances of prisons towards a fight against crime and violence are considerable; at the very least, there is a strong case for more carefully monitored experimentation of this kind.

Reduction of risk factors

Chapter 4 has argued that this approach is essentially about two related strands of activity: initiatives to address issues in relation to those groups in society who are more likely to become offenders (particularly young men), and actions to help those groups who are likely to become victims of crime (particularly women). There has also been a growing emphasis on victim-support initiatives of several kinds. This approach recognizes that in a world of limited resources, it is important to target major problem areas such as these. It is therefore not surprising to find that activities of this nature are common in strategic processes designed to address crime and violence.

Women's rights and measures against violence have also to be reflected in the law, as in many contexts legislation is still very wanting in terms of protecting women from violence

■ Targeting youthful offenders: Recruitment and educational policy issues

With respect to the first strand of activities, many of the initiatives seek to target youth either in ways that deflect their energy and interests into other activities or offer various kinds of work experience and training. This combination of approaches is evident in Toronto's programme of crime prevention through social development and the strategies adopted in Kingston (Jamaica), both of which were discussed in Chapter 4. It is important, however, that thinking about problems of this nature does not only begin at the time when young people leave school because, as Chapter 3 has demonstrated, children as young as six years are recruited into gangs. Even if young people have not already committed themselves to criminal activities by the time they leave school, there is still a considerable possibility that the role models they seek to emulate are from the criminal fraternity.

One of the most important developments in this field is the need for closer and more effective liaison between the work of educational services and work that targets young people in order to try to prevent them from offending so that, as much as possible, the transition between the two is seamless. Evidence suggests that this is often not the case. However, there is considerable scope for closer and more effective coordination. A typical example is where school sports and cultural facilities are, in effect, locked up in the evenings, at weekends and during school holidays – and, yet, projects to divert the energy of young people towards sporting and cultural activities at these very same times struggle for access to facilities. Very often, the explanation for locking up these facilities relates, understandably, to concerns about the security of school premises.

But these problems are capable of being resolved locally and in ways that take up a small fraction of the cost involved in duplicating these facilities, or of the cost to society of crime and violence perpetrated by young people that might have been capable of being deflected through the community use of these facilities. Another issue that is commonly faced is how young people manage the transition from school to work, where again there is considerable scope to improve cooperation between schools, local employers and youth-related services. The aims of these sorts of activities would be to improve work experience and training opportunities of many types, and to emphasize both the importance and the value of an economically active lifestyle in preference to one dominated by crime and violence.

■ Preventing violence against women

In relation to the prevention of violence against women, the key element of importance is the fact that such violence needs to be perceived as a serious issue by policy-makers and leaders at all levels. A systemic approach to tackling violence against women needs to be developed and deployed. This should strengthen the understanding of the impacts and causes of gender-based violence, as well as identify vulnerabilities, and systematically address them. Awareness and sensitization tools are therefore of key importance. Women's rights and measures against violence have also to be reflected in the law, as in many contexts legislation is still very wanting in terms of protecting women from violence. In terms of interventions, in many contexts, the priority would have to be sensitization of policy-makers and access of women to decision-making processes. The development of specific tools and interventions to address vulnerability in different contexts is also important. Other interventions of relevance should target underlying factors, such as conceptions of masculinity, cultural definitions of women's roles and rights in society, capacity of law enforcement and other actors to carry out early interventions and to deal with offenders.

■ Women's safety audits

One of the frequently used tools to support the prevention of violence against women in the African Safer Cities programmes is the women's safety audit. The example from Durban (Box 4.9) demonstrated both the value of the specific suggestions that emerged from the process and the process itself.[21] As valuable as these process-related benefits are, they need to be followed through so that commitments to action are made by the key players and are then put into practice. This is often not just about doing specific things, but is also about getting the process of governance in partnership with local communities to take this seriously in its everyday actions and practices. The Durban experience suggests that this process of embedding action can be the most difficult element in implementing the results of a women's safety audit, but that it is also one of the most important elements.

■ Reducing crime and violence to make a difference in people's lives

It is important to remember that actions of the kind discussed in this section are not just about tackling some of the most difficult problems in many cities in terms of crime and violence, but are also about making a difference to the lives of individuals. Some of the most encouraging stories in the struggle against crime and violence in Diadema (São Paulo), for example, are of young people whose lives have been changed for the better through opportunities provided and taken to develop cultural or sporting interests that would otherwise have been very difficult to pursue.[22] It is very easy to forget this kind of individual dimension to change, especially, perhaps, when looking at problems that exist on a large scale. Nevertheless, changes of this kind are about making a positive difference to the lives of identifiable individuals and are not just the broader abstractions inevitably expressed in formal evaluations, important, of course, though these are.

As with all of the other policy responses reviewed here, it is important that initiatives regarding the reduction of risk factors are carefully evaluated so that more is known about what works, and under what circumstances, so that other cities can learn from these experiences. It seems likely, however, that initiatives of this kind will continue to be important elements of many programmes because they are about tackling fundamental problems, some of which are deeply embedded in the economic, social, cultural and political circumstances of societies. Some of these, such as endemic violence against women, can be seen not just as crime and violence issues, but also as basic issues of human rights.

Non-violent resolution of conflicts

As Chapter 4 has argued, the non-violent resolution of conflicts can be seen as a philosophical approach that has been put into practice in many related fields, but has not seen very much specific application in tackling crime and violence. Consequently, there is, as yet, only limited evidence that can be drawn upon in discussing what its future role might be in programmes of this nature. This situation might be improving. For example, Chapter 4 noted, in passing, some American evidence of its successful application to problems in schools. Furthermore, there is evidence from the Kingston case study of programmes of this nature being instituted as part of a wide range of initiatives, in which the Jamaican government has been a major player.[23] Three components of this work – the Dispute Resolution Foundation, the Peace and Love in Society programmes and the Police Mediation Unit – in their various ways offer mediation training to community members, police, teachers, lay magistrates and youth. They also develop programmes to teach non-violent conflict resolution in schools and communities, and they have incorporated peace education as part of their regular activities. The key question here is this: can approaches that emphasize the non-violent resolution of conflicts play an effective part in addressing the problems of crime and violence? The answer to this question, in the absence of reliable evidence, must be that it would be worth exploring the scope for this, perhaps in the first instance on an experimental basis that is carefully evaluated and reported upon.

It is important that initiatives regarding the reduction of risk factors are carefully evaluated so that more is known about what works, and under what circumstances, so that other cities can learn from these experiences

Two examples that relate to problem areas already discussed might be particularly appropriate in this context. The first is as part of managing the transition of young people from a school environment to the world of work and other social, community or sporting activities. This would be particularly appropriate where young people have already come across approaches of this nature in their school lives: it would represent a continuation of something that is familiar, rather than introducing something completely new.

The second example relates to efforts to tackle the problem of prisons becoming 'universities for crime'. This needs to be seen alongside programmes to improve prison conditions and to enhance rehabilitation efforts, rather than as a substitute for initiatives of this kind. The argument here is that this issue needs to be tackled not just for the benefits to the lives of individual prisoners that would arise, but also because of the general benefits to communities from reducing rates of recidivism.

This problem needs to be addressed by rethinking attitudes regarding what the purpose of a prison sentence is, and by reconsidering the nature of the prison experience to place greater emphasis on rehabilitation and ensuring that resources are available to support these activities. This, in itself, might be seen as a controversial approach in some quarters, and the suggestion that non-violent approaches to conflict resolution might have a part to play in such an approach would probably add to this among those who see imprisonment as being primarily about punishment. But evidence seems to suggest that existing prison regimes in many parts of the world are not working and that alternative approaches need to be considered.

Evidence seems to suggest that existing prison regimes in many parts of the world are not working and that alternative approaches need to be considered

Strengthening social capital

Chapter 4 adopted a relatively broad-based definition of social capital, which encompasses efforts to improve the ability of people, groups and communities, as a whole, to challenge problems of crime and violence, as well as the provision of community facilities that facilitate or provide more opportunities for processes of this nature. This approach therefore includes the idea that public realm improvements, and the provision of better facilities in areas such as culture and sport, can also contribute to reducing crime and violence, as well as being of value in their own right to local communities by adding to quality of life.

Strengthening educational opportunities and providing means to smooth the path from school to work...are vital components of many programmes that address the problems of youth in rapidly growing cities

It is clear that the strengthening social capital has an important part to play in strategies to tackle crime and violence

The fundamental maintenance issue

A critical issue in many initiatives of this nature, however, is that of maintenance. Typically, this can be problematic because while the provision of new facilities usually involves finding capital resources for investment at a particular time, their ongoing maintenance usually involves locating revenue resources to, for example, pay people to carry out essential tasks continuously. This often seems to be trickier than the initial task of raising capital resources precisely because it is a continuing commitment that has not always been clearly thought through at the time of initiating the project. Where maintenance fails, facilities then become neglected, vandalized or underutilized. There is the risk that this can actually undermine the good work done up until then and send out very negative messages about the communities in which such facilities are located and the level of care for that community by the people who live there. This argument is akin to that of the 'broken windows theory', which states that the negative signals sent out by environmental problems of the type often caused by lack of maintenance convey messages that an environment is not cared for and, consequently, invites crime.

Creating social capital and reducing crime through educational opportunities and programmes

One of the most basic ways of creating social capital is by encouraging young people to attend school regularly in order to develop skills that are relevant to the world of work. Programmes of this nature are important to the social development of the individual since the likelihood is that someone who missed many years of schooling will be permanently disadvantaged and may turn to crime in the absence of perceived alternatives. Typically, strengthening educational opportunities and providing means to smooth the path from school to work through initiatives such as work experience, training and apprenticeships are vital components of many programmes that address the problems of youth in rapidly growing cities.

The need for programmes of this nature that provide alternatives for young people to a life of crime in a city like Kingston (Jamaica) is, in part, illustrated by the fact that 53 per cent of the murders recorded between 1997 and 2005 were committed by males aged 25 and under.[24] Many of the young people involved in crime come from Kingston's inner city communities, which are characterized by low levels of employment, established gang activities and an associated culture of violence.[25] Consequently, part of the response has been to tackle the problems of poverty and social marginalization that are the breeding grounds for these problems. A specific illustration of this approach is in the Fletchers Land community in downtown Kingston, where the Citizens Security and Justice Programme has initiated long-term creation of social capital and short-term training of individuals. These have included remedial education, mentoring programmes, identifying jobs and skills training, dispute resolution, homework programmes, continuing education services, and parenting workshops.

Creating social capital and reducing insecurity through innovative infrastructure development: Nairobi's Adopt a Light initiative

Defining social capital more broadly to include not just the capacity of communities to address issues of crime and violence themselves, but also the provision of community infrastructure that helps communities in this regard, carries with it the likelihood that some elements that fall within this definition are likely to be expensive. There are ways in which issues of this nature can be addressed without being totally dependent upon the public budget. One of these is the use of sponsorship. An example of this is the Nairobi Adopt a Light initiative, which is part of the Safer Nairobi Initiative that sought to address the widespread feelings of insecurity brought about by poor or non-existent street lighting. Here, in order to fill an important gap in public service provision by improving street lighting in major streets and by adding high-mast lighting into Nairobi's slum districts, sponsors are invited to pay an agreed annual sum to adopt a light pole in return for their advertisement being hoisted on that pole. This project has been well received by firms and advertisers since its commencement in August 2002.

The use of sponsorship, in this instance, enabled more to be done than would have been the case if reliance had been solely on public budgets. A project of this nature also illustrates the point that many activities fall into several categories since in one sense this could be seen as a classic CPTED project, as well as something that is about improving community safety infrastructure as a basis for getting the community more actively involved in the fight against crime.

It is clear that strengthening social capital has an important part to play in strategies to tackle crime and violence, and that its resource challenges can be tackled by thinking creatively and by working across traditional boundaries between sectors. The effect of strengthening what is available to a community in terms of physical infrastructure may also have a positive effect on the dynamics of community responses to crime. Although this is hard to calculate in individual cases if it does result in strengthening the will of communities to fight against unacceptable behaviour, then that is undoubtedly a very significant added benefit of this approach.

EMERGING POLICY TRENDS

Chapter 4 identified six emerging policy trends that are discussed in more detail below:

1 the move away from the idea that crime prevention and tackling violence are essentially matters for the police and the criminal justice system, and towards the idea that these are complex phenomena with a range of causes that require broad-based responses. The emergence of crime prevention as a specific concern of urban policy and urban actors is an indication of such a shift;

2 as an important part of this process, four of the six groupings of policy responses to crime and violence (see the previous section on 'Scope for the continuing development of key policy responses') have attracted particular interest: enhancing urban safety and security through effective urban planning, design and governance; community-based approaches; reducing risk factors; and strengthening social capital;
3 the move away from *ad hoc* initiatives and towards more programmatic approaches encompassing some or all of the approaches described above, backed by broad strategies and detailed understanding of the issues on the ground;
4 the use of the partnership mechanism as a key vehicle for delivering programmes of this nature;
5 the growing recognition of the need to adapt solutions to local circumstances, rather than to borrow uncritically from elsewhere;
6 the growing acceptance of the need for honest evaluation of initiatives and for publicizing such material.

Before undertaking this task, however, it is important to make the point that it does not follow automatically that just because something has been identified as a policy trend, it is inherently desirable. There are several reasons why something might become a 'policy trend', one of which is the process of emulating something else in the desperate search to find some action to undertake. Another is the observable point that some policy ideas do become fashionable for a period of time. Thus, in order to assess the merits or otherwise of these trends in relation to particular circumstances, the following discussion includes a brief analysis of the strengths and limitations of each trend in question.

Broadening the range of responses to problems of crime and violence

The first trend identified is the move away from the *traditional* reliance on the police and the criminal justice system towards the idea that crime and violence are complex phenomena that require broad-based responses. For ease of reference, these added approaches will be referred to as *non-traditional*. The reasons for this policy trend are complex; but two related lines of argument are outlined here.

The first is that in many countries the traditional approaches were seen as increasingly struggling to tackle crime and violence effectively in societies that were becoming more complex and less reliant on historic family and community structures. Thus, there has been a growing need over the last 30 or 40 years to explore other approaches that could complement the work of the police and the criminal justice system. This does not imply that traditional work has remained largely unchanged during the time in which other approaches have been explored, although there have been criticisms about inflexibility and slowness to change in this context. The growing police interest in CPTED in some parts of the world and the increasing adoption of community policing models can both be seen as illustrations of adaptations of this kind that have been taking place. Nevertheless, it became clear that this search for alternative ways of tackling what was widely seen as an increasingly sophisticated problem was not confined to changes within the police and the criminal justice system, but also needed to encompass other areas outside of them.

The second reason why this policy trend has taken root is that it has been recognized that the nature of the response must be congruent with the nature of the problem. Thus, the growing recognition that criminal behaviour and opportunity are often a function of economic and social circumstances, as well as the recognition that technological developments have assisted criminals, as well as the process of fighting crime, have together seen the development of more broadly based approaches to tackling crime and violence.

The main strength of this approach of broadening the range of responses is that it appears to be appropriate to the task in hand. To use a simple example: if it is, indeed, the case that the likelihood that young people will embark upon a life of crime is related at least in part to both educational opportunity and to effective processes of transition between school and work, then measures that seek to address these issues head on are more likely to be successful than the traditional work of the police and the criminal justice services. A related strength is that, by definition, broadening the range of responses to problems of crime and violence also extends the numbers of people and groups who are involved in processes of this kind, and thus adds to both the range of possible responses they might identify and to the numbers of people who are prepared to participate in implementing chosen actions.

In many countries the traditional approaches were seen as increasingly struggling to tackle crime and violence effectively in societies that were becoming more complex and less reliant on historic family and community structures

These are real strengths, although they also represent challenges in the sense that the process of ensuring that these theoretical advantages are always captured, in practice, is a complex one in terms of issues such as forms of partnership operation, seeking agreements for all affected parties, including local communities, and effective coordination. The main weakness of this approach is that it can deflect attention from measures to ensure that the police and the criminal justice system are fully 'fit for purpose'; indeed, it can be seen as downgrading the importance of these traditional services in the ever widening search for alternatives. It is very important that the approach adopted does not see this as being about alternatives to efficient and effective police and criminal justice systems, but rather sees it as being about the identification of complementary activities that are simply more appropriate for the particular challenge being addressed than expecting the police and the criminal justice system to do what they are not primarily designed to do.

Available evidence from the experience of African cities in establishing Safer Cities projects indicates that tackling problems in these 'traditional' areas of the police and the criminal justice systems is vitally important, and that it is necessary to look for, and to encourage, change in areas where existing practices may be contributing to the problem rather than its solution.[27] Two very difficult illustrations of this point are the fight against corruption and the need to tackle the extent to which prisons in some countries[28] have become finishing schools for crime, rather than places where criminals can be rehabilitated. Both of these involve issues that cannot be resolved at the city level, although in both instances it is at the level of the individual city where many of their adverse consequences are felt.

Thus, the approach here needs to be one of continuing to find policies and practices that are appropriate to tackle both the symptoms and the causes of crime and violence in cities. Because many of these are socio-economic in nature, and are about much more than simply the criminal intentions of some human beings, it is likely that the range of solutions that continue to be seen to be appropriate will be broadly based and probably will in future be more comprehensive than has been seen to date. But within these approaches, the traditional functions of the police and the criminal justice system are of vital importance, and it is essential that they are fully involved in the agreed actions, fully aware of their own roles within them and of how these relate to other roles, and constantly reviewed to ensure that they remain 'fit for purpose'.

The extent to which non-traditional approaches to crime and violence have now become well established is illustrated by the main areas of activity promoted via UNHabitat's Safer Cities approach

Developing policies and practices in 'non-traditional' areas

Of the six broad groups of policy responses to crime and violence discussed in the section on 'Scope for the continuing development of key policy responses', one (strengthening formal criminal justice and policing) represents the 'traditional' approach[29] and the other five are the main non-traditional policy responses. Since this section has already discussed what was involved in the development of these policy responses, the focus of this discussion is on the process of broadening out policy development in non-traditional areas, rather than on the content of these policy packages. Four of these are commonly found in contemporary strategies to tackle crime and violence; but a fifth (the non-violent resolution of conflicts) seems to be much less commonly utilized.

The nine case studies prepared in support of the part of this Global Report that focuses on crime and violence reflect this balance, with the strategies evident in Bradford,[30] Durban,[31] Kingston,[32] Nairobi[33] and Toronto,[34] and, to a lesser extent, New York[35] and Rio de Janeiro,[36] exemplifying this broadly based approach, and the work on developing the Safer Cities Programme for Port Moresby[37] also going in this direction. The only one of these that appears to contain an explicit programme designed around the theme of non-violent approaches to conflict resolution is the strategy adopted for Kingston (Jamaica). Available evidence suggests that this strategy, as a whole, has contributed to the recent reductions of crime and violence in Jamaica,[38] although it is often difficult to be clear about what elements of success can be attributed to individual initiatives when several different initiatives are being implemented more or less simultaneously.

The Kingston case is interesting because apart from its innovative elements, such as the work on non-violent approaches, it also includes significant measures to improve police performance. In addition, it contains an example of measures to target gang operations via *Operation Kingfish*, which has been successful in recovering firearms, ammunition and other equipment from gangs operating in the illicit drugs trade,[39] and which can also be seen as a development of the 'traditional' role of the police and criminal justice systems. The lesson that this experience reinforces is the point that the process of exploring 'non-traditional' approaches to crime and violence is not an alternative to seeking improvements in traditional areas, but rather should be seen as a complement to it.

The extent to which non-traditional approaches to crime and violence have now become well established is illustrated by the main areas of activity promoted via UN-Habitat's Safer Cities approach, which are summarized in Box 10.4.

What Box 10.4 shows is a mix of traditional and non-traditional approaches, with a strong emphasis on process issues, an emphasis on the leadership role of local authorities working in collaboration with a wide range of partners, and recognition of the need to build capacities in order to make people and processes more effective. This does not neglect traditional approaches, including the need to support new and alternative forms of justice and policing; but it recognizes that reliance on these alone would offer a very limited approach to what are seen as major and deep-seated problems both for many urban communities and the citizens who inhabit them and for the process of urban governance.

Box 10.4 The place of non-traditional approaches to crime and violence in UN-Habitat Safer Cities programmes

UN-Habitat Safer Cities Programme activities target three main types of prevention:

- situational prevention – crime prevention through environmental design (CPTED);
- institutional prevention – support to new and alternative forms of justice and policing;
- social prevention – actions aimed particularly at groups at risk.

In addition, the following are the other significant areas of activity:

- promoting local authority leadership and responsibility for urban safety as part of good urban governance;
- supporting crime prevention partnerships and initiatives implemented in collaboration with local authorities, the criminal justice system, the private sector and civil society in order to address urban insecurity issues successfully and in sustainable ways;
- building city networks to share knowledge, expertise and good practices that can be replicated in other cities and regions;
- conducting training and capacity-building for local authorities and other stakeholders;
- disseminating lessons learned in collaboration with partners in the North and South.

Source: UN-Habitat, undated, p3

The move away from *ad hoc* initiatives and towards more programmatic approaches

As has been previously discussed, urban crime is rarely a one-dimensional phenomenon. It is therefore unlikely that it will be challenged effectively by single *ad hoc* initiatives. This does not imply that carefully chosen and well-targeted initiatives have nothing to contribute. But the recognition of the deep-seated and multidimensional nature of the problem has led to a growing emphasis on more programmatic approaches, which seek to address not merely the symptoms and effects of crime and violence, but also its causes. The UN-Habitat Safer Cities Programme is one example of such an approach. A second example is the approach to be found in England as a result of the 1998 Crime and Disorder Act, which required local Crime and Disorder Reduction Partnerships to prepare three-year rolling strategies to address the issues revealed by a careful audit of crime and violence in the locality.[40]

There are several characteristics that appear to be important in making approaches of this nature successful:

- a careful audit of the main crime and violence issues that are experienced in the locality that needs to be repeated periodically;
- an approach to tackling these issues that has both clear strategic intentions and specific action plans/programmes;
- effective public consultation practices and a good level of community support for the proposed actions that includes opportunities for direct action by communities, where appropriate;
- a partnership framework that draws key stakeholders together, generates real commitment from them, and encourages them to address how their own mainstream activities can support this work;
- a long-term perspective in recognition of the fact that it is unlikely that all problems will be resolved quickly, together with a commitment to achieve some early successes in order to generate some momentum for the process;
- an innovative approach to providing resources for programme work that does not just rely on what will inevitably be limited public budgets, but creatively explores a range of possible sources;
- a firm commitment to evaluation and the publication of results on a regular basis so that the programme can be adjusted, where necessary, in the light of experience.

Not all programmes display these characteristics; indeed, it is important to recognize that they are not all easily attained. In particular, the recognition that this must be seen as a long-term commitment to tackling problems that will not easily be eradicated does not sit easily with much shorter-term political and electoral cycles. It is also clear that many programmes have been limited by the resources available to them not just in terms of finance, but in terms of expertise. It should also be remembered that criminal communities often do not just stand by while their hegemony is being challenged; thus, programmes need to constantly adapt as the nature of the problem changes. All of this underlies the point that this should not be seen as an easy road. Nevertheless, there is ample evidence from around the world that programmatic approaches have much to offer, not just in tackling problems of crime and violence, but in terms of engaging people from many walks of life and across all sectors to address these problems.

The use of the partnership mechanism

If properly used, partnerships can be helpful and effective. But as the discussion in Chapter 4 has shown, the process of partnership by itself is not a universal panacea since partnership needs to be seen both as a specific tool and as a more general philosophy about the importance of working together. There are examples of successful partnerships and there are also examples of partnerships that achieve very little. This sub-section explores what partnerships set out to do, who is involved and with whom they seek to engage, and how effectively they are able to go beyond mere discussion and undertake meaningful action. Key questions in this context include:

- Who is involved in the partnership and who is not? How is membership determined, and what sort of commitment to the partnership process does membership entail?
- How is the partnership process led and how broadly accepted is that process of leadership? If leadership sits with the political or executive leadership of the local authority, does this carry with it a commitment to ensure that the aims of the partnership are supported in the everyday work of the authority?
- What sorts of resources are available to the partnership to enable it to undertake its work? Can the partnership seek to add to these in a variety of ways?
- How does the partnership see its relationships with the various sectors that are active in the local community – public, private, voluntary and community? Does it have a communications strategy which ensures that it is not only committed to keeping people up to date with what it is doing, but also listens to what they are saying? If members of the community wish to engage with or access the work of the partnership, is this easy for them to do?
- Is this a partnership with clear terms of reference that allow it to go beyond discussion and into action? Is it clear just what it and other organizations are responsible for, and what the lines of communication are between these bodies?
- Has it achieved a strong level of buy-in for what it is doing from all sectors, and does it keep checking this from time to time? Is it willing to review what it has been doing in the light of feedback from these processes?
- Is the partnership committed to evaluation processes as a standard arm of its activity, and does it carefully discuss the results of such evaluations and make adjustments in the light of them?
- What is the distribution of power within the partnership? Can all partnership members, irrespective of their backgrounds, influence what the partnership does, or is it, in practice, dominated by a small number of members who are seen as holding the most powerful positions?
- Is the partnership willing to challenge existing orthodoxies if there is evidence that they may be part of the problem, or is it unwilling to step on what it regards as

There have been many examples of projects that have been implemented in a locality because they have been seen elsewhere and have been copied...without any understanding of the extent to which the apparent success of the project was dependent upon a particular set of local circumstances

the territory of key members of the partnership? The significance of this goes back to the issue of the motivations of some partnership members. Are they there primarily to make an unbiased contribution to the work of the partnership, which includes the possibility of change within their own organizations, or are they principally there to defend their territories, which they see as being threatened by the partnership process?

- Does the partnership genuinely add value to what was done previously? Is this added value measurable, or is there a widely held view that the partnership is mainly a 'talking shop' that adds very little in real terms?

These ten questions do not deal with every issue about the work of partnerships; but they are derived from many of the main criticisms that have been made about partnerships. Consequently, careful consideration of these questions should help partnerships to structure themselves and their work in ways that help them to overcome many of these criticisms. Underlying all of this is the question of commitment. Are people truly committed to partnership processes because they see them as having the potential to add value to existing methods of working, even if this challenges their existing political or executive territories? Or is this process merely fashionable window dressing, which is not going to be allowed to operate in challenging ways but is merely there to give the impression of change and modernity? The will to make partnership work for the benefits that it is capable of bringing, rather than to confine it to the margins by refusing to allow it to challenge existing orthodoxies and territories, is of fundamental importance. This is, in particular, a challenge to local authority leaderships since they often find themselves in leadership roles in relation to the process of partnership and thus need to set the tone for what the partnership is and what it could become.

The importance of evaluation has come to be more widely recognized, and more programmes funded with public money have undertaken and published evaluations as a condition of receiving support

Adaptation to local circumstances, rather than uncritical borrowing

There have been many examples of projects that have been implemented in a locality because they have been seen elsewhere and have been copied, sometimes without any proper evaluation of the original project and almost always without any understanding of the extent to which the apparent success of the project was dependent upon a particular set of local circumstances. It is easy, in one sense, to see the superficial attractions of an approach of this nature – it may appear to offer a quick fix, it certainly gives the impression of action being taken, and it appears to short-circuit the learning process. Many projects of this nature, however, have proved not to be as successful as was hoped, and from this experience has come a greater willingness to recognize that borrowing what appear to be good ideas must be dependent upon an understanding of the particular context in which they were originally applied and a recognition of the necessity to think carefully about how they might need to be adapted to local circumstances. These circumstances might be physical, political, cultural, resource or skills based, or of many other types. Indeed, a simple list such as this underlines the need for care when undertaking such activities since any one or a combination of these activities could be sufficient to make something that is apparently very effective in one locality more doubtful in another.

A good example of this is the difficulty often experienced in applying ideas from the developed West to the developing world. For example, the British approach to integrating planning for crime prevention within planning processes may be seen as a useful model. But this has happened over a long period of time in a planning system that is now well established and in a police force that has adopted CPTED as one of the areas where it will offer crime prevention advice and in so doing will liaise with planners. Even so, there are limitations in terms of what it has yet achieved and there are areas of controversy between police, planners and the development community that remain unresolved.[41]

There are also important issues about training, about buy-in to this philosophy, and about how well connected this thinking is with other policy drives. None of these things would necessarily stop other localities from going down this road or from trying to learn from the British experience. But they all should cause people to stop and think carefully about how to do this in their local context where the likelihood is that many or even all of these characteristics may be different. In particular, how to fit such an approach into local planning systems given their stages of development, how to develop capacity among planners and the police in order to make something like this effective, and how to generate acceptance of an approach of this nature given the other priorities of planning systems are important questions that need careful thought.

The importance of evaluation

A major review of crime prevention programmes in the US that was published in 1997 concluded that 'Many crime prevention initiatives work. Others don't. Most programmes have not yet been evaluated with enough scientific evidence to draw conclusions.'[42]

The situation has probably improved: the importance of evaluation has come to be more widely recognized, and more programmes funded with public money have undertaken and published evaluations as a condition of receiving support.[43] Nevertheless, the case for evaluation still needs to be made because there is much that is done in this field that is either not evaluated, is assessed in the most perfunctory manner or is declared to be successful without much (if any) evidence to support such a claim. The review by UN-Habitat of the experience of delivering Safer Cities strategies in African cities[44] not only reinforces this point, but also focuses on the different kinds of evaluative activity needed at various stages of the Safer Cities process. These are as follows:

- at the stage of the initial assessment of the issues;
- when thinking about whether the strategy actually seeks to address the issues identified as fully and as effectively as possible;

- whether goals are being achieved;
- whether individual projects are succeeding given the different timeframes to which they relate;
- whether the implementation process is effective;
- whether partnership structures continue to be fit for purpose; and
- whether the partnership process itself is operating appropriately.[45]

The importance of identifying this multiplicity of evaluation activities is that it sees evaluation not just as a set of activities at the end of the process, but as something that is integral to the process itself at several stages, and which probably operates as a series of iterations, rather than as a linear process.

This is an important corrective to the all-too-common view that evaluation is something that only happens at the end of the process. The fact that there are many different types of evaluation, and that these can contribute in various ways to an effective process on an ongoing basis, challenges this view. The experience of evaluation activities also suggests that these are best done if they are built into the process from the beginning, with the intention to evaluate systematically helping to structure how the process and its various stages are conceived. An important point that is by no means always recognized is that valuable lessons can be learned from what has not gone well, as well as what has succeeded. Indeed, it can be argued that the need to identify what is not working as quickly as possible in order that consideration can be given to changing it is one of the most important tasks of evaluation, especially when it is seen not just as a task to be carried out at the end of a process, but as something integral to that process at several stages.

This often raises issues about what gets published by way of evaluative material, especially on websites, where there seems to be a tendency not to include material about what has not worked well for what appear to be public relations reasons. It is understandable that organizations will look at their websites in this manner in the contemporary world; but they do need to reflect on how credible this stance is among those stakeholders who are aware that there have been issues and expect them to be covered in published evaluative material. It is also more helpful for outsiders looking at material of this nature in an attempt to learn from it to see a 'warts and all' presentation. The fact that these are still relatively rare, and that a presentation which only highlights the positive aspects is much more common, may have contributed to the phenomenon discussed above of the uncritical borrowing of ideas from elsewhere. The need, therefore, is to move towards honest, open and transparent reporting – and if organizations find this difficult from a public relations perspective, one action that they can consider is publishing alongside such material a statement of how they intend to address the issues raised.

THE CHALLENGES OF IMPLEMENTATION

One of the most important considerations for any partnership is the need to think carefully about how what it wants to do can be effectively implemented in the particular circumstances of its remit. As a consequence, one of the early issues to be faced in such situations is an identification of what the barriers to implementation might be and how they might be overcome. This must be about the local situation since implementation is about making something work in a specific context. The key question here is how can things be made to work? This relates to the previous discussion about adapting to local circumstances, rather than uncritical borrowing, since without careful consideration of the particular circumstances in which something is going to be applied, there can be no guarantee that what has worked well elsewhere can be transplanted effectively.

Having underlined the importance of locality, this section looks at five implementation challenges that are commonly faced and which are more thematic in nature. These are defining appropriate institutional structures for action; involving and mobilizing local communities; capacity-building at the local level; integrating crime prevention into urban development; and effective international support for initiatives against crime and violence. Each of these is discussed in turn.

Defining appropriate institutional structures for action

In most instances, the appropriate local player to take the lead on actions against crime and violence at the urban scale will be the local authority. Not only will it have a large number of service functions that it can bring to bear on these problems and a resource base that can be used to address them,[46] but it will also see itself as having a central responsibility for the quality of life in its area and for the welfare of its citizens. If these reasons were not enough by themselves to explain why local authorities can normally be found in leading roles in relation to urban initiatives against crime and violence, it is also likely that the local authority will attach considerable importance to the representational role that it plays on behalf of its city.

To enable it to do all of these things well, it will need to be in regular touch with its citizens and its businesses, to be an effective communicator and provider of information, and to be responsive to the feedback that it receives through these channels. In order to do these things, it will almost certainly have to work with a wide range of other local stakeholders, and as has already been argued, in practice this often leads to the creation of formal partnership mechanisms to provide vehicles for activities of this nature. All of these things help to explain why local authorities increasingly accept that taking a lead in fighting against urban crime and violence is an integral part of their approach to providing good governance for their locality.[47] And they also help to explain why leadership in these terms comes not merely from the executive arms of local authorities, but also often from their political arms. It is no coincidence in this context that it was African city mayors who were instrumental in taking the action that led to the establishment by UN-Habitat of the Safer Cities Programme.

Role of local authorities

It is, however, important to recognize that local authorities cannot do it all. Their powers and their resources are finite, and other players in the local environment are simply better at doing some things than local authorities. This is one of the reasons why, increasingly, partnership approaches have emerged as the most appropriate vehicle for addressing problems of crime and violence. It is not necessary for local authorities to be in the forefront of providing leadership for partnerships, and there are many examples of respected local players who are not from the local authority who do this, and do it very well. But what is critical is that the local authorities, whether playing leadership roles or not, are fully supportive of the work of their partnerships. This means not just making formal statements of support for specific actions, but also being willing to align their own policies, practices and budgets with the work of the partnership so that this becomes part of their mainstream work, rather than a marginal extra. If this means changes for the local authority, they should be willing to embrace change if it enables crime and violence to be tackled more effectively. The relationship between the partnership that is tackling crime and violence and the local authority is probably the single most important relationship of all; and both the partnership and the local authority need to recognize this for what it is and to put the time and effort into this relationship to ensure that it is an effective one.

Increasingly, partnership approaches have emerged as the most appropriate vehicle for addressing problems of crime and violence

The spirit of partnerships

It is worth emphasizing that partnerships are most likely to flourish if their members take on board what might be described as 'the spirit of partnership'. This means that partners commit to the enterprise, rather than to the defence of their own territories; that everyone is treated as an equal; that partners seek to promote the aims and objectives of the partnership not just when they are sitting around the table, but also in their everyday working and community lives; and that contributions are valued according to their quality and not their source. Many of the difficulties that partnerships have experienced have probably arisen at least, in part, because key partners have not fully adopted the spirit of partnership, which inevitably lessens the likelihood that the model will achieve its full potential. Thus, it is important to acknowledge that partnerships are much more than simple coordination mechanisms, and that they represent an attempt to do much better through joint working than individuals and organizations are capable of doing in isolation. To maximize the likelihood of this happening, however, it is necessary for all partners to recognize and to commit to the spirit of partnership whole heartedly.

Structural problems affecting partnerships

There are two common structural problems affecting the work of partnerships and the local authority's contributions to them. The first is the problem of the boundaries of jurisdictions, and the second is the difficulties that national governments can experience in committing to partnerships that effectively require them to give priority to particular localities. The problem of the boundaries of jurisdictions is a common one that takes many forms. Typically, the local government structure of large urban areas is a fragmented one, which often involves several local authorities covering different parts of the city that may well involve two tiers of government each having responsibility for particular services. Similarly, the basis on which the police operate does not follow the same set of boundaries and is often commanded at a broader spatial scale than that of the individual city. It is also known that problems of crime and violence do not respect local government or police administrative boundaries. All of this can combine to present real issues for the structuring of partnerships to tackle urban crime and violence; realistically, it is unlikely that structural changes to produce a much better set of boundaries will solve these problems in the short term.

This situation requires a considerable amount of pragmatism in many quarters and it can also test sorely what has been discussed about the spirit of partnership. Often, a practical way forward starts from an acknowledgement that there may be more than one spatial scale that is appropriate here, so that broad strategic issues covering the scale of a whole conurbation may need different partnership structures than interventions in individual communities experiencing particular kinds of problems. This can make the structure of partnerships in the area very complex, and it almost certainly will raise issues about how the various partnerships relate to each other; but it may well be a partnership structure that is both achievable and congruent with the real world situation. The need here is to reach agreements about ways forward relatively quickly, and not to let the difficulties of this process get in the way of what the real task is, which is addressing the problems of crime and violence. It is probably helpful to acknowledge that there is no such thing as a perfect structure, and that what matters most is getting something that works and that partners are prepared to commit to as quickly as possible, rather than to wrangle endlessly about alternative approaches.

The difficulty that governments often have with committing to individual spatial partnerships is not usually a political one, but is more often the problem that government departments or ministries are simply not set up in ways that enable spatial differentiation of this kind. So a typical problem for them would be when they are asked to do something that they regard as being inconsistent with their general policies and practices, or when they are asked to adjust their budgets in order to make more resources available to a particular area than would normally occur. They can also have real difficulties with how they are represented in particular spatial partnerships since it can be genuinely difficult for someone from one ministry to represent the full range of governmental interests. It can be equally unhelpful for people from several ministries to be in attendance, not least because it tends to give the impression that government coordination is poor and that these are people defending ministerial fiefdoms, rather than committing to the spirit of partnership.

At the same time, it is easy to understand why the idea of having central government representation on such partnerships is likely to be an attractive one. In practice, central government services frequently have a part to play in the fight against crime and violence in a particular locality, and partnerships will often want to raise issues with central governments about how policies and practices might be changed in order to aid their work. There is no single correct answer to this, not least because the structure of central government departments or ministries itself might make a difference to how an issue of this nature could be tackled. For example, a governmental structure with regional arms might find this easier than a structure that consists solely of nationally focused organizations. Sometimes this creates the view that the national government level will not be incorporated within partnerships looking at specific localities. But, occasionally, ways of enabling this to happen have been found. The important issue for central governments, whatever view they take about this particular matter, is that they should be supportive of the work of partnerships and should be prepared to look in an unbiased way at how they can help, whether this comes at them as a result of partnership membership or as a result of a direct approach to them by a partnership.

This represents the kinds of challenges that many partnerships have had to overcome. The primary test is whether a partnership mechanism can be put together that will work effectively in the local circumstances and will be seen, in particular, to be adding real value to what otherwise would have been achieved. Partnerships can achieve this; of that, there is no doubt. But the creation of a partnership structure is not of itself a guarantee that this will happen. More than anything else, what is probably needed is people who are committed to the idea that they need to work with each other and with the affected local communities in order to be effective – people who, in other words, embrace the spirit of partnership.

Involving and mobilizing local communities

In just the same way that people need to embrace the idea of what has been called 'the spirit of partnership' in order for partnerships to deliver to their full potential, so it is in terms of involving and mobilizing local communities. The central concern here is that the value of this kind of action needs to be fully understood and fully committed to, and not undertaken as an act of tokenism or in the most minimal ways. In a phrase, action to tackle problems of crime and violence should be 'done with' local communities rather than 'done to' them. This means many different things in different circumstances, which have to take into account both a differential willingness and a differential ability to take part in activities of this nature. It will also vary according to the types of actions to be taken, although the broad philosophy about the importance of community involvement as a principle is a common element. This is well put in relation to efforts to tackle domestic violence in Africa:

> *Effective projects aimed at changing harmful beliefs and practices in a community must engage and be led by members of that community. Organizations can play an important facilitative and supportive role; yet the change must occur in the hearts and minds of community members themselves.*[48]

This gets to the heart of why community involvement is so central to work in the field of crime and violence. Essentially, what action to address crime and violence is seeking to achieve is changing human behaviour for the better, and while there are potentially a large number and a wide variety of contributions to this endeavour, much of this comes down to the various ways that exist of making an impact on individuals. This is often achieved at least as much through the influence of families and household members, neighbours and regular social contacts as it is through the formal mechanisms of public policy. Not only can engaging with local communities in developing and implementing programmes be seen in terms of people's rights as citizens, but it also makes sense in terms of working towards successful outcomes to help mobilize people who are best placed to make a difference because they are closest to these target individuals. This is unlikely, in practice, to prove as straightforward as this may sound; but the principle really is as simple as this.

Action to tackle problems of crime and violence should be 'done with' local communities rather than 'done to' them

What does accepting the philosophy of 'doing with' rather than 'doing to' mean for partnerships and other implementing bodies in seeking to involve and mobilize local communities in taking action against crime and violence? The suggestion here is that this requires them to make at least the following three commitments from the beginning:

- A commitment to go down the road of community involvement with all that this will entail. This includes a willingness to trust local people even when that trust is not always immediately repaid.
- A commitment to support communities and individuals in a range of ways during the implementation process. For example, programmes seeking to address domestic violence need to accept the possibility that confronting this issue might, in some cases, cause violence to increase in the first instance. Consequently, it is important not only to pursue programmes of this nature, but also to offer appropriate victim support and, possibly, tough police intervention as well.
- A commitment to improve community capacity to take a leading role not as a one-off activity, but as part of an ongoing programme. Training and development activities need to be available not just to partnership members and public officials engaged in the process of implementation, but also to a wide range of community groups and individuals. There is inevitably an element of upfront cost in this; but the pay-back is in terms of community members who are both willing and able to play active roles in the process.

Capacity-building at the local level

One of the most important tasks that partnerships and other implementing agencies need to undertake as an early part of the process of tackling crime and violence is an assessment of the extent to which what they want to do might be limited by the capacities of the relevant organizations and individuals. This should be followed up by a programme designed to address capacity limitations over a reasonable period of time. Put differently, implementing organizations need to audit the skills available to them in relation to what they want to do and to put in place actions to tackle the deficiencies identified. This may need to be seen as a process that will take a reasonable amount of time; in the short term, there may be limits on what can be achieved. The critical issue is the need to recognize the relationship between what the implementing body wishes to do and the human capacity that is available to get this done effectively. The failure to take cognisance of this partly accounts for why programmes in this field sometimes struggle.

Discovering from an audit process of this kind that there is a shortage of the appropriate skills typically raises two types of issues. The first relates to resource – are the resources available to bring in more people with the necessary skills and experience? The second is a staff development issue – can existing staff be helped in sufficient numbers to develop the required skills? These are not mutually exclusive alternatives, but they may well operate over different timeframes, with the former approach probably being quicker. Very often, the resources are simply not available for wholesale programmes of recruitment in order to bring in the required skills; as a result, for many organizations, staff development is a necessary component of seeking to develop new functions or to undertake new initiatives. A judicious combination of bringing skills in from the outside and improving existing staff capabilities is often the response to this situation. But most organizations with limited budgets would probably take the view that investing in staff development is a better long-term option than relying on imported skills, even though the latter, in the short term, might enable action to be undertaken more quickly.

Many determinants of crime and violence are local in context and are better tackled through local interventions

For example, the decision to pay more attention to the principles of CPTED in managing new development and in tackling the crime problems experienced by existing development will require people in the architecture, planning and police communities who are knowledgeable about these issues and have practical experience of working in these fields. Internationally, but not always locally, expertise of this kind is available and can be brought into organizations by various means in order to kick-start programmes of this nature. One example of initiatives of this kind might be relatively short-term international secondments of skilled and experienced professionals. But in-service training programmes can also help to develop a cadre of people who build up these skills over a period of time. Programmes that seek to link these two elements in appropriate ways so that external expertise is used not just to begin work in the field, but also to institute training programmes that can then be expanded upon by their early participants, may have much to offer in these terms.

Over time, activities of this kind can develop relationships with the formal structure of skills and qualifications development in a country so that they become part of its more formal awards programmes, often through further or higher education institutions or professional bodies. But it is likely that the focus will be on the more immediate benefits of capacity development. One of the most valuable learning tools in this context is the initial work being undertaken to implement programmes so that there are benefits from these activities not just in terms of the specific achievements, but also in the opportunities they offer in developing the skills of those who either participate in these processes or observe them at close hand. The kinds of skills that are important here include not just direct hands-on skills, but also reflective skills, so that people are able to think about what is going well or badly, and to consider appropriate action as a consequence.

It also needs to be acknowledged that capacity development issues permeate the work both of local authorities and of partnerships at all levels; thus, the potential scale of this challenge may be daunting. To take just four groups of stakeholders by way of illustration, the development needs of different groups of professionals; partnership members; the local development community and its various agents; and members of community groups may all be different, not just from each other, but also within each of these groups. It is very unlikely that a partnership would be able to put in place a single programme that could tackle all of these differing needs at the same time. But what a partnership could do in this situation is to acknowledge the nature and the extent of this task, commit itself to addressing it over a reasonable period of time, and make a start on what it is able to do immediately. In making decisions on matters of this nature, the partnership will want to take into account the benefits that will ensue not just to its own immediate operations, but also to the capacities of various stakeholders (including community members and groups) to contribute more effectively in implementing the overall strategy.

Improving capacity should be seen by partnerships and other implementing bodies as seeking to establish a continuous trajectory of improvement. In the UN-Habitat Safer Cities Programme, this responsibility is often carried out through the Safer Cities coordinator (who will also need training for this role), who is able to draw on some training modules that have already been developed by UN-Habitat for particular issues.[49] The ability to do things such as this is one of the real benefits of a programmatic approach because it means that cities that have decided to undertake Safer Cities projects can learn directly in this way from the accumulated experience of Safer Cities work elsewhere.

Integrating crime prevention into urban development

Many determinants of crime and violence are local in context and are better tackled through local interventions. The impacts of crime and violence are also to a large extent local. It is therefore quite understandable that crime and violence are increasingly becoming subjects of concern for urban development interventions and policies. There are various ways of achieving this, and the role that local authorities play is important in this respect. Specifically, it is important to systematically include crime and violence among issues to be analysed when assessing urban development and investment needs, as well as in relation to the formulation of City Development Strategies. Similarly, development interventions and policies should be subjected, as much as possible, to crime impact assessment. Although integrated and comprehensive tools to assess crime impacts have not been fully developed, social impact assessment and the *ex-ante* evaluation of physical developments in terms of their vulnerability to crime or responsiveness to criteria of prevention through environmental design could become routine.

Another means for working towards increased integration of the issue would be the involvement of the police and its knowledge and experience in the formulation of policies and projects. The experience of the UK in relation to the collaboration between the police and planning authorities, or the positive role played by police authorities and individual officers in the consultative processes promoted by UN-Habitat Safer Cities Programme, indicate the potential of such collaboration. This will also assist in changing the negative perception of the police, and would respond to the need for partnership that the police itself often expresses in relation to crime prevention.

Such integration requires more accurate and in-depth analytical capacities and information, the development of local capacity, and a systematic analysis of the relationships between service provision, social and economic urban policies, and planning, with crime prevention. Such relations are complex and, to some extent, debatable and have to be clarified locally. Integration will also require the development of tools and the necessary guidelines. Indeed, there are to date still very few training and academic programmes that provide training geared towards such integration.

Effective international support for initiatives against crime and violence

International support of various kinds can help cities in the developing world to improve their ability to effectively implement measures that address problems of crime and violence. This kind of direct assistance should be seen as part of a package, which also includes continuing and strengthening international cooperation in tackling certain kinds of crime, where very often their worst consequences are most felt in cities. For example, as Chapters 3 and 4 have discussed, the trafficking of drugs, arms and people into prostitution are all matters where international cooperation is vitally important, and where, in practice, the consequences of a failure to stop illegal activities of this nature will be experienced on the streets of cities of both the Western world and the rapidly urbanizing developing world. It is important that support activities continue and develop across this full spectrum. But the following discussion develops, in particular, arguments about the scope for direct international support targeted at particular cities.

In terms of direct action to help specific cities, several examples have already been given of projects that are of considerable benefit. For example, funding from the US has been a very significant factor in recent efforts to mount projects tackling aspects of crime and violence in Kingston (Jamaica).[50] The Netherlands has contributed to Safer Cities projects in Johannesburg, Durban and Dar es Salaam (where the government of Sweden has also been a contributor).[51] Canada has helped with the process of updating the pre-existing review of the experience of Safer Cities projects in Africa.[52] These are a few examples of how international assistance can help the effort to tackle crime and violence in rapidly developing cities. Targeted assistance of this nature is not only immediately beneficial to the recipient city, but it also gives the donating organization confidence that the funding will be used in the specified manner and will not be filtered off for other uses, including corrupt activities, which has been a big issue in relation to international funding.

It is important to systematically include crime and violence among issues to be analysed when assessing urban development and investment needs

One particular type of international support that can be very helpful is in the field of training and staff development. There are already several good examples of this practice. For example, as part of its support for the reform of the Jamaica Constabulary Force since 2000, the UK government has been providing financial resources on a significant scale – UK£2.5 million in the first three-year period, a further UK£2.4 million for the three years from August 2005, and a further UK£750,000 announced in October 2005, mainly to support international police officers working alongside Jamaica's force in addressing issues of serious crime. This latter element has included Metropolitan Police officers working directly with their Jamaican counterparts, as well as training being offered by the Metropolitan Police to the Jamaica Constabulary Force.[53] The relationship between the Jamaica Constabulary Force and the UK's Metropolitan Police suggests there can be particular advantages in this relationship existing on a continuous rather than an *ad hoc* basis since this offers the opportunity of progressive improvement rather than short-term gains. This arrangement was also of direct value to the UK in the sense that it helped to stem the flow of criminal activity from Jamaica to the UK.[54] Bearing in mind the international nature of some criminal activity, this is a dimension that should not be ignored when considering such arrangements.

International support of various kinds can help cities in the developing world to improve their ability to effectively implement measures that address problems of crime and violence

Mentoring projects can also help in this situation and may well be an appropriate form of follow-up to initial training periods. If initiatives of this kind concentrate not just on skills development, but also on helping to develop a cadre of people capable of training others in their locality, this can be a very cost-effective form of assistance with considerable long-term benefits. It should also be said that the benefits of approaches of this nature can be two way since this can also be a useful development opportunity for the individual seconded and from which the employing organization would also subsequently benefit. There is clearly scope for more initiatives of this kind because capacity-building is one of the significant problem areas that many crime and violence initiatives face in parts of the world where few, if any, of these kinds of activities have taken place previously.

IMPLICATIONS FOR THE UN-HABITAT SAFER CITIES PROGRAMME

The experience of the Safer Cities Programme to date is that more cities in various parts of the world are signing up to it after its initial concentration in African cities.[55] The available evidence suggests that those cities that have chosen to participate in the programme have benefited from that choice, although this is not to say that their problems of crime and violence have all been successfully addressed.[56] This gives rise to three kinds of challenges:

The experience of the Safer Cities Programme to date is that more cities in various parts of the world are signing up to it after its initial concentration in African cities

- Can more cities that could benefit from involvement in the programme be encouraged to choose to do so?
- Is it possible to speed up the process in individual cities so that more can be achieved quickly?
- Are there any significant modifications to the programme that should be considered in the light of accumulated experience?

These challenges are in some ways interrelated; but for ease of presentation, they will be discussed separately below.

Continuing development of the programme

There can be little doubt that the answer to the first challenge – will more cities benefit from this approach? – must, in the broadest sense, be 'yes'. Reading the account of the cities that have already chosen to go along this path suggests that they are typical of many other cities that have not done so; and as such, in principle, the same kinds of benefits that participating cities have obtained ought to be achievable in other cities as well. Of course, if cities do not believe that this is an appropriate model for addressing their problems of crime and violence, then that is a matter of their choice. Perhaps UN-Habitat could contribute to debates of this nature by promoting the benefits of the Safer Cities Programme more forcefully, particularly by using stories from participating cities that demonstrate these benefits. Of themselves, such actions raise resource questions for the programme as a whole, and also for UN-Habitat in terms of its role both in overall programme management and in contributing to individual city projects, especially in their early phases. This may be one area where the scale of international financial and practical support available could really make a difference.

It should also be remembered that the Safer Cities approach is not in the territory of the quick fix

Can progress with individual Safer Cities programmes be accelerated?

The rate of progress with individual Safer Cities projects depends mainly upon the local situation. In some cases, this means that it is relatively slow, given that the pace at which individual city projects are able to proceed varies. This is undoubtedly related, in part, to capacity-building issues since the capacity to deliver is one of the key factors in the rate of local progress. This needs to be seen in the context of the problems being addressed, particularly where rates of crime and violence are high and/or growing. It also needs to be related to the expectations of stakeholders, particularly to what is needed to maintain their commitment, support and enthusiasm since these are vital ingredients of a successful process. Thus, whether or not individual programmes are moving fast enough really ought to be a local judgement. Nevertheless, there is scope for the individual cities that have been moving slowly to learn from the cities that have been moving more quickly, and in order for this to happen there is scope for developing existing experience-sharing arrangements.

But it should also be remembered that the Safer Cities approach is not in the territory of the quick fix. Rather, it is about gaining a thorough understanding of the problem, working towards recognition of the importance of getting the right machinery in place, generating full and necessary engagement with the process from all sectors, and building capacity. It is also important that these things are properly embedded within the working relationships between partners in order to ensure that beneficial change is long term. All of this is likely to take time, and since the challenge each one poses will be different from one city to another, it is likely that these time periods will also vary. While there is a *prima facie* case for speeding up the process, especially in cities where it has been slow, this should be seen in the context of the situation on the ground in individual cities, rather than by developing a standardized view of what the pace of projects ought to be.

Should the Safer Cities approach be adapted in the light of experience?

A useful starting point for considering this issue is by examining the major problems that have been experienced, to date, in implementing strategies in Safer Cities projects. These are summarized in Box 10.5, which draws on the experience of African cities since these are, as yet, the most advanced in utilizing the Safer Cities model.[57]

The first thing to note in Box 10.5 is that some of the points reflect the difficulties in making partnership models work, which are by no means unique to this programme. These issues about the experience of partnership have been discussed earlier; in particular, they have contributed to the 'checklist' of ten groups of questions that should be asked about partnerships, generated in the section on 'Emerging policy trends'. It is also quite common to find that 'process' issues in this area can be challenging. It is therefore not wholly surprising that some partnerships have struggled with translating broad goals into action plans. Similarly, it is not an uncommon experience that organizations sometimes marginalize experimental or pilot projects, which they see as challenging their traditional ways of doing things.

Perhaps one way of addressing these 'process' issues is to think about how Safer Cities partnerships might themselves be paired with partnerships in other parts of the world that have relevant experience to offer, and which can help them to overcome some of these challenges by drawing on their own experiences and playing a mentoring role. Just as cities across the world benefit in these terms by being 'twinned' with other cities, so too could partnerships benefit from similar arrangements. The points about the importance of capacity-building and of the open and accessible reporting of evaluative work have already been made earlier. Encouraging developments in these areas ought to be helpful not just in its own right, but also in helping the Safer Cities partnership process in individual cities. The difficulty of relating individual initiatives in Safer Cities programmes to national and even international initiatives in these fields is important, and a willingness to address issues of this nature is one of the ways in which national governments can improve their contributions to particular place-based partnerships. As far as the resources available for Safer Cities projects are concerned, there is no getting away from the fact that resource availability affects both what UN-Habitat can do in relation to the programme as a whole, and what can be done in individual cities. It is, of course, a matter for individual jurisdictions to decide whether they wish to do anything about this situation; but the challenges of urbanization are among the greatest faced by humanity, and within this the drive for safer cities is of considerable significance to the quality of life. There is also scope, as some of the examples have demonstrated, for help both in terms of financial resources and expertise to be made available to individual partnerships. This is a very effective way in which the Safer Cities process can be moved forward.

On the basis of this quick review, however, none of these points suggests that there is anything basically wrong with the Safer Cities model. They merely indicate that there is more that could be done to help overcome some of the operational difficulties being experienced in trying to put into practice something that is inherently quite complex and difficult.

Options for scaling up and enhancing the impact of the Safer Cities Programme

There are two broad areas where the impact of the programme could possibly be enhanced. These are: at city level, in terms of direct impact on local insecurity; and at the international level, where the programme could increase its impact on partners and actors that can deliver at the local level or provide enabling frameworks for local-level action.

The scope of institutional change and reform should indeed be considered as paramount for sustainability of actions and impacts as well as the development of local capacities among key actors. Both are ways to enhance impact of individual initiatives. A third important strategy to increase impact is to look at leveraging large-scale investment in support of the implementation of local crime prevention strategies. This report has identified in some detail areas of planning and service delivery that are considered as providing an important contribution to the prevention of crime in cities. Accessing resources for such types of investment is crucial for the larger-scale impact of Safer Cities processes at local levels.

Box 10.5 Major difficulties encountered in implementing Safer Cities strategies in African cities, to date

The 2006 review of progress with Safer Cities programmes in African cities itemized eight difficulties encountered in implementing strategies:

- the necessity to translate general goals into a concrete and targeted action plan geared towards short-, medium- and long-term benefits;
- the complexity of creating and implementing projects involving several partners;
- the experimental or pilot nature of several initiatives, which is quite often marginal to the traditional ways of doing things by the involved institutions and organizations;
- limited financial resources available for the municipality or the partners to ensure the implementation of such initiatives;
- limited resources and technical capacities of the municipal services in several countries working on implementing decentralization policies;
- the difficulty of anchoring these initiatives to larger national and international programmes addressing poverty and exclusion, good governance, decentralization, social development, women, children, youth and family support, and criminal justice system modernization;
- insufficient partnerships blocking the development of a joint approach to safety and prevention, and making coordination very difficult; and
- limited access to information on good or promising practices.

Source: UN-Habitat, 2006e, p26

The strategic focus of the Safer Cities Programme in a new global context

The first ten years have been dedicated to establishing the programme, assuring its position on the international scene as a global knowledge base, and supporting local actors in their crime prevention policies. Since its inception, the environment in which the programme works has evolved considerably. On one hand, there is an increasing and diversified demand for security, for which the traditional level of state intervention would appear to be insufficient. On the other hand, there is growing awareness among global institutions responsible for supporting sustainable social and economic development that development cannot be achieved independently from the rule of law and everyday security. Local, regional and national authorities and organizations and civil society, as well as international organizations, constitute today the universe of actors concerned with prevention and the fight against crime. These new circumstances require a reinvigoration of the Safer Cities Programme, highlighting its strategic role as a normative and evaluation facility, in addition to its operational functions.

CONCLUDING REMARKS: WAYS FORWARD

Positive ways forward to address the problems of crime and violence in urban areas, particularly in the rapidly growing urban areas of the developing world, can be summarized as follows:

- The 'traditional' approach to these problems, which is to see them as being the primary responsibility of the police and the criminal justice system, has increasingly been replaced by an approach that recognizes the necessity for a broad-based response. There is considerable scope for further developing this approach.

- Nonetheless, it is important that the police and the criminal justice system are 'fit for purpose' in the modern world, and are seen as key contributors to the fight against crime and violence. Improvements in these 'traditional' areas should be seen as being complementary to the new approaches being developed in 'non-traditional' fields, and appropriate linkages should be developed between all of these activities.
- The main 'non-traditional' fields where the development of fresh policy responses has taken place comprise the following:
  - the idea that urban safety and security can be enhanced through effective urban planning, design and governance;
  - the development of community-based approaches to enhancing urban safety and security;
  - developing ways of reducing the key risk factors by focusing on groups most vulnerable to crime, especially young people and women; and
  - strengthening social capital through initiatives that look to develop the ability of individuals and communities themselves to respond to problems of crime and violence, provide economic, social, cultural and sporting opportunities, and improve the environment in ways that assist these processes.
- Less attention has, as yet, been paid to applying the idea of the non-violent resolution of conflicts. However, there is scope for the further exploration of this idea.
- The combination of several of these approaches into a systematic programme, driven by a broad strategy and based upon a careful understanding of the local context, seems more likely to be successful than the *ad hoc* application of individual initiatives.
- The preferred mechanism to support this approach is usually the partnership mechanism; but to be fully effective, partnerships need to address a series of questions about their operation, and partners need to buy fully into 'the spirit of partnership'.
- The transfer of ideas from elsewhere can be very valuable; but it needs to be thought about carefully in the particular circumstances in which the ideas will be applied. It cannot be assumed that ideas that have worked in one part of the world will necessarily work successfully elsewhere. There are no one-size-fits-all solutions, and there is no substitute for a careful study of the particular situation in order to determine the most appropriate course of action.
- A greater level of commitment to evaluation as a process that can contribute to partnerships working at several points in time and on several levels is still required, and there needs to be more open reporting of evaluation results, including in areas where problems have been experienced. The work of partnerships should be seen as a learning process, to which both the results of evaluative work and the operational experiences of people directly involved in the process of implementation can make a considerable contribution.
- The best institutional structures for implementing programmes are likely to be those that succeed in getting the key players involved in delivery in ways that commit them to the programme, as well as ways that explore how the mainstream work of their own agencies can contribute to the overall effectiveness of the programme's initiatives. Local authorities will often be the most appropriate leaders of such structures.
- Local communities need to be as fully involved as possible in these processes, not only in terms of consultation, but also as generators and implementers of projects.
- Capacity-building is a fundamental part of work at the local level to tackle crime and violence. The approach adopted to capacity-building activities needs to be as broadly based as possible and should include the idea of capacity-building for professional groups, partnership members and local community members.
- International support has a key role to play in action against crime and violence in the cities of the developing world, as well as continuing to develop cooperative measures in tackling the international dimensions of crime. This can also include targeted financial support for particular initiatives, help with capacity-building, availability of appropriate expertise through secondment, and assistance with various types of mentoring. In addition, norms, guidelines, and reporting requirements could be developed to assist and facilitate the promotion of such interventions.
- The UN-Habitat Safer Cities Programme needs to engage more cities than it has done to date and, where possible, to help speed up the process in cities that have proved to be slow in getting to grips with the problems. There are several things that might help in this context; but one important issue is resource availability both for the programme as a whole and for projects in individual cities. Further international support could be of considerable value in this context as well.

There are many parts of the world where crime and violence are at completely unacceptable levels, and where citizens find their daily lives blighted all too frequently by experiences of this kind

There can be no doubt that this represents a very challenging agenda. There are many parts of the world where crime and violence are at completely unacceptable levels, and where citizens find their daily lives blighted all too frequently by experiences of this kind. It is also clear that many cities are being held back in their development by the adverse consequences of crime and violence, and the reputation that these bring with them, which, in turn, affects their ability as cities to invest in improving the quality of life of their citizens. In all of these areas, the challenge is to improve the situation as quickly and as effectively as possible so that freedom from crime and violence becomes the realistic expectation of citizens. In particular, this agenda represents a huge challenge to those cities that can expect large-scale growth in the coming decades if that growth is not to be associated with crime and violence on a scale with which city authorities struggle to cope. The propositions that have been summarized above do not represent an easy solution to these problems: in truth, there is no such thing. But they offer hope that this problem is capable of being addressed effectively so that urban crime and violence, if not eradicated, can at least be contained in the 21st century.

NOTES

1 See Colquhoun, 2004; Schneider and Kitchen, 2007.
2 This issue of the relationship between design decisions and future pressures on police resources seems to have been little studied in the literature; but if it is the case that one kind of design approach will lead to a different experience of crime in the future than will another, then it is a factor to be taken into account.
3 Kitchen, 2005.
4 Poyner, 2006.
5 One of the best-known examples of this is in the work of Coleman (1990), who coined the phrase 'design disadvantagement' for the features she saw in the developments she studied, which in her view created opportunities for crime and violent behaviour.
6 There is some evidence from the field of premises liability litigation in the US to the effect that this issue is beginning to have an impact on court decisions. It remains to be seen whether, and if so to what extent, this will spread to other parts of the world; but if it does, it could well have a powerful impact on designers and developers. See Schneider and Kitchen, 2007.
7 Morton and Kitchen, 2005.
8 There are several examples of African cities that illustrate this point that are summarized in UN-Habitat, 2006e.
9 The elements summarized in this paragraph are discussed in more detail in the Bradford case study undertaken for this volume (Kitchen, 2007).
10 See UN-Habitat, 2006g.
11 Schneider and Kitchen, 2007.
12 This work is summarized in Box 4.2.
13 This would certainly be the conclusion to be drawn from the literature on these processes in developed countries, although there are also extensive debates about both the strengths and the limitations of this approach. See Innes and Booher, 2004.
14 Kingston case study undertaken for this Global Report by Gray, 2007.
15 Elements of this same process of transition can also be seen in the case study material presented in Chapter 4 on the role of the police in helping to reduce crime and violence in Diadema, São Paulo, and also in the development of a stronger community orientation for the police as part of a series of measures to address crime and violence and Kingston (Jamaica).
16 This is also a strong feature of the reactions to the prison system in Port Moresby (Papua New Guinea).
17 UN-Habitat, 2006g, p8.
18 Boamah and Stanley, 2007.
19 Esser, 2004.
20 *Ibid*.
21 Zambuko and Edwards, 2006.
22 Manso et al, 2005.
23 Gray, 2007.
24 *Ibid*.
25 *Ibid*.
26 UN-Habitat, 2006g, p16.
27 *Ibid*, p32.
28 The example of Papua New Guinea has already been cited by Boamah and Stanley, 2007.
29 The Hong Kong case study undertaken for this Global Report illustrates the processes of change in policing that have taken place in those particular circumstances (Broadhurst et al, 2007).
30 Kitchen, 2007.
31 Zambuko and Edwards, 2006.
32 Gray, 2007.
33 Masese, 2007.
34 Thompson and Gartner, 2007.
35 Macedo, 2007.
36 Zaluar, 2007.
37 Boamah and Stanley, 2007.
38 Gray, 2007.
39 *Ibid*.
40 The example of the work of one of these partnerships is discussed in Kitchen (2007).
41 Morton and Kitchen, 2005.
42 Sherman et al, 1997.
43 UN-Habitat, 2006g, p27.
44 *Ibid*, pp26–28.
45 *Ibid*, pp26–28.
46 The resources available to local authorities in various parts of the world to enable them to discharge their mainstream functions are variable, with some local authorities having in an absolute sense a much stronger resource base than others.
47 UN-Habitat, 2006g, pp15–16.
48 Michau and Naker, 2003, p14.
49 UN-Habitat, undated, pp8–9.
50 Gray, 2007.
51 UN-Habitat Safer Cities website, http://unhabitat.org/programmes/safercities/projects.asp.
52 UN-Habitat, 2006g.
53 News announcement at http://news.bbc.co.uk/1/hi/world/americas/4300240.stm.
54 *Ibid*.
55 The progress with individual projects can be reviewed at http://www.unhabitat.org/programmes/safercities/projects.asp.
56 UN-Habitat, 2006g.
57 As yet, the Port Moresby Safer Cities Programme is still in its early stages.

CHAPTER 11

ENHANCING TENURE SECURITY AND ENDING FORCED EVICTIONS

The objective is to ... guarantee that all persons, everywhere, can enjoy appropriate degrees of secure tenure throughout their lives

Ensuring that everyone enjoys the legal and physical protections provided by security of tenure will continue to be one of the major challenges facing policy- and law-makers in the coming years. Chapter 5 reviewed some of the current trends on secure tenure, while Chapter 6 explored a cross-section of some of the key policy responses that have been employed to address the problem of tenure insecurity throughout the world today. This chapter expands on the findings in Chapter 6 and offers a series of proposals designed to strengthen the prospects of security of tenure by focusing on the human rights dimensions of a status that is increasingly seen as an enforceable human right.

A range of efforts are under way dedicated to tackling the global security of tenure crisis. From the Global Campaign on Secure Tenure to the work of Cities Alliance and others, and the countless efforts of non-governmental organizations (NGOs) and community-based organizations (CBOs), numerous organizations are now actively seeking to expand tenure protection around the globe. And yet, given the massive scale of the problem, to date these efforts have effectively only begun to scratch the surface. Much work thus remains to be done if the goal of security of tenure for all is to be achieved. Moreover, there is a need to work towards the integration of the many diverse and often competing approaches to providing tenure security (see Chapters 5 and 6). The objective is to address the issue of security of tenure in the most effective, just and rights-consistent manner in order to guarantee that all persons, everywhere, can enjoy appropriate degrees of secure tenure throughout their lives.

A new ... approach to security of tenure ... must combine the laws and principles of human rights and jurisprudence with the best of the tried and tested approaches to secure tenure

In many respects, the eventual outcome of these discussions will be highly determinative of the shape of cities in the future. Whichever approach ends up influencing policy-makers from the international to the national and local levels will have considerable ramifications not only for the current generation of hundreds of millions of people living under the constant threat of forced eviction and other threats because of their insecurity of tenure, but also for future generations, as well.[1] As shown above, there is considerable evidence, for instance, that freehold title-based approaches to the conferral of security of tenure, while possessing many positive features, may, in fact, result in greater numbers of people being forced into situations of tenure insecurity, both now and certainly in the future. Conversely, continuing to embrace the *status quo* will also surely lead to increased levels of insecure tenure. While various approaches presented in the past have been criticized as overly simplistic and potentially harmful to the rights of the poor, it seems timely to consider whether more flexible and innovative approaches to secure tenure or some other path might stand the best chance of achieving the most desired outcome.

This chapter provides an overview of the main elements of a human-rights based approach, focusing on a comprehensive understanding of the interrelationships between housing, land and property rights. It calls for enhanced efforts to support and develop innovative approaches to tenure, taking into account the wide range of experiences from all over the world, and it calls for enhanced efforts to combat homelessness. This is followed by a discussion of the roles and potential contributions of local authorities and an overview of how the obligations of non-state actors can be strengthened and clarified. The last part of the chapter provides a set of recommendations for future action to end forced evictions and enhance security of tenure.

A HUMAN RIGHTS–HUMAN SECURITY APPROACH TO SECURITY OF TENURE

What is needed in the coming years, therefore, is a new, more nuanced approach to security of tenure. Such a new approach must combine the laws and principles of human rights and jurisprudence with the best of the tried and tested approaches to secure tenure (i.e. those that have actually yielded the most concrete results in practice): formal and informal, legal and illegal, and modern and customary. Thus, it must incorporate the positive attributes of each view of tenure within a consolidated package – a new and more refined set of measures that can be employed to steadily increase the degree to which security of tenure is enjoyed by everyone. The eventual emergence of such an integral approach to the question of tenure should be given serious consideration by governments and international agencies. Such an approach may stand the best chance yet of gaining and maintaining tenure security for the world's poorest and most vulnerable groups.

But if such an approach is to be embraced, why would an integrated approach, based on human rights, be any better than what has been attempted in the past? First, it is important because states are already legally bound by a whole series of human rights obligations. Second, when access to secure tenure is viewed through the lens of human rights – or the bundle of rights and entitlements that protect people from being arbitrarily or unlawfully removed from their homes and lands, and the protections that this legal regime is designed to provide to every human being – it becomes clear that the right to security of tenure is perhaps denied to more people than any other basic human right, with the possible exception of the right to water.[2] Thus, the pressing need to address these questions as rights violations adds increased urgency to the global quest for security of tenure.

While approaching security of tenure from such a rights-based approach is still relatively uncommon, many developments point in this direction. The Global Campaign for Secure Tenure, for instance, has recognized the importance of taking human rights approaches in achieving secure tenure, and has stressed the absolute primacy of human rights in this regard.[3] All states have voluntarily ratified international human rights instruments that legally bind them to certain actions, many of which include specific obligations to recognize and protect rights, such as the right to secure tenure. The principles of a human rights-based approach are, in fact, found – albeit providing varied levels of protection – within the existing law of most countries. These principles may not always be subject to full compliance or enforcement; but as legal principles, there is no disputing the fact that they are in place. Indeed, all legal systems – common law, civil law, Roman–Dutch law, Islamic law (see Box 11.1), customary law and others – address the question of tenure and the degrees of security accorded to each type of recognized and informal tenure arrangements. Much research on security of tenure, however, only touches lightly on the question of law and its role in the conferral of security tenure, and even less so on the human rights dimensions (which are also legal in nature) of this question. It is important to ask why states have not more frequently embraced human rights tools to support wider access to tenure. International human rights law, for instance, stipulates that governments need to respect, protect and fulfil housing, land and property rights by 'taking steps' to the 'maximum of available resources' to ensure the 'progressive realization' of all rights, including the right to security of tenure.

Moreover, addressing security of tenure as a human rights issue is somewhat trickier than many other rights. The main reason is that local conditions must always be taken into account in determining both the diagnosis and the remedy to prevailing conditions of tenure insecurity. This is not often the case with rights such as freedom from torture, a fair trial and other rights for which more universally applicable remedies may be easier to identify and implement.

Box 11.1 Islamic law and security of tenure

In the work to develop a new integrated human rights-based approach to realizing the right to secure tenure, the explicit recognition of an extensive range of property rights in Islam should be taken into consideration:

> *Property rights are not only well established under Islamic law, they are indisputably one of the five foundational principles of Islamic society. Understanding the nature and scope of property rights in Islamic society could further secure tenure as the land rights framework emerges from divine edict and the sayings and examples of the Prophet.*

The concept of property rights in Islamic economics has implications far beyond the material domain as it lays stress on responsibility, poverty alleviation and redistribution. Islamic doctrines engage with entitlement to land rights for a broad range of beneficiaries, including women, children, landless and minorities. The repeated Islamic emphasis on obligations regarding philanthropy, fairness and poverty alleviation are influential in land rights argumentation based on a holistic, authentic, moral, ethical and legal land rights code.

Source: UN-Habitat, 2005e, pp13–14

While to an extent true of all rights, the importance of strong political support for security of tenure within all housing sectors is vital to ensuring that everyone has fully enforceable security of tenure rights.

The right to security of tenure is perhaps denied to more people than any other basic human right

The legal and normative basis for security of tenure as a human right

If security of tenure is to be treated as a right, it is clear that a range of existing human rights, viewed as an integral whole, form the legal and normative basis for the existence of this right. While numerous rights form the foundation upon which the right to security of tenure rests, it is perhaps the right to adequate housing, the right to be protected against forced evictions, the right not to be arbitrarily deprived of one's property, the right to privacy and respect for the home, and the right to housing and property restitution that are most fundamental. These rights are briefly outlined in the following sections.

■ The right to adequate housing

The right to adequate housing was first recognized in the Universal Declaration of Human Rights in 1948 and subsequently reaffirmed in various international legal standards (see Box 11.2). While international human rights law widely recognizes various manifestations of housing rights, the International Covenant on Economic, Social and Cultural Rights (ICESCR) contains perhaps the most significant international legal source of the right to adequate housing:

The right to adequate housing was first recognized in the Universal Declaration of Human Rights in 1948

> *The States Parties to the present Covenant recognize the right of everyone to an adequate standard of living for himself and his family, including adequate food, clothing and housing, and to the continuous improvement of living conditions.*[4]

Box 11.2 The right to housing in international law

The right to housing is recognized in a range of international legal instruments, including *inter alia*:

- 1948: Universal Declaration of Human Rights (Article 25(1));
- 1961: International Labour Organization (ILO) Recommendation No 115 on Workers' Housing;
- 1965: International Convention on the Elimination of All Forms of Racial Discrimination (Article 5(e)(iii));
- 1976: International Covenant on Economic, Social and Cultural Rights (Article 11(1));
- 1979: Convention on the Elimination of All Forms of Discrimination Against Women (Article 14(2));
- 1989: Convention on the Rights of the Child (Article 27(3));
- 1990: International Convention on the Protection of the Rights of All Migrant Workers and Members of Their Families (Article 43(1)(d));
- 2007: Convention on the Rights of Persons with Disabilities (Article 28).

The practice of forced eviction ... constitutes a gross violation of a broad range of human rights

As noted above, many states have incorporated references to the right to housing in their national constitutions. Moreover, all states have domestic legislation in place recognizing at least some of the requirements associated with the right to adequate housing. Laws governing property relations, landlord and tenant arrangements, non-discrimination rights in the housing sector, access to services, land administration and a range of other legal areas can be found in all states. Among other things, those entitled to this right are legally assured to housing that is adequate. Adequacy has specifically been defined to include security of tenure; availability of services, materials, facilities and infrastructure; affordability; habitability; accessibility; location; and cultural adequacy.[5]

Governmental obligations derived from this right include duties to take measures to confer security of tenure (and consequent protection against arbitrary or forced eviction and/or arbitrary confiscation or expropriation of housing); to prevent discrimination in the housing sphere; to ensure equality of treatment and access vis-à-vis housing; to protect against racial discrimination; to guarantee housing affordability; and many others.[6] Moreover, there is a duty incumbent upon those exercising powers of governance to promote access to, and provision of, housing resources suited to the needs of the disabled, the chronically ill, migrant workers, the elderly, and refugees and internally displaced persons (IDPs).

Every human being ... have the right to be protected against being arbitrarily displaced from his or her home or place of habitual residence

> *States parties must give due priority to those social groups living in unfavourable conditions by giving them particular consideration. Policies and legislation should correspondingly not be designed to benefit already advantaged social groups at the expense of others.*[7]

Finally, and perhaps most importantly, international law requires governments to take steps to progressively realize housing (and other) rights:

> *Each State Party to the present Covenant undertakes to take steps ... to the maximum of its available resources, with a view to achieving progressively the full realization of the rights recognized in the present Covenant by all appropriate means, including particularly the adoption of legislative measures.*[8]

The right to be protected against forced evictions

Building on the legal foundations of the right to adequate housing (and other related rights), many internationally negotiated documents assert that forced evictions constitute a gross violation of human rights. As a result, in 1993, the then United Nations Commission on Human Rights urged all states to confer security of tenure on those currently without these protections.[9] This was followed up in 2004 with an even more unequivocal resolution on the prohibition of forced evictions,[10] which reaffirmed:

> *... that the practice of forced eviction that is contrary to laws that are in conformity with international human rights standards constitutes a gross violation of a broad range of human rights, in particular the right to adequate housing.*

This resolution also urged governments:

> *... to undertake immediately measures, at all levels, aimed at eliminating the practice of forced eviction by, inter alia, repealing existing plans involving forced evictions as well as any legislation allowing for forced evictions, and by adopting and implementing legislation ensuring the right to security of tenure for all residents, [and to] protect all persons who are currently threatened with forced eviction and to adopt all necessary measures giving full protection against forced eviction, based upon effective participation, consultation and negotiation with affected persons or groups.*

The United Nations Guiding Principles on Internal Displacement adopt a similar perspective and state clearly that 'Every human being shall have the right to be protected against being arbitrarily displaced from his or her home or place of habitual residence'.[11] The United Nations Committee on Economic, Social and Cultural Rights' (CESCR's) General Comment No 7, examined earlier, is perhaps the most detailed statement interpreting the view of international law in this area, stating that 'forced evictions are *prima facie* incompatible with the requirements of the Covenant and can only be justified in the most exceptional circumstances, and in accordance with the relevant principles of international law'.[12] In addition, rights such as the right to freedom of movement and the corresponding right to choose one's residence, the right to be free from degrading or inhuman treatment and others are being increasingly interpreted to protect people against forced evictions.[13]

The more recently adopted Principles on Housing and Property Restitution for Refugees and Displaced Persons (the Pinheiro Principles) is even clearer in establishing rights against displacement (see Box 11.3).[14]

The right not to be arbitrarily deprived of one's property

The right not to be arbitrarily deprived of one's property is closely related to the issue of forced eviction. The Universal Declaration of Human Rights, which was adopted in 1948, guarantees everyone the right to own property alone, as well as in association with others, and prohibits the arbitrary deprivation of property.[15] Such rights are widely addressed throughout human rights law, although 'property rights' as such, are – perhaps surprisingly for many readers – not found within the two (legally binding) international covenants on human rights, which became law in those states that have ratified them as from 1976.

While some have argued that this omission was essentially a technical mistake, the vote of the drafting body of seven 'against' to six 'for', with five abstentions, of whether or not to include a specific article on property within the ICESCR, clearly shows that unanimity on this question was not apparent at the time of the drafting of these cornerstone international human rights treaties.[16] In identifying the reasons for the exclusion of property rights from these texts, it appears that questions of definition, scope and issues surrounding interference with property, the circumstances under which the right of the state to expropriate property could be legitimately exercised and the question of compensation each contributed to preventing widespread agreement.

The right to privacy and respect for the home

The widely recognized rights to privacy and respect for the home are fundamental human rights protections that can also be linked directly to security of tenure. Privacy is, in fact, one of the elements of adequacy identified by the CESCR,[17] as well as by governments in both the Global Strategy for Shelter to the Year 2000 and the Habitat Agenda.

The safeguards against arbitrary and unlawful interference with the home found in Article 8 of the European Convention on Human Rights, for instance, have been frequently relied upon by claimants before the European Court on Human Rights in cases seeking protection of housing rights, as well as related housing and property restitution rights. Closely related to the practice of forced eviction, according to jurisprudence, any interference with these rights can only be justified if they are carried out in accordance with law, in pursuit of a legitimate social aim in the public interest and subject to the payment of just and satisfactory compensation.

Both owner-occupied and rental housing falls under the protections offered by the right to privacy provisions under the European Court on Human Rights. Under the case law of the European Court on Human Rights, one's 'home' can even be a place that a person neither owns nor rents, but

Box 11.3 The Pinheiro Principles: Provision against evictions

- Principle 5.1: Everyone has the right to be protected against being arbitrarily displaced from his or her home, land or place of habitual residence.
- Principle 5.2: States should incorporate protections against displacement into domestic legislation, consistent with international human rights and humanitarian law and related standards, and should extend these protections to everyone within their legal jurisdiction or effective control.
- Principle 5.3: States shall prohibit forced eviction, demolition of houses and destruction of agricultural areas, and the arbitrary confiscation or expropriation of land as a punitive measure or as a means or method of war.
- Principle 5.4: States shall take steps to ensure that no one is subjected to displacement by either state or non-state actors. States shall also ensure that individuals, corporations and other entities within their legal jurisdiction or effective control refrain from carrying out or otherwise participating in displacement.

Source: United Nations Documents E/CN.4/Sub.2/2005/17 and E/CN.4/Sub.2/2005/17/Add.1

nonetheless resides in. Moreover, the court has repeatedly determined Article 8 cases more on the basis of the factual situation of a resident of a particular home than exclusively on the legal status of the rights holder concerned. Both of these trends are important for dwellers in the informal sector, and for their relevance for treating security of tenure as a human right.[18]

The Universal Declaration of Human Rights ... guarantees everyone the right to own property ..., and prohibits the arbitrary deprivation of property

The right to housing and property restitution

Over the past several decades, intergovernmental agencies, government officials, the United Nations and NGO field staff, and others working in protection or support capacities with refugees and IDPs have become increasingly involved in efforts to secure durable rights-based solutions to all forms of displacement based on the principle of voluntary repatriation. During more recent years, the idea of voluntary repatriation and return have expanded into concepts involving not simply the return to one's country for refugees or one's city or region for IDPs, but the return to, and reassertion of, control over one's original home, land or property (i.e. the process of housing and property restitution).

As a result of these developments, since the early 1990s several million refugees and IDPs have recovered and re-inhabited their original homes, lands and properties through restitution processes, while smaller numbers have accepted compensation in lieu of return.[19] These efforts have been played out from Bosnia-Herzegovina and Afghanistan to South Africa, and from Tajikistan to Guatemala, Mozambique and beyond. This historic change in emphasis from what were essentially humanitarian-driven responses, to voluntary repatriation, to more rights-based approaches, to return is increasingly grounded in the principle of restorative justice and of restitution as a legal remedy that can support refugees and IDPs in their choice of a durable solution (whether return, resettlement or local integration). As noted above, the recently approved Pinheiro Principles expand and clarify the rights of all refugees and displaced persons (including evictees) 'to have restored to them any housing, land and/or property of which they were arbitrarily or unlawfully deprived'.[20]

The ... rights to privacy and respect for the home are fundamental human rights protections

Box 11.4 Defining human security

The former United Nations Secretary-General Kofi Annan has said:

> *Human security in its broadest sense embraces far more than the absence of violent conflict. It encompasses human rights, good governance, access to education and health care and ensuring that each individual has opportunities and choices to fulfil his or her own potential. Every step in this direction is also a step towards reducing poverty, achieving economic growth and preventing conflict. Freedom from want, freedom from fear and freedom of future generations to inherit a healthy natural environment – these are the interrelated building blocks of human and, therefore, national security.*

Source: Commission on Human Security, 2003

Security of tenure goes beyond property rights

Examining security of tenure within the context of the above-mentioned recognized human rights also meshes well with treating security of tenure as a core element within the concept of human security. This implies taking a more all-encompassing vision of human rights as they relate to the tenure issue (see Box 11.4). Nobel Peace Prize winner Jody Williams makes the link between human rights, human security and property rights in a 2006 article, where she questions the efficacy of a property rights (title-based) approach to solving the security of tenure crisis:

A focus on property rights alone may serve ... to justify a grossly unfair and unequal status quo

> *But it remains to be seen how extracting one right – the right to property – can possibly be ... a long-term solution to meeting the complex needs of the poor. Meeting those needs for the long term would require addressing the political, social, cultural and economic factors (on both the national and international levels) that created the gross inequalities in the first place and exacerbates them in a globalized world, thus depriving the poor of human dignity and the full realization of their human rights.*[21]

The question thus becomes whether the concept of 'property rights' is adequate

This is an important point, for in the realm of housing and land policy (as also discussed in Chapters 5 and 6), property rights approaches have often proven inadequate in fully achieving the objective of universal access to a place to live in peace and dignity. Indeed, on their own, property rights are often seen to undermine the pursuit of this goal. In some situations, a focus on property rights alone may serve (as a concept, as well as in law, policy and practice) to justify a grossly unfair and unequal *status quo*. In other instances, what are referred to as property rights are confused with housing and land rights, effectively usurping them in an effort to give an impression that all residentially related human rights requirements can be met via property rights.

The term 'housing, land and property rights' ensures that all residential sectors are included in legal analyses and in the development of plans, policies and institutions

As such, the question thus becomes whether the concept of 'property rights' is adequate for addressing the multifaceted questions relating to both land and housing, and the inadequate living conditions facing such a large portion of humanity. Can property rights in and of themselves address the increasingly inequitable distribution of land in developing countries? Can programmes solely supporting property rights lead to increasingly higher levels of enjoyment of all rights related to the conditions in which one lives? Most controversially, perhaps, does a purely property rights approach help those without rights to actually achieve them?

In certain instances, the recognition of property rights has proven to be an important element or step in developing a legal system based upon the rule of law. The effective enforcement of property rights requires clear and transparent rules, as well as a functioning and independent judiciary – elements that are considered fundamental for the promotion and protection of human rights and the rule of law. But while property rights could play a role in triggering the emergence of a human rights friendly environment, one can question, in the longer term, the impact of a system relying primarily on property rights for the full realization of all human rights. In practical terms, within the real world, do property rights actually protect only those who already possess property? And what is their significance for those hundreds of millions of people who do not possess these rights within the formal legal system?

Housing, land and property (HLP) rights

As one means of addressing these questions and, in effect, of overcoming the limitations of the concept of 'property rights', the more inclusive terminology of housing, land and property (HLP) rights has been suggested as a far better (and, again, integral) term with which to describe the residential dimensions of the property question, set within a human rights framework.[22] Treating what are traditionally referred to as 'property rights' as the more all-encompassing 'HLP rights' promotes a unified and evolutionary approach to human rights and all of their associated residential dimensions. Moreover, such an approach – grounded deeply in the indivisibility and interdependence of all rights – allows all of the rights just noted to be viewed as a consolidated whole in broad support of security of tenure initiatives. The term 'housing, land and property rights' ensures that all residential sectors are included in legal analyses and in the development of plans, policies and institutions addressing the legal and physical conditions in which people in all societies live. Working with HLP rights also ensures that the terminology used in one country to describe the rights possessed by everyone (e.g. 'housing rights') is treated as the human rights equivalent of terms such as 'property rights' or 'land rights', and vice-versa. Using only the term 'property rights' can very easily result in the exclusion of certain sectors (tenants, co-operative dwellers, informal-sector dwellers without secure tenure, women, vulnerable groups, nomads, indigenous peoples and others), inequitable treatment and, far too often, outright discrimination. In contrast, the term 'HLP rights' is universally relevant within all legal and political systems, and resonates in both developed and developing countries.

While HLP rights are each unique and complex legal and human rights concepts, they are, at the same time, closely related to one another and, to a certain degree, overlap. In general terms:

- Housing rights are the rights of 'everyone' to have access to a safe, secure, affordable and habitable home.
- Land rights cover those rights related directly to the land itself as distinct from purely the structure built on the land in question.
- Property rights concern the exclusive user and ownership rights over a particular dwelling or land parcel.

Each of these terms is important; but none of them captures in their entirety the full spectrum of rights associated with the right to a place to live in peace and dignity, including the right to security of tenure. For the purposes of the security of tenure process, therefore – and because historical, political, cultural and other distinctions between countries with respect to what have also more broadly been called 'residential' rights are so extensive – HLP rights seems a more comprehensive term for describing the numerous residential dimensions of these questions from the perspective of human rights law. What people in one country label as 'land rights' may be precisely the same thing as what citizens of another country call 'housing rights'. 'Property rights' in one area may greatly assist in protecting the rights of tenants, while in another place property rights are used to justify mass forced evictions. Many more examples could be given; but the important point here is simply that the composite term HLP rights probably captures the notion of 'home' or 'place of habitual residence' better than other possible terms.

A term such as HLP rights may confuse some and frustrate others; but it is difficult to imagine how an integral approach to security of tenure can emerge within human rights law unless the impasse between housing rights, property rights and land rights is broken and allowed to properly evolve. This new terminology embraces all of the different approaches to this question, not necessarily favouring one or the other, but incorporating the best, most pro-human rights elements of each into a new vision of human rights as they relate to the places and conditions in which people live. The new terminology may assist greatly in finding new ways to integrate rights with security of tenure.

In addition and, more specifically, linked to the question of eviction, it may also be time to consider looking for new ways to define people's rights not to be evicted in a more positive and affirmative manner. Since all human rights are to be treated equally, in an interdependent and indivisible manner (see Box 11.5), it may be useful to expand discussions on what could be called a *right to security of place*. This right exemplifies the convergence of civil, political, economic, social and cultural rights and places three forms of security into an indispensable human rights framework:

- It encapsulates the notion of physical security, protection of physical integrity and safety from harm, and guarantees that basic rights will be respected.
- It incorporates all dimensions of human security – or the economic and social side of the security equation.
- It recognizes the importance of tenure rights (for tenants, owners and those too poor to afford to rent or buy a home) and the crucial right to be protected against any arbitrary or forced eviction from one's home.

This manifestation of security intrinsically links to housing rights concerns during times of peace and to housing rights issues arising in the midst of armed conflict and humanitarian disasters. It recognizes that everyone has an enforceable and defendable right to physical security and rights to housing, property and land, including rights to security of tenure. As with 'HLP rights', a right to security of place makes no presumption that one form of tenure is to be necessarily preferred over another, but the 'right to security of place' would go beyond security of tenure alone. The stability of the home would form the starting point from which supplementary rights emerge. Such a right to security of place would strengthen the rights of all dwellers within the informal sector by providing a conceptual means to plug the gap in the attention and institutional protection given to those forced from their homes due to forced evictions and development-induced displacement.

Treating HLP rights simultaneously as human rights concerns and development concerns is both practical and has universally applicability

An integral, comprehensive approach based on the notion of HLP rights holds the best promise for marshalling resources and assets towards improving the lives of lower-income groups. Treating HLP rights simultaneously as human rights concerns and development concerns is both practical and has universal applicability. In fact, this approach can provide one of the clearest examples of how a rights-based approach to development actually looks in practice and how security of tenure can be treated increasingly as a core human rights issue. A human rights–human security approach to secure tenure has the potential to significantly improve the prospects of security of tenure being an attribute of everyone's life. The essential issue, however, is that the approach has to be applied seriously and wisely by governments – both local and national – and must be supported solidly by the international community and civil society. To achieve this will be no small feat, as few rights, if any, are as widely denied as the right to security of tenure.

By treating security of tenure as part of the broader human rights equation, we automatically incorporate dimensions of security, rights, remedies and justice

This view, though perhaps seemingly distant from a human rights perspective on the issue, in fact reflects the key point. At the end of the day, what matters most is not necessarily the formality associated with the tenure levels enjoyed by dwellers, but the *perception* of security, both *de facto* and *de jure*, that comes with that tenure. By treating security of tenure as part of the broader human rights equation, we automatically incorporate dimensions of security, rights, remedies and justice to the analysis.

Box 11.5 The indivisibility of human rights

All human rights are universal, indivisible and interdependent and interrelated … it is the duty of States, regardless of their political, economic and cultural systems, to promote and protect all human rights and fundamental freedoms.

Source: Vienna Declaration and Programme of Action, para 5

Moreover, and in turn, we open up – rather than close – the avenues through which security of tenure (in a manner fully consistent with human rights) can be provided. The explicit human rights dimensions of security of tenure have not been long on the international agenda; but they are there now and need to be used as the basis for improving the prospects for secure tenure so that this right can be enjoyed universally and sustainably by everyone, everywhere.

Flexible ... approaches to ... security of tenure are more advisable than approaches grounded in ideology

THE NEED FOR INNOVATIVE APPROACHES TO TENURE

The major lesson learned from a variety of tenure initiatives taken in preceding decades is simply that flexible and innovative approaches to providing security of tenure are more advisable than approaches grounded in ideology and the generation of capital. Such a view is increasingly shared by researchers and practitioners, as well as by international organizations. The World Bank, for example, who earlier advocated title-based approaches, states that:

> *Tenure security, one of the key goals of public land policies, can be achieved under different modalities of land ownership. Instead of an often ideological stance in favor of full private ownership rights, long-term secure tenure and transferable leases will convey many of the same benefits to owners and may be preferable where full ownership rights and titles would be too politically controversial or too costly.*[23]

Tenure systems exist within a continuum in which even pavement dwellers may enjoy a degree of legal protection

Any successful initiative to provide tenure will need to be based on a recognition that innovation is required for many reasons, not the least of which is the fact that there are many diverse types of tenure and varying degrees of legality and *de facto* and *de jure* protection associated with both. Although a variety of tenure types was listed in Chapter 5, the 'reality is that tenure systems exist within a continuum in which even pavement dwellers may enjoy a degree of legal protection'.[24] Furthermore, in practice, there are numerous sub-markets between those with the highest and the lowest levels of tenure security. The majority of urban dwellers in developing countries have some form of *de facto* security to the housing and land that they occupy. The actual legal status of their housing and land occupancy may not even be clear to the occupants themselves. What matters in the everyday life of the majority of urban dwellers is their *perception* of security. Everything else being equal, if the residents themselves in one location consider the risks of eviction to be marginal, their level of security of tenure is, indeed, higher than that of others who perceive higher eviction risks.

Granting of full title to 'owners' in settlement upgrading schemes tends to lead to market evictions of tenants

Experience shows that settlements upgrading approaches, which include the granting of full freehold title, may, in fact, result in an increase in informal settlements rather than a decrease. This may occur because granting such titles implies that households acquire an asset that can be sold at a high price in the formal land market. Many households may thus be encouraged to sell, realize the capital value, and move on to another informal settlement, perhaps even hoping to repeat the process. Furthermore, as noted above, traditional slum upgrading approaches also tend to ignore the situation of tenants. Granting of full title to 'owners' in settlement upgrading schemes tends to lead to market evictions of tenants. Again, the result is often the same: the poorest are forced to relocate to other informal settlements.

The main question faced is thus how to increase security of tenure without forcing the poor to relocate to more peripheral locations where lack of employment opportunity may further enhance their poverty. Although no universally applicable answers to these questions exist, experience indicates that the main focus should be on providing forms of tenure that are sufficiently secure to ensure protection from eviction.[25] At the same time, HLP rights and regulatory frameworks should cater for multipurpose use of their dwellings (i.e. support the development of home-based and other small-scale enterprises)[26] and ensure access to basic services.

So, which types of tenure provide such levels of security? Again, there are no universally applicable answers. In addition to the most obvious solution (i.e. a moratorium on forced evictions; see below), several options have been successfully employed. Among these are temporary occupation licences, communal or individual leases, community land trusts, communal ownership, customary tenure, and others that are detailed below.

A recent UK Department for International Development (DFID)-funded survey explored innovative ways of providing secure tenure to the urban poor by examining unique methods of tenure provision. The survey revealed that certificates of use or occupancy, community land trusts and other forms of what could be called intermediate forms of tenure provide a valuable means of increasing legitimacy. Furthermore, the existence of these approaches also provides valuable breathing space for local governments, while the administrative capability to record and clarify rights is improved. The survey also exposed that tenure issues cannot be isolated from other related policies of urban land management and that it is important not to put all of one's eggs in one or two baskets. It is essential to offer a wide range of tenure options so that the diverse and changing needs of households can be met on a long-term basis through competition.[27] Linking innovative approaches such as these with HLP rights and the right to security of place could truly create the basis for an entirely new approach to ensuring security of tenure for all.

A range of innovative approaches to providing tenure is used in Brazil. One of these – '*use concessions*' – is a measure through which the government transfers the right to use property for residential purposes to families settled in public areas without the transfer of property title. Use concession can be an appropriate measure in establishing the collective occupation of areas such as *favelas*. These measures can provide the population with security of tenure and impede forced eviction, and can also be a mechanism guaranteeing the social purpose of a public area, thus avoiding real estate speculation since such public areas are not 'privatized'.

Similarly, '*special social interest zones*' can now be declared in urban areas in Brazil. These zones are efficient tools for municipalities to avoid forced evictions. The main candidates to be defined as such zones are urban areas occupied by *favelas*, *cortiços*,[28] collective residences, popular subdivisions, and vacant and underutilized urban areas. Such zones are typically declared in areas where there are a high number of landownership conflicts or housing that will result in forced evictions of low-income groups. Once such areas have been identified, municipal law can define them to be special social interest zones. This provides legal guarantees to social groups living within the zone and recognizes these as residential areas for low-income groups. Based on this tool, judges can deliver judgements in favour of these social groups when they consider requests for eviction and removal of families occupying public or private areas. They can then establish a process of negotiation between the owner of the area, the residents and the government to regulate the legal situation of the population and promote improvement of these areas. Some Brazilian municipalities – such as Recife, Diadema, Porto Alegre, Santos and Santo Andre – have utilized this land regulation tool to combat forced evictions.

Thailand is another country where innovative tenure options have been introduced to address the concerns of low-income groups. Low-income residents of Bangkok experience one of the main effects of globalization and urbanization, increasing pressures for more 'efficient' use of land in inner-city areas. Box 11.6 provides an example of such attempted 'development' in Bangkok. Despite local government efforts to evict and relocate the community of Pom Mahakan, the residents were able to resist eviction and obtain security of tenure in a negotiated settlement that included elements of *land sharing*. The experience of this community exemplifies how development can be achieved in a process incorporating both human rights and community design/development concerns.

'Special social interest zones' ... are efficient tools for municipalities to avoid forced evictions

On the basis of the wisdom associated with innovative approaches to the security of tenure question, it is appropriate to consider a 'twin-track' approach to improving tenure security. First, implementation of such innovative approaches can improve living conditions for current slum dwellers. And, second, the *revision of regulatory frameworks* can reduce the need for future slums by significantly improving access to legal land and housing.[29] The latter is perhaps even more important than the former as urban growth

The revision of regulatory frameworks can reduce the need for future slums by ... improving access to legal land and housing

Box 11.6 Eviction prevention in Pom Mahakan, Bangkok

In Pom Mahakan in Bangkok (Thailand), a community of about 300 residents in the Rattanakosin area of the city has been successfully resisting eviction for several years. This area of the city is the original settlement of Bangkok, and today there are some 200,000 people who live and work in Rattanakosin.

Historically, there have been a number of plans to develop the area, and the most recent set of plans, ratified by the Bangkok Metropolitan Administration in 2001, began to have a progressively destructive impact on the security of tenure for many of the communities who make the Rattanakosin area their home. The plan – *The Master Plan for Land Development: Ratchadamnoen Road and Surrounding Area* – was partly motivated by the 1997 economic crash and the consequent desire to capture more tourism income for the city of Bangkok.

Rattanakosin – with the Grand Palace and Wat Po as international attractions – was the main focus of this tourism initiative. The master plan was meant to 'beautify' this local environment essentially as a tourist attraction and, in so doing, to improve property values (most of Rattanakosin is Crown Land administered by the Crown Property Bureau). The idea was that if the city was made more attractive, tourists would stay longer and thus leave more money behind, speeding the economic recovery of Bangkok.

Thus, in January 2003, the city planning department posted eviction notices on all the houses in Pom Mahakan. The residents were told to vacate their homes and were offered relocation to a place 45 kilometres away, on the outskirts of Bangkok. The evictions were spearheaded by the governor of Bangkok, supported by the Board of the Bangkok Metropolitan Administration, the Crown Property Bureau, the National Economic and Social Development Board and other organizations, such as the Tourism Authority of Thailand.

Despite this pressure, residents began holding protests, building barricades and organizing a night-watch system. They also acted pre-emptively. Assisted by a coalition of academics based at the local university, non-governmental organizations (NGOs) and human rights activists, they put forward a highly innovative land-sharing plan as an alternative to eviction and relocation. The plan included the renovation of the older buildings and the integration of the residences within a historical park. The residents even started implementing part of this plan, and many outsiders rallied to the call to support them in this process.

Despite the above efforts, in August 2003 an administrative court ruled that the eviction was legal and could go ahead. In January 2004, the authorities started work on the unoccupied areas of Pom Mahakan. The authorities repeatedly announced their intention to evict the entire community. Some lost hope and left; but the majority continued their attempts to negotiate with the authorities and to put forward alternatives.

Eventually, although after yet another attempt to implement the evictions, the governor finally agreed to resolve the issue through negotiations. On 19 December 2005, the governor confirmed that negotiations between the community, the Bangkok Metropolitan Administration and other stakeholders had resulted in an agreement to preserve and develop the area as an 'antique wooden house community'.

This agreement led to the development of a community plan that included preservation and rehabilitation of existing buildings and landscape in the community. Furthermore, it was agreed that the people will stay where they are and that the funds that had been allocated to the park development would go to the community improvements that the community itself had planned.

Pom Mahakan now has security of tenure.

Source: Bristol, 2007b

continues unabated. As noted earlier, the Millennium Development Goal (MDG) of improving the lives of 100 million slum dwellers by 2020 does, indeed, pale in comparison with the projected urban population growth of some 2 billion between 2000 and 2020 (see also Box 6.1).[30]

The creative use of *regulation* and *regulatory audits* has also been suggested as an innovative way of promoting improvements in the urban landscape and increasing tenure security. Developed as a means for promoting the upgrading of existing informal settlements, this approach seeks to strengthen regulatory frameworks to better benefit the poor. Among the positive aspects of regulation are that it allows orderly land development and efficient land management; attracts and guides inward local investment; maximizes public revenues; protects the environment and public health; mitigates the impact of disasters; helps the poor access improved housing, services and credit; protects occupants from unscrupulous developers; minimizes harmful externalities; and allows for common land uses. Conversely, the negative aspects of regulation include the dangers of over-regulating and, therefore, discouraging investment; imposing regulations, standards or administrative procedures that increase costs to levels that many people cannot afford; failing to reflect the cultural priorities of different groups, especially in the ways in which people perceive and use dwellings and open space; institutionalizing corruption through fees for non-enforcement; and creating overlapping or contradictory conditions that expose developers or individuals to the risk of conforming to one regulation or standard and therefore of contravening another.[31]

The creative use of regulation and regulatory audits has ... been suggested as an innovative way of ... increasing tenure security

Few would argue against the view that the universal enjoyment of housing rights remains a very long-term proposition

COMBATING HOMELESSNESS AND PROTECTING THE RIGHTS OF HOMELESS PEOPLE

As discussed above, the international legal foundations of the human right to adequate housing are designed to ensure access to a secure, adequate and affordable home for all people in all countries. The long recognition of this right under international human rights law, however, has yet to sufficiently influence national policy, law and practice on housing rights; as a result, few rights are denied as frequently, on such a scale and with the degree of impunity as housing rights. Whether in terms of outright homelessness, forced evictions and other forms of displacement; life-threatening, unhealthy and dangerous living conditions; the destruction of homes during armed conflict; systematic housing discrimination against certain vulnerable groups (particularly women); campaigns of 'ethnic cleansing'; or any number of other circumstances where housing rights are denied, few would argue against the view that the universal enjoyment of housing rights remains a very long-term proposition.

States are obliged to respect, protect and fulfil all human rights, including the housing rights of homeless persons

In essence, states are obliged to respect, protect and fulfil all human rights, including the housing rights of homeless persons. The obligation to respect human rights requires states to refrain from interfering with the enjoyment of rights. As noted, housing rights are violated if a state engages in arbitrary forced evictions. The obligation to protect requires states to prevent violations of such rights by third parties, such as landlords or private developers. If the exercise of these two obligations does not result in the access by everyone to an adequate home, then the obligation to fulfil becomes relevant, requiring states to take appropriate legislative, administrative, budgetary, judicial and other measures towards the full realization of such rights. Thus, the failure of states to take such steps, to the maximum of its available resources, to achieve the universal enjoyment of housing rights, would not comply with human rights principles.[32] So, while states are not necessarily required to build homes for the entire population, they are required to undertake a whole range of steps, both positive and negative in nature, grounded in human rights law, which are designed to ensure the full realization of all human rights, including the right to adequate housing by the homeless.

At the same time, there are a number of states that have accepted the fundamental legal responsibility of providing an adequate home to certain specifically identified homeless groups. There are laws and jurisprudence in several states, indicating that under certain circumstances, the state is legally required to provide particular individuals or groups with adequate housing in an expedient manner:

- In Finland, the law requires local government authorities to provide housing resources for the severely handicapped under certain circumstances. Furthermore, local governments are required to rectify inadequate housing conditions or, as the case may be, to provide for housing when inadequate or non-existent housing causes the need for special child welfare or constitutes a substantial hindrance to rehabilitating the child or the family.[33]
- In the UK, local city councils are required to provide adequate accommodation to homeless families and persons 'in priority need' (see Box 11.7).
- In Germany, two additional legal duties are added to the legal framework relating to the rights of the homeless. First, the law provides that social welfare payments may be used to pay rent arrears in order to maintain the dwelling and to prevent homelessness. Second, it proclaims that individuals (including the homeless) who have special social difficulties that they cannot themselves overcome may claim assistance to avert, eliminate or ease particular difficulties – including measures to help procure and maintain a dwelling.[34]

In addition to these national-level rights of the homeless, many states approach housing requirements, at least in a *de facto* manner, in terms of providing housing to the homeless following natural disasters, and to refugees and displaced persons, and while perhaps not invariably accepting such duties in law, in practice temporary (and sometimes permanent) homes are provided. Interestingly, the ICESCR is now

Box 11.7 The UK Homeless Persons Act

Section 65: *Duties to persons found to be homeless:*

1 This section has effect as regards the duties owed by the local housing authority to an applicant where they are satisfied that he is homeless.

2 Where they are satisfied that he has a priority need and are not satisfied that he became homeless intentionally, they shall ... secure that accommodation becomes available for his occupation.

3 Where they are satisfied that he has a priority need but are also satisfied that he became homeless intentionally, they shall:

- secure that accommodation is made available for his occupation for such period as they consider will give him a reasonable opportunity of securing accommodation for his occupation; and
- furnish him with advice and such assistance as they consider appropriate in the circumstances in any attempts he may make to secure that accommodation becomes available for his occupation.

Section 66: *Duties to persons found to be threatened with homelessness:*

1 This section has effect as regards the duties owed by the local housing authority to an applicant where they are satisfied that he is threatened with homelessness.

2 Where they are satisfied that he has a priority need and are not satisfied that he become threatened with homelessness intentionally, they shall take reasonable steps to secure that accommodation does not cease to be available for his occupation.

Section 69:

1 A local housing authority may perform any duty under section 65 or 68 (duties to persons found to be homeless) to secure that accommodation becomes available for the occupation of a person by:

- making available suitable accommodation held by them under Part II (provision of housing) or any enactment; or
- securing that he obtains suitable accommodation from some other person; or
- giving him such advice and assistance as will secure that he obtains suitable accommodation from some other person.

Source: 1985 UK Housing Act (amended) (Homeless Persons Act)

also seen to provide similar protections to all persons who have faced forced eviction, notwithstanding the rationale behind the eviction in question. The CESCR clearly asserts that evictions 'should not result in rendering individuals homeless',[35] thus making it incumbent on governments to guarantee that people who are evicted – whether illegally or in accordance with the law – are to be ensured some form of alternative housing.

Many have questioned whether or not states that have housing rights obligations are legally required to provide, in a substantive sense, adequate housing directly to homeless persons and families or even to the entire population. Indeed, this comparatively minor issue in the overall housing rights domain has unfortunately often dominated debates on the legal status of housing rights. Critics of housing rights have often equated 'the human right to adequate housing' with the immediate duty of governments to substantively provide a house to anyone who requests it to do so. This overly literal translation of the term, however, reflects neither general state practice or the interpretation given to this right under international law, although there are, as will be shown, specific instances where the direct provision of housing is envisaged. CESCR attests that while states are required to 'take whatever steps are necessary' to achieve the full realization of the right to adequate housing, it also stipulates that 'Measures designed to satisfy a state party's obligations in respect of the right to adequate housing may reflect whatever mix of public- and private-sector measures [are] considered appropriate.'[36]

No state has ever, or could ever, hope to construct adequate housing for the entire population, and the advocacy of such approaches verges on the absurd. No government, no United Nations institution and no NGOs back this approach to implementing housing rights. Rather, a perspective is required whereby a collective effort by all relevant actors leads as rapidly as possible to the enjoyment by all persons of an adequate home as a right. Ultimately, there is a growing recognition that a continuum of rights approaches is the most likely method to result in protecting the rights of the homeless and the inadequately housed. Coupled with this approach is the growing view that the provision of appropriate forms of security of tenure can act as an important means of preventing homelessness and, conversely, that insufficient tenure security can far too easily become the cause of homelessness. Human rights law and the rights that this system of law provides in support of housing rights and against forced eviction is developing rapidly in this regard, and the manner by which it can be used to protect against eviction is particularly noteworthy.

No state has ever, or could ever, hope to construct adequate housing for the entire population

Very few local governments have adopted policies that explicitly draw on human rights and none, at present, use international human rights to inform their planning and programming

Despite ... decentralization policies ... land management still tends to depend upon central or federal governments

Box 11.8 Brazil's City Statute

The City Statute, or the Brazilian Federal Law on Urban Development, was adopted in 2001. It defines the framework, principles and instruments to regulate the use of land for social purposes, the recognition of informal settlements as part of the city and the subject of rights, the democratic participation in urban management, and the empowerment of the municipalities as the main local agents entitled to regulate land usage and occupation.

One of the major components of the City Statute is that it includes provisions to simplify the regularization of informal land occupations. Before the adoption of this law, the regularization process in São Paulo included 80 steps, making approval of informal settlements virtually impossible, thus ensuring that the expansion of settlements could only occur in irregular ways. The City Statute thus allows for the decentralization of urban planning, thereby facilitating the work of municipal governments in developing local plans.

The City Statute is particularly innovative by introducing clear regulations governing democratic participation of civil society in urban planning and management. The municipalities must arrange their decision-making procedures in such a way that all the concerned parties can participate directly in the process of designing public policy, as well as in the subsequent management of programmes on housing, land and urban planning, which result from such policies. In essence, the statute empowers local government, through laws, urban planning and management tools, to determine how best to balance individual and collective interests in urban land.

The statute seeks to deter speculation and non-use of urban land (through taxation) so that land can be freed to provide housing space for the urban poor. Among many unique elements of the statute is the envisaged use of adverse possession rights (see Articles 8 and 9 below) to establish secure tenure and to enforce the social function of urban property. Yet, it should be noted that despite the City Statute, the poor remain excluded from official entitlements such as identity cards and social services.

Several articles of the City Statute provide the basis for perhaps the first legislative recognition in any country of the essential 'right to the city' as a basic element of citizenship and human rights:

- Article 2 states that the purpose of the urban policy is to support development of the social functions of the city and of urban property through a number of guidelines, including guaranteeing the right to sustainable cities. This is understood as the right to urban land, housing, environmental sanitation, urban infrastructure, transportation and public services, and to work and leisure for current and future generations.
- Article 8 entitles local governments to expropriate unused urban land after a period of five years if the obligation of the owner of the land to subdivide, build or use the property is not met.
- Article 9 entitles anyone who has possession of an urban area or building of less than 250 square metres for five years or more the right to title of dominion. The main provisions are that the land or building has been in the possession uninterruptedly and without contestation; that they use it for their own or their family's residence; and that the claimant is not the owner of any other real estate. The article also states that title will be conferred to men or women alike irrespective of their marital status; that the same possessor can only make use of this adverse possession entitlement once in their lives; and that the title can be transferred through inheritance.

Source: Estatuto das Cidades-Lei Federal no 10.257, 10 July 2001 (City Statute); Polis, 2002; Commission on Legal Empowerment of the Poor, 2006b, pp5–6

SUPPORTING THE VITAL ROLE OF LOCAL GOVERNMENT

The role of local government in diagnosing security of tenure conditions and then acting to provide security of tenure to all, within the shortest possible timeframe, is a vitally important component of any successful security of tenure policy. However, security of tenure is not the only concern of public bodies at the municipal level; local government responsibilities the world over are expanding, with many local governments effectively inundated with new powers and responsibilities, including the provision of services related to health, education, housing, water supply, policing, taxation and other matters. Its relevance to political empowerment, citizen involvement and delivery of public services has meant that local government has become a major arena of policy formulation. It is estimated that such processes are under way in some 80 per cent of all developing and transition countries.[37]

However, while the localization of governance has many positive features, weak and under-resourced local governments are far more common than those with the political will and financial basis for remedying tenure insecurity. One of the major problems, from the perspective of urban security and safety, is that very few local governments have adopted policies that explicitly draw on human rights and none, at present, use international human rights to inform their planning and programming. There are, however, signs of positive developments in this regard as some local governments have joined up in the Cities for Human Rights movement, which is working towards the development of a Charter of Human Rights in the City. Other local governments are developing their own city charters.[38]

Yet, despite the fact that decentralization policies in many countries have led to the transfer of responsibilities for urban management to local governments, land management still tends to depend upon central or federal governments. In general, national governments are still responsible for the regulation of land tenure, taxation systems and the registration of property rights and transactions. Furthermore, the administration of these tends to fall under the responsibility of regional delegations of central government agencies, rather than that of local governments. The main problem with this central government control over land management, however, is that they 'generally lack the financial and administrative resources to ensure effective implementation of their policies throughout the country. At the same time, intermediate-level management agencies with genuine decision-making power are generally weak or absent.'[39] The City Statute in Brazil is one example of how local governments can more effectively play a supportive role in expanding tenure security (see Box 11.8).

STRENGTHENING AND CLARIFYING THE HUMAN RIGHTS OBLIGATIONS OF NON-STATE ACTORS

The legal obligations emerging under human rights law have advanced considerably during recent years. Whereas human rights law has traditionally been seen largely as a set of rules governing the acts and omissions of states (see Boxes 6.17 and 6.18), in fact, this legal domain creates a very considerable degree of obligations requiring non-state actors to act in accordance with internationally recognized human rights principles. In terms of security of tenure, this would be particularly relevant both to companies and individuals capable of infringing upon the security of tenure rights and related rights of individuals and groups. Principle 1 of the United Nations Global Compact, a standard initiated by the former United Nations Secretary-General Kofi Annan and agreed to by various world business leaders, commits companies to 'support and respect the protection of international human rights within their sphere of influence'. The scope of the obligations accepted by companies under the Global Compact includes commitments ensuring rights to basic health, education and housing (if operations are located in areas where these are not provided). The website explaining the nature of the compact explicitly declares that the intent of those who support the compact is to 'prevent the forcible displacement of individuals, groups or communities' and to 'protect the economic livelihood of local communities'.[40]

Some companies have begun making tentative steps in the direction of preventing evictions. For instance, for several years BP has been refining its approach to involuntary resettlement and developing project management techniques that actively seek to prevent the economic and, especially, the physical displacement of communities in areas of operation. The aspiration of the company is not to physically displace communities against their will. It seeks to create active dialogue with communities who may be displaced, and to work in partnership with them to develop mutually acceptable solutions. It commits to ensure that their human rights are not threatened by project activities.[41]

The principle of corporate complicity in human rights abuses has also gained added credence in recent years, and may assist in clarifying the responsibilities of companies with respect to evictions and security of tenure. Complicity can take three forms:

Box 11.9 Private-sector companies and human rights violations

In describing the direct responsibility for evictions in Sudan, Human Rights Watch points the finger at the failure of one oil company to voice human rights concerns linked to the government's policy of forced displacement of civilians in areas allocated for oil extraction:

> *From the beginning of its involvement in Sudan ...* [the company] *resolutely refused to speak out against or to seriously investigate the Sudanese government's policy of forcibly displacing civilians from areas designated for oil extraction and the human rights abuses that have been an essential element of this policy. Yet, under modern concepts of corporate responsibility that ...* [the company] *claims to endorse, it had a responsibility to ensure that its business operations did not depend upon, or benefit from, gross human rights abuses such as those that have been committed by the government and its proxy forces in Sudan ...* [the company's] *complicity in the government's abuses was not limited to its inaction in the face of the continued displacement campaign rolling through the oil areas. Its activities in some cases assisted forcible displacement and attacks on civilians. For example, it allowed government forces to use ...* [its] *airfield and road infrastructure in circumstances in which it knew or should have known that the facilities would be used to conduct further displacement and wage indiscriminate or disproportionate military attacks and/or targeted civilians and civilian objects.*

Source: Amnesty International, 1998, pp81–82, 88

- *Direct complicity.* This occurs when a company knowingly assists a state in violating human rights. An example of this occurs when a company assists in the forced relocation of peoples in circumstances related to business activity.
- *Beneficial complicity.* This suggests that a company benefits directly from human rights abuses committed by someone else. For example, violations committed by security forces, such as the suppression of a peaceful protest against business activities or the use of repressive measures while guarding company facilities, are often cited in this context.
- *Silent complicity.* This describes the way in which human rights advocates see the failure by a company to raise the question of systematic or continuous human rights violations in its interactions with the appropriate authorities. For example, inaction or acceptance by companies of systematic discrimination in employment law against particular groups on the grounds of ethnicity or gender could bring accusations of silent complicity.[42]

The United Nations Global Compact ... commits companies to support and respect the protection of international human rights

The principle of corporate complicity in human rights abuses has ... gained added credence in recent years

Amnesty International urges all companies to establish procedures to ensure that all operations are examined for their potential impact on human rights and for their safeguards to ensure that company staff are never complicit in human rights abuses.[43] Some companies which have been viewed as directly complicit in forced evictions have been singled out by respected human rights NGOs (see Box 11.9).

Box 11.10 The Habitat Agenda: Recommendations on secure tenure

To facilitate access to land and security of tenure for all socio-economic groups, governments at the appropriate levels, including local authorities, should:

(a) Adopt an enabling legal and regulatory framework … to stimulate partnerships with the private business and community sectors, specifying recognized types of land tenure and prescribing procedures for the regularization of tenure …

(b) Provide institutional support, accountability and transparency of land management, and accurate information on landownership, land transactions and current and planned land use.

(c) Explore innovative arrangements to enhance the security of tenure, other than full legalization …

(d) Promote measures to ensure that women have equal access to credit for buying, leasing or renting land, and equal protection for the legal security of tenure of such land.

(f) Encourage, in particular, the participation of community and non-governmental organizations.

Source: Habitat Agenda, para 79

CONCLUDING REMARKS: RECOMMENDATIONS FOR FUTURE ACTION

It is crucial to recognize the forced evictions paradox that exists today, … a firm normative framework for addressing forced evictions exists …, and yet the scale of eviction continues to grow

There is no doubt that considerable progress has been made in recent years on the question of security of tenure. Policy at all levels has changed in important ways; as a result, taking all legal domains into account, there is today more legal (and *de facto*) protection against arbitrary and unlawful forced evictions than ever before. Furthermore, there is greater recognition than ever that forced evictions are *prima facie* human rights violations. Governments, international organizations, NGOs and other civil society actors are increasingly showing resolve and commitment to enable ever larger numbers of people to have access to appropriate forms of tenure security. It is widely agreed that security of tenure can be addressed in a pro-poor manner, and there is also widespread agreement that this does not happen automatically and that special care thus needs to be taken to address the concerns of the poor and other vulnerable groups in this regard.

At the same time, there is a compelling need to move the security of tenure agenda forward. We still cannot underestimate the scale of forced evictions or of market-based evictions. Furthermore, it is crucial to recognize the forced evictions paradox that exists today, where a firm normative framework for addressing forced evictions exists and is constantly being improved, and yet the scale of eviction continues to grow. We need to recognize that there are no universal solutions to providing security of tenure and that challenges in this regard tend to be solved in different manners in different locations. Rather, the goal must be to identify appropriate forms of secure tenure. Depending upon circumstances, there are a number of such acceptable forms of secure tenure in addition to the often presented ideal of individual title, and the merits of innovative policies are clear. There is also a pressing need for better monitoring and better data on security of tenure and forced evictions, and a necessity to simplify the process of providing security of tenure, but in ways that are acceptable to the communities involved and fully consistent with human rights principles.

As noted above, a whole range of international agreements are highlighting the importance of security of tenure. Many of these are presenting specific recommendations for action. Perhaps the most prominent of these international agreements is the Habitat Agenda (see Box 11.10). Indicative of the increasing focus on security of tenure, a myriad of other declarations and statements have been adopted by a range of organizations and conferences during the last decade. The main perspective of most of these statements is that the 'illegal' city, far from being an eyesore in need of eradication or eviction, is the core of better cities, which are more responsive to the rights and needs of people. Convincingly, there seems to be a general agreement on the importance of security of tenure and that the informal housing sector is realistically the only housing sector currently capable of providing land and dwellings to lower-income groups. There is also widespread agreement that the conditions in which the urban poor are forced to live are wholly unacceptable – whether in moral, ethical or human rights terms – and that much more needs to be done to provide lower-income groups with greater protection from abuse and insecurity. All would agree that a huge infusion of financial resources dedicated to expanding security of tenure protections are required, and new ways need to be developed to mobilize these from as many sources as possible. The Bathurst and Fukuoka declarations are fairly typical of such statements (see Boxes 11.11 and 11.12). Both declarations provide quite a comprehensive coverage of the types of actions that governments and other stakeholders should take to make security of tenure a reality for everyone.

In view of the fact that a myriad of recommendations has already been presented on how to achieve the goals of enhancing security of tenure and ending forced evictions, the focus of this Global Report is to attempt to reconcile the various recommendations made in the past. The main focus of this report is that an integral approach grounded in HLP

Box 11.11 The Bathurst Declaration on Land Administration for Sustainable Development

The Bathurst Declaration was adopted in 1999 at a workshop organized by the International Federation of Surveyors (FIG). The workshop was attended by representatives of a wide range of international organizations and other participants. The declaration recommends a global commitment to:

1 *[Provide] effective legal security of tenure and access to property for all men and women, including indigenous peoples, those living in poverty and other disadvantaged groups …*

8 *Improve security of tenure, access to land and to land administration systems through policy, institutional reforms and appropriate tools with special attention paid to gender, indigenous populations, the poor and other disadvantaged groups. In many nations, this will entail particular efforts in areas under customary or informal tenure and in urban areas where population growth is fast and deficiencies are most prevalent.*

Source: FIG, 1999

Box 11.12 The Fukuoka Declaration

The Fukuoka Declaration was adopted in 2001 at a seminar on securing land for the urban poor. The declaration asserted that:

1. *Secure tenure is a major contribution to the alleviation of poverty, to advancing sustainable livelihoods, to improving choices and opportunities for men and women; for accessing services; and for the recognition of the citizenship of the urban poor and the rights that go with such citizenship.*
2. *The fundamental principle of secure tenure endorsed by all Governments at the City Summit is a culture of governance and a legal and administrative system that prevents forced and arbitrary evictions from land and homes; provides effective redress for those who are so evicted whether by public agencies or private interests; and a fair hearing before, and alternative accommodation in the event of, any eviction or relocation that is adjudged to be necessary in the public interest.*
3. *Governments must adopt policies and where necessary reform legal and administrative systems to enable women to have access to land and credit through market processes; to inherit land; and to achieve secure tenure of land in ways which are no less favourable than those which apply to men. Policies must address historical imbalances which have disadvantaged women in relation to their access to land.*
4. *Secure tenure embraces a range of relationships between humankind and land. Governments must adopt policies and adapt administrative and legal systems to give recognition and endorsement to relationships based on customary tenure; practices and tenurial relationships developed by the urban poor themselves; communal forms of tenure; intermediate, flexible and innovative forms of tenure which are less than freehold tenure.*
5. *The participation of the urban poor is central to any proposed solutions to the challenges of developing policies and programmes to ensure secure tenure; governance systems must be adapted to facilitate and actively assist the urban poor to contribute to the development and the implementation of policies and programmes to that end.*

Source: UN-Habitat and ESCAP, 2002

rights is one such way of unifying the various approaches to providing security of tenure.

Clearly, much more needs to be accomplished in the quest for secure tenure for all. And, as discussed above, there are, in fact, hundreds of measures that can be instigated today to strengthen ongoing processes in support of security of tenure and against forced eviction. With hundreds of millions of people still living without security of tenure, clearly renewed action is required. The following sub-sections thus outline some areas for priority action for what will obviously be a long and arduous journey

Housing, land and property (HLP) rights-based housing and urban policies

For a start, there is a need for housing policies that are more consciously pro-poor and pro-human rights. Such a policy can be developed in its generic dimensions at the international level and subsequently applied within nations everywhere. A framework for such policies is outlined in Table 11.1. This comprehensive framework includes relevant elements from international law, including prohibition of any forms of discrimination, with provisions recommended by human settlements practitioners, all of which have direct implications for enhancing security of tenure or ending forced evictions. It should be noted that the steps indicated may not be applicable in all locations.

Support the awareness-raising work of local institutions and organizations

Experience from all over the world highlights the importance of local institutions and actors when it comes to protecting the housing rights of the poor. NGOs and CBOs in particular play essential roles in awareness-raising about HLP rights at national and local levels. Without their efforts, the number of people evicted during the last decades would have been considerably higher. In many instances such organizations are the only support mechanism available to slum dwellers when they are threatened by forced eviction. Even if there are laws protecting the housing rights of slum dwellers, this is not much help to people who are unaware of their rights, or unable to make use of appeals mechanisms where such do exist. International cooperation activities should thus increasingly encourage the formation of, enhance the capacities of and/or support the activities of such local organizations or institutions.

Even if there are laws protecting the housing rights of slum dwellers, this is not much help to people who are unaware of their rights, or unable to make use of appeals mechanisms where such do exist

Promoting residential justice

Every year, millions of people end up as refugees, IDPs and evictees, whether due to development projects, city beautification schemes, armed conflict, natural and human-made disasters, or other factors. Virtually all of these individuals are entirely innocent victims of circumstances beyond their control, and for many their wish to return to their original homes is never achieved. And, yet, every legal system on Earth – especially international law – clearly gives all human rights victims the right to an effective remedy – a means of

Table 11.1

A framework for developing housing, land and property (HLP) rights-based housing and urban policies

Goal		Steps
1	Prevent any detrimental discrimination with respect to housing	• Prohibit all forms of housing discrimination in law. • Strictly enforce such provisions with respect to tenancy and sale agreements. • Prevent any actual or perceived attempt at neighbourhood segregation.
2	Increase the scale of enjoyment of the right to security of tenure	• Develop quick and affordable measures for conferring title to slums and popular settlements currently without security of tenure. • Make public commitments to allow existing communities to continue to exist. • Expand national land and housing registration systems to allow for the inclusion of new tenure rights of the poor.
3	Ensure affordable housing to all	• Introduce or expand housing subsidy programmes to ensure that low-income groups are not forced to spend a disproportionate percentage of their income on satisfying housing requirements. • Develop rent regulation policies to protect low-income groups against unreasonable rent increases that they cannot afford.
4	Increase public expenditure on low-income housing programmes	• Ensure that public expenditure is commensurate to national housing requirements. • Ensure that a reasonable portion of international development assistance, as appropriate, is earmarked for housing construction or improvements.
5	Identify and allocate affordable land for low-income housing settlements	• Set annual benchmarks for identifying land for eventual use and/or allocation to low-income groups. • Develop longer-term plans for land allocation and distribution (particularly of state land) with a view to accurately addressing future housing needs.
6	Cease arbitrary forced evictions and other displacements	• Prohibit, in law, the practice of arbitrary forced evictions and other displacement. • Rescind any existing eviction plans. • Provide restitution and/or compensation to individuals subjected to arbitrary forced evictions or displacement in the past.
7	Provide infrastructure to existing low-income settlements	• Allocate sufficient public funds to providing infrastructure, including roads, water and sanitation systems, drainage, lighting and emergency life-saving systems. • Provide subsidies and/or incentives to the private sector to provide relevant infrastructure and services.
8	Encourage the formation of community-based organizations	• Promote community organizing as a key means of neighbourhood and housing improvement. • Protect the rights of community-based organizations to act in a manner that they deem fit to achieve improvements in housing and neighbourhood living conditions.
9	Promote housing finance programmes for the poor	• Provide assistance to low-income groups and encourage them to develop self-controlled housing finance and savings programmes.
10	Ensure the protection of all women's rights	• Ensure that women's rights to inherit housing, land and property are fully respected.
11	Promote special programmes for groups with special needs	• Develop special housing policies for vulnerable and other groups with particular housing needs, including the disabled, the elderly, minorities, indigenous peoples, children and others.
12	Provide stimulants to the private sector to construct low-income housing	• Develop tax credit programmes and other stimulants for the private sector to encourage the construction of low-income housing.

Recent developments ... will enable the international community to hold those ordering forced evictions and other housing rights violations accountable

obtaining justice by undoing the circumstances that resulted in their current housing predicament. This principle, however, is still too rarely applied to the displaced.

Renewed energy to achieve the restoration and the restitution of the housing rights of the world's 50 million or more displaced persons would considerably strengthen the seriousness accorded to security of tenure rights. Whenever refugees and IDPs themselves express a wish to return to their original homes, international standards now clearly provide for rights entitling them to reclaim, repossess and re-inhabit these homes.

If HLP rights are to be taken seriously, there are strong grounds on which to discourage the impunity almost invariably enjoyed by violators of these rights

Applying international criminal law to forced evictions

Although violations of housing, land and property rights are not always considered as seriously as violations of other human rights, recent developments involving the prosecution of war criminals and those who have committed crimes against humanity will enable the international community to hold those ordering forced evictions and other housing rights violations accountable. Armed conflicts result in thousands and sometimes millions of individuals being forcibly evicted from their homes or forced to flee their homes for their own safety, despite protections under international humanitarian law expressly prohibiting such evictions unless the security of the inhabitants can only be assured through temporary displacement.[44]

Since the violent conflicts in the Balkans, Rwanda, East Timor and elsewhere, considerable attention has been devoted to creating international courts and commissions entrusted with bringing those individuals responsible for war crimes and crimes against humanity to justice. The statutes of the International Criminal Court, and the international tribunals on the former Yugoslavia and Rwanda each provide the legal basis necessary to prosecute persons responsible for crimes of 'destruction or appropriation of property', 'destruction of cities', 'inhumane acts' or 'ordering the displacement of the civilian population'. The Rome Statute of the International Criminal Court declares forcible transfer as a crime against humanity.

As such, HLP rights violations carried out during armed conflicts or those generally subject to the jurisdiction of the various mechanisms developed to prosecute war criminals can now act as one of the grounds on which to base complaints for HLP (or residential) justice. If HLP rights are to be taken seriously, there are strong grounds on which to discourage the impunity almost invariably enjoyed by violators of these rights. Whether it is those who advocate ethnic cleansing, those who sanction violent and illegal forced evictions, those who call for laws and policies that clearly result in homelessness, or those who fail to end systematic discrimination against women in the land and housing sphere – all those promoting such violations should be held accountable. The recommendations in 2005 by the United Nations Special Envoy on *Operation Murambatsvina* in

Zimbabwe are indicative of this trend, as she recommends that the government 'should hold to account those responsible for the injury caused by the operation' (see Box 5.14).

A global moratorium on forced evictions

Examples the world over have shown that forced evictions are not an inevitable consequence of economic development, nor are they the necessary price of progress or an adjunct to civic infrastructure improvements. Forced evictions are a largely preventable source of inconceivable human anguish. While some evictions may be impossible to avoid (under exceptional circumstances), the overwhelming majority of the forced evictions already carried out and those that are planned can be prevented and ultimately made unnecessary. An initial global moratorium on forced evictions, therefore, over a period of five years could be one concrete means for ending a practice that patently violates a range of recognized human rights.

United Nations member states could proclaim such a moratorium at a future United Nations General Assembly session. During the five-year moratorium period, each state would cease carrying out forced evictions, review domestic legislation on these practices, carry out any legislative reform required to adequately protect people against forced eviction, all the while taking a series of well-financed and concerted series of steps to confer security of tenure on all of the world's communities currently without such protections. This initial five-year period would see national security of tenure action plans developed in all member states. Such plans could be coordinated by initiatives such as the Global Campaign for Secure Tenure and would involve more positive and suitable approaches to security of tenure emerging, combined with renewed commitments and resources dedicated to the improvement of existing homes and communities.

A global mechanism to monitor the realization of housing rights

As noted in Chapter 6, there is a glaring lack of accurate and comprehensive data on security of tenure and forced evictions. Similarly, there is also a scarcity of data on other components of the right to adequate housing. This is so despite the fact that all state parties to the ICESCR are required, by international law, to submit such data to the CESCR every five years (see Box 5.4). Several different efforts are already under way to collect such data, including as part of the effort to report on the implementation of the MDG on improving the lives of 100 million slum dwellers by 2020. Yet, it is time for the establishment of a mechanism to collect a comprehensive set of data on the progressive realization of HLP rights. The effort to design and implement a set of housing rights indicators by the United Nations Housing Rights Programme (see Box 5.5) is an important step in this direction since it gives advocates and governments alike information needed to establish benchmarks, evaluate success (and failure) and implement effective policies.

A global moratorium on forced evictions ... could be one concrete means for ending a practice that ... violates a range of ... human rights

Perhaps the time for addressing this in a more compressive manner has arrived, with the ongoing reform of the human rights framework and mechanisms within the United Nations system, including that of treaty bodies, in general, and the reporting procedure, in particular. It has been argued that use of appropriate indicators for assessing human rights implementation could contribute to streamlining the reporting process, make it more transparent and effective, reduce the reporting burden, and, above all, improve follow-up on the recommendations and concluding observations of the CESCR at the national level. The ongoing work of the United Nations Housing Rights Programme regarding the development of housing rights indicators is a good start and should be supported, particularly in the context of developing a comprehensive mechanism for continuous monitoring of the progressive realization of all human rights.

It is time for the establishment of a mechanism to collect a comprehensive set of data on the progressive realization of HLP rights

NOTES

1 See, for instance, COHRE, 2006.
2 See CESCR, General Comment No 15.
3 UN-Habitat, 2004b.
4 ICESCR, Article 11(1).
5 CESCR, General Comment No 4, para 8. For an in-depth analysis of the right to adequate housing, see UN-Habitat and OHCHR, 2002.
6 CESCR, General Comment No 4.
7 *Ibid*, para 11.
8 ICESCR, Article 2(1).
9 Commission on Human Rights, Resolution 1993/77.
10 Commission on Human Rights, Resolution 2004/28.
11 UN Document E/CN.4/1998/53/Add.2, Principle 6.
12 CESCR, General Comment No 7, para 18. See also UN-Habitat and OHCHR, 2002.
13 See United Nations Human Rights Committee, General Comment No 27, para 7.
14 Approved in 2005 by the United Nations Sub-Commission on the Protection and Promotion of Human Rights. See also FAO et al (2007) for practical ways of implementing the Pinheiro Principles.
15 Universal Declaration of Human Rights, Article 17.
16 Schabas, 1991.
17 CESCR, General Comment No 4, para 7.
18 Buyse, 2006.
19 See Leckie (2003b), which provides an overview of more than 12 restitution initiatives.
20 UN Documents E/CN.4/Sub.2/2005/17, Principle 2.1. Additional relevant provisions can be found throughout Principles 2 and 10.
21 Williams, 2006, p173.
22 Leckie, 2005a.
23 World Bank, 2003b, p186.
24 Payne, 2001b, p8.
25 Payne, 2005.
26 UNCHS and ILO, 1995.
27 Payne, 2002.
28 A *favela* is an informal settlement, normally found in the periphery of the city. In contrast, *cortiços* are overpopulated high rises.
29 Payne, 2005.
30 United Nations, 2005.
31 Payne and Majale, 2004.
32 1998 Maastricht Guidelines on Violations of Economic, Social and Cultural Rights.
33 Karapuu and Rosas, 1990 (Act No 380/1987, Article 8(2) and Child Welfare Act No 683/1983, respectively).
34 1994 German Federal Welfare Assistance Act, sections 15(a) and 72, respectively.
35 CESCR, General Comment No 7, para 16.
36 *Ibid*, para 14.
37 International Council on Human Rights Policy, 2005.
38 *Ibid*.
39 Durand-Lasserve, 1998, p242.
40 See www.unglobalcompact.org/AboutTheGC/TheTenPrinciples/principle1.html.
41 See www.bp.com/sectiongenericarticle.do?categoryId=9013904&contentId=7026915.
42 Clapham, 2006.
43 *Ibid*, p222.
44 See, for example, Article 49 of the Geneva Convention Relative to the Protection of Civilian Persons in Time of War, and Article 17 of Protocol II to the Geneva Convention.

CHAPTER

12

MITIGATING THE IMPACTS OF DISASTERS

This Global Report has shown that there is no shortage of evidence for the negative impacts of natural and human-made disasters on human life, property and the environment in urban areas. Rapid urbanization is, in turn, fast becoming a force shaping who, where and when disaster strikes. Economic development planning and urban management systems that lead to inequality, poverty and poor governance also accumulate disaster risk in urban areas. Changing hazard landscapes, partly caused by urban growth, but also linked to environmental change, further contribute to the need for a dynamic set of tools and approaches with which to reduce risk and enhance resilience in urban areas.

Rapid urbanization is ... fast becoming a force shaping who, where and when disaster strikes

This chapter examines future policy directions in disaster risk reduction. It concentrates on policies that can contribute towards effective disaster preparedness and prevention and improved processes of relief, recovery and reconstruction post-disaster. At heart, these are agendas for increasing the disaster resilience of local communities, civil society and government organizations. Policies and practices at the city, national, regional and international levels are identified, and the factors underlying their success examined. The need to reduce human vulnerability, incorporate disaster risk reduction within national planning, and the requirement for this to be built on interdisciplinary and inter-sectoral collaboration drive the central concerns of this chapter.

The chapter starts by reviewing existing international frameworks for supporting national- and city-level risk reduction initiatives. Specific policy concerns for risk reduction are then outlined, including land-use planning, the design of disaster-resistant buildings and infrastructure, early warning and emergency response, and reconstruction. The role of participatory and inclusive strategies and polices in mitigating disaster impacts is subsequently considered.

INTERNATIONAL FRAMEWORKS FOR ACTION

Urban development and disaster risk reduction are two critical agendas for international development policy and action. Increasing numbers of people and resources based in urban locations, and growing numbers of people affected by disasters, have led to the integration of the disaster risk reduction agenda in major international frameworks of action. This section examines the ways in which urban disaster risk affects progress towards achieving the Millennium Development Goals (MDGs), the overarching framework influencing international and national development policy. An assessment is then presented of the Habitat Agenda and the Hyogo Framework for Action, 2005–2015, two international agreements adopted by the majority of governments. Both set out programmes of action to reduce urban disaster risk. Some of the barriers that hinder the integration of disaster risk reduction policies on the ground are also examined.

The Millennium Development Goals (MDGs)

The MDGs provide an international framework for development work that extends to disaster management. The MDGs are empowered by the Millennium Declaration,[1] which calls for the international community to

> *intensify cooperation to reduce the number and effects of natural and man-made disasters* (IV, 23, v)

and to:

> *... spare no effort to ensure that children and all civilian populations that suffer disproportionately the consequences of natural disasters, genocide, armed conflicts and other humanitarian emergencies are given every assistance and protection so that they can resume normal life as soon as possible.* (VI, 26)

During 2001, a road map for the implementation of the United Nations Millennium Declaration[2] was released that prioritized the following agenda for risk reduction:

- developing early warning systems, vulnerability mapping, technological transfer and training;
- supporting interdisciplinary and inter-sectoral partnerships, improved scientific research on the causes of natural disasters and better international cooperation to

Box 12.1 National initiatives to integrate urban disaster risk reduction and the Millennium Development Goals (MDGs)

With international support, national planning for urban development has begun to integrate disaster risk reduction and the Millennium Development Goals (MDGs). The following cases are indicative of such integrated work.

MDG 1: Eradicating extreme poverty and hunger.
In India, the Self-Employed Women's Association (SEWA), a trade union representing low-income informal-sector women workers, offers its members a variety of micro-insurance packages. Over ten years, 2000 women have received US$327,400 in claims. Following the 2001 Gujarat earthquake, SEWA provided insurance benefits and microfinance to regenerate destroyed livelihoods, homes, working capital and assets. Within two weeks, SEWA's insurance team surveyed over 2500 insured members' claims of damage and asset loss, mainly destruction of houses.

MDG 2: Universal primary education.
Colombia has linked achieving MDG 2 directly with seismic vulnerability analysis of a school building programme in the capital city, Bogotá. This programme was developed by Proyectos y Diseños Ltda[6] in April 2000. The programme developed a risk evaluation methodology that staff in the Education Ministry were trained to implement. Primary evaluations were then conducted in all schools to determine seismic vulnerability. Priorities among individual schools were subsequently assigned according to available budgets. In some cases, more detailed vulnerability analyses and structural retrofitting studies were conducted.

MDG 3: Promoting gender equality and empowering women.
In Armenia, the non-governmental organization (NGO) Women for Development has partnered other agencies in a national survey for seismic protection and has worked towards including seismic protection courses in school curricula. This has enabled the inclusion of education games and contributed to a greater acceptance of women's participation as specialists in a wide range of disaster reduction and response activities where men traditionally dominate, including vulnerability and impact surveying, academic work, emergency services and civil protection.

MDG 6: Combating infectious diseases.
Tajikistan has integrated this goal with risk reduction through the Dushanbe Water Contamination Response Programme sponsored by the European Commission's Humanitarian Aid Department (ECHO). This programme aims to improve the access of targeted health facilities to safe and potable water supply in the capital city, as well as their disease outbreak response capacity. The programme directly addresses MDG 6, which deals with the containment of infectious diseases, by increasing preparedness and response levels in case of a possible disaster. It seeks to build community capacity for self-management of health needs by improving public awareness in the prevention of water-borne diseases.

MDG 7: Ensuring environmental sustainability.
As part of its efforts towards meeting target 11, which is on slums, UN-Habitat is active in applying inclusive strategies to support slum upgrading and, where appropriate, as a mechanism for risk reduction. In Mozambique, rapid unplanned urbanization has brought flood-prone land into residential use in Maputo, a city where more than 70 per cent of the population live in slums. Here, slum upgrading has fostered risk reduction. The wider programme supported training and capacity-building, participatory land-use planning and physical interventions at the local level. Local government and community groups, as well as state ministries, participated. This inclusive approach was instrumental in leading to the revision of planning regulations, and a movement away from dealing with floods through reactive emergency management, towards a more proactive and developmental approach.

MDG 8: Developing global partnerships for development.
In Turkey, in partnership with the World Bank, ProVention Consortium has been promoting best practice examples of disaster mitigation and future cost reductions through measures such as a US$505 million reconstruction loan to Turkey that included measures to update and enforce building codes. Poor quality construction was responsible for many of the lives lost during the 1999 Marmara earthquake. The reconstruction programme will introduce better planning for land use (possible links to MDGs) and requires compulsory insurance for housing. Emergency response management will also be upgraded.

Source: ISDR, undated a, undated b; Spaliviero, 2006

reduce the impact of climate variables, such as El Niño and La Niña;

- encouraging governments to address the problems created by megacities, the location of settlements in high-risk areas and other human-made determinants of disasters;
- encouraging governments to incorporate disaster risk reduction within national planning processes, including building codes.

Disaster risk reduction cuts across each of the eight MDGs, but is not identified as a separate target for action. This has reduced the visibility of risk reduction to some degree. However, the importance of integrating risk reduction with safeguard gains from disaster loss has become increasingly apparent. A number of international organizations – such as the United Nations International Strategy for Disaster Reduction (ISDR),[3] the UK Department for International Development (DFID)[4] and the United Nations Development Programme (UNDP)[5] – have reviewed the ways in which risk reduction can contribute towards meeting the MDGs.

The ISDR has surveyed disaster risk reduction strategies that have been designed purposely to contribute to meeting individual MDG targets. Box 12.1 presents some of these findings that draw from urban projects and programmes. In addition to direct contributions towards achieving individual MDGs, reducing disaster impacts frees up resources, including overseas development aid.

... disasters are a serious impediment to meeting the MDGs

In 2005, progress towards meeting the MDGs was reviewed by the independent United Nations Millennium Project.[7] The resulting report recognizes that disasters are a serious impediment to meeting the MDGs. It calls for the mainstreaming of risk reduction strategies within MDG-based poverty reduction strategies. The report recommends four pathways for achieving better integration, all of which have relevance for urban disaster risk reduction:

- *Investment in disaster-proof infrastructure, including the application of disaster standards in new building and retrofitting existing buildings and infrastructure.* This is a particularly important task for rapidly growing cities since uncontrolled urban growth increases vulnerability to disasters. Risk assessments, land-use planning and construction standards are identified as key components of any urban risk reduction strategy.
- *The protection of livelihoods.* Social safety nets to safeguard livelihoods and lives during slow-onset disaster or during protected periods of recovery are supported, with employment guarantees and micro-finance schemes suggested as appropriate for urban contexts.
- *Governments investment in building and strengthening national and local early warning systems to monitor conditions and provide advance warning of potential disasters.* Surveillance systems can include field monitoring, remote sensing and meteorological forecasting. Public information campaigns are important for raising awareness of the risks of natural disasters and adequate responses.
- *Emergency preparedness and contingency plans are needed to minimize loss and maximize efficiency and equity in post-disaster relief and reconstruction.* Plans should include strategies for evacuation, emergency safety zones, insurance schemes, and the pre-location and financing of humanitarian resources for rapid distribution. As part of their contingency plans, governments must establish mechanisms for delivering emergency services after a disaster has occurred, especially immediate healthcare, to prevent the outbreak of diseases among displaced populations. Developed countries should establish a far more systematic financial mechanism for disaster response, including contingent credit investments for individual countries.

The Habitat Agenda ... includes disaster risk reduction amongst its commitments for action

Box 12.2 The Habitat Agenda: International commitments for action to reduce urban disaster risk

The following commitments directly address disaster risk reduction. Many other commitments for action impact indirectly upon vulnerability and risk through targeting urban poverty, infrastructure and service provision, pollution, land-use planning and urban governance.

Commitment 40 (l):

Promoting shelter and supporting basic services and facilities for education and health for the homeless, displaced persons, indigenous people, women and children who are survivors of family violence, persons with disabilities, older persons, victims of natural and man-made disasters and people belonging to vulnerable and disadvantaged groups, including temporary shelter and basic services for refugees.

Commitment 43 (z):

Preventing man-made disasters, including major technological disasters, by ensuring adequate regulatory and other measures to avoid their occurrence, and reducing the impacts of natural disasters and other emergencies on human settlements, inter alia, through appropriate planning mechanisms and resources for rapid people-centred responses that promote a smooth transition from relief, through rehabilitation, to reconstruction and development, taking into account cultural and sustainable dimensions; and rebuilding disaster-affected settlements in a manner that reduces future disaster-related risks and makes the rebuilt settlements accessible to all.

Source: Habitat Agenda, 1996

The Habitat Agenda

The 1996 Istanbul Declaration on Human Settlements[8] endorses 'the universal goals of ensuring adequate shelter for all and making human settlements safer, healthier and more liveable, equitable, sustainable and productive'. In particular, paragraph 4 reaffirms commitment to integrated urban development:

> *To improve the quality of life within human settlements, we must combat the deterioration of conditions that, in most cases, particularly in developing countries, have reached crisis proportions. To this end, we must address comprehensively ... planning; growing insecurity and violence; environmental degradation; and increased vulnerability to disasters.*

This integrated approach to urbanization presented in the Habitat Agenda is entirely compatible with disaster risk reduction, which takes disaster risk to be a product of the unsustainable trends identified in paragraph 4 of the Istanbul Declaration. The United Nations General Assembly Resolution S25.2 of 9 June 2001[9] reaffirmed that the Istanbul Declaration and the Habitat Agenda provide the basic framework for future sustainable human settlements development.

The Habitat Agenda is the sister document to the Istanbul Declaration and the main political document directing international work on urban development. The document recognizes the World Conference on Natural Disaster Reduction (which took place in Yokohama, in 1994) and includes disaster risk reduction among its commitments for action (see Box 12.2). In addition to commitments, some 31 recommendations are made that cover all aspects of disaster risk reduction, including building partnerships between local organizations, government and the international community; risk mapping (including hazardous waste); investing in human capital for risk management; emergency planning; early warning; land-use planning, including the location of dangerous industrial plants; recognizing the needs of women and children; and planning for reconstruction.

As the leading United Nations agency for human settlements issues, UN-Habitat has a commitment to reduce disaster risk and build this into the reconstruction of human settlements. It seeks to influence partners and, in particular, to provide guidance at the national level, as well as through urban professional practice. Building on the commitments of the Habitat Agenda and on dialogue with its partners during the second and third World Urban Forums (2004 and 2006, respectively), UN-Habitat has developed a conceptual Framework for Sustainable Relief and Reconstruction. This framework identifies priority areas for action in making urban areas more resilient in the face of disaster risk (see Box 12.3).

Box 12.3 The UN-Habitat Framework for Sustainable Relief and Reconstruction

The Framework for Sustainable Relief and Reconstruction is the key guide used by UN-Habitat to support humanitarian agencies and local and national governments, and to refine the practice of building back better. The framework builds on UN-Habitat's experience and strength in assisting local capacity development in pre-disaster preparedness and mitigation and in post-disaster response and reconstruction.

The aim of the framework is to promote reconstruction and risk reduction strategies that promote longer-term sustainable development gains, as well as reduce disaster risk in human settlements. Consultation with partners has led to the elaboration of seven key thematic areas of the framework:

Disaster mitigation and vulnerability reduction

Often, the root causes of vulnerability are known, but they are seldom addressed. When building a culture of prevention, one needs to overcome preferences for short- over long-term development options and to demonstrate the cost effectiveness of risk reduction over post-disaster reconstruction. The framework recommends integrating disaster risk reduction within national and local development and poverty reduction plans, emphasizing risk reduction in human settlements rather than reconstruction as the mode of managing disaster risk, as well as the need for cross-sectoral working.

Land and property administration

Housing, land and property rights are major challenges in reconstruction. This is often exacerbated by the disintegration of institutions governing and protecting land and property rights after disaster and can increase social tension and add to conflict. Restitution problems requiring resolution have challenged reconstruction following the 2004 Indian Ocean Tsunami, Hurricane Katrina in 2005 and the 2005 South Asian earthquake.

Longer-term shelter strategies

It is vital to consider the long-term consequences of post-disaster shelter and infrastructure. The importing of prefabricated dwellings proves a cheap and easily transportable short-term solution; but construction standards are often culturally inappropriate, environmentally unsustainable or not built to hazard-resistant standards. The transition from temporary to permanent housing continues to take too long and, in some cases, is never achieved. Part of the resolution of this challenge lies in planning for long-term recovery at the initial relief stage. This will also enable the more efficient use of emergency resources.

Local economic recovery

Even after disaster, affected communities have many resources and skills that can be used as a base to rebuild the local economy. Recovery and reconstruction interventions, especially those in the shelter and infrastructure sectors, provide a real opportunity for local economic recovery, and even for increasing the local skill and experience base. Re-establishing small-scale production, support for local market development and skill training can all be part of shelter reconstruction programmes.

Public participation and good governance

Disaster risk reduction and reconstruction are opportunities for engaging civil society actors in development. Effective risk reduction can utilize participatory vulnerability and risk assessments to shape local preparedness and response planning. Inclusive decision-making in recovery that includes women will be more likely to identify opportunities and challenges for 'building back better'. The local government is best positioned to coordinate public participation, and a first step is to strengthen the capacity of local government in community development, disaster preparedness and recovery planning.

Partnerships

Making best use of the limited resources available for risk reduction and reconstruction is facilitated through the building of partnerships between all stakeholders (local, national and international), the public sector, civil society and the private sector, including the media. Partnerships allow individual organizations to contribute from positions of strength and can control overlapping functions. Partnerships can also be a pathway for transferring skills and for developing relationships that contribute to development in addition to reconstruction and risk reduction work.

Capacity-building

The integration of development and disaster management at the points of preparedness and recovery provide opportunities for skills enhancement, knowledge transfer and the building of confidence that can empower local actors, especially women. Capacity-building is often supported by legislation and national or local vulnerability reduction plans that help to move the focus of risk management away from a narrow interest in building standards and engineering techniques to embrace the social, economic and institutional aspects of life that shape disaster risk.

The opportunities for moving towards more sustainable relief and reconstruction methods outlined in this framework are designed to be compatible with the objectives of the Hyogo Framework for Action.

Source: UN-Habitat, 2006a, 2006d

The Hyogo Framework for Action, 2005–2015

International action for disaster risk reduction is given direction by the Hyogo Framework for Action, 2005–2015: Building the Resilience of Nations and Communities to Disaster.[10] The framework identifies five general priorities for action:

- Ensure that disaster risk reduction is a national and local priority with a strong institutional basis for implementation.
- Enhance early warning through improvements in the identification, assessment and monitoring of disaster risks.
- Use knowledge, innovation and education to build a culture of safety and resilience at all levels.
- Reduce the underlying risk factors that are currently built into development paths.
- Strengthen disaster preparedness for effective response at all levels.

The Hyogo Framework recognizes unplanned urbanization as a key factor driving increasing global vulnerability and losses to natural and human-made disasters. Detailed urban-specific recommendations encourage two priority actions for urban development and land-use planning:

The Hyogo Framework recognizes unplanned urbanisation as a key factor driving increasing global vulnerability and losses to...disasters

> *Institutions dealing with urban development should provide information to the public on disaster reduction options prior to constructions, land purchase or land sale.* (Section 3, i (f))
>
> *Incorporate disaster risk assessments into the urban planning and management of disaster-prone human settlements, [particularly] highly populated areas and quickly urbanizing settlements. The issues of informal or non-permanent housing and the location of housing in high-risk areas should be addressed as priorities, including in the framework of urban poverty reduction and slum-upgrading programmes.* (Section 4, iii (n))

In addition, international organizations are encouraged to support states in building and maintaining urban search and rescue capacity, mainly through the development of mechanisms to mainstream disaster risk reduction into development financing and assistance for urban development.

Recommendations for action also include many cross-cutting themes that apply to urban, but also to peri-urban and rural, contexts. These include human resource development, early warning, emergency planning, and partnerships between local, national and international actors.

The UN-Habitat Framework on Sustainable Relief and Reconstruction ... identifies future opportunities for ... integrating disaster risk reduction and urban development

Plans for implementing the Hyogo Framework have been agreed and explicitly acknowledge the need to break the negative spiral of poverty, accelerated urbanization, environmental degradation and disaster.[11] Work is required at national and international levels to build the institutional structures that can take the Hyogo Framework forward. A survey of progress made at the national level in 2006 indicates that some good progress has already been made.[12] A total of 60 governments have designated focal points with responsibility for implementing the framework and 40 countries have reported concrete disaster risk reduction activities. Examples of reported national-level progress are as follows:

- The strengthening of national institutions for risk reduction has been the area where most progress has been achieved, to date. In many countries, this is a first step in building the organizational infrastructure from which more targeted initiatives can be developed. Examples of progress include work in Argentina, where the Ministry of Federal Planning, Public Investments and Services has embarked on a two-year national programme to mainstream disaster risk reduction at the national, provincial and local levels as part of an overall Federal Land-Use Planning Strategy. In El Salvador, authorities have developed a National Action Plan for Disaster Risk Reduction. In Uganda, disaster reduction has been mainstreamed into a national Poverty Eradication Plan. Nepal has designed a national strategy and comprehensive national plan on disaster reduction. Indonesia has prepared a comprehensive disaster management law on response, risk mitigation and recovery for all hazards. Bolivia included disaster risk reduction in its national development plan. Cuba is implementing a policy of risk assessment in all of its development initiatives.
- National risk assessment and early warning programmes have also been developed. There is increasing investment in seismic hazard monitoring capacity in several Central Asian countries. Thailand, the Maldives and ten countries in East Africa with coastal settlements have strengthened their capacities in flood and tsunami early-warning and response systems.
- Efforts by governments aimed at building a culture of awareness through public education and information programmes include disaster reduction in national curricula (e.g. in Indonesia and Kazakhstan). In China, promoting awareness through schools is complemented by public awareness campaigns focusing on communities and villages. There are also many examples of graduate and postgraduate studies that have integrated disaster risk reduction. One example is the University of the West Indies in Jamaica.
- A national policy to reduce underlying risk factors is essential, but requires strong political will. Some laudable progress has already been made by India through creating a training programme for safer construction. Cuba and Grenada have also developed programmes for safer construction. In Simeulue Island (Indonesia), community knowledge has been used in the design of local regulations and the promotion of forest and mangrove conservation.
- The challenge of integrating risk reduction within emergency recovery plans has already been met by Bolivia and Guatemala. Elsewhere, while integration has not yet been achieved, progress has been made on strengthening disaster preparedness and response planning in Comoros, China, the Islamic Republic of Iran and Tajikistan. Pakistan has developed a national scheme for volunteers and Cuba, the Dominican Republic, Haiti and Jamaica have initiatives to increase their preparedness and response capacity.

Integrating disaster risk reduction and urban development

Progress is being made in bringing together urban development, disaster risk reduction and humanitarian action. The UN-Habitat Framework on Sustainable Relief and Reconstruction is a key document in this process. Here, UN-Habitat identifies future opportunities for working with the international community, local authorities and communities in integrating disaster risk reduction and urban development. The vision of sustainable relief and reconstruction encompasses all phases of disaster management, from prevention through relief to recovery, and aims to provide a

Box 12.4 Integrating disaster risk reduction, urban planning and housing in El Salvador

Since Hurricane Mitch in 1998 and earthquakes in 2001, development and housing organizations in El Salvador have begun to integrate risk reduction within their programmes and projects. Increased work at the municipal level, greater focus on participation and changes in housing finance during the 1990s triggered the adoption of new operational approaches in providing social housing. Changes in the delivery of housing were accompanied by the uptake of new tools that have enabled an integrated risk reduction approach. Key among these tools have been:

Risk checklists for improved housing quality control. These were introduced after the earthquakes of 2001 to fill a gap in national construction legislation and enforcement.

Risk maps and assessments. Guidelines for local risk mapping have been available since 1992, but have only been applied comprehensively by municipalities since the recent disasters. Maps have been used for local awareness-raising and in digitized format for land-use planning.

Strategic frameworks. A strategic framework for integrated housing and risk reduction was introduced by the Fundación Salvadoreña de Apoyo Integral (FUSAI)[13] in 2004. Within this plan, housing is repositioned and is no longer seen as a final goal, but as a component that, with other activities, can contribute towards sustainable development. Guidelines for integrated land-use planning and risk reduction were also introduced by the German Government's International Development Agency, the Deutsche Gesellschaft für Technische Zusammenarbeit (GTZ) in 2003.

Risk indicators. These have been developed with the aim of building a more quantitative instrument to aid policy decision-making, supported by the Inter-American Development Bank.

To enable the implementation of integrated projects, some organizations have adapted their internal structures and other new organizations have been created. Existing organizations have broadened their mandates to incorporate new collaborations. This is also reflected in statements in strategic plans and the creation of focal points for risk reduction inside urban planning and housing organizations. Since 2001, legislative changes have included the updating of laws and regulations for construction and urban planning; the integration of risk reduction within national housing policy and within a draft policy for land use; change in government housing finance; and the integration of risk reduction within municipal land-use and related enactments.

Source: Warmsler, 2006a

conceptual framework for broadening the portfolios of humanitarian and development actors.

Yet, key challenges to a more integrated and sustainable approach persist, perpetuated by institutional structures at all levels. International progress on joint funding for sustainable reconstruction is tangible but slow. At the municipal level, challenges vary, but include differences in institutional capacity and political will. Box 12.4 presents the findings of a review of innovations in El Salvador that have overcome some of these barriers and enabled a more integrated approach to risk reduction.

It has been argued that the failure to integrate risk reduction and urban development starts with overly specialized training, which serves to compartmentalize disaster management and urban planning, rather than foster a culture of interdisciplinarity.[14] This is exacerbated when urban planners have limited post-disaster experience, until their city is hit by a disaster, although city exchanges and training in post-conflict reconstruction can help to overcome this challenge. This disciplinary and experiential gap is all too often translated into the absence of urban development professionals from disaster response and reconstruction efforts, particularly in the planning and management of temporary housing. This misses an opportunity for disaster response to integrate the knowledge of local urban planning professionals.

Professional separation results in the use of different working priorities, concepts and terminologies that maintain barriers between the different professionals.[15] Institutional differences and competition for funding breeds scepticism about the tools and capacities of other disciplines. Urban planning is criticized for predominantly employing a physical/engineering approach, often related to expensive large-scale engineering measures, which has only limited relevance to the language and working priorities of risk reduction. Potential for developing more integrated, interdisciplinary risk reduction projects is further limited by donors' separate budget lines for development and emergency relief.[16]

Ways beyond the impasse in communication between disaster management and urban development professionals are opening up; but more work is needed. International organizations, as well as national and local governments, can develop internal mechanisms to foster interaction between these practitioner communities. Funding cycles for reconstruction and relief projects are often rapid and target specific aspects of reconstruction, rather than taking an integrated approach. This undermines capacity for building integrated teams. At the national level, legal structures for risk reduction and urban planning are frequently separate, absent or lack national–municipal collaboration.

...the failure to integrate risk reduction and urban development starts with overly specialized training

RISK REDUCTION THROUGH LAND-USE PLANNING

Effective land-use planning requires evidence-based and transparent decision-making. Without up-to-date and accurate information, as well as clear decision-making criteria, effective urban development planning becomes difficult.

Land-use planning for risk reduction needs appropriate tools and must be set within a supportive and responsive urban governance regime.

Because of the scale of resources and the number of people whose lives can be affected by land-use planning, strong governance systems are required to protect the legitimacy of decisions and to maximize compliance. Legal instruments and capacity for oversight and enforcement are also required to support implementation. Implementation and the quality of planning decision-making are often strongest when strategies are inclusive. Governance systems that include local voices and foster individual and local responsibility for safe land use, and that can support local, decentralized leadership, can be more effective than overly centralized regimes. This is particularly the case where rapid urbanization has stretched capacity for oversight and enforcement, and where centralized approaches are not practical. A balance must be kept between decentralized responsibility and the maintenance of minimum standards for safe land-use planning. This is a difficult balance to get right and a large part of the recipe for success surrounds the generation and distribution of information and knowledge on land use, vulnerability and hazard, and the development and use of more inclusive decision-support tools.

Re-planning the city to design out risks inherited from past planning decisions is important

The advantages of inclusive strategies for urban risk reduction are discussed later in this chapter. This section concentrates on actions driven by municipalities and local government, although a common theme for success is partnership with other local actors, international organizations, the state and the private sector. Land-use planning needs to face a number of challenges, some of which were discussed in Chapter 8. Key future challenges include the following:

Participatory GIS can enable the extension of risk management and urban land-use planning into informal and slum settlements

- The global proliferation of slums calls for innovative land-use planning procedures. Providing frameworks for more participatory planning and extending planning into informal settlements can help to build resilience in the face of risk from natural and human-made hazards. Integrated projects and programmes for slum upgrading emerged during the 1990s, and these provide a background of experience for innovation built on inclusive planning.[17]
- Re-planning the city to design out risks inherited from past planning decisions is important. Examples of this include planning for buffer zones (using mangroves, salt marshes and river floodplains to absorb hazard); and preventing the establishment of major industrial and port facilities on reclaimed land in cities at risk from earthquake that may be prone to liquefaction, such as Kingston (Jamaica) and Kobe (Japan).
- Planning for risk reduction in the city region in a way that recognizes that the city is not an isolated system and will be at risk from disaster in its hinterland is also very important. It is the hinterland that provides inputs and a sink for wastes produced by the city. Examples of where this approach has been recognized include Mexico City and New Delhi. This approach also concedes that the economy of the city drives environmental change in its hinterland, so that urban areas are partly responsible for peri-urban and rural risk. Examples of this include environmental degradation caused by fuelwood extraction for charcoal and the degradation of floodplains caused by the extraction of gravel from riverbeds for the construction industry.
- Yet another challenge is planning for global risk reduction – for example, by reducing dependency upon private or collective car use in order to mitigate climate change, as well as atmospheric pollution and accident rates in cities. Land-use patterns that bring residential, educational, recreational, commercial and employment activities closer together can make a major contribution to reducing the pollution footprint of cities.[18]

In the following sub-sections, opportunities for improving planning performance and examples of practice that point towards future directions in land-use planning which can integrate disaster risk reduction are reviewed. These are areas of innovation that will improve the effectiveness and accountability of land-use planning across the range of challenges that lie ahead. Pathways for building resilience within urban planning through innovations in data collection, management and analysis, as well as through decision-support tools and institutional reform, are examined.

Data collection, management and analysis

Technological innovation provides new opportunities for collecting and manipulating data on hazard, human vulnerability and disaster impacts. Geographic information systems (GIS) and organized data collection systems both offer scope to improve the evidence base for urban planning. Box 12.5 offers experience in the use of GIS for risk mapping gained by Gesellschaft für Technische Zusammenarbeit (GTZ).[19]

During recent years, technological advances in GIS have led to the development and improvement of numerous instruments and methods for physical hazard mapping and analysis. In contrast, the integration of social, economic and environmental variables within GIS models, risk maps and risk analysis, generally, still remains a challenge. It is in this area where improvements might be looked for in the future. Better integration of social, economic and environmental variables within GIS and risk models might be achieved through more systematic formal data collection systems managed by municipalities. Participatory GIS (P-GIS), in particular, can generate relevant socio-economic and environmental data that may serve as an input for risk models and plans. P-GIS combines participatory methodologies with GIS technologies in order to involve communities in the production of spatial data on hazards. P-GIS can thus engage local stakeholders in land-use planning and risk management and contribute to efforts to decentralize planning. The involvement of local actors opens scope for better communication and strengthens local monitoring of the impacts of risk reduction policies.[20] In this way, P-GIS can enable the extension of risk management and urban land-use planning into informal and slum settlements.

The process of quantifying local knowledge through P-GIS can further enhance the position of communities when they negotiate with outside agencies. For example, when assessments are conducted before and after external interventions, the success or failure of plans can be made equally transparent to local and external stakeholders.[21] P-GIS can thus contribute to reaching consensus on the state of local urban environments and on arriving at targets for land-use planning that integrates risk reduction.

P-GIS has become established as a tool in risk management for urban planning within richer cities; but scarcity of human resources and technical capacity have meant that it has received more limited application as a strategic tool in cities at risk from disaster in middle- and low-income countries. P-GIS is an important opportunity not to be missed as it provides a mechanism for generating basic data on hazard, vulnerability and loss when centralized data is not available, which is predominantly the case in low-income urban communities at risk. This said, the comprehensive use of P-GIS is likely to prove costly to implement and maintain, and may not be achievable in many poorer cities over the short and medium term.

The methodology used in GIS is to construct individual maps for specific social or environmental variables, such as income class, housing quality or altitude. Individual maps can then be layered on top of one another to identify risk as a result of different combinations of vulnerability and hazard variables. In this way, GIS is useful for identifying sites of special concern (which may vary over time in response to economic and environmental cycles) or areas of potential land-use or social conflict.

For long-term analysis of trends in vulnerability and impacts, regular and consistent data collection systems are required. There are few examples of such systematic data collection systems operating among marginalized and at-risk populations in urban settlements. Box 12.6 presents the experience of the Monitoring, Mapping and Analysis of Disaster Incidents in South Africa (MANDISA) database operating in squatter settlements in Cape Town (South Africa), with a focus on fire hazard loss data collection.

Box 12.5 Using geographic information systems (GIS) for risk mapping

The Deutsche Gesellschaft für Technische Zusammenarbeit (GTZ) recommends the following multi-method approach to risk mapping using geographic information systems (GIS).

First, use existing records to identify the areas potentially affected by a hazard of interest. Supplement these with analysis of aerial and satellite images and surveys among the population affected. In the case of very extensively flood-prone areas (e.g. Mozambique), hazard-prone areas might be delineated using satellite images (Landsat Thematic Mapper). Second, collected data is entered manually or using GIS on topographical maps to a scale of 1:20,000 to 1:100,000 or larger. Depending upon the hazard type, more or less intensive use is made of satellite and aerial images as a data source, together with GIS as an analytical instrument. To determine hazard frequency, it is necessary to study aerial images from as long a time span as possible, mostly on a scale of 1:15,000 to 1:30,000 (for small-scale flooding), and possibly supplemented with National Aeronautics and Space Administration Agency (NASA) and/or landscape photos.

Source: Kohler et al, 2004

Cost–benefit analysis

Cost-benefit analysis allows a comparison to be made between the costs and benefits of an investment decision. Benefits are defined as anything that improves human well-

Box 12.6 Monitoring, Mapping and Analysis of Disaster Incidents in South Africa (MANDISA): An urban fire inventory for small disasters in Cape Town, South Africa

In 1999, the Disaster Mitigation for Sustainable Livelihoods Programme at the University of Cape Town developed the Monitoring, Mapping and Analysis of Disaster Incidents in South Africa (MANDISA). This initiative was developed in collaboration with a range of local partners and aims to monitor incidents of urban fire, many of which often fall under the radar of disaster managers.

MANDISA covers the Cape Metropolitan Area and has data from 1990 onwards. Data is collected from multiple sources (e.g. fires services, social services, the Red Cross and newspapers), and is managed and presented in text as well as geographic information system (GIS) formats, allowing for both spatial and temporal analysis of many different disaster types, with differing impacts and scales.

Overall, the number of fires, most including one or, at most, a small number of dwellings, has increased rapidly from 1250 events per year between 1990 and 1999, to 3667 events per year between 2000 and 2002 (i.e. a doubling of the ten-year reported pattern in three years). This evidence has prompted local government officials to consider risk more seriously in their development planning. An analysis of the distribution of fire incidents between planned and unplanned settlements (1990–1999) in Guguletu, a township, shows that fires in the informal housing sector constituted 86 per cent, with only 11 per cent occurring in formal housing areas.

MANDISA is the first African-generated disaster events database that has allowed the geo-referencing of these very small and local events. This capability has provided a database to support legal reform for disaster management.

Key challenges revealed by MANDISA are as follows:

- Determining the accurate trigger, particularly of an informal dwelling fire, is highly problematic. Since all of the data is provided by emergency and relief records, there is complete reliance on the first responders to identify the trigger. In the case of fires, the emergency and fire services are increasingly unable to ascertain the trigger, and therefore report the trigger unknown.
- The limited analytic capability of those involved in disaster management, as well as those in development planning, has delayed uptake, buy-in and use of the information generated.

Source: Disaster Mitigation for Sustainable Livelihoods Programme, University of Cape Town, South Africa, www.egs.uct.ac.za/dimp

being. There is a wide variety of cost–benefit tools and these are frequently applied in decision-making in urban infrastructure development. Most methodologies include a three-stage process. First, the costs and benefits of an investment are identified. If a quantitative methodology is used, a common metric and numerical value must be assigned to each cost and benefit. Second, future costs and benefits are discounted to allow for the comparison of future and current values. Third, a decision criterion is applied to determine which is greater, the costs or benefits of a proposed investment. Recent efforts have applied the cost–benefit analysis approach to measure the pros and cons of land-use decisions and the relative merits of investing in hazard mitigation.

Cost-benefit analysis offers a methodology to help determine the optimum allocation of resources to reduce disaster risk

Despite some growing evidence of the utility of cost–benefit analysis as an aid to land-use decision-making for risk reduction, it is still not routinely used to determine the comparative advantage of investing in disaster prevention, preparedness and mitigation infrastructure investments. Cost-benefit analysis offers a methodology to help determine the optimum allocation of resources to reduce disaster risk. Where cost–benefit analysis has been undertaken, there is now a growing body of evidence to show empirically the cost effectiveness of investing in risk reduction. For example, a comparison of different disaster prevention measures undertaken against floods and volcanic hazard in the Philippines calculated benefits of between 3.5 and 30 times the project costs.[22] The Philippines case is based only on direct losses. Box 12.7 presents additional measures of the benefit of proactive investment in risk reduction, which have been calculated using a range of cost–benefit methodologies.

Disaster risk is ... not included in the majority of evaluations for urban planning decisions

Disaster risk is similarly not included in the majority of evaluations for urban planning decisions.[23] This increases the chance of projects being damaged or destroyed by natural and human-made hazards. Where investment funds have to be borrowed internationally, this increases debt while running the risk of losing the investment. The scale of this problem is seen in the increasing number of disaster reconstruction projects that international development banks, and mainly the World Bank, have supported during the last two decades. It is hoped that increasing the awareness of disaster risk through tools such as cost–benefit analysis will prevent reconstruction investments from also becoming subject to disaster. The need to adapt to climate change places additional pressure on the necessity of integrating disaster risk within development planning decision-making.

The variable frequency and severity of natural and technological hazard events and any associated human disasters present a challenge to cost–benefit analysis, although a number of statistical methods can be employed to measure the uncertainty that this brings to calculations.[24] Cost-benefit analysis is further constrained by the need to reduce inputs to a common metric that usually requires putting a monetary value on all costs and benefits, including human life and injuries. This is a challenge for any comparative assessments between places with different land uses – for example, in attempting to measure relative returns from an investment that increases security in a business district or a low-income housing area. The former land use will have far higher economic value; but the latter provides life-support services, some of which (shelter and access to basic services) can be quantified in economic terms, as well as social and ecological services (a sense of identity and community) that cannot be easily represented. More generally, methods for deriving values for human life, and also for other intangibles such as environmental quality or women's empowerment, are hotly contested. One approach is to ask people how much they are willing to pay to protect a certain asset, or how much they would be willing to receive in compensation if an asset was lost. The latter methodology routinely provides values an order of magnitude higher. This serves to indicate the vulnerability of cost–benefit analysis to manipulation or misinterpretation. Part of the solution to this is not to use cost–benefit analysis as a stand-alone tool to determine decisions, but rather to provide supporting evidence for decision-making alongside other non-economic inputs.[25]

Box 12.7 Revealing the advantages of disaster risk reduction through cost–benefit analysis

The World Bank and US Geological Survey calculated that economic losses worldwide from disasters during the 1990s could have been reduced by US$20 billion if US$40 million had been invested in mitigation and preparedness.

In China, investments of US$3.15 billion in flood control measures over 40 years are believed to have averted potential losses of US$12 billion.

In Viet Nam, 12,000 hectares of mangroves planted by the Red Cross to protect 110 kilometres of sea dikes costs US$1.1 million, but has reduced the costs of dike maintenance by US$7.3 million per year, in addition to protecting 7750 families living behind the dikes.

A study on Jamaica and Dominica calculated that the potential avoided losses compared with the costs of mitigation when building infrastructure, such as ports and schools, would have been between two and four times. For example, a year after constructing a deepwater port in Dominica, Hurricane David, in 1979, necessitated reconstruction costs equivalent to 41 per cent of the original investment; while building the port to a standard that could resist such a hurricane would have increased basic costs by only about 12 per cent.

In Darbhanga district in North Bihar (India), a cost–benefit analysis of disaster mitigation and preparedness interventions suggests that for every Indian rupee spent, 3.76 rupees of benefits were realized.

Source: DFID, 2005

Institutional reform

Appropriate institutional arrangements define the relationships, responsibilities and power of stakeholders in disaster and its management. The movement from managing risk through emergency relief and response towards a more proactive pre-disaster orientation requires institutional change. Development actors are better placed and have more appropriate skills than emergency response experts in achieving disaster risk reduction. Humanitarian actors and those involved in disaster reconstruction also need to integrate development planning within their work. These two shifts require a change in the distribution of responsibilities for risk management. This is likely to be accompanied by adjustments in budgets and in policy. Institutional arrangements can help in co-coordinating such changes

Box 12.8 Elements of successful reform for disaster risk reduction legislation

A recent study by Tearfund has reviewed the processes leading to the successful reform of national disaster risk reduction legislation. The following recommendations draw from this report, and together emphasize the need for strong leadership, a commitment to participation in the process of drafting legislation, and clarity in the required roles and outcomes of local-level actors, who include local authorities:

- Reform requires sustained high-level political support.
- Reform is greatly facilitated by high-level political support and a well-placed policy champion with technical knowledge, skill, commitment and creative initiative.
- The leadership of the reform process must be explicitly committed to broad stakeholder consultation.
- Review of the pre-reform policy and legislative context is necessary to understand the pre-existing mandates of agencies. As far as possible, legislation should fit into existing government planning cycles and procedures for implementation and monitoring.
- External facilitators can enable the reform process. Since disaster risk reduction is a fairly new policy area, it can easily be perceived as a threat or as duplicating existing policy and budget lines. In addition, the need to build high-level and cross-sectoral support is challenging for sectoral actors. International expertise or neutral, but informed, national actors, such as academics, may be well placed to act as technical advisers for dialogue.
- Create a clear identity for disaster risk reduction. Disaster risk reduction is developmental and should clearly be seen as a separate policy area from relief-oriented disaster management.
- Align new legislation with international best practice and use terminology consistent with contemporary global thinking.
- Develop an implementation plan during the development of legislation. This should clearly demarcate responsibilities, timelines for action, agreed benchmarks and protocols for review.
- Legislation must explicitly state required outcomes at the community level, such as local early warning systems or community-based disaster-contingency plans.
- Monitor performance and implementation. As risk changes in character, the nature and tasks of frontline policy actors will also change and legislation needs to be able to reflect this change to empower disaster risk reduction.

Source: Pelling and Holloway, 2006

(through legislation) and in enabling learning (through international and South–South partnerships).

Many cities have a solid base of legislation for urban risk management, including legislation to enforce land-use planning, construction standards and industrial risk management. The challenge at this level is to implement and enforce legislation. It is at the level of national legislation for disaster management policy and planning where there is most scope for clarifying legislation that can support city-level planning.

A review of legislation in Central America found that while progress was made after Hurricane Mitch, in 1998, in introducing new legislation, urban concerns were not fully addressed.[26] In particular, links between disaster management and urban management were not strong, leading to a missed opportunity to enhance urban planning as a risk reduction tool. Coordination across levels and sectors of government is essential to prevent blind spots in national or urban risk assessment and policy development that would cause unseen risk to accumulate, often at the local scale. Box 12.8 presents recent work by Tearfund that identifies common characteristics of successful legislative reform processes.

Disaster risk continues to grow despite existing legislative frameworks for urban risk reduction. This is a direct product of failure to implement legislative duties. This, in turn, is a product of financial and human resource shortages, as well as cultural norms, which undermine the effectiveness of legal regimes. There are a number of ways in which implementation can be maximized. Those who will eventually have responsibility for policing or implementing urban planning law should be consulted in the drafting of legislation.

Disaster risk continues to grow despite existing legislative frameworks for urban risk reduction

Urban- and national-level legislative reform has usefully engaged with international forums for risk reduction. The Habitat Agenda, which promotes the need to improve the quality of human settlements through solidarity, cooperation and partnerships, and the ISDR, which can act to provide information on good practice or facilitate South–South learning, are examples of this.

Regional cooperation can be similarly useful in promoting successful reform and implementation of risk reduction in urban planning. The Asian Urban Disaster Mitigation Program (AUDMP)[27] and the African Urban Risk Analysis Network[28] have been instrumental in sharing information on risk reduction and building communities of practice for urban professionals working on risk reduction in their respective regions.

Technological and engineering expertise is available in most cities to design buildings and infrastructure for disaster-proofing

DESIGNING DISASTER-RESISTANT BUILDINGS AND INFRASTRUCTURE

> *US$1 invested in construction saves US$40 if the building has to be rebuilt after an earthquake; US$1 invested in retrofitting saves US$8.*[29]

This estimate of the economic benefits of safe construction and retrofitting in Turkey is compelling. Technological and engineering expertise is available in most cities to design buildings and infrastructure for disaster-proofing. When development projects fail, this is more a reflection of failures in oversight and demand-side pressures, such as a desire for modern over indigenous design, even when indigenous housing has been proven through experience to offer disaster resistance, or of a desire for cost-cutting, even when this knowingly leads to the exclusion of disaster resistant design features.

Where inappropriate development has led to the accumulation of disaster risk, retrofitting can offer a way of improving the resilience of a city's buildings

Professional bodies have begun to develop guidelines for good practice in designing disaster-resilient critical infrastructure and this offers a great potential for information exchange and refinements, in practice, to reduce risk. An example is work by the Pan-American Health Organization (PAHO) and the World Health Organization (WHO), which offers guidelines for promoting disaster mitigation in new health facilities. Many of the recommendations would apply to other infrastructure. The goal of these guidelines is to incorporate risk reduction tools within project cycles, including pre-investment activities, project design, construction and maintenance.[30]

Future pathways for building resilience in the city through designing disaster-resilient buildings and infrastructure include tools for better integrating disaster risk within project management; efforts to engage with the public to rethink housing design choices; and support by international and national agencies, as well as the private sector, for partnerships with artisan builders to promote good practice in disaster-proof construction locally.

In slums ... incentives to improve the safety of buildings are particularly limited

Aid agencies and construction oversight

Multilateral and bilateral development aid agencies can influence the location, timing and content of investments in infrastructure through their stated policy priorities. However, these agencies often do not have their own guidelines or engineering standards and procedures with which to ensure that investments are disaster resistant. Rather, this service is decentralized and local standards and practices are used. Aid donors rarely become involved in design. This is especially so in indirect investments such as social investment funds, where detailed budget decisions and design criteria are generally set at the national level.

Given the high profile of schools and health service infrastructure during urban disaster events, and particularly during earthquakes, the lack of oversight in construction through social investment funds suggests an area for future policy consideration. There is also scope for agencies to provide some momentum for international comparison and reform of local building standards where these are not appropriate.

A recent review of donor behaviour observes that publicly constructed infrastructure is exempt from building codes in many countries.[31] Where codes are followed, they are often inadequate, particularly in multi-hazard contexts. Donors usually view the responsibility for construction standards as resting with governments.

Retrofitting

Where inappropriate development has led to the accumulation of disaster risk, retrofitting can offer a way of improving the resilience of a city's buildings. Opportunities for retrofitting are often constrained. Despite the small marginal costs of retrofitting in most instances, where works are perceived by owners to be unduly disruptive, they are unlikely to be entered into voluntarily. Similarly, if costs of retrofitting are considered to be high in relation to perceived risk, voluntary action will be limited. Where building owners are not prepared to retrofit buildings, tenants have little power and are often denied rights to invest in the upgrading of the property they rent. This includes tenants of private and public landlords. In slums lacking landownership, incentives to improve the safety of buildings are particularly limited.

Retrofitting has been encouraged by insurance companies by offering incentives such as reduced premiums, or the stick of only insuring those properties meeting basic standards of construction. Municipal governments may also offer advice, technical support and sometimes grants to encourage private owners to upgrade building safety, and can integrate retrofitting within urban plans for disaster management. This is most likely to be undertaken where local authorities are contemplating urban redevelopment schemes in which disaster risk reduction has been integrated. Retrofitting is being tackled on three fronts by the Tokyo Metropolitan government (see Box 12.9).[32]

Whereas the Tokyo Metropolitan government has taken a spatial planning approach to retrofitting, Quito (Ecuador) has followed a sectoral path. The National Polytechnic School in Quito has undertaken an evaluation of school construction standards in the city. Many design weaknesses were revealed in this study, which led to a revised code of standards for schools that have now been classified as critical facilities.[33]

Box 12.9 City government support for retrofitting: Tokyo Metropolitan government

Tokyo is highly exposed to earthquake hazard. Many neighbourhoods in the city are densely built, with wood being a common building material. Consequently, fire risk is high and has caused large losses following urban earthquakes. To reduce risk, a Promotional Plan for a Disaster Resilient City was formulated in 1997. The plan aims to strengthen the resilience of Tokyo's buildings through retrofitting and the redesign of urban neighbourhoods. It has three important components:

- The designation by the Tokyo Metropolitan government of areas for redevelopment into disaster-resistant zones has made it possible to subsidize retrofitting for fire safety. Financial assistance is available for the retrofitting of old wooden lease apartments.
- As a basis for planning and retrofitting, the Tokyo Metropolitan Earthquake Disaster Countermeasure Ordinance and the Tokyo Metropolitan Earthquake Disaster Prevention Plan call for a diagnosis of the earthquake resistance of public buildings constructed before 1981. This will include fire stations, police stations, schools and hospitals that will need to function as bases for information, rescue and relief in the event of a major earthquake.
- The Building Earthquake-Resistance Diagnosis System provides a consultation service for privately owned buildings.

Source: Tokyo Metropolitan Government, Bureau of Urban Development, undated

Indigenous buildings

Non-engineered or indigenous structures are dominant in many cities around the world. For instance, almost 90 per cent of Kathmandu's buildings are non-engineered.[34] Although indigenous construction techniques are not always inferior to modern ones, in many disasters, especially those associated with earthquakes, it is the non-engineered or indigenous buildings that are most damaged and that kill the most people.[35] Indigenous styles are not of themselves inherently dangerous. Where traditional building skills persist and are valued by contractors, and where good quality materials are used, indigenous building techniques can be hazard-proof, as well as retain local built heritage. Unfortunately, under rapid urbanization, the majority of non-engineered structures have not been built to such high standards.

Indigenous buildings are considered by some to fall outside the scope of engineering science. However, this view is changing and offers an opportunity for partnerships between engineers, artisan builders and low-income households to improve building safety. New knowledge is a necessary component of a comprehensive strategy for improving the quality of indigenous buildings, most of which are constructed outside the formal housing and planning systems. In addition to a lack of knowledge, indigenous housing is made unsafe by a lack of financial resources and the number of competing demands on household budgets, many of which require more immediate attention than disaster risk-proofing.

Given the constraints of poverty and the reality of competing demands, complete seismic resistance in indigenous housing may not be attainable. However, improvements to enhance security can be made to ensure that key buildings will not suffer complete collapse and that damage incurred will be of a type that can be quickly repaired. These are the aims of the National Information Centre of Earthquake Engineering in India,[36] which has undertaken research on improved security for indigenous buildings in fried-brick, stone, wood, earth and non-engineered reinforced concrete. Engineering advice is available in the report *Guidelines for Earthquake Resistant Non-Engineered Construction* produced by the National Information Centre.[37] Growing interest among engineers in research and the training of builders, architects and planners in safe building design for non-engineered structures offer major opportunities for safer cities.

Training

Universities and technical institutes have long been at the forefront of disaster risk reduction through research and teaching on design aspects for disaster-resilient cities. But more can be done. There are opportunities for integrating disaster awareness within curricula, even for non-specialist degrees. This is a mechanism for fostering awareness of disaster risk reduction as a cross-cutting concern for all seeking careers in urban development, engineering design, project management, housing and urban planning. Box 12.10 describes some of the initiatives of the Asian Disaster Preparedness Centre (ADPC), which has a long track record in professional training for urban disaster risk reduction.

The potential for e-learning opens much additional scope for professional training in design for risk reduction. The United Nations Disaster Management Training Programme[38] was launched in 1990. The programme is delivered at distance, but promotes national and regional workshops. Since 1990, more than 70 workshops have been organized, benefiting approximately 6000 participants in developing and transitional countries. The workshops have supported national efforts to revise national disaster management plans and legislation and to create and strengthen national and United Nations disaster management teams. They have generated follow-up training events that disseminate learning to community levels, and have led to the initiation of technical projects supported by the UNDP, other partner agencies and donor governments. It is notable in this programme that urban disaster risk is not flagged as a priority for action, although many generic issues are covered that would benefit those engaged in urban risk management. Individual universities also coordinate disaster management training courses, often with distance learning components.

There are opportunities for integrating disaster awareness within curricula, even for non-specialist degrees

Climate change, building and infrastructure design

The Intergovernmental Panel on Climate Change (IPCC) expects climate change to affect urban populations through rising sea levels, increased hazard from tropical cyclones, flooding, landslides, heat and cold waves, as well as challenges of urban water quality and storage. Changing physical parameters require adaptation in building and infrastructure design.[39] Cities in low- and middle-income countries are doubly at risk. Many cities are located in tropical and subtropical climatic zones where climatic hazards are already a constraint on development, and face extreme financial and technical constraints and limited adaptive capacity. The location of large urban centres in coastal areas exposed to hydro-meteorological hazards is a significant risk factor.

Box 12.10 Professional training in urban risk management: The Asian Disaster Preparedness Centre (ADPC) story

Through educational work and professional training, the Asian Disaster Preparedness Centre (ADPC) has helped to incorporate disaster risk reduction aims and techniques within related disciplines such as engineering, environmental management, hydrology and planning. In Asia, the ADPC engages with a number of universities and lists 15 specialist centres for disaster research in the region among its network. The centre also works in partnership with the European Union (EU).

The ADPC offers e-learning programmes on disaster risk reduction. South–South learning has also been facilitated by the centre and delivered by national partners. For example, the Prince of Songkhla University and the University of Chiang Mai in Thailand undertook training in risk assessment with planners from the people's Democratic Republic of Lao's Urban Research Institute.

In addition, the ADPC offers a range of short courses for professionals on a regular basis. Courses include earthquake vulnerability for cities, flood risk management, technological risk management, urban fire risk management, urban disaster mitigation, land-use planning and risk management, as well as hospital preparedness for emergencies.

Source: ADPC, 2005

Indeed, 21 of the 33 cities that are projected to have a population of 8 million or more by 2015 are located in coastal zones.[40]

Perhaps most challenging of all is sea-level rise. The scale of risk is enormous:[41]

- In Japan, a 1 metre sea-level rise would expand areas at risk 2.7 times to 2339 square kilometres, and increase population and assets at risk to 4.1 million and 109 trillion Japanese yen,[42] respectively.
- In Egypt, a 50 centimetre sea-level rise would affect 2 million people and 214,000 jobs, and would result in the loss of US$35 billion in land value, property and tourism income.
- In Poland, a 1 metre sea-level rise would cause US$30 billion of land to be lost to the sea, and put US$18 billion of assets and land at risk of flooding. It is estimated that coastal protection would cost US$6 billion.

The greatest challenge is to … ensure that early warnings are communicated and acted on in a timely manner

Adapting now to future climate change is difficult because of the uncertainty in forecasting and a tendency for conservative estimates of future change. This makes it difficult to identify design targets for adaptation. Some basic principles for successful adaptation have been proposed. For example, to be successful, adaptations must be consistent with economic development, be environmentally and socially sustainable over time, and be equitable.[43] In cities where the institutional architecture for natural disaster risk reduction is in place, this is a strong base for adapting to climate change.[44]

Mitigating greenhouse gas emissions in cities requires immediate and aggressive action alongside adaptation work. There is great scope for future work in enabling mitigation through improved urban design. One direction to begin research and development might be in those areas where mitigation also offers a financial opportunity. Examples include improved building materials and energy efficiency to reduce costs; transport demand management to reduce congestion and the health impacts of transport; and the promotion of renewable or alternative energy generation, such as methane recuperation from landfills for use in local energy generation schemes.[45] Many local authorities already play leadership roles by reviewing purchasing and energy conservation policy. The Cities for Climate Protection Campaign, coordinated by ICLEI-Local Governments for Sustainability, has enlisted over 650 cities worldwide, each of which has demonstrated willingness to integrate climate mitigation within its decision-making processes.[46]

Urban settlements offer opportunities as well as challenges for early warning

STRENGTHENING EARLY WARNING SYSTEMS

There is always scope for greater investment and innovation in the technical aspects of early warning systems, and there remain many cities exposed to hazard without an early warning system. The greatest challenge is to link existing technical capacity with people-centred approaches which ensure that early warnings are communicated and acted on in a timely manner. As indicated in Box IV.1, failure to communicate and provide effective ways for people to prepare for disaster was evidenced during Hurricane Katrina in New Orleans (US) in 2005, when a mixture of alienation from authority and a lack of resources contributed to the high numbers of people who were neither evacuated nor adequately prepared for the event.[47]

Integrating 'top-down' and 'bottom-up' approaches

Connecting technical expertise to people at risk requires that early warning systems are built from the bottom up (sensitive to the contexts in which they will be useful), as well as from the top down (being accurate and effective with their use of information). The fusion of top-down scientific and bottom-up people-centred approaches can maximize the trust that those at risk place in the system. Not only the message but also the messenger needs to be trusted for people to take action.

An important challenge in improving the outputs of early warning systems is to bring the right team of stakeholders together – politicians, hazard experts, disaster managers, the media and community members all have a role to play. To help build trust in Jamaica, mayors chair local Disaster Committees, thereby adding legitimacy to any warnings that might be issued from hazard technicians. There is also a policy of avoiding the 'blame game'. It is accepted that early warning is not an exact science and that wrong decisions may be made. A professional approach to analysing why wrong decisions have been made, rather than a recriminatory approach, helps to reduce pressure on decision-makers.[48]

The challenge of cities

Environmental change associated with urban expansion into new hazard zones, or with the local consequences of global environmental change, coupled with social and demographic change in cities, generates uncertainty for early warning. New hazards and vulnerabilities may emerge, generating risk that is unrecognized until disaster strikes. This was partly the case in the European heat wave of 2003.

Urban settlements offer opportunities as well as challenges for early warning. The density of settlement and strength of social relations in cities indicate that messages of early warning and preparedness will diffuse quickly. This observation is a little more difficult to maintain in cities that are home to diverse migrant communities, or where social class and demographic factors can cause some to be isolated from mainstream society. As noted in Chapter 7, it was the isolated elderly who were most vulnerable to heat shock in Europe and the US. In each of these cases, isolation from mainstream society is a feature of vulnerability that can also lead to exclusion from systems of early warning and advice on preparedness and evacuation. Linguistic barriers, poverty and lifestyle habits mean that access to messages communicated through the mainstream media is limited. While

Box 12.11 Early warning in a multi-hazard risk environment: Experience from Mexico

Mexico is exposed to a wide range of hazards. For example, Mexico City is at risk from earthquakes, volcanoes and floods, while settlements in the south, west and east of the country may also be exposed to hurricane and storm surge hazards. Recognizing the need to build risk reduction into development, Mexico has produced a national development plan and a *National Risks Atlas* as a basis for risk and development planning. Funds for emergency management and for disaster prevention are available.

Early warning systems for volcanic eruptions and tropical storms are coordinated by national civil protection authorities, while earthquake early warning is coordinated by a civil association. Each system relies upon close collaboration between federal, state and municipal levels for the timely communication of warnings. Warnings are sent using a simple three-tier 'traffic light' indicator system for severity of risk. This prevents confusion along the communication chain. Multiple methods of communication are available to help spread warning messages, including telephone and pager messaging, the internet and local civil authorities. The traffic light system indicates severity and also triggers actions to be taken by civil protection agencies, as well as by the population.

Lessons learned from the Mexican experience are:

- While it is appropriate for different agencies to be involved with early warning and response for particular hazards, it is useful to have a coordinating body (the National Civil Protection Authority in Mexico's case).
- Coordination between state and local levels is essential.
- There should be consistency in the ways in which warnings for different hazards are presented.
- Different alert levels for different hazards should be clearly defined and should correspond with specific actions to be taken by named authorities and the public.
- The traffic light system has proven effective as a communication tool.
- Warning systems and responses should be tested.

Source: Guevara, 2006

information spread through word of mouth may be effective, little research has been undertaken on the effectiveness of social networks as an information system for early warning and preparedness among marginalized urban populations.

Cities often face multiple hazards and present a complex distribution of vulnerabilities and capacities. This presents a challenge for early warning, which has developed as a linear science where single hazard types are monitored. The integration of multiple hazard monitoring systems is a current challenge for urban disaster risk managers. Data requirements are beyond the current capacity of many municipalities. Simple multi-hazard risk assessments presented in GIS are perhaps a first step; but investment in monitoring equipment and communication systems that can reach the most vulnerable are proving more difficult to achieve. Box 12.11 presents a reflection on the status of Mexico's early warning systems, which have to cope with a multi-hazard environment.

Knowledge for action

Experience shows that, following a warning, in order for action to be effective, knowledge on what preparedness actions to take is needed by people at risk and emergency services. This section discusses the potential for developing two strategies for building capacity: public education and participatory mapping.

Knowledge of hazards and resources is essential for successful evacuation. Box 12.12 recounts experiences from the evacuation system put into operation for Hurricane Rita during 2005, which made landfall on the Texas–Louisiana border on the Gulf Coast of the US. This was the fourth most intensive Atlantic hurricane recorded and caused US$10 billion in damages and 120 deaths. This case study underlines the importance for advance preparation to enable the best actions to follow from scientific information and early warnings.

Public information campaigns can seek to target the general population and have dedicated strategies for reaching less accessible social groups – for example, by presenting material in multiple languages. Successful public information campaigns also often include working with key community groups to disseminate messages, and to build, in advance, the cooperative relationships that are the bedrock of an effective disaster response. Key groups include schools, businesses, community groups, fire and police departments, local governments and the media.

The media can be very helpful in educating the public on disaster preparedness and recovery programmes after disaster strikes. However, disaster managers frequently complain that the media distorts information, often sensationalizing warnings or turning disasters into a spectacle. Forging links with local and national media and individual journalists and reporters is time consuming, but is valuable in fostering more responsible media coverage of disasters.

The integration of multiple hazard monitoring systems is a current challenge for urban disaster risk managers

Innovative media strategies include the use of radio soap opera (*Radionovelas*) to promote hurricane preparedness, the creation and broadcasting, by the International Federation of Red Cross and Red Crescent Societies (IFRC) and the European Union (EU), of calypso-style songs on the subject of disaster preparedness in Central America, and a weekly 15-minute radio programme on humanitarian concerns from Nepal Red Cross.[49] Some of the most successful innovations, such as *Radionovelas*, combine media messages with hands-on workshops or self-led exercises. The *Radionovelas* initiative has, to date, been delivered in Central America with 20-minute programmes being delivered each day over a month during the hurricane season.[50]

Many aspects of participatory risk mapping have been discussed already both in Chapter 8 and earlier in this chapter; but an additional benefit of this tool is that local actors are able to share information with one another and external actors to help identify where vulnerable people, such as the frail or isolated elderly, live. If evacuation becomes necessary, this data is useful for planning and

Box 12.12 Lessons learned for knowledge management and evacuation planning during Hurricane Rita, US (2005)

Whereas Hurricane Katrina's evacuation plan functioned relatively well for motorists, but failed to serve people who depend upon public transport, Hurricane Rita's evacuation plan failed because of excessive reliance on automobiles, resulting in traffic congestion and local fuel shortages.

Three days before Hurricane Rita made landfall, an evacuation plan that would see over 1 million people leave their homes was begun. On 21 September 2005, a staggered evacuation order was announced for Galveston County and city. The system of staggered evacuation and the designation of particular evacuation routes and destination cities for different zones of the county and city were aimed at preventing traffic congestion. Evaluations of the evacuation have identified a number of communication failures and weaknesses.

Training and planning needs to include those local authorities involved in evacuation. This can help, for example, in streamlining traffic control to reduce congestion, and in the provision of sanitary facilities and primary healthcare along evacuation routes. Public education is needed to inform people of evacuation routes and destinations, and to provide advice on the need to prepare adequately for long journey times by taking adequate water, food, medications, etc.

Conflicting information from state and media weather bulletins and approaches to providing information led to confusion. At times, the media sensationalized the nature of the hazard, adding unnecessarily to tension. This had an exaggerated impact, given the recent nature of Hurricane Katrina. Elected officials need to take control and act as figure heads to reassure people and project a sense of responsibility.

A number of recommendations have come from reviews of communication and information flow during the Rita evacuation. While communication between state and local government was good, there was a disconnection between public agencies and the people. This needs to be improved. Simple actions, such as providing more roadside signs about fuel and water, have been proposed, as has a statewide public education programme.

Source: Gutierrez, 2005

implementing assisted evacuation. Participatory risk mapping can also be used to identify local resources, including evacuation routes and buildings that can be converted into public shelters.

For the majority of residents in many cities, resources are not available for long distance evacuation; so local plans based on local knowledge can help to bring order and clarity. An additional advantage to decentralized planning is the capacity for local plans to be implemented even if national or city-wide communications and plans fail. However, the most effective local systems do not operate in isolation. Liaisons between adjacent communities and with city or national disaster planning authorities can improve the performance of early warning and action through exposure to the experiences of other communities and national standards of good practice.

...reconstruction governance is made complicated by ad hoc legislative and institutional frameworks generating uncoordinated and fragmented action

IMPROVING EMERGENCY RESPONSE AND RECONSTRUCTION

Urban areas offer specific challenges for emergency response and recovery (see also Chapter 7). Key challenges for emergency responders include:

- The existence of the majority of settlements in cities of developing countries outside the formal and legal system: at best, there are restricted land rights and documentation.
- The mobility of responders can be inhibited by large quantities of debris. Consequently, in some cases, communities may not receive adequate medical supplies, food, water and security for weeks.
- Public services may be inadequate, such as, for instance, the lack of available water through the public distribution system for fire fighting.
- Secondary disasters (such as fires, toxic spills and other industrial accidents) complicate and hinder rescue efforts (e.g. fire, smoke, gases).
- Information management for decision-making becomes more complicated and difficult in larger settlements.

From the perspective of emergency services, resilience can be built into risk management through making use of redundant capacity. In cities exposed to frequent events, spare capacity should be extended to mobilize materials, such as medical stock, temporary accommodation, equipment, and mobile water and sanitation units. Capacity can also be extended by involving community actors and the wider civil society in first-response planning and training. The Iranian Red Crescent has promoted disaster-response training, with over 1.2 million people trained.[51]

Coordination of emergency response efforts between different urban sectors remains a key challenge. It is particularly important to synchronize response efforts that involve critical services such as medical assistance, electricity and water services. The case of Nanning City's Urban Emergency Response Centre in China illustrates the mechanisms for establishing an integrated disaster response system (see Box 12.13)

Post-disaster recovery is also challenged, particularly if this period is to make the most of its opportunity for 'building back better' to reduce risk and integrate development within reconstruction. The gap in funding and planning between response, recovery and development continues. On the ground, reconstruction governance is made complicated by *ad hoc* legislative and institutional frameworks generating uncoordinated and fragmented action. There is no agency devoted to housing reconstruction, and very few of the major non-governmental organizations (NGOs) working in relief would claim to specialize here. UN-Habitat's increasing involvement in reconstruction is a progressive indication of the positive contribution to be made by developmental actors. Future improvements in recovery and reconstruction might come from approaches that build on local and national capaci-

Box 12.13 Integrated Urban Emergency Response Centre, Nanning, China

Nanning City is located in southwest China, with a population of 1.7 million and a built area of 170 square kilometres. The city has experienced rapid urbanization over the last decade, with its population growing by 172 per cent. This has been accompanied by increased threats to safety and security, including natural and human-made disasters. The old emergency response system, characterized by fragmented agencies, was poorly adapted to the changing environment of the city. Thus, the city established an Emergency Response Center, a successful example of an integrated emergency response system.

The Center, the first of its kind in China, started to provide emergency services in November 2001 by integrating telephone calls for the Police Service (110), Fire Service (119), Ambulance Service (120), Traffic Accident (122), Mayor's Hot Line (12345), and other emergency response systems for flood, earthquake, water, electricity and gas supplies. To prevent emergencies and disasters, and to minimize their impact, the Center has prepared numerous prevention and emergency response programmes for natural disasters, public health, management of dangerous chemicals, housing safety, school safety and public space safety. This Center, consisting of 15 sub-units, has the following technical capabilities:

- to identify immediately, with the support of GIS and GPS systems, the location of incoming calls from among nearly 1 million landline telephones, and display the distribution of all police units;
- to identify the location of available rescue resources and make the best choice of response;
- to transmit voice, image and document information between the Center and the site of the emergency;
- to monitor, record and intervene traffic conditions;
- to set up temporary command stations at emergency sites and provide commanding and communication serves by deploying emergency mobile communication vehicles; and
- to record all relevant voice and digital information for each case for further search.

The Center has improved the overall efficiency and coverage of emergency responses in the city, particularly rescue services. The experience of the Center shows that a municipal government can successfully mobilize stakeholders and use modern technologies to create a safer living environment for its residents.

Source: Nanning Municipal Government, 2007

ties, and which experiment with more decentralized planning and programming that builds on pre-disaster risk reduction.

Speed and sustainability in shelter provision

A longstanding tension in reconstruction is between the demands of delivering basic needs, including shelter, quickly, and the desire for sustainability, which requires greater participation and a longer time commitment. Fair and efficient distribution of housing that provides a basis for economic development and resilience building is repeatedly undermined by a rapid and fragmented approach to shelter reconstruction, which does not consider the economic, social and environmental consequences of reconstruction decisions.

Part of this challenge is conceptual and lies in the very nature of housing, which, unlike other relief items such as food aid or medicine, is a significant, long-term and non-consumable asset. While the logic for humanitarian actors to lead in the post-disaster provision of life-saving medical care is clear, this is less so for settlement reconstruction, which is, at heart, a developmental activity requiring the skills and knowledge of housing and urban development specialists. Reconstruction in Bam during 2003 – one of the first times that UN-Habitat had been formally consulted on post-natural disaster reconstruction planning – shows that the integration of development within shelter reconstruction is rare.[52]

The disconnection between shelter reconstruction and development is perhaps also partly a reason for the many instances where temporary shelter is not replaced and becomes, *de facto*, permanent. In Santo Domingo (the Dominican Republic), public confidence in the ability of the state to adequately deliver reconstruction following Hurricane Georges in 1998 was severely undermined by the knowledge that many still remained in 'temporary' housing built after Hurricane David struck in 1979. In extensive disasters, a scarcity of large construction firms can lead to the creation of virtual monopolies, forcing up prices to exorbitant levels and creating a long waiting time for completion. The long waiting period for temporary housing following Hurricane Katrina has contributed to anxiety and financial hardship among those affected.

A longstanding tension in reconstruction is between the demands of delivering basic needs... and the desire for sustainability...

An awareness of the opportunity for shelter provision to contribute to longer-term development has stimulated some reappraisal by humanitarian and development agencies of the processes through which shelter is provided. It is important that, as far as possible, those people whose homes have been lost or damaged in disaster are involved in repair and reconstruction. This saves costs, provides a mechanism for transferring new or improved construction skills and can bolster the local economy. Time and again, survivors of disaster express a preference for working on reconstruction, rather than being made to receive aid in temporary camps. Where possible, survivors should be allowed to return to the sites of their former occupation and begin reconstruction as soon as possible. Where the costs of reconstruction are affordable, this can further enable survivors to take over the process of providing their own shelter.

Where settlements have suffered great damage or been shown, through disaster, to be at unacceptable levels of hazard exposure, settlement planning and, in extreme cases, relocation will still be required. This opens a rare opportunity for progressive land-use and ownership planning, including the extension of basic services for those people who may previously have lived on the margins of urban life. It is commonplace for landownership to be disputed in the aftermath of a disaster, which is made worse by a lack of documentation or the destruction of local public offices that held records. Networked electronic databases of citizen identity and property ownership can help. In areas with high land values (such as inner-city and coastal locations), there is pressure for redevelopment and a risk that customary landownership and use will not be recognized in redevelopment. Oversight of reconstruction planning and the legal empowerment of those affected by disaster can help to maintain a more level playing field in discussions of post-disaster planning. It is especially important that the rights of the poor, women and orphans are recognized in this process.

Participation of beneficiaries in shelter reconstruction enhances the appropriateness of housing

Closing the gap between emergency shelter, shelter in recovery and longer-term development is important. Human shelter should be recognized as a foundational aspect of building resilient communities. Working with people at risk to achieve sustainable shelter in both pre- and post-disaster contexts requires action to strengthen institutions, including those that govern entitlements to landownership. It is also important that sustainable shelter is maintained within the context of local economic development and poverty reduction over the long term.

A recent review of shelter reconstruction identifies much scope for positive reform and innovation.[53] The review argues for flexibility and the participation of all stakeholders, particularly beneficiary communities, if housing reconstruction is to fulfil its potential as a mechanism for enhancing social and economic development. To do this, agencies should try to avoid standard one-size-fits-all approaches to housing. Flexibility in design should allow structures to be adapted to meet a variety of cultural needs and expectations.

Participation of beneficiaries in shelter reconstruction enhances the appropriateness of housing. For example, involving women in house design can correct misconceptions about family life and thus prevent inappropriate interventions, such as the design of nuclear houses for extended families. Active participation can also help to improve local skills and industry, re-establish social networks and relationships, and promote psychological recovery. Disaster survivors almost always would prefer to be engaged in reconstruction than be made passive recipients of aid in refugee camps.

The most provocative question raised by a number of authors commenting on the Indian Ocean Tsunami is why relief agencies should contemplate doing housing reconstruction at all.[54] Why not meet the need for shelter through temporary provision and leave more permanent solutions to the developmental sector, private businesses or the government, once the immediate, acute disaster phase has passed? UN-Habitat's *Sustainable Relief and Reconstruction* proposal recognizes that the transition from relief to reconstruction is not always clear on the ground. This is especially so following large events with widespread losses, such as the 2004 Indian Ocean Tsunami, the 2005 South Asian earthquake, and Hurricanes Katrina or Mitch in 2005 and 1998, respectively. Different places and communities will be at different stages of recovery; so some degree of overlap is unavoidable. The roots of reconstruction lie in relief, so that long-term reconstruction and economic recovery should begin while post-emergency actions are being undertaken. This enables strategic investments to be made during emergency and relief stages.

Box 12.14 Natural disaster training to build trust in Bosnia Herzegovina

The political separation of Bosnia and Herzegovina into two subdivisions is not reflected in the physical landscape. Both flooding and earthquake risk can impact upon both sides of the border. The Assistance to Casualties 2004 exercise has turned this challenge into an opportunity for collaboration. The exercise simulated an earthquake measuring 7.3 on the Mercalli scale (approximately 4 on the Richter scale) in the Doboj/Gračanica area, a village close to the boundary line that separates Bosnia and Herzegovina's two political subdivisions.

The drill involved fire fighting, de-mining, bridge building and aerial observation, and was organized and executed under the supervision of the Organization for Security and Cooperation in Europe (OSCE).

The training exercise was aimed at demonstrating the country's capability to cooperate and carry out a military-led emergency relief operation. It was the first of its kind involving military units from both entities and more than 400 staff, including civil protection agencies.

One of the goals was to provide a system of protection and rescue through coordinated alerting, observation, evaluation and decision-making. Fire fighters from both regions were called in to deal with a blaze in a brick factory. This was followed by a search and rescue operation to recover casualties from the Usora River and mine fields in the area and the construction of a bridge across the River Bosna. Special rescue units were flown in by helicopter to bring the 'victims' to the nearest hospital in Doboj municipality. The successful coordination of services from both administrations demonstrated the capacity for joint disaster response efforts and is one step in building resilience in this frontier territory.

Source: OSCE, 2004

Disaster response training

Human-made and natural hazards and the resultant disasters often cross administrative boundaries. Planning for effective and timely response not only benefits from collaboration between adjacent political and administrative units, but offers an opportunity to build trust and cooperation. This is particularly the case in adjacent countries recovering from political or military tensions, or in countries rebuilding national identity following civil conflict. Box 12.14 describes a collaborative natural disaster training exercise that included emergency response and military units from the government of Bosnia and Herzegovina, the Federation of Bosnia and Herzegovina, and the Republika Srpska.

Insurance and urban reconstruction

Chapter 8 discussed the challenges of international financing for disaster management and noted the increased willingness of donors to take the challenges of reconstruction seriously. Putting financial mechanisms in place before a disaster strikes can enable a more speedy and independent recovery. Innovations in financial aspects of risk management have been most active around the potential for insurance and risk off-setting through hedge funds at the national and international levels, and through the potential offered by micro-insurance at the household and individual levels. Both are reviewed here.

The uptake of risk transfer understandably remains low in developing countries as insurance demand generally rises with per capita income (up to a certain level). In developed countries, insurance cover for loss from disasters may be restricted, as illustrated in the aftermath of the Kobe earthquake in 1995 (see Box 12.15). Recently, however, a number of novel schemes have been implemented or are under implementation. These include, at the macro level, private–public insurance partnerships administered together with national governments, international financial institutions and the private sector, and risk transfer for public liabilities.[55] For example, the World Bank's Commodity Risk Management Group is establishing a Global Index Insurance Facility to assist in providing reinsurance.[56] The Inter-American Development Bank (IDB) and the Organization of American States (OAS) have also been providing support for insurance and hedging products.

The Mexico City earthquake of 1985 revealed a financing gap, with few residential properties having insurance cover. Today, the World Bank and Mexico take a three-step approach to financial risk management: identification of risks, mitigation investment, and the transfer of residual risk to insurance companies and capital markets.[57] This has led to a strengthening of the insurance sector and its regulatory regime; the establishing of a broad-based pooled catastrophe fund with efficient risk transfer tools; the promotion of public insurance policies linked to programmes for loss reduction in the uninsured sectors; and the strengthening of procedures for risk assessment and enforcement of structural measures, such as zoning and building code compliance.[58]

Micro-insurance can assist poorer urban residents to meet their immediate needs during and after a disaster through emergency loans or the release of savings. It can also support clients in reconstruction through helping businesses where productive assets or stock have been lost, or for repairs to be done on homes. Research by the World Bank shows clearly the range of options available for relief and reconstruction.[59] For both of these stages, planning ahead is critical. Policies, procedures, practices and systems need to be in place and understood by clients and managers before a disaster. It is quite difficult to design and roll out new products immediately after a natural disaster event.

Post-disaster loans are riskier than those provided in stable times. Refinanced loans will need to be structured so that the business being financed can generate enough cash to service both loans, while still allowing the borrower to care for her or his family. This will require greater focus by the loan officer on clients' cash flow, collateral and personal character. In some circumstances, it may be necessary to decline a loan application where a second loan may over-indebt the borrower. Applications from those who have not previously held a loan should be viewed with caution as capacity and experience to repay immediately following a crisis may be limited. When successful, post-disaster microfinance can kick-start development. The Asociación de Consultores para el Desarrollo de la Pequeña, Mediana y Micro Empresa (ACODEP), a microfinance organization based in Nicaragua, focused on micro-enterprise loans pre-disaster, but following Hurricane Mitch, established a new housing loan product in response called *Mi Vivenda* ('My House'). In total, 2700 households took advantage of this product. The housing loan is now offered as a regular loan product and has reached a high level of demand.[60]

Box 12.15 Insurance policies and disaster loss in Kobe, Japan

In 1995, the Kobe earthquake in Japan caused over US$100 billion in damages and resulted in the destruction of 150,000 buildings. Insured losses, however, were limited to around US$6 billion. The absence of a comprehensive insurance cover in this wealthy country is a consequence of the restrictive provisions of the national insurance sector and several key features of Japanese insurance policies:

- Basic homeowners' fire insurance policies do not cover fires resulting from earthquakes.
- Owners may purchase a limited earthquake rider, with the indemnity covering 30 to 50 per cent of the structure's replacement value, up to a maximum of US$100,000.
- Claims were categorized into three groups: total loss, half loss and less than half. If damage was categorized as half loss, payout would be 15 to 20 per cent of the replacement value.
- Contents were not covered unless they were totally destroyed.

In addition to the specificities of these insurance policies, only 7 per cent of homeowners nationally have such earthquake riders, and at the time of the earthquake in Kobe, coverage was less than 3 per cent of homeowners.

During reconstruction, lack of insurance may well have contributed to the economic pressures that led some homeowners, especially the poor and elderly, to join many renters in moving from high-value city centre property. The elderly and lower-income families comprised a large portion of residents in city centre neighbourhoods that were heavily affected by the earthquake. For many, it was easier to sell their properties to speculators and move elsewhere than to borrow towards rebuilding. Renters, likewise, found it easier to move elsewhere than wait for housing to be reconstructed in their former neighbourhoods. The result was a movement of property from vulnerable groups into the speculation sector, with potential impacts on land use and values that could, in turn, reduce land and housing access and equity in the city.

Source: Orr, 2007

Revisiting governance for relief and reconstruction

During the last 25 years, coordination has become a prominent feature of multilateral assistance during and after emergencies. Today, coordination takes up considerable time and effort for all humanitarian actors. Contemporary relief and reconstruction operations are large in scope and include numerous agencies responding to a broad range of needs. Perhaps the first such large-scale event was the humanitarian response to Hurricane Mitch in 1998, which directly affected more than 3 million people as it swept across Honduras, Nicaragua, El Salvador, Guatemala and Belize.[61]

Micro-insurance can assist poorer urban residents to meet their immediate needs during and after a disaster

While the United Nations system and large international NGOs have developed coordination architecture (as exemplified by the United Nations Office for the Coordination of Humanitarian Affairs, or OCHA) and codes of practice (such as the Sphere Standards[62]), the multitude of small and sometimes temporary civil society actors who have come to prominence during recent disasters, such as the Indian Ocean Tsunami, largely lie outside of these arrangements and lines of accountability. The contemporary presence of such a large number of partners, each one with its own identity, culture, mandate, capacity, funding sources and operating style, is possibly the one main factor making coordination an absolutely essential feature of today's humanitarian operations. But for coordination to be successful, an underlying tension between two directions of

Box 12.16 Community participation: Lessons from the Maharashtra Emergency Earthquake Rehabilitation Programme, India

On 30 September 1993, an earthquake struck the Indian state of Maharashtra, killing about 8000 people and damaging some 230,000 houses. To guide reconstruction, the government of Maharashtra and the World Bank created the Maharashtra Emergency Earthquake Rehabilitation Programme (MEERP). MEERP identified 52 villages that needed to be relocated and 1500 villages (190,000 families) that needed their homes to be reconstructed, repaired or strengthened, but on the same site.

In the relocation sites, beneficiaries were not directly involved in construction, but were heavily engaged in the decision-making stages, including the selection of beneficiaries, the identification of relocation sites, the layout of the village, the design of houses and the provision of amenities. Final decisions were taken in plenary meetings of the whole village. During the construction stage, only the village-level committee and community participation consultants were involved with the project management unit. Once the construction was completed, houses were allotted to beneficiaries in open consultation with the entire village.

In communities undergoing reconstruction or repair, homeowners took on the responsibility of repairing, retrofitting and strengthening their houses, with materials and financial and technical assistance from the government. The project management unit opened a bank account for each of the 190,000 eligible homeowners, who received coupons for construction materials. A junior engineer appointed at the village level provided technical assistance to ensure that the houses were earthquake resistant. Each village formed a beneficiary committee to work with the project management unit. In most villages, these committees consisted of women's self-help groups. Training programmes were organized in villages with large numbers of beneficiaries, where residents were informed of their entitlements and the processes to be followed.

After 18 months, the programme had taken on the dimensions of a housing movement. As MEERP progressed, community participation became increasingly accepted as an effective method for resolving problems during the reconstruction process. It also had a positive effect on communities insofar as involving local people helped them to overcome their trauma.

In addition to housing work, some agencies also tackled social issues, such as schooling. Over time, MEERP became a people's project. The participatory process opened many informal channels of communication between ordinary people and the government. Beneficiaries became aware of their entitlements and worked hard within the process to secure them. Individuals who felt that their grievances were not addressed appropriately at the local level approached the district authorities and the government in Mumbai.

Source: Barakat, 2003

accountability for intermediary humanitarian actors needs to be resolved. First, and most important, is downward accountability to the survivors of disaster. Second is accountability to donors or the government agencies, private companies or individuals who provide funds for specific work to be undertaken. Tensions set up by these necessary lines of accountability contribute towards gaps, overlaps and competition between agencies on the ground. This leads to losses in the efficiency and equity of programmes and can undermine local governance structures.

Perhaps most fundamental is that humanitarian actors should review the extent to which their interventions contribute to local development agendas and build resilience by adding to local skill, knowledge and resource bases. In a review of the tsunami reconstruction, it was found that generous levels of funding created obstacles for field-level learning as a consequence of requirements for upward accountability. Upward accountability is resource intensive and expensive. It relies upon skilled professionals to report back on local actions.[63]

If reconstruction and development are to be genuinely linked, then those involved in reconstruction need to think hard about who sets the agenda, and about how best their actions can contribute to local and national visions and plans for development. But concerted effort will be required. The Stockholm Conference in 1999 set out a framework for the US$9 billion in international reconstruction aid for Central America following Hurricane Mitch, but this has arguably led to little improvement in socio-economic status or environmental security in the region.[64] More recently, in Sri Lanka, a Road Map for Disaster Management, co-sponsored by the Government of Sri Lanka Ministry for Disaster Management and the UNDP, was issued in 2005. This provides a framework for integrating disaster risk reduction within development planning.[65] The central involvement of national government in the planning stage of the road map is a good example of growing partnerships between national and international actors in reconstruction governance.

THE ROLE OF PARTICIPATORY AND INCLUSIVE STRATEGIES AND POLICIES

Building resilience into urban development is a challenge that requires the application of participatory and inclusive strategies. The task of participatory and inclusive strategies is to identify what every actor and asset in the city can contribute to shape and implement sound disaster risk management. The fact that everyone, even children, has a role to play is demonstrated well in Armenia, where disaster risk education is promoted in schools and through the mass media. This initiative is led by a women's development group that emphasizes disaster mitigation and focuses on mothers and teachers fostering seismic protection skills among children.[66]

Trends in urban governance over the last 20 years have opened up the range of actors with stakes in development. Structural adjustment and associated social impact amelioration policies, and, more recently, Poverty Reduction Strategy Papers (PRSPs) have brought civil society and the private sector alongside government as actors in urban development. The experience of urban development, to date, has many examples of collaborative and participatory approaches. These will not be reviewed here.[67] Rather, this section examines three emerging themes for disaster risk reduction that offer scope for enhancing the inclusiveness of disaster management within urban development planning: inclusive planning, the role of education in awareness-raising and the potential of the private sector.

Inclusive planning

Inclusive planning opens space for wide participation and engagement with the planning process. The aspect of inclusive planning that is, perhaps, most developed, and where most experience lies is the incorporation of local actors within disaster preparedness, relief and reconstruction projects. Many techniques exist for bringing multiple stakeholders together to generate more open and transparent planning processes.[68] The Earthquake Safe Shimla Initiative coordinated by the Indian NGO Sustainable Environment and Ecological Development Society is typical in concluding that bringing communities and local government together in partnership delivers better results than a recipient–provider relationship.[69] The huge potential for inclusive reconstruction planning is exemplified in Box 12.16 through an account of the Maharashtra Emergency Earthquake Rehabilitation Programme in India.

As mentioned earlier in Box 12.1, UN-Habitat is using inclusive strategies for slum upgrading in Maputo (Mozambique) and is integrating flood risk reduction in the process.[70] Through the inclusion of multiple actors, including community groups, as well as through participatory land-use planning and reform of planning regulations, flood risk is now seen and responded to as a problem of development and not one for humanitarian relief.

Local conflict over land rights following a disaster can also be mediated through the use of inclusive approaches. As part of disaster preparedness programmes, customary landownership and use rights can usefully be catalogued. These will require regular updating, but are invaluable post-disaster. Where no records are available, rapid participatory reviews of land use and landownership are less open to disruption and corruption than exercises conducted without open participation or, at a later date, during reconstruction. In addition to physical outputs that reduce risk, institutional benefits of participatory approaches have included the establishment of a transparent decision-making process that helps to resolve local conflict over land rights.

Inclusive planning also presents opportunities to identify resources used in everyday urban life that can contribute to disaster preparedness, response or reconstruction. Existing, local civil society, business or government networks can be piggybacked for raising awareness of disaster risk and planning for disaster or for disseminating disaster warnings. Box 12.17 describes actions taken in the state of Texas (US), which is exposed to hurricanes. Here, school buildings and buses are used for evacuation and shelter during hurricanes. This is common practice in many US states and other countries and points the way for other imaginative uses of everyday resources to build resilience through their overlapping uses.

Box 12.17 Education centres as evacuation resources for the US Gulf Coast

School buses have long been used to support evacuation during hurricanes. Following Hurricanes Katrina and Rita, where evacuation planning has been criticized, strategies for the Gulf Coast have been re-evaluated, with greater emphasis put on pre-disaster planning to improve the effectiveness with which school resources can be used in evacuations.

It is estimated that in a hurricane evacuation of the Texas Gulf Coast area, aside from those requiring support because of medical or special needs assistance, there might be as many as 190,000 citizens requiring pubic evacuation because they have no access to private transportation or have insufficient funds for fuel, lodging, etc.

In March 2006, the Governor's Division of Emergency Management in Texas issued an executive order including a directive that requires public education institutes to assist in transportation and shelter operations. School districts have been asked to draw up a plan to provide school buses, drivers and shelter facilities in the event of a hurricane threatening the Texas Gulf Coast. This directive applies to inland, as well as coastal, schools.

School district plans are coordinated with the regional unified command structure of the local council of government. Plans need to identify the right people to be on call in an emergency and must provide this information to local emergency responders. Depending upon the severity of the hurricane threat and the population of the area, the need for school buses and drivers from outside the area affected by a hurricane could range from several hundred to more than a thousand.

Hurricane season is mostly during the summer when students do not attend school. This makes it easier to use schools as shelters, but more difficult to contact and raise drivers and other support staff. Staff directories and an agreement by staff that they are willing to work during emergencies can help to overcome this challenge. Plans also need to consider how a school closure will be managed should the school become a shelter during teaching time.

Source: Governor's Division of Emergency Management, Texas, www.txdps.state.tx.us/dem/pages/index.htm

Inclusive planning opens space for ... the incorporation of local actors within disaster preparedness, relief and reconstruction projects

Inclusive planning is often criticized for requiring more time and resources than more directed planning. However, the experience of UN-Habitat in Mozambique illustrates that inclusive planning can increase time and cost effectiveness. This is achieved through transparent decision-making that reduces conflict and the facilitation of access to local knowledge, avoiding reliance on contracted technical field surveys.[71]

Local conflict over land rights following a disaster can ... be mediated through the use of inclusive approaches

Among other challenges facing inclusive planning is the charge that most initiatives are inherently local and can only contribute in a limited way to larger structural concerns that shape poverty, vulnerability and risk. Initiatives focus on resolving the symptoms of a problem (e.g. poor housing, lack of local institutions and inadequate services) without addressing the root causes of risk (e.g. macro-economic restructuring and lack of political will). However, deliberative techniques can enable participation to feed into policy decision-making.

Deliberative processes can be used either for instrumental ends or for genuine citizen empowerment. They can open political space for debate about wider questions of ethics, values and their links with issues of justice, morality and rights in development or risk management decision-making. Techniques used include citizens' juries, citizens' panels, committees, consensus conferences, scenario workshops, deliberative polling, focus groups, multi-criteria mapping, public meetings, rapid and participatory urban appraisal, and visioning exercises.

Informal education ... offers a key opportunity for empowering those at risk...

Recent examples of deliberative planning feeding into decision-making for risk governance have included the setting of air quality standards and regulation in Santiago (Chile); citizen involvement in the location of a hazardous waste facility in Alberta (Canada); urban environmental assessment in Greenpoint, New York (US); and, a citizens' panel to feed into a decision on where to locate a waste disposal site in Canton Aargau (Switzerland).[72] All of these activities provide scope for local communities to be involved in planning decisions that shape their exposure to human-made hazard and potential disaster.

Deliberative techniques can take time and this is a potential source of exclusion for those who are poor or have little time to spare. Care needs to be taken to ensure that women burdened with domestic, child caring and other tasks can still engage in the process. Guidelines for deliberative and inclusive processes have been proposed by the UK-based Institute of Public Policy Research.[73] Despite the wide application of deliberative methods, there has been little systematic analysis of the interaction of these methods with the wider policy process that they claim to influence.[74]

Box 12.18 World Disaster Reduction Campaign: Disaster Risk Reduction Begins at School

Faced with the huge challenge of responding to urban disaster risk, it is difficult to know where to start. One leading priority should be to make public infrastructure safe for those who use it today and as a legacy for the future. Protecting schools adds security and can build human resources when undertaken as part of an integrated programme of education and skill development in addition to structural safety.

The need for risk reduction initiatives for schools is clear. In 2006, 160 schools were destroyed during an earthquake in Iran, and a mudslide on Leyte Island in the Philippines covered a single school but killed more than 200 children. In 2005, the South Asian earthquake led to over 16,000 children being killed when schools collapsed.

The 2006–2007 World Disaster Reduction Campaign: Disaster Risk Reduction Begins at School is led by the United Nations International Strategy for Disaster Reduction (ISDR) in partnership with the United Nations Educational, Scientific and Cultural Organization (UNESCO), the United Nations Children's Fund (UNICEF), ActionAid International and the International Federation of Red Cross and Red Crescent Societies (IFRC). It seeks to promote disaster reduction education in school curricula, and to improve school safety by encouraging the application of construction standards that can withstand any kind of natural hazard.

The campaign was launched in June 2006 and during this year brought attention to school safety through press briefings and workshops with journalists, academics and policy-makers. Activities have taken place in Kathmandu (Nepal), Nairobi (Kenya), Panama City (Panama), Bali (Indonesia), Geneva (Switzerland), Paris (France) and Wuppertal (Germany).

Source: ISDR, www.unisdr.org/eng/public_aware/world_camp/2006-2007/wdrc-2006-2007.htm

Education for awareness-raising and self-reliance

Education provides a key resource to make risk reduction strategies more inclusive. A little over half of the countries reporting to the United Nations World Conference on Disaster Reduction in 2005 stated that their education systems included some form of disaster-related teaching. Mexico, Romania and New Zealand mandate, by law, the teaching of disaster-related subjects in their schools.

A very recent review of the potential of education systems to raise awareness and skills for disaster risk reduction reports that many school curricula already focus on hazards through earth science, and also practise preparedness and drills; but few schools integrate the two and few develop their own local curriculum to reflect local risk contexts.[75] Greater still is the unmet potential for schools to connect learning with practice in the local community.

School curricula vary greatly. Some provide excellent training in earth and climate science, but do not focus on locally experienced hazards. In other cases, they focus exclusively on one recent disaster. On the tsunami-affected coast of Thailand, new curricula focus exclusively on tsunami, despite more common hazards being coastal storms, floods and forest fire.

In Cuba, disaster preparedness, prevention and response are part of all school curricula. This is supported by the Cuban Red Cross, which provides teaching material, and is reinforced by training courses and disaster drills for parents in the workplace, as well as by radio and television broadcasts. The impacts of such holistic education can be seen, in part, in Cuba's exceptional record in protecting human life in recent hurricanes.[76] In Ecuador, Civil Defence is involved in training on appropriate actions to be taken by teachers and students in case of emergency for both earthquakes and volcanic eruption. These programmes were put to the test during recent active periods of Pichincha and Reventador volcanoes.

In New Delhi (India), 500 schools have developed school disaster plans as a result of the work of school committees composed of the zone education officer, the principal, teachers, parents, the head boy and the head girl. Mock drills are held in the selected schools. The children also learn life-saving skills.[77]

Informal education also offers a key opportunity for empowering those at risk, not only children, but adults too. Informal education can be promoted alongside formal services, where these exist, to target vulnerable groups who may be excluded from formal education through poverty or social inequality. Two successful pathways are to develop community and popular media programmes. Community delivery works well where programmes are built onto existing community organizations and networks. The advantage of this approach is that people can learn from experience and the example of others. Using the popular media can reach more people and be cost effective in these terms, but has less lasting impressions compared to community-delivered programmes of education. Opportunities for combining popular media with local activities offer perhaps the greatest scope for informal education to reduce risk.

In conclusion, education can:

- Provide a sense of continuity and normalcy after disaster. The United Nations Educational, Scientific and Cultural Organization (UNESCO), the United Nations Children's Fund (UNICEF) and a number of NGOs, such as Save the Children, are already active in this field.
- Challenge preconceptions about who is most at risk and who can reduce risk in the community. In particular, education can challenge gender and age stereotypes.
- Reach out to the 325 million children worldwide who live on the street or work full time and have no contact with formal education.

Some progress in meeting these challenges and a potential mechanism for sharing lessons learned will come from the ISDR 2006–2007 World Disaster Reduction Campaign: Disaster Risk Reduction Begins at School (see Box 12.18).[78] Driven by an understanding that every school that collapses killing children or destroying resources was once a development project, this campaign aims to inform and mobilize governments, communities and individuals to ensure that disaster risk reduction is fully integrated within school curricula in high-risk countries and that school buildings are built or retrofitted to withstand natural hazards.

Including the private sector

The private sector is a major actor in shaping the opportunities and risks of urban life. Public–private partnerships and foreign direct investment have increased the stake and responsibility of international capital in urban infrastructure provision and economic development. Despite this growing influence, there is little evidence of a proactive engagement with disaster risk reduction among the private sector that goes beyond charity donations for recovery. Even this is by no means to be taken for granted. The generosity of many businesses following the Indian Ocean Tsunami in 2004 has been followed by doubt among business donors over the transparency of relief and reconstruction mechanisms managed by non-governmental and governmental actors alike, with potential for a backlash against donations for disaster response and recovery.

The business case for involvement in disaster risk reduction is largely built upon corporate social responsibility. The most active industrial sector is insurance, with a growing number of companies going beyond offering advice to providing financial incentives and training for safe construction and disaster response.[79] There are also a small number of global engineering and urban planning companies that have provided services as part of a corporate social responsibility package during reconstruction. Arup, an engineering firm, for example, provided urban planning expertise to the Government of Turkey following the Marmara earthquake in 1999. Twenty experts worked for six months to develop a city master plan. The experience also enabled planners from Turkey and overseas to exchange ideas on reconstruction in an earthquake-prone region.[80] The majority of recorded cases of corporate support come from the US, with some examples from the Philippines and the Caribbean.[81] There is clearly great scope for private-sector involvement in cities outside these areas.

From a business perspective, successful prevention activity can reduce risks to operations, suppliers, trading and customers, and reinforce good will towards a company. One of the most important ways in which business could contribute is by working to reduce vulnerability among at-risk populations within their sphere of influence. Responsible business practice can include putting in place measures to protect employees, their homes and families from the effects of disasters. Business relationships also provide a level for change. Giving preference to suppliers who themselves follow a corporate social responsibility code, and endeavouring not to leave suppliers in the event of temporary disruption following a disaster event, are examples of the kind of positive engagement with risk reduction that corporations could be encouraged to consider.

...there is little evidence of a proactive engagement with disaster risk reduction amongst the private sector...

The corporate social responsibility case for disaster prevention is held back by a lack of empirical evidence. Analysis is needed of the impacts of disasters on business, of the contribution that business involvement can make to disaster prevention, and of the costs and benefits of that involvement to establish the most effective actions that businesses can take.

Strategies for encouraging corporate social responsibility for risk reduction might include partnerships between business and humanitarian actors. Where this relationship already exists, there is some evidence that business has recognized the strategic value of supporting risk reduction. Examples of partnerships include:

- TNT and Citigroup working in partnership with the World Food Programme;
- Nike and Microsoft in partnership with the UNHCR and the IFRC;
- UPS in partnership with CARE;
- FedEx in partnership with the American Red Cross;
- Ericsson in partnership with the United Nations and the IFRC; and
- DHL in partnership with the OCHA and the UNDP.

The business case for involvement in disaster risk reduction is largely built upon corporate social responsibility

Small- and medium-sized businesses are also becoming involved, often through their local chamber of commerce or other local business associations.[82]

CONCLUDING REMARKS

Increasing numbers of urban dwellers have to live with the threat and experience of natural and human-made disasters. Often, but not always, disaster risk is greatest among the poorest. This chapter has examined core pathways through which resilience to disaster risk is, and can be, strengthened in cities. There is a good degree of overlap between these routes to security and also with pro-poor urban development and urban policies that aim to reduce the environmental damage of urbanization.

For all aspects of disaster risk reduction, inclusive and participatory strategies and policies can offer scope for building empowerment, self-reliance and accountability among those who make decisions, strengthening the resilience of communities and cities. Participation is not a panacea and it is as vulnerable to capture from vested interests as other approaches to development. There are many examples of partnerships, including local or national government and civil society; but the private sector also has much to offer. This potential has not yet been realized in urban risk reduction, with corporate social responsibility being limited to emergency relief.

NOTES

1 General Assembly Resolution A/RES/55/2 (*adopted* 18 September 2000).
2 United Nations, 2001b.
3 See www.unisdr.org/eng/mdgs-drr/link-mdg-drr.htm.
4 See www.dfid.gov.uk/pubs/files/drr-scoping-study.pdf.
5 See www.undp.org/bcpr/disred/rdr.htm.
6 Projects and Designs Ltd.
7 See www.unmillennium project.org/reports/fullreport.htm.
8 See www.unhabitat.org/down loads/docs/2072_61331_ist-dec.pdf.
9 UN-Habitat, 2001.
10 The United Nations Conference on Disaster Reduction in 2005 culminated in the adoption of the Hyogo Framework for Action; see www.unisdr.org/eng/hfa/docs/HFA-brochure-English.pdf.
11 United Nations, 2006.
12 *Ibid*.
13 Salvadorian Foundation of Integral Support.
14 Warmsler, 2006b.
15 Bull-Kamanga et al, 2003.
16 DFID, 2005.
17 UN-Habitat, 2003d.
18 Re-planning the city to reduce the amount of distances that people and goods travel also needs to consider the potential risks of placing industrial facilities close to other land uses (e.g. residential, educational and recreational risks).
19 The German government's international development agency.
20 Forrester et al, undated.
21 Quan et al, 1998.
22 Dedeurwaerdere, 1998.
23 Mechler, 2003.
24 Sensitivity analysis randomly varies input variables to study the sensitivity of outputs to these changes. Where frequency data on return periods and severity exists, more sophisticated probabilistic analysis can be undertaken. See, for example, the US Federal Emergency Management Agency Mitigation Benefit-Cost Analysis Toolkit, available from www.fema.gov/government/grant/bca.shtm#1.
25 Venton and Venton, 2004.
26 Gavidia and Crivellari, 2006.
27 The AUDMP aims to reduce the disaster vulnerability of urban populations, infrastructure, critical facilities and shelter in targeted cities throughout Asia. It has demonstration projects in nine countries, coordinated from its headquarters in Bangkok. See www.adpc.net/AUDMP/audmp.html.
28 The African Urban Risk Analysis Network is a network of African-based universities and NGOs conducting research and undertaking local activities that attempt to reduce disaster risks in African cities. The network was initiated in 2003, with founding institutes from Algeria, Ghana, Kenya, Senegal, South Africa and Tanzania. See www.auranafrica.?org.
29 Bursa, 2004.
30 Conchesco, 2003.
31 Benson and Twigg, 2004.
32 Tokyo Metropolitan Government, Bureau of Urban Development, undated.
33 ISDR, 2005a.
34 Dixit, 2006.
35 ISDR, 2005a.
36 See www.nicee.org/IAEE_English.php.
37 IAEE, 1986.
38 See www.undmtp.org/about.htm.
39 IPCC, 2001.
40 *Ibid*.
41 *Ibid*.
42 Approximately US$34 billion, US$459 billion and US$917 billion, respectively.
43 Munasinhge, 2000.
44 Schipper and Pelling, 2006.
45 Bigio, 2003.
46 See www.iclei.org/index.php?id=800.
47 Bohannon, 2005.
48 McQuaid and Marshall, 2005.
49 IFRC, 2005a, 2005b.
50 To listen to the *Radionovela* episodes over the internet, access www.eird.org/esp/radionovela/?radionove-tiempos-hist-una.htm.
51 Bijan Daftari, head of Relief and Rescue Organization, Red Crescent Society of the Islamic Republic of Iran, Tehran, in GIGnos Institute, undated.
52 DFID, 2005.
53 Barakat, 2003.
54 Christoplos, 2006.
55 Pelling, 2006.
56 ProVention Consortium Brief, undated.
57 Kreimer et al, 1999.
58 Guerra-Fletes and Williams, 2006.
59 Miamidian et al, 2005.
60 Pantoja, 2002.
61 Calvi-Parisetti and Kiniger-Passigli, 2002.
62 See www.sphereproject.org.
63 Christoplos, 2006.
64 See, for example, Christian Aid, (undates) www.christian-aid.org.uk/indepth/9910inde/indebt1.htm.
65 Disaster Management Centre, 2005.
66 Wisner, 2006.
67 For a review of the opportunities and challenges facing participatory urban development, see also Riley and Wakely (2005). See also the journal *Environment and Urbanization* for many examples of participatory approaches to urban development, poverty alleviation and environmental management.
68 Hamdi and Goethert, 1997.
69 Gupta et al, 2006.
70 Spaliviero, 2006.
71 *Ibid*.
72 Holmes and Scoones, 2000.
73 See www.ippr.org.
74 Pimbert and Wakeford, 2001.
75 Wisner, 2006.
76 IFRC, 2005b.
77 UNDP, 2005.
78 See www.unisdr.org/eng/public_aware/world_camp/2006-2007/wdrc-2006-2007.htm.
79 Pelling, 2003.
80 Twigg, 2001.
81 *Ibid*.
82 Warhurst, 2006.

PART VI
SUMMARY OF CASE STUDIES

INTRODUCTION

A series of case studies was commissioned by UN-Habitat specifically for this Global Report on each of the three threats to urban safety and security addressed in the report (i.e. crime and violence, insecurity of tenure and forced evictions, and natural and human-made disasters). For each of these threats – covered in Parts II, III and IV of the report, respectively – case studies illustrate empirical conditions and trends; as well as effective policy responses. An attempt has been made to ensure adequate coverage of all of the world's geographic regions.

This part contains summaries of 25 of these case studies. The original case studies may be found, in full, at UN-Habitat's website (www.unhabitat.org). Many of the illustrative boxes contained in the different chapters of this report are based on these case studies, while some of the experiences described in the case studies – including related empirical evidence – are also directly integrated within the text of the chapters.

A typical illustrative box in this report uses only a portion of the full case study, so that the 'full story' of the experience on which the box is based may not be apparent to the reader. The summaries contained in this part thus provide the reader with a fuller picture of the experiences described in the illustrative boxes, including the geographical and socio-economic context of the case; the full scope of the experience described; and the main conclusions or lessons from the case.

THE HUMAN SECURITY PERSPECTIVE

Enhancing urban safety and human security in Asia through the United Nations Trust Fund for Human Security

In March 1999, the Government of Japan and the United Nations Secretariat launched the United Nations Trust Fund for Human Security (UNTFHS), from which the Commission on Human Security prepared the *Human Security Now* report in 2003 as a contribution to the United Nations Secretary-General's plea for progress on the goals of 'freedom from want' and 'freedom from fear'. The main objective of the UNTFHS is to advance the operational impact of the human security concept, particularly in countries and regions where the insecurities of people are most manifest and critical, such as in areas affected by natural and human-made disasters.

Growing inequalities between the rich and the poor, as well as social, economic and political exclusion of large sectors of society, make the security paradigm increasingly complex. Human security has broadened to include such conditions as freedom from poverty and access to work, education and health. This, in turn, has necessitated a change in perspective, from state-centred security to people-centred security. To ensure human security as well as state security, particularly in conflict and post-conflict areas where institutions are often fragile and unstable, rebuilding communities becomes an absolute priority to promote peace and reconciliation.

With the rapid urbanization of the world's population, human security as protecting 'the vital core of all human lives in ways that enhance human freedoms and human fulfilment' increasingly means providing the conditions of livelihood and dignity in urban areas. Living conditions are crucial for human security since an inadequate dwelling, insecurity of tenure and insufficient access to basic services all have a strong negative impact on the lives of the urban population, particularly the urban poor. Spatial discrimination and social exclusion limit or undermine the rights to the city and to citizenship.

In this context, UN-Habitat is coordinating three UNTFHS programmes in Afghanistan, northeast Sri Lanka and Phnom Penh, the capital city of Cambodia, all focusing on informal settlements upgrading. On the assumption that community empowerment is crucial for reconstructing war-affected societies, all programmes have adopted the community action planning method – a community-based consultative planning process – and have established community development councils as the most effective approach to improving living conditions and human security in informal settlements.

Upgrading informal settlements in three cities in Afghanistan

The programme's main objective is to improve the urban environment in informal settlements by:

- providing security of tenure and adequate access to basic infrastructure; and
- empowering the communities to directly implement specific projects and to negotiate with central and municipal agencies.

Since its inception in 2005, the programme has been implemented in 48 settlements in Mazar-e-Sharif (Balkh Province) to the north, Jalalabad (Nangarhar Province) to the east and Kandahar to the south, with an average of three projects per settlement. Local projects are carried out with the direct involvement of community development councils and through the community action planning approach.

The programme addresses the issue of human security by improving the conditions of the urban environment, empowering local communities and fostering local economic development.

■ Rebuilding communities in northeast Sri Lanka

The programme aims to restore the human dignity of the urban poor through community empowerment and the provision of basic infrastructure. It was launched in the aftermath of the peace agreements with the Liberation Tamil Tigers Elam; but its implementation took place after the conflict had resumed. The programme seeks to empower poor communities in improving their living environment through community development councils and their integration within the urban context, following the destruction of the physical and socio-economic fabric from both conflict and the 2004 Indian Ocean Tsunami. The programme has supported a range of physical improvements and social projects, including savings-and-loan operations, drainage and road paving, community centres, public markets, libraries and children's playgrounds. The programme is being implemented in ten settlements in the north-eastern cities of Jaffna, Kilinochchi, Batticaloa and Kattankudy, all conflict- and natural disaster-affected areas largely excluded from government interventions and post-tsunami international aid.

■ Partnership for Urban Poverty Reduction in Phnom Penh, Cambodia

The Partnership for Urban Poverty Reduction was set up to strengthen the self-confidence, enhance the competence and raise the dignity of communities living in the slum and squatter settlements of Phnom Penh by reducing their vulnerability, poverty and social exclusion. A Community Human Security Fund helps the communities to implement a community action plan based on their own priorities. Most projects focus on community-based infrastructure, such as concrete lanes, drainage and footbridges, primarily benefiting the women and children of more than 30,000 families, or approximately 150,000 slum dwellers.

Lessons learned

The contribution to human security, and the dignity upon which this concept is based, in Afghanistan, northeast Sri Lanka and Phnom Penh provided by UNTFHS is grounded primarily on:

- addressing the different aspects of vulnerability in war-affected areas through a multi-sectoral approach and;
- a seamless transition from a protection-centred to an empowerment-centred perspective, through community organization.

CRIME AND VIOLENCE

Effective crime prevention strategies and engagement with the planning process in Bradford, UK

Bradford is a city in northern England that is part of the West Yorkshire conurbation. Its population is just over 475,000 and since World War II it has been characterized by a high rate of inward migration (by UK comparative standards) from the Indian subcontinent and particularly from Pakistan. Just over 20 per cent of the population declared their religion as Muslim, Sikh or Hindu at the 2001 census, with Muslims making up just fewer than 90 per cent of this group.

These characteristics make Bradford one of the UK's most ethnically diverse cities, and this is important in shaping how it approaches issues of crime and violence, especially since major riots in July 2001, which saw significant confrontations between Muslim youths and the police, resulting in considerable property damage and approximately 300 people injured.

As far as the experience of crime is concerned, the evidence appears to suggest that Bradford has seen some improvements during recent years, although in an absolute sense the city's crime rate of about 150 recorded crimes per 1000 people in 2003/2004 would still be regarded as being quite high in many parts of the world. The city's crime audit for 2004 estimated that overall crime levels had fallen by around 16 per cent between 2001/2002 and 2003/2004, once account has been taken of a nationally driven change in the way that crimes were recorded by the police. The city's crime figures suggest that crime rates in Bradford are slightly higher than the average for England and Wales; but they are lower than for most of the other large cities in England outside London when calculated as rates per 1000 people, where the average was approximately 170 recorded crimes per 1000 people.

The trends in relation to the main types of crime between 2001/2002 and 2003/2004 were as follows:

- Domestic burglary fell by 28 per cent. The figure for 2004/2005 was just over 8 per 1000 people.
- Vehicle crime (both theft of vehicles and theft from vehicles) fell by just under 25 per cent. The figure for 2004/2005 was just under 19 per 1000 people.
- Robbery fell by 42 per cent. The figure for 2004/2005 was just under 1 per 1000 people.
- Violent crime apparently increased by 133 per cent, although this figure needs to be treated with caution. It is likely that the true rise in violent crime is very much smaller than this bare statistic would suggest, although it does seem that crimes of violence are on the increase. During 2004/2005 there were 23 incidents of violence and just over 1 of sexual offences per 1000 individuals.

Hate crime (consisting of racial and homophobic crime and domestic abuse) also appears to be increasing, although this is mainly because reported incidents of domestic abuse (which make up 90 per cent of recorded hate crimes) rose by 29 per cent.

Bradford has a partnership approach for addressing issues of crime and violence that follows the model established by the 1998 Crime and Disorder Act, and which appears to have been able to put in place a strategy and a series of action plans that have contributed to the fall in crime. The current strategic priorities for this strategy, which is rolled forward every three years, are visible responses both to environmental quality issues and to the provision in communities of a uniformed presence, support for vulnerable people, the prevention of crime and law enforcement. This is also closely related to the overall community strategy for the city, in which securing public safety for a multicultural community is a major issue.

In addition, Bradford has also taken the British idea of getting the planning system to address crime prevention quite a long way, with a clear policy statement in a recently approved development plan, a commitment to the further development of this thinking in the preparation of more detailed guidance, a history of effective work by the police architectural liaison service, and some solid achievements on the ground (see Box 4.6).

All of these things make Bradford an interesting case of effective crime prevention strategies and of engagement with the planning process. At the same time, this case also demonstrates some of the difficulties involved in going down these roads, since this has by no means always been a smooth journey. In particular, there is still a distance to go before a consensus could be said to have been reached within the city's planning and development community about what constitutes good practice in this field. As a consequence, the case is useful not just as a demonstration of a highly structured approach to tackling crime and violence, but also as an illustration of some of the issues that arise from such an approach.

Effective crime prevention in Durban, South Africa

South Africa experienced soaring crime levels during the last years of apartheid, which continue unabated into the ten years of democracy. Crime in Durban, the largest city in the KwaZulu-Natal Province, increased by 13 per cent between 2001 and 2005, with more than 190,000 cases of crime between 2004 and 2005. Crime statistics from the South African Police Services Information Analysis Centre show that burglary at residential premises, other forms of theft, common assault, robbery with aggravating circumstances, assault with the intent to inflict grievous bodily harm, and theft out of or from motor vehicles are among the leading forms of crime, constituting 60 per cent, 18 per cent, 9 per cent, 8 per cent, 6 per cent and 5.9 per cent, respectively, of the total crime, While total crime, in general, has increased in Durban, there have been noticeable decreases in particular forms of crime, such as theft of motor vehicles and motorcycles, burglary at business premises and arson, which have reduced by 10 per cent, 2 per cent, 1.5 per cent and 1 per cent, respectively, between 2001 and 2005. On the obverse, sharp increases in crimes such as burglary at residential areas, common robbery and drug-related crimes have increased by 47 per cent, 4 per cent and 2 per cent, respectively, contributing to increased crime in Durban.

As a response, city officials have forged development negotiations, peace pacts and partnerships as mechanisms to prevent crime in Durban. These efforts are an attempt to strengthen community-based involvement in the development process of the new South Africa, a notion that aligns well with the concept of participatory democracy. Key issues in Durban are centred around creating and carrying out partnership processes, the problems (and value) of incorporating the informal sector within crime prevention efforts, targeting programmes for vulnerable groups, and crafting effective social and environmental design initiatives.

The Safer Cities Steering Committee, consisting of city councillors, public officials and South African Police Services and Business against Crime members, was established to guide project development. A research advisory group was established to advise on research, information-gathering, analysis and best practices, mainly in the area of 'social' crime prevention, focusing on violence against women, victim support, youth development and understanding the causes of violence. While most of these initiatives are still in their infancy, results prove to be positive. In 2003, the new Ethekwini Municipality Safety and Crime Prevention Strategy was developed and adopted by council as part of a five-year strategic plan of action. The Durban Safer Cities Strategy brings different role-players together in a prevention partnership. Three pillars of the strategy include:

- effective policing and crime prevention;
- targeted 'social' crime prevention; and
- crime prevention through environmental design.

These initiatives also include:

- community police forums;
- business against crime partnerships;
- education, including a strategy on school safety;
- extensive inner-city CCTV networks monitored by municipal police;
- Durban suburban crime prevention strategies; and
- use of women's safety audits.

While these initiatives have not eradicated crime, they have, to a greater extent, contained it. Clearly, the challenges are overwhelming and, to have any impact at all, there is a strong need to coordinate exceedingly well and to build strong alliances across society. This should include strong links with relevant government departments, business, media, civil society (including churches), traditional leaders and healers, as well as communities.

Several lessons have emerged from Durban's experience, the most notable of which include the following:

- There is still a lack of coordination between government departments on safety and security. Consequently, developing mechanisms for coordinated action is a necessary step if crime and violence prevention programmes are to be implemented effectively.

- The effective implementation of crime prevention programmes is necessary if confidence in public authorities is to be achieved and maintained.
- Despite government's commitment to prioritize crime, there are still no timeframes or performance indicators in place to monitor service delivery. Measurement of performance is crucial in programme delivery and evaluation.
- The importance of directly involving the business community in crime prevention and reduction programmes, such as the Business against Crime initiative, is clear. This initiative has created an alliance with various business sectors in the Durban area so that their different safety needs can be identified and presented to the South African Police Services and the Durban City Police.
- It is important to harness the strong points and value of the informal sector and unemployed youths as part of local crime prevention efforts, such as the Traders against Crime and youth car guards initiatives. The Traders against Crime initiative has been quite successful: traders and street vendors know their areas very well and, as such, can easily spot criminal elements and criminal activity and report these to the relevant authorities.
- It is important to target vulnerable groups, such as women and children, in crime and violence prevention programmes.
- Women safety audits for the purpose of obtaining first-hand knowledge about crime and violence are also important: such knowledge affects specific groups.
- While the problems of crime in transitional or emerging democracies are significant, they can be tackled by concerted public and private initiatives.

Crime and violence in Hong Kong, China

Hong Kong has become one of the world's safest metropolises. Compared to other cities, Hong Kong's crime rate is very low, especially for offences such as burglary, car theft and robbery, as well as offences notable for their sensitivity to environmental and situational determinants. This low rate of crime is supported by the results of the periodic crime victimization surveys undertaken by both the government and the United Nations. Hong Kong's anti-crime efforts and support of law enforcement are reflected in the relatively high incarceration rate (176.8 per 100,000 individuals in 2005) and a large police service (486.6 police per 100,000 individuals in 2000). The police force has long been equipped with extensive 'stop and search' powers since the colonial period. An average of 10 per cent of public expenditure is devoted to security.

Hong Kong has not always been safe and suffered several civil disturbances during the 1950s and 1960s, and crime rates for homicide and robbery were not particularly low compared to other countries in the same period. Indeed, Hong Kong's crime rates continued to rise throughout the 1960s and 1970s as the colony underwent rapid modernization and the proportion of the youthful population surged. Positive attitudes to the reporting of crime have been associated with the demise of the symbiosis between organized crime (triads) and elements of the police, following special anti-corruption measures. This also contributed to increases in the *reported* crime rate during this period. Crime rates, however, reached a plateau during the 1980s and thereafter have generally declined.

The labour- and Cultural Revolution-inspired disturbances of the 1950s and 1960s initiated social welfare responses from the British colonial government, which hitherto had long upheld a 'minimal state doctrine' and unfettered 'free trade'. The 1970s marked the start of genuine localization and transformation of the Hong Kong Police from an alien force that served British colonial hegemony to one that served the Hong Kong community. After the transfer of sovereignty to the People's Republic of China in 1997, the Hong Kong Police operated in the context of the 'one country, two systems' arrangements for the new Hong Kong Special Administrative Region of the People's Republic of China (see Box 4.8 for details).

Cultural factors such as utilitarian familism, Confucianism and extended kinship structures are often cited as contributing factors to the low crime rates in Hong Kong. The pervasive family-oriented traditions of the Chinese and public attitudes favour a government hostile to crime and corruption and are generally supportive of severe punishment to adult offenders. Familism also amplifies the shaming effect of offending because it is shared by the entire family. Confucianism also privileges order over individual rights and thus promotes *communitarianism*, where the emphasis is on collective interests.

Although the death penalty was abolished in 1992, Hong Kong had been a *de facto* abolitionist jurisdiction since the 1960s. Nevertheless, many offences, such as firearm-related offences, often result in lengthy sentences when compared to sentences given in Western countries. Furthermore, strict gun laws have effectively reduced firearm robbery to fewer than five events per year, and not a single incident of domestic violence was perpetuated with a firearm during the past five years.

The overall reduction in official crime matched the declining population group aged 15 to 29 – the age group that usually accounts for the majority of the crime committed. The proportion of the 15 to 29 age group decreased by 15 per cent in 2005, while overall crime and violent crime decreased by 25 per cent and 43.1 per cent, respectively.

The densely populated nature of urban high-rise living in Hong Kong also provides higher levels of natural or informal surveillance by facilitating the presence of capable guardians and reduces the opportunity for crime. The availability of attractive wealthy targets within the city has a limited stimulus on crime opportunity due to the large numbers of private security officers employed (1872 per 100,000 individuals). In addition, advanced crime prevention technologies, including CCTV, are installed in public housing, public recreational areas and crime hotspots, and these serve to reduce a potential offender's willingness to commit crime.

Various measures that attempted to bring the public and state together in fighting crime have been successfully implemented since the late 1960s. The continual localization and professionalization of the Hong Kong police also overcame the challenge caused by the rising proportion of at-risk youths during the 1970s and the cross-border crime wave that struck during the late 1980s and early 1990s.

Hong Kong's service-oriented policing, however, faces new challenges. The challenges are not only about the threat of transnational crime and traditional crime and its evolution in cyberspace, but about the demand for proactive action on domestic violence – where the would-be guardians may be the perpetrators. This requires balancing the role of state intervention in family disputes with heightened respect for civil rights, while at the same time ensuring that social services and police collaborate. However, with an increasingly ageing population, more attention will be needed to curb the growing incidence of crime against the elderly.

The low crime rate observed in Hong Kong is a result of a complicated mixture of cultural traditions, proactive crime prevention and the emergence of a legitimate 'consensus' style of law enforcement. Thus, family-oriented Confucianist values, a large professionalized and localized police force that focuses on a client–services approach, strict gun laws, successful cooperative suppression of cross-border crime, high levels of formal or informal supervision, proactive efforts against organized crime and corruption, and severe punishment for the convicted all serve to reduce opportunity for crime.

Trends in crime and violence in Kingston, Jamaica

Kingston is the capital of Jamaica, with a geographic coverage of 430.7 square kilometres. The 1991 population census showed that 538,000 persons lived in the Kingston Metropolitan Area (KMA), and in 2001 that number had increased to 651,880. At the end of 2005, Jamaica's population stood at 2,660,700. In other words, the KMA accounted for 21.52 per cent of the population in 1991, compared to 24.5 per cent in 2001, which represents a population growth rate for the KMA of 2.3 per cent – more than four times higher than the overall population growth rate for Jamaica. The KMA has limited access to land, leading to environmental problems such as squatting and the unsustainable use of natural resources. There are considerable strains on the environment resulting from rapid population growth, inadequate housing, waste management and improper drainage in some areas.

The KMA is characterized by many inner-city communities and informal settlements with predominantly high unemployment levels, inadequate infrastructure and social services, proliferation of gang violence, and drug use and trafficking, as well as poverty. The greater KMA remains the most criminally active and dangerous area in Jamaica. It experiences various forms of violent crimes, such as murder, assaults, shootings and robberies. Kingston has the highest rate of murder of the three major urban areas in Jamaica.

Over the past three decades there has been a general increase in murders in Jamaica. In 1970, the country's homicide rate was 8.1 per 100,000 individuals. By 2002, it had increased to 40 per 100,000, and by 2005, it had risen to 64 per 100,000, making Jamaica one of the countries with the highest murder rates in the world. Between 1998 and 2005, the Jamaican police reported 8993 murders – approximately 76 per cent of these murders occurred in the KMA.

In view of the escalating levels of crime and its destabilizing impacts, the Government of Jamaica has initiated several social programmes at the national, parish and community levels in partnership with several international agencies such as the IDB, the Canadian International Development Agency, DFID, USAID, the EU and the World Bank.

Utilizing a collaborative approach, the Jamaican government, in conjunction with several international and local partners, has developed various initiatives and programmes to address the policy-making process, social problems and crime and violence in the country. A multilevel approach has been employed by the Ministry of National Security involving police crime-fighting initiatives and numerous community safety and security programmes that operate mainly in Kingston. At the national level, *Operation Kingfish* was launched in 2004 as a major anti-crime initiative. With the assistance of international partners, *Operation Kingfish* has been successful in its mandate of dismantling gangs within the Kingston corporate area and has recovered numerous firearms and ammunition and equipment used in drug trafficking.

At the community level, two success stories particularly stand out. These are Fletcher's Land and Grants Pen, where social intervention programmes include initiatives such as remedial education, mentoring programmes, identifying job and skills training, dispute resolution, homework programmes, continuing education services and parenting workshops. These initiatives have brought about some short-term success. For instance, the community of Grants Pen had not recorded a single murder during 2006 until the point when this case study was drafted, whereas previously it had been regarded as one of the most volatile communities in Kingston.

One of the key lessons from crime fighting and crime prevention initiatives in Kingston is that the people should be the key focus of such initiatives. Furthermore, a collaborative approach with international agencies, government institutions and non-governmental organizations (NGOs) can prove effective in reducing crime and violence. While it should be noted that Kingston's programmes cannot be applied, as a whole, to all other urban areas since these programmes have not been assessed, the approach used can be duplicated by other urban areas by using the following principles:

- Use crime prevention approaches that operate at the grassroots level, where the common citizen can see, feel and react to issues. Generally, Jamaica had success at the tactical and conceptual levels, but it was not much felt by the citizenry.
- Utilize a prescriptive approach rather than a reactive approach, which fails to attack the root of the problem. Community needs must be assessed through consulta-

tions with key stakeholders and solutions must be determined with inputs from the relevant stakeholders.

- Engage the community in all levels of planning and development to ensure the successful implementation of policing strategies and social intervention programmes/initiatives. Communities must buy into the process and be recognized as partners in maintaining their own security.
- Invest in human capital. The outcomes of many social interventions programmes indicate that investing in the individual bears greater results than investing in structures. Evaluating investment in people might be difficult; however, it serves to reinforce the work of social intervention programmes in countries that face economic and social challenges such as Jamaica.

Crime and violence trends in Nairobi, Kenya

Over the last two decades, violent crimes such as armed robbery, murder, mugging, car jacking, housebreaking, physical and sexual assault and other forms of violent crime have been on the increase in Nairobi. Other forms of offences include commercial and property crimes such as burglaries. Firearms trafficking – a consequence of civil wars in neighbouring countries – is a major contributor to crime and violence in Nairobi.

Criminal youth gangs are increasingly becoming a growing phenomenon in Nairobi. The largest proportion of crime in Kenya is committed by youths, and over 50 per cent of convicted prisoners in the country are aged between 16 and 25 years. This makes it imperative to address youth crime as a special focus of crime prevention strategy. Two groups have been identified for illustrative purposes in this respect. These are the *Mungiki* movement and youth who live and work on the streets (see Box 3.5). While these groups are not necessarily criminal in all their interactions with the broader society, their association with crime, both real and perceived, is such that they warrant special attention.

The *Mungiki* movement, with membership said to range between 200,000 and 2 million, is one of the most significant youth groups in Kenya in terms of its propensity for extreme violence and the potential for developing into a highly disruptive force in society. The group came into the limelight during the late 1990s, when media reports highlighted groups of youths donning dreadlocks, taking unusual oaths and engaging in traditional prayers that involved the sniffing of snuff. *Mungiki* then posed as a traditional religious group interested in reintroducing and promoting the traditional way of life among the Kikuyu people. The group unmistakably drew its inspiration from the Mau-Mau movement of Kenya's struggle for independence from Britain during the 1950s. With time, it has transformed itself into probably the most organized and feared criminal group, with deep anti-establishment characteristics.

In order to put the violence unleashed by the movement in proper perspective, a few examples are provided:

- In March 2002, *Mungiki* was implicated in the massacre of 23 people in Kariobangi (Nairobi) and were also involved in stripping women wearing mini-skirts and trousers naked.
- In January 2003, the movement was linked to the death of 23 people in the outskirts of Nakuru.
- Thereafter, in April 2003, over 50 armed *Mungiki* members allegedly attacked a *matatu* (minibuses) crew in Kayole estate in Nairobi and killed five people in the same area.
- In November 2006, there was a resurgence of *Mungiki* violence in the Mathare slums of Nairobi. This resulted in several deaths and scores of injuries, the displacement of many people, the wanton destruction of property and the disruption of livelihoods.

The violent confrontations of November 2006 were a good pointer to *Mungiki*'s transformation into an organized crime group with considerably deep roots in its areas of operation.

The feeling that the movement is, in part, motivated by economic gain is rife. While accurate information of the economic activities of the movement are not available, owing to its covert nature, several indicators point to the movement being engaged in lucrative 'business' activities. Among these activities are the forceful management of *matatu* stages, levying illegal taxes and extorting protection money from large sections of Nairobi's informal settlements. Working in a tight, disciplined manner, *Mungiki* has taken over the provision of security, water and electricity in various slums in Nairobi. By 'taxing' residents of informal settlements, 'providing security', presiding over kangaroo courts and meting out their own form of justice, *Mungiki* has, in effect, been functioning as a parallel government at the local level.

In addition to the *Mungiki* movement, the growing population living and working in the streets of Nairobi and other Kenyan urban areas is a matter of major security and general development concern for the affected areas (see Box 3.2). Over the years, the number of street children has been on the rise. There were approximately 115 street children in 1975. By 1990, this had grown to 17,000. In 2001, the number of street children countrywide was estimated to be 250,000. With older street dwellers included, the total number increases to 300,000. The bulk of such street dwellers are found in Nairobi, which, at present, has a conservative estimate of 60,000 street people.

The issue of street families as an important factor in the city's security is both real and perceived. It is real in that street families are involved in criminal activities, which include drug peddling and prostitution, as well as theft of mobile phones, vehicle lights and side mirrors, and other valuables from pedestrians and motorists. Older street persons are also known to be involved in more serious crime, such as muggings and rape. Consequently, the public generally perceives street persons as criminals, thieves, drug addicts and eyesores who should be removed from the streets.

In an effort to address the challenge posed by street people and the pressure from city residents for the government to act regarding this challenge, the Kenya government established the Street Families Rehabilitation Trust Fund. The trust's mandate is to coordinate rehabilitation activities for street families in Kenya, educate the public, mobilize resources and manage a fund to support rehabilitation activities, among other functions.

The fund has made important progress in its mandate during the period of its existence. Among its key achievements are:

- spearheading the establishment of affiliate committees in major towns to oversee local activities of the rehabilitation of street people;
- overseeing capacity-building initiatives among service providers in providing basic psycho-social rehabilitation services;
- facilitating entry into school for rehabilitated street children; and
- facilitating the provision of vocational training for rehabilitated street youth.

Although an important headway has been made in the period of the fund's existence, there is still plenty of work to be done before proper mechanisms for managing the challenge of street people can be put in place.

Effective crime prevention in New York, US

New York City, following a national trend, has had declining crime rates for 30 years. Midtown Manhattan, once a popular entertainment district in the city, started a period of decline during the late 1960s that led to neglect, abandonment and increased criminal activity. Successive city administrations implemented policies to improve law enforcement with good results; but other aspects needed to be addressed, as well. During the 1980s, private non-profit groups decided to get involved and a period of redevelopment, restoration and revitalization was initiated. Bryant Park was one of the catalysts for this process.

The redevelopment of Bryant Park was entrusted to a non-profit group formed especially to restore, maintain and manage the park. The city, private sponsors and businesses in the area formed a partnership, providing channels for public input regarding redesign and redevelopment. Certain areas within the park had been appropriated by criminals. Most tourists, business people working in the area and patrons of the adjacent library, particularly women, avoided the park. The park's design detached it from its surroundings with the intention of providing a place of respite from the urban chaos; however, this isolation turned it into the perfect hiding place for derelicts.

Several public–private partnerships were established during the 1980s to aid in revitalization efforts. Some groups opposed these management agreements even though local government retained its authority over the public areas. Despite these concerns, these partnerships proved effective in not only restoring public areas, but also in maintaining order and, thus, working in the public interest to increase security for everyone. Using a Business Improvement District Strategy whereby commercial property owners imposed a surtax on themselves to pay for such things as security and physical improvements, two public–private coalitions supported the regeneration of the park over a sustained period of time. The effort included a redesign of the many physical elements of the park that were thought to have contributed to its demise as a public place. This included natural and built surveillance obstacles, pathways, obstructed entrances and the generally enclosed nature of the site that cut it off from the surrounding city. This effort was also supported by New York mayors and by the police, who had made it a policy to reclaim public space for public use.

Even though Bryant Park had been an important public place in the city for more than 100 years, its periods of decline had prevented citizens from enjoying it and had allowed part of the public realm to become a breeding ground for criminal activities. Today, the park is a desirable destination; it has also become self-sufficient since it is the only park in the city that does not receive any public funding. The existence of public spaces such as the restored Bryant Park confirms that even large and dense urban places such as New York City can offer their citizens the opportunity to enjoy public spaces. These opportunities are part of what makes cities sustainable in the long term.

Bryant Park is, indeed, a success story. Reclaiming a public space that had been hijacked by drug pushers and users and making it accessible to thousands of people on a daily basis is a considerable achievement. The decline in crime afforded by the restoration of Bryant Park is undeniable and is verified by police data and citizen reports. Evidence suggests that city administrators would not have been able to accomplish this feat on their own. By most accounts, the participation of private businesses and citizens made it all possible. Public–private partnerships proved efficient and effective in restoring and managing not only Bryant Park, but several public spaces in New York and elsewhere.

The spatial changes in the park have made it welcoming to any citizen or visitor passing by. The homeless continue to be welcome as long as they abide by park regulations and behave in a manner that is acceptable to the majority of the people benefiting from the public space. In terms of physical and design-induced changes, Bryant Park also serves as a model. Inspired by William H. Whyte's philosophy of urban space and his understanding of how social behaviour is influenced by it, the park's design proves that simple elements can be used to great effect.

A combination of physical changes and increased law enforcement can be credited with Bryant Park's rebirth. An important lesson to be learned is that a better understanding of all the issues that factor into making not only public space, but entire cities, safe, comfortable and desirable is needed. When people are willing to be creative, tolerant and innovative, institutional and economic barriers can be surpassed.

The Bryant Park experience also shows that sustained efforts are necessary. Restoration projects that only address one aspect of the myriad of problems usually comprising degraded areas do not yield the same benefits. The physical environment is an important component of any redevelopment project; but urban design can only create the enabling environment for a successful public space. Other initiatives that ensure economic vitality, absence of crime, continued sources of revenue, and close attention to maintenance and management are indispensable. Only by combining design ingenuity with other continuous efforts can a public space be created and sustained.

Crime and violence trends in Port Moresby, Papua New Guinea

Port Moresby is the capital city of Papua New Guinea – the biggest developing country in the Pacific region. The city is infamously known for its high crime rate. The escalating high levels of rape, robbery and murder have earned Port Moresby the dubious distinction of being the worst city in which to live in the world by the *Economist* magazine for 2002 and 2005.

The main types of crimes committed in Port Moresby, in order of frequency, are burglary, petty crime, assault, car jacking, drug dealing, property crimes, rape, violence and vandalism. About 48 per cent of crimes in Port Moresby involve a high level of violence, compared to other cities in Papua New Guinea where violence is used in 25 to 30 per cent of crimes. The use of violence in crime creates a feeling of fear among the population. Nearly one quarter of crimes committed involve the use of weapons such as guns, knives, swords or blades. Young people are the main perpetrators of crime, as most of the first offences and the relatively serious offences are committed by young males between the ages of 15 and 20. The most common type of first offence is petty crime (which includes theft, pick pocketing, shoplifting and bag snatching). The widespread substance abuse, especially among the youth, often contributes to increased levels of criminal activities and street brawls.

Apart from the types of crime noted above, domestic violence, particularly against women, is endemic. Gang rape and assault on women are rapidly increasing. However, most communities and households view violence against women as a private matter and therefore very few victims report them. Consequently, very few cases are prosecuted even though domestic violence is regarded as a crime in Papua New Guinea. Even when victims of domestic violence report such assault to relatives, it is usually frowned upon and the victim does not receive any sympathy.

The impact of crime and violence on Port Moresby affects the whole of Papua New Guinea. The surge in crime causes residents to feel very unsafe: entire suburbs in the city are known to be unsafe and even the police are reluctant to respond to calls for help. The cost of crime to the nation in terms of its impact on tourism, cost of security and health services is enormous.

The causes of escalating levels of crime in Port Moresby are many and varied. But there seems to be a general agreement that crime and violence in Papua New Guinea are caused by five main factors – namely, a general lack of economic opportunities; the drive to acquire material wealth; the inability of law enforcement institutions to address criminal behaviour in the city effectively; a general decline of traditional cultural practices that assist with conflict resolutions and the maintenance of law and order; and the abuse of the *wantok* system and the impact of urbanization – *wantok* literally means 'people who speak your language'.

It is estimated that the formal sector provides fewer than 10 per cent of jobs in the country. In addition, Papua New Guinea as a country has adopted the laws and regulations of the State of Queensland (Australia) – its colonial power. The supplanting of laws and regulations that are much suited to developed economies has made it impossible for the informal sector to develop effectively. The strict enforcement of regulations relating to public health, building codes and taxation have stifled the growth and expansion of the informal sector.

Migration to Port Moresby and internal urban growth have contributed to the growth and expansion of squatter settlements; yet, the relevant authorities have failed to give due recognition to squatter settlements in the city and provide basic services and support to enable the migrants to integrate within the city. This has, in part, given rise to discontent and resentment of authority, and the flourishing of organized gang activity, which provides support and 'employment' opportunities for many migrants in the city.

The declining use of conflict resolution mechanisms in urban areas compels individuals to use their *wantoks* to resolve disputes. It is not uncommon to hear *wantoks* using community justice (a payback system). Abuse of the *wantok* system has created an environment that breeds ethnic tensions, especially within the squatter settlements, and often results in increased violence.

Law enforcement and the criminal justice institutions are largely unable to cope with the level of criminal activities in the city due to lack of equipment and poor training, which contribute to them being considered unprofessional and incapable of stemming the tide of criminal activities in the city.

The complexity of the causes and types of crime shows that policies and programmes aimed at addressing crime and violence in Port Moresby should foster a strong partnership between the government, NGOS and the community. The international community also has a key role to play in providing better training and equipment, and in supporting partnership approaches. In addition, there is the need to systematically approach crime reduction and prevention from a holistic framework with maximum support from the grassroots level. The challenge facing the city with regard to dealing with crime and criminal behaviour is enormous; but it is not insurmountable. It requires strong commitment and collective determination to tackle the problem and to instil confidence among residents, investors and tourists alike.

Crime and violence trends in Rio de Janeiro, Brazil

The city of Rio de Janeiro, Brazil's former capital between 1688 and 1960 and second major city, exhibited a remarkable increase in crime rates from 1980 onwards, despite decreases in population growth of 2 per cent in 1980 and 0.4 per cent in 2000. While there were some improvements in urban infrastructure in some of the poorest areas of the city – the shantytowns – these continued to grow at a rate of 2.4 per cent in 2000. Then, the city had 5,857,904 inhabitants, of which 1,094,922 lived in subnormal urban agglomerations, an official definition for the popular term *favelas*, where a heterogeneous, but mainly poor, population resides. This has been a common scenario in major Brazilian cities since the early years of the 20th century due to accelerated and chaotic urbanization, or urbanization without industrialization or sufficient economic development to provide employment for the migrants.

Rio de Janeiro's homicide rate tripled from 20.5 per 100,000 individuals in 1982 to 61.2 per 100,000 in 1989, when it reached its peak, following the expansion of cocaine trafficking and use. From then on, it has been around 50 per 100,000 individuals, with the lowest rate in 2001 being 45.3 per 100,000, but up again in 2002. While homicide rates for young men aged 14 to 25 escalated from 30 per 100,000 in 1980 to 54.5 per 100,000 in 2002, the rate among older men remained stable, from 21.3 per 100,000 to 21.7 per 100,000 during the same period. Nationwide, 90 per cent or more of murder cases involve males, while 10 per cent or less relate to women.

Violent crimes, particularly homicides, are more common in *favelas* and distant poor districts. This corresponds to differences in inequality within the city, and the lack of social and state control, especially policing, in the more distant areas. It is, however, difficult to compare official rates of homicides in different districts or *favelas* of Rio de Janeiro because the lack of property rights translates into the lack of addresses. Fearing being discriminated against as *favelados*, people give non-existing addresses or addresses in adjacent districts. Moreover, since police repression is stronger against *favelados*, bodies are dumped in neighbouring districts, thereby increasing their homicide rates remarkably. Murder rates in Rio de Janeiro often vary with socio-economic and racial characteristics. For instance, blacks, low-income households and less educated people have a greater proportion of relatives, friends and neighbours killed.

Vulnerability, especially for young men who have the highest unemployment rates, growth of the informal sector and irregular dwellings do not fully account for the growth of homicides during the 1980s and 1990s. New forms of criminal business affected informal markets, transforming them into gateways not only for selling stolen, smuggled or counterfeit goods, but also for trafficking illegal drugs. This increased the number of murders in so far as the illegality of the drug business made the use of guns inevitable. During the 1980s, trafficking gangs started to dominate some *favelas*, and traffickers expanded their operations. As armed mobs appeared, death squads or militias were formed in order to eliminate those identified as bandits.

Although the proportion of people who have handguns is small in Brazilian cities, criminal groups defy the rule of law because guns can be easily obtained. Drug gangs have transient skirmishes to dispute the territory where their markets are located. As a result of the ensuing military local control, the drug lords restrict the movements of dwellers and governmental agents.

Possession of guns follows the dynamics of small networks of peers. Youths display firearms to gain the respect and admiration of their peers and to avoid being victimized by those who carry them. Using guns is a learned behaviour. Where there is a high concentration of handguns, youths believe that they will have military, juridical and personal protection inside the gangs, where they learn to be ruthless and to kill.

Policing with a focus on the control of illegal gun use could diminish homicide rates. But the foci of prevention policies are improved schooling, providing stipends to augment family income, and sponsoring sport and cultural programmes. The idea behind the latter programmes is that the symbolic dimensions of belonging and identity are more important to youths than income. Yet, these social programmes remain fragmented and low scale. Their main impacts on youths who become involved with them are to increase personal health and grooming, to increase paternal responsibility, to increase dialogue within the family and to increase pride in those who are working hard to make progress.

Multi-age neighbourhood projects should be encouraged as much as the new projects that develop global identities related to hip hop and funk music. Traditional forms of community association, such as Schools of Samba, Carnival Blocs and soccer teams have always fulfilled a socializing function. Since trauma resulting from violence is collective, mobilizing families and different generations will be more successful.

But cultural projects will thrive if there are public policies creating more jobs and employment for youths, and reducing access to guns with gun-oriented patrolling. New prevention strategies should link police and neighbourhoods, including those inside *favelas*, based on respect for civil rights.

Effective crime prevention in Toronto, Canada

Toronto, with a population of 2.7 million people, is Canada's largest city. It lies on the north-western shore of Lake Ontario, the easternmost of the Great Lakes. One of the most ethnically diverse cities in the world, Toronto is home to people from over 200 nations who speak more than 100 languages and dialects. It is also one of Canada's primary immigrant reception centres, welcoming nearly 70,000 newcomers each year. The resulting cultural diversity is reflected in the numerous ethnic neighbourhoods and enclaves in the city.

Although Toronto is a relatively safe city, it is facing challenges with crime and violence in some neighbourhoods and among some segments of the population. For example, while the overall risk of homicide victimization in Toronto has been relatively stable over the last decade, the city has become more dangerous for some people and less so for others. Over this period, female victimization rates decreased, while male rates increased slightly, and the average age of homicide victims declined. Toronto's black population has faced much higher rates of homicide victimization than non-blacks since at least the early 1990s. Just as there is evidence indicating that the risk of homicide and other serious violence in Toronto is unequally distributed across social groups, there is also some evidence to suggest that incidents of serious violent crime tend to cluster in particular neighbourhoods.

The changing nature of who is at risk of homicide victimization and the contexts in which this violence tends to occur have guided the development of a host of crime prevention and violence reduction policies in Toronto over the past several years (see Box 4.7 for details).

For example, in early 2004, the City of Toronto established its Community Safety Plan (CSP), a toolbox of crime prevention initiatives designed to improve public safety in those neighbourhoods where violent crime is thought to cluster. The CSP emphasizes collaborative efforts that work across authority and agency boundaries with respect to the development and evaluation of social policy. The CSP is based on a strategic model that rests on the twin pillars of crime prevention through social development and CPTED. While recognizing the central role that policing plays in the control of crime, the CSP also argues that in order to be successful, enforcement-based strategies must be balanced with preventative approaches that address the root causes of crime and violence.

Among the more prominent policy developments have been the introduction of spatially targeted or area-based interventions aimed at specific neighbourhoods in Toronto. The privileging of such initiatives stems from the recognition that the causes of crime are rooted in a complex mix of social and structural factors that can vary across urban neighbourhoods. As such, the CSP emphasizes that solutions cannot be of the 'one-size-fits-all' variety, but rather that resources and support be tailored to address the specific needs of each neighbourhood.

It is, as yet, difficult to comment on the efficacy of recent crime prevention initiatives implemented in Toronto's neighbourhoods for the simple reason that many are new and have yet to be subject to evaluation. Criminological research has consistently highlighted the importance of evaluating and monitoring the effects of crime prevention initiatives to ensure that they are having the desired impact. Careful programme evaluation and monitoring are also important in light of the limited resources that are available for investment in crime prevention and reduction programmes – thus, an understanding of what programmes and interventions are the most effective use of scarce resources is important from a cost–benefit perspective.

Furthermore, although a multi-agency or 'partnership' approach to community safety has been widely endorsed in Toronto, it appears that crime prevention strategies and initiatives are more segmented and compartmentalized than they are collaborative. Research on partnerships and crime prevention has demonstrated that conflicts and tensions often emerge among different parties incorporated within partnership structures. Therefore, policy-makers in Toronto will face some challenges with respect to fostering an environment that is conducive to the development of inter-organizational trust and collaboration.

On the whole, crime prevention initiatives in Toronto appear to be one facet of more generalized public policy aimed at empowering 'distressed' neighbourhoods and fostering the growth of healthy and self-governing communities. Research has shown that 'non-crime' policies – for example, building neighbourhood-level social and economic capital, increasing levels of community cohesion, and promoting collective action among residents – may, in fact, have important effects on crime. As such, if the obstacles to interagency collaboration outlined above are addressed early on, it may well be that the integration of crime-targeted interventions with more general policies that address social and structural deficits will have lasting effects on crime and violence in Toronto's neighbourhoods.

SECURITY OF TENURE AND FORCED EVICTIONS

Positive policies and legal responses to enhance security of tenure in Brazil

Brazil is one of the most urbanized countries in the world, with 85 per cent of its population, or some 162 million people, living in cities or towns. According to official statistics, some 30 million people migrated from rural to urban areas between 1970 and 1990. The lack of available urban land forced millions of Brazilians to live in cardboard or tin shacks in the urban slums known as *favelas* or *vilas*. Many other low-income Brazilians live in *cortiços*: collective, often dilapidated, multi-family buildings with poor access to basic sanitation and infrastructure.

This was the situation when the period of military dictatorship ended in 1984. The 1988 Brazilian constitution introduced institutional and legal processes for the democratization of the state. The new constitution recognized the right of citizens to participate in formulating and implementing public policy. It thus opened up possibilities of resolving a range of problems stemming from social inequality in Brazilian cities. The constitution also recognized the municipalities as autonomous members of the federation, alongside the states and the union itself. The case of Brazil during the last two decades is thus a story of decentralization and increased participation of social movements and NGOs. This is framed in a historical context where democracy and human rights are increasingly being considered by the national government and its institutions. From the perspective of increasing security of tenure, this gave rise to national policies and programmes aimed at regularizing and upgrading urban slums, including issues related to the utilization of vacant public and private land, the occupation of vacant buildings, the acquisition of informal land, etc.

The City Statute – the Federal Law on Urban Development, adopted in 2001 – introduced a range of legal instruments that address landownership regularization and slum upgrading (see Box 11.8). It also guaranteed protection against forced evictions through the adoption of the legal instruments of urban adverse possession and the 'special social interest zones'. The latter recognize informal settlements as part of the city and provide special regulations for land use and occupation.

Many social movements, NGOs, academic institutions, professional entities, workers' unions and social organizations have actively engaged in the processes made possible by the new constitution, the City Statute and other new legislation. These range from the elaboration of participatory municipal master plans to the implementation of national public policies. As a result, many programmes and investments have been discussed, implemented and monitored with the direct participation of a range of civil society organizations.

The main policy initiatives arising out of these new pieces of legislation were the National Programme to Support Sustainable Urban Land Regularization (*Programa Papel Passado*) and the National Social Housing System, which identified the limits, possibilities and challenges to implementing comprehensive and integrated social housing projects (see also Box 6.27). Both programmes were designed in accordance with the principles and guidelines contained in the City Statute, and provide for the implementation of the instruments regulated by this new legislation.

The former programme, created in 2003 to provide support to states and municipalities and to regularize union property, seeks to grant landownership titles to households living in informal settlements. The programme also attempts to provide financial and technical support to states and municipalities for the purpose of implementing land regularization and social housing projects. The National Social Housing System was created to regulate an institutional and financial scheme designed to support different social housing projects, including the participation of states, municipalities and NGOs. Its introduction implies that Brazil now has a comprehensive social housing system that can support and fund social housing and land regularization projects.

However, even with the introduction of these two programmes, the achievement of concrete results – such as the provision and registration of landownership titles, the effective support from states and municipalities to housing projects, and the empowerment of communities and social movements – is still a challenge. Many institutional, legal and political obstacles still need to be removed, both at the national and at local levels, before the integration of socio-environmental polices and legislation can adequately benefit the regularization of urban informal settlements.

Brazil has enshrined in its national legislation most housing rights laid down in the international human rights instruments. Even so, this has not always resulted in more or better access to adequate housing and land for the poor. It is thus appropriate to call on the courts to protect the right to adequate housing more effectively, and to consider and apply international human rights law directly when deciding cases involving rights of possession, forced evictions and land conflicts affecting vulnerable urban residents. Within the Brazilian legal system, the civil code has traditionally been applied by the judiciary to give privilege to full ownership rather than possession in those cases where there is a conflict between the two. These decisions undermine the fulfilment of the social function of property and the application of instruments to protect security of tenure, which are enshrined in the City Statute.

For housing rights to be fully respected, it is essential to obtain recognition from public officials that consideration of human rights is a key objective in the application of urban and housing policies. The Brazilian experience shows that social participation is possible and that it results in fruitful outcomes, when all relevant stakeholders engage together in actions based on a consistent and strategic urban-political platform.

The struggle for tenure in Cambodia

In October 2006, the Australian television network ABC aired a piece on mass evictions occurring in Phnom Penh, which recorded this observation from the US ambassador to Cambodia:

> *There's too many land disputes, too many rich people, greedy companies. Property is really the key to prosperity and freedom and once people are not secure in what they own, everything else falls apart.*

This statement is a good summary of the importance of land to the poor in Cambodia. If the growing disputes over land and the resulting evictions of thousands of households from the city are to end, efforts must be made to better understand the motivation and pressures creating these tragic events. From this, possible alternatives may be found.

In assessing these events it is also essential to understand the legal context of urban settlements in Cambodia since everyone who returned to Phnom Penh after the collapse of the Khmer Rouge regime was a squatter (see also Chapter 5). Thus, among the important revisions to the 1992 Land Law adopted in 2001 was a clarification of adverse possession rights. Under the revised law, Article 30 allowed any person who had occupied a piece of land peacefully and without contest for five years or more to request definitive title to the land. While this provided the prospect of title for many urban residents, there were still many obstacles for them to overcome. These included a general lack of awareness about the process of requesting title; the cost of such requests; the process and costs of appeals; the corruption of the bureaucracy and the courts; and the lack of access to the legal process, particularly when disputes occurred.

Throughout 2006 and early 2007, evictions took place at a rapid rate in both urban and rural areas of the country. There was a pattern to these evictions: companies, often owned by prominent national and local politicians, used the police and the army to evict people from land that, under the 2001 Land Law, should have been theirs. In urban Cambodia, particularly in Phnom Penh, additional pressure came from companies demanding land for development purposes. In general, increasing competition for land, increasing land values, and urban planning pressures linked to beautification and gentrification were all involved.

The residents of 'Group 78', who faced eviction in 2006, were just one of many examples (see Box 5.6). In their case, many residents already had documents issued by the local authorities recognizing their legal occupation of the land. Despite this, they were to be relocated to the outskirts of the city because the land was needed to 'contribute to city beautification and development'. In order to fight for their security of tenure, such urban residents need support.

However, such support has not come from any level of the Cambodian government – national or local. Nor has this support come from international funding agencies. Support was provided by United Nations agencies and from individual embassies in Phnom Penh, such as that exemplified by the US ambassador's statement. The bulk of support for the potential evictees did, however, come from local NGOs and, to some extent, international NGOs, such as Human Rights Watch and the Asian Human Rights Commission. Human Rights Watch, for example, sent an open letter to development agencies pointing out that they needed to do a better job of providing benchmarks for international assistance. These benchmarks would include the observance by all levels of the Cambodian government of human rights, transparency and good governance. They also pointed out that the agencies forming the consultative group for Cambodia should also support civil society directly.

In addition to the recommendations made by Human Rights Watch, there are a number of other steps that could be taken by communities under threat of evictions to enhance their security of tenure:

- *Awareness-raising.* There is a need to enhance the access of all urban residents to information on procedures for registration of tenure rights, for appeals and for redress. Information is also needed about available land, urban planning proposals and private development proposals.
- *Planning alternatives.* Once information is available to them, communities can begin to formulate alternative plans to those presented by local authorities or private developers. Such alternative plans are an essential negotiating tool.
- *Coordination.* The Housing Rights Task Force requires greater support in coordinating the efforts of local and international NGOs.
- *International support.* There is potential for increased leverage based on international support, particularly where the media can publicize activities widely.

In all of this, it must be emphasized that information and the process of information-gathering itself can be a powerful tool for organizing communities.

Security of housing tenure in the People's Republic of China

Within five years after the founding of the People's Republic of China in 1949, a rural land reform and the nationalization of the urban building stock had virtually solved the historic problem of endemic insecurity of tenure to land and housing. With the deepening of economic reforms, begun in 1978, problems of insecure tenure have gradually re-emerged in both urban and rural areas.

In the cities, newly installed governments commandeered the building stock and apportioned it, in a largely egalitarian manner, to meet the most pressing needs of the local economy and population. Crowding, including bathrooms and kitchens shared by multiple (and sometimes dozens of) families were endemic in large cities such as Shanghai, Guangzhou and Tianjin. On the positive side, however, rents were affordable and evictions were rare. Low rents did, however, make it almost impossible to maintain the quality of the housing or to invest in upgrading of infrastructure or new housing. By the early 1980s, a consensus emerged within government on the need to make housing self-financing (i.e. to remove it from the urban employment welfare package).

Yet, this did not change the fact that housing remained a resource drain for most cities. Neither state, nor collective enterprises, nor government agencies could pay wages that allowed rents to cover the full costs of improved housing. Gradual salary and rent increases during the 1990s helped to lay the ground for the 1998 instruction to halt the distribution of housing as a welfare good. Instead, occupiers of publicly owned housing were required to buy the apartments they occupied or to pay the market rent. With much of the existing state-owned housing stock being offered at bargain prices, housing sales soared by the year 2000. In parallel, purchases of commercial real estate, including luxury housing, grew rapidly, in step with China's burgeoning economy.

In the meantime, reforms in the agricultural sector dating from the late 1970s helped to kick-start what was to become a massive exodus of workers from rural areas. Many of these moved into the fast-growing coastal cities filling the ranks of construction workers, maids, street sweepers, factory hands in export industries, and most of the other hard, dirty and low-paid jobs that permanent city residents frowned upon. Numbering just a few million in the early 1980s, migrant workers in the cities today may total as many as 200 million. Many of these have been forced off their land, often illegally and violently, to make way for growing cities and new economic activities (see Box 5.11).

Once in the cities, migrant workers' security of tenure became and remains the weakest of any group of Chinese citizen (see also Box 5.17). While they may comprise as much as one quarter of the long-term population in China's major cities, only about 2 per cent of them own their housing. Many such migrants are housed by their employers, enjoying shelter only for the duration of their work. Others rent rooms in illegally constructed or dilapidated buildings that are likely to eventually be demolished by authorities. Even for migrants with steady jobs, average incomes of US$2 to $4 per day do not permit access to formal housing arrangements, leaving them vulnerable to forced evictions.

In contrast to the situation of urban-based migrants, 77 per cent of the officially registered urban residents had become homeowners by the year 2000. Many among them had been moved, sometimes forcefully and/or illegally, from older housing units that were to be destroyed to make way for grand-scale urban renewal. Formal tallies of forced evictions do not exist; but those for 'demolition removals' often do. In Shanghai, over the ten-year period ending in 2003, the housing units of some 820,000 households were torn down, directly affecting 2.3 million people. In Beijing, between 1991 and 2008, the corresponding figures were roughly 673,000 and 2 million. To a lesser extent, these experiences are repeated in fast-growing cities across China (see also Box 5.7).

Massive urban redevelopment is one of the drivers of rapid economic growth in China. With the privatization of housing, urban households with formal-sector employment have moved from spending approximately 1 per cent of their, albeit, low incomes in 1990 to more than 40 per cent of their much higher incomes today. However, the incomes of the elderly, infirm, low-skilled and large numbers of workers laid off from state enterprises have not kept pace with those in formal employment. These comprise a significant part of the new urban poor. Even if they receive compensation when they are evicted from their old substandard, but affordable, accommodation, they cannot afford to live in a new one. Instead, they move to another low-rent apartment in the private market. Here they compete with migrants for the shrinking stock of substandard, but affordable, housing. If they live long enough, they may even be evicted again.

China's leaders recognize the seriousness of the problem of ensuring adequate housing for all urban residents. The government is seeking to use market and non-market methods to rein in the explosive increases in housing costs, to build or purchase from the market rental housing for the lowest-income strata, and to offer subsidized housing to help middle-income households purchase their first homes. Low-income (rental) housing, along with subsidized commercial housing, will be located adjacent to the major mass transit arteries, as is being planned for Beijing and has been implemented, to some extent, in Shanghai. While such accommodation may be at some distance from city centres, the new communities are being designed to offer convenient access to full health, educational, commercial and recreational infrastructure. Expanding the coverage of the housing provident fund and instituting support to help low-income families obtain mortgages, along with measures to fully integrate migrant worker housing needs within formal urban housing plans, are recognized as important problems, but have yet to see major policy initiatives taken up by lawmakers. Moreover, the supply of affordable housing through formal channels will fall far below the need for at least the next few years.

A place to live: A case study of the Ijora-Badia community in Lagos, Nigeria

In 1973, the residents of a sprawling old settlement known as Oluwole village in central Lagos were evicted to make room for the construction of Nigeria's National Arts Theatre. Following largely uncoordinated protests by the residents, the federal authorities retrospectively paid paltry sums as compensation to some of the evictees for their demolished homes. Other evictees who insisted on resettlement were allocated vacant plots of land in Ijora-Badia, located less than 1 kilometre away.

Except for allocation papers issued to some of the relocated households by the federal government, there was no evidence of their title to the newly allocated lands. By the early 1990s, Ijora-Badia, like many other informal settlements, had become a choice place to live for many who could not afford the cost of living in formal sections of the city. It had also become a highly attractive frontier marked for demolition and eventual upscale development by affluent developers. Ijora-Badia's poor were expendable and undeserving of the land.

In July 1996, residents of 15 Lagos slum communities, with a total population of 1.2 million people, learned of plans by the Lagos state government to forcibly evict them from their homes and businesses as part of the US$85 million World Bank-funded Lagos Drainage and Sanitation Project (LDSP). In 1997, bulldozers and eviction officials backed by heavily armed police and military personnel invaded Ijora-Badia and demolished the homes of over 2000 people as part of the LDSP demonstration project.

While bulldozers tore down and flattened houses and property, armed security men harassed, brutalized and arrested residents who attempted to salvage personal effects from their homes. These officials also extorted monies from residents desperate to secure their freedom or gain access to pick up their possessions. The terror unleashed on these residents was heightened by the suddenness of the attack that found mostly women, children and old people at home to bear the brunt.

Prior to the July 1996 eviction announcement, a civil society organization, the Social and Economic Rights Action Center (SERAC), was already working within the Ijora-Badia community, providing basic human rights education and helping the community to strengthen its capacity to communicate with various government institutions.

In an effort to address the eviction threat, SERAC increased its support to Ijora-Badia and other targeted slum communities. Working with community leaders, women, youth and associations, the organization designed and implemented various initiatives and activities, including outreach and sensitization meetings; focus group discussions; onsite legal clinics and training workshops; the creative use of local and international media; as well as posters and handbills that were widely disseminated within and beyond the target communities. More experienced leaders and organizers from similar communities – such as Maroko, which was demolished in July 1990 – were brought in to share their organizing and mobilizing knowledge and experience, and to inspire the leaders and people of Ijora-Badia.

These efforts helped many in the community to gain a new perception of themselves as persons imbued with certain rights that are protected by both national and international law. They also learned that the government and the World Bank had certain legal obligations to them whether or not they had valid legal title to their lands. They learned that the World Bank and the government were under duty to consult with them and to ensure their active participation in the LDSP's design and implementation, as well as to provide adequate notice, compensation, resettlement and rehabilitation to them should forced eviction become inevitable in order to accomplish the project's purposes.

Following a series of consultations and investigations, the government of Lagos renewed its effort to forcibly evict the Ijora-Badia community in July 2003. Now, however, the residents were better organized, mobilized and determined to keep their homes. On 29 July 2003, a demolition squad escorted by heavily armed police officers destroyed a part of the Ijora-Badia settlement, but had to pull back momentarily due to vehement resistance.

On 1 August 2003, SERAC filed a lawsuit on behalf of the Ijora-Badia residents seeking to enforce their fundamental rights, as well as an order of injunction restraining the relevant authorities from continuing with the community's destruction pending a resolution of the matter by the courts. On 19 August 2003, the court granted leave to the applicants to apply to enforce their fundamental rights.

In disregard of the pending lawsuit and the order of leave, the Lagos state government again attacked Ijora-Badia on 19 October 2003. Bulldozers backed by heavily armed police officers destroyed houses and other structures and left over 3000 people homeless, mostly women and children.

In a dramatic turn of events, however, research revealed that a significant portion of the Ijora-Badia lands had been acquired by the federal government of Nigeria in 1929 for the use and benefit of the Nigeria Railway Company. This finding had profound implications for the community and the Lagos state government. In a SERAC-backed petition to the federal minister for housing and urban development, the Ijora-Badia community ascribed responsibility to the federal government for the many violations committed against them by the Lagos state government and demanded immediate action to save their homes and land. In an uncharacteristically swift reaction, the minister notified the Lagos state government of its legal ownership of the Ijora-Badia land and directed the Lagos state government to keep away from Ijora-Badia while accepting responsibility to upgrade and redevelop Ijora-Badia for the benefit of its people.

An urban slice of pie: The Prevention of Illegal Eviction from and Unlawful Occupation of Land Act in South Africa

The first democratically elected parliament of South Africa adopted a constitution with a bill of rights in 1996. The bill of rights included a range of justiciable socio-economic rights, including the right to housing, all of which were to be 'respected, protected, promoted and fulfilled'. The adoption of the new constitution offered hope to thousands of homeless and landless South Africans, who looked forward to the fulfilment of their rights to land and housing (see also Chapter 6).

After the abolishment of apartheid, millions of people were able to move about freely for the first time, leading to a rapid increase in the level of urbanization. Furthermore, the democratically elected government committed itself to return land to those who had been dispossessed on the grounds of their race and local government, and pledged itself to deliver basic services to the majority of the poor. The government made it clear that South Africa's history had for too long been one of dispossession and dislocation. In excess of 3 million people had been forcibly removed to enforce spatial racial segregation. The apartheid regime had bulldozed black communities and moved them away from the centre of every one of its cities and most towns.

Shortly after the introduction of the new constitution, the courts started grappling with its impact on tenure issues. The key court cases centred on evictions: the new constitution, in effect, banned evictions without a court order made out after considering all relevant circumstances. In a dramatic shift from old cases – where an assertion of ownership was sufficient to obtain eviction – a new court ruling held that landlords/owners had to plead all relevant circumstances, otherwise cases were to be dismissed by the courts.

As a result of the new constitution, the new parliament adopted a series of new legislation (see Box 6.25). Prominent among these was the Prevention of Illegal Evictions from and Unlawful Occupation of Land Act (PIE), which was passed in 1998. In fact, most of the land-related cases that have reached the higher courts in South Africa during the last decade have dealt with PIE's impact on the lives of people living illegally on land in urban areas. The new act protected illegal occupants from the evictions of old and prescribed new procedures for carrying out evictions.

A flurry of cases followed across the country, adopting or rejecting the greater burden being placed on the owner, and the new legislation, particularly PIE, came to play a significant role. Further statutory interpretations ensured that, in all cases, potential evictees (often previously evicted without ever having seen court papers) had to be advised expressly of their right to legal representation; furthermore, the courts ruled that they were entitled to legal representation whenever they faced substantial injustice. Landlords (and courts) initially believed that this legislation regarding 'illegal evictions and unlawful occupations' dealt only with the hundreds of thousands of people living in desperate conditions in informal settlements. However, after a long series of court cases, it was clarified that this protective approach should be applied to all unlawful occupants, including those who had not paid rent or their mortgage, and who had therefore become unlawful occupants. These new court cases were, in fact, developing a substantive rights jurisprudence and were not merely interpreting procedural protections.

The next key shift occurred with the *Grootboom* case (see also Box 6.26), where the Constitutional Court, while not following the High Court's order that shelter should be mandatory for children – held that in failing to provide for those most desperately in need, an otherwise reasonable local authority housing policy was still in breach of the constitution.

The Grootboom community had brought an application to the High Court in Cape Town seeking an order that the government provide 'adequate basic temporary shelter or housing to them and their children pending their obtaining permanent accommodation; or basic nutrition, shelter, healthcare and social services to the respondents who are children'. The High Court ordered that the children (on the basis of children's rights enshrined in the constitution) and their parents were entitled to housing and certain services. On appeal by the state, the Constitutional Court did not follow the lower court's approach. It confirmed the justiciability of socio-economic rights contained in the constitution. Secondly, it declined, on the basis that there was insufficient evidence before it, to determine a minimum core in respect of the right to housing. It then considered the City of Cape Town's housing policy and held that it appeared reasonable, save that it did not provide relief for those 'who have no access to land, no roof over their heads, and were living in intolerable conditions or crisis situations' – and thus declared the policy to be unconstitutional.

The *Grootboom* decision was greeted with great acclaim, and pressure was brought to bear on all local authorities to ensure that housing policies as set out in the integrated development programmes of each of the local authorities would make provision for those most desperately in need. The Constitutional Court has since considered these issues in even greater depth in the *Port Elizabeth Municipality* case and the *Modderklip* case (see Box 6.26).

The PIE undoubtedly made it more difficult for owners, in general, and authorities in urban areas, in particular, to evict people 'in desperate need with nowhere else to go'. It has strengthened legal protections for poor people and has also enhanced their bargaining position when faced with nowhere else to live, other than on someone else's land without permission. The new legislation has protected poor people against mass evictions and has put extra pressure on local governments to develop policies for those most 'desperately in need', and, accordingly, has ensured that more land is made available for low-cost housing. There have been significant policy advantages to the poor flowing from these court cases. Property owners and lending banks have been less than enamoured with the courts' interpretation and have brought pressure for amendments. The Department of Housing has recently announced plans to amend the PIE and other housing legislation.

Strategies for survival: Security of tenure in Bangkok

The story of the Pom Mahakan community in inner-city Bangkok (Thailand) and its fight against eviction exemplifies one of the major threats to security of tenure for poor and marginalized people all over the world (see also Box 11.6). The threat is urban planning, or, more specifically, development pressures that include tourism, gentrification and the regulation of land use. The Pom Mahakan case also exemplifies how communities can develop strategies to counteract such threats. It highlights how it is important to understand the source of a threat in order to respond effectively to it.

For the last 150 years or more, this community of nearly 300 people had existed at the edge of Rattanakosin Island – the original settlement of Bangkok, dating from the mid 1700s – between the *klong* (canal) and one of the last remaining pieces of the old city wall. The community is also located just next to two of Bangkok's other major tourist attractions: Wat Saket (Golden Mount Temple) and the old fort (Pom Mahakan).

When a master plan was approved for Rattanakosin Island in 2002, the impetus was to improve the prospects for tourism in the area. In doing this, the plan called for a dramatic increase of parklands, particularly around existing monuments, temples, the royal palace, the canals and the Chao Phraya River.

Because of its location, the Pom Mahakan community, living on a piece of land some 50 metres wide and 150 metres long, had been facing the threat of eviction long before the Rattanakosin master plan. The city had always seen this location as a future park where tourists could sit and view Wat Saket from across the *klong*. With this view surrounded by the historical setting of the old fort and the wall of the city, in the minds of the city planners, it had long been an ideal place for a park.

Understandably, then, Pom Mahakan was the first of Rattanakosin's communities to be targeted for beautification. In January 2003, the city planning department posted eviction notices on all the houses in the community. Pom Mahakan was simply going to be the first in a long line of evictions in aid of the master plan to beautify Rattanakosin. Behind it were the forces of gentrification and tourism, as well as arguments about the preservation of national history, environmental protection and economic development.

In November 2002, as a result of the persistent insecurity of tenure faced by the residents of Pom Mahakan, the Community Organizations Development Institute (CODI) brought a group of architecture students from one of the local universities to the community. The idea was that the students, working in close collaboration with the Pom Mahakan residents, should develop alternative planning proposals for their community's improvement. When the city authorities issued the eviction notices, these alternative plans became part of the residents' argument against the eviction process. Their argument, however, needed more than an alternative plan. They had to respond to the master plan and what motivated it – namely, the establishment of a park. The issues that were included in their argument with the city authorities comprised the following:

- *History:* an understanding of how to view history and historical preservation. Is it the artefacts and/or architecture alone, or are people included? Is it only 'official' history, or is vernacular history included?
- *Development:* an understanding of the process of development – how decisions are made and who makes them.
- *Costs/benefits:* an understanding of who benefits from

development and who pays. Was the city authority evicting these people simply for tourism? Should it be the community alone who pays the cost of tourism?

- *Parks:* an understanding of the use of urban parks and how they work. Can parks be designed with housing? There was ample precedent for this.
- *Environment:* the ways in which the basic conflict between green and brown issues is resolved (i.e. parks or housing). Must this kind of choice be made?
- *Rights:* an understanding of human rights and the 'right to the city' – the right to space, to land and access to services.
- *Conflict resolution:* the manner in which conflict can be avoided in the development process.
- *Gentrification:* does the community have the right to be part of overall economic development in the city, and if so, how?

In developing these arguments, the community was able to create alliances with other communities and other interest groups. This proved to be essential to their ultimate success. Along with alliances with other communities facing eviction, the Pom Mahakan residents were able to add academics in a number of disciplines. Along with the architecture students, law, political science, anthropology, landscape architecture, and planning faculty and students were involved, not only locally but nationally and internationally. In addition to the academics, the National Human Rights Commission supported the community's claim to the extent that it pushed the city authority into acceding to the commission's demand that it postpone the eviction process. Furthermore, the Centre on Housing Rights and Evictions (COHRE), an international NGO, helped the community engage the United Nations High Commission for Human Rights.

All of these arguments – historical, economic and cultural – along with the fact that they had an alternative to the official plan, led the city officials, under a new governor elected in 2004, to rethink their plan. Finally, a contract was signed in early 2006 between the city and the community to have the architecture faculty of a local university complete a report that would allow for the community's design to be realized. That report was completed in September 2006, and the renovations of the park and the Pom Mahakan community were expected to begin in 2007.

Security of tenure in Istanbul: The triumph of the 'self-service city'

Turkey is perhaps the only developing country in the world to have successfully accommodated massive rural-to-urban migration through the creation of stable and well-serviced neighbourhoods. The country has done this with no major planning interventions, minimal investment in traditional government-built social housing and, in fact, almost no government action. What is more, these high-quality urban neighbourhoods have grown even though Turkey has a complex system of land tenure. With many basic concepts deriving from the Ottoman era, outsiders often find Turkey's land laws mystifying (see Box III.1).

The key to Turkey's success in housing its new urban arrivals is the fact that some of these vestigial laws give migrants the ability to build on unused or undesirable land on the urban periphery. Squatters in Turkey often build on land that has no single private owner and is held, instead, in either an undifferentiated shared title or by various government agencies. The squatter communities are able to survive and thrive because inhabitants have been particularly savvy in using two obscure local laws that help them to prevent their homes from being demolished. The first – Turkey's so-called '*gecekondu* law' – guarantees that people who build overnight without being caught cannot be evicted without due process of the law. In other words, they cannot be evicted without a court fight. To make use of this law, many squatters engage in a cat-and-mouse game with local authorities, building and having their homes demolished several times before succeeding in surviving the night and therefore gaining the right to a court hearing. Over the years, the Turkish government has issued periodic amnesties, essentially making many of the original 'built-overnight' communities quasi-legal (see Box 6.5).

The second law gives communities of more than 2000 people the right to petition the federal government in order to be recognized as legal municipal entities. Communities can register as a *belediye* (municipality) or an *ilçe* (district). The technical requirements are different, but the result is the same: access to politics. When squatter communities become a *belediye* or an *ilçe*, they gain the right to organize elections and create a local government. In a giant city such as Istanbul, every resident – in legal as well as 'illegal' neighbourhoods – is actually a citizen represented by two elected governments: the *Büyük Şehir*, or 'big city,' and the *belediye*. Every resident has two mayors: one from the big city and one from the small. The local government, in turn, can exert control over many aspects of land use, can pass and implement local plans, and can even collect revenues to fund government services. And if the local politicians are particularly savvy, they can negotiate with the bigger cities in which they are located to expand infrastructure and city services. This 'access to politics' has allowed squatters to create self-governing cities that are often more desirable places in which to live than the 'housing projects' built by the government for low-income groups.

Sultanbeyli, far out on the Asian side of the city, is a good example. A mere cluster of a few dozen houses three decades ago, Sultanbeyli today is a full-fledged squatter city of 300,000 residents led by a popularly elected mayor who heads a city government that provides many essential public services. Sultanbeyli became a *belediye* in 1989 and an *ilçe* in 1992, and using those powers, the district has successfully negotiated with one of the big city government's agencies to fund a US$90 million project to run water and sewer pipes to every home.

This squatter area has declared that it will seek to recreate itself as a legal community through selling private titles to its residents. But some squatters fear that establishing private property in land will increase costs and, ultimately, destabilize their communities (see Box III.1). Without squatting, many of the inhabitants in such communities would either be homeless or hungry. Rents in Asian-side areas of Istanbul near Sultanbeyli and Sarıgazi are close to US$62 per month. This is more than half the income of many of the squatters and, at that price, they would not have enough money to feed their families. With Istanbul continuing to grow, it is quite possible that selling private titles could set off a frenzy of speculation in Sultanbeyli. Illegal ownership, while perhaps legally precarious, is possibly safer for poor people because they don't have to go into debt to build their houses. They build what they can afford and when they can afford it.

Today, Turkey is under pressure to modernize its land tenure system as it seeks to join the EU. Perhaps in acknowledgement of this, the government has intensified efforts to demolish certain squatter neighbourhoods in Ankara and Istanbul and to replace them with social housing. Nevertheless, the country should not ignore the successes of the 'self-service' system pioneered by the squatters. Without landownership, squatters have nonetheless built stable and desirable modern neighbourhoods. Their achievements should be studied closely to see if they offer a much more cost-effective and desirable form of urban development.

With its experiment in sensible self-building, Turkey is perhaps the only country in the world to have successfully integrated urban migrants and squatters within the maelstrom of its cities. As many countries around the world are facing massive urban expansion, Turkey's squatters could become a model for developing nations around the globe.

NATURAL AND HUMAN-MADE DISASTERS

Lessons in risk reduction from Cuba

Cuba sits squarely in the path of hurricanes blowing up from the Caribbean into the Gulf of Mexico. According to the Cuban National Information Agency, Cuba faced 48 hyrdo-meteorological disasters between 1985 and 2000. A major hurricane hits the country every few years, as a result of which homes are destroyed, coastal areas flooded and agricultural production damaged; but very few people die. Between 1996 and 2002, six hurricanes hit Cuba: Lili (a category 2 hurricane) in 1996, Georges (a category 3 to 4) in 1998, Irene (a category 1) in 1999, Michelle (a category 4) in 2001, and Isidore and Lili in 2003 (both category 2). The total number of fatalities in Cuba for these six hurricanes was 16 people out of the total 665 deaths they collectively caused in the affected countries. Despite being a small poor country with few resources, Cuba has successfully curtailed the number of deaths from frequent and violent hurricanes.

Central to Cuba's successful risk reduction is the government's stated priority to save lives during a hurricane (see also Box 8.15). The country's risk reduction system supports this commitment through a range of disaster mitigation, preparedness and response activities. Disaster mitigation at the national level is facilitated through laws and legal frameworks, as well as land-use regulations, building codes and physical planning. The research and monitoring activities of the Cuban Institute of Meteorology further reinforce disaster mitigation initiatives. Disaster preparedness is coordinated at the national level by the High Command of the National Civil Defence. Preparedness activities successfully build on governmental and administrative structures already in place. Moreover, Cuba has developed an effective communication system for disaster preparedness that emphasizes:

- a clear decision-making structure for disaster preparedness and response that everyone understands;
- political will to act on and disseminate information to the general population through designated public communication channels;
- a clear, consistent and easily understood package of information on the progress of a hazard and the measures to safeguard lives;
- alternative systems of communication in case power lines are affected by a hazard.

A particularly noteworthy aspect of Cuba's disaster risk reduction system is its emphasis on enhancing community-level disaster risk reduction capacity through cultivating a 'culture of safety'. Key aspects of Cuba's community-level risk reduction efforts include:

- *Education:* the Cuban government constantly reinforces education on risk reduction through the formal education system, the workplace and public education. Disaster prevention, preparedness and response are part of all school curricula and many university curricula. Routine training on risk reduction is provided in institutions and workplaces. The media runs programmes and broadcasts regular messages about risk reduction, disaster mitigation and preparedness.
- *Community organization and social capital:* Cuba is a highly organized society with dense social networks that provide ready-made networks of communication. People may have memberships in several mass organizations and professional organizations that intersect and cross over neighbourhood, professional and workplace spheres. Such social organization builds knowledge and creates cohesion among different groups and actors, which strongly enhances cooperation in times of emergencies.
- *Community risk mapping:* community-level risk mapping is the mortar in the wall of Cuba's risk reduction system. It is undertaken by people who live in the neighbourhood, such as the family doctor or representatives of mass organizations. It involves identifying those who will need additional assistance during evacuation and persons who could provide such assistance. The Committee for the Defence of the Revolution at the neighbourhood level collates this information for incorporation within annual community emergency plans. In turn, information gathered at all levels is used to update Cuba's national emergency plans every year.
- *The national simulation exercise (the Metereo):* risk reduction capacity is reinforced by the annual simula-

tion exercise. Once a year, at the end of May, before the hurricane season starts, Cubans participate in their respective ministries, schools, workplaces and hospitals in a two-day training exercise in hurricane risk reduction. The first day consists of simulation exercises to rehearse disaster scenarios, while the second day focuses on preparation activities.

Cuba's disaster response is organized into four phases: 72 hours before the disaster; 48 hours before the disaster; the hurricane period; and recovery in the post-disaster period. The government packages messages and information relevant to each phase in clear, consistent and easily recognized formats. For each phase, there are consistent instructions about what measures to take and what to expect. These have been clearly assimilated by the entire population, including school children. These are taught in schools and workplaces, explained in Red Cross training activities and reinforced through the media.

Within a context of limited resources, the Cuban risk reduction system has been very effective, as demonstrated by the surprisingly low numbers of hurricane-related deaths. This calls for a reassessment of the often assumed advantage of wealthy countries in protecting lives during emergencies. There are increasingly compelling reasons for other governments and organizations to learn from the Cuban example, especially those with fewer resources and in need of an effective, low-cost, low-technology risk reduction system.

Vulnerabilities exposed: The 2004 Indian Ocean Tsunami

The Indian Ocean Tsunami of 26 December 2004 transcended the world's imagination for natural disaster. Just before 8:30 am local time on 26 December 2004, tsunami waves with maximum heights ranging from 2 to 15 metres began to hit coastlines in the Indian Ocean. The Sumatra–Andaman earthquake, of magnitude 9.0 on the Richter scale and with an epicentre off the west coast of Sumatra (Indonesia) set off the waves that directly hit 12 countries. From Southeast Asia to Africa, tsunami waves consumed entire towns, infrastructure collapsed, response plans fell apart and millions of survivors were left unaided to search for food, water, shelter and loved ones. More than 180,000 people died, over 40,000 went missing and in excess of 1.7 million were displaced. Total estimated economic damage from the tsunami exceeds US$10 billion. Losses in fishing, agriculture and tourism industries, as well as informal-sector economic activities, paralysed livelihoods among affected populations, with serious negative impacts on national economic growth. In the agricultural sector, the tsunami affected close to 130,000 farmers in Aceh (Indonesia); ruined 39,035 hectares of cropped area and killed over 31,000 livestock in India; and flooded over 23,000 acres of cultivated land in Sri Lanka. In Thailand, the tourism sector lost more than 120,000 jobs and estimates suggest tourism industry losses of around US$25 million per month.

During the tsunami, staggering human losses were recorded among specific sub-groups due to socio-economic factors. Women made up one such vulnerable group (see also Box 7.6). Children are another group hit hard by the tsunami and for whom efforts are being made to 'build back better'. For example, Zahira College in southern Sri Lanka saw 100 students, the principal and 5 teachers die, and 90 students lost one or both parents. Although the school is operating on relief supplies, by 2007 a new facility with more space for recreation and computing, a library, separate girls' and boys' bathrooms, and boarding facilities for teachers will provide more support and prospects for students.

The over-reliance on a few economic sectors worsened economic vulnerability during the tsunami. Dependence upon a few large industrial sectors – fishing, agriculture and tourism – for the majority of employment in tsunami-affected localities, and the lack of protection of those industries against such a hazard, compounded the devastation – not only causing large economic losses, but also reducing capacities to regain normalcy and recover afterwards. For instance, almost 75 per cent of the total fishing fleet was damaged or destroyed in Sri Lanka, where artisanal fishery is an important source of fish for local markets and industrial fishery is the major economic activity. Environmental damage to reefs and changes in winds, currents and populations of fish were also reported.

The phenomenal physical damage that occurred as a result of the tsunami was also a consequence of poor physical preparedness in affected areas. The built environment could not resist the tsunami's force, leaving victims unprotected – without shelter, safe water, communication or access to help. In Indonesia, for example, the tsunami severely damaged already poor infrastructure, increasing the event's casualties, and hindering relief and recovery. Before the tsunami, 67 per cent of roads were damaged, increasing to 72 per cent afterwards. Infrastructure damage in Thailand, including of piers, bridges, culverts, roads, dikes and public utilities, amounted to more than US$26 million. Total shelter losses across India, Indonesia, Sri Lanka and the Maldives numbered over 580,000 houses (severely damaged or destroyed).

Inadequate institutional preparedness further exacerbated loss from the tsunami in several contexts. Although the tsunami was identified, early warning information either failed to reach communities at risk or was transmitted too late. For instance, lives could have been saved in India as the tsunami took two hours to make land there after striking Indonesia; but there were no established communication networks or organizational infrastructure to deliver the warning to the people at the coast. In some places, such as Kanyakumari district in Tamil Nadu (India), the situation was made worse by the fact that concerned officials were away for Christmas.

In response to the colossal destruction of the tsunami, the world is implementing the largest ever reconstruction effort, involving 124 international NGOs and 430 local NGOs, as well as donor and United Nations agencies. Tsunami aid across the world reached over US$13.5 billion. The international community's response received praise for the unprecedented aid sent to assist tsunami relief and recovery. However, it also drew criticism for lack of coordination, supply-driven irrelevant or redundant activities and inputs, competitive 'bidding' for client victims, and poor understanding of community needs. In many cases, local populations were never consulted on what and how they wanted the resources spent, as a result of which misunderstandings on needs and strategies to meet them ensued.

Fortunately, international and national bodies from governments, the private sector and NGOs are responding to these criticisms, including those resulting from failures in coordination. The development of international aid tracking systems is one method that seeks to streamline and improve accountability in international assistance. In Thailand, the Thailand International Development Cooperation Agency, with support from the United Nations Development Programme (UNDP), has implemented the Development Assistance Database. This government-owned clearinghouse for information on technical assistance projects in the country is designed to aid long-term recovery by keeping updated information on technical assistance projects. By improving information availability and consolidation, the Development Assistance Database provides the opportunity to identify unmet needs and redundancy, make informed decisions about priorities and coordinate among actors at different levels.

The tsunami illustrated the profound vulnerabilities of human settlements around the Indian Ocean. The disaster was not a catastrophic anomaly, but rather a looming prospect linked to failures in resilience and, more specifically, weak human security, physical and institutional preparedness, and the interaction of these weaknesses. As the tsunami recovery process continues to unfold, efforts increasingly aim to build back better and there are signs of success.

Disaster response and adaptation in Kobe, Japan

Kobe, a city of roughly 1.5 million people, is located in the Hanshin region of western Japan, which produces around 10 per cent of the country's total gross national product (GNP). At 5:46 am on 17 January 1995, an earthquake of magnitude 7.2 occurred on the northern tip of Awaji Island, heavily damaging structures as far away as 70 kilometres. Within this area was much of metropolitan Kobe.

The disaster left 6300 dead, 150,000 buildings destroyed, 300,000 people homeless and caused direct economic losses of US$200 billion, making it one of the costliest earthquakes on record. The indirect economic losses resulting from disrupted commerce and industry in Kobe and its economic hinterland, which stretches into Southeast Asia, are thought to significantly exceed direct losses. Exacerbating the situation was the severity of damage to the city's lifelines. Transportation, gas and water services were disrupted, and Kobe's power and communication systems were heavily damaged.

While the earthquake itself was of a formidable magnitude, the resulting catastrophe was a combination of several risk factors. Geological conditions exacerbated loss given the soft, water-saturated soils of the city, which led to structural damage and landslides from soil liquefaction. Kobe is also located on a narrow strip of land between the Osaka Bay and the Rokko Mountains. The collapse of elevated roads and railways severed all major transportation lines within this narrow corridor.

The built environment of the city further aggravated damage from the earthquake. Most lifelines and infrastructure were built prior to the implementation of more rigorous codes and performed poorly during the earthquake. Housing in Kobe was particularly vulnerable to damage since an estimated 60 per cent consisted of traditional wooden dwellings with heavy tiled roofs supported by light frames, a design created with storms in mind but ill suited for earthquakes. Thus, housing constituted 95 per cent of the building damage and accounted for more than 50 per cent of the total value of the damage in the Hanshin region, leaving hundreds of thousands of residents in need of temporary shelter. Like many older cities, central areas had narrow streets with very dense populations – around 6000 to 12,000 people per square kilometre. Moreover, the City of Kobe's development pattern had drawn investment, and people, away from inner areas, thus exacerbating the degree of dilapidation and neglect.

Socio-economic polarization, which had already begun to manifest itself within the geography of the city well before the earthquake, was an additional factor that increased vulnerability in Kobe. The destruction was concentrated in low-income areas of the inner city, where residents tended to be the elderly, working class citizens or students living in low-cost houses. This is reflected in the death rates – 53 per cent of those killed were more than 60 years old, and rates for persons in their mid 20s were also comparatively high. The inner-city areas also had communities of immigrant labourers and *buraku*, a 'historically untouchable caste'. Vulnerability within specific neighbourhoods and communities had been allowed to continue unaddressed by policy-makers, and arguably remained unaddressed throughout the recovery process. Middle-class families tended to live outside the city centre, where newer higher-quality housing existed.

In the period after the earthquake, the government of Japan constructed 48,000 temporary housing units to house 100,000 people. Within the heavily damaged centre, city parks and schools were used for temporary shelters. However, the majority of shelters were placed in the outer areas of the city on vacant land or parking lots, two hours away by bus or train. Preference was given to the elderly and disabled, who accounted for 60 per cent of the population in the camps, as well as to single parents. Despite good intentions, moving the elderly and disabled to temporary housing in the outlying areas of the city separated an especially vulnerable population from their families and services. Temporary shelters officially closed after eight months, although housing needs were still unmet for thousands of displaced persons. As a result, many resorted to makeshift shelters in tents or under tarps, or relocated altogether to other cities. Many could not rely on insurance payments to rebuild their homes due to restricted policies (see also Box 12.15).

Housing recovery in Kobe was, for the most part, left to market forces rather than government programmes. Instead, the government focused on large infrastructural projects. Economic pressures led the poor, elderly and renters to move away from high-value city centre locations by selling their property to speculators rather than borrowing money for rebuilding. Those who did attempt to repair or reconstruct their homes within the inner city faced the difficult task of working within the physical limitations of the area, while also meeting the demands of new building regulations. The government prohibited permanent reconstruction in about half of the heavily affected areas. In lots where reconstruction was attempted, compliance with the Building Standards Act was mandatory. New buildings were required to be adjacent to a road at least 4 metres wide and of a building-to-site area ratio of 60 per cent or less. Because of the density and narrow streets of the area, it was often impossible for the rebuilt structure to match the former house's building area or floor area, and in some instances it was impossible to construct anything at all since more than half of the lots were adjacent to very narrow roads.

While city-wide measures are highly positive, the benefits of the housing recovery programme were not reaped by those most in need. The city of Kobe as a space has recovered in most sectors; but many victims of the earthquake have not recovered. Many of those displaced have never returned. Diasporas of disaster give a false impression of success by eliminating those most in need from the scope of concern. Following such calamitous events, holistic recovery requires recognizing that the city has, at least temporarily, been scattered beyond its boundaries.

Learning from the Mexico City earthquake

A series of powerful earthquakes struck Mexico City from 19 to 20 September 1985. The first tremor hit at 7:19 am, lasting for nearly two minutes and registered 8.1 on the Richter scale. Dozens of smaller but powerful after-shocks continued to consume the city, culminating in a final 7.5 magnitude quake, 36 hours after the first tremor. Even for this natural hazard-prone urban centre, the 1985 earthquake struck with an unprecedented force. The ensuing disaster killed between 3050 and 10,000 people, injured between 14,000 and 50,000, and caused overall economic losses of an estimated US$4 billion. The earthquakes destroyed thousands of modern and antiquated buildings and damaged 100,000 more. This destruction left 2 million of Mexico City's 18 million residents homeless.

Earthquakes pose an ever-present threat to Mexico City. Mexico is one of the world's most seismically active countries, sitting atop the intersection of five tectonic plates. Located in the centre of the country directly above these faults, Mexico City is particularly vulnerable to any seismic movements and has suffered a recorded 340 earthquakes in the vicinity since Aztec times. Moreover, the city is partially built on a lakebed of unstable saturated mud and clay soils and is responsible for the city's ongoing subsidence of up to 40 centimetres per year in some areas. The city's sinking compromises buildings' structural integrity and increases their vulnerability to seismic movements. Such geological factors contribute to increased earthquake risk and amplify earthquake impacts.

The housing sector suffered the worst damage from the 1985 earthquake. A year before the earthquake, planners estimated that the city faced a housing shortage equivalent to 30 per cent of the existing stock. High rural–urban migration, low wages, rent control policies and high urban construction costs, among other factors, had resulted in inadequate housing development and maintenance by both the private and public sectors. This forced city dwellers to overcrowd the available housing, thereby rendering it less safe for habitation.

Among housing damaged by the earthquake, large multi-storey apartment buildings that accommodated hundreds of residents and smaller apartment buildings called *viviendas* suffered the most. Multi-storey government buildings constructed during the 1950s and 1960s as low-cost alternatives had offered a solution to Mexico's ongoing housing shortage. Yet, decades later, the oversized structures proved to be among the most vulnerable to the earthquake's force, killing thousands of inhabitants and leaving thousands more homeless. Post-quake analysis revealed that the use of substandard construction materials and loose adherence to building standards contributed to the devastating collapses. The hard hit *viviendas* were typically old and in poor condition, often lacking basic plumbing and sanitation services. The poor state of some of these structures could be attributed to 'absentee' landlords who had long neglected their properties, citing rent-control policies that removed market incentives for landlords to maintain or rehabilitate buildings.

No residential losses had insurance coverage, forcing the government and citizens to bear the brunt of responsibility for financing housing reconstruction. On 4 October 1985, the Mexican government formed the National Reconstruction Commission, which developed four government housing programmes. A total of 94,893 housing units were repaired, upgraded or built anew under these four programmes. However, the public felt that the government response paid greater attention to the middle-class areas of the city, rather than the poorer downtown tenement areas. Some of the reconstruction policies and programmes implemented also reproduced pre-existing inequities that had previously created and perpetuated many of the city's vulnerabilities. Moreover, ambiguities in ownership and tenure and private landlords' refusal to invest in what they considered worthless properties meant that many damaged apartment buildings remained in their state of disrepair.

NGOs partly filled the gaps left by the government in disaster response activities. Community organizations also stepped in to meet citizen's needs and independently contributed over 7000 new housing units (both reconstruction and repair). NGOs and community groups partnered with the government projects to help realize the housing objectives, but opposed those interventions which seemed to work against citizens' interests. These organizations worked to combat the reinforcement of social inequities perpetuated through government-sponsored housing reconstruction. They also lobbied for rebuilding and rehabilitation within existing residential communities instead of removing citizens to peripheral areas.

In the two decades since the earthquake, Mexico has taken significant steps towards addressing risks related to earthquakes and other hazards. Many of these are technological advancements in earthquake monitoring, plans to improve structural resistance to earthquake tremors and citizen readiness programmes. Motivated by active community involvement during the 1985 recovery, the government has added mechanisms to incorporate citizens' voices within public debate and decision-making. Furthermore, Mexico has established monitoring and warning systems to detect earthquakes, volcanoes and tropical storms, such as the 1991 Seismic Alert System (SAS). The international community has also directed attention to Mexico City's disaster risk. For example, the World Bank is involved in disaster risk assessment in Mexico and supports risk mitigation efforts.

Reducing vulnerability in Mexico City is a perennial challenge. While many risk factors that exacerbated the effects of the 1985 earthquake have been addressed, new vulnerabilities constantly emerge. The rapid spread of informal settlements that do not follow building codes and laws, and spatial polarization of the poor, are some factors that continue to undermine resilience to disasters. If a similarly powerful earthquake hits Mexico City again, it is probable that there will be an enormous death toll and significant structural damage. Despite their dynamism and recurrence, hazards in Mexico City are predictable. The key to increasing the city's resilience is to understand vulnerability as an evolving and interdependent process, which must constantly be reassessed, and to simultaneously mitigate multiple disaster risks at multiple levels.

Living with floods in Mozambique

International media coverage of 23-year-old Caroline Mabuiango giving birth to daughter Rosita while clinging to a tree limb high above the raging waters that had swallowed the earth gave a human face to the devastating flooding that tormented Mozambique from October 1999 into March 2000. Carolina, one of 15 people who sought refuge for three days in a Mafurra tree, was one of the survivors. Others, like her grandmother, could not withstand the driving rains and were swept away by the merciless waters. While flooding in Mozambique was not a new phenomenon, the disaster known as 'the 2000 floods' was the most severe the country had experienced in 50 years. The Mozambican government calculated that the flooding killed at least 700 people, displaced 650,000 and left 1 million in urgent need of nutritional and/or medical assistance. Overall, the floods affected 4.5 million, about one quarter of Mozambique's total population, by destroying land, property and disrupting livelihoods. Moreover, the floods had a devastating impact on several of Mozambique's small but growing urban centres, the location of more than 70 per cent of all related deaths.

As a predominantly rural country with several small- to medium-sized urban and peri-urban centres, Mozambique's experience emphasized the relevance and interconnectedness of urban safety to wider national and even regional preparedness strategies. While the 2000 floods primarily debilitated rural Mozambique, there were far reaching consequences for the country's urban centres. The floods' destruction of over 66 per cent of Mozambique's crops, 140,000 hectares of farming and grazing land, agricultural equipment and irrigation systems and the death or serious injury of hundreds of thousands of livestock decimated the food supply, drove up prices and made all urban areas, even those unaffected by the floods, vulnerable to hunger. At the same time, by incapacitating the country's transportation infrastructure, the floods prevented the delivery of food to urban areas from neighbouring countries. The floods also caused significant direct loss of life, livelihoods, economic assets and physical infrastructure in Mozambique's urban centres (see also Box 7.2).

Complex risk factors expose Mozambique to the threat of flooding. The country's many rivers, extensive river basins and dams contribute to the physical vulnerability of the country to flooding. More than 50 per cent of Mozambique's territory is located in international river basins so that physical hazards are regional in nature and cannot be managed by the country on its own. Poor land-use practices in areas within and surrounding Mozambique's cities exacerbate the severity of the damage from floods. Extensive deforestation has been identified as a key contributing factor that magnified the impact of the 2000 floods. Disregard of land-use plans led to the construction of buildings in hazard-prone locations. Poor urban residents living in informal settlements were especially vulnerable to the impacts of the floods. Mozambique's vulnerability to flooding should also be seen in the context of extremely low human development, post-conflict reconstruction and high debt accumulated throughout prolonged conflict and the subsequent implementation of structural adjustment initiatives.

Despite its minimal resources, Mozambique has demonstrated a willingness to invest in the mitigation of future disasters and, together with the international community, is responding to lessons learned from the 2000 floods. Post-flood interventions have been both structural and institutional. Since the 2000 floods, additional dams, such as the Moamba on the Incomati River, the Mapai on the Limpopo River and the Mepanda Uncua on the Zambezi River, have been built. Many hydrometric stations have been upgraded and hydrological sites modernized, enabling more data collection and sharing among relevant actors. Institutionally, government departments such as the National Disaster Management Institution and the Coordinating Council for Disaster Management have been expanded and given a stronger mandate to provide emergency response and enforce policies, respectively. The removal of political jurisdictions and increased transparency are expected to help avoid miscommunication and to enable vital information to be shared quickly among relevant departments.

In 2006, the government reported significant progress in disaster risk reduction efforts. Most notable had been experiences of floods one year after the 2000 floods.

Prolonged and intense rains returned to Mozambique at the end of 2000 and the beginning of 2001, resulting in serious flooding during February and March 2001 in central provinces. This flood affected 500,000 people and displaced 223,000. Before the flooding began, essential government agencies received training and delivered 5100 tonnes of food to flood-prone areas in December 2000 in preparation for the 2001 rainy season. While the flooding itself was less severe than the 2000 disaster, country-level actors, including government agencies, international donors and institutions, and civil society organizations had integrated lessons learned from 2000 within their disaster systems and contingency plans. The international community also responded quickly to calls for aid, providing 93 per cent of the country's appeal by mid 2001.

Vulnerability to monsoon flooding in Mumbai, India

On 26 July 2005, the deep-seated vulnerability of Mumbai's deteriorating infrastructure, weak planning and implementation of the government's disaster mitigation strategy, and overwhelming socio-economic inequalities showed through in the face of disastrous monsoon rains and flooding. As India's heaviest recorded rainfall, Mumbai was battered with 2.89 inches of rain in the city centre and 37.2 inches in surrounding suburban areas in one single day.

The aged and poorly maintained drainage systems throughout Mumbai exacerbate flood risk in the city. The city's centre has an over 100-year-old drainage system with cracked pipelines that frequently leak into drinking water pipelines. During the monsoon season, when the rains raise the sea-water level, these pipelines flood with water, mixing with street sewage and leading to the closing of streets every year. Due to the pressure to create housing for the growing population and incentives of high real estate profits, the development of suburban areas has not been accompanied by the necessary infrastructural facilities. There are open sewers throughout this area that are usually clogged with waste and are closed due to road expansion and construction. This area is home to both new government development and the largest portion of the city's slum dweller population residing on the Mithi River's banks. In fact, 70 per cent of the Mithi River's embankments are occupied by informal settlements.

Growing flood risk in Mumbai is also associated directly and indirectly with rapid urban population growth. The population of the city and its surrounding suburban areas increased by 38 per cent, from approximately 12,420,600 in 1991 to approximately 20 million by the end of 2005. Mumbai alone takes in 350 families every day. While urban populations are expanding, it has become more difficult for state and municipal governments to house and provide services for the growing populations. Thus, over half of Mumbai's 12 million people live in informal settlements or slums.

Due to poor land regulations and policies, the majority of Mumbai's slums are located in areas that are most prone to flooding during times of heavy rainfall and high tides. Thus, slum dwellers experience the brunt of natural disasters. The encroachment of slums on vital drainage areas further limits the capacity of the city to ensure effective drainage both prior to and following heavy rains. The overwhelming accumulation of new and stagnant rain water inevitably spills over into relatively dry areas of the city. By not addressing chronic drainage and sanitation problems in Mumbai's slums, the entire city is exposed to devastating flooding during the monsoon season.

Mumbai actually had a Disaster Management Plan (DMP), prepared by the Relief and Rehabilitation Division of the Government of Maharashtra, in place prior to the July 2005 floods. The Mumbai DMP provides a risk assessment and vulnerability analysis that recognizes flooding as a major risk to the city and identifies vulnerable locations and communities. However, studies note that the plan was never enacted in a way that could prevent the 2005 floods. In the decade that elapsed since the DMP was developed, no action was taken to alleviate the pinpointed risks and chronic problems that the plan identified. The government had not devised or implemented a plan of action to repair and maintain working drainage systems, new housing options for slum dwellers living in flood-prone areas or sound land policies to address the city's overpopulation.

Following the floods, a committee was set up to manage relief efforts for the crisis. The committee deployed army, air force and navy personnel for search-and-rescue operations, heavily relying on the assistance of non-governmental and community-based organizations. Relief efforts included the removal of 100,000 tonnes of garbage and 15,321 cattle carcasses, in addition to the provision of food grains, chlorine tablets for safe drinking water and oral rehydration solutions. The government released public health advisories and distributed 133 medical teams to prevent the spread of infectious diseases, such as cholera and gastroenteritis. A commitment was also made to provide financial assistance of US$22 for each of the approximately 842,185 destitute persons. Furthermore, a week after the deluge, the Mithi River Authority was created to address risk associated with the river and the surrounding area. A major component of the authority's responsibility was to remove the encroachment of slum dwellings upon the river and to improve the area's drainage system. However, neither of these responses initiated by the government called for the active involvement of citizens or non-governmental urban planning engineers and professionals.

As a megacity, Mumbai's large physical area, growing population and complex social factors make the development and implementation of disaster management plans inherently difficult. The size and dynamic nature of the city increases the liability to disaster risks. The existing physical hazards and correlating social conditions exacerbate Mumbai's vulnerability to flooding.

The Dutch experience in flood management

Since the establishment of the earliest settlements in the area, the people of The Netherlands have struggled with the ever present threat of flooding in the cities and towns of their low-lying region. Over half of the land area of The Netherlands is below sea level, and in the south-western part lies the marshy delta of three big rivers: the Rhine, Meuse and Scheldt. Although this geography provides fertile soil and easy access to the seas and waterways, these areas are also subject to the dangers of river flooding and of the ebb and flow of the sea.

Creative innovation and the adaptation of new technologies for water management have enabled the Dutch to successfully mitigate risk, prospering despite the natural hazards posed by the surrounding waters. To protect themselves against flood risks, the Dutch have built an elaborate system of dikes and drainage mechanisms. The earliest forms of water management came about in the 12th century as the Dutch reclaimed, or drained and elevated, land covered by water. Although the vulnerability to flooding of The Netherland's most important settlements and infrastructure made water management of paramount importance, it was not until the formation of the national water authority, the Rijkswaterstaat, during the late 18th century that water management was handled by a structured government authority. Prior to this time, the task of building dikes and waterways was left largely to individual villages and communities. Local reclamation efforts, at least until the 16th century, consisted of simple technologies, such as building dwelling mounds (higher ground) and basic dikes and polder systems to artificially manage the water flow. Technical innovation, fuelled mainly by trial and error, nonetheless occurred during this time as water management and land reclamation efforts grew to accommodate increased transportation and agricultural demands.

By the late 1930s and early 1940s, there was ongoing research to determine the strength of the next big storm surge and to establish the country's greatest vulnerabilities. The predictions revealed that the barriers in place at the time would not be sufficient and that greater protections would be necessary. These warnings went unheeded. With the disastrous flooding of 1916 having occurred decades earlier, the attention of the government and greater public was instead devoted to rebuilding the dikes that had been destroyed during World War II. On 1 February 1953, a strong storm in the North Sea, coupled with exceptionally high spring tides, led to a breach of the dikes protecting the southwest part of the country. The resulting flooding killed 1835 people. Approximately 200,000 hectares of land (535,575 acres) were flooded, and 26,000 homes and 300 farms were destroyed. The total damage amounted to about 5 per cent of the country's gross domestic product (GDP), a devastating blow to a nation recovering from World War II.

The 1953 flooding was one of the worst disasters ever to strike The Netherlands, and was the result both of an unusually powerful storm and an inability to conceive and prepare for it. The storm was of the strength and severity seen only once every 500 years. The Dutch infrastructure was simply not built in anticipation of such a fierce storm. The government deemed the risk too remote to justify the enormous expense required to raise and strengthen the then existing dikes. Once the storm surge reached The Netherlands, the elaborate system of dikes and pumps gave way. Entire villages were submerged as water cascaded over the tops of the dikes. In all, 80 breaches were recorded, some of them 180 metres wide. It was later found that many kilometres of dikes needed serious repair or replacement. Just as the Dutch government failed to imagine a storm strong enough to overpower the dikes, so too did the Dutch people, whose unquestioning trust in The Netherlands waterways authority and the dikes led to low levels of preparedness for flooding and the inability to communicate the dangers either before or during the flooding.

The Delta Commission was formed shortly after the floods to determine a course of action. The commission put forth the Delta Act, passed by the government in 1957, which proposed shortening the coastline and called for the construction of a series of primary and secondary dams to strengthen flood defences. The Delta Project was the first comprehensive approach designed to address the vulnerabilities of the nation. The scope and technological vision of the project rank it among the greatest engineering feats ever accomplished by any country. There were two major technological accomplishments of this project. The first was the Eastern Scheldt Dam, which is one of the most highly regarded water management structures in the country. The construction of the dam was met with public protests over negative ecological consequences; but these were resolved through a willingness to incorporate a dialogue on the process surrounding the project. The second major technological accomplishment of the Delta Project was the Maeslant Barrier. Like the Eastern Scheldt Dam, the Maeslant Barrier was a technological breakthrough, capable of mitigating flooding during storms without hindering Rotterdam's commercial linkages to the North Sea.

Whereas the Delta Project aimed to control the waters with human-made barriers, new policies were implemented during the late 1990s that prioritized reducing risks rather than controlling and taming the rivers, as had been done in the past. Risks and vulnerabilities had increased over the years due to weakened river barriers and changes brought by urbanization in adjacent areas. The Netherlands government also realized that cooperation with countries upstream was essential in preserving their own cities and interests.

The Dutch case demonstrates, first and foremost, an ongoing process of institutional learning. The flood of 1953 came from the storm at sea, but later flooding during the 1990s was the result of river levels rising inland. The history of Dutch water management reflects the realization that the security of Dutch cities is contingent upon the management of ecological processes in the hinterlands (see also Box 8.10).

Implementing a national response plan for Hurricane Katrina in New Orleans, US

On 29 August 2005, Hurricane Katrina devastated New Orleans and much of the Gulf Coast of the US. The hurricane unleashed its fury on the Gulf Coast, sustaining maximum wind speeds of up to 195 kilometres per hour and a storm-eye radius of 48 kilometres. Although the storm lost momentum prior to landfall, a category 3 storm still inundated New Orleans and much of the surrounding region. Within five hours of landfall, several sections of the levee system in New Orleans were breached and 80 per cent of the city was under water. Residents unable to leave the city prior to Katrina's landfall were either stranded in their residences, in temporary shelters, or died. Katrina's estimated death toll in the Gulf Coast region was approximately 1100 people and hundreds of thousands were displaced throughout the country.

Nine months prior to the hurricane, in December 2004, the Department of Homeland Security (DHS) authored the National Response Plan (NRP) that outlined a system of coordination between local, state and federal disaster responses. The plan defined the roles and responsibilities of each key player in the event of an emergency. However, as seen through the Katrina experience, there were major emergency preparation and coordination failures.

Post-Katrina investigations have clearly illustrated shortcomings in implementing the NRP, mostly at the federal (rather than the state and local) level. As was discovered by the Select Bipartisan Committee that investigated preparation for and response to Hurricane Katrina, the federal government failed to recognize the magnitude of Katrina's potential impacts, project future needs, fully engage the president and respond in a proactive and timely manner. The incorporation of the Federal Emergency Management Administration (FEMA) within the DHS and the coordination plan laid out in the NRP created an additional bureaucratic layer separating the president further from direct contact with FEMA and, consequently, with the individuals immediately involved with disaster management. Hence, key decisions became the responsibility of the secretary of the DHS, rather than the director of FEMA. The following are cited by the Bipartisan Committee as key actions that the DHS implemented too late or not at all:

- *The designation of an incident of national significance (INS).* As spelled out in the NRP, an incident of national significance is an impending event, which due to its potential magnitude, requires coordination between the three levels of government to mobilize and implement an effective response that will minimize the impact and help to save lives. As Hurricane Katrina was meteorologically well documented more than 50 hours prior to landfall, and the impact of a category 3 storm in the Gulf Coast region was also widely known, it should have been considered as an INS. By establishing this disaster as an INS, a better-organized response plan could have been implemented at least two days prior to landfall.
- *The authority to convene the Interagency Incident Management Group (IIMG).* When an INS is declared, the IIMG, a federal-level multi-agency group, convenes. The IIMG acts as an advisory group to the Secretary of Homeland Security and refers information to the White House. The role of the IIMG is to provide the executive branch of the federal government with information pertaining to the coordination and management of a disaster, in addition to acting as a key strategic partner providing guidance to the secretary of homeland security and to the White House. The IIMG did not convene until Tuesday evening after landfall, clearly too late to coordinate a federal response.
- *The designation of the principal federal officer.* A principal federal officer was not designated by the DHS for Hurricane Katrina. This federal officer acts as the local focal person for DHS while an INS evolves. The officer's responsibility is to coordinate and facilitate all managerial responsibilities of the secretary of homeland security on the ground in addition to any federal support/response. Furthermore, an officer is expected to provide real-time insight into the changing events on the ground, in order for the federal government to better monitor the situation. Had a principal federal officer been in position, this officer would have been able to keep DHS and the additional partners at the federal level abreast of the rapidly evolving situation.
- *The invocation of the National Response Plan's Catastrophic Incident Annex.* The annex, which serves to shift the federal response from a reactive response to a proactive one, was not implemented. If the DHS had implemented the annex, the response to Hurricane Katrina would have been very different. The Bipartisan Committee further showed that the government rather responded in a reactive fashion that is not appropriate for disasters of Katrina's magnitude.

The experience of implementing the NRP in response to Hurricane Katrina clearly illustrates the challenges of coordinating disaster risk reduction activities at various levels within a federal system of governance. Where a national disaster management system is over-ridden with multiple levels of responsibilities and bureaucracy, preparedness and response efforts are at risk of being obstructed.

PART VII
STATISTICAL ANNEX

■ General disclaimer

The designations employed and presentation of the data do not imply the expression of any opinion whatsoever on the part of the Secretariat of the United Nations concerning the legal status of any country, city or area or of its authorities, or concerning the delimitation of its frontiers or boundaries.

TECHNICAL NOTES

The Statistical Annex comprises 25 tables covering such broad statistical categories as demography, households, housing, housing infrastructure, economic and social indicators. Taking into account the theme of the 2007 Global Report, this Statistical Annex highlights as much as possible safety and security issues. The Annex is divided into three sections presenting data at the regional, country and city levels. Tables A.1 to A.5 present regional-level data grouped by selected criteria of economic and development achievements, as well as geographic distribution. Tables B.1 to B.13 contain country-level data and Tables C.1 to C.7 are devoted to city-level data. Data have been compiled from various international sources, from national statistical offices and from the United Nations.

EXPLANATION OF SYMBOLS

The following symbols have been used in presenting data throughout the Statistical Annex:

Category not applicable ..
Data not available ...
Magnitude zero –

COUNTRY GROUPINGS AND STATISTICAL AGGREGATES

World major groupings

More developed regions: All countries and areas of Europe and Northern America, as well as Australia, Japan and New Zealand.

Less developed regions: All countries and areas of Africa, Latin America, Asia (excluding Japan) and Oceania (excluding Australia and New Zealand).

Least developed countries (LDCs): The United Nations currently designates 50 countries as LDCs: Afghanistan, Angola, Bangladesh, Benin, Bhutan, Burkina Faso, Burundi, Cambodia, Cape Verde, Central African Republic, Chad, Comoros, Democratic Republic of the Congo, Djibouti, Equatorial Guinea, Eritrea, Ethiopia, Gambia, Guinea, Guinea-Bissau, Haiti, Kiribati, Lao People's Democratic Republic, Lesotho, Liberia, Madagascar, Malawi, Maldives, Mali, Mauritania, Mozambique, Myanmar, Nepal, Niger, Rwanda, Samoa, Sao Tome and Principe, Senegal, Sierra Leone, Solomon Islands, Somalia, Sudan, Timor-Leste, Togo, Tuvalu, Uganda, United Republic of Tanzania, Vanuatu, Yemen, Zambia.

Landlocked developing countries (LLDCs): Afghanistan, Armenia, Azerbaijan, Bhutan, Bolivia, Botswana, Burkina Faso, Burundi, Central African Republic, Chad, Ethiopia, Kazakhstan, Kyrgyzstan, Lao People's Democratic Republic, Lesotho, Malawi, Mali, Mongolia, Nepal, Niger, Paraguay, Republic of Moldova, Rwanda, Swaziland, Tajikistan, TFYR of Macedonia, Turkmenistan, Uganda, Uzbekistan, Zambia, Zimbabwe.

Small island developing states (SIDS):[1] Antigua and Barbuda, Bahamas, Barbados, Belize, Cape Verde, Comoros, Cuba, Dominica, Dominican Republic, Fiji, Grenada, Guinea-Bissau, Guyana, Haiti, Jamaica, Kiribati, Maldives, Marshall Islands, Mauritius, Micronesia (Federated States of), Nauru, Palau, Papua New Guinea, Saint Kitts and Nevis, Saint Lucia, Samoa, Sao Tome and Principe, Seychelles, Singapore, Solomon Islands, Saint Vincent and the Grenadines, Suriname, Timor-Leste, Tonga, Trinidad and Tobago, Tuvalu, Vanuatu; American Samoa, Anguilla, Aruba, British Virgin Islands, Cook Islands, French Polynesia, Guam, Montserrat, Netherlands Antilles, New Caledonia, Niue, Puerto Rico, United States Virgin Islands.

United Nations Regional Groups[2]

African States: Algeria, Angola, Benin, Botswana, Burkina Faso, Burundi, Cameroon, Cape Verde, Central African Republic, Chad, Comoros, Congo, Côte d'Ivoire, Democratic Republic of the Congo, Djibouti, Egypt, Equatorial Guinea, Eritrea, Ethiopia, Gabon, Gambia, Ghana, Guinea, Guinea-Bissau, Kenya, Lesotho, Liberia, Libyan Arab Jamahiriya, Madagascar, Malawi, Mali, Mauritania, Mauritius, Morocco, Mozambique, Namibia, Niger, Nigeria, Rwanda, Sao Tome and Principe, Senegal, Seychelles, Sierra Leone, Somalia, South Africa, Sudan, Swaziland, Togo, Tunisia, Uganda, United Republic of Tanzania, Zambia, Zimbabwe.

Asian States: Afghanistan, Bahrain, Bangladesh, Bhutan, Brunei Darussalam, Cambodia, China, Cyprus, Democratic People's Republic of Korea, Fiji, India, Indonesia, Iran, Iraq, Japan, Jordan, Kazakhstan, Kuwait, Kyrgyzstan, Lao People's Democratic Republic, Lebanon, Malaysia, Maldives, Marshall

Islands, Micronesia, Mongolia, Myanmar, Nauru, Nepal, Oman, Pakistan, Palau, Papua New Guinea, Philippines, Qatar, Republic of Korea, Samoa, Saudi Arabia, Singapore, Solomon Islands, Sri Lanka, Syrian Arab Republic, Tajikistan, Thailand, Tonga, Turkmenistan, Tuvalu, United Arab Emirates, Uzbekistan, Vanuatu, Viet Nam, Yemen.

Eastern European States: Albania, Armenia, Azerbaijan, Belarus, Bosnia and Herzegovina, Bulgaria, Croatia, Czech Republic, Georgia, Hungary, Latvia, Lithuania, Poland, Republic of Moldova, Romania, Russian Federation, Serbia and Montenegro, Slovakia, Slovenia, TFYR Macedonia, Ukraine.

Latin American and Caribbean States: Antigua and Barbuda, Argentina, Bahamas, Barbados, Belize, Bolivia, Brazil, Chile, Colombia, Costa Rica, Cuba, Dominica, Dominican Republic, Ecuador, El Salvador, Grenada, Guatemala, Guyana, Haiti, Honduras, Jamaica, Mexico, Nicaragua, Panama, Paraguay, Peru, Saint Kitts and Nevis, Saint Lucia, Saint Vincent and the Grenadines, Suriname, Trinidad and Tobago, Uruguay, Venezuela.

Western Europe and other States: Andorra, Australia, Austria, Belgium, Canada, Denmark, Finland, France, Germany, Greece, Iceland, Ireland, Israel, Italy, Liechtenstein, Luxembourg, Malta, Monaco, Netherlands, New Zealand, Norway, Portugal, San Marino, Spain, Sweden, Switzerland, Turkey, United Kingdom.

Countries in the Human Development aggregates[3]

High human development (*HDI 0.800 and above*):[4] Argentina, Australia, Austria, Bahamas, Bahrain, Barbados, Belgium, Brunei Darussalam, Bulgaria, Canada, Chile, Hong Kong SAR of China, Costa Rica, Croatia, Cuba, Cyprus, Czech Republic, Denmark, Estonia, Finland, France, Germany, Greece, Hungary, Iceland, Ireland, Israel, Italy, Japan, Kuwait, Latvia, Lithuania, Luxembourg, Malta, Mexico, Netherlands, New Zealand, Norway, Panama, Poland, Portugal, Qatar, Republic of Korea, Saint Kitts and Nevis, Seychelles, Singapore, Slovakia, Slovenia, Spain, Sweden, Switzerland, Tonga, Trinidad and Tobago, United Arab Emirates, United Kingdom, United States, Uruguay.

Medium human development (*HDI 0.500–0.799*):[5] Albania, Algeria, Antigua and Barbuda, Armenia, Azerbaijan, Bangladesh, Belarus, Belize, Bhutan, Bolivia, Bosnia and Herzegovina, Botswana, Brazil, Cambodia, Cape Verde, China, Colombia, Comoros, Congo, Dominica, Dominican Republic, Ecuador, Egypt, El Salvador, Equatorial Guinea, Fiji, Gabon, Georgia, Ghana, Grenada, Guatemala, Guyana, Honduras, India, Indonesia, Iran (Islamic Republic of), Jamaica, Jordan, Kazakhstan, Kyrgyzstan, Lao People's Democratic Republic, Lebanon, Libyan Arab Jamahiriya, Malaysia, Maldives, Mauritius, Mongolia, Morocco, Myanmar, Namibia, Nepal, Nicaragua, Occupied Palestinian Territories, Oman, Pakistan, Papua New Guinea, Paraguay, Peru, Philippines, Republic of Moldova, Romania, Russian Federation, Saint Lucia, Saint Vincent and the Grenadines, Samoa, Sao Tome and Principe, Saudi Arabia, Solomon Islands, South Africa, Sri Lanka, Sudan, Suriname, Syrian Arab Republic, Tajikistan, TFYR Macedonia, Thailand, Timor-Leste, Togo, Tunisia, Turkey, Turkmenistan, Uganda, Ukraine, Uzbekistan, Vanuatu, Venezuela, Viet Nam, Zimbabwe.

Low human development (*HDI 0.500 and below*):[6] Angola, Benin, Burkina Faso, Burundi, Cameroon, Central African Republic, Chad, Côte d'Ivoire, Democratic Republic of the Congo, Djibouti, Eritrea, Ethiopia, Gambia, Guinea, Guinea-Bissau, Haiti, Lesotho, Kenya, Madagascar, Malawi, Mali, Mauritania, Mozambique, Niger, Nigeria, Rwanda, Senegal, Sierra Leone, Swaziland, United Republic of Tanzania, Yemen, Zambia.

Countries in the income aggregates[7]

The World Bank classifies all member economies and all other economies with population of more than 30,000. In the 2006 World Development Report, economies are divided among income groups according to 2004 GNI per capita, calculated using the World Bank Atlas method. The groups are:

High income: Andorra, Aruba, Australia, Austria, Bahamas, Bahrain, Belgium, Bermuda, Brunei Darussalam, Canada, Cayman Islands, Channel Islands, Cyprus, Denmark, Faeroe Islands, Finland, France, French Polynesia, Germany, Greece, Greenland, Guam, Hong Kong SAR of China, Iceland, Ireland, Isle of Man, Israel, Italy, Japan, Kuwait, Liechtenstein, Luxembourg, Macao SAR of China, Malta, Monaco, Netherlands, Netherlands Antilles, New Caledonia, New Zealand, Norway, Portugal, Puerto Rico, Qatar, Republic of Korea, San Marino, Saudi Arabia, Singapore, Slovenia, Spain, Sweden, Switzerland, United Arab Emirates, United Kingdom, United States, United States Virgin Islands.

Upper-middle income: American Samoa, Antigua and Barbuda, Argentina, Barbados, Belize, Botswana, Chile, Costa Rica, Croatia, Czech Republic, Dominica, Estonia, Equatorial Guinea, Gabon, Grenada, Hungary, Latvia, Lebanon, Libyan Arab Jamahiriya, Lithuania, Malaysia, Mauritius, Mexico, Northern Mariana Islands, Oman, Palau, Panama, Poland, Russian Federation, Seychelles, South Africa, Slovakia, Saint Kitts and Nevis, Saint Lucia, Saint Vincent and the Grenadines, Trinidad and Tobago, Turkey, Uruguay, Venezuela.

Lower-middle income: Albania, Algeria, Angola, Armenia, Azerbaijan, Belarus, Bolivia, Bosnia and Herzegovina, Brazil, Bulgaria, Cape Verde, China, Colombia, Cuba, Djibouti, Dominican Republic, Ecuador, Egypt, El Salvador, Fiji, Georgia, Guatemala, Guyana, Honduras, Iraq, Iran (Islamic Republic of), Jamaica, Jordan, Indonesia, Kazakhstan, Kiribati, Maldives, Marshall Islands, Micronesia (Federated States of), Morocco, Namibia, Occupied Palestinian Territories, Paraguay, Peru, Philippines, Romania, Samoa,

Serbia and Montenegro, Sri Lanka, Suriname, Swaziland, Syrian Arab Republic, TFYR Macedonia, Thailand, Tonga, Tunisia, Turkmenistan, Ukraine, Vanuatu.

Low income: Afghanistan, Bangladesh, Benin, Bhutan, Burkina Faso, Burundi, Cambodia, Cameroon, Central African Republic, Chad, Comoros, Congo, Côte d'Ivoire, Democratic People's Republic of Korea, Democratic Republic of the Congo, Eritrea, Ethiopia, Gambia, Ghana, Guinea, Guinea-Bissau, Haiti, India, Kenya, Kyrgyzstan, Lao People's Democratic Republic, Liberia, Lesotho, Madagascar, Malawi, Mali, Mauritania, Mongolia, Mozambique, Myanmar, Nepal, Nicaragua, Niger, Nigeria, Pakistan, Papua New Guinea, Republic of Moldova, Rwanda, Sao Tome and Principe, Senegal, Sierra Leone, Solomon Islands, Somalia, Sudan, Tajikistan, Timor-Leste, Togo, Uganda, United Republic of Tanzania, Uzbekistan, Viet Nam, Yemen, Zambia, Zimbabwe.

Sub-regional aggregates

Africa

Eastern Africa: Burundi, Comoros, Djibouti, Eritrea, Ethiopia, Kenya, Madagascar, Malawi, Mauritius, Mozambique Réunion, Rwanda, Seychelles, Somalia, Uganda, United Republic of Tanzania, Zambia, Zimbabwe.

Middle Africa: Angola, Cameroon, Central African Republic, Chad, Congo, Democratic Republic of the Congo, Equatorial Guinea, Gabon, Sao Tome and Principe.

Northern Africa: Algeria, Egypt, Libyan Arab Jamahiriya, Morocco, Sudan, Tunisia, Western Sahara.

Southern Africa: Botswana, Lesotho, Namibia, South Africa, Swaziland.

Western Africa: Benin, Burkina Faso, Cape Verde, Côte d'Ivoire, Gambia, Ghana, Guinea, Guinea-Bissau, Liberia, Mali, Mauritania, Niger, Nigeria, Saint Helena, Senegal, Sierra Leone, Togo.

Asia

Eastern Asia: China, China, Hong Kong SAR, China, Macao SAR, Democratic People's Republic of Korea, Japan, Mongolia, Republic of Korea.

South-central Asia: Afghanistan, Bangladesh, Bhutan, India, Iran (Islamic Republic of), Kazakhstan, Kyrgyzstan, Maldives, Nepal, Pakistan, Sri Lanka, Tajikistan, Turkmenistan, Uzbekistan.

Southeastern Asia: Brunei Darussalam, Cambodia, Democratic Republic of East Timor, Indonesia, Lao People's Democratic Republic, Malaysia, Myanmar, Philippines, Singapore, Thailand, Viet Nam.

Western Asia: Armenia, Azerbaijan, Bahrain, Cyprus, Georgia, Iraq, Israel, Jordan, Kuwait, Lebanon, Occupied Palestinian Territory, Oman, Qatar, Saudi Arabia, Syrian Arab Republic, Turkey, United Arab Emirates, Yemen

Europe

Eastern Europe: Belarus, Bulgaria, Czech Republic, Hungary, Poland, Republic of Moldova, Romania, Russian Federation, Slovakia, Ukraine.

Northern Europe: Channel Islands, Denmark, Estonia, Faeroe Islands, Finland, Iceland, Ireland, Isle of Man, Latvia, Lithuania, Norway, Sweden, United Kingdom.

Southern Europe: Albania, Andorra, Bosnia and Herzegovina, Croatia, Gibraltar, Greece, Holy See, Italy, Malta, Portugal, San Marino, Serbia and Montenegro, Slovenia, Spain, TFYR Macedonia.

Western Europe: Austria, Belgium, France, Germany, Liechtenstein, Luxembourg, Monaco, Netherlands, Switzerland.

Latin America and the Caribbean

Caribbean: Anguilla, Antigua and Barbuda, Aruba, Bahamas, Barbados, British Virgin Islands, Cayman Islands, Cuba, Dominica, Dominican Republic, Grenada, Guadeloupe, Haiti, Jamaica, Martinique, Montserrat, Netherlands Antilles, Puerto Rico, Saint Kitts and Nevis, Saint Lucia. Saint Vincent and the Grenadines, Trinidad and Tobago, Turks and Caicos Islands, United States Virgin Islands.

Central America: Belize, Costa Rica, El Salvador, Guatemala, Honduras, Mexico, Nicaragua, Panama.

South America: Argentina, Bolivia, Brazil, Chile, Colombia, Ecuador, Falkland Islands (Malvinas), French Guiana, Guyana, Paraguay, Peru, Suriname, Uruguay, Venezuela.

Northern America

Bermuda, Canada, Greenland, Saint-Pierre and Miquelon, United States.

Oceania

Australia/New Zealand: Australia, New Zealand.

Melanesia: Fiji, New Caledonia, Papua New Guinea, Solomon Islands, Vanuatu.

Micronesia: Guam, Kiribati, Marshall Islands, Micronesia (Federated States of), Nauru, Northern Mariana Islands, Palau.

Polynesia: American Samoa, Cook Islands, French Polynesia, Niue, Pitcairn, Samoa, Tokelau, Tonga, Tuvalu, Wallis and Futuna Islands.

NOMENCLATURE AND ORDER OF PRESENTATION

Tables A.1 to A.5 contain regional, income and development aggregates data. Tables B.1 to B.13 and C.1 to C.7 contain national- and city-level data, respectively. In these tables, the countries or areas are listed in English alphabetical order within the macro-regions of Africa, Asia, Europe, Latin America, Northern America and Oceania. Countries or area names are presented in the form commonly used within the United Nations Secretariat for statistical purposes. Due to space limitations, the short name is used – for example, the United Kingdom of Great Britain and Northern Ireland is referred to as 'United Kingdom'.

DEFINITION OF TERMS

Assault: Physical attack against the body of another person, including battery but excluding indecent assault. Some criminal or penal codes distinguish between aggravated assault and simple assault, depending on the degree of resulting injury.

Automobile theft: The removal of a motor vehicle without the consent of the owner of the vehicle.

Bribery: Requesting and/or accepting material or personal benefits, or the promise thereof, in connection with the performance of a public function for an action that may or may not be a violation of law and/or promising as well as giving material or personal benefits to a public officer in exchange for a requested favor.

Burglary: Unlawful entry into someone else's premises with the intention to commit a crime.

Control of corruption: The extent to which public power is exercised for private gain, including both petty and grand forms of corruption, as well as 'capture' of the state by elites and private interests.

Drug-related crimes: Intentional acts that involve the cultivation, production, manufacture, extraction, preparation, offering for sale, distribution, purchase, sale, delivery on any terms whatsoever, brokerage, dispatch, dispatch in transit, transport, importation, exportation and possession of internationally controlled drugs.

Embezzlement: The wrongful appropriation of another person's property that is already in the possession of the person doing the appropriating.

Expenditure on health: This covers expenditure on health services (preventive and curative), family planning activities, nutrition activities and emergency aid designated for health, but does not include provision of water and sanitation.

Fraud: The acquisition of another person's property by deception.

Gini index: This measures the extent to which the distribution of income (or, in some cases, consumption expenditure) among individuals or households within an economy deviates from a perfectly equal distribution. A Lorenz curve plots the cumulative percentages of total income received against the cumulative number of recipients, starting with the poorest individual or household. The Gini index measures the area between the Lorenz curve and a hypothetical line of absolute equality, expressed as a percentage of the maximum area under the line. Thus, a Gini index of 0 represents perfect equality, while an index of 100 implies absolute inequality.

Government effectiveness: The quality of public services, the quality of the civil service and the degree of its independence from political pressures, the quality of policy formulation and implementation, and the credibility of the government's commitment to such policies.

GNI per capita (PPP): This is gross national income divided by midyear population and converted to international dollars using purchasing power parity rates.

Hospital beds: Include inpatient beds available in public, private, general, and specialized hospitals and rehabilitation centres. In most cases, beds for both acute and chronic care are included.

Household: The concept of household is based on the arrangements made by persons, individually or in groups, for providing themselves with food or other essentials for living. A household may be either:

- A one-person household – that is to say, a person who makes provision for his or her own food or other essentials for living without combining with any other person to form a part of a multiperson household; or
- A multiperson household – that is to say, a group of two or more persons living together who make common provision for food or other essentials for living. The persons in the group may pool their incomes and may, to a greater or lesser extent, have a common budget; they may be related or unrelated persons or constitute a combination of persons both related and unrelated. This concept of household is known as the 'housekeeping' concept. It does not assume that the number of households and housing units is equal. Although the concept of housing unit implies that it is a space occupied by one household, it may also be occupied by more than one household or by a part of a household (for example, two nuclear households that share one housing unit for economic reasons or one household in a polygamous society routinely occupying two or more housing units).

Improved drinking water coverage: This is an indicator expressed as the percentage of people using improved drinking water sources or delivery points (listed below). Improved drinking water technologies are more likely to provide safe drinking water than those characterized as unimproved. Improved drinking water sources: Piped water into dwelling, plot or yard; Public tap/standpipe; Tubewell/borehole; Protected dug well; Protected spring; Rainwater collection. Unimproved drinking water sources: Unprotected dug well; Unprotected spring; Cart with small tank/drum; Bottled water[8]; Tanker-truck; Surface water (river, dam, lake, pond, stream, canal, irrigation channels)

Improved sanitation coverage: This is an indicator expressed as the percentage of people using improved sanitation facilities (listed below). Improved sanitation facilities are more likely to prevent human contact with human excreta than unimproved facilities. Improved sanitation facilities: Flush or pour–flush to: piped sewer system, septic tank, pit latrine; Ventilated improved pit latrine; Pit latrine with slab; Composting toilet. Unimproved sanitation facilities: Flush or pour–flush to elsewhere[9]; Pit latrine without slab or open pit; Bucket; Hanging toilet or hanging latrine; No facilities or bush or field.

Intentional homicide: Death deliberately inflicted on a person by another person, including infanticide.

Land inequality: This measures the extent to which the distribution of land among individuals or households within an economy deviates from a perfectly equal distribution.

Level of urbanization: Percentage of the population residing in places classified as urban. Urban and rural settlements are defined in the national context and vary among countries (the definitions of urban are generally national definitions incorporated within the latest census).

Life expectancy at birth: Number of years a newborn infant would live if prevailing patterns of mortality at the time of birth were to stay the same throughout the child's life.

Motor vehicles: Include cars, buses and freight vehicles but not two-wheelers. Roads refer to motorways, highways, main or national roads, and secondary or regional roads. A motorway is a road specially designed and built for motor traffic that separates the traffic flowing in opposite directions.

Natural Disaster: A serious disruption triggered by a natural hazard causing human, material, economic or environmental losses, which exceed the ability of those affected to cope.

Natural Hazard: Natural processes or phenomena occurring in the biosphere that may constitute a damaging event. Hazardous events vary in magnitude, frequency, duration, area of extent, speed of onset, spatial dispersion and temporal spacing. In tables, natural hazards refer exclusively to earthquake, tropical cyclone, flood and drought.

Non-intentional homicide: Death not deliberately inflicted on a person by another person. This includes the crime of manslaughter but excludes traffic accidents that result in the death of persons.

Persons in housing units: Number of persons resident in housing units.

Persons prosecuted: Alleged offenders prosecuted by means of an official charge, initiated by the public prosecutor or the law enforcement agency responsible for prosecution.

Police staff: Police personnel or law enforcement personnel in public agencies whose principal functions are the prevention, detection and investigation of crime and the apprehension of alleged offenders. Data concerning support staff (secretaries, clerks etc.) are not excluded.

Political stability and absence of violence: Perceptions of the likelihood that the government will be destabilized or overthrown by unconstitutional or violent means, including domestic violence and terrorism.

Poor households: Percentage of women and men-headed households situated below the locally defined poverty line. The poverty line is usually an 'absolute' poverty line, taken as the income necessary to afford a minimum nutritionally adequate diet, plus essential non-food requirements, for a household of a given size.

Population, total: Mid-year population estimates for the world, region, countries or areas. The Population Division of the United Nations Department of Economic and Social Affairs updates, every two years, population estimates and projections by incorporating new data, new estimates and new analyses of data on population, fertility, mortality and international migration. Data from new population censuses and/or demographic surveys are used to verify and update old estimates of population or demographic indicators, or to make new ones and to check the validity of the assumptions made in the projections. Total population refers to the estimates and projections (medium variant) of the total population for each country region and major area. Annual growth rate, calculated by UN-Habitat, refers to the average annual percentage change of population during the indicated period for each country, major regions and global totals. The formula used throughout the Annex is as follows: $r = [(1/t) \times \ln(A2/A1)] \times 100$, where 'A1' is a value at any given year; 'A2' is a value at any given year later than the year of 'Al'; 't' is the year interval between 'Al' and 'A2'; and 'ln' is the natural logarithm function.

Population affected by conflicts: This refers to percentage of total population affected by armed conflicts. **Armed conflict:** A contested incompatibility that concerns government and/or territory where the use of armed force between two parties, of which at least one is the government of a state, results in at least 25 battle related deaths.

Population, urban and rural: Mid-year estimates and projections (medium variant) of the population residing in human settlements classified as urban or rural.

Poverty definitions: *National poverty rate:* Percentage of the population living below the national poverty line. National estimates are based on population-weighted subgroup estimates from household surveys. Survey year is the year in which the underlying data were collected. *Population below US$1 a day and Population below US$2 a day:* Percentages of the population living on less than US$1.08 a day and US$2.15 a day at 1993 international prices (equivalent to US$1 and US$2 in 1985 prices, adjusted for purchasing power parity).

Prevalence of HIV, 15-49 age group: The percentage of population aged 15-49 years who are infected with HIV.

Prosecution staff: Prosecution personnel - a government official whose duty is to initiate and maintain criminal proceedings on behalf of the state against persons accused of committing a criminal offence. In some countries, a prosecutor is a member of a separate agency, in others, a prosecutor is a member of the police or judiciary.

Rape: Sexual intercourse without valid consent by one of the parties involved.

Refugees, asylum-seekers and others concern: Data are provided by governments based on their own definitions and methods of collection. Total asylum-seekers, refugees and others of concern to the United Nations High Commissioner for Refugees (UNHCR) include the following. *Refugees:* Persons recognized as refugees under the international conventions, in accordance with the UNHCR Statute; persons allowed to stay on humanitarian grounds and those granted temporary protection. Asylum-seekers: Persons whose application for refugee status is pending in the asylum procedure or who are otherwise registered as asylum-seekers. The total number of asylum-seekers is underestimated due to a lack of data from a number of countries. Returned refugees: Refugees who have returned to their country of origin during the year. Internally displaced persons (IDPs): Persons who are displaced within their country and to whom UNHCR extends protection or assistance, generally pursuant to a special request by a competent organ of the United Nations. Returned IDPs: IDPs of concern to UNHCR who have returned to their place of origin during the year. Stateless Person: Any person who is not considered as a national by any state through its nationality legislation or constitution. This definition refers mainly to *de jure* stateless persons but also includes *de facto* stateless persons as well as persons who have difficulties establishing their nationality. Refugees and asylum seekers by place of origin excludes stateless persons.

Regulatory quality: The ability of the government to formulate and implement sound policies and regulations that permit and promote private sector development.

Roads: Motorways, highways, main or national roads, and secondary or regional roads. A motorway is a road specially designed and built for motor vehicles that separates the traffic flowing in opposite directions. *Total road network:* Includes motorways, highways and main or national roads, secondary or regional roads, and all other roads in a country. *Paved roads:* Roads surfaced with crushed stone (macadam) and hydrocarbon binder or bitumized agents, with concrete or with cobblestones, as a percentage of all of the country's roads measured in length.

Robbery: The theft of property from a person, overcoming resistance by force or threat of force.

Rule of law: The extent to which agents have confidence in and abide by the rules of society, and in particular the quality of contract enforcement, the police, and the courts, as well as the likelihood of crime and violence.

Slum dwellers: Individuals residing in housing with one or more of the following conditions: inadequate drinking water; inadequate sanitation; poor structural quality/durability of housing; overcrowding; and insecurity of tenure.

Theft: The removal of property without the property owner's consent. Theft excludes burglary and housebreaking as well as theft of a motor vehicle. Some criminal and penal codes distinguish between grand and petty theft, depending on the value of the goods and property taken from their rightful owner.

Transport used for work trips: Percentage of work trips undertaken by private car; train, tram or ferry; bus or minibus; other (motorcycle, bicycle and other non-motorized modes). When several modes of transport are used for a given trip, the principal mode is selected.

Travel time: Average time in minutes for a one-way work trip. This is an average over all modes of transport.

Urban agglomerations and capital cities: The term 'urban agglomeration' refers to the population contained within the contours of a contiguous territory inhabited at urban density levels without regard to administrative boundaries. It usually incorporates the population in a city or town plus that in the suburban areas lying outside of but being adjacent to the city boundaries. Whenever possible, data classified according to the concept of urban agglomeration are used. However, some countries do not produce data according to the concept of urban agglomeration but use instead that of metropolitan area or city proper. If possible, such data are adjusted to conform to the concept of urban agglomeration. When sufficient information is not available to permit such an adjustment, data based on the concept of city proper or metropolitan area are used. The sources listed online indicate whether data were adjusted to conform to the urban agglomeration concept or whether a different concept was used. Table C.1 contains revised estimates and projections for all urban agglomerations comprising 750,000 or more inhabitants.

Urban population: This is the midyear population of areas defined as urban in each country and reported to the United Nations. Estimates of the world's urban population would change significantly if China, India, and a few other populous nations were to change their definition of urban centers. According to China's State Statistical Bureau, by the end of 1996 urban residents accounted for about 43 percent of China's population, while in 1994 only 20 percent of the population was considered urban. In addition to the continuous migration of people from rural to urban areas, one of the main reasons for this shift was the rapid growth in the hundreds of towns reclassified as cities in recent years. Because the estimates in the table are based on national definitions of what constitutes a city or metropolitan area, cross-country comparisons should be made with caution.

Voice and accountability: The extent to which a country's citizens are able to participate in selecting their government, as well as freedom of expression, freedom of association, and a free media.

Wastewater treated: Percentage of all wastewater undergoing some form of treatment.

Water consumption: Average consumption of water in litres per day per person for all domestic uses (excludes industrial use) in settlements.

Water supply system: 'Housing units with piped water inside the housing unit' refers to the existence of water pipes within the walls that constitute a housing unit. Water can be piped from a community source – that is, one that is subject to inspection and control by public authorities. Water can also be piped into the unit from a private source, such as a pressure tank, a pump or some other installation. The category 'piped water outside unit, but within 200 metres' refers to units where the piped water is not available to occupants within the unit they reside in, but is accessible within the range of 200 metres, assuming that access to piped water within that distance allows occupants to provide water for household needs without being subjected to extreme effort. 'Other' refers to units that do not have access to piped water at all, whose occupants depend upon springs or wells, or to units where piped water is located beyond 200 metres.

NOTES

1. Including 37 UN members and 14 non-UN members/associate members of regional commissions.
2. All members of the United Nations General Assembly arranged in Regional Groups. According to the *United Nations Handbook 2003* (2003), this grouping is unofficial and has been developed to take account of the purposes of General Assembly Resolutions 1991 (XVIII) (1963), 33/138 (1978) and 2847 (XXVI) (1971). The US is not a member of any regional group, but attends meetings of the Western European and Other States Group (WEOG) as an observer and is considered to be a member of that group for electoral purposes. Turkey participates fully in both the Asian and WEOG groups, but for electoral purposes is considered a member of WEOG only. Israel became a full member of WEOG on a temporary basis on 28 May 2000. As of 31 May 2002, Estonia and Kiribati were not members of any regional group. In addition to member states, there is also a non-member state, the Holy See, which has observer status in the United Nations. By General Assembly Resolution 52/250 (1998), the General Assembly conferred upon Palestine, in its capacity as observer, additional rights and privileges of participation. These included, *inter alia*, the right to participation in the general debate of the General Assembly, but did not include the right to vote or to put forward candidates.
3. As classified by the United Nations Development Programme (UNDP); see *Human Development Report 2005* for detail.
4. 57 countries or areas.
5. 88 countries or areas.
6. 32 countries or areas.
7. As classified by the World Bank; see *World Development Report 2006* (World Bank, 2005) for detail.
8. Bottled water is considered improved only when the household uses water from an improved source for cooking and personal hygiene.
9. Excreta are flushed to plot, open sewer, a ditch, or other location.

SOURCES OF DATA

The Statistical Tables have been compiled from the following UN-Habitat databases:
Human Settlements Statistics Database,
Global Urban Observatory (GUO) Database,
CitiBase, and UN-Habitat Household Projections Project.

In addition, various statistical publications from the United Nations and other international organizations have been used. These include:

International Road Federation (IRF) (1999) *World Road Statistics 1997.* Geneva.

International Road Federation (IRF) (2005) *World Road Statistics 2004*. Geneva.

Organisation for Economic Co-operation (OECD) *International Development Statistics*, CD-ROM, various years. Paris.

United Nations (2001) *Compendium of Human Settlements Statistics 2001*. United Nations, New York.

UNDP (2006) *Human Development Report.* Oxford University Press, New York.

UNDP (2004) *A Global Report. Reducing Disaster Risk: A Challenge for Development.* UNDP, New York.

United Nations Population Division (2006) *World Urbanization Prospects: The 2005 Revision*. United Nations, New York.

UNHCR (United Nations High Commission for Refugees) (2006) *2005 Global Refugee Trends, Statistical Overview of Populations of Refugees, Asylum-Seekers, Internally Displaced Persons, Stateless Persons, and Other Persons of Concern to UNHCR.* UNHCR, Geneva, Available at:

United Nations Human Settlements Programme (UN-Habitat) (2002) *Global Urban Indicators Database 2*. UN-Habitat, Nairobi.

UNICEF/WHO (2006) *Meeting the MDG Drinking Water and Sanitation Target: The Urban and Rural Challenge of the Decade*. World Health Organization and UNICEF, Geneva

United Nations Office on Drug and Crime. The Seventh United Nations Survey on Crime Trends and the Operations of Criminal Justice Systems (1999 – 2000); The Eighth United Nations Survey on Crime Trends and the Operations of Criminal Justice Systems (2001 - 2002) available at:

World Bank (2005) *Governance Matters V*, available at: http://www.worldbank.org/wbi/governance/press-2005indicators/

World Bank (2005) *World Development Indicators 2005.* World Bank, Washington, DC

World Bank (2006) *World Development Indicators, 2006*. World Bank, Washington DC.

World Health Organization (WHO), United Nations Children's Fund (UNICEF) and Water Supply and Sanitation Collaborative Council (2000) *Global Water Supply and Sanitation Assessment, 2000 Report*. WHO and UNICEF, Geneva and New York.

WHO/UNICEF Joint Monitoring Programme for Water Supply and Sanitation (2004). *Meeting the MDG Drinking Water and Sanitation Target: a Mid-term Assessment of Progress*. WHO/UNICEF, Geneva.

DATA TABLES

TABLE A.1

Population

	Total population			Level of urbanization			Urban population			Rural population		
	Estimates and projections (000)		Rate of change 2000–2030 (%)	Estimates and projections (%)		Rate of change 2000–2030 (%)	Estimates and projections (000)		Rate of change 2000–2030 (%)	Estimates and projections (000)		Rate of change 2000–2030 (%)
	2000	2030		2000	2030		2000	2030		2000	2030	
World	6,085,572	8,199,104	0.99	46.7	59.9	0.83	2,844,802	4,912,553	1.82	3,240,771	3,286,551	0.05
World Major Aggregates												
More Developed Regions	1,193,354	1,250,658	0.16	73.2	80.8	0.33	874,039	1,011,061	0.49	319,315	239,597	-0.96
Less Developed Regions	4,892,218	6,948,446	1.17	40.3	56.1	1.11	1,970,763	3,901,492	2.28	2,921,456	3,046,954	0.14
Least Developed Countries	673,524	1,281,335	2.14	24.7	40.9	1.68	166,203	523,627	3.83	507,321	757,707	1.34
Landlocked Developing Countries	337,978	633,419	2.09	26.0	36.3	1.11	87,958	230,119	3.21	250,020	403,300	1.59
Small Island Developing States	49,987	68,026	1.03	52.6	60.9	0.49	26,305	41,441	1.52	23,682	26,585	0.39
United Nations Regional Groups												
African States	812,466	1,463,493	1.96	36.2	50.7	1.12	294,392	742,188	3.08	518,074	721,305	1.10
Asian States	3,588,671	4,754,851	0.94	36.3	53.5	1.29	1,303,536	2,541,696	2.23	2,285,135	2,213,155	-0.11
Eastern European States	352,389	304,883	-0.48	66.4	72.3	0.28	233,936	220,367	-0.20	118,453	84,516	-1.13
Latin American and Caribbean States	522,929	722,377	1.08	75.4	84.3	0.37	394,212	608,968	1.45	128,717	113,409	-0.42
Western European And Other States	518,251	579,983	0.38	75.2	82.2	0.30	389,732	476,769	0.67	128,520	103,215	-0.73
Human Development Aggregates												
High Human Development	1,188,416	1,354,589	0.44	75.7	83.3	0.32	899,834	1,128,224	0.75	288,582	226,365	-0.81
Medium Human Development	4,264,077	5,639,873	0.93	40.6	56.7	1.11	1,731,120	3,198,371	2.05	2,532,957	2,441,502	-0.12
Low Human Development	533,379	1,025,382	2.18	30.4	47.0	1.46	161,899	481,978	3.64	371,480	543,404	1.27
Income Aggregates												
High Income	955,957	1,096,982	0.46	76.5	83.9	0.31	731,116	920,010	0.77	224,841	176,972	-0.80
Middle Income	2,937,207	3,577,609	0.66	50.6	68.7	1.02	1,484,806	2,457,546	1.68	1,452,401	1,120,063	-0.87
Upper-middle Income	565,094	650,483	0.47	71.4	80.2	0.39	403,284	521,872	0.86	161,810	128,611	-0.77
Lower-middle Income	2,372,113	2,927,126	0.70	45.6	66.1	1.24	1,081,522	1,935,674	1.94	1,290,591	991,452	-0.88
Low Income	2,190,228	3,521,372	1.58	28.6	43.5	1.40	626,913	1,532,068	2.98	1,563,315	1,989,304	0.80
Geographic Aggregates												
Africa	812,466	1,463,493	1.96	36.2	50.7	1.12	294,392	742,188	3.08	518,074	721,305	1.10
Eastern Africa	255,681	492,698	2.19	20.7	33.7	1.61	53,041	165,913	3.80	202,640	326,785	1.59
Middle Africa	96,040	207,223	2.56	37.4	54.9	1.28	35,899	113,786	3.85	60,141	93,437	1.47
Northern Africa	175,051	269,743	1.44	48.9	64.1	0.90	85,540	172,855	2.34	89,510	96,887	0.26
Southern Africa	52,069	55,323	0.20	53.9	68.6	0.81	28,053	37,956	1.01	24,016	17,367	-1.08
Western Africa	233,624	438,506	2.10	39.3	57.4	1.26	91,858	251,678	3.36	141,766	186,828	0.92
Asia	3,675,799	4,872,472	0.94	37.1	54.1	1.26	1,363,035	2,636,623	2.20	2,312,764	2,235,850	-0.11
Eastern Asia	1,479,233	1,655,077	0.37	40.4	62.5	1.46	597,490	1,034,427	1.83	881,742	620,650	-1.17
South-central Asia	1,484,624	2,197,640	1.31	29.4	42.9	1.26	437,035	943,816	2.57	1,047,589	1,253,825	0.60
South-eastern Asia	518,867	700,930	1.00	39.6	61.2	1.45	205,621	428,630	2.45	313,246	272,299	-0.47
Western Asia	193,075	318,826	1.67	63.6	72.1	0.41	122,888	229,750	2.09	70,187	89,076	0.79
Europe	728,463	698,140	-0.14	71.7	78.3	0.29	522,108	546,462	0.15	206,355	151,678	-1.03
Eastern Europe	304,636	258,264	-0.55	68.3	73.7	0.25	208,145	190,443	-0.30	96,491	67,821	-1.18
Northern Europe	94,157	102,977	0.30	83.4	87.4	0.15	78,530	89,971	0.45	15,627	13,006	-0.61
Southern Europe	146,081	147,342	0.03	65.4	74.3	0.43	95,539	109,542	0.46	50,542	37,800	-0.97
Western Europe	183,589	189,558	0.11	76.2	82.6	0.27	139,894	156,506	0.37	43,695	33,052	-0.93
Latin America	522,929	722,377	1.08	75.4	84.3	0.37	394,212	608,968	1.45	128,717	113,409	-0.42
Caribbean	37,456	45,524	0.65	62.1	72.6	0.52	23,273	33,036	1.17	14,183	12,488	-0.42
Central America	136,039	193,104	1.17	68.8	77.6	0.41	93,528	149,935	1.57	42,510	43,169	0.05
South America	349,434	483,749	1.08	79.4	88.1	0.35	277,410	425,996	1.43	72,024	57,752	-0.74
Northern America	314,968	400,079	0.80	79.1	86.7	0.30	249,242	346,918	1.10	65,725	53,160	-0.71
Oceania	30,949	42,543	1.06	70.5	73.8	0.15	21,813	31,394	1.21	9,135	11,149	0.66
Australia/New Zealand	22,890	29,873	0.89	86.9	91.5	0.17	19,895	27,331	1.06	2,995	2,542	-0.55
Melanesia	6,935	11,142	1.58	19.2	27.6	1.21	1,332	3,073	2.79	5,603	8,068	1.22
Micronesia	505	757	1.35	65.7	76.6	0.51	332	580	1.86	173	177	0.07
Polynesia	619	771	0.73	41.1	53.2	0.85	255	410	1.59	364	361	-0.03

Sources: United Nations, Department of Economic and Social Affairs, Population Division, 2006. Figures in regional, income or development aggregates are calculated on the basis of country/area level data from Tables B.1, B.2 and B.3.

Note: Lists of countries/areas in aggregates are presented in the Technical Notes.

TABLE A.2

Number of Urban Agglomerations

	Number of agglomerations Estimates and projections			Distribution of urban population by size of agglomerations			Population Estimates and projections		
				(%)	(%)	(%)	(000)	(000)	(000)
Size of urban agglomeration	1985	2000	2015	1985	2000	2015	1985	2000	2015
World									
10 million or more	7	17	22	5.27	8.42	9.41	104,507	239,655	359,238
5 to 10 million	21	28	39	7.71	6.80	7.15	152,932	193,583	272,960
1 to 5 million	223	335	460	21.08	22.35	23.83	418,255	635,867	910,092
500 000 to 1 million	299	403	494	10.39	9.78	9.08	206,194	278,271	346,789
Fewer than 500 000	...	...	...	55.54	52.64	50.54	1,101,787	1,497,425	1,929,945
More Developed Regions									
10 million or more	4	5	5	8.55	9.77	9.61	66,662	85,377	90,795
5 to 10 million	4	6	10	4.19	4.78	7.12	32,637	41,786	67,267
1 to 5 million	86	97	101	21.40	21.91	21.15	166,859	191,524	199,859
500 000 to 1 million	110	117	129	9.56	9.03	9.24	74,515	78,929	87,255
Fewer than 500 000	...	...	...	56.31	54.51	52.88	439,086	476,423	499,623
Less Developed Regions									
10 million or more	3	12	17	3.14	7.83	9.34	37,844	154,278	268,442
5 to 10 million	17	22	29	9.99	7.70	7.16	120,295	151,797	205,693
1 to 5 million	137	238	359	20.88	22.55	24.71	251,396	444,343	710,232
500 000 to 1 million	189	286	365	10.94	10.11	9.03	131,679	199,342	259,534
Fewer than 500 000	...	...	...	55.05	51.81	49.76	662,701	1,021,002	1,430,322
Least Developed Countries									
10 million or more	—	1	1	—	6.11	5.61	—	10,159	16,842
5 to 10 million	—	1	4	—	3.03	8.73	—	5,042	26,218
1 to 5 million	10	21	35	22.29	22.51	22.85	19,570	37,414	68,644
500 000 to 1 million	12	19	28	9.11	7.54	6.70	8,000	12,534	20,129
Fewer than 500 000	...	...	...	68.60	60.80	56.12	60,242	101,053	168,573
Africa									
10 million or more	—	1	2	—	3.53	6.13	—	10,391	29,279
5 to 10 million	1	2	2	5.07	4.57	3.21	8,328	13,464	15,326
1 to 5 million	20	34	58	21.02	22.12	25.89	34,547	65,131	123,637
500 000 to 1 million	27	41	68	10.65	9.62	9.93	17,509	28,322	47,443
Fewer than 500 000	...	...	...	63.26	60.15	54.84	103,970	177,083	261,882
Eastern Africa									
10 million or more	—	—	—	—	—	—	—	—	—
5 to 10 million	—	—	—	—	—	—	—	—	—
1 to 5 million	3	9	13	13.05	26.47	30.30	3,612	14,038	28,216
500 000 to 1 million	6	4	8	14.87	**World**				
10 million or more	7	17	22	5.27	8.42	9.41	104,507	239,655	359,238
5 to 10 million	21	28	39	7.71	6.80	7.15	152,932	193,583	272,960
1 to 5 million	223	335	460	21.08	22.35	23.83	418,255	635,867	910,092
500 000 to 1 million	299	403	494	10.39	9.78	9.08	206,194	278,271	346,789
Fewer than 500 000	...	...	...	55.54	52.64	50.54	1,101,787	1,497,425	1,929,945
More Developed Regions									
10 million or more	4	5	5	8.55	9.77	9.61	66,662	85,377	90,795
5 to 10 million	4	6	10	4.19	4.78	7.12	32,637	41,786	67,267
1 to 5 million	86	97	101	21.40	21.91	21.15	166,859	191,524	199,859
500 000 to 1 million	110	117	129	9.56	9.03	9.24	74,515	78,929	87,255
Fewer than 500 000	...	...	...	56.31	54.51	52.88	439,086	476,423	499,623
Less Developed Regions									
10 million or more	3	12	17	3.14	7.83	9.34	37,844	154,278	268,442
5 to 10 million	17	22	29	9.99	7.70	7.16	120,295	151,797	205,693
1 to 5 million	137	238	359	20.88	22.55	24.71	251,396	444,343	710,232
500 000 to 1 million	189	286	365	10.94	10.11	9.03	131,679	199,342	259,534
Fewer than 500 000	...	...	...	55.05	51.81	49.76	662,701	1,021,002	1,430,322
Least Developed Countries									
10 million or more	—	1	1	—	6.11	5.61	—	10,159	16,842
5 to 10 million	—	1	4	—	3.03	8.73	—	5,042	26,218
1 to 5 million	10	21	35	22.29	22.51	22.85	19,570	37,414	68,644
500 000 to 1 million	12	19	28	9.11	7.54	6.70	8,000	12,534	20,129
Fewer than 500 000	...	...	...	68.60	60.80	56.12	60,242	101,053	168,573
Africa									
10 million or more	—	1	2	—	3.53	6.13	—	10,391	29,279
5 to 10 million	1	2	2	5.07	4.57	3.21	8,328	13,464	15,326
1 to 5 million	20	34	58	21.02	22.12	25.89	34,547	65,131	123,637
500 000 to 1 million	27	41	68	10.65	9.62	9.93	17,509	28,322	47,443
Fewer than 500 000	...	...	...	63.26	60.15	54.84	103,970	177,083	261,882
Eastern Africa									
10 million or more	—	—	—	—	—	—	—	—	—
5 to 10 million	—	—	—	—	—	—	—	—	—
1 to 5 million	3	9	13	13.05	26.47	30.30	3,612	14,038	28,216
500 000 to 1 million	6	4	8	14.87	4.54	6.48	4,115	2,407	6,031
Fewer than 500 000	...	...	...	72.08	69.00	63.23	19,949	36,597	58,885
Middle Africa									
10 million or more	—	—	—	—	—	—	—	—	—
5 to 10 million	—	1	1	—	14.04	14.18	—	5,042	9,304
1 to 5 million	2	4	9	21.43	16.70	27.20	4,122	5,994	17,845
500 000 to 1 million	5	8	11	15.63	15.71	12.12	3,007	5,639	7,952
Fewer than 500 000	...	...	...	62.94	53.55	46.49	12,110	19,224	30,500

TABLE A.2

continued

Size of urban agglomeration	Number of agglomerations Estimates and projections			Distribution of urban population by size of agglomerations			Population Estimates and projections		
				(%)	(%)	(%)	(000)	(000)	(000)
	1985	2000	2015	1985	2000	2015	1985	2000	2015
Northern Africa									
10 million or more	—	1	1	—	12.15	10.43	—	10,391	13,138
5 to 10 million	1	—	1	15.26	—	4.78	8,328	—	6,022
1 to 5 million	5	6	8	17.54	19.45	16.00	9,573	16,637	20,152
500 000 to 1 million	4	8	19	5.11	6.65	10.19	2,790	5,690	12,829
Fewer than 500 000	...	...	...	62.09	61.75	58.60	33,884	52,822	73,805
Southern Africa									
10 million or more	—	—	—	—	—	—	—	—	—
5 to 10 million	—	—	—	—	—	—	—	—	—
1 to 5 million	4	5	7	36.67	40.02	50.37	6,382	11,227	16,821
500 000 to 1 million	3	2	1	11.35	6.61	1.86	1,975	1,855	622
Fewer than 500 000	...	...	...	51.98	53.37	47.77	9,047	14,971	15,952
Western Africa									
10 million or more	—	—	1	—	—	10.12	—	—	16,141
5 to 10 million	—	1	—	—	9.17	—	—	8,422	—
1 to 5 million	6	10	21	23.88	18.76	25.46	10,858	17,236	40,603
500 000 to 1 million	9	19	29	12.37	13.86	12.55	5,622	12,731	20,008
Fewer than 500 000	...	...	...	63.75	58.21	51.88	28,980	53,469	82,740
Asia									
10 million or more	3	9	13	6.09	9.66	11.05	50,995	131,686	217,699
5 to 10 million	13	17	23	10.49	8.75	8.16	87,832	119,232	160,865
1 to 5 million	97	166	244	21.45	22.61	23.81	179,591	308,118	469,091
500 000 to 1 million	128	195	241	10.81	9.99	8.71	90,522	136,228	171,655
Fewer than 500 000	...	...	...	51.15	48.99	48.26	428,126	667,769	950,904
Eastern Asia									
10 million or more	2	3	5	11.21	9.85	10.41	40,654	58,858	87,298
5 to 10 million	5	8	8	9.62	9.91	7.22	34,882	59,214	60,595
1 to 5 million	57	93	133	27.29	29.27	31.77	99,009	174,901	266,509
500 000 to 1 million	65	109	121	12.83	12.78	10.58	46,545	76,355	88,748
Fewer than 500 000	...	...	...	39.06	38.19	40.02	141,682	228,162	335,759
South-central Asia									
10 million or more	1	5	5	3.64	14.13	14.04	10,341	61,764	89,450
5 to 10 million	4	5	8	10.07	6.82	9.08	28,587	29,793	57,871
1 to 5 million	18	42	66	13.94	15.76	18.38	39,578	68,895	117,077
500 000 to 1 million	49	51	71	12.22	8.34	7.72	34,692	36,466	49,202
Fewer than 500 000	...	...	...	60.12	54.94	50.77	170,680	240,118	323,401
South-eastern Asia									
10 million or more	—	1	2	—	5.38	9.25	—	11,065	29,739
5 to 10 million	3	2	5	16.74	7.92	9.24	18,955	16,282	29,717
1 to 5 million	9	13	17	17.37	15.45	10.17	19,668	31,778	32,697
500 000 to 1 million	9	16	23	5.23	5.21	5.01	5,923	10,716	16,113
Fewer than 500 000	...	...	...	60.65	66.03	66.32	68,658	135,781	213,211
Western Asia									
10 million or more	—	—	1	—	—	6.49	—	—	11,211
5 to 10 million	1	2	2	7.00	11.35	7.34	5,407	13,944	12,680
1 to 5 million	13	18	28	27.63	26.48	30.56	21,336	32,544	52,809
500 000 to 1 million	5	19	26	4.35	10.33	10.18	3,361	12,692	17,593
Fewer than 500 000	...	...	...	61.01	51.84	45.44	47,106	63,708	78,533
Europe									
10 million or more	—	1	1	—	1.93	2.07	—	10,103	11,022
5 to 10 million	3	4	5	5.18	5.42	6.57	25,352	28,293	34,994
1 to 5 million	45	48	45	16.66	15.12	13.85	81,544	78,940	73,787
500 000 to 1 million	77	77	84	10.52	9.76	10.57	51,525	50,938	56,299
Fewer than 500 000	...	...	...	67.64	67.77	66.94	331,157	353,834	356,539
Eastern Europe									
10 million or more	—	1	1	—	4.85	5.61	—	10,103	11,022
5 to 10 million	1	1	1	4.27	2.51	2.73	8,580	5,214	5,375
1 to 5 million	21	22	18	15.84	14.14	12.76	31,853	29,426	25,088
500 000 to 1 million	27	28	34	9.01	8.67	11.63	18,114	18,042	22,857
Fewer than 500 000	...	...	...	70.88	69.84	67.27	142,517	145,360	132,221
Northern Europe									
10 million or more	—	—	—	—	—	—	—	—	—
5 to 10 million	1	1	1	10.33	10.47	10.31	7,667	8,225	8,618
1 to 5 million	6	7	8	13.78	13.94	14.81	10,228	10,944	12,378
500 000 to 1 million	11	11	10	10.52	10.11	8.59	7,814	7,942	7,179
Fewer than 500 000	...	...	...	65.37	65.48	66.29	48,535	51,419	55,399
Southern Europe									
10 million or more	—	—	—	—	—	—	—	—	—
5 to 10 million	—	1	2	—	5.40	10.72	—	5,162	11,143
1 to 5 million	10	9	8	30.12	24.15	18.25	26,743	23,077	18,960
500 000 to 1 million	17	18	19	12.56	12.37	12.03	11,151	11,821	12,499
Fewer than 500 000	...	...	...	57.32	58.07	59.00	50,886	55,479	61,300
Western Europe									
10 million or more	—	—	—	—	—	—	—	—	—
5 to 10 million	1	1	1	7.26	6.93	6.63	9,105	9,692	9,858
1 to 5 million	8	10	11	10.14	11.08	11.68	12,719	15,493	17,362
500 000 to 1 million	22	20	21	11.51	9.39	9.26	14,447	13,133	13,764

TABLE A.2

continued

Size of urban agglomeration	Number of agglomerations Estimates and projections			Distribution of urban population by size of agglomerations			Population Estimates and projections		
				(%)	(%)	(%)	(000)	(000)	(000)
	1985	2000	2015	1985	2000	2015	1985	2000	2015
Fewer than 500 000	...	...	...	71.10	72.61	72.42	89,219	101,576	107,620
Latin America and the Caribbean									
10 million or more	2	4	4	10.02	14.67	13.36	27,504	57,816	68,268
5 to 10 million	3	3	4	8.80	4.85	5.77	24,135	19,101	29,502
1 to 5 million	26	44	63	18.16	21.68	25.87	49,827	85,475	132,169
500 000 to 1 million	34	51	57	8.62	8.96	8.03	23,648	35,339	41,014
Fewer than 500 000	...	...	...	54.40	49.84	46.97	149,240	196,481	240,000
Caribbean									
10 million or more	—	—	—	—	—	—	—	—	—
5 to 10 million	—	—	—	—	—	—	—	—	—
1 to 5 million	3	4	4	27.83	34.48	35.89	4,782	8,024	10,175
500 000 to 1 million	2	1	3	8.30	2.49	6.77	1,427	579	1,918
Fewer than 500 000	...	...	...	63.86	63.04	57.34	10,971	14,670	16,257
Central America									
10 million or more	1	1	1	22.01	19.32	17.65	14,109	18,066	21,568
5 to 10 million	—	—	—	—	—	—	—	—	—
1 to 5 million	3	12	21	9.80	20.95	29.49	6,283	19,592	36,033
500 000 to 1 million	13	21	24	13.66	15.39	14.36	8,759	14,393	17,548
Fewer than 500 000	...	...	...	54.53	44.35	38.50	34,960	41,477	47,047
South America									
10 million or more	1	3	3	6.94	14.33	12.96	13,395	39,749	46,700
5 to 10 million	3	3	4	12.50	6.89	8.19	24,135	19,101	29,502
1 to 5 million	20	28	38	20.08	20.86	23.85	38,763	57,859	85,960
500 000 to 1 million	19	29	30	6.97	7.34	5.98	13,463	20,367	21,548
Fewer than 500 000	...	...	...	53.51	50.59	49.03	103,309	140,334	176,696
Northern America									
10 million or more	2	2	2	12.95	11.90	10.95	26,008	29,659	32,970
5 to 10 million	1	2	5	3.63	5.41	10.72	7,285	13,494	32,273
1 to 5 million	31	37	44	31.94	34.32	32.12	64,163	85,531	96,731
500 000 to 1 million	31	39	42	10.54	11.01	9.71	21,185	27,443	29,239
Fewer than 500 000	...	...	...	40.95	37.36	36.51	82,258	93,115	109,949
Oceania									
10 million or more	—	—	—	—	—	—	—	—	—
5 to 10 million	—	—	—	—	—	—	—	—	—
1 to 5 million	4	6	6	49.26	58.10	55.42	8,583	12,672	14,678
500 000 to 1 million	2	—	2	10.36	—	4.30	1,805	—	1,139
Fewer than 500 000	...	...	...	40.38	41.91	40.29	7,035	9,142	10,670
Australia/New Zealand									
10 million or more	—	—	—	—	—	—	—	—	—
5 to 10 million	—	—	—	—	—	—	—	—	—
1 to 5 million	4	6	6	53.28	63.70	61.76	8,583	12,672	14,678
500 000 to 1 million	2	—	2	11.21	—	4.79	1,805	—	1,139
Fewer than 500 000	...	...	...	35.51	36.30	33.45	5,720	7,223	7,950
Melanesia									
10 million or more	—	—	—	—	—	—	—	—	—
5 to 10 million	—	—	—	—	—	—	—	—	—
1 to 5 million	—	—	—	—	—	—	—	—	—
500 000 to 1 million	—	—	—	—	—	—	—	—	—
Fewer than 500 000	...	...	...	100.00	100.00	100.00	900	1,332	1,938
Micronesia									
10 million or more	—	—	—	—	—	—	—	—	—
5 to 10 million	—	—	—	—	—	—	—	—	—
1 to 5 million	—	—	—	—	—	—	—	—	—
500 000 to 1 million	—	—	—	—	—	—	—	—	—
Fewer than 500 000	...	...	...	100.00	100.00	100.00	217	332	460
Polynesia									
10 million or more	—	—	—	—	—	—	—	—	—
5 to 10 million	—	—	—	—	—	—	—	—	—
1 to 5 million	—	—	—	—	—	—	—	—	—
500 000 to 1 million	—	—	—	—	—	—	—	—	—
Fewer than 500 000	...	...	...	100.00	100.00	100.00	198	255	322

Source: United Nations, Department of Economic and Social Affairs, Population Division, 2006

TABLE A.3

Shelter Indicators

	Total number of households						Water and sanitation coverage					
	Estimates and projections (000)		5-year increment (000)				Improved drinking water (%)		Improved sanitation (%)		Household connections (%)	
	2000	2030	2005-2010	2010-2015	2015-2020	2020-2025	1990	2004	1990	2004	1990	2004
World	1,568,693	2,653,762	192,576	184,059	182,630	175,921	78	83	49	59	49	54
World Major Aggregates												
More Developed Regions	469,276	601,034	28,355	23,216	19,623	16,936	100	99	100	99	97	97
Less Developed Regions	1,099,417	2,052,728	164,221	160,843	163,007	158,985	71	80	35	50	37	44
Least Developed Countries	121,848	288,339	21,915	24,267	28,942	33,586	52	62	28	39	12	14
Landlocked Developing Countries	65,128	142,717	9,991	11,469	13,492	15,702	56	69	32	47	24	27
Small Island Developing States	12,209	19,694	1,374	1,291	1,227	1,184	84	83	71	70	44	53
United Nations Regional Groups												
African States	163,509	387,272	32,596	32,827	37,107	42,760	61	71	38	46	24	29
Asian States	833,654	1,458,357	113,795	109,915	107,996	98,854	82	80	61	67	41	46
Eastern European States	133,688	145,841	5,606	1,983	710	-212	94	93	96	88	77	77
Latin American and Caribbean States	128,557	226,806	17,208	16,856	16,514	15,893	84	90	70	79	64	76
Western European and Other States	197,992	264,277	12,625	11,724	10,403	9,360	99	99	98	99	96	99
Human Development Aggregates												
High Human Development	438,856	602,758	30,996	28,999	25,978	23,774	98	98	96	97	92	92
Medium Human Development	982,469	1,691,491	130,896	124,509	119,645	111,792	78	82	58	66	43	52
Low Human Development	129,199	319,586	28,062	27,787	31,558	36,335	50	61	30	38	13	14
Income Aggregates												
High Income	364,139	496,742	24,972	23,471	20,943	19,087	100	100	100	100	97	97
Middle Income	785,958	1,314,779	98,271	91,251	88,643	83,619	86	87	76	80	60	70
Upper-middle Income	179,399	261,869	16,221	13,937	13,396	12,297	93	91	86	85	69	82
Low-middle Income	606,560	1,052,909	82,050	77,314	75,247	71,322	80	83	66	74	50	58
Low Income	416,993	839,039	69,093	69,083	72,773	72,922	55	64	28	39	15	19
Geographic Aggregates												
Africa	163,509	387,272	32,596	32,827	37,107	42,760	61	71	38	46	24	29
Eastern Africa	50,046	121,636	8,711	10,296	12,505	14,913	58	65	36	44	22	21
Middle Africa	19,897	58,675	4,549	5,730	6,930	8,323	40	59	19	33	8	15
Northern Africa	30,060	57,110	4,789	4,680	4,771	4,580	80	85	67	75	50	56
Southern Africa	15,120	25,358	3,235	873	566	633	78	82	42	43	28	39
Western Africa	48,386	124,495	11,311	11,249	12,334	14,312	50	63	24	34	10	14
Asia	854,279	1,493,623	116,256	112,485	110,510	101,175	82	83	59	68	46	53
Eastern Asia	431,691	737,806	57,263	53,201	53,875	48,049	83	86	62	66	57	70
South-central Asia	265,789	480,182	38,296	39,002	36,686	34,181	74	76	42	56	31	29
South-eastern Asia	119,989	201,746	15,345	14,526	13,453	12,095	82	77	57	64	29	36
Western Asia	36,809	73,889	5,352	5,756	6,496	6,849	87	91	76	84	69	78
Europe	289,818	340,219	13,533	8,836	6,404	4,640	99	99	99	96	95	92
Eastern Europe	119,901	130,818	5,179	1,730	616	-266	98	93	96	91	87	80
Northern Europe	39,990	54,891	2,692	2,615	2,407	2,332	99	99	99	95	94	95
Southern Europe	51,855	61,276	2,150	1,639	1,162	833	98	98	97	96	89	88
Western Europe	78,053	93,211	3,511	2,850	2,218	1,742	100	100	100	100	100	100
Latin America	128,557	226,806	17,208	16,856	16,514	15,893	84	90	70	79	64	76
Caribbean	10,216	15,543	1,041	942	872	785	92	92	86	88	67	74
Central America	30,456	55,358	4,199	4,372	4,366	4,132	79	90	56	69	61	78
South America	87,847	155,838	11,962	11,537	11,272	10,972	81	89	69	79	63	77
Northern America	122,085	188,393	11,849	11,894	10,903	10,249	100	100	100	100	100	97
Oceania	10,445	17,448	1,135	1,161	1,192	1,203	83	84	76	79	49	56
Australia/New Zealand	8,769	14,325	929	939	941	920	100	100	100	100	...	...
Melanesia	1,447	2,774	184	198	228	266	50	54	56	50	20	21
Micronesia	106	162	10	13	11	7	85	88	63	70	25	36
Polynesia	123	187	12	11	11	10	96	95	86	95	50	66

Source: UN-Habitat, 2006. Figures in regional, income or development aggregates are calculated on the basis of country/area level data from Tables B.4 and B.5.

Note: Lists of countries/areas in aggregates are presented in the Technical Notes.

TABLE A.4

Income and Health

	Gross national income per capita PPP		Poverty		Expenditure on health		Physicians per 100,000	Prevalence of HIV population aged 15-49 (%)		Life expectancy at birth (years)	
	US$	US$	below $1/day (%)	below $2/day (%)	% of GDP (%)	per capita Int $				Male	Female
	2003	2004	1993/2003		2003	2003	1993/2003	2001	2003	2004	2004
World Total	8,394	8,760	18.9	48.7	6	718.9	1.24	1.2	1.2	64	68
World Major Aggregates											
More Developed Regions	24,616	26,364	...	...	9.7	2,739	2.98	0.2	0.3	73	79
Less Developed Regions	4,405	4,760	22.1	55.4	5.1	235	0.83	1.3	1.4	63	67
Least Developed Countries	1,235	1,354	39.1	78.7	4.7	51	0.15	4.4	4.7	51	54
Landlocked Developing Countries	1,732	1,893	31.5	70.0	5.7	89	0.79	7.2	7.0	51	53
Small Island Developing States	6,210	7,331	...	...	6.1	309	1.96	1.1	1.1	65	70
United Nations Regional Groups											
African States	2,266	2,422	34.7	64.5	5.2	119	0.28	9.3	9.2	51	53
Asian States	5,160	5,651	21.9	59.0	4.9	266	0.84	0.3	0.3	66	69
Eastern European States	8,499	9,401	2.4	13.6	6.1	566	3.43	0.5	0.6	64	74
Latin American and Caribbean States	7,260	7,829	9.9	25.6	6.9	532	1.61	1.2	1.2	69	75
Western European and Other States	24,129	26,136	...	...	9.1	2,334	2.99	0.2	0.2	76	81
Human Development Aggregates											
High Human Development	25,725	27,543	...	...	9.9	2,828	2.71	0.4	0.4	75	81
Medium Human Development	4,480	4,872	19.2	52.8	5.1	233	0.98	2.3	2.2	65	69
Low Human Development	947	1,036	46.0	77.6	4.8	45	0.16	6.8	6.4	47	49
Income Aggregates											
High Income	29,463	31,472	...	...	10.5	3,346	2.72	0.4	0.3	76	82
Middle Income	5,917	6,473	11.0	36.0	5.6	354	1.33	2.5	2.4	68	73
Upper-middle Income	9,076	9,978	5.2	16.4	6.5	620	2.51	3.1	2.9	66	73
Low-middle Income	5,165	5,639	12.4	40.7	5.4	291	1.05	2.0	2.0	68	73
Low Income	2,037	2,177	34.2	74.5	4.3	64	0.46	4.6	4.3	52	54
Geographic Aggregates											
Africa	2,266	2,422	34.7	64.5	5.2	119	0.28	9.3	9.2	51	53
Eastern Africa	938	1,057	38.0	76.0	5.4	46	0.08	7.9	8.7	47	49
Middle Africa	1,095	1,273	27.1	57.4	4.0	36	0.12	5.8	5.8	43	47
Northern Africa	...	4,244	<3	27.8	5.0	202	0.64	0.4	0.5	65	69
Southern Africa	9,805	10,362	22.8	45.0	8.1	622	0.70	29.6	28.3	46	49
Western Africa	1,167	1,217	58.5	84.2	4.9	56	0.19	2.9	2.8	47	48
Asia	5,090	5,558	20.3	54.9	5.0	274	0.87	0.2	0.3	66	69
Eastern Asia	7,361	8,029	14.3	40.3	5.8	470	1.19	0.1	0.1	71	75
South-central Asia	2,905	3,115	30.8	75.1	4.5	100	0.65	0.1	0.2	61	63
South-eastern Asia	4,286	4,606	7.4	38.6	3.7	163	0.35	0.7	0.7	65	70
Western Asia	6,687	8,010	...	...	5.8	416	1.52	0.1	0.1	66	71
Europe	18,570	20,254	...	...	7.9	1,655	3.39	0.2	0.3	71	79
Eastern Europe	8,785	9,696	2.4	13.6	6.0	585	3.54	0.5	0.6	63	74
Northern Europe	27,015	30,148	...	...	8.1	2,370	2.65	0.2	0.3	75	81
Southern Europe	22,084	24,416	...	...	8.4	1,790	3.51	0.2	0.2	78	83
Western Europe	27,695	29,405	...	...	10.4	2,960	3.42	0.2	0.2	76	82
Latin America	7,260	7,829	9.9	25.6	6.9	532	1.61	1.2	1.2	69	75
Caribbean	4,440	4,696	...	...	6.5	252	2.25	2.2	2.2	66	71
Central America	8,066	8,655	13.0	30.9	6.4	534	1.79	0.8	0.8	71	76
South America	7,332	7,934	8.8	23.7	7.1	566	1.47	0.6	0.5	68	75
Northern America	36,744	38,828	...	...	14.1	5,446	2.52	0.4	0.4	75	80
Oceania	21,194	21,892	...	...	7.3	2,091	1.88	0.2	0.3	74	78
Australia/New Zealand	27,094	28,021	...	...	8.3	2,710	2.45	0.1	0.1	78	82
Melanesia	2,489	2,699	...	...	3.5	139	0.06	0.4	0.6	60	64
Micronesia	...	...	...	...	13.0	361	0.47	...	...	64	68
Polynesia	...	...	...	...	6.1	251	0.55	...	...	68	74

Source: Figures in regional, income or development aggregates are calculated on the basis of country/area level data from Tables B.1, B.11 and B.12.

Note: Lists of countries/areas in aggregates are presented in the Technical Notes.

TABLE A.5

Safety Indicators

	Population exposed to disasters				Loss of lives due to disasters		Population affected by conflicts	Refugees and asylum seekers (2005) by place of	
	Annual average 1980–2000				Annual average 1980–2000		1980–2000	asylum	origin
	Cyclones (000)	Droughts (000)	Earthquakes (000)	Floods (000)	(000)	per million	(%)	(000)	(000)
World Total	1,813,390.4	129,882.9	111,998.2	510,476.7	66.7	12.6	13.1	10,273.4	10,273.4
World Major Aggregates									
More Developed Regions	320,088.3	—	43,079.4	44,563.3	1.1	1.0	0.7	2,765.5	758.8
Less Developed Regions	1,493,302.1	129,882.9	68,918.8	465,913.4	65.5	15.9	14.5	7,507.9	9,514.6
Least Developed Countries	163,152.0	8,525.1	3,539.3	72,070.7	36.2	69.4	29.1	3,396.9	6,542.6
Landlocked Developing Countries	4,589.5	3,782.6	3,981.5	27,030.8	37.6	61.0	28.8	2,238.6	4,059.5
Small Island Developing States	16,961.3	436.9	1,645.5	9,972.6	0.2	4.3	0.0	19.3	55.4
United Nations Regional Groups									
African States	16,527.5	9,744.4	2,425.5	16,782.3	27.3	43.0	23.6	3,300.7	4,079.0
Asian States	1,692,788.2	109,792.8	78,229.8	402,406.0	32.6	10.6	13.0	3,926.2	4,379.6
Eastern European States	—	—	2,703.7	9,371.1	1.4	3.9	0.4	438.0	1,015.6
Latin American and Caribbean States	99,560.4	10,345.7	22,237.8	65,347.6	3.8	8.6	9.8	48.6	256.1
Western European and Other States	4,514.2	—	6,401.4	16,569.7	1.3	2.6	1.5	2,010.0	185.1
Human Development Aggregates									
High Human Development	424,015.9	—	51,405.8	64,154.0	1.8	1.6	0.5	2,631.4	203.4
Medium Human Development	1,456,140.7	122,096.6	65,298.9	430,244.2	31.2	8.5	7.5	4,380.4	4,073.1
Low Human Development	22,640.9	6,297.0	290.3	14,485.6	19.9	46.4	13.3	2,496.3	4,738.1
Income Aggregates									
High Income	357,737.7	—	41,316.0	44,349.9	1.1	1.2	1.0	2,815.0	130.9
Middle Income	946,182.3	75,424.8	66,498.1	267,310.0	12.4	4.7	16.1	2,320.4	3,175.4
Upper-middle Income	74,357.2	—	14,012.9	26,537.0	3.3	6.6	2.0	269.0	506.6
Low-middle Income	871,825.0	75,424.8	52,485.2	240,773.0	9.1	4.3	35.4	2,051.3	2,668.7
Low Income	598,877.6	54,458.2	10,930.0	209,408.6	53.2	30.1	29.7	5,137.6	6,966.6
Geographic Aggregates									
Africa	16,527.5	9,744.4	2,425.5	16,782.3	27.3	43.0	23.6	3,300.7	4,079.0
Eastern Africa	16,474.4	6,417.7	256.9	5,940.5	19.5	98.5	19.0	1,059.7	1,403.8
Middle Africa	—	514.1	—	848.5	0.2	2.1	30.0	557.8	948.8
Northern Africa	—	2,478.9	2,086.1	2,857.8	7.4	25.6	19.0	1,095.5	1,095.5
Southern Africa	34.7	—	82.5	1,600.1	0.1	2.2	30.1	183.4	68.8
Western Africa	18.4	333.8	—	5,535.3	0.2	1.0	19.8	404.3	562.4
Asia	1,691,486.8	109,355.8	80,211.8	405,216.4	34.8	11.0	8.9	4,150.4	5,177.6
Eastern Asia	843,033.5	27,618.4	34,349.6	123,520.6	15.5	11.5	0.0	307.2	145.8
South-central Asia	492,964.2	43,513.7	9,550.4	198,638.8	14.7	12.0	6.6	2,916.2	3,420.3
South-eastern Asia	355,489.1	38,223.8	32,530.3	79,063.7	2.2	5.0	26.0	197.0	651.2
Western Asia	—	—	3,781.5	3,993.3	2.3	15.0	13.7	729.9	960.3
Europe	—	—	5,197.6	20,744.8	0.5	0.6	0.8	1,973.7	757.6
Eastern Europe	—	—	1,666.4	8,180.9	0.2	0.5	...	35.3	268.7
Northern Europe	—	—	—	450.5	0.0	0.1	1.1	507.7	10.9
Southern Europe	—	—	3,065.3	5,435.3	0.3	2.0	0.9	216.7	477.1
Western Europe	—	—	465.9	6,678.1	0.0	0.1	...	1,214.1	0.9
Latin America	99,560.4	10,345.7	22,237.8	65,347.6	3.8	8.6	9.8	48.6	256.1
Caribbean	15,327.9	—	—	8,274.2	0.2	4.8	...	1.2	86.5
Central America	76,518.4	—	10,569.1	8,271.1	1.7	15.2	9.1	18.0	72.6
South America	7,714.1	10,345.7	11,668.6	48,802.3	1.9	6.5	16.9	29.5	97.1
Northern America	89,407.2	0.0	6,745.8	11,251.1	0.3	0.9	...	716.8	1.1
Oceania	5,815.6	436.9	1,925.6	1,726.3	0.0	4.4	...	82.5	2.0
Australia/New Zealand	4,514.2	0.0	280.2	1,641.9	0.0	0.5	...	72.5	0.1
Melanesia	1,301.4	436.9	1,645.5	84.4	0.0	5.6	...	10.0	1.8
Micronesia	...	...	...	...	0.0	0.7	...	—	—
Polynesia	...	...	...	...	0.0	8.1	...	—	—

Sources: Figures in regional, income or development aggregates are calculated on the basis of country/area level data from UNDP, 2005; and Tables B.7 and B.8 of this Report.

Note: Lists of countries/areas in aggregates are presented in the Technical Notes.

TABLE B.1

Total Population Size and Rate of Change

	Total population									Population density (people/km²)	
	Estimates and projections					Rate of change					
	(000) 1990	(000) 2000	(000) 2010	(000) 2020	(000) 2030	(%) 1990–2000	(%) 2000–2010	(%) 2010–2020	(%) 2020–2030	2004	2030
WORLD	5,279,519	6,085,572	6,842,923	7,577,889	8,199,104	1.42	1.17	1.02	0.79	49	63
AFRICA	635,685	812,466	1,006,905	1,228,276	1,463,493	2.45	2.15	1.99	1.75		
Algeria	25,291	30,463	35,420	40,624	44,706	1.86	1.51	1.37	0.96	14	19
Angola	10,532	13,841	18,327	23,777	30,050	2.73	2.81	2.60	2.34	11	21
Benin	5,178	7,197	9,793	12,717	15,820	3.29	3.08	2.61	2.18	62	119
Botswana	1,429	1,754	1,729	1,671	1,642	2.05	-0.14	-0.34	-0.17	3	3
Burkina Faso	8,532	11,292	15,314	20,305	26,199	2.80	3.05	2.82	2.55	45	91
Burundi	5,670	6,486	9,099	12,263	15,930	1.34	3.39	2.98	2.62	286	605
Cameroon	11,651	14,856	17,685	20,361	22,821	2.43	1.74	1.41	1.14	35	50
Cape Verde	355	451	567	690	808	2.38	2.29	1.96	1.58	119	200
Central African Republic	3,000	3,777	4,333	4,960	5,572	2.31	1.37	1.35	1.16	6	8
Chad	6,055	8,216	11,130	14,881	19,751	3.05	3.04	2.90	2.83	7	15
Comoros[1]	527	699	907	1,130	1,357	2.83	2.61	2.19	1.84	276	499
Congo	2,484	3,438	4,633	6,363	8,551	3.25	2.98	3.17	2.96	11	24
Côte d'Ivoire	12,657	16,735	19,777	23,339	26,883	2.79	1.67	1.66	1.41	54	81
Dem. Republic of the Congo	37,764	50,052	67,129	90,022	117,494	2.82	2.94	2.93	2.66	24	50
Djibouti	558	715	859	1,015	1,200	2.47	1.85	1.66	1.67	31	50
Egypt	55,673	67,285	81,133	94,834	107,056	1.89	1.87	1.56	1.21	69	101
Equatorial Guinea	353	449	563	693	836	2.40	2.26	2.07	1.88	18	32
Eritrea	3,038	3,557	5,128	6,584	8,138	1.58	3.66	2.50	2.12	44	86
Ethiopia	51,040	68,525	86,998	107,681	128,979	2.95	2.39	2.13	1.80	70	119
Gabon	957	1,272	1,498	1,709	1,907	2.84	1.63	1.32	1.10	5	7
Gambia	936	1,316	1,706	2,070	2,439	3.41	2.60	1.94	1.64	145	250
Ghana	15,479	19,867	24,312	28,789	33,075	2.50	2.02	1.69	1.39	93	142
Guinea	6,217	8,434	10,485	13,371	16,492	3.05	2.18	2.43	2.10	33	59
Guinea-Bissau	1,016	1,366	1,835	2,479	3,317	2.96	2.96	3.01	2.91	55	123
Kenya	23,430	30,689	38,956	49,563	60,606	2.70	2.39	2.41	2.01	57	102
Lesotho	1,593	1,788	1,768	1,718	1,663	1.15	-0.11	-0.28	-0.33	60	56
Liberia	2,136	3,065	3,800	5,042	6,655	3.61	2.15	2.83	2.78	171	350
Libyan Arab Jamahiriya	4,334	5,306	6,439	7,538	8,345	2.02	1.93	1.58	1.02	3	4
Madagascar	12,045	16,195	21,151	26,584	32,317	2.96	2.67	2.29	1.95	30	53
Malawi	9,459	11,512	14,348	17,816	21,687	1.96	2.20	2.17	1.97	119	204
Mali	8,894	11,647	15,617	20,904	27,413	2.70	2.93	2.92	2.71	10	21
Mauritania	2,030	2,645	3,520	4,473	5,482	2.64	2.86	2.40	2.03	3	5
Mauritius[2]	1,057	1,186	1,298	1,384	1,443	1.15	0.91	0.64	0.41	842	1001
Morocco	24,696	29,231	33,832	38,327	42,016	1.69	1.46	1.25	0.92	69	93
Mozambique	13,429	17,911	21,620	25,508	29,604	2.88	1.88	1.65	1.49	24	37
Namibia	1,398	1,894	2,132	2,384	2,641	3.04	1.18	1.12	1.02	2	3
Niger	8,472	11,782	16,430	22,585	30,637	3.30	3.33	3.18	3.05	10	22
Nigeria	90,557	117,608	145,991	175,798	204,465	2.61	2.16	1.86	1.51	154	244
Réunion	604	724	838	931	1,007	1.82	1.46	1.05	0.79	...	...
Rwanda	7,096	8,025	10,125	12,352	14,368	1.23	2.33	1.99	1.51	341	553
Saint Helena[3]	5	5	5	6	6	-0.99	0.58	0.92	0.62	...	...
São Tomé and Príncipe	117	140	174	209	241	1.80	2.22	1.80	1.44	167	271
Senegal	7,977	10,343	13,082	15,970	18,678	2.60	2.35	2.00	1.57	54	88
Seychelles	72	77	84	91	97	0.69	0.87	0.81	0.56	188	229
Sierra Leone	4,078	4,509	6,132	7,740	9,650	1.00	3.08	2.33	2.21	76	142
Somalia	6,674	7,012	9,590	12,336	15,304	0.49	3.13	2.52	2.16	16	32
South Africa	36,877	45,610	47,819	48,100	48,405	2.13	0.47	0.06	0.06	38	40
Sudan	26,066	32,902	40,254	47,536	54,511	2.33	2.02	1.66	1.37	14	21
Swaziland	865	1,023	1,010	983	973	1.67	-0.12	-0.28	-0.10	187	179
Togo	3,961	5,364	6,977	8,731	10,486	3.03	2.63	2.24	1.83	91	159
Tunisia	8,219	9,563	10,639	11,604	12,379	1.51	1.07	0.87	0.65	64	79
Uganda	17,758	24,309	34,569	50,572	72,078	3.14	3.52	3.80	3.54	132	335
United Republic of Tanzania	26,231	34,763	41,838	49,265	56,178	2.82	1.85	1.63	1.31	41	61
Western Sahara	218	300	429	627	728	3.16	3.60	3.78	1.49	...	...
Zambia	8,377	10,702	12,673	15,128	17,706	2.45	1.69	1.77	1.57	14	22
Zimbabwe	10,565	12,595	13,402	14,144	14,700	1.76	0.62	0.54	0.39	34	39
ASIA	**3,168,616**	**3,675,799**	**4,130,383**	**4,553,791**	**4,872,472**	**1.48**	**1.17**	**0.98**	**0.68**		
Afghanistan	14,606	23,735	35,642	48,032	63,424	4.85	4.07	2.98	2.78	...	...
Armenia	3,545	3,082	2,981	2,952	2,843	-1.40	-0.33	-0.10	-0.38	108	101
Azerbaijan	7,212	8,143	8,741	9,384	9,713	1.21	0.71	0.71	0.34	100	116
Bahrain	493	672	791	910	1,016	3.10	1.63	1.40	1.11	1022	1479
Bangladesh	104,047	128,916	154,960	181,180	205,641	2.14	1.84	1.56	1.27	1079	1592
Bhutan	1,642	1,938	2,414	2,950	3,460	1.66	2.20	2.00	1.59	19	32
Brunei Darussalam	257	333	414	491	561	2.60	2.17	1.70	1.34	69	109
Cambodia	9,738	12,744	15,530	18,580	21,313	2.69	1.98	1.79	1.37	77	118
China[4]	1,155,305	1,273,979	1,354,533	1,423,939	1,446,453	0.98	0.61	0.50	0.16	139	154
China, Hong Kong SAR[5]	5,704	6,637	7,416	8,080	8,610	1.51	1.11	0.86	0.64	6569	8140
China, Macao SAR[6]	372	444	476	509	531	1.75	0.71	0.67	0.41	265	311
Cyprus	681	786	881	972	1,051	1.44	1.14	0.98	0.78	84	109
Dem. People's Republic of Korea	19,690	21,862	22,907	23,722	24,375	1.05	0.47	0.35	0.27	189	208
Georgia	5,460	4,720	4,299	4,059	3,755	-1.46	-0.93	-0.58	-0.78	65	54
India	849,415	1,021,084	1,183,293	1,332,032	1,449,078	1.84	1.47	1.18	0.84	363	484
Indonesia	181,414	209,174	235,755	255,853	270,844	1.42	1.20	0.82	0.57	120	148
Iran (Islamic Republic of)	56,674	66,365	74,283	85,036	92,253	1.58	1.13	1.35	0.81	41	54

TABLE B.1

continued

	Total population									Population density (people/km²)	
	Estimates and projections					Rate of change					
	(000) 1990	(000) 2000	(000) 2010	(000) 2020	(000) 2030	(%) 1990–2000	(%) 2000–2010	(%) 2010–2020	(%) 2020–2030	2004	2030
Iraq	18,515	25,075	32,534	40,522	48,797	3.03	2.60	2.20	1.86	58	105
Israel	4,514	6,084	7,315	8,296	9,156	2.99	1.84	1.26	0.99	313	436
Japan	123,537	127,034	128,457	126,713	122,566	0.28	0.11	-0.14	-0.33	351	337
Jordan	3,254	4,972	6,338	7,556	8,672	4.24	2.43	1.76	1.38	61	96
Kazakhstan	16,500	15,033	14,802	14,883	14,556	-0.93	-0.16	0.05	-0.22	6	6
Kuwait	2,143	2,230	3,047	3,698	4,296	0.40	3.12	1.94	1.50	138	232
Kyrgyzstan	4,395	4,952	5,567	6,094	6,431	1.19	1.17	0.90	0.54	27	33
Lao People's Dem. Republic	4,132	5,279	6,604	8,014	9,389	2.45	2.24	1.94	1.58	25	40
Lebanon	2,741	3,398	3,773	4,140	4,428	2.15	1.05	0.93	0.67	445	555
Malaysia	17,845	22,997	27,532	31,474	34,720	2.54	1.80	1.34	0.98	77	108
Maldives	216	290	371	461	547	2.97	2.47	2.17	1.70	998	1759
Mongolia	2,216	2,497	2,813	3,137	3,381	1.19	1.19	1.09	0.75	2	3
Myanmar	40,753	47,724	52,801	57,054	60,629	1.58	1.01	0.77	0.61	76	94
Nepal	19,114	24,431	29,891	35,679	41,424	2.45	2.02	1.77	1.49	176	274
Occupied Palestinian Territory	2,154	3,150	4,330	5,694	7,171	3.80	3.18	2.74	2.31	564	1117
Oman	1,843	2,442	2,863	3,481	4,053	2.81	1.59	1.96	1.52	9	14
Pakistan	111,698	142,648	175,178	211,703	246,322	2.45	2.05	1.89	1.51	197	312
Philippines	61,104	75,766	90,048	103,266	114,080	2.15	1.73	1.37	1.00	278	389
Qatar	467	606	894	1,036	1,158	2.60	3.88	1.47	1.11	58	99
Republic of Korea	42,869	46,779	48,566	49,393	49,161	0.87	0.37	0.17	-0.05	488	505
Saudi Arabia	16,379	21,484	27,664	34,024	40,132	2.71	2.53	2.07	1.65	11	18
Singapore	3,016	4,017	4,590	4,986	5,265	2.87	1.33	0.83	0.55	6470	8022
Sri Lanka	17,786	19,848	21,557	22,902	23,667	1.10	0.83	0.61	0.33	301	347
Syrian Arab Republic	12,843	16,813	21,432	26,029	29,983	2.69	2.43	1.94	1.41	97	156
Tajikistan	5,303	6,159	6,992	8,216	9,237	1.50	1.27	1.61	1.17	46	65
Thailand	54,639	61,438	66,785	71,044	73,827	1.17	0.83	0.62	0.38	122	142
Timor-Leste	740	722	1,244	1,713	2,173	-0.25	5.44	3.20	2.38	62	158
Turkey	57,300	68,234	78,081	86,774	93,876	1.75	1.35	1.06	0.79	93	121
Turkmenistan	3,668	4,502	5,163	5,811	6,270	2.05	1.37	1.18	0.76	10	13
United Arab Emirates	1,868	3,247	5,035	6,144	7,225	5.53	4.39	1.99	1.62	51	100
Uzbekistan	20,515	24,724	28,578	32,515	35,329	1.87	1.45	1.29	0.83	63	85
Viet Nam	66,206	78,671	89,718	99,928	108,128	1.73	1.31	1.08	0.79	252	328
Yemen	12,086	17,937	24,502	32,733	41,499	3.95	3.12	2.90	2.37	37	75
EUROPE	721,390	728,463	725,786	714,959	698,140	0.10	-0.04	-0.15	-0.24		
Albania	3,289	3,062	3,216	3,420	3,512	-0.72	0.49	0.61	0.27	116	130
Andorra	52	66	68	67	66	2.31	0.26	-0.09	-0.24	136	134
Austria	7,729	8,096	8,248	8,320	8,333	0.46	0.19	0.09	0.01	98	100
Belarus	10,266	10,029	9,484	8,939	8,314	-0.23	-0.56	-0.59	-0.73	47	40
Belgium	9,967	10,304	10,495	10,573	10,588	0.33	0.18	0.07	0.01	344	351
Bosnia and Herzegovina	4,308	3,847	3,935	3,827	3,639	-1.13	0.23	-0.28	-0.50	75	70
Bulgaria	8,718	7,997	7,446	6,859	6,243	-0.86	-0.71	-0.82	-0.94	70	56
Channel Islands[7]	142	147	152	158	164	0.33	0.36	0.36	0.37	745	823
Croatia	4,517	4,505	4,532	4,367	4,164	-0.03	0.06	-0.37	-0.48	81	75
Czech Republic	10,306	10,267	10,158	9,932	9,525	-0.04	-0.11	-0.23	-0.42	132	123
Denmark	5,140	5,340	5,502	5,624	5,752	0.38	0.30	0.22	0.23	127	135
Estonia	1,584	1,367	1,309	1,272	1,221	-1.47	-0.43	-0.29	-0.41	32	29
Faeroe Islands	47	46	49	51	54	-0.39	0.62	0.60	0.39	34	39
Finland[8]	4,986	5,177	5,307	5,409	5,453	0.37	0.25	0.19	0.08	17	18
France	56,735	59,278	61,535	62,954	63,712	0.44	0.37	0.23	0.12	109	115
Germany	79,433	82,344	82,701	82,283	81,512	0.36	0.04	-0.05	-0.09	237	234
Gibraltar	27	28	28	28	28	0.30	0.13	0.03	-0.09	...	...
Greece	10,160	10,975	11,205	11,217	11,119	0.77	0.21	0.01	-0.09	86	86
Holy See[9]	1	1	1	1	1	0.22	-0.03	0.00	-0.26	...	...
Hungary	10,365	10,226	9,961	9,628	9,221	-0.14	-0.26	-0.34	-0.43	109	99
Iceland	255	281	307	330	349	0.99	0.88	0.71	0.58	125	152
Ireland	3,515	3,801	4,422	4,893	5,249	0.78	1.51	1.01	0.70	58	75
Isle of Man	70	77	76	75	74	0.89	-0.07	-0.10	-0.16	135	131
Italy	56,719	57,715	58,176	57,132	55,423	0.17	0.08	-0.18	-0.30	196	188
Latvia	2,713	2,373	2,248	2,129	1,981	-1.34	-0.54	-0.54	-0.72	37	32
Liechtenstein	29	33	36	39	41	1.25	0.92	0.73	0.61	213	260
Lithuania	3,698	3,500	3,358	3,214	3,029	-0.55	-0.41	-0.44	-0.59	55	48
Luxembourg	378	435	494	552	612	1.42	1.27	1.11	1.04	174	236
Malta	360	392	411	426	434	0.84	0.47	0.37	0.18	400	437
Monaco	30	33	37	42	46	1.02	1.12	1.14	1.01	159	214
Netherlands	14,952	15,898	16,592	17,007	17,303	0.61	0.43	0.25	0.17	480	513
Norway[10]	4,241	4,502	4,730	4,960	5,190	0.60	0.49	0.47	0.45	15	17
Poland	38,111	38,649	38,359	37,712	36,254	0.14	-0.08	-0.17	-0.39	125	118
Portugal	9,983	10,225	10,712	10,902	10,933	0.24	0.47	0.18	0.03	114	120
Republic of Moldova	4,364	4,275	4,160	4,054	3,856	-0.21	-0.27	-0.26	-0.50	128	117
Romania	23,207	22,117	21,287	20,396	19,285	-0.48	-0.38	-0.43	-0.56	95	84
Russian Federation	148,370	146,560	140,028	133,101	125,325	-0.12	-0.46	-0.51	-0.60	8	7
San Marino	24	27	29	30	31	1.09	0.79	0.35	0.13	463	515
Serbia and Montenegro	10,156	10,545	10,478	10,335	10,114	0.38	-0.06	-0.14	-0.22	80	77
Slovakia	5,256	5,400	5,400	5,350	5,189	0.27	-0.00	-0.09	-0.31	110	106
Slovenia	1,926	1,967	1,959	1,917	1,842	0.21	-0.04	-0.22	-0.40	99	93
Spain	39,303	40,717	43,993	44,419	44,008	0.35	0.77	0.10	-0.09	83	87
Sweden	8,559	8,877	9,168	9,488	9,769	0.37	0.32	0.34	0.29	22	24

TABLE B.1

continued

	Total population									Population density (people/km²)	
	Estimates and projections					Rate of change					
	(000) 1990	(000) 2000	(000) 2010	(000) 2020	(000) 2030	(%) 1990–2000	(%) 2000–2010	(%) 2010–2020	(%) 2020–2030	2004	2030
Switzerland	6,834	7,167	7,301	7,368	7,410	0.48	0.18	0.09	0.06	187	192
TFYR Macedonia[11]	1,909	2,010	2,046	2,057	2,027	0.51	0.18	0.05	-0.14	81	81
Ukraine	51,891	49,116	44,128	39,609	35,052	-0.55	-1.07	-1.08	-1.22	83	62
United Kingdom	56,761	58,670	60,517	62,491	64,693	0.33	0.31	0.32	0.35	247	269
LATIN AMERICA AND THE CARIBBEAN	443,747	522,929	598,771	666,955	722,377	1.64	1.35	1.08	0.80		
Anguilla	9	11	13	15	16	2.19	1.53	1.21	0.80	...	...
Antigua and Barbuda	63	77	87	96	104	1.89	1.25	1.05	0.74	182	238
Argentina	32,581	36,896	40,738	44,486	47,534	1.24	0.99	0.88	0.66	14	17
Aruba	66	92	103	108	112	3.27	1.15	0.48	0.31	521	613
Bahamas	255	301	344	385	420	1.68	1.33	1.12	0.86	32	43
Barbados	257	266	273	278	278	0.34	0.25	0.17	-0.00	632	655
Belize	186	242	296	345	386	2.66	2.01	1.52	1.12	12	18
Bolivia	6,669	8,317	10,031	11,638	13,034	2.21	1.87	1.49	1.13	8	12
Brazil	149,394	173,858	198,497	219,193	235,505	1.52	1.33	0.99	0.72	21	27
British Virgin Islands	17	21	23	26	27	2.18	1.27	0.91	0.66	...	...
Cayman Islands	26	40	49	53	56	4.12	2.01	0.86	0.63	745	1001
Chile	13,179	15,412	17,134	18,639	19,779	1.57	1.06	0.84	0.59	21	26
Colombia	34,970	42,120	48,930	55,046	60,153	1.86	1.50	1.18	0.89	44	59
Costa Rica	3,076	3,929	4,665	5,276	5,795	2.45	1.72	1.23	0.94	80	110
Cuba	10,537	11,125	11,379	11,432	11,182	0.54	0.23	0.05	-0.22	103	103
Dominica	72	78	83	90	95	0.77	0.67	0.81	0.53	95	114
Dominican Republic	7,090	8,265	9,522	10,676	11,626	1.53	1.42	1.14	0.85	183	243
Ecuador	10,272	12,306	14,192	16,026	17,520	1.81	1.43	1.22	0.89	48	64
El Salvador	5,110	6,280	7,461	8,550	9,517	2.06	1.72	1.36	1.07	321	452
Falkland Islands (Malvinas)	2	3	3	3	3	3.98	0.56	0.45	0.22	...	...
French Guiana	116	164	209	254	296	3.45	2.42	1.95	1.52	...	...
Grenada	96	102	110	127	141	0.52	0.84	1.39	1.07	...	...
Guadeloupe	391	430	462	480	492	0.95	0.73	0.38	0.25	...	...
Guatemala	8,894	11,166	14,213	17,527	20,698	2.28	2.41	2.10	1.66	116	194
Guyana	729	744	751	725	676	0.20	0.10	-0.36	-0.70	4	4
Haiti	6,867	7,939	9,145	10,328	11,371	1.45	1.41	1.22	0.96	312	421
Honduras	4,867	6,424	7,997	9,533	10,883	2.78	2.19	1.76	1.32	64	99
Jamaica	2,369	2,585	2,703	2,785	2,801	0.87	0.45	0.30	0.06	246	262
Martinique	360	386	401	405	399	0.69	0.39	0.09	-0.14	...	...
Mexico	84,296	100,088	113,271	124,652	133,221	1.72	1.24	0.96	0.66	54	68
Montserrat	11	4	5	5	5	-10.09	1.97	0.69	0.37	...	...
Netherlands Antilles	191	176	188	198	205	-0.82	0.69	0.50	0.35	277	317
Nicaragua	3,960	4,959	6,066	7,179	8,116	2.25	2.02	1.68	1.23	46	69
Panama	2,411	2,950	3,509	4,027	4,488	2.02	1.73	1.38	1.08	41	58
Paraguay	4,219	5,470	6,882	8,341	9,747	2.60	2.30	1.92	1.56	15	24
Peru	21,753	25,952	30,063	34,250	37,931	1.76	1.47	1.30	1.02	22	30
Puerto Rico	3,528	3,835	4,060	4,242	4,361	0.83	0.57	0.44	0.28	277	310
Saint Kitts and Nevis	41	40	45	50	54	-0.06	1.08	1.03	0.83	131	171
Saint Lucia	138	154	168	180	187	1.15	0.81	0.70	0.38	268	317
Saint Vincent and the Grenadines	109	116	122	125	123	0.59	0.51	0.26	-0.16	278	291
Suriname	402	434	462	478	479	0.77	0.62	0.34	0.02	3	3
Trinidad and Tobago	1,215	1,285	1,324	1,345	1,332	0.56	0.30	0.16	-0.10	258	265
Turks and Caicos Islands	12	19	28	31	33	5.19	3.74	0.96	0.66	...	...
United States Virgin Islands	104	111	112	109	104	0.69	0.06	-0.20	-0.53	333	311
Uruguay	3,106	3,342	3,575	3,767	3,916	0.73	0.68	0.52	0.39	19	22
Venezuela	19,735	24,418	29,076	33,450	37,176	2.13	1.75	1.40	1.06	30	42
NORTHERN AMERICA	283,361	314,968	346,062	375,000	400,079	1.06	0.94	0.80	0.65		
Bermuda	60	63	65	66	66	0.50	0.33	0.13	0.00	1280	1329
Canada	27,701	30,689	33,680	36,441	39,052	1.02	0.93	0.79	0.69	3	4
Greenland	56	56	58	59	60	0.11	0.26	0.26	0.18	0	0
Saint-Pierre-et-Miquelon	6	6	6	7	7	-0.12	0.57	0.91	0.64	...	...
United States of America	255,539	284,154	312,253	338,427	360,894	1.06	0.94	0.80	0.64	32	39
OCEANIA	26,721	30,949	35,017	38,909	42,543	1.47	1.23	1.05	0.89		
American Samoa	47	58	72	85	99	2.04	2.14	1.72	1.48	285	458
Australia[12]	16,873	19,071	21,201	23,317	25,238	1.22	1.06	0.95	0.79	3	4
Cook Islands	18	19	18	17	16	0.25	-0.64	-0.45	-0.64	...	...
Fiji	724	811	878	920	952	1.14	0.80	0.46	0.34	46	53
French Polynesia	195	236	274	307	333	1.89	1.50	1.14	0.79	67	90
Guam	134	155	182	206	227	1.49	1.59	1.22	1.00	298	418
Kiribati	72	90	109	128	147	2.21	1.95	1.63	1.37	134	208
Marshall Islands	47	52	73	94	113	0.98	3.30	2.57	1.87	174	343
Micronesia (Fed. States of)	96	107	114	117	115	1.06	0.60	0.30	-0.21	181	191
Nauru	9	12	14	16	17	2.53	1.72	0.93	0.65	...	...
New Caledonia	171	215	257	296	331	2.30	1.78	1.40	1.12	13	19
New Zealand	3,411	3,818	4,172	4,425	4,635	1.13	0.89	0.59	0.46	15	18
Niue	2	2	2	2	2	-2.09	-0.55	0.84	0.55	...	...
Northern Mariana Islands	44	70	91	104	116	4.52	2.63	1.39	1.04	161	248
Palau	15	19	21	22	22	2.35	0.62	0.51	0.31	43	48
Papua New Guinea	4,114	5,299	6,450	7,602	8,784	2.53	1.97	1.64	1.44	12	18
Pitcairn	0	0	0	0	0	0.45	0.00	0.00	-1.09	...	...
Samoa	161	177	189	190	189	0.95	0.62	0.06	-0.05	63	66

TABLE B.1

continued

	Total population									Population density (people/km²)	
	Estimates and projections					Rate of change					
	(000) 1990	(000) 2000	(000) 2010	(000) 2020	(000) 2030	(%) 1990–2000	(%) 2000–2010	(%) 2010–2020	(%) 2020–2030	2004	2030
Solomon Islands	317	419	537	653	762	2.79	2.50	1.95	1.54	17	29
Tokelau	2	1	1	2	2	-0.78	0.46	0.93	0.61	...	...
Tonga	94	100	103	103	98	0.59	0.31	-0.06	-0.44	141	137
Tuvalu	9	10	11	11	12	0.77	0.46	0.45	0.45	...	...
Vanuatu	149	191	232	273	313	2.48	1.91	1.65	1.36	18	28
Wallis and Futuna Islands	14	15	17	19	22	0.78	1.10	1.46	1.09	...	...

Sources: United Nations, Department of Economic and Social Affairs, Population Division, 2006; World Bank, 2006; WHO, 2006.

Notes:

(1) Including the island of Mayotte.
(2) Including Agalega, Rodrigues and Saint Brandon.
(3) Including Ascension and Tristan da Cunha.
(4) For statistical purposes, the data for China do not include Hong Kong and Macao Special Administrative Regions (SAR) of China.
(5) As of 1 July 1997, Hong Kong became a Special Administrative Region (SAR) of China.
(6) As of 20 December 1999, Macao became a Special Administrative Region (SAR) of China.
(7) Including the islands of Guernsey and Jersey.
(8) Including Åland Islands.
(9) Refers to the Vatican City State.
(10) Including Svalbard and Jan Mayen islands.
(11) The former Yugoslav Republic of Macedonia.
(12) Including Christmas Island, Cocos (Keeling) Islands and Norfolk Island.

TABLE B.2

Urban and Rural Population Size and Rate of Change

	Urban population							Rural population						
	Estimates and projections (000)				Rate of change (%)			Estimates and projections (000)				Rate of change (%)		
	2000	2010	2020	2030	2000–2010	2010–2020	2020–2030	2000	2010	2020	2030	2000–2010	2010–2020	2020–2030
WORLD	2,844,802	3,474,571	4,177,106	4,912,553	2.00	1.84	1.62	3,240,771	3,368,353	3,400,783	3,286,551	0.39	0.10	-0.34
AFRICA	294,392	407,900	556,191	742,188	3.26	3.10	2.88	518,074	599,004	672,085	721,305	1.45	1.15	0.71
Algeria	18,220	23,553	29,190	34,081	2.57	2.15	1.55	12,243	11,867	11,435	10,625	-0.31	-0.37	-0.73
Angola	6,920	10,366	14,900	20,487	4.04	3.63	3.18	6,920	7,961	8,877	9,563	1.40	1.09	0.74
Benin	2,762	4,126	6,021	8,519	4.01	3.78	3.47	4,435	5,667	6,697	7,301	2.45	1.67	0.86
Botswana	934	1,058	1,131	1,195	1.25	0.66	0.55	820	671	541	448	-2.00	-2.16	-1.89
Burkina Faso	1,869	3,116	5,218	8,512	5.11	5.16	4.89	9,423	12,199	15,088	17,686	2.58	2.13	1.59
Burundi	557	1,059	1,919	3,314	6.43	5.95	5.46	5,930	8,041	10,344	12,616	3.05	2.52	1.98
Cameroon	7,428	10,411	13,445	16,320	3.38	2.56	1.94	7,428	7,273	6,915	6,501	-0.21	-0.50	-0.62
Cape Verde	241	346	464	585	3.61	2.95	2.31	210	221	226	223	0.52	0.20	-0.10
Central African Republic	1,421	1,686	2,105	2,696	1.71	2.22	2.48	2,356	2,647	2,855	2,875	1.16	0.76	0.07
Chad	1,921	3,075	5,048	8,146	4.71	4.96	4.78	6,295	8,056	9,833	11,605	2.47	1.99	1.66
Comoros[1]	237	367	539	748	4.38	3.85	3.29	462	541	591	609	1.56	0.89	0.30
Congo	2,005	2,878	4,221	6,060	3.61	3.83	3.62	1,433	1,755	2,141	2,491	2.03	1.99	1.51
Côte d'Ivoire	7,204	9,343	12,313	15,893	2.60	2.76	2.55	9,531	10,435	11,025	10,991	0.91	0.55	-0.03
Dem. Republic of the Congo	14,936	23,641	37,835	57,757	4.59	4.70	4.23	35,116	43,488	52,187	59,737	2.14	1.82	1.35
Djibouti	596	757	919	1,104	2.40	1.94	1.83	119	102	96	96	-1.52	-0.67	0.06
Egypt	28,596	35,468	45,229	57,682	2.15	2.43	2.43	38,689	45,665	49,604	49,375	1.66	0.83	-0.05
Equatorial Guinea	174	223	300	413	2.49	2.94	3.21	275	339	393	423	2.12	1.46	0.74
Eritrea	632	1,106	1,808	2,798	5.59	4.91	4.37	2,924	4,021	4,776	5,340	3.19	1.72	1.12
Ethiopia	10,210	15,094	22,917	34,949	3.91	4.18	4.22	58,315	71,904	84,764	94,031	2.09	1.65	1.04
Gabon	1,020	1,288	1,517	1,728	2.34	1.63	1.30	253	209	192	179	-1.88	-0.87	-0.70
Gambia	646	992	1,347	1,732	4.29	3.06	2.52	670	714	724	707	0.64	0.14	-0.24
Ghana	8,743	12,532	16,844	21,420	3.60	2.96	2.40	11,124	11,780	11,946	11,655	0.57	0.14	-0.25
Guinea	2,618	3,704	5,534	8,014	3.47	4.02	3.70	5,816	6,781	7,837	8,478	1.53	1.45	0.79
Guinea-Bissau	406	551	814	1,281	3.06	3.91	4.53	960	1,285	1,665	2,036	2.91	2.59	2.01
Kenya	6,056	8,640	13,169	20,027	3.55	4.21	4.19	24,634	30,315	36,394	40,579	2.08	1.83	1.09
Lesotho	319	355	424	517	1.07	1.78	1.97	1,469	1,413	1,294	1,146	-0.39	-0.88	-1.21
Liberia	1,663	2,337	3,424	4,904	3.40	3.82	3.59	1,402	1,462	1,618	1,751	0.42	1.01	0.79
Libyan Arab Jamahiriya	4,410	5,554	6,662	7,512	2.31	1.82	1.20	897	884	877	833	-0.14	-0.09	-0.51
Madagascar	4,211	5,955	8,673	12,713	3.47	3.76	3.82	11,984	15,195	17,911	19,604	2.37	1.64	0.90
Malawi	1,737	2,797	4,470	6,920	4.76	4.69	4.37	9,775	11,551	13,346	14,766	1.67	1.44	1.01
Mali	3,245	5,207	8,354	12,996	4.73	4.73	4.42	8,402	10,410	12,550	14,417	2.14	1.87	1.39
Mauritania	1,058	1,459	2,033	2,835	3.22	3.32	3.33	1,587	2,062	2,440	2,647	2.62	1.69	0.81
Mauritius[2]	506	556	638	752	0.95	1.38	1.63	680	742	746	691	0.88	0.05	-0.77
Morocco	16,106	20,957	25,973	30,528	2.63	2.15	1.62	13,125	12,875	12,353	11,488	-0.19	-0.41	-0.73
Mozambique	5,499	8,307	11,794	15,885	4.12	3.51	2.98	12,411	13,313	13,714	13,719	0.70	0.30	0.00
Namibia	614	810	1,060	1,361	2.78	2.68	2.50	1,281	1,321	1,324	1,280	0.31	0.02	-0.34
Niger	1,911	2,926	4,803	8,259	4.26	4.96	5.42	9,871	13,504	17,782	22,378	3.13	2.75	2.30
Nigeria	51,657	76,141	104,296	134,898	3.88	3.15	2.57	65,950	69,850	71,502	69,567	0.57	0.23	-0.27
Réunion	651	788	891	971	1.91	1.23	0.86	73	50	40	37	-3.80	-2.17	-0.88
Rwanda	1,105	2,422	4,130	6,053	7.84	5.34	3.82	6,919	7,704	8,223	8,315	1.07	0.65	0.11
Saint Helena[3]	2	2	2	3	0.65	1.86	1.99	3	3	3	3	0.54	0.25	-0.57
São Tomé and Príncipe	75	108	144	179	3.74	2.84	2.14	65	66	65	63	0.13	-0.18	-0.33
Senegal	4,203	5,611	7,521	9,936	2.89	2.93	2.78	6,140	7,470	8,449	8,741	1.96	1.23	0.34
Seychelles	39	47	56	64	1.68	1.79	1.42	38	38	36	32	-0.04	-0.57	-0.96
Sierra Leone	1,669	2,723	4,025	5,743	4.89	3.91	3.55	2,840	3,409	3,715	3,907	1.83	0.86	0.50
Somalia	2,332	3,593	5,309	7,634	4.32	3.91	3.63	4,680	5,997	7,027	7,670	2.48	1.58	0.88
South Africa	25,948	29,505	32,017	34,523	1.28	0.82	0.75	19,662	18,314	16,083	13,882	-0.71	-1.30	-1.47
Sudan	11,873	18,204	25,287	33,080	4.27	3.29	2.69	21,030	22,049	22,249	21,431	0.47	0.09	-0.37
Swaziland	239	258	297	360	0.77	1.44	1.92	785	753	685	612	-0.41	-0.94	-1.12
Togo	1,963	3,050	4,470	6,147	4.41	3.82	3.19	3,401	3,926	4,261	4,339	1.44	0.82	0.18
Tunisia	6,062	7,148	8,251	9,291	1.65	1.43	1.19	3,501	3,491	3,353	3,089	-0.03	-0.40	-0.82
Uganda	2,943	4,613	8,096	14,886	4.50	5.62	6.09	21,366	29,956	42,476	57,192	3.38	3.49	2.97
United Republic of Tanzania	7,755	11,038	15,659	21,720	3.53	3.50	3.27	27,008	30,800	33,606	34,458	1.31	0.87	0.25
Western Sahara	273	395	582	681	3.69	3.87	1.58	26	35	45	47	2.68	2.72	0.27
Zambia	3,724	4,526	5,891	7,922	1.95	2.64	2.96	6,979	8,147	9,237	9,785	1.55	1.25	0.58
Zimbabwe	4,252	5,127	6,213	7,454	1.87	1.92	1.82	8,343	8,275	7,931	7,246	-0.08	-0.42	-0.90
ASIA	1,363,035	1,755,006	2,191,963	2,636,623	2.53	2.22	1.85	2,312,764	2,375,377	2,361,828	2,235,850	0.27	-0.06	-0.55
Afghanistan	5,050	8,838	14,262	22,997	5.60	4.79	4.78	18,685	26,804	33,770	40,428	3.61	2.31	1.80
Armenia	2,006	1,899	1,924	1,964	-0.55	0.13	0.20	1,076	1,082	1,028	879	0.06	-0.51	-1.56
Azerbaijan	4,145	4,534	5,104	5,754	0.90	1.19	1.20	3,998	4,208	4,280	3,959	0.51	0.17	-0.78
Bahrain	636	772	896	1,004	1.94	1.49	1.13	36	19	14	13	-6.27	-3.34	-0.83
Bangladesh	29,900	42,292	59,525	82,064	3.47	3.42	3.21	99,016	112,668	121,655	123,577	1.29	0.77	0.16
Bhutan	186	309	501	774	5.06	4.83	4.35	1,752	2,105	2,449	2,686	1.84	1.51	0.92
Brunei Darussalam	237	313	389	462	2.78	2.17	1.71	96	101	101	99	0.47	0.06	-0.22
Cambodia	2,155	3,540	5,496	7,882	4.97	4.40	3.61	10,590	11,989	13,084	13,431	1.24	0.87	0.26
China[4]	455,800	608,587	757,766	872,671	2.89	2.19	1.41	818,180	745,945	666,173	573,781	-0.92	-1.13	-1.49
China, Hong Kong SAR[5]	6,637	7,416	8,080	8,610	1.11	0.86	0.64	—	—	—	—	..	..	..
China, Macao SAR[6]	444	476	509	531	0.71	0.67	0.41	—	—	—	—	..	..	..
Cyprus	540	619	709	803	1.37	1.36	1.25	247	262	263	248	0.61	0.04	-0.58
Dem. People's Republic of Korea	13,156	14,517	16,092	17,638	0.98	1.03	0.92	8,706	8,391	7,630	6,737	-0.37	-0.95	-1.24
Georgia	2,487	2,266	2,250	2,268	-0.93	-0.07	0.08	2,233	2,033	1,808	1,487	-0.93	-1.17	-1.96
India	282,480	356,388	457,619	589,957	2.32	2.50	2.54	738,604	826,904	874,413	859,121	1.13	0.56	-0.18
Indonesia	87,861	126,570	160,087	186,723	3.65	2.35	1.54	121,314	109,185	95,766	84,121	-1.05	-1.31	-1.30
Iran (Islamic Republic of)	42,606	51,625	62,962	71,827	1.92	1.99	1.32	23,759	22,658	22,074	20,426	-0.47	-0.26	-0.78
Iraq	17,008	21,667	27,491	34,810	2.42	2.38	2.36	8,066	10,867	13,031	13,987	2.98	1.82	0.71

TABLE B.2

continued

	Urban population							Rural population						
	Estimates and projections (000)				Rate of change (%)			Estimates and projections (000)				Rate of change (%)		
	2000	2010	2020	2030	2000–2010	2010–2020	2020–2030	2000	2010	2020	2030	2000–2010	2010–2020	2020–2030
Israel	5,563	6,709	7,651	8,519	1.87	1.31	1.08	521	606	645	636	1.51	0.62	-0.13
Japan	82,794	85,830	88,450	90,350	0.36	0.30	0.21	44,240	42,627	38,263	32,216	-0.37	-1.08	-1.72
Jordan	3,998	5,318	6,538	7,673	2.85	2.07	1.60	974	1,020	1,017	1,000	0.47	-0.03	-0.17
Kazakhstan	8,460	8,677	9,258	9,738	0.25	0.65	0.51	6,573	6,125	5,625	4,818	-0.71	-0.85	-1.55
Kuwait	2,190	2,998	3,644	4,241	3.14	1.95	1.52	40	49	53	55	2.04	0.78	0.32
Kyrgyzstan	1,753	2,040	2,447	2,968	1.52	1.82	1.93	3,199	3,527	3,648	3,463	0.98	0.34	-0.52
Lao People's Dem. Republic	995	1,493	2,210	3,197	4.06	3.92	3.69	4,283	5,110	5,804	6,192	1.77	1.27	0.65
Lebanon	2,922	3,292	3,669	3,987	1.19	1.08	0.83	476	481	471	441	0.12	-0.22	-0.65
Malaysia	14,209	19,778	24,592	28,435	3.31	2.18	1.45	8,788	7,753	6,882	6,284	-1.25	-1.19	-0.91
Maldives	80	119	175	247	3.99	3.87	3.44	210	252	286	300	1.82	1.25	0.47
Mongolia	1,413	1,616	1,905	2,220	1.35	1.64	1.53	1,084	1,197	1,232	1,161	0.99	0.29	-0.60
Myanmar	13,375	17,906	23,366	29,337	2.92	2.66	2.28	34,349	34,895	33,688	31,292	0.16	-0.35	-0.74
Nepal	3,281	5,446	8,537	12,679	5.07	4.49	3.96	21,149	24,445	27,143	28,746	1.45	1.05	0.57
Occupied Palestinian Territory	2,251	3,120	4,217	5,538	3.26	3.01	2.72	899	1,210	1,476	1,633	2.97	1.99	1.01
Oman	1,748	2,053	2,553	3,094	1.61	2.18	1.92	694	810	928	959	1.54	1.36	0.33
Pakistan	47,284	64,812	90,440	122,572	3.15	3.33	3.04	95,364	110,366	121,263	123,751	1.46	0.94	0.20
Philippines	44,360	59,771	74,633	87,488	2.98	2.22	1.59	31,406	30,277	28,633	26,592	-0.37	-0.56	-0.74
Qatar	576	857	999	1,122	3.98	1.54	1.16	31	37	37	36	1.96	-0.18	-0.24
Republic of Korea	37,246	39,793	41,572	42,406	0.66	0.44	0.20	9,533	8,772	7,821	6,754	-0.83	-1.15	-1.47
Saudi Arabia	17,155	22,705	28,651	34,609	2.80	2.33	1.89	4,330	4,959	5,373	5,523	1.36	0.80	0.28
Singapore	4,017	4,590	4,986	5,265	1.33	0.83	0.55	—	—	—	—	..	..	..
Sri Lanka	3,118	3,262	3,870	5,064	0.45	1.71	2.69	16,730	18,296	19,032	18,603	0.89	0.39	-0.23
Syrian Arab Republic	8,416	11,089	14,444	18,277	2.76	2.64	2.35	8,397	10,343	11,585	11,706	2.08	1.13	0.10
Tajikistan	1,594	1,695	2,125	2,868	0.61	2.26	3.00	4,565	5,297	6,091	6,369	1.49	1.40	0.45
Thailand	19,134	22,682	27,644	33,791	1.70	1.98	2.01	42,304	44,103	43,400	40,036	0.42	-0.16	-0.81
Timor-Leste	177	357	583	886	7.01	4.91	4.19	545	887	1,130	1,287	4.87	2.42	1.30
Turkey	44,176	54,382	64,179	72,968	2.08	1.66	1.28	24,059	23,698	22,596	20,908	-0.15	-0.48	-0.78
Turkmenistan	2,031	2,485	3,129	3,757	2.02	2.31	1.83	2,471	2,678	2,681	2,513	0.80	0.01	-0.65
United Arab Emirates	2,512	3,872	4,804	5,820	4.33	2.16	1.92	735	1,163	1,340	1,406	4.58	1.42	0.48
Uzbekistan	9,212	10,557	13,007	16,304	1.36	2.09	2.26	15,512	18,021	19,508	19,025	1.50	0.79	-0.25
Viet Nam	19,101	25,866	34,631	45,162	3.03	2.92	2.66	59,570	63,852	65,297	62,966	0.69	0.22	-0.36
Yemen	4,559	7,207	11,389	17,299	4.58	4.58	4.18	13,377	17,295	21,343	24,200	2.57	2.10	1.26
EUROPE	522,108	528,889	537,145	546,462	0.13	0.15	0.17	206,355	196,896	177,814	151,678	-0.47	-1.02	-1.59
Albania	1,279	1,580	1,924	2,201	2.12	1.97	1.35	1,783	1,636	1,496	1,311	-0.86	-0.90	-1.32
Andorra	61	60	59	58	-0.11	-0.29	-0.16	5	7	9	8	3.88	1.40	-0.78
Austria	5,327	5,496	5,759	6,089	0.31	0.47	0.56	2,769	2,753	2,561	2,243	-0.06	-0.72	-1.33
Belarus	7,020	7,074	7,024	6,795	0.08	-0.07	-0.33	3,009	2,410	1,915	1,519	-2.22	-2.30	-2.32
Belgium	10,006	10,215	10,316	10,358	0.21	0.10	0.04	298	280	257	230	-0.61	-0.88	-1.11
Bosnia and Herzegovina	1,663	1,913	2,111	2,244	1.40	0.99	0.61	2,184	2,022	1,716	1,395	-0.77	-1.64	-2.07
Bulgaria	5,506	5,311	5,104	4,859	-0.36	-0.40	-0.49	2,490	2,135	1,755	1,384	-1.54	-1.96	-2.38
Channel Islands[7]	45	47	52	60	0.45	0.97	1.51	102	105	106	104	0.32	0.08	-0.23
Croatia	2,505	2,617	2,688	2,771	0.44	0.27	0.30	2,001	1,914	1,679	1,393	-0.44	-1.31	-1.87
Czech Republic	7,597	7,471	7,452	7,427	-0.17	-0.03	-0.03	2,671	2,688	2,480	2,099	0.06	-0.80	-1.67
Denmark	4,544	4,745	4,928	5,126	0.43	0.38	0.39	796	757	696	626	-0.49	-0.85	-1.06
Estonia	948	908	908	914	-0.44	0.01	0.07	419	402	364	306	-0.42	-0.99	-1.72
Faeroe Islands	17	19	22	26	1.55	1.48	1.65	29	29	29	27	0.05	-0.04	-0.71
Finland[8]	3,164	3,271	3,482	3,750	0.33	0.62	0.74	2,012	2,036	1,927	1,703	0.12	-0.55	-1.24
France	44,907	47,860	50,518	52,799	0.64	0.54	0.44	14,371	13,675	12,436	10,913	-0.50	-0.95	-1.31
Germany	61,801	62,521	63,618	65,202	0.12	0.17	0.25	20,543	20,181	18,665	16,309	-0.18	-0.78	-1.35
Gibraltar	28	28	28	28	0.13	0.03	-0.09	—	—	—	—	..	..	..
Greece	6,454	6,689	7,036	7,492	0.36	0.51	0.63	4,521	4,516	4,181	3,627	-0.01	-0.77	-1.42
Holy See[9]	1	1	1	1	-0.03	0.00	-0.26	—	—	—	—	..	..	..
Hungary	6,603	6,805	6,959	7,016	0.30	0.22	0.08	3,622	3,156	2,669	2,204	-1.38	-1.68	-1.91
Iceland	260	286	310	331	0.97	0.80	0.65	22	21	20	19	-0.32	-0.52	-0.68
Ireland	2,248	2,742	3,222	3,695	1.99	1.61	1.37	1,553	1,680	1,671	1,554	0.78	-0.05	-0.72
Isle of Man	40	40	41	43	-0.02	0.24	0.47	37	36	35	32	-0.13	-0.48	-0.95
Italy	38,797	39,769	40,516	41,319	0.25	0.19	0.20	18,918	18,407	16,616	14,104	-0.27	-1.02	-1.64
Latvia	1,615	1,533	1,493	1,457	-0.53	-0.26	-0.24	758	716	636	524	-0.57	-1.18	-1.94
Liechtenstein	5	5	6	8	0.41	1.56	2.77	28	31	33	33	1.00	0.59	0.15
Lithuania	2,344	2,231	2,179	2,154	-0.50	-0.24	-0.11	1,155	1,128	1,036	874	-0.24	-0.85	-1.69
Luxembourg	365	406	455	515	1.09	1.12	1.24	71	88	97	97	2.16	1.03	0.02
Malta	366	396	416	426	0.79	0.50	0.22	26	14	10	8	-5.84	-3.80	-1.82
Monaco	33	37	42	46	1.12	1.14	1.01	—	—	—	—	..	..	..
Netherlands	12,209	13,749	14,706	15,328	1.19	0.67	0.41	3,688	2,844	2,301	1,975	-2.60	-2.12	-1.53
Norway[10]	3,425	3,683	3,943	4,250	0.72	0.68	0.75	1,077	1,048	1,016	939	-0.27	-0.30	-0.79
Poland	23,853	24,099	24,774	25,362	0.10	0.28	0.23	14,796	14,261	12,939	10,892	-0.37	-0.97	-1.72
Portugal	5,562	6,503	7,238	7,809	1.56	1.07	0.76	4,663	4,210	3,664	3,124	-1.02	-1.39	-1.59
Republic of Moldova	1,971	1,995	2,138	2,266	0.12	0.69	0.58	2,303	2,165	1,916	1,591	-0.62	-1.22	-1.86
Romania	12,076	11,632	11,841	12,175	-0.37	0.18	0.28	10,041	9,654	8,555	7,110	-0.39	-1.21	-1.85
Russian Federation	107,502	101,597	97,384	94,825	-0.56	-0.42	-0.27	39,058	38,431	35,717	30,500	-0.16	-0.73	-1.58
San Marino	25	29	30	31	1.34	0.44	0.15	2	0	0	0	-15.60	-10.93	-4.64
Serbia and Montenegro	5,444	5,595	5,924	6,349	0.27	0.57	0.69	5,101	4,883	4,411	3,765	-0.44	-1.02	-1.58
Slovakia	3,038	3,066	3,199	3,358	0.09	0.42	0.49	2,362	2,333	2,151	1,831	-0.12	-0.81	-1.61
Slovenia	998	1,016	1,059	1,117	0.18	0.42	0.53	969	943	857	725	-0.27	-0.95	-1.68
Spain	31,052	34,049	35,253	36,052	0.92	0.35	0.22	9,665	9,944	9,166	7,956	0.28	-0.81	-1.42
Sweden	7,456	7,749	8,137	8,543	0.39	0.49	0.49	1,421	1,418	1,351	1,226	-0.02	-0.49	-0.97
Switzerland	5,241	5,623	5,919	6,159	0.70	0.51	0.40	1,927	1,677	1,449	1,251	-1.39	-1.46	-1.47

TABLE B.2

continued

	Urban population							Rural population						
	Estimates and projections (000)				Rate of change (%)			Estimates and projections (000)				Rate of change (%)		
	2000	2010	2020	2030	2000–2010	2010–2020	2020–2030	2000	2010	2020	2030	2000–2010	2010–2020	2020–2030
TFYR Macedonia[11]	1,304	1,479	1,595	1,645	1.26	0.75	0.31	705	567	462	382	-2.17	-2.06	-1.90
Ukraine	32,979	30,401	28,406	26,361	-0.81	-0.68	-0.75	16,137	13,727	11,204	8,691	-1.62	-2.03	-2.54
United Kingdom	52,423	54,549	56,932	59,621	0.40	0.43	0.46	6,247	5,968	5,559	5,073	-0.46	-0.71	-0.92
LATIN AMERICA AND THE CARIBBEAN	394,212	473,561	546,342	608,968	1.83	1.43	1.09	128,717	125,210	120,613	113,409	-0.28	-0.37	-0.62
Anguilla	11	13	15	16	1.53	1.21	0.80	—	—	—	—	..	..	..
Antigua and Barbuda	29	36	46	57	2.33	2.51	2.07	48	51	50	47	0.54	-0.13	-0.67
Argentina	32,903	37,025	41,011	44,299	1.18	1.02	0.77	3,993	3,713	3,475	3,235	-0.73	-0.66	-0.71
Aruba	43	48	53	59	1.19	0.88	1.04	49	55	56	53	1.12	0.11	-0.45
Bahamas	268	315	357	394	1.63	1.26	0.98	34	29	28	26	-1.35	-0.56	-0.75
Barbados	133	152	172	188	1.35	1.23	0.90	133	121	106	90	-0.98	-1.32	-1.67
Belize	116	146	184	229	2.36	2.31	2.15	127	150	160	157	1.67	0.68	-0.22
Bolivia	5,143	6,675	8,265	9,799	2.61	2.14	1.70	3,174	3,356	3,373	3,235	0.56	0.05	-0.42
Brazil	141,159	171,757	196,182	214,603	1.96	1.33	0.90	32,699	26,740	23,012	20,902	-2.01	-1.50	-0.96
British Virgin Islands	12	15	18	20	2.31	1.74	1.31	9	8	8	7	-0.33	-0.73	-0.96
Cayman Islands	40	49	53	56	2.01	0.86	0.63	—	—	—	—	..	..	..
Chile	13,246	15,250	16,958	18,246	1.41	1.06	0.73	2,166	1,884	1,681	1,532	-1.39	-1.14	-0.93
Colombia	29,989	36,308	42,528	48,298	1.91	1.58	1.27	12,131	12,622	12,518	11,855	0.40	-0.08	-0.54
Costa Rica	2,318	3,001	3,656	4,277	2.58	1.97	1.57	1,611	1,664	1,621	1,518	0.33	-0.27	-0.66
Cuba	8,410	8,512	8,578	8,648	0.12	0.08	0.08	2,714	2,867	2,853	2,534	0.55	-0.05	-1.19
Dominica	55	62	70	77	1.15	1.27	0.93	22	21	20	18	-0.63	-0.69	-1.04
Dominican Republic	5,160	6,710	8,130	9,303	2.63	1.92	1.35	3,105	2,812	2,546	2,322	-0.99	-0.99	-0.92
Ecuador	7,420	9,255	11,199	13,004	2.21	1.91	1.49	4,885	4,937	4,826	4,516	0.10	-0.23	-0.66
El Salvador	3,668	4,577	5,575	6,640	2.21	1.97	1.75	2,613	2,884	2,975	2,877	0.99	0.31	-0.33
Falkland Islands (Malvinas)	3	3	3	3	1.36	0.72	0.31	0	0	0	0	-6.38	-4.01	-1.74
French Guiana	123	160	200	241	2.58	2.24	1.87	41	49	54	55	1.90	0.94	0.14
Grenada	31	34	43	57	0.86	2.37	2.74	70	76	83	84	0.83	0.91	0.07
Guadeloupe	428	461	480	492	0.76	0.38	0.25	2	1	0	0	-9.23	-4.83	-1.55
Guatemala	5,039	7,030	9,584	12,550	3.33	3.10	2.70	6,127	7,184	7,943	8,148	1.59	1.00	0.25
Guyana	213	214	226	250	0.06	0.54	1.01	531	537	499	426	0.12	-0.74	-1.58
Haiti	2,827	3,846	5,057	6,372	3.08	2.74	2.31	5,112	5,299	5,271	4,999	0.36	-0.05	-0.53
Honduras	2,850	3,906	5,172	6,568	3.15	2.81	2.39	3,575	4,091	4,361	4,315	1.35	0.64	-0.11
Jamaica	1,339	1,479	1,642	1,801	0.99	1.05	0.92	1,245	1,224	1,142	1,000	-0.17	-0.69	-1.33
Martinique	378	394	398	393	0.41	0.11	-0.12	8	8	7	6	-0.64	-1.03	-1.32
Mexico	74,761	87,588	99,803	110,260	1.58	1.31	1.00	25,327	25,683	24,849	22,961	0.14	-0.33	-0.79
Montserrat	0	1	1	1	4.55	2.39	2.82	3	4	4	4	1.60	0.37	-0.21
Netherlands Antilles	122	135	149	161	1.03	0.98	0.78	54	53	49	44	-0.14	-0.82	-1.12
Nicaragua	2,836	3,697	4,677	5,660	2.65	2.35	1.91	2,122	2,370	2,502	2,456	1.10	0.54	-0.18
Panama	1,941	2,624	3,233	3,752	3.02	2.09	1.49	1,009	884	794	736	-1.32	-1.08	-0.75
Paraguay	3,027	4,232	5,593	7,012	3.35	2.79	2.26	2,443	2,650	2,748	2,735	0.81	0.36	-0.05
Peru	18,575	22,158	26,128	30,060	1.76	1.65	1.40	7,378	7,906	8,121	7,871	0.69	0.27	-0.31
Puerto Rico	3,630	4,010	4,218	4,343	1.00	0.51	0.29	205	49	23	19	-14.26	-7.59	-2.15
Saint Kitts and Nevis	13	15	18	23	0.96	1.91	2.44	27	30	32	32	1.13	0.57	-0.17
Saint Lucia	43	47	55	67	0.82	1.60	2.04	111	121	125	119	0.81	0.32	-0.44
Saint Vincent and the Grenadines	52	58	66	72	1.23	1.21	0.93	64	64	59	51	-0.11	-0.71	-1.51
Suriname	313	349	377	393	1.11	0.77	0.39	121	112	100	86	-0.75	-1.14	-1.54
Trinidad and Tobago	139	184	244	316	2.78	2.82	2.62	1,146	1,140	1,102	1,016	-0.05	-0.34	-0.81
Turks and Caicos Islands	8	13	15	18	4.13	1.80	1.81	11	15	16	15	3.44	0.21	-0.59
United States Virgin Islands	103	106	105	101	0.34	-0.08	-0.47	8	5	4	3	-4.38	-3.07	-2.10
Uruguay	3,053	3,309	3,523	3,694	0.81	0.63	0.47	289	266	244	222	-0.81	-0.89	-0.94
Venezuela	22,245	27,601	32,279	36,094	2.16	1.57	1.12	2,172	1,475	1,171	1,082	-3.87	-2.31	-0.79
NORTHERN AMERICA	249,242	284,289	317,346	346,918	1.32	1.10	0.89	65,725	61,773	57,654	53,160	-0.62	-0.69	-0.81
Bermuda	63	65	66	66	0.33	0.13	0.00	—	—	—	—	..	..	..
Canada	24,366	27,179	29,990	32,942	1.09	0.98	0.94	6,323	6,501	6,450	6,110	0.28	-0.08	-0.54
Greenland	46	49	51	53	0.58	0.53	0.39	10	9	8	7	-1.31	-1.30	-1.28
Saint-Pierre-et-Miquelon	5	5	6	7	0.61	1.01	0.77	1	1	1	1	0.23	0.06	-0.61
United States of America	224,763	256,991	287,232	313,851	1.34	1.11	0.89	59,391	55,262	51,195	47,043	-0.72	-0.76	-0.85
OCEANIA	21,813	24,925	28,119	31,394	1.33	1.21	1.10	9,135	10,091	10,790	11,149	1.00	0.67	0.33
American Samoa	51	67	81	94	2.60	1.92	1.56	6	5	4	4	-2.56	-1.34	-0.20
Australia[12]	16,624	18,892	21,135	23,183	1.28	1.12	0.92	2,448	2,309	2,182	2,055	-0.58	-0.56	-0.60
Cook Islands	12	13	13	13	0.60	0.24	-0.21	7	5	4	3	-3.48	-2.67	-2.45
Fiji	392	469	540	612	1.80	1.42	1.25	419	409	379	339	-0.23	-0.77	-1.11
French Polynesia	124	142	165	196	1.35	1.56	1.67	112	133	142	137	1.66	0.68	-0.36
Guam	145	173	197	219	1.76	1.32	1.06	11	10	9	9	-1.04	-0.73	-0.40
Kiribati	39	56	76	96	3.75	2.99	2.39	51	53	53	51	0.33	-0.04	-0.30
Marshall Islands	34	49	67	85	3.60	3.04	2.40	18	23	27	28	2.69	1.51	0.43
Micronesia (Fed. States of)	24	26	29	35	0.75	1.32	1.67	83	88	88	80	0.56	-0.02	-0.92
Nauru	12	14	16	17	1.72	0.93	0.65	—	—	—	—	..	..	..
New Caledonia	133	169	205	243	2.34	1.98	1.69	82	89	91	88	0.79	0.21	-0.31
New Zealand	3,271	3,620	3,897	4,148	1.01	0.74	0.62	547	552	528	487	0.09	-0.44	-0.81
Niue	1	1	1	1	1.15	2.41	1.95	1	1	1	1	-1.54	-0.36	-0.87
Northern Mariana Islands	65	86	100	112	2.84	1.50	1.10	5	4	4	4	-1.00	-1.06	-0.44
Palau	13	14	16	17	0.69	0.79	0.75	6	6	6	5	0.47	-0.19	-0.95
Papua New Guinea	699	901	1,258	1,876	2.53	3.34	4.00	4,599	5,549	6,344	6,907	1.88	1.34	0.85
Pitcairn	—	—	—	—	..	..	..	0	0	0	0	0.00	0.00	-1.09
Samoa	39	44	51	63	1.29	1.51	1.99	139	145	139	126	0.43	-0.43	-0.93
Solomon Islands	66	100	150	223	4.16	4.09	3.94	353	438	503	540	2.15	1.39	0.70

TABLE B.2

continued

	Urban population							Rural population						
	Estimates and projections (000)				Rate of change (%)			Estimates and projections (000)				Rate of change (%)		
	2000	2010	2020	2030	2000–2010	2010–2020	2020–2030	2000	2010	2020	2030	2000–2010	2010–2020	2020–2030
Tokelau	—	—	—	—	..	..	..	1	1	2	2	0.46	0.93	0.61
Tonga	23	26	31	36	1.22	1.67	1.59	77	77	72	62	0.02	-0.72	-1.46
Tuvalu	5	5	6	7	1.37	1.44	1.46	5	5	5	4	-0.39	-0.66	-0.97
Vanuatu	42	59	85	119	3.55	3.58	3.40	150	172	189	194	1.40	0.89	0.29
Wallis and Futuna Islands	—	—	—	—	..	..	..	15	17	19	22	1.10	1.46	1.09

Source: United Nations, Department of Economic and Social Affairs, Population Division, 2006

Notes:

(1) Including the island of Mayotte.
(2) Including Agalega, Rodrigues and Saint Brandon.
(3) Including Ascension and Tristan da Cunha.
(4) For statistical purposes, the data for China do not include Hong Kong and Macao Special Administrative Regions (SAR) of China.
(5) As of 1 July 1997, Hong Kong became a Special Administrative Region (SAR) of China.
(6) As of 20 December 1999, Macao became a Special Administrative Region (SAR) of China.
(7) Including the islands of Guernsey and Jersey.
(8) Including Åland Islands.
(9) Refers to the Vatican City State.
(10) Including Svalbard and Jan Mayen islands.
(11) The former Yugoslav Republic of Macedonia.
(12) Including Christmas Island, Cocos (Keeling) Islands and Norfolk Island.

TABLE B.3

Urbanization and Urban Slum Dwellers

	Level of urbanization						Urban slum dwellers							
	Estimates and projections (%)				Rate of change (%)		Estimates and projections (000)				% of urban population		Slum projection Target 11 (000)	
	1990	2000	2010	2020	1990-2010	2010-2020	1990	2001	2010	2020	1990	2001	2010	2020
WORLD	43.0	46.7	50.8	55.1	0.83	0.82	714,972	912,918	1,115,002	1,392,416	...	31.6	1,070,494	1,292,065
AFRICA	32.0	36.2	40.5	45.3	1.18	1.11	122,692	187,563	270,948	413,846	...	61.3	260,941	388,529
Algeria	52.1	59.8	66.5	71.9	1.22	0.77	1,508	2,101	2,755	3,725	11.8	11.8	2,649	3,474
Angola	37.1	50.0	56.6	62.7	2.10	1.02	2,193	3,918	6,300	10,677	83.1	83.1	6,077	10,075
Benin	34.5	38.4	42.1	47.3	1.00	1.17	1,288	2,318	3,749	6,394	80.3	83.6	3,617	6,035
Botswana	41.9	53.2	61.2	67.6	1.89	1.00	311	466	650	939	59.2	60.7	625	879
Burkina Faso	13.8	16.5	20.3	25.7	1.94	2.33	987	1,528	2,185	3,250	80.9	76.5	2,104	3,047
Burundi	6.3	8.6	11.6	15.6	3.09	2.96	294	394	501	653	83.3	65.3	481	608
Cameroon	40.7	50.0	58.9	66.0	1.84	1.15	2,906	5,064	7,977	13,217	62.1	67.0	7,693	12,459
Cape Verde	44.1	53.4	61.0	67.3	1.62	0.98	106	193	314	540	70.3	69.6	303	510
Central African Republic	36.8	37.6	38.9	42.4	0.28	0.87	1,038	1,455	1,919	2,610	94.0	92.4	1,845	2,435
Chad	20.8	23.4	27.6	33.9	1.42	2.05	1,218	1,947	2,856	4,373	99.3	99.1	2,751	4,106
Comoros	28.2	33.8	40.4	47.7	1.81	1.66	91	151	228	361	61.7	61.2	220	340
Congo	54.3	58.3	62.1	66.3	0.67	0.66	1,050	1,852	2,945	4,930	84.5	90.1	2,840	4,650
Côte d'Ivoire	39.7	43.0	47.2	52.8	0.86	1.11	2,532	4,884	8,361	15,194	50.5	67.9	8,074	14,381
Dem. Republic of the Congo	27.8	29.8	35.2	42.0	1.18	1.77	5,366	7,985	11,054	15,865	51.9	49.5	10,637	14,846
Djibouti	76.0	83.3	88.1	90.6	0.74	0.28	...	...	...	...	...	...	...	...
Egypt	43.5	42.5	43.7	47.7	0.03	0.87	14,087	11,762	10,148	8,613	57.5	39.9	9,671	7,733
Equatorial Guinea	34.8	38.8	39.7	43.3	0.66	0.86	112	201	323	547	89.1	86.5	311	516
Eritrea	15.8	17.8	21.6	27.5	1.56	2.41	342	510	707	1,016	69.9	69.9	680	950
Ethiopia	12.6	14.9	17.4	21.3	1.59	2.04	5,984	10,159	15,665	25,347	99.0	99.4	15,102	23,866
Gabon	69.1	80.1	86.0	88.8	1.09	0.31	357	688	1,174	2,129	56.1	66.2	1,134	2,015
Gambia	38.3	49.1	58.1	65.0	2.09	1.12	155	280	455	781	67.0	67.0	439	737
Ghana	36.5	44.0	51.5	58.5	1.73	1.27	4,083	4,993	5,886	7,067	80.4	69.6	5,647	6,540
Guinea	28.0	31.0	35.3	41.4	1.15	1.58	1,145	1,672	2,278	3,213	79.6	72.3	2,192	3,003
Guinea-Bissau	28.1	29.7	30.0	32.8	0.32	0.90	210	371	591	990	93.4	93.4	570	934
Kenya	18.2	19.7	22.2	26.6	0.98	1.81	3,985	7,605	12,905	23,223	70.4	70.7	12,460	21,972
Lesotho	17.2	17.8	20.1	24.7	0.78	2.06	168	337	596	1,121	49.8	57.0	576	1,062
Liberia	45.3	54.3	61.5	67.9	1.53	0.99	632	788	943	1,153	70.2	55.7	905	1,068
Libyan Arab Jamahiriya	78.6	83.1	86.3	88.4	0.47	0.24	1,242	1,674	2,138	2,806	35.2	35.2	2,055	2,612
Madagascar	23.6	26.0	28.2	32.6	0.89	1.47	2,562	4,603	7,434	12,664	90.9	92.9	7,172	11,953
Malawi	11.6	15.1	19.5	25.1	2.58	2.53	1,033	1,590	2,262	3,348	94.6	91.1	2,178	3,138
Mali	23.3	27.9	33.3	40.0	1.79	1.81	1,968	3,361	5,208	8,474	94.1	93.2	5,022	7,981
Mauritania	39.7	40.0	41.4	45.4	0.22	0.92	827	1,531	2,534	4,437	94.3	94.3	2,446	4,193
Mauritius	43.9	42.7	42.8	46.1	-0.12	0.74	...	...	...	...	...	...	...	...
Morocco	48.4	55.1	61.9	67.8	1.23	0.90	4,457	5,579	6,705	8,223	37.4	32.7	6,435	7,621
Mozambique	21.1	30.7	38.4	46.2	3.00	1.85	2,722	5,841	10,909	21,842	94.5	94.1	10,549	20,753
Namibia	27.7	32.4	38.0	44.5	1.59	1.57	155	213	276	368	42.3	37.9	265	343
Niger	15.4	16.2	17.8	21.3	0.73	1.77	1,191	2,277	3,869	6,972	96.0	96.2	3,736	6,597
Nigeria	35.0	43.9	52.2	59.3	1.99	1.29	24,096	41,595	55,732	76,749	80.0	79.2	57,422	76,943
Réunion	81.2	89.9	94.0	95.7	0.73	0.17	...	...	...	...	...	...	...	...
Rwanda	5.4	13.8	23.9	33.4	7.43	3.35	296	437	601	857	82.2	87.9	579	802
Saint Helena	41.6	39.2	39.5	43.4	-0.25	0.94	–	–	...	...	...	...	...	...
São Tomé and Príncipe	43.6	53.4	62.2	69.0	1.77	1.04	–	1	...	...	...	...	...	...
Senegal	39.0	40.6	42.9	47.1	0.48	0.93	2,276	3,555	5,120	7,679	77.6	76.4	4,930	7,203
Seychelles	49.3	51.0	55.3	61.1	0.58	0.99	–	1	...	...	...	...	...	...
Sierra Leone	30.1	37.0	44.4	52.0	1.94	1.58	1,107	1,642	2,266	3,243	90.9	95.8	2,181	3,034
Somalia	29.7	33.3	37.5	43.0	1.17	1.39	1,670	2,482	3,433	4,923	96.3	97.1	3,304	4,606
South Africa	52.0	56.9	61.7	66.6	0.85	0.76	8,207	8,376	8,517	8,677	46.2	33.2	8,147	7,930
Sudan	26.6	36.1	45.2	53.2	2.65	1.62	5,708	10,107	16,131	27,118	86.4	85.7	15,560	25,580
Swaziland	22.9	23.3	25.5	30.3	0.53	1.72	...	...	...	...	...	...	...	...
Togo	30.1	36.6	43.7	51.2	1.87	1.58	796	1,273	1,870	2,866	80.9	80.6	1,801	2,691
Tunisia	59.6	63.4	67.2	71.1	0.60	0.57	425	234	144	84	9.0	3.7	136	71
Uganda	11.1	12.1	13.3	16.0	0.93	1.82	1,806	3,241	5,231	8,904	93.8	93.0	5,047	8,403
United Republic of Tanzania	18.9	22.3	26.4	31.8	1.67	1.86	5,601	11,031	19,205	35,561	99.1	92.1	18,551	33,685
Western Sahara	88.5	91.2	92.0	92.8	0.19	0.09	–	5	...	...	...	...	...	...
Zambia	39.4	34.8	35.7	38.9	-0.49	0.87	2,284	3,136	4,065	5,423	72.0	74.0	3,907	5,053
Zimbabwe	29.0	33.8	38.3	43.9	1.39	1.38	116	157	202	266	4.0	3.4	194	247
ASIA	31.9	37.1	42.5	48.1	1.43	1.25	420,415	533,385	648,605	806,731	...	...	622,664	748,388
Afghanistan	18.3	21.3	24.8	29.7	1.52	1.80	2,458	4,945	8,760	16,536	98.5	98.5	8,464	15,676
Armenia	67.5	65.1	63.7	65.2	-0.29	0.23	...	...	...	...	...	...	...	...
Azerbaijan	53.7	50.9	51.9	54.4	-0.18	0.48	...	...	...	...	...	...	...	...
Bahrain	88.1	94.6	97.6	98.5	0.51	0.09	0	12	...	...	...	...	...	...
Bangladesh	19.8	23.2	27.3	32.9	1.61	1.85	18,988	30,403	44,687	68,553	87.3	84.7	43,047	64,378
Bhutan	7.2	9.6	12.8	17.0	2.90	2.83	61	70	78	88	70.0	44.1	75	81
Brunei Darussalam	65.8	71.1	75.7	79.3	0.70	0.48	3	5	7	9	...	...	6	9
Cambodia	12.6	16.9	22.8	29.6	2.96	2.61	870	1,696	2,929	5,375	71.7	72.2	2,829	5,089
China	27.4	35.8	44.9	53.2	2.47	1.69	137,929	178,256	219,878	277,616	43.6	37.8	211,141	257,793
China, Hong Kong SAR	99.5	100.0	100.0	100.0	0.02	0.00	113	139	163	196	...	...	156	181
China, Macao SAR	99.8	100.0	100.0	100.0	0.01	0.00	7	9	10	12	...	...	10	11
Cyprus	66.8	68.6	70.3	73.0	0.26	0.38	...	...	...	...	...	...	...	...
Dem. People's Republic of Korea	58.4	60.2	63.4	67.8	0.41	0.68	117	95	80	67	...	...	77	60
Georgia	55.2	52.7	52.7	55.4	-0.23	0.51	...	...	...	...	...	...	...	...
India	25.5	27.7	30.1	34.4	0.82	1.32	131,174	158,418	184,868	219,466	60.8	55.5	177,332	202,950
Indonesia	30.6	42.0	53.7	62.6	2.81	1.53	17,964	20,877	23,608	27,064	32.2	23.1	22,632	24,965
Iran (Islamic Republic of)	56.3	64.2	69.5	74.0	1.05	0.63	17,094	20,406	23,587	27,707	51.9	44.2	22,621	25,603
Iraq	69.7	67.8	66.6	67.8	-0.23	0.18	6,825	9,026	11,346	14,630	56.7	56.7	10,899	13,604

TABLE B.3

continued

	Level of urbanization						Urban slum dwellers							
	Estimates and projections (%)				Rate of change (%)		Estimates and projections (000)				% of urban population		Slum projection Target 11 (000)	
	1990	2000	2010	2020	1990-2010	2010-2020	1990	2001	2010	2020	1990	2001	2010	2020
Israel	90.4	91.4	91.7	92.2	0.07	0.06	81	113	148	199	...	...	142	186
Japan	63.1	65.2	66.8	69.8	0.29	0.44	...	...	...	...	...	...	...	...
Jordan	72.2	80.4	83.9	86.5	0.75	0.31	388	623	920	1,416	16.5	15.7	886	1,330
Kazakhstan	56.3	56.3	58.6	62.2	0.20	0.59	...	...	...	...	...	...	...	...
Kuwait	98.0	98.2	98.4	98.6	0.02	0.02	60	56	53	50	...	...	51	45
Kyrgyzstan	37.8	35.4	36.6	40.1	-0.15	0.91	...	...	...	...	...	...	...	...
Lao People's Dem. Republic	15.4	18.9	22.6	27.6	1.91	1.99	422	705	1,073	1,711	...	...	1,034	1,610
Lebanon	83.1	86.0	87.2	88.6	0.24	0.16	1,142	1,602	2,112	2,872	66.1	66.1	2,031	2,679
Malaysia	49.8	61.8	71.8	78.1	1.83	0.84	177	262	361	515	50.0	50.0	347	482
Maldives	25.8	27.5	32.1	38.0	1.08	1.70	–	–	–	–	...	...	...	...
Mongolia	57.0	56.6	57.5	60.7	0.04	0.55	866	940	1,006	1,084	68.5	64.9	963	995
Myanmar	24.9	28.0	33.9	41.0	1.55	1.89	3,105	3,596	4,056	4,635	31.1	26.4	3,888	4,275
Nepal	8.9	13.4	18.2	23.9	3.61	2.72	1,574	2,656	4,077	6,562	96.9	92.4	3,930	6,177
Occupied Palestinian Territory	67.9	71.5	72.1	74.1	0.30	0.28	–	1,333	...	...	–	60.0	...	...
Oman	65.4	71.6	71.7	73.3	0.46	0.23	671	1,214	1,972	3,379	60.5	60.5	1,902	3,190
Pakistan	30.6	33.1	37.0	42.7	0.96	1.44	26,416	35,627	45,507	59,730	78.7	73.6	43,728	55,602
Philippines	48.8	58.5	66.4	72.3	1.54	0.85	16,346	20,183	23,984	29,053	54.9	44.1	23,015	26,904
Qatar	92.2	94.9	95.8	96.5	0.19	0.07	8	11	13	17	...	...	13	16
Republic of Korea	73.8	79.6	81.9	84.2	0.52	0.27	11,728	14,385	17,002	20,470	37.0	37.0	16,313	18,948
Saudi Arabia	76.6	79.8	82.1	84.2	0.35	0.26	2,385	3,609	5,066	7,382	19.8	19.8	4,876	6,914
Singapore	100.0	100.0	100.0	100.0	0.00	0.00	–	–	–	–	...	...	...	...
Sri Lanka	17.2	15.7	15.1	16.9	-0.64	1.11	899	597	428	295	24.8	13.6	406	258
Syrian Arab Republic	48.9	50.1	51.7	55.5	0.28	0.70	629	892	1,187	1,630	10.4	10.4	1,141	1,522
Tajikistan	31.5	25.9	24.2	25.9	-1.32	0.65	...	...	...	...	...	...	...	...
Thailand	29.4	31.1	34.0	38.9	0.72	1.36	1,998	253	47	7	19.5	2.0	42	2
Timor-Leste	20.8	24.5	28.7	34.0	1.60	1.71	1	7	28	140	...	...	28	136
Turkey	59.2	64.7	69.6	74.0	0.81	0.60	7,997	8,011	8,022	8,035	23.3	17.9	7,671	7,332
Turkmenistan	45.1	45.1	48.1	53.9	0.33	1.12	...	...	...	...	...	...	...	...
United Arab Emirates	79.1	77.4	76.9	78.2	-0.14	0.17	32	46	62	86	...	...	59	80
Uzbekistan	40.1	37.3	36.9	40.0	-0.41	0.80	...	...	...	...	...	...	...	...
Viet Nam	20.3	24.3	28.8	34.7	1.77	1.84	8,100	9,197	10,204	11,453	60.5	47.4	9,779	10,548
Yemen	20.9	25.4	29.4	34.8	1.70	1.68	1,787	3,110	4,892	8,092	67.5	65.1	4,717	7,628
EUROPE	70.6	71.7	72.9	75.1	0.16	0.31	...	...	...	...	...	...	...	...
Albania	36.4	41.8	49.1	56.2	1.49	1.35	...	...	...	...	...	...	...	...
Andorra	94.8	92.3	89.0	87.2	-0.31	-0.20	...	...	...	...	...	...	...	...
Austria	65.8	65.8	66.6	69.2	0.06	0.38	...	...	...	...	...	...	...	...
Belarus	66.4	70.0	74.6	78.6	0.58	0.52	...	...	...	...	...	...	...	...
Belgium	96.4	97.1	97.3	97.6	0.05	0.02	...	...	...	...	...	...	...	...
Bosnia and Herzegovina	39.2	43.2	48.6	55.2	1.07	1.26	...	...	...	...	...	...	...	...
Bulgaria	66.4	68.9	71.3	74.4	0.36	0.42	...	...	...	...	...	...	...	...
Channel Islands	31.4	30.5	30.8	32.7	-0.10	0.61	...	...	...	...	...	...	...	...
Croatia	54.0	55.6	57.8	61.6	0.33	0.64	...	...	...	...	...	...	...	...
Czech Republic	75.2	74.0	73.5	75.0	-0.11	0.20	...	...	...	...	...	...	...	...
Denmark	84.8	85.1	86.2	87.6	0.08	0.16	...	...	...	...	...	...	...	...
Estonia	71.1	69.4	69.3	71.4	-0.13	0.29	...	...	...	...	...	...	...	...
Faeroe Islands	30.6	36.3	39.9	43.6	1.33	0.89	...	...	...	...	...	...	...	...
Finland	61.4	61.1	61.6	64.4	0.02	0.43	...	...	...	...	...	...	...	...
France	74.1	75.8	77.8	80.2	0.25	0.31	...	...	...	...	...	...	...	...
Germany	73.4	75.1	75.6	77.3	0.15	0.22	...	...	...	...	...	...	...	...
Gibraltar	100.0	100.0	100.0	100.0	0.00	0.00	...	...	...	...	...	...	...	...
Greece	58.8	58.8	59.7	62.7	0.07	0.50	...	...	...	...	...	...	...	...
Hungary	65.8	64.6	68.3	72.3	0.18	0.56	...	...	...	...	...	...	...	...
Iceland	90.8	92.3	93.2	94.0	0.13	0.08	...	...	...	...	...	...	...	...
Ireland	56.9	59.1	62.0	65.9	0.43	0.60	...	...	...	...	...	...	...	...
Isle of Man	51.7	51.8	52.1	53.9	0.03	0.34	...	...	...	...	...	...	...	...
Italy	66.7	67.2	68.4	70.9	0.12	0.37	...	...	...	...	...	...	...	...
Latvia	69.3	68.1	68.2	70.1	-0.08	0.28	...	...	...	...	...	...	...	...
Liechtenstein	16.9	15.1	14.4	15.6	-0.81	0.83	...	...	...	...	...	...	...	...
Lithuania	67.6	67.0	66.4	67.8	-0.09	0.20	...	...	...	...	...	...	...	...
Luxembourg	80.9	83.8	82.2	82.4	0.08	0.02	...	...	...	...	...	...	...	...
Malta	90.4	93.4	96.5	97.7	0.33	0.12	...	...	...	...	...	...	...	...
Monaco	100.0	100.0	100.0	100.0	0.00	0.00	...	...	...	...	...	...	...	...
Netherlands	68.7	76.8	82.9	86.5	0.94	0.43	...	...	...	...	...	...	...	...
Norway	72.0	76.1	77.9	79.5	0.39	0.21	...	...	...	...	...	...	...	...
Poland	61.3	61.7	62.8	65.7	0.13	0.45	...	...	...	...	...	...	...	...
Portugal	47.9	54.4	60.7	66.4	1.18	0.90	...	...	...	...	...	...	...	...
Republic of Moldova	46.8	46.1	48.0	52.7	0.13	0.95	...	...	...	...	...	...	...	...
Romania	54.3	54.6	54.6	58.1	0.03	0.61	...	...	...	...	...	...	...	...
Russian Federation	73.4	73.4	72.6	73.2	-0.06	0.08	...	...	...	...	...	...	...	...
San Marino	90.1	93.5	98.7	99.6	0.46	0.09	...	...	...	...	...	...	...	...
Serbia and Montenegro	50.9	51.6	53.4	57.3	0.24	0.71	...	...	...	...	...	...	...	...
Slovakia	56.5	56.3	56.8	59.8	0.03	0.51	...	...	...	...	...	...	...	...
Slovenia	50.4	50.8	51.9	55.3	0.15	0.63	...	...	...	...	...	...	...	...
Spain	75.4	76.3	77.4	79.4	0.13	0.25	...	...	...	...	...	...	...	...
Sweden	83.1	84.0	84.5	85.8	0.09	0.14	...	...	...	...	...	...	...	...
Switzerland	68.4	73.1	77.0	80.3	0.59	0.42	...	...	...	...	...	...	...	...
TFYR Macedonia	57.8	64.9	72.3	77.5	1.12	0.70	...	...	...	...	...	...	...	...

TABLE B.3

continued

	Level of urbanization						Urban slum dwellers							
	Estimates and projections (%)				Rate of change (%)		Estimates and projections (000)				% of urban population		Slum projection Target 11 (000)	
	1990	2000	2010	2020	1990-2010	2010-2020	1990	2001	2010	2020	1990	2001	2010	2020
Ukraine	66.8	67.1	68.9	71.7	0.16	0.40	...	...	...	...	...	...	...	...
United Kingdom	88.7	89.4	90.1	91.1	0.08	0.11	...	...	...	...	...	...	...	...
LATIN AMERICA AND THE CARIBBEAN	70.9	75.4	79.1	81.9	0.54	0.35	110,837	127,566	143,116	162,626	35.4	31.9	137,174	149,913
Anguilla	100.0	100.0	100.0	100.0	0.00	0.00	3	5	7	10	40.6	40.6	7	9
Antigua and Barbuda	35.4	37.3	41.6	48.1	0.80	1.46	2	2	2	2	6.9	6.9	2	2
Argentina	87.0	89.2	90.9	92.2	0.22	0.14	8,597	10,964	13,379	16,690	30.5	33.1	12,844	15,486
Aruba	50.3	46.7	46.9	48.8	-0.35	0.40	1	1	2	2	...	...	1	2
Bahamas	83.6	88.8	91.5	92.8	0.45	0.14	4	5	7	8	...	...	6	8
Barbados	44.8	49.9	55.7	61.8	1.09	1.05	1	1	2	2	...	...	1	2
Belize	47.5	47.7	49.4	53.5	0.20	0.79	48	69	92	127	54.2	62.0	88	119
Bolivia	55.6	61.8	66.5	71.0	0.90	0.65	2,555	3,284	4,032	5,064	70.0	61.3	3,871	4,701
Brazil	74.8	81.2	86.5	89.5	0.73	0.34	49,806	51,676	53,259	55,074	45.0	36.6	50,958	50,392
British Virgin Islands	50.2	57.3	63.6	69.1	1.18	0.83	0	0	1	1	...	...	1	1
Cayman Islands	100.0	100.0	100.0	100.0	0.00	0.00	1	1	1	2	...	...	1	2
Chile	83.3	85.9	89.0	91.0	0.33	0.22	432	1,143	2,534	6,136	4.0	8.6	2,456	5,868
Colombia	68.7	71.2	74.2	77.3	0.38	0.40	6,239	7,057	7,806	8,732	26.0	21.8	7,480	8,039
Costa Rica	50.7	59.0	64.3	69.3	1.19	0.74	195	313	461	710	11.9	12.8	444	667
Cuba	73.4	75.6	74.8	75.0	0.10	0.03	156	169	180	194	...	...	173	178
Dominica	67.7	71.1	74.6	78.1	0.49	0.46	8	7	6	6	16.6	14.0	6	5
Dominican Republic	55.2	62.4	70.5	76.2	1.22	0.78	2,327	2,111	1,950	1,785	56.4	37.6	1,861	1,615
Ecuador	55.1	60.3	65.2	69.9	0.84	0.69	1,588	2,095	2,629	3,382	28.1	25.6	2,525	3,144
El Salvador	49.2	58.4	61.3	65.2	1.10	0.61	1,126	1,386	1,644	1,986	44.7	35.2	1,577	1,839
Falkland Islands (Malvinas)	74.5	85.8	92.9	95.4	1.10	0.27	...	...	...	...	...	...	...	...
French Guiana	74.5	75.1	76.4	78.6	0.12	0.29	11	16	23	32	12.9	12.9	22	30
Grenada	32.2	31.0	31.0	34.2	-0.19	0.98	2	2	3	3	6.9	6.9	3	3
Guadeloupe	98.5	99.6	99.8	99.9	0.07	0.01	27	30	33	36	6.9	6.9	31	33
Guatemala	41.1	45.1	49.5	54.7	0.92	1.00	2,192	2,884	3,609	4,632	65.8	61.8	3,467	4,305
Guyana	29.5	28.6	28.5	31.2	-0.18	0.90	12	14	16	18	4.9	4.9	15	16
Haiti	29.5	35.6	42.1	49.0	1.78	1.52	1,728	2,574	3,568	5,128	84.9	85.7	3,434	4,799
Honduras	40.3	44.4	48.8	54.3	0.97	1.05	488	638	793	1,012	24.0	18.1	762	940
Jamaica	49.4	51.8	54.7	59.0	0.51	0.75	356	525	721	1,026	29.2	35.7	693	959
Martinique	97.6	97.8	98.0	98.2	0.02	0.02	6	7	8	9	...	...	8	8
Mexico	72.5	74.7	77.3	80.1	0.33	0.35	13,923	14,692	15,353	16,123	23.1	19.6	14,694	14,771
Montserrat	12.5	11.0	14.3	16.9	0.64	1.71	...	...	...	...	...	...	...	...
Netherlands Antilles	68.3	69.3	71.7	75.3	0.24	0.48	1	2	2	2	...	...	2	2
Nicaragua	53.1	57.2	60.9	65.1	0.69	0.67	1,638	2,382	3,237	4,550	80.7	80.9	3,114	4,253
Panama	53.9	65.8	74.8	80.3	1.64	0.71	397	505	615	766	30.8	30.8	591	711
Paraguay	48.7	55.3	61.5	67.1	1.17	0.87	756	797	832	873	36.8	25.0	796	800
Peru	68.9	71.6	73.7	76.3	0.34	0.34	8,979	12,993	17,581	24,601	60.4	68.1	16,911	22,988
Puerto Rico	72.2	94.6	98.8	99.5	1.57	0.07	50	59	68	80	...	...	66	74
Saint Kitts and Nevis	34.6	32.8	32.4	35.4	-0.33	0.88	1	1	1	1	...	...	1	1
Saint Lucia	29.3	28.0	28.0	30.6	-0.24	0.90	6	7	8	9	11.9	11.9	7	8
Saint Vincent and the Grenadines	40.6	44.4	47.8	52.6	0.81	0.96	2	3	4	6	...	...	4	6
Suriname	68.3	72.1	75.6	79.0	0.51	0.43	18	22	25	29	6.9	6.9	24	27
Trinidad and Tobago	8.5	10.8	13.9	18.1	2.43	2.66	292	310	326	344	34.7	32.0	312	315
Turks and Caicos Islands	42.6	43.5	45.2	49.1	0.30	0.84	...	...	...	...	...	...	...	...
United States Virgin Islands	87.7	92.6	95.3	96.5	0.41	0.12	1	4	13	49	...	...	13	47
Uruguay	89.0	91.3	92.5	93.5	0.20	0.11	191	62	24	9	6.9	2.0	23	6
Venezuela	84.0	91.1	94.9	96.5	0.61	0.16	6,664	8,738	10,906	13,952	40.7	40.7	10,475	12,967
NORTHERN AMERICA	75.4	79.1	82.1	84.6	0.43	0.30	...	...	...	...	...	...	...	...
Bermuda	100.0	100.0	100.0	100.0	0.00	0.00	...	...	...	...	...	...	...	...
Canada	76.6	79.4	80.7	82.3	0.26	0.20	...	...	...	...	...	...	...	...
Greenland	79.7	81.6	84.3	86.5	0.28	0.27	8	9	9	9	18.5	18.5	8	8
Saint-Pierre-et-Miquelon	88.9	88.9	89.3	90.2	0.02	0.10	1	1	...	...	8.7	8.7	...	...
United States of America	75.3	79.1	82.3	84.9	0.44	0.31	...	...	...	...	...	...	...	...
OCEANIA	70.3	70.5	71.2	72.3	0.06	0.15	...	...	...	...	...	...	...	...
American Samoa	80.9	88.8	93.0	94.8	0.69	0.20	...	...	...	...	...	...	...	...
Australia	85.4	87.2	89.1	90.6	0.21	0.17	...	...	...	...	...	...	...	...
Cook Islands	56.9	65.2	73.8	79.0	1.30	0.68	...	...	...	...	...	...	...	...
Fiji	41.6	48.3	53.4	58.8	1.25	0.96	...	...	...	...	...	...	...	...
French Polynesia	55.9	52.4	51.6	53.8	-0.40	0.42	...	...	...	...	...	...	...	...
Guam	90.8	93.2	94.7	95.7	0.21	0.10	...	...	...	...	...	...	...	...
Kiribati	35.0	43.0	51.5	59.0	1.93	1.35	...	...	...	...	...	...	...	...
Marshall Islands	64.7	65.8	67.8	71.1	0.24	0.47	...	...	...	...	...	...	...	...
Micronesia (Fed. States of)	25.8	22.3	22.7	25.1	-0.65	1.02	...	...	...	...	...	...	...	...
Nauru	100.0	100.0	100.0	100.0	0.00	0.00	...	...	...	...	...	...	...	...
New Caledonia	59.6	61.9	65.5	69.4	0.47	0.57	...	...	...	...	...	...	...	...
New Zealand	84.7	85.7	86.8	88.1	0.12	0.15	...	...	...	...	...	...	...	...
Niue	30.9	33.7	39.9	46.7	1.28	1.57	...	...	...	...	...	...	...	...
Northern Mariana Islands	89.8	93.3	95.3	96.3	0.30	0.11	...	...	...	...	...	...	...	...
Palau	69.6	69.6	70.1	72.1	0.03	0.28	...	...	...	...	...	...	...	...
Papua New Guinea	13.1	13.2	14.0	16.5	0.30	1.70	...	...	...	...	...	...	...	...
Pitcairn	0.0	0.0	0.0	0.0	..	..	...	...	...	...	...	...	...	...
Samoa	21.2	21.9	23.4	27.1	0.49	1.45	...	...	...	...	...	...	...	...
Solomon Islands	13.7	15.7	18.6	23.0	1.52	2.14	...	...	...	...	...	...	...	...
Tokelau	0.0	0.0	0.0	0.0	..	..	...	...	...	...	...	...	...	...

TABLE B.3

continued

	Level of urbanization						Urban slum dwellers							
	Estimates and projections (%)				Rate of change (%)		Estimates and projections (000)				% of urban population		Slum projection Target 11 (000)	
	1990	2000	2010	2020	1990-2010	2010-2020	1990	2001	2010	2020	1990	2001	2010	2020
Tonga	22.7	23.2	25.3	30.1	0.55	1.73	...	...	...	...	...	...	...	...
Tuvalu	40.7	46.0	50.4	55.6	1.08	0.98	...	...	...	...	...	...	...	...
Vanuatu	18.7	21.7	25.6	31.0	1.56	1.93	...	...	...	...	...	...	...	...
Wallis and Futuna Islands	0.0	0.0	0.0	0.0	..	..	...	...	...	...	...	...	...	...

Sources: UN Population Division, 2006; UN-Habitat, 2006

TABLE B.4

Households: Total Number and Rate of Change

	Estimates and projections (000)				Annual rate of change (%)			Five-year increment (000)				
	2000	2010	2020	2030	2000–2010	2010–2020	2020–2030	2005–2010	2010–2015	2015–2020	2020–2025	2025–2030
WORLD	1,568,693	1,939,206	2,305,895	2,653,762	2.12	1.73	1.41	192,576	184,059	182,630	175,921	171,946
AFRICA	163,509	225,572	295,506	387,272	3.22	2.70	2.70	32,596	32,827	37,107	42,760	49,006
Algeria	4,807	5,953	7,348	8,461	2.14	2.11	1.41	584	672	723	636	477
Angola	2,873	4,039	5,893	8,572	3.41	3.78	3.75	684	843	1,011	1,211	1,468
Benin	1,244	1,852	2,581	3,583	3.97	3.32	3.28	323	341	387	458	544
Botswana	397	417	417	442	0.48	-0.00	0.60	-5	-5	5	11	15
Burkina Faso	1,544	1,906	2,391	3,022	2.10	2.27	2.34	183	223	261	299	332
Burundi	1,483	2,235	3,386	5,079	4.11	4.15	4.06	542	535	616	741	953
Cameroon	3,309	4,481	5,858	7,683	3.03	2.68	2.71	595	650	727	840	986
Cape Verde	96	134	185	241	3.31	3.22	2.67	20	24	27	29	28
Central African Republic	785	984	1,231	1,574	2.26	2.24	2.46	107	115	132	158	185
Chad	1,195	1,562	2,079	2,861	2.68	2.86	3.19	172	228	289	351	430
Comoros	99	140	190	257	3.49	3.06	3.04	21	23	27	32	35
Congo	821	1,249	2,009	3,214	4.20	4.75	4.70	238	333	427	535	670
Côte d'Ivoire	3,233	4,117	5,321	7,119	2.42	2.57	2.91	523	541	663	838	961
Dem. Republic of the Congo	10,462	14,614	22,349	33,795	3.34	4.25	4.14	2,682	3,482	4,253	5,125	6,321
Djibouti	150	182	234	308	1.95	2.52	2.75	22	23	29	34	40
Egypt	13,178	17,974	22,988	27,469	3.10	2.46	1.78	2,605	2,540	2,474	2,340	2,142
Equatorial Guinea	102	143	202	282	3.36	3.44	3.34	23	27	31	37	44
Eritrea	671	1,118	1,618	2,335	5.11	3.70	3.67	205	229	272	325	392
Ethiopia	13,475	17,963	24,213	32,899	2.87	2.99	3.07	2,398	2,848	3,401	4,006	4,681
Gabon	321	400	500	624	2.19	2.23	2.22	43	46	54	58	66
Gambia	166	240	321	420	3.70	2.93	2.67	36	39	43	47	51
Ghana	4,092	5,537	7,243	9,397	3.02	2.69	2.60	754	822	884	1,005	1,148
Guinea	1,266	1,572	2,171	3,014	2.17	3.23	3.28	226	274	325	389	454
Guinea-Bissau	156	218	306	438	3.31	3.40	3.59	33	40	48	59	73
Kenya	7,385	11,396	16,672	23,681	4.34	3.81	3.51	2,239	2,433	2,844	3,288	3,720
Lesotho	342	348	347	363	0.18	-0.02	0.44	-3	-3	2	6	9
Liberia	298	611	821	1,293	7.16	2.96	4.54	87	81	130	214	258
Libyan Arab Jamahiriya	747	899	1,012	1,180	1.85	1.18	1.53	73	54	59	72	96
Madagascar	3,332	4,382	5,990	7,775	2.74	3.13	2.61	572	799	810	847	938
Malawi	1,836	1,684	1,773	2,352	-0.86	0.51	2.83	-76	-50	139	267	312
Mali	1,894	2,599	3,672	5,262	3.17	3.45	3.60	375	481	591	726	865
Mauritania	369	482	618	784	2.66	2.48	2.38	58	65	71	79	86
Mauritius	286	323	354	375	1.22	0.93	0.56	17	19	12	11	9
Morocco	5,558	6,928	8,380	9,706	2.20	1.90	1.47	716	683	769	700	625
Mozambique	2,937	3,248	3,504	4,109	1.01	0.76	1.59	108	63	193	276	329
Namibia	353	421	461	532	1.77	0.92	1.42	23	15	26	33	38
Niger	1,435	1,860	2,484	3,325	2.60	2.89	2.91	230	293	331	387	454
Nigeria	29,542	44,636	59,643	78,522	4.13	2.90	2.75	7,815	7,277	7,730	8,800	10,080
Réunion	205	261	317	367	2.45	1.94	1.45	29	30	26	25	24
Rwanda	1,523	2,779	3,722	5,057	6.01	2.92	3.07	396	434	509	606	729
São Tomé and Príncipe	29	38	52	69	2.82	2.98	2.85	5	6	7	8	9
Senegal	1,013	1,350	1,793	2,331	2.87	2.84	2.62	184	213	231	254	284
Seychelles	15	17	20	23	1.29	1.42	1.57	1	1	1	2	2
Sierra Leone	928	1,448	1,983	2,755	4.45	3.14	3.29	222	248	287	352	420
Somalia	882	1,259	1,754	2,516	3.56	3.31	3.61	211	219	275	345	418
South Africa	13,813	21,269	22,646	23,697	4.32	0.63	0.45	3,196	855	523	570	481
Sudan	3,699	4,543	5,687	7,151	2.06	2.25	2.29	591	554	590	681	783
Swaziland	216	272	294	323	2.32	0.78	0.96	24	11	11	13	16
Togo	1,108	1,554	2,165	2,990	3.38	3.32	3.23	240	288	323	377	448
Tunisia	2,019	2,438	2,726	2,987	1.89	1.12	0.91	201	155	133	136	125
Uganda	4,451	6,088	9,697	15,823	3.13	4.66	4.90	1,050	1,539	2,070	2,706	3,420
United Republic of Tanzania	6,200	7,133	8,280	9,600	1.40	1.49	1.48	480	562	586	627	692
Western Sahara	52	80	126	154	4.41	4.46	2.03	19	21	24	15	13
Zambia	1,943	2,277	2,811	3,587	1.58	2.11	2.44	144	232	302	357	418
Zimbabwe	3,173	3,918	4,669	5,492	2.11	1.75	1.62	352	358	393	418	406
ASIA	854,279	1,075,088	1,298,083	1,493,623	2.30	1.88	1.40	116,256	112,485	110,510	101,175	94,365
Afghanistan	4,233	6,924	9,968	13,781	4.92	3.64	3.24	1,362	1,422	1,623	1,834	1,979
Armenia	595	561	527	494	-0.59	-0.62	-0.66	-10	-13	-21	-18	-16
Azerbaijan	1,644	1,842	2,006	2,091	1.14	0.85	0.41	122	113	51	43	42
Bahrain	109	132	151	159	1.88	1.38	0.49	12	12	8	4	3
Bangladesh	24,091	32,564	40,085	48,219	3.01	2.08	1.85	4,114	3,462	4,059	4,224	3,911
Bhutan	338	439	578	734	2.62	2.74	2.39	57	67	71	75	81
Brunei Darussalam	55	68	79	84	2.15	1.46	0.58	7	6	4	3	2
Cambodia	2,522	3,545	4,744	6,065	3.41	2.91	2.46	560	577	622	637	684
China	359,971	457,410	556,704	645,544	2.40	1.96	1.48	53,907	50,353	48,940	45,247	43,594
China, Hong Kong SAR	1,897	2,472	2,905	3,303	2.65	1.61	1.28	264	229	204	201	197
China, Macao SAR	144	201	246	279	3.33	2.02	1.25	26	24	21	17	15
Cyprus	200	233	255	270	1.51	0.90	0.60	16	13	9	8	8
Dem. People's Rep. of Korea	6,377	6,682	9,320	10,832	0.47	3.33	1.50	122	114	2,524	756	756
Georgia	1,276	1,130	1,073	1,005	-1.21	-0.52	-0.66	-36	-28	-30	-32	-36
India	187,291	236,239	286,164	323,136	2.32	1.92	1.22	25,618	26,338	23,586	20,426	16,546
Indonesia	51,321	63,040	72,655	79,749	2.06	1.42	0.93	5,821	5,102	4,514	3,761	3,333
Iran (Islamic Republic of)	14,854	20,433	25,130	29,037	3.19	2.07	1.44	2,582	2,729	1,969	1,930	1,977
Iraq	2,953	3,599	4,629	6,280	1.98	2.52	3.05	338	383	646	779	873
Israel	1,626	2,095	2,494	2,815	2.54	1.74	1.21	226	215	184	172	149
Japan	48,643	53,396	56,323	58,147	0.93	0.53	0.32	2,047	1,550	1,377	1,128	697
Jordan	486	661	861	1,105	3.07	2.65	2.49	88	94	106	118	126

TABLE B.4

continued

	Estimates and projections (000)				Annual rate of change (%)			Five-year increment (000)				
	2000	2010	2020	2030	2000–2010	2010–2020	2020–2030	2005–2010	2010–2015	2015–2020	2020–2025	2025–2030
Kazakhstan	5,291	5,800	6,298	6,692	0.92	0.82	0.61	267	268	230	206	188
Kuwait	295	462	555	631	4.51	1.84	1.28	76	52	42	39	37
Kyrgyzstan	986	1,093	1,208	1,256	1.03	1.00	0.39	64	66	49	29	19
Lao People's Dem. Republic	955	1,273	1,682	2,191	2.88	2.79	2.64	179	200	210	235	273
Lebanon	644	753	877	1,013	1.57	1.52	1.45	55	58	66	68	69
Malaysia	4,909	6,536	8,394	9,756	2.86	2.50	1.50	825	979	878	752	610
Maldives	41	57	76	101	3.34	2.85	2.89	9	9	10	12	13
Mongolia	499	624	708	766	2.23	1.26	0.79	69	49	34	29	28
Myanmar	10,351	12,573	14,079	15,591	1.94	1.13	1.02	933	727	779	784	728
Nepal	4,355	5,831	7,676	9,995	2.92	2.75	2.64	794	868	977	1,120	1,199
Occupied Palestinian Territory	597	864	1,206	1,641	3.71	3.33	3.08	142	158	184	206	229
Oman	345	403	483	594	1.55	1.82	2.07	41	37	44	52	59
Pakistan	14,229	18,753	25,004	32,572	2.76	2.88	2.64	2,533	2,955	3,295	3,666	3,903
Philippines	15,619	20,837	27,359	33,336	2.88	2.72	1.98	2,775	3,122	3,401	3,186	2,791
Qatar	107	153	167	180	3.56	0.90	0.73	12	8	6	7	6
Republic of Korea	14,161	16,104	17,760	18,936	1.29	0.98	0.64	828	881	776	671	504
Saudi Arabia	2,882	3,660	4,623	5,910	2.39	2.34	2.46	370	430	534	603	684
Singapore	820	893	932	904	0.85	0.43	-0.30	35	33	6	-8	-19
Sri Lanka	4,077	4,665	5,016	5,294	1.35	0.73	0.54	241	182	170	148	130
Syrian Arab Republic	2,659	3,764	4,829	6,019	3.47	2.49	2.20	589	511	555	603	588
Tajikistan	1,099	1,277	1,527	1,768	1.50	1.79	1.47	104	110	141	130	111
Thailand	15,850	18,895	21,054	22,944	1.76	1.08	0.86	1,487	1,125	1,035	980	909
Timor-Leste	167	317	469	626	6.41	3.91	2.88	87	77	75	76	81
Turkey	16,169	20,725	25,258	29,336	2.48	1.98	1.50	2,111	2,240	2,293	2,133	1,944
Turkmenistan	610	674	784	898	0.99	1.51	1.36	37	37	73	62	52
United Arab Emirates	1,102	1,726	2,019	2,283	4.49	1.57	1.23	194	153	140	135	129
Uzbekistan	4,294	5,184	6,107	6,698	1.88	1.64	0.92	516	489	433	320	271
Viet Nam	17,421	22,643	27,151	30,500	2.62	1.82	1.16	2,637	2,579	1,930	1,689	1,660
Yemen	3,122	4,885	7,885	12,064	4.48	4.79	4.25	1,007	1,320	1,680	1,931	2,248
EUROPE	289,818	318,242	333,482	340,219	0.94	0.47	0.20	13,533	8,836	6,404	4,640	2,097
Albania	641	659	715	736	0.27	0.82	0.29	28	32	24	13	8
Andorra	23	26	27	27	0.90	0.43	0.16	1	1	0	0	0
Austria	3,271	3,602	3,865	4,036	0.96	0.71	0.43	165	150	114	93	78
Belarus	3,070	3,155	3,038	2,916	0.27	-0.38	-0.41	29	-41	-77	-65	-57
Belgium	4,319	4,731	5,058	5,291	0.91	0.67	0.45	206	183	144	122	111
Bosnia and Herzegovina	1,233	1,364	1,393	1,395	1.01	0.21	0.02	52	21	8	2	1
Bulgaria	3,194	3,233	3,128	2,985	0.12	-0.33	-0.47	16	-39	-66	-66	-77
Channel Islands	62	71	79	87	1.26	1.12	0.99	4	4	4	4	4
Croatia	1,636	1,753	1,739	1,714	0.69	-0.08	-0.15	40	-4	-9	-12	-13
Czech Republic	4,385	4,661	4,785	4,787	0.61	0.26	0.01	134	101	23	11	-8
Denmark	2,492	2,676	2,913	3,096	0.72	0.85	0.61	101	123	115	103	79
Estonia	570	636	661	678	1.11	0.38	0.25	41	10	14	5	12
Faeroe Islands	19	23	26	29	1.52	1.35	1.00	2	2	2	1	1
Finland	2,248	2,484	2,671	2,806	1.00	0.73	0.49	114	104	83	70	65
France	24,257	26,840	28,779	30,321	1.01	0.70	0.52	1,254	1,062	876	796	746
Germany	35,942	38,209	39,520	39,921	0.61	0.34	0.10	1,214	789	521	271	131
Greece	4,023	4,542	4,858	5,078	1.21	0.67	0.44	221	174	142	119	100
Hungary	4,053	4,188	4,256	4,217	0.33	0.16	-0.09	68	57	12	-8	-30
Iceland	111	132	156	179	1.78	1.62	1.37	11	12	12	12	11
Ireland	1,249	1,596	1,856	2,140	2.45	1.51	1.42	153	130	131	139	145
Isle of Man	33	35	38	40	0.83	0.66	0.46	1	1	1	1	1
Italy	22,706	24,559	25,796	26,264	0.78	0.49	0.18	877	741	496	320	148
Latvia	877	922	906	887	0.49	-0.16	-0.22	27	1	-16	-12	-7
Liechtenstein	14	16	18	20	1.56	1.22	0.93	1	1	1	1	1
Lithuania	1,245	1,353	1,392	1,391	0.84	0.28	-0.00	54	30	9	1	-2
Luxembourg	167	206	247	290	2.08	1.83	1.58	20	21	21	21	21
Malta	133	151	167	181	1.32	0.97	0.80	9	8	7	7	6
Monaco	14	17	20	23	1.77	1.63	1.34	1	2	1	1	1
Netherlands	6,863	7,781	8,634	9,190	1.26	1.04	0.62	466	463	389	311	245
Norway	2,004	2,255	2,562	2,845	1.18	1.28	1.05	137	156	151	149	134
Poland	13,013	13,806	13,759	13,461	0.59	-0.03	-0.22	276	67	-114	-131	-167
Portugal	3,778	4,252	4,607	4,859	1.18	0.80	0.53	210	192	163	134	119
Republic of Moldova	1,219	1,302	1,305	1,286	0.65	0.03	-0.15	43	11	-8	-12	-7
Romania	7,881	8,364	8,369	8,267	0.59	0.01	-0.12	265	54	-49	-51	-51
Russian Federation	65,614	74,459	77,186	75,920	1.26	0.36	-0.17	4,124	1,595	1,132	335	-1,601
Serbia and Montenegro	3,380	3,632	3,760	3,877	0.72	0.35	0.31	107	72	56	54	62
Slovakia	2,037	2,225	2,308	2,335	0.88	0.37	0.11	86	62	22	22	5
Slovenia	716	774	792	791	0.78	0.23	-0.01	26	12	6	1	-3
Spain	13,041	14,766	15,393	15,711	1.24	0.42	0.20	561	373	254	180	138
Sweden	4,269	4,806	5,378	5,789	1.19	1.12	0.74	301	314	258	212	199
Switzerland	3,206	3,562	3,893	4,119	1.06	0.89	0.56	184	180	151	125	101
TFYR Macedonia	543	587	619	642	0.78	0.53	0.37	19	16	16	14	10
Ukraine	15,434	15,675	15,281	14,642	0.16	-0.25	-0.43	139	-136	-259	-300	-338
United Kingdom	24,813	28,132	31,505	34,924	1.26	1.13	1.03	1,745	1,730	1,644	1,647	1,772
LATIN AMERICA AND THE CARIBBEAN	128,557	162,556	195,925	226,806	2.35	1.87	1.46	17,208	16,856	16,514	15,893	14,988
Antigua and Barbuda	21	26	31	35	2.16	1.75	1.32	3	3	2	2	2
Argentina	10,518	12,510	14,727	16,842	1.73	1.63	1.34	1,043	1,091	1,125	1,089	1,026
Aruba	25	31	35	38	2.06	1.17	0.89	3	2	2	2	2

TABLE B.4

continued

	Estimates and projections (000)				Annual rate of change (%)			Five-year increment (000)				
	2000	2010	2020	2030	2000–2010	2010–2020	2020–2030	2005–2010	2010–2015	2015–2020	2020–2025	2025–2030
Bahamas	69	75	83	86	0.89	0.91	0.40	3	4	3	2	1
Barbados	84	92	99	103	0.96	0.66	0.40	4	4	3	2	2
Belize	49	65	88	106	2.94	2.96	1.92	8	11	11	10	9
Bolivia	1,614	2,012	2,478	2,947	2.20	2.09	1.73	209	226	241	238	231
Brazil	46,222	58,891	69,580	79,434	2.42	1.67	1.32	6,193	5,497	5,192	5,031	4,823
Chile	4,188	5,315	6,525	7,682	2.38	2.05	1.63	603	605	606	591	566
Colombia	8,735	11,341	14,222	16,944	2.61	2.26	1.75	1,337	1,451	1,431	1,385	1,337
Costa Rica	1,002	1,397	1,775	2,164	3.33	2.39	1.98	196	190	187	193	196
Cuba	4,025	4,681	5,219	5,529	1.51	1.09	0.58	356	297	241	174	136
Dominica	21	25	29	32	1.58	1.50	1.11	2	2	2	2	2
Dominican Republic	2,033	2,626	3,249	3,824	2.56	2.13	1.63	314	317	307	292	282
Ecuador	3,023	4,019	5,127	6,178	2.85	2.44	1.86	518	552	556	543	507
El Salvador	1,678	2,277	2,978	3,734	3.05	2.68	2.26	308	345	355	380	376
French Guiana	41	58	76	95	3.43	2.73	2.20	9	9	9	9	9
Grenada	28	33	41	48	1.75	2.09	1.65	4	4	4	4	4
Guadeloupe	132	151	166	179	1.33	0.99	0.76	9	8	7	7	6
Guatemala	1,757	2,282	2,969	3,719	2.62	2.63	2.25	286	325	362	376	374
Guyana	157	162	156	143	0.31	-0.37	-0.89	1	-1	-5	-7	-7
Haiti	1,528	1,969	2,382	2,861	2.54	1.90	1.83	239	200	213	222	257
Honduras	1,175	1,651	2,237	2,827	3.40	3.04	2.34	256	288	298	297	293
Jamaica	507	514	510	485	0.14	-0.07	-0.51	1	1	-5	-11	-14
Martinique	124	138	149	154	1.13	0.73	0.35	7	6	5	3	2
Mexico	23,251	28,985	34,677	39,358	2.20	1.79	1.27	2,854	2,887	2,806	2,528	2,153
Netherlands Antilles	55	65	76	86	1.71	1.56	1.20	5	6	5	5	5
Nicaragua	814	1,117	1,526	1,964	3.16	3.12	2.52	163	195	214	220	218
Panama	731	975	1,237	1,486	2.88	2.38	1.83	127	131	131	127	122
Paraguay	1,159	1,675	2,294	3,017	3.68	3.14	2.74	275	300	319	347	377
Peru	5,714	7,205	8,775	10,175	2.32	1.97	1.48	781	791	780	737	663
Puerto Rico	1,167	1,310	1,465	1,607	1.16	1.11	0.93	68	77	78	75	67
Saint Lucia	42	50	58	63	1.72	1.39	0.97	4	4	4	3	3
Saint Vincent and the Grenadines	32	37	40	42	1.42	0.95	0.43	3	2	2	1	1
Suriname	108	121	131	136	1.11	0.84	0.35	3	6	4	3	2
Trinidad and Tobago	293	329	334	334	1.15	0.14	0.01	14	5	0	-1	1
United States Virgin Islands	30	33	35	35	0.97	0.50	0.06	2	1	1	0	0
Uruguay	1,025	1,149	1,281	1,405	1.15	1.09	0.92	65	64	68	64	60
Venezuela	5,343	7,112	9,004	10,840	2.86	2.36	1.86	927	946	946	942	894
NORTHERN AMERICA	122,085	145,062	167,859	188,393	1.72	1.46	1.15	11,849	11,894	10,903	10,249	10,285
Bermuda	26	30	33	35	1.45	0.98	0.68	2	2	1	1	1
Canada	12,504	15,337	18,072	20,714	2.04	1.64	1.36	1,408	1,424	1,312	1,303	1,338
Greenland	23	26	29	32	1.37	1.11	0.86	2	2	1	1	1
United States of America	109,531	129,667	149,721	167,609	1.69	1.44	1.13	10,437	10,467	9,587	8,943	8,944
OCEANIA	10,445	12,686	15,040	17,448	1.94	1.70	1.49	1,135	1,161	1,192	1,203	1,205
American Samoa	12	16	21	25	2.64	2.43	2.06	2	2	2	2	2
Australia	7,340	8,918	10,559	12,175	1.95	1.69	1.42	802	819	822	808	809
Fiji	155	179	194	207	1.44	0.83	0.62	11	9	7	7	5
French Polynesia	54	67	80	89	2.13	1.72	1.09	7	6	6	5	4
Guam	35	40	47	51	1.43	1.69	0.81	3	4	3	2	2
Kiribati	20	24	30	33	1.78	2.10	1.19	2	3	3	2	2
Marshall Islands	12	16	22	26	3.13	3.04	1.68	2	3	3	2	2
Micronesia (Fed. States of)	24	25	27	26	0.44	0.77	-0.39	1	1	1	0	-1
New Caledonia	56	70	86	100	2.27	2.07	1.45	7	8	8	7	6
New Zealand	1,411	1,672	1,909	2,127	1.69	1.32	1.08	126	119	118	111	107
Northern Mariana Islands	16	20	24	26	2.47	1.86	0.86	2	2	2	1	1
Papua New Guinea	1,133	1,424	1,783	2,257	2.28	2.25	2.36	150	164	195	232	243
Samoa	35	39	43	47	0.97	1.00	0.93	2	2	2	2	2
Solomon Islands	69	92	120	151	2.99	2.59	2.33	12	13	14	15	16
Tonga	22	23	25	25	0.81	0.65	0.15	1	1	1	0	0
Vanuatu	35	42	50	58	2.01	1.73	1.51	4	4	4	4	4

Source: UN-Habitat, 2006 updates.

TABLE B.5

Environmental Infrastructure

	Improved drinking water coverage						Household connection to improved drinking water						Improved sanitation coverage					
	Total (%)		Urban (%)		Rural (%)		Total (%)		Urban (%)		Rural (%)		Total (%)		Urban (%)		Rural (%)	
	1990	2004	1990	2004	1990	2004	1990	2004	1990	2004	1990	2004	1990	2004	1990	2004	1990	2004
AFRICA																		
Algeria	94	85	99	88	89	80	49	41	66	74	46	58	88	92	99	99	77	82
Angola	36	53	23	75	40	40	0	6	1	15	0	1	29	31	61	56	18	16
Benin	63	67	73	78	57	57	7	12	18	25	1	2	12	33	32	59	2	11
Botswana	93	95	100	100	88	90	24	46	40	62	13	28	38	42	61	57	21	25
Burkina Faso	38	61	61	94	34	54	4	6	24	31	1	0	7	13	32	42	3	6
Burundi	69	90	97	92	67	77	3	5	32	42	1	1	44	36	42	47	44	35
Cameroon	50	66	77	86	31	44	12	14	26	25	2	2	21	48	43	63	7	33
Cape Verde	...	80	...	86	...	73	...	25	...	41	4	4	...	43	...	61	...	19
Central African Republic	52	75	74	93	39	61	2	4	4	9	0	0	23	27	34	47	17	12
Chad	19	42	41	41	13	43	2	4	10	10	0	2	7	9	28	24	2	4
Comoros	93	86	98	92	91	82	31	14	50	31	23	4	32	33	62	41	20	29
Congo	...	58	...	84	...	27	...	28	...	49	4	4	...	27	...	28	...	25
Côte d'Ivoire	69	84	73	97	67	74	21	21	47	48	4	5	21	37	37	46	10	29
Dem. Republic of the Congo	43	46	90	82	25	29	25	10	89	32	0	1	16	30	53	42	1	25
Djibouti	72	73	76	76	59	59	25	16	41	41	5	5	79	82	88	88	50	50
Egypt	94	98	97	99	92	97	61	85	89	99	40	74	54	70	70	86	42	58
Equatorial Guinea	...	43	...	45	...	42	4	8	12	17	0	0	...	53	...	60	...	46
Eritrea	43	60	62	74	39	57	6	9	40	42	0	0	7	9	44	32	0	3
Ethiopia	23	22	81	81	15	11	0	5	2	32	0	0	3	13	13	44	2	7
Gabon	...	88	95	95	...	47	...	45	...	52	...	8	...	36	...	37	...	30
Gambia	...	82	95	95	...	77	...	12	...	39	3	3	...	53	...	72	...	46
Ghana	55	75	86	88	37	64	16	19	40	37	2	4	15	18	23	27	10	11
Guinea	44	50	74	78	34	35	9	11	31	28	1	1	14	18	27	31	10	11
Guinea-Bissau	...	59	...	79	...	49	...	5	...	15	0	0	...	35	...	57	...	23
Kenya	45	61	91	83	30	46	23	28	59	52	11	12	40	43	48	46	37	41
Lesotho	...	79	...	92	...	76	4	16	18	53	1	8	37	37	61	61	32	32
Liberia	55	61	85	72	34	52	11	0	21	1	3	0	39	27	59	49	24	7
Libyan Arab Jamahiriya	71	...	72	...	68	...	54	...	54	...	55	...	97	97	97	97	96	96
Madagascar	40	46	80	77	27	35	7	6	28	16	1	2	14	32	27	48	10	26
Malawi	40	73	90	98	33	68	7	7	44	29	2	2	47	61	64	62	45	61
Mali	34	50	50	78	29	36	2	11	8	29	0	2	36	46	50	59	32	39
Mauritania	38	53	32	59	43	44	12	25	20	32	5	13	31	34	42	49	22	8
Mauritius	100	100	100	100	100	100	100	100	100	100	100	100	...	94	95	95	...	94
Morocco	75	81	94	99	58	56	41	57	75	86	9	17	56	73	87	88	27	52
Mozambique	36	43	83	72	24	26	8	8	33	18	1	2	20	32	49	53	12	19
Namibia	57	87	99	98	42	81	29	48	83	77	10	33	24	25	70	50	8	13
Niger	39	46	62	80	35	36	3	8	19	35	0	0	7	13	35	43	2	4
Nigeria	49	48	80	67	33	31	14	9	32	15	4	3	39	44	51	53	33	36
Rwanda	59	74	88	92	57	69	1	8	24	34	0	1	37	42	49	56	36	38
Saint Helena	...	...	...	...	...	...	...	...	...	...	...	...	...	...	...	...	...	...
Senegal	65	76	89	92	49	60	22	46	50	75	4	17	33	57	53	79	19	34
Seychelles	88	88	100	100	75	75	88	88	100	100	75	75	...	...	...	...	100	100
Sierra Leone	...	57	...	75	...	46	...	12	...	30	1	1	...	39	...	53	...	30
Somalia	...	29	...	32	...	27	1	1	3	3	0	0	...	26	...	48	...	14
South Africa	83	88	98	99	69	73	55	64	87	87	24	32	69	65	85	79	53	46
Sudan	64	70	85	78	57	64	34	26	75	46	19	13	33	34	53	50	26	24
Swaziland	...	62	...	87	...	54	...	23	...	52	...	14	...	48	...	59	...	44
Togo	50	52	81	80	37	36	4	4	14	12	0	0	37	35	71	71	24	15
Tunisia	81	93	95	99	62	82	61	74	87	94	26	38	75	85	96	96	70	72
Uganda	44	60	80	87	40	56	3	1	24	7	0	0	42	43	54	54	41	41
United Republic of Tanzania	46	62	85	85	35	49	10	18	33	43	3	3	47	47	52	53	45	43
Zambia	50	58	86	90	27	40	23	16	53	41	3	2	41	55	63	59	31	52
Zimbabwe	78	81	100	98	69	72	34	32	97	91	8	5	50	53	69	63	42	47
ASIA																		
Afghanistan	4	39	10	63	3	31	1	4	6	15	0	0	3	34	7	49	2	29
Armenia	...	92	99	99	...	80	87	86	97	97	68	66	...	83	96	96	...	61
Azerbaijan	68	77	82	95	51	59	43	47	66	76	16	19	...	54	...	73	...	36
Bahrain	...	...	100	100	...	...	...	...	100	100	...	...	...	...	100	100	...	...
Bangladesh	72	74	83	82	69	72	6	6	28	24	0	0	20	39	55	51	12	35
Bhutan	...	62	...	86	...	60	...	...	...	81	...	...	...	70	...	65	...	70
Cambodia	...	41	...	64	...	35	...	9	...	36	...	2	...	17	...	53	...	8
China	70	77	99	93	59	67	48	69	81	87	36	57	23	44	64	69	7	28
Cyprus	100	100	100	100	100	100	100	100	100	100	100	100	100	100	100	100	100	100
Dem. People's Republic of Korea	100	100	100	100	100	100	...	77	...	81	...	71	...	59	...	58	...	60
Georgia	80	82	91	96	67	67	50	57	75	85	19	28	97	94	99	96	94	91
India	70	86	89	95	64	83	19	19	53	47	8	8	14	33	45	59	3	22
Indonesia	72	77	92	87	63	69	10	17	27	30	2	6	46	55	65	73	37	40
Iran (Islamic Republic of)	92	94	99	99	84	84	84	...	96	96	69	...	83	...	86	...	78	...
Iraq	83	81	97	97	50	50	76	74	94	94	33	33	81	79	95	95	48	48
Israel	100	100	100	100	100	100	100	100	100	100	98	98	...	...	100	100	...	...
Japan	100	100	100	100	100	100	95	96	98	98	91	91	100	100	100	100	100	100
Jordan	97	97	99	99	91	91	94	93	97	96	87	81	93	93	97	94	82	87
Kazakhstan	87	86	97	97	73	73	62	62	89	89	27	27	72	72	87	87	52	52
Kyrgyzstan	78	77	98	98	66	66	47	45	79	79	27	27	60	59	75	75	51	51
Lao People's Dem. Republic	...	51	...	79	...	43	...	14	...	44	6	6	...	30	...	67	...	20
Lebanon	100	100	100	100	100	100	...	98	100	100	...	85	...	98	100	100	...	87
Malaysia	98	99	100	100	96	96	...	94	98	98	...	87	...	94	...	95	...	93
Maldives	96	83	100	98	95	76	20	22	77	76	0	0	...	59	100	100	...	42

TABLE B.5

continued

	Improved drinking water coverage						Household connection to improved drinking water						Improved sanitation coverage					
	Total (%)		Urban (%)		Rural (%)		Total (%)		Urban (%)		Rural (%)		Total (%)		Urban (%)		Rural (%)	
	1990	2004	1990	2004	1990	2004	1990	2004	1990	2004	1990	2004	1990	2004	1990	2004	1990	2004
Mongolia	63	62	87	87	30	30	28	28	49	49	1	1	...	59	...	75	...	37
Myanmar	57	78	86	80	47	77	5	6	18	16	1	2	24	77	48	88	16	72
Nepal	70	90	95	96	67	89	6	17	41	52	3	11	11	35	48	62	7	30
Occupied Palestinian Territory	...	92	94	94	...	88	...	81	...	88	...	64	...	73	...	78	...	61
Oman	80	...	85	...	73	...	25	...	35	...	8	...	83	...	97	97	61	...
Pakistan	83	91	95	96	78	89	25	27	60	49	10	15	37	59	82	92	17	41
Philippines	87	85	95	87	80	82	24	45	41	58	8	23	57	72	66	80	48	59
Qatar	100	100	100	100	100	100	...	...	100	100	...	...	100	100	100	100	100	100
Republic of Korea	...	92	97	97	...	71	...	84	96	96	...	39	...	...	...	...	...	...
Saudi Arabia	90	...	97	97	63	...	89	...	97	97	60	...	...	...	100	100	...	...
Singapore	100	100	100	100	..	..	100	100	100	100	..	..	100	100	100	100	..	..
Sri Lanka	68	79	91	98	62	74	11	10	36	32	4	4	69	91	89	98	64	89
Syrian Arab Republic	80	93	94	98	67	87	69	84	92	96	46	72	73	90	97	99	50	81
Tajikistan	...	59	...	92	...	48	...	34	...	79	...	20	...	51	...	70	...	45
Thailand	95	99	98	98	94	100	28	38	70	85	11	16	80	99	95	98	74	99
Timor-Leste	...	58	...	77	...	56	...	12	...	28	...	11	...	36	...	66	...	33
Turkey	85	96	92	98	74	93	62	92	70	96	51	83	85	88	96	96	70	72
Turkmenistan	...	72	...	93	...	54	...	53	...	81	...	29	...	62	...	77	...	50
United Arab Emirates	...	...	...	...	...	...	...	...	...	...	...	...	97	98	98	98	93	95
Uzbekistan	94	82	99	95	91	75	59	46	88	83	40	25	51	67	69	78	39	61
Viet Nam	65	85	90	99	59	80	9	24	40	73	1	6	36	61	58	92	30	50
Yemen	71	67	84	71	68	65	35	23	67	59	26	10	32	43	82	86	19	28
EUROPE																		
Albania	96	96	99	99	94	94	...	69	96	96	...	47	...	91	99	99	...	84
Andorra	100	100	100	100	100	100	...	...	100	100	...	...	100	100	100	100	100	100
Austria	100	100	100	100	100	100	100	100	100	100	100	100	100	100	100	100	100	100
Belarus	100	100	100	100	100	100	...	71	...	89	...	25	...	84	...	93	...	61
Belgium	...	...	100	100	...	...	100	...	100	100	90	...	...	...	...	...	...	...
Bosnia and Herzegovina	97	97	99	99	96	96	...	85	95	95	...	77	...	95	99	99	...	92
Bulgaria	99	99	100	100	97	97	89	90	97	97	72	72	100	100	100	100	100	100
Croatia	100	100	100	100	100	100	...	83	...	95	...	65	100	100	100	100	100	100
Czech Republic	100	100	100	100	100	100	...	95	97	97	...	91	99	98	99	99	97	97
Denmark	100	100	100	100	100	100	100	100	100	100	100	100	...	...	...	...	...	...
Estonia	100	100	100	100	99	99	80	90	92	97	51	73	97	97	97	97	96	96
Finland	100	100	100	100	100	100	92	97	96	100	85	92	100	100	100	100	100	100
France	100	100	100	100	100	100	99	100	100	100	95	100	...	...	...	...	...	...
Germany	100	100	100	100	100	100	100	100	100	100	97	97	100	100	100	100	100	100
Greece	...	...	...	...	...	...	84	...	91	...	73	...	...	...	...	...	...	...
Hungary	99	99	100	100	98	98	86	94	94	95	73	91	...	95	100	100	...	85
Iceland	100	100	100	100	100	100	100	100	100	100	100	100	100	100	100	100	100	100
Ireland	...	...	100	100	...	...	98	98	99	99	96	96	...	...	...	...	...	...
Italy	...	...	100	100	...	...	99	99	100	100	96	96	...	...	...	...	...	...
Latvia	99	99	100	100	96	96	...	81	...	93	...	59	...	78	...	82	...	71
Lithuania	...	...	...	...	...	...	76	80	89	92	49	56	...	...	...	...	...	...
Luxembourg	100	100	100	100	100	100	100	100	100	100	98	98	...	...	...	...	...	...
Malta	100	100	100	100	100	100	99	100	100	100	96	96	...	...	100	100	...	...
Monaco	100	100	100	100	..	..	100	100	100	100	..	..	100	100	100	100	..	..
Netherlands	100	100	100	100	100	100	98	100	100	100	95	100	100	100	100	100	100	100
Norway	100	100	100	100	100	100	100	100	100	100	100	100	...	...	...	...	...	...
Poland	...	...	100	100	...	...	88	98	97	99	73	96	...	...	...	...	...	...
Portugal	...	...	...	...	...	...	72	...	97	97	50	...	...	...	...	...	...	...
Republic of Moldova	...	92	97	97	...	88	...	41	...	78	...	9	...	68	...	86	...	52
Romania	...	57	...	91	...	16	...	49	...	79	...	13	...	...	...	89	...	...
Russian Federation	94	97	97	100	86	88	76	82	86	93	49	52	87	87	93	93	70	70
Serbia and Montenegro	93	93	99	99	86	86	81	82	98	98	64	64	87	87	97	97	77	77
Slovakia	100	100	100	100	100	100	95	96	99	99	89	93	99	99	100	100	98	98
Spain	100	100	100	100	100	100	99	99	99	99	99	99	100	100	100	100	100	100
Sweden	100	100	100	100	100	100	100	100	100	100	100	100	100	100	100	100	100	100
Switzerland	100	100	100	100	100	100	100	100	100	100	99	99	100	100	100	100	100	100
Ukraine	...	96	99	99	...	91	...	76	...	89	...	48	...	96	...	98	...	93
United Kingdom	100	100	100	100	100	100	100	100	100	100	98	98	...	...	...	...	...	...
LATIN AMERICA AND THE CARIBBEAN																		
Anguilla	...	60	...	60	..	..	...	45	...	45	..	..	99	99	99	99	..	..
Antigua and Barbuda	...	91	95	95	...	89	...	84	...	90	...	79	...	95	98	98	...	94
Argentina	94	96	97	98	72	80	69	79	76	83	22	45	81	91	86	92	45	83
Aruba	100	100	100	100	100	100	100	100	100	100	100	100	...	...	...	...	...	...
Bahamas	...	97	98	98	...	86	...	70	...	69	...	80	100	100	100	100	100	100
Barbados	100	100	100	100	100	100	...	...	98	100	...	...	100	100	99	99	100	100
Belize	...	91	100	100	...	82	...	81	92	99	...	63	...	47	...	71	...	25
Bolivia	72	85	91	95	49	68	53	73	78	90	22	44	33	46	49	60	14	22
Brazil	83	90	93	96	55	57	74	79	90	91	28	17	71	75	82	83	37	37
British Virgin Islands	98	98	98	98	98	98	97	97	97	97	97	97	100	100	100	100	100	100
Chile	90	95	98	100	49	58	86	91	98	99	25	38	84	91	91	95	52	62
Colombia	92	93	98	99	78	71	77	86	94	96	41	51	82	86	95	96	52	54
Costa Rica	...	97	100	100	...	92	...	92	99	99	...	81	...	92	...	89	97	97
Cuba	...	91	95	95	...	78	65	74	77	82	31	49	98	98	99	99	95	95
Dominica	...	97	100	100	...	90	...	87	98	98	...	58	...	84	...	86	...	75
Dominican Republic	84	95	98	97	66	91	63	80	85	92	35	62	52	78	60	81	43	73

TABLE B.5

continued

	Improved drinking water coverage						Household connection to improved drinking water						Improved sanitation coverage					
	Total (%)		Urban (%)		Rural (%)		Total (%)		Urban (%)		Rural (%)		Total (%)		Urban (%)		Rural (%)	
	1990	2004	1990	2004	1990	2004	1990	2004	1990	2004	1990	2004	1990	2004	1990	2004	1990	2004
Ecuador	73	94	82	97	61	89	55	68	74	82	32	45	63	89	77	94	45	82
El Salvador	67	84	87	94	48	70	45	64	74	81	16	38	51	62	70	77	33	39
French Guiana	...	84	...	88	...	71	...	79	...	83	...	65	...	78	...	85	...	57
Grenada	...	95	97	97	...	93	...	82	...	93	...	75	97	96	96	96	97	97
Guadeloupe	...	98	98	98	...	93	...	98	98	98	...	75	...	64	...	64	...	61
Guatemala	79	95	89	99	72	92	49	76	70	89	34	65	58	86	73	90	47	82
Guyana	...	83	...	83	...	83	...	53	...	66	...	45	...	70	...	86	...	60
Haiti	47	54	60	52	42	56	9	11	27	24	2	3	24	30	25	57	23	14
Honduras	84	87	92	95	79	81	58	75	82	91	42	62	50	69	77	87	31	54
Jamaica	92	93	98	98	86	88	61	70	88	92	33	46	75	80	86	91	64	69
Mexico	82	97	89	100	64	87	77	90	86	96	52	72	58	79	75	91	13	41
Montserrat	100	100	100	100	100	100	...	...	98	98	...	...	96	96	96	96	96	96
Nicaragua	70	79	91	90	46	63	53	60	85	84	16	27	45	47	64	56	24	34
Panama	90	90	99	99	79	79	85	86	96	96	72	72	71	73	89	89	51	51
Paraguay	62	86	81	99	44	68	30	58	60	82	2	25	58	80	72	94	45	61
Peru	84	83	89	89	41	65	57	71	75	82	16	39	52	63	69	74	15	32
Saint Kitts and Nevis	99	99	99	99	99	99	...	71	...	72	...	72	96	96	96	96	96	96
Saint Lucia	98	98	98	98	98	98	...	75	...	75	...	75	...	89	...	89	...	89
Saint Vincent and the Grenadines	...	...	...	...	...	93	...	...	...	...	...	73	...	...	...	...	96	96
Suriname	...	92	98	98	...	73	...	81	...	91	...	48	...	94	99	99	...	76
Trinidad and Tobago	92	91	93	92	89	88	77	77	81	80	68	67	100	100	100	100	100	100
Turks and Caicos Islands	100	100	100	100	100	100	...	68	...	78	...	60	...	96	98	98	...	94
Uruguay	...	98	98	98	...	93	...	96	97	97	...	84	100	100	100	100	99	99
Venezuela	...	83	...	85	...	70	...	81	79	84	...	61	...	68	...	71	...	48
NORTHERN AMERICA																		
Canada	100	100	100	100	99	99	...	88	100	100	...	38	100	100	100	100	99	99
United States of America	100	100	100	100	100	100	100	100	100	100	100	100	100	100	100	100	100	100
OCEANIA																		
Australia	100	100	100	100	100	100	...	...	...	...	...	...	100	100	100	100	100	100
Cook Islands	94	94	99	98	87	88	...	...	...	...	...	...	94	100	100	100	91	100
Fiji	...	47	...	43	...	51	...	20	...	32	...	7	68	72	87	87	55	55
French Polynesia	100	100	100	100	100	100	98	98	99	99	96	96	98	98	99	99	97	97
Guam	100	100	100	100	100	100	...	...	...	...	...	...	99	99	99	99	98	98
Kiribati	49	65	76	77	33	53	25	36	46	49	13	22	25	40	33	59	21	22
Marshall Islands	96	87	95	82	97	96	...	...	...	...	...	...	74	82	88	93	51	58
Micronesia (Fed. States of)	88	94	93	95	86	94	...	...	...	...	...	...	29	28	54	61	20	14
New Zealand	97	...	100	100	82	...	...	...	100	100	...	...	...	...	...	...	88	...
Niue	100	100	100	100	100	100	...	100	100	100	...	80	100	100	100	100	100	100
Northern Mariana Islands	98	99	98	98	100	97	...	...	93	...	...	35	84	95	85	94	78	96
Palau	80	85	73	79	98	94	...	...	...	...	...	10	67	80	76	96	54	52
Papua New Guinea	39	39	88	88	32	32	11	11	61	61	4	4	44	44	67	67	41	41
Samoa	91	88	99	90	89	87	...	57	...	74	...	52	98	100	100	100	98	100
Solomon Islands	...	70	...	94	...	65	11	14	76	76	1	1	...	31	98	98	...	18
Tokelau	94	88	..	..	94	88	0	0	..	..	0	0	39	78	..	..	39	78
Tonga	100	100	100	100	100	100	...	75	...	72	...	76	97	97	98	98	96	96
Tuvalu	91	93	92	94	89	92	...	...	...	...	...	...	78	90	83	93	74	84
Vanuatu	60	60	93	86	53	52	38	39	80	74	28	28	...	50	...	78	...	42

Source: UNICEF and WHO, 2006

TABLE B.6

Transport Safety and Transport Infrastructure

	Road safety					Roads			Motor vehicles		Railways			Port traffic	Air	
	per 10,000 vehicles		per 100,000 population			total	passengers	goods hauled	number per 1000		route	passengers	goods hauled	TEU	passengers	freight
	injury rate 1996	fatality rate 1996	injury rate 1996	fatality rate 1996	fatality rate 2004	(km) 1999–2003	m-p-km 1999–2003	m-t-km 1999–2003	1990	2003	km 1999–2004	m-p-km 1999–2004	m-t-km 1999–2004	(000) 2004	(000) 2004	m-t-km 2004
AFRICA																
Algeria	237	24	124	13	...	104,000	...	...	55	...	3,572	950	1,945	311	3,236	21
Angola	...	...	...	...	...	51,429	166,045	4,709	19	...	2,761	...	...	...	223	64
Benin	100	14	53	7	...	6,787	...	...	3	...	438	66	86	...	46	7
Botswana	791	62	355	28	...	25,233	...	...	18	92	888	171	842	...	214	0
Burkina Faso	...	...	...	...	...	12,506	...	...	4	...	622	...	...	...	62	0
Burundi	...	...	...	...	...	14,480	...	...	...	...	...	...	...	...	...	...
Cameroon	329	52	39	6	...	80,932	...	...	10	...	974	308	1,115	...	358	23
Cape Verde	1,640	112	172	12	...	...	...	...	...	...	...	...	...	...	...	...
Central African Republic	3,104	339	16	2	...	23,810	...	...	1	...	...	...	...	...	46	7
Chad	144	7	6	0	...	33,400	...	...	2	...	...	...	...	...	46	7
Comoros	...	8	...	2	...	...	...	...	...	...	...	...	...	...	...	...
Congo	170	23	33	5	...	12,800	...	...	18	...	1,026	76	307	...	52	0
Côte d'Ivoire	...	...	...	...	...	50,400	...	...	24	...	639	148	129	670	46	7
Dem. Republic of the Congo	...	...	...	...	...	157,000	...	...	...	...	4,499	140	491	...	95	7
Egypt	100	20	37	7	...	64,000	...	...	29	...	5,150	40,837	4,188	1,422	4,584	248
Eritrea	...	...	...	...	...	4,010	...	...	1	...	306	...	...	...	...	...
Ethiopia	853	195	13	3	...	33,856	219,113	2,456	1	2	...	...	...	...	1,403	117
Gabon	235	28	86	10	...	32,333	...	...	32	...	650	92	1,949	...	433	62
Gambia	...	...	...	...	...	3,742	16	...	13	8	...	...	...	...	...	...
Ghana	621	73	48	6	...	47,787	...	...	8	...	977	85	242	...	96	7
Guinea	1,111	121	58	6	...	44,348	...	...	4	...	837	...	...	...	...	...
Guinea-Bissau	...	...	...	...	...	4,400	...	...	7	...	...	...	...	...	...	...
Kenya	558	64	80	9	...	63,942	...	22	12	11	1,917	226	1,399	...	2,005	193
Lesotho	439	87	82	16	...	5,940	...	...	11	...	...	...	...	...	...	...
Liberia	...	...	...	...	...	10,600	...	...	14	...	490	...	...	...	...	...
Libyan Arab Jamahiriya	...	...	150	21	...	83,200	...	...	165	...	2,757	...	...	...	850	0
Madagascar	105	3	6	0	...	49,827	...	...	6	...	883	10	12	...	514	13
Malawi	700	193	39	11	...	28,400	...	...	4	...	710	25	88	...	114	1
Mali	177	16	8	1	...	15,100	...	...	3	...	733	196	189	...	46	7
Mauritania	...	...	...	...	...	7,660	...	...	10	...	717	...	...	...	128	0
Mauritius	375	15	318	13	...	2,015	...	...	59	119	...	...	...	382	1,089	220
Morocco	...	...	212	10	...	57,694	...	18	37	45	1,907	2,614	5,535	561	3,004	62
Mozambique	...	...	...	...	...	30,400	...	...	4	...	2,072	137	808	...	299	5
Namibia	...	9	38	8	...	42,237	47	591	71	82	...	...	...	...	281	56
Niger	...	...	...	...	...	10,100	...	...	6	...	...	...	...	...	46	7
Nigeria	166	65	20	8	...	194,394	...	...	30	...	3,505	973	39	513	682	10
Rwanda	...	...	...	...	...	12,000	...	...	2	...	...	...	...	...	...	...
Senegal	710	64	103	9	...	13,576	...	...	11	14	906	138	371	...	421	0
Sierra Leone	199	21	16	2	...	11,300	...	...	10	4	...	...	...	...	16	8
Somalia	...	...	...	...	...	22,100	...	...	2	...	...	...	...	...	...	...
South Africa	217	17	341	27	25	362,099	...	434	139	144	20,047	10,001	106,549	2,675	9,876	930
Sudan	...	...	...	...	...	11,900	...	...	9	...	5,478	32	889	...	476	41
Swaziland	251	44	179	31	...	3,594	...	...	66	83	301	...	...	...	90	0
Togo	...	...	...	...	...	7,520	...	...	24	...	568	...	...	...	46	7
Tunisia	...	...	...	...	...	18,997	...	16,611	48	88	1,909	1,242	2,173	...	1,940	20
Uganda	497	122	33	8	...	70,746	...	...	2	5	259	...	218	...	46	27
United Republic of Tanzania	879	111	40	5	...	78,891	...	...	5	...	2,600	471	1,351	...	248	2
Zambia	235	39	60	10	...	91,440	...	...	14	...	1,273	186	554	...	49	0
Zimbabwe	252	17	161	11	...	97,267	...	...	32	50	...	...	...	...	238	17
ASIA																
Afghanistan	...	...	...	...	...	34,789	...	...	3	...	...	...	...	...	150	8
Armenia	1,277	279	43	10	...	7,633	1,867	280	5	...	711	48	452	...	510	7
Azerbaijan	65	20	32	10	10	27,016	9,862	53,738	52	57	2,122	584	6,980	...	1,007	34
Bahrain	128	3	377	10	10	...	...	...	...	...	...	...	...	...	...	...
Bangladesh	71	45	3	2	...	239,226	...	...	1	1	2,745	...	...	625	1,647	180
Bhutan	10	4	2	1	...	...	...	...	...	...	...	...	...	...	...	...
Brunei Darussalam	22	4	125	22	3	...	...	...	...	...	...	...	...	...	...	...
Cambodia	29	3	15	2	...	12,323	201	308	...	30	650	45	92	...	163	4
China	57	26	13	6	8	1,809,829	769,560	709,950	5	15	61,015	551,196	1,828,548	74,540	119,789	8,188
China, Hong Kong SAR	...	...	326	5	...	1,831	...	...	66	79	...	...	...	...	17,893	6,932
Cyprus	...	...	610	17	...	...	...	...	...	...	...	...	...	...	...	...
Dem. People's Republic of Korea	...	...	...	...	...	31,200	...	...	...	...	5,214	...	...	...	95	2
Georgia	40	10	37	9	14	20,247	4,987	22,500	107	63	1,565	401	5,065	...	203	3
India	104	20	32	6	8	3,851,440	...	...	4	9	63,221	541,208	381,241	4,267	23,797	689
Indonesia	15	8	11	6		368,360	...	...	16	...	...	...	...	5,567	26,785	434
Iran (Islamic Republic of)	58	6	47	5	39	178,152	...	...	34	...	6,405	10,012	18,182	1,221	12,234	98
Iraq	...	...	...	...	...	45,550	...	...	14	...	2,339	570	1,682	...	...	...
Israel	308	3	834	9	8	17,237	...	...	210	284	493	1,423	1,173	1,608	4,954	1,355
Japan	112	1	749	8	6	1,177,278	955,412	312,028	469	582	20,060	242,300	22,200	15,938	103,116	8,938
Jordan	524	19	357	13	...	7,364	...	...	60	99	291	...	522	...	1,660	254
Kazakhstan	107	20	87	17		258,029	55,676	382	76	96	13,770	11,816	163,420	...	843	13
Kuwait	...	...	...	...	...	4,450	...	...	474	332	...	...	...	...	2,317	224
Kyrgyzstan	228	41	75	14	...	18,500	5,274	797	44	38	424	50	561	...	246	5
Lao People's Dem. Republic	...	8	...	4	...	32,620	1,290	121	9	...	...	...	...	...	276	2
Lebanon	22	2	74	8	9	7,300	...	...	321	...	401	...	...	299	1,087	85

TABLE B.6

continued

	Road safety					Roads			Motor vehicles		Railways			Port traffic	Air	
	per 10,000 vehicles		per 100,000 population			total	passengers	goods hauled	number per 1000		route	passengers	goods hauled	TEU	passengers	freight
	injury rate 1996	fatality rate 1996	injury rate 1996	fatality rate 1996	fatality rate 2004	(km) 1999–2003	m-p-km 1999–2003	m-t-km 1999–2003	1990	2003	km 1999–2004	m-p-km 1999–2004	m-t-km 1999–2004	(000) 2004	(000) 2004	m-t-km 2004
Malaysia	63	8	229	31	21	71,814	...	...	124	254	1,667	1,931	1,224	11,264	19,268	2,599
Mongolia	113	30	41	11	...	49,250	761	1,889	21	41	1,810	1,073	6,452	...	318	6
Myanmar	...	36	...	2	...	27,966	2,028	9,493	2	...	...	...	...	...	1,408	3
Nepal	...	...	...	4	...	15,905	...	...	...	...	59	...	...	...	449	7
Oman	213	16	306	24	...	32,800	...	...	130	...	...	...	...	2,516	3,267	235
Pakistan	37	17	7	3	...	254,410	209,959	...	6	8	7,791	23,911	5,004	1,102	5,097	402
Philippines	15	2	6	1	...	200,037	...	...	10	34	...	...	...	3,673	7,406	301
Qatar	...	...	...	...	19	...	...	...	...	...	...	...	...	...	...	...
Republic of Korea	297	11	782	28	...	97,252	9,404	565	79	304	3,129	28,641	10,641	14,299	33,390	7,969
Saudi Arabia	109	14	166	21	...	152,044	...	...	165	...	1,390	364	1,173	3,186	14,943	957
Singapore	105	4	221	7	...	3,165	...	...	130	135	...	...	...	21,311	17,718	7,193
Sri Lanka	218	25	92	11	...	97,286	21,067	...	21	34	...	...	...	2,221	2,416	300
Syrian Arab Republic	187	36	54	11	...	91,795	589	...	26	36	2,798	635	1,924	...	1,141	20
Tajikistan	...	...	45	10	...	27,767	...	...	3	...	617	41	1,087	...	498	6
Thailand	25	10	73	28	...	57,403	...	...	46	...	4,044	10,092	3,422	4,856	20,625	1,869
Turkey	202	11	167	9	13	354,421	163,327	152,163	50	90	8,697	5,237	9,332	2,942	12,516	369
Turkmenistan	...	...	...	...	...	24,000	...	...	...	...	2,523	1,118	6,437	...	1,779	17
United Arab Emirates	...	...	...	...	...	1,088	...	...	121	...	...	...	...	8,662	14,314	3,734
Uzbekistan	...	...	...	...	...	81,600	...	...	...	...	4,126	2,163	18,428	...	1,588	83
Viet Nam	41	11	29	7	...	215,628	18,116	4,772	...	...	2,600	4,376	2,682	2,139	5,050	217
Yemen	126	24	43	8	...	67,000	...	...	34	...	...	...	...	377	995	60
EUROPE																
Albania	24	24	8	8	9	18,000	197	...	11	70	447	89	32	...	189	0
Austria	125	2	704	13	11	133,718	82,330	26,411	421	545	5,801	8,375	19,047	...	7,619	502
Belarus	47	11	73	17	17	93,055	10,739	12,710	61	168	5,498	13,893	40,331	...	274	1
Belgium	137	3	672	13	...	149,757	118,340	32,450	423	527	3,536	8,676	8,725	7,293	3,265	713
Bosnia and Herzegovina	...	...	232	19	...	21,846	...	332	114	...	1,032	53	293	...	73	0
Bulgaria	30	4	88	12	13	102,016	8,596	...	163	335	4,259	2,628	5,212	...	476	3
Croatia	167	7	339	15	14	28,588	3,716	8,241	...	324	2,726	1,213	2,733	...	1,336	2
Czech Republic	80	3	368	13	14	127,672	90,055	475	246	391	9,511	6,553	16,214	...	4,219	41
Denmark	44	2	185	10	7	71,847	61,258	17,766	368	424	2,141	5,390	1,888	998	6,429	175
Estonia	32	4	106	15	13	56,849	2,299	6,364	211	386	959	192	9,567	...	510	1
Finland	39	2	181	8	7	78,216	67,300	27,800	441	450	5,741	3,352	10,105	1,308	7,201	325
France	56	3	291	14	9	891,290	744,900	266,500	494	596	29,246	74,014	45,121	3,947	48,583	5,584
Germany	108	2	602	11	7	231,581	1,062,700	227,197	405	578	34,729	70,286	77,640	12,458	82,156	8,064
Greece	61	4	302	20	15	116,470	5,889	18,360	248	435	2,449	1,668	588	1,878	9,277	58
Hungary	81	5	234	13	13	159,568	13,300	12,505	212	313	8,000	7,380	8,713	...	2,546	24
Iceland	108	1	576	4	8	...	...	...	...	...	...	...	...	...	...	...
Ireland	73	3	271	13	10	95,736	39,440	6,500	270	447	1,919	1,582	399	925	34,783	124
Italy	75	2	460	11	12	479,688	759,200	184,756	529	610	16,235	46,768	21,581	8,473	35,932	1,393
Latvia	89	11	174	22	22	69,919	2,550	2,324	135	329	2,270	810	16,877	...	594	1
Liechtenstein	...	...	...	...	17	...	...	...	...	...	...	...	...	...	...	...
Lithuania	58	7	141	18	21	78,893	20,982	11,462	160	397	1,782	443	11,637	...	448	1
Luxembourg	60	3	370	17	11	...	...	...	...	...	...	...	...	...	...	...
Malta	...	...	198	4	3	...	...	...	...	...	...	...	...	...	...	...
Netherlands	14	2	67	7	5	116,500	193,900	481	405	427	2,811	14,097	4,026	8,482	25,304	4,773
Norway	53	1	274	6	6	91,916	56,573	13,614	458	527	4,077	2,477	2,668	...	13,230	177
Poland	63	6	185	17	15	423,997	29,996	85,989	168	354	19,576	18,626	47,847	428	3,493	77
Portugal	154	5	671	21	11	72,600	98,328	20,470	222	463	2,849	3,415	2,675	866	9,052	237
Republic of Moldova	...	...	71	13	9	12,730	1,640	1,577	53	78	1,120	355	2,715	...	201	1
Romania	25	9	34	13	17	198,817	5,283	25,350	72	168	10,844	8,633	14,262	...	1,338	5
Russian Federation	101	14	141	20	24	537,289	164	5,702	87	174	85,542	157,100	1,664,300	1,368	25,949	1,416
Serbia and Montenegro	97	7	180	12	9	45,290	...	...	137	...	3,809	...	...	...	1,414	6
Slovakia	90	5	218	12	11	42,993	32,981	16,859	194	286	3,660	2,227	9,675	...	825	0
Slovenia	100	5	390	20	14	38,400	1,065	6,305	306	490	1,229	764	3,462	...	765	3
Spain	65	3	316	14	12	666,292	397,117	132,868	360	558	14,395	20,237	14,117	7,810	45,529	1,043
Sweden	49	1	235	6	5	424,981	105,834	37,048	464	504	9,895	5,544	13,122	934	11,539	257
Switzerland	62	1	375	9	7	71,220	94,622	26,100	491	553	3,378	12,869	9,313	...	9,279	1,090
TFYR Macedonia	112	5	172	8	8	8,684	...	...	132	...	699	94	426	...	211	0
Ukraine	...	...	37	6	15	169,739	40,131	24,387	63	137	22,011	51,726	233,961	...	1,924	23
United Kingdom	132	1	539	6	5	392,342	666,000	159,000	400	442	16,514	42,626	20,700	7,481	86,055	5,698
LATIN AMERICA AND THE CARIBBEAN																
Argentina	4	12	6	18	...	215,471	...	...	181	181	35,754	...	...	1,252	6,851	115
Bahamas	124	4	563	18	...	...	...	...	...	...	...	...	...	...	...	...
Barbados	334	4	691	9	...	...	...	...	...	...	...	...	...	...	...	...
Belize	349	34	317	31	...	...	...	...	...	...	...	...	...	...	...	...
Bolivia	48	5	27	3	...	60,762	...	...	41	10	3,698	...	...	...	1,853	24
Brazil	124	10	200	17	...	1,724,929	...	...	88	170	30,403	...	...	5,059	35,264	1,499
Chile	323	12	364	13	...	79,604	...	...	81	136	2,035	820	1,935	1,474	5,464	1,094
Colombia	366	55	140	21	...	112,988	...	...	39	51	3,154	...	...	1,073	8,965	1,079
Costa Rica	225	5	311	8	...	35,889	...	...	87	185	848	...	...	734	884	10
Cuba	132	20	85	13	...	60,856	...	...	37	...	4,382	...	...	...	773	33
Dominican Republic	...	...	...	...	...	12,600	...	...	75	...	1,743	...	...	537	...	...
Ecuador	120	21	54	10	...	43,197	10,276	5,170	35	53	966	...	...	564	478	1
El Salvador	404	31	148	11	...	10,029	...	...	33	...	283	...	...	...	2,535	25

TABLE B.6

continued

	Road safety					Roads			Motor vehicles		Railways			Port traffic	Air	
	per 10,000 vehicles		per 100,000 population			total	passengers	goods hauled	number per 1000		route	passengers	goods hauled	TEU	passengers	freight
	injury rate 1996	fatality rate 1996	injury rate 1996	fatality rate 1996	fatality rate 2004	(km) 1999–2003	m-p-km 1999–2003	m-t-km 1999–2003	1990	2003	km 1999–2004	m-p-km 1999–2004	m-t-km 1999–2004	(000) 2004	(000) 2004	m-t-km 2004
Guatemala	...	...	...	...	...	14,095	...	...	21	57	886	...	...	817	...	...
Guyana	...	...	217	20	...	...	...	...	...	...	...	...	...	...	...	...
Haiti	...	...	...	...	...	4,160	...	...	8	...	...	...	...	...	...	...
Honduras	92	26	30	9	...	13,600	...	...	22	61	699	...	...	556	...	...
Jamaica	...	...	...	...	15	18,700	...	...	52	...	272	...	...	1,361	2,008	38
Mexico	25	3	36	4	...	349,038	399,000	195,200	119	201	26,656	...	...	1,906	21,240	403
Nicaragua	219	28	80	10	...	18,658	...	...	19	39	6	...	...	...	61	1
Panama	314	15	335	16	...	11,643	...	...	75	107	355	...	...	2,429	1,501	34
Paraguay	304	4	155	2	...	29,500	...	...	27	88	441	...	...	...	373	0
Peru	4	2	13	9	...	78,672	...	72	128	46	2,123	...	...	696	2,666	200
Puerto Rico	...	...	...	24,023	...	10	295	...	96	...	...	1,671	...	...	...	...
Saint Lucia	189	12	195	13	...	...	...	...	...	...	...	...	...	...	...	...
Trinidad and Tobago	13	20	...	8,320	...	...	117	...	...	...	...	440	1,132	42	...	...
Uruguay	90	33	58	22	...	8,983	...	...	138	...	2,993	...	...	302	564	0
Venezuela	591	58	117	12	...	96,155	...	...	93	...	433	...	32	921	4,592	2
NORTHERN AMERICA																
Canada	134	2	771	10	9	1,408,900	...	184,774	605	577	49,422	3,122	323,600	3,926	40,701	1,657
United States of America	163	2	1,281	16	15	6,378,154	...	1,599,754	758	808	141,961	...	2,200,123	35,613	678,111	37,450
OCEANIA																
Australia	16	2	93	11	8	811,601	...	...	530	...	9,474	1,347	41,314	5,130	41,597	1,898
Fiji	129	10	145	11	...	...	...	...	...	...	...	...	...	...	...	...
New Zealand	70	2	457	14	11	92,662	...	...	524	730	3,898	...	3,853	1,615	11,305	749
Papua New Guinea	168	25	44	7	...	19,600	...	...	27	...	...	...	...	...	759	23
Samoa	...	...	62	6	...	...	...	...	...	...	...	...	...	...	...	...
Tonga	36	52	7	10	...	...	...	...	...	...	...	...	...	...	...	...

Sources: World Bank, 2006; Road Federation, 2004

Notes:

TEU - Container capacity is measured in twenty-foot equivalent units

m-p-k million passenger- km

m-t-k million ton-km

TABLE B.7

International Migrants and Internally Displaced Persons

	By Country of Asylum				By Country of Origin			Internally displaced persons		International migrants		
	Refugees 2005	Asylum seekers 2005	Returned refugees 2005	Stateless persons 2005	Refugees 2005	Asylum seekers 2005	Returned refugees 2005	Displaced 2005	Returned 2005	percentage 1995	percentage 2000	percentage 2005
WORLD	8,394,373	773,492	1,105,544	2,381,886	8,394,373	773,492	1,105,544	6,616,791	519,430	2.9	2.9	3.0
AFRICA										2.5	2.0	1.9
Algeria[1]	94,101	306	1	–	12,006	1,391	1	–	–	1.1	0.8	0.7
Angola	13,984	885	53,771	–	215,777	8,352	53,771	–	–	0.3	0.3	0.4
Benin	30,294	1,695	–	–	411	272	–	–	–	2.4	1.9	2.1
Botswana	3,109	47	–	–	4	11	–	–	–	2.4	3.2	4.5
Burkina Faso	511	784	–	–	607	211	–	–	–	4.7	5.1	5.8
Burundi	20,681	19,900	68,248	–	438,663	8,268	68,248	11,500	–	4.8	1.2	1.3
Cameroon	52,042	6,766	–	–	9,016	4,860	–	–	–	1.2	1.0	0.8
Cape Verde	–	–	–	–	5	14	–	–	–	2.4	2.3	2.2
Central African Republic	24,569	1,960	74	–	42,890	1,843	74	–	–	2.0	1.9	1.9
Chad	275,412	68	1,447	–	48,400	3,113	1,447	–	–	1.1	1.3	4.5
Comoros	1	–	–	–	61	516	–	–	–	8.6	8.7	8.4
Congo	66,075	3,486	346	–	24,413	8,174	346	–	–	5.8	6.4	7.2
Côte d'Ivoire	41,627	2,443	2	–	18,303	6,356	2	38,039	–	15.7	14.0	13.1
Dem. Republic of the Congo	204,341	138	39,050	–	430,625	55,962	39,050	–	–	4.6	1.4	0.9
Djibouti	10,456	19	–	–	503	218	–	–	–	5.8	4.0	2.6
Egypt	88,946	11,005	–	96	6,291	2,329	–	–	–	0.3	0.3	0.2
Equatorial Guinea	–	–	–	–	477	59	–	–	–	0.9	1.0	1.2
Eritrea	4,418	1,591	1	–	143,594	4,034	1	–	–	0.4	0.4	0.3
Ethiopia	100,817	209	147	–	65,293	16,235	147	–	–	1.3	1.0	0.7
Gabon	8,545	4,843	–	–	81	57	–	–	–	14.7	16.5	17.7
Gambia	7,330	602	–	–	1,678	662	–	–	–	13.3	14.1	15.3
Ghana	53,537	5,496	1	–	18,432	2,351	1	–	–	5.9	7.6	7.5
Guinea	63,525	3,808	3	–	5,820	3,277	3	–	–	11.6	8.7	4.3
Guinea-Bissau	7,616	166	–	–	1,050	250	–	–	–	2.7	1.4	1.2
Kenya	251,271	16,460	–	–	4,620	11,444	–	–	–	1.3	1.1	1.0
Lesotho	–	–	–	–	6	7	–	–	–	0.3	0.3	0.3
Liberia	10,168	29	70,288	–	231,114	6,000	70,288	237,822	260,744	9.3	5.2	1.5
Libyan Arab Jamahiriya[2]	12,166	200	–	–	1,535	769	–	–	–	10.5	10.5	10.6
Madagascar	4,240	5,331	–	–	203	19	–	–	–	0.4	0.4	0.3
Malawi	–	–	–	–	101	3,849	–	–	–	3.2	2.4	2.2
Mali	11,233	1,833	–	–	520	353	–	–	–	0.6	0.4	0.3
Mauritania	632	92	–	–	31,651	2,304	–	–	–	5.1	2.4	2.1
Mauritius	–	–	–	–	27	18	–	–	–	1.0	1.3	1.7
Morocco	219	1,843	–	4	2,920	463	–	–	–	0.4	0.4	0.4
Mozambique	1,954	4,015	–	–	104	371	–	–	–	1.6	2.0	2.1
Namibia	5,307	1,073	53	–	1,226	41	53	–	–	7.5	7.5	7.1
Niger	301	48	–	–	655	591	–	–	–	1.4	1.0	0.9
Nigeria	9,019	420	7,401	–	22,098	14,039	7,401	–	–	0.6	0.6	0.7
Réunion	–	–	–	–	–	–	–	–	–	11.9	14.6	18.1
Rwanda	45,206	4,301	9,854	–	100,244	15,880	9,854	–	–	1.1	1.1	1.3
Saint Helena	–	–	–	–	–	–	–	–	–	14.4	19.4	24.8
São Tomé and Príncipe	–	–	–	–	24	–	–	–	–	5.6	5.2	4.8
Senegal	20,712	2,629	–	–	8,671	1,850	–	–	–	3.5	2.9	2.8
Seychelles	–	–	–	–	40	10	–	–	–	5.5	5.9	6.1
Sierra Leone	59,965	177	210	–	40,447	5,950	210	–	–	1.3	1.0	2.2
Somalia	493	98	11,952	–	394,760	30,467	11,952	400,000	–	0.3	0.3	3.4
South Africa	29,714	140,095	–	–	268	165	–	–	–	2.6	2.2	2.3
Sudan	147,256	4,425	18,525	–	693,267	13,476	18,525	841,946	–	3.8	2.6	1.8
Swaziland	760	256	–	–	13	5	–	–	–	4.0	4.1	4.4
Togo	9,287	420	3	–	51,107	7,479	3	3,000	6,000	3.8	3.3	3.0
Tunisia	87	26	–	–	3,129	365	–	–	–	0.4	0.4	0.4
Uganda	257,256	1,809	24	–	34,170	4,313	24	–	–	2.9	2.2	1.8
United Republic of Tanzania	548,824	307	–	–	1,544	5,250	–	–	–	3.7	2.6	2.1
Western Sahara	–	–	–	–	90,652	24	–	–	–	1.1	1.1	1.0
Zambia	155,718	146	–	–	151	481	–	–	–	2.8	3.3	2.4
Zimbabwe	13,850	118	–	–	10,793	17,326	–	–	–	5.4	5.2	3.9
ASIA										1.4	1.4	1.4
Afghanistan[3]	32	14	752,084	–	1,908,052	14,035	752,084	142,505	17,044	0.2	0.2	0.1
Armenia	219,550	70	–	–	13,965	4,352	–	–	–	14.1	10.2	7.8
Azerbaijan	3,004	115	1	2,300	233,675	4,125	1	578,545	–	3.7	2.0	2.2
Bahrain	15				41	27	–	–	–	37.5	37.8	40.7
Bangladesh	21,098	58	–	250,000	7,294	10,166	–	–	–	0.9	0.8	0.7
Bhutan	–	–	–	–	106,537	1,110	–	–	–	0.5	0.5	0.5
Brunei Darussalam	–	–	–	–	49	–	–	–	–	29.6	31.2	33.2
Cambodia	127	68	–	–	17,806	860	–	–	–	1.0	1.9	2.2
China	301,041	84	–	–	124,021	19,394	–	–	–	0.0	0.0	0.0
China, Hong Kong SAR	1,934	1,097	–	–		17	–	–	–	39.3	40.7	42.6
China, Macao SAR	–	–	–	–	9	7	–	–	–	54.4	54.2	55.9
Cyprus	701	13,067	–	1	5	4	–	–	–	7.6	10.2	13.9
Dem. People's Republic of Korea	–	–	–	–	288	78	–	–	–	0.2	0.2	0.2
Georgia	2,497	8	41	1,289	7,301	3,011	41	234,249	398	0.7	0.7	0.6
India	139,283	303	–	–	16,275	12,193	–	–	–	5.0	4.6	4.3
Indonesia	89	58	135	–	34,384	4,498	135	–	–	0.7	0.6	0.5
Iran (Islamic Republic of)	716,403	140	68	–	262,142	34,441	56,155	1,200,000	196,000	0.1	0.2	0.1
Iraq	50,177	1,948	56,155	130,000	98,722	12,894	68	–	–	4.0	3.5	2.8

TABLE B.7

continued

	By Country of Asylum				By Country of Origin			Internally displaced persons		International migrants		
	Refugees 2005	Asylum seekers 2005	Returned refugees 2005	Stateless persons 2005	Refugees 2005	Asylum seekers 2005	Returned refugees 2005	Displaced 2005	Returned 2005	percentage 1995	percentage 2000	percentage 2005
Israel	609	939	–	–	632	626	–	–	–	0.6	0.6	0.1
Japan	1,941	533	–	–	13	56	–	–	–	35.7	37.1	39.6
Jordan	965	16,570	–	9	1,789	670	–	–	–	1.0	1.3	1.3
Kazakhstan	7,265	65	–	50,576	4,316	608	–	–	–	37.7	39.1	39.0
Kuwait	1,523	203	–	80,000	381	73	–	–	–	20.8	19.1	16.9
Kyrgyzstan	2,598	498	–	100,000	3,122	371	–	–	–	58.7	62.2	62.1
Lao People's Dem. Republic	33,693	10,838	–	–	24,442	354	–	–	–	10.5	7.5	5.5
Lebanon	1,078	1,450	–	–	18,323	2,003	–	–	–	0.5	0.5	0.4
Malaysia	–	–	–	–	394	182	–	–	–	18.7	18.5	18.4
Maldives	–	–	–	–	13	4	–	–	–	5.6	6.1	6.5
Mongolia	–	2	–	581	654	642	–	–	–	1.2	1.1	1.0
Myanmar	–	–	92	236,495	164,864	41,135	92	–	–	0.3	0.3	0.3
Nepal	126,436	1,272	–	400,000	2,065	2,425	–	–	–	0.3	0.2	0.2
Occupied Palestinian Territory[1]	–	–	3	–	349,673	1,066	3	–	–	2.9	2.9	3.0
Oman	7	4			12	8	–	–	–	46.0	44.7	45.4
Pakistan	1,084,694	3,426	1	–	29,698	16,458	1	–	–	26.3	24.8	24.4
Philippines	96	42	–	–	465	867	–	–	–	3.2	3.0	2.1
Qatar	46	28	–	–	11	7	–	–	–	0.3	0.4	0.5
Republic of Korea	69	519	–	–	268	318	–	–	–	77.2	76.0	78.3
Saudi Arabia	240,701	212	–	70,000	151	71	–	–	–	1.3	1.2	1.2
Singapore	3	1	–	–	39	28	–	–	–	24.7	23.9	25.9
Sri Lanka	106	121	2,700	–	108,059	4,238	2,700	324,699	27,185	28.5	33.6	42.6
Syrian Arab Republic	26,089	1,898	19	300,000	16,281	7,004	19	–	–	2.3	2.0	1.8
Tajikistan	1,018	22	40	–	54,753	149	40	–	–	5.4	5.4	5.2
Thailand	117,053	32,163	–	–	424	217	–	–	–	5.3	5.4	4.7
Timor-Leste	3	10			251	3	–	–	–	1.0	1.4	1.6
Turkey	2,399	4,872	21	–	170,131	11,316	21	–	–	1.9	1.8	1.8
Turkmenistan	11,963	2	–	–	820	176	–	–	–	6.2	5.4	4.6
United Arab Emirates	104	79	–	–	30	16	–	–	–	70.5	70.4	71.4
Uzbekistan	43,950	587	–	–	8,323	1,475	–	–	–	6.4	5.5	4.8
Viet Nam	2,357	–	179	15,000	358,248	1,695	179	–	–	0.0	0.0	0.0
Yemen	81,937	798	6	–	1,325	419	6	–	–	1.5	1.4	1.3
EUROPE										7.6	8.0	8.8
Albania	56	35	–	–	12,702	2,579	–	–	–	2.3	2.5	2.6
Andorra	–	–	–	–	9	3	–	–	–	77.6	77.9	77.9
Austria	21,230	40,710	–	500	66	4	–	–	–	8.9	11.4	15.1
Belarus	725	56	–	9,983	8,857	1,431	–	–	–	12.4	12.8	12.2
Belgium	15,282	18,913	–	237	95	22	–	–	–	9.0	8.5	6.9
Bosnia and Herzegovina	10,568	215	1,273	–	109,930	1,815	1,273	182,747	5,164	2.1	2.5	1.0
Bulgaria	4,413	805	–	–	–	–	–	–	–	0.6	1.3	1.3
Channel Islands	–	–	–	–	4,254	1,217	–	–	–	39.8	42.7	45.8
Croatia	2,927	8	5,261	20	119,148	214	5,261	4,804	2,736	15.4	13.7	14.5
Czech Republic	1,802	924	–	–	3,589	203	–	–	–	4.4	4.4	4.4
Denmark	44,374	509	–	446	12	7	–	–	–	4.8	5.7	7.2
Estonia	7	8	–	136,000	743	135	–	–	–	21.3	18.3	15.0
Faeroe Islands	–	–	–	–	–	–	–	–	–	9.1	10.2	11.4
Finland	11,809	–	–	726	5					62.0	2.6	3.0
France	137,316	11,700	–	835	286	56	–	–	–	10.5	10.6	10.7
Germany[4]	700,016	71,624	–	9,476	78	63	–	–	–	11.1	11.9	12.3
Gibraltar	–	–	–	–	–	–	–	–	–	30.5	28.3	26.4
Greece	2,390	8,867	–	–	331	43	–	–	–	5.1	6.7	8.8
Hungary	8,046	684	–	49	3,519	257	–	–	–	2.8	2.9	3.1
Iceland	293	29	–	53	7	2	–	–	–	3.9	5.6	7.8
Ireland	7,113	2,414	–	–	21	4	–	–	–	7.3	10.1	14.1
Isle of Man	–	–	–	–	–	–	–	–	–	49.6	47.4	48.3
Italy	20,675	–	–	886	217	23	–	–	–	2.6	2.8	4.3
Latvia	11	9	–	418,638	2,430	123	–	–	–	28.5	22.7	19.5
Liechtenstein	150	60	–	–	–	–	–	–	–	37.8	35.6	33.9
Lithuania	531	55	–	8,708	1,448	188	–	–	–	7.5	6.1	4.8
Luxembourg	1,822	–	–	–	1	–	–	–	–	33.4	36.9	37.4
Malta	1,939	149	–	–	5	2	–	–	–	1.9	2.2	2.7
Monaco	–	–	–	–	0	3	–	–	–	68.0	68.9	68.9
Netherlands	118,189	14,664	–	6,500	159	42	–	–	–	9.0	9.8	10.1
Norway	43,034	–	–	941	15	1	–	–	–	5.3	6.6	7.4
Poland	4,604	1,627	–	74	19,641	612	–	–	–	2.5	2.1	1.8
Portugal	363	–	–	–	74	127	–	–	–	5.3	6.2	7.3
Republic of Moldova	84	148	–	1,530	12,063	576	–	–	–	10.9	11.1	10.5
Romania	2,056	264	–	400	11,492	1,129	–	–	–	0.6	0.6	0.6
Russian Federation	1,523	292	162	71,155	102,965	14,316	162	170,544	1,677	7.9	8.1	8.4
San Marino	–	–	–	–	1	3	–	–	–	34.9	34.1	33.5
Serbia and Montenegro	148,264	33	5,828	–	189,850	18,132	5,828	246,391	2,482	7.2	6.6	4.9
Slovakia	368	2,707	–	–	791	203	–	–	–	2.1	2.2	2.3
Slovenia	251	185	–	445	155	21	–	–	–	10.2	8.9	8.5
Spain	5,374	–	–	18	49	27	–	–	–	2.5	4.0	11.1
Sweden	74,915	15,702	–	5,299	75	10	–	–	–	10.3	11.2	12.4
Switzerland	48,030	14,428	–	28	16	2	–	–	–	21.0	21.8	22.9
TFYR Macedonia	1,274	723	–	2,200	8,599	706	–	–	–	5.8	6.2	6.0

TABLE B.7

continued

	By Country of Asylum				By Country of Origin			Internally displaced persons		International migrants		
	Refugees 2005	Asylum seekers 2005	Returned refugees 2005	Stateless persons 2005	Refugees 2005	Asylum seekers 2005	Returned refugees 2005	Displaced 2005	Returned 2005	percentage 1995	percentage 2000	percentage 2005
Ukraine	2,346	1,618	1	70,077	84,213	2,670	1	–	–	13.7	14.1	14.7
United Kingdom	293,459	13,400	–	205	135	63	–	–	–	7.3	8.1	9.1
LATIN AMERICA AND THE CARIBBEAN										1.3	1.2	1.2
Anguilla	–	–	–	–	–	–	–	–	–	31.4	36.2	41.8
Antigua and Barbuda	–	–	–	–	13	11	–	–	–	19.9	20.7	22.4
Argentina	3,074	825	–	–	856	292	–	–	–	4.6	4.2	3.9
Aruba	–	–	–	–	–	–	–	–	–	21.2	22.7	24.6
Bahamas	–	–	–	–	11	8	–	–	–	10.2	9.9	9.8
Barbados	–	–	–	–	8	21	–	–	–	8.7	9.2	9.7
Belize	624	14	–	–	8	24	–	–	–	13.7	14.2	15.0
Bolivia	535	3	–	–	2	3	–	–	–	0.9	1.1	1.3
Brazil	3,458	195	–	91	269	353	–	–	–	0.5	0.4	0.3
British Virgin Islands	–	–	–	–	370	593	–	–	–	43.2	40.9	38.3
Cayman Islands	–	–	–	–		2	–	–	–	42.2	37.7	35.8
Chile	806	107	–	–	938	92	–	–	–	0.9	1.2	1.4
Colombia	155	41	5	9	60,415	19,754	5	2,000,000	–	0.3	0.3	0.3
Costa Rica[2]	11,253	223	–	–	178	133	–	–	–	6.6	7.9	10.2
Cuba	706	32	1	–	19,000	1,683	1	–	–	0.8	0.7	0.7
Dominica	–	–	–	–	30	46	–	–	–	4.1	4.8	5.7
Dominican Republic	–	–	–	–	67	79	–	–	–	1.5	1.6	1.8
Ecuador	10,063	2,489	–	–	770	287	–	–	–	0.8	0.8	0.9
El Salvador	49	1	–	–	4,281	45,205	–	–	–	0.5	0.4	0.3
Falkland Islands (Malvinas)	–	–	–	–	–	–	–	–	–	46.6	52.6	70.2
French Guiana	–	–	–	–	–	–	–	–	–	47.0	45.0	44.9
Grenada	–	–	–	–	152	103	–	–	–	5.9	7.8	10.5
Guadeloupe	391	3	–	–	3,379	31,850	–	–	–	18.1	19.4	20.8
Guatemala	–	–	–	–	–	–	–	–	–	0.5	0.4	0.4
Guyana	–	–	–	–	406	387	–	–	–	0.3	0.2	0.1
Haiti	22	50	–	–	13,542	13,519	–	–	–	0.3	0.3	0.4
Honduras	–	–	–	–	535	1,227	–	–	–	0.5	0.4	0.4
Jamaica	–	–	–	–	450	290	–	–	–	0.8	0.7	0.7
Martinique	–	–	–	–	–	–	–	–	–	12.2	14.1	16.3
Mexico	3,229	161	–	–	2,313	12,614	–	–	–	0.5	0.5	0.6
Montserrat	–	–	–	–	–	–	–	–	–	17.8	4.7	2.5
Netherlands Antilles	–	–	–	–	–	–	–	–	–	23.6	26.3	26.5
Nicaragua	227	1	44	–	1,463	4,426	44	–	–	0.6	0.6	0.5
Panama	1,730	433	–	6	42	58	–	–	–	2.7	2.9	3.2
Paraguay	50	8	–	–	44	35	–	–	–	3.8	3.2	2.7
Peru	848	336	3	–	4,865	1,649	3	–	–	0.2	0.2	0.1
Puerto Rico	–	–	–	–	–	–	–	–	–	9.5	10.0	10.6
Saint Kitts and Nevis	–	–	–	–	31	1	–	–	–	10.3	10.6	10.4
Saint Lucia	–	–	–	–	99	201	–	–	–	4.3	4.8	5.4
Saint Vincent and the Grenadines	–	–	–	–	279	355	–	–	–	4.9	6.5	8.7
Suriname	–	–	–	–	29	21	–	–	–	1.8	1.4	1.2
Trinidad and Tobago	–	–	–	–	63	209	–	–	–	3.6	3.2	2.9
Turks and Caicos Islands	–	–	–	–	–	2	–	–	–	15.6	14.0	11.9
United States Virgin Islands	–	–	–	–	–	–	–	–	–	30.9	31.4	32.7
Uruguay	121	9	–	–	111	62	–	–	–	2.9	2.7	2.4
Venezuela	408	5,912	–	–	2,590	2,832	–	–	–	4.6	4.2	3.8
NORTHERN AMERICA										11.2	12.8	13.5
Bermuda	–	–	–	–	–	–	–	–	–	26.8	27.6	29.3
Canada	147,171	20,552	–	–	122	36	–	–	–	17.1	18.1	18.9
Greenland	–	–	–	–	–	–	–	–	–	19.2	20.4	21.5
Saint-Pierre-et-Miquelon	–	–	–	–	–	–	–	–	–	18.7	20.9	23.3
United States of America[5]	379,340	169,743	–	–	683	263	–	–	–	10.6	12.2	12.9
OCEANIA										17.5	16.3	15.2
American Samoa	–	–	–	–	–	–	–	–	–	39.4	35.7	31.4
Australia	64,964	1,822	–	–	44	4	–	–	–	22.7	21.4	20.3
Cook Islands	–	–	–	–	–	–	–	–	–	13.7	15.3	17.0
Fiji	–	–	–	–	1,379	373	–	–	–	3.2	3.2	3.2
French Polynesia	–	–	–	–	1	–	–	–	–	1.9	2.0	2.0
Guam	–	–	–	–	–	–	–	–	–	13.1	13.0	13.1
Kiribati	–	–	–	–	33	5	–	–	–	56.6	62.2	66.9
Marshall Islands	–	–	–	–	–	–	–	–	–	2.9	2.7	2.6
Micronesia (Fed. States of)		–	–	–	–	1	–	–	–	3.1	3.1	2.7
Nauru	–	–	–	–		3	–	–	–	39.3	37.4	36.1
New Caledonia	–	–	–	–		7	–	–	–	20.0	19.0	18.2
New Zealand	5,307	396	–	–	4	5	–	–	–	20.0	18.5	15.9
Niue	–	–	–	–	–	–	–	–	–	10.0	8.7	7.6
Northern Mariana Islands	–	–	–	–	–	–	–	–	–	8.7	7.3	6.5
Palau	–	–	–	–	1	–	–	–	–	12.9	13.5	15.2
Papua New Guinea	9,999	4	–	–	23	21	–	–	–	0.7	0.5	0.4
Pitcairn	–	–	–	–	–	–	–	–	–	9.0	8.8	9.0
Samoa	–	–	–	–	–	3	–	–	–	4.1	4.5	5.0
Solomon Islands	–	–	–	–	27	11	–	–	–	1.0	0.8	0.7
Tokelau	–	–	–	–	–	–	–	–	–	13.2	12.8	12.5

TABLE B.7

continued

	By Country of Asylum				By Country of Origin			Internally displaced persons		International migrants		
	Refugees	Asylum seekers	Returned refugees	Stateless persons	Refugees	Asylum seekers	Returned refugees	Displaced	Returned		percentage	
	2005	2005	2005	2005	2005	2005	2005	2005	2005	1995	2000	2005
Tonga	–	–	–	–	4	10	–	–	–	2.3	1.6	1.1
Tuvalu	–	–	–	–	–	–	–	–	–	3.2	3.1	3.1
Vanuatu	–	–	–	–	–	–	–	–	–	1.0	0.7	0.5
Wallis and Futuna Islands	–	–	–	–	–	–	–	–	–	11.9	12.6	13.4

Sources: UNHCR, 2006; United Nations, 2006

Notes:

1 According to the Government of Algeria, there are an estimated 165,000 Sahrawi refugees in Tindouf camps.
2 2004 data for Costa Rica (asylum-seekers) and the Libyan Arab Jamahiriya (refugees and asylum-seekers).
3 UNHCR figures for Pakistan only include Afghans living in camps who are assisted by UNHCR. According to the 2005 government census of Afghans in Pakistan and subsequent voluntary repatriation during the year, there are an additional 1.5 million Afghans living outside camps, some of whom may be refugees. Those Afghans living outside camps receive no UNHCR assistance except access to UNHCR-facilitated voluntary repatriation.
4 With the introduction of the new Immigration Act in 2005, the Central Aliens Register now encompasses new residence categories and simultaneously refines previous ones, allowing for a better differentiation of refugee statistics. The refugee data included in this table refers to 15 December 2005. 5 UNHCR's method of estimating the refugee population in the United States is currently under review due to newly available information. As a result, the estimated refugee population in the country might increase significantly as of 2006.

TABLE B.8

Major Disaster Incidents, 1980–2000

	Cyclones			Droughts			Earthquakes			Floods			Population affected by conflicts 1980–2000
	Number of events 1980–2000	Loss of lives 1980–2000		Number of events 1980–2000	Loss of lives 1980–2000		Number of events 1980–2000	Loss of lives 1980–2000		Number of events 1980–2000	Loss of lives 1980–2000		
	Annual average	Annual average	Per million	Annual average	Annual average	Per million	Annual average	Annual average	Per million	Annual average	Annual average	Per million	Annual average
WORLD													
AFRICA													
Algeria	...	...	...	...	...	...	0.38	137.19	5.79	0.71	13.33	0.50	37.0
Angola	...	...	...	...	...	...	...	...	...	0.24	1.38	0.11	79.0
Benin	...	...	...	...	...	...	...	...	...	0.48	4.67	0.91	–
Botswana	...	...	...	...	...	...	...	...	...	0.14	1.48	1.07	–
Burkina Faso	...	...	...	...	...	...	...	...	...	0.24	2.10	0.23	–
Burundi	...	...	...	0.1	0.29	0.05	...	...	...	0.10	0.57	0.10	16.0
Cameroon	...	...	...	...	...	...	...	...	...	0.24	1.76	0.13	–
Cape Verde	0.1	1.52	5.07	...	...	...	...	...	...	...	...	...	–
Central African Republic	...	...	...	...	...	...	...	...	...	0.24	0.33	0.09	3.6
Chad	...	...	...	0.33	142.86	27.87	...	...	...	0.29	4.00	0.63	43.0
Comoros	0.19	2.81	5.97	...	...	...	...	...	...	...	...	...	–
Congo	...	...	...	...	...	...	...	...	...	0.14	0.10	0.03	6.0
Côte d'Ivoire	...	...	...	...	...	...	...	...	...	0.10	1.33	0.10	–
Dem. Republic of the Congo	...	...	...	...	...	...	...	...	...	0.19	3.05	0.07	18.0
Djibouti	...	...	...	...	...	...	...	...	...	0.19	8.57	18.26	23.4
Egypt	...	...	...	...	...	...	0.1	27.19	0.45	0.14	28.95	0.48	–
Eritrea													70.0
Ethiopia	...	...	...	0.57	14,303.19	286.24	...	...	...	1.00	27.14	0.50	24.0
Gambia	...	...	...	...	...	...	...	...	...	0.10	2.52	2.09	–
Ghana	...	...	...	...	...	...	...	...	...	0.19	9.95	0.60	–
Guinea	...	...	...	0.14	0.57	0.1	...	...	...	...	...	...	–
Kenya	...	...	...	0.29	4.05	0.16	...	...	...	0.24	12.86	0.50	–
Lesotho	...	...	...	...	...	...	...	...	...	0.14	1.90	1.19	–
Liberia	...	...	...	...	...	...	...	...	...	0.05	0.48	0.19	28.0
Madagascar	0.71	48.81	3.87	0.24	9.52	0.78	...	...	...	...	...	...	–
Malawi	...	...	...	...	...	...	0.05	0.43	0.05	0.43	23.33	2.36	–
Mali	...	...	...	...	...	...	...	...	...	0.29	1.81	0.18	–
Mauritania	...	...	...	0.33	106.81	57.86	...	...	...	...	...	...	–
Morocco	...	...	...	...	...	...	...	...	...	0.33	39.62	1.40	–
Mozambique	0.33	22.1	1.41	0.43	4,764.29	357.06	...	...	...	0.33	41.33	2.66	46.0
Namibia	...	...	...	...	...	...	...	...	...	0.29	4.57	0.47	40.0
Niger	...	...	...	...	...	...	...	...	...	0.62	12.67	0.12	–
Rwanda	...	...	...	...	...	...	...	...	...	0.05	2.29	0.34	23.0
Senegal											6.0		
Sierra Leone	...	...	...	...	...	...	...	...	...	0.05	0.57	0.14	24.0
Somalia	...	...	...	0.24	29.57	4.14	...	...	...	0.52	117.62	15.38	3.0
South Africa	...	...	...	...	...	...	0.14	1.62	0.05	0.67	54.71	1.38	22.0
Sudan	...	...	...	0.48	7,142.86	294.05	...	...	...	0.57	15.52	0.57	65.0
Swaziland	0.05	2.52	4.04	...	...	...	...	...	...	...	...	...	–
Togo	...	...	...	...	...	...	...	...	...	0.19	0.14	0.04	–
Tunisia	...	...	...	...	...	...	...	...	...	0.14	8.43	1.13	–
Uganda	...	...	...	0.29	5.48	0.29	0.14	0.33	0.02	0.14	7.05	0.36	45.0
United Republic of Tanzania	...	...	...	...	...	...	0.05	0.05	0	0.71	22.00	0.77	–
Zimbabwe	...	...	...	...	...	...	...	...	...	0.10	5.05	0.41	–
ASIA													
Afghanistan	...	...	...	...	...	...	0.81	399.95	2480	0.76	420.57	24.63	98.0
Armenia	...	...	...	...	...	...	0.05	1190.48	343.96	0.05	0.19	0.05	–
Azerbaijan	...	...	...	...	...	...	0.14	1.52	0.19	0.19	0.76	0.10	0.8
Bangladesh	3.43	7,467.62	64.02	...	...	...	0.19	1.38	0.01	2.00	461.95	4.11	4.0
Bhutan	...	...	...	...	...	...	...	...	...	0.10	10.57	5.44	–
Cambodia	...	...	...	...	...	...	...	...	...	0.29	48.52	4.08	75.0
China	6.9	428.38	0.37	0.86	161.9	0.14	2.1	92.24	0.08	5.57	1490.57	1.32	–
Cyprus	...	...	...	...	...	...	0.05	0.1	0.13	...	...	...	–
Dem. People's Republic of Korea	...	...	...	0.1	12,857.14	579.43	...	...	...	0.29	28.14	1.35	–
Georgia	...	...	...	...	...	...	0.14	13.29	2.44	0.14	4.81	0.90	–
India	2.76	1,022.52	1.24	0.38	19.52	0.02	0.67	576.52	0.73	3.86	1313.24	1.55	3.0
Indonesia	...	...	...	0.29	60.29	0.34	1.62	193.24	1.04	2.48	120.29	0.67	1.0
Iran (Islamic Republic of)	...	...	...	...	...	...	1.43	2,250.81	38.68	1.90	131.19	2.20	22.0
Iraq													71.0
Israel	...	...	...	...	...	...	...	...	...	0.10	0.52	0.09	99.0
Japan	1.95	39.29	0.32	...	...	...	1.14	281.29	2.31	0.62	30.71	0.25	–
Jordan	...	...	...	...	...	...	...	...	...	0.10	0.81	0.26	–
Kazakhstan	...	...	...	...	...	...	0.1	0.05	0	0.10	0.48	0.03	–
Kuwait	...	...	...	...	...	...	...	...	...	0.05	0.10	0.06	–
Kyrgyzstan	...	...	...	...	...	...	0.1	2.76	0.62	0.10	0.10	0.02	–
Lao People's Dem. Republic	0.19	2.67	0.6	...	...	...	...	...	...	0.43	3.29	0.75	6.0
Lebanon													25.0
Malaysia	0.1	12.86	0.6	...	...	...	...	...	...	0.43	4.43	0.24	–
Myanmar	...	...	...	...	...	...	...	...	...	0.29	9.05	0.20	74.0
Nepal	...	...	...	...	...	...	0.1	38.52	2.42	0.90	199.38	10.92	–
Pakistan	0.62	53.9	0.46	0.05	6.81	0.05	0.62	30.95	0.3	0.95	200.38	1.77	–
Philippines	5.57	863.19	14.35	0.24	0.38	0.01	0.57	120.57	2.03	1.76	75.71	1.22	100.0
Republic of Korea	1	71.52	1.67	...	...	...	...	...	...	0.71	51.95	1.19	–
Sri Lanka	...	...	...	...	...	...	...	...	...	1.29	27.62	1.62	65.0

TABLE B.8

continued

	Cyclones			Droughts			Earthquakes			Floods			Population affected by conflicts 1980–2000
	Number of events 1980–2000	Loss of lives 1980–2000		Number of events 1980–2000	Loss of lives 1980–2000		Number of events 1980–2000	Loss of lives 1980–2000		Number of events 1980–2000	Loss of lives 1980–2000		
	Annual average	Annual average	Per million	Annual average	Annual average	Per million	Annual average	Annual average	Per million	Annual average	Annual average	Per million	Annual average
Syrian Arab Republic													4.0
Tajikistan													15.0
Thailand	0.71	30.24	0.54	...	...	...	...	...	...	1.33	78.52	1.37	11.0
Turkey	...	...	...	...	...	...	0.76	949.86	15.58	0.67	20.90	0.36	3.0
Uzbekistan	...	...	...	...	...	...	0.1	0.43	0.02	...	...	...	–
Viet Nam	2.24	435.24	6.4	...	...	...	...	...	...	1.00	137.90	1.98	10.0
Yemen	...	...	...	...	...	...	0.1	72.29	6.9	0.52	46.71	3.65	4.0
EUROPE													
Albania	...	...	...	...	...	...	0.14	0.05	0.02	0.19	0.71	0.22	–
Austria	...	...	...	...	...	...	...	...	...	0.29	0.90	0.12	–
Belarus	...	...	...	...	...	...	...	...	...	0.10	0.10	0.01	–
Belgium	...	...	...	...	...	...	0.1	0.1	0.01	0.29	0.33	0.03	–
Bosnia and Herzegovina													27.0
Croatia													4.0
Czech Republic	...	...	...	...	...	...	...	...	...	0.05	1.38	0.13	–
France	...	...	...	...	...	...	...	...	...	1.10	5.29	0.09	–
Germany	...	...	...	...	...	...	0.05	0.05	0	0.38	1.00	0.01	–
Greece	...	...	...	...	...	...	0.62	11.29	1.11	0.19	1.19	0.11	–
Hungary	...	...	...	...	...	...	...	...	...	0.24	0.43	0.04	–
Ireland	...	...	...	...	...	...	...	...	...	0.10	0.14	0.04	–
Italy	...	...	...	...	...	...	0.52	225.71	3.98	0.57	14.00	0.24	–
Norway	...	...	...	...	...	...	...	...	...	0.10	0.05	0.01	–
Poland	...	...	...	...	...	...	...	...	...	0.24	2.95	0.08	–
Portugal	...	...	...	...	...	...	...	...	...	0.19	3.33	0.34	–
Republic of Moldova	...	...	...	...	...	...	...	...	...	0.14	2.67	0.62	–
Romania	...	...	...	...	...	...	0.14	0.52	0.02	0.43	9.24	0.41	–
Russian Federation	...	...	...	...	...	...	0.29	95.29	0.65	1.33	9.24	0.06	–
Slovakia	...	...	...	...	...	...	...	...	...	0.10	2.67	0.49	–
Spain	...	...	...	...	...	...	...	...	...	0.52	8.38	0.21	–
Switzerland	...	...	...	...	...	...	...	...	...	0.14	0.10	0.01	–
Ukraine	...	...	...	...	...	...	...	...	...	0.29	3.00	0.06	–
United Kingdom	...	...	...	...	...	...	...	...	...	0.43	0.48	0.01	2.0
Yugoslavia	...	...	...	...	...	...	...	...	...	0.38	3.90	0.38	
LATIN AMERICA AND THE CARIBBEAN													
Argentina	...	...	...	...	...	...	0.05	0.29	0.01	1.19	11.14	0.34	–
Belize	0.1	0.67	3.01	...	...	...	...	...	...	...	...	...	–
Bolivia	...	...	...	...	...	...	0.14	5.95	0.86	0.48	14.48	2.27	–
Brazil	...	...	...	0.43	0.95	0.01	0.05	0.05	0	2.19	99.33	0.67	–
Chile	...	...	...	...	...	...	0.24	9.48	0.73	0.57	16.48	1.21	–
Colombia	0.14	1.48	0.05	...	...	...	0.48	85.05	2.34	1.14	47.90	1.34	100.0
Costa Rica	0.19	4.29	1.22	...	...	...	0.33	2.52	0.85	0.38	1.67	0.51	–
Cuba	...	...	...	...	...	...	...	...	...	0.71	5.00	0.47	–
Dominican Republic	0.38	19.19	2.68	...	...	...	...	...	...	0.29	3.00	0.42	–
Ecuador	...	...	...	...	...	...	0.43	28.33	2.75	0.38	30.62	2.92	–
El Salvador	0.19	23.43	3.9	...	...	...	0.1	53.33	11.23	0.33	26.76	4.92	44.0
Guatemala	0.05	18.29	1.69	...	...	...	0.24	1.71	0.2	0.43	38.24	4.02	76.0
Haiti	0.29	81.24	11.63	...	...	...	...	...	...	0.81	11.90	1.72	–
Honduras	0.19	702.29	139.65	...	...	...	...	...	...	0.62	30.62	6.09	–
Jamaica	0.24	3.14	1.34	...	...	...	...	...	...	0.24	3.43	1.45	–
Mexico	1.57	80.76	0.93	...	...	...	0.76	427.24	5.05	1.10	121.19	1.41	–
Nicaragua	0.33	162.57	37.39	...	...	...	0.14	8.86	2.05	0.24	2.52	0.60	33.0
Panama	...	...	...	...	...	...	0.05	1.43	0.58	0.29	0.81	0.32	–
Paraguay	...	...	...	...	...	...	...	...	...	0.38	3.62	0.85	–
Peru	...	...	...	...	...	...	0.62	13	0.62	1.10	97.62	4.56	70.0
Puerto Rico	...	...	...	...	...	...	...	...	...	0.10	24.67	7.07	–
Saint Vincent and the Grenadines	...	...	...	...	...	...	...	...	...	0.14	0.14	1.37	–
Trinidad and Tobago	...	...	...	...	...	...	...	...	...	0.10	0.24	0.19	–
Venezuela	0.1	5.14	0.26	...	...	...	0.14	4.62	0.25	0.67	1439.62	68.30	–
NORTHERN AMERICA													
Canada	...	...	...	...	...	...	...	...	...	0.52	1.52	0.05	–
United States of America	12.14	222.86	0.86	...	...	...	0.48	6.52	0.03	3.48	24.19	0.09	–
OCEANIA													
Australia	2.38	4.43	0.26	...	...	...	0.14	1.1	0.07	1.10	4.43	0.26	...
Fiji	0.67	5.71	7.99	...	...	...	...	...	...	0.14	1.57	2.10	...
New Zealand	0.29	0.48	0.13	...	...	...	0.05	0.05	0.01	1.10	0.29	0.09	...
Papua New Guinea	0.1	2.24	0.52	0.14	4.67	1.16	0.33	3.1	0.83	0.24	2.76	0.72	...

Source: United Nations Development Programme, 2005

Notes: Number of earthquakes: these include events equal or greater than a magnitude of 5.5 on the Richter scale.

TABLE B.9

Income and Health

	Gross national income PPP		Expenditure on health				Health services				Prevalence of HIV Population aged 15–49 (%)		Life expectancy at birth (years)	
	$/capita 2003	$/capita 2004	% of GDP	% of total gov exp	per capita		Hospital beds per 10000		Physicians per 1000		2001	2003	Male 2004	Female 2004
					US$	Int $								
			2003	2003	2003	2003	no.	year	no	year				
WORLD	8394	8,760												
AFRICA														
Algeria	5,940	6,260	4.1	10.0	89	186	...		1.13	2002	0.0	0.1	69	72
Angola	1,890	2,030	2.8	5.3	26	49	...		0.08	1997	3.7	3.9	38	42
Benin	1,110	1,120	4.4	9.8	20	36	...		0.04	2004	1.9	1.9	52	53
Botswana	7,960	8,920	5.6	7.5	232	375	...		0.40	2004	38.0	37.3	40	40
Burkina Faso	1,180	1,220	5.6	12.7	19	68	...		0.06	2004	4.3	1.8	47	48
Burundi	620	660	3.1	2.0	3	15	...		0.03	2004	6.2	6.0	42	47
Cameroon	1,980	2,090	4.2	8.0	37	64	...		0.19	2004	7.0	5.5	50	51
Cape Verde	...	5,650	4.6	11.1	78	185	...		0.49	2004	...	...	67	71
Central African Republic	1,080	1,110	4.0	12.4	12	47	...		0.08	2004	13.5	13.5	40	41
Chad	1,100	1,420	6.5	10.5	16	51	...		0.04	2004	4.9	4.8	45	48
Comoros	...	...	2.7	6.4	11	25	...		0.15	2004	...	...	62	67
Congo	710	750	2.0	4.3	19	23	...		0.20	2004	5.3	4.9	53	55
Côte d'Ivoire	1,390	1,390	3.6	5.0	28	57	...		0.12	2004	6.7	7.0	41	47
Dem. Republic of the Congo	640	680	4.0	5.4	4	14	...		0.11	2004	4.2	4.2	42	47
Djibouti	...	2,270	5.7	10.5	47	72	16	2000	0.18	2004	...		54	57
Egypt	3,940	4,120	5.8	8.2	55	235	22	2003	0.54	2003	0.0	0.0	66	70
Equatorial Guinea	...	7,400	1.5	7.0	96	179	...		0.30	2004	1.3	1.3	42	44
Eritrea	1,110	1,050	4.4	4.0	8	50	...		0.05	2004	2.8	2.7	58	62
Ethiopia	710	810	5.9	9.6	5	20	...		0.03	2003	4.1	4.4	49	51
Gabon	...	5,600	4.4	12.8	196	255	...		0.29	2004	6.9	8.1	55	59
Gambia	...	...	8.1	13.9	21	96	...		0.11	2003	1.2	1.2	55	59
Ghana	2,190	2,280	4.5	5.0	16	98	...		0.15	2004	3.1	2.2	56	58
Guinea	2,100	2,130	5.4	4.9	22	95	...		0.11	2004	2.8	3.2	52	55
Guinea-Bissau	...	...	5.6	6.9	9	45	...		0.12	2004	1.4	1.4	45	48
Kenya	1,020	1,050	4.3	7.2	20	65	...		0.14	2004	8.0	6.7	51	50
Lesotho	3,120	3,210	5.2	9.5	31	106	...		0.05	2003	29.6	28.9	39	44
Liberia	...	...	4.7	17.6	6	17	...		0.03	2004	5.1	5.9	39	44
Libyan Arab Jamahiriya	...	...	4.1	5.9	171	327	39	2002	1.29	1997	0.1	0.3	70	75
Madagascar	800	830	2.7	9.3	8	24	...		0.29	2004	1.3	1.7	55	59
Malawi	600	620	9.3	9.1	13	46	...		0.02	2004	14.3	14.2	41	41
Mali	960	980	4.8	9.2	16	39	...		0.08	2004	1.8	1.9	44	47
Mauritania	2,010	2,050	4.2	14.3	17	59	...		0.11	2004	0.5	0.6	55	60
Mauritius	...	11,870	3.7	9.2	172	430	...		1.06	2004	0.1	...	69	75
Morocco	3,950	4,100	5.1	6.0	72	218	9	2003	0.51	2004	0.0	...	69	73
Mozambique	1,070	1,160	4.7	10.9	12	45	...		0.03	2004	12.1	12.2	44	46
Namibia	6,620	6,960	6.4	12.4	145	359	...		0.30	2004	21.3	21.3	52	55
Niger	820	830	4.7	12.4	9	30	...		0.03	2004	1.1	1.2	42	41
Nigeria	900	930	5.0	3.2	22	51	...		0.28	2003	5.5	5.4	45	46
Rwanda	1,290	1,300	3.7	7.2	7	32	...		0.05	2004	5.1	5.1	44	47
São Tomé and Príncipe	...	...	8.6	11.1	34	93	...		0.49	2004	...	...	57	60
Senegal	1,660	1,720	5.1	9.3	29	58	...		0.06	2004	0.8	0.8	54	57
Seychelles		15,590	5.9	10.2	522	599	...		1.51	2004	...	...	67	78
Sierra Leone	530	790	3.5	7.9	7	34	...		0.03	2004	3.7	...	37	40
Somalia	...	...	...	...	...	...	4	1997	0.04	1997	0.5	...	43	45
South Africa	10,270	10,960	8.4	10.2	295	669	...		0.77	2004	20.9	15.6	47	49
Sudan	...	1,870	4.3	9.1	21	54	7	2003	0.22	2004	1.9	2.3	56	60
Swaziland	...	4,970	5.8	10.9	107	324	...		0.16	2004	38.2	38.3	36	39
Togo	1,500	1,690	5.6	9.3	16	62	...		0.04	2004	4.3	4.1	52	56
Tunisia	6,840	7,310	5.4	7.2	137	409	21	2003	1.34	2004	0.0	0.0	70	74
Uganda	1,440	1,520	7.3	10.7	18	75	...		0.08	2004	5.1	4.1	48	51
United Republic of Tanzania	610	660	4.3	12.7	12	29	...		0.02	2002	9.0	7.0	47	49
Zambia	850	890	5.4	11.8	21	51	...		0.12	2004	16.7	15.6	40	40
Zimbabwe	2,180	2,180	7.9	9.2	40	132	...		0.16	2004	24.9	24.6	37	34
ASIA														
Afghanistan	...	...	6.5	7.3	11	26	4	2001	0.19	2001	...	...	42	42
Armenia	3,770	4,217	6.0	5.4	55	302	44	2004	3.59	2003	0.1	0.1	65	72
Azerbaijan	3,380	3,830	3.6	2.8	32	140	83	2003	3.55	2003	0.0	...	63	68
Bahrain		18,070	4.1	8.8	555	813	28	2003	1.09	2004	...	...	73	75
Bangladesh	1,870	1,980	3.4	5.8	14	68	3	2001	0.26	2004	0.0	...	62	63
Bhutan	...	...	3.1	7.6	10	59	16	2001	0.05	2004	...	...	62	65
Brunei Darussalam	...	...	3.5	5.2	466	681	26	2003	1.01	2000	...	...	76	78
Cambodia	2,060	2,180	10.9	11.8	33	188	6	2004	0.16	2000	2.7	2.6	51	58
China	4,990	5,530	5.6	9.7	61	278	23	2004	1.06	2001	0.1	0.1	70	74
China, Hong Kong SAR	28,810	31,510	...	...	...	...	...	...	...	...	0.1	0.1	76	83
China, Macao SAR		21,880	...	...	...	...	...	...	...	...	...	...	77	82
Cyprus		22,330	6.4	7.0	1038	1143	43	2003	2.34	2002	...	...	77	82
Dem. People's Republic of Korea			5.8	7.3	<1	74	132	2002	3.29	2003	...	...	65	68
Georgia	2,540	2,930	4.0	4.7	35	174	41	2004	4.09	2003	0.0	0.1	70	77
India	2,880	3,100	4.8	3.9	27	82	7	1998	0.60	2005	0.8	0.9	61	63
Indonesia	3,210	3,460	3.1	5.1	30	113	6	1998	0.13	2003	0.1	0.1	65	68
Iran (Islamic Republic of)	7,190	7,550	6.5	10.3	131	498	16	2001	0.45	2004	0.0	0.1	68	72
Iraq	...	...	2.7	4.2	23	64	13	2003	0.66	2004	0.0	0.0	51	61

TABLE B.9

continued

	Gross national income PPP		Expenditure on health				Health services				Prevalence of HIV Population aged 15–49 (%)		Life expectancy at birth (years)	
	$/capita 2003	$/capita 2004	% of GDP	% of total gov exp	per capita		Hospital beds per 10000		Physicians per 1000		2001	2003	Male 2004	Female 2004
					US$ 2003	Int $ 2003								
			2003	2003			no.	year	no	year				
Israel	19,200	23,510	8.9	11.4	1514	1911	61	2004	3.82	2003	...	0.1	78	82
Japan	28,620	30,040	7.9	16.8	2662	2244	129	2001	1.98	2002	0.0	0.0	79	86
Jordan	4,290	4,640	9.4	8.9	177	440	17	2004	2.03	2004	0.0	0.0	69	73
Kazakhstan	6,170	6,980	3.5	9.0	73	315	78	2004	3.54	2003	0.1	0.2	56	67
Kuwait	17,870	19,510	3.5	6.1	580	567	21	2003	1.53	2001	...	...	76	78
Kyrgyzstan	1,660	1,840	5.3	9.0	20	161	53	2004	2.51	2003	0.0	0.1	59	67
Lao People's Dem. Republic	1,730	1,850	3.2	6.2	11	56	11	2003	...		0.0	0.1	58	60
Lebanon	4,840	5,380	10.2	8.4	573	730	30	2002	3.25	2001	0.1	0.1	68	72
Malaysia	8,940	9,630	3.8	6.9	163	374	19	2003	0.70	2000	0.4	0.4	69	74
Maldives	...	...	6.2	13.8	136	364	23	2003	0.92	2004	...	...	66	68
Mongolia	1,800	2,020	6.7	10.3	33	140	73	2003	2.63	2002	0.0	0.0	61	69
Myanmar	...	...	2.8	2.5	394	51	6	2000	0.36	2004	1.0	1.2	56	63
Nepal	1,420	1,470	5.3	7.9	12	64	2	2001	0.21	2004	0.4	0.5	61	61
Occupied Palestinian Territory													71	75
Oman	...	13,250	3.2	7.0	278	419	22	2004	1.32	2004	0.1	0.1	71	77
Pakistan	2,060	2,160	2.4	2.6	13	48	7	2003	0.74	2004	0.1	0.1	62	63
Philippines	4,640	4,890	3.2	5.9	31	174	11	2002	0.58	2000	0.0	0.0	65	72
Qatar	...	...	2.7	6.7	862	685	24	2002	2.22	2001	...	...	76	75
Republic of Korea	17,930	20,400	5.6	8.9	705	1074	89	2004	1.57	2003	0.0	0.0	73	80
Saudi Arabia	12,850	14,010	4.0	9.4	366	578	22	2001	1.37	2004	...	...	68	74
Singapore	24,180	26,590	4.5	7.7	964	1156	28	2004	1.40	2001	0.2	0.2	77	82
Sri Lanka	3,730	4,000	3.5	6.5	31	121	29	2000	0.55	2004	0.0	0.0	68	75
Syrian Arab Republic	3,430	3,550	5.1	6.3	59	116	15	2003	1.40	2001	...	0.0	70	74
Tajikistan	1,040	1,150	4.4	4.8	11	71	63	2004	2.03	2003	0.0	0.0	62	64
Thailand	7,450	8,020	3.3	13.6	76	260	22	1999	0.37	2000	1.7	1.5	67	73
Timor-Leste	...	...	9.6	7.7	39	125	...		0.10	2004	...	...	61	66
Turkey	6,690	7,680	7.6	13.9	257	528	26	2004	1.35	2003	...	...	69	73
Turkmenistan	5,840	6,910	3.9	12.7	89	221	49	2004	4.18	2002	...	0.0	56	65
United Arab Emirates	...	21,000	3.3	8.0	661	623	22	2002	2.02	2001	...	...	76	79
Uzbekistan	1,720	1,860	5.5	7.6	21	159	53	2004	2.74	2003	0.0	0.1	63	69
Viet Nam	2,490	2,700	5.4	5.6	26	164	23	2003	0.53	2001	0.3	0.4	69	74
Yemen	820	820	5.5	6.0	32	89	6	2003	0.33	2004	0.1	0.1	57	61
EUROPE														
Albania	4,700	5,070	6.5	9.2	118	366	30	2004	1.31	2002	...	...	69	74
Andorra	...	...	7.1	33.7	2039	2453	28	2004	3.70	2003	...	...	77	83
Austria	24,610	31,790	7.5	10.0	2358	2306	83	2003	3.38	2003	0.2	0.3	76	82
Belarus	6,010	6,900	5.5	8.3	99	570	107	2004	4.55	2003	...	...	63	74
Belgium	28,930	31,360	9.4	12.4	2796	2828	68	2004	4.49	2002	0.2	0.2	75	81
Bosnia and Herzegovina	6,320	7,430	9.5	11.4	168	327	30	2004	1.34	2003	0.0	0.0	70	77
Bulgaria	7,610	7,870	7.5	10.1	191	573	61	2004	3.56	2003	...	0.1	69	76
Croatia	10,710	11,670	7.8	13.8	494	838	55	2004	2.44	2003	0.0	0.0	72	79
Czech Republic	15,650	18,400	7.5	12.7	667	1302	85	2004	3.51	2003	0.1	0.1	73	79
Denmark	31,213	31,550	9.0	13.5	3534	2762	40	2003	2.93	2002	0.2	0.2	75	80
Estonia	12,480	13,190	5.3	11.2	366	682	58	2004	4.48	2000	0.7	1.1	66	78
Finland	27,100	29,560	7.4	11.2	2307	2108	69	2004	3.16	2002	0.1	0.1	75	82
France	27,460	29,320	10.1	14.2	2981	2902	76	2003	3.37	2004	0.4	0.4	76	83
Germany	27,460	27,950	11.1	17.6	3204	3001	86	2004	3.37	2003	0.1	0.1	76	82
Greece	19,920	22,000	9.9	10.1	1556	1997	47	2000	4.38	2001	0.2	0.2	77	82
Hungary	13,780	15,670	8.4	12.1	684	1269	78	2004	3.33	2003	0.0	0.1	69	77
Iceland		32,360	10.5	18.3	3821	3110	75	2002	3.62	2004	0.1	...	79	83
Ireland	30,450	33,170	7.3	17.2	2860	2496	35	2004	2.79	2004	0.1	0.1	75	81
Italy	26,760	27,860	8.4	12.8	2139	2266	41	2003	4.20	2004	0.5	0.5	78	84
Latvia	10,130	11,850	6.4	9.4	301	678	77	2004	3.01	2003	0.5	0.6	66	76
Lithuania	11,090	12,610	6.6	14.7	351	754	84	2004	3.97	2003	0.1	0.1	66	78
Luxembourg	...	61,220	6.8	13.7	4112	3680	68	2003	2.66	2003	...	...	76	81
Malta	...	18,720	9.3	15.5	1104	1436	46	2004	3.18	2003	...	...	76	81
Monaco	...	...	9.7	17.5	4587	4487	196	1995	...		...	...	78	85
Netherlands	28,600	31,220	9.8	12.4	3088	2987	46	2002	3.15	2003	0.2	0.2	77	81
Norway	37,300	38,550	10.3	17.6	4976	3809	43	2004	3.13	2003	0.1	0.1	77	82
Poland	11,450	12,640	6.5	9.8	354	745	55	2003	2.47	2003	...	0.1	71	79
Portugal	17,980	19,250	9.6	14.1	1348	1791	36	2003	3.42	2003	0.4	0.4	74	81
Republic of Moldova	1,750	1,930	7.2	11.8	34	177	64	2004	2.64	2003	0.1	0.2	64	71
Romania	7,140	8,190	6.1	10.9	159	540	66	2004	1.90	2003	0.0	0.0	68	76
Russian Federation	8,920	9,620	5.6	9.3	167	551	99	2004	4.25	2003	0.7	1.1	59	72
San Marino	...	...	7.5	21.0	2957	3133	...		...		...	...	79	84
Serbia and Montenegro	...	...	9.6	16.0	181	373	60	2002	2.06	2002	0.2	0.2	70	75
Slovakia	13,420	14,370	5.9	13.2	360	777	70	2004	3.18	2003	...	0.0	70	78
Slovenia	19,240	20,730	8.8	13.8	1218	1669	48	2004	2.25	2002	0.0	0.0	73	81
Spain	22,020	27,070	7.7	13.7	1541	1853	37	2004	3.30	2003	0.6	0.7	77	83
Sweden	26,620	29,770	9.4	13.6	3149	2704	30	2004	3.28	2002	0.1	0.1	78	83
Switzerland	32,030	35,370	11.5	19.4	5035	3776	59	2003	3.61	2002	0.4	0.4	78	83
TFYR Macedonia	6,720	6,480	7.1	17.1	161	389	49	2001	2.19	2001	0.0	0.0	69	76
Ukraine	5,410	6,250	5.7	10.2	60	305	87	2004	2.95	2003	1.2	1.4	62	73
United Kingdom	27,650	31,460	8.0	15.8	2428	2389	40	2003	2.30	1997	0.2	0.2	76	81

TABLE B.9

continued

	Gross national income PPP		Expenditure on health				Health services				Prevalence of HIV Population aged 15–49 (%)		Life expectancy at birth (years)	
	$/capita 2003	$/capita 2004	% of GDP	% of total gov exp	per capita		Hospital beds per 10000		Physicians per 1000		2001	2003	Male 2004	Female 2004
			2003	2003	US$ 2003	Int $ 2003	no.	year	no	year				
LATIN AMERICA AND THE CARIBBEAN														
Antigua and Barbuda	...	10,360	4.5	10.8	426	477	24	2004	0.17	1999	...	...	70	75
Argentina	10,920	12,460	8.9	14.7	305	1067	41	2000	3.01	1998	0.7	0.7	71	78
Bahamas	...	16,140	6.4	13.9	1121	1220	34	2003	1.05	1998	2.3	...	70	76
Barbados	...	15,060	6.9	11.1	691	1050	73	2003	1.21	1999	...	...	71	78
Belize	...	6,510	4.5	5.0	174	309	13	2004	1.05	2000	1.2	...	65	72
Bolivia	2,450	2,590	6.7	11.9	61	176	10	2004	1.22	2001	0.1	0.1	63	66
Brazil	7,480	8,020	7.6	10.3	212	597	26	2002	1.15	2000	0.6	0.7	67	74
Chile	9,810	10,500	6.1	12.7	282	707	25	2003	1.09	2003	0.3	0.3	74	81
Colombia	6,520	6,820	7.6	20.5	138	522	12	2004	1.35	2002	0.5	0.5	68	77
Costa Rica	9,040	9,530	7.3	22.8	305	616	14	2003	1.32	2000	0.6	0.6	75	80
Cuba	...	...	7.3	11.2	211	251	49	2004	5.91	2002	0.0	0.1	75	80
Dominica	...	5,250	6.3	11.6	212	320	39	2003	0.50	1997	...	...	72	76
Dominican Republic	6,210	6,750	7.0	12.8	132	335	22	2004	1.88	2000	1.5	1.0	64	70
Ecuador	3,440	3,690	5.1	8.7	109	220	14	2003	1.48	2000	0.3	0.3	70	75
El Salvador	4,890	4,980	8.1	22.0	183	378	7	2004	1.24	2002	0.6	0.7	68	74
Grenada	...	7,000	6.7	12.4	289	473	57	2004	0.50	1997	...	...	66	69
Guatemala	4,060	4,140	5.4	15.3	112	235	5	2003	0.90	1999	1.1	1.1	65	71
Guyana	...	4,110	4.8	11.6	53	283	29	2001	0.48	2000	2.3	...	62	64
Haiti	1,630	1,680	7.5	23.8	26	84	8	2000	0.25	1998	5.5	5.6	53	56
Honduras	2,580	2,710	7.1	16.8	72	184	10	2002	0.57	2000	1.6	1.8	65	70
Jamaica	3,790	3,630	5.3	4.5	164	216	18	2004	0.85	2003	0.8	1.2	70	74
Mexico	8,950	9,590	6.2	11.7	372	582	10	2003	1.98	2000	0.3	0.3	72	77
Nicaragua	2,400	3,300	7.7	11.7	60	208	9	2004	0.37	2003	0.2	0.2	67	71
Panama	6,310	6,870	7.6	16.2	315	555	18	2004	1.50	2000	0.7	0.9	73	78
Paraguay	4,740	4,870	7.3	14.2	75	301	12	2002	1.11	2002	0.4	0.5	70	74
Peru	5,090	5,370	4.4	10.7	98	233	11	2004	1.17	1999	0.4	0.5	69	73
Saint Kitts and Nevis	...	11,190	5.3	11.4	467	670	60	2004	1.19	1997	...	...	69	72
Saint Lucia	...	5,560	5.0	10.3	221	294	29	2003	5.17	1999	...	...	71	77
Saint Vincent and the Grenadines	...	6,250	6.1	11.0	194	384	45	2004	0.87	1997	...	...	66	73
Suriname	...	...	7.9	10.4	182	309	31	2004	0.45	2000	0.9	...	65	70
Trinidad and Tobago	...	11,180	3.9	5.9	316	532	33	2003	0.79	1997	3.0	3.2	67	73
Uruguay	7,980	9,070	9.8	6.3	323	824	19	2003	3.65	2002	0.3	0.3	71	79
Venezuela	4,740	5,760	4.5	6.4	146	231	9	2003	1.94	2001	0.6	0.7	72	78
NORTHERN AMERICA														
Canada	29,740	30,660	9.9	16.7	2669	2989	36	2003	2.14	2003	0.3	0.3	78	83
United States of America	37,500	39,710	15.2	18.5	5711	5711	33	2003	2.56	2000	0.6	0.6	75	80
OCEANIA														
Australia	28,290	29,200	9.5	17.7	2519	2874	40	2003	2.47	2001	0.1	0.1	78	83
Cook Islands	...	...	3.8	9.6	294	425	39	2004	0.78	2001	...	...	70	75
Fiji	...	5,770	3.7	7.8	104	220	26	1999	0.34	1999	0.0	...	66	71
Kiribati	...	...	13.1	7.8	96	253	15	2004	0.30	1998	...	...	63	67
Marshall Islands	...	...	13.1	14.4	255	477	21	1999	0.47	2000	...	...	60	64
Micronesia (Fed. States of)	...	...	6.4	8.8	147	270	31	2000	0.60	2000	...	...	68	71
Nauru	...	...	12.3	8.8	798	763	59	2004	...		...	...	58	65
New Zealand	21,120	22,130	8.1	17.2	1618	1893	60	2002	2.37	2001	0.1	0.1	77	82
Niue	...	...	9.7	9.3	655	153	73	2003	...		...	...	68	74
Palau	...	...	9.7	15.2	607	798	50	1998	1.11	1998	...	...	67	70
Papua New Guinea	2,240	2,300	3.4	10.9	23	132	...		0.05	2000	0.4	0.6	58	61
Samoa	...	...	5.4	20.1	94	209	36	2004	0.70	1999	...	...	66	70
Solomon Islands	...	1,760	4.8	9.4	28	87	22	1999	0.13	1999	...	...	66	70
Tonga	...	7,220	6.5	21.2	102	300	113	2004	0.34	2001	...	...	71	70
Tuvalu	...	...	6.1	6.0	142	74	19	2003	0.55	2002	...	...	61	62
Vanuatu	...	2,790	3.9	12.9	54	110	19	2003	0.11	1997	...	...	67	69

Sources: World Bank, 2004; World Bank, 2006; WHO, 2006; UNDP, 2005

TABLE B.10

Poverty and Inequality

	Inequality					National poverty line				International poverty line						
	Income/consumption inequality			Land inequality											Below $1/day	Below $2/day
			Gini index		Gini index		Rural %	Urban %	Total %		Rural %	Urban %	Total %		%	%
AFRICA																
Algeria	1995	c	0.35		...	1995	10.0	14.7	22.6	1998	16.6	7.3	12.2	1995	<2	11.8
Benin	2003	c	0.36		...	1995	25.2	28.5	26.5	1999	33.0	23.3	29.0		...	...
Botswana	1995	c	0.63		...	...	...	...	...		...	...	...		...	...
Burkina Faso	2003	c	0.38	1993	0.42	1994	51.0	10.4	44.5	1998	51.0	16.5	45.3	1998	44.9	81.0
Burundi	1998	c	0.42		...	1990	36.0	43.0	36.4		...	...	...	1998	54.6	87.6
Cameroon	2001	c	0.45		...	1996	59.6	41.4	53.3	2001	49.9	22.1	40.2	2001	17.1	50.6
Central African Republic	1993	c	0.61				...	...	...	...	...	...	...	1993	66.6	84.0
Chad			...		...	1996	67.0	63.0	64.0	...	...	...			...	...
Côte d'Ivoire	2002	c	0.45		...		...	...	...		...	...	...	2002	14.8	48.8
Egypt	2000	c	0.34	1990	0.65	1996	23.3	22.5	22.9	2000	...	...	16.7	2000	3.1	43.9
Eritrea			...		...	1994	...	...	53.0		...	...	...		...	...
Ethiopia	2000	c	0.30	2001	0.47	1996	47.0	33.3	45.5	2000	45.0	37.0	44.2	2000	23.0	77.8
Gambia	1998	c	0.48		...		...	...	...		...	...	...		...	...
Ghana	1999	c	0.41		...	1992	...	...	50.0	1999	49.9	18.6	39.5	1999	44.8	78.5
Guinea	2003	c	0.39		...	1994	...	...	40.0		...	...	...		...	...
Guinea-Bissau	1993	c	0.40	1988	0.62		...	...	...		...	...	...		...	...
Kenya	1997	c	0.44		...	1994	47.0	29.0	40.0	1997	53.0	49.0	52.0	1997	22.8	58.3
Lesotho	1998	c	0.63	1990	0.49		...	...	...		...	...	...		...	...
Madagascar	2001	c	0.46		...	1997	76.0	63.2	73.3	1999	76.7	52.1	71.3	2001	61.0	85.1
Malawi	1998	c	0.50	1993	0.52	1991	...	...	54.0	1998	66.5	54.9	65.3	1998	41.7	76.1
Mali	2001	c	0.39		...		...	...	...	1998	75.9	30.1	63.8	1994	72.3	90.6
Mauritania	2000	c	0.38		...	1996	65.5	30.1	50.0	2000	61.2	25.4	46.3	2000	25.9	63.1
Morocco	1998	c	0.38	1996	0.62	1991	18.0	7.6	13.1	1999	27.2	12.0	19.0	1999	<2	14.3
Mozambique	1997	c	0.40		...	1997	71.3	62.0	69.4		...	...	...	1996	37.9	78.4
Namibia	1997	c	0.71	1997	0.36		...	...	...		...	...	...	1993	34.9	55.8
Niger	1995	c	0.51		...	1993	66.0	52.0	63.0		...	...	...	1995	60.6	85.8
Nigeria	2003	c	0.41		...	1985	49.5	31.7	43.0	1993	36.4	30.4	34.1	2003	70.8	92.4
Rwanda			...		...	1993	...	...	51.2	2000	65.7	14.3	60.3	2000	51.7	83.7
Senegal	1995	c	0.40	1998	0.50	1992	40.4	23.7	33.4		...	...	...	1995	22.3	63.0
Sierra Leone			...		...	1989	...	...	82.8	2004	79.0	56.4	70.2	1989	57.0	74.5
South Africa	2000	c	0.58		...		...	...	...		...	...	...	2000	10.7	34.1
Togo			...		...	1988	...	...	32.3		...	...	...		...	...
Tunisia	2000	c	0.40	1993	0.70	1990	13.1	3.5	7.4	1995	13.9	3.6	7.6	2000	<2	6.6
Uganda			...	1991	0.59	1993	...	...	55.0	1997	...	...	44.0		...	...
United Republic of Tanzania	2001	c	0.35		...	1991	40.8	31.2	38.6	2001	38.7	29.5	35.7	1991	48.5	72.5
Zambia	1998	c	0.53		...	1996	82.8	46.0	69.2	1998	83.1	56.0	72.9	1998	63.7	87.4
Zimbabwe	1995	c	0.58		...	1991	35.8	3.4	25.8	1996	48.0	7.9	34.9	1996	56.1	83.0
ASIA																
Armenia	2003	c	0.26		...	1999	50.8	58.3	55.1	2001	48.7	51.9	50.9	2003	<2	31.1
Azerbaijan	2001	c	0.36		...	1995	...	...	68.1	2001	42.0	55.0	49.0	2001	3.7	33.4
Bangladesh	2000	c	0.31	1996	0.62	1996	55.2	29.4	51.0	2000	53.0	36.6	49.8	2000	36.0	82.8
Cambodia	1997	c	0.40		...	1997	40.1	21.1	36.1	1999	40.1	13.9	35.9	1997	34.1	77.7
China	2001	c	0.45		...	1996	7.9	<2	6.0	1998	4.6	<2	4.6	2001	16.6	46.7
Georgia	2002	c	0.38		...	1997	9.9	12.1	11.1		...	...	...	2001	2.7	15.7
India	2000	c	0.33		...	1994	37.3	32.4	36.0	2000	30.2	24.7	28.6	2000	35.3	80.6
Indonesia	2000	c	0.34	1993	0.46	1996	...	...	15.7	1999	...	...	27.1	2002	7.5	52.4
Iran (Islamic Republic of)	1998	c	0.43		...		...	...	...		...	...	...	1998	<2	7.3
Israel	2001	c	0.35		...		...	...	...		...	...	...		...	...
Japan	1993	y	0.25	1995	0.59		...	...	...		...	...	...		...	...
Jordan	2002	c	0.39	1997	0.78	1991	...	...	15.0	1997	...	...	11.7	2002	<2	6.5
Kazakhstan	2003	c	0.30		...	1996	39.0	30.0	34.6		...	...	...	2003	<2	24.9
Kyrgyzstan	2002	c	0.29		...	2000	56.4	43.9	52.0	2001	51.0	41.2	47.6	2002	<2	24.7
Lao People's Dem. Republic	1998	c	0.35	1999	0.39	1993	48.7	33.1	45.0	1998	41.0	26.9	38.6	1998	26.3	73.2
Malaysia	1997	y	0.49		...	1989	...	...	15.5		...	...	...	1997	<2	9.3
Mongolia	1998	c	0.30		...	1995	33.1	38.5	36.3	1998	32.6	39.4	35.6	1998	27.0	74.9
Nepal	1996	c	0.36	1992	0.45	1996	44.0	23.0	42.0		...	...	...	1996	39.1	80.9
Pakistan	2001	c	0.27	1990	0.57	1993	33.4	17.2	28.6	1999	35.9	24.2	32.6	2001	17.0	73.6
Philippines	2000	c	0.46	1991	0.55	1994	53.1	28.0	40.6	1997	50.7	21.5	36.8	2000	15.5	47.5
Republic of Korea	1998	y	0.32	1990	0.34		...	...	...		...	...	...	2002	<2	<2
Singapore	1998	y	0.43		...		...	...	...		...	...	...		...	...
Sri Lanka	2002	c	0.38		...	1991	22.0	15.0	20.0	1996	27.0	15.0	25.0	2002	5.6	41.6
Tajikistan	2003	c	0.32		...		...	...	...		...	...	...	2003	7.4	42.8
Thailand	2002	c	0.40	1993	0.47	1990	...	...	18.0	1992	15.5	10.2	13.1	2000	<2	32.5
Timor-Leste	2001	c	0.37		...		...	...	...		...	...	...		...	...
Turkey	2002	c	0.37	1991	0.61		...	...	...		...	...	...	2002	4.8	24.7
Turkmenistan	1998	c	0.41		...		...	...	...		...	...	...	1998	12.1	44.0
Uzbekistan	2000	c	0.27		...		...	...	...	2000	30.5	22.5	27.5	2000	17.3	71.7
Viet Nam	2002	c	0.35	1994	0.53	1998	45.5	9.2	37.4	2002	35.6	6.6	28.9		...	...
Yemen	1998	c	0.33		...	1998	45.0	30.8	41.8		...	...	...	1998	15.7	45.2
EUROPE																
Albania	2002	c	0.31	1998	0.84		...	...	...	2002	29.6	19.8	25.4	2002	<2	11.8
Austria	1997	y	0.28	2000	0.59		...	...	...		...	...	...		...	...
Belarus	2000	c	0.30		...		...	...	...	2000	...	...	41.9	2000	<2	<2
Belgium	2000	y	0.26	2000	0.56		...	...	...		...	...	...		...	...
Bosnia and Herzegovina	2001	c	0.25		...		...	...	...	2002	19.9	13.8	19.5		...	...
Bulgaria	2003	c	0.28		...	1997	...	...	36.0	2001	...	...	12.8	2003	<2	6.1

TABLE B.10

continued

	Inequality					National poverty line				International poverty line						
	Income/consumption inequality			Land inequality												
			Gini index		Gini index		Rural %	Urban %	Total %		Rural %	Urban %	Total %		Below $1/day %	Below $2/day %
Croatia	2001	c	0.29		...		...	...	...		...	...	...	2001	<2	<2
Czech Republic	1996	y	0.25	2000	0.92		...	...	...		...	...	...	1996	<2	<2
Denmark	1997	y	0.27	2000	0.51		...	...	...		...	...	...		...	...
Estonia	1998	c	0.32	2001	0.79		...	...	...		...	...	...		...	...
Finland	2000	y	0.25	2000	0.27		...	...	...		...	...	...		...	...
France	1994	y	0.31	2000	0.58		...	...	...		...	...	...		...	...
Germany	2000	y	0.28	2000	0.63		...	...	...		...	...	...		...	...
Greece	1998	c	0.36	2000	0.59		...	...	...		...	...	...		...	...
Hungary	2002	c	0.24		...	1993	...	...	14.5	1997	...	...	17.3	2002	<2	<2
Italy	2000	c	0.31	2000	0.73		...	...	...		...	...	...		...	...
Latvia	1998	c	0.34	2001	0.58		...	...	...		...	...	...	1998	<2	11.5
Lithuania	2000	c	0.29		...		...	...	...		...	...	...	2000	<2	6.9
Luxembourg	2000	y	0.29	2000	0.48		...	...	...		...	...	...		...	...
Netherlands	1999	y	0.29	2000	0.57		...	...	...		...	...	...		...	...
Norway	2000	y	0.27	1999	0.18		...	...	...		...	...	...		...	...
Poland	2002	c	0.31	2002	0.69	1993	...	...	23.8		...	...	...	2002	<2	<2
Portugal	1997	y	0.39	2000	0.74		...	...	...		...	...	...	1994	<2	<2
Republic of Moldova	2001	c	0.36		...	1997	26.7	19.3	23.3		...	...	...	2001	21.8	64.1
Romania	2002	c	0.28		...	1994	27.9	20.4	21.5		...	...	...	2002	<2	14.0
Russian Federation	2002	c	0.32		...	1994	...	...	30.9		...	...	...	2002	<2	7.5
Serbia and Montenegro	2003	c	0.28		...		...	...	...		...	...	...		...	...
Slovakia	1996	y	0.26		...		...	...	...		...	...	...	1996	<2	2.9
Slovenia	1998	c	0.28	1991	0.62		...	...	...		...	...	...	1998	<2	<2
Spain	2000	y	0.35	2000	0.77		...	...	...		...	...	...		...	...
Sweden	2000	y	0.25	2000	0.32		...	...	...		...	...	...		...	...
Switzerland	1992	y	0.31	1990	0.50		...	...	...		...	...	...		...	...
TFYR Macedonia	2003	c	0.36		...		...	...	...		...	...	...		...	...
Ukraine	1999	y	0.29		...	1995	...	...	31.7		...	...	...	1999	2.9	45.7
United Kingdom	1999	y	0.34	2000	0.66		...	...	...		...	...	...		...	...
LATIN AMERICA AND THE CARIBBEAN																
Argentina	2001	y	0.51	1988	0.83	1995	...	28.4	...	1998	...	29.9	...	2001	3.3	14.3
Bolivia	2002	y	0.58		...	1997	77.3	53.8	63.2	1999	81.7	50.6	62.7	1999	14.4	34.3
Brazil	2001	y	0.59	1996	0.85	1996	54.0	15.4	23.9	1998	51.4	14.7	22.0	2001	8.2	22.4
Chile	2000	y	0.51		...	1996	...	...	19.9	1998	...	...	17.0	2000	<2	9.6
Colombia	1999	y	0.54	2001	0.80	1995	79.0	48.0	60.0	1999	79.0	55.0	64.0	1999	8.2	22.6
Costa Rica	2000	y	0.46		...	1992	25.5	19.2	22.0		...	...	...	2000	2.0	9.5
Dominican Republic	1997	y	0.47		...	1992	49.0	19.3	33.9	1998	42.1	20.5	28.6	1998	<2	<2
Ecuador	1998	y	0.54		...	1994	47.0	25.0	35.0		...	...	...	1998	17.7	40.8
El Salvador	2002	y	0.50		...	1992	55.7	43.1	48.3		...	...	...	2000	31.1	58.0
Guatemala	2000	y	0.58		...	1989	71.9	33.7	57.9	2000	74.5	27.1	56.2	2000	16.0	37.4
Guyana	1998	y	0.45		...		...	...	...		...	...	...		...	...
Haiti	2001	y	0.68		...	1987	...	...	65.0	1995	66.0	...	...	2001	67.0	83.3
Honduras	1999	y	0.52	1993	0.66	1992	46.0	56.0	50.0	1993	51.0	57.0	53.0	1999	20.7	44.0
Jamaica	2001	c	0.42		...	1995	37.0	18.7	27.5	2000	25.1	12.8	18.7	2000	<2	13.3
Mexico	2002	y	0.49		...	1988	...	...	10.1		...	...	...	2000	9.9	26.3
Nicaragua	2001	c	0.40	2001	0.72	1993	76.1	31.9	50.3	1998	68.5	30.5	47.9	2001	45.1	79.9
Panama	2000	c	0.55	2001	0.52	1997	64.9	15.3	37.3		...	...	...	2000	7.2	17.6
Paraguay	2001	y	0.55	1991	0.93	1991	28.5	19.7	21.8		...	...	...	2002	16.4	33.2
Peru	2000	c	0.48	1994	0.86	1994	67.0	46.1	53.5	1997	64.7	40.4	49.0	2000	18.1	37.7
Saint Lucia	1995	c	0.44		...		...	...	...		...	...	...		...	...
Trinidad and Tobago	1992	c	0.39		...		...	...	...		...	...	...		...	...
Uruguay	2000	y	0.43	2000	0.79		...	...	...		...	...	...	2000	<2	3.9
Venezuela	2000	y	0.42	1997	0.88		...	...	...		...	...	...	2000	9.9	32.1
NORTHERN AMERICA																
Canada	2000	y	0.33	1991	0.64		...	...	...		...	...	...		...	...
United States of America	2000	y	0.38	1997	0.76		...	...	...		...	...	...		...	...
OCEANIA																
Australia	1994	y	0.32		...		...	...	...		...	...	...		...	...
New Zealand	1997	y	0.37		...		...	...	...		...	...	...		...	...
Papua New Guinea			...		...	1996	41.3	16.1	37.5		...	...	...		...	...

Source: World Bank, 2006

Note: While 'c' indicates that data refer to consumption inequality, 'y' indicates that data refer to income inequality. The inequality data for Argentine and Uruguay in this table refer to urban.

TABLE B.11

Governance Indicators

	Voice and accountability		Political stability		Government effectiveness		Regulatory quality		Rule of law		Control of corruption		Corruption perceptions index	
	1996	2005	1996	2005	1996	2005	1996	2005	1996	2005	1996	2005	2000	2005
WORLD														
AFRICA														
Algeria	-1.23	-0.92	-2.92	-1.09	-0.60	-0.37	-0.81	-0.63	-0.67	-0.71	-0.35	-0.43	...	2.8
Angola	-1.50	-1.15	-2.35	-0.82	-1.33	-0.96	-1.46	-1.24	-1.50	-1.28	-1.06	-1.09	1.7	2.0
Benin	0.70	0.34	0.98	0.31	-0.02	-0.69	0.12	-0.55	-0.05	-0.59	...	-1.00	...	2.9
Botswana	0.69	0.68	0.66	0.94	0.45	0.79	0.60	0.76	0.76	0.70	0.45	1.10	6.0	5.9
Burkina Faso	-0.54	-0.37	-0.41	-0.05	-0.71	-0.60	-0.38	-0.47	-0.81	-0.54	-0.32	0.06	3.0	3.4
Burundi	-1.34	-1.15	-2.00	-1.65	-0.98	-1.34	-1.33	-1.22	-0.24	-1.17	...	-0.86	...	2.3
Cameroon	-1.12	-1.19	-1.18	-0.34	-1.11	-0.90	-0.83	-0.76	-1.24	-1.02	-1.17	-1.15	2.0	2.2
Cape Verde	0.86	0.83	0.98	0.88	-0.07	-0.11	-0.60	-0.21	0.04	0.21	...	0.21	...	...
Central African Republic	-0.21	-1.15	-0.24	-1.13	-0.92	-1.47	-0.31	-1.23	-0.24	-1.29	...	-1.08	...	...
Chad	-0.83	-1.25	-0.91	-1.34	-0.66	-1.13	-0.01	-0.94	-0.24	-1.23	...	-1.22	...	1.7
Comoros	-0.18	-0.28	0.98	-0.36	-0.66	-1.63	-0.74	-1.63	...	-0.96	...	-0.93	...	...
Congo	-1.33	-0.71	-0.93	-1.24	-1.19	-1.31	-0.84	-1.20	-1.33	-1.42	-0.86	-1.01	...	2.1
Côte d'Ivoire	-0.25	-1.50	0.02	-2.49	0.05	-1.38	-0.13	-0.95	-0.74	-1.47	0.46	-1.23	2.7	1.9
Dem. Republic of the Congo	-1.29	-1.64	-2.00	-2.40	-1.72	-1.64	-2.24	-1.66	-1.89	-1.76	-2.13	-1.34	...	2.3
Djibouti	-0.85	-0.84	0.17	-0.74	-1.09	-0.85	-0.02	-0.86	...	-0.87	...	-0.64	...	...
Egypt	-0.80	-1.15	-0.64	-0.90	-0.30	-0.35	-0.05	-0.47	0.19	0.02	0.14	-0.42	3.1	3.4
Equatorial Guinea	-1.56	-1.71	-0.64	0.21	-1.51	-1.42	-0.97	-1.31	...	-1.33	...	-1.79	...	1.9
Eritrea	-1.17	-1.83	0.23	-0.72	-0.34	-0.98	-0.16	-1.84	-0.24	-0.81	...	-0.37	...	2.6
Ethiopia	-0.68	-1.10	-0.90	-1.48	-0.55	-0.97	-1.31	-1.09	-0.32	-0.77	-1.05	-0.79	3.2	2.2
Gabon	-0.61	-0.71	-0.43	0.22	-1.02	-0.63	-0.53	-0.26	-0.36	-0.48	-1.32	-0.61	...	2.9
Gambia	-1.43	-0.72	-0.03	0.18	-0.34	-0.65	-1.56	-0.42	0.20	-0.29	0.41	-0.70	...	2.7
Ghana	-0.41	0.41	-0.11	0.16	0.05	-0.09	0.00	-0.14	-0.17	-0.23	-0.49	-0.38	3.5	3.5
Guinea	-1.21	-1.18	-1.53	-1.11	-1.11	-1.03	-0.00	-0.92	-1.13	-1.11	0.41	-0.84	...	...
Guinea-Bissau	-0.61	-0.31	-0.79	-0.51	-0.55	-1.46	0.14	-1.11	-1.65	-1.33	-1.05	-1.08	...	...
Kenya	-0.56	-0.12	-0.65	-1.16	-0.64	-0.78	-0.43	-0.32	-0.83	-0.94	-1.12	-1.01	2.1	2.1
Lesotho	-0.04	0.28	0.78	0.31	0.09	-0.29	-0.72	-0.55	-0.36	-0.19	...	-0.15	...	3.4
Liberia	-1.48	-0.92	-2.71	-1.45	-1.80	-1.36	-3.00	-1.70	-2.22	-1.60	-1.78	-1.08	...	2.2
Libyan Arab Jamahiriya	-1.53	-1.93	-1.78	0.30	-0.82	-0.96	-1.75	-1.44	-1.05	-0.73	-0.95	-0.89	...	2.5
Madagascar	0.21	-0.01	-0.07	0.18	-0.95	-0.12	-0.08	-0.27	-0.90	-0.15	0.41	0.00	...	2.8
Malawi	-0.50	-0.45	-0.16	0.15	-0.67	-0.78	-0.39	-0.58	-0.25	-0.35	-1.05	-0.85	4.1	2.8
Mali	0.26	0.47	0.45	0.06	-0.72	-0.46	0.12	-0.50	-0.83	-0.12	-0.32	-0.29	...	2.9
Mauritania	-0.91	-1.09	0.51	-0.31	0.14	-0.19	-0.69	-0.14	-0.66	-0.54	...	-0.26	...	...
Mauritius	0.82	0.92	0.92	0.90	0.62	0.60	0.14	0.32	0.67	0.79	0.54	0.32	4.7	4.2
Morocco	-0.70	-0.76	-0.60	-0.43	-0.05	-0.20	0.11	-0.39	0.14	-0.10	0.26	-0.09	4.7	3.2
Mozambique	-0.26	-0.06	-0.59	0.04	-0.54	-0.34	-1.07	-0.60	-1.29	-0.72	-0.54	-0.68	2.2	2.8
Namibia	0.46	0.36	0.62	0.50	0.25	0.09	-0.03	0.11	0.32	-0.01	0.85	0.06	5.4	4.3
Niger	-0.47	-0.06	-0.25	-0.56	-1.07	-0.79	-0.96	-0.53	-1.31	-0.82	-0.32	-0.83	...	2.4
Nigeria	-1.57	-0.69	-1.75	-1.77	-1.26	-0.92	-1.02	-1.01	-1.26	-1.38	-1.28	-1.22	1.2	1.9
Réunion	...	1.25	...	0.48	...	1.02	...	1.09	...	1.15	...	0.78	...	...
Rwanda	-1.48	-1.32	-1.46	-1.21	-1.24	-1.05	-1.11	-0.73	-0.24	-1.00	...	-0.81	...	3.1
São Tomé and Príncipe	0.84	0.56	0.98	0.61	-0.66	-0.75	-0.38	-0.84	...	-0.63	...	-0.77	...	...
Senegal	-0.23	0.30	-0.78	-0.07	-0.32	-0.15	-0.53	-0.30	-0.22	-0.26	-0.40	-0.23	3.5	3.2
Seychelles	0.06	-0.04	0.98	0.84	-0.71	-0.05	-1.19	-0.09	...	0.21	...	0.01	...	4.0
Sierra Leone	-1.45	-0.38	-2.47	-0.48	-0.60	-1.20	-0.51	-0.94	-1.08	-1.12	-1.78	-0.99	...	2.4
Somalia	-1.98	-1.89	-2.40	-2.51	-1.80	-2.21	-3.00	-2.35	-1.75	-2.36	-1.78	-1.74	...	2.1
South Africa	0.62	0.82	-1.17	-0.10	0.53	0.84	0.16	0.59	0.31	0.19	0.70	0.54	5.0	4.5
Sudan	-1.74	-1.84	-2.82	-2.05	-1.34	-1.30	-1.70	-1.29	-1.52	-1.48	-1.16	-1.40	...	2.1
Swaziland	-1.35	-1.28	-0.04	-0.04	-0.39	-0.84	-0.01	-0.44	0.35	-0.75	...	-0.60	...	2.7
Togo	-1.14	-1.23	-0.72	-1.22	-0.75	-1.38	0.36	-0.81	-1.29	-1.07	-1.05	-0.70	...	...
Tunisia	-0.60	-1.13	0.04	0.12	0.49	0.43	0.29	-0.07	0.02	0.21	-0.03	0.13	5.2	4.9
Uganda	-0.71	-0.59	-1.35	-1.32	-0.39	-0.48	0.14	0.01	-0.93	-0.74	-0.54	-0.87	2.3	2.5
United Republic of Tanzania	-0.85	-0.31	-0.20	-0.37	-1.20	-0.37	-0.35	-0.51	-0.75	-0.47	-1.10	-0.73	2.5	2.9
Zambia	-0.23	-0.35	-0.66	0.02	-0.75	-0.94	0.31	-0.62	-0.40	-0.62	-1.04	-0.82	3.4	2.6
Zimbabwe	-0.37	-1.65	-0.38	-1.58	-0.03	-1.42	-0.81	-2.20	-0.28	-1.47	-0.11	-1.24	3.0	2.6
ASIA														
Afghanistan	-1.60	-1.28	-2.06	-2.12	...	-1.20	...	-1.63	-1.25	-1.68	...	-1.37	...	2.5
Armenia	-0.63	-0.64	0.19	-0.22	-0.39	-0.17	-0.81	0.12	-0.51	-0.46	-0.69	-0.64	2.5	2.9
Azerbaijan	-1.16	-1.16	-0.62	-1.21	-1.17	-0.73	-1.20	-0.52	-0.91	-0.84	-1.03	-1.01	1.5	2.2
Bahrain	-1.02	-0.85	-0.79	-0.28	0.61	0.42	0.60	0.69	0.70	0.71	0.10	0.64	...	5.8
Bangladesh	-0.40	-0.50	-0.87	-1.65	-0.77	-0.90	-0.41	-1.07	-0.74	-0.87	-0.49	-1.18	...	1.7
Bhutan	-1.47	-1.05	0.78	1.01	0.25	0.33	0.06	-0.11	-1.25	0.52	...	0.84	...	...
Brunei Darussalam	-1.04	-1.04	1.08	1.13	1.09	0.56	3.34	0.95	0.66	0.45	0.41	0.25	...	...
Cambodia	-0.76	-0.94	-1.39	-0.44	-0.66	-0.94	-0.31	-0.62	-0.97	-1.13	-1.00	-1.12	...	2.3
China	-1.36	-1.66	-0.10	-0.18	0.15	-0.11	-0.15	-0.28	-0.50	-0.47	0.00	-0.69	3.1	3.2
China, Hong Kong SAR	0.49	0.26	0.08	1.19	1.93	1.63	1.75	1.89	1.67	1.50	1.64	1.68	7.7	8.3
China, Macao SAR	...	0.37	...	1.27	...	1.29	...	1.09	...	0.78	...	0.55	...	...
Cyprus	1.01	1.03	0.44	0.29	1.17	1.16	0.82	1.31	0.57	0.85	1.72	0.69	...	5.7
Dem. People's Republic of Korea	-1.92	-2.06	-1.64	-0.12	-0.89	-1.82	-2.19	-2.31	-1.10	-1.15	-0.32	-1.32	...	...
Georgia	-0.58	-0.27	-0.95	-0.80	-0.45	-0.47	-0.92	-0.54	-0.90	-0.82	-1.12	-0.57	...	2.3
India	0.23	0.35	-1.03	-0.85	-0.45	-0.11	-0.13	-0.34	-0.06	0.09	-0.32	-0.31	2.8	2.9
Indonesia	-1.22	-0.21	-0.66	-1.42	0.08	-0.47	0.22	-0.45	-0.41	-0.87	-0.49	-0.86	1.7	2.2
Iran (Islamic Republic of)	-1.16	-1.43	-0.63	-1.14	-0.36	-0.77	-1.45	-1.49	-0.83	-0.76	-0.88	-0.47	...	2.9
Iraq	-1.80	-1.47	-3.06	-2.82	-1.30	-1.64	-2.39	-1.61	-1.63	-1.81	-1.45	-1.27	...	2.2
Israel	1.03	0.61	-0.70	-1.16	1.49	0.95	1.12	0.89	1.14	0.76	1.62	0.76	6.6	6.3
Japan	1.02	0.94	0.82	0.94	1.33	1.16	0.71	1.17	1.56	1.33	1.34	1.24	6.4	7.3
Jordan	-0.22	-0.74	0.18	-0.31	0.13	0.08	0.10	0.16	0.15	0.43	-0.09	0.33	4.6	5.7
Kazakhstan	-1.08	-1.19	-0.28	0.03	-1.03	-0.71	-0.32	-0.47	-0.79	-0.79	-0.90	-0.94	3.0	2.6
Kuwait	-0.25	-0.47	-0.01	0.11	0.17	0.39	0.20	0.43	0.61	0.67	0.70	0.84	...	4.7

TABLE B.11

continued

	Voice and accountability		Political stability		Government effectiveness		Regulatory quality		Rule of law		Control of corruption		Corruption perceptions index	
	1996	2005	1996	2005	1996	2005	1996	2005	1996	2005	1996	2005	2000	2005
Kyrgyzstan	-0.55	-1.03	0.54	-1.21	-0.53	-0.91	-0.28	-0.67	-0.75	-1.07	-0.84	-1.06	...	2.3
Lao People's Dem. Republic	-1.18	-1.54	0.98	-0.27	-0.07	-1.09	-1.22	-1.21	-1.42	-1.12	-1.00	-1.10	...	3.3
Lebanon	-0.50	-0.72	-0.60	-1.14	-0.34	-0.30	0.27	-0.28	-0.32	-0.36	-0.18	-0.39	...	3.1
Malaysia	-0.11	-0.41	0.77	0.49	0.75	1.01	0.80	0.50	0.80	0.58	0.57	0.27	4.8	5.1
Maldives	-1.07	-1.09	0.17	0.76	-0.02	0.18	0.21	0.50	...	0.33	...	-0.28	...	...
Mongolia	0.32	0.36	0.54	0.92	-0.50	-0.35	-0.71	-0.32	0.43	-0.26	0.41	-0.55	...	3.0
Myanmar	-1.80	-2.16	-1.29	-1.00	-1.20	-1.61	-1.18	-2.19	-1.38	-1.56	-1.25	-1.44	...	1.8
Nepal	0.09	-1.19	-0.58	-2.36	-0.39	-0.97	-0.26	-0.59	-0.41	-0.81	-0.29	-0.71	...	2.5
Occupied Palestinian Territory	-1.64	-1.22	...	-1.69	...	-1.13	...	-1.14	...	-0.52	...	-1.09	...	2.6
Oman	-0.68	-0.94	0.55	0.82	0.67	0.47	0.46	0.49	1.08	0.72	0.15	0.69	...	6.3
Pakistan	-1.06	-1.23	-1.41	-1.68	-0.39	-0.53	-0.54	-0.60	-0.49	-0.81	-1.04	-1.01	...	2.1
Philippines	0.11	0.01	-0.33	-1.11	0.22	-0.07	0.40	-0.02	-0.16	-0.52	-0.41	-0.58	2.8	2.5
Qatar	-0.91	-0.75	0.76	0.83	0.62	0.55	0.28	0.20	0.91	0.87	-0.05	0.82	...	5.9
Republic of Korea	0.65	0.74	-0.08	0.43	0.63	1.00	0.58	0.77	0.77	0.73	0.61	0.47	4.0	5.0
Saudi Arabia	-1.30	-1.72	-0.48	-0.70	-0.25	-0.38	-0.13	-0.01	0.71	0.20	-0.33	0.23	...	3.4
Singapore	0.35	-0.29	1.17	1.08	2.31	2.14	1.95	1.79	2.10	1.83	2.38	2.24	9.1	9.4
Sri Lanka	-0.28	-0.26	-1.91	-1.25	-0.33	-0.41	0.41	-0.12	0.24	0.00	-0.23	-0.31	...	3.2
Syrian Arab Republic	-1.45	-1.67	-0.74	-0.91	-0.69	-1.23	-0.80	-1.22	-0.58	-0.42	-0.75	-0.59	...	3.4
Tajikistan	-1.50	-1.17	-2.80	-1.35	-1.54	-1.06	-1.89	-1.05	-1.47	-0.99	-1.76	-1.08	...	2.1
Thailand	-0.05	0.07	-0.06	-0.55	0.58	0.40	0.42	0.38	0.45	0.10	-0.33	-0.24	3.2	3.8
Timor-Leste	...	0.18	...	-0.69	...	-0.97	...	-1.09	...	-0.55	...	-0.77	...	...
Turkey	-0.47	-0.04	-1.40	-0.54	-0.16	0.27	0.44	0.18	-0.02	0.07	0.10	0.08	3.8	3.5
Turkmenistan	-1.77	-1.95	0.15	-0.34	-1.47	-1.57	-2.60	-1.95	-1.26	-1.41	-1.54	-1.30	...	1.8
United Arab Emirates	-0.74	-1.08	0.73	0.61	0.59	0.55	0.90	0.44	0.74	0.58	0.22	1.13	...	6.2
Uzbekistan	-1.47	-1.76	-0.16	-1.91	-1.07	-1.20	-1.40	-1.71	-1.08	-1.31	-1.05	-1.07	2.4	2.2
Viet Nam	-1.39	-1.60	0.17	0.34	-0.28	-0.31	-0.48	-0.64	-0.55	-0.45	-0.68	-0.76	2.5	2.6
Yemen	-0.99	-1.07	-1.09	-1.61	-0.73	-0.94	-0.69	-0.83	-1.10	-1.10	-0.25	-0.63	...	2.7
EUROPE														
Albania	-0.40	0.08	-0.10	-0.68	-0.49	-0.49	-0.04	-0.27	-0.37	-0.84	0.07	-0.76	...	2.4
Andorra	1.39	1.26	...	1.38	...	1.29	...	1.33	...	1.03	...	1.25	...	...
Austria	1.39	1.24	1.12	0.98	1.99	1.60	1.27	1.52	1.95	1.87	1.81	1.99	7.7	8.7
Belarus	-1.10	-1.68	-0.18	0.01	-1.30	-1.19	-1.09	-1.53	-1.07	-1.04	-0.99	-0.90	4.1	2.6
Belgium	1.44	1.31	0.69	0.66	1.93	1.65	1.17	1.24	1.62	1.47	1.23	1.45	6.1	7.4
Bosnia and Herzegovina	-1.28	-0.11	-0.64	-0.78	...	-0.53	-2.10	-0.53	-0.24	-0.74	...	-0.32	...	2.9
Bulgaria	0.11	0.59	-0.08	0.16	-0.64	0.23	-0.02	0.63	-0.14	-0.19	-0.71	-0.05	3.5	4.0
Croatia	-0.57	0.51	0.02	0.32	-0.30	0.44	-0.07	0.45	-0.58	0.00	-0.51	0.07	3.7	3.4
Czech Republic	1.01	1.01	0.86	0.69	0.52	0.94	1.00	1.04	0.60	0.70	0.65	0.42	4.3	4.3
Denmark	1.69	1.51	1.01	0.91	2.09	2.12	1.37	1.69	2.00	1.99	2.44	2.23	9.8	9.5
Estonia	0.72	1.05	0.60	0.68	0.53	1.03	1.23	1.43	0.30	0.82	0.07	0.88	5.7	6.4
Finland	1.67	1.49	1.22	1.48	2.04	2.07	1.26	1.74	2.05	1.96	2.43	2.39	10.0	9.6
France	1.46	1.28	0.82	0.33	1.94	1.46	1.04	1.09	1.62	1.35	1.53	1.40	6.7	7.5
Germany	1.51	1.31	1.07	0.67	2.01	1.51	1.31	1.38	1.86	1.76	1.92	1.92	7.6	8.2
Greece	0.93	0.95	0.16	0.35	0.82	0.66	0.76	0.91	0.74	0.66	0.42	0.40	4.9	4.3
Hungary	1.02	1.10	0.54	0.79	0.39	0.79	0.45	1.11	0.62	0.70	0.70	0.63	5.2	5.0
Iceland	1.40	1.38	1.01	1.58	1.56	2.20	0.23	1.67	1.67	2.10	1.93	2.49	9.1	9.7
Ireland	1.44	1.41	0.99	1.08	1.70	1.63	1.41	1.56	1.73	1.63	2.01	1.70	7.2	7.4
Italy	1.05	1.00	0.47	0.21	0.93	0.60	0.62	0.94	0.85	0.51	0.52	0.41	4.6	5.0
Latvia	0.46	0.89	0.54	0.83	-0.34	0.68	0.45	1.03	0.14	0.43	-0.59	0.33	3.4	4.2
Liechtenstein	1.39	1.26	...	1.38	...	1.57	...	1.58	...	1.03	...	1.25	...	...
Lithuania	0.71	0.90	0.44	0.88	-0.16	0.85	0.28	1.13	-0.19	0.46	-0.12	0.26	4.1	4.8
Luxembourg	1.45	1.34	1.23	1.41	2.34	1.94	1.47	1.79	1.75	1.96	1.97	1.84	8.6	8.5
Malta	1.06	1.18	1.13	1.34	-0.23	0.95	0.43	1.24	-0.00	1.38	0.41	1.04	...	6.6
Monaco	1.12	0.96	...	0.99	...	-0.12	...	...	...	0.83	...	...	...	...
Netherlands	1.66	1.45	1.27	0.80	2.44	1.95	1.49	1.64	1.91	1.78	2.33	1.99	8.9	8.6
Norway	1.71	1.45	1.23	1.22	2.13	1.99	1.17	1.46	2.07	1.99	2.19	2.04	9.1	8.9
Poland	0.95	1.04	0.40	0.23	0.50	0.58	0.38	0.82	0.42	0.32	0.46	0.19	4.1	3.4
Portugal	1.27	1.32	1.08	0.94	1.03	1.03	1.20	1.20	1.32	1.10	1.34	1.13	6.4	6.5
Republic of Moldova	-0.28	-0.49	-0.37	-0.65	-0.82	-0.75	0.04	-0.43	-0.25	-0.59	-0.21	-0.76	2.6	2.9
Romania	-0.04	0.36	0.31	0.03	-0.88	-0.03	-0.59	0.17	-0.34	-0.29	-0.18	-0.23	2.9	3.0
Russian Federation	-0.43	-0.85	-1.17	-1.07	-0.79	-0.45	-0.64	-0.29	-0.90	-0.84	-0.78	-0.74	2.1	2.4
San Marino	1.39	1.16	...	1.10	...	-0.50	...	...	...	0.83	...	...	...	...
Serbia and Montenegro	-1.45	0.12	-1.29	-0.91	-0.71	-0.31	-1.45	-0.53	-1.26	-0.81	-0.98	-0.55	1.3	2.8
Slovakia	0.34	1.04	0.36	0.69	0.17	0.95	0.30	1.16	0.07	0.41	0.46	0.43	3.5	4.3
Slovenia	0.95	1.08	0.88	0.94	0.52	0.99	0.45	0.86	0.47	0.79	1.15	0.88	5.5	6.1
Spain	1.10	1.12	0.37	0.38	1.70	1.40	0.99	1.25	1.19	1.13	0.85	1.34	7.0	7.0
Sweden	1.66	1.41	1.17	1.18	2.05	1.93	1.16	1.47	2.00	1.84	2.38	2.10	9.4	9.2
Switzerland	1.67	1.43	1.39	1.26	2.53	2.03	1.25	1.47	2.14	2.02	2.30	2.12	8.6	9.1
TFYR Macedonia	-0.13	0.03	0.03	-1.04	-0.29	-0.28	-0.23	-0.20	-0.62	-0.38	-1.06	-0.50	...	2.7
Ukraine	-0.46	-0.26	-0.45	-0.39	-0.87	-0.42	-0.63	-0.26	-0.73	-0.60	-0.79	-0.63	1.5	2.6
United Kingdom	1.34	1.30	0.82	0.34	2.33	1.70	1.58	1.53	1.91	1.69	2.08	1.94	8.7	8.6
LATIN AMERICA AND THE CARIBBEAN														
Anguilla	...	0.81	...	1.20	...	1.56	...	1.09	...	1.67	...	1.25	...	...
Antigua and Barbuda	0.12	0.54	...	0.80	...	0.48	...	0.60	...	0.73	...	0.78	...	...
Argentina	0.55	0.43	0.23	-0.26	0.65	-0.27	0.73	-0.64	0.24	-0.56	-0.12	-0.44	3.5	2.8
Aruba	...	1.03	...	1.37	...	1.29	...	0.85	...	0.88	...	1.25	...	...
Bahamas	1.05	1.14	0.97	0.83	0.43	1.28	0.66	0.99	0.76	1.33	0.41	1.32	...	...
Barbados	1.18	1.12	0.98	1.18	...	1.17	0.30	1.00	-0.33	1.22	...	1.17	...	6.9
Belize	1.05	0.92	0.71	0.31	-0.39	0.13	0.10	0.09	0.66	0.02	...	-0.22	...	3.7
Bolivia	0.03	-0.09	-0.38	-1.15	-0.62	-0.80	0.76	-0.53	-0.71	-0.78	-0.93	-0.81	2.7	2.5

TABLE B.11

continued

	Voice and accountability		Political stability		Government effectiveness		Regulatory quality		Rule of law		Control of corruption		Corruption perceptions index	
	1996	2005	1996	2005	1996	2005	1996	2005	1996	2005	1996	2005	2000	2005
Brazil	0.16	0.36	-0.43	-0.13	-0.25	-0.09	0.12	0.08	-0.31	-0.41	-0.10	-0.28	3.9	3.7
British Virgin Islands	...	...	...	1.50	...	...	...	...	...	...	...	...	...	...
Cayman Islands	...	0.81	...	1.20	...	1.29	...	1.33	...	0.88	...	1.25	...	...
Chile	0.89	1.04	0.52	0.85	1.20	1.26	1.36	1.40	1.22	1.20	1.40	1.34	7.4	7.3
Colombia	-0.13	-0.32	-1.50	-1.79	0.17	-0.09	0.44	0.05	-0.51	-0.71	-0.45	-0.22	3.2	4.0
Costa Rica	1.32	0.99	0.66	0.76	0.11	0.30	0.59	0.61	0.60	0.54	0.84	0.38	5.4	4.2
Cuba	-1.46	-1.87	-0.28	0.03	-0.29	-0.94	-0.76	-1.75	-0.79	-1.14	0.03	-0.26	...	3.8
Dominica	1.22	1.12	...	1.00	-0.87	0.57	-0.23	0.75	...	0.66	...	0.68	...	...
Dominican Republic	-0.05	0.20	-0.44	0.05	-0.37	-0.41	0.16	-0.27	-0.57	-0.66	-0.34	-0.66	...	3.0
Ecuador	-0.00	-0.16	-0.85	-0.83	-0.98	-1.01	0.00	-0.83	-0.45	-0.84	-0.79	-0.81	2.6	2.5
El Salvador	-0.30	0.26	-0.33	-0.14	-0.53	-0.30	0.69	0.12	-0.53	-0.37	-0.80	-0.39	4.1	4.2
French Guiana	...	0.37	...	0.21	...	0.75	...	0.85	...	0.88	...	0.78	...	...
Grenada	0.99	0.84	0.98	0.49	-0.55	0.26	-0.16	0.36	...	0.32	...	0.68	...	...
Guadeloupe	...	...	...	1.50	...	...	...	...	...	...	...	...	...	...
Guatemala	-0.71	-0.37	-1.40	-0.89	-0.53	-0.70	0.11	-0.26	-0.70	-1.04	-1.02	-0.98	...	2.5
Guyana	0.85	0.49	-0.05	-0.38	-0.23	-0.52	0.28	-0.38	-0.03	-0.80	-0.32	-0.58	...	2.5
Haiti	-0.54	-1.41	-0.49	-1.91	-1.16	-1.39	-1.31	-1.17	-1.29	-1.62	-1.05	-1.45	...	1.8
Honduras	-0.43	-0.14	-0.59	-0.78	-1.07	-0.64	-0.31	-0.44	-0.90	-0.78	-1.03	-0.67	...	2.6
Jamaica	0.49	0.57	0.43	-0.33	-0.35	-0.12	0.52	0.24	-0.26	-0.55	-0.34	-0.50	...	3.6
Martinique	...	0.59	...	1.20	...	0.75	...	0.85	...	0.88	...	0.78	...	...
Mexico	-0.30	0.29	-0.66	-0.29	-0.20	-0.01	0.48	0.33	-0.17	-0.48	-0.35	-0.41	3.3	3.5
Netherlands Antilles	...	0.59	...	0.86	...	1.02	...	0.85	...	0.88	...	1.25	...	...
Nicaragua	-0.28	-0.01	-0.86	-0.16	-0.64	-0.78	-0.19	-0.31	-0.73	-0.70	-0.14	-0.62	...	2.6
Panama	0.27	0.52	0.13	-0.05	-0.38	0.11	0.55	0.25	0.21	-0.11	-0.53	-0.27	...	3.5
Paraguay	-0.46	-0.19	-0.26	-0.62	-0.92	-0.83	0.75	-0.77	-0.56	-1.00	-0.52	-1.19	...	2.1
Peru	-0.81	0.04	-1.08	-1.08	-0.11	-0.60	0.49	0.10	-0.40	-0.77	-0.09	-0.49	4.4	3.5
Puerto Rico	...	1.03	0.58	0.72	1.43	1.01	0.88	1.01	0.71	0.62	1.29	1.10	...	...
Saint Kitts and Nevis	1.00	0.87	...	1.29	-0.28	1.00	-0.16	1.14	...	0.82	...	1.00	...	...
Saint Lucia	1.07	1.04	0.98	1.10	0.30	1.12	-0.16	1.14	...	0.82	...	1.15	...	...
Saint Vincent and the Grenadines	1.08	1.04	0.98	1.14	-0.28	1.07	-0.23	1.14	...	0.82	...	1.00	...	...
Suriname	-0.12	0.74	0.43	0.26	-0.89	-0.04	-0.68	-0.46	-0.88	-0.15	-0.32	0.05	...	3.2
Trinidad and Tobago	0.72	0.44	0.45	-0.05	0.37	0.29	0.44	0.65	0.31	-0.07	0.37	0.01	...	3.8
Turks and Caicos Islands	...	...	...	1.50	...	...	...	...	...	...	...	...	...	...
United States Virgin Islands	...	1.03	...	0.52	...	1.29	...	1.09	...	1.15	...	0.78	...	...
Uruguay	0.72	0.99	0.62	0.64	0.71	0.53	0.92	0.26	0.49	0.43	0.50	0.78	...	5.9
Venezuela	-0.00	-0.50	-0.88	-1.22	-0.78	-0.83	-0.19	-1.15	-0.72	-1.22	-0.76	-1.00	2.7	2.3
NORTHERN AMERICA														
Bermuda	...	1.03	...	0.79	...	1.02	...	1.33	...	0.88	...	1.25	...	...
Canada	1.39	1.32	0.82	0.91	2.03	1.92	1.15	1.57	1.84	1.81	2.34	1.92	9.2	8.4
Greenland	...	...	...	1.50	...	...	...	...	...	...	...	...	...	...
United States of America	1.48	1.19	0.82	0.06	2.06	1.59	1.39	1.47	1.76	1.59	1.87	1.56	7.8	7.6
OCEANIA														
American Samoa	...	0.59	...	0.74	...	0.21	...	0.36	...	1.15	...	0.78	...	...
Australia	1.68	1.32	1.01	0.82	2.00	1.88	1.25	1.58	1.85	1.80	2.02	1.95	8.3	8.8
Cook Islands	...	...	...	...	...	0.23	...	...	...	...	...	...	...	...
Fiji	-0.14	0.18	0.71	0.29	-0.07	-0.09	-0.52	-0.35	0.05	-0.25	...	-0.60	...	4.0
French Polynesia	...	...	...	0.65	...	...	...	...	...	...	...	...	...	...
Guam	...	0.59	...	0.74	...	0.21	...	0.60	...	1.15	...	0.78	...	...
Kiribati	1.13	0.87	...	1.38	-0.34	-0.50	-0.38	-0.98	...	0.76	...	0.22	...	...
Marshall Islands	1.18	1.19	...	1.10	...	-0.96	...	-0.77	...	-0.27	...	-0.43	...	...
Micronesia (Fed. States of)	1.14	1.11	...	1.08	...	-0.09	...	0.19	...	0.72	...	-0.28	...	...
Nauru	0.84	1.03	...	1.10	...	-0.44	...	...	...	0.83	...	...	...	...
New Caledonia	-0.24	...	-0.93	-0.21	0.43	...	0.39	...	-0.81	...	-1.05	...	...	...
New Zealand	1.61	1.39	1.07	1.20	2.46	1.90	1.70	1.66	2.05	1.95	2.42	2.24	9.4	9.6
Niue	...	...	...	...	...	-0.44	...	...	...	...	...	...	...	...
Palau	...	1.19	...	1.10	...	-0.76	...	...	...	-0.07	...	...	...	...
Papua New Guinea	0.09	-0.05	-1.41	-0.81	-0.60	-0.96	-0.75	-0.86	-0.38	-0.92	-0.27	-1.08	...	2.3
Samoa	0.72	0.62	...	1.10	-0.34	0.35	-0.23	0.01	...	1.09	...	0.17	...	...
Solomon Islands	1.02	0.27	0.98	-0.05	-1.03	-0.69	-1.26	-1.05	...	-0.90	...	0.02	...	...
Tonga	-0.08	-0.16	...	0.53	-0.23	-0.48	-0.16	-0.69	...	0.45	...	-1.28	...	...
Tuvalu	1.39	1.04	...	1.38	...	0.23	...	-0.37	...	1.20	...	-0.15	...	...
Vanuatu	0.45	0.60	0.98	1.27	-0.23	-0.33	-0.09	0.05	...	0.53	...	0.26	...	...

Sources: World Bank, 2006b; Transparency International, 2005

Note: Corruption perceptions index (or 'CPI Score) relates to perceptions of the degree of corruption as seen by business people, risk analysts and the general public. CPI Score ranges between 10 (highly clean) and 0 (highly corrupt).

TABLE B.12

Recorded Crime Data

Rates are per 100 000 population (latest available data)

	Police staff		Recorded crimes														
	Year		grand total	intent homicide commit	intent homicide attempt	non-int homicide	assault	rape	robbery	major theft	theft	automob theft	burglary	fraud	embez-zlement	drug offence	bribery
WORLD																	
AFRICA																	
Côte d'Ivoire	2000	...	437.91	4.07	...	2.86	...	2.06	...	27.85	82.86	18.51	...	18.84	0.28	2.25	...
Mauritius	1999	735.10	3,239.87	1.96	1.02	0.43	972.58	2.47	97.50	52.03	936.14	...	138.62	79.36	42.15	167.15	1.45
Mauritius	2000	755.98	3,030.25	2.19	1.43	0.17	909.17	2.28	98.30	41.06	803.62	...	133.54	77.06	45.10	208.49	0.59
Morocco	2001	142.84	928.50	0.44	0.40	0.68	159.96	3.42	0.01	23.59	222.85	5.49	...	9.45	0.04	53.96	0.14
Morocco	2002	141.62	957.13	0.48	0.46	0.67	156.34	3.42	0.01	22.79	219.85	5.14	...	12.16	0.06	57.57	0.23
Namibia	2001	...	...	6.33	...	1.70	...	14.09	...	...	...	2.93	...	...	...	...	...
Namibia	2002	...	...	6.35	...	1.91	...	14.41	...	...	...	3.02	...	...	...	...	...
Seychelles	1999	...	5,369.24	3.75	...	...	910.91	122.45	69.97	...	1,007.12	...	980.88	162.44	...	246.16	...
Seychelles	2000	...	...	7.39	...	...	861.75	78.79	65.25	...	...	...	279.45	...	...	313.92	...
South Africa	2001	222.08	5,848.82	47.77	69.83	24.42	1,173.57	121.16	96.00	...	1,977.14	216.15	869.79	130.46	...	118.05	...
South Africa	2002	224.02	5,918.73	47.53	79.08	24.70	1,210.38	115.61	100.56	...	2,054.96	205.39	868.80	124.01	...	118.67	...
Swaziland	1999	231.49	4,741.48	88.48	29.82	34.04	1,300.48	122.22	241.30	1,044.37	1,188.36	...	817.68	37.27	...	79.85	...
Swaziland	2000	231.29	4,802.49	88.61	26.32	26.41	1,356.84	121.24	259.14	1,093.78	1,251.87	...	810.05	40.10	...	84.50	...
Tunisia	2001	...	1,242.68	1.26	1.75	0.32	360.16	3.49	216.46	68.80	240.68	12.22	...	19.34	0.98	8.80	0.96
Tunisia	2002	...	1,332.94	1.22	1.49	0.20	365.23	3.13	194.97	76.69	262.71	17.28	...	23.56	1.39	8.33	0.70
Zambia	1999	121.93	681.92	10.85	1.46	1.27	233.87	3.17	40.72	255.76	255.76	9.98	116.11	4.83	...	3.92	9.54
Zambia	2000	126.75	588.38	7.89	0.90	0.31	219.08	2.97	26.72	217.52	217.52	7.84	97.68	3.46	...	4.00	6.76
Zimbabwe	1999	146.86	2,794.51	7.04	2.34	4.36	706.32	47.23	72.60	1,243.94	1,243.94	13.27	441.70	43.27	57.17	50.35	2.41
Zimbabwe	2000	162.98	2,786.93	7.24	2.65	7.69	738.59	44.18	94.09	1,265.00	1,265.00	10.65	438.73	39.79	60.06	54.23	2.65
ASIA																	
Armenia	1999	...	264.56	4.10	...	...	...	0.61	3.31	...	80.40	...	2.74	18.42	5.45	12.63	0.74
Armenia	2000	...	316.80	3.34	...	...	...	0.74	4.26	...	96.32	...	2.42	20.40	5.94	12.70	0.95
Azerbaijan	2001	403.74	180.09	2.69	1.23	0.20	2.44	0.51	21.08	0.25	25.74	0.90	...	16.59	2.06	28.39	0.67
Azerbaijan	2002	402.28	189.92	2.59	1.26	0.09	2.12	0.48	24.79	0.22	19.81	0.99	...	13.63	1.71	26.80	0.21
China	1999	...	179.95	...	...	...	7.42	3.15	15.89	52.78	115.79	...	...	7.46	...	...	...
China	2000	...	288.68	...	...	...	9.59	2.84	24.59	...	188.39	35.74	91.25	12.11	...	...	...
China, Hong Kong SAR	1999	501.55	1,188.28	0.86	0.13	0.07	119.21	1.35	54.16	232.54	432.19	38.31	135.89	64.64	...	33.42	45.98
China, Hong Kong SAR	2000	486.57	1,185.70	0.56	0.10	0.07	109.61	1.53	50.51	244.24	449.76	41.25	131.96	74.89	...	34.02	49.24
Cyprus	2001	624.84	1,683.97	0.92	1.05	0.39	146.25	2.37	42.76	94.61	150.20	129.43	105.26	33.64	...	52.30	0.66
Cyprus	2002	618.17	1,702.35	0.26	0.78	...	155.82	1.70	53.60	123.92	208.50	131.90	160.52	26.14	...	56.99	0.92
Georgia	1999	254.50	281.61	4.86	2.89	0.96	11.94	0.70	5.69	2.01	85.73	6.47	34.39	6.27	5.37	27.21	0.86
Georgia	2000	229.04	299.14	4.76	3.64	0.80	9.71	0.94	6.69	...	89.91	4.86	37.52	4.40	7.50	33.26	0.92
India	1998	104.00	181.51	3.94	3.12	0.38	24.07	1.55	3.23	...	29.38		12.17	3.91	1.65	1.86	0.38
India	1999	103.50	176.82	3.72	2.97	0.39	23.68	1.55	2.85	...	27.25	5.98	11.15	4.15	1.55	2.02	0.36
Indonesia	1999	...	...	1.01	...	0.19	7.96	0.64	33.12	...	...	16.07	...	...	4.48	3.33	1.59
Indonesia	2000	...	...	1.05	...	0.20	8.84	0.65	29.17	...	...	13.84	...	...	4.77	3.35	2.73
Japan	2001	179.48	2,153.40	...	0.53	0.16	40.06	1.75	16.18	...	1,842.39	49.81	...	33.93	1.57	21.78	...
Japan	2002	182.23	2,244.39	...	0.59	0.15	43.86	1.85	11.77	...	1,869.83	49.29	...	38.92	1.69	20.82	...
Kazakhstan	1999	455.36	...	...	...	...	...	...	...	...	...	...	...	...	...	...	...
Kazakhstan	2000	463.73	...	...	...	...	...	...	...	...	...	...	...	...	...	...	...
Kyrgyzstan	1999	347.51	821.26	8.90	...	...	4.28	5.86	30.94	...	395.37	2.94	...	32.91	27.57	71.11	3.15
Kyrgyzstan	2000	340.33	785.76	8.40	...	...	4.23	6.53	30.46	...	371.92	3.32	...	23.52	24.19	72.00	3.11
Kuwait	2001	906.11	864.44	1.71	3.12	1.89	98.55		129.67	99.69	238.20	...	...	5.58	0.22	...	1.19
Kuwait	2002	1,116.11	831.19	0.99	2.66	1.37	90.08		113.94	107.22	245.88	...	...	6.01	0.82	...	0.56
Malaysia	1999	351.02	745.00	2.59	0.23	...	...	6.42	60.57		259.70	227.25	158.31	9.66	18.49	54.04	...
Malaysia	2000	353.58	717.48	2.36	0.18	...	...	5.19	63.07	...	235.54	239.82	141.26	8.58	18.08	58.81	...
Maldives	2001	99.64	2,291.43	2.50	0.71	...	135.36	1.79	158.16	15.00	468.93	76.79	15.00	199.29	89.29	85.36	1.07
Maldives	2002	104.53	2,448.08	2.79	1.05	...	182.23	0.70	146.57	23.69	621.95	129.27	23.69	205.57	95.47	102.09	...
Myanmar	2001	143.05	41.24	0.25	0.03	1.56	18.09	0.44	1.31	0.60	7.98	0.04	0.02	4.06	2.66	6.07	0.02
Myanmar	2002	141.35	37.51	0.19	0.01	1.42	16.52	0.46	0.82	0.88	7.69	0.06	0.01	3.20	2.08	5.88	0.01
Nepal	2001	196.91	40.89	2.56	1.00	5.10	...	0.45	131.33	...	1.46	...	...	0.27	...	0.95	...
Nepal	2002	192.67	36.78	3.42	0.53	5.54	...	0.65	132.49	...	0.91	...	...	0.31	...	0.83	...
Oman	2001	...	...	0.52	0.40	0.40	32.45	4.40	160.03	...	179.26	20.78	0.00	5.77	0.40	12.83	0.08
Oman	2002	...	...	0.59	0.12	0.51	28.25	4.53	148.50	...	188.38	16.67	0.00	7.64	0.24	9.73	0.35
Pakistan	1999	...	1.94	0.05	0.09	...	0.14	0.04	0.09	0.12	0.29	0.06	0.19	0.17	0.03	0.30	0.00
Pakistan	2000	...	2.23	0.05	0.07	...	0.15	0.04	0.06	0.04	0.22	0.05	0.15	0.16	0.04	0.29	0.01
Philippines	2000	147.81	105.96	7.59	5.40	3.25	...	4.06	7.78	9.86	...	...	...	...	...	...	...
Philippines	2002	141.34	107.30	8.20	5.41	3.24	0.08	...	...	...	...	...	...	...	...	...	...
Qatar	1999	...	996.62	0.53	1.42	1.59	51.67	1.59	1.24	...	125.64	10.62	42.65	10.09	...	42.29	1.24
Qatar	2000	...	998.14	0.17	0.68	1.03	55.91	2.05	0.68	...	130.11	4.27	51.29	12.31	...	44.62	
Republic of Korea	1999	193.09	3,358.00	2.12	...	7.33	22.40	13.14	10.42	...	128.60	...	6.52	375.61	52.83	9.04	18.93
Republic of Korea	2000	190.72	3,262.62	2.02	...	7.90	31.55	12.98	9.56	...	144.96	...	6.40	287.96	40.56	9.85	2.21
Saudi Arabia	2001	...	374.84	0.87	0.52	0.24	66.56	0.22	...	...	174.23	76.89	0.34	2.61	4.21	...	...
Saudi Arabia	2002	...	386.54	0.92	0.76	0.24	63.35	0.27	...	...	181.32	85.52	0.06	3.39	4.22	...	...
Singapore	1999	314.85	1,318.24	1.01	...	0.18	12.58	3.14	16.78	189.63	484.67	54.38	39.52	36.34	15.01	116.04	2.78
Singapore	2000	324.22	1,202.61	0.92	0.10	0.12	13.29	3.04	11.52	178.72	419.64	41.09	24.71	36.44	12.97	105.08	3.81
Sri Lanka	1999	176.53	...	...	...	...	...	6.89	26.06	...	87.38	...	67.74	...	...	...	...
Sri Lanka	2000	178.40	...	...	...	...	...	6.20	23.95	...	76.21	...	65.29	...	...	...	...
Thailand	1999	376.90	964.72	8.39	7.16	0.48	...	6.53	1.43	...	93.13	4.77	23.38	10.73	19.67	396.38	0.20
Thailand	2000	354.94	930.99	8.47	7.81	0.38	...	6.62	1.29	...	95.13	5.40	21.78	11.25	21.16	428.92	0.85
Turkey	1999	247.35	475.55	...	...	2.40	81.52	1.00	2.16	...	138.96	27.86	...	19.21	...	5.14	0.39
Turkey	2000	253.96	438.72	...	...	3.33	81.91	1.93	2.50	...	128.88	22.90	...	16.38	...	5.28	0.49
Yemen	1999	...	97.16	6.02	5.05	1.12	20.34	0.26	1.03	0.61	29.75	6.27	0.65	2.46	0.09	0.35	...
Yemen	2000	...	137.52	3.98	4.55	0.74	5.80	0.46	...	...	41.55	4.69	...	3.76	...	0.77	...

TABLE B.12

continued

Rates are per 100 000 population (latest available data)

	Police staff		Recorded crimes														
	Year		grand total	intent homicide commit	intent homicide attempt	non-int homicide	assault	rape	robbery	major theft	theft	automob theft	burglary	fraud	embezzlement	drug offence	bribery
EUROPE																	
Albania	2001	424.52	149.11	6.64	9.99	0.32	17.72	1.63	8.17	...	39.62	5.36	968.45	2.04	...	10.86	0.03
Albania	2002	380.54	168.35	5.68	7.40	0.51	17.59	1.43	6.98	...	41.97	6.29	1,141.86	1.21	...	7.94	0.16
Austria	2001	311.43	6,034.16	0.87	1.10	1.49	371.05	7.15	2.21	67.07	2,001.52	71.46	...	309.42	34.44	272.19	0.29
Austria	2002	305.08	6,863.95	0.81	1.29	1.35	392.35	7.77	2.23	71.40	2,423.15	68.20	...	389.24	36.39	278.60	2.44
Belarus	2001	...	1,125.27	9.72	1.78	0.77	19.86	7.49	66.68	45.14	525.95	16.63	267.66	27.10	0.00	43.46	9.74
Belarus	2002	...	1,338.71	9.96	1.95	0.94	21.32	8.59	66.66	50.92	600.77	19.57	260.23	22.43	0.02	53.43	11.89
Belgium	2001	...	9,240.04	1.80	4.18	0.22	580.64	22.50	114.75	...	3,529.71	...	778.43	101.45	76.47	390.92	0.72
Belgium	2002	357.50	9,421.74	1.50	4.27	0.40	597.65	23.57	109.06	...	3,559.86	...	798.57	93.17	77.53	395.39	0.56
Bulgaria	1998	...	1,986.05	4.61	2.82	1.20	40.66	9.34	54.43	...	658.37	96.97	530.82	79.62	26.14	9.25	1.11
Bulgaria	1999	...	1,767.00	3.98	3.30	1.15	40.08	9.02	49.27	...	572.43	94.35	402.10	94.32	30.54	9.84	1.38
Bulgaria	2000	...	1,823.38	4.07	2.14	1.37	37.76	7.26	52.23	...	583.00	138.13	483.11	84.51	25.30	5.19	0.53
Croatia	2001	514.25	2,185.39	1.86	4.01	0.07	99.31	3.88	5.52	315.17	556.99	49.80	479.78	96.93	2.78	215.35	14.03
Croatia	2002	446.23	2,281.14	1.79	4.17	0.18	121.03	3.70	4.97	306.09	600.54	53.84	498.05	80.31	1.86	242.31	9.63
Czech Republic	2001	447.80	3,507.21	2.29	...	0.44	69.50	5.50	59.56	...	1,389.19	230.23	617.83	232.61	91.79	35.17	1.99
Czech Republic	2002	458.48	3,650.04	2.29	...	0.48	72.05	6.40	60.25	...	1,363.88	256.28	706.21	249.22	78.37	37.84	1.68
Denmark	2001	...	8,831.69	0.97	2.74	0.19	188.09	9.20	122.68	...	3,397.87	549.80	1,772.92	133.50	12.22	16.59	0.09
Denmark	2002	192.09	9,137.07	1.04	3.03	0.19	192.22	9.30	83.01	...	3,483.94	541.51	1,920.64	140.17	11.97	19.59	0.07
Estonia	1999	258.46	3,716.75	11.32	3.10	0.72	30.00	4.25	354.66	...	743.36	177.04	1,717.50	95.91	31.01	21.42	3.68
Estonia	2000	265.38	4,221.99	10.45	3.36	1.97	33.60	5.33	347.26	...	1,038.86	169.61	1,699.85	131.63	35.79	115.49	4.75
Finland	2001	159.46	9,949.40	3.01	7.07	0.64	526.77	8.85	69.36	6.90	2,104.47	435.29	1,472.82	264.61	58.98	286.60	1.33
Finland	2002	160.09	10,005.65	2.54	7.16	0.52	538.99	10.60	71.36	7.56	2,180.77	444.60	1,400.60	300.15	62.38	266.53	1.31
France	1999	205.46	6,088.51	1.63	1.78	...	162.52	13.58	35.94	2,483.47	3,843.90	506.92	631.53	162.87	...	173.79	...
France	2000	211.01	6,403.82	1.78	1.89	...	180.79	14.36	41.26	2,580.14	3,963.83	511.95	629.87	242.08	...	176.11	...
Germany	2001	...	7,729.42	1.05	2.15	1.06	146.17	9.58	32.58	...	3,678.76	91.59	1,248.98	1,124.95	...	299.42	4.74
Germany	2002	303.17	7,888.23	1.11	2.12	1.00	153.87	10.44	33.36	...	3,817.23	85.60	1,279.85	1,123.59	...	304.22	3.92
Greece	1999	...	2,367.80	1.48	1.42	0.40	68.25	2.28	19.50	4.60	542.22	162.77	351.88	6.40	...	63.73	...
Greece	2000	...	969.65	0.76	0.65	0.18	31.34	1.08	7.86	1.48	235.84	80.06	149.99	3.69	...	33.30	...
Hungary	2001	283.16	4,571.45	2.49	1.51	0.20	107.75	5.78	13.83	49.00	1,573.28	91.12	672.42	350.23	83.31	43.33	8.21
Hungary	2002	286.57	4,141.96	2.00	1.54	0.24	115.97	5.89	11.27	43.40	1,451.34	82.23	578.21	248.85	49.50	47.11	7.81
Iceland	2001	285.11	19,043.26	0.35	1.77	0.35	492.55	18.09	65.95	...	2,490.07	...	1,013.12	143.62	26.60	323.05	0.35
Iceland	2002	289.79	21,211.97	1.41	0.35	–	447.18	26.06	69.35	...	2,597.89	...	1,129.58	157.04	35.56	350.00	0.00
Ireland	1998	302.67	2,306.76	1.02	0.13	0.35	255.74	7.87	102.83	24.14	1,129.26	371.58	693.16	83.41	1.02	161.21	0.05
Ireland	1999	305.38	2,166.15	1.01	0.16	0.24	264.42	5.81	64.34	20.63	826.55	395.82	614.13	40.75	1.01	190.22	0.03
Italy	2001	555.68	3,749.81	1.23	2.52	0.88	53.19	4.24	5.03	...	2,258.65	408.88	317.99	67.47	...	62.46	...
Italy	2002	558.99	3,868.17	1.12	2.70	0.63	49.75	4.41	5.49	...	2,262.52	403.13	293.69	94.17	...	65.81	...
Latvia	2001	451.21	2,165.41	9.28	0.89	0.85	34.89	5.13	120.19	62.40	1,216.49	117.38	523.27	29.33	23.95	35.18	3.05
Latvia	2002	441.62	2,109.88	9.15	1.11	0.47	37.72	4.53	130.73	54.53	1,161.68	121.69	526.60	24.51	20.19	26.90	2.01
Lithuania	2001	349.20	2,276.42	10.14	0.72	0.69	39.78	5.05	69.77	263.01	1,407.09	167.20	248.33	52.84	31.30	29.84	3.04
Lithuania	2002	336.64	2,670.68	8.45	0.58	0.66	48.08	5.42	96.62	330.18	1,216.75	164.77	201.47	58.72	33.50	27.01	1.67
Luxembourg	2001	282.05	5,146.82	1.36	10.00	–	265.45	5.68	8.93	...	1,665.00	133.86	658.64	5.91	1.59	244.77	0.00
Luxembourg	2002	294.37	5,866.22	0.90	12.84	0.45	299.10	8.78	18.12	...	1,922.52	129.50	664.86	38.51	4.28	297.52	0.68
Malta	2001	447.59	4,032.66	1.52	1.77	...	189.11	2.28		...	2,119.49	214.68	...	146.84	...	97.97	...
Malta	2002	452.39	4,287.91	1.51	3.02	1.51	207.30	1.26		...	2,297.48	178.09	...	144.58	...	85.89	...
Netherlands	2001	203.17	8,464.47	1.23	9.36	...	303.55	10.76	42.72	...	4,732.09	218.45	571.69	143.01	53.30	64.72	...
Netherlands	2002	212.35	8,813.57	0.97	9.84	...	325.33	11.16	46.56	...	4,782.74	219.18	639.52	152.15	54.98	78.56	...
Norway	1999	240.94	7,083.50	0.83	1.48	1.05	294.15	10.47	38.07	1,602.85	4,217.20	467.78	107.11	253.14	48.97	924.42	...
Norway	2000	247.92	7,349.61	1.09	1.51	0.91	327.92	12.36	39.66	1,557.36	4,281.34	519.68	117.95	273.77	54.00	987.09	...
Poland	2001	260.79	3,597.44	2.01	1.40	0.40	81.10	6.05	171.48	0.62	660.86	153.87	842.88	238.74	...	75.64	6.03
Poland	2002	258.98	3,672.89	1.87	1.22	0.44	81.00	6.13	170.60	0.51	683.34	140.39	796.77	248.00	...	94.63	6.30
Portugal	2001	455.85	2,149.78	...	0.42	1.59	219.52	3.68	15.47	...	1,329.91	257.62	227.53	59.75	14.63	45.95	0.88
Portugal	2002	449.80	2,145.62	...	0.36	1.90	229.71	4.25	13.57	...	1,453.85	300.28	210.36	47.97	13.50	36.93	1.11
Republic of Moldova	2001	314.54	885.95	8.36	1.36	0.44	26.04	4.43	34.66	30.40	479.18	16.46	50.61	27.40	...	44.43	3.84
Republic of Moldova	2002	323.53	853.16	7.99	1.43	0.45	27.92	4.79	29.76	23.29	426.23	14.38	36.38	25.55	...	58.31	2.30
Romania	2001	199.35	1,519.16	2.66	2.65	...	58.00	5.66	23.00	...	425.36	8.37	78.45	84.07	18.98	2.98	56.73
Romania	2002	207.83	1,400.02	2.52	2.18	...	49.94	5.62	26.19	...	326.37	5.50	53.87	69.35	14.26	5.79	49.09
Russian Federation	1999	...	2,055.99	19.27	2.06	1.04	...	5.01	95.19	...	968.36	18.80	...	57.30	33.23	148.19	4.67
Russian Federation	2000	...	2,022.17	19.80	2.00	1.15	...	4.78	90.68	...	897.31	17.88	...	55.80	36.70	166.83	4.83
Slovakia	2001	385.67	1,729.93	2.40	...	...	77.47	3.14	27.26	3.72	426.47	94.61	437.57	60.27	25.64	19.35	1.54
Slovakia	2002	376.39	1,996.15	2.57	...	...	89.25	3.18	25.36	2.88	509.65	89.14	409.67	139.28	44.62	20.80	2.58
Slovenia	2001	360.24	4,049.52	1.42	2.53	2.18	111.79	5.01	461.80	43.50	1,446.13	43.40	748.71	227.52	21.75	292.97	3.54
Slovenia	2002	364.15	4,159.73	1.83	2.65	2.04	127.34	4.99	503.79	44.65	1,450.31	47.35	800.66	271.69	24.90	284.27	3.56
Spain	1999	295.01	2,441.08	1.16	1.63	0.18	224.70	14.86	1,332.23	232.02	1,414.71	352.69	68.28	41.11	12.64	31.44	0.14
Spain	2000	292.80	2,337.39	1.25	1.77	0.24	228.99	14.34	1,258.89	248.92	1,365.92	340.72	60.39	39.14	11.02	27.93	0.13
Sweden	2001	181.25	13,372.98	1.88	8.15	2.29	668.55	23.43	31.20	...	7,496.75	675.11	1,326.56	397.13	21.16	364.35	...
Sweden	2002	180.96	13,836.67	2.45	8.15	2.38	690.62	24.47	33.54	...	7,694.69	687.47	1,352.92	411.41	23.22	425.87	...
Switzerland	2001	205.84	3,811.24	2.42	1.23	...	79.77	6.28	10.18	...	1,677.39	888.41	793.46	144.48	31.42	637.75	...
Switzerland	2002	203.66	4,219.90	2.92	1.74	...	83.99	6.64	11.29	...	1,995.53	899.47	834.32	141.66	35.38	674.91	...
TFYR Macedonia	1999	473.18	1,113.63	1.88	2.48	0.05	10.36	1.98	11.01	547.94	724.49	17.35	...	28.66	1.98	14.53	3.77
TFYR Macedonia	2000	481.98	975.58	2.31	3.79	0.20	10.14	1.33	14.57	434.27	662.48	14.92	...	23.49	1.33	21.27	1.97
Ukraine	1999	...	1,119.67	8.52	0.75	0.74	9.65	2.58	42.65	118.55	351.58	6.41	...	32.22	21.32	85.35	4.66
Ukraine	2000	...	1,118.37	8.93	0.78	0.68	10.63	2.33	43.29	120.10	357.58	6.39	...	29.56	21.38	92.03	4.59
United Kingdom	2001	252.21	10,399.77	1.76	2.89	0.02	970.52	17.95	148.45	...	4,142.20	614.72	1,592.82	582.18	30.66	268.69	1.82
United Kingdom	2002	257.60	11,014.38	2.03	3.08	0.03	1,222.18	22.62	145.87	...	4,299.76	587.84	1,606.34	604.75	30.65	309.68	2.25

TABLE B.12

continued

Rates are per 100 000 population (latest available data)

	Year	Police staff	Recorded crimes														
			grand total	intent homicide commit	intent homicide attempt	non-int homicide	assault	rape	robbery	major theft	theft	automob theft	burglary	fraud	embez-zlement	drug offence	bribery
LATIN AMERICA AND THE CARIBBEAN																	
Argentina	2001	...	3,258.76	8.43	2.46	12.22	509.94	9.09	1,061.06	...	870.22	...	...	...	...	42.48	...
Argentina	2002	...	3,674.70	9.47	2.36	10.33	509.79	8.32	1,288.10	...	1,060.08	...	...	...	...	42.51	...
Barbados	1999	505.86	3,833.06	8.64	3.38	93.58	561.86	25.56	155.59	214.22	941.45	105.98	1,086.14	97.71	...	369.81	...
Barbados	2000	516.48	4,085.39	7.49	3.00	103.00	576.78	25.47	160.30	149.44	870.04	83.52	1,109.74	85.39	...	546.44	...
Bolivia	2001	214.45	435.80	3.74	10.15	...	57.26	13.90	87.78	...	58.74	36.06	6.88	38.59	1.54	38.40	0.22
Bolivia	2002	219.83	353.48	2.82	6.44	...	52.71	10.53	85.13	...	52.73	45.65	10.27	28.16	0.05	44.70	0.28
Colombia	1999	247.96	538.83	58.69	47.42	...	64.55	4.55	64.75	12.15	20.13	79.49	47.50	4.23	3.99	40.13	0.02
Colombia	2000	215.50	506.36	62.74	51.77	...	59.62	4.40	58.01	10.27	15.74	78.33	31.62	2.91	2.95	49.61	0.01
Chile	2001	192.87	3,572.80	...	...	0.10	278.27	8.91	...	...	317.44	31.91	121.13	29.31	48.12	1.68	0.00
Chile	2002	193.02	3,810.36	...	...	1.17	356.50	8.99	...	...	373.80	38.04	330.10	30.48	51.89	2.08	0.00
Costa Rica	2001	265.22	1,076.37	6.64	2.87	15.00	57.99	14.25	...	296.95	479.16	113.12	...	53.03	4.26	24.97	0.49
Costa Rica	2002	256.82	1,021.39	6.44	2.92	14.00	57.94	16.06	26.97	277.09	442.92	111.24	...	46.91	6.52	27.88	0.63
Dominica	2000	605.48	10,763.01	2.74	...	...	95.89	32.88	78.08	3,108.22	3,121.92	98.63	1,776.71	43.84	...	369.86	...
El Salvador	2001	256.51	841.81	34.98	3.41	0.60	91.08	12.97	41.58	224.54	279.44	54.91	0.00	17.44	4.68	...	0.00
El Salvador	2002	251.66	697.55	31.54	2.87	0.75	70.78	13.12	40.78	176.50	224.17	47.83	7.73	14.21	3.15	...	0.47
Guatemala	1999	221.14	200.48	23.92	...	...	42.38	2.91	74.52	...	...	56.41	...	...	...	...	...
Guatemala	2000	233.63	239.63	25.47	...	...	47.38	3.21	101.29	...	...	62.04	...	...	...	...	...
Jamaica	1999	276.64	1,600.62	32.97	38.69	...	443.17	48.69	92.36	105.98	253.71	16.72	98.49	86.45	...	392.97	0.39
Jamaica	2000	267.11	1,488.34	33.69	39.31	...	411.43	49.53	88.53	98.94	187.50	9.80	92.14	43.64	...	451.84	0.72
Mexico	2001	451.02	1,521.93	13.94	...	17.44	260.41	13.05	63.00		116.74	150.66	...	54.64	...	23.38	...
Mexico	2002	491.79	1,503.71	13.04	...	15.87	251.91	14.26	55.02		112.47	139.86	...	61.47	...	23.40	...
Panama	2001	528.41	756.51	10.56	...	...	105.35	6.39	126.45	321.71	321.71	20.85	...	10.63	...	57.09	...
Panama	2002	518.88	716.26	9.56	...	...	108.23	7.21	127.24	298.47	298.47	19.25	...	8.88	...	50.48	...
Paraguay	1999	...	109.76	11.83	3.77	9.05	...	54.34	5.09	71.49	...	23.23	...	15.32	1.60	1.53	...
Paraguay	2000	...	79.75	12.05	5.51	10.06	...	57.35	4.97	51.35	...	25.53	...	21.03	1.00	1.16	...
Peru	2001	...	600.69	4.91	...	...	110.66	22.50	129.04	179.94	179.94	7.05	29.09	22.92	20.24	14.76	...
Peru	2002	...	604.21	4.25	...	...	99.92	22.31	125.05	198.47	198.47	7.10	26.91	20.77	19.85	16.30	...
Uruguay	2001	529.71	3,598.86	6.31	2.27	1.44	318.97	7.60	...	...	1,961.46	112.96	261.43	46.47	48.03	23.49	0.33
Uruguay	2002	540.70	3,987.21	6.46	2.95	1.13	313.72	9.02	...	...	2,234.51	134.39	332.76	35.97	58.46	25.50	0.60
Venezuela	1999	...	1,042.05	25.21	...	...	...	13.23	144.41	268.89	...	...	...	47.37	17.50	37.37	0.15
Venezuela	2000	...	975.89	33.15	...	...	...	12.11	144.52	211.58	...	...	...	48.52	16.99	11.17	0.13
NORTHERN AMERICA																	
Canada	2001	183.63	8,050.38	0.67	2.33	0.15	762.36	77.36	489.42	67.06	2,189.16	542.42	899.11	278.25	...	287.61	...
Canada	2002	186.28	8,025.37	1.67	2.17	0.19	750.18	77.64	17.95	63.40	2,195.25	514.97	876.52	290.91	...	295.23	...
United States of America	2001	325.17	4,162.61	5.62	...	...	...	31.85	332.65	978.64	2,485.74	430.53	741.81	...	...	...	...
United States of America	2002	326.37	4,118.76	5.62	...	...	...	32.99	305.92	969.14	2,445.80	432.12	746.22	...	...	...	...
OCEANIA																	
Australia	1999	220.89	1.81	1.89	1.41	706.69	74.23	118.98	29.16	3,223.99	681.85	2,188.08	...	...	...	...	...
Australia	2000	218.99	1.57	2.04	1.54	735.02	81.41	121.43	38.85	3,514.65	724.45	2,275.34	...	...	...	...	...
New Zealand	2001	181.60	444.51	1.16	0.80	0.23	810.67	21.64	4.28	0.00	3,335.20	542.62	1,533.57	513.97	2.71	640.20	0.23
New Zealand	2002	181.90	464.22	1.29	1.04	0.28	807.62	26.88	6.54	0.00	3,407.77	592.13	1,511.32	553.62	2.28	602.87	0.33
Papua New Guinea	1999	113.73	274.34	8.99	...	...	26.61	31.92	67.10	18.50	18.50	29.31	53.20	8.07	...	12.70	...
Papua New Guinea	2000	106.47	259.10	9.06	...	...	26.34	25.24	66.16	20.23	20.23	14.87	51.03	8.13	...	16.69	...

Sources: UNODC, 2002; UNODC, 2005

TABLE B.13

Conviction Statistics

Rates are per 100 000 population (latest available data)

		Prosecution staff	Persons convicted														
			grand total	intent homicide commit	intent homicide attempt	non-int homicide	assault	rape	robbery	major theft	theft	automob theft	burglary	fraud	embez-zlement	drug offence	bribery
WORLD																	
AFRICA																	
Egypt	1999	25.36	…	3.38	2.87	1.97	1.84	…	3.39	…	…	…	…	…	0.82	28.32	0.84
Egypt	2000	27.96	…	3.86	3.88	3.58	3.02	…	3.42	…	…	…	…	…	1.75	40.53	1.92
Ethiopia	2001	0.22	3.16	0.34	0.20	0.23	…	0.02	0.54	0.00	0.04	…	…	0.61	0.01	0.01	0.03
Ethiopia	2002	0.23	4.46	0.46	0.23	0.58	…	0.06	0.75	0.01	0.07	…	…	0.63	0.00	0.01	0.02
South Africa	2001	4.91	…	…	…	…	…	…	…	…	…	…	…	…	…	…	…
South Africa	2002	5.58	…	…	…	…	…	…	…	…	…	…	…	…	…	…	…
Swaziland	1999	…	1,285.37	2.75	0.49	0.39	446.90	5.20	25.50	255.62	274.95	…	117.90	1.28	…	43.16	…
Swaziland	2000	…	1,333.88	0.96	0.96	0.19	420.57	3.16	25.17	248.13	265.65	…	125.65	0.57	…	50.33	
Zambia	1999	0.21	33.26	1.34	0.03	…	9.22	0.60	1.96	10.24	28.57	0.18	2.89	0.53	…	2.28	3.34
Zambia	2000	0.18	19.28	0.97	0.07	…	5.03	0.47	1.06	5.38	9.44	0.38	1.74	0.43	…	1.30	1.11
Zimbabwe	1999	1.32	598.58	1.00	1.88	1.81	80.98	10.72	13.76	54.26	152.51	2.99	82.94	53.48	55.42	23.14	6.53
Zimbabwe	2000	1.37	620.60	1.03	1.73	1.71	83.67	10.02	18.00	81.06	175.81	4.29	97.91	86.64	56.15	28.13	13.89
ASIA																	
Afghanistan	2001	…	1.91	0.18	…	0.21	0.39	0.18	0.26	0.59	0.85	0.18	0.32	0.07	0.05	0.08	0.04
Afghanistan	2002	…	9.23	0.77	…	0.92	0.38	0.94	3.02	0.21	0.75	0.14	0.25	0.16	0.13	0.47	0.54
Armenia	1999	…	171.95	3.13	…	0.21	…	0.55	1.42	…	34.10	…	2.55	4.71	2.89	11.63	0.32
Armenia	2000	…	178.52	2.68	…	0.18	…	0.42	2.05	…	31.08	…	1.66	5.89	3.68	10.60	0.74
Azerbaijan	2001	…	168.76	2.81	…	0.02	…	0.33	…	…	18.83	0.55	…	3.69	3.27	23.38	0.07
Azerbaijan	2002	…	173.62	2.86	…	0.12	…	0.32	…	…	15.25	0.59	…	4.76	3.27	24.17	0.09
China	1999	13.50	48.19	…	…	0.08	5.43	2.01	7.45	…	16.18	…	…	1.32	0.57	2.69	0.69
China	2000	13.59	50.78	…	…	0.09	5.81	1.93	7.72	…	14.91	…	…	1.35	0.65	2.61	0.77
China, Hong Kong SAR	1999	…	300.30	0.30	0.04	0.60	24.80	0.24	7.95	…	100.73	…	8.21	6.59	…	23.48	1.10
China, Hong Kong SAR	2000	…	313.56	0.16	0.01	0.32	24.50	0.16	8.34	…	106.00	…	8.17	5.28	…	21.16	1.57
Cyprus	2001	3.42	9,090.54	…	…	0.39	55.58	0.26	3.29	0.13	59.53	…	19.84	…	0.79	26.15	0.13
Cyprus	2002	3.40	7,849.15	0.13	0.39	0.92	73.86	0.26	1.44	0.26	61.44	…	31.90	…	0.39	17.25	…
Georgia	1999	20.58	158.70	4.64	…	0.54	11.48	0.90	4.80	0.30	42.54	2.63	…	…	…	16.68	0.04
Georgia	2000	18.93	164.89	3.94	…	0.56	10.01	0.44	4.42	0.68	43.83	1.13	…	2.05	…	18.49	0.36
India	1998	…	59.53	2.10	1.54	0.22	6.36	0.38	1.02	…	4.58	…	1.83	0.50	0.25	0.83	0.07
India	1999	…	60.58	2.14	1.77	0.22	7.33	0.44	1.16	…	4.46	0.84	1.82	0.60	0.33	0.80	0.07
Indonesia	1999	…	…	0.84	…	2.21	…	0.90	…	…	18.66	…	…	0.97	1.05	0.88	0.19
Indonesia	2000	…	…	0.91	…	1.77	…	1.05	…	…	14.00	…	…	1.01	0.91	2.40	0.11
Japan	2001	1.81	55.16	…	…	…	9.60	…	1.16	…	…	…	0.49	3.40	0.52	11.97	0.12
Japan	2002	1.82	58.20	…	…	…	11.07	…	1.25	…	…	…	0.57	3.71	0.65	11.39	0.15
Kazakhstan	1999	13.42	…	…	…	…	…	…	…	…	…	…	…	…	…	…	…
Kazakhstan	2000	21.84	…	…	…	…	…	…	…	…	…	…	…	…	…	…	…
Kyrgyzstan	1999	12.05	362.87	7.40	…	…	…	5.47	…	…	125.66	…	8.67	…	…	46.15	
Kyrgyzstan	2000	12.19	410.34	9.50	…	…	…	6.10	…	…	152.04	…	8.61	…	…	51.72	
Malaysia	1999	…	194.03	0.21	…	0.53	3.15	1.10	3.44	19.32	9.75	20.11	6.79	1.42	2.69	56.93	2.82
Malaysia	2000	…	192.22	0.20	…	0.34	2.67	0.69	2.72	17.15	10.35	18.87	5.23	1.14	2.64	53.58	3.43
Maldives	2001	7.14	…	…	…	…	…	…	…	…	…	…	…	…	…	…	…
Maldives	2002	6.27	…	…	…	…	…	…	…	…	…	…	…	…	…	…	…
Myanmar	2001	2.36	35.04	1.38	0.07	1.37	10.61	1.15	0.24	4.13	7.23	0.00	1.08	1.42	0.74	9.49	0.06
Myanmar	2002	2.44	32.48	1.38	0.03	1.16	10.52	1.07	0.13	3.93	7.17	0.01	1.04	1.15	0.83	7.78	0.02
Nepal	2001	0.95	…	…	…	…	…	…	…	…	…	…	…	…	…	…	…
Nepal	2002	0.93	…	…	…	…	…	…	…	…	…	…	…	…	…	…	…
Oman	2001	12.27	…	…	…	…	…	…	…	…	…	…	…	…	…	…	…
Oman	2002	11.74	…	…	…	…	…	…	…	…	…	…	…	…	…	…	…
Pakistan	1999	0.00	…	…	…	…	…	…	…	…	…	…	…	…	…	…	…
Pakistan	2000	0.00	…	…	…	…	…	…	…	…	…	…	…	…	…	…	…
Qatar	1999	6.02	437.08	…	…	…	16.63	…	1.06	38.05	…	…	14.86	8.85	…	…	7.26
Qatar	2000	5.98	446.24	…	…	…	20.69	…	0.17	24.45	…	…	16.76	…	…	…	0.17
Republic of Korea	1999	2.42	380.12	…	…	…	8.32	4.18	3.48	…	28.03	…	0.53	44.49	6.91	10.32	3.13
Republic of Korea	2000	2.51	370.70	…	…	…	8.77	4.05	3.00	…	28.02	…	0.47	40.85	5.74	9.75	2.03
Saudi Arabia	2001	6.05	274.76	2.95	…	…	36.20	…	…	…	30.99	…	…	…	…	50.12	…
Saudi Arabia	2002	6.60	273.58	3.66	…	…	37.79	…	…	…	27.11	…	…	…	…	49.46	…
Singapore	1999	3.57	279.98	0.05	…	0.20	2.88	0.03	0.86	38.08	54.40	1.29	2.00	2.28	1.64	…	2.78
Singapore	2000	3.78	292.71	…	0.02	0.07	2.89	0.07	0.97	38.43	55.85	2.36	1.72	0.52	0.75	…	3.81
Syrian Arab Republic	1998	…	926.64	…	…	…	…	…	68.15	…	…	…	…	…	…	…	…
Syrian Arab Republic	1999	…	614.82	…	…	…	…	…	65.75	…	…	…	…	…	…	…	…
Thailand	1999	3.31	414.21	4.32		6.76	18.71	5.09	2.11		43.91	…	…	2.33	2.32	328.67	…
Thailand	2000	3.23	…	…	…	…	…	…	…	…	…	…	…	…	…	…	…
Turkey	2002	4.66	45.11	5.96		0.35	2.78	2.42	3.43		6.35			0.97	0.42	4.17	0.11
EUROPE																	
Albania	2001	11.33	135.89	5.27	4.63	0.06	2.23	0.16	3.38	19.41	20.18	0.57	0.54	2.08	–	8.52	0.03
Albania	2002	11.75	138.73	8.03	3.94	0.32	2.41	0.22	2.86	21.02	9.14	0.60	1.84	1.56	–	6.92	–
Belarus	2001	19.69	505.01	8.27	0.99	0.76	22.77	3.14	20.62	62.92	199.79	9.58	…	8.19	12.29	22.48	1.21
Belarus	2002	19.65	540.31	8.75	1.11	0.72	34.72	3.19	14.03	57.39	179.66	10.57	…	7.00	9.78	26.10	1.67
Belgium	2001	…	1,529.23	1.26	0.74	3.93	41.86	4.43	…	…	98.89	…	…	20.52	…	38.51	0.28
Belgium	2002	…	1,362.96	1.82	0.93	3.98	39.73	3.99	…	…	88.35	…	…	18.29	…	38.06	0.31
Bulgaria	1998	…	340.00	1.39	0.71	0.98	7.97	1.84	12.47	…	195.88	3.04	…	4.97	5.41	0.97	0.39
Bulgaria	1999	10.43	358.08	2.14	0.45	0.88	7.71	2.52	11.21	…	158.39	3.40	…	4.36	4.69	1.45	0.32
Bulgaria	2000	11.29	372.29	1.73	0.51	1.22	13.93	2.16	16.60	…	186.43	4.21	…	6.16	7.20	2.84	0.47

TABLE B.13

continued

Rates are per 100 000 population (latest available data)

		Prosecution staff	Persons convicted														
			grand total	intent homicide commit	intent homicide attempt	non-int homicide	assault	rape	robbery	major theft	theft	automob theft	burglary	fraud	embez-zlement	drug offence	bribery
Croatia	2000	8.58	393.90	4.04	1.71	0.53	6.19	1.30	4.68	42.26	44.61	0.05	...	19.18	3.61	47.37	1.00
Czech Republic	2001	9.32	588.63	1.45	...	...	27.90	1.37	12.59	...	158.71	...	37.07	61.21	29.49	10.30	1.12
Czech Republic	2002	9.70	638.15	1.53	...	...	29.86	1.44	14.13	...	153.98	...	37.89	82.71	28.77	11.45	1.34
Denmark	2001	11.29	275.54	0.41	0.26	...	71.84	1.16	11.63	...	37.62	10.17	29.24	...	...	7.67	...
Denmark	2002	11.18	251.53	0.39	0.19	...	71.36	1.19	12.21	...	35.41	11.50	28.27	...	...	9.71	...
Estonia	1999	10.82	633.60	9.23	0.36	1.23	21.27	2.67	66.49	...	43.77	16.95	285.07	15.22	11.90	10.31	1.44
Estonia	2000	11.47	749.53	8.04	0.29	0.88	19.28	2.85	79.33	...	52.59	17.38	266.84	19.14	11.54	23.52	3.14
Finland	2001	6.78	3,979.68	1.83	1.95	...	193.66	0.96	10.58	11.72	734.43	...	...	82.65	15.61	123.65	0.08
Finland	2002	6.92	3,447.37	2.10	2.04	...	185.96	1.21	10.31	10.31	567.40	...	...	74.59	15.58	142.09	0.08
France	1999	2.67	999.56	1.00	...	1.24	90.11	3.15	0.72	1.02	167.20	...	...	11.51	4.07	41.15	0.54
France	2000	2.75	984.79	0.84	...	1.17	89.93	2.97	0.75	0.98	158.26	...	...	11.02	3.99	38.91	0.47
Germany	2001	...	628.08	0.24	0.10	0.83	65.40	2.28	11.11	8.61	148.41	...	18.52	121.61	11.04	55.83	0.44
Germany	2002	6.24	633.88	0.15	0.12	0.79	70.21	2.40	11.56	8.88	152.65	...	19.04	117.99	11.33	55.27	0.46
Iceland	2001	12.06	729.79	1.06	–	1.42	66.67	2.84	4.26	123.05	123.05	24.11	7.09	18.79	6.74	209.57	–
Iceland	2002	11.97	814.79	0.70	0.35	2.11	63.73	4.23	5.28	130.99	130.99	23.94	14.79	25.35	7.75	221.13	0.35
Ireland	1998	1.59	...	...	...	...	...	1.24	...	...	...	...	...	...	...	...	...
Ireland	1999	1.79	...	...	...	...	...	1.28	...	...	...	...	...	...	...	...	...
Italy	2001	3.77	414.48	1.24	0.65	...	11.21	2.57	13.21	...	79.07	...	...	5.98	2.71	40.79	1.10
Italy	2002	3.68	383.41	1.38	0.57	...	12.30	2.72	12.29	...	64.13	...	...	6.25	2.93	36.90	0.73
Latvia	2001	24.42	537.47	4.54	0.25	1.14	23.40	2.92	32.26	74.90	125.14	...	107.21	5.04	6.02	10.85	0.76
Latvia	2002	24.25	539.56	5.90	0.43	0.64	26.99	2.61	36.31	67.54	113.69	...	106.46	7.87	7.44	23.87	0.86
Lithuania	2001	23.55	600.66	25.53	...	...	...	...	...	327.80	...	...	...	...	...	19.01	1.44
Lithuania	2002	24.65	573.36	25.34	...	...	...	...	...	307.64	...	...	...	...	...	17.38	1.56
Luxembourg	2001		1,063.64	2.05	0.68	1.14	8.64	3.18	20.68	48.18	18.64	1.59	0.45	22.50	10.23	60.91	–
Luxembourg	2002		966.89	0.90	1.13	1.58	80.86	2.25	22.97	53.60	13.51	13.29	19.37	27.93	9.01	72.97	0.45
Malta	2001	455.92	...	1.52	...	...	...	1.27	...	...	8.61	...	...	1.27	...	18.73	...
Malta	2002	1.63	...	1.26	...	...	...	1.76	...	...	13.60	...	...	0.50	...	16.37	...
Netherlands	2001	3.56	633.35	...	...	0.09	...	2.04	22.41	...	...	...	...	24.22	8.93	43.96	0.02
Netherlands	2002	3.63	660.57	...	...	0.04	...	2.27	24.43	...	...	...	...	20.92	8.02	53.90	0.02
Norway	1999	...	263.50	0.47	0.13	0.94	29.39	0.70	4.04	48.21	72.96	5.81	0.78	28.99	4.66	62.33	...
Norway	2000	...	240.08	0.47	0.13	1.02	25.85	0.56	4.70	41.15	63.48	4.97	0.76	24.49	5.14	57.85	...
Poland	2001	13.98	815.23	1.47	0.46	0.55	...	2.38	26.02		68.51	4.79	78.05	58.15	0.13	11.13	1.63
Poland	2002	14.29	...	...	...	...	...	...	...	...	...	...	...	...	...	...	...
Portugal	2001	10.53	595.45	1.95	0.94	6.64	58.38	2.41	10.58	36.79	52.90	1.19	9.58		0.59	38.24	0.37
Portugal	2002	10.81	607.64	...	...	...	...	...	...	...	...	...	...	...	...	...	...
Republic of Moldova	2001	17.28	401.36	9.30	...	...	8.38	3.14	19.44	8.83	208.69	2.53	...	3.68	12.76	11.33	0.52
Republic of Moldova	2002	18.07	442.70	7.99	...	...	7.47	4.16	22.37	8.74	216.15	2.94	...	3.83	14.62	14.12	0.96
Romania	2001	9.15	370.01	5.01	1.95	7.93	14.39	3.27	13.04	...	141.80	0.55	...	10.57	4.58	1.20	1.50
Romania	2002	9.16	366.88	5.76	2.30	8.61	14.11	2.91	12.72	...	135.95	1.65	...	11.07	4.52	1.94	1.61
Russian Federation	1999	30.01	837.85	12.84	...	0.80	...	4.68	44.03	...	405.18	15.05	...	12.02	9.52	74.17	1.04
Russian Federation	2000	30.39	810.71	13.30	...	...	...	4.41	44.33	...	409.90	12.47	...	11.18	10.34	67.89	1.05
Slovakia	2001	12.33	430.54	1.47	0.22	0.41	53.23	1.21	12.21	124.61	126.36	1.80	25.97	26.03	11.66	10.80	0.50
Slovakia	2002	12.68	448.08	1.45	0.39	0.41	51.57	1.17	11.75	124.80	135.36	0.71	23.54	35.81	14.31	8.70	0.76
Slovenia	2001	8.04	384.22	1.01	...	0.15	36.12	3.44	4.50	3.14	51.59	5.11	45.12	29.69	2.88	15.58	0.86
Slovenia	2002	8.30	424.59	1.07	...	0.31	37.07	4.58	5.09	4.94	60.44	4.74	42.67	36.20	3.11	17.72	0.31
Spain	1999	...	253.64	0.27	...	0.88	...	2.08	79.52	9.30	...	6.94		3.76	2.93	17.27	0.10
Spain	2000	3.67	...	...	...	...	...	...	...	...	...	...	...	...	...	...	...
Sweden	2001	8.19	622.37	0.99	...	1.16	81.05	1.25	8.10	11.52	79.24	15.98	...	12.53	2.64	48.10	0.03
Sweden	2002	7.91	636.17	1.01	...	1.21	83.30	1.27	10.04	11.89	81.05	16.86	...	12.61	2.55	51.64	0.15
Switzerland	2001	...	1,283.23	1.41	...	2.14	27.19	1.76	7.87	...	134.35	...	...	19.91	24.99	99.88	0.03
Switzerland	2002	...	1,319.60	0.99	...	1.51	28.66	1.40	8.55	...	147.24	...	...	18.86	23.50	103.20	0.16
TFYR Macedonia	1999	8.38	382.70	2.08	0.10	0.35	32.62	1.24	5.65	44.67	...	7.68	89.04	10.26	4.02	7.19	1.14
TFYR Macedonia	2000	8.47	366.08	1.62	...	0.20	28.66	1.03	5.22	38.16	...	6.25	89.32	11.23	3.25	97.64	0.94
Ukraine	1999	...	445.37	7.31	...	0.49	5.05	2.17	17.07	6.56	116.48	3.64	...	4.93	0.04	49.21	0.88
Ukraine	2000	...	466.47	8.17	...	0.66	5.13	1.83	16.75	5.18	131.63	2.81	...	5.41	0.03	51.70	1.02
United Kingdom	2001	11.18	2,370.55	0.57	0.17	0.51	142.74	0.99	12.76	...	211.96	26.27	47.78	31.12	0.28	80.59	–
United Kingdom	2002	12.68	2,394.67	0.56	0.11	0.51	130.98	1.13	13.20	...	186.67	24.59	45.90	27.71	...	83.60	...
LATIN AMERICA AND THE CARIBBEAN																	
Argentina	2001	...	63.72	...	...	...	...	...	...	...	...	...	...	...	...	...	...
Argentina	2002	...	70.01	...	...	...	...	...	...	...	...	...	...	...	...	...	...
Barbados	1999	3.01		6.39	1.88		11.27	16.91	8.64	...		...	9.02	...	...	1.88	...
Barbados	2000	3.00		7.87	2.62		18.73	13.11	7.87	...		...	5.62	...	...	5.62	...
Bolivia	2001	...	30.80	1.16	0.26	0.21	1.44	3.48	4.90	...	0.93	...	...	1.30	1.03	11.20	0.06
Bolivia	2002	...	59.28	2.25	0.27	0.64	4.22	2.82	6.62	...	2.40	...	...	1.98	1.67	16.06	0.20
Colombia	1998	44.69	194.52	7.88	...	1.63	21.94	...	...	...	37.57	...	...	0.76	...	13.32	...
Colombia	1999	42.24	250.97	8.35	...	1.87	23.97	...	...	...	53.57	...	...	0.90	...	18.01	...
Chile	2001	1.21	1,302.97	2.62	...	2.06	29.31	3.93	33.27	...	12.56	0.02	2.54	3.22	2.46	9.50	0.06
Chile	2002	1.59	722.82	3.57	...	2.73	30.18	4.42	32.54	0.03	16.95	0.12	6.06	2.52	2.03	19.59	0.04
Dominica	2000	2.74	...	...	...	...	...	...	...	...	...	...	...	...	...	...	...
Dominican Republic	1999	3.93	68.50	1.01	0.33	2.56		1.76	17.54			...	...	2.66	...	11.87	...
Dominican Republic	2000	4.59	41.11	0.78	0.10	1.77		1.23	9.26			...	...	1.40	...	6.31	...
El Salvador	2001	10.30	31.59	6.61	0.95	0.41	5.21	5.10	11.32	1.85	1.85	...	...	2.54	0.02	3.00	0.06
El Salvador	2002	10.33	36.06	6.69	1.18	0.58	3.52	4.66	11.49	2.12	2.12	...	...	1.99	0.28	1.95	0.03

TABLE B.13

continued

Rates are per 100 000 population (latest available data)

		Prosecution staff	Persons convicted														
			grand total	intent homicide commit	intent homicide attempt	non-int homicide	assault	rape	robbery	major theft	theft	automob theft	burglary	fraud	embez-zlement	drug offence	bribery
Guatemala	1999	18.08	276.23	28.38	...	10.40	2.74	16.21	53.09	43.14	89.99	...	...	8.23	12.14	26.26	3.32
Guatemala	2000	18.74	306.97	25.91	...	13.25	4.88	16.48	80.26	46.33	109.38	...	...	7.98	12.20	41.84	5.26
Mexico	2001	1.98	...	...	...	...	...	...	...	...	...	...	...	...	...	...	...
Peru	2001	13.27	...	...	...	...	...	...	...	...	...	...	...	...	...	...	...
Peru	2002	14.19	...	...	...	...	...	...	...	...	...	...	...	...	...	...	...
Venezuela	1999	...	56.55	18.44	...	0.01	0.32	2.92	22.22	3.30	3.58	...	...	0.24	0.00	8.21	0.05
Venezuela	2000	...	17.74	6.43	...	0.01	0.04	0.57	7.52	0.59	0.63	...	...	0.05	...	2.18	...
NORTHERN AMERICA																	
Canada	2001	11.61	1,040.70	0.56	0.22	...	159.41	8.74	15.61	...	110.84	...	45.58	42.13	...	71.21	...
Canada	2002	...	1,049.63	0.55	0.39	...	164.69	8.71	16.50	...	108.73	...	46.34	42.82	...	65.51	...
OCEANIA																	
Australia	2002	...	77.40	2.35	...	...	...	8.06	10.18	...	4.16	...	11.22	5.62	...	10.25	
New Zealand	2001	...	...	0.39	0.26	0.77	211.70	6.06	9.97	...	164.42	26.54	74.26	62.61	1.70	162.48	0.13
New Zealand	2002	...	...	0.61	0.33	0.74	199.82	5.43	9.55	...	155.60	25.36	71.06	60.02	1.47	150.98	0.08
Papua New Guinea	1999	0.58	3.66	3.10	0.60	...	0.86	3.14	0.46	0.62	...	0.20	...	0.04	...	...	0.84
Papua New Guinea	2000	0.55	3.96	4.29	0.72	...	1.21	2.65	0.60	1.05	...	...	...	1.01	...	...	0.23

Sources: UNODC, 2002; UNODC, 2005

TABLE C.1

Urban Agglomerations: Population Size and Rate of Change

		Estimates and Projections (000)						Annual rate of change (%)					Share in urban population (%)	
		1990	1995	2000	2005	2010	2015	1990–1995	1995–2000	2000–2005	2005–2010	2010–2015	1990	2015
AFRICA														
Algeria	El Djazaïr (Algiers)	1,908	2,295	2,754	3,200	3,576	3,924	3.69	3.65	3.00	2.22	1.86	14.49	14.86
Algeria	Wahran (Oran)	647	675	706	765	852	944	0.86	0.91	1.60	2.15	2.05	4.91	3.58
Angola	Luanda	1,568	1,953	2,322	2,766	3,303	3,904	4.39	3.46	3.50	3.55	3.34	40.08	31.23
Burkina Faso	Ouagadougou	594	689	771	926	1,170	1,489	2.95	2.24	3.68	4.66	4.82	50.47	36.93
Cameroon	Douala	931	1,155	1,432	1,761	2,076	2,350	4.30	4.30	4.14	3.29	2.48	19.63	19.69
Cameroon	Yaoundé	754	948	1,192	1,485	1,760	1,995	4.59	4.59	4.39	3.39	2.51	15.89	16.72
Chad	N'Djaména	477	579	707	888	1,097	1,374	3.88	3.99	4.56	4.24	4.51	37.85	35.08
Congo	Brazzaville	704	830	986	1,173	1,390	1,653	3.31	3.44	3.47	3.40	3.47	52.14	47.34
Côte d'Ivoire	Abidjan	2,102	2,535	3,055	3,577	4,032	4,525	3.74	3.73	3.16	2.40	2.30	41.79	42.13
Dem. Republic of the Congo	Kinshasa	3,644	4,397	5,042	6,049	7,526	9,304	3.76	2.74	3.64	4.37	4.24	34.69	30.92
Dem. Republic of the Congo	Kolwezi	712	901	1,047	1,270	1,599	1,998	4.70	3.00	3.87	4.60	4.46	6.78	6.64
Dem. Republic of the Congo	Lubumbashi	700	838	971	1,179	1,484	1,856	3.59	2.95	3.88	4.61	4.47	6.66	6.17
Dem. Republic of the Congo	Mbuji-Mayi	606	726	843	1,024	1,291	1,616	3.63	2.97	3.90	4.63	4.49	5.77	5.37
Egypt	Al-Iskandariyah (Alexandria)	3,063	3,277	3,506	3,770	4,109	4,518	1.35	1.35	1.45	1.72	1.90	12.66	11.30
Egypt	Al-Qahirah (Cairo)	9,061	9,707	10,391	11,128	12,041	13,138	1.38	1.36	1.37	1.58	1.74	37.44	32.85
Ethiopia	Addis Ababa	1,791	2,157	2,494	2,893	3,407	4,078	3.72	2.90	2.97	3.27	3.60	27.80	21.98
Ghana	Accra	1,197	1,415	1,674	1,981	2,321	2,666	3.35	3.35	3.38	3.16	2.77	21.21	18.21
Ghana	Kumasi	696	909	1,187	1,517	1,818	2,095	5.34	5.34	4.90	3.62	2.84	12.33	14.31
Guinea	Conakry	892	1,044	1,222	1,425	1,669	2,001	3.16	3.14	3.07	3.17	3.62	51.13	44.14
Kenya	Mombasa	476	572	686	817	974	1,181	3.65	3.65	3.49	3.53	3.85	11.16	11.09
Kenya	Nairobi	1,380	1,755	2,233	2,773	3,326	4,001	4.81	4.81	4.33	3.64	3.70	32.32	37.57
Liberia	Monrovia	535	644	776	936	1,129	1,357	3.73	3.73	3.73	3.75	3.68	55.32	47.81
Libyan Arab Jamahiriya	Banghazi	612	799	945	1,114	1,273	1,399	5.34	3.36	3.27	2.67	1.88	17.97	22.79
Libyan Arab Jamahiriya	Tarabulus (Tripoli)	1,500	1,678	1,877	2,098	2,326	2,533	2.24	2.24	2.23	2.06	1.71	44.05	41.29
Madagascar	Antananarivo	948	1,169	1,361	1,585	1,853	2,182	4.20	3.04	3.04	3.12	3.28	33.40	30.47
Mali	Bamako	746	910	1,110	1,368	1,700	2,117	3.96	3.97	4.19	4.34	4.38	35.98	32.04
Morocco	Dar-el-Beida (Casablanca)	2,682	2,951	3,043	3,138	3,294	3,570	1.91	0.62	0.62	0.97	1.61	22.44	15.20
Morocco	Fès	685	785	870	963	1,069	1,184	2.72	2.04	2.04	2.09	2.05	5.74	5.04
Morocco	Marrakech	578	681	755	837	931	1,032	3.26	2.07	2.07	2.12	2.07	4.84	4.40
Morocco	Rabat	1,174	1,379	1,507	1,647	1,808	1,991	3.22	1.77	1.77	1.87	1.93	9.83	8.48
Mozambique	Maputo	776	921	1,095	1,320	1,586	1,872	3.43	3.46	3.74	3.67	3.32	27.37	18.80
Niger	Niamey	431	542	680	850	1,049	1,308	4.55	4.55	4.45	4.23	4.41	33.12	35.21
Nigeria	Benin City	738	831	937	1,055	1,203	1,394	2.39	2.39	2.39	2.62	2.94	2.33	1.55
Nigeria	Ibadan	1,782	1,978	2,195	2,437	2,742	3,152	2.08	2.09	2.08	2.36	2.78	5.62	3.51
Nigeria	Kaduna	961	1,083	1,220	1,375	1,566	1,812	2.39	2.39	2.39	2.61	2.91	3.03	2.02
Nigeria	Kano	2,095	2,360	2,658	2,993	3,405	3,920	2.38	2.38	2.38	2.58	2.82	6.61	4.36
Nigeria	Lagos	4,764	6,373	8,422	10,886	13,717	16,141	5.82	5.58	5.13	4.62	3.26	15.02	17.96
Nigeria	Maiduguri	598	673	758	854	973	1,129	2.37	2.37	2.37	2.62	2.96	1.89	1.26
Nigeria	Ogbomosho	623	712	818	941	1,089	1,268	2.68	2.79	2.79	2.93	3.04	1.96	1.41
Nigeria	Port Harcourt	680	766	863	972	1,108	1,284	2.38	2.38	2.38	2.62	2.95	2.15	1.43
Nigeria	Zaria	592	667	752	847	967	1,121	2.39	2.39	2.39	2.63	2.97	1.87	1.25
Rwanda	Kigali	219	320	497	779	1,146	1,544	7.57	8.83	8.96	7.73	5.96	57.02	47.79
Senegal	Dakar	1,384	1,606	1,862	2,159	2,478	2,819	2.97	2.97	2.95	2.76	2.58	44.54	43.34
Sierra Leone	Freetown	532	609	698	799	924	1,098	2.72	2.72	2.72	2.91	3.44	43.29	33.02
Somalia	Muqdisho (Mogadishu)	945	1,080	1,189	1,320	1,545	1,855	2.67	1.92	2.09	3.16	3.65	47.74	42.20
South Africa	Cape Town	2,155	2,394	2,715	3,083	3,316	3,401	2.10	2.52	2.54	1.45	0.51	11.23	11.07
South Africa	Durban	1,723	2,081	2,370	2,631	2,804	2,876	3.77	2.60	2.10	1.27	0.51	8.98	9.36
South Africa	Ekurhuleni (East Rand)	1,531	1,894	2,326	2,817	3,118	3,212	4.26	4.11	3.83	2.03	0.59	7.98	10.46
South Africa	Johannesburg	1,898	2,265	2,732	3,254	3,574	3,674	3.53	3.75	3.50	1.87	0.56	9.89	11.96
South Africa	Port Elizabeth	828	911	958	999	1,040	1,070	1.93	1.00	0.84	0.79	0.57	4.31	3.48
South Africa	Pretoria	911	951	1,084	1,271	1,392	1,439	0.85	2.61	3.19	1.81	0.67	4.75	4.68
South Africa	Vereeniging	743	800	897	1,027	1,113	1,150	1.48	2.30	2.69	1.61	0.67	3.87	3.74
Sudan	Al-Khartum (Khartoum)	2,360	3,242	3,949	4,518	5,178	6,022	6.35	3.95	2.69	2.73	3.02	34.02	27.71
Togo	Lomé	622	810	1,053	1,337	1,639	1,969	5.27	5.26	4.76	4.08	3.67	52.18	52.88
Uganda	Kampala	755	912	1,097	1,319	1,612	2,054	3.79	3.68	3.69	4.02	4.84	38.38	33.87
United Republic of Tanzania	Dar es Salaam	1,316	1,668	2,116	2,676	3,260	3,831	4.75	4.75	4.70	3.95	3.23	26.56	29.07
Zambia	Lusaka	757	902	1,073	1,260	1,408	1,564	3.49	3.49	3.20	2.23	2.10	22.95	30.53
Zimbabwe	Harare	1,047	1,255	1,379	1,515	1,650	1,788	3.62	1.89	1.87	1.71	1.61	34.20	31.64
ASIA														
Afghanistan	Kabul	1,432	1,616	1,963	2,994	3,753	4,666	2.41	3.90	8.44	4.52	4.35	53.59	41.67
Armenia	Yerevan	1,175	1,142	1,111	1,103	1,102	1,102	-0.55	-0.55	-0.15	-0.01	-0.00	49.12	57.89
Azerbaijan	Baku	1,733	1,766	1,803	1,856	1,910	1,977	0.37	0.42	0.58	0.57	0.69	44.74	41.21
Bangladesh	Chittagong	2,023	2,565	3,271	4,114	4,914	5,707	4.75	4.86	4.59	3.55	2.99	9.84	11.36
Bangladesh	Dhaka	6,526	8,217	10,159	12,430	14,625	16,842	4.61	4.24	4.03	3.25	2.82	31.73	33.53
Bangladesh	Khulna	900	1,066	1,264	1,494	1,754	2,048	3.40	3.40	3.35	3.21	3.09	4.37	4.08
Bangladesh	Rajshahi	484	576	668	775	907	1,062	3.50	2.95	2.99	3.14	3.17	2.35	2.12
Cambodia	Phnum Pénh (Phnom Penh)	594	836	1,160	1,364	1,664	2,057	6.84	6.55	3.25	3.98	4.24	48.40	46.19
China	Anshan, Liaoning	1,442	1,496	1,552	1,611	1,704	1,864	0.74	0.74	0.74	1.12	1.81	0.46	0.27
China	Anshun	658	709	763	822	896	992	1.49	1.49	1.49	1.71	2.04	0.21	0.15
China	Anyang	617	686	763	849	948	1,057	2.13	2.13	2.13	2.20	2.17	0.20	0.15
China	Baoding	595	728	890	1,042	1,206	1,356	4.03	4.03	3.15	2.92	2.35	0.19	0.20
China	Baotou	1,229	1,426	1,655	1,920	2,210	2,473	2.97	2.98	2.97	2.81	2.26	0.39	0.36
China	Beijing	7,362	8,486	9,782	10,717	11,741	12,850	2.84	2.84	1.83	1.83	1.81	2.33	1.87
China	Bengbu	695	748	805	867	944	1,045	1.47	1.47	1.47	1.70	2.03	0.22	0.15
China	Benxi	938	958	979	1,000	1,046	1,144	0.43	0.43	0.43	0.90	1.79	0.30	0.17
China	Changchun	2,192	2,446	2,730	3,046	3,400	3,765	2.19	2.19	2.19	2.20	2.04	0.69	0.55
China	Changde	1,180	1,258	1,341	1,429	1,543	1,700	1.28	1.28	1.28	1.54	1.93	0.37	0.25

TABLE C.1

continued

		Estimates and Projections (000)						Annual rate of change (%)					Share in urban population (%)	
		1990	1995	2000	2005	2010	2015	1990–1995	1995–2000	2000–2005	2005–2010	2010–2015	1990	2015
China	Changsha, Hunan	1,329	1,667	2,091	2,451	2,832	3,169	4.53	4.53	3.18	2.89	2.25	0.42	0.46
China	Changzhou, Jiangsu	730	883	1,068	1,249	1,445	1,623	3.81	3.81	3.13	2.91	2.33	0.23	0.24
China	Chengdu	2,955	3,403	3,919	4,065	4,266	4,637	2.82	2.82	0.73	0.97	1.67	0.93	0.68
China	Chifeng	987	1,065	1,148	1,238	1,348	1,490	1.51	1.51	1.51	1.71	2.00	0.31	0.22
China	Chongqing	3,123	4,342	6,037	6,363	6,690	7,258	6.59	6.59	1.05	1.00	1.63	0.99	1.06
China	Dalian	2,472	2,658	2,858	3,073	3,335	3,664	1.45	1.45	1.45	1.64	1.88	0.78	0.53
China	Dandong	661	716	776	841	921	1,021	1.61	1.61	1.61	1.81	2.06	0.21	0.15
China	Daqing	997	1,167	1,366	1,594	1,842	2,067	3.15	3.15	3.09	2.90	2.30	0.32	0.30
China	Datong, Shanxi	1,277	1,392	1,518	1,763	2,038	2,285	1.73	1.73	2.99	2.90	2.29	0.40	0.33
China	Dongguan, Guangdong	1,737	2,559	3,770	4,320	4,850	5,370	7.75	7.75	2.72	2.32	2.04	0.55	0.78
China	Foshan	429	569	754	888	1,027	1,156	5.63	5.63	3.26	2.92	2.37	0.14	0.17
China	Fushun, Liaoning	1,388	1,410	1,433	1,456	1,516	1,653	0.32	0.32	0.32	0.81	1.73	0.44	0.24
China	Fuyu, Jilin	945	984	1,025	1,068	1,133	1,244	0.81	0.81	0.81	1.19	1.87	0.30	0.18
China	Fuzhou, Fujian	1,396	1,710	2,096	2,453	2,834	3,172	4.06	4.06	3.15	2.89	2.25	0.44	0.46
China	Guangzhou, Guangdong	3,918	5,380	7,388	8,425	9,447	10,420	6.34	6.34	2.62	2.29	1.96	1.24	1.52
China	Guilin	557	666	795	929	1,075	1,210	3.55	3.55	3.12	2.92	2.36	0.18	0.18
China	Guiyang	1,665	2,208	2,929	3,447	3,980	4,446	5.65	5.65	3.26	2.87	2.21	0.53	0.65
China	Haerbin	2,991	3,209	3,444	3,695	4,003	4,392	1.41	1.41	1.41	1.60	1.85	0.95	0.64
China	Handan	1,092	1,201	1,321	1,535	1,775	1,992	1.90	1.90	3.00	2.90	2.31	0.35	0.29
China	Hangzhou	1,476	1,887	2,411	2,831	3,269	3,656	4.91	4.91	3.21	2.88	2.24	0.47	0.53
China	Hefei	1,100	1,342	1,637	1,916	2,214	2,481	3.98	3.98	3.14	2.89	2.28	0.35	0.36
China	Hengyang	702	783	873	973	1,087	1,211	2.17	2.17	2.17	2.22	2.16	0.22	0.18
China	Heze	1,200	1,238	1,277	1,318	1,388	1,519	0.62	0.62	0.62	1.04	1.80	0.38	0.22
China	Hohhot	938	1,142	1,389	1,625	1,878	2,107	3.92	3.92	3.14	2.90	2.30	0.30	0.31
China	Huai'an	1,113	1,154	1,198	1,243	1,315	1,441	0.74	0.74	0.73	1.13	1.83	0.35	0.21
China	Huaibei	536	627	733	858	995	1,121	3.14	3.14	3.14	2.96	2.38	0.17	0.16
China	Huainan	1,228	1,289	1,353	1,420	1,515	1,664	0.97	0.97	0.97	1.30	1.87	0.39	0.24
China	Hunjiang	722	746	772	798	843	925	0.67	0.67	0.67	1.09	1.87	0.23	0.14
China	Huzhou	1,028	1,083	1,141	1,203	1,288	1,417	1.05	1.05	1.05	1.37	1.90	0.33	0.21
China	Jiamusi	660	750	853	969	1,099	1,230	2.56	2.56	2.56	2.52	2.25	0.21	0.18
China	Jiaozuo	605	670	742	822	915	1,019	2.05	2.05	2.05	2.14	2.16	0.19	0.15
China	Jiaxing	741	806	877	954	1,047	1,160	1.68	1.68	1.68	1.86	2.06	0.23	0.17
China	Jilin	1,320	1,596	1,928	2,255	2,606	2,918	3.79	3.79	3.13	2.89	2.26	0.42	0.43
China	Jinan, Shandong	2,404	2,512	2,625	2,743	2,914	3,184	0.88	0.88	0.88	1.21	1.78	0.76	0.46
China	Jining, Shandong	871	954	1,044	1,143	1,260	1,397	1.81	1.81	1.81	1.95	2.07	0.28	0.20
China	Jinxi, Liaoning	1,350	1,605	1,908	2,268	2,658	2,988	3.46	3.46	3.46	3.17	2.34	0.43	0.44
China	Jinzhou	736	795	858	925	1,010	1,118	1.52	1.53	1.52	1.74	2.03	0.23	0.16
China	Jixi, Heilongjiang	835	871	908	947	1,006	1,106	0.83	0.83	0.83	1.21	1.89	0.26	0.16
China	Kaifeng	693	741	793	848	918	1,015	1.34	1.34	1.34	1.60	2.00	0.22	0.15
China	Kaohsiung	1,380	1,424	1,469	1,515	1,595	1,744	0.62	0.62	0.62	1.03	1.79	0.44	0.25
China	Kunming	1,612	2,045	2,594	2,837	3,095	3,406	4.75	4.76	1.79	1.74	1.92	0.51	0.50
China	Langfang	591	648	711	780	861	957	1.84	1.85	1.84	1.99	2.12	0.19	0.14
China	Lanzhou	1,618	1,830	2,071	2,411	2,785	3,117	2.47	2.47	3.04	2.89	2.25	0.51	0.46
China	Leshan	1,070	1,094	1,118	1,143	1,197	1,308	0.44	0.44	0.44	0.91	1.78	0.34	0.19
China	Lianyungang	537	605	682	768	865	968	2.38	2.38	2.38	2.39	2.23	0.17	0.14
China	Liaoyang	640	681	725	773	835	922	1.26	1.26	1.26	1.54	2.00	0.20	0.14
China	Linfen	583	647	719	799	891	994	2.11	2.11	2.11	2.18	2.17	0.18	0.15
China	Linyi, Shandong	1,740	1,834	1,932	2,035	2,177	2,387	1.04	1.04	1.04	1.35	1.84	0.55	0.35
China	Liuan	1,380	1,464	1,553	1,647	1,771	1,948	1.18	1.18	1.18	1.46	1.90	0.44	0.28
China	Liupanshui	827	905	989	1,149	1,329	1,494	1.79	1.79	3.00	2.91	2.34	0.26	0.22
China	Liuzhou	751	950	1,201	1,409	1,630	1,829	4.69	4.69	3.19	2.91	2.31	0.24	0.27
China	Luoyang	1,202	1,334	1,481	1,644	1,830	2,031	2.09	2.09	2.09	2.14	2.09	0.38	0.30
China	Luzhou	412	706	1,208	1,447	1,673	1,878	10.75	10.76	3.60	2.90	2.31	0.13	0.27
China	Mianyang, Sichuan	876	1,004	1,152	1,322	1,509	1,689	2.75	2.75	2.75	2.65	2.25	0.28	0.25
China	Mudanjiang	751	868	1,004	1,171	1,355	1,522	2.91	2.91	3.07	2.91	2.34	0.24	0.22
China	Nanchang	1,262	1,516	1,822	2,188	2,585	2,913	3.67	3.67	3.67	3.33	2.39	0.40	0.43
China	Nanchong	619	1,029	1,712	2,046	2,364	2,649	10.18	10.18	3.56	2.89	2.27	0.20	0.39
China	Nanjing, Jiangsu	2,611	3,013	3,477	3,621	3,813	4,151	2.87	2.87	0.81	1.04	1.70	0.83	0.61
China	Nanning	1,159	1,421	1,743	2,040	2,357	2,641	4.08	4.08	3.15	2.89	2.27	0.37	0.39
China	Nantong	470	597	759	891	1,031	1,160	4.79	4.80	3.20	2.92	2.37	0.15	0.17
China	Nanyang, Henan	375	753	1,512	1,830	2,115	2,371	13.95	13.96	3.81	2.90	2.29	0.12	0.35
China	Neijiang	1,289	1,338	1,388	1,441	1,525	1,670	0.74	0.74	0.74	1.13	1.82	0.41	0.24
China	Ningbo	1,142	1,331	1,551	1,810	2,092	2,345	3.06	3.06	3.08	2.90	2.29	0.36	0.34
China	Pingdingshan, Henan	997	949	904	861	854	921	-0.98	-0.98	-0.98	-0.16	1.51	0.32	0.13
China	Pingxiang, Jiangxi	569	664	775	905	1,047	1,178	3.09	3.09	3.08	2.92	2.36	0.18	0.17
China	Qingdao	2,102	2,381	2,698	2,817	2,977	3,248	2.50	2.50	0.86	1.11	1.74	0.66	0.47
China	Qinhuangdao	519	646	805	944	1,092	1,229	4.40	4.40	3.17	2.92	2.36	0.16	0.18
China	Qiqihaer	1,401	1,466	1,535	1,607	1,712	1,877	0.92	0.92	0.92	1.26	1.84	0.44	0.27
China	Quanzhou	480	745	1,158	1,377	1,592	1,788	8.81	8.81	3.47	2.91	2.32	0.15	0.26
China	Shanghai	8,205	10,423	13,243	14,503	15,790	17,225	4.79	4.79	1.82	1.70	1.74	2.59	2.51
China	Shangqiu	245	574	1,349	1,650	1,908	2,140	17.08	17.08	4.02	2.90	2.30	0.08	0.31
China	Shantou	885	1,054	1,255	1,495	1,756	1,980	3.50	3.50	3.50	3.22	2.40	0.28	0.29
China	Shenyang	4,655	4,627	4,599	4,720	4,952	5,377	-0.12	-0.12	0.52	0.96	1.65	1.47	0.78
China	Shenzhen	875	2,304	6,069	7,233	8,114	8,958	19.36	19.37	3.51	2.30	1.98	0.28	1.31
China	Shijiazhuang	1,372	1,634	1,947	2,275	2,628	2,943	3.50	3.50	3.11	2.89	2.26	0.43	0.43
China	Suining, Sichuan	1,260	1,305	1,352	1,401	1,481	1,621	0.71	0.71	0.71	1.11	1.82	0.40	0.24
China	Suzhou, Anhui	258	623	1,509	1,849	2,137	2,396	17.67	17.68	4.06	2.90	2.28	0.08	0.35
China	Suzhou, Jiangsu	875	1,077	1,326	1,553	1,795	2,014	4.16	4.16	3.16	2.90	2.30	0.28	0.29

TABLE C.1

continued

		Estimates and Projections (000)						Annual rate of change (%)					Share in urban population (%)	
		1990	1995	2000	2005	2010	2015	1990–1995	1995–2000	2000–2005	2005–2010	2010–2015	1990	2015
China	Taian, Shandong	1,413	1,472	1,534	1,598	1,696	1,858	0.82	0.82	0.82	1.19	1.82	0.45	0.27
China	Taichung	754	838	930	1,033	1,151	1,281	2.10	2.10	2.10	2.17	2.14	0.24	0.19
China	Taipei	2,711	2,676	2,640	2,606	2,651	2,863	-0.26	-0.26	-0.26	0.35	1.54	0.86	0.42
China	Taiyuan, Shanxi	2,225	2,274	2,521	2,794	3,104	3,434	0.44	2.06	2.06	2.10	2.02	0.70	0.50
China	Tangshan, Hebei	1,485	1,590	1,703	1,825	1,977	2,176	1.38	1.38	1.37	1.60	1.93	0.47	0.32
China	Tianjin	5,804	6,246	6,722	7,040	7,468	8,119	1.47	1.47	0.92	1.18	1.67	1.83	1.18
China	Tianmen	1,484	1,545	1,609	1,676	1,777	1,946	0.81	0.81	0.81	1.18	1.82	0.47	0.28
China	Tianshui	1,040	1,090	1,143	1,199	1,279	1,405	0.95	0.95	0.95	1.29	1.88	0.33	0.21
China	Tongliao	674	729	790	855	935	1,036	1.59	1.59	1.59	1.79	2.06	0.21	0.15
China	Ürümqi (Wulumqi)	1,161	1,417	1,730	2,025	2,340	2,621	3.99	3.99	3.15	2.89	2.27	0.37	0.38
China	Weifang	1,152	1,257	1,372	1,498	1,646	1,822	1.75	1.75	1.75	1.89	2.03	0.36	0.27
China	Wenzhou	604	1,056	1,845	2,212	2,556	2,862	11.16	11.16	3.63	2.89	2.26	0.19	0.42
China	Wuhan	3,833	5,053	6,662	7,093	7,542	8,204	5.53	5.53	1.26	1.23	1.68	1.21	1.20
China	Wuhu, Anhui	553	619	692	774	868	969	2.24	2.24	2.24	2.29	2.20	0.18	0.14
China	Wuxi, Jiangsu	1,009	1,192	1,410	1,646	1,903	2,135	3.35	3.35	3.10	2.90	2.30	0.32	0.31
China	Xiamen	639	1,124	1,977	2,371	2,739	3,066	11.28	11.29	3.64	2.89	2.26	0.20	0.45
China	Xi'an, Shaanxi	2,873	3,271	3,725	3,926	4,178	4,559	2.60	2.60	1.05	1.24	1.75	0.91	0.67
China	Xiangfan, Hubei	492	649	855	1,006	1,164	1,310	5.53	5.53	3.25	2.92	2.35	0.16	0.19
China	Xiantao	1,361	1,415	1,470	1,528	1,618	1,772	0.77	0.77	0.77	1.15	1.82	0.43	0.26
China	Xianyang, Shaanxi	737	835	946	1,072	1,212	1,355	2.50	2.50	2.50	2.47	2.22	0.23	0.20
China	Xingyi, Guizhou	593	651	715	785	868	965	1.86	1.87	1.86	2.00	2.12	0.19	0.14
China	Xining	698	770	849	987	1,142	1,284	1.96	1.96	3.01	2.92	2.35	0.22	0.19
China	Xinxiang	613	687	770	863	968	1,081	2.27	2.28	2.27	2.31	2.20	0.19	0.16
China	Xinyang	273	571	1,195	1,450	1,677	1,882	14.76	14.76	3.87	2.90	2.31	0.09	0.28
China	Xinyu	608	685	772	870	981	1,096	2.39	2.39	2.39	2.39	2.22	0.19	0.16
China	Xuanzhou	769	795	823	851	900	987	0.68	0.68	0.68	1.10	1.86	0.24	0.14
China	Xuzhou	944	1,247	1,648	1,960	2,284	2,566	5.58	5.58	3.46	3.06	2.32	0.30	0.37
China	Yancheng, Jiangsu	497	580	677	789	914	1,029	3.09	3.09	3.08	2.93	2.38	0.16	0.15
China	Yantai	838	1,188	1,684	1,991	2,301	2,578	6.98	6.98	3.35	2.89	2.28	0.27	0.38
China	Yibin	685	743	805	872	954	1,058	1.61	1.61	1.61	1.80	2.06	0.22	0.15
China	Yichang	492	589	704	823	953	1,073	3.58	3.58	3.12	2.92	2.38	0.16	0.16
China	Yichun, Heilongjiang	882	849	816	785	785	849	-0.78	-0.78	-0.78	-0.00	1.57	0.28	0.12
China	Yichun, Jiangxi	836	876	917	961	1,025	1,127	0.93	0.93	0.93	1.29	1.90	0.26	0.16
China	Yinchuan	502	632	795	932	1,079	1,214	4.60	4.60	3.19	2.92	2.36	0.16	0.18
China	Yingkou	572	630	694	764	847	942	1.93	1.94	1.93	2.06	2.14	0.18	0.14
China	Yiyang, Hunan	1,062	1,140	1,223	1,313	1,425	1,572	1.41	1.41	1.41	1.64	1.97	0.34	0.23
China	Yongzhou	946	960	976	991	1,032	1,128	0.31	0.31	0.31	0.82	1.77	0.30	0.16
China	Yuci	467	555	660	785	921	1,042	3.46	3.46	3.46	3.21	2.46	0.15	0.15
China	Yueyang	1,078	995	918	847	821	880	-1.60	-1.61	-1.60	-0.63	1.38	0.34	0.13
China	Yulin, Guangxi	667	779	909	1,060	1,227	1,379	3.09	3.09	3.08	2.92	2.35	0.21	0.20
China	Zaozhuang	1,793	1,889	1,990	2,096	2,242	2,458	1.04	1.04	1.04	1.34	1.84	0.57	0.36
China	Zhangjiakou	720	803	897	1,001	1,120	1,248	2.20	2.20	2.20	2.25	2.17	0.23	0.18
China	Zhanjiang	1,049	1,185	1,340	1,514	1,709	1,905	2.45	2.45	2.45	2.42	2.17	0.33	0.28
China	Zhaotong	620	670	724	783	855	948	1.56	1.56	1.56	1.77	2.06	0.20	0.14
China	Zhengzhou	1,752	2,081	2,472	2,590	2,738	2,989	3.44	3.44	0.93	1.11	1.75	0.55	0.44
China	Zhenjiang, Jiangsu	490	581	688	803	930	1,047	3.39	3.39	3.10	2.92	2.38	0.16	0.15
China	Zhuhai	331	518	809	963	1,114	1,254	8.94	8.94	3.48	2.92	2.36	0.11	0.18
China	Zhuzhou	585	713	868	1,016	1,176	1,322	3.95	3.95	3.14	2.92	2.35	0.19	0.19
China	Zibo	2,484	2,640	2,806	2,982	3,209	3,517	1.22	1.22	1.22	1.46	1.84	0.79	0.51
China	Zigong	977	1,012	1,049	1,087	1,149	1,260	0.71	0.71	0.71	1.11	1.84	0.31	0.18
China	Zunyi	392	516	679	799	924	1,041	5.50	5.50	3.25	2.92	2.38	0.12	0.15
China, Hong Kong SAR	Hong Kong[1]	5,677	6,187	6,637	7,041	7,416	7,764	1.72	1.41	1.18	1.04	0.92	100.00	100.00
Dem. People's Rep. of Korea	Hamhung	678	724	769	804	833	864	1.32	1.21	0.90	0.71	0.73	5.90	5.67
Dem. People's Rep. of Korea	N'ampo	580	806	1,016	1,102	1,142	1,182	6.58	4.63	1.63	0.70	0.69	5.05	7.75
Dem. People's Rep. of Korea	P'yongyang	2,473	2,863	3,194	3,351	3,439	3,531	2.93	2.19	0.96	0.51	0.53	21.51	23.14
Georgia	Tbilisi	1,224	1,160	1,100	1,047	1,024	1,021	-1.07	-1.07	-0.99	-0.44	-0.06	40.61	45.39
India	Agra	933	1,095	1,293	1,511	1,702	1,892	3.20	3.32	3.12	2.39	2.12	0.43	0.47
India	Ahmadabad	3,255	3,790	4,427	5,120	5,716	6,298	3.04	3.11	2.91	2.20	1.94	1.50	1.56
India	Aligarh	468	554	653	763	862	963	3.39	3.29	3.11	2.45	2.21	0.22	0.24
India	Allahabad	830	928	1,035	1,152	1,277	1,420	2.23	2.17	2.14	2.07	2.12	0.38	0.35
India	Amritsar	726	844	990	1,151	1,296	1,444	3.00	3.20	3.02	2.38	2.15	0.34	0.36
India	Asansol	727	891	1,065	1,257	1,423	1,584	4.06	3.56	3.32	2.48	2.15	0.34	0.39
India	Aurangabad	568	708	868	1,048	1,197	1,336	4.38	4.09	3.78	2.66	2.19	0.26	0.33
India	Bangalore	4,036	4,744	5,567	6,462	7,216	7,939	3.23	3.20	2.98	2.21	1.91	1.86	1.97
India	Bareilly	604	664	722	787	867	966	1.87	1.67	1.72	1.95	2.16	0.28	0.24
India	Bhopal	1,046	1,228	1,426	1,644	1,842	2,045	3.21	3.00	2.84	2.28	2.10	0.48	0.51
India	Bhubaneswar	395	504	637	790	912	1,020	4.90	4.69	4.30	2.87	2.25	0.18	0.25
India	Chandigarh	564	667	791	928	1,049	1,170	3.36	3.40	3.19	2.46	2.19	0.26	0.29
India	Chennai (Madras)	5,338	5,836	6,353	6,916	7,545	8,280	1.78	1.70	1.70	1.74	1.86	2.46	2.05
India	Coimbatore	1,088	1,239	1,420	1,618	1,806	2,005	2.60	2.73	2.61	2.20	2.09	0.50	0.50
India	Delhi	8,206	10,092	12,441	15,048	16,983	18,604	4.14	4.18	3.80	2.42	1.82	3.78	4.62
India	Dhanbad	805	915	1,046	1,189	1,328	1,477	2.56	2.67	2.57	2.21	2.13	0.37	0.37
India	Durg-Bhilainagar	670	780	905	1,043	1,172	1,305	3.03	2.98	2.83	2.32	2.16	0.31	0.32
India	Faridabad	593	779	1,018	1,298	1,509	1,685	5.47	5.35	4.85	3.02	2.20	0.27	0.42
India	Ghaziabad	492	675	928	1,236	1,461	1,634	6.30	6.38	5.73	3.34	2.23	0.23	0.41
India	Guwahati (Gauhati)	564	675	797	932	1,052	1,174	3.60	3.32	3.13	2.44	2.18	0.26	0.29
India	Gwalior	706	779	855	940	1,039	1,156	1.97	1.88	1.89	2.00	2.14	0.33	0.29
India	Hubli-Dharwad	639	705	776	855	946	1,054	1.95	1.93	1.94	2.02	2.16	0.30	0.26

TABLE C.1

continued

		Estimates and Projections (000)						Annual rate of change (%)					Share in urban population (%)	
		1990	1995	2000	2005	2010	2015	1990–1995	1995–2000	2000–2005	2005–2010	2010–2015	1990	2015
India	Hyderabad	4,193	4,825	5,445	6,115	6,749	7,420	2.81	2.42	2.32	1.97	1.90	1.93	1.84
India	Indore	1,088	1,314	1,597	1,913	2,172	2,413	3.77	3.91	3.61	2.54	2.10	0.50	0.60
India	Jabalpur	879	981	1,100	1,231	1,366	1,519	2.19	2.29	2.24	2.09	2.12	0.41	0.38
India	Jaipur	1,478	1,826	2,259	2,747	3,130	3,470	4.23	4.26	3.91	2.61	2.06	0.68	0.86
India	Jalandhar	502	588	694	811	916	1,023	3.16	3.31	3.12	2.45	2.20	0.23	0.25
India	Jamshedpur	817	938	1,081	1,238	1,387	1,542	2.75	2.84	2.71	2.26	2.13	0.38	0.38
India	Jodhpur	654	743	842	951	1,061	1,181	2.54	2.51	2.43	2.19	2.16	0.30	0.29
India	Kanpur	2,001	2,294	2,641	3,018	3,363	3,718	2.73	2.82	2.67	2.17	2.01	0.92	0.92
India	Kochi (Cochin)	1,103	1,229	1,340	1,463	1,609	1,785	2.17	1.73	1.76	1.91	2.08	0.51	0.44
India	Kolkata (Calcutta)	10,890	11,924	13,058	14,277	15,548	16,980	1.82	1.82	1.78	1.71	1.76	5.02	4.21
India	Kota	523	604	692	789	883	986	2.89	2.71	2.61	2.27	2.19	0.24	0.24
India	Kozhikode (Calicut)	781	835	875	924	1,007	1,119	1.33	0.94	1.09	1.71	2.12	0.36	0.28
India	Lucknow	1,614	1,906	2,221	2,566	2,872	3,180	3.33	3.06	2.88	2.26	2.04	0.74	0.79
India	Ludhiana	1,006	1,183	1,368	1,571	1,759	1,954	3.24	2.91	2.77	2.26	2.10	0.46	0.49
India	Madurai	1,073	1,132	1,187	1,254	1,365	1,514	1.07	0.95	1.10	1.69	2.07	0.49	0.38
India	Meerut	824	975	1,143	1,328	1,494	1,662	3.36	3.18	3.00	2.36	2.13	0.38	0.41
India	Mumbai (Bombay)	12,308	14,111	16,086	18,196	20,036	21,869	2.73	2.62	2.47	1.93	1.75	5.67	5.43
India	Mysore	640	708	776	852	942	1,049	2.01	1.85	1.87	2.00	2.15	0.30	0.26
India	Nagpur	1,637	1,849	2,089	2,350	2,606	2,885	2.44	2.44	2.35	2.07	2.03	0.75	0.72
India	Nashik	700	886	1,117	1,381	1,588	1,769	4.71	4.63	4.23	2.79	2.17	0.32	0.44
India	Patna	1,087	1,331	1,658	2,029	2,320	2,578	4.05	4.40	4.03	2.69	2.11	0.50	0.64
India	Pune (Poona)	2,430	2,978	3,655	4,409	5,000	5,524	4.07	4.09	3.75	2.52	1.99	1.12	1.37
India	Raipur	453	553	680	824	942	1,053	4.00	4.13	3.82	2.69	2.22	0.21	0.26
India	Rajkot	638	787	974	1,185	1,357	1,513	4.21	4.26	3.92	2.70	2.18	0.29	0.38
India	Ranchi	607	712	844	989	1,118	1,247	3.21	3.39	3.18	2.45	2.18	0.28	0.31
India	Salem	574	647	736	834	932	1,039	2.38	2.58	2.50	2.22	2.18	0.27	0.26
India	Solapur	613	720	853	1,002	1,132	1,263	3.20	3.41	3.20	2.46	2.18	0.28	0.31
India	Srinagar	730	833	954	1,087	1,216	1,353	2.62	2.72	2.61	2.24	2.14	0.34	0.34
India	Surat	1,468	1,984	2,699	3,557	4,166	4,623	6.01	6.16	5.52	3.16	2.08	0.68	1.15
India	Thiruvananthapuram	801	853	885	926	1,006	1,118	1.25	0.73	0.92	1.65	2.11	0.37	0.28
India	Tiruchirappalli	705	768	837	915	1,009	1,123	1.71	1.74	1.78	1.96	2.14	0.33	0.28
India	Vadodara	1,096	1,273	1,465	1,675	1,872	2,077	2.99	2.81	2.68	2.22	2.09	0.51	0.52
India	Varanasi (Benares)	1,013	1,106	1,199	1,303	1,432	1,589	1.75	1.62	1.67	1.88	2.09	0.47	0.39
India	Vijayawada	821	914	999	1,094	1,206	1,341	2.14	1.79	1.81	1.95	2.12	0.38	0.33
India	Visakhapatnam	1,018	1,168	1,309	1,465	1,625	1,804	2.73	2.29	2.24	2.08	2.09	0.47	0.45
Indonesia	Bandung	2,460	2,896	3,448	4,126	4,786	5,338	3.26	3.49	3.59	2.96	2.19	4.43	3.70
Indonesia	Bogor	596	625	683	805	942	1,064	0.94	1.78	3.27	3.16	2.42	1.08	0.74
Indonesia	Jakarta	7,650	9,161	11,065	13,215	15,206	16,822	3.60	3.78	3.55	2.81	2.02	13.79	11.65
Indonesia	Malang	620	698	807	964	1,129	1,273	2.40	2.88	3.57	3.16	2.39	1.12	0.88
Indonesia	Medan	1,537	1,699	1,931	2,287	2,661	2,981	2.01	2.56	3.39	3.03	2.27	2.77	2.06
Indonesia	Palembang	1,032	1,212	1,442	1,733	2,022	2,270	3.20	3.48	3.68	3.09	2.31	1.86	1.57
Indonesia	Pekalongan	420	550	713	881	1,034	1,167	5.40	5.17	4.23	3.22	2.41	0.76	0.81
Indonesia	Semarang	804	795	832	967	1,130	1,273	-0.21	0.90	3.00	3.11	2.39	1.45	0.88
Indonesia	Surabaya	2,061	2,252	2,536	2,992	3,473	3,883	1.77	2.37	3.31	2.99	2.23	3.72	2.69
Indonesia	Surakarta	578	599	649	762	893	1,008	0.70	1.61	3.23	3.16	2.43	1.04	0.70
Indonesia	Tegal	550	650	774	933	1,094	1,233	3.34	3.49	3.74	3.17	2.40	0.99	0.85
Indonesia	Ujung Pandang	816	926	1,074	1,284	1,501	1,688	2.53	2.98	3.57	3.12	2.35	1.47	1.17
Iran (Islamic Republic of)	Ahvaz	685	784	871	960	1,051	1,152	2.69	2.10	1.96	1.80	1.84	2.15	2.01
Iran (Islamic Republic of)	Esfahan	1,094	1,230	1,381	1,535	1,679	1,836	2.33	2.33	2.11	1.80	1.78	3.43	3.20
Iran (Islamic Republic of)	Karaj	693	903	1,063	1,223	1,354	1,483	5.30	3.25	2.82	2.02	1.83	2.17	2.58
Iran (Islamic Republic of)	Kermanshah	608	675	750	827	905	994	2.11	2.09	1.95	1.82	1.86	1.90	1.73
Iran (Islamic Republic of)	Mashhad	1,680	1,854	1,990	2,134	2,307	2,515	1.97	1.41	1.40	1.56	1.72	5.26	4.38
Iran (Islamic Republic of)	Qom	622	744	888	1,035	1,150	1,261	3.56	3.55	3.05	2.10	1.85	1.95	2.20
Iran (Islamic Republic of)	Shiraz	946	1,030	1,124	1,222	1,331	1,456	1.70	1.74	1.67	1.70	1.80	2.97	2.54
Iran (Islamic Republic of)	Tabriz	1,058	1,165	1,274	1,387	1,510	1,651	1.91	1.79	1.71	1.69	1.79	3.32	2.88
Iran (Islamic Republic of)	Tehran	6,365	6,687	6,979	7,314	7,807	8,432	0.99	0.86	0.94	1.30	1.54	19.94	14.68
Iraq	Al-Basrah (Basra)	474	631	759	837	926	1,028	5.71	3.68	1.97	2.02	2.08	3.67	4.21
Iraq	Al-Mawsil (Mosul)	736	889	1,056	1,234	1,407	1,565	3.78	3.44	3.12	2.62	2.14	5.70	6.42
Iraq	Baghdad	4,092	4,598	5,200	5,904	6,593	7,242	2.34	2.46	2.54	2.20	1.88	31.70	29.68
Iraq	Irbil (Erbil)	536	644	773	925	1,070	1,195	3.65	3.65	3.60	2.90	2.22	4.16	4.90
Israel	Hefa (Haifa)	582	775	888	992	1,043	1,104	5.74	2.73	2.22	1.00	1.13	14.26	15.32
Israel	Tel Aviv-Yafo (Tel Aviv-Jaffa)	2,026	2,442	2,752	3,012	3,256	3,453	3.73	2.39	1.81	1.56	1.17	49.68	47.92
Japan	Fukuoka-Kitakyushu	2,487	2,619	2,716	2,800	2,830	2,834	1.04	0.73	0.61	0.22	0.02	3.19	3.25
Japan	Hiroshima	1,986	2,040	2,044	2,044	2,045	2,045	0.54	0.04	0.01	0.00	0.00	2.55	2.34
Japan	Kyoto	1,760	1,804	1,806	1,805	1,805	1,805	0.49	0.02	-0.00	-0.00	-0.00	2.26	2.07
Japan	Nagoya	2,947	3,055	3,122	3,179	3,200	3,202	0.71	0.44	0.36	0.13	0.01	3.78	3.67
Japan	Osaka-Kobe	11,035	11,052	11,165	11,268	11,305	11,309	0.03	0.20	0.18	0.07	0.01	14.16	12.96
Japan	Sapporo	2,319	2,476	2,508	2,530	2,538	2,539	1.31	0.26	0.17	0.06	0.01	2.98	2.91
Japan	Sendai	2,021	2,135	2,184	2,224	2,239	2,240	1.09	0.46	0.36	0.13	0.01	2.59	2.57
Japan	Tokyo	32,530	33,587	34,450	35,197	35,467	35,494	0.64	0.51	0.43	0.15	0.02	41.75	40.69
Jordan	Amman	851	985	1,132	1,292	1,461	1,615	2.91	2.79	2.64	2.46	2.00	36.23	27.21
Kazakhstan	Almaty	1,080	1,108	1,137	1,156	1,164	1,183	0.52	0.51	0.33	0.14	0.31	11.63	13.19
Kuwait	Al Kuwayt (Kuwait City)	1,392	1,105	1,549	1,810	2,099	2,341	-4.62	6.76	3.12	2.96	2.19	66.27	70.33
Kyrgyzstan	Bishkek	635	703	766	798	841	902	2.03	1.72	0.81	1.04	1.41	38.26	40.46
Lebanon	Bayrut (Beirut)	1,293	1,268	1,487	1,777	1,941	2,055	-0.39	3.19	3.57	1.77	1.13	56.72	58.95
Malaysia	Kuala Lumpur	1,120	1,213	1,306	1,405	1,534	1,696	1.58	1.47	1.47	1.74	2.02	12.60	7.61
Mongolia	Ulaanbaatar	572	661	764	863	932	999	2.90	2.90	2.44	1.54	1.39	45.23	56.84
Myanmar	Mandalay	630	712	809	924	1,054	1,192	2.43	2.56	2.66	2.63	2.45	6.22	5.80

TABLE C.1

continued

		Estimates and Projections (000)						Annual rate of change (%)					Share in urban population (%)	
		1990	1995	2000	2005	2010	2015	1990–1995	1995–2000	2000–2005	2005–2010	2010–2015	1990	2015
Myanmar	Rangoon	2,897	3,233	3,634	4,107	4,635	5,184	2.20	2.34	2.45	2.42	2.24	28.58	25.24
Nepal	Kathmandu	398	509	644	815	1,028	1,280	4.92	4.70	4.71	4.65	4.38	23.52	18.67
Pakistan	Faisalabad	1,520	1,804	2,140	2,494	2,877	3,326	3.43	3.41	3.07	2.85	2.90	4.45	4.34
Pakistan	Gujranwala	848	1,019	1,224	1,440	1,668	1,937	3.69	3.66	3.24	2.95	2.98	2.48	2.53
Pakistan	Hyderabad	950	1,077	1,221	1,392	1,605	1,864	2.51	2.52	2.62	2.85	2.98	2.78	2.43
Pakistan	Karachi	7,147	8,467	10,020	11,608	13,252	15,155	3.39	3.37	2.94	2.65	2.68	20.93	19.78
Pakistan	Lahore	3,970	4,653	5,448	6,289	7,201	8,271	3.17	3.16	2.87	2.71	2.77	11.63	10.79
Pakistan	Multan	953	1,097	1,263	1,452	1,675	1,944	2.82	2.82	2.78	2.87	2.98	2.79	2.54
Pakistan	Peshawar	769	905	1,066	1,240	1,436	1,669	3.27	3.26	3.03	2.93	3.00	2.25	2.18
Pakistan	Rawalpindi	1,087	1,286	1,520	1,770	2,045	2,371	3.36	3.34	3.05	2.89	2.95	3.18	3.09
Philippines	Cebu	612	661	721	799	902	1,006	1.53	1.75	2.05	2.42	2.19	2.05	1.49
Philippines	Davao	854	1,001	1,152	1,327	1,511	1,680	3.17	2.81	2.82	2.59	2.13	2.87	2.50
Philippines	Manila	7,973	9,401	9,950	10,686	11,799	12,917	3.30	1.13	1.43	1.98	1.81	26.75	19.18
Republic of Korea	Goyang	241	493	744	1,040	1,183	1,210	14.28	8.25	6.69	2.59	0.44	0.76	2.97
Republic of Korea	Ich'on	1,785	2,271	2,464	2,620	2,695	2,712	4.82	1.62	1.23	0.56	0.13	5.64	6.65
Republic of Korea	Kwangju	1,122	1,249	1,346	1,436	1,483	1,499	2.16	1.49	1.30	0.64	0.21	3.54	3.68
Republic of Korea	Pusan	3,778	3,813	3,673	3,554	3,529	3,534	0.18	-0.75	-0.66	-0.14	0.03	11.94	8.67
Republic of Korea	Seongnam	534	842	911	955	981	994	9.10	1.59	0.93	0.55	0.26	1.69	2.44
Republic of Korea	Soul (Seoul)	10,544	10,256	9,917	9,645	9,554	9,545	-0.55	-0.67	-0.56	-0.19	-0.02	33.31	23.41
Republic of Korea	Suwon	628	748	932	1,134	1,228	1,248	3.50	4.42	3.91	1.59	0.33	1.98	3.06
Republic of Korea	Taegu	2,215	2,434	2,478	2,511	2,538	2,551	1.88	0.36	0.26	0.22	0.10	7.00	6.26
Republic of Korea	Taejon	1,036	1,256	1,362	1,453	1,500	1,516	3.85	1.62	1.30	0.64	0.21	3.27	3.72
Republic of Korea	Ulsan	673	945	1,011	1,056	1,084	1,097	6.80	1.36	0.87	0.52	0.24	2.13	2.69
Saudi Arabia	Ad-Dammam	409	533	639	766	904	1,025	5.30	3.63	3.62	3.32	2.51	3.26	4.00
Saudi Arabia	Al-Madinah (Medina)	529	669	795	944	1,107	1,251	4.69	3.45	3.45	3.18	2.45	4.22	4.88
Saudi Arabia	Ar-Riyadh (Riyadh)	2,325	3,035	3,567	4,193	4,863	5,438	5.33	3.23	3.23	2.96	2.24	18.54	21.21
Saudi Arabia	Jiddah	1,742	2,200	2,509	2,860	3,244	3,612	4.66	2.63	2.62	2.52	2.15	13.89	14.09
Saudi Arabia	Makkah (Mecca)	856	1,033	1,168	1,319	1,488	1,661	3.76	2.45	2.45	2.41	2.20	6.83	6.48
Singapore	Singapore	3,016	3,478	4,017	4,326	4,590	4,815	2.85	2.88	1.48	1.19	0.96	100.00	100.00
Syrian Arab Republic	Dimashq (Damascus)	1,691	1,849	2,035	2,272	2,559	2,872	1.79	1.92	2.20	2.38	2.30	26.91	22.61
Syrian Arab Republic	Halab (Aleppo)	1,554	1,870	2,212	2,520	2,840	3,185	3.70	3.37	2.61	2.39	2.29	24.73	25.07
Syrian Arab Republic	Hims (Homs)	565	680	806	923	1,048	1,183	3.70	3.40	2.72	2.53	2.43	8.99	9.31
Thailand	Krung Thep (Bangkok)	5,888	6,106	6,332	6,593	6,963	7,439	0.73	0.73	0.81	1.09	1.32	36.63	29.79
Turkey	Adana	907	1,011	1,123	1,245	1,364	1,471	2.18	2.10	2.06	1.82	1.50	2.67	2.48
Turkey	Ankara	2,561	2,842	3,179	3,573	3,914	4,191	2.08	2.25	2.33	1.82	1.37	7.55	7.06
Turkey	Bursa	819	981	1,180	1,414	1,591	1,718	3.62	3.69	3.61	2.36	1.54	2.41	2.89
Turkey	Gaziantep	595	710	844	992	1,111	1,202	3.54	3.47	3.23	2.26	1.58	1.75	2.02
Turkey	Istanbul	6,552	7,665	8,744	9,712	10,546	11,211	3.14	2.63	2.10	1.65	1.22	19.32	18.87
Turkey	Izmir	1,741	1,966	2,216	2,487	2,728	2,929	2.43	2.39	2.31	1.85	1.42	5.13	4.93
Turkey	Konya	508	610	734	871	980	1,061	3.66	3.69	3.42	2.34	1.60	1.50	1.79
United Arab Emirates	Dubayy (Dubai)	473	650	938	1,330	1,537	1,688	6.36	7.35	6.98	2.89	1.88	32.00	39.03
Uzbekistan	Tashkent	2,072	2,104	2,137	2,181	2,284	2,460	0.30	0.30	0.42	0.92	1.49	25.18	21.10
Viet Nam	Hà Noi	3,126	3,424	3,752	4,164	4,703	5,320	1.82	1.83	2.09	2.43	2.47	23.31	17.73
Viet Nam	Hai Phòng	1,474	1,585	1,704	1,873	2,120	2,411	1.45	1.46	1.89	2.48	2.58	10.99	8.04
Viet Nam	Thành Pho Ho Chí Minh (Ho Chi Minh City)	3,996	4,296	4,621	5,065	5,698	6,436	1.45	1.46	1.84	2.36	2.43	29.80	21.45
Yemen	Sana'a'	653	1,034	1,365	1,801	2,339	2,931	9.18	5.55	5.54	5.23	4.52	25.83	32.25
EUROPE														
Belarus	Minsk	1,607	1,649	1,694	1,778	1,875	1,903	0.52	0.54	0.97	1.06	0.30	23.56	26.92
Belgium	Bruxelles-Brussel	962	960	964	1,012	1,050	1,062	-0.04	0.09	0.98	0.74	0.21	10.01	10.34
Bulgaria	Sofiya (Sofia)	1,191	1,191	1,164	1,093	1,063	1,059	0.01	-0.46	-1.26	-0.56	-0.07	20.57	20.32
Czech Republic	Praha (Prague)	1,210	1,197	1,181	1,171	1,183	1,186	-0.21	-0.28	-0.17	0.20	0.05	15.61	15.91
Denmark	København (Copenhagen)	1,338	1,358	1,079	1,088	1,094	1,098	0.30	-4.61	0.17	0.10	0.08	30.67	22.72
Finland	Helsinki	872	943	1,019	1,091	1,120	1,135	1.57	1.56	1.35	0.54	0.26	28.46	33.75
France	Bordeaux	699	730	763	790	808	822	0.88	0.87	0.71	0.45	0.33	1.66	1.67
France	Lille	961	984	1,007	1,029	1,048	1,063	0.47	0.47	0.43	0.36	0.29	2.29	2.16
France	Lyon	1,265	1,313	1,362	1,403	1,428	1,446	0.74	0.73	0.59	0.36	0.24	3.01	2.94
France	Marseille-Aix-en-Provence	1,305	1,331	1,357	1,382	1,404	1,421	0.39	0.39	0.37	0.32	0.24	3.11	2.89
France	Nice-Cannes	854	874	894	914	931	946	0.46	0.46	0.44	0.38	0.30	2.03	1.92
France	Paris	9,331	9,510	9,692	9,820	9,856	9,858	0.38	0.38	0.26	0.07	0.00	22.21	20.03
France	Toulouse	654	714	778	830	854	868	1.75	1.74	1.27	0.57	0.33	1.56	1.76
Germany	Berlin	3,434	3,471	3,392	3,389	3,389	3,389	0.22	-0.46	-0.02	0.00	0.00	5.89	5.38
Germany	Hamburg	1,652	1,708	1,715	1,740	1,752	1,755	0.66	0.08	0.29	0.14	0.03	2.84	2.79
Germany	Köln (Cologne)	954	966	966	965	961	961	0.25	-0.00	-0.02	-0.07	-0.01	1.64	1.53
Germany	München (Munich)	1,229	1,236	1,211	1,263	1,296	1,303	0.12	-0.41	0.83	0.52	0.12	2.11	2.07
Greece	Athínai (Athens)	3,070	3,122	3,179	3,230	3,248	3,251	0.34	0.37	0.31	0.11	0.02	51.34	47.49
Greece	Thessaloniki	746	771	797	820	832	841	0.66	0.67	0.58	0.29	0.21	12.48	12.28
Hungary	Budapest	2,005	1,893	1,787	1,693	1,664	1,655	-1.15	-1.15	-1.08	-0.35	-0.10	29.39	24.02
Ireland	Dublin	916	946	989	1,037	1,107	1,186	0.65	0.87	0.96	1.30	1.38	45.82	39.76
Italy	Milano (Milan)	3,063	3,020	2,985	2,953	2,939	2,937	-0.28	-0.23	-0.22	-0.10	-0.01	8.09	7.31
Italy	Napoli (Naples)	2,208	2,218	2,232	2,245	2,251	2,252	0.09	0.13	0.12	0.05	0.01	5.83	5.61
Italy	Palermo	844	850	855	859	862	862	0.14	0.12	0.11	0.05	0.01	2.23	2.15
Italy	Roma (Rome)	3,450	3,425	3,385	3,348	3,332	3,330	-0.14	-0.24	-0.22	-0.10	-0.01	9.12	8.29
Italy	Torino (Turin)	1,775	1,733	1,694	1,660	1,644	1,642	-0.48	-0.45	-0.41	-0.18	-0.02	4.69	4.09
Netherlands	Amsterdam	1,053	1,102	1,126	1,147	1,173	1,201	0.90	0.43	0.38	0.45	0.48	10.26	8.42
Netherlands	Rotterdam	1,047	1,078	1,092	1,101	1,118	1,143	0.57	0.26	0.17	0.30	0.44	10.20	8.00
Norway	Oslo	684	729	774	802	825	842	1.28	1.19	0.72	0.55	0.42	22.41	22.15
Poland	Kraków (Cracow)	735	748	756	763	766	767	0.35	0.21	0.19	0.08	0.02	3.15	3.14

TABLE C.1

continued

		Estimates and Projections (000)						Annual rate of change (%)					Share in urban population (%)	
		1990	1995	2000	2005	2010	2015	1990–1995	1995–2000	2000–2005	2005–2010	2010–2015	1990	2015
Poland	Lódz	836	825	799	776	765	764	-0.26	-0.64	-0.59	-0.26	-0.02	3.58	3.13
Poland	Warszawa (Warsaw)	1,628	1,652	1,666	1,680	1,686	1,687	0.29	0.17	0.16	0.07	0.01	6.97	6.91
Portugal	Lisboa (Lisbon)	2,537	2,600	2,672	2,761	2,890	3,005	0.49	0.55	0.65	0.92	0.78	53.04	43.62
Portugal	Porto	1,164	1,206	1,254	1,309	1,380	1,443	0.72	0.77	0.86	1.06	0.89	24.33	20.94
Romania	Bucuresti (Bucharest)	1,757	2,054	2,009	1,934	1,941	1,942	3.13	-0.44	-0.76	0.07	0.01	13.94	16.58
Russian Federation	Chelyabinsk	1,130	1,109	1,088	1,068	1,057	1,055	-0.38	-0.38	-0.37	-0.20	-0.04	1.04	1.06
Russian Federation	Kazan	1,094	1,099	1,103	1,108	1,110	1,111	0.08	0.08	0.08	0.04	0.01	1.01	1.12
Russian Federation	Krasnoyarsk	910	911	911	912	912	912	0.02	0.02	0.01	0.01	0.00	0.84	0.92
Russian Federation	Moskva (Moscow)	9,053	9,563	10,103	10,654	10,967	11,022	1.10	1.10	1.06	0.58	0.10	8.31	11.10
Russian Federation	Nizhniy Novgorod	1,420	1,375	1,331	1,289	1,268	1,264	-0.65	-0.65	-0.63	-0.34	-0.06	1.30	1.27
Russian Federation	Novosibirsk	1,430	1,428	1,426	1,425	1,424	1,424	-0.03	-0.03	-0.02	-0.01	-0.00	1.31	1.43
Russian Federation	Omsk	1,144	1,140	1,136	1,132	1,130	1,129	-0.07	-0.07	-0.07	-0.04	-0.01	1.05	1.14
Russian Federation	Perm	1,076	1,044	1,014	985	970	967	-0.59	-0.59	-0.57	-0.31	-0.05	0.99	0.97
Russian Federation	Rostov-na-Donu (Rostov-on-Don)	1,022	1,041	1,061	1,081	1,091	1,093	0.38	0.38	0.36	0.20	0.03	0.94	1.10
Russian Federation	Samara	1,244	1,208	1,173	1,141	1,124	1,121	-0.58	-0.58	-0.56	-0.31	-0.05	1.14	1.13
Russian Federation	Sankt Peterburg (Saint Petersburg)	5,019	5,116	5,214	5,312	5,365	5,375	0.38	0.38	0.37	0.20	0.03	4.61	5.42
Russian Federation	Saratov	901	890	878	868	862	861	-0.25	-0.25	-0.24	-0.13	-0.02	0.83	0.87
Russian Federation	Ufa	1,078	1,063	1,049	1,035	1,028	1,027	-0.27	-0.27	-0.26	-0.14	-0.02	0.99	1.03
Russian Federation	Volgograd	999	1,005	1,010	1,016	1,019	1,019	0.11	0.11	0.10	0.06	0.01	0.92	1.03
Russian Federation	Voronezh	880	867	854	842	836	834	-0.30	-0.30	-0.29	-0.16	-0.03	0.81	0.84
Russian Federation	Yekaterinburg	1,350	1,326	1,303	1,281	1,270	1,268	-0.35	-0.35	-0.34	-0.18	-0.03	1.24	1.28
Serbia and Montenegro	Beograd (Belgrade)	1,162	1,150	1,128	1,106	1,094	1,100	-0.22	-0.38	-0.38	-0.22	0.10	22.50	19.17
Spain	Barcelona	4,101	4,313	4,548	4,795	4,998	5,057	1.01	1.06	1.06	0.83	0.24	13.85	14.56
Spain	Madrid	4,414	4,751	5,162	5,608	5,977	6,086	1.47	1.66	1.66	1.28	0.36	14.90	17.52
Spain	Valencia	776	783	790	797	806	813	0.20	0.18	0.18	0.21	0.18	2.62	2.34
Sweden	Göteborg	729	761	793	827	854	867	0.86	0.81	0.84	0.64	0.30	10.25	10.94
Sweden	Stockholm	1,487	1,561	1,652	1,708	1,745	1,760	0.97	1.13	0.67	0.43	0.17	20.91	22.22
Switzerland	Zürich (Zurich)	929	1,002	1,074	1,144	1,183	1,200	1.52	1.39	1.26	0.67	0.28	19.86	20.77
Ukraine	Dnipropetrovs'k	1,162	1,119	1,077	1,036	1,007	998	-0.77	-0.77	-0.77	-0.58	-0.16	3.36	3.40
Ukraine	Donets'k	1,097	1,061	1,026	992	967	960	-0.67	-0.67	-0.67	-0.51	-0.14	3.17	3.27
Ukraine	Kharkiv	1,586	1,534	1,484	1,436	1,400	1,390	-0.66	-0.66	-0.66	-0.50	-0.14	4.58	4.73
Ukraine	Kyiv (Kiev)	2,574	2,590	2,606	2,672	2,738	2,757	0.13	0.13	0.50	0.49	0.14	7.43	9.39
Ukraine	Odesa	1,092	1,064	1,037	1,010	990	985	-0.52	-0.52	-0.52	-0.39	-0.11	3.15	3.35
Ukraine	Zaporizhzhya	873	847	822	798	780	775	-0.60	-0.60	-0.60	-0.45	-0.13	2.52	2.64
United Kingdom	Birmingham	2,301	2,291	2,285	2,280	2,279	2,279	-0.09	-0.05	-0.04	-0.01	0.00	4.57	4.10
United Kingdom	Glasgow	1,217	1,186	1,171	1,159	1,157	1,162	-0.52	-0.26	-0.21	-0.02	0.08	2.42	2.09
United Kingdom	Liverpool	831	829	818	810	810	816	-0.05	-0.26	-0.20	0.01	0.13	1.65	1.47
United Kingdom	London	7,654	7,908	8,225	8,505	8,607	8,618	0.65	0.79	0.67	0.24	0.02	15.20	15.49
United Kingdom	Manchester	2,282	2,262	2,243	2,228	2,223	2,223	-0.18	-0.16	-0.14	-0.05	-0.00	4.53	3.99
United Kingdom	Newcastle upon Tyne	877	883	880	879	882	887	0.14	-0.07	-0.04	0.06	0.12	1.74	1.59
United Kingdom	West Yorkshire	1,449	1,468	1,495	1,519	1,530	1,534	0.27	0.36	0.32	0.14	0.06	2.88	2.76
LATIN AMERICA AND THE CARIBBEAN														
Argentina	Buenos Aires	10,513	11,154	11,847	12,550	13,067	13,396	1.18	1.21	1.15	0.81	0.50	37.10	34.27
Argentina	Córdoba	1,200	1,275	1,348	1,423	1,492	1,552	1.21	1.11	1.08	0.95	0.79	4.24	3.97
Argentina	Mendoza	759	802	838	876	917	956	1.11	0.88	0.88	0.90	0.84	2.68	2.45
Argentina	Rosario	1,084	1,121	1,152	1,186	1,231	1,280	0.68	0.55	0.57	0.74	0.78	3.82	3.27
Argentina	San Miguel de Tucumán	611	666	722	781	830	868	1.71	1.63	1.57	1.22	0.89	2.16	2.22
Bolivia	La Paz	1,062	1,267	1,390	1,527	1,692	1,864	3.53	1.85	1.89	2.05	1.94	28.65	24.96
Bolivia	Santa Cruz	616	833	1,054	1,320	1,551	1,724	6.04	4.69	4.51	3.22	2.11	16.63	23.08
Brazil	Baixada Santista[2]	1,184	1,319	1,468	1,638	1,810	1,940	2.15	2.14	2.18	2.00	1.39	1.06	1.05
Brazil	Belém	1,129	1,393	1,748	2,043	2,335	2,524	4.20	4.54	3.11	2.68	1.55	1.01	1.37
Brazil	Belo Horizonte	3,548	4,093	4,659	5,304	5,941	6,354	2.86	2.59	2.59	2.27	1.34	3.18	3.44
Brazil	Brasília	1,863	2,257	2,746	3,341	3,938	4,282	3.84	3.92	3.92	3.29	1.67	1.67	2.32
Brazil	Campinas	1,693	1,975	2,264	2,634	3,003	3,239	3.08	2.74	3.02	2.62	1.51	1.52	1.75
Brazil	Cuiabá	510	606	686	770	857	923	3.43	2.49	2.31	2.12	1.50	0.46	0.50
Brazil	Curitiba	1,829	2,138	2,494	2,908	3,320	3,581	3.12	3.07	3.07	2.65	1.51	1.64	1.94
Brazil	Florianópolis	503	609	734	934	1,142	1,262	3.85	3.72	4.81	4.03	2.01	0.45	0.68
Brazil	Fortaleza	2,226	2,554	2,875	3,237	3,598	3,850	2.75	2.37	2.37	2.12	1.35	1.99	2.08
Brazil	Goiânia	1,132	1,356	1,608	1,898	2,189	2,372	3.61	3.41	3.31	2.85	1.61	1.01	1.28
Brazil	Grande São Luís	672	775	876	990	1,106	1,192	2.83	2.45	2.45	2.22	1.50	0.60	0.65
Brazil	Grande Vitória	1,052	1,221	1,398	1,613	1,829	1,974	2.97	2.72	2.85	2.51	1.53	0.94	1.07
Brazil	João Pessoa	652	741	827	918	1,012	1,087	2.54	2.21	2.09	1.95	1.43	0.58	0.59
Brazil	Maceió	660	798	952	1,116	1,281	1,391	3.77	3.55	3.17	2.76	1.64	0.59	0.75
Brazil	Manaus	955	1,159	1,392	1,645	1,898	2,059	3.87	3.68	3.33	2.86	1.63	0.85	1.11
Brazil	Natal	692	800	910	1,035	1,161	1,253	2.89	2.58	2.58	2.31	1.52	0.62	0.68
Brazil	Norte/Nordeste Catarinense[3]	603	709	815	936	1,059	1,146	3.22	2.78	2.78	2.47	1.58	0.54	0.62
Brazil	Pôrto Alegre	2,934	3,236	3,505	3,795	4,096	4,342	1.96	1.59	1.59	1.52	1.17	2.63	2.35
Brazil	Recife	2,690	2,958	3,230	3,527	3,830	4,070	1.90	1.76	1.76	1.65	1.21	2.41	2.20
Brazil	Rio de Janeiro	9,595	10,174	10,803	11,469	12,170	12,770	1.17	1.20	1.20	1.19	0.96	8.59	6.91
Brazil	Salvador	2,331	2,644	2,968	3,331	3,695	3,950	2.53	2.31	2.31	2.07	1.34	2.09	2.14
Brazil	São Paulo	14,776	15,948	17,099	18,333	19,582	20,535	1.53	1.39	1.39	1.32	0.95	13.22	11.11
Brazil	Teresina	614	706	789	872	958	1,029	2.77	2.24	2.00	1.88	1.42	0.55	0.56
Chile	Santiago	4,616	4,983	5,326	5,683	5,982	6,191	1.53	1.33	1.30	1.02	0.69	42.06	38.33
Colombia	Barranquilla	1,241	1,396	1,658	1,857	2,042	2,191	2.35	3.45	2.26	1.90	1.40	5.17	5.55
Colombia	Bucaramanga	658	776	921	1,019	1,116	1,201	3.30	3.41	2.03	1.81	1.46	2.74	3.04
Colombia	Cali	1,574	1,829	2,237	2,514	2,767	2,963	3.00	4.03	2.33	1.92	1.37	6.55	7.51
Colombia	Cartagena	572	667	829	954	1,067	1,152	3.09	4.34	2.80	2.24	1.54	2.38	2.92
Colombia	Cucuta	530	637	760	852	939	1,012	3.68	3.52	2.28	1.96	1.50	2.21	2.57

TABLE C.1

continued

		Estimates and Projections (000)						Annual rate of change (%)					Share in urban population (%)	
		1990	1995	2000	2005	2010	2015	1990–1995	1995–2000	2000–2005	2005–2010	2010–2015	1990	2015
Colombia	Medellín	2,155	2,403	2,814	3,058	3,304	3,522	2.18	3.16	1.67	1.54	1.28	8.97	8.93
Colombia	Santa Fé de Bogotá	4,905	5,751	6,964	7,747	8,416	8,932	3.18	3.83	2.13	1.66	1.19	20.42	22.65
Costa Rica	San José	737	867	1,032	1,217	1,374	1,506	3.25	3.48	3.29	2.43	1.84	47.30	45.22
Cuba	La Habana (Havana)	2,108	2,183	2,187	2,189	2,159	2,151	0.69	0.04	0.02	-0.27	-0.08	27.28	25.19
Dominican Republic	Santo Domingo	1,522	1,665	1,834	2,022	2,240	2,449	1.80	1.93	1.96	2.04	1.78	38.88	32.87
Ecuador	Guayaquil	1,572	1,808	2,077	2,387	2,709	2,975	2.80	2.78	2.78	2.53	1.87	27.77	29.07
Ecuador	Quito	1,088	1,217	1,357	1,514	1,680	1,839	2.25	2.18	2.18	2.09	1.80	19.22	17.96
El Salvador	San Salvador	970	1,142	1,353	1,517	1,662	1,807	3.27	3.39	2.29	1.83	1.67	38.54	35.69
Guatemala	Ciudad de Guatemala (Guatemala City)	803	839	908	984	1,103	1,269	0.89	1.57	1.62	2.28	2.81	21.95	15.39
Haiti	Port-au-Prince	1,134	1,427	1,766	2,129	2,460	2,785	4.60	4.26	3.74	2.89	2.48	56.05	62.81
Honduras	Tegucigalpa	578	677	793	927	1,075	1,230	3.16	3.16	3.14	2.96	2.68	29.48	27.22
Mexico	Acapulco de Juárez	598	681	726	769	816	864	2.61	1.27	1.17	1.18	1.14	0.98	0.92
Mexico	Aguascalientes	552	631	736	859	981	1,059	2.69	3.07	3.10	2.64	1.53	0.90	1.13
Mexico	Ciudad de México (Mexico City)	15,311	16,790	18,066	19,411	20,688	21,568	1.84	1.47	1.44	1.27	0.83	25.07	23.01
Mexico	Ciudad Juárez	809	997	1,239	1,540	1,841	2,008	4.19	4.34	4.35	3.57	1.73	1.32	2.14
Mexico	Culiacán	606	690	750	812	876	931	2.60	1.67	1.60	1.51	1.23	0.99	0.99
Mexico	Guadalajara	3,011	3,431	3,697	3,968	4,237	4,456	2.61	1.50	1.41	1.31	1.01	4.93	4.75
Mexico	León de los Aldamas	961	1,127	1,293	1,481	1,665	1,785	3.19	2.75	2.72	2.33	1.39	1.57	1.90
Mexico	Mérida	664	765	849	939	1,028	1,097	2.83	2.07	2.01	1.82	1.30	1.09	1.17
Mexico	Mexicali	607	690	771	860	949	1,015	2.57	2.22	2.20	1.96	1.35	0.99	1.08
Mexico	Monterrey	2,594	2,961	3,267	3,596	3,914	4,140	2.65	1.97	1.92	1.70	1.13	4.25	4.42
Mexico	Puebla	1,699	1,932	1,888	1,824	1,801	1,861	2.57	-0.46	-0.69	-0.25	0.65	2.78	1.99
Mexico	Querétaro	561	671	798	947	1,094	1,185	3.58	3.45	3.43	2.89	1.60	0.92	1.26
Mexico	San Luis Potosí	665	774	857	946	1,034	1,103	3.04	2.05	1.97	1.79	1.29	1.09	1.18
Mexico	Tijuana	760	1,017	1,297	1,649	2,003	2,194	5.82	4.86	4.79	3.90	1.82	1.25	2.34
Mexico	Toluca de Lerdo	835	981	1,420	1,545	1,669	1,770	3.22	7.39	1.69	1.55	1.17	1.37	1.89
Mexico	Torreón	882	954	1,012	1,072	1,136	1,200	1.55	1.18	1.15	1.16	1.10	1.45	1.28
Mexico	Tuxtla Gutierrez	294	372	539	788	1,067	1,209	4.72	7.41	7.61	6.06	2.49	0.48	1.29
Nicaragua	Managua	735	870	1,021	1,165	1,312	1,461	3.37	3.21	2.64	2.36	2.15	34.97	34.94
Panama	Ciudad de Panamá (Panama City)	847	953	1,072	1,216	1,379	1,527	2.36	2.36	2.51	2.52	2.04	65.24	51.93
Paraguay	Asunción	928	1,140	1,457	1,858	2,264	2,606	4.12	4.92	4.86	3.95	2.81	45.16	53.20
Peru	Arequipa	564	640	724	819	915	994	2.54	2.46	2.46	2.22	1.65	3.76	4.12
Peru	Lima	5,825	6,456	6,811	7,186	7,590	8,026	2.06	1.07	1.07	1.10	1.12	38.87	33.29
Puerto Rico	San Juan	1,539	1,855	2,237	2,605	2,758	2,791	3.74	3.74	3.04	1.15	0.23	60.44	67.65
Uruguay	Montevideo	1,274	1,299	1,285	1,264	1,260	1,277	0.38	-0.21	-0.33	-0.06	0.27	46.12	37.34
Venezuela	Barquisimeto	742	828	923	1,029	1,143	1,243	2.18	2.18	2.18	2.10	1.67	4.48	4.14
Venezuela	Caracas	2,767	2,816	2,864	2,913	2,988	3,144	0.35	0.34	0.34	0.51	1.02	16.70	10.47
Venezuela	Maracaibo	1,351	1,603	1,901	2,255	2,639	2,911	3.41	3.42	3.41	3.14	1.97	8.15	9.69
Venezuela	Maracay	766	881	1,015	1,168	1,333	1,463	2.82	2.82	2.82	2.65	1.85	4.62	4.87
Venezuela	Valencia	1,129	1,462	1,893	2,451	3,090	3,499	5.17	5.17	5.16	4.64	2.48	6.81	11.65
NORTHERN AMERICA														
Canada	Calgary	738	809	953	1,058	1,142	1,193	1.84	3.26	2.09	1.55	0.87	3.48	4.18
Canada	Edmonton	831	859	947	1,015	1,075	1,118	0.67	1.95	1.39	1.14	0.79	3.92	3.92
Canada	Montréal	3,154	3,305	3,471	3,640	3,787	3,897	0.94	0.98	0.95	0.79	0.57	14.87	13.65
Canada	Ottawa-Gatineau	918	988	1,079	1,156	1,216	1,262	1.48	1.74	1.39	1.01	0.75	4.33	4.42
Canada	Toronto	3,807	4,197	4,747	5,312	5,737	5,938	1.95	2.46	2.25	1.54	0.69	17.95	20.80
Canada	Vancouver	1,559	1,789	2,040	2,188	2,309	2,389	2.75	2.63	1.40	1.07	0.69	7.35	8.37
United States of America	Atlanta	2,184	2,781	3,542	4,304	4,682	4,864	4.84	4.84	3.89	1.69	0.76	1.14	1.79
United States of America	Austin	569	720	913	1,107	1,212	1,271	4.73	4.73	3.86	1.82	0.95	0.30	0.47
United States of America	Baltimore	1,849	1,962	2,083	2,205	2,316	2,410	1.19	1.19	1.14	0.98	0.80	0.96	0.88
United States of America	Boston	3,428	3,726	4,049	4,361	4,585	4,751	1.66	1.66	1.48	1.00	0.71	1.78	1.74
United States of America	Bridgeport-Stamford	714	799	894	987	1,053	1,103	2.25	2.25	1.98	1.30	0.93	0.37	0.41
United States of America	Buffalo	955	966	977	999	1,043	1,091	0.23	0.23	0.44	0.86	0.90	0.50	0.40
United States of America	Charlotte	461	596	769	946	1,041	1,093	5.10	5.10	4.15	1.92	0.98	0.24	0.40
United States of America	Chicago	7,374	7,839	8,333	8,814	9,186	9,469	1.22	1.22	1.12	0.83	0.61	3.83	3.48
United States of America	Cincinnati	1,335	1,419	1,508	1,599	1,683	1,755	1.22	1.22	1.18	1.02	0.85	0.69	0.64
United States of America	Cleveland	1,680	1,734	1,789	1,855	1,939	2,019	0.63	0.63	0.72	0.88	0.82	0.87	0.74
United States of America	Columbus, Ohio	950	1,040	1,138	1,236	1,310	1,370	1.81	1.81	1.64	1.18	0.89	0.49	0.50
United States of America	Dallas-Fort Worth	3,219	3,665	4,172	4,655	4,941	5,121	2.59	2.59	2.19	1.20	0.72	1.67	1.88
United States of America	Dayton	616	659	706	754	798	837	1.37	1.37	1.32	1.14	0.95	0.32	0.31
United States of America	Denver-Aurora	1,528	1,747	1,998	2,239	2,389	2,489	2.68	2.68	2.28	1.30	0.82	0.79	0.91
United States of America	Detroit	3,703	3,804	3,909	4,034	4,192	4,342	0.54	0.54	0.63	0.77	0.71	1.92	1.59
United States of America	Hartford	783	818	853	894	940	984	0.86	0.86	0.92	1.01	0.92	0.41	0.36
United States of America	Honolulu	635	676	720	767	810	850	1.27	1.27	1.24	1.11	0.95	0.33	0.31
United States of America	Houston	2,922	3,353	3,849	4,320	4,596	4,767	2.76	2.76	2.31	1.24	0.73	1.52	1.75
United States of America	Indianapolis	921	1,063	1,228	1,387	1,487	1,554	2.87	2.87	2.44	1.39	0.89	0.48	0.57
United States of America	Jacksonville, Florida	742	811	886	961	1,020	1,069	1.78	1.78	1.62	1.20	0.93	0.39	0.39
United States of America	Kansas City	1,233	1,297	1,365	1,437	1,510	1,576	1.02	1.02	1.03	0.99	0.86	0.64	0.58
United States of America	Las Vegas	708	973	1,335	1,720	1,912	2,001	6.34	6.34	5.07	2.11	0.91	0.37	0.73
United States of America	Los Angeles-Long Beach-Santa Ana	10,883	11,339	11,814	12,298	12,738	13,095	0.82	0.82	0.80	0.70	0.55	5.66	4.81
United States of America	Louisville	757	810	866	924	977	1,023	1.34	1.34	1.29	1.11	0.92	0.39	0.38
United States of America	Memphis	829	899	976	1,053	1,115	1,167	1.64	1.64	1.51	1.16	0.91	0.43	0.43
United States of America	Miami	3,969	4,431	4,946	5,434	5,739	5,940	2.20	2.20	1.88	1.09	0.69	2.06	2.18
United States of America	Milwaukee	1,228	1,269	1,311	1,361	1,425	1,488	0.65	0.65	0.75	0.92	0.86	0.64	0.55
United States of America	Minneapolis-St. Paul	2,087	2,236	2,397	2,556	2,688	2,795	1.38	1.39	1.29	1.00	0.78	1.09	1.03
United States of America	Nashville-Davidson	577	660	755	848	909	954	2.69	2.69	2.32	1.41	0.96	0.30	0.35
United States of America	New Orleans	1,039	1,024	1,009	1,010	1,049	1,096	-0.30	-0.30	0.04	0.74	0.89	0.54	0.40
United States of America	New York-Newark	16,086	16,943	17,846	18,718	19,388	19,876	1.04	1.04	0.95	0.70	0.50	8.36	7.29

TABLE C.1

continued

		Estimates and Projections (000)						Annual rate of change (%)					Share in urban population (%)	
		1990	1995	2000	2005	2010	2015	1990–1995	1995–2000	2000–2005	2005–2010	2010–2015	1990	2015
United States of America	Oklahoma City	711	729	748	773	811	850	0.51	0.51	0.66	0.95	0.94	0.37	0.31
United States of America	Orlando	893	1,020	1,165	1,306	1,397	1,461	2.66	2.66	2.28	1.35	0.90	0.46	0.54
United States of America	Philadelphia	4,725	4,938	5,160	5,392	5,615	5,806	0.88	0.88	0.88	0.81	0.67	2.46	2.13
United States of America	Phoenix-Mesa	2,025	2,437	2,934	3,416	3,677	3,822	3.71	3.71	3.04	1.47	0.78	1.05	1.40
United States of America	Pittsburgh	1,681	1,717	1,755	1,806	1,883	1,962	0.43	0.43	0.58	0.84	0.82	0.87	0.72
United States of America	Portland	1,181	1,372	1,595	1,810	1,941	2,025	3.01	3.01	2.53	1.39	0.85	0.61	0.74
United States of America	Providence	1,047	1,111	1,178	1,248	1,314	1,374	1.18	1.18	1.15	1.04	0.88	0.54	0.50
United States of America	Richmond	696	757	822	888	942	987	1.66	1.66	1.53	1.18	0.93	0.36	0.36
United States of America	Riverside-San Bernardino	1,178	1,336	1,516	1,690	1,803	1,882	2.53	2.53	2.17	1.30	0.86	0.61	0.69
United States of America	Sacramento	1,104	1,244	1,402	1,555	1,657	1,731	2.39	2.39	2.07	1.28	0.87	0.57	0.64
United States of America	Salt Lake City	792	840	890	943	995	1,042	1.17	1.17	1.16	1.07	0.92	0.41	0.38
United States of America	San Antonio	1,134	1,229	1,333	1,436	1,518	1,585	1.62	1.62	1.49	1.12	0.87	0.59	0.58
United States of America	San Diego	2,356	2,514	2,683	2,852	2,994	3,110	1.30	1.30	1.22	0.97	0.77	1.22	1.14
United States of America	San Francisco-Oakland	2,961	3,095	3,236	3,385	3,534	3,666	0.89	0.89	0.90	0.86	0.74	1.54	1.35
United States of America	San Jose	1,376	1,457	1,543	1,631	1,715	1,789	1.14	1.14	1.12	1.00	0.84	0.72	0.66
United States of America	Seattle	2,206	2,453	2,727	2,989	3,165	3,289	2.12	2.12	1.84	1.14	0.77	1.15	1.21
United States of America	St. Louis	1,950	2,014	2,081	2,159	2,254	2,346	0.65	0.65	0.74	0.86	0.79	1.01	0.86
United States of America	Tampa-St. Petersburg	1,717	1,886	2,072	2,252	2,383	2,481	1.88	1.88	1.67	1.12	0.81	0.89	0.91
United States of America	Tucson	582	649	724	798	852	893	2.18	2.18	1.93	1.31	0.96	0.30	0.33
United States of America	Virginia Beach	1,286	1,341	1,397	1,460	1,531	1,598	0.83	0.83	0.88	0.95	0.85	0.67	0.59
United States of America	Washington, D.C.	3,376	3,651	3,949	4,238	4,451	4,613	1.57	1.57	1.41	0.98	0.71	1.76	1.69
OCEANIA														
Australia	Adelaide	1,046	1,074	1,102	1,134	1,179	1,230	0.53	0.51	0.58	0.77	0.84	7.26	6.15
Australia	Brisbane	1,329	1,486	1,624	1,758	1,866	1,946	2.24	1.77	1.59	1.19	0.84	9.22	9.73
Australia	Melbourne	3,117	3,257	3,433	3,626	3,796	3,933	0.88	1.05	1.10	0.91	0.71	21.63	19.66
Australia	Perth	1,160	1,273	1,373	1,474	1,560	1,627	1.87	1.51	1.42	1.13	0.85	8.05	8.14
Australia	Sydney	3,632	3,839	4,078	4,331	4,540	4,701	1.11	1.21	1.20	0.95	0.70	25.20	23.50
Austria	Wien (Vienna)	2,096	2,127	2,158	2,260	2,352	2,379	0.29	0.29	0.92	0.80	0.24	41.22	42.40
New Zealand	Auckland	870	976	1,063	1,148	1,208	1,240	2.30	1.71	1.55	1.01	0.53	30.09	32.99

Source: United Nations, Department of Economic and Social Affairs, Population Division, 2006

Notes:

(1) As of 1 July 1997, Hong Kong became a Special Administrative Region (SAR) of China.

(2) Including Santos.

(3) Including Joinville.

TABLE C.2

Population of Capital Cities (2005)

AFRICA		(000)
Algeria	El Djazaïr (Algiers)	3,200
Angola	Luanda	2,766
Benin	Cotonou[1]	719
Benin	Porto-Novo[1]	242
Botswana	Gaborone	210
Burkina Faso	Ouagadougou	926
Burundi	Bujumbura	447
Cameroon	Yaoundé	1,485
Cape Verde	Praia	117
Central African Republic	Bangui	541
Chad	N'Djaména	888
Comoros	Moroni	44
Congo	Brazzaville	1,173
Côte d'Ivoire	Abidjan[2]	3,577
Côte d'Ivoire	Yamoussoukro[2]	490
Dem. Republic of the Congo	Kinshasa	6,049
Djibouti	Djibouti	555
Egypt	Al-Qahirah (Cairo)	11,128
Equatorial Guinea	Malabo	96
Eritrea	Asmera	551
Ethiopia	Addis Ababa	2,893
Gabon	Libreville	556
Gambia	Banjul	381
Ghana	Accra	1,981
Guinea	Conakry	1,425
Guinea-Bissau	Bissau	367
Kenya	Nairobi	2,773
Lesotho	Maseru	172
Liberia	Monrovia	936
Libyan Arab Jamahiriya	Tarabulus (Tripoli)	2,098
Madagascar	Antananarivo	1,585
Malawi	Lilongwe	676
Mali	Bamako	1,368
Mauritania	Nouakchott	637
Mauritius	Port Louis	146
Morocco	Rabat	1,647
Mozambique	Maputo	1,320
Namibia	Windhoek	289
Niger	Niamey	850
Nigeria	Abuja	612
Réunion	Saint-Denis	137
Rwanda	Kigali	779
Saint Helena	Jamestown	1
São Tomé and Príncipe	São Tomé	4,193
Senegal	Dakar	1,106
Seychelles	Victoria	799
Sierra Leone	Freetown	4,326
Somalia	Muqdisho (Mogadishu)	400
South Africa	Bloemfontein[3]	3,083
South Africa	Cape Town[3]	1,271
South Africa	Pretoria[3]	5,608
Sudan	Al-Khartum (Khartoum)	4,518
Swaziland	Mbabane[4]	73
Togo	Lomé	1,337
Tunisia	Tunis	734
Uganda	Kampala	1,319
United Republic of Tanzania	Dodoma	168
Western Sahara	El Aaiún	185
Zambia	Lusaka	1,260
Zimbabwe	Harare	1,515

ASIA		(000)
Afghanistan	Kabul	2,994
Armenia	Yerevan	1,103
Azerbaijan	Baku	1,856
Bahrain	Al-Manamah (Manama)	162
Bangladesh	Dhaka	12,430
Bhutan	Thimphu	85
Brunei Darussalam	Bandar Seri Begawan	64
Cambodia	Phnum Pénh (Phnom Penh)	1,364
China	Beijing	10,717
China, Hong Kong SAR	Hong Kong[5]	7,041
China, Macao SAR	Macao[6]	460
Cyprus	Lefkosia (Nicosia)	211
Dem. People's Republic of Korea	P'yongyang	3,351
Georgia	Tbilisi	1,047
India	Delhi[7]	15,048
Indonesia	Jakarta	13,215
Iran (Islamic Republic of)	Tehran	7,314
Iraq	Baghdad	5,904
Israel	Jerusalem	711
Japan	Tokyo	35,197
Jordan	Amman	1,292
Kazakhstan	Astana	331
Kuwait	Al Kuwayt (Kuwait City)	1,810
Kyrgyzstan	Bishkek	798
Lao People's Dem.	Vientiane	702
Republic Lebanon	Bayrut (Beirut)	1,777
Malaysia	Kuala Lumpur[8]	1,405
Maldives	Male	89
Mongolia	Ulaanbaatar	863
Myanmar	Rangoon	4,107
Nepal	Kathmandu	815
Occupied Palestinian Territory	Ramallah	63
Oman	Masqat	565
Pakistan	Islamabad	736
Philippines	Manila	10,686
Qatar	Ad-Dawhah (Doha)	357
Republic of Korea	Soul (Seoul)	9,645
Saudi Arabia	Ar-Riyadh (Riyadh)	2,159
Singapore	Singapore	424
Sri Lanka	Colombo[9]	119
Sri Lanka	Sri Jayewardenepura Kotte[9]	26
Syrian Arab Republic	Dimashq (Damascus)	2,272
Tajikistan	Dushanbe	549
Thailand	Krung Thep (Bangkok)	6,593
Timor-Leste	Dili	156
Turkey	Ankara	3,573
Turkmenistan	Ashgabat	711
United Arab Emirates	Abu Zaby (Abu Dhabi)	597
Uzbekistan	Tashkent	2,181
Viet Nam	Hà Noi	4,164
Yemen	Sana'a'	1,801

EUROPE		(000)
Albania	Tiranë (Tirana)	388
Andorra	Andorra la Vella	22
Austria	Wien (Vienna)	2,260
Belarus	Minsk	1,778
Belgium	Bruxelles-Brussel	1,012
Bosnia and Herzegovina	Sarajevo	380
Bulgaria	Sofiya (Sofia)	1,093
Channel Islands	St. Helier	29
Croatia	Zagreb	689
Czech Republic	Praha (Prague)	1,171
Denmark	København (Copenhagen)	1,088
Estonia	Tallinn	392
Faeroe Islands	Tórshavn	18
Finland	Helsinki	1,091
France	Paris	9,820
Germany	Berlin	3,389
Gibraltar	Gibraltar	28
Greece	Athínai (Athens)	3,230
Holy See	Vatican City	1
Hungary	Budapest	1,693
Iceland	Reykjavík	185
Ireland	Dublin	1,037
Isle of Man	Douglas	27
Italy	Roma (Rome)	3,348
Latvia	Riga	729
Liechtenstein	Vaduz	5
Lithuania	Vilnius	553
Luxembourg	Luxembourg-Ville	77
Malta	Valletta	210
Monaco	Monaco	35
Netherlands	Amsterdam[10]	1,147
Netherlands	The Hague[10]	729
Norway	Oslo	802
Poland	Warszawa (Warsaw)	1,680
Portugal	Lisboa (Lisbon)	2,761
Republic of Moldova	Chisinau	598
Romania	Bucuresti (Bucharest)	1,934
Russian Federation	Moskva (Moscow)	10,654
San Marino	San Marino	57
Serbia and Montenegro	Beograd (Belgrade)	25
Slovakia	Bratislava	263
Slovenia	Ljubljana	61
Spain	Madrid	652
Sweden	Stockholm	1,708
Switzerland	Bern	357
TFYR Macedonia	Skopje[11]	475
Ukraine	Kyiv (Kiev)	2,672
United Kingdom	London	8,505

LATIN AMERICA AND THE CARIBBEAN		(000)
Anguilla	The Valley	1
Antigua and Barbuda	St. John's	32
Argentina	Buenos Aires	12,550
Aruba	Oranjestad	30
Bahamas	Nassau	233
Barbados	Bridgetown	142
Belize	Belmopan	14
Bolivia	La Paz[12]	1,527
Bolivia	Sucre[12]	227
Brazil	Brasília	3,341
British Virgin Islands	Road Town	13
Cayman Islands	George Town	26
Chile	Santiago	5,683
Colombia	Santa Fé de Bogotá	7,747
Costa Rica	San José	1,217
Cuba	La Habana (Havana)	2,189
Dominica	Roseau	14
Dominican Republic	Santo Domingo	2,022
Ecuador	Quito	1,514
El Salvador	San Salvador	1,517
Falkland Islands (Malvinas)	Stanley	2
French Guiana	Cayenne	59
Grenada	St.George's	32
Guadeloupe	Pointe-à-Pitre	19
Guatemala	Ciudad de Guatemala (Guatemala City)	984
Guyana	Georgetown	134
Haiti	Port-au-Prince	2,129
Honduras	Tegucigalpa	927
Jamaica	Kingston	576
Martinique	Fort-de-France	91
Mexico	Ciudad de México (Mexico City)	19,411
Montserrat	Brades Estate[13]	1
Montserrat	Plymouth[13]	0
Netherlands Antilles	Willemstad	125
Nicaragua	Managua	1,165
Panama	Ciudad de Panamá (Panama City)	1,216
Paraguay	Asunción	1,858
Peru	Lima	7,186
Puerto Rico	San Juan	2,605
Saint Kitts and Nevis	Basseterre	13
Saint Lucia	Castries	13
Saint Vincent and the Grenadines	Kingstown	41
Suriname	Paramaribo	268
Trinidad and Tobago	Port of Spain	52
Turks and Caicos Islands	Grand Turk	4
United States Virgin Islands	Charlotte Amalie	52
Uruguay	Montevideo	1,264
Venezuela	Caracas	2,913

TABLE C.2

continued

NORTHERN AMERICA		(000)			(000)			(000)
Bermuda	Hamilton	1	Greenland	Nuuk (Godthåb)	15	United States of America	Washington, D.C.	4,238
Canada	Ottawa-Gatineau[14]	1,156	Saint-Pierre-et-Miquelon	Saint-Pierre	5			
OCEANIA		**(000)**			**(000)**			**(000)**
American Samoa	Pago Pago	55	Nauru	Nauru	14	Solomon Islands	Honiara	1,320
Australia	Canberra	381	New Caledonia	Nouméa	149	Tokelau[18]		
Cook Islands	Rarotonga[15]	13	New Zealand	Wellington	346	Tonga	Nuku'alofa	25
Fiji	Greater Suva	219	Niue	Alofi	1	Tuvalu	Funafuti	5
French Polynesia	Papeete	130	Northern Mariana Islands	Saipan[17]	75	Vanuatu	Port Vila	36
Guam	Hagåtña	144	Palau	Koror	14	Wallis and Futuna Islands	Matu-Utu	1
Kiribati	Tarawa[16]	47	Papua New Guinea	Port Moresby	289			
Marshall Islands	Majuro	27	Pitcairn	Adamstown	0			
Micronesia (Fed. States of)	Palikir	7	Samoa	Apia	4			

Sources: United Nations, Department of Economic and Social Affairs, Population Division, 2006

Notes:

Table presents data on population of capital cities of countries as well as areas that are included in the World Urbanization Prospects.

(1) Porto-Novo is the constitutional capital; Cotonou is the seat of government.

(2) Yamoussoukro is the capital, Abidjan is the seat of government.

(3) Pretoria is the administrative capital, Cape Town is the legislative capital and Bloemfontein is the judicial capital.

(4) Mbabane is the administrative capital, Lobamba is the legislative capital.

(5) As of 1 July 1997, Hong Kong became a Special Administrative Region (SAR) of China.

(6) As of 20 December 1999, Macao became a Special Administrative Region (SAR) of China.

(7) The capital is New Delhi, included in the urban agglomeration of Delhi. The population of New Delhi was estimated at 294,783 in the year 2001.

(8) Kuala Lumpur is the financial capital, Putrajaya is the administrative capital.

(9) Colombo is the commercial capital, Sri Jayewardenepura Kotte is the administrative and legislative capital.

(10) Amsterdam is the capital, The Hague is the seat of government.

(11) The former Yugoslav Republic of Macedonia.

(12) La Paz is the capital and the seat of government; Sucre is the legal capital and the seat of the judiciary.

(13) Due to volcanic activity, Plymouth was abandoned in 1997. The government premises have been established at Brades Estate.

(14) The capital is Ottawa.

(15) The capital is Avarua, located on the island of Rarotonga; the estimated population refers to the island of Rarotonga. Population estimates for Avarua have not been made available.

(16) The capital is Bairiki, located on the island of Tarawa; the estimated population refers to the island of South Tarawa. Population estimates for Bairiki have not been made available.

(17) The capital is Garapan, located on the island of Saipan; the estimated population refers to the island of Saipan. The population of Garapan was estimated at 3,588 in the year 2000. Government offices are located in Capitol Hill.

(18) There is no capital in Tokelau. Each atoll (Atafu, Fakaofo and Nukunonu) has its own administrative centre.

TABLE C.3

Household Living Conditions in Selected Cities

			Persons per room in housing unit									Distribution of household size by housings units								Total number*
			1	2	3	4	5	6	7	8+	Average	1 (%)	2 (%)	3 (%)	4 (%)	5 (%)	6 (%)	7 (%)	8+ (%)	
AFRICA																				
Egypt[1]	Alexandria	1996	3.5	2.0	1.4	1.1	0.9	...	...	...	1.3	5.7	12.4	38.5	31.4	12.0	...	...	...	3,321,844
Egypt[1]	Cairo	1996	3.5	2.0	1.4	1.0	0.8	...	...	...	1.2	7.0	11.5	37.3	33.4	10.8	...	...	...	6,735,172
Egypt[1]	Giza	1996	3.6	2.1	1.4	1.0	0.8	...	...	...	1.2	4.7	9.0	39.5	37.1	9.7	...	...	...	2,203,688
Egypt[1]	Shubra El-Kheima	1996	3.7	2.2	1.5	1.1	1.0	...	...	...	1.4	5.6	10.1	44.8	35.0	4.5	...	...	...	869,853
ASIA																				
Azerbaijan	Baku	1998	2.1	1.6	1.5	1.5	...	...	...	...	1.6	9.5	36.5	41.2	12.8	...	...	...	...	1,721,372
Azerbaijan	Giandja	1998	3.0	2.1	1.9	1.8	...	...	...	...	2.1	18.9	35.4	30.5	15.2	...	...	...	...	279,043
Azerbaijan[2]	Mingecheviz	1998	2.1	1.7	1.6	1.9	...	...	...	...	1.7	6.5	30.2	37.2	26.1	...	...	...	...	86,294
Azerbaijan	Sumgait	1998	2.7	2.1	1.7	1.6	...	...	...	...	2.0	15.1	39.1	40.8	5.0	...	...	...	...	320,731
Cyprus[3]	Larnaka	1992	1.3	0.7	0.6	0.7	0.7	0.6	0.6	0.5	0.6	0.2	1.6	3.2	17.1	30.8	31.5	10.4	4.9	59,832
Cyprus[3]	Limassol	1992	1.3	0.8	0.7	0.7	0.7	0.6	0.5	0.5	0.6	0.2	1.4	5.2	14.5	29.9	36.6	7.9	4.2	135,469
Cyprus[3]	Nicosia	1992	1.2	0.7	0.6	0.6	0.6	0.6	0.5	0.5	0.6	0.1	1.2	3.1	11.9	25.9	34.5	16.3	6.9	175,310
Cyprus[3]	Patos	1992	1.3	0.8	0.7	0.7	0.7	0.6	0.5	0.5	0.7	0.4	2.4	5.5	14.2	26.6	35.0	11.1	4.7	32,251
Pakistan[4]	Islamabad	1998	4.4	3.0	2.1	1.7	1.3	1.2	...	...	2.0	11.7	28.6	25.4	13.9	7.5	12.7	...	...	524,359
Syrian Arab Republic[3]	Aleppo	1994	4.6	3.0	2.2	1.7	1.4	1.2	1.1	1.4	2.1	5.5	25.1	32.7	20.5	9.2	4.2	1.3	1.3	2,959,053
Syrian Arab Republic[3]	Damascus	1994	4.0	2.5	1.9	1.5	1.3	1.2	1.2	1.6	1.7	3.8	16.4	27.2	24.2	14.5	6.8	2.4	3.9	1,384,017
Syrian Arab Republic[3]	Homs	1994	4.4	2.9	2.2	1.8	1.5	1.4	1.4	1.5	2.0	3.3	18.7	29.5	26.1	13.1	5.1	1.5	2.3	1,205,785
Syrian Arab Republic[3]	Lattakia	1994	3.9	2.5	1.9	1.5	1.3	1.2	1.1	1.0	1.7	4.9	18.4	31.4	26.4	11.7	4.0	1.2	1.7	741,372
Turkey[3]	Adana	1994	3.5	2.2	1.5	1.1	1.0	0.8	...	0.8	1.4	1.4	12.3	54.0	28.4	3.2	0.2	...	0.2	1,018,248
Turkey[3]	Ankara	1994	5.5	1.8	1.4	1.1	0.9	0.8	...	0.6	1.2	0.4	7.2	35.2	53.0	2.2	0.2	...	1.8	2,669,550
Turkey[3]	Istanbul	1994	4.0	2.0	1.3	1.1	1.0	1.1	...	0.5	1.2	0.6	9.1	45.7	37.1	4.3	1.9	...	1.0	7,362,804
Turkey[3]	Izmir	1994	3.6	1.9	1.3	0.9	0.8	0.8	...	1.0	1.1	0.7	11.2	41.6	39.7	2.2	0.7	...	1.3	1,902,831
EUROPE																				
Finland[5]	Espoo	1998	1.2	0.8	0.9	0.8	0.7	0.6	0.5	...	0.8	5.3	19.2	28.4	26.8	13.5	4.1	1.8	...	201,335
Finland[5]	Helsinki	1998	1.2	0.8	0.8	0.7	0.6	0.5	0.4	...	0.8	14.5	30.2	27.6	17.9	6.7	1.8	0.7	...	523,443
Finland[5]	Tampere	1998	1.2	0.8	0.8	0.7	0.6	0.6	0.5	...	0.8	10.9	29.5	27.9	20.2	7.6	2.2	0.8	...	185,796
Finland[5]	Turku	1998	1.2	0.8	0.7	0.7	0.6	0.5	0.4	...	0.8	12.3	29.4	25.8	18.3	6.5	1.9	0.9	...	165,042
Netherlands	Amsterdam	1998	1.0	0.6	0.5	0.6	0.6	0.5	0.3	0.4	0.6	4.0	16.2	35.0	29.7	9.3	3.6	1.2	0.9	706,100
Netherlands	Rotterdam	1998	1.1	0.6	0.5	0.6	0.6	0.6	0.5	0.3	0.6	1.8	9.4	31.7	32.9	16.7	4.5	1.8	1.3	555,600
Netherlands	The Hague	1998	1.0	0.6	0.6	0.6	0.6	0.5	0.4	0.4	0.6	1.9	10.7	26.5	33.8	15.1	5.8	2.6	3.5	437,200
Netherlands	Utrecht	1998	1.1	0.6	0.5	0.6	0.5	0.4	0.3	0.3	0.5	6.1	9.0	22.6	33.7	19.8	5.6	2.0	1.1	218,700
Poland[6]	Krakow	1995	...	1.1	1.0	0.9	0.8	...	...	...	0.9	...	18.1	32.6	36.2	13.1	...	...	...	719,520
Poland[6]	Lodz	1995	...	1.0	0.8	0.8	0.8	...	...	...	0.8	...	24.9	42.6	24.2	8.3	...	...	...	811,652
Poland[6]	Warsaw	1995	...	1.0	0.9	0.8	0.8	...	...	...	0.9	...	19.1	33.7	35.5	11.7	...	...	...	1,635,557
Poland[6]	Wroclaw	1995	...	1.1	0.9	0.8	0.8	...	...	...	0.9	...	16.4	28.7	31.4	23.5	...	...	...	618,469
United Kingdom[2]	London	1996	1.1	0.6	0.5	0.5	0.5	0.5	0.5	0.4	0.5	0.6	2.5	9.5	20.1	26.3	20.6	9.3	11.0	7,050,000
LATIN AMERICA AND CARIBBEAN																				
Brazil[2]	Belo Horizonte	1998	2.3	1.5	1.1	0.9	0.8	0.7	0.6	0.5	0.7	0.6	2.6	7.2	14.0	19.2	17.2	14.3	24.9	3,978,856
Brazil[2]	Brasília	1998	2.2	1.5	1.1	0.8	0.8	0.7	0.6	0.5	0.7	1.4	4.5	6.7	12.4	20.5	17.8	12.5	24.3	1,927,737
Brazil[2]	Rio de Janeiro	1998	2.3	1.2	1.0	0.7	0.7	0.6	0.5	0.4	0.6	0.7	2.0	6.7	18.5	36.2	17.5	7.9	10.4	10,382,082
Brazil[2]	São Paulo	1998	2.8	1.6	1.1	0.9	0.8	0.6	0.6	0.5	0.7	0.6	4.3	14.5	18.9	24.4	14.3	7.8	15.1	17,119,420
Colombia[7]	Barranquilla	1993	3.6	2.2	1.6	1.3	1.1	1.0	...	...	1.3	7.6	14.7	18.8	22.0	18.0	19.0	...	...	988,657
Colombia[7]	Bogotá	1993	3.0	1.9	1.3	1.0	0.9	0.8	...	...	1.2	13.6	20.8	17.2	20.2	12.8	15.3	...	...	4,934,591
Colombia[7]	Cali	1993	3.0	1.9	1.4	1.1	0.9	0.8	...	...	1.2	11.3	15.4	16.7	21.3	17.3	17.9	...	...	1,666,378
Colombia[7]	Medellín	1993	3.2	1.9	1.3	1.0	0.9	0.8	...	...	1.1	6.9	13.1	16.7	20.2	18.4	24.7	...	...	1,621,489
Nicaragua	Jinotepe	1995	4.8	2.6	2.0	1.5	1.3	1.1	0.8	0.9	1.8	10.3	28.2	26.1	16.6	9.4	5.1	2.3	2.0	25,034
Nicaragua	Leon	1995	5.0	2.7	2.0	1.6	1.4	1.1	1.1	0.9	2.3	26.1	30.1	22.4	12.0	5.2	2.4	0.9	1.0	123,687
Nicaragua	Managua	1995	4.6	2.6	1.9	1.5	1.3	1.1	1.0	0.9	2.2	25.5	28.2	23.2	13.4	5.8	2.4	0.8	0.6	862,240
Nicaragua	Matagalpa	1995	4.8	2.6	1.9	1.6	1.3	1.1	1.0	0.9	2.0	17.6	28.8	25.2	15.6	6.7	3.1	1.6	1.4	59,349
Saint Lucia[8]	Castries	1999	...	...	...	...	...	...	...	...	...	6.9	23.7	25.0	22.3	13.0	5.5	3.7	...	13,179
Saint Lucia[8]	Gros Islet	1999	...	...	...	...	...	...	...	...	...	4.5	22.0	24.7	24.4	14.4	5.6	4.5	...	3,656
Saint Lucia[8]	Soufriere	1999	...	...	...	...	...	...	...	...	...	6.6	20.5	20.2	24.7	19.0	6.1	2.9	...	1,905
Saint Lucia[8]	Vieux-Fort	1999	...	...	...	...	...	...	...	...	...	7.2	21.1	26.6	24.6	12.1	5.0	3.4	...	3,097
Uruguay	Montevideo	1996	2.7	1.4	1.0	0.9	0.8	0.7	0.6	0.7	1.0	7.3	17.6	32.7	23.0	10.7	4.5	1.9	2.2	1,282,277
Uruguay	Paysandu	1996	3.1	1.6	1.2	0.9	0.8	0.7	0.6	0.6	1.1	9.3	15.6	30.1	24.7	12.8	4.5	1.6	1.4	73,737
Uruguay	Rivera	1996	2.8	1.5	1.1	0.9	0.8	0.7	0.6	0.5	1.0	7.7	15.7	30.9	25.7	12.0	4.8	1.8	1.4	62,391
Uruguay	Salto	1996	3.5	1.9	1.2	1.0	0.9	0.7	0.6	0.6	1.2	8.0	14.2	30.9	27.6	11.8	4.1	1.9	1.5	92,030
NORTHERN AMERICA																				
Canada	Calgary	1996	1.2	0.7	0.5	0.5	0.5	0.4	0.4	0.4	0.4	0.4	1.2	4.2	8.2	13.7	14.8	15.1	42.5	813,925
Canada	Montreal	1996	1.1	0.6	0.5	0.5	0.5	0.5	0.4	0.4	0.5	0.6	1.5	5.3	14.6	22.6	18.6	13.5	23.3	3,272,810
Canada	Ottawa	1996	1.2	0.7	0.5	0.5	0.5	0.5	0.4	0.4	0.4	0.5	1.4	5.3	9.6	13.8	16.8	16.9	35.7	994,110
Canada	Toronto	1996	1.3	0.9	0.6	0.6	0.5	0.5	0.5	0.5	0.5	1.0	2.7	7.7	11.2	13.1	14.8	13.9	35.6	4,218,470

Source: UNSO and UNCHS (Habitat), 2001

Notes

* Data for 'Total number' refer to the number of persons resident in housing units.

1 Data for the category 5 rooms refer to housing units with 5+ rooms.

2 Data as reported; the total differs from the sum of categories.

3 The total differs form the sum of categories and that difference refers to the category not stated.

4 Data for total occupied housing units and total number of occupants are provisional and are estimated based on advanced sample tabulation of census data. Data for the category 6 rooms refer to housing units with 6+ rooms.

5 Data as reported; the total differs from the sum of categories. The category 7 rooms refer to 7+ rooms.

6 Data for the category 2 rooms also include housing units with one room. Data for category 5 rooms refer to to housing units with 5+ rooms.

7 Data for the category 6 rooms refer to housing units with 6+ rooms.

8 Estimated data. The category 7 rooms refer to housing units with 7+ rooms.

TABLE C.4

Housing Indicators in Selected Cities (1998)

		Housing rights					Housing price to income* (ratio)	Rent to income** (ratio)	Access to water*** (%)	Household connection**** (%)			
		Legal provisions+		Impediments to women++ x = none o = some + = considerable									
		A	B	A	B	C				A	B	C	D
AFRICA													
Algeria	Algiers	Yes	Yes	x	x	x	...	...	...	...	...	...	...
Benin	Cotonou	Yes	No	o	o	x	...	...	70.0	45.0	13.0	50.0	18.6
Benin	Parakou	Yes	No	o	o	x	2.9	36.3	90.0	20.0	3.4	45.3	...
Benin	Porto-Novo	Yes	No	o	o	x	2.9	...	85.0	35.0	...	60.0	6.4
Botswana	Gaborone	No	No	o	o	o	...	...	100.0	...	...	...	...
Burkina Faso	Bobo-Dioulasso	Yes	Yes	...	...	...	...	...	72.0	24.0	...	29.3	5.7
Burkina Faso	Koudougou	Yes	Yes	...	...	...	...	...	79.0	30.0	...	25.8	7.4
Burkina Faso	Ouagadougou	Yes	Yes	...	...	...	...	...	77.0	30.0	...	47.1	10.7
Burundi	Bujumbura	Yes	Yes	o	+	o	7.5	...	95.0	25.8	61.7	56.7	18.9
Cameroon	Douala	Yes	Yes	o	+	o	13.4	...	84.4	34.2	1.2	94.9	9.4
Cameroon	Yaounde	Yes	Yes	o	+	o	...	...	84.4	34.2	1.2	94.9	9.4
Central African Republic	Bangui	Yes	No	o	o	+	...	...	30.0	30.6	...	17.8	11.1
Chad	N'Djamena	Yes	Yes	o	x	+	...	21.0	22.0	42.0	...	13.3	6.0
Congo	Brazzaville	Yes	No	+	+	o	...	...	96.6	55.5	0.1	52.3	18.4
Congo	Pointe-Noire	Yes	No	o	o	+	...	...	74.3	66.5	3.1	43.6	12.0
Côte d'Ivoire	Abidjan	Yes	Yes	x	x	o	18.0	9.9	92.1	26.3	14.6	40.7	5.0
Côte d'Ivoire	Yamoussoukro	Yes	Yes	+	+	x	...	...	79.0	7.9	5.7	10.5	6.6
Dem. Rep. of Congo	Kinshasa	Yes	Yes	x	o	o	...	...	72.3	72.3	...	66.2	1.2
Egypt	Ismailia	Yes	Yes	x	x	x	5.4	21.0	99.6	99.6	95.5	99.8	80.0
Egypt	Tanta	Yes	Yes	x	x	x	23.1	25.3	...	...	...	...	...
Ethiopia	Addis Ababa	Yes	Yes	x	x	x	...	...	...	32.3	0.0	49.4	15.7
Gabon	Libreville	Yes	Yes	o	o	o	...	...	60.0	55.0	...	95.0	45.0
Gabon	Port-Gentil	Yes	No	+	+	+	...	...	...	48.0	...	...	...
Gambia	Banjul	Yes	No	x	x	x	11.4	12.4	79.0	22.5	12.4	24.0	...
Ghana	Accra	Yes	No	x	x	x	14.0	21.1	...	...	...	...	...
Ghana	Kumasi	Yes	No	x	x	x	11.6	20.8	65.0	65.0	...	95.0	51.0
Guinea	Conakry	Yes	Yes	x	o	x	...	...	79.5	29.7	32.3	53.8	5.6
Kenya	Kisumu	Yes	Yes	o	o	x	8.5	...	93.3	38.0	31.0	49.0	...
Kenya	Mombasa	Yes	Yes	o	o	x	...	...	100.0	...	...	...	...
Kenya	Nairobi	Yes	Yes	o	o	x	...	...	...	...	...	...	...
Lesotho	Maseru	Yes	No	+	x	o	...	...	70.0	41.0	10.0	13.0	10.0
Liberia	Monrovia	Yes	Yes	x	x	x	28.0	...	46.0	..	..	..	..
Libyan Arab Jamahiriya	Tripoli	Yes	Yes	x	x	x	0.8	...	97.0	97.0	89.9	99.0	6.3
Madagascar	Antananarivo	Yes	Yes	x	x	x	13.9	30.0	89.0	38.5	27.5	73.0	14.5
Malawi	Lilongwe	Yes	Yes	x	o	..	...	...	60.0	65.0	12.0	50.0	10.0
Mali	Bamako	Yes	Yes	o	o	x	...	...	82.3	38.4	1.5	61.2	3.0
Mauritania	Nouakchott	Yes	No	x	x	x	5.4	...	16.0	...	...	...	...
Morocco	Casablanca	Yes	Yes	o	o	o	...	...	95.0	83.0	93.0	91.0	...
Morocco	Rabat	Yes	Yes	o	o	o	...	...	95.9	92.8	97.2	52.0	...
Mozambique	Maputo	Yes	Yes	+	x	x	20.0	...	49.6	21.8	25.6	37.8	13.6
Namibia	Windhoek	Yes	Yes	o	o	x	...	...	97.0	97.0	90.0	...	...
Niger	Maradi	Yes	Yes	o	x	+	...	...	...	14.6	...	14.1	...
Niger	Niamey	Yes	Yes	o	x	+	...	...	...	33.2	...	51.0	3.7
Nigeria	Ibadan	...	...	x	x	x	...	...	25.7	25.7	12.1	41.4	...
Nigeria	Lagos	...	...	x	x	x	...	...	25.7	...	...	41.4	...
Rwanda	Kigali	Yes	Yes	x	+	x	11.4	...	79.0	36.0	20.0	57.0	6.0
Senegal	Bignona	Yes	No	o	x	o	2.5	5.8	38.9	17.6	..	25.3	8.0
Senegal	Dakar	Yes	Yes	x	x	x	3.5	14.6	91.4	77.0	43.1	89.3	40.8
Senegal	Thies	Yes	No	o	x	o	2.9	17.3	64.1	57.2	1.2	74.2	12.8
South Africa	Durban	Yes	Yes	...	...	...	...	...	...	...	...	...	...
South Africa	East Rand	Yes	Yes	o	o	...	...	...	20.0	40.0	43.0	38.0	...
South Africa	Port Elizabeth	Yes	Yes	...	...	...	10.6	...	100.0	74.0	73.0	...	...
Togo	Lome	Yes	Yes	x	x	x	...	8.3	80.0	...	70.0	51.0	18.0
Togo	Sokode	Yes	Yes	x	x	x	1.4	7.1	70.0	6.0	45.0	31.0	10.0
Tunisia	Tunis	Yes	Yes	x	x	x	5.0	20.3	97.4	75.2	47.2	94.6	26.8
Uganda	Entebbe	Yes	Yes	o	+	o	10.4	...	56.0	48.0	13.0	42.0	...
Uganda	Jinja	Yes	Yes	o	+	o	15.4	6.0	78.0	65.0	43.0	55.0	5.0
Zimbabwe	Bulawayo	Yes	Yes	x	x	x	...	...	100.0	100.0	100.0	98.0	...
Zimbabwe	Chegutu	Yes	No	x	x	x	3.4	...	...	100.0	68.0	9.0	3.0
Zimbabwe	Gweru	Yes	No	x	o	x	...	...	100.0	100.0	100.0	90.0	60.9
Zimbabwe	Harare	Yes	Yes	o	o	x	...	...	100.0	100.0	100.0	88.0	42.0
Zimbabwe	Mutare	Yes	No	x	x	x	...	...	100.0	88.0	88.0	74.0	4.0
ASIA													
Armenia	Yerevan	No	No	...	...	...	4.0	6.6	97.9	97.9	98.0	100.0	88.1
Bangladesh	Chittagong	Yes	Yes	x	x	x	8.1	9.2	100.0	44.0	...	95.0	...
Bangladesh	Dhaka	Yes	Yes	x	x	x	16.7	...	99.1	60.0	22.0	90.0	7.0
Bangladesh	Sylhet	Yes	Yes	x	x	x	6.0	...	100.0	28.8	...	93.0	39.6
Bangladesh	Tangail	Yes	Yes	x	x	x	13.9	4.6	100.0	11.6	...	90.0	11.5
Cambodia	Phnom Penh	Yes	No	o	o	o	8.9	...	85.4	44.7	74.9	75.5	40.0
Georgia	Tbilisi	...	...	x	x	x	9.4	...	91.9	...	98.0	100.0	57.9
India	Alwar	Yes	Yes	...	...	...	...	...	...	...	...	...	...
India	Bangalore	Yes	Yes	x	x	x	13.8	...	82.9	22.5	20.8	98.3	44.5
India	Chennai	Yes	Yes	x	x	x	7.7	14.6	94.0	51.3	55.5	...	60.4
India	Delhi	Yes	Yes	+	+	+	...	...	78.6	58.5	55.0	82.2	0.0
India	Mysore	Yes	Yes	x	x	x	4.7	26.1	92.5	44.4	68.0	82.8	33.6

TABLE C.4

continued

		Housing rights					Housing price to income* (ratio)	Rent to income** (ratio)	Access to water*** (%)	Household connection**** (%)			
		Legal provisions+		Impediments to women++ x = none o = some + = considerable									
		A	B	A	B	C				A	B	C	D
Indonesia	Bandung	Yes	Yes	x	x	x	7.6	...	90.0	...	55.0	99.0	...
Indonesia	Jakarta	Yes	Yes	x	x	x	14.6	...	91.4	50.3	64.8	99.0	...
Indonesia	Semarang	Yes	Yes	x	x	x	...	...	89.7	34.0	...	85.2	...
Indonesia	Surabaya	Yes	Yes	x	x	x	3.4	19.0	94.3	40.9	55.8	89.2	70.8
Iraq	Baghdad	No	No	x	x	x	...	...	...	...	...	...	...
Japan	Tokyo	Yes	Yes	x	x	x	5.6	2.5	100.0	100.0	100.0	100.0	99.2
Jordan	Amman	Yes	Yes	x	x	x	6.1	16.7	98.0	97.7	81.3	98.5	62.0
Kazakhstan	Astana	Yes	No	x	x	x	8.6	9.9	94.3	84.1	83.9	100.0	58.3
Kuwait	Kuwait	Yes	Yes	x	x	x	6.5	27.8	100.0	100.0	98.0	100.0	98.0
Kyrgyzstan	Bishkek	Yes	Yes	x	x	x	...	...	75.0	29.7	23.3	99.9	19.8
Lao PDR	Vientiane	Yes	Yes	x	x	x	23.2	10.0	95.0	87.0	...	100.0	86.8
Lebanon	Sin El Fil	Yes	Yes	x	x	x	8.3	28.6	80.0	80.0	30.0	98.0	80.0
Malaysia	Penang	Yes	Yes	x	x	x	7.2	4.9	99.9	99.1	...	100.0	98.0
Mongolia	Ulaanbaatar	Yes	Yes	x	x	x	7.8	...	90.3	60.0	60.0	100.0	90.0
Myanmar	Yangon	No	No	x	x	x	8.3	15.4	95.0	77.8	81.2	85.0	17.3
Nepal	Butwal	Yes	No	x	x	x	10.3	...	80.0	33.7	...	80.0	10.0
Nepal	Pokhara	Yes	No	x	x	x	21.6	34.0	80.0	41.4	...	75.0	11.3
Occupied Palestine Territory	Gaza	Yes	Yes	+	+	o	5.4	...	...	85.4	37.9	99.0	37.7
Oman	Muscat	Yes	Yes	x	x	x	...	...	80.0	80.0	90.0	89.0	53.0
Pakistan	Karachi	No	No	+	+	+	13.7	...	89.5	82.4	85.0	98.4	...
Pakistan	Lahore	No	No	+	+	+	7.1	23.3	100.0	96.4	78.0	97.1	70.0
Philippines	Cebu	Yes	Yes	x	x	x	13.3	...	98.2	41.4	92.3	80.0	25.0
Qatar	Doha	No	No	x	x	x	...	...	...	...	...	...	...
Republic of Korea	Hanam	Yes	Yes	o	o	o	3.7	13.9	81.1	81.1	67.9	100.0	100.0
Republic of Korea	Pusan	Yes	Yes	o	o	o	4.0	...	99.9	97.9	69.4	100.0	100.0
Republic of Korea	Seoul	Yes	Yes	o	o	o	5.7	...	99.9	99.9	98.6	100.0	...
Singapore	Singapore	Yes	No	x	x	x	3.1	2.0	100.0	100.0	100.0	100.0	100.0
Sri Lanka	Colombo	Yes	Yes	o	x	x	...	...	...	22.9	76.0	96.0	26.0
Syrian Arab Rep.	Damascus	Yes	Yes	x	x	x	10.3	...	98.4	98.4	71.0	95.0	9.9
Thailand	Bangkok	Yes	No	x	x	x	8.8	22.2	...	99.0	100.0	99.8	59.7
Thailand	Chiang Mai	Yes	No	o	o	o	6.8	25.0	99.0	95.0	60.0	100.0	75.0
Turkey	Ankara	Yes	Yes	x	x	x	4.5	24.0	97.0	97.0	98.5	100.0	...
Vietnam	Hanoi	Yes	Yes	x	x	x	...	...	100.0	70.0	50.0	100.0	60.0
Vietnam	Ho Chi Minh	Yes	Yes	x	x	x	...	...	90.0	59.0	30.0	99.7	21.2
Yemen	Sana'a	Yes	Yes	x	x	x	...	...	30.4	30.4	9.4	96.0	...
EUROPE													
Albania	Tirana	Yes	Yes	x	x	x	...	...	62.6	62.6	...	99.5	12.6
Belarus	Minsk	Yes	Yes	x	x	x	...	...	...	99.3	98.4	100.0	87.2
Bosnia and Herzegovina	Sarajevo	No	No	x	x	x	...	...	95.0	95.0	90.0	100.0	...
Bulgaria	Bourgas	Yes	Yes	x	x	x	5.1	3.9	100.0	100.0	93.0	100.0	144.4
Bulgaria	Sofia	Yes	Yes	x	x	x	13.2	...	100.0	95.4	90.5	100.0	89.0
Bulgaria	Troyan	Yes	Yes	x	x	x	3.7	2.0	100.0	99.0	82.0	100.0	44.8
Bulgaria	Veliko Tarnovo	Yes	Yes	x	x	x	5.4	3.3	100.0	98.4	97.6	100.0	96.0
Croatia	Zagreb	Yes	Yes	o	o	o	7.8	...	98.0	97.5	96.9	99.7	94.0
Czech Republic	Brno	Yes	Yes	x	x	x	...	...	99.5	99.5	95.6	100.0	68.5
Czech Republic	Prague	Yes	Yes	x	x	x	...	...	100.0	98.9	99.7	100.0	99.5
Estonia	Riik	Yes	Yes	x	x	x	...	...	91.6	91.6	90.2	98.0	55.0
Estonia	Tallinn	Yes	Yes	x	x	x	6.4	7.0	98.0	98.1	98.1	100.0	85.5
Germany	Berlin	...	...	...	...	...	...	...	100.0	99.9	...	...	...
Germany	Cologne	...	...	...	...	...	4.3	...	100.0	100.0	...	...	...
Germany	Duisburg	...	...	...	...	...	3.2	...	100.0	100.0	...	...	...
Germany	Erfurt	...	...	...	...	...	2.6	...	100.0	100.0	...	...	...
Germany	Freiburg	...	...	...	...	...	...	...	100.0	100.0	...	...	...
Germany	Leipzig	...	...	...	...	...	3.2	...	100.0	100.0	...	...	...
Germany	Wiesbaden	...	...	...	...	...	...	...	100.0	100.0	...	...	...
Hungary	Budapest	Yes	No	x	x	x	3.6	11.8	100.0	98.3	90.7	100.0	84.0
Italy	Aversa	...	...	x	x	x	3.5	...	100.0	...	...	...	...
Latvia	Riga	No	No	x	x	x	4.7	0.9	99.9	95.0	93.0	99.9	90.0
Lithuania	Vilnius	No	Yes	o	x	x	20.0	...	89.4	89.4	89.1	100.0	77.0
Netherlands	Amsterdam	...	...	...	...	...	7.8	17.5	100.0	100.0	100.0	100.0	...
Netherlands	Eindhoven	...	...	x	x	x	5.6	16.5	100.0	100.0	100.0	100.0	...
Netherlands	Meppel	...	...	x	x	x	4.5	15.9	100.0	100.0	100.0	100.0	...
Poland	Bydgoszcz	Yes	Yes	x	x	x	4.3	18.8	94.9	94.6	87.1	100.0	84.9
Poland	Gdansk	Yes	Yes	x	x	x	4.4	7.4	100.0	98.7	94.0	99.6	56.2
Poland	Katowice	Yes	Yes	x	x	x	1.7	5.2	100.0	99.1	94.4	100.0	75.2
Poland	Poznan	Yes	Yes	x	x	x	5.8	18.4	100.0	94.9	96.4	99.9	85.5
Republic of Moldova	Chisinau	Yes	Yes	o	o	+	...	...	100.0	100.0	95.0	100.0	83.0
Russian Federation	Astrakhan	Yes	Yes	x	x	x	5.0	13.8	100.0	81.0	79.0	100.0	51.0
Russian Federation	Belgorod	Yes	Yes	x	x	x	4.0	6.4	100.0	90.0	89.0	100.0	51.0
Russian Federation	Kostroma	Yes	Yes	x	x	x	6.9	12.4	100.0	88.0	84.0	100.0	46.3
Russian Federation	Moscow	Yes	Yes	x	x	x	5.1	5.2	100.0	99.8	99.8	100.0	100.0
Russian Federation	Nizhny Novgorod	Yes	Yes	x	x	x	6.9	7.8	100.0	98.4	98.0	100.0	63.7
Russian Federation	Novomoscowsk	Yes	Yes	x	x	x	4.2	7.1	100.0	99.0	93.0	100.0	62.0
Russian Federation	Omsk	Yes	Yes	x	x	x	3.9	12.8	100.0	87.0	87.0	100.0	41.0
Russian Federation	Pushkin	Yes	Yes	x	x	x	9.6	7.2	100.0	99.0	99.0	100.0	89.0
Russian Federation	Surgut	Yes	Yes	x	x	x	4.5	8.8	100.0	98.4	98.4	100.0	50.1

TABLE C.4

continued

		Housing rights					Housing price to income* (ratio)	Rent to income** (ratio)	Access to water*** (%)	Household connection**** (%)			
		Legal provisions+		Impediments to women++ x = none o = some + = considerable									
		A	B	A	B	C				A	B	C	D
Russian Federation	Veliky Novgorod	Yes	Yes	x	x	x	3.4	11.1	100.0	97.0	96.7	100.0	51.1
Serbia and Montenegro	Belgrade	Yes	Yes	x	x	..	13.5	...	99.0	95.0	86.0	99.6	86.0
Slovenia	Ljubljana	Yes	Yes	x	x	x	7.8	17.3	100.0	100.0	100.0	100.0	97.0
Spain	Madrid	Yes	Yes	x	x	x	...	...	100.0	...	...	...	...
Spain	Pamplona	Yes	Yes	x	x	x	...	...	100.0	100.0	...	100.0	...
Sweden	Amal	Yes	Yes	x	x	x	2.9	...	100.0	100.0	100.0	100.0	...
Sweden	Stockholm	Yes	Yes	x	x	x	6.0	...	100.0	100.0	100.0	100.0	...
Sweden	Umea	Yes	Yes	x	x	x	5.3	...	100.0	100.0	100.0	100.0	...
Switzerland	Basel	Yes	Yes	o	x	x	12.3	19.4	100.0	100.0	100.0	100.0	99.0
United Kingdom	Belfast	...	Yes	o	x	x	3.6	6.9	100.0	100.0	100.0	100.0	...
United Kingdom	Birmingham	...	Yes	x	x	x	3.4	12.5	100.0	100.0	100.0	100.0	...
United Kingdom	Cardiff	...	Yes	o	x	x	3.2	13.2	100.0	100.0	100.0	100.0	...
United Kingdom	Edinburgh	...	Yes	o	x	x	3.5	11.7	100.0	100.0	100.0	100.0	...
United Kingdom	London	...	Yes	o	x	x	4.7	15.6	100.0	100.0	100.0	100.0	...
United Kingdom	Manchester	...	Yes	o	x	x	3.0	12.3	100.0	100.0	100.0	100.0	...
LATIN AMERICA AND THE CARIBBEAN													
Argentina	Buenos Aires	Yes	No	...	...	...	5.1	...	100.0	100.0	98.1	100.0	70.4
Argentina	Comodoro Rivadavia	Yes	No	x	x	x	...	...	99.0	98.0	93.0	99.9	...
Argentina	Córdoba	Yes	No	x	x	x	6.8	5.4	100.0	98.7	40.1	99.3	80.0
Argentina	Rosario	Yes	No	x	x	x	5.7	...	...	97.8	66.8	92.9	75.7
Barbados	Bridgetown	Yes	Yes	x	x	x	4.4	...	100.0	98.0	4.5	99.0	78.0
Belize	Belize City	Yes	No	o	x	o	...	...	...	...	...	...	...
Bolivia	Santa Cruz de la Sierra	Yes	Yes	x	x	x	...	...	47.4	52.6	33.3	97.7	59.1
Brazil	Belém	Yes	Yes	x	x	x	...	...	...	...	...	...	...
Brazil	Icapui	Yes	Yes	x	x	x	4.5	9.6	85.0	88.0	...	90.0	33.0
Brazil	Maranguape	Yes	Yes	x	x	x	...	...	90.0	73.0	...	...	...
Brazil	Porto Alegre	Yes	Yes	x	x	x	...	...	99.0	99.0	87.0	100.0	...
Brazil	Recife	Yes	Yes	x	x	x	12.5	25.9	97.1	89.3	41.0	99.8	29.1
Brazil	Rio de Janeiro	Yes	Yes	x	x	x	...	...	...	87.7	79.8	10.0	...
Brazil	São Paulo	Yes	Yes	x	x	x	...	24.3	98.0	98.0	95.0	99.9	78.9
Chile	Gran Concepcion	Yes	No	x	x	x	...	...	100.0	99.7	90.7	95.0	69.1
Chile	Santiago de Chile	Yes	No	x	x	x	...	...	100.0	100.0	99.2	99.2	72.8
Chile	Tome	Yes	No	x	x	x	...	...	78.4	91.7	51.9	98.0	57.6
Chile	Valparaiso	Yes	No	x	x	o	...	...	98.0	98.0	91.8	97.0	62.5
Chile	Vina del mar	Yes	No	x	x	x	...	...	97.1	97.1	97.0	98.0	64.9
Colombia	Armenia	Yes	Yes	o	x	x	5.0	...	100.0	90.0	50.0	98.7	97.1
Colombia	Marinilla	Yes	Yes	x	x	x	8.5	...	100.0	97.7	92.8	100.0	65.0
Colombia	Medellín	Yes	Yes	x	x	x	...	...	99.9	99.9	98.5	99.5	86.9
Cuba	Baracoa	Yes	Yes	x	x	x	...	...	89.0	83.0	3.0	93.0	32.0
Cuba	Camaguey	Yes	Yes	x	x	x	...	...	72.0	72.0	47.0	97.0	...
Cuba	Cienfuegos	Yes	Yes	x	x	x	4.0	...	100.0	100.0	73.0	100.0	8.7
Cuba	Havana	Yes	Yes	x	x	x	8.5	...	100.0	100.0	85.0	100.0	14.0
Cuba	Pinar Del Rio	Yes	Yes	x	x	x	...	...	...	97.0	48.0	99.6	...
Cuba	Santa Clara	Yes	Yes	x	x	x	...	...	95.0	95.0	42.0	99.7	43.2
Dominican Republic	Santiago de los Caballeros	Yes	Yes	x	x	x	...	...	80.0	75.0	80.0	...	71.0
Ecuador	Ambato	Yes	Yes	x	x	x	...	...	85.0	89.5	80.5	90.6	86.8
Ecuador	Cuenca	Yes	Yes	o	o	o	4.6	...	98.0	96.8	92.2	97.0	48.0
Ecuador	Guayaquil	Yes	Yes	x	x	o	3.4	16.1	77.0	70.0	42.0	99.0	44.0
Ecuador	Manta	Yes	Yes	o	o	o	...	28.0	70.0	70.0	52.0	98.0	40.0
Ecuador	Puyo	Yes	Yes	x	x	x	2.1	15.8	89.4	80.0	30.0	90.0	60.0
Ecuador	Quito	Yes	Yes	x	x	x	2.4	13.3	89.4	85.0	70.0	96.2	55.3
Ecuador	Tena	Yes	Yes	x	x	o	1.6	...	80.0	80.0	60.0	...	...
El Salvador	San Salvador	No	No	+	+	+	3.5	37.0	81.5	81.5	79.7	97.7	70.1
Guatemala	Quetzaltenango	Yes	Yes	o	x	o	4.3	...	90.0	60.0	55.0	80.0	40.0
Jamaica	Kingston	No	No	...	...	...	...	...	...	96.6	...	88.1	...
Jamaica	Montego Bay	No	No	...	...	...	...	...	78.0	78.0	...	86.0	...
Mexico	Ciudad Juarez	Yes	Yes	x	x	x	1.4	...	92.0	89.2	77.0	96.0	45.0
Nicaragua	Leon	...	...	...	...	...	...	...	...	78.2	...	83.8	20.6
Panama	Colon	Yes	Yes	x	x	o	14.2	24.5	100.0	...	...	...	...
Paraguay	Asuncion	Yes	No	o	x	x	10.7	...	...	46.2	8.2	86.4	17.0
Peru	Cajamarca	Yes	No	x	x	x	3.9	34.9	86.0	86.0	69.0	81.0	38.0
Peru	Huanuco	Yes	Yes	x	x	x	30.0	24.0	54.0	57.0	28.0	80.0	32.0
Peru	Huaras	Yes	Yes	x	x	+	6.7	...	90.0	...	...	71.0	...
Peru	Iquitos	Yes	Yes	x	x	o	5.6	...	72.5	72.5	60.3	82.3	62.3
Peru	Lima	Yes	Yes	o	x	x	8.7	...	81.1	75.2	71.5	99.0	...
Peru	Tacna	Yes	Yes	...	...	...	4.0	...	87.0	64.6	58.3	73.7	15.8
Peru	Tumbes	Yes	Yes	x	x	x	...	29.0	85.0	60.0	35.0	80.0	25.0
Uruguay	Montevideo	Yes	No	x	x	x	5.6	31.1	99.3	97.6	79.1	99.7	75.1
NORTHERN AMERICA													
Canada	Hull	Yes	Yes	x	x	x	...	18.7	100.0	100.0	100.0	100.0	100.0
United States	Atlanta	Yes	Yes	x	x	x	2.10	29.0	99.8	99.6	100.0	100.0	90.3
United States	Birmingham-USA	Yes	Yes	x	x	x	...	24.0	99.8	99.8	100.0	100.0	...
United States	Boston	Yes	Yes	x	x	x	2.90	31.0	100.0	99.9	100.0	100.0	...
United States	Des Moines	Yes	Yes	x	x	x	...	...	...	...	...	...	...
United States	Hartford	Yes	Yes	x	x	x	2.50	29.0	99.8	100.0	100.0	100.0	90.0
United States	Minneapolis-St. Paul	Yes	Yes	x	x	x	2.10	28.0	100.0	99.8	100.0	100.0	100.0

TABLE C.4

continued

		Housing rights					Housing price to income* (ratio)	Rent to income** (ratio)	Access to water*** (%)	Household connection**** (%)			
		Legal provisions+		Impediments to women++ x = none o = some + = considerable									
		A	B	A	B	C				A	B	C	D
United States	New York	Yes	Yes	x	x	x	2.70	28.0	100.0	100.0	100.0	100.0	96.0
United States	Providence	Yes	Yes	x	x	x	2.50	29.0	100.0	99.9	100.0	100.0	...
United States	Salt Lake	Yes	Yes	x	x	x	2.80	27.0	100.0	100.0	100.0	99.9	...
United States	San Jose	Yes	Yes	x	x	x	...	...	100.0	99.9	100.0	100.0	...
United States	Seattle	Yes	Yes	x	x	x	3.00	28.0	100.0	100.0	100.0	100.0	92.1
United States	Tampa	Yes	Yes	x	x	x	2.10	30.0	100.0	100.0	100.0	100.0	...
United States	Washington	Yes	Yes	x	x	x	2.30	26.0	100.0	100.0	100.0	99.9	...
OCEANIA													
Samoa	Apia	Yes	Yes	x	x	x	10.0	36.0	69.0	60.0	...	98.0	96.0

Source: UN-Habitat (2002), Global Urban Indicators Database 2.

Notes:

\+ Responses (yes/no) to the questions:
(A) Does the Constitution or national law promote the full and progressive realisation of the right to adequate housing?
(B) Does it include protections against eviction?.

++ Responses (none/some/considerable) to the questions:
(A) Are there impediments to women owning land?
(B) Are there impediments to women inheriting land and housing?
(C) Are there impediments to women taking mortgages in their own name?

* Ratio of the median free-market price of a dwelling unit and the median annual household income.

** Per cent ratio of the median annual rent of a dwelling unit and the median annual household income of renters.

*** Percentage of households with access to water within 200 meters.

**** Percentage of households residing in housing units that are connected to:
(A) Piped water
(B) Sewerage
(C) Electricity
(D) Telephone

TABLE C.5

Environmental and Transport Indicators in Selected Cities (1998)

		Local environmental planning*			Transport use for work trip**				Travel time per work trip	Disaster prevention and mitigation measures***		
		A	B	C	Car (%)	Train (%)	Bus (%)	Other (%)	(minutes)	A	B	C
AFRICA												
Algeria	Algiers	Yes	Yes	No	...	...	...	...	...	Yes	Yes	Yes
Benin	Cotonou	Yes	No	No	90.0	–	–	10.0	...	Yes	Yes	Yes
Benin	Parakou	Yes	No	No	80.0	–	–	20.0	45	Yes	Yes	Yes
Benin	Porto-Novo	Yes	No	No	83.0	–	–	17.0	50	Yes	Yes	Yes
Botswana	Gaborone	No	No	No	...	...	...	...	...	No	No	No
Burkina Faso	Bobo-Dioulasso	No	No	No	...	...	...	...	...	No	No	No
Burkina Faso	Koudougou	No	No	No	...	...	...	...	...	No	No	No
Burkina Faso	Ouagadougou	No	Yes	No	63.4	–	2.2	34.4	...	Yes	Yes	No
Burundi	Bujumbura	No	No	Yes	12.4	–	48.2	39.4	25	Yes	No	Yes
Cameroon	Douala	Yes	Yes	Yes	...	...	...	...	40	Yes	No	No
Cameroon	Yaounde	Yes	Yes	Yes	30.0	–	42.3	27.7	45	Yes	No	Yes
Central African Republic	Bangui	Yes	Yes	Yes	3.7	–	66.3	30.0	60	No	No	No
Chad	N'Djamena	No	No	No	17.0	–	35.0	48.0	...	Yes	Yes	Yes
Congo	Brazzaville	No	No	Yes	19.0	–	55.0	26.0	20	Yes	Yes	Yes
Congo	Pointe-Noire	No	No	Yes	8.0	–	55.0	37.0	30	Yes	Yes	Yes
Côte d'Ivoire	Abidjan	Yes	No	No	...	...	...	...	45	Yes	Yes	No
Côte d'Ivoire	Yamoussoukro	Yes	No	No	...	...	...	...	20	Yes	Yes	No
Dem. Rep. of Congo	Kinshasa	Yes	Yes	Yes	13.0	42.0	30.0	15.0	57	Yes	Yes	Yes
Egypt	Ismailia	Yes	Yes	Yes	...	...	...	...	30	No	No	No
Egypt	Tanta	Yes	Yes	No	...	...	...	...	50	No	No	No
Ethiopia	Addis Ababa	No	No	No	4.2	–	12.6	83.3	...	Yes	No	Yes
Gabon	Libreville	No	No	No	–	55.0	25.0	20.0	30	Yes	Yes	Yes
Gabon	Port-Gentil	No	No	No	...	...	...	...	45	Yes	Yes	Yes
Gambia	Banjul	No	No	No	19.5	–	54.9	25.6	22	Yes	Yes	Yes
Ghana	Accra	Yes	Yes	Yes	34.7	4.0	50.0	11.3	21	Yes	Yes	Yes
Ghana	Kumasi	Yes	Yes	Yes	22.2	0.6	50.0	27.2	21	Yes	Yes	Yes
Guinea	Conakry	Yes	No	Yes	22.0	–	25.5	52.5	45	Yes	Yes	Yes
Kenya	Kisumu	Yes	Yes	Yes	21.1	–	43.5	35.5	24	No	No	No
Kenya	Mombasa	Yes	Yes	Yes	2.1	–	47.0	50.9	20	Yes	No	Yes
Kenya	Nairobi	Yes	Yes	Yes	6.0	1.0	70.0	23.0	57	No	No	No
Lesotho	Maseru	Yes	Yes	No	3.0	–	47.0	50.0	15	Yes	Yes	Yes
Liberia	Monrovia	Yes	Yes	Yes	10.0	–	80.0	10.0	60	Yes	No	Yes
Libyan Arab Jamahiriya	Tripoli	Yes	Yes	No	81.0	–	18.0	1.0	20	Yes	Yes	Yes
Madagascar	Antananarivo	Yes	Yes	Yes	7.0	–	60.0	33.0	60	Yes	Yes	Yes
Malawi	Lilongwe	Yes	No	No	6.0	–	27.0	67.0	5	Yes	No	Yes
Mali	Bamako	No	No	No	24.9	–	12.2	62.9	30	Yes	No	Yes
Mauritania	Nouakchott	No	No	No	16.5	–	45.0	38.5	50	Yes	Yes	No
Morocco	Casablanca	Yes	Yes	No	...	...	...	...	30	Yes	Yes	Yes
Morocco	Rabat	Yes	Yes	No	40.0	–	40.0	20.0	20	Yes	Yes	Yes
Mozambique	Maputo	No	No	Yes	6.5	–	80.0	13.5	60	Yes	No	No
Namibia	Windhoek	No	No	Yes	...	...	...	...	20	Yes	No	Yes
Niger	Maradi	Yes	Yes	Yes	...	...	...	...	15	No	No	Yes
Niger	Niamey	Yes	Yes	Yes	...	...	...	...	30	No	No	Yes
Nigeria	Ibadan	Yes	No	Yes	45.0	0.5	45.0	9.5	45	Yes	Yes	Yes
Nigeria	Lagos	Yes	No	Yes	51.0	2.5	45.5	...	60	Yes	Yes	Yes
Rwanda	Kigali	No	Yes	Yes	12.0	–	32.0	56.0	45	Yes	No	No
Senegal	Bignona	Yes	Yes	Yes	1.7	–	–	98.3	10	Yes	Yes	Yes
Senegal	Dakar	Yes	Yes	Yes	8.1	1.3	77.2	13.4	30	No	No	No
Senegal	Thies	Yes	Yes	Yes	18.2	–	59.3	22.6	12	Yes	Yes	Yes
South Africa	Durban	No	No	No	...	...	...	...	...	No	No	No
South Africa	East Rand	Yes	Yes	Yes	...	...	...	...	...	Yes	No	Yes
South Africa	Port Elizabeth	No	No	No	52.4	1.8	45.8	–	35	No	No	No
Togo	Lome	Yes	Yes	No	45.0	–	40.0	15.0	30	Yes	Yes	Yes
Togo	Sokode	Yes	Yes	No	60.0	–	10.0	30.0	15	Yes	Yes	Yes
Tunisia	Tunis	Yes	Yes	Yes	...	...	...	...	...	Yes	No	Yes
Uganda	Entebbe	No	No	No	35.0	–	65.0	–	20	No	No	Yes
Uganda	Jinja	Yes	No	Yes	18.0	–	49.0	33.0	12	Yes	Yes	Yes
Zimbabwe	Bulawayo	Yes	Yes	Yes	22.8	–	74.9	2.3	15	Yes	Yes	Yes
Zimbabwe	Chegutu	No	No	No	19.0	–	20.0	61.0	22	Yes	No	Yes
Zimbabwe	Gweru	Yes	No	Yes	...	...	...	...	15	Yes	No	Yes
Zimbabwe	Harare	No	No	No	18.0	–	32.0	50.0	45	Yes	Yes	Yes
Zimbabwe	Mutare	Yes	No	No	12.0	–	70.0	18.0	20	Yes	No	Yes
ASIA												
Armenia	Yerevan	Yes	Yes	Yes	2.0	11.5	72.5	14.0	30	No	No	No
Bangladesh	Chittagong	Yes	Yes	No	4.0	1.0	25.0	70.0	45	Yes	Yes	Yes
Bangladesh	Dhaka	Yes	Yes	No	4.6	0.0	9.2	86.2	45	Yes	Yes	Yes
Bangladesh	Sylhet	Yes	Yes	No	1.3	–	10.0	88.7	50	Yes	Yes	Yes
Bangladesh	Tangail	Yes	Yes	No	...	...	...	...	30	Yes	Yes	No
Cambodia	Phnom Penh	No	No	No	87.3	–	0.2	12.5	45	Yes	Yes	Yes
Georgia	Tbilisi	Yes	Yes	No	...	...	...	...	...	No	Yes	No
India	Alwar	No	No	No	...	...	...	...	...	No	No	No
India	Bangalore	Yes	Yes	No	39.6	–	35.7	24.7	30	Yes	No	Yes
India	Chennai	Yes	No	No	42.0	11.0	25.0	22.0	23	Yes	No	Yes
India	Delhi	No	No	No	24.6	0.4	62.0	13.0	...	No	No	No
India	Mysore	Yes	No	No	39.1	–	0.1	60.8	20	No	No	No
Indonesia	Bandung	No	Yes	Yes	82.0	...	...	...	30	Yes	No	No
Indonesia	Jakarta	No	Yes	Yes	...	...	...	...	...	Yes	No	Yes
Indonesia	Semarang	No	Yes	Yes	...	...	...	...	...	Yes	No	Yes

TABLE C.5

continued

		Local environmental planning*			Transport use for work trip**				Travel time per work trip	Disaster prevention and mitigation measures***		
		A	B	C	Car (%)	Train (%)	Bus (%)	Other (%)	(minutes)	A	B	C
Indonesia	Surabaya	Yes	No	No	80.0	–	17.8	2.2	35	Yes	No	Yes
Iraq	Baghdad	No	No	No	...	...	...	...	...	No	No	No
Japan	Tokyo	Yes	Yes	Yes	...	...	...	...	45	Yes	Yes	Yes
Jordan	Amman	Yes	No	Yes	51.0	–	21.0	28.0	25	No	No	No
Kazakhstan	Astana	Yes	Yes	Yes	30.0	28.0	34.0	8.0	27	No	No	No
Kuwait	Kuwait	Yes	Yes	Yes	68.0	–	21.0	11.0	10	Yes	Yes	Yes
Kyrgyzstan	Bishkek	Yes	Yes	Yes	5.0	35.4	59.6	0.0	35	Yes	Yes	Yes
Lao PDR	Vientiane	Yes	Yes	No	41.8	–	2.1	56.1	27	Yes	Yes	Yes
Lebanon	Sin El Fil	No	Yes	No	25.0	–	50.0	25.0	10	No	No	Yes
Malaysia	Penang	Yes	No	Yes	42.0	–	55.0	3.0	40	Yes	Yes	Yes
Mongolia	Ulaanbaatar	Yes	Yes	Yes	10.0	21.0	59.0	10.0	30	Yes	Yes	Yes
Myanmar	Yangon	No	No	Yes	16.7	3.7	65.0	14.7	45	Yes	Yes	Yes
Nepal	Butwal	No	Yes	No	10.0	–	15.0	75.0	15	Yes	Yes	No
Nepal	Pokhara	Yes	Yes	No	11.0	–	14.0	75.0	20	Yes	No	Yes
Occupied Palestinian Territory	Gaza	Yes	No	No	...	...	...	...	...	No	No	No
Oman	Muscat	Yes	Yes	Yes	...	...	...	...	20	Yes	Yes	Yes
Pakistan	Karachi	Yes	No	No	16.5	–	41.0	39.5	...	No	No	No
Pakistan	Lahore	Yes	No	No	...	...	...	...	...	No	No	No
Philippines	Cebu	Yes	No	Yes	...	...	...	...	35	Yes	Yes	Yes
Qatar	Doha	No	No	No	...	...	...	...	...	No	No	No
Republic of Korea	Hanam	Yes	Yes	Yes	...	...	...	...	...	Yes	Yes	Yes
Republic of Korea	Pusan	Yes	Yes	No	37.1	6.6	32.5	23.8	42	Yes	Yes	Yes
Republic of Korea	Seoul	No	Yes	Yes	20.1	32.3	38.8	8.8	60	Yes	Yes	Yes
Singapore	Singapore	No	Yes	Yes	25.1	14.5	38.7	21.7	30	Yes	Yes	Yes
Sri Lanka	Colombo	Yes	No	Yes	23.7	8.1	65.0	3.2	25	Yes	Yes	Yes
Syrian Arab Rep.	Damascus	Yes	Yes	Yes	15.0	–	32.6	52.4	40	No	No	No
Thailand	Bangkok	No	Yes	No	58.7	1.0	27.0	13.3	60	Yes	Yes	Yes
Thailand	Chiang Mai	Yes	No	No	94.1	–	5.0	0.9	30	No	Yes	No
Turkey	Ankara	Yes	Yes	No	20.0	6.3	...	15.9	32	No	Yes	No
Viet Nam	Hanoi	No	No	No	64.4	–	2.0	33.6	30	Yes	Yes	Yes
Viet Nam	Ho Chi Minh	No	No	No	74.0	–	2.0	24.0	25	Yes	Yes	Yes
Yemen	Sana'a	Yes	Yes	No	20.0	–	78.0	2.0	20	No	No	No
EUROPE												
Albania	Tirana	No	No	Yes	...	...	...	...	25	No	No	No
Belarus	Minsk	No	No	No	...	...	...	...	...	No	No	Yes
Bosnia and Herzegovina	Sarajevo	Yes	Yes	Yes	...	57.0	43.0		12	Yes	No	No
Bulgaria	Bourgas	Yes	Yes	Yes	6.0	0.1	61.0	33.0	32	Yes	Yes	Yes
Bulgaria	Sofia	Yes	Yes	Yes	21.0	26.0	53.0	–	32	Yes	Yes	Yes
Bulgaria	Troyan	Yes	Yes	No	18.0	–	44.0	38.0	22	Yes	Yes	Yes
Bulgaria	Veliko Tarnovo	Yes	Yes	No	2.4	–	45.8	51.8	30	Yes	Yes	Yes
Croatia	Zagreb	Yes	Yes	Yes	37.5	35.9	20.4	6.2	31	Yes	Yes	Yes
Czech Republic	Brno	Yes	Yes	Yes	25.0	29.0	21.0	25.0	25	Yes	No	Yes
Czech Republic	Prague	No	No	No	33.0	–	54.5	12.5	22	Yes	No	Yes
Estonia	Riik	Yes	Yes	Yes	...	...	...	...	...	Yes	Yes	Yes
Estonia	Tallin	Yes	Yes	Yes	...	...	...	...	35	Yes	Yes	Yes
Germany	Berlin	No	No	No	...	...	...	...	...	No	No	No
Germany	Cologne	No	No	No	...	...	...	...	...	No	No	No
Germany	Duisburg	No	No	No	...	...	...	...	...	No	No	No
Germany	Erfurt	No	No	No	...	...	...	...	...	No	No	No
Germany	Freiburg	No	No	No	...	...	...	...	...	No	No	No
Germany	Leipzig	No	No	No	...	...	...	...	...	No	No	No
Germany	Wiesbaden	No	No	No	...	...	...	...	...	No	No	No
Hungary	Budapest	Yes	No	Yes	...	...	...	...	...	No	No	No
Italy	Aversa	Yes	No	Yes	...	...	...	...	...	No	No	No
Latvia	Riga	Yes	No	Yes	...	...	...	...	...	Yes	Yes	Yes
Lithuania	Vilnius	No	No	No	22.3	29.1	23.2	25.5	37	Yes	Yes	Yes
Netherlands	Amsterdam	No	No	No	...	...	...	...		No	No	No
Netherlands	Eindhoven	No	No	No	...	...	...	...		No	No	No
Netherlands	Meppel	No	No	No	...	...	...	...	...	No	No	No
Poland	Bydgoszcz	No	No	Yes	42.5	10.5	24.0	...	18	Yes	Yes	Yes
Poland	Gdansk	Yes	Yes	Yes	43.0	32.9	23.4	0.7	20	Yes	Yes	Yes
Poland	Katowice	No	Yes	Yes	46.2	9.4	19.9	24.6	36	Yes	Yes	Yes
Poland	Poznan	Yes	Yes	No	33.0	30.0	21.0	16.0	25	Yes	Yes	Yes
Republic of Moldova	Chisinau	Yes	No	Yes	15.0	–	80.0	5.0	23	Yes	Yes	Yes
Russian Federation	Astrakhan	Yes	Yes	Yes	16.0	31.0	35.0	18.0	35	Yes	No	Yes
Russian Federation	Belgorod	Yes	Yes	Yes	...	...	...	...	25	Yes	Yes	Yes
Russian Federation	Kostroma	Yes	Yes	Yes	5.0	19.5	48.0	27.5	20	Yes	Yes	Yes
Russian Federation	Moscow	Yes	Yes	Yes	15.0	63.7	21.0	0.3	62	Yes	Yes	Yes
Russian Federation	Nizhny Novgorod	Yes	Yes	Yes	17.0	37.3	41.7	4.0	35	Yes	Yes	Yes
Russian Federation	Novomoscowsk	Yes	Yes	Yes	5.0	22.5	38.9	33.6	25	Yes	Yes	Yes
Russian Federation	Omsk	Yes	Yes	Yes	9.5	16.5	69.0	5.0	43	Yes	Yes	No
Russian Federation	Pushkin	Yes	Yes	Yes	6.0	–	60.2	33.8	15	Yes	Yes	Yes
Russian Federation	Surgut	No	No	No	1.5	–	81.0	17.5	57	Yes	Yes	Yes
Russian Federation	Veliky Novgorod	Yes	Yes	Yes	9.5	–	75.0	15.5	30	Yes	Yes	Yes
Serbia and Montenegro	Belgrade	Yes	No	Yes	12.5	18.8	53.0	...	40	No	No	No
Slovenia	Ljubljana	Yes	Yes	Yes	43.0	0.1	20.0	36.9	30	Yes	Yes	No
Spain	Madrid	Yes	Yes	Yes	60.0	–	16.0	24.0	32	No	No	No
Spain	Pamplona	Yes	Yes	No	...	...	...	...	...	Yes	No	Yes
Sweden	Amal	Yes	Yes	Yes	...	...	...	...	...	Yes	Yes	Yes

TABLE C.5

continued

		Local environmental planning*			Transport use for work trip**				Travel time per work trip	Disaster prevention and mitigation measures***		
		A	B	C	Car (%)	Train (%)	Bus (%)	Other (%)	(minutes)	A	B	C
Sweden	Stockholm	Yes	Yes	Yes	35.1	34.5	13.8	16.6	28	Yes	Yes	Yes
Sweden	Umea	Yes	Yes	Yes	...	...	...	...	16	Yes	Yes	Yes
Switzerland	Basel	Yes	Yes	Yes	...	...	...	...	...	Yes	Yes	No
United Kingdom	Belfast	No	No	No	...	...	...	...	...	No	No	No
United Kingdom	Birmingham	No	No	No	73.9	1.4	9.1	15.6	20	No	No	No
United Kingdom	Cardiff	No	No	No	81.0	0.3	5.7	13.0	20	No	No	No
United Kingdom	Edinburgh	No	No	No	69.9	2.4	13.0	14.7	20	No	No	No
United Kingdom	London	No	No	No	...	...	...	...	24	No	No	No
United Kingdom	Manchester	No	No	No	71.8	1.9	8.1	18.0	19	No	No	No
LATIN AMERICA AND THE CARIBBEAN												
Argentina	Buenos Aires	Yes	Yes	Yes	33.5	16.4	42.2	...	42	Yes	No	Yes
Argentina	Comodoro Rivadavia	Yes	Yes	Yes	44.0	–	36.0	20.0	29	Yes	No	Yes
Argentina	Córdoba	Yes	Yes	Yes	26.5	2.9	40.9	...	32	Yes	Yes	Yes
Argentina	Rosario	No	Yes	Yes	...	...	...	...	22	Yes	No	No
Barbados	Bridgetown	Yes	Yes	Yes	...	...	...	...	...	Yes	Yes	No
Belize	Belize City	No	No	Yes	...	...	...	...	...	No	No	No
Bolivia	Santa Cruz de la Sierra	No	Yes	No	...	...	...	...	29	Yes	Yes	No
Brazil	Belém	No	No	No	...	...	...	...	...	No	No	No
Brazil	Icapui	Yes	No	No	6.0	...	1.0	93.0	30	No	No	No
Brazil	Maranguape	No	No	No	5.0	–	30.0	...	20	Yes	Yes	Yes
Brazil	Porto Alegre	Yes	Yes	Yes	...	...	...	...	...	Yes	No	Yes
Brazil	Recife	Yes	Yes	Yes	28.6	1.8	44.2	25.4	35	Yes	Yes	Yes
Brazil	Rio de Janeiro	Yes	Yes	Yes	...	...	...	...	...	Yes	No	Yes
Brazil	São Paulo	Yes	Yes	Yes	42.0	6.0	37.0	15.0	40	Yes	No	Yes
Chile	Gran Concepcion	Yes	Yes	Yes	19.6	–	56.5	23.9	35	Yes	No	Yes
Chile	Santiago de Chile	Yes	Yes	Yes	14.1	4.0	55.8	26.2	38	No	No	Yes
Chile	Tome	No	No	No	...	...	...	...	...	No	Yes	No
Chile	Valparaiso	No	No	No	42.0	19.0	36.0	3.0	...	No	No	No
Chile	Vina del mar	Yes	Yes	Yes	...	...	...	...	...	No	No	Yes
Colombia	Armenia	Yes	No	No	31.0	–	41.9	27.2	60	Yes	Yes	Yes
Colombia	Marinilla	Yes	Yes	Yes	14.3	–	18.4	67.3	15	Yes	Yes	Yes
Colombia	Medellín	Yes	Yes	Yes	21.9	4.8	33.1	40.2	35	Yes	Yes	No
Cuba	Baracoa	Yes	Yes	Yes	...	...	...	...	...	No	No	No
Cuba	Camaguey	Yes	Yes	Yes	2.5	–	2.1	95.4	60	No	No	No
Cuba	Cienfuegos	Yes	Yes	Yes	...	...	...	...		No	No	No
Cuba	Havana	Yes	Yes	Yes	6.5	1.0	57.1	35.4		No	No	No
Cuba	Pinar Del Rio	Yes	Yes	Yes	...	...	...	...		No	No	No
Cuba	Santa Clara	Yes	Yes	Yes	30.3	3.2	4.1	62.4	48	No	No	No
Dominican Republic	Santiago de los Caballeros	Yes	Yes	Yes	...	...	...	...	30	Yes	No	Yes
Ecuador	Ambato	Yes	Yes	No	...	...	...	...	...	Yes	Yes	Yes
Ecuador	Cuenca	Yes	Yes	No	...	...	...	...	25	No	No	Yes
Ecuador	Guayaquil	No	Yes	No	10.7	–	89.3	–	45	Yes	Yes	Yes
Ecuador	Manta	No	Yes	No	...	...	...	...	30	Yes	Yes	Yes
Ecuador	Puyo	No	No	No	...	...	...	...	15	Yes	No	Yes
Ecuador	Quito	Yes	Yes	No	...	...	...	...	33	Yes	Yes	No
Ecuador	Tena	Yes	Yes	No	...	...	...	...	5	Yes	Yes	Yes
El Salvador	San Salvador	Yes	Yes	Yes	29.0	...	...	2.0	...	No	No	No
Guatemala	Quetzaltenango	No	No	Yes	...	...	...	...	15	Yes	No	Yes
Jamaica	Kingston	Yes	Yes	Yes	...	...	...	...	...	No	No	No
Jamaica	Montego Bay	Yes	No	Yes	...	...	...	...	...	No	No	No
Mexico	Ciudad Juarez	No	Yes	Yes	51.3	–	23.7	25.0	23	Yes	No	Yes
Nicaragua	Leon	Yes	Yes	No	...	...	56.0	...	15	No	No	No
Panama	Colon	Yes	Yes	Yes	...	...	...	...	15	No	No	No
Paraguay	Asuncion	Yes	Yes	No	49.8	...	...	...	25	Yes	Yes	Yes
Peru	Cajamarca	Yes	Yes	No	22.0	...	20.0	58.0	20	No	No	No
Peru	Huanuco	No	Yes	No	17.5	...	45.0	...	20	Yes	No	No
Peru	Huaras	No	Yes	No	...	...	...	...	15	No	No	No
Peru	Iquitos	No	Yes	Yes	35.0	–	25.0	40.0	10	Yes	Yes	Yes
Peru	Lima	Yes	Yes	Yes	16.9	–	82.2	0.9	...	Yes	No	Yes
Peru	Tacna	Yes	Yes	Yes	37.5	...	66.0	1.0	25	No	No	Yes
Peru	Tumbes	Yes	Yes	No	25.0	...	...	5.0	20	Yes	Yes	Yes
Trinidad and Tobago	Port of Spain	No	No	No	56.2	–	43.8	–	...	No	No	No
Uruguay	Montevideo	No	No	Yes	26.9	–	59.6	13.5	45	Yes	No	Yes
NORTHERN AMERICA												
Canada	Hull	Yes	Yes	Yes	73.3	–	16.3	10.4	...	Yes	Yes	Yes
United States of America	Atlanta	Yes	Yes	Yes	...	...	...	...	26	Yes	Yes	Yes
United States of America	Birmingham-USA	Yes	Yes	Yes	...	...	...	...	23	Yes	Yes	Yes
United States of America	Boston	Yes	Yes	Yes	...	...	...	...	25	Yes	Yes	Yes
United States of America	Des Moines	Yes	Yes	Yes	...	...	...	...	18	Yes	Yes	Yes
United States of America	Hartford	Yes	Yes	Yes	...	...	...	...	21	Yes	Yes	Yes
United States of America	Minneapolis-St. Paul	Yes	Yes	Yes	...	...	...	...	21	Yes	Yes	Yes
United States of America	New York	Yes	Yes	Yes	...	...	...	...	35	Yes	Yes	Yes
United States of America	Providence	Yes	Yes	Yes	...	...	...	...	19	Yes	Yes	Yes
United States of America	Salt Lake	Yes	Yes	Yes	...	...	...	...	20	Yes	Yes	Yes
United States of America	San Jose	Yes	Yes	Yes	...	...	...	...	23	Yes	Yes	Yes
United States of America	Seattle	Yes	Yes	Yes	...	...	...	...	24	Yes	Yes	Yes
United States of America	Tampa	Yes	Yes	Yes	...	...	...	...	22	Yes	Yes	Yes
United States of America	Washington	Yes	Yes	Yes	...	...	...	...	30	Yes	Yes	Yes

TABLE C.5

continued

		Local environmental planning*			Transport use for work trip**				Travel time per work trip	Disaster prevention and mitigation measures***		
		A	B	C	Car (%)	Train (%)	Bus (%)	Other (%)	(minutes)	A	B	C
OCEANIA												
Samoa	Apia	Yes	No	Yes	...	...	...	...	...	No	Yes	No

Source: UN-Habitat (2002), Global Urban Indicators Database 2.

Notes

* Table contains responses (Yes/No) to the following questions:

A. Has the city established a long-term strategic planning initiative for sustainable development, involving key partners?

B. Is this process institutionalized and/or has there been any legislative change to support cities to engage in sustainable development planning processes?

C. Is the city implementing local environmental action plans involving key partners?

** Car = private car. Train = train, tram or ferry. Bus = bus or minibus. Other = motorcycle, bicycle, and other non-motorised modes. When several modes of transport are used for a given trip, the following hierarchy is used to determine the principal mode: (1) train; (2) tram or ferry; (3) bus or minibus; (4) car; (5) taxi or motocycle; (6) bicycle or other non-motorized modes.

*** Responses (Yes/No) to the following questions:

In the city, are there:

A. building codes ?

B. hazard mapping ?

C. natural disaster insurance for public and private buildings ?

TABLE C.6

Environmental Infrastructure in Selected Cities (1998)

		Waste water treated	Solid waste disposal (%)						Water consumption (litre/person/day)		Median price of water (US$/m^3)
			Incinerated	Sanitary landfill	Open damp	Recycled	Burned openly	Other	A	B	
AFRICA											
Algeria	Algiers	80.0	...	...	...	...	...	...	150.0	100.0	0.08
Benin	Cotonou	70.0	–	–	75.0	20.0	–	5.0	36.4	...	0.39
Benin	Parakou	...	–	–	90.0	5.0	–	5.0	60.4	...	0.39
Benin	Porto-Novo	...	–	–	70.0	25.0	–	5.0	26.4	...	0.39
Botswana	Gaborone	95.0	–	–	99.0	1.0	–	–	239.0	...	...
Burkina Faso	Bobo-Dioulasso	...	...	...	...	...	...	...	27.0	...	...
Burkina Faso	Koudougou	...	...	...	...	...	...	...	27.0	...	...
Burkina Faso	Ouagadougou	18.5	7.0	–	55.0	12.0	25.0	1.0	39.0	...	...
Burundi	Bujumbura	21.3	–	15.0	33.4	–	27.4	24.2	82.4	30.0	0.08
Cameroon	Douala	5.0	0.6	65.4	26.0	8.0	–	–	40.0	20.0	0.33
Cameroon	Yaounde	24.2	0.3	66.9	31.0	1.8	–	–	40.0	15.0	0.33
Central African Republic	Bangui	0.1	–	–	80.0	–	20.0	–	55.0	30.0	3.33
Chad	N'Djamena	20.9	...	76.0	...	–	45.0	–	17.5	10.0	2.50
Congo	Brazzaville	...	–	0.8	40.0	16.2	38.0	5.0	30.0	25.0	...
Congo	Pointe-Noire	...	0.8	5.3	23.2	26.2	36.1	8.4	30.0	25.0	...
Côte d'Ivoire	Abidjan	45.0	10.0	–	72.0	3.0	–	15.0	40.0	20.0	1.19
Côte d'Ivoire	Yamoussoukro	25.0	–	–	100.0	–	–	–	37.0	...	0.48
Dem. Rep. of Congo	Kinshasa	...	5.8	15.9	15.5	4.9	32.5	18.5	25.0	20.0	...
Egypt	Ismailia	35.0	–	–	80.0	–	–	20.0	444.0	...	0.03
Egypt	Tanta	...	...	...	...	...	...	...	259.0	...	...
Ethiopia	Addis Ababa	...	–	10.8	21.8	–	–	67.4	16.9	...	...
Gabon	Libreville	44.0	–	70.0	10.0	–	15.0	5.0	160.0	120.0	0.57
Gabon	Port-Gentil	25.0	–	65.0	6.0	–	25.0	4.0	160.0	120.0	0.60
Gambia	Banjul	...	–	96.0	–	–	2.5	1.5	9.3	6.8	1.20
Ghana	Accra	0.0	...	...	...	...	...	...	9.0	6.5	1.20
Ghana	Kumasi	...	–	98.0	–	–	0.8	1.2	9.1	6.3	0.75
Guinea	Conakry	...	5.0	70.0	15.0	5.0	5.0	–	20.0	...	...
Kenya	Kisumu	65.0	–	–	30.0	–	7.0	63.0	20.0	...	...
Kenya	Mombasa	49.5	–	55.0	–	–	–	45.0	16.0	10.0	...
Kenya	Nairobi	52.0	...	25.0	...	1.0	3.0	1.3	17.7	...	2.18
Lesotho	Maseru	...	...	...	...	...	...	...	40.0	...	0.23
Liberia	Monrovia	0.0	–	–	100.0	–	–	–	30.0	...	0.03
Libyan Arab Jamahiriya	Tripoli	40.0	–	15.0	65.0	20.0	–	–	404.0	...	0.05
Madagascar	Antananarivo	...	...	...	...	...	...	...	...	...	0.12
Malawi	Lilongwe	0.0	...	...	22.0	...	3.0	...	100.0	60.0	...
Mali	Bamako	...	–	2.0	95.0	–	–	3.0	54.0	31.0	...
Mauritania	Nouakchott	...	3.0	...	28.0	1.0	6.0	2.0	35.0	20.0	0.62
Morocco	Casablanca	...	3.0	7.0	90.0	–	–	–	...	...	0.72
Morocco	Rabat	...	7.0	8.0	85.0	–	–	–	...	...	0.60
Mozambique	Maputo	5.0	–	–	100.0	–	–	–	67.0	...	0.41
Namibia	Windhoek	100.0	3.0	92.5	–	4.5	–	–	139.0	30.0	0.79
Niger	Maradi	...	...	...	...	...	...	...	24.0	...	0.34
Niger	Niamey	...	...	...	...	...	...	...	45.0	...	0.34
Nigeria	Lagos	...	...	...	...	...	...	...	45.0	22.5	...
Rwanda	Kigali	20.0	–	–	16.0	–	84.0	–	81.0	29.0	1.00
Senegal	Bignona	0.0	–	–	100.0	–	–	–	44.0	...	0.12
Senegal	Dakar	3.5	–	–	100.0	–	–	–	70.5	...	0.61
Senegal	Thies	0.0	–	–	100.0	–	–	–	44.0	...	0.18
South Africa	East Rand	80.0	...	...	...	...	...	...	113.0	...	...
South Africa	Port Elizabeth	...	0.1	99.9	–	–	–	–	110.0	25.0	2.39
Togo	Lome	...	–	–	25.0	–	10.0	65.0	73.0	...	0.33
Togo	Sokode	0.0	–	–	100.0	–	–	–	7.0	4.0	0.40
Tunisia	Tunis	83.0	2.0	80.0	12.0	5.0	1.0	–	...	...	0.30
Uganda	Entebbe	30.0	2.0	–	75.0	–	20.0	3.0	25.0	...	1.60
Uganda	Jinja	30.0	1.5	34.0	35.0	2.5	17.0	10.0	100.0	40.0	0.50
Zimbabwe	Bulawayo	80.0	1.0	65.0	2.0	5.0	...	1.0	87.0	...	...
Zimbabwe	Chegutu	69.0	5.0	–	75.0	3.0	15.0	2.0	160.0	...	0.63
Zimbabwe	Gweru	95.0	6.0	40.0	13.0	16.0	4.0	21.0	100.0	...	...
Zimbabwe	Harare	...	...	...	...	...	...	...	...	...	0.10
Zimbabwe	Mutare	100.0	–	97.7	–	2.3	–	–	139.0	...	...
ASIA											
Armenia	Yerevan	35.7	–	–	35.0	–	65.0	–	250.0	50.0	0.10
Bangladesh	Chittagong	0.0	...	...	70.0	0.5	...	...	96.0	48.0	0.09
Bangladesh	Dhaka	...	–	–	50.0	35.0	–	15.0	160.0	...	0.50
Bangladesh	Sylhet	0.0	...	...	45.0	0.5	...	...	96.0	48.0	1.37
Bangladesh	Tangail	0.0	–	–	83.0	–	–	17.0	...	...	...
Cambodia	Phnom Penh	0.0	–	–	74.0	15.0	5.0	6.0	...	...	0.21
Georgia	Tbilisi	0.0	...	...	...	...	...	...	...	...	0.19
India	Bangalore	82.9	–	–	60.8	14.5	–	24.7	68.8	40.0	0.20
India	Chennai	70.0	–	–	100.0	–	–	–	70.0	45.0	0.08
India	Delhi	73.2	–	99.5	–	–	–	0.5	136.0	45.0	...
India	Mysore	13.0	–	–	100.0	–	–	–	124.2	80.0	0.06
Indonesia	Bandung	23.4	–	78.6	–	–	16.3	5.1	130.0	...	0.85
Indonesia	Jakarta	15.7	–	77.7	–	–	–	22.3	161.6	...	0.18
Indonesia	Semarang	0.0	–	74.3	–	–	–	25.7	137.4	...	0.09
Indonesia	Surabaya	0.0	–	70.0	–	30.0	–	–	138.6	34.7	0.85
Japan	Tokyo	...	78.0	8.6	0.1	10.3	–	3.0	84.0	...	...
Jordan	Amman	54.3	–	100.0	–	–	–	–	84.0	...	0.53
Kazakhstan	Astana	93.0	...	...	...	...	...	...	...	...	0.23

TABLE C.6

continued

		Waste water treated	Solid waste disposal (%) Incinerated	Sanitary landfill	Open damp	Recycled	Burned openly	Other	Water consumption (litre/person/day) A	B	Median price of water (US$/m³)
Kuwait	Kuwait	...	9.0	82.0	2.0	–	2.0	5.0	379.0	...	1.26
Kyrgyzstan	Bishkek	15.0	–	–	100.0	–	–	–	135.0	...	0.04
Lao PDR	Vientiane	20.0	...	...	...	...	...	...	161.0	...	0.06
Lebanon	Sin El Fil	...	–	82.0	–	6.0	–	12.0	...	...	...
Malaysia	Penang	20.0	10.0	–	80.0	10.0	–	–	384.0	...	0.08
Mongolia	Ulaanbaatar	96.0	5.0	5.0	90.0	–	–	–	160.0	3.2	0.32
Myanmar	Yangon	0.0	–	–	86.0	14.0	–	–	160.0	50.0	0.81
Nepal	Butwal	0.0	...	...	94.0	6.0	...	...	75.0	...	0.03
Nepal	Pokhara	0.0	–	–	76.7	15.9	7.4	–	80.0	...	0.03
Occupied Palestine Territory	Gaza	...	...	...	...	...	...	...	80.0	...	0.41
Pakistan	Karachi	10.0	–	–	51.0	12.0	20.0	17.0	132.0	63.0	0.25
Pakistan	Lahore	0.0	–	70.0	25.0	–	5.0	–	320.0	...	0.09
Philippines	Cebu	...	–	100.0	–	–	–	–	225.0	...	0.50
Republic of Korea	Hanam	80.8	3.0	67.0	–	30.0	–	–	286.0	...	0.33
Republic of Korea	Pusan	69.4	14.5	41.2	–	44.3	–	–	384.0	...	0.35
Republic of Korea	Seoul	98.6	5.0	57.0	–	38.0	–	–	409.0	...	0.33
Singapore	Singapore	100.0	66.3	33.7	–	–	–	–	166.2	...	0.32
Sri Lanka	Colombo	10.0	–	–	100.0	–	–	–	...	...	0.03
Syrian Arab Rep.	Damascus	3.0	4.0	46.0	6.0	21.0	16.0	7.0	270.0	...	0.20
Thailand	Bangkok	...	–	99.0	–	–	–	1.0	352.0	...	0.19
Thailand	Chiang Mai	70.0	2.0	98.0	–	–	–	–	200.0	100.0	0.45
Turkey	Ankara	80.0	–	–	92.0	0.8	0.8	6.5	138.0	...	1.06
Vietnam	Hanoi	...	–	65.0	–	15.0	–	20.0	100.0	...	0.90
Vietnam	Ho Chi Minh	...	...	...	...	...	...	...	200.0	...	...
Yemen	Sana'a	30.0	–	–	95.0	5.0	–	–	75.0	40.0	0.90
EUROPE											
Albania	Tirana	...	–	–	–	–	100.0	–	130.0	...	0.05
Belarus	Minsk	100.0	–	100.0	–	–	–	–	358.0	...	...
Bosnia and Herzegovina	Sarajevo	...	...	...	...	...	...	...	165.0	...	0.90
Bulgaria	Bourgas	93.0	–	100.0	–	–	–	–	112.0	...	0.35
Bulgaria	Sofia	94.0	–	0.2	77.0	22.8	–	–	150.0	...	0.17
Bulgaria	Troyan	...	–	–	73.0	9.0	4.0	14.0	121.0	...	0.10
Bulgaria	Veliko Tarnovo	50.0	–	–	94.0	6.0	–	–	114.0	...	0.22
Croatia	Zagreb	...	–	–	85.0	13.0	–	2.0	145.3	...	0.67
Czech Republic	Brno	100.0	100.0	–	–	–	–	–	131.8	...	0.78
Czech Republic	Prague	...	...	...	...	...	...	...	110.0	...	0.81
Estonia	Riik	...	...	...	...	...	...	...	144.0	...	...
Estonia	Tallinn	99.6	–	23.9	74.3	–	–	1.8	138.0	...	0.51
Germany	Berlin	100.0	...	...	...	...	...	...	178.0	...	0.20
Germany	Cologne	100.0	...	...	...	...	...	...	247.0	...	0.20
Germany	Duisburg	100.0	...	...	...	...	...	...	200.0	...	0.23
Germany	Erfurt	97.5	...	...	...	...	...	...	210.0	...	0.30
Germany	Freiburg	100.0	...	...	...	...	...	...	203.0	...	0.19
Germany	Leipzig	100.0	...	...	...	...	...	...	200.0	...	0.23
Germany	Wiesbaden	99.7	...	...	...	...	...	...	188.0	...	0.35
Hungary	Budapest	87.5	64.7	35.3	–	–	–	–	184.0	...	0.35
Italy	Aversa	90.0	–	–	98.8	1.2	–	–	...	...	3.00
Latvia	Riga	83.3	–	–	92.0	–	–	8.0	166.0	...	0.57
Lithuania	Vilnius	53.9	...	...	...	...	...	...	73.0	...	0.77
Netherlands	Amsterdam	...	–	1.0	–	30.0	69.0	–	...	...	2.87
Netherlands	Eindhoven	...	–	1.0	–	30.0	69.0	–	...	...	1.98
Netherlands	Meppel	...	–	1.0	–	30.0	69.0	–	...	...	1.76
Poland	Bydgoszcz	28.4	–	–	99.8	0.2	–	–	133.9	...	0.29
Poland	Gdansk	100.0	0.0	–	96.5	3.5	–	–	129.9	...	0.34
Poland	Katowice	67.0	–	–	85.0	1.5	–	13.5	149.0	...	0.54
Poland	Poznan	78.0	1.1	...	81.7	17.2	...	...	145.0	...	0.32
Republic of Moldova	Chisinau	71.2	...	...	...	...	...	...	...	...	0.25
Russian Federation	Astrakhan	92.0	–	–	86.4	13.6	–	–	200.0	...	0.08
Russian Federation	Belgorod	95.9	...	5.0	89.0	...	...	...	200.0	...	0.05
Russian Federation	Kostroma	95.9	–	–	86.1	13.9	–	–	250.0	...	0.04
Russian Federation	Moscow	98.1	1.2	66.2	24.0	8.0	0.6	–	235.0	...	...
Russian Federation	Nizhny Novgorod	97.6	–	–	90.2	9.8	–	–	230.0	...	0.05
Russian Federation	Novomoscowsk	97.0	–	–	97.1	2.9	–	–	225.0	...	0.09
Russian Federation	Omsk	89.0	–	–	100.0	–	–	–	300.0	...	0.07
Russian Federation	Pushkin	100.0	–	–	90.0	10.0	–	–	220.0	...	0.15
Russian Federation	Surgut	93.2	–	–	100.0	–	–	–	320.0	...	0.40
Russian Federation	Veliky Novgorod	95.0	–	2.0	97.0	1.0	–	–	325.0	...	0.04
Serbia and Montenegro	Belgrade	20.0	–	–	99.3	0.7	–	–	385.0	...	0.13
Slovenia	Ljubljana	98.0	–	92.0	–	8.0	–	–	179.0	...	0.28
Spain	Madrid	100.0	–	46.0	–	54.0	–	–	172.5	...	0.73
Spain	Pamplona	79.0	1.8	82.0	–	16.2	–	–	136.1	...	0.38
Sweden	Amal	100.0	–	71.0	–	29.0	–	–	143.0	...	1.98
Sweden	Stockholm	100.0	74.0	1.0	–	25.0	–	–	198.0	...	1.49
Sweden	Umea	100.0	78.0	1.0	–	21.0	–	–	153.0	...	1.75
Switzerland	Basel	100.0	58.0	27.0	–	15.0	–	–	380.0	...	...
United Kingdom	Belfast	...	–	–	–	4.0	–	96.0	...	...	...
United Kingdom	Birmingham	100.0	53.0	43.0	–	4.0	–	–	...	...	...
United Kingdom	Cardiff	...	–	95.0	–	5.0	–	–	...	...	...
United Kingdom	London	...	23.0	72.0	–	5.0	–	–	...	...	...
United Kingdom	Manchester	...	–	92.0	–	3.0	–	5.0	...	...	...

TABLE C.6

continued

		Waste water treated	Solid waste disposal (%) Incinerated	Sanitary landfill	Open damp	Recycled	Burned openly	Other	Water consumption (litre/person/day) A	B	Median price of water (US$/m³)
LATIN AMERICA AND THE CARIBBEAN											
Argentina	Buenos Aires	0.0	–	100.0	–	–	–	–	270.0	...	...
Argentina	Comodoro Rivadavia	10.0	–	–	100.0	–	–	–	440.0	...	0.35
Argentina	Córdoba	49.1	0.1	99.6	–	0.3	–	–	340.0	...	0.36
Argentina	Rosario	0.6	0.1	71.9	25.2	–	2.7	–	171.8	...	0.17
Barbados	Bridgetown	7.0	...	...	...	...	...	...	230.0	...	0.75
Bolivia	Santa Cruz de la Sierra	53.0	2.0	60.0	30.0	2.0	2.0	3.0	122.0	...	...
Brazil	Icapui	...	–	–	75.0	–	15.0	10.0	120.0	...	0.67
Brazil	Maranguape	...	–	96.0	2.0	2.0	–	–	150.0	...	0.45
Brazil	Porto Alegre	...	...	92.0	...	7.6	...	0.4	202.4	...	0.51
Brazil	Recife	33.0	...	75.0	24.0	1.0	...	...	185.0	...	0.72
Brazil	Rio de Janeiro	...	...	73.2	–	22.0	0.7	4.1	209.0	...	...
Brazil	São Paulo	...	–	99.0	–	1.0	–	–	159.6	108.7	0.52
Chile	Gran Concepcion	5.7	–	100.0	–	–	–	–	179.0	30.0	0.28
Chile	Santiago de Chile	3.3	–	100.0	–	–	–	–	...	...	0.34
Chile	Tome	57.0	–	91.6	–	2.2	0.8	5.4	144.0	...	0.20
Chile	Valparaiso	100.0	–	100.0	–	–	–	–	166.3	...	0.45
Chile	Vina del mar	92.9	–	89.0	3.0	8.0	–	–	170.0	12.0	0.46
Colombia	Armenia	0.0	–	–	96.0	–	–	4.0	...	...	0.58
Colombia	Marinilla	...	–	88.5	–	11.5	–	–	125.5	...	...
Colombia	Medellín	...	–	75.0	7.0	10.0	3.0	5.0	141.5	...	0.18
Cuba	Baracoa	...	–	–	100.0	–	–	–	225.0	...	1.00
Cuba	Camaguey	...	–	–	100.0	–	–	–	203.0	...	...
Cuba	Cienfuegos	2.2	–	80.0	20.0	–	–	–	230.0	...	0.85
Cuba	Havana	...	–	100.0	–	–	–	–	100.0	...	1.30
Cuba	Pinar Del Rio	...	10.0	60.0	10.0	–	20.0	–	125.0	...	...
Cuba	Santa Clara	...	–	70.0	30.0	–	–	–	225.0	...	...
Dominican Republic	Santiago de los Caballeros	80.0	...	...	100.0	...	100.0	...	...	...	...
Ecuador	Ambato	0.0	–	–	95.0	5.0	–	–	220.0	...	0.11
Ecuador	Cuenca	82.0	–	88.0	–	5.0	–	7.0	246.0	...	...
Ecuador	Guayaquil	9.0	–	94.0	0.3	0.3	1.2	4.2	244.0	109.0	0.51
Ecuador	Manta	...	...	...	...	...	...	...	40.5	...	0.66
Ecuador	Puyo	...	–	–	90.0	10.0	–	–	420.0	...	0.04
Ecuador	Quito	...	–	–	70.0	20.0	–	10.0	...	...	...
Ecuador	Tena	0.0	–	–	90.0	5.0	–	5.0	190.0	...	0.11
El Salvador	San Salvador	...	–	81.1	18.9	–	–	–	...	...	...
Guatemala	Quetzaltenango	...	–	60.0	30.0	5.0	5.0	–	120.0	...	0.16
Jamaica	Kingston	20.0	...	...	...	...	...	...	...	...	...
Jamaica	Montego Bay	15.0	...	...	...	...	...	...	...	...	...
Mexico	Ciudad Juarez	...	–	89.0	2.0	8.0	1.0	–	336.4	...	0.26
Panama	Colon	0.0	–	90.0	10.0	–	–	–	496.0	...	0.21
Paraguay	Asuncion	0.0	0.2	...	...	4.0	...	91.0	200.0	90.0	0.40
Peru	Cajamarca	62.0	–	95.0	1.5	–	–	3.5	160.0	...	0.64
Peru	Huanuco	...	–	100.0	–	–	–	–	...	...	...
Peru	Huaras	...	–	–	100.0	–	–	–	120.0	...	0.33
Peru	Iquitos	...	–	64.0	15.0	–	8.0	13.0	119.8	...	0.23
Peru	Lima	4.0	–	57.0	34.0	7.0	2.0	–	108.0	...	0.34
Peru	Tacna	64.0	–	–	50.0	–	50.0	–	201.0	90.0	0.43
Peru	Tumbes	...	70.0	...	...	...	20.0	10.0	150.0	...	0.59
Trinidad and Tobago	Port of Spain	...	...	...	...	...	...	...	...	...	...
Uruguay	Montevideo	34.0	0.2	–	99.8	–	–	–	173.1	...	0.62
NORTHERN AMERICA											
Canada	Hull	100.0	–	91.9	–	8.1	–	–	397.0	...	0.29
United States	Atlanta	...	...	...	...	...	...	...	403.0	...	...
United States	Birmingham-USA	...	...	...	...	...	...	...	393.0	...	...
United States	Boston	...	...	...	...	...	...	...	252.0	...	...
United States	Des Moines	...	...	...	...	...	...	...	226.0	...	...
United States	Hartford	...	...	...	...	...	...	...	284.0	...	...
United States	Minneapolis-St. Paul	...	...	...	...	...	...	...	281.0	...	...
United States	New York	...	...	...	...	...	...	...	448.0	...	...
United States	Providence	...	...	...	...	...	...	...	246.0	...	...
United States	Salt Lake	...	...	...	...	...	...	...	668.0	...	...
United States	San Jose	...	...	...	...	...	...	...	343.0	...	...
United States	Seattle	...	...	...	...	...	...	...	476.0	...	...
United States	Tampa	...	...	...	...	...	...	...	327.0	...	...
United States	Washington	...	...	...	...	...	...	...	396.0	...	...
OCEANIA											
Samoa	Apia	0.0	...	...	...	...	...	...	...	...	0.10

Source: UN-Habitat (2002), Global Urban Indicators Database 2

Note: * Consumption of water in litres per day per person, for all domestic uses (excludes industrial use): A = city average, B = average in informal settlements.

TABLE C.7

Urban Safety and Governance Indicators in Selected Cities (1998)

		Urban violence*						Reported crime (rate per 1000)			Local government transparency and accountability**			
		A	B	C	D	E	F	homicide	rape	thefts	A	D	C	D
AFRICA														
Algeria	Algiers	Yes	No	Yes	Yes	Yes	No	...	...	...	Yes	Yes	Yes	Yes
Benin	Cotonou	Yes	No	Yes	Yes	Yes	No	0.02	0.04	3.20	Yes	Yes	Yes	Yes
Benin	Parakou	Yes	No	Yes	Yes	Yes	No	0.09	0.06	3.30	Yes	Yes	Yes	Yes
Benin	Porto-Novo	Yes	No	Yes	Yes	Yes	No	0.02	0.03	3.38	Yes	Yes	Yes	Yes
Botswana	Gaborone	No	No	Yes	Yes	No	No	0.18	0.79	0.85	Yes	Yes	Yes	Yes
Burkina Faso	Bobo-Dioulasso	No	No	No	No	No	No	...	...	...	No	No	No	No
Burkina Faso	Koudougou	No	No	No	No	No	No	...	...	...	No	No	No	No
Burkina Faso	Ouagadougou	No	No	Yes	Yes	Yes	Yes	0.01	0.03	4.90	Yes	Yes	No	No
Burundi	Bujumbura	No	No	No	Yes	Yes	No	0.50	0.64	8.70	No	Yes	Yes	No
Cameroon	Douala	No	No	Yes	Yes	Yes	Yes	...	...	...	Yes	Yes	Yes	Yes
Cameroon	Yaounde	No	No	Yes	Yes	Yes	Yes	...	...	0.20	Yes	Yes	Yes	Yes
Central African Republic	Bangui	Yes	Yes	Yes	Yes	Yes	Yes	0.52	0.21	4.00	No	Yes	No	No
Chad	N'Djamena	No	Yes	Yes	Yes	Yes	No	1.00	...	25.00	Yes	Yes	Yes	Yes
Congo	Brazzaville	Yes	Yes	Yes	No	No	Yes	...	...	...	No	Yes	Yes	Yes
Congo	Pointe - Noire	Yes	No	No	No	Yes	Yes	...	8.00	16.00	No	Yes	Yes	No
Côte d'Ivoire	Abidjan	Yes	Yes	No	Yes	Yes	No	...	...	...	Yes	Yes	Yes	Yes
Côte d'Ivoire	Yamoussoukro	Yes	No	No	Yes	Yes	No	...	...	7.00	Yes	Yes	Yes	Yes
Dem. Rep. of Congo	Kinshasa	No	No	Yes	Yes	Yes	Yes	...	...	...	No	Yes	Yes	No
Egypt	Ismailia	No	Yes	Yes	Yes	Yes	Yes	...	...	...	Yes	Yes	Yes	No
Egypt	Tanta	No	No	Yes	Yes	Yes	Yes	...	...	...	Yes	Yes	Yes	No
Ethiopia	Addis Ababa	No	No	No	No	No	No	...	...	...	No	No	No	No
Gabon	Libreville	Yes	No	No	Yes	Yes	No	...	...	...	No	Yes	Yes	Yes
Gabon	Port-Gentil	Yes	No	No	Yes	Yes	No	...	...	...	No	No	No	No
Gambia	Banjul	No	No	Yes	Yes	Yes	Yes	...	...	...	Yes	Yes	Yes	Yes
Ghana	Accra	No	No	Yes	Yes	Yes	Yes	10.00	23.00	15.00	Yes	Yes	Yes	Yes
Ghana	Kumasi	No	No	Yes	Yes	Yes	Yes	9.00	21.00	16.00	Yes	Yes	Yes	Yes
Guinea	Conakry	Yes	Yes	No	No	Yes	No	0.01	0.00	0.00	Yes	Yes	Yes	Yes
Kenya	Kisumu	No	Yes	No	Yes	Yes	Yes	0.18	0.18	1.00	No	Yes	Yes	Yes
Kenya	Mombasa	No	Yes	No	Yes	Yes	Yes	...	...	...	No	Yes	Yes	Yes
Kenya	Nairobi	No	Yes	No	Yes	Yes	Yes	...	...	...	No	Yes	Yes	Yes
Lesotho	Maseru	No	Yes	No	Yes	Yes	No	...	...	...	No	No	No	No
Liberia	Monrovia	No	No	Yes	Yes	Yes	Yes	...	...	...	Yes	No	Yes	Yes
Libyan Arab Jamahiriya	Tripoli	No	No	Yes	Yes	Yes	Yes	13.00	40.00	173.00	Yes	Yes	Yes	Yes
Madagascar	Antananarivo	Yes	No	Yes	Yes	Yes	Yes	...	...	...	No	Yes	Yes	Yes
Malawi	Lilongwe	No	Yes	No	Yes	Yes	No	...	...	...	Yes	Yes	Yes	Yes
Mali	Bamako	Yes	No	No	Yes	Yes	Yes	0.07	0.05	0.21	Yes	Yes	Yes	No
Mauritania	Nouakchott	No	No	No	No	No	No	...	...	1.00	Yes	Yes	Yes	Yes
Morocco	Casablanca	No	No	Yes	Yes	Yes	Yes	...	...	...	Yes	Yes	Yes	Yes
Morocco	Rabat	No	No	Yes	Yes	Yes	Yes	...	...	...	Yes	Yes	Yes	Yes
Mozambique	Maputo	Yes	Yes	No	Yes	Yes	Yes	...	...	...	No	No	No	No
Namibia	Windhoek	No	No	Yes	Yes	Yes	Yes	24.00	4.00	36.00	Yes	Yes	Yes	Yes
Niger	Maradi	No	No	Yes	Yes	Yes	No	...	...	...	No	No	Yes	No
Niger	Niamey	No	No	No	No	No	No	...	...	...	Yes	No	No	No
Nigeria	Ibadan	No	No	Yes	Yes	Yes	Yes	...	...	...	Yes	Yes	Yes	Yes
Nigeria	Lagos	No	No	Yes	Yes	Yes	Yes	...	...	...	Yes	Yes	Yes	Yes
Rwanda	Kigali	Yes	No	No	Yes	Yes	Yes	...	...	14.00	No	Yes	Yes	No
Senegal	Bignona	Yes	No	No	No	Yes	No	0.06	...	7.93	Yes	Yes	Yes	No
Senegal	Dakar	Yes	No	No	No	Yes	No	0.06	...	7.93	Yes	Yes	Yes	No
Senegal	Thies	Yes	No	No	No	Yes	No	0.06	...	7.93	Yes	Yes	Yes	No
South Africa	Durban	No	No	No	No	No	No	...	...	...	No	No	No	No
South Africa	East Rand	No	No	No	No	No	No	...	...	...	No	No	No	No
South Africa	Port Elizabeth	Yes	No	Yes	No	No	No	...	...	...	No	No	No	No
Togo	Lome	No	No	Yes	Yes	Yes	No	...	...	...	Yes	Yes	Yes	No
Togo	Sokode	No	No	Yes	Yes	Yes	No	...	...	...	Yes	Yes	Yes	No
Tunisia	Tunis	No	No	Yes	Yes	Yes	Yes	...	...	...	Yes	Yes	Yes	No
Uganda	Entebbe	No	No	Yes	Yes	Yes	Yes	18.00	4.00	28.50	Yes	Yes	Yes	No
Uganda	Jinja	No	Yes	Yes	Yes	Yes	Yes	...	...	...	Yes	Yes	Yes	Yes
Zimbabwe	Bulawayo	No	No	Yes	Yes	Yes	Yes	...	...	...	Yes	Yes	Yes	No
Zimbabwe	Chegutu	No	No	Yes	Yes	Yes	Yes	...	...	...	Yes	Yes	Yes	Yes
Zimbabwe	Gweru	No	No	Yes	Yes	Yes	Yes	1.00	...	18.00	Yes	Yes	Yes	Yes
Zimbabwe	Harare	No	No	Yes	Yes	Yes	Yes	...	...	...	Yes	Yes	Yes	Yes
Zimbabwe	Mutare	No	No	No	Yes	Yes	Yes	...	...	...	Yes	Yes	Yes	Yes
ASIA														
Armenia	Yerevan	No	No	No	Yes	Yes	No	0.08	...	...	No	No	No	No
Bangladesh	Chittagong	No	No	No	Yes	Yes	Yes	...	...	...	Yes	Yes	Yes	No
Bangladesh	Dhaka	Yes	No	No	Yes	Yes	Yes	...	...	1.00	No	No	No	No
Bangladesh	Sylhet	No	No	No	Yes	Yes	Yes	...	...	...	Yes	Yes	Yes	No
Bangladesh	Tangail	No	No	Yes	Yes	Yes	Yes	...	...	...	Yes	Yes	No	No
Cambodia	Phnom Penh	Yes	Yes	Yes	Yes	Yes	Yes	0.17	0.01	0.03	No	Yes	Yes	No
Georgia	Tbilisi	No	No	No	No	No	No	...	...	...	No	Yes	No	Yes
India	Alwar	No	No	No	No	No	No	...	...	...	No	No	No	No
India	Bangalore	No	Yes	No	Yes	Yes	No	...	...	2.00	Yes	Yes	Yes	Yes
India	Chennai	No	No	No	Yes	Yes	Yes	...	...	...	Yes	Yes	Yes	Yes
India	Delhi	No	No	No	No	No	No	...	...	...	No	No	No	No
India	Mysore	No	No	No	Yes	Yes	Yes	...	...	1.00	Yes	Yes	Yes	Yes
Indonesia	Bandung	No	No	No	Yes	Yes	No	0.16	0.01	2.23	Yes	Yes	Yes	No
Indonesia	Jakarta	No	Yes	No	Yes	Yes	Yes	0.00	0.00	0.20	Yes	Yes	Yes	Yes
Indonesia	Semarang	No	No	No	Yes	Yes	No	0.02	0.01	0.23	Yes	Yes	Yes	Yes

TABLE C.7

continued

		Urban violence*						Reported crime (rate per 1000)			Local government transparency and accountability**			
		A	B	C	D	E	F	homicide	rape	thefts	A	D	C	D
Indonesia	Surabaya	No	Yes	Yes	Yes	Yes	Yes	0.01	0.01	0.21	Yes	Yes	Yes	Yes
Iraq	Baghdad	No	No	No	No	No	No	...	...	...	No	No	No	No
Japan	Tokyo	No	Yes	Yes	Yes	Yes	Yes	...	...	...	Yes	Yes	Yes	Yes
Jordan	Amman	No	No	Yes	Yes	Yes	Yes	0.02	0.02	1.88	Yes	Yes	Yes	No
Kazakhstan	Astana	No	Yes	Yes	Yes	Yes	Yes	0.22	0.05	4.40	No	Yes	Yes	Yes
Kuwait	Kuwait	No	No	Yes	Yes	Yes	Yes	...	...	...	Yes	Yes	Yes	Yes
Kyrgyzstan	Bishkek	Yes	No	No	Yes	Yes	No	0.06	0.25	...	No	Yes	Yes	Yes
Lao People Dem. Rep.	Vientiane	No	No	No	No	Yes	No	...	...	...	Yes	Yes	Yes	No
Lebanon	Sin El Fil	No	No	Yes	Yes	Yes	Yes	...	...	...	Yes	Yes	Yes	Yes
Malaysia	Penang	No	Yes	Yes	Yes	Yes	Yes	...	...	...	Yes	Yes	Yes	Yes
Mongolia	Ulaanbaatar	Yes	Yes	No	Yes	Yes	Yes	0.10	0.25	7.39	Yes	Yes	Yes	Yes
Myanmar	Yangon	No	No	Yes	Yes	Yes	Yes	...	...	...	Yes	Yes	Yes	Yes
Nepal	Butwal	No	Yes	No	Yes	Yes	No	0.51	0.05	0.11	Yes	Yes	Yes	No
Nepal	Pokhara	No	Yes	No	Yes	Yes	No	0.11	...	0.02	Yes	Yes	Yes	No
Occupied Palestinian Territory	Gaza	No	No	Yes	Yes	Yes	Yes	8.00	9.00	...	Yes	Yes	Yes	Yes
Oman	Muscat	No	No	No	Yes	Yes	Yes	...	...	...	Yes	Yes	Yes	Yes
Pakistan	Karachi	Yes	No	No	No	No	No	0.18	...	1.01	Yes	Yes	No	No
Pakistan	Lahore	Yes	Yes	No	No	Yes	No	0.07	0.03	0.02	Yes	Yes	No	No
Philippines	Cebu	No	Yes	Yes	Yes	Yes	Yes	0.24	0.02	0.53	Yes	Yes	Yes	Yes
Qatar	Doha	No	No	No	No	No	No	...	...	...	No	No	No	No
Republic of Korea	Hanam	No	Yes	Yes	Yes	Yes	Yes	...	...	...	Yes	Yes	Yes	Yes
Republic of Korea	Pusan	No	Yes	Yes	Yes	Yes	Yes	0.05	0.26	4.18	Yes	Yes	Yes	Yes
Republic of Korea	Seoul	No	Yes	Yes	Yes	Yes	Yes	0.04	0.24	3.19	Yes	Yes	Yes	No
Singapore	Singapore	No	No	Yes	Yes	Yes	Yes	0.01	0.03	0.14	Yes	Yes	Yes	Yes
Sri Lanka	Colombo	No	No	Yes	Yes	Yes	Yes	20.40	...	47.50	Yes	Yes	Yes	Yes
Syrian Arab Rep.	Damascus	No	No	No	Yes	Yes	No	...	...	...	Yes	Yes	Yes	Yes
Thailand	Bangkok	Yes	Yes	Yes	Yes	Yes	No	0.80	0.70	3.00	Yes	Yes	No	Yes
Thailand	Chiang Mai	No	No	No	No	Yes	No	0.15	0.10	5.50	No	No	No	No
Turkey	Ankara	No	No	Yes	Yes	Yes	Yes	0.05	0.03	0.17	Yes	Yes	Yes	No
Viet Nam	Hanoi	No	No	Yes	Yes	Yes	Yes	...	...	...	No	Yes	Yes	Yes
Viet Nam	Ho Chi Minh	No	Yes	Yes	Yes	Yes	Yes	0.03	0.03	2.00	No	Yes	Yes	Yes
Yemen	Sana'a	No	No	No	Yes	Yes	Yes	...	...	1.00	Yes	Yes	Yes	Yes
EUROPE														
Albania	Tirana	Yes	Yes	No	Yes	Yes	Yes	...	...	...	No	No	No	No
Belarus	Minsk	No	No	No	Yes	Yes	No	...	...	5.00	No	No	No	No
Bosnia and Herzegovina	Sarajevo	No	No	Yes	Yes	Yes	Yes	...	8.00	...	Yes	Yes	Yes	No
Bulgaria	Bourgas	Yes	Yes	Yes	Yes	Yes	Yes	0.07	0.20	33.34	Yes	Yes	Yes	Yes
Bulgaria	Sofia	Yes	No	No	Yes	Yes	No	0.04	0.05	11.32	No	No	No	No
Bulgaria	Troyan	No	No	No	No	Yes	No	0.03	1.00	9.00	Yes	Yes	No	No
Bulgaria	Veliko Tarnovo	Yes	No	No	Yes	Yes	No	0.08	0.15	16.40	Yes	Yes	Yes	Yes
Croatia	Zagreb	No	No	Yes	Yes	Yes	Yes	0.10	...	4.00	Yes	Yes	Yes	Yes
Czech Republic	Brno	Yes	No	Yes	Yes	Yes	Yes	0.04	0.08	40.46	Yes	Yes	Yes	Yes
Czech Republic	Prague	No	No	Yes	Yes	Yes	Yes	0.05	0.10	67.98	Yes	Yes	Yes	Yes
Estonia	Riik	No	Yes	Yes	Yes	Yes	No	...	...	...	No	No	No	No
Estonia	Tallinn	No	Yes	Yes	Yes	Yes	No	...	1.00	44.00	Yes	Yes	Yes	Yes
Germany	Berlin	No	No	No	No	No	No	...	...	...	No	No	No	No
Germany	Cologne	No	No	No	No	No	No	...	...	...	No	No	No	No
Germany	Duisburg	No	No	No	No	No	No	...	...	...	No	No	No	No
Germany	Erfurt	No	No	No	No	No	No	...	...	...	No	No	No	No
Germany	Freiburg	No	No	No	No	No	No	...	...	...	No	No	No	No
Germany	Leipzig	No	No	No	No	No	No	...	...	...	No	No	No	No
Germany	Wiesbaden	No	No	No	No	No	No	...	...	...	No	No	No	No
Hungary	Budapest	Yes	Yes	No	Yes	No	Yes	0.06	0.04	25.79	No	No	No	No
Italy	Aversa	No	Yes	Yes	Yes	Yes	Yes	...	...	...	Yes	Yes	Yes	Yes
Latvia	Riga	No	No	No	Yes	Yes	Yes	0.11	0.02	8.45	Yes	Yes	Yes	Yes
Lithuania	Vilnius	No	Yes	Yes	Yes	Yes	No	...	...	18.00	Yes	Yes	Yes	Yes
Moldova	Chisinau	Yes	No	Yes	Yes	Yes	No	1.00	...	13.00	Yes	No	No	Yes
Netherlands	Amsterdam	No	No	No	Yes	Yes	No	...	...	...	No	No	No	No
Netherlands	Eindhoven	No	No	No	Yes	Yes	No	...	...	...	No	No	No	No
Netherlands	Meppel	No	No	No	Yes	Yes	No	...	...	...	No	No	No	No
Poland	Bydgoszcz	No	Yes	Yes	Yes	Yes	Yes	0.02	0.04	9.20	Yes	Yes	Yes	Yes
Poland	Gdansk	Yes	No	Yes	Yes	Yes	No	0.03	0.05	13.58	Yes	Yes	Yes	Yes
Poland	Katowice	No	Yes	Yes	Yes	Yes	Yes	0.05	0.04	8.20	Yes	Yes	Yes	Yes
Poland	Poznan	Yes	Yes	Yes	Yes	Yes	Yes	0.03	0.05	7.20	Yes	Yes	Yes	Yes
Russian Federation	Astrakhan	No	No	Yes	Yes	Yes	No	0.20	0.10	10.70	Yes	Yes	Yes	Yes
Russian Federation	Belgorod	No	No	No	Yes	Yes	No	...	...	5.70	Yes	Yes	Yes	Yes
Russian Federation	Kostroma	No	No	Yes	Yes	Yes	No	0.20	0.10	14.70	No	No	No	No
Russian Federation	Moscow	No	No	Yes	Yes	Yes	No	0.10	0.00	2.20	Yes	Yes	Yes	Yes
Russian Federation	Nizhny Novgorod	No	No	Yes	Yes	Yes	No	0.40	0.10	19.00	Yes	Yes	Yes	Yes
Russian Federation	Novomoscowsk	No	No	Yes	Yes	Yes	No	0.20	...	5.60	Yes	Yes	Yes	Yes
Russian Federation	Omsk	No	No	Yes	Yes	Yes	No	0.20	0.10	9.40	Yes	Yes	Yes	Yes
Russian Federation	Pushkin	No	No	Yes	Yes	Yes	No	0.20	...	9.70	Yes	Yes	Yes	Yes
Russian Federation	Surgut	No	No	Yes	Yes	Yes	No	0.20	0.10	15.40	Yes	Yes	Yes	Yes
Russian Federation	Veliky Novgorod	No	No	Yes	Yes	Yes	No	0.20	0.10	9.70	Yes	Yes	Yes	Yes
Serbia and Montenegro	Belgrade	No	No	Yes	Yes	Yes	Yes	...	...	...	No	Yes	Yes	Yes
Slovenia	Ljubljana	No	Yes	Yes	Yes	Yes	Yes	0.04	0.03	34.56	Yes	Yes	Yes	Yes
Spain	Madrid	No	Yes	Yes	Yes	Yes	Yes	...	...	35.00	Yes	Yes	Yes	No
Spain	Pamplona	No	No	Yes	Yes	Yes	Yes	...	...	2.00	Yes	Yes	Yes	Yes
Sweden	Amal	No	Yes	Yes	Yes	Yes	Yes	0.00	0.00	49.00	Yes	Yes	Yes	Yes

TABLE C.7

continued

		Urban violence*						Reported crime (rate per 1000)			Local government transparency and accountability**			
		A	B	C	D	E	F	homicide	rape	thefts	A	D	C	D
Sweden	Stockholm	No	Yes	Yes	Yes	Yes	Yes	...	...	129.00	Yes	Yes	Yes	Yes
Sweden	Umea	No	Yes	Yes	Yes	Yes	Yes	...	...	58.00	Yes	Yes	Yes	Yes
Switzerland	Basel	No	Yes	Yes	Yes	Yes	Yes	0.01	0.10	59.62	No	Yes	Yes	Yes
United Kingdom	Belfast	No	No	No	No	No	No	0.06	...	48.08	No	No	No	No
United Kingdom	Birmingham	No	No	No	No	No	No	0.03	0.35	51.00	No	No	No	No
United Kingdom	Cardiff	No	No	No	No	No	No	0.03	...	58.00	No	No	No	No
United Kingdom	Edinburgh	No	No	No	No	No	No	0.02	...	51.74	No	No	No	No
United Kingdom	London	No	No	No	No	No	No	0.02	...	54.00	No	No	No	No
United Kingdom	Manchester	No	No	No	No	No	No	0.05	...	85.30	No	No	No	No
LATIN AMERICA AND THE CARIBBEAN														
Argentina	Buenos Aires	No	No	Yes	Yes	Yes	Yes	...	...	...	Yes	Yes	Yes	Yes
Argentina	Comodoro Rivadavia	Yes	No	Yes	Yes	Yes	Yes	0.03	0.01	0.96	Yes	Yes	Yes	Yes
Argentina	Cordoba	Yes	Yes	No	No	No	No	...	...	18.20	Yes	Yes	Yes	Yes
Argentina	Rosario	No	Yes	Yes	Yes	No	Yes	...	...	4.00	Yes	Yes	Yes	Yes
Barbados	Bridgetown	No	No	Yes	Yes	Yes	Yes	0.03	0.21	0.40	No	No	No	No
Belize	Belize City	No	No	Yes	Yes	Yes	No	...	...	...	Yes	Yes	Yes	Yes
Bolivia	Santa Cruz de la Sierra	Yes	Yes	Yes	No	No	Yes	0.06	0.68	3.78	Yes	Yes	Yes	Yes
Brazil	Belem	No	No	No	No	No	No	...	...	...	No	Yes	Yes	No
Brazil	Icapui	No	No	No	No	No	No	...	...	...	Yes	Yes	Yes	Yes
Brazil	Maranguape	Yes	Yes	Yes	Yes	Yes	Yes	...	...	...	No	Yes	Yes	Yes
Brazil	Porto Alegre	Yes	Yes	Yes	Yes	No	Yes	...	0.90	35.90	Yes	Yes	Yes	Yes
Brazil	Recife	Yes	Yes	Yes	Yes	Yes	Yes	...	...	...	Yes	Yes	Yes	No
Brazil	Rio de Janeiro	Yes	Yes	Yes	Yes	Yes	Yes	4.00	...	54.00	Yes	Yes	Yes	No
Brazil	Santo Andre/ Sao Paulo	Yes	Yes	Yes	Yes	Yes	Yes	0.71	0.05	13.79	Yes	Yes	Yes	Yes
Chile	Gran Concepcion	No	Yes	Yes	Yes	Yes	Yes	8.00	19.00	...	Yes	Yes	Yes	No
Chile	Santiago de Chile	Yes	Yes	Yes	Yes	Yes	Yes	0.04	0.12	6.17	Yes	Yes	Yes	Yes
Chile	Tome	No	No	No	No	No	No	0.02	0.06	3.21	No	Yes	Yes	No
Chile	Valparaiso	Yes	Yes	Yes	Yes	Yes	No	0.01	0.02	6.56	Yes	Yes	Yes	No
Chile	Vina del Mar	No	Yes	No	Yes	Yes	Yes	0.02	0.05	3.00	Yes	Yes	Yes	Yes
Colombia	Armenia	Yes	Yes	Yes	Yes	Yes	Yes	...	...	...	Yes	Yes	Yes	Yes
Colombia	Marinilla	Yes	Yes	Yes	Yes	Yes	Yes	0.99	0.14	2.18	Yes	Yes	Yes	Yes
Colombia	Medellin	Yes	Yes	Yes	Yes	Yes	No	1.51	0.09	14.41	Yes	Yes	Yes	No
Cuba	Baracoa	No	No	No	No	No	No	...	...	...	No	No	Yes	No
Cuba	Camaguey	No	No	No	No	No	No	...	...	...	No	No	Yes	No
Cuba	Cienfuegos	No	No	No	No	No	No	...	...	...	No	No	Yes	No
Cuba	Ciudad Habana	No	No	No	No	No	No	...	...	...	No	No	Yes	No
Cuba	Pinar del Rio	No	No	No	No	No	No	...	...	...	No	No	No	No
Cuba	Santa Clara	No	No	No	No	No	No	...	...	...	No	No	Yes	No
Dominican Republic	Santiago de los Caballeros	Yes	No	No	Yes	Yes	No	...	...	...	No	Yes	No	No
Ecuador	Ambato	Yes	Yes	Yes	Yes	Yes	Yes	0.17	0.08	1.23	Yes	Yes	Yes	Yes
Ecuador	Cuenca	No	Yes	Yes	No	No	Yes	0.03	0.03	0.33	Yes	Yes	Yes	Yes
Ecuador	Guayaquil	Yes	No	Yes	Yes	Yes	Yes	0.23	0.13	6.22	Yes	Yes	Yes	No
Ecuador	Manta	Yes	No	Yes	Yes	Yes	No	...	...	...	No	No	Yes	Yes
Ecuador	Puyo	No	Yes	Yes	No	Yes	No	0.15	0.15	2.46	Yes	Yes	Yes	Yes
Ecuador	Quito	Yes	Yes	Yes	Yes	Yes	Yes	0.03	0.06	1.49	Yes	Yes	Yes	Yes
Ecuador	Tena	No	No	Yes	Yes	Yes	Yes	0.28	0.24	2.19	Yes	Yes	Yes	No
El Salvador	San Salvador	Yes	Yes	Yes	Yes	Yes	No	...	...	...	No	No	No	No
Guatemala	Quetzaltenango	Yes	Yes	No	Yes	Yes	Yes	...	8.00	...	Yes	Yes	Yes	Yes
Jamaica	Kingston	No	Yes	No	No	No	Yes	...	...	...	No	No	No	No
Jamaica	Montego Bay	No	No	No	No	No	No	...	...	...	No	No	No	No
Mexico	Ciudad Juarez	Yes	No	Yes	Yes	Yes	Yes	0.18	0.22	8.17	Yes	Yes	Yes	Yes
Nicaragua	Leon	No	No	Yes	Yes	Yes	No	0.22	0.94	5.60	No	No	No	No
Panama	Colon	No	Yes	Yes	Yes	Yes	Yes	...	...	...	No	Yes	Yes	No
Paraguay	Asuncion	No	No	Yes	No	No	Yes	0.26	0.07	0.10	Yes	Yes	Yes	No
Peru	Cajamarca	No	Yes	No	No	Yes	No	...	1.00	10.00	Yes	Yes	Yes	No
Peru	Huanuco	Yes	Yes	Yes	Yes	Yes	Yes	...	...	...	Yes	Yes	Yes	No
Peru	Huaras	No	No	Yes	Yes	Yes	Yes	...	...	...	Yes	Yes	Yes	Yes
Peru	Iquitos	Yes	No	Yes	Yes	Yes	No	...	...	...	Yes	Yes	Yes	Yes
Peru	Lima	Yes	Yes	Yes	Yes	Yes	Yes	...	...	...	Yes	Yes	Yes	Yes
Peru	Tacna	No	No	Yes	No	Yes	Yes	2.00	2.00	9.00	Yes	Yes	Yes	Yes
Peru	Tumbes	No	No	Yes	Yes	Yes	Yes	4.00	2.00	21.00	No	Yes	Yes	No
Trinidad and Tobago	Port of Spain	No	No	No	No	No	No	20.00	57.00	...	No	No	No	No
Uruguay	Montevideo	Yes	Yes	No	Yes	Yes	Yes	0.08	0.31	20.89	Yes	Yes	Yes	No
NORTHERN AMERICA														
Canada	Hull	No	No	Yes	Yes	Yes	Yes	0.00	0.00	14.40	Yes	Yes	No	Yes
USA	Atlanta	Yes	Yes	Yes	Yes	Yes	Yes	0.03	0.01	10.00	Yes	Yes	Yes	Yes
USA	Birmingham	Yes	Yes	Yes	Yes	Yes	Yes	0.03	0.01	10.00	Yes	Yes	Yes	Yes
USA	Boston	Yes	Yes	Yes	Yes	Yes	Yes	0.03	0.01	10.00	Yes	Yes	Yes	Yes
USA	Des Moines	Yes	Yes	Yes	Yes	Yes	Yes	0.03	0.01	10.00	Yes	Yes	Yes	Yes
USA	Hartford	Yes	Yes	Yes	Yes	Yes	Yes	0.03	0.01	10.00	Yes	Yes	Yes	Yes
USA	Minneapolis-St. Paul	Yes	Yes	Yes	Yes	Yes	Yes	0.03	0.01	10.00	Yes	Yes	Yes	Yes
USA	New York	Yes	Yes	Yes	Yes	Yes	Yes	0.03	0.01	10.00	Yes	Yes	Yes	Yes
USA	Providence	Yes	Yes	Yes	Yes	Yes	Yes	0.03	0.01	10.00	Yes	Yes	Yes	Yes
USA	Salt Lake	Yes	Yes	Yes	Yes	Yes	Yes	0.03	0.01	10.00	Yes	Yes	Yes	Yes
USA	San Jose	Yes	Yes	Yes	Yes	Yes	Yes	0.03	0.01	10.00	Yes	Yes	Yes	Yes
USA	Seattle	Yes	Yes	Yes	Yes	Yes	Yes	0.03	0.01	10.00	Yes	Yes	Yes	Yes
USA	Tampa	Yes	Yes	Yes	Yes	Yes	Yes	0.03	0.01	10.00	Yes	Yes	Yes	Yes
USA	Washington	Yes	Yes	Yes	Yes	Yes	Yes	0.03	0.01	10.00	Yes	Yes	Yes	Yes

TABLE C.7

continued

		Urban violence*						Reported crime (rate per 1000)			Local government transparency and accountability**			
		A	B	C	D	E	F	homicide	rape	thefts	A	D	C	D
OCEANIA														
Samoa	Apia	No	Yes	No	Yes	Yes	Yes	0.06	0.05	0.55	No	No	No	No

Source: UN-Habitat (2002), Global Urban Indicators Database 2.

Note:

* Responses (yes/no) to the following questions: At the city level, are there:
(A) areas considered as dangerous or inaccessible to the police?
(B) Violence at school?
(C) Domestic violence prevention policy?
(D) Crime prevention policy?
(E) Weapon control policy?
(F) Assistance programme(s)?

** Responses (yes/no) to the following questions: Are there:
(A) Regular in dependent auditing of municipal accounts?
(B) Published contracts and tenders for municipal services?
(C) Sanctions against faults of civil servants?
(D) Laws on disclosure of potential conflicts of interest?

REFERENCES

ABC TV (2006) 'Cambodia evictions', Foreign Correspondent Series 16, Episode 15, Broadcast on 10 October 2006. Transcript and video available at www.abc.net.au/foreign/content/2006/s1754763.htm

Abney, G. and L. Hill (1966) 'Natural disasters as a political variable: The effect of a hurricane on an urban election', *American Political Science Review* **60**(4): 974–981

ACHR (Asian Coalition for Housing Rights) (2001) 'Building an urban poor people's movement in Phnom Penh, Cambodia', *Environment and Urbanization* **13**: 61–72, http://eau.sagepub.com/cgi/reprint/13/2/61.pdf

ActionAid (2006) *Climate Change, Urban Flooding and the Rights of the Urban Poor in Africa*, ActionAid International, www.actionaid.org/wps/content/documents/Urban%20Flooding%20Africa%20Report_10112006_182953.pdf

Adams, R. A., Jr. (2003) *International Migration, Remittances, and the Brain Drain: A Study of 24 Labor-Exporting Countries*, Policy Research Working Paper 3069, World Bank, Poverty Reduction and Economic Management Network, wwwwds.worldbank.org/servlet/WDSContentServer/WDSP/IB/2003/07/08/000094946_03062104301450/Rendered/PDF/multi0page.pdf

ADB (Asian Development Bank) (2002) *Technical Assistance for Road Safety in the Association of Southeast Asian Nations*, ADB, www.adb.org/Documents/TARs/REG/tar_stu_36046.pdf

Adger, W. N. (1999) 'Social vulnerability to climate change and extremes in coastal Vietnam', *World Development* **27**(2): 249–269

Adinkrah, M. (2005) 'Vigilante homicides in contemporary Ghana', *Journal of Criminal Justice* **33**: 413–427

ADPC (Asian Disaster Preparedness Centre) (2004) *Community-Based Disaster Risk Management Field Practitioners' Handbook*, ADPC, Bangkok, accessed from www.proventionconsortium.org/themes/default/pdfs/CRA/CBDRM2004_meth.pdf

ADPC (2005) *A Primer: Disaster Risk Management in Asia*, ADPC, Bangkok

Aeron-Thomas, A. (2003) *Community Traffic Policing Scoping Study*, TRL Report PR/INT/265/2003, TRL, London

Aeron-Thomas, A., G. Jacobs, B. Sexton, G. Gururaj and F. Rahman (2004) *The Involvement and Impact of Road Crashes on the Poor: Bangladesh and India Case Studies*, TRL, Crowthorne, UK

Afukaar, F. K., P. Antwi and S. Ofosu-Amah (2003) 'Pattern of road traffic injuries in Ghana: Implications for control', *Injury Control and Safety Promotion* **10**: 69–76

AIDMI (All India Disaster Mitigation Institute) (2006) 'Shelter security in Kashmir: A central aspect of long-term recovery', *Southasiadisasters.net*, issue 22, www.proventionconsortium.org/themes/default/pdfs/AIDMI_Dec06.pdf

Alemika, E. O. and I. C. Chukwuma (2005) *Criminal Victimization and Fear of Crime in Lagos Metropolis, Nigeria*, Cleen Foundations Monograph Series No 1, www.cleen.org/LAGOS%20CRIME%20SURVEY.pdf

Alexander, D. (1989) 'Urban landslides', *Progress in Physical Geography* **13**: 157–191

Allen, F. G. (1997) 'Vigilante justice in Jamaica: The community against crime', *International Journal of Comparative and Applied Criminal Justice* **21**: 1–12

Allen, T. (2000) *The Right to Property in Commonwealth Constitutions*, Cambridge University Press, Cambridge

Alston, P. (1993) 'Excerpts from a speech to the plenary of the World Conference on Human Rights', reprinted in *Terra Viva*, 22 June 1993

Alwang, J., P. B. Siegel and S. L. Jorgensen (2001) *Vulnerability: A View from Different Disciplines*, Social Protection Discussion Paper, No 0115, World Bank, Washington, DC

Amnesty International (1998) *Human Rights Principles for Companies*, AI Index ACT 70/01/98, London

Amnesty International and COHRE (Centre on Housing Rights and Evictions) (2006) 'Forced evictions reach crisis levels in Africa: More than 3 million evicted since 2000', Presss release, 4 October 2006, www.cohre.org

Anderson, M. (1990) 'Analyzing the costs and benefits of natural disaster responses in the context of development', *Environment Working paper*, No 29, World Bank, Washington, DC

Andrienko, Y. (2002) 'Crime, wealth and inequality: Evidence from international crime victim surveys', Centre for Economic and Financial Research, Moscow, www.cepr.org/meets/wkcn/7/756/papers/andrienko.pdf

Angel, S. (2000) *Housing Policy Matters: A Global Analysis*, Oxford University Press, Oxford

Angel, S., S. C. Sheppard, D. L. Civco, R. Buckley, A. Chabaeva, L. Gitlin, A. Kraley, J. Parent and M. Perlin (2005) *The Dynamics of Global Urban Expansion*, World Bank, Washington, DC

Anti-Corruption (undated) 'Namibia's zero tolerance for corruption campaign', www.anticorruption.info/cam_info.htm

Anti-Corruption Gateway for Europe and Eurasia (undated) 'Understanding corruption', www.nobribes.org/en/reference_centre/understanding_corruption/default.asp

Appadurai, A. (2006) *Fear of Small Numbers: An Essay on the Geography of Anger*, Duke University Press, Durham and London

Appiahene-Gyamfi, J. (2003) 'Urban crime trends and patterns in Ghana: The case of Accra', *Journal of Criminal Justice* **31**: 13–23

Arimah, B. C. (2005) 'What drives infrastructure spending in cities of developing countries?', *Urban Studies* **42**(8): 1345–1368

Arizaga, C. (2005) *El mito de Communidad en la Cuidad Mundializada: Estilos de Vida y Nuevas Clases Medias en Urbanizaciones Cerradas*, Ediciones El Cielo Por Asalto, Buenos Aires

Asian Coalition for Housing Rights and Third World Network (1989) *Battle for Housing Rights in Korea: Report of the South Korea Project of the Asian Coalition for Housing Rights*, ACHR, Bangkok

Asian Urban Disaster Mitigation Programme (2001) *Naga City Disaster Mitigation Plan*, Working Paper No 5, www.adpc.net/audmp/library/work_papers/ph1.pdf

Asian Urban Disaster Mitigation Programme (undated) *Creating Safer Communities: Sri Lanka Urban Multi-Hazard Mitigation Project*, www.adpc.net/AUDMP/sri.html

Astill, J. (2004) 'Iran considers moving capital from quake zone', *The Guardian*, 6 January 2004, www.guardian.co.uk/naturaldisasters/story/0,7369,1116676,00.html

Atlas, R. and W. LeBlanc (1994) 'Environmental barriers to crime', *Ergonomics in Design*, October: 9–16

Baker, B. (2002) 'When the Bakassi boys came: Eastern Nigeria confronts vigilantism', *Journal of Contemporary African Studies* **20**: 223–244

Balbo, M. and G. Guadagnoli (2007) 'Enhancing urban safety and human security: UNTFHS projects implemented by UN-Habitat in Afghanistan, Cambodia and Sri Lanka ', unpublished paper prepared for UN-Habitat

Balbus, I. (1973) *The Dialectics of Legal Repression*, Russell Sage Foundation, New York

Banarji, G. (1997) 'The impact of modern warfare: The case of Iraq, in J. Beall (ed.) *A City for All, Valuing Difference and Working with Diversity*, Zed Books: London, pp194–199.

Banerjee, B. (2002) 'Security of tenure in Indian cities', in A. Durand-Lasserve and L. Royston (eds) *Holding Their Ground: Secure Land Tenure for the Urban Poor in Developing Countries*, Earthscan, London, pp37–58

Bankoff, G., G. Frerks and D. Hilhorst (eds) (2004) *Mapping Vulnerability: Disasters, Development and People*, Earthscan, London and Sterling, Virginia

Barakat, S. (2003) *Housing Reconstruction After Conflict and Disaster*, Humanitarian Practice Network Paper No 43, Humanitarian Practice Network, Overseas Development Institute, London, www.odihpn.org/documents/networkpaper043.pdf

Barber, B. R. (1996) *Jihad vs McWorld: How Globalism and Tribalism are Reshaping the World*, Ballentine Books, New York

Barclay, G., C. Tavares, S. Kenny, A. Siddique and E. Wilby (2003) *International Comparisons of Criminal Justice Statistics 2001*, Research, Development and Statistics Directorate, Home Office, London, www.csdp.org/research/hosb1203.pdf

Barker, J. (2003) *The No-Nonsense Guide to Terrorism*, Verso in association with *New Internationalist*, London

Barr, R. and K. Pease (1990) 'Crime placement, displacement, and deflection', *Crime and Justice* **12**: 277–318

Barrios, S., L.Bertinelli and E. Strobl (2006) 'Climatic change and rural–urban migration: The case of sub-Saharan Africa', *Journal of Urban Economics*, **60**: 357–371

Barter, P. (2001) Linkages between Transport and Housing for the Urban Poor: Policy Implications and Alternatives, UN-Habitat Discussion Paper, www.unhabitat.org/categories.asp?catid=373

Bastos, Y. G. L., S. M. de Andrade, D. A. Soares and T. Matsuo (2005) 'Seat belt and helmet use among victims of traffic accidents in a city of southern Brazil, 1997–2000', *Public Health* **119**: 930–932

Baxi, U. (1982) 'Taking suffering seriously: Social action litigation in the Supreme Court of India', *Review of the International Commission of Jurists* **29**: 37–49

BBC News (2001) 'Smugglers jailed over Chinese deaths', http://news.bbc.co.uk/2/hi/europe/1325778.stm

BBC News (2003) 'Nigeria remembers deadly barracks blast', January, http://news.bbc.co.uk/1/hi/world/africa/2698081.stm

BBC News (2006a) 'Homebuyers "face growing worries"', http://news.bbc.co.uk/2/hi/business/5365934.stm

BBC News (2006b) 'Scores dead in Mumbai train bombs', http://news.bbc.co.uk/1/hi/world/south_asia/5169332.stm

Beall, J. (2006) 'Cities, terrorism and development', *Journal of International Development* **18**: 105–120

Beavon, D. J. K., P. L. Brantingham and P. J. Brantingham (1994) *The Influence of Street Networks on the Patterning of Property Offenses*, www.popcenter.org/Library/CrimePrevention/Volume%2002/06beavon.pdf

Benevides, M., and R. F. Ferreira (1991) 'Popular responses and urban violence: Lynching in Brazil', in M. K. Huggins (eds) *Vigilantism and the State in Modern Latin America*, Praeger, New York, pp33–45

Benson, C. and Twigg, J. (2004) *Measuring Mitigation: Methodologies for Assessing Natural Hazard Risks and the Net Benefits of Mitigation: A Scoping Study*, ProVention Consortum, Geneva

Bern, C. (1993) 'Risk factors for mortality in the Bangladesh cyclone of 1991', *Bulletin of the World Heath Organization* **71**(11): 73–78

Bhattachatya, S. (2003) 'European heatwave caused 35,000 deaths', *New Scientist*, 10 October

Bigio, A. G. (2003) 'Cities and climate change' in A. Kreimer, M. Arnold and A. Carlin (eds) *Building Safer Cities: The Future of Disaster Risk*, Disaster Risk Management Series, No 3, World Bank, Washington, DC, pp91–100

Billing, K. (2006) 'Building back better: Post-crisis economic recovery and development', *Habitat Debate* **12**(4): 14

Blaikie, P., T. Cannon, I. Davis and B. Wisner (1994) *At Risk: Natural Hazards, People's Vulnerability and Disasters*, Routledge, London

Blakely, E. J. and M. G. Snyder (1999) *Fortress America: Gated Communities in the United States*, Brookings Institution Press, Washington, DC

Blandy, S. (2005) *Housing Responses to a Less then Perfect World: Where Do Gated Communities Fit In?* Public presentation at Sheffield Hallam University Sheffield, England, 12 October 2005

Blandy, S., D. F. Lister, R. Atkinson and J. Flint (2003) *Gated Communities: A Systematic Review of the Research Evidence*, CNR Paper 12: 1–65, www.bris.ac.uk/sps/cnrpaperspdf/cnr12pap.pdf

Boamah, S. and J. Stanley (2007) 'Conditions and trends in crime and violence: The case of Port Moresby, Papua New Guinea', Unpublished case study prepared for *Global Report on Human Settlements 2007*

Bohannon, J. (2005) 'Disasters: Searching for lessons from a bad year', *Science*, 23 December, **310** (5756): 1883

Boisteau, C. and Y. Pedrazzini (2006) 'Urban violence and security policies: Local public and private practices for securing the urban space: Action-oriented research in Barcelona and Bogota', Panel presentation, Third Session of the World Urban Forum, Vancouver, June 2006

Bombay First (2003) *Vision Mumbai: Transforming Mumbai into a World-Class City: A Summary of Recommendations*, Bombay First and McKinsey and Company, Mumbai

Boonyabancha, S. (2005) 'Baan Mankong: Going to scale with "slum" and squatter upgrading in Thailand', *Environment and Urbanization* **17**(1): 21–46

Bosshard, P. and S. Lawrence (2006) *The World Bank's Conflicted Corruption Fight*, International Rivers Network, www.irn.org/programs/finance/index.php?id=060511worldbank.html#note3

Bram, J., J. Orr and C. Rapaport (2002) 'Measuring the effects of the September 11 attack on New York City', *Federal Reserve Bank of New York Economic Policy Review*, November, pp5–20

Brantingham, P. J. and P. L. Brantingham (1991) *Environmental Criminology*, Waveland Press, Prospect Heights, Illinois

Bray, M. (2003) *Adverse Effects of Private Supplementary Tutoring: Dimensions, Implications and Government Responses*, UNESCO, http://unesdoc.unesco.org/images/0013/001330/133039e.pdf

Breteche, J. and A. Steer (2006) 'Land titles in Aceh: So much hope but more action needed', *Jakarta Post*, 2 December, www.reliefweb.int/rw/RWB.NSF/db900SID/KHII–6WT7NX?OpenDocument

Briceno-Leon, R. (1999) 'Violence and the right to kill: Public perceptions from Latin America', Paper presented at the workshop Rising Violence and the Criminal Justice Response in Latin America: Toward an Agenda for Collaborative Research in the 21st Century, University of Texas, Austin, 6–9 May 1999, cited in C. Moser (ed) (2004) 'Urban violence and insecurity: An introductory roadmap', *Environment and Urbanization* **16**(2): 3–16

Briceno-Leon, R. and V. Zubillaga (2002) 'Violence and globalization in Latin America', *Current Sociology* **50**(1): 19–31

Bristol, G. (2007a) 'Cambodia: The struggle for tenure', Unpublished case study prepared for *Global Report on Human Settlements 2007*

Bristol, G. (2007b) 'Strategies for survival: Security of tenure in Bangkok', Unpublished case study prepared for *Global Report on Human Settlements 2007*

Broadhurst, R. G, L. K. Wa, and C. C. Yee (2007) 'Trends in crime and violence: The case of Hong Kong, China', Unpublished case study prepared for *Global Report on Human Settlements 2007*

Bromley, D. W. (2005) 'The empty promises of formal titles: Creating Potempkin villages in the tropics', www.desotowatch.net/?module=Articles;action=Article.publicOpen;ID=2935

Bronfenbrenner, U. (1988) 'Toward an experimental ecology of human development', *American Psychologist* **32**(5): 13–31

Brown, H. A. (1994) *Economics of Disaster with Special Reference to the Jamaican Experience*, Working Paper No 2, Centre for Environment and Development, University of the West Indies, Mona Campus, Jamaica

Brunetti, A., G. Kisunko and B. Weder (undated) *Institutional Obstacles to Doing Business: Region by Region Results from a Worldwide Survey of the Private Sector*, Policy Research Working Paper No 1759, World Bank, Washington, DC

Budd, T. (1999) *Findings from the British Crime Survey*, Information and Publications Group, Home Office, London Issue 4/99, www.homeoffice.gov.uk/rds/pdfs/hosb499.pdf

Bukurura, S. H. (1993). 'Vigilantism in Tanzania', in M. Findlay and U. Zvekic (eds) *Alternative Policing Styles: Cross-Cultural Perspectives*, Kluwer, Boston, pp131–137

Bull-Kamanga, L., K. Diagne, A. Lavell, E. Leon, F. Lerise, H. MacGregor, A. Maskrey, M. Meshack, M. Pelling, H. Reid, D. Satterthwaite, J. Songsore, K. Westgate and A. Yitambe (2003) 'From everyday hazards to disasters: The accumulation of risk in urban areas', *Environment and Urbanization* **15**(1): 193–203

Burgess, E. W. and M. McKenzie (1925) *The City*, University of Chicago Press, Chicago, IL

Bursa, M. (2004) 'Policies and practices in Turkey', Paper presented at an International Seminar on Policies and Practices in the Management of Seismic Risks in Urban Areas, 16–18 November, Tehran, www.gignos.ch/reps/Tehran.pdf

Buscaglia, E. and J. van Dijk (2003) 'Controlling organized crime and corruption in the public sector', *Forum on Crime and Society* **3**(1, 2): 3–34

Butler, B. and S. Purchase (2004) 'Personal networking in Russian post soviet life', *Research and Practice in Human Resource Management* **12**(1): 34–60

Buvinic, M. and A. Morrison (1999) *Violence as an Obstacle to Development*, Inter-American Development Bank, Washington, DC

Buvinic, M., A. R. Morrison and M. Shifter (1999) 'Violence in the Americas: A framework for action', in A. R. Morrison and M. L. Biehl (eds) *Too Close to Home: Domestic Violence in the Americas*, Inter-American Development Bank, Washington, DC, ppxi–xiii

Buyse, A. (2006) 'Strings attached: The concept of "home" in the case law of the European Court of Human Rights', *European Human Rights Law Review* **3**: 294–307

Cai, Y. (2003) 'Collective ownership or cadres' ownership? The non-agricultural use of farmland in China', *China Quarterly* **175**: 662–680

Caldeira, T. (2000) *City of Walls: Crime, Segregation, and Citizenship in São Paulo*, University of California Press, Berkeley, CA

Calvi-Parisetti, P. and D. Kiniger-Passigli (2002) *Coordination in Crisis Response and Reconstruction*, ILO Press, Geneva, www.gignos.ch/reps/coordination.pdf

Carreño, Martha-Liliana, Omar D. Cardona and Alex H. Barbat (2007) 'Urban seismic risk evaluation: A holistic approach', *Natural Hazards* **40**(1): 137–172

Carter, J. (2006) *Residents of Rio's Favelas Face Diverse Risks*, Worldwatch Institute, www.worldwatch.org/node/4756

Casa Alianza UK (undated) 'Giving street children back their childhood', www.casa-alianza.org.uk/

Caulfield, C. (1998) *Masters of Illusion: The World Bank and the Poverty of Nations*, Pan Books, Macmillan, London

CEN (Comité Européen du Normalisation) (2003) *Prevention of Crime – Urban Planning and Design –*

Part 2: Urban Planning, ENV 14383–2, CEN Management Centre, Brussels, Belgium

Center for Family Policy and Research (2006) *The State of Children and Families: 2000*, www.missouri.edu/~cfprwww/MOchildfam06.pdf

Cernea, M. (1996) 'Public policy responses to development: Induced population displacements', *Economic and Political Weekly* **31**(24): 1515–1523

Chang, H. J. (2003) *Kicking Away the Ladder: Development Strategy in Historical Perspective*, Anthem Press, London

Chege, L. W., C. J. Irene, R. Nadelman and B. Orr (2007) 'Living with floods in Mozambique: Urban impact in a context of chronic disaster', Unpublished case study prepared for *Global Report on Human Settlements 2007*

Chitere, P. O. and T. N. Kibual (2006) Efforts to Improve *Road Safety in Kenya: Achievements and Limitations of Reforms in the Matatu Industry*, Discussion Paper DP/081/2006, Institute of Policy Analysis and Research, Kenya, www4.worldbank.org/afr/ssatp/Resources/CountryDocuments/Road-Safety-Kenya-IPAR.pdf

Christian Aid (undated) 'In debt to disaster: What happened to Honduras after Hurricane Mitch?', www.christian-aid.org.uk/indepth/9910inde/indebt1.htm

Christoplos, I. (2006) *Links between Relief, Rehabilitation and Development in the Tsunami Response*, Tsunami Evaluation Coalition, www.tsunami-evaluation.org

Chua, A. (2003) *World on Fire: How Exporting Free Market Democracy Breeds Ethnic Hatred and Global Instability*, Random House, New York

Cicolella, P. (1999) 'Globalizacion y dualizacion en la Region Metropolitana de Buenos Aires. Grandes inversions y reestructuracion socioterritorial en los anos 90', *Estudios Urbanos y Regionales (EURE)* **25**(76), Instituto de Estudios Urbanos, Facultad de Arquitectura y Bellas Artes, Pontificia Universidad Catolica de Chile, Santiago de Chile

Cities Alliance (2003) *Annual Report*, Washington, DC

Clapham, A. (2006) *Human Rights Obligations of Non-State Actors*, Oxford University Press, Oxford

Clark, D. (2000) 'World urban development: Processes and patterns at the end of the twentieth century', *Geography* **85**(1): 15–23

Clarke, R. V. (1997) *Situational Crime Prevention: Successful Case Studies*, 2nd edition, Harrrow and Heston, Albany, NY

Clarke, R.V. (2003) 'Closing streets and alleys to reduce crime: Should you go down this road? Problem-oriented guides for police response', *Response Guides Series*, No 2, US Department of Justice, Office of Community Oriented Policing Services, Washington, DC, www.popcenter.org/Responses/PDFs/Closing_alleys_and_streets.pdf

Clarke, R. V. and M. Felson (1993) *Routine Activity and Rational Choice: Advances in Criminology Theory*, Transaction Publishers, New Brunswick, NJ

Clichevsky, N. (2003) 'Urban land markets and disasters: Floods in Argentina's cities', in A. Kreimer, M. Arnold and A. Carlin (eds) *Building Safer Cities: The Future of Disaster Risk*, Disaster Risk Management Series No 3, World Bank, Washington, DC, pp165–176

Cohen, M. A. (1974) *Urban Policy and Political Conflict in Africa: A Study of the Ivory Coast*, University of Chicago Press, Chicago, IL

Cohen, M., B. Ruble, J. Tulchin and A. Garland (eds) (1996) *Preparing the Urban Future: Global Pressures and Local Forces*, The Woodrow Wilson Center Press and the Johns Hopkins University Press, Baltimore

COHRE (Centre on Housing Rights and Evictions) (1999) *Forced Evictions and Human Rights: A Manual for Action*, Sources No 3, COHRE, Geneva

COHRE (2000) *Successfully Resisting Forced Eviction: Case Studies*, COHRE, Geneva

COHRE (2002) *Forced Evictions: Violations of Human Rights*, Global Survey No 8, COHRE, Geneva

COHRE (2003) *Forced Evictions: Violations of Human Rights*, Global Survey No 9, COHRE, Geneva

COHRE (2006) *Forced Evictions: Violations of Human Rights*, Global Survey No 10, COHRE, Geneva

Coker, A. L., K. E. Davis, I. Arias, S. Desai, M. Sanderson, H. M. Brandt and P. H. Smith (2002) 'Physical and mental health effects of intimate partner violence for men and women', *American Journal of Preventive Medicine* **23**(4): 260–268

Collier, P. and A. Hoeffler (2004) 'Murder by numbers: Comparisons and inter-relationships between homicide and war', www.csae.ox.ac.uk/conferences/2004-GPRaHDiA/papers/3m–HoefflerCollier–CSAE2004.pdf

Collins, D. C. A. and R. A. Kearns (2005) 'Geographies of inequality: Child pedestrian injury and walking school buses in Auckland, New Zealand', *Social Science and Medicine* **60**: 61–69

Colquhoun, I. (2004) *Design out Crime: Creating Safe and Sustainable Communities,* Architectural Press, Oxford

Commission for Global Road Safety (2006) *Make Roads Safe: A New Priority for Sustainable Development, Commission for Global Road Safety*, www.makeroadssafe.org/documents/make_roads_safe_low_res.pdf

Commission on Human Security (2003) *Human Security Now: Protecting and Empowering People*, New York

Commission on Legal Empowerment of the Poor (2006a) *Overview Paper*, http://legalempowerment.undp.org/pdf/Overview.pdf

Commission on Legal Empowerment of the Poor (2006b) *Report from South America (Brazil)*, http://legalempowerment.undp.org/pdf/SouthAmerica_report.pdf

Comte, S., M. Wardman and G. Whelan (2000) 'Drivers' acceptance of automatic speed limiters: Implications for policy and implementation', *Transport Policy* **7**: 259–267

Conchesco T. G. (2003) *Protecting New Health Facilities from Natural Disasters: Guidelines for the Promotion of Disaster Mitigation, PAHO/WHO*, Washington, DC

Consortium for Street Children (2003) *Frequently Asked Questions*, www.streetchildren.org.uk/

Cornelius, W. A. (1969) 'Urbanization as an agent in Latin American political instability: The case of Mexico', *American Political Science Review* **63**(3): 833–857

Cousins, B., T. Cousins, D. Hornby, R. Kingwill, L. Royston and W. Smit (2005) 'Will formalising property rights reduce poverty in South Africa's "second economy"?', *Policy Brief: Debating Land Reform, Natural Resources and Poverty*, No 18, PLAAS, Cape Town, South Africa

Cozens, P. M., T. Pascoe and D. Hillier (2004) 'Critically reviewing the theory and practice of secured-by-design for residential new-build housing in Britain', *Crime Prevention and Community Safety* **6**(1): 13–29

Cross, J. A. (2001) 'Megacities and small towns: Different perspectives on hazard vulnerability', *Environmental Hazards* **3**(2): 63–80

Cukier, W. and Seidel, V. (2005) *The Global Gun Epidemic*, Greenwood, Westport, CT

Currie, J. and Tekin, E. (2006) *Does Child Abuse Cause Crime?* NBER Working Papers 12171, National Bureau of Economic Research, Inc, Cambridge, MA

Cyclists' Touring Club (2002) *Best Value in Implementing Cycling Policy*, www.ctc.org.uk/DesktopDefault.aspx?TabID=4384

Dagens Nyheter (2002) *Dagens Nyheter*, Swedish daily newspaper, Stockholm, March, reproduced in World Press Review, vol 49, no 3

Davies, J., S. Sandstrom, A. Shorrocks and E. Wolff (2006) *The World Distribution of Household Wealth*, United Nations University World Institute for Development Economics Research (UNU–WIDER), www.wider.unu.edu/research/2006-2007/2006-2007-1/wider-wdhw-launch-5-12-2006/wider-wdhw-report-5-12-2006.pdf

Davis, A., A. Quimby, W. Odero, G. Gururaj and M. Hijar, (2003) *Improving Safety by Reducing Impaired Driving in Developing Countries: A Scoping Study*, TRL Unpublished Project Report PR/INT/724/03.TRL, Crowthorne, UK

Davis, M. (2006a) *Planet of Slums*, Verso, London

Davis, M. (2006b) 'Who is killing New Orleans', *The Nation*, 10 April 2006, pp11–20

De Cesare, D. (1997) 'De la Guerra Civil a la Guerra de Pandillas: Crecimiento de las Pandillas de Los Angeles en El Salvador', in *Proceedings of PAHO Adolescent and Youth Gang Violence Prevention Workshop*, 7–9 May, San Salvador, PAHO, Washington, DC

de Soto, H. (2000) *The Mystery of Capital: Why Capitalism Triumphs in the West and Fails Everywhere Else*, Black Swan Books, London

Decker, D., D. Shichor and R. O'Brien (1982) *Urban Sructure and Victimization*, Lexington Books, Lexington, MA

Dedeurwaerdere, A. (1998) *Cost-Benefit Analysis for Natural Disaster Management: A Case Study in the Philippines*, CRED, University of Louvain, Brussels, Belgium

Deininger, K. (2003) *Land Policies for Growth and Poverty Reduction: A World Bank Policy Research Report*, World Bank, Washington, DC and Oxford University Press, Oxford and New York

del Frate, A. (2003) 'The voice of victims of crime: Estimating the true level of conventional crime', *Forum on Crime and Society* **3**(1, 2): 127–140

Delgado, J., M. E. Ramirez-Cardich, and R. H. Gilam (2002) 'Risk factors for burns in children: Crowding poverty and poor maternal education', *Injury Prevention* **8**(1): 38–41

Denner, J., D. Kirby, K. Coyle and C. Brindis (2001) 'The protective role of social capital and cultural norms in Latino communities: A study of adolescent births', *Hispanic Journal of Behavioral Sciences* **23**(1): 3–21

DETR (Department of the Environment, Transport and the Regions) (2000) *Our Towns and Cities: The Future: Delivering an Urban Renaissance*, HMSO (Her Majesty's Stationery Office), London

Devereux, S. (1999) *Making Less Last Longer: Informal Safety Nets in Malawi*, IDS Discussion Paper 373, Institute for Development Studies, Sussex, UK

DFID (Department for International Development) (2005) *Disaster Risk Reduction: A Development Concern*, DFID, London

DFID (2006) *Reducing the Risk of Disasters: Helping to Achieve Sustainable Poverty Reduction in a Vulnerable World: A DFID Policy Paper*, DFID, London

Diamond, J. (2005) *Collapse: How Societies Decide to Fail or Succeed*, Viking Books, New York

Dill, K. and M. Pelling (2006) *Case Studies of Natural Disasters and Political Change*, Working Paper No 1, Department of Geography, King's College London, London

Dilley, M., R. S.Chen, U. Deichmann, A. L. Lerner-Lam, M. Arnold, J. Agwe, P. Buys, O. Kjekstad, B. Lyon, and G. Yetman (2005) *Natural Disaster Hotspots: A Global Risk Analysis*, World Bank, Washington, DC, www.proventionconsortium.org/?pageid=37&publicationid=38#38

Dimitriou, H. T. (2006) 'Towards a generic sustainable urban transport strategy for middle-sized cities in Asia: Lessons from Ningbo, Kanpur and Solo', *Habitat International* **30**(4):1082–1099

Disaster Management Centre (2005) *Towards a Safer Sri Lanka: A Road Map for Disaster Risk Management*, Ministry for Disaster Management, Colombo, Sri Lanka

Dixit, A. (2006) *Community-Centered Earthquake Mitigation and Preparedness: Experience from Nepal*, www.janathakshan.org/sapd/pdf/AmodDixitNepal.pdf

DoE (UK Department of the Environment) (1994) *Planning Out Crime*, Circular 5/94, HMSO, London

Dossal, M. (2005) 'A master plan for the city', *Economic and Political Weekly*, 3 September

Dowdney, L. (2003) 'Neither war nor peace: International comparisons of children and youth in organized armed violence', COAV Viva Rio, ISER and IANSA

Dowdney, L. (2005) *Neither War nor Peace: International Comparisons of Children and Youth in Organized Armed Violence. Children and Youth in Organized Armed Violence (COAV)*, Rio de Janeiro, www.coav.org.br

DTLR (Department of Transport, Local Government and the Regions) (2001) *Planning: Delivering a Fundamental Change*, DTLR, London

Duchrow, U. and F. J. Hinkelammert (2004) *Property for People, Not for Profit*, Zed Books, London

Durand-Lasserve, A. (1998) 'Law and urban change in developing countries: Trends and issues', in E. Fernandes and A. Varley (eds) *Illegal Cities: Law and Urban Change in Developing Countries*, Zed Books, London, pp176–190

Durand-Lasserve, A. (2006) 'Market-driven evictions and displacements: Implications for perpetuation of informal settlements in developing countries', in M. Huchzermeyer and A. Karam (eds) *Informal Settlements: A Perpetual Challenge?*, UCT Press, Cape Town

Durand-Lasserve, A. and L. Royston (2002) 'International trends and country contexts: From tenure regularization to tenure security', in A. Durand-Lasserve and L. Royston (eds) *Holding Their Ground: Secure Land Tenure for the Urban Poor in Developing Countries*, Earthscan, London, pp1–26

ECA (Economic Commission for Africa) and WHO (World Health Organization) (2007) Accra Declaration, Ministerial Roundtable, African Road Safety Conference, Accra, Ghana, 8 February 2007, www.fiafoundation.com/resources/documents/1406060961ministerialdeclarationofroadsafetyconferenceaccra.pdf

Eck, J. (1997) 'Preventing crime at places', in L. W. Sherman, D. C. Gottfredson, D. C. Mackenzie, J. Eck, P. Reuter and S. D. Bushway (eds) *Preventing Crime:*

What Works, What Doesn't, What's Promising, National Institute of Justice Research, Department of Justice, Washington, DC

Eck, J. E. and J. Wartell (1996) *Reducing Crime and Drug Dealing by Improving Place Management: A Randomized Experiment*, Report to the San Diego Police Department, Crime Control Institute, Washington, DC

ECLAC (United Nations Economic Commission for Latin America and the Caribbean) (2004) *Grenada, Macro Socio-Economic Assessment of the Damages Caused by Hurricane Ivan*, www.eclac.cl/portofspain/noticias/noticias/7/19587/gndreport3%20rev.pdf

Eisner, M. (2003) 'Long-term historical trends in violent crime', *Crime and Justice: A Review of Research* **30**: 83–142

Ekblom, P. (1997) 'Gearing up against crime: A dynamic framework to help designers keep up with the adaptive criminal in a changing world', *International Journal of Risk, Security and Crime Prevention* **2**(4): 249–265

Enarson, E. (2000) *Gender Issues in Natural Disasters: Talking Points and Research Needs*, ILO InFocus Programme on Crisis Response and Reconstruction Workshop, Geneva, 3–5 May 2000, www.gdnonline.org/resources/ilo–talking.doc

Enarson, E. and B. Morrow (eds) (1997) *The Gendered Terrain of Disasters: Through Woman's Eyes*, Praeger, New York

Esnal, L. (2006) 'La inseguridad en Brasil ahora oblige a vivir blindado', *La Nacion*, Buenos Aires, 11 June

Esser, D. (2004) 'The city as arena, hub and prey: Patterns of violence in Kabul and Karachi', *Environment & Urbanization* **16**(2): 31–38

European Commission (2001) *European Transport policy for 2020: Time to Decide*, Office for Official Publications of the European Communities, Luxembourg

Eversole, R., R. Routh and L. Ridgeway (2004) 'Crime and violence prevention in an urban indigenous community', *Environment and Urbanization* **16**(4): 73–82

Eviction Watch India (2003) *A Report on Evictions in India's Major Cities*, Combat Law Publication, Indore

Fafchamps, M. and Moser, C. (2003) 'Crime, isolation and law enforcement', *Journal of African Economies* **12**(4): 625–671

Fajnzylber, P., D. Lederman and N. Loayza (2002) 'Inequality and violent crime', *Journal of Law and Economics* **45**: 1–40

FAO (Food and Agriculture Organization of the United Nations) (2005) *Access to Rural Land and Land Administration after Violent Conflicts*, FAO Land Tenure Studies 8, FAO, Rome

FAO, Norwegian Refugee Council, Office for the Coordination of Humanitarian Affairs, Office of the United Nations High Commissioner for Human Rights, UN-Habitat, Office of the United Nations High Commissioner for Refugees (2007) *Housing and Property Restitution for Refugees and Displaced Persons. Implementing the 'Pinheiro Principles'*, International Training Centre of the ILO, Turin, Italy

Farrington, D. P. and B. C. Welsh (2002) *Effects of Improved Street Lighting on Crime: A Systematic Review*, Research Study 251, Home Office, London

Farvacque-Vitkovic, C., L. Godin, H. Leroux, F. Verdet and R. Chavez, (2005) *Street Addressing and the Management of Cities*, World Bank, Washington, DC

FBI (Federal Bureau of Investigations) (2004) 'Crime in the United States 2004' United States Department of Justice, www.fbi.gov/ucr/cius_04/offenses_reported/index.html

Felson, M. (1986) 'Linking criminal choices, routine activities, informal control, and criminal outcomes', in D. B. Cornish and R. V. Clarke (eds), *The Reasoning Criminal*, Springer Verlag, New York, pp119–128

Felson, M. (2002) *Crime in Everyday Life*, 3rd edition, Sage, Thousand Oaks, CA

FIG (International Federation of Surveyors) (1999) *The Bathurst Declaration on Land Administration for Sustainable Development*, www.fig.net/pub/figpub/pub21/figpub21.htm

Fitzpatrick, D. (2006) 'Evolution and chaos in property rights systems: The Third World tragedy of contested areas', *Yale Law Journal* **115**: 996–1049

Flood, J. (2001) *Istanbul +5: Analysis of the data collection*, Report for UNCHS (Habitat)

Florida Department of Education (2003) *Florida Safe School Design Guidelines: Strategies to Enhance Security and Reduce Vandalism*, Florida Department of Education, Tallahassee, www.firn.edu/doe/edfacil/safeschools.htm

Florida Legislature (2006) *2006 Florida Statutes*, Title XI, Intergovernmental Programs, Part IV, Neighborhood Improvement Districts, Chapter 163.501, The Safe Neighborhoods Act, www.leg.state.fl.us/statutes/index.cfm?App_mode=Display_Statute&Search_String=&URL=Ch0163/SEC502.HTM&Title=->2006->Ch0163->Section%20502#0163.502

Fordham, M. (2003) 'Gender, disaster and development: The necessity for integration', in M. Pelling (ed) *Natural Disasters and Development in a Globalizing World*, Routledge, London, pp57–74

Fordham, M. (2006) 'Please don't raise gender now: We're in an emergency!', in International Federation of the Red Cross and Red Crescent Societies' (ed) *World Disasters Report 2006*, Eurospan, London

Forrester, J., H. Cambridge and S. Cinderby (undated) *The Value and Role of GIS to Planned Urban Management and Development in Cities in Developing Countries*, Stockholm Environment Institute (SEI) and University of York, www.iapad.org/publications/ppgis/research_paper-99_01.pdf

Fourie, C. (2001) 'Land and property registration at the crossroads: A time for more relevant approaches', *Habitat Debate* **7**(3): 16

Fox, N. P. (2002) 'A guideline for developing a management system for municipal integrated development planning in KwaZulu-natal', Paper presented at the Planning Africa 2002 Conference, Durban, South Africa, 18–20 September 2002, www.saplanners.org.za/SAPC/papers/Fox_20.pdf

Freeman, P. K. (2004) 'Allocation of post-disaster reconstruction financing to housing', *Building Research and Information* **32**(5): 427–437

Freudenheim (1980) cited in J. M. Albala-Bertrand (1993) *Political Economy of Large Natural Disasters: With Special Reference to Developing Countries*, Clarendon Press, Oxford

Friedmann, J. (1992) *Empowerment: The Politics of Alternative Development*. Blackwell, London

Galster, G. (1999) *Econometric Model of the Urban Opportunity Structure: Cumulative Causation among City Markets, Social Problems, and Undeserved Areas*, Diane Publishing Company, Chicago, IL

Galtung, J. (1969) 'Violence, peace and peace research', *Journal of Peace Research* **6**(3): 167–191

Gartner, R. (1990) 'The victims of homicide: A temporal and cross-national comparison', *American Sociological Review* **55**: 92–106

Gauteng Provincial Legislature (1998) *Rationalisation of Local Government Affairs Act*, Gauteng Province, South Africa

Gavidia, J. and A. Crivellari (2006) 'Legislation as vulnerability factor', *Open House International* **31**(1): 84–89

Gaviria, A. (2002) 'Assessing the effects of corruption and crime on firm performance: Evidence from Latin America', *Emerging Markets Review* **3**(3): 245–268

Gaviria, A. and C. Pages (2002) 'Patterns of crime victimization in Latin American cities' *Journal of Development Economics*, **67**:181–203

General Secretariat Central American Integration System (1999) *Reconstruction and Transformation of Central America after Hurricane Mitch*, www.sica.int/sgsica

Gentleman, A. (2007) 'Police ignore serial killings in Delhi slum, exposing unequal justice for India's poor', *New York Times*, 7 January: 8

GHI (GeoHazards International) (2001) *Global Earthquake Safety Initiative Final Report*, www.geohaz.org/contents/publications/gesi–report%20with%20prologue.pdf

Gibbons, S. (2002) 'The costs of urban property crime', Lincoln Institute of Land Policy, Conference paper, www.lincolninst.edu/pubs/dl/556_gibbons.pdf

GIGnos Institute (undated) *Report of an International Seminar on Policies and Practices in the Management of Seismic Risks in Urban Areas*, www.gignos.ch/reps/Tehran.pdf

Gimode, E. A. (2001) 'An anatomy of violent crime and insecurity in Kenya: The case of Nairobi, 1985–1999', *Africa Development* **26**(1–2): 295–335

Glaeser, E. L. and B. Sacerdote (1999) 'Why is there more crime in cities?', *Journal of Political Economy* **107**(6): 225–258

Glaeser, E. L. and J. E. Shapiro (2002) 'Cities and warfare: The impact of terrorism on urban form', *Journal of Urban Economics* **51**: 205–224

Gold, P. (2000) *Traffic Safety: Using Engineering to Reduce Accidents*, Inter-American Development Bank, Washington, DC

Goldstein, D. (2004) *The Spectacular City, Violence and Performance in Urban Bolivia*, Duke University Press, Durham, North Carolina

Gommes, R., J. du Guerny, F. Nachtergaele and R. Brinkman (1998) 'Potential impacts of sea-level rise on populations and agriculture', SD Dimension, Sustainable Development Department, Food and Agriculture Organizations (FAO), March 1998, www.fao.org/sd/Eldirect/Elre0046.htm

Gonsalves, C. (2005) 'The right to housing: The preserve of the rich', *Housing and ESC Rights Litigation Quarterly* **1**(2): 1–32

Gonsalves, C. (2007) 'The right to housing: The Indian experience', Unpublished case study prepared for *Global Report on Human Settlements 2007*

Goodrich, J. N. (2002) 'September 11, 2001 attack on America: A record of the immediate impacts and reactions in the US travel and tourism industry', *Tourism Management* **23**: 573–580

Government of Maharashtra, Department of Relief and Rehabilitation (undated) *Mumbai Disaster Management Plan*, http://mdmu.maharashtra.gov.in/pages/Mumbai/mumbaiplanShow.php

Government of Western Australia (2004) *Preventing Crime: State Community Safety and Crime Prevention Strategy*, Office of Crime Prevention, Perth, www.crimeprevention.wa.gov.au

Gray, S. (2007) 'Trends in urban crime and violence: The case of Kingston, Jamaica', Unpublished case study prepared for *Global Report on Human Settlements 2007*

Greening, L., S. J. Dollinger and G. Pitz (1996) 'Adolescents' perceived risk and personal experience with natural disasters: An evaluation of cognitive heuristics', *Acta Psychologica* **91**(1): 27–38

GRSP (Global Road Safety Partnership) (undated) *Moving Ahead: Emerging Lessons*, GRSP, Switzerland, www.grsproadsafety.org/

Guerra-Fletes, F. F. and A. William (2006) 'Mexico disaster recovery', *Financial Times*, 23 February

Guevara, E. (2006) 'Monitoring and warning systems for natural phenomena: The Mexican experience', Paper presented at the Third International Conference on Early Warning, Bonn, 27–29 March 2006, www.ewc3.org/UK/symposium/default.asp

Guha-Sapir, D. (1997) 'Women in the front line', *UNESCO Courier*, October: 27–29

Guha-Sapir, D., D. Hargitt and P. Hoyois (2004) *Thirty Years of natural Disasters 1974–2003: The Numbers*, Presses University of Brussels, Belgium

Gupta, M., A. Sharma and R. Kaushik (2006) 'Saving Shimla, north India, from the next earthquake', *Open House International* **31**(1): 90–97

Gurr, T. (1981) 'Historical trends in violent crime: A critical review of the evidence', *Crime and Justice* **3**: 295–353

Gutierrez, F. E. (2005) *Hurricane Katrina Lessons Learned*, Harris County Office of Homeland Security and Emergency Management, www.ukresilience.info/

Gutman, M. (2006) *Revista Veinte-Tres*, Buenos Aires

Haeringer, P. (1969) *Quitte ou Double: Les Chances de l'Agglomeration Abidjanaise*, ORSTOM, Abidjan

Hagedorn, J. M. (2005) 'The global impact of gangs', *Journal of Contemporary Criminal Justice* **21**(2): 153–169

Hagedorn, J. M. and B. Rauch (2004) 'Variations in urban homicide', UIC Great Cities Institute, www.uic.edu/cuppa/cityfutures/papers/webpapers/cityfuturespapers/session3_2/3_2variations.pdf

Haggart, K. and Y. Chongqing (2003) 'Reservoirs of repression', China Rights Forum, 16 April, www.threegorgesprobe.org/tgp/print.cfm?ContentID=7007

Haines, R. and G. Wood (2002) 'Unemployment, marginalization and survival in greater east London', *Development Southern Africa* **19**(4): 573–581

Hamdi, N. and R. Goethert (1997) *Action Planning for Cities: A Guide for Community Practice*, Earthscan, London

Hamermesh, D. S. (1998) *Crime and the Timing of Work*, Working Paper 6613, National Bureau of Economic Research, Boston, MA

Hampton, C. (1982) *Criminal Procedure*, Sweet and Maxwell, London

Hansen, J. (2006) 'Can we avoid dangerous human-made climate change?', *Social Research* **73**(3): 949–974

Hardoy, J. E., D. Mitlin and D. Satterthwaite (2001) *Environmental Problems in an Urbanizing World*, Earthscan, London

Hardoy, J. E. and D. Satterthwaite (1989) *Squatter Citizen: Life in the Urban Third World*, Earthscan, London

Harris, N. (1995) 'Bombay in a global economy, structural adjustment and the role of cities', *Cities* **12**:175–184

Hartman, C. and G. D. Squires (eds) (2006) *There Is No Such Thing as a Natural Disaster: Race, Class, and Katrina*, Routledge, New York

Harvey, D. (2000) *Spaces of Hope*, University of California Press, New York

Hasan, A. (2003) 'Karachi mass transit system: What we can learn from others', Urban Resource Centre, www.urckarachi.org/mass.htm

Hedley, D., M. Phiri and L. Bull-Kamanga (2002) 'PROSPECT (Programme of Support for Poverty Elimination and Community Transformation), urban vulnerability and governance: Lusaka Zambia', in C. Nomdo and E. Coetzee (eds) *Urban Vulnerability: Perspectives from Southern Africa*, Oxfam, Oxford, and Peri Peri, South Africa

Helmke, G. and S. Levitsky (2004) 'Informal institutions and comparative politics: A research agenda', *Perspective on Politics* **2**(4): 725–740

Hensher, D. A. (2007) 'Sustainable public transport systems: Moving towards a value for money and network-based approach and away from blind commitment', *Transport Policy* **14**: 98–102

Hewitt, K. (1997) *Regions of Risk: A Geographical Introduction to Disasters*, Addison Wesley Longman, Harlow, Essex

Hijar, M., E. Vasquez-Vela and C. Arreola-Rissa (2003) 'Pedestrian traffic injuries in Mexico', *Injury Control and Safety Promotion* **10**: 37–43

Hillier, B. (2004) 'Can streets be made safe?', *Urban Design International* **9**(1): 31–45

Hindustan Times (2005) 'Slums to be relocated', *Hindustan Times*, 16 September

Holmes, T. and I. Scoones (2000) *Participatory Environmental Policy Processes: Experiences from North and South*, IDS Working Paper No 113, University of Sussex, UK

Holmgren, P., A. Holmgren and J. Ahlner (2005) 'Alcohol and drugs in drivers fatally injured in traffic accidents in Sweden during the years 2000–2002', *Forensic Science International* **151**: 11–17

Holzman, R. and S. Jorgensen (2000) *Social Risk Management: A Conceptual Framework for Social Protection and Beyond*, Social Protection Discussion Paper No 0006, World Bank, Washington, DC, www.worldbank.org/sp

Housing and Property Directorate/Housing and Property Claims Commission (2005) *Annual Report 2005 (with Statistical Update)*, Housing and Property Directorate/Housing and Property Claims Commission, Kosovo

Howell, J. C. and S. H. Decker (1999) 'The youth gangs, violence and drugs connection', US Department of Justice, Office of Juvenile Justice and Delinquency Prevention, www.ncjrs.gov/pdffiles1/93920.pdf

HRW (Human Rights Watch) (undated a) 'Women's rights: Stop violence against women in Pakistan', http://hrw.org/campaigns/pakistan/forms.htm

HRW (undated b) 'Background on child trafficking in Togo' http://hrw.org/reports/2003/togo0403/togo0303-03.htm

Hsieh, C. C. and M. D. Pugh (1993) 'Poverty, income inequality, and violent crime: A meta-analysis of recent aggregate data studies', *Criminal Justice Review* **18**(2): 182–202

Huggins, C. and J. Clover (eds) (2005) *From the Ground Up: Land Rights, Conflict and Peace in Sub-Saharan Africa*, Institute for Security Studies, South Africa

Huggins, C. and B. M. Ochieng (2005) 'Paradigms, processes and practicalities of land reform in post-conflict sub-Saharan Africa', in C. Huggins and J. Clover (eds) *From the Ground Up: Land Rights, Conflict and Peace in Sub-Saharan Africa*, Institute for Security Studies, South Africa, pp27–54

Hulchanski, J. D. (2007) 'Warning: Do not come to Canada for affordable housing or security of tenure (unless you have lots of money)', Unpublished case study prepared for *Global Report on Human Settlements 2007*

Humansecurity-cites.org (2007) *Human Security for an Urban Century: Local Challenges, Global Perspectives*, Human Security Policy Division, Vancouver

Humantrafficking.org (2005) *Child Beggars in Thailand: A Lucrative Business*, www.humantrafficking.org/updates/91

Humantrafficking.org (undated) 'Approaches to combating trafficking', www.humantrafficking.org/content/combat_trafficking

Hummel, T. (2001) *Land Use Planning in Safer Transportation Network Planning*, Institute for Road Safety Research, Leidschendam

Huntington, S. (1996) *The Clash of Civilizations and the Making of World Order*, Simon and Schuster, New York

Huq, S. (1999) 'Environmental hazards in Dhaka', in J. K. Mitchell (ed) *Crucibles of Hazards: Mega-Cities and Disasters in Transition*, UNU Press, Tokyo, pp119–137

IAEE (International Association for Earthquake Engineering) (1986) *Guidelines for Earthquake Resistant Non-Engineered Construction*, www.nicee.org/IAEE_English.php

IFRC (International Federation of Red Cross and Red Crescent Societies) (1999) *World Disasters Report 1999*, Edigroup, Switzerland

IFRC (2001) *World Disasters Report 2001*, IFRC, Geneva

IFRC (2003) *World Disasters Report 2003*, IFRC, Geneva

IFRC (2005a) 'Humanitarian media coverage in the digital age', *World Disasters Report 2005*, IFRC, Geneva

IFRC (2005b) *World Disasters Report*, IFRC, Geneva

Imparto, I. (2002) 'Security of tenure in São Paulo', in A. Durand-Lasserve and L. Royston (eds) *Holding Their Ground: Secure Land Tenure for the Urban Poor in Developing Countries*, Earthscan, London

Indian People's Human Rights Commission (2000) *Crushed Homes, Lost Lives: The Story of the Demolitions in the Sanjay Gandhi National Park*, P. A. Sebastian, Mumbai

Innes, J. E. and D. E. Booher (2004) 'Reframing public participation: Strategies for the 21st century', *Planning Theory and Practice* **5**(4): 419–436

Institute for Security Studies (2002) *Attitudes to Firearms and Crime in Nairobi: Results of a City Survey*, ISS Paper 59, Institute for Security Studies, Pretotia

Institute of Civil Engineers (1999) *Megacities: Reducing Vulnerability to Natural Disasters*, ICE, London

International Action Network on Small Arms (undated a) 'Bringing the global gun crisis under control: Summary', www.iansa.org/media/releases/IANSA-report-summary.pdf

International Action Network on Small Arms (undated b) 'Women affected by gun violence speak out', www.iansa.org/women/documents/survivors-for-web.pdf

International Council on Human Rights Policy (2005) *Local Government and Human Rights: Doing Good Service*, International Council on Human Rights Policy, Geneva

Interpol (2006) *Interpol at Work: Annual Report 2005*, Interpol, www.interpol.int/Public/ICPO/InterpolAtWork/iaw2005.pdf

IOM (International Organization for Migration) (undated) *The Nature of Human Trafficking*, www.iom.int/jahia/page676.html

IPCC (Intergovernmental Panel on Climate Change) (2001) *Climate Change 2001: Impacts, Adaptations and Vulnerability*, Contribution of Working Group II to the Third Assessment Report of the Intergovernmental Panel on Climate Change, Cambridge University Press, New York

IRIN (Integrated Regional Information Networks) News (2007a) *India: Human Trafficking in the Northeast Fuelling HIV/AIDS – Report*, www.irinnews.org/report.asp?ReportID=53386&SelectRegion=Asia&SelectCountry=INDIA

IRIN News (2007b) 'Sudan: Displaced caught in the crossfire', *IRIN News*, 10 February 2007, IRIN web special on internal displacement, OCHA, www.irinnews.org/webspecials/idp/rSudan.asp

ISDR (United Nations International Strategy for Disaster Risk Reduction) (2003) *Activities Report on the Collaboration Agreement between the ISDR and DGR of the EU*, ISDR

ISDR (2004a) *Living with Risk: A Review of Global Disaster Reduction Initiatives*, www.unisdr.org/eng/about_isdr/bd-lwr-2004-eng.htm

ISDR (2004b) *Early Warning as a Matter of Policy: The Conclusions of the Second International Conference on Early Warning*, 16–18 October 2003, Bonn, Germany, ISDR, Geneva

ISDR (2005a) *Living with Risk: A Review of Global Risk Reduction Initiatives*, ISDR, Geneva

ISDR (2005b) 'Algeria: Disaster risk reduction discussed at national land use planning meeting', *ISDR Informs*, **6**: 3, December 2005, www.unisdr.org/africa/af-informs/issue6/Issue6-2006-english-ISDR-informs-part2.pdf

ISDR (2006a) *Global Survey of Early Warning Systems*, ISDR, Geneva, www.unisdr.org/ppew/info-resources/ewc3/Global-Survey-of-Early-Warning-Systems.pdf

ISDR (2006b) *Integrating Early Warning into Relevant Policies*, www.unisdr.org/ppew/info–resources/docs/ewcii-Policy_brief.pdf

ISDR (undated a) *Millennium Development Goals and Disaster Risk Reduction: Summary of Country Practices and Examples*, www.unisdr.org/eng/mdgs-drr/summary-countries.htm

ISDR (undated b) *Millennium Development Goals and Disaster Risk Reduction: Review of 8 MDGs: Relevance for Disaster Risk Reduction and Vice-Versa*, www.unisdr.org/eng/mdgs–drr/review–8mdgs.htm

Ismail, A. (ed) (2004) *The Story of SKAA: Sind Kathci Abadis Authority*, City Press, Karachi

Jacobs, G., A. Aeron-Thomas and A. Astrop (1999) Estimating Global Road Fatalities, TRL Report 445, Transport Research Laboratory, Berkshire, UK

Jacobs, J. (1961) *The Death and Life of Great American Cities*, Vintage Books, New York

Jacquemin, A. R. A. (ed) (1999) *Urban Development and New Towns in the Third World: Lessons from the New Bombay Experience*, Ashgate, Aldershot

Jasanoff, S. (ed) (1994) *Learning from Disaster: Risk Management After Bhopal*, University of Pennsylvania Press, Philadelphia

Jeffrey, C. R. (1977) *Crime Prevention through Environmental Design*, 2nd edition, Sage, Beverly Hills

Jeffrey, P. (2000) 'Lives saved in Caracas slum', cited in D. Sanderson (2000) 'Cities, disasters and livelihoods', *Environment and Urbanization* **12**(2): 93–102

Jejeebhoy, S. J. and R. J. Cook (1997) 'State accountability for wife-beating: The Indian challenge', *Lancet* **3**(49): 110–112

Jing, J. (1997) 'Rural resettlement: Past lessons for the Three Gorges Project', *China Journal* **38**: 65–92

Kahanovitz, S. (2007) 'An urban slice of pie: The "Prevention of Illegal Eviction From and Unlawful Occupation of Land Act" in South Africa', Unpublished case study prepared for *Global Report on Human Settlements 2007*

Kaldor M., H. K. Anheier and M. Galsius (2004) *Global Civil Society 2004/05*, Russell Sage, New York

Kanji, N., L. Cotula, T. Hilhorst, C. Toulmin and W. Witten (2005) *Research Report 1: Can Land Registration Serve Poor and Marginalized Groups? Summary Report*, International Institute for Environment and Development, London

Karapuu, H. and A. Rosas (1990) 'Economic, social and cultural rights in Finland', in A. Rosas (ed) *International Human Rights Norms in Domestic Law: Finnish and Polish Perspectives*, Finnish Lawyers' Publishing Company, Helsinki

Kasperson, J. X., R. E. Kasperson and B. L. Turner (1996) *Regions at Risk: Comparisons of Threatened Environments*, United Nations University Press, Washington, DC

Kerr, R.A. (2006) 'A worrying trend of less ice, higher seas', *Science* **311**: 1698–1701

Kershaw, C., N. Chivite-Matthews, C. Thomas and R. Aust (2001) *The 2001 British Crime Survey: First Results, England and Wales*, Home Office Statistical Bulletin, www.homeoffice.gov.uk/rds/pdfs/hosb1801.pdf

Khayesi, M. (2003) 'Liveable streets for pedestrians in Nairobi: The challenge of road traffic accidents', in J. Whitelegg and G. Haq (eds) *The Earthscan Reader on World Transport, Policy and Practice*, Earthscan, London, pp35–41

Kingham, S., J. Dickinson and S. Copsey (2001) 'Travelling to work: Will people move out of their cars?', *Transport Policy* **8**: 151–160

Kitchen, T. E. (2005) 'New urbanism and CPTED in the British planning system: Some critical reflections', *Journal of Architectural and Planning Research* **22**(4): 342–357

Kitchen, T. (2007) 'Effective crime prevention strategies and engagement with the planning process: The case of Bradford, England', Unpublished case study prepared for *Global Report on Human Settlements 2007*

Kitchen, T. E. and R. H. Schneider (2005) 'Crime and the design of the built environment: Anglo-American comparisons of policy and practice', in J. Hillier and E. Rooksby (eds) *Habitus: A Sense of Place* Ashgate, Aldershot, pp258–282

Klein, R. J. T., R. J. Nicholls, and F. Thomalla (2003) 'The resilience of coastal megacities to weather-related hazards', in A. Kriemer, M. Arnold and A. Carlin (eds), *Building Safer Cities, The Future of Disaster Risk*, Disaster Risk Management Series No 3, World Bank, Washington, DC

Klinenberg, E. (2002a) *A Social Autopsy of Disaster in Chicago*, University of Chicago Press, London

Klinenberg, E. (2002b) *Heat Wave: A Social Ecology of Disaster in Chicago*, University of Chicago Press, Chicago, IL and London

Knowles, P. (2003a) 'Designs on crime', *Police Review* **18**: 22–23

Knowles, P. (2003b) 'The cost of policing new urbanism', *Community Safety Journal* **2**(4): 33–37

Koenig, M. A., R. Stephenson, S. Ahmed, S. J. Jejeebhoy and J. Campbell (2006) 'Individual and contextual determinants of domestic violence in North India', *America Journal of Public Health* **96**(1): 132–138

Kohler, A., S. Jülich, and L. Bloemertz (2004) *Guidelines for Risk Analysis: A Basis for Disaster Risk Management GTZ*, www.gtz.de/en/themen/uebergreifende-themen/krisenpraevention/5152.htm

Kopits. E. and M. Cropper (2003) 'Traffic fatalities and economic growth', Policy Research Working Paper, No. 3035, World Bank, Washington, DC

Kreimer, A., M. Arnold and A. Carlin (eds) (2003) *Building Safer Cities: The Future of Disaster Risk*, Disaster Risk Management Series No 3, World Bank, Washington, DC

Kreimer, A., A. Margaret, C. Barham, P. Freeman, R. Gilbert, F. Krimgold, R. Lester, J. D. Pollner and T. Vogt (1999) *Managing Disaster Risk in Mexico: Market Incentives for Mitigation Investment*, World Bank, Washington, DC

Kreimer, A. and A. Munasinghe (1992) *Environmental Management and Urban Vulnerability*, World Bank Discussion Paper No 168, World Bank, Washington, DC

Krkoska, L. and K. Robeck (2006) *The Impact of Crime on the Enterprise Sector: European Bank for Reconstruction and Development*, Working Paper 97, www.ebrd.org/pubs/econo/wp0097.pdf

Krug, E., L. Dahlberg, J. Mercy, A. Zwi and R. Lozano (2002) 'The way forward: Recommendations for action', in WHO (ed) *World Report on Violence and Health*, WHO, Geneva, www.who.int/violence_injury_prevention/violence/world_report/en/full_en.pdf

La Oferta (2006) 'Truck driver found guilty in 19 immigrants' deaths', www.laoferta.com/index.php?option=com_content&task=view&id=3023&Itemid=38

La Vigne, N. G. (1996) 'Safe transport: Security by design on the Washington metro', in R. Clarke (ed) *Preventing Mass Transit Crime*, Criminal Justice Press, Monsey, NY, www.popcenter.org/Library/CrimePrevention/Volume%2006/05%20nancy.pdf

LaFree, G. (2002) 'Criminology and democracy', *Criminologist* **19**: 33–35

LaFree, G. and Tseloni, A. (2006) 'Democracy and crime: A multilevel analysis of homicide trends on forty-four countries, 1950–2000', *The Annals of the American Academy of Political and Social Science* **605**: 25–49

Lanza, S. G. (2003) 'Flood hazard threat on cultural heritage in the town of Genoa (Italy)', *Journal of Cultural Heritage* **4**: 159–167

Lavell, A. (2005) cited in B. Wisner, V. Ruiz, A. Lavell and L. Meyreles (2005) 'Run, tell your neighbour! Hurricane warning in the Caribbean', International Federation of the Red Cross and Red Crescent Societies (ed) *World Disasters Report*, Eurospan, London

Leckie, S. (2003a) *Addressing Housing, Land and Property Rights in Post-Conflict Settings: A Preliminary Framework for Post-Conflict Iraq*, Report prepared for UNOPS (United Nations Office for Project Services), OHCHR (Office of the United Nations High Commissioner for Human Rights) and UNHCR, Baghdad

Leckie, S. (ed) (2003b) *Returning Home: Housing and Property Restitution Rights for Refugees and Displaced Persons: Volume 1*, Transnational Publishers, Ardsley, NY

Leckie, S. (2005a) *Housing, Land and Property Rights in Post-Conflict Societies: Proposals for a New United Nations Institutional Policy Framework*, Legal and Protection Policy Research Series No 5 (PPLA/2005/01), Department of International Protection, UNHCR, Geneva, www.unhcr.org/doclist/protect/3e5210567.html

Leckie, S. (2005b) 'The great land theft', *Forced Migration Review*, July: 15–16

Leckie, S. (ed) (forthcoming) *UN Peace Operations and Housing, Land and Property Rights: Proposals for Reform*, University of Cambridge Press, Cambridge

Lemard, G. and D. Hemenway (2006) 'Violence in Jamaica: An analysis of homicides', *Injury Prevention* **12**: 15–18, http://ip.bmjjournals.com/cgi/content/full/12/1/15

Levitt, S. (2004) 'Understanding why crime fell in the 1990s: Four factors that explain the decline and six that do not', *Journal of Economic Perspectives* **18**(1): 163–190

Linnerooth-Bayer J. and A. Amendola (2000) 'Global change, natural disasters, and loss-sharing: Issues of efficiency and equity', *The Geneva Papers on Risk and Insurance: Issues and Practice* **25**(2)

Litman, T. (2005) 'Terror, transit and public safety: Evaluating the risks', *Journal of Public Transit* **8**(4): 33–46, http://www.vtpi.org/transitrisk.pdf

Lock, P. (2006) 'Crime and violence: Global economic parameters', Keynote address at the Geothe-Institut in Johannesburg, www.libertysecurity.org/article940.html

Lodhi, A. Q. and C. Tilly (1973) 'Urbanization, crime and collective violence in 19th century France', *American Journal of Sociology* **19**(2): 296–318

Londono, J. L. and R. Guerrero (1999) *Violencia en America Latina: Epidemiologia y Costos*, IDB Working Paper R-375, IDB, Washington, DC

Loukaitou-Sideris, A. (1999), 'Hot spots of bus stop crime: The importance of environmental attributes', *Journal of the American Planning Association* **65**(4): 395–411

Luo, M. (2006) 'Crisis in housing adds to miseries of Iraq mayhem', *New York Times*, 29 December

Macedo, J. (2007) 'Effective strategies of crime prevention: The case of New York City, USA', Unpublished case study prepared for *Global Report on Human Settlements 2007*

Manso, B. P., M. Faria and N. Gail (2005) 'Diadema democracy 3: Frontier violence and civilization in São Paulo's periphery', Braudel papers, www.braudel.org.br/novo/publicacoes/bp/bp37_en.pdf

Marques, L. O. (2007) 'Positive policies and legal responses to enhance security of tenure in Brazil', Unpublished case study prepared for *Global Report on Human Settlements 2007*

Marris, P. (1961) *Family and Social Change in an African City*, Routledge and Kegan Paul, London

Masese, G. (2007) 'Conditions and trends in urban crime: The case of Nairobi', Unpublished case study prepared for *Global Report on Human Settlements 2007*

Mayhew, P. (2003) *Counting the Costs of Crime in Australia*, No 247, Australian Institute of Criminology, www.crimeprevention.wa.gov.au/html/publications/AIC-Trends&IssuesCountingtheCostsofCrimeinAustralia–2003.pdf

Mboup, G. and M. Amuyunzu-Nyamongo (2005) 'Getting the right data: Helping municipalities help women', *Habitat Debate* **11**(1): 9

Mboya, T. (2002) 'Crime in Nairobi: Results of a citywide victim survey. Nairobi: Habitat safer cities programme', *Safer Cities Series* **4**: 132

McAuslan, P. (2002) 'Tenure and the law: The legality of illegality and the illegality of legality', in G. Payne (ed) *Land, Rights and Innovation: Improving Tenure Security for the Urban Poor*, ITDG Publishing, London, pp23–38

McCarney, P. and R. E. Stren (eds) (2003) *Governance on the Ground: Innovations and Discontinuities in the Developing World*, Johns Hopkins University Press and the Woodrow Wilson International Center for Scholars, Baltimore

McGranahan, G., D. Balk and D. Anderson (2007) 'The rising tide: Assessing the risks of climate change and human settlements in low elevation coastal zones', *Environment and Urbanization* **19**(1): 17–37

McGranahan, G., P. Jacobi, J. Songsore, C. Suradi, and M. Kjellén (2001) *The Citizens at Risk: From Urban Sanitation to Sustainable Cities*, Earthscan, London

McGregor, G., M. Pelling, T. Wolf and S. Gosling (2006) *The Social Impact of Heat Waves*, Report for the UK Environment Agency

McQuaid, J. and B. Marshall (2005) 'Evidence points to man-made disaster', *New Orleans' Times–Picayune*, 8 December

Mechler, R. (2003) 'Natural disaster risk and cost–benefit analysis', in A. Kreimer, M. Arnold and A. Carlin (eds) *Building Safer Cities: The Future of Disaster Risk*, Disaster Risk Management Series, No 3, World Bank, Washington, DC, pp45–56

Miamidian, E., M. Arnold, K. Burritt and M. Jacquand (2005) *Surviving Disasters and Supporting Recovery: A Guidebook for Microfinance Institutions*, Working Paper Series, No 10, Hazard Management Unit, World Bank, Washington, DC

Michau, L. and D. Naker (2003) *Mobilising Communities to Prevent Domestic Violence: A Resource Guide for Organisations in East and Southern Africa*, Raising Voices, Kampala

Microenterprise Best Practice (undated) *Pre-Disaster Planning to Protect Microfinance Clients*, MBP, www.gdrc.org/icm/disasters/rapid_onset_brief_7.pdf

Milliot, M. (2004) 'Urban growth, travel practices and evolution of road safety', *Journal of Transport Geography* **12**: 207–218

Ministry of Foreign Affairs, Canada (2006) 'Freedom from fear in urban spaces', Discussion Paper, Human Security Research and Outreach Program, Ottawa

Ministry of the Environment, Republic of Indonesia (undated) *Rapid Environmental Impact Assessment*, www.benfieldhrc.org/disaster_studies/rea/banda_aceh.pdf

Mitchell, J. K. (1999) *Crucibles of Hazards: Mega-Cities and Disasters in Transition*, United Nations University Press, Tokyo

Mohan, D. (2002a) 'Road Safety in Less-Motorized Environments: Future Concerns', *International Journal of Epidemiology* **31**(3): 527–532

Mohan, D. (2002b) 'Traffic safety and health in Indian cities', *Journal of Transport and Infrastructure* **9**: 79–94

Monkkonen, E. (2001a) 'Homicide: Explaining America's exceptionalism', *American Historical Review* **111**: 76–94

Monkkonen, E. (2001b) *Murder in New York City*, University of California Press, Berkeley and Los Angeles

Morbidity and Mortality Weekly Report (2004) *Homicide Trends and Characteristics – Brazil 1980–2002*, Centers for Disease Control, 5 March 2004 **53**(08): 169–171, www.cdc.gov/mmwr/preview/mmwrhtml/mm5308a1.htm#fig1

Morka, F. C. (2007) 'A place to live: A case study of the Ijora–Badia community Lagos, Nigeria', Unpublished case study prepared for *Global Report on Human Settlements 2007*

Morley, S. A. (1998) *The Impact of the Macroeconomic Environment on Urban Poverty*, ECLAC, Santiago

Morrison, A. R., and M. B. Orlando (1999) 'Social and economic costs of domestic violence: Chile and Nicaragua', in A. R. Morrison and M. L. Biehl (eds) *Too Close to Home: Domestic Violence in the Americas*, New York, IDB, Washington, DC, pp51–80

Morton, C. O. N. and T. E. Kitchen (2005) 'Crime prevention and the British planning system: Operational relationships between planners and police' *Planning Practice and Research* **20**(4): 419–431

Moser, C. O. N. (1996) *Confronting Crisis: A Comparative Study of Household Responses to Poverty and Vulnerability in Four Poor Urban Communities*, World Bank, Washington, DC

Moser, C. O. N. (1998) 'The asset vulnerability framework: Reassessing urban poverty reduction strategies', *World Development* **26**(1): 1–19

Moser, C. O. N. (2004) 'Urban violence and insecurity: An introductory roadmap', *Environment and Urbanization* **16**(2): 3–16

Moser, C. O. N. and J. Holland (1997a) 'Confronting crisis in Chawama, Lusaka Zambia', *Household Responses to Poverty and Vulnerability*, Vol 4, Urban Programme Management Policy Paper 24

Moser, C. O. N. and J. Holland (1997b) *Urban Poverty and Violence in Jamaica*, World Bank, Washington, DC

Moser, C. O. N. and C. McIlwaine (1999) 'Participatory urban appraisal and its application for research on violence', *Environment and Urbanization* **11**(2): 203–226

Moser, C. O. N. and C. McIlwaine (2004) *Encounters with Violence in Latin America: Urban Poor Perceptions from Colombia and Guatemala*, Routledge, London and New York

Moser, C. and E. Schrader (1999) *A Conceptual Framework for Violence Reduction*, World Bank, Washington, DC.

Moser, C. and A. Winton (2002) *Violence in the Central American Region: Towards an Integrated Framework for Violence Reduction*, ODI (Overseas Development Institute) Working Paper No 171, ODI, London

Moser, C. O. N., A. Winton and A. Moser (2005) 'Violence, fear and insecurity among the urban poor in Latin America', in M. Fay (ed) *The Urban Poor in Latin America*, World Bank, Washington, DC

Munasinhge, M. (2000) 'Development, equity and sustainability (DES) and climate change', in R. Pachauri, T. Taniguchi and K. Tanaka (eds) *Guidance Papers on the Cross Cutting Issues of the Third*

Assessment Report of the IPCC, Intergovernmental Panel on Climate Change, Geneva, Switzerland, pp69–110

Munich Re (2004) *Megacities: Megarisks: Trends and Challenges for Insurance and Risk Management*, Munich Re, www.munichre.com/publications/302–04271_en.pdf

Mura, P., C. Chatelain, V. Dumestre, J. M. Gaulier, M. H. Ghysel, C. Lacriox, M. F. Kergueris, M. Lhermitte, M. Moulsma, G. Pepin, F. Vincent and P. Kintz (2006) 'Use of drugs of abuse in less than 30-year-old drivers killed in a road crash in France: A spectacular increase for cannabis, cocaine and amphetamines', *Forensic Science International* **160**: 168–172

Mycoo, M. (2006) 'The retreat of the upper and middle classes to gated communities in the poststructural adjustment era: The case of Trinidad', *Environment and Planning A* **38**: 131–148

Nanning Municipal Government (2007) 'Faster, better and safer: The introduction of Nanning city Emergency Communication Center', paper prepared for *Global Report on Human Settlements 2007*

National Counterterrorism Center (2005) 'A chronology of significant international terrorism for 2004', http://www.tkb.org/documents/Downloads/NCTC_Report.pdf

National Crime Prevention Centre (2005) *Overview of Funding Programs*, National Crime Prevention Centre, Ottawa, Networks on the Patterning of Property Offenses, www.publicsafety.gc.ca/prg/cp/index-en.asp

National Labour Committee, El Salvador (2001) *Salvador Earthquake: From Poverty to Misery*, www.nlcnet.org

Nedoroscik, J. A. (1997) *The City of the Dead: A History of Cairo's Cemetery Communities*, Bergin and Garvey, Westport, CT

Neuwirth, R. (2007) 'Security of tenure in Istanbul: The triumph of the "self service city"', Unpublished case study prepared for *Global Report on Human Settlements 2007*

New Scientist (2002) 'Fresh evidence on Bhopal disaster', *New Scientist*, 4 December

New York City (undated) *New York City Marshalls*, Department of Investigation, www.nyc.gov/html/doi/html/marshals/marshal_main.html

Newman, O. (1973) *Defensible Space: Crime Prevention through Urban Design*, Macmillan, New York

Ngugi, M. (2005) 'Dream come true for slum dwellers', *The Standard*, 26 April, Nairobi

Nicholls, R. J. (2004) 'Coastal megacities and climate change', *GeoJournal* **37**(3): 369–379

Nisbett R. E. and D. Cohen (1996) *Culture of Honor: The Psychology of Violence in the South*, Westview, Boulder, CO

Norris, F. H. (undated) *Risk Factors for Adverse Outcomes in Natural and Human-Caused Disasters: A Review of Empirical Literature*, National Centre for Posttraumatic Stress Disorder (PTSD), Factsheet, US Department of Veterans Affairs, www.ncptsd.va.gov/ncmain/ncdocs/fact_shts/fs_riskfactors.html?opm=1&rr=rr49&srt=d&echorr=true

Nuttall, C., E. DeCourcey and I. Rudder (2002) *The Barbados Crime Survey 2002: International Comparisons*, Barbados Statistical Department, http://barbados.gov.bb/Docs/AG–barbados crimesurvey2002.pdf

Nwankwo, L. N. (2005) 'The birth and death of a local initiative: Challenges of and lessons from the "Bakassi" vigilante group in southeastern Nigeria', *Local Environment* **11**(1): 95–108

O'Rourke, T. D., A. J. Lembo, L. K. Nozick and A. L. Bonneau (2006) 'Resilient infrastructure: Lessons from the WTC', *Crisis Response*, **2**(2): 50–51

OAS (Organization of American States) (2001) *Hazard Resistant Housing*, www.oas.org/pgdm/document/safe_hse.htm

OAS (2003) *Hurricane Resistant Home Improvement in the OECS*, www.oas.org/cdmp/hrhip/

Odero, W., M. Khayesi and P. M. Heda (2003) 'Road traffic injuries in Kenya: Magnitude, causes and status of intervention', *Injury Control and Safety Promotion* **10**: 53–61

ODPM (Office of the Deputy Prime Minister) (2004) 'Safer places: The planning system and crime prevention', www.communities.gov.uk/pub/724/SaferPlacesThePlanningSystemandCrimePrevention_id1144724.pdf

ODPM (2005a) *Planning Policy Statement 1: Delivering Sustainable Development*, ODPM, London

ODPM (2005b) *Sustainable Communities: People, Places and Prosperity*, ODPM, London

ODPM and the Home Office (2004) *Safer Places: The Planning System and Crime Prevention*, HMSO, London

Office on Violence against Women (2000) *Victims of Violence and Trafficking Prevention Act of 2000*, US Department of Justice, Washington, DC

Okwebah, D. and D. Wabala (2007) '100,000 reasons to be afraid' *Sunday Nation*, March

Olivira, M. G. G. and R. Denaldi (1999) 'Community participation in relocation programmes: The case of slum *Sacadura Cabral* in Santo André, Brazil', *Open House International* **24**(3): 24–32

Ongkittikul, S. and H. Geerlings (2006) Opportunities for *Innovation in Public Transport: Effects of Regulatory Reforms on Innovative Capabilities, Transport Policy*, **13**: 283–293

ORG (Operations Research Group) (1994) *Household Travel Surveys in Delhi*, ORG, Delhi

Orr, B. (2007) 'Kobe: Disaster response and adaptation', Unpublished case study prepared for *Global Report on Human Settlements 2007*

Orr, B., A. Stodghill and L. Candu (2007) 'The Dutch experience: A history of institutional learning', Unpublished case study prepared for *Global Report on Human Settlements 2007*

OSCE (Organization for Security and Cooperation in Europe) (2004) *Responding to Natural Disaster in Bosnia and Herzegovina*, www.osce.org/item/193.html

Oxfam International (2005a) *The Tsunami's Impact on Women: Oxfam Briefing Note*, Oxfam International, www.oxfam.org.uk/what_we_do/issues/conflict_disasters/downloads/bn_tsunami_women.pdf

Oxfam International (2005b) *A Place to Stay, A Place to Live, Oxfam Briefing Note*, www.oxfam.org.uk/what_we_do/issues/conflict_disasters/downloads/bn_tsunami_shelter.pdf

Özerdem, A. and S. Barakat (2000) 'After the Marmara earthquake: Lessons for avoiding short cuts to disasters', *Third World Quarterly* **21**(93): 425–439

PAHO (Pan-American Health Organization) (undated) *Gender and Natural Disasters*, Women Health and Development Program Fact Sheet, www.paho.org/English/DPM/GPP/GH/genderdisasters.pdf

Pantoja, E. (2002) *Microfinance and Disaster Risk Management: Experiences and Lessons Learned*,

World Bank, www.proventionconsortium.org/files/microfinance_drm.pdf

Parker, T. (2003) 'Beware the pitfalls of adverse possession', in *The Property Newsletter of Foot Anstey Sargent*, Devon, October

Patel, S., C. d'Cruz and S. Burra (2002) 'Beyond evictions in a global city: People-managed resettlement in Mumbai', *Environment and Urbanization* **10**(2): 149–159

Pawlowski, J. (2005) 'Forced evictions of Cambodia's poor', *Human Rights Tribune* **11**(3), www.hri.ca/tribune/onlineissue/V11-3-2005/Evictions_in_Cambodia.html

Payne, G. (1997) *Urban Land Tenure and Property Rights in Developing Countries: A Review*, Intermediate Technology Publications/ODA, London

Payne, G. (2001a) 'Book review: The mystery of capital. Why capitalism triumphs in the West and fails everywhere else: Hernando de Soto', *Habitat Debate* **7**(3): 23

Payne, G. (2001b) 'Innovative approaches to tenure', *Habitat Debate* **7**(1): 8

Payne, G. (2001c) 'Settling for more: Innovative approaches to tenure for the urban poor', in UN–Habitat and ESCAP (ed) *Seminar on Securing Land for the Urban Poor*, Fukuoka, Japan, 2–4 October

Payne, G. (2001d) 'The impact of regulation on the livelihoods of the poor', Paper presented at the International Workshop on Regulatory Guidelines for Urban Upgrading, 17–18 May, Bourton-on-Dunsmore

Payne, G. (2001e) 'Urban land tenure policy options: Titles or rights?' *Habitat International* **25**(3): 415–429

Payne, G. (ed) (2002) *Land, Rights and Innovation: Improving Tenure Security for the Urban Poor*, ITDG Publishing, London

Payne, G. (2005) 'Getting ahead of the game: A twin-track approach to improving existing slums and reducing the need for future slums', *Environment and Urbanization* **17**(1), pp133–145

Payne, G. and M. Majale (2004) *The Urban Housing Manual: Making Regulatory Frameworks Work for the Poor*, Earthscan, London

Peacock, W. G., S. D. Brody and W. Highfield (2005) 'Hurricane risk perceptions among Florida's single family homeowners', *Landscape and Urban Planning* **73**(2–3), 120–135

Pearce, T., D. A. C Maunder, T. C. Mbara and D. M. Babu (1998) Road Safety for Buses, CODATU (Coopération pour le Développement et l'Amélioration des Transports Urbains et Périurbains) VIII Conference, Cape Town, South Africa, September 1998

Pelling, M. (1997) 'What determines vulnerability to floods: A case study in Georgetown, Guyana', *Environment and Urbanization* **9**(1): 203–226

Pelling, M. (2003) *The Vulnerability of Cities: Natural Disasters and Social Resilience*, Earthscan, London and Sterling, Virginia

Pelling, M. (2006) *Incentives for Reducing Risk: The ProVention Forum Report 2006*, ProVention Consortium, Geneva, www.proventionconsortium.org/themes/default/pdfs/Forum06_Report.pdf

Pelling, M. (Forthcoming) 'Learning from others: Scope and Challenges for Participatory Disaster Risk Assessment', *Disasters*

Pelling, M. and Holloway, A. (2006) *Legislation for Mainstreaming Disaster Risk Reduction*, Tearfund, London

Pelling, M., A. Özerdem and S. Barakat (2002) 'The macro-economic impact of disasters', *Progress in Development Studies* **2**(4): 283–305

Pettis, M. (2003) *The Volatility Machine: Emerging Economies and the Threat of Financial Collapse*, Oxford University Press, New York

Pimbert, M. and T. Wakeford (2001) 'Overview: Deliberative Democracy and Citizen Empowerment', *PLA Notes*, IIED, 40: 23–28

Plan International (2005) *Denied an Identity*, www.plan-international.org/identity/registrationindisasters

Platt, H. (2005) *Shock Cities: The Environmental Transformation and Reform of Manchester and Chicago.* University of Chicago Press, Chicago, IL

Polis (2002) *The Statute of the City: New Tools for Assuring the Right to the City in Brazil*, Polis, São Paulo, Brazil

Pottier, L., T. Wichmann, M. Gujrati, J. Lindsay and B. Orr (2007) 'Tangshan and Cape Town: Top-down and bottom-up planning for disaster', Unpublished case study prepared for *Global Report on Human Settlements 2007*

Poyner, B. (1983) *Design against Crime: Beyond Defensible Space*, Butterworths, London

Poyner, B. (2006) *Crime-Free Housing in The 21st Century*, UCL Jill Dando Institute of Crime Science, London

Prefecture of São Paulo (2003) *The Regularization of Allotments in the Municipal District of São Paulo*, São Paulo, Brazil

ProVention Consortium (undated) *Risk Transfer and Private Sector*, www.proventionconsortium.org/?pageid=19

Pucher, J., N. Korattyswaropam, N. Mittal and N. Ittyerah (2005) 'Urban transport crises in India', *Transport Policy* **12**: 185–198

Quan, J., A. Martin and J. Pender (1998) *Issues and Methods in the Joint Application of GIS and Participatory Enquiry in Natural Resources Research: Assessment of Available Literature and Project Information Natural Resources Institute*, University of Greenwich, London

Quarantelli, E. L. (2003) *Urban Vulnerability to Disasters in Developing Countries: Managing Risks*, in A. Kreimer, M. Arnold and A. Carlin (eds), *Building Safer Cities: The Future of Disaster Risk*, World Bank, Washington, DC

Rao, V. (1997) 'Wife-beating in rural south India: A qualitative and econometric analysis', *Social Science and Medicine* **44**:1169–1180

Rashid, S. F. (2000) 'The poor in Dhaka City: Their struggles and coping strategies during the floods of 1998', *Disasters* **24**(3): 240–253

Rawal, V., R. Desai and D. Jadeja (2006) *Assessing Post–Tsunami Housing Reconstruction in Andaman and Nicobar Islands*, Society for Andaman and Nicobar Ecology, ActionAid, Housing and Land Rights Network, and Tsunami Rehabilitation Information Network (TRINet), www.hic-sarp.org/Tsunami%20Reconstruction.pdf

Revi, A. (2005) 'Lessons from the deluge', *Economic and Political Weekly*, 3 September

Reza, A., J. A. Mercy and E. Krug (2001) 'Epidemiology of violent deaths in the world', *Injury Prevention* **7**: 104–111, cited in E. Monkkonen (2006) 'Homicide: explaining America's exceptionalism', *American Historical Review* **111**: 76–94

Riley, E. and P. Wakely (2005) *Communities and Communication: Building Urban Partnership*, ITDG, Rugby, UK

Robben, A. and C. Nordstrom (1995) 'The anthropology and ethnography of violence and sociopolitical conflict', in C. Nordstrom and A. Robben (eds) *Fieldwork under Fire*, University of California Press, Berkeley, CA, pp1–23

Robert, B., J. P. Sabourin, M. Glaus, F. Petit, and M. H. Senay (2003) 'A new structural approach for the study of domino effects between life support networks', in A. Kreimer, M. Arnold and A. Carlin (eds) *Building Safer Cities: The Future of Disaster Risk*, Disaster Risk Management Series No 3, World Bank, Washington, DC, pp245–272

Rodgers, D. (1999) *Youth Gangs and Violence in Latin America and the Caribbean: A Literature Review*, Latin America and Caribbean Region Development Working Paper No 4, Urban Peace Program Series, World Bank, Washington, DC

Rodgers, D. (2003) *Dying for It: Gangs, Violence and Social Change in Urban Nicaragua*, Working Paper No 35, Crises States Programme, Development Research Centre, www.Zcrisisstates.com/download/wp/wp35.pdf

Rodgers, D. (2005) *Urban Segregation from Below: Drugs, Consumption, and Primitive Accumulation in Managua, Nicaragua*, Working Paper No 71, Crisis States Research Centre, London School of Economics, London

Rojas, E., J. R. Cuadrado-Roura and J. M. Fernández (eds) (2006) *Gobernar las Metropolis*, Banco Inter-Americano del Desarrollo and Universidad de Alcala, Washington, DC

Rose, D. (2006) 'Deportees linked to crime wave', *Jamaica Gleaner*, 13 September, www.jamaicagleaner.com/gleaner/20060913/lead/lead5.html

Rowbottom, S. (2007) 'The Indian Ocean tsunami: Vulnerabilities exposed … opportunities to seize', Unpublished case study prepared for *Global Report on Human Settlements 2007*

Roy, A. (1999) 'The greater common good', www.narmada.org/gcg/gcg.html

Royston, L. (2002) 'Security of urban tenure in South Africa: Overview of policy and practice', in A. Durand-Lasserve and L. Royston (eds) *Holding Their Ground: Secure Land Tenure for the Urban Poor in Developing Countries*, Earthscan, London

Sampson, R. J. and J. D. Wooldredge (1986) 'Evidence that high crime rates encourage migration away from central cities', *Sociology and Social Research* **70**: 310–314

Sanderson, D. (1997) 'Reducing risk as a tool for urban improvement: The Caqueta ravine, Lima, Peru'. *Environment and Urbanization* **9**(1): 251–262

Sanderson, D. (2000) 'Cities, Disasters and Livelihoods', *Environment and Urbanization* **12**(2): 93–102

Sanin, F. G. and A. M. Jaramillo (2004) 'Crime, (counter) insurgency and the privatization of security: The case of Medellin, Colombia', *Environment and Urbanization* **16**(2): 17–30

Satterthwaite, D. (2006) 'Climate change and cities', *Sustainable Development Opinion*, International Institute for Environment and Development, London

Saunders, P. and R. Taylor (2002) *The Price Of Prosperity: The Economic and Social Costs of Unemployment*, UNSW Press, Sydney

Save the Children (2006) *Back to School after the Quake*, Media briefing, www.savethechildren.org.uk/scuk_cache/scuk/cache/cmsattach/3976_b2sch.pdf

Schabas, W. A. (1991) 'The omission of the right to property in the international covenants', *4 Hague Yearbook of International Law*, Martinus Nijhoff, Dordrecht, pp135–170

Schauer, E. J. and E. M. Wheaton (2006) 'Sex trafficking into the United States: A literature review', *Criminal Justice Review* **31**(2): 146–169

Scherer, A. (2005) 'Why people who face losing their homes in legal proceedings must have a right to counsel', in *Cardozo Public Law, Policy and Ethics Journal* **3**(3): 669–732

Schipper, L. and M. Pelling (2006) 'Disaster risk, climate change and international development: Scope and challenges for integration', *Disasters* **30**(1): 19–38

Schneider, R. H. (2003) 'American anti-terrorism planning and design strategies: Applications for Florida growth management, comprehensive planning and urban design', *University of Florida Journal of Law and Public Policy* **15**(1): 129–154

Schneider, R. H. and T. Kitchen (2002) *Planning for Crime Prevention: A Trans-Atlantic Perspective*, Routledge, London

Schneider, R. H. and T. Kitchen (2007) *Crime Prevention and the Built Environment,* Routledge, London

Schwartz, A. E, S. Susin and I. Voicu (2003) 'Has falling crime driven New York City's real estate boom?', *Journal of Housing Research* **15**(1): 101–135

Schweitzer, J. H., J. W. Kim and J. R. Mackin (1999) 'The impact of the built environment on crime and fear of crime in urban neighborhoods', *Journal of Urban Technology* **6**(3): 59–73

Seabrook, J. (1996) *In the Cities of the South*, Verso, London

Sen, A. (1982) *Poverty and Famines: An Essay on Entitlement and Deprivation*, Clarendon Press, Oxford

Sen, A. (2000) *Development as Freedom*, Random House, New York

Shack and Slum Dwellers International (2004) *Baan Mankong: The National Programme for Upgrading and Secure Tenure in Thailand's Cities*, www.sdinet.org/documents/doc8.htm

Sharma, M., I. Burton, M. van Aalst, M. Dilley and G. Acharya (2000) *Reducing Vulnerability to Environmental Variability*, Background Paper to the World Bank's Environmental Strategy, World Bank, Washington, DC

Sharma, A. and M. Gupta (1998) 'Reducing urban risk, India', TDR project progress report, Sustainable Environment and Ecological Development Society, Delhi

Sharma, S. (2001) Director of the Energy Environment Group, New Delhi, Note to the Mountain Forum: Asia e-list mf-asia@lyris.bellanet.org

Shaw, M. (2002) *Crime and Policing in Post-Apartheid South Africa: Transforming under Fire*, Indiana University Press, Bloomington, IN

Shaw, M., J. van Dijk and W. Rhomberg (2003) 'Determining trends in global crime and justice: An overview of results from the United Nations survey of crime trends and operations of criminal justice systems', *Forum on Crime and Society* **3**(1, 2): 35–63

Sherman, L. W (1995) 'Hot spots of crime and criminal careers of places', in J. E. Eck and D. Wisburd (eds) *Crime and Place*, Criminal Justice Press, Monsey, NY, pp35–52

Sherman, L. W., D. C. Gottfredson, D. C. Mackenzie, J. Eck, P. Reuter and S. D. Bushway (1997) *Preventing Crime: What Works, What Doesn't, What's Promising*, National Institute of Justice Research, US Department of Justice, Washington, DC

Shiozaki, Y., E. Nishikawa, and T. Deguchi (eds) (2005) *Lessons from the Great Hanshin Earthquake*, Creates-Kamogawa Publishers accessed from www.shinsai.or.jp/hrc-e/publish/lessons_ghe

Shorter, A. and E. Onyancha (1999) *Street Children in Africa: A Nairobi Case Study*, Pauline's Publications, Nairobi

Shrivastava, P. (1996) 'Long-term recovery from the Bhopal crisis', in J. K. Mitchell (ed) *The Long Road to Recovery: Community Response to Industrial Disaster*, United Nations University Press, Tokyo, pp121–147

Sim, L. L., L. C. Malone-Lee and K. H. L. Chin (2001) 'Integrating land use and transport planning to reduce work-related travel: A case study of Tampines Regional Centre in Singapore', *Habitat International* **25**: 399–414

Simmel, G. (1950) 'The metropolis and mental life', in K. Wolff (ed) *The Sociology of Georg Simmel*, Free Press, Glencoe, IL (originally published in 1903 as *Die Grosstädte und das Geistesleben*, Petermann, Dresden)

Simone, A. M. (2005) *For the City Yet to Come: Changing African Life in Four Cities*, Duke University Press, Durham

Sinclair, G. and C. Mills (2003) 'US gang links – study shows deportees criminal connections', *Jamaica Gleaner*, 21 October, www.jamaica-gleaner.com/gleaner/20031021/lead/lead1.html

Sivaramkrishnan, K. C. and L. Green (1986) *Metropolitan Management: The Asian Experience*, Oxford University Press for the World Bank's Economic Development Institute, New York and Oxford

Small Arms Survey (2002) Counting the Human Cost, Geneva Graduate Institute of International Studies, Oxford University Press, www.cdi.org/program/document.cfm?DocumentID=2996

Small Arms Survey (2006a) 'Few options but the gun: Angry young men', www.smallarmssurvey.org/files/sas/publications/year_b_pdf/2006/2006SASCh12–full_en.pdf

Small Arms Survey (2006b) 'Jumping the gun: Armed violence in Papua New Guinea', www.smallarmssurvey.org/files/sas/publications/year_b_pdf/2006/2006SASCh7_summary_en.pdf

Sofia Echo.com (2006) 'Corruption and human trafficking hinder Bulgaria's EU entry', www.sofiaecho.com/article/corruption-and-human-trafficking-hinder-bulgarias-eu-entry/id_15314/catid_69

Soja, E. (2001) *Postmetropolis: Critical Studies of Cities and Regions*, Blackwell, Oxford

South Africa Cities Network (2006) *State of the Cities Report 2006*, www.sacities.net/2006/state_of_cities_2006.stm

South Durban Community Environmental Alliance (2003a) *Department of Agriculture and Environmental Affairs (DAEA) Minister Restrained from Approving Mondi Biotrace Combuster*, www.h-net.org/~esati/sdcea/pr6may03.html

South Durban Community Environmental Alliance (2003b) *Judge Declared Dodgy Decision a Nullity*, www.h-net.org/~esati/sdcea/pr9july03.html

Spaliviero, M. (2006) 'Integrating slum upgrading and vulnerability reduction in Mozambique', *Open House International* **31**(1): 106–115

Srinivasan, S. and P. Rogers (2005) 'Travel behaviour of low-income residents: Studying two contrasting locations in the city of Chennai, India', *Journal of Transport Geography* **13**: 265–274

Stecko, S. and N. Barber (2007) 'Exposing vulnerabilities: Monsoon floods in Mumbai, India', Unpublished case study prepared for *Global Report on Human Settlements 2007*

Stephens, C. (1996) 'Healthy cities or unhealthy islands? The health and social implications of urban inequality', *Environment and Urbanization* **8**: 9–30

Stephens, C., I. Timaeus, M. Akerman, S. Avle, P. B. Maia, P. Campanario, B. Doe, L. Lush, D. Tetteh and T. Harpham (1994) *Environment and Health in Developing Countries: An Analysis of Intra-Urban Differentials Using Existing Data*, London School of Hygiene and Tropical Medicine, London

Stiglitz, J. (2002) 'The lessons of Argentina for development in Latin America', in M. Cohen and M. Gutman (eds) *Argentina in Collapse? The Americas Debate*, New School and the International Institute for Environment and Development, America Latina, Buenos Aires, pp151–170

Stohl, R. (2005) *Fighting the Illicit Trafficking in Small Arms*, Center for Defense Information, www.cdi.org/program/document.cfm?DocumentID=2996

Stren, R. E. and M. Polese (eds) (2000) *The Social Sustainability of Cities*, University of Toronto Press, Toronto, Ontario

Svampa, M. (2001) *Los Que Ganaron: La Vida en los Countries y Barrios Privadas*, Editorial Biblos, Buenos Aires

Svampa, M. (2005) *La Sociedad Excluyente: La Argentina Bajo el Signo de Neo-Liberalismo*, Taurus, Buenos Aires

Swiss Re (2007) *Natural Catastrophes and Man-Made Disasters in 2006: Low Insured Losses*, Swiss Reinsurance Company, Zurich, Switzerland

Synergy Project (2002) *Children on the Brink 2002: A Joint Report on Orphan Estimates and Program Strategies*, USAID, July, Washington, DC

Taboroff, J. (2003) 'Natural disasters and urban cultural heritage: A reassessment', in A. Kreimer, M. Arnold and A. Carlin (eds) *Building Safer Cities: The Future of Disaster Risk*, Disaster Risk Management Series No 3, World Bank, Washington, DC, pp233–239

Taipei Times (2006) 'Tsunami rumor triggers panic', *Taipei Times*, 20 July: 5

Tannerfeldt, G. and P. Ljung (2006) *More Urban, Less Poor: An Introduction to Urban Development and Management*, Earthscan, London and Sterling, Virginia

Tanzi, V. (1998) 'Corruption around the World: Causes, consequences, scope and cures', *IMF Staff Papers* **45**(4), December

Tanzi, V. and H. Davoodi (1997) *Corruption, Public Investment, and Growth*, IMF Working paper No 97/139, International Monetary Fund, Washington, DC

Taylor, R. B. (1999) *Crime Grime, Fear and Decline: A Longitudinal Look*, US Department of Justice, Office of Justice Programs, National Institute of Justice, Washington, DC

Tewarie, B. (2006) *Stop the Crime, to Stop Brain Drain, to Save our Country*, Chagnaus (Trinidad and Tobago) Chamber of Commerce, www.sta.uwi.edu/principal/documents/Stop%20the%20Crime.pdf

Thachuk, K. L. (2001) 'The sinister underbelly: Organized crime and terrorism', in R. Kugler and E. Frost (eds) *The Global Century: Globalization and National Security*, NDU Press, Washington, DC

Thompson, M. (2007) 'Lessons in risk reduction from Cuba', Unpublished case study prepared for *Global Report on Human Settlements 2007*

Thompson, S. K. and R. Gartner (2007) 'Effective strategies of crime prevention: The case of Toronto, Canada', Unpublished case study prepared for *Global Report on Human Settlements 2007*

Tibaijuka, A. K. (2005) *Report of the Fact-Finding Mission to Zimbabwe to Assess the Scope and Impact of Operation Murambatsvina by the UN Special Envoy on Human Settlements Issues in Zimbabwe*, www.unhabitat.org/downloads/docs/1664_96507_ZimbabweReport.pdf

Tibaijuka, A. K. (2006) 'A message from the executive director', *Habitat Debate* **12**(4): 2

Tilley, C. (2002) 'Violence, terror and politics as usual', *Boston Review* **27**(3, 4), http://bostonreview.net/BR27.3/tilly.html

Times of India (2006) 'Gun for trouble', *Times of India*, 15 September, http://timesofindia.indiatimes.com/articleshow/1992299.cms

Tiwari, G. T. (2002) 'Meeting the challenge of social economic diversity in cities: A case study of Delhi, India', *Cities* **19**(2): 95–103

Tokyo Metropolitan Government, Bureau of Urban Development (undated) 'Urban Disaster Prevention Project', www.toshiseibi.metro.tokyo.jp/plan/pe-010.htm

Town, S., C. Davey and A. Wootton (2003) *Design against Crime: Secure Urban Environments by Design: Guidance for the Design of Residential Areas*, University of Salford, Salford

Transparency International (2005a) *Report on the Transparency International Global Corruption Barometer 2000*, Transparency International, Berlin

Transparency International (2005b) *Corruption Perceptions Index*, www.transparency.org/policy_research/surveys_indices/cpi/2005.

Transparency International (undated) 'Hungarian chapter: Definitions of corruption', www.c3.hu/~tihun/eng/corr/corr.htm

Tsunami Evaluation Coalition (2006) *Synthesis Report*, TEC, www.tsunami-evaluation.org

Tunstall, S. M., C. L. Johnson and E. C. Penning-Rowsell (2004) 'Flood hazard management in England and Wales: From land drainage to flood risk management', Paper presented at the World Congress on Natural Disaster Mitigation, New Delhi, 19–21 February, www.fhrc.mdx.ac.uk/resources/docs_pdfs/India%20paper%20final%20version.pdf

Turner, J. F. C. and R. Fichter, (1972) *Freedom to Build: Dweller Control of the Housing Process*, Macmillan Company, New York

Twigg, J. (2001) *Corporate Social Responsibility and Disaster Reduction: A Global Overview*, Benfield Hazard Research Centre, University College London, www.benfieldhrc.org/disaster_studies/csr/csr_overview.pdf

Twigg, J. (2004) 'Disaster risk reduction', *Good Practice Review*, no 9, Humanitarian Practice Network, ODI, London

Tyler, P. E. (1994) 'China proposes huge aqueduct to Beijing area', *New York Times*, 19 July

UN Millennium Project (2005) *A Home in the City*, United Nations Millennium Project, Task Force on Improving the Lives of Slum Dwellers, Earthscan, London, www.unmillenniumproject.org/documents/slumdwellers-complete.pdf

UNCHS (United Nations Centre for Human Settlements (Habitat)) (1993) *Provision of Travelway Space for Urban Public Transport in Developing Countries*, UNCHS, Nairobi

UNCHS (2000a) *Informal Transport in the Developing World*, UNCHS, Nairobi

UNCHS (2000b) *Strategies to Combat Homelessness*, UNCHS, Nairobi

UNCHS and ILO (International Labour Office) (1995) *Shelter Provision and Employment Generation*, UNCHS and ILO, Nairobi and Geneva

UNCRD (United Nations Centre for Regional Development) (1995) *A Call to Arms: Report of the 17 January Great Hanshin Earthquake*, UNCRD Discussion Paper, 95–2, Nagoya, Japan

UNDP (United Nations Development Programme) (2003) *Regional Forum Report Mitch +5*, UNDP and CEPREDENAC, www.undp.org/bcpr/disred/documents/regions/america/m5regforum/report.pdf

UNDP (2004) *Reducing Disaster Risk: A Challenge for Development*, UNDP, New York

UNDP (2005) *Delhi Schools get Ready with Disaster Management Plans*, UNDP–BCPR, www.undp.org/bcpr/disred/documents/news/2005/may/india240505.pdf?OpenDocument&rc=3&cc=geo

UNDP (2006a) 'UNDP and ECOWAS launch small arms control programme', http://content.undp.org/go/newsroom/june–2006/undp–ecowas–small–arms.en

UNDP (2006b) *Human Development Report*, UNDP, Palgrave Macmillan, New York

UNDRCO (United Nations Disaster Relief Coordinator) (1991) *Mitigating Natural Disaster Phenomena, Effects and Options: A Manual for Policy Makers and Planners*, United Nations, New York

UNEP (United Nations Environment Programme) (2005) *Environmental Management and Disaster Preparedness: Lessons Learnt from the Tokage Typhoon in Japan*, UNEP, Kenya

UNEP and UN-Habitat (2005) 'Climate change and role of cities: Involvement influence implementation', http://www.unhabitat.org/pmss/getPage.asp?page=promoView&promo=2226

UNESCO (United Nations Educational, Scientific and Cultural Organization) (2002) *Best Practices of Non-Violent Conflict Resolution In and Out-of-School: Some Examples*, UNESCO, Paris, http://unesdoc.unesco.org/images/0012/001266/126679e.pdf

UN-Habitat (United Nations Human Settlements Programme) (2001) *Declaration on Cities and other Human Settlements*, UN-Habitat, www.unhabitat.org/content.asp?cid=2071&catid=1&typeid=25&subMenuId=0

UN-Habitat (2002) *International Instruments on Housing Rights*, UNHRP Report No 2, UN-Habitat, Nairobi, www.unhabitat.org/list.asp?typeid=48&catid=282&subMenuID=58

UN–Habitat (2003a) *Guide to Monitoring Target 11: Improving the lives of 100 million slum dwellers: Progress towards the Millennium Development Goals*, UN-Habitat, Nairobi

UN-Habitat (2003b) *Guidelines on How to Undertake a National Campaign for Secure Tenure*, UN-Habitat, Nairobi

UN-Habitat (2003c) *Rental Housing: An Essential Option*

for the Urban Poor in Developing Countries, UN-Habitat, Nairobi

UN-Habitat (2003d) *The Challenge of Slums: Global Report on Human Settlements 2003*, Earthscan, London

UN-Habitat (2003e) *Monitoring Housing Rights: Developing a Set of Indicators to Monitor the Full and Progressive Realisation of the Human Right to Adequate Housing*, UNHRP Working Paper No 1, UN-Habitat, Nairobi

UN-Habitat (2003f) *Water and Sanitation in the World's Cities*, Earthscan, London

UN-Habitat (2004a) *Global Campaign for Secure Tenure: Concept Paper*, 2nd edition, UN-Habitat, Nairobi

UN-Habitat (2004b) *Urban Indicators Guidelines: Monitoring the Habitat Agenda and the Millennium Development Goals*, http://ww2.unhabitat.org/programmes/guo/documents/urban_indicators_guidelines.pdf, UN-Habitat, Nairobi

UN-Habitat (2005a) *Compilation of Selected United Nations Documents on Housing Rights*, 2nd edition, UNHRP Report No 6, UN-Habitat, Nairobi

UN-Habitat (2005b) *Compilation of United Nations Resolutions on Housing Rights*, 2nd edition, UNHRP Report No 5, UN-Habitat, Nairobi

UN-Habitat (2005c) *Financing Urban Shelter: Global Report on Human Settlements 2005*, Earthscan, London

UN-Habitat (2005d) *Forced Evictions: Towards Solutions*, First Report of the Advisory Group on Forced Evictions to the Executive Director of UN-Habitat, AGFE and UN-Habitat, Nairobi

UN-Habitat (2005e) *Islamic Land Theories and Their Application*, Islam, Land and Property Research Series No 1, UN-Habitat, Nairobi

UN-Habitat (2005f) *Responding to the Challenges of an Urbanising World: UN-Habitat Annual Report 2005*, UN-Habitat, Nairobi

UN-Habitat (2006a) 'A new start: The paradox of crisis', *Habitat Debate* **12**(4)

UN-Habitat (2006b) 'Information by country', www.unhabitat.org/categories.asp?catid=2

UN-Habitat (2006c) *Urban Safety: A Review: A Collective Challenge for Sustainable Human Settlements in Africa*, UN-Habitat, Nairobi

UN-Habitat (2006f) *Progress Report on Removing Discrimination against Women in Respect of Property and Inheritance Rights*, Tools on Improving Women's Secure Tenure, Series 1, No 2, UN-Habitat, Nairobi

UN-Habitat (2006d) *Sustainable Relief and Reconstruction: From Conceptual Framework into Operational Reality*, UN-Habitat, Nairobi

UN-Habitat (2006e) *State of the World's Cities 2006/2007: The Millennium Development Goals and Urban Sustainability*, Earthscan, London

UN-Habitat (2007) *Forced Evictions: Towards Solutions*, Second report of the Advisory Group on Forced Evictions to the Executive Director of UN-Habitat, AGFE and UN-Habitat, Nairobi

UN-Habitat (forthcoming) *Housing Rights Indicators: Measuring the Progressive Realization of the Right to Adequate Housing*, UNHRP Working Paper No 2, UN-Habitat, Nairobi

UN-Habitat (undated) *Making Cities Safer from Crime: The Safer Cities Programme, UN-Habitat: Activities Brief*, UN-Habitat, Nairobi

UN-Habitat and ESCAP (United Nations Economic and Social Commission for Asia and the Pacific) (2002) *Seminar on Securing Land for the Urban Poor*, Fukuoka Japan, 2–4 October 2001

UN-Habitat and OHCHR (Office of the United Nations High Commission on Human Rights) (2002) *Housing Rights Legislation*, UNHRP Report No 1, UN-Habitat and OHCHR, Nairobi, www.unhabitat.org/list.asp?typeid=48&catid=282&subMenuID=58

UN-Habitat and UNDP (2002) *Crime in Nairobi: Results of a Citywide Victim Survey*, Safer Cities Series No 2, UN-Habitat/ITDG, Nairobi

UNICEF (United Nations Children's Fund) (2006) *The State of the World's Children 2006: Excluded and Invisible*, www.unicef.org/sowc06/pdfs/sowc06_fullreport.pdf

United Nations (1998) *Principles and Recommendation for Population and Housing Censuses*, Statistical Papers, Series M No 67/Rev.1, Sales No E.98.XVII. 8, New York

United Nations (2001a) *Crime and Development in Africa*, United Nations Office on Drugs and Crime, www.unodc.org/pdf/African_report.pdf

United Nations (2001b) *Road Map towards the Implementation of the United Nations Millennium Declaration*, Report of the Secretary-General to the 56th Session of the General Assembly, www.un.org/documents/ga/docs/56/a56326.pdf

United Nations (2002) *United Nations Guidelines for the Prevention of Crime – 2002*, www.e-oca.net/Resources/Special%20Documents/UNguidelines.pdf

United Nations (2005) *World Urbanization Prospects: The 2005 Revision*, Population Division, Department of Economic and Social Affairs, New York, www.un.org/esa/population/publications/WUP2005/2005wup.htm

United Nations (2006) *Global Survey of Early Warning Systems*, www.unisdr.org/ppew/info-resources/ewc3/Global-Survey-of-Early-Warning-Systems.pdf

United Nations (undated) *Backgrounder 8. Survival in the Cities: Urban Poverty and Urban Development*, www.un.org/cyberschoolbus/habitat/background/bg8.asp

Unnithan, N. P. and H. P. Whitt (1992) 'Inequality, economic development and lethal violence: A cross national analysis of suicide and homicide', *International Journal of Comparative Sociology* **33**: 182–196

UNODC (2000) *Convention against Transnational Organized Crime*, General Assembly Resolution 55/25, www.undoc.org/undoc/crime_cicp_convention.html

UNODC (2002) *Results of a Pilot Survey of Forty Selected Organized Criminal Groups in Sixteen Countries*, United Nations Office on Drugs and Crime, Vienna

UNODC (2004) *The Global Programme against Corruption: UN Anti-Corruption Toolkit*, 3rd edition, United Nations Office on Drugs and Crime, Vienna, www.unodc.org/pdf/corruption/publications_toolkit_sep04.pdf

UNODC (2005a) *Crime and Development in Africa*, United Nations Office on Drugs and Crime, Vienna, www.unodc.org/pdf/African_report.pdf

UNODC (2005b) *Eighth United Nations Survey of Crime Trends and Operations of Criminal Justice Systems*, United Nations Office on Drugs and Crime, Vienna, www.unodc.org/pdf/crime/eighthsurvey/5678svc.pdf

UNODC (2006a) *2006 World Drug Report, Volume 1: Analysis*, United Nations Office on Drugs and Crime, Vienna, www.unodc.org/pdf/WDR_2006/wdr2006_volume1.pdf

UNODC (2006b) *Trafficking in Persons: Global Patterns*, United Nations Office on Drugs and Crime, Vienna, www.unodc.org/pdf/traffickinginpersons_report_2006ver2.pdf

US Department of Justice, Office of Justice Programmes, Office of Juvenile Justice and Delinquency Prevention, (1997) *Conflict Resolution*, Fact Sheet 55, OJJDP, Washington, DC

US Department of Justice (2006) *Preliminary Semiannual Uniform Crime Report, January – June 2006*, www.fbi.gov/ucr/prelim06/index.html

US State Department (2001) *Fact Sheet: Arms and Conflict in Africa*, www.state.gov/s/inr/rls/fs/2001/4004.htm

Vale L. J. and T. J. Campanella (2005) *The Resilient City: How Modern Cities Recover from Disaster*, Oxford University Press, Oxford and New York

van Dijk, J. and P. van Vollenhoven (2006) 'Organized crime and collective victimization', Paper presented at the International Conference on Corruption and Organized Crime: Bridging Criminal and Economic Policies, Centre for the Study of Democracy, Sofia, Bulgaria, 23–24 June, www.tilburguniversity.nl/intervict/lezingJvD210606.pdf

van Ness, D. (2005) 'Doing one thing well: Applying restorative justice to a specific crime', www.restorativejustice.org/resources/docs/vanness26

Vanderschueren, F. (1996) 'From violence to justice and security in cities', *Environment and Urbanization* **8**(1): 93–112

Vanderschueren, F. (2000) 'Prevention of urban crime: Safer cities concept note', Paper presented at Africities 2000 Summit, 15–21 May, Windhoek, Namibia

Vasconcellos, E. A. (2005) 'Urban change, mobility and transport in São Paulo', *Transport Policy* **12**: 91–104

Vecvagars, K. (2006) 'Valuing damage and losses in cultural assets after a disaster: Concept paper and research options', *Estudios y Perspectivas*, Series, No 56, CEPAL (Comisión Económica para América Latina), Santiago, Chile

Venton, C. C. and Venton, P. (2004) *Disaster Preparedness Programmes in India: A Cost Benefit Analysis*, Humanitarian Practice Network Paper No 49, Humanitarian Practice Network, ODI, London

Viva Rio (2005) 'Women and girls in contexts of armed violence: A case study on Rio de Janeiro', Paper presented to the Second Biennial Meeting of States on the Implementation of the United Nations Programme of Action on Small Arms and Light Weapons, New York, 11–14 July

Volunteer Brazil (undated) Welcome to helping street kids, http://volunteerbrazil.com/streetkidsproject.html

Walker, A., C. Kershaw and S. Nicholas (2006) *British Crime Survey 2005–2006*, www.homeoffice.gov.uk/rds/pdfs06/hosb1206.pdf

Walton, J. and D. Seddon (1994) *Free Markets and Food Riots: The Politics of Global Adjustment*, Blackwell, Oxford

Warah, R. (2007) 'It's a city under siege by murderous gangs', *Daily Nation*, February

Warhurst, A. (2006) *Disaster Prevention: A Role for Business?*, ProVention Consortium, Geneva, www.proventionconsortium.org/themes/default/pdfs/business_case_DRR.pdf

Warmsler, C. (2006a) 'Integrating risk reduction, urban planning and housing: Lessons from El Salvador', *Open House International* **31**(1): 71–83

Warmsler, C. (2006b) 'Mainstreaming risk reduction in urban planning and housing: A challenge for international aid organizations', *Disasters* **30**(2): 151–177

Washington, W. (2007) 'Considering citizens in disaster plans, preparedness, and recovery: Hurricane Katrina and the levee breeches, an ethnography in New Orleans', Unpublished case study prepared for *Global Report on Human Settlements 2007*

Weber, A. (1899) *The Growth of Cities in the Nineteenth Century*, Columbia University Press, New York

Wei, S. J. (1999) *Corruption in Economic Development – Beneficial Grease, Minor Annoyance, or Major Obstacle*, Policy Research Working Paper Series 2048, World Bank, Washington, DC

Wells, P. (2007) 'Deaths and injuries from car accidents: An intractable problem?', *Journal of Cleaner Production* **15**(11–12): 1116–1121

Westendorff, D. (2007) 'Security of housing tenure in the People's Republic of China: Background, trends and issues', Unpublished case study prepared for *Global Report on Human Settlements 2007*

WHO (World Health Organization) (2001) 'Street children and drug abuse: Social and health consequences', www.drugabuse.gov/PDF/StreetChildren.pdf

WHO (2002) *World Health Report on Violence and Health*, WHO, Geneva, www.who.int/violence_injury_prevention/violence/world_report/en/full_en.pdf

WHO (2004a) *The Economic Dimensions of Interpersonal Violence*, WHO, Geneva

WHO (2004b) *World Report on Road Traffic Injury Prevention*, WHO, Geneva

WHO (2005) 'Child abuse and neglect', www.who.int/violence_injury_prevention/violence/neglect/en/

WHO (2007) *Youth and Road Safety*, WHO, Geneva

Willemot, Y. (2006) 'Building a future for street children in the Central African Republic', www.unicef.org/infobycountry/car_34714.html

Williams, J. (2006) 'Human rights, property rights and human security', in H. de Soto and F. Cheneval (eds) *Realizing Property Rights*, Swiss Human Rights Book, vol 1, Rüffer and Rub, Bern, pp166–174

Willoughby, C. (2001) 'Singapore's motorization policies, 1960–2000', *Transport Policy* **8**: 125–139

Winton, A. (2004) 'Young people's views on how to tackle gang violence in "post conflict" Guatemala', *Environment and Urbanization* **16** (4): 83–100

Wilson, S. (1978) 'Vandalism and defensible space on London housing estates', in R. V. Clark (ed) *Tackling Vandalism*, Her Majesty's Stationery Office, London, http://72.14.209.104/search?q=cache:cyTleLy48V8J:www.popcenter.org/Problems/Supplemental_Material/graffiti/Clarke_1978.pdf+clarke+tackling+vandalism&hl=en&ct=clnk&cd=6&gl=us

Wirth, L. (1938) 'Urbanism as a way of life' *American Journal of Sociology* **44**: 3–24

Wisner, B. (1999) 'There are worse things than earthquakes: Hazard vulnerability and mitigation capacity in Greater Los Angeles', in J. K. Mitchell (ed) *Crucibles of Hazard: Mega-Cities and Disasters in Transition*, United Nations University Press, Tokyo, pp375–427

Wisner, B. (2001) 'Disasters: What the United Nations and its world can do', *Global Environmental Change B: Environmental Hazards* **3**(3–4): 125–127

Wisner, B. (2006) *Let Our Children Teach Us!*, ISDR, Geneva

Wisner, B., P. Blaikie, T. Cannon, and I. Davis (2004) *At Risk: Natural Hazards, People's Vulnerability and Disasters*, Routledge, London

Wisner, B., V. Ruiz, A. Lavell and L. Meyreles (2005) 'Run, tell your Neighbour! Hurricane warning in the Caribbean', *World Disasters Report 2005*, International Federation of the Red Cross and Red Crescent Societies, Geneva

WMO (World Meteorological Organization) (2002) *Guide on Public Understanding and Response to Warnings*, WMO, Geneva

World Bank (1975) *Housing Policy Paper*, World Bank, Washington, DC

World Bank (1993a) *China: Involuntary Resettlement*, World Bank, Washington, DC

World Bank (1993b) *World Development Report 1993: Investing in Health*, World Bank, Washington, DC

World Bank (2001) *Operational Policy 4.12: Involuntary Resettlement*, World Bank, Washington, DC

World Bank (2003a) *Jamaica – The Road to Sustained Growth*, World Bank Country Economic Memorandum, Report No 26088-JM

World Bank (2003b) *Land Policies for Growth and Poverty Reduction: A World Bank Policy Research Report*, World Bank and Oxford University Press, Oxford

World Bank (2003c) 'The global crisis of youth unemployment', http://web.worldbank.org/WBSITE/EXTERNAL/NEWS/0,,contentMDK:20123817~menuPK:34459~pagePK:34370~piPK:34424~theSitePK:4607,00.html

World Bank (2005) *Lessons from Natural Disasters and Emergency Reconstruction*, Operations Evaluation Department, www.worldbank.org/oed/disasters/lessons_from_disasters.pdf

World Bank (2006a) *Hazards of Nature, Risks to Development: An IEG Evaluation of World Bank Assistance for Natural Disasters*, World Bank, Washington, DC

World Bank (2006b) *Operational Policy 4.12: Involuntary Resettlement*, http://go.worldbank.org/WTA1ODE7T0

World Bank (2006c) *World Development Indicators*, World Bank, Washington, DC

World Bank (2006d) *Doing Business in 2006: Creating Jobs*, World Bank, Washington, DC, www.doingbusiness.org/documents/2006-Sub_Saharan.pdf

World Fact Book 2006 (2006) www.cia.gov/cia/publications/factbook/fields/2119.html

Yonder, A. with S. Ackar and P. Gopalan (2005) *Women's Participation in Disaster Relief and Recovery*, Journal No 22, Population Council, New York

Yong, C., T. Kam-ling, F. Chen, Z. Gao, Q. Zou and Z. Chan (1988) *The Great Tangshan Earthquake of 1976: An Anatomy of Disaster*, State Seismological Bureau, People's Republic of China, China, p128

Zaluar, A. (1997) 'Gangues, galeras e quadrilhas: Globalização, juventude e violência', in H. Vianna (ed) *Galeras Cariocas: Territórios de Conflictos e Encontros Culturais*, Editora UFRJ, Rio de Janeiro, Brazil

Zaluar, A. (2007) 'Conditions and trends in urban crime and violence: The case of Rio de Janeiro, Brazil', Unpublished case study prepared for *Global Report on Human Settlements 2007*

Zambuko, O. and Edwards, C. (2007) 'Effective strategies of crime prevention: The case of Durban, South Africa', Unpublished case study prepared for *Global Report on Human Settlements 2007*

Zheng, Y. (2006) 'A preliminary evaluation of the impact of local accident information on the public perception of road safety', *Reliability Engineering and System Safety* **92**: 1170–1182

Ziccardi, A. (1991) *Las Obras Publicas de la Ciudad de Mexico (1976–1982), Politica Urbana e Industria de la Construccion*, UNAM, Mexico City

International Covenants, Conventions and Declarations

Convention on the Elimination of All Forms of Discrimination against Women, *adopted* by General Assembly Resolution 34/180 of 18 December 1979, *entry into force* 3 September 1981

Convention on the Rights of Persons with Disabilities, *adopted* by General Assembly Resolution 61/106 of 13 December 2006 (*not yet in force*)

Convention on the Rights of the Child, *adopted* by General Assembly Resolution 44/25 of 20 November 1989, *entry into force* 2 September 1990

European Convention on Human Rights (Convention for the Protection of Human Rights and Fundamental Freedoms), ETS no 005, *entry into force* 3 September 1953

Geneva Convention Relative to the Protection of Civilian Persons in Time of War, *adopted* 12 August 1949, *entry into force* 21 October 1950

International Covenant on Civil and Political Rights, *adopted* by General Assembly Resolution 2200A (XXI) of 16 December 1966, *entry into force* 23 March 1976

ICESCR (International Covenant on Economic, Social and Cultural Rights), *adopted* by General Assembly Resolution 2200A (XXI) of 16 December 1966, *entry into force* 3 January 1976

ILO Recommendation No 115 Concerning Worker's Housing, *adopted* 28 June 1961

International Convention on the Elimination of All Forms of Racial Discrimination, *adopted* by General Assembly Resolution 2106 (XX) of 21 December 1965, *entry into force* 4 January 1969

International Convention on the Protection of the Rights of All Migrant Workers and Members of Their Families, *adopted* by General Assembly Resolution 45/158 of 18 December 1990 (*not yet in force*)

Protocol Additional to the Geneva Conventions of 12 August 1949, and Relating to the Protection of Victims of Non-International Armed Conflicts (Protocol II), *adopted* 8 June 1977, *entry into force* 7 December 1978

Protocol to Prevent, Suppress and Punish Trafficking in Persons, Especially Women and Children, Supplementing the United Nations Convention against Transnational Organized Crime, *entry into force* 25 December 2003

Universal Declaration of Human Rights, *adopted* by General Assembly Resolution 217 A (III) of 10 December 1948

Interpretative Texts of International Covenants/ Conventions

'Maastricht Guidelines on Violations of Economic, Social and Cultural Rights' (1998) in *Human Rights Quarterly* **20**(3): 691–704

United Nations Committee on Economic, Social and Cultural Rights (CESCR)

'General Comment No. 2: International technical assistance measures (Article 22 of the Covenant)', *adopted* at the fourth session, 1990

'General Comment No. 4: The right to adequate housing (Article 11 (1) of the Covenant)', *adopted* at the sixth session, 1991

'General Comment No. 7: The right to adequate housing (Article 11 (1) of the Covenant): Forced evictions', *adopted* at the 16th session, 1997

'General Comment No 15: The right to water (Articles 11 and 12 of the Covenant)', *adopted* at the 29th session, 2002

United Nations Human Rights Committee

'General Comment No 16: Article 17 (Right to privacy)', *adopted* at the 32nd session, 1988

'General Comment No 27: Article 12 (Freedom of movement)' *adopted* at the 67th session, 1999

Declarations/Programmes of Actions of United Nations Conferences

Agenda 21, *adopted* at the United Nations Conference on Environment and Development (Rio de Janerio, Brazil, 3–14 June 1992), *endorsed* by General Assembly Resolution 47/190 of 22 December 1992

Copenhagen Declaration on Social Development, *adopted* at the World Summit for Social Development, March 1995, Copenhagen

Global Strategy for Shelter to the Year 2000, *adopted* by the United Nations General Assembly in Resolution 43/181 on 20 December 1988

Habitat Agenda and Istanbul Declaration, *adopted* at the Second United Nations Conference on Human Settlements (Habitat II) (Istanbul, 3–14 June 1996), *endorsed* by General Assembly Resolution 51/177 of 16 December 1996

Millennium Declaration, *adopted* by General Assembly Resolution 55/2 of 18 September 2000

Vancouver Declaration on Human Settlements and the Vancouver Action Plan, *adopted* at Habitat: United Nations Conference on Human Settlements, (Vancouver, Canada, 31 May–11 June 1976)

Vienna Declaration and Programme of Action, *adopted* at the World Conference on Human Rights (Vienna, Austria, 14–25 June, 1993)

United Nations Resolutions and Other Documents

General Assembly (A/...)

General Assembly Resolution 401 (V): 'Land Reform' (*adopted* 20 November 1950)

A/RES/55/2. Resolution 55/2: 'United Nations Millennium Declaration' (*adopted* 18 September 2000)

A/RES/58/289. Resolution 58/289: 'Improving Global Road Safety' (*adopted* 11 May 2004)

A/RES/60/5. Resolution 60/5: 'Improving Global Road Safety' (*adopted* 1 December 2005)

A/60/181. 'The Global Road Safety Crisis: Progress on the Implementation of General Assembly Resolution 58/289, Note by the Secretary-General'

Security Council (S/...)

S/2001/1015. Enclosure: *Report of the Panel of Experts pursuant to Security Council Resolution 1343 (2001), paragraph 19, concerning Liberia*, www.un.org/Docs/sc/committees/Liberia2/1015e.pdf

S/2004/616. *The Rule of Law and Transitional Justice in Conflict and Post-Conflict Societies*, Report of the Secretary-General, Available from www.un.org/Docs/sc/sgrep04.html

Committee on Economic, Social and Cultural Rights (E/C.12/...)

E/C.12/1990/8. 'Revised guidelines regarding the form and contents of reports to be submitted by states parties under articles 16–17 of the Covenant on Economic, Social and Cultural Rights', in *Report of the Fifth Session of the Committee on Economic, Social and Cultural Rights*, 26 November–14 December 1990, pp88–110

Commission on Human Rights (E/CN.4/...)

E/CN.4/RES/1993/77. Resolution 1993/77: 'Forced evictions' (*adopted* 10 March 1993)

E/CN.4/1998/53/Add.2. 'Guiding Principles on Internal Displacement', Addendum 2 to 'Internally displaced persons' the *Report of the Representative of the Secretary-General, Mr Francis M. Deng*, Submitted pursuant to Commission on Human Rights Resolution 1997/39

E/CN.4/RES/2004/28. Resolution 2004/28: 'Prohibition of forced eviction' (*adopted* 10 April 2004)

Sub-Commission on the Promotion and Protection of Human Rights under the Commission on Human Rights (E/CN.4/Sub.2/...)

E/CN.4/Sub.2/1993/8. *Study Concerning the Right to Restitution, Compensation and Rehabilitation for Victims of Gross Violations of Human Rights and Fundamental Freedoms*, Final report submitted by Theo van Boven, Special Rapporteur

E/CN.4/Sub.2/1997/7. *Expert Seminar on the Practice of Forced Evictions (Geneva, 11–13 June 1997)*, Report of the Secretary-General

E/CN.4/Sub.2/2005/17. *Housing and Property Restitution in the Context of the Return of Refugees and Internally Displaced Persons*, Final report of the Special Rapporteur, Paulo Sérgio Pinheiro

E/CN.4/Sub.2/2005/17/Add.1. *Explanatory Notes on the Principles on Housing and Property Restitution for Refugees and Displaced Persons*, Final report of the Special Rapporteur, Paulo Sérgio Pinheiro

International Human Rights Instruments (HRI/MC)

HRI/MC/2006/7. *Report on Indicators for Monitoring Compliance with International Human Rights Instruments*, Eighteenth meeting of chairpersons of the human rights treaty bodies, Geneva, 22–23 June 2006. Fifth inter-committee meeting of the human rights treaty bodies Geneva, 19–21 June 2006

United Nations Commission on Human Settlements (HS/C)

HS/C/15/INF.7. *Towards a Housing Rights Strategy: Practical Contributions by UNCHS (Habitat) on Promoting, Ensuring and Protecting the full Realization of the Human Right to Adequate Housing*

Relevant Court Decisions

Ahmedabad Municipal Corporation v *Nawab Khan Gulab Khan & Ors* (1997) 11 SCC 121

Akdivar and others v *Turkey*, European Court on Human Rights, Reports 1996–IV (99/1995/605/693), Decided on 16 September 1996

Chapman v *United Kingdom*, 10 BHRC 48, Decided by European Court of Human Rights on 18 January 2001

Connors v *United Kingdom*, European Court of Human Rights, Application no 66746/01, Decided on 27 May 2004

Cyprus v *Turkey*, Applications 6780/74 and 6950/75, Report of the Commission, paras 208–210, *European Human Rights Reports* **4**, p482

Francis Coralie Mullin v *The Administrator, Union Territory of Delhi, All India Reporter* 1981 SC 746

Government of the Republic of South Africa and Others v *Grootboom and Others*, 2000(11) BCLR1169 (CC); 2001(1) SA46 (CC)

Grootboom v *Oostenberg Municipality and Others*, 2000(3) BCLR277 (C)

Maneka Gandhi v *Union of India* (1978) 1 SCC 248

'Modderklip' (*Modder East Squatters, Greater Benoni City Council* v *Modderklip Boerdery (Pty) Ltd.*), SCA 187/03, Decided by South Africa's Supreme Court of Appeal on 27 May 2004

'Modderklip' (*President of the Republic of South Africa, the Minister of Safety and Security, the Minister of Agriculture and Land Affairs, the National Commissioner of Police* v *Modderklip Boerdery (Pty) Ltd*), SCA 213/03

Olga Tellis v *Bombay Municipal Corporation* (1985) 3 SCC 545

Phocas v *France*, European Court of Human Rights, Reports 1996–II, Decided on 23 April 1996

Port Elizabeth Municipality v *Various Occupiers*, 2005 (1) SA 217 (CC)

Ram Prasad v *Chairman, Bombay Port Trust*, AIR 89 S.C.R. 1306, Decided on 29 March 1989

Social and Economic Rights Action Center and the Center for Economic and Social Rights v *Nigeria*, Communication 155/96

Spadea and Scalabrino v *Italy*. 12868/87 [1995] ECHR 35, Decided by European Court of Human Rights on 28 September 1995

Zubani v *Italy*, European Court of Human Rights, Reports 1996–IV, Decided on 7 August 1996

INDEX